A COMPARATIVE HANDBOOK

BLACK AFRICA

A COMPARATIVE HANDBOOK

Donald George Morrison

Robert Cameron Mitchell
John Naber Paden

Second Edition

A WASHINGTON INSTITUTE BOOK

PARAGON HOUSE
NEW YORK

IRVINGTON PUBLISHERS, INC.
NEW YORK

Co-Published in the United States and Canada by

Paragon House   Irvington Publishers, Inc.
90 Fifth Avenue   740 Broadway
New York, NY 10011   New York, NY 10003

For availability outside the U.S. and Canada, write to Irvington Publishers, Inc. at the above address.

A Washington Institute Book

Library of Congress Cataloging-in-Publication Data

Morrison, Donald George.
    Black Africa.

    Bibliography: p.
    1. Africa, Sub-Saharan. I. Mitchell, Robert Cameron.
II. Paden, John N. III. Title.
DT352.8.M67 1989   967   89-2879
ISBN 0-88702-042-9

BLACK AFRICA was formerly announced as ISBN 0-8290-1246-X (Vol. 1) and 0-8290-1247-8 (Vol. 2).
The contents of both these volumes are being published instead as Part I and Part II of the present edition of
BLACK AFRICA.

10 9 8 7 6 5 4 3 2 1

Printed in the United States of America

About The Authors

Donald George Morrison holds a joint appointment in the Harvard University Office of Information Technology and the Boston University African Studies Center. He has held faculty appointments at M.I.T., Northwestern University and York University, Canada, where he was Director of the Methods & Analysis Section, Institute of Behavioural Research. He was also Director of the Center for Social Science Computation Research at the University of Washington and was Director of the Computing Center at the University of Ibadan, Nigeria. He received his Ph.D. in Political Science from M.I.T.

Robert Cameron Mitchell is Senior Staff Sociologist at Resources for the Future. He has held faculty positions at Northwestern University and Swarthmore College. He received his Ph.D. in Sociology from Northwestern University.

John Naber Paden is Clarence J. Robinson Professor of International Studies at George Mason University. He was previously Director of the Program of African Studies and Professor of Political Science at Northwestern University. He received his Ph.D. in Political Science from Harvard University.

THE BLACK AFRICA DATA BASE

by Donald George Morrison with Robert Cameron Mitchell and John Naber Paden

---

The complete data base, containing more than five times the data selected to be printed in Black Africa: A Comparative Handbook is now available. The data base contains over 3,000 variables coded for each of 41 black African states, as well as data on the background of elites, the cultural characteristics of ethnic groups, and information on urban centers.

The BLACK AFRICA data base is now available on disks for use in desktop computers. This data includes three major components. The first is the data that appears in this book in the form that it appears. Indeed, the tables in the book were generated by this data. The second set of data includes data associated with the data in this book. That data is of several types. The first type is typically data that is of the same form as that included but for different years or forms of aggregation.

The second type will be of considerable interest to those studying political systems in a disaggregated form. It includes data collected at levels of aggregation different than as published. For example, detailed annual data on many kinds of instability events is included. These data along with other data on urban areas and ethnic groups will be of interest to those studying subnational forces in these countries.

The third kind of data is later data for any of the measures included in the first two sets. This data and its distribution on disk for analysis will allow us to keep users current as time increases the data available to us. The data will be distributed in a standard form (ASCII) which can be read by most word processors and most data or statistical analysis programs on desktop or microcomputers. Therefore, such packages as SPSS-PC, BMOP-PC, SAS-PC, SYSTAT, etc. and WORD PERFECT, WORD, WORDSTAR, etc., can be used to access the data files. Also, the FORTRAN program that creates the tables in the book is included. The users may also want to add countries to the coverage which would be straightforward.

The data base is updated perpetually so that whenever the disk is ordered, it will always contain the latest available data. For most purposes, an update every six months will be sufficient. Approximately half the data will change in that time period. When ordering, be sure to specify IBM 3 1/2 or 5 1/4 inch disks, or Macintosh disks.

BLACK AFRICA Data Base — $80.00
Subscription — 4 disks, one with your initial order and then
3 disks, one every 6 months thereafter—$240.00 (save $80.00)

Please order from:
IRVINGTON PUBLISHERS, INC.
740 Broadway, New York, New York 10003

Prices subject to change without notice.

Abbreviated Table of Contents: Part I

Part II

Detailed Table of Contents
Part I

Detailed Table of Contents
Part II

List of Abbreviations

Africa   Jeune Afrique. *Africa*   New York: Africana, annual.

Africa Contemporary Record   Colin Legum, ed. *Africa Contemporary Record: Annual Survey and Documents.* Exeter, England: Africa Research Limited, annual.

AID Economic Data Book   United States Agency for *International Development. Office of Program and Policy Division. AID Economic Data Book: Africa.* AID 3/00/0309. Washington, D.C.: Clearinghouse, December 1967. Subsequent editions issued irregularly and noted by date.

Démographie Comparée   Francis Gendreau. *Centres Urbains.* Afrique Noire, Madagascar, Comores, démographie comparée, vol. 2. Paris: Délégation Générale Recherche Scientifique et Technique, 1966.

ECA Statistical Bulletin   United Nations, Economic Commission for Africa. *Statistical Bulletin for Africa.* Addis Ababa: Economic Commission for Africa.

Étude Monographique   *Étude Monographique de trente et un pays africains.* 4 vols. Paris: Union Africaine et Malgache de Coopération Économique, 1964.

Europa Yearbook   *The Europa Yearbook.* Vol. 2, Africa, London: Europa Publications, annual.

Overseas Business Reports 166   *Overseas Business Reports.* Washington, D.C.: Bureau of Commerce, 1966. Issued separately by country.

Statesman's Yearbook   S. H. Steinberg, ed. *Statesman's Yearbook.* New York: St. Martin's Press, annual.

UA   *Urban Agglomeration.*

UN Demographic Yearbook   United Nations. *Demographic Yearbook.* New York: United Nations, annual.

UN Statistical Yearbook   United Nations. *Statistical Yearbook.* New York: United Nations, annual.

UNESCO Statistical Yearbook   United Nations Educational, Scientific and Cultural Organization. *Statistical Yearbook.* Paris: UNESCO, annual.

World Bank Atlas   International Bank for Reconstruction and Finance. *World Bank Atlas: Population, Per Capita Product and Growth Rates.* Washington, D.C.: International Bank for Reconstruction and Finance, annual.

World Bank Tables 1980   Baltimore: Johns Hopkins University Press, 1980, first edition in 1976. It is expected that it will be updated about every four years.

Accelerated Development in sub-Saharan Africa   Washington, D.C.: World Bank, 1982

World Factbook   Washington, D.C.: National Foreign Assessment Center, 1981

List of Tables and Figures
Part I

List of Tables and Figures
Part II

Preface to the Second Edition

The decision to publish this new edition of *Black Africa* reflects the sanguine and, hopefully, accurate impression of the authors and the publisher that the 1972 version of the book was of interest to a fairly general public and to the academic community interested in contemporary African affairs. That interest is marked at least by the evidence that the first edition was sold quickly; that information from the book has been used in the work of a number of professional students of African affairs, and that the book's reception by academic reviewers was generally favorable and, more to the point, emphasized a need for future revisions, including corrections and more up to date information. Thus inspired by the market and by the academy, we present this new edition. It is necessary, however, to indicate briefly the scope of the revisions incorporated in this new volume, lest it be anticipated that all the deficiencies of the first volume are now corrected, and that our intentions are more encyclopedic than they in fact are.

First, the geographical coverage of the book has been expanded to include Angola, Djibouti, Equatorial Guinea, Guinea-Bissau, Madagascar, Mozambique, Namibia, Swaziland, and Zimbabwe. We have still not included North African countries "separated" by the Sahara and by historical experience from the rest of Black Africa. Again, as in the first volume, we must stress that this "separation" is far from absolute, and that the regional homogeneity of the sample of African countries we include is really an empirically unsubstantiated assumption. We still hope that with future collaboration from other scholars with expertise in these areas, and with the necessary research funding, we may be able to give complete continental coverage in the future.

Second, we have tried so far as possible in this volume to provide comparative date which give a more adequate explanation of temporal change. Essentially we have tried wherever possible in Part I to produce aggregate data for the periods 1955, 1961, 1966, 1972 and 1977, and to extend the coverage of Part II to 1982. It will be evident that we are not always successful in realizing this intention, but the greater historical detail of the present volume constitutes, nevertheless, a substantial improvement.

Third, we have made some marginal extensions of the conceptual base of the information collected in this volume. In particular, we have attempted to provide information on the economic structure of these nations, and on their international situation, in greater detail than in the previous volume. This reflects an effort to go beyond the theoretical emphasis on problems of national integration that guided our earlier work. In pursuit of this objective, we have chosen to collapse the chapter structure of Part I of the earlier edition into the fewer but more integrated sections in this present volume. In the new sections, more substantive commentary on the interpretation of the date is given, although no attempt is made to give an exhaustive account of theories and empirical generalizations pertaining to the substantive topics treated in Part I.

Finally, substantial additions to the essays in the present volume have been made, where three original essays now appear on theoretical and methodological issues. In the first of these new essays, the reliability of aggregate data on Black African nations is explored with an extensive comparative analysis of different data bases now available. In a second new essay, a macro-analytic model of politcal instability in Black African states is summarized, which is evaluated with illustrative aggregate data. The intention here is not only to make a substantive contribution to the literature on the particular problem of political stability, but to provide also a general indication of the uses and utility of data presented in this book. Finally, a new essay on the structure of the existing data bank from which this book is derived is presented with an indication of future developments in computer assisted archiving procedures that we hope will allow for more flexible and efficient access to information on African states.

Finally, we have to extend the list of those to whom we were indebted in the first volume, although, of course, this revised edition owes much to them as well. We are particularly indebted for assistance in the development of this revised edition to the Rockefeller Foundation from whom Morrison received support for a visiting appointment at the University of Ibadan, Nigeria, where he had opportunities to develop the data base. At the University of Ibadan, the late Professor Billy Dudley was responsible for direct and indirect assistance to this enterprise.

Much of the earlier work on this book was done with

Michael Stevenson. Unfortunately, his other commitments were such that he withdrew from active participation in the project, but not before he had made important contributions to this work which should be acknowledged here. We are grateful also to the Canada Council for a small grant to Stevenson to finance the collection and analysis of new data relevant to the question of the relationship between economic and political developments in Black Africa. For work under that grant, we are grateful to Mr. Samuel Ifejika and to Mr. Don Coward, graduate students at York University and the University of Toronto, who will see some of the fruits of their labor reflected in this volume. Also, at York University, we are grateful to the Senate Small Grants Committee for financial assistance in support of the preparation of this manuscript; to the Master and Fellows and Ms. Anjie Williams of Bethune College for office space and secretarial assistance to this project; and to Mirka Ondracek, John Tibert and Jim Wert, at the Institute for Behavioural Research, for assistance with data mangagement and analysis.

At M.I.T. Ann Fryling carried a substantial part of the burden of updating the data. The Political Science department housed the data collection and Sandra Miller typed much of the manuscript. In these times of financial constraint in the univesity community, it is important to note that this new volume was produced with only small amounts of research grant assistance, and our debts to these individuals and institutions have been correspondingly greater than we can indicate by this brief acknowledgment.

At the University of Washington where work on this manuscript was completed there are many debts. First, institutional support from the University with computer funds, office space from the Department of Sociology, and general support from the Center for Social Science Computation and Research which I headed were all essential to the completion of this work. Individually, there were many key actors. The book was typeset using the University's typesetting equipment by Richard de Canio, a doctoral student in English, who mastered a complex and powerful computerized system to set the often complex tables in the book. Douglas Adams pasted up the galleys and proofed much of the work. There were many research assistants gathering data including Binh Chau, Tich Ha Vuong, Ho Phi Li, Diep Hoa Le, Brian Ha, and Bradley Esparza. We thank them all.

D.G.M.
and
R.C.M.
J.N.P.

Introduction

Background on Black Africa

Since January 1, 1956, when Sudan became an independent state, thirty-seven other Black African countries have celebrated the end of colonial rule.* Together with the ancient country of Ethiopia and the century-old Republic of Liberia these new states have brought Black Africa dramatically into the world's consciousness.

The independent Black African countries fill the Southern three quarters of the African continent (except for South Africa). This is an extremely compact continent whose smooth coastline has few natural harbors. Its interior is a vast plateau broken by the great river systems of the Nile, Niger, and Zaire rivers and the great Rift valley in Eastern Africa. Transversed by the equator, its climate varies widely. Only a relatively small portion of the continent, the Zaire basin and parts of West Africa, have rain forests with jungle foliage. Vast savannah grasslands characterize much of the continent's interior. It was under conditions like this that earliest man is thought to have evolved in Africa some two million years ago.

To the north, across the vast Sahara desert, lie the nations of North Africa. Although relatively distinct in culture and religion from Black Africa, caravans have traversed the far from impenetrable Sahara for centuries, facilitating both trade and culture contact. To the south lie two countries culturally similar to the independent black nations but now still under the control of minority white regimes: South Africa and Namibia (South West Africa). We have included Namibia in this edition because its independence is expected soon.

In order to understand Black Africa's dynamic response to modernization it is important to realize that the traditional culture of its people was principally tribal rather than peasant. This means that the basis of social organization lies in kinship units larger than the immediate family rather than in villages and the immediate family; that the land rights are held typically by groups such as clans, lineages (people tracing their relationship to a common ancestor), or extended families (kin groups larger than the parent-children unit) rather than by individuals; that political authority often involves checks and balances ensuring to some degree the consent of the governed rather than being vested in a relatively absolute ruler; that traditional African religion involves local cults and ceremonies rather than a universal religion; that villages or homesteads rather than cities are the characteristic places of residence; and that culture is transmitted by oral rather than written tradition.

Table 1 Dates of Independence for Forty-One Independent Black African States.

Country	Date of Independence
Ethiopia	Ancient Country
Liberia	July 26, 1847
Sudan	Jan. 1, 1956
Ghana	Mar. 6, 1957
Guinea	Oct. 2, 1958
Cameroon	Jan. 1, 1960
Togo	Apr. 27, 1960
Madagascar	June 26, 1960
Zaire	June 30, 1960
Somalia	July 1, 1960
Benin (formerly Dahomey)	Aug. 1, 1960
Niger	Aug. 3, 1960
Upper Volta	Aug. 5, 1960
Ivory Coast	Aug. 7, 1960
Chad	Aug. 11, 1960
Central African Republic	Aug. 13, 1960
Congo	Aug. 15, 1960
Gabon	Aug. 17, 1960
Senegal	Aug. 20, 1960
Mali	Sept. 22, 1960
Nigeria	Oct. 1, 1960
Mauritania	Nov. 28, 1960
Sierra leone	Apr. 27, 1961
Tanzania	Dec. 9, 1961
Burundi	July 1, 1962
Rwanda	July 1, 1962
Uganda	Oct. 9, 1962
Kenya	Dec. 12, 1963
Malawi	July 6, 1964
Zambia	Oct. 27, 1964
Gambia	Feb. 18, 1965
Botswana	Sept. 30, 1966
Lesotho	Oct. 4, 1966
Swaziland	Sept. 6, 1968
Equatorial Guinea	Oct. 12, 1968
Guinea-Bissau	Sept. 10, 1974
Mozambique	June 25, 1975
Angola	Nov. 11, 1975
Djibouti	June 27, 1977
Zimbabwe	April 18, 1980
Namibia	Not yet independent

*Not including islands such as Sao Tome, Cape Verde and the Comoros.

These generalizations admit to some exceptions, of course. To name a few, the rural Amhara people in central Ethiopia have a way of life that is more peasant than tribal. Those areas where Islam has become the dominant religion, such as parts of northern Nigeria, northern Sudan, and Somalia, have a universal religion at the heart of their culture. Finally, before the Western impact, the Yoruba in Nigeria had cities of up to 100,000 population although the vast majority of these city dwellers were farmers.

Within the tribal framework, the diversity of the traditional culture of the 800 or more African peoples is very large. Some peoples are nations of fifteen million like the Yoruba of Nigeria, while others are just a few thousand strong. Some have complex state political systems, while at the other extreme there are peoples with minimal political institutions above the authority of the family. Although inheritance in most African peoples passes through the father's line (patrilineal), a significant number of peoples are matrilineal. A herding way of life centered around cattle characterizes some peoples such as the Bororo Fulani of West Africa and the Masai of East Africa, but most peoples are settled on the land and follow an agricultural way of life. A small number of peoples such as the pygmies of the Zaire forests and the Bushmen of the Kalahari desert in Botswana and Namibia follow the ancient hunting and gathering way of life.

African culture has never been static. For millenia the continent has known migrations, wars, cultural innovation, and cultural diffusion. With the Western colonial impact of the nineteenth century the tempo of change quickened. The major colonial powers were the British, French, Belgians, Portuguese and, until the end of World War I, the Germans. They arbitrarily divided the continent into large political units and imposed Western culture. Following the initial resistance and a period of hesitancy, most African peoples responded in a dramtic fashion—crowding the primary and secondary schools, migrating to the cities in search of jobs, and sacrificing to send the most brilliant students to universities overseas and, later, at home. It is in this context of traditional tribal cultures responding to the forces of modernization and political change that the new states of Africa have come into being.

Scope of the Handbook

George H.T. Kimble has written, "The darkest thing about Africa has always been our ignorance of it." True as this statement is, the Western desire to learn about Africa has a long history. Although the ancients were not able to explore the interior of Africa, Ptolemy's geography (A.D. 125—155) summarized the results of numerous voyages along its perimeter.[1] In the nineteenth century, the Victorians were fascinated by the puzzle of the origins of the Nile and the Niger rivers and acclaimed the explorers who finally "discovered" these origins. Now that Black African countries are members of the United Nations and an important part of the world community of nations, both Africans and non-Africans are seeking more knowledge about contemporary Africa.

This Handbook is designed to assist the study of independent Black African nations by making available in readily accessible form comparable data on a wide range of topics. Although the reader interested in a specific country will find much that is of interest to him in this book, we have prepared the volume especially to encourage the comparative study of these nations.

We identify as "Black Africa" the forty sub-Saharan countries that were sovereign states as of this writing, and which were governed by Black Africans. We also include Namibia which appears likely to be independent soon. This is not to argue that there is a "White Africa," but only to indicate that territories governed by white minorities, and the North African states are not considered comparable for the purposes of this Handbook. As of this book's time of writing, active liberation movements were ongoing in South Africa, and the South African-controlled territory of Namibia. We hope that future editions of this Handbook will be able to include additional countries just as this edition includes nine additional countries over the first edition.

This Handbook is not intended to be a distillation of all available data dealing with Black Africa. Rather, it is designed to provide reliable information to facilitate the enterprise of comparative political, economic and social analysis and inquiry, and therefore, the development of theory and empirically verified generalization. This information was collected not because "it was there," but because it seemed important to the study of problems in the development of nations.

The African National Integration Project at M.I.T. and earlier at York University, out of which this edition of the Handbook has developed, was designed to investigate problems of conflict, national integration, social mobilization and political change. Countries, we argue, are political systems that are functionally equivalent units of analysis in that they have in common properties of territoriality, citizenship, and sovereignty. Changes in the boundaries of national territory, in the opportunities and obligations of citizens, and in the coerciveness and justice of the exercise of sovereignty seemed to be critical problems in the lives of men and women throughout Africa, and it seemed desirable to attempt to discover empirical regularities or generalizations about the development of nations. We were especially interested in two related processes of state-building: the degree to which national political systems are radically altered by violent breakdowns in the authority relationships between different segments of the population, and the degree to which elements of national populations become politically unified in increasing contact, cooperation, and consensus. In the organization and substance of this book, therefore, we give special attention to the requirements for a theoretical analysis of African political development. For a further discussion of the theoretical context of the data collection, see Cross-National Research, Chapters 1 and 2

Organization and Handbook

In Cross-National Research on Africa: Issues and Context, we discuss some of the important methodological issues in the comparative analysis of Black African states. These include an elaboration of our theoretical focus, the relevance and peculiar problems of generalizations based on cross-national research, the treatment of ethnicity in comparative research on Africa, and the reliability of aggregate data such as those we present in this book. The chapter on ethnic units (Chapter 4) provides a detailed discussion of the system of ethnic classification used in Part II.

Part I, Comparative Profiles, presents over 150 tables containing nearly 300 indicators which are not only of intrinsic interest but also necessary to the measurement of concepts and the testing of theory. In general, the data are based on existing, quantitative information, which have been checked for consistency between different sources; in some cases indices were constructed for concepts believed to be theoretically important, but for which there was no available quantitative measure.

Part II, Country Profiles, gives information about each country's ethnic, linguistic, urban, and political situation in the independence period. Where the index construction in Part I has required extensive aggregation from smaller units for each country, the country profiles give the original data for each unit. For example, as an index for urbanization in Part I. We include the percentage of population in cities of 20,000 people or more (Table 1.11). In the country profiles, each of these cities is listed with its population. This same pattern is followed for pluralism and political development. Part II also includes a map and selected bibliliography for each country.

The present Handbook is a selection of material from a larger data base[2]—a selection which represents the most reliable and significant data we have presently available. While there have been major improvements in the availability of data on Africa since the first edition much effort remains if data describing Africa is to be readily available. Our hope is that any errors and omissions will be isolated in critical readings of this book and that the work in its present form will stimulate greater international cooperation in the collection and sharing of information about Africa.[3] This hope is based not only on the assumption that the systematic collection, evaluation, and open publication of information is the essence of scholarship, but also on the feeling that this kind of enterprise is ultimately rewarding to Africans themselves. From the vantage point of African nations and their citizens, the development of national autonomy depends on being able to get information, as power depends on having information and being able to use it.

> A society or community that is to steer itself must continue to receive a full flow of three kinds of information: first, information about the world outside; second, information from the past, with a wide range of recall and recombination; and third, information about itself and its own parts. Let any one of these three streams be long interrupted, such as by oppression or secrecy, and the society becomes an automaton, a walking corpse. It loses control over its own behavior, not only of some of its parts, but also eventually at its very top.[4]

This Handbook, then, represents an attempt to provide comparative information—i.e., information about a country, which in its very presentation, is information about a "world" of countries outside. As it is analyzed, modified, and added to, this information may make some contribution to the potential autonomy of African nations. That, at least, is the intention of this book.

Notes

[1]Robert I. Rotberg, A Political History of Tropical Africa (New York: Harcourt Brace, 1965), pp. 3—33.

[2]The data base developed by the African National Integration Project contains over 3,000 variables coded for each of 41 black African states, as well as data on the background of elites, the cultural characteristics of ethnic groups, and information on urban centers.

The data base is available from Irvington Publishers, Inc. 740 Broadway, Suite 905, New York, New York 10003. Also, see Morrison et. al., 1974, "Information on African Political Systems: the African National Integration Project Data Bank", Social Science Information 13.6 (December), pp.109–123 and Chapter 5, Part III.

[3]The authors would be most grateful if readers finding any errors would bring them to our attention. Communications should be addressed to Donald G. Morrison, Harvard University, Office for Information Technology, 1730 Cambridge Street, Cambridge, MA 02138.

[4]Karl W. Deutsch, the Nerves of Government (New York: Free Press, 1963), p. 129.

Part I

Comparative Profiles

Introduction

Part I presents data on over 300 variables in 154 tables for 41 Black African countries. By "variable" is meant a measurable aspect of these countries which varies over a range of possibilities such as telephones per 10,000 population (Table 4.20) which varied in 1977 from 10 to 620 across the countries represented in this book. The variables are grouped by topic into six chapters. Each chapter includes: (a) a brief discussion of the topic and its theoretical importance for an understanding of contemporary Black Africa, (b) references to some of the recent and most important references on the topic, (c) an explanation of the selection of variables,* and (d) an evaluation of the data sources for these variables plus, if possible, our assessment of the reliability of the data. Chapters in this section are not intended to interpret the meaning of the data patterns themselves, however.

Each of the tables presents the data for one or more variables. These data consist of the values for each country on those variables plus a variety of summary statistics. Many readers will consult the table simply for the values. Consulting Table 4.20, for instance, they will learn that Namibia had the highest number of telephones per 10,000 population (620) in 1977. The statistics, however, provide additional useful information about the distribution of the values for that variable showing, for instance, that Gabon's value of 600 is far above the mean of 84.7 telephones per 10,000 population.

In Figure 1.1, Table 3.4 is reprinted as a sample table. Each element of the table is explained in detail so that the reader may use all the information in the tables, if he wishes, to aid in the interpretation of the data.

Guide to Reading the Tables in Part I

(A)=*Title*: The table title describes the variable and the year(s). In this case the variable is the consumer price index (with 1970 = 100) and the years are 1977, 1972, 1967 and 1960.
(B)=*Definition*: When it is necessary to define the variable more precisely and less ambiguously, additional information is given here.
(C)=*Sources*: The principal source is listed first. When subsidiary sources are used or additional information is given about particular countries, the countries involved are listed. The general source for Table 3.4 data is the

---

A

TABLE 3.4 Consumer Price Index 1977 (A), 1972 (B), 1967 (C) and 1960 (D).

B

Definition: Ratio of prices in the given years to prices in 1970 times 100.
Note: There are considerable variations in the population base used and the inclusion of goods in the calculation of this index and reference to the source would be appropriate for users of this data.

G
I

```
Range =           583.90
Mean =            230.19
Standard Deviation =          116.99
```

Population Percent		Rank	Country Name	A	Range Decile	B	C	D
Cum.	Country							
8.29	8.29	1.0	Zaire	714.7	1	122.5	56.9	82.0
11.80	3.51	2.0	Ghana	633.9	2	114.8	83.6	48.4
15.75	3.95	3.0	Uganda	434.0	5	112.3	84.3	65.0
36.75	21.00	4.0	Nigeria	281.6	8	120.1	80.2	66.4
38.70	1.95	5.0	Angola	251.2		14.1	10.5	9.9
44.94	6.24	6.0	Sudan	246.0	9	115.0	94.9	71.7
46.81	1.87	7.0	Mali	245.2		130.0		
48.17	1.36	8.0	Rwanda	236.7		103.6	95.7	
48.33	.16	9.0	Gabon	224.6		107.5	91.4	104.0
53.49	5.16	10.0	Tanzania	224.0		112.8	92.7	81.9
58.09	4.60	11.5	Kenya	219.6		109.8	98.1	82.7
59.42	1.33	11.5	Niger	219.6		114.4	92.0	75.8
60.17	.75	13.0	Togo	216.5		114.9	90.5	
61.81	1.64	14.0	Senegal	211.7		110.0	93.7	77.9
64.03	2.22	15.0	Ivory Coast	206.5		95.5	83.7	69.1
65.68	1.65	16.0	Zambia	201.7		111.7	85.8	65.8
66.14	.46	17.0	Mauritania	199.2		116.3	87.9	65.8
66.31	.17	18.0	Gambia	198.6		106.0	91.8	83.0
68.72	2.41	19.0	Cameroon	197.7		110.1	93.9	86.0
69.30	.58	20.0	Central Afri. R	193.0		116.7	91.5	62.2
69.53	.23	21.5	Botswana	192.9		112.5	91.2	76.2
69.91	.38	21.5	Lesotho	192.9		112.5	91.2	76.1
70.90	.99	23.0	Sierra Leone	191.0		103.8	88.8	66.7
71.43	.53	24.0	Liberia	189.1	10	103.6	87.3	92.0
72.46	1.03	25.0	Somalia	183.1		96.5	90.2	65.3
72.91	.45	26.0	Congo	179.0		114.3	95.8	66.9
82.62	9.71	27.0	Ethiopia	178.4		79.7	89.4	66.0
82.78	.16	28.0	Swaziland	175.8		103.5	91.9	
84.06	1.28	29.0	Burundi	174.6		107.8	90.8	
87.05	2.99	30.0	Mozambique	172.0		124.0	111.0	100.0
88.71	1.66	31.0	Malawi	170.7		112.1	82.2	68.3
91.19	2.48	32.0	Madagascar	168.8		111.4	92.8	88.0
92.53	1.34	33.0	Chad	167.6		109.3	88.0	62.3
94.50	1.97	34.0	Upper Volta	167.5		99.2	89.9	71.3
95.50	1.00	35.0	Benin	166.6		106.8	87.9	
97.76	2.26	36.0	Zimbabwe	160.1		106.0	95.7	96.0
97.86	.10	37.0	Equatorial Guinea	130.8				10.8

F J K E H

```
DATA NOT AVAILABLE OR NOT APPLICABLE
FOR THE FOLLOWING COUNTRIES                 D

Djibouti     Guinea     Guinea-Bissau  Namibia
```

C

SOURCE: *World Tables 1980* Economic Data Sheet 1.

L

World Tables 1980, second edition (Whose full reference is given in the List of Abbreviations). The data also comes from the publication *Accelerated Development in Sub Saharan Africa* (Washington, D.C.: World Bank, 1981)

(D)=*Data Not Available or Not Applicable*: Whenever data is unavailable on a variable for any of the countries covered in this Handbook or the variable is not applicable for a given country, the names of the missing countries are listed here.

(E)=(A): The data in this column are the values for the variable for each country. The 633.9 and 114.8 figures opposite Ghana indicate that Ghana's consumer price index in 1977 was 6.339 times the index in 1970 (i.e. it cost more than six times as much for the same basket of goods in 1977 as it did in 1970 in cedis, the Ghanaian currency) and in 1972 it cost 1.148 times as much as in 1970. The unit of measurement (e.g. percent or millions of U.S. dollars, etc.) is always specified in the table title. In some cases the measure has no units as in the case of a price index such as in this table.

If additional data appears in the table the columns for this data are headed by letters (B, C, D, etc.) which refer to the variables listed in the tables with parentheses indicating the column in which the variable's data occurs.

(F)=*Rank*: The countries are listed in the table in rank order from those which have the highest value on the variable to those which have the lowest value. This column gives the rank of every country on the variable. It shows that Zaire is highest, Sierra Leone, twenty-third, and Equatorial Guinea thirty-seventh out of 37 countries in terms of the growth of consumer prices from 1970 to 1977. Note that a different base period would lead to different rankings. Countries which have equal values, are given the same rank. This is calculated as the average of the ranks which they cover. In the case of Botswana and Lesotho these ranks are 21 and 22. The average is 21.5 which is the rank given to each.

The next four statistics provide a simple summary of some aspects of the distribution of the values for the 37 countries in the table. They are all expressed in the original measurement units, in this case a dimensionless index.

(G)=*Range*: This is the distance between the highest and the lowest value of the variable and shows the limits within which all measurements fall. In this case the distance between Zaire's 714.7 and Equatorial Guinea's 130.8 gives a range of 583.90.

(H)=*Range Decile*: The numbers in this column show which countries fall into which decile (or tenth) of the range. In this case the range is 583.90 so each decile is 58.39. Each country in Table 3.4, whose value is between 714.7 (highest value) and 656.3 (lowest value within one decile of the highest value) is in the first de-

cile of the range, etc Thus Zaire is the only country in the first decile (value714.7. There is one country in the second decile (Ghana) and no country in the third or fourth decile while Uganda is in the fifth decile, etc. A glance at the range decile column will show how evenly or unevenly the countries are distributed across the range. For instance, when the country having the highest value is in decile 1 and the country with the next highest value is in decile 8, the distribution across the range is highly uneven. In the case of Table 3.4 the distribution across the range is skewed with most countries approximately doubling prices over the seven year period while a few had very substantial inflation.

(I)=*Mean*: The mean may be thought of as the central tendency of the distribution. It is that number about which deviations in one direction equals deviations in the other. It is calculated by taking the sum of all the values (in column E) and dividing them by the total number of values (in this case by 37). The mean for Table 3.4 is 230.19. In cases where the distribution is skewed, the countries with values closest to the mean will be closer to the top or the bottom of the rank ordered countries.

(J)=*Standard Deviation*: This is an index of variability or how the values depart from the central tendency or the mean of a distribution. It is the square root of the variance for a distribution. For Table 3.4 the standard deviation is 116.99. The higher the standard deviation relative to the mean, the greater the countries' dissimilarity as a whole.

As an aid in interpreting the data, the remaining two sets of figures give information about the size of each country relative to the other countries covered by this Handbook.

(K)=*Country Population Percent*: The figures in this column give the percent each country's population is of the total population for all the countries. Adding the 1980 population figures for all the countries we get a value for the total population for the 41 countries covered in this Handbook. The figures in this column show that Congo's population comprises one half of one percent of the total (.45) while Nigeria's people comprises 21 percent of the total. A glance at this column will show such things as whether the smaller countries are grouped at the top or the bottom of a distribution. In the case of Table 3.4 the distribution by size of country population is relatively uniform, although there is a tendency for the lower values to be held by smaller countries. The country population percent is also a useful reminder of absolute values. In a table presented in Chapter 4 (4.20), "Telephones per 10,000 Population, 1977, 1972, 1967 and 1963" Congo has a higher value than Nigeria. Of course the more populous Nigeria had a much larger number of telephones (121,000) in 1977 than Congo (12,000), but

Congo has a much greater figure relative to its population (90 per 10,000 population for Congo versus 20 per 10.000 for Nigeria).

(L)=*Cumulative Population Percent*: The figures in this column give the country population percent (K) in a cumulative fashion beginning with the country population percent in the country with the highest value. At every point in the distribution of the value it shows the percentage of the total Black African population accounted for by those countries which hold that value or a higher one. For example, the countries in Table 3.4 that have a value of 251 or higher account for 38.7 percent of the total population of all the countries in the table. The figure of 97.86 opposite Equatorial Guinea in this column shows that the 37 countries for which data were available on this variable account for 97.86 percent of the total population.

Notes

*A total of over 300 variables are presented in the six chapters of Part I. These are a selection from a much larger data base on Black Africa. Generally in selecting the data for inclusion in this Handbook we have been guided by the principle that data readily available elsewhere should not be included in *that form* in this Handbook. Instead we try to provide sufficient references to the literature so that the user might locate those data and we go on to present either other data, or these data in another form such as percent increase or per capita. Some variables are included in the same form for the sake of completeness. however. This data set is available from Irvington Publishers, 740 Broadway, New York, N.Y. 10003.

1. Ecology, Demography, Urbanization

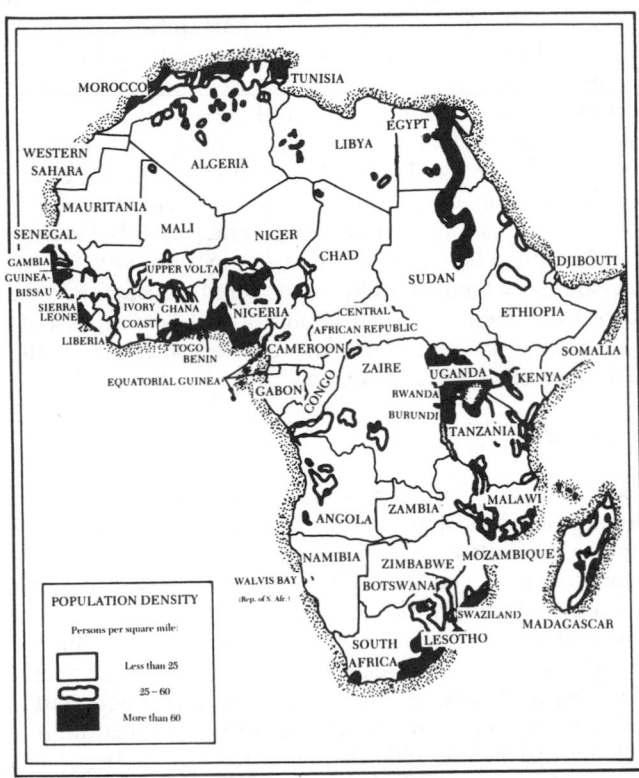

POPULATION DENSITY

Persons per square mile:

Less than 25

25 – 60

More than 60

Characteristics of the physical environment, the human population, and their mutual interaction in any society are fundamental to comparative analysis. However, many such characteristics are among the more difficult phenomena to measure with reasonable accuracy, particularly in less developed countries.

This chapter presents data on aspects of the ecology, demography and urbanization in black African states that are amenable to reasonably accurate cross-national measurement. These variables characterize only the most basic parameters of the African situation, however. Readers are referred to recent geographies dealing with Africa as a whole,[1] and the increasing number of single country geographies, which provide more detailed data on the ecology of Black Africa. Works on African demography provide a sophisticated review of the state of African population studies.[2]

Tropical Africa (excluding the Republic of South Africa) has been described by William Hance[3] in topographical terms as a plateau continent, possessing few good natural harbors, with narrow coastal plains where two-fifths of the continent is steppe or desert and one-third savanna.

Agriculture and herding remain the principal economic pursuits of the vast majority of Africans. About three-fifths of the total cultivated area of tropical Africa is devoted to subsistence farming. However, the soils in the rainforest and savanna areas are poorly structured leached lactosols which require careful cultivation. Neither land nor solar radiation are lacking, however. Only inadequacies in technique and deficiencies in rainfall stand in the way of abundant agricultural productivity.[4] The forests (Africa has about one sixth of the world's forest areas) represent an important and valuable resource which has been only modestly exploited to date. Cattle and the well-known African wildlife constitute very large faunal resources, and the fisheries are expanding.

The mineral exploitation potential and the availability of energy resources for export and for supplying power to indigenous manufacturing industries vary widely from country to country. Iron ore is mined in Angola, Mauritania, Guinea, Sierra Leone, Swaziland, and Liberia and coal deposits are either exploited or known to exist in at least six of the countries discussed in this Handbook. There are important copper mines in Zambia, Uganda, and Zaire; tin mines in Nigeria and Zaire; bauxite reserves in Guinea, Sierra Leone, and Ghana; manganese mines in Gabon; and commercial production of diamonds in Sierra Leone, Liberia, Tanzania, Namibia, Lesotho, Zaire, Angola, Botswana, and the Central African Republic. As of 1982, most of these mines and most of the presently known potential mineral resources were in South, West and Equatorial Africa. Since few areas of Black Africa have had thorough geological surveys, new discoveries may be expected in the future, however.

Africa has the greatest water power potential in the world. Add to this the possession of some of the world's major known reserves of uranium ore (which could fuel nuclear power stations), large petroleum discoveries in Nigeria, major commercial oil fields in Gabon, Congo, Angola, Zaire, lesser but growing fields in Cameroon, Ghana and Ivory Coast and considerable potential in other parts of West Africa, plus the natural gas fields in

Nigeria, and a promising energy picture emerges. The major drawback is the shortage of coking coal, necessary for the production of iron and steel, and the unequal distribution of fuel resources between the various countries.

Ecology

We have limited our presentation of data on the ecology of Africa to three variables: (1) Area of the Country in Square Kilometers, (2) Acres of Agricultural Land per Capita, and (3) a Non-Agricultural Development Potential Index (Tables 1.1—1.3). Further variables could have been included on other aspects of land use, but even these relatively simple variables present serious reliability problems. For instance, the area of African countries is seemingly a straightforward variable which is highly amenable to measurement. Nevertheless, the United Nations and its agency, the Economic Commission for Africa, give slightly different figures for Mali, Botswana, and Mauritania, and other sources offer even more divergent estimates. This dilemma is resolved without solving it by presenting in Table 1.1 a UN figure in square kilometers as the measure of size.[5] In the country sections of Part II the size of each country is given in square miles along with the names of those American states which in combination approximate the same land area.

With the second ecological variable, agricultural land per capita, the reliability problems become quite serious. Norton Ginsburg in his *Atlas of Economic Development* labeled this variable "highly suspect for many of the poorer countries"[6] because reliable information is difficult to obtain and the definitions of "cultivated" and "potentially cultivatable" land are open to different interpretations. This problem has been considerably exacerbated because of the serious droughts in the 1970s stretching across the central third of Africa from Senegal to Somalia. In our data-gathering operations we located three other measures of this variable (or variables very similar to it, such as "cultivated land in hectares per capita"). In a factor analysis of all our ecological and demographic data, the four variables fell on three different factors instead of the same factor, indicating a definite multidimensionality, and probable low reliability, instead of the hoped-for unidimensionality. Since, with a few exceptions, we did not have access to special information that would allow us to resolve these difficulties or to improve upon existing data, we took our data from a single source. Of course, this variable does not take into account the quality and character of the land involved, but it provides a rough comparative indicator of agricultural potential.

The third variable in this set is qualitative, originally based upon a series of assessments by William A. Hance

of certain aspects of the non-agricultural potential of the countries included in this Handbook. Hance, in his book *African Economic Development*, surveys the development of Black Africa, country by country. He summarizes this discussion in a table which rates each country on a number of factors which inhibit development (overpopulation, aridity, remoteness, etc.) and also on various short- and medium-run opportunities for development. We present a variable which is the sum of the scores for each country on the short- and medium-run opportunities for non-agricultural development in the following areas: forestry, fishing, mining, hydropower, and manufacturing. The rankings on this variable give a rough ordering of the development potential of these countries. Qualitative and judgemental as this variable is, it has the advantage of coming from a readily accessible source which contains a detailed justification for these judgements. The 1972 and 1977 data represents the authors' attempt to update Hance's analysis on the basis of more recent information.

Demography

The populations of these countries constitute a human resource of utmost importance. Development planning requires accurate data regarding population size and its characteristics in order to allocate national resources in a manner consistent with national goals. These data are not less vital in theoretical research which must account for variations in systemic scale. It will be noted that many variables contained in this Handbook have been standardized by population size for greater unit comparability. Although population counts of one kind or another have been undertaken in Black Africa for several decades, it is only since about 1960 that enumerations using modern census techniques have been widely used.[7] Even by 1982 some countries had not undertaken full censuses, although most of these countries have used the technique of the sample survey. This was first introduced to Africa in 1948, and was subsequently adopted by most of the former French colonies as well as by Zaire and Sudan. Most of the countries which have not had a census are currently planning them.

Since the building of an accurate demographic data base in Africa has just begun, the reliability of various important demographic measures such as birth rate, death rate, infant mortality rate, size of the labor force, etc., are generally low and extremely variable across these countries. In this Handbook we have restricted ourselves to the inclusion of an estimate for population size, an estimated rate of population increase, a population density indicator, and measures of the European population as percent of total population.

As with other demographic features, population size is difficult to measure with reasonable accuracy. A successful census is an enormous bureaucratic undertaking that requires the availability of highly specialized technicians and statisticians, and a considerable expenditure of funds. It also requires the cooperation of the population. In the colonial era, census undercounts commonly resulted because people feared taxation or otherwise misunderstood the purpose of the census. In the contemporary post-independence era the opposite may hold true as the rewards of parliamentary representation, national prestige, and resource allocation threaten to bias the results towards overcounts. While in general, the pre-independence censuses had been undercounts, the governments of Sierra Leone, Sudan, and Liberia unexpectedly found that their populations had been overestimated.

Nigeria is a dramatic example of the contemporary threat of overcounting. The first census to be taken in the 1960s (1962) was branded fraudulent and scrapped. Regional officials had allegedly conspired to preserve or change the political balance in their favor by inflating their returns. A second census, taken the next year with similar returns, was accepted by politicians but not by demographers because it indicated an exceedingly high and irregular growth rate. Thus, although the United Nations reported the official figure of sixty-one million for 1967, a non-governmental study of Nigerian human resource development based its analysis on an estimate of fifty million[8] Most international agencies report 1975 estimates of Nigerian population of about 60—61 million while the annulled 1973 census had a preliminary figure of nearly 80 million. The *gap* between these two recent estimates exceeds the summed *total* populations of 15 of the countries reported on in this Handbook!

Migratory movements, mostly of a seasonal variety, have a significant influence on the populations of several African countries which is difficult to take into account. For example, the inland countries of West Africa—Mali, Burkino Faso, and Niger—supply seasonal migrants to coastal countries, especially to Ghana, Nigeria, and Ivory Coast. In the 1960 Ghana census, 12 percent of the population were immigrant aliens. If the census had been taken earlier in the year the figure would have been even higher since many of the immigrants had returned to their home countries after the harvest (before the March-April date of the census).[9] Hance estimates that Ivory Coast annually receives about 200,000 semi-permanent immigrants from both Mali and Guinea, and 400,000 from Burkino Faso—equivalent to about one-fourth of her total labor force. Mining and industrial locations in Zim-

babwe and South Africa attract migrants from Zambia and especially Malawi in Central Africa, and one-sixth of the working force in Zambia itself are immigrants.[10] Mozambique, Lesotho, Botswana, and Swaziland are also major contributors to the South African labor force although these sources are declining in importance.

Another category of immigrants are political refugees. According to the *Statesman's Yearbook 1975—76* the following countries had received refugees, some of them in very substantial numbers: (in 1974) Zaire 1,500,000 (1,000,000 from Angola, others from Rwanda and Burundi), Tanzania (in 1966) (12,000 from Mozambique, 13,500 from Rwanda, others from Zaire), Uganda (in 1966,) 155,000 (55,000 from Sudan, 67,000 from Rwanda, and 33,000 from Zaire), and Zambia (in 1966,) 6,500 (from Angola and Mozambique). This sea of misery has only expanded since those figures were published. The population size data are from the Population Reference Bureau in Washington which reports on unpublished United Nations material.[11] Census dates have been gathered from several sources including the annuals, *U.N. Demographic Yearbook* and *Africa South of the Sahara*.

The measure of population density (Table 1.5) shows the comparatively low density which characterizes the African continent, which has about 22 percent of the world's land area and only 9—10 percent of world population. Australia is the only continent that has a lower population density. However, to understand the meaning of population density in terms of over- or underpopulation we must take into account the relatively low carrying-capacity of much of African land including the "arable" portions. William Hance has reviewed the arguments, pro and con, regarding Africa's "underpopulation" and seems to feel that the danger lies in the direction of overpopulation in the habitable zones if the expected high population growth rates are experienced.[12]

A population growth rate consists of the balance of in- and out-migration and the rate of natural increase (births minus deaths). Although we present a rate of population increase variable (Table 1.6), it should be noted that its reliability is not very high. Having compared two independent attempts to estimate mortality and fertility by demographers at Princeton Unviersity and at the Economic Commission for Africa, J.C. Caldwell[13] concludes that fertility in tropical Africa is "very high, but not quite uniformly so." Mortality rates are falling, "perhaps rapidly." With the mortality transition and without a fertility transition as yet, Africa is in the early phase of rapidly accelerating population growth.[14] One consequence of this situation is that more than two-fifths of the population in most African countries are under fifteen years of age.

The size of the European population is an important variable reflecting the differential colonial impact in these countries. That even a relatively small percentage of Europeans can exert a dominant neo-colonial influence is illustrated by the case of Gabon in the early 1960s, which has been described by the former American ambassador to that country.[15] Table 1.7 presents data for the mid-1920s and recent data on European populations (1960 and 1970); these data are generally representative of the early colonial period, the independence period, and a later period in which the new regime's attitudes towards European residents can be expected to have had some effect.

Since the European populations in the forty-one countries were mostly small and under the direct control of the colonial regimes, the data on them is likely to be relatively reliable, even for earlier periods. The definition of "European" complicates the reliability of the variable, however: Indian or Levantine residents may be counted separately from "whites" in one country, such as Kenya, and together with them in another, such as Nigeria.

Urban Patterns

Africa is at once the least urbanized and the fastest urbanizing of the world's continents. According to United Nations data for the entire continent (including North and South Africa), the percent of the population residing in localities of 20,000 and more inhabitants in 1960 was 13 percent, as compared with Asia's 17 percent and Latin America's 32 percent.[16] In terms of urban growth, however, African cities have been growing at a very high rate and by 1970 nearly 20 percent of black Africa's population were living in urban areas. One hundred years ago there were only two cities approaching a population of 100,000 in the countries considered in this Handbook,[17] while by 1975 there were eighty-seven cities of this size or greater, and more than thirty-one million Black Africans resided in towns of 20,000 or more.[18]

The recency of the growth of large settlements should not obscure the fact that cities have been an important aspect of African history for a thousand years or more. Although relatively small by present-day standards, cities such as Kano, Timbuktu, Gao, Oyo, and Mombasa developed as important centers of trade and political power at various times from the eleventh through the nineteenth centuries.[19]

Contemporary urbanization in Africa is one of the key components of the modernization process and an important aspect of political development.[20] Cities require a societal level of agricultural production adequate to produce a surplus to support the non-agricultural urban population.[21] Large cities are typically the center of international trade, communication, and local manufacture. The capital city, which is usually the largest as well, may stand both as a referent or symbol of national identity, and as a source of mass media dissemination which operates to instill nationalistic sentiments and values.

The city exerts its influence on and through its inhabitants. African urban residents, relatively independent as they are from the land and from their traditional social matrix, tend to acquire aspects of a new way of life and to modify their traditional world view.[22] The effect of urban life on the society as a whole is multiplied by the close ties African city dwellers maintain with their village or homesteads. Most African city dwellers are first-generation migrants who participate in urban associations made up of people from the same village or area; they return "home" regularly, and provide hospitality for fellow villagers who visit the city. Through these influences African cities exert an influence far beyond their administrative boundaries.

The effect of urban life upon city dwellers should not be exaggerated, however. In earlier writings on African urbanization there was a tendency to suppose that the change to urban living by migrants from rural areas brought about an extreme individualism, a loss of traditional identity or "detribalization," and thus a tendency to feel normless or rootless.[23] Studies now show that this analysis of the effects of urban living was distorted. There certainly are serious social problems in many overcrowded African cities and these will probably become more prominent as the ranks of the unemployed schooldropouts increase and concentrate in the cities. Nevertheless, the resiliency of African culture has led to the spontaneous development of new forms of urban social organization, such as friendly societies and ethnic associations, which mitigate the harshness of the new environment and relate the newcomers to their ethnic group identity in new ways.[24] The extended family, moreover, has tended to retain its importance despite the relative dispersion of its members both geographically and socially, although this may decline over time.[25]

African cities may be differentiated in terms of function (administrative, mining, port, etc.), history (traditional, colonial, post-colonial), location (West Africa, East Africa, etc.), as well as size. The variables presented in this chapter treat all cities alike, however, taking account only of size and that in a relatively limited manner. Nevertheless, the recent founding of most African cities and their general characteristic of serving as loci for rapidly expanding economic and/or political and administrative activities suggests that they share important underlying uniformities. This homogeneity is evidenced by the failure of the few modern African cities built upon traditional urban bases, such as Kumasi or Kano, to develop into what Hoselitz has called "parasitic cities." This type of city, common in Asia, has a traditional foundation and tends in the modern era to live off the areas surrounding it and to resist reorganization of any kind. Brian Berry studied Kumasi, a large city in Ghana that might be expected by Hoselitz's notions to develop parasitic characteristics. He found that even Kumasi had made a "smooth rapid transition" to a specialized commercial economy which was more generative than parasitic.[26]

Concepts and Definitions

What criterion shall be evoked for defining one population agglomeration in Africa as an "urban unit" and another as "not an urban unit"? Arguments are made that the distinctive thing about a city is not its size but its style of life or its mode of social and economic organization. Given the limited availability of data on African cities, the criterion for our purposes will have to be one of size only. But what population size is the most appropriate urban cut-off point? Kingsley Davis used a minimum population of 100,000 as his operational definition for a metropolitan area in an examination of world urban patterns,[27] while the UN has used 20,000 as the urban cut-off point in some comparative studies. Individual countries, of course, vary widely in the size definition of "urban" used in their statistical reports. Davis' criterion is too large to be useful for Africa where eleven of these forty-one countries have no urban units as large as 100,000, while the official criterion of the countries themselves is too variable to be of comparative value. We have decided for purposes of reliability and comparability to use the UN minimum population of 20,000 in calculating the index of urban population as a percent of total population. By contemporary European and American standards a non-suburban town of 20,000 may seem more village than urban in character, but in Africa today most towns with populations of 20,000 exhibit a distinctly non-traditional way of life.

Having taken a population of 20,000 as the lower limit for a definition of an urban center, the problem that next presents itself is the basis for defining the boundary of the urban unit. For instance, according to the 1959 Uganda census, the population of the administratively defined area of Kampala City was 46,735, while the population of the larger urban area including the contiguous, densely populated areas such as Mengo was actually about 122,000. Sometimes the opposite situation occurs. Kumasi was reported by the *UN Demographic Yearbook*

to have a population of 249,000 in 1966, but according to information from a specialist on Ghanaian urbanization this figure is for an administrative unit, the Kumasi Municipal Council area, which contains a considerable rural area. This source suggested a figure of 180,000 as more representative of the actual population of what we might call the Kumasi urban agglomeration.

Our approach to the boundary problem has been to use the existing definitions of urban places, and where UN data differentiates between cities and urban agglomeration[28] figures, we use the latter figure on the supposition that this reflects the reality of an urbanized area spreading beyond city administrative boundaries in a way similar to the use of the Metropolitan Area definition in the United States. Examples of cities affected in this manner are Banjul, Accra, Conakry, Abidjan, Nairobi, Bamako, Lome, and Kampala. The various indices of urbanization which are presented here are selected from a number of possible indices as those most appropriate, given the data available. With the exception of the index of urban concentration their meaning is self-evident. This index indicates the population size dominance of the capital city in a country (Table 1.14).

Population size dominance is often related to administrative, political and economic dominance as well.[29] There are various ways to calculate primacy indexes. The method used here gives the population of the city as a percentage of the total population of the four largest cities.[30] In the cases where there were fewer than four cities over 20,000 in population, the index was calculated using the population of the two or three cities which reached this size. In a few instances we have included cities just below the 20,000 minimum population since they would probably have exceeded that figure by the time of publication.

Reliability

Reliability is a serious problem for African urban data. The ideal data source is a modern census taken in the year for which our data are presented—i.e., 1955, 1965, 1972, or 1977 for the variables on cities 20,000 or more (Tables 1.09—1.12). Rarely have our model year and a modern census come into juxtaposition in such a fortuitous way, however. Failing a modern census, a sophisticated and well executed sample survey in the same year would be virtually as reliable, but again these have rarely coincided with our years. Thus we have had to do interpolations or extrapolations from the latest available data on urban populations, or had to rely on other scholars' estimates. Since our approach for the four time periods has varied, we discuss each in turn in order to give the reader a sense of the reliability of the data and information regarding an alternate data source.

1955 Urban Population (Table 1.09).

For this variable we relied primarily upon two existing data sources. The first is the Ginsburg *Atlas of Economic Development*, which gives data on this variable for the entire world, including all of Africa. The Ginsburg data were derived from work done for the Berkeley International Population and Urban Research Center. These data have the advantage of providing estimates for a single year. Unfortunately the Ginsburg Atlas presents data for the French African federations as a whole instead of for their constituent countries. It was necessary to consult a second data source, the French publication *Demographie Comparee*, for comparable data for each of the former French African countries. This invaluable source presents a table showing the growth of every city of 10,000 and above for French Africa from 1915 to 1960. This source does not extrapolate between estimates, however. Thus, Abidjan is shown as having a population of 121,000 for 1955—1959 and then in 1960 the population jumps to 180,000. Where necessary, we have interpolated between points in arriving at our 1955 urban estimates.[31] The reliability of these data cannot be stated with any degree of precision but, since the census and sample survey data for the 1950's are generally not up to modern standards, it must be assumed to be only moderate and all the data for this variable should be regarded as estimates.

Urban Population 1965, 1972 and 1977 (Table 1.10).

Data for this table were gathered from a wide variety of sources, country by country, including wherever possible the most recent census or sample survey which provided urban population data. The sources for the ca. 1977 data are presented for each country in Part II of this edition, and the sources for the 1965 data were presented in part II of the 1st edition of *Black Africa*. In general the reliability for these data should be significantly greater than for the 1955 data because many of the countries have had modern censuses or special sample surveys of urban populations in recent years. This has been less true of the former French colonies, thus introducing a possible source of systematic error. Furthermore, given the extremely rapid growth rate of many African cities, attempts to estimate the population of a city from census data three or even two years old can be a hazardous business. This is why the variable is given as "ca. 1965." Data available only for 1966, for example, were calculated on the basis of 1966 population estimates rather than trying to estimate the 1965 urban population. A similar procedure was used for 1972 and 1977 data. Given these problems, these data also should be considered as estimates.

The existence of an alternative data source for some of the countries allowed a partial check on our data and suggests that our cautionary statements on reliability are well founded. This source is the preliminary version of a report by the United Nations Economic Commission for Africa (ECA).[32] It contains data on the percentage of the country's population living in cities with 20,000 or more population for a variety of years, the years chosen being based upon the availability of data. Thus Benin has data for 1955 and 1961, while Gambia's data is for 1951 and 1964. The ECA estimates are based upon the *UN Demographic Yearbooks* and "national publications," and individual city totals are not given, making a detailed comparison impossible. Of the seven possible comparisons of ECA data with our 1955 data, all on former French countries, six show our estimates to be lower than the ECA estimate, the average difference being 30 percent. For the three possible 1965 comparisons, none involving former French countries, our estimates were higher in two of the three cases by an average of 20 percent. There are a variety of possible explanations for these differences, involving conjectures about the ECA methodology, which could account for the difference, apart from the obvious explanation that one is based on inaccurate data.[33] None of these can be proved without further information about the ECA data which is unavailable to us. Correlations between our estimates of urban population percentages (1972) and those reported by the U.S. Agency for International Development and the UN ECA are .78 and .81 respectively. Since the definition of urbanization varies from country to country in these reports this appears reasonably satisfactory.[34]

Notes

[1]R. J. Harrison Church, et al., *Africa and the Islands* (New York: John Wiley, 1965); William A. Hance, *The Geography of Modern Africa*, 3rd edition (New York: Columbia University Press, 1980); George H. T. Kimble, *Tropical Africa*, 2 vols. (New York: The Twentieth Century Fund, 1960); P. Ady, ed., *Oxford Regional Economic Atlas—Africa* (Oxford: Clarendon Press, 1965); L. Dudley Stamp, *Africa: A Study in Tropical Development*, 3rd ed. (New York: Wiley, 1972) and R. Mansell Prothero, ed., *People and Land in Africa South of the Sahara* (New York: Oxford University Press, 1972). It is clear, however, that these will be in need of revision or replacement as the recent censuses, changes in the environment, increases in knowledge of mineral deposits, and advances in economic development take place. One major source of change is the serious drought in the Sahelian region during the 1970's as well as a continuing drought in Ethiopia and So-

malia which has had a profound influence on the ecology of a major area of Africa; see D. J. Rogers *A Bibliography of African Ecology* (Westport: Greenwood Press 1979). Also see P. Paylore *Desertification: a World Bibliography* (Tuscon: University of Arizona, 1976) on this subject. For individual country geographies see the country references in Part II.

[2]J. C. Caldwell and C. Okonjo, *The Population of Tropical Africa* (London: Longmans, 1968); R. P. Mass and R. J. A. Rathbone, eds., *The Population Factor in African Studies* (London: University of London Press, 1975); William Brass, et al., *The Demography of Tropical Africa* (Princeton, N.J.: Princeton University Press, 1968); and R. B. Tabbarah, "Toward a Theory of Demographic Development," *Economic Development and Cultural Change* 19, 2 (1971), pp. 257—76.

[3]William A. Hance, *African Economic Development*, 2nd ed. (New York: Praeger, 1967).

[4]Pierre Gourou, "Agriculture in the African Tropics: The Observations of a Geographer," in *Africa*, ed., P. J. McEwan (London: Oxford University Press, 1968), pp. 128—38. Among other discussions of African agriculture see: William Allan, *The African Husbandman* (Edinburgh: Oliver and Boyd, 1965); Rene Dumont, *False Start in Africa* (New York: Praeger, 1966); David Hapgood and Max F. Millikan, *No Easy Harvest: The Dilemma of Agriculture in Under-Developed Countries* (Boston: Little, Brown, 1967). Also see the recent works on the problems of maintaining the environment: D. F. Owen, *Man's Environmental Predicament* (London: Oxford University Press, 1973); and M. F. Thomas and G. W. Whittington, *Environment and Land Use in Africa* (New York: Harper and Row, 1972).

[5]*U.N. Statistical Yearbook, 1973.*

[6]Norton Ginsburg, *Atlas of Economic Development* (Chicago: University of Chicago Press, 1961), p. 46.

[7]Complete house-to-house censuses had been carried out, however, as early as 1948. Frank Lorimer, "Introduction," in *The Demography of Tropical Africa*, eds., William Brass, *et al.*, p. 5. Various census reports and summaries are often available and can be useful. Sources such as the *U.N. Demographic Yearbook* provide discussions on census reliabilities as do contributors to Brass et al. An important study of a controversial census is, I. I. Ekanem, *The 1963 Nigerian Census: A Critical Appraisal* (Benin City, Nigeria: Ethiope, 1972).

[8]Education and World Affairs, *Nigerian Human Resource, Development and Utilization* (New York: Education and World Affairs, 1967), p. 18.

[9]B. Gil, "Immigration into Ghana and Its Contribution in Skill," in U.N. Department of Economic and Social Affairs, *Proceedings of the World Population Conference*, v. 4 (New York: United Nations, 1967), p. 202. In late 1969 the Ghanaian government expelled many of the estimated two million aliens then resident in the country. Also see S. Amin, ed., *Modern Migration in Western Africa* (London: Oxford University Press, 1975) for commentary on migration in West Africa.

[10]C. A. L. Myburgh, "Migration in Relationship to the Economic Development of Rhodesia, Zambia and Malawi," in *ibid.*, p. 216, and William A. Hance, *Population, Migration, and Urbanization in Africa* (New York: Columbia University Press, 1970), pp. 128—208. Other sources on migration can be found in the following bibliography: M. Aghassian "Les migrations en Afrique au sud du Sahara: bibliographie selective" pp. 101—18 in *Migrations Africaines* (Paris: F. Maspero, 1976); L. G. Davis *Migration to African Cities: an Introductory Survey.* (Monticello, Ill.: Council of Planning Librarians, 1976); and *Les*

Migration dans Sept Etats d'Afrique de l'Ouest (Abidjan: INADES-documentation, 1977).

[11]For a useful discussion of the United Nations' population data reliability see C. L. Taylor and M. Hudson, *World Handbook of Social and Political Indicators* (New Haven: Yale University Press, 1972).

[12]William A. Hance, "The Race Between Population and Resources," *Africa Report*, 13 (January 1968): 6—12; and Hance, *Population, Migration, and Urbanization in Africa*, pp. 43—127. More recent studies include the World Bank report, *Population Policies and Economic Development* (Washington, D. C. : World Bank, 1975), and S. H. Ominde and C. N. Ejiogu, *Population Growth and Economic Development in Africa* (London: Heinemann, 1974). Also see E. M. Drives, *World Population Policy: An Annotated Bibliography* (Lexington: Heath, 1972); J. C. Caldwell, et al., eds., *Population Growth and Socioeconomic Change in West Africa* (New York: Columbia University Press, 1975); B. Valquist, *Nutrition: A Priority in African Development* (Stockholm: Almquist and Wicksell, 1972); and J. M. May and D. L. McClellan, *The Ecology of Malnutrition in Eastern Africa and Four Countries of Western Africa* (New York: Hafner, 1970).

[13]J. C. Caldwell, "The Demographic Situation," in Caldwell and Okonjo, *The Population of Tropical Africa*, pp. 8—15. Of the two different estimates of population growth mentioned, the estimate given in this Handbook conforms more to the Economic Commission for Africa estimates, which are generally higher than the Princeton estimates.

[14]In the next decades, Africa may achieve the highest population growth rate of the world's regions. R. K. Som, "Some Demographic Indicators for Africa," in Caldwell and Okonjo, *op. cit.*, p. 197.

[15]Charles and Alice Darlington, *African Betrayal* (New York: David McKay Co., 1967). For another example see R. Cruse O'Brien, *White Society in Black Africa: The French of Senegal* (Evanston, Ill.: Northwestern University Press, 1972).

[16]United Nations Economic Commission for Africa, "Size and Growth of Urban Population in Africa," in *The City in Newly Developed Countries*, ed., Gerald Breese (Englewood Cliffs, N.J.: Prentice-Hall, 1969), pp. 128—45.

[17]All further references to Africa in this chapter are restricted to the countries reviewed in this Handbook unless otherwise indicated.

[18]Africa experienced a 30 percent increase in population in localities of 20,000 or more (1950—1960) as compared with the world (19 percent) and North America (14 percent), Economic Commission for Africa, *Urban Population in Africa*, p. 128, and over a 75 percent increase in urban population from 1965—1972 (See Table 1.10).

[19]We cannot assume that urbanization in some form would not have continued without exogenous influences. Some difference of opinion exists among scholars, however, as to whether these population centers can qualify as "cities." While the criteria of size and density were met, social heterogeneity and functional specialization were not characteristic of some, and unified political authority and common institutions were not present in others. For discussions of traditional urbanism in Africa see Hilda Kuper, ed., *Urbanization and Migration in West Africa* (Berkeley: University of California Press, 1965), pp. 1—22; William Bascom, "Urbanization among the Yoruba," *American Journal of Sociology*, 60 (1955): 445—454; Horace Miner, *The Primitive City of Timbuctoo* (Princeton University Press, 1953), and "The Folk Urban Continuum," *American Sociological Review*, 17 (1952): 529—537; P. C. Lloyd, A. L. Mabogunje, and B. Awe, eds., *The City of Ibadan* (Cambridge: Cambridge University Press, 1967); Eva Krapf-Askari, *Yoruba*

Towns and Cities (Oxford: Clarendon Press, 1969).

[20]Daniel Lerner, *The Passing of Traditional Society* (New York: Free Press, 1958): pp. 54—65. Karl W. Deutsch has suggested measures of urbanization to assess rates of social mobilization, a process in which traditional "economic and psychological commitments are eroded or broken and people become available for new patterns of socialization and behavior." Karl W. Deutsch, "Social Mobilization and Political Development," *American Political Science Review*, 55 (1961): 493—514. See also Akin Mabogunje, "Urbanization and Change" in *The African Experience*, eds., John Paden and Edward Soja (Evanston, Ill.: Northwestern University Press, 1970).

[21]For additional discussion of the pre-conditions for urbanization see Gideon Sjoberg, *The Preindustrial City* (New York: Free Press, 1960): pp. 25—49. Two additional prerequisites cited by Sjoberg are a favorable ecological base and a complex social organization. Serious problems exist and may intensify in the next decade should the rate of urbanization outstrip the capacity of developing economies to absorb non-agricultural manpower. It should be noted that some urban areas, most notably many cities in Western Nigeria, have a high percentage of farmers who live in the city during non-farming times of the year. Many cities in the Sahelian region as well as elsewhere have considerable seasonal variation in their populations because of this phenomenon.

[22]In addition to contributions by Breese and Kuper, *op. cit.*, the following are some of the major works on urbanization in Africa: A. L. Epstein, "Urbanization and Social Change in Africa," *Current Anthropology*, 8 (1967): 275—296; Horace Miner, ed., *The City in Modern Africa* (New York: Praeger, 1967); Kenneth Little, *West African Urbanization* (New York: Cambridge University Press, 1965); Philip M. Hauser and Leo F. Schnore, eds., *The Study of Urbanization* (New York: John Wiley, 1967); Leo Van Hoey, "The Coercive Process of Urbanization: The Case of Niger," pp. 15—32; and Dennis McElrath, "Societal Scale and Social Differentiation: Accra, Ghana," pp. 33—52, in *The New Urbanization*, eds., Scott Greer, *et al.* (New York: St. Martin's Press, 1968); and William A. Hance, *Population, Migration, and Urbanization in Africa* (New York: Columbia University Press, 1970). Studies of the contemporary characteristics and dynamics of specific cities include Richard J. Peterec, *Dakar and West African Economic Development* (New York: Columbia University Press, 1967); Claude Meillassoux, *Urbanization of an African Community, Voluntary Associations in Bamako* (Seattle: University of Washington Press, 1968); Valdo Pons, *Stanleyville, An African Urban Community under Belgian Administration* (New York: Oxford University Press, 1969); and Harm J. de Bilj, *Mombasa, an African City* (Evanston, Ill.: Northwestern University Press, 1968). A study of the urbanization of a particular country is Akin L. Mabogunje, *Urbanization in Nigeria* (New York: Africana, 1969). William J. Hanna and Judith Hanna, *Urban Dynamics in Black Africa* 2nd edition, (Hawthorne, N.Y.: Aldine, 1980), is a useful synthesis of the literature which includes a substantial bibliography. Another bibliography with nearly 3000 entries indexed by country and city is H.I. Ajaegbu's *African Urbanization: A Bibliography* (London: International African Institute, 1972). Other studies include H. Wolpe, *Urban Politics in Nigeria: A Study of Port Harcourt* (Berkeley: University of California Press, 1974); J. Hutton, ed., *Urban Challenge in East Africa* (Nairobi: East Africa Publishing, 1972); M. Kilson, *African Urban Kinsmen* (London: Hurst, 1975); G. Bjeren, *Some Theoretical and Methodological Aspects of the Study of African Urbanization* (Stockholm: Scandinavian Institute of African Studies, 1971); M. A. Cohen,

Urban Policy and Political Conflict in Africa: A Study of the Ivory Coast (Chicago: University of Chicago Press, 1974); Kenneth Little, *Some Aspects of African Urbanization South of the Sahara*, McCaleb module in anthropology (Reading, Mass.: Addison-Wesley, 1971); P. H. Baker, *Urbanization and Political Change: The Politics of Lagos 1917—1967* (Berkeley: University of California Press, 1974); E. P. Skinner, *African Urban Life: The Transformation of Ouagadougou* (Princeton: Princeton University Press, 1973); P. M. Gutkind, "From the Energy of Despair to the Anger of Despair: The Transition from Social Circulation to the Political Consciousness among the Urban Poor in Africa," *Canadian Journal of African Studies*, II, 2 (1973), pp. 179—98; R. Stren, "Urban Policy in Africa: A Political Analysis," *African Studies Review*, XV, 3 (Dec. 1972), pp. 489—516; S. El-Shakhs, *Urbanization, National Development and Regional Planning in Africa* (New York: Praeger, 1974); K. L. Little, *Urbanization as a Social Process in Contemporary Africa*, (London: Routledge and Kegan Paul, 1974); M. Peil, "The Common Man's Reaction to Nigerian Urban Government," *African Affairs*, 74, 296 (July 1975), pp. 300—313 and Marc Howard Ross, *The Political Integration of Urban Squatters* (Evanston, Ill.: Northwestern University Press, 1973). Other sources can be found in the following bibliographies: S. A. Hallaron *Urbanization in the Developing Nations* (Monticello, Ill.: Council of Planning Librarians 1976); Obudho, R. A. and El-Shakhs, eds., *Development of Urban Systems in Africa* (New York: Praeger, 1979); L. G. Davis *Urban Growth Development and Planning of African Towns and Cities* (Monticello, Ill.: Council for Planning Libraries, 1977); B. Buick, *Squatter Settlements in Developing Countries* (Canberra: Australian National University, Res. School of Pacific Studies, 1975).

[23]For an example of this perspective see G. Malengrean, "Observations on the Orientations of Sociological Researches in African Urban Centers, with Reference to the Situation in the Belgian Congo," in *Social Implications of Industrialization and Urbanization in Africa South of the Sahara*, International African Institute (Paris: UNESCO, 1956): pp. 624—38.

[24]Peter Marris, *Family and Social Change in an African City* (Evanston, Ill.: Northwestern University Press, 1961); Kenneth Little, *West African Urbanization: A Study of Voluntary Associations in Social Change* (New York: Cambridge University Press, 1965) and Marc Howard Ross, *Grass Roots in an African City: Political Behavior in Nairobi* (Cambridge, MA: M.I.T. Press, 1975).

[25]Peter C. W. Gutkind, "African Urban Family Life and the Urban System," in *Urbanism, Urbanization, and Change: Comparative Perspectives*, eds., Paul Meadows and Ephraim Mizruchi, (Reading, Mass.: Addison-Wesley, 1969), pp. 215—22; Joan Aldous, "Urbanization, the Extended Family and Kinship Ties in West Africa," *Social Forces* 51 (October 1962): 6—12.

[26]Brian J. L. Berry, "Urban Growth and the Economic Development of Ashanti," in *Urban Systems and Economic Development*, F. R. Pitts, ed., (Eugene: University of Oregon School of Business Administration, 1962), pp. 53—64.

[27]The original study by Davis was International Urban Research, *The World's Metropolitan Areas* (Berkeley: University of California Press, 1959). A volume which contains much data on Africa, all compiled independently of our data-gathering effort, is Kingsley Davis, *World Urbanization 1950—1970, Volume I: Basic Data for Cities, Countries, and Regions*, Population Monograph Series No. 4 (Berkeley, Ca.: Institute of International Studies, 1969).

[28]"The urban agglomeration has been defined as including the suburban fringe or thickly settled territory lying outside of, but adjacent to, the city boundaries." *UN Demographic Yearbook 1966*, p. 24.

[29]For example, Dakar, Senegal, with 16 percent of the country's population, has over 70 percent of the country's commercial workers, consumes 35 percent of the country's electric power production, etc. Hance, *Population, Migration, and Urbanization*, p. 209. See on primate cities: Arnold S. Linsky, "Some Generalizations Concerning Primate Cities," *Annals of the Association of American Geographers*, 55 (1965): 506—13. Surrinder K. Mehta, "Some Demographic and Economic Correlates of Primate Cities: A Case for Revaluation," in *The City in Newly Developing Countries*, ed. Gerald Breese, pp. 295—308.

[30]This is the method used in Norton Ginsburg, ed., *Atlas of Economic Development* (Chicago: University of Chicago Press, 1961). For an alternative method see Harley L. Browning and Jack P. Gibbs, "Some Measures of Demographic and Spatial Relationships Among Cities," in *Urban Research Methods*, ed. Jack P. Gibbs (New York: Van Nostrand, 1961), pp. 436—461.

[31]A difference in procedure which may account for some systematic variation between the two data sources is the fact that we used our own national population estimates for 1955 in computing the percentage figure for the former French countries while the Ginsburg data were already in percent form. Since our national population estimates are calculated on the most recent data available, and since the earlier estimates of many African nations' populations are regarded as underestimates, the result may be an overestimation of the level of urbanism in the non-French countries. This is predicated on the assumption that the urban counts in the earlier censuses were more accurate than the total counts, thus a relatively "true" count of the cities' population was used with an underestimated population base. It is not possible to know the extent to which this may in fact have been the case.

[32]United Nations Economic Commission for Africa, *Urban Population in Africa*.

[33]For the 1955 discrepancies, the effect of using different population bases in calculating the percent figures may have lowered our estimates in the way outlined in the previous footnote. The largest differences for 1955 were for Guinea (60 percent) and Congo (34 percent). The 1965 differences may in part be attributed to the fact that the ECA data for Botswana and Gambia are for the year preceding our estimates.

[34]See *AID Economic Data Book 1973* and *U.S. Economic Commission for Africa Statistical Yearbook 1972*.

TABLE 1.1   Area of Country, 1980.

Definition: Total area enclosed within the natural boundaries, including that covered by water. Value is in thousands of square kilometers.

```
Range    =    2495.00
Mean     =     562.49
Standard Deviation =        587.81
```

Population Percent Cum.	Country	Rank	Country Name	A	Range Decile
6.24	6.24	1.0	Sudan	2506	1
14.53	8.29	2.0	Zaire	2345	
15.87	1.34	3.0	Chad	1284	5
17.20	1.33	4.0	Niger	1267	
19.15	1.95	5.0	Angola	1247	6
21.02	1.87	6.0	Mali	1240	
30.73	9.71	7.0	Ethiopia	1222	
31.19	.46	8.0	Mauritania	1031	
36.35	5.16	9.0	Tanzania	945	7
57.35	21.00	10.0	Nigeria	924	
57.64	.29	11.0	Namibia	824	
60.63	2.99	12.0	Mozambique	783	
62.28	1.65	13.0	Zambia	753	8
63.31	1.03	14.0	Somalia	638	
63.89	.58	15.0	Central African R	623	
64.12	.23	16.0	Botswana	600	
66.60	2.48	17.0	Madagascar	587	
71.20	4.60	18.0	Kenya	583	
73.61	2.41	19.0	Cameroon	475	9
75.87	2.26	20.0	Zimbabwe	391	
76.32	.45	21.0	Congo	342	
78.54	2.22	22.0	Ivory Coast	322	
80.51	1.97	23.0	Upper Volta	274	
80.67	.16	24.0	Gabon	268	
82.24	1.57	25.0	Guinea	246	10
85.75	3.51	26.0	Ghana	239	
89.70	3.95	27.0	Uganda	236	
91.34	1.64	28.0	Senegal	197	
93.00	1.66	29.0	Malawi	118	
94.00	1.00	30.0	Benin	113	
94.53	.53	31.0	Liberia	111	
95.52	.99	32.0	Sierra Leone	72	
96.27	.75	33.0	Togo	57	
96.46	.19	34.0	Guinea-Bissau	36	
96.84	.38	35.0	Lesotho	30	
98.12	1.28	36.5	Burundi	28	
98.22	.10	36.5	Equatorial Guinea	28	
99.58	1.36	38.0	Rwanda	26	
99.68	.10	39.0	Djibouti	23	
99.84	.16	40.0	Swaziland	17	
100.00	.17	41.0	Gambia	11	

SOURCE: *UN Statistical Yearbook 1979*, Table 18. See Part II, Country Profiles, for country area in square miles.

TABLE 1.2   Acres of Agricultural Land per Capita, 1972.

Comment: These figures are rough estimates and are based on varying definitions of agricultural (arable) land. For the sake of consistency a single source was used.

```
Range    =     14.83
Mean     =      2.20
Standard Deviation =        2.82
```

Population Percent Cum.	Country	Rank	Country Name	A	Range Decile
1.65	1.65	1.0	Zambia	14.83	1
3.52	1.87	2.0	Mali	9.69	4
4.10	.58	3.0	Central African R	7.70	5
5.43	1.33	4.0	Niger	6.06	6
13.72	8.29	5.0	Zaire	4.72	7
15.06	1.34	6.0	Chad	4.55	
15.59	.53	7.0	Liberia	2.93	9
16.58	.99	8.0	Sierra Leone	2.84	
18.22	1.64	9.0	Senegal	2.62	
20.63	2.41	10.0	Cameroon	2.56	
22.20	1.57	11.0	Guinea	2.55	
22.95	.75	12.0	Togo	2.29	
24.92	1.97	13.0	Upper Volta	1.89	
27.14	2.22	14.0	Ivory Coast	1.75	
27.43	.29	15.0	Namibia	1.74	
27.53	.10	16.0	Equatorial Guinea	1.65	
32.69	5.16	17.0	Tanzania	1.56	
36.20	3.51	18.0	Ghana	1.25	10
37.20	1.00	19.5	Benin	1.22	
37.36	.16	19.5	Swaziland	1.22	
37.55	.19	21.0	Guinea-Bissau	1.16	
38.00	.45	22.0	Congo	1.11	
38.46	.46	23.0	Mauritania	1.01	
48.17	9.71	24.5	Ethiopia	.93	
54.41	6.24	24.5	Sudan	.93	
54.58	.17	26.0	Gambia	.91	
57.06	2.48	27.0	Madagascar	.88	
78.06	21.00	28.0	Nigeria	.83	
79.09	1.03	29.0	Somalia	.72	
79.47	.38	30.0	Lesotho	.70	
83.42	3.95	31.0	Uganda	.69	
85.68	2.26	32.0	Zimbabwe	.68	
87.34	1.66	33.0	Malawi	.60	
88.62	1.28	34.0	Burundi	.59	
89.98	1.36	35.0	Rwanda	.58	
90.21	.23	36.5	Botswana	.56	
90.37	.16	36.5	Gabon	.56	
93.36	2.99	38.0	Mozambique	.52	
95.31	1.95	39.0	Angola	.34	
99.91	4.60	40.0	Kenya	.31	
100.00	.10	41.0	Djibouti	.0	

SOURCES: *U.S. AID Economic Data Book* 1973; A.I.D. *Africa: Economic Growth* (October 1974: Washington D.C.)
Note: The prolonged drought, particularly in the early 1970's, in the Sahelian region (including Senegal, Mauritania, Mali, Niger, Nigeria, Upper Volta, and Chad) and in Ethiopia and Somalia may have permanently destroyed the delicate ecological balance in large areas of grassland which have now become arid desert-like areas. The following countries have over 50 percent of their land in pasture and meadow: Angola, Botswana, Cameroon, Chad, Congo, Ethiopia, Gabon, Gambia, Kenya, Lesotho, Madagascar, Mali, Mauritania, Mozambique, Niger, Nigeria, Rwanda, Somalia, Sudan, Swaziland, Tanzania, Togo, Uganda, Upper Volta, Zaire, and Zambia. Ghana figure is for area under crops only.

TABLE 1.3 Non-Agricultural Development Potential Index, ca. 1977 (A), ca. 1972 (B) and ca. 1967 (C).

Definition: Summation of rankings on "short— and medium—run opportunities for development" in (a) forestry, (b) fishing, (c) mining, (d) hydropower, and (e) manufacturing. Scores can be roughly interpreted as follows:

4—7	Poor
8—11	Fair
12—14	Good
15—17	Excellent

Range =   13.00
Mean =   10.10
Standard Deviation =   3.66

Population Percent Cum.	Country	Rank	Country Name	A	Range Decile	B	C
.16	.16	2.0	Gabon	17	1	16	16
21.16	21.00	2.0	Nigeria	17		17	16
23.42	2.26	2.0	Zimbabwe	17		17	17
25.37	1.95	5.0	Angola	16		15	12
27.78	2.41	5.0	Cameroon	16		15	13
30.00	2.22	5.0	Ivory Coast	16		15	14
30.53	.53	7.5	Liberia	14	3	15	13
32.18	1.65	7.5	Zambia	14		14	14
32.63	.45	9.5	Congo	13	4	13	12
36.14	3.51	9.5	Ghana	13		14	12
38.62	2.48	12.0	Madagascar	12		12	12
41.61	2.99	12.0	Mozambique	12		11	11
49.90	8.29	12.0	Zaire	12		16	15
54.50	4.60	15.0	Kenya	11	5	11	10
54.79	.29	15.0	Namibia	11		11	11
54.95	.16	15.0	Swaziland	11		11	10
55.18	.23	19.0	Botswana	10	6	9	5
56.75	1.57	19.0	Guinea	10		14	14
58.39	1.64	19.0	Senegal	10		10	8
64.63	6.24	19.0	Sudan	10		8	7
68.58	3.95	19.0	Uganda	10		12	10
69.58	1.00	24.5	Benin	9	7	9	7
70.16	.58	24.5	Central African R	9		9	5
71.82	1.66	24.5	Malawi	9		9	8
72.81	.99	24.5	Sierra Leone	9		9	8
77.97	5.16	24.5	Tanzania	9		12	9
78.72	.75	24.5	Togo	9		9	6
80.06	1.34	29.5	Chad	8		6	4
80.23	.17	29.5	Gambia	8		6	5
80.69	.46	29.5	Mauritania	8		9	9
82.02	1.33	29.5	Niger	8		7	4
82.12	.10	33.5	Djibouti	7	8	7	7
91.83	9.71	33.5	Ethiopia	7		9	8
92.21	.38	33.5	Lesotho	7		7	4
94.08	1.87	33.5	Mali	7		7	5
95.36	1.28	37.5	Burundi	5	10	5	4
95.46	.10	37.5	Equatorial Guinea	5		7	7
95.65	.19	37.5	Guinea-Bissau	5		4	4
97.01	1.36	37.5	Rwanda	5		5	5
98.04	1.03	40.5	Somalia	4		4	4
100.00	1.97	40.5	Upper Volta	4		4	4

SOURCES: (1967) William A. Hance, *African Economic Development* (New York: Praeger, 1967), pp. 290—291. Authors' estimates for Botswana, Lesotho, Equatorial Guinea, Guinea-Bissau, Swaziland and Madagascar.
(1972 and 1977) Authors' estimates using the procedures from Hance, *African Economic Development, Ibid.*

TABLE 1.4 Estimated Population in Millions; 1980 (A); Year of Latest Census (B).

Definition: Year of latest census also includes year of sample survey if no census has been taken. Last two digits of the year are given.

Range =   72.30
Mean =   8.45
Standard Deviation =   12.54

Population Percent Cum.	Country	Rank	Country Name	A	Range Decile	B
21.00	21.00	1.0	Nigeria	72.6	1	77
30.71	9.71	2.0	Ethiopia	33.6	6	
39.00	8.29	3.0	Zaire	28.7	7	70
45.24	6.24	4.0	Sudan	21.6	8	73
50.40	5.16	5.0	Tanzania	17.8		74
55.00	4.60	6.0	Kenya	15.9		69
58.95	3.95	7.0	Uganda	13.7	9	69
62.46	3.51	8.0	Ghana	12.1		70
65.45	2.99	9.0	Mozambique	10.3		80
67.93	2.48	10.0	Madagascar	8.6		75
70.34	2.41	11.0	Cameroon	8.3		76
72.60	2.26	12.0	Zimbabwe	7.8		69
74.82	2.22	13.0	Ivory Coast	7.6		75
76.77	1.95	14.5	Angola	6.8	10	70
78.74	1.97	14.5	Upper Volta	6.8		75
80.61	1.87	16.0	Mali	6.5		76
82.27	1.66	18.0	Malawi	5.7		77
83.91	1.64	18.0	Senegal	5.7		76
85.56	1.65	18.0	Zambia	5.7		69
87.13	1.57	20.0	Guinea	5.4		72
88.46	1.33	21.0	Niger	5.3		77
89.82	1.36	22.0	Rwanda	4.7		78
91.16	1.34	23.0	Chad	4.6		68
92.44	1.28	24.0	Burundi	4.4		71
93.47	1.03	25.0	Somalia	3.6		75
94.47	1.00	26.0	Benin	3.5		79
95.46	.99	27.0	Sierra Leone	3.4		74
96.21	.75	28.0	Togo	2.6		70
96.79	.58	29.0	Central African R	2.0		75
97.32	.53	30.0	Liberia	1.9		74
97.78	.46	31.0	Mauritania	1.7		77
98.23	.45	32.0	Congo	1.5		74
98.61	.38	33.0	Lesotho	1.3		76
98.90	.29	34.0	Namibia	1.0		70
99.13	.23	35.0	Botswana	.8		81
99.30	.17	37.0	Gambia	.6		73
99.49	.19	37.0	Guinea-Bissau	.6		79
99.65	.16	37.0	Swaziland	.6		76
99.81	.16	39.0	Gabon	.5		72
99.91	.10	40.5	Djibouti	.3		76
100.00	.10	40.5	Equatorial Guinea	.3		60

SOURCES: *World Population 1977* (Washington, D. C.: U.S. Dept. of Commerce Bureau of the Census, 1978). Census dates are reported in the Country Profiles—Part II of the book and are derived from United Nations sources, *Africa South of the Sahara*, and individual country reports. In the case of Nigeria, the 1973 census was abrogated by the government and its final results never published, so that 1963 is taken as the last census.

TABLE 1.5   Population Density, 1980.

Definition: Value is persons per square kilometer. Area estimates include inland waters.

Range =   180.00
Mean =   32.85
Standard Deviation =   37.30

Population Percent Cum.	Country Percent	Rank	Country Name	A	Range Decile
1.36	1.36	1.0	Rwanda	181	1
2.64	1.28	2.0	Burundi	158	2
4.29	1.65	3.0	Zambia	82	6
25.29	21.00	4.0	Nigeria	79	
26.32	1.03	5.0	Somalia	61	7
30.27	3.95	6.0	Uganda	58	
30.44	.17	7.0	Gambia	54	8
33.95	3.51	8.0	Ghana	51	
35.61	1.66	9.0	Malawi	49	
36.60	.99	10.0	Sierra Leone	48	
37.35	.75	11.0	Togo	46	
37.73	.38	12.0	Lesotho	44	
37.89	.16	13.0	Swaziland	33	9
38.89	1.00	14.0	Benin	31	
40.53	1.64	15.0	Senegal	29	
50.24	9.71	16.5	Ethiopia	27	
54.84	4.60	16.5	Kenya	27	
56.81	1.97	18.0	Upper Volta	25	
59.03	2.22	19.0	Ivory Coast	24	
60.60	1.57	20.0	Guinea	22	
61.06	.46	21.0	Mauritania	21	
63.32	2.26	22.0	Zimbabwe	20	
68.48	5.16	23.0	Tanzania	19	10
70.89	2.41	24.5	Cameroon	18	
71.08	.19	24.5	Guinea-Bissau	18	
71.61	.53	26.0	Liberia	17	
74.09	2.48	27.0	Madagascar	15	
74.19	.10	28.0	Djibouti	14	
77.18	2.99	29.0	Mozambique	13	
77.28	.10	30.5	Equatorial Guinea	12	
85.57	8.29	30.5	Zaire	12	
91.81	6.24	32.0	Sudan	9	
93.76	1.95	34.0	Angola	5	
94.21	.45	34.0	Congo	5	
96.08	1.87	34.0	Mali	5	
97.42	1.34	36.5	Chad	4	
98.75	1.33	36.5	Niger	4	
99.33	.58	38.0	Central African R	3	
99.49	.16	39.0	Gabon	2	
99.72	.23	40.5	Botswana	1	
100.00	.29	40.5	Namibia	1	

SOURCE: Population data from Table 1.4; area data from Table 1.1.

TABLE 1.6   Estimated Percent Rate of Population Increase, Average Annual (A), 1970—1977 (B), 1960—1970

Definition: Rate of population increase is obtained by subtracting the death rate from the birth rate and adding the net immigration rate.

Range =   5.00
Mean =   2.64
Standard Deviation =   .75

Population Percent Cum.	Country Percent	Rank	Country Name	A	Range Decile	B
2.22	2.22	1.0	Ivory Coast	6.0	1	3.8
6.82	4.60	2.0	Kenya	3.8	5	3.5
7.35	.53	3.0	Liberia	3.4	6	3.2
9.61	2.26	4.0	Zimbabwe	3.3		3.9
9.78	.17	5.5	Gambia	3.1		3.2
11.44	1.66	5.5	Malawi	3.1		2.8
14.95	3.51	9.0	Ghana	3.0	7	2.4
16.52	1.57	9.0	Guinea	3.0		2.9
21.68	5.16	9.0	Tanzania	3.0		2.7
25.63	3.95	9.0	Uganda	3.0		3.7
27.28	1.65	9.0	Zambia	3.0		2.8
28.28	1.00	13.0	Benin	2.9		2.6
28.57	.29	13.0	Namibia	2.9		2.0
29.93	1.36	13.0	Rwanda	2.9		2.6
31.26	1.33	15.0	Niger	2.8		3.3
31.71	.45	17.0	Congo	2.7		2.1
32.17	.46	17.0	Mauritania	2.7		2.5
40.46	8.29	17.0	Zaire	2.7		2.0
61.46	21.00	20.5	Nigeria	2.6		2.5
63.10	1.64	20.5	Senegal	2.6		2.5
69.34	6.24	20.5	Sudan	2.6		2.3
70.09	.75	20.5	Togo	2.6		2.7
79.80	9.71	25.5	Ethiopia	2.5	8	2.4
82.28	2.48	25.5	Madagascar	2.5		2.2
84.15	1.87	25.5	Mali	2.5		2.4
85.14	.99	25.5	Sierra Leone	2.5		2.2
86.17	1.03	25.5	Somalia	2.5		2.4
86.33	.16	25.5	Swaziland	2.5		2.2
86.71	.38	29.0	Lesotho	2.4		2.0
88.66	1.95	31.0	Angola	2.3		1.6
88.76	.10	31.0	Djibouti	2.3		2.0
91.75	2.99	31.0	Mozambique	2.3		2.4
94.16	2.41	34.0	Cameroon	2.2		1.8
94.74	.58	34.0	Central African R	2.2		2.2
96.08	1.34	34.0	Chad	2.2		1.9
96.31	.23	36.5	Botswana	1.9	9	1.9
97.59	1.28	36.5	Burundi	1.9		2.4
97.69	.10	38.0	Equatorial Guinea	1.7		1.4
99.66	1.97	39.0	Upper Volta	1.6		1.6
99.85	.19	40.0	Guinea-Bissau	1.5	10	-.6
100.00	.16	41.0	Gabon	1.0		.6

SOURCE: *World Tables: The Second Edition (1980)*—Data Sheet I section.

TABLE 1.7 Percent European Population, ca. 1970(A), ca. 1960(B), and ca. 1926 (C).

Definition: "European" includes all whites. For 1926—Cameroon includes the European population of Douala only, Ghana includes British Togoland.

Range = 12.97
Mean = 1.35
Standard Deviation = 2.76

Population Percent		Rank	Country Name	A	Range Decile	B	C
Cum.	Country						
.29	.29	1.0	Namibia	13.00	1	14.10	1.14
.39	.10	2.0	Djibouti	11.70	2	14.10	
2.34	1.95	3.0	Angola	5.71	6	3.58	1.61
5.33	2.99	4.5	Mozambique	3.50	8	1.53	1.02
7.59	2.26	4.5	Zimbabwe	3.50		1.53	3.73
7.75	.16	6.0	Gabon	3.14		1.12	.17
7.91	.16	7.0	Swaziland	2.33	9	1.95	1.98
9.55	1.64	8.0	Senegal	1.22	10	2.00	.36
9.78	.23	9.0	Botswana	1.15		.80	.69
10.78	1.00	10.0	Benin	1.14		1.25	.06
11.23	.45	11.0	Congo	1.00		1.56	.13
13.45	2.22	12.0	Ivory Coast	.88		.56	.07
15.32	1.87	13.0	Mali	.76		.19	.06
19.92	4.60	14.0	Kenya	.73		.37	.34
20.50	.58	15.0	Central African R	.46		.40	.10
22.98	2.48	16.0	Madagascar	.45		1.50	.50
23.17	.19	17.5	Guinea-Bissau	.40		.50	.10
24.50	1.33	17.5	Niger	.40		.31	.02
24.60	.10	19.0	Equatorial Guinea	.37		2.87	.29
27.01	2.41	20.5	Cameroon	.34		.42	.07
30.96	3.95	20.5	Uganda	.34		.17	.05
31.49	.53	22.0	Liberia	.32		.20	.01
37.73	6.24	23.5	Sudan	.31		.27	.09
46.02	8.29	23.5	Zaire	.31		.84	.26
47.68	1.66	25.0	Malawi	.20		.17	.08
48.67	.99	26.0	Sierra Leone	.19		.09	.07
49.05	.38	27.0	Lesotho	.18		.28	.34
52.56	3.51	28.5	Ghana	.16		.16	.07
53.02	.46	28.5	Mauritania	.16		.21	.04
54.36	1.34	30.5	Chad	.13		.10	.03
75.36	21.00	30.5	Nigeria	.13		.10	.02
85.07	9.71	32.0	Ethiopia	.12		.13	.03
86.35	1.28	33.5	Burundi	.11		.07	.01
91.51	5.16	33.5	Tanzania	.11		.22	.13
93.08	1.57	35.0	Guinea	.10		.06	.10
93.25	.17	36.0	Gambia	.08		.33	.10
94.28	1.03	37.5	Somalia	.07		.24	.13
95.03	.75	37.5	Togo	.07		.14	.08
97.00	1.97	39.0	Upper Volta	.06		.09	.02
98.65	1.65	40.0	Zambia	.05		2.31	.54
100.00	1.36	41.0	Rwanda	.03		.15	.02

SOURCES: (1960) Unless otherwise indicated, data source is an official government census report. *Cameroon, Central African Republic, Gabon, Liberia, Mali, Mauritania, Niger*: Outre-mer 1958 (Paris: Republique Francaise, Ministere d'Outre-mer, Service des Statistics, 1960); *Nigeria, Somalia*: Francisco H. Blasco, *Africa Tercer Mundo* (Barcelona: Corona, 1966); *Sierra Leone, Tanzania*: U.N. Statistical Yearbook 1961—61; *Burundi, Rwanda*: Office de l'Information et des Relations Publique du Congo Belge et du Ruanda-Urundi, *Ruanda-Urundi Geography and History* (Brussels: 1960), p. 52; *Ghana*: Walter Birmingham et al., eds., *A Study of Contemporary Ghana*, Vol. 2 (London: Allen and Unwin, 1967); *Benin*: includes all non-indigenous population; *Burundi, Guinea, Rwanda*: for the main urban centers only; *Ivory Coast*: 1965 figure; *Chad*: Guide Afrique Equatoriale 1962-63; *Zaire*: Howard M. Epstein, ed., *Revolt in Congo 1900-1964* (New York: Facts on File, 1965) p. 173; *Zambia*: George Kay, *A Social Geography of Zambia* (London: University of London Press, 1967); *Botswana, Burundi, Cameroon, Chad, Congo, Benin, Gambia, Guinea, Ivory Coast, Kenya, Lesotho, Malawi, Mali, Mauritania, Nigeria, Rwanda, Senegal, Sierra Leone, Somalia, Sudan, Tanzania, Upper Volta*: extrapolations on a straight line basis were made for these countries. *Madagascar*: Junod, *African Handbook*.

(1970)Various U.S. State Department publications, principally the State Department. *Background Notes* on the various countries; *Rwanda, Upper Volta, Togo, Kenya, Equatorial Guinea, Gabon*: Statesman's Yearbook 1970—71 and 1971—72.

(1926) D. Martens and O. Karstedt, *The African Handbook*, 2nd ed. (London: Allen and Unwin, 1938). Population data for the years indicated is from Appendix 5. *Central African Republic, Congo, Gabon*: J. Brummelkamp, *Social Geografie van Afrika*, Vol. 2 (Groningen: J. B. Wolters, 1930); *Liberia*: R. P. Strong, ed., *The African Republic of Liberia and the Belgian Congo* (Cambridge: Harvard University Press, 1930), pp. 42—44; *Angola, Equatorial Guinea, Madagascar, Mozambique, Swaziland*: Statesman's Yearbook, various editions. Data is for 1926 except for: *Botswana, Gambia, Sierra Leone*: 1921; *Ethiopia, Swaziland*: 1927; *Liberia, Mozambique, Nigeria, Tanzania, Zambia*: 1928; *Cameroon, Benin, Equatorial Guinea, Kenya, Lesotho, Malawi, Somalia, Togo, Uganda, Upper Volta*: 1929; *Zaire*: 1930; *Ghana*: 1930; *Central African Republic, Guinea, Mali*: 1926 estimates were made by extrapolating between 1920 and 1930 data; *Angola, Swaziland, Madagascar*: Statesman's Yearbook, various years.

TABLE 1.8   Index of Urban Concentration 1977 (A), 1972 (B), 1965 (C).

Definition: The Herfindahl—Hirschman index.

```
Range =          .95
Mean =           .53
Standard Deviation =       .27
```

Population Percent Cum.	Country	Rank	Country Name	A	Range Decile	B	C
1.28	1.28	4.5	Burundi	1.00	1	1.00	1.00
1.38	.10	4.5	Djibouti	1.00		1.00	1.00
1.55	.17	4.5	Gambia	1.00		1.00	1.00
1.74	.19	4.5	Guinea-Bissau	1.00		1.00	1.00
2.12	.38	4.5	Lesotho	1.00		1.00	1.00
2.65	.53	4.5	Liberia	1.00		1.00	1.00
2.94	.29	4.5	Namibia	1.00		1.00	1.00
4.30	1.36	4.5	Rwanda	1.00		1.00	1.00
5.29	.99	9.0	Sierra Leone	.83	2	.75	.74
7.51	2.22	10.0	Ivory Coast	.71	4	.52	.42
9.08	1.57	11.0	Guinea	.65		.65	
10.95	1.87	12.0	Mali	.61	5	.53	.39
14.90	3.95	13.0	Uganda	.59		.54	.49
15.06	.16	14.0	Gabon	.58		.58	.54
15.81	.75	15.0	Togo	.57		.57	.68
15.91	.10	16.0	Equatorial Guinea	.56		.56	.51
20.51	4.60	17.0	Kenya	.52	6	.47	.42
22.17	1.66	18.5	Malawi	.51		.57	
22.63	.46	18.5	Mauritania	.51		.41	
22.79	.16	20.0	Swaziland	.50		.35	.26
24.74	1.95	21.0	Angola	.47		.47	
25.19	.45	22.5	Congo	.45		.48	.35
30.35	5.16	22.5	Tanzania	.45		.32	.22
32.83	2.48	24.0	Madagascar	.42	7	.42	.18
34.16	1.33	25.0	Niger	.39		.32	.30
35.80	1.64	26.0	Senegal	.38		.38	.32
36.38	.58	28.0	Central African R	.37		.37	.28
39.37	2.99	28.0	Mozambique	.37		.37	.36
41.34	1.97	28.0	Upper Volta	.37		.38	.39
44.85	3.51	30.0	Ghana	.35		.35	.30
47.11	2.26	31.0	Zimbabwe	.33	8	.35	.35
56.82	9.71	32.0	Ethiopia	.32		.42	.37
57.85	1.03	33.0	Somalia	.31		.31	.30
58.85	1.00	34.0	Benin	.30		.42	.35
60.19	1.34	35.0	Chad	.29		.42	.38
68.48	8.29	36.0	Zaire	.27		.51	
70.89	2.41	37.0	Cameroon	.23	9	.24	.25
71.12	.23	39.0	Botswana	.18		.34	.26
77.36	6.24	39.0	Sudan	.18		.18	.16
79.01	1.65	39.0	Zambia	.18		.14	.14
100.00	21.00	41.0	Nigeria	.05		.05	.05

SOURCES: On the index's definition see Rein Taagepera "Inequality, Concentration, Imbalance" *Political Methodology* 6, 3 1978—9, 275—92. The data comes from Part II of this Handbook.

TABLE 1.9   Estimated Percent of Population in Cities of 20,000 and More, ca. 1955.

Definition: It is not always clear whether the populations given for the largest cities are for urban agglomerations or for the political entity only. It is presumed that the data does not include surrounding population. Since a large number of countries had such a low level of urbanization, data is presented to one decimal point. The reliability of the data is not high, so only the whole percentages should be taken as relatively reliable.

```
Range =          48.40
Mean =            5.77
Standard Deviation =       8.14
```

Population Percent Cum.	Country	Rank	Country Name	A	Range Decile
.10	.10	1.0	Djibouti	48.4	1
.55	.45	2.0	Congo	17.7	7
.65	.10	3.0	Equatorial Guinea	16.0	
2.29	1.64	4.0	Senegal	14.8	
4.55	2.26	5.0	Zimbabwe	14.0	8
6.20	1.65	6.0	Zambia	11.4	
27.20	21.00	7.0	Nigeria	9.4	9
27.37	.17	8.0	Gambia	8.3	
35.66	8.29	9.0	Zaire	8.0	
36.24	.58	10.0	Central African R	7.4	
39.75	3.51	11.0	Ghana	6.4	
42.23	2.48	12.0	Madagascar	6.2	
44.18	1.95	13.0	Angola	6.0	
44.47	.29	14.0	Namibia	5.8	
46.69	2.22	15.0	Ivory Coast	5.3	
52.93	6.24	16.0	Sudan	5.0	
55.34	2.41	17.5	Cameroon	4.7	10
55.50	.16	17.5	Gabon	4.7	
56.50	1.00	19.0	Benin	4.2	
57.53	1.03	20.0	Somalia	3.9	
62.13	4.60	21.0	Kenya	3.8	
63.12	.99	22.0	Sierra Leone	3.1	
63.87	.75	23.0	Togo	2.8	
66.86	2.99	24.0	Mozambique	2.4	
67.39	.53	25.5	Liberia	2.2	
69.26	1.87	25.5	Mali	2.2	
70.83	1.57	27.0	Guinea	2.1	
72.17	1.34	28.5	Chad	2.0	
74.14	1.97	28.5	Upper Volta	2.0	
83.85	9.71	30.0	Ethiopia	1.7	
89.01	5.16	31.0	Tanzania	1.5	
92.96	3.95	32.0	Uganda	.9	
94.29	1.33	33.0	Niger	.8	
95.57	1.28	34.0	Burundi	.7	
97.23	1.66	35.0	Malawi	.6	
97.46	.23	38.5	Botswana	0	
97.65	.19	38.5	Guinea-Bissau	0	
98.03	.38	38.5	Lesotho	0	
98.49	.46	38.5	Mauritania	0	
99.85	1.36	38.5	Rwanda	0	
100.00	.16	38.5	Swaziland	0	

SOURCES: Leo F. Schnore, "Economic Development and Urbanization: An Ecological Approach," data republished in N. Ginsburg, *Atlas of Economic Development* (Chicago: University of Chicago, 1961), p. 34. The Schnore data uses his own population estimates while the *Démographie Comparée* data was used with the 1955 population estimates given in Appendix 5 (first edition). Cameroon, Chad, Congo, Benin, Gabon, Guinea, Ivory Coast, Mali, Niger, Senegal, Togo, Upper Volta: *Démographie Comparée* (1966); *Nigeria*: Schnore figure adjusted by population estimate for Nigeria in Appendix 5 (first edition); *Botswana, Lesotho, Guinea-Bissau, Swaziland, Rwanda, Mauritania*: no city over 20,000; *Equatorial Guinea*: based on extrapolation from 1965 (24%) and 1960 (20%); *Angola*: U.S. Army Area Handbook for Angola, p. 63.

TABLE 1.10 Estimated Percent of Population in Cities of 20,000 and More, ca. 1977 (A), 1972 (B) and 1965 (C).

Definition: Largest cities' population is for urban agglomeration if this figure is available. Cities whose population is slightly below 20,000 according to earlier data are included if their population was expected to pass 20,000 by the urbanization date. The complete list of cities for ca. 1965 is given by country in Part II of the first edition. The complete list of cities for circa 1977 data is given in Part II of this edition.

Range = 48.00
Mean = 17.05
Standard Deviation = 10.76

Population Percent Cum.	Country	Rank	Country Name	A	Range Decile	B	C
.10	.10	1.0	Djibouti	50	1	53	81
.26	.16	2.0	Gabon	40	3	24	18
.71	.45	3.0	Congo	37		32	30
2.36	1.65	4.0	Zambia	36		30	20
2.94	.58	5.0	Central African R	31	4	22	18
3.97	1.03	6.0	Somalia	29	5	22	14
24.97	21.00	7.0	Nigeria	28		23	14
26.61	1.64	8.0	Senegal	27		27	24
28.83	2.22	9.0	Ivory Coast	26	6	21	14
28.93	.10	10.0	Equatorial Guinea	25		24	24
29.10	.17	11.5	Gambia	22		16	13
37.39	8.29	11.5	Zaire	22		17	12
40.90	3.51	13.0	Ghana	20	7	20	16
41.13	.23	14.0	Botswana	19		10	3
43.54	2.41	16.0	Cameroon	17		15	9
45.11	1.57	16.0	Guinea	17		15	7
47.37	2.26	16.0	Zimbabwe	17		10	8
48.36	.99	18.0	Sierra Leone	15	8	12	7
50.31	1.95	21.0	Angola	14		11	9
51.31	1.00	21.0	Benin	14		11	10
52.65	1.34	21.0	Chad	14		9	6
52.84	.19	21.0	Guinea-Bissau	14		14	10
53.30	.46	21.0	Mauritania	14		7	1
55.78	2.48	24.5	Madagascar	13		13	9
56.53	.75	24.5	Togo	13		14	8
57.06	.53	26.0	Liberia	12		9	9
58.93	1.87	28.5	Mali	11	9	6	6
65.17	6.24	28.5	Sudan	11		10	7
65.33	.16	28.5	Swaziland	11		11	6
67.30	1.97	28.5	Upper Volta	11		5	4
71.90	4.60	31.5	Kenya	10		9	7
74.89	2.99	31.5	Mozambique	10		8	6
75.18	.29	33.0	Namibia	9		9	8
80.34	5.16	34.0	Tanzania	8		6	5
90.05	9.71	35.5	Ethiopia	7		6	5
91.38	1.33	35.5	Niger	7		5	4
93.04	1.66	37.0	Malawi	6	10	4	3
94.32	1.28	38.5	Burundi	4		2	2
94.70	.38	38.5	Lesotho	4		3	2
96.06	1.36	40.5	Rwanda	2		1	1
100.00	3.95	40.5	Uganda	2		5	3

TABLE 1.11 Average Annual Rate of Increase in Percent of the Population in Cities of 20,000 or More Inhabitants, 1965—77 (A) and 1955—65 (B).

Definition: This is the growth of the percent of the population in all cities over 20,000 in population from 1965 (1955) to 1977 (1965). Cities are included if they were over the population minimum by the end of the period.

Range = 146.50
Mean = 9.22
Standard Deviation = 20.88

Population Percent Cum.	Country	Rank	Country Name	A	Range Decile	B
.46	.46	1.0	Mauritania	108.0	1	20.0
2.33	1.87	2.0	Mali	69.0	3	17.3
2.56	.23	3.0	Botswana	44.4	5	13.1
4.53	1.97	4.0	Upper Volta	14.6	7	10.0
5.87	1.34	5.0	Chad	11.1		20.0
6.03	.16	6.0	Gabon	10.2		28.3
7.02	.99	7.0	Sierra Leone	9.5		12.6
8.05	1.03	8.0	Somalia	8.9		25.9
9.33	1.28	11.0	Burundi	8.3		18.6
9.71	.38	11.0	Lesotho	8.3		10.0
11.37	1.66	11.0	Malawi	8.3		40.0
32.37	21.00	11.0	Nigeria	8.3		4.9
33.73	1.36	11.0	Rwanda	8.3		27.5
36.14	2.41	14.0	Cameroon	7.4		9.5
38.36	2.22	15.0	Ivory Coast	7.1		16.4
38.52	.16	16.0	Swaziland	6.9		14.2
40.17	1.65	17.0	Zambia	6.7		7.5
41.50	1.33	18.0	Niger	6.3		40.0
42.08	.58	19.0	Central African R	6.0		14.3
42.25	.17	20.0	Gambia	5.8		6.3
45.24	2.99	21.0	Mozambique	5.6		17.1
45.99	.75	22.0	Togo	5.2	8	18.6
51.15	5.16	23.0	Tanzania	5.0		23.3
52.72	1.57	24.0	Guinea	4.9		23.3
58.96	6.24	25.0	Sudan	4.8		4.0
67.25	8.29	26.0	Zaire	3.8		5.0
71.85	4.60	27.0	Kenya	3.6		8.4
72.85	1.00	28.5	Benin	3.3		13.8
73.04	.19	28.5	Guinea-Bissau	3.3		13.8
74.99	1.95	30.0	Angola	3.0		4.6
75.52	.53	31.0	Liberia	2.8		30.9
78.00	2.48	32.0	Madagascar	2.6		4.5
87.71	9.71	33.0	Ethiopia	2.4		19.4
91.22	3.51	34.0	Ghana	2.1		15.0
91.67	.45	35.0	Congo	1.9		6.9
91.96	.29	36.5	Namibia	1.0		3.8
93.60	1.64	36.5	Senegal	1.0		6.2
93.70	.10	38.0	Equatorial Guinea	.3		5.0
95.96	2.26	39.0	Zimbabwe	-.5		2.9
99.91	3.95	40.0	Uganda	-2.8		23.3
100.00	.10	41.0	Djibouti	-38.5	10	68.0

SOURCE: See Tables 1.09 and 1.10.

SOURCES: (1965) *U.N. Demographic Yearbook 1967* and various other sources listed in Part II (first edition). *Zaire*: Estimate, 1965 data unavailable. *Angola*: Interpolation between 1960 and 1972. *Madagascar*: Estimate from 1960 and 1972 data. *Mozambique*: Estimated by interpolation between 1957 and 1972 data. Botswana: No cities over 20,000 in 1965; cities with over 20,000 at a later date are used as basis for this calculation.

(1972) *U.N. Demographic Yearbook 1973* and *1974*; *Africa South of the Sahara, 1973, 1974,* and *1975*; and various other sources as cited in Part II. 1972 population estimates taken by decrementing 1975 figures from *1975 World Population Data Sheet* (Washington D.C.: Population Reference Bureau, 1975).

(1977) See urban sections in Part II.

TABLE 1.12   Number of Cities, 20,000 or More in Population per Million National Population, 1977 (A), 1972 (B), and 1965 (C).

```
Range =              6.64
Mean =               1.66
Standard Deviation =        1.53
```

Population Percent Cum.	Country	Rank	Country Name	A	Range Decile	B	C
.23	.23	1.0	Botswana	6.9	1	4.6	1.9
.33	.10	2.0	Equatorial Guinea	6.2	2	6.7	8.0
.91	.58	3.0	Central African R	4.3	4	4.5	4.6
1.01	.10	4.0	Djibouti	4.0	5	10.1	11.8
1.17	.16	5.0	Swaziland	3.9		2.1	0
1.33	.16	6.0	Gabon	3.8		3.8	4.1
1.78	.45	7.0	Congo	2.8	7	4.1	3.4
2.24	.46	8.0	Mauritania	2.7		1.6	0
23.24	21.00	9.0	Nigeria	2.6		2.3	2.7
23.41	.17	10.5	Gambia	1.8	8	2.1	2.8
24.44	1.03	10.5	Somalia	1.8		2.0	2.2
26.08	1.64	12.0	Senegal	1.8		1.7	1.9
27.73	1.65	13.0	Zambia	1.7		1.8	2.2
28.48	.75	14.0	Togo	1.7		1.4	1.3
28.67	.19	15.0	Guinea-Bissau	1.6		1.5	2.2
30.01	1.34	16.0	Chad	1.6		1.0	1.1
31.01	1.00	17.0	Benin	1.6	9	1.1	1.5
33.42	2.41	18.0	Cameroon	1.4		1.6	1.8
35.68	2.26	19.0	Zimbabwe	1.1		1.2	1.3
39.19	3.51	20.0	Ghana	1.1		1.3	1.5
39.48	.29	21.0	Namibia	1.1		1.2	1.5
41.70	2.22	22.0	Ivory Coast	1.0		1.1	1.4
43.65	1.95	23.0	Angola	.9		1.0	1.1
46.13	2.48	24.0	Madagascar	.9	10	1.0	1.1
48.00	1.87	25.5	Mali	.8		1.0	1.0
49.33	1.33	25.5	Niger	.8		.9	1.0
50.90	1.57	27.5	Guinea	.8		.7	.8
51.28	.38	27.5	Lesotho	.8		.9	0
56.44	5.16	29.0	Tanzania	.7		.9	.9
64.73	8.29	30.0	Zaire	.6		.7	.7
65.72	.99	31.5	Sierra Leone	.6		1.1	.9
67.69	1.97	31.5	Upper Volta	.6		.7	.7
68.22	.53	33.0	Liberia	.6		.8	.9
69.88	1.66	34.0	Malawi	.6		.4	.5
76.12	6.24	35.0	Sudan	.6		.9	.9
77.48	1.36	36.0	Rwanda	.5		.3	.3
82.08	4.60	37.5	Kenya	.4		.5	.4
85.07	2.99	37.5	Mozambique	.4		.5	.6
94.78	9.71	39.0	Ethiopia	.4		.4	.4
98.73	3.95	40.0	Uganda	.3		.5	.4
100.00	1.28	41.0	Burundi	.2		.3	.3

TABLE 1.13   Population of Largest City, in Thousands, ca. 1977 (A), 1972 (B) and 1966 (C).

Definition: Population is given, where applicable, for urban agglomeration. Original data from earlier or later years were adjusted to provide a 1966 estimate. A similar procedure is followed for the 1977 and 1972 data. The capital is the largest city in all countries except Cameroon and Swaziland, see Part II for details.

```
Range =              2540.00
Mean =               512.07
Standard Deviation =         568.43
```

Population Percent Cum.	Country	Rank	Country Name	A	Range Decile	B	C
8.29	8.29	1.0	Zaire	2570	1	1600	1000
29.29	21.00	2.0	Nigeria	2500		1600	1000
39.00	9.71	3.0	Ethiopia	1400	5	912	640
41.22	2.22	4.0	Ivory Coast	1300	6	750	405
47.46	6.24	5.0	Sudan	1000	7	740	463
50.97	3.51	6.0	Ghana	936		800	600
52.54	1.57	7.0	Guinea	850		525	180
54.18	1.64	8.0	Senegal	840		700	520
58.78	4.60	9.0	Kenya	776	8	600	396
60.73	1.95	10.0	Angola	700		538	375
65.89	5.16	11.5	Tanzania	600		425	255
68.15	2.26	11.5	Zimbabwe	600		490	300
70.56	2.41	13.0	Cameroon	560		310	220
73.04	2.48	14.0	Madagascar	546		367	300
74.69	1.65	15.0	Zambia	520	9	348	170
75.72	1.03	16.0	Somalia	470		315	170
77.59	1.87	17.0	Mali	420		210	170
80.58	2.99	18.5	Mozambique	400		450	282
84.53	3.95	18.5	Uganda	400		348	175
85.11	.58	20.0	Central African R	330		200	160
86.10	.99	21.0	Sierra Leone	320		496	148
86.55	.45	22.0	Congo	310		230	167
87.89	1.34	23.0	Chad	300		179	120
88.64	.75	24.0	Togo	229	10	232	129
90.30	1.66	25.0	Malawi	222		120	110
91.63	1.33	26.0	Niger	210		102	55
92.16	.53	27.0	Liberia	199		140	89
93.16	1.00	28.0	Benin	196		175	115
95.13	1.97	29.0	Upper Volta	180		130	78
96.41	1.28	30.0	Burundi	163		82	74
96.57	.16	31.0	Gabon	150		87	53
97.03	.46	32.0	Mauritania	140		48	15
97.13	.10	33.0	Djibouti	125		74	70
97.30	.17	34.0	Gambia	97		75	43
98.66	1.36	35.0	Rwanda	90		27	15
98.95	.29	36.0	Namibia	85		70	50
99.14	.19	37.0	Guinea-Bissau	84		70	70
99.24	.10	38.0	Equatorial Guinea	60		48	23
99.62	.38	39.0	Lesotho	47		29	18
99.85	.23	40.0	Botswana	40		23	12
100.00	.16	41.0	Swaziland	30		30	14

SOURCES: Cities are listed with sources by country in Part II: 1965 (first edition), and 1977 and 1972 (this edition).

SOURCES: *U.N. Demographic Yearbook 1967 and 1973* and other sources. See Part II for information on individual cities and sources. 1966 data see first edition and 1977 and 1972 data see this edition.

TABLE 1.14 Primacy of Capital City; 1977 (A), 1972 (B) and 1966 (C).

Definition: Population of the capital city divided by the sum of the population of the four largest cities (including the capital): multiplied by 100. Where fewer than four cities are 20,000 or above in population, divided by the population of the two or three largest cities. In countries where only the capital city had a population of 20,000 or more, the index is defined as 100. Where urban agglomeration data is available, it is used. The higher the index value, the greater the primacy.

```
Range =            72.00
Mean =             68.27
Standard Deviation =        20.98
```

Population Percent Cum.	Country	Rank	Country Name	A	Range Decile	B	C
1.28	1.28	4.0	Burundi	100	1	100	100
1.38	.10	4.0	Djibouti	100		100	100
1.55	.17	4.0	Gambia	100		100	100
1.74	.19	4.0	Guinea-Bissau	100		100	100
2.12	.38	4.0	Lesotho	100		100	100
2.65	.53	4.0	Liberia	100		100	100
2.94	.29	4.0	Namibia	100		100	100
3.93	.99	8.0	Sierra Leone	91	2	61	85
5.50	1.57	9.0	Guinea	84	3	84	78
6.86	1.36	10.0	Rwanda	81		100	100
8.81	1.95	11.5	Angola	79		72	69
13.97	5.16	11.5	Tanzania	79		65	59
15.84	1.87	13.0	Mali	77	4	71	63
16.42	.58	15.5	Central African R	74		61	59
26.13	9.71	15.5	Ethiopia	74		71	69
28.35	2.22	15.5	Ivory Coast	74		75	66
29.10	.75	15.5	Togo	74		80	100
29.26	.16	18.5	Gabon	73		71	66
33.21	3.95	18.5	Uganda	73		70	75
34.85	1.64	20.5	Senegal	72		68	73
41.09	6.24	20.5	Sudan	72		73	69
42.43	1.34	22.0	Chad	68	5	62	56
42.89	.46	23.0	Mauritania	67		56	100
45.37	2.48	24.0	Madagascar	65		66	69
46.70	1.33	25.0	Niger	63	6	49	44
51.30	4.60	26.5	Kenya	62		63	58
54.29	2.99	26.5	Mozambique	62		59	62
62.58	8.29	28.0	Zaire	61		60	61
63.61	1.03	29.0	Somalia	59		57	55
84.61	21.00	30.0	Nigeria	58		50	43
88.12	3.51	31.0	Ghana	57		62	64
90.38	2.26	32.0	Zimbabwe	55	7	50	45
90.83	.45	33.0	Congo	54		60	60
90.99	.16	34.0	Swaziland	50		39	100
92.96	1.97	35.0	Upper Volta	49	8	44	46
94.61	1.65	36.0	Zambia	38	9	36	33
94.84	.23	37.0	Botswana	36		36	100
97.25	2.41	38.0	Cameroon	32	10	33	26
97.35	.10	39.5	Equatorial Guinea	29		32	50
99.01	1.66	39.5	Malawi	29		30	13
100.00	1.00	41.0	Benin	28		32	31

SOURCES: (1965) *U.N. Demographic Yearbook 1967* and other sources. See Part II, first edition, for detailed information by country. *Congo, Guinea, Upper Volta*: index calculated on three cities; *Gabon, Malawi, Sierra Leone, Uganda*: index calculated on two cities; *Sudan*: Khartoum, Khartoum North and Omdurman have been treated as a single primate city.
(1972) Sources as cited in Part II.
(1977) Sources as cited in Part II.

TABLE 1.15 Average Annual Percent Increase in the Captial City Population, 1966 to 1977 (A) and 1950 to 1967 (B).

Definition: Population of capital city in 1977, which includes urban agglomeration data where applicable, divided by the population of the capital city in 1966 minus one and times 100. A similar procedure is followed for the change from 1950 to 1967.

```
Range =            59.00
Mean =             15.10
Standard Deviation =        12.03
```

Population Percent Cum.	Country	Rank	Country Name	A	Range Decile	B
.46	.46	1.0	Mauritania	62	1	60
.69	.23	2.0	Botswana	51	2	60
2.35	1.66	3.0	Malawi	40	4	7
3.92	1.57	4.0	Guinea	34	5	24
5.25	1.33	5.5	Niger	26	7	33
6.61	1.36	5.5	Rwanda	26		2
8.83	2.22	7.0	Ivory Coast	22		16
10.48	1.65	8.0	Zambia	19	8	7
10.64	.16	9.0	Gabon	17		20
11.67	1.03	10.0	Somalia	16		7
11.77	.10	11.5	Equatorial Guinea	15		4
12.15	.38	11.5	Lesotho	15		15
14.56	2.41	14.0	Cameroon	14	9	9
15.90	1.34	14.0	Chad	14		15
17.77	1.87	14.0	Mali	14		5
22.93	5.16	16.5	Tanzania	13		10
31.22	8.29	16.5	Zaire	13		8
52.22	21.00	19.0	Nigeria	12		11
56.17	3.95	19.0	Uganda	12		13
58.14	1.97	19.0	Upper Volta	12		8
59.42	1.28	23.5	Burundi	11		19
59.59	.17	23.5	Gambia	11		7
60.12	.53	23.5	Liberia	11		5
61.11	.99	23.5	Sierra Leone	11		4
67.35	6.24	23.5	Sudan	11		9
67.51	.16	23.5	Swaziland	11		22
68.09	.58	27.0	Central African R	10		8
68.54	.45	29.5	Congo	9		4
78.25	9.71	29.5	Ethiopia	9		5
78.44	.19	29.5	Guinea-Bissau	9		10
80.70	2.26	29.5	Zimbabwe	9		14
82.65	1.95	32.5	Angola	8	10	11
87.25	4.60	32.5	Kenya	8		10
87.35	.10	34.5	Djibouti	7		8
88.10	.75	34.5	Togo	7		17
90.58	2.48	36.5	Madagascar	6		4
90.87	.29	36.5	Namibia	6		4
91.87	1.00	39.0	Benin	5		8
95.38	3.51	39.0	Ghana	5		20
97.02	1.64	39.0	Senegal	5		3
100.00	2.99	41.0	Mozambique	3		16

SOURCES: (1950 to 1967) *U.N. Demographic Yearbook 1967* and other sources listed in Part II, first edition, by country.
(1966 to 1977) See Part II, second edition.
Mauritania, Botswana: Capital is a new city. The measure is arbitrarily taken as 60 for each year during the period. *Malawi*: has changed its capital from Zomba to Lilongwe. We use Lilongwe in these calculations.

2. Cultural Pluralism

The three major types of cultural pluralism in Black Africa are those based on differences in language, religion and ethnicity. We will consider each of these in this chapter.

In the tradition of J. S. Furnivall, the term *cultural pluralism* is used to refer to the extent to which national populations are divided into mutually exclusive and culturally distinctive groups.[1] He was describing the social structure of tropical colonies in which the inhabitants participated in the colonial economic market but lived otherwise in relatively separate societies with distinct values, customs and institutions. So conceptualized, cultural pluralism was seen as a threat to political integration and stability in the post-colonial period. There is a considerable body of political theory that suggests that modernization and social mobilization tend to produce social and political disruption and instability by exacerbating the latent conflicts between segments of culturally plural populations, and by reinforcing the pre-existing lines of cultural segregation with overlapping cleavages based on new patterns of economic stratification.[2] In various and complex ways, however, the types of pluralism may overlap, creating cross-cutting cleavages. For example, in Nigeria some of the Yoruba share a common religion with the Hausa, Islam. These cross-cutting cleavages generally develop from voluntary identification with universal religions, the use of *lingua francas* and the shared values and customs of particular ethnic groups, and have the potential of moderating conflict between culturally plural groups. The complexity of the patterns of language, religion and ethnicity in Black African states which are described below should caution against facile references to "tribalism" in the examination of contemporary African affairs.

a. Language Pluralism

Language Distribution and Classification

According to Knappert,[3] there are over one thousand indigenous languages in the forty-one countries included in this Handbook. Many linguists estimate the actual number to be somewhat higher. Language distribution is difficult to assess in Africa because scholars disagree on whether a particular designation refers to the dialect of a language, a single language, or a group of closely related languages. A number of classification schemes have been proposed. Most tend to follow one or the other of two major organizing principles: (1) etiological or historical relatedness between languages (exemplified in the work of Westermann and Bryan,[4] and Guthrie[5]); (2) typologies based on similarities between languages (exemplified in the work of Dalby, Greenberg[6] and the Voegelins[7]). A good deal of controversy has surrounded the issue of classification, but such literature[8] will not be reviewed in this Handbook. For our purpose, to illustrate the idea of language families, we selected the Greenberg classification. This classification, which first appeared in 1955, and then in revised form (with fewer over-all categories) in 1963, has come to be widely accepted. We also report the more recent coding scheme by Dalby in the country sections of Part II.

The Greenberg classification identifies four major language families (or "macro-phyla," according to the Voegelins), which may be regarded as roughly comparable in degree of comprehensiveness to the "Indo-European" language family (which includes such widely different languages as Russian, Persian, English and Hindi-Urdi). The four language families are: (I) Congo-Kordofanian, which includes both the Bantu of East and Central Africa, as well as most of the languages of West Africa; (II) Nilo-Saharan, which groups such languages of the Sudanic belt as Songhai and Kanuri together with the several Nilotic northeastern languages; (III) Afro-Asiatic, including Arabic, the Semitic languages of Ethiopia, the Berber languages of North Africa, ancient Egyptian (now extinct), and Hausa; and (IV) Khoisan, which includes the languages of a few very small societies such as the Bushmen and Hottentots (now extinct).

The basis of the Greenberg classification is typological: i.e., a comparison of basic vocabulary and grammatical elements between the various African languages for similarity of sound (phonology) and meaning or function (semantics and morphology). The major sections within each of the four language families are summarized in Figure 2.1. Notice that Bantu languages form only a sub-category in the Benue-Congo section of Congo-Kordofania. Although Guthrie and Dalby suggest major families within the Bantu languages,[9] we have not made such distinctions in our coding of language families. In Part II of this Handbook, every language group which constitutes 5 percent or more of the population within each language

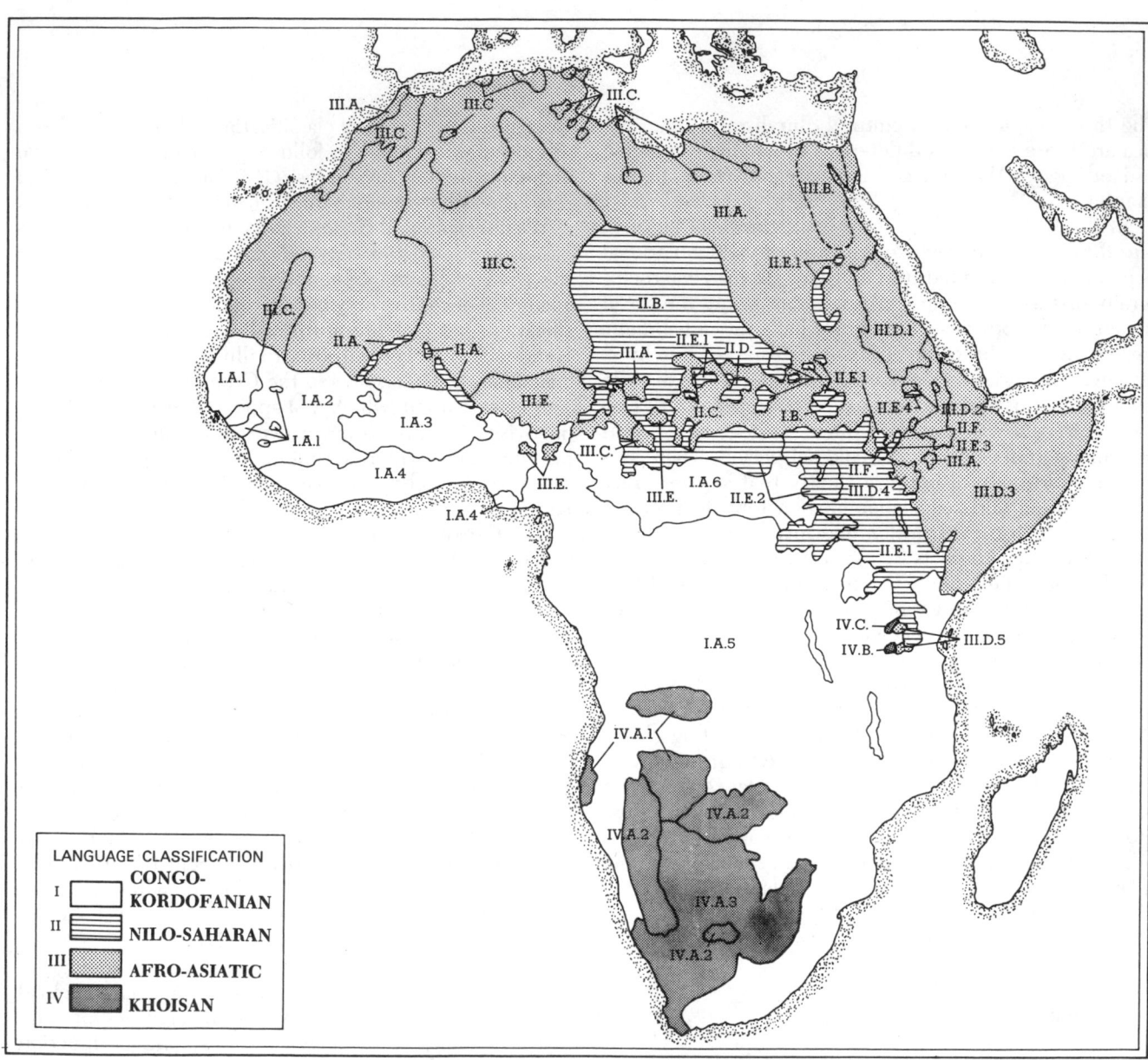

LANGUAGE CLASSIFICATION

I   **CONGO-KORDOFANIAN**

II   **NILO-SAHARAN**

III   **AFRO-ASIATIC**

IV   **KHOISAN**

Figure 2.1   Language Families of Africa: Greenberg's 1963 Classification

Language Family *(macro-phylum)*	*Major Sections* *(phyla/families)*	*Examples of individual languages or groups*
I. Congo-Kordofanian	A. Niger-Congo	
	A-1. West Atlantic	Fulani, Wolof, Serer, Temme, Limba, Soninke, Malinké, Bambara, Kpellé,
	A-2. Mande	Senoufo, Mossi, Grusi, Kabré, Bargu, Kru, Bété, Bassa, Ewé, Akan, Yoruba,
	A-3. Voltaic (Gur)	Bantu family, Tiv, Ibibio, Basa, Mbum, Gbaya, Banda, Mbaka, Sango
	A-4. Kwa ("others")	
	A-5. Benue-Congo	
	A-6. Adamawa	
	B. Kordofanian	
	B-1. Koalib	Kanderma
	B-2. Tegali	Rashad
	B-3. Talodi	Lafofa
	B-4. Tumtum	Tuleshi
	B-5. Katla	Tima
II. Nilo-Saharan	A. Songhai	
	B. Saharan	Kanuri (Kanembu)
	C. Maban	Maba
	D. Fur	
	E. Chari-Nile	
	E-1. Eastern Sudanic	Nubian group, Nilotic family, (Acholi, Lango, Nuer)
	E-2. Central Sudanic	
	E-3. Berua	
	E-4. Kunama	
	F. Koman	Koma
III. Afro-Asiatic	A. Semitic	Arabic
	B. Egyptian	
	C. Berber	
	D. Cushitic	
	D-1. Northern Cushitic	Beja
	D-2. Central Cushitic	Bogo
	D-3. Eastern Cushitic	Saho-Afar, Somali, Galla
	D-4. Western Cushitic	Janjero
	D-5. Southern Cushitic	Burungi
	E. Chad	Hausa, Bana, Banana (Masa)
IV. Khoisan	A. South African Khoisan	(Not significant in the countries contained in this Handbook)
	A-1. Northern South African Khoisan	
	A-2. Central South African Khoisan	
	A-3. Southern South African Khoisan	
	B. Sandawe	
	C. Hatsa	

family and major sub-sections are listed in Figure 2.

Language and National Integration

The relationship between language patterns and national integration has been explored by a number of scholars.[10] The distinction between a nation-state and a multinational state most commonly revolves around the issue of language. Many scholars have used language pluralism as a measure of cultural diversity within a country. Banks and Textor[11] suggest two such measures: (a) "linguistic homogeneity" (countries with 85 percent of the adult population speaking a common language are coded as homogenous); (b) speakers of dominant language as percentage of population. Adelman and Morris[12] use language diversity as the major indicator of national integration. Anderson, von der Mehden, and Young[13] use an ordinal scale to show the degree of linguistic pluralism within a country. When language distribution is viewed from a national context in Africa there is a tremendous range between those countries which have only one or two languages, and those which have up to two hundred. In this Handbook we present three variables on language homogeneity (Tables 2.1—2.3).

Yet quite apart from the actual number of languages within a state is the issue of the number of language families, which is probably some measure of the "degree of language corpus distance"[14] within a country (Table 2.4). According to Kloss:

> It would seem that close linguistic kinship facilitates collaboration and mutual understanding between the leading ethnic nationalities, whereas fundamental linguistic distance tends to make for mutual distrust and to be an obstacle (though not an insurmountable one) to a national feeling of belonging together.[15]

This hypothesis may be tested within the African context. At the first view, some countries which appear to have a large number of languages, such as the Central African Republic, Congo, or Tanzania, actually contain languages which are all of a single sub-category (IA6, IA5, and IA5 respectively) while countries such as Mauritania (which has had several severe language riots and disturbances have a more limited number of languages which nevertheless represent different macro-phyla (IIIA and IA1). On the other hand, countries such as Nigeria which have a large number of languages can have compound language problems since virtually all major African language families and sub-categories are represented.

Within the African context, political leaders are clearly aware of the significance of language to national integration. Some have even suggested that all internal administrative districts within the state follow linguistic lines.[16]

At this point the question of *lingua francas*, or "languages of wider communication,"[17] becomes extremely important (Table 2.5). A leading Tanzanian newspaper writes: "A common indigenous language in the modern nation state is a powerful factor for unity. Cutting across tribal and ethnic lines, it promotes a feeling of a single community. In Tanzania we have been blessed with such a language—Swahili."[18] In most African states there exist languages of wider communication, although to date relatively little research has been done on lingua francas or multi-lingualism.[19] In many of the states with a high level of linguistic pluralism a non-indigenous European language has become the dominant *lingua franca* as well as the official language of the country. These non-indigenous language are omitted from our discussion in what follows, however.

For purposes of this volume, we have defined a *lingua franca* as a second language which is spoken by 5 percent or more of the population. In terms of potential for wider communication, we would suggest that the degree of standardization of a language or *lingua franca* is of prime importance (Table 2.6). If language standardization has reached a stage where widespread publishing is possible, the communications potential is greater than in cases where orthographies have not been devised. Most of the major languages of Africa are becoming standardized, particularly those languages which exist in more than one country (e.g., Hausa and Swahili). It is clear that governmental policy regarding language patterns is important to national integration (Table 2.7). Policy regarding use of official languages, languages of mass media, and languages of education, is central to the processes of national communication and cooperation.[20]

The Formulation of Language Variables

Many social scientists have suggested the importance of language classification variables. Barrett[21] has coded the ethnic groups for each country on a dichotomous language-family variable (Bantu, non-Bantu). In Part II of this Handbook, we have included data on language pluralism within the capital cities of the forty-one African states when available. (The capital city context may be more relevant to certain types of social science analysis than the national context.

In formulating variables dealing with language pluralism in Africa it is important to recognize the limitations of source materials. Both Adelman and Morris, and Banks and Textor draw almost exclusively for their African language data on MacDougald.[22] This study was done in the 1940's and besides being incomplete for several African countries, its reliability is questionable. In all cases, it is important to recognize when scholars are using ethnic distribution data as a surrogate for language distribution data and vice versa.

The variables we have chosen to formulate and include in this Handbook may be divided into two categories: (1) language distribution, and (2) national communications potential. Language distribution refers to the total number of distinct languges within a country (Table 2.3), the degree to which a single language predominates—including both percent of total population (Table 2.1) and relationship to second largest language (Table 2.2), and the degree to which languages within a country are part of the same, or different language families (Table 2.4).

National communications potential in vernacular languages refers to the types, if any, of *lingua franca* within a country (Table 2.5), the extent of standardization of the major languages (Table 2.6), and governmental policy with regard to use of vernaculars in communications, education, and government (Table 2.7). It should be noted that we have not included exoglossic (i.e., non-indigenous) language variables (such as degree of literacy in French or English) since such data is contained in the education section.

With regard to the future formulation of national language policy variables, it is clear that time-series data will be of special importance although these changes will probably be slow. The language policies of most countries in Africa have changed over time, and the timing of these changes may well be correlated with other important events within the countries. In Nigeria, for example, the *number* of vernacular languages used in education and broadcasting changed in 1960, 1966, 1967, again after the ending of the civil war, and during the subsequent increase in the number of states.

Data Sources and Reliability

On the question of language distribution within a country, there is a wide difference of opinion among scholars. The three major comprehensive attempts to code dominant language as percent of total population have been MacDougald (1944),[23] Knappert (1965),[24] and Rustow (1968).[25] Not only is there considerable variation in the estimates (see Figure 2.2), but in eight countries (Cameroon, C.A.R., Gabon, Ivory Coast, Kenya, Sierra Leone, Tanzania, and Zaire) there is a lack of agreement as to which is the dominant language.

Part of this lack of coding congruence is probably definitional since Rustow is apparently referring to languages as the equivalent of ethnic groups, while Knappert is apparently referring to speakers of a given language (including second-language speakers). We have adopted the latter procedure. Thus, in at least twenty-six out of forty-one countries, the dominant language is—at least to some extent—a *lingua franca* within the country, and hence is invariably larger than the "ethnic group" who may speak it as a mother tongue. Our estimates of whether a dominant language acts as a *lingua franca* are based on individual country studies of language distribution (cited in Part II) and on our own estimates. These estimates should be regarded as rough approximations unless they are based on census results.

Our estimates of the degree of standardization of dominant languages (first or second language) are also based on

Figure 2.2 Estimated Reliability of Major Language (Inter-coder Estimates of Major Language as Percent of Total Population)*

Country	Language	MacDougald Estimate	Knappert Estimate	Rustow Estimate	Range of Estimate**
1. Botswana	Tswana		100%	69%	31%
2. Burundi	Rundi	84%	100	28	72
3. Chad	Arabic		40	33	7
4. Congo	Kongo		40	50	10
5. Benin	Fon	51	50	58	8
6. Ethiopia	Amharic	61	71	49	22
7. Gambia	Mandingo		100	46***	54
8. Ghana	Akan	62	57	44	18
9. Guinea	Fulani	62	33	39	29

*Includes all the countries in the first half (alphabetically ordered) of the first edition's thirty-two country sample, except those where there was no agreement on choice of primary language.

**Average range of estimate is 28 percent.

***Includes Malinke-Bambara-Dyula.

country-specific literature. In his discussion of a standardization criterion , Kloss[26] provides some paradigms from the African context. He regards French as a "mature standard language," Luganda as a "young standard language," Somali as an "unstandardized alphabetized language" until recently when a Roman script alphabet was adopted, and Galla as a "pre-literate language." We have coded only four African languages as "mature standard languages": Arabic, Amharic, Swahili, and Hausa. As the UNESCO studies of language distribution and characteristics in Africa become available, it may be possible to refine the distinctions between African languages on such matters as standardization of orthography, extent of vernacular literature, and range/number of vocabulary words. The world-wide language survey[27] directed by Kloss should yield valuable data on the African countries.

Our judgements as to official language policy within the African countries are also approximations, especially since such policies may change over time or may be "unofficial." In general, the French-speaking areas have not used vernacular languages in education, but in the post-independence period they have used vernaculars in broadcasting. English-speaking areas have been receptive to using the vernacular in government, education, and mass media. The regional and/or national official languages of each country are cited in Part II.

b. Religious Pluralism

The three major religious traditions in contemporary Africa are African traditional religions, Islam, and Christianity. Traditional religion, which consists of a wide variety of localized religious practices and beliefs, is presently declining in institutional vigor and importance, giving way to Islam and Christianity. The underlying philosophy or world view[28] common to African traditional religions has by no means shared in this decline, however. It persists in important ways such as the African adaptations of Islam and Christianity, the continued demand for the divinatory powers, witchcraft protection, and healing skills of traditional practioners, and in aspects of the new African culture.

Islam[29] has been an important religious influence in Africa south of the Sahara, especially since the days of Ibn Yasin, an eleventh-century Muslim missionary who established himself among the Berbers in present-day Mauritania. Christianity[30] has an even longer history of contact back to the fourth-century introduction of Coptic Christianity to the Kingdom of Axum (present-day Ethiopia). The Ethiopian Orthodox Church remains today the most important Christian Church in Ethiopia.

The centuries-long contact between Roman Catholic Portugal and Central and West Africa which began in the fifteenth century was ultimately unsuccessful in establishing a lasting mission. A sustained Christian missionary effort on the part of Protestants and Roman Catholics ultimately occurred in the nineteenth century. Today the northern part of Black Africa is heavily Muslim while certain countries to the south, such as Gabon, Zaire, Lesotho, and Malawi, have Christian majorities. Present indications suggest an accelerated movement towards these two major world religions so that by the end of the 1980's avowed adherents of traditional African religion will be a very small minority in Black Africa.

Islam and Christianity have been important forces for change in Africa. Each embodies a distinctive universalistic culture which it transmits to its converts through the teachings of its religious leaders, its religious ceremonies, and special experiences such as the Muslim pilgrimage to Mecca. Christianity, as the religion of the colonial powers, came to enjoy high prestige with those Africans who aspired to elite positions in the modern social structure. One of the special attractions of Christianity was the widespread network of mission schools. Developed from the beginning of missionary work in each area so as to instruct the new believers in the Bible, these schools quickly broadened to serve a wider clientele, providing a full curriculum and attracting financial support from the colonial governments. As a consequence, the colonial governments, especially the British, opened relatively few secular government schools. Until independence it was not uncommon to find that 60—75 percent of the schools in a country were owned by the churches.[31] Islam, of course, offers Koranic instruction through local Koranic schools, and a few Islamic secondary schools are operated by reform Islamic brotherhoods.

One of the few quantitative cross-national studies of a sample of African nations examined the effect of Christianity in ten mainly English-speaking countries concluded that Christian missionaries have been an important cause of social mobilization.[32] Although the conclusions of this study have been called into question on methodological grounds,[33] the relationship of religion to social change in Africa remains one of considerable interest.

The pattern of the relationship between religion and politics in contemporary Africa is far from clear at this point in the development of African nations. In most African countries thus far Christianity and Islam have avoided direct confrontations with the state, but the cases of Guinea, Senegal, Malawi and Ghana suggest a certain potential for political opposition on the part of religious groups and leaders. On the other hand, the Is-

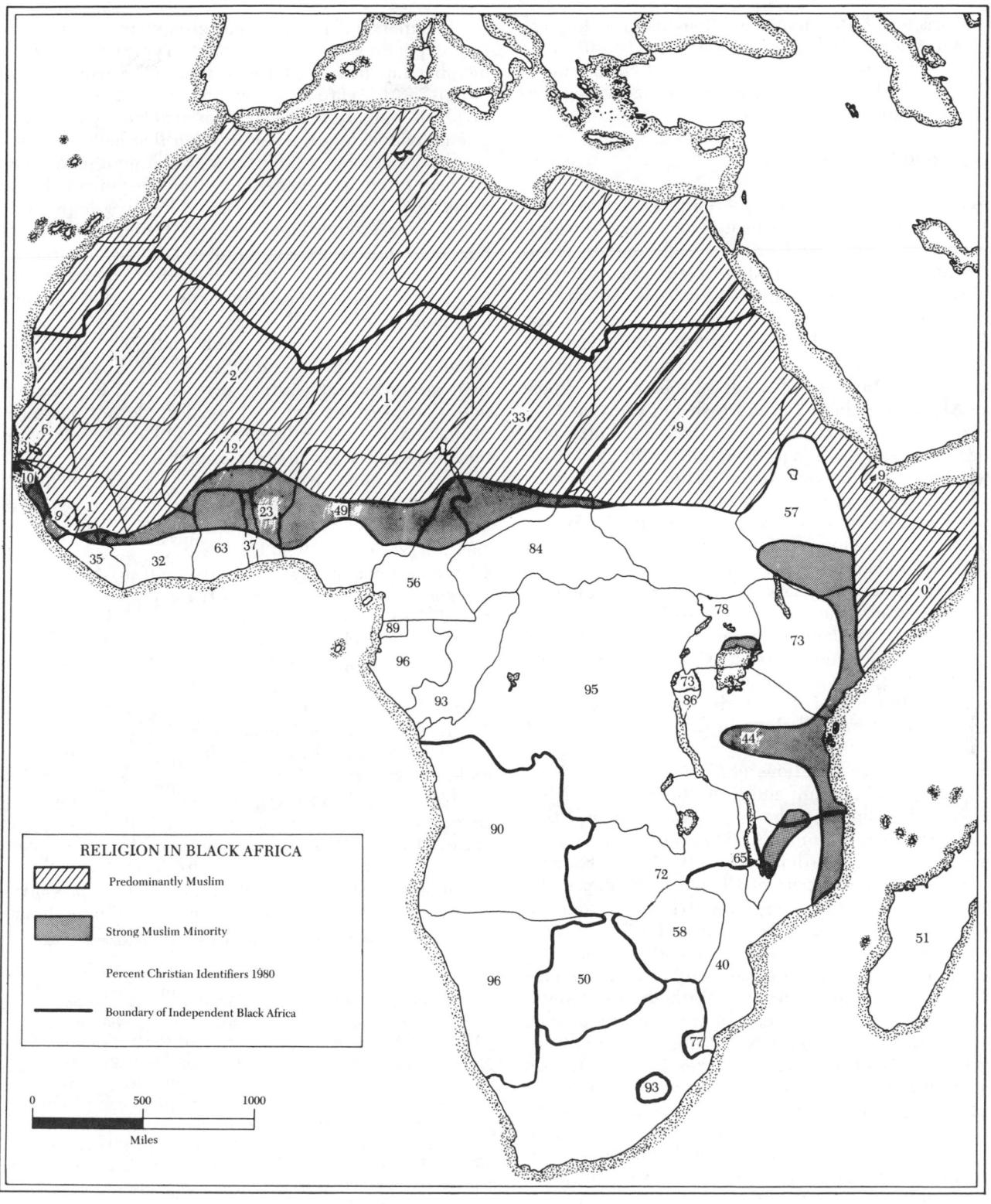

RELIGION IN BLACK AFRICA

▨	Predominantly Muslim
▩	Strong Muslim Minority
56	Percent Christian Identifiers 1980
▬	Boundary of Independent Black Africa

0　　　500　　　1000

Miles

lamic character of Mauritania and Somalia probably contributes to the political integration of these countries. In countries where there is no one dominant faith, religion has the potential for acting as a cross-cutting cleavage between ethnic groups.

Concepts and Definitions

In order to satisfactorily employ a religion as a variable in the analysis of African societies it is necessary to understand how Muslims and Christians differentiate themselves. Islam, to the non-Muslim, often appears to be a monolithic, homogenous entity. Actually it contains important divisions between the various legal schools, the Sufi brotherhoods, the believers and the nonbelievers in a Mahdi (i.e., a messiah), and the reformed and conservative groups. Only two of the legal schools are important in Africa: the Maliki in the North and West, and the Shafi'i on the eastern coast. Among the many Sufi brotherhoods in Africa, the Tijaniyya and the Qadiriyya are especially important in West Africa. Claimants to the position of Mahdi (a messianic leader) have occasionally appeared in Islamic Africa, most notably in the Sudan. The Pakistani Ahmadiyya Muslim group, which considers the late Ghulam Ahman to have been the Mahdi, also undertakes active missionary work in Africa.[34] Although much of African Islam is very conservative, reform groups exist, particularly in urban settings where they show a concern for modernizing Islamic education and the role of women. Unfortunately, data are unavailable on a cross-national basis for Muslim sub-groupings and we are unable to include them in the variables for this section.

The three major traditions of Christianity are Othodoxy, Roman Catholicism, and Protestantism. The Ethiopian Orthodox Church is the major expression of Orthodoxy in Africa, while Roman Catholicism is represented by various missionary orders such as the White Fathers. With the exception of part of Eritrea in Ethiopia, the Catholic areas in our sample of countries are under the authority of *Propaganda Fide* in Rome. Protestantism is divided into a large number of denominations. These denominations may be further grouped into the "main line" mission denominations such as the Methodists and Anglicans, the "third force" or sect-type mission groups such as the Seventh Day Adventists and the Church of God, and the African independent churches.[35] The latter are Christian groups which either broke away from the mission churches or spontaneously emerged as a response to the work of African Christian diviner-healers or prophets. Data are available for most of the Christian subgroupings, a small section of which is presented in Tables 2.10, 2.11, 2.13, 2.15, and 2.16.

"Membership" in a religious group has various meanings depending upon the context. Typically the official membership figures of the various Christian religious groups in Africa are far below the aggregate claims of individuals who are polled in a national survey or census. The individual tells the census taker that he is a "Protestant" or "Catholic" in the sense of stating a preference. He may rarely or never occupy a pew—perhaps he has never ever been baptized. The Christian groups themselves, on the other hand, generally count as full members only those who have fulfilled certain requirements (such as confirmation). Even when they label a broader category of people as "catechumens" or as the "Christian community," they still reserve these labels for people who have demonstrated their religious preference through their actions in enrolling as catechumens and/or their attendance at church services. It is important to note that Muslims and traditionalists do not make this distinction: in these religions the individual's self-definition is the sole criterion for "membership."

In this Handbook we will make a basic distinction for the Christian groups, between these two types of involvement or identification with religion in terms of: (a) *Identifiers*, or those who claim a traditional, Muslim, or Christian identity (as in a census), and (b) *Affiliators*, a category applicable *only to Christianity*, which denotes those claimed by the Christian groups themselves as members, catechumens, or adherents. Our "affiliators" category is comparable to the "total Christian community" claimed by each Protestant denomination in the *World Christian Handbook*,[36] a major source for data. The most comparable Roman Catholic category for affiliators is the sum of their "Catholics" (baptized, including children) and their "catechumens" (under instructions for baptism) categories.[37] Although we will not do so here, it is possible to break the Protestant data into categories of affiliators such as communicants or "full members," and catechumens or inquirers. In Africa the catechumen category is typically swollen out of proportion compared to other parts of the world because the Roman

Figure 2.3   Estimates of Christians in Ghana and Nigeria, 1960s

	Beetham's Data on "Percent Christian"[1]	Christian Affiliators[2]	Christian Identifiers[3]
Ghana	36% (c. 1964)	17% (1962)	43% (1960)
Nigeria	8 (c. 1964)	6 (1962)	35 (1963)

[1]T. A. Beetham. *Christianity in Africa* (London: Pall Mall, 1965).

[2]*World Christian Handbook 1962* (London: World Dominion Press, 1963). This source presents official Protestant and Roman Catholic reports on membership (full members plus catechumens).

[3]Ghana Census, 1960, and Nigerian Census, 1963.

Catholic Church, and many Protestant churches do not baptize polygynists.

All too often the presentation of data on Christianity in Africa fails to make this important distinction between identifiers and affiliators and the reader is left uncertain as to how the author defines membership. Figure 2.3 illustrates this problem and shows the marked differences between national data and affiliators and identifiers. T. A. Beetham's book reports data identified as "percent Christian" and footnoted as being based on "official Roman Catholic and Protestant statistics." In fact, only the Nigerian figure resembles the official Christian data. His Ghanaian figure is much closer to the figure reported in the Ghanaian 1960 census. The difference in years between the figures cannot account for this great a difference.

Data Sources and Reliability

The best source for data on religious *identifiers* are official censuses or sample surveys. Unfortunately religion is not always included in African censuses (nor in the U.S. census for that matter), so for the most part other authorities have to be relied upon in making estimates of identifiers. These authorities' reliability is impossible to estimate, but an overall error margin of 10 percent or more may be assumed at the present time. It should also be noted that some countries show an enormous growth rate for Christianity since 1966. Such changes must be treated with caution even though the source is the only consistent one available.

The *affiliation* category for the Christian data presents a more hopeful situation with regard to data reliability. The annual church membership reports compiled by the national church authorities represent one of the most extensive statistical operations in Africa, and provide a relatively thorough and consistent data base. There are many chances for misreporting and nonreporting in this operation, however, as anyone knows who has tried to collect religious data on the local level in Africa.

The Roman Catholic membership figures are published annually, diocese by diocese (but not by country), for the entire world in *Annuario Pontificio* (Vatican City). Compilations on the national level for Africa are made by the International Fides Service and have been published in *Ready Information about Africa*,[38] *Bilan du Monde*,[39] and the Protestant *World Christian Handbook*.[40] The sources of bias in the Roman Catholic reporting process are unknown.

Protestant data are published periodically in the *World Christian Handbook*. The *Handbook* obtains its data by sending questionaires to all Protestant denomina-

tions requesting data on a number of categories. It publishes these data in country tables which list each denomination and their reported data. Until recently the reliability of the *Handbook's* data left much to be desired.[41] Errors of considerable magnitude, such as its 1957 report that the Free Presbyterian Church of Scotland had one thousand ordained pastors in the Republic of South Africa whereas in fact they had only one, found publication with alarming frequency. Churches were sometimes counted more than once when multiple reports were received under variations of the church's name.[42] Finally, no attempt was made to include the African independent churches, thus ignoring several million African Christians. Gross errors of this sort were eliminated from the 1968 *Handbook*, by its new African editor, David B. Barrett. Future editions of the *Handbook* are to be combined with the Roman Catholic *Bilan du Monde*, and Barrett and his co-editors have made serious efforts to improve the comprehensiveness and reliability of the African data in the new *World Christian Handbook* (Nairobi:Oxford University Press, 1982).

The Data

The first five tables, 2.8—2.12, give estimates of the percentage of the population who identify (as defined above) with Islam, Christianity, Protestantism, Roman Catholicism and traditional religion. These estimates correspond to the statements in other reference books that 50 percent of the population in a country is Muslim, 32 percent is Christian, etc. The figures given here vary from the available estimates in standard international reference works, sometimes considerably. Since they are based on the most recent data as detailed in the source notes to the tables, overall they should provide a more satisfactory estimate, but the reader should keep the suggested error margin of at least 10 percent in mind.

Although there are sources for Christian *affiliators* which present data over time,[43] nothing comparable was available for Christian, Muslim and traditional *identifiers* until Barrett's new *World Christian Handbook* appeared in 1982. The Christian affiliator data sources for the years prior to World War II suffer from two weaknesses, however. Their reliability is very hard to assess since they give totals for each country but do not break these totals down to the component denominations. Second, their coverage is poor — they only present data for about 21 of our 41 countries.

In an attempt to overcome these weaknesses we present data on mission stations per million population in 1925 (Table 2.13). The data source is a map which clearly locates these stations. [44] The decison to use mission stations instead of members or missionaries per million population reduces the validity of the variable somewhat, but it can be argued that the mission stations were important indicators of the Christian presence in Africa at that time. Hildegard Johnson has described the role of the mission station in this regard:

> ...With their chapels, residences, dormitories, schools, dispensaries, gardens, utility buildings, water-supply systems, and good access roads they stand in great contrast with their immediate surroundings. In the confrontation of European with African ways of life these stations have been for the missionaries a refuge, a symbol of achievement, and a home; for the Africans they have been strongholds of alien ways from religion to agriculture.[45]

Variables which indicate change are highly desirable and we present a change variable for growth in membership in the major groupings from 1970 to 1980 (Table 2.16). Detailed denominational change rates can be calculated from the *World Christian Encyclopedia*.[46]

Only two recent variables on the level of Christian adherence are included here because many of these variables are available in the *World Christian Encyclopedia* and were also published in the second edition of the *World Handbook of Social and Political Indicators*.[47] Because the data for an estimate of total Christian affiliators has only recently become available,[48] however, we present that variable (Table 2.14) and also Barrett's estimate of the number of adherents of the African Independent Churches (Table 2.15).

c. Ethnic Pluralism

An operational definition of ethnic pluralism is *the degree of variation in the cultural characteristics of ethnic groups in a nation*. The critical empirical problems in this definition are the identification of what we call "ethnic units" (not to be confused with identity groups or "tribes"), and the description of their cultural characteristics in quantitative form.[49] Because of the complexity and novelty of our ethnic unit approach, we include a full discussion of the rationale and procedure used in identifying the ethnic units in Chapter 4 of Sect. A of this Handbook. In addition, a list of ethnic units, with a description of their constituent identity groups or "tribes," and their population size, is given for each country in the sections entitled "Ethnic Patterns" in Part II of the Handbook. In this chapter we assume a familiarity with these other sections of the Handbook.

It was necessary, both for the identification of ethnic units, and for the measurement of cultural pluralism as we have operationally defined it, to specify dimensions of cultural variation in human populations, and to construct measures, relating to these dimensions, which could describe the specific cultural characteristics of each of our

ethnic units. Initially the dimensions that were selected were: (a) *marriage* (variables which indicate processes of inter-group alliances based on marriage, also those variables which indicate the composition of family groups); (b) *descent* (variables which indicate how kinship and lineage obligations and loyalties are organised); (c) *community organization* (variables such as stratification and settlement patterns); and (d) *authority*[51] (variables which indicate the nature of authority and the levels at which it exists within the political community; also processes by which authority changes hands).

In addition, because of the close correlation between environmental constraints (or ecological factors) and social behavior, we selected certain variables which indicated the basic *economic structure*[52] of the ethnic units. Levels of agricultural development and/or animal husbandry have frequently been used by anthropologists to typologize ethnic units, (e.g., "hunters and gatherers," "pastoralists," settled agriculturalists, etc.). On the basis of these guidelines, eighteen variables were formulated to reflect the above dimensions. These measures were structured on ordinal scales[53] which are summarized in Figure 2.4.

Figure 2.4   Summary Definitions of Selected Variables

I. *Descent*

1. MATRILINEALITY:	Presence and type of matrilineal kin groups: an ordinal continuum extending from an absence of matrilineal exogamy and kin groups to the presence of matrilineal exogamy and the most inclusive matrilineal kin groups.
2. PATRILINEALITY:	Presence and type of patrilineal kin groups: an ordinal continuum extending from an absence of patrilineal exogamy to the most inclusive patrilineal kin groups.
3. MARITAL RESIDENCE:	Prevailing pattern of marital residence: an ordinal scale ranging from matrilocality, through residence with or near a male relative, to patrilocality.
4. DESCENT:	Principles of reckoning *descent* assumes continuum from matrilineality through double descent to patrilineality.

II. *Economic Structure*

5. HUSBANDRY: Dependence on animal husbandry refers to the percentage of time devoted to this activity. (0—100 percent).

6. AGRICULTURE: Dependence on agriculture refers to the percentage of time devoted to this activity. (0—100 percent)

7. SETTLEMENT: Settlement patterns refers to the *permanence* and complexity of community settlements, ranging from migratory to permanent/complex.

III. *Social Stratification*

8. HIERARCHY: Hierarchy above family refers to the number of *levels of community structure* above the family, ranging from stateless groupings, to petty chiefdoms, to tribal chiefdoms.

9. CLASSES: Class stratification refers to the *degree and type of class differentiation*, ranging from absence of class to complex stratification.

10. CASTES: Caste stratification refers to the *degree and type of caste differentiation*, ranging from absence of caste to complex stratification.

IV. *Social Scale*

11. FAMILY: Family organization refers to the *scale of the prevailing unit* of domestic or familial organization, ranging from large extended families to nuclear families.

12. HIERARCHY: Number of levels of hierarchy in the local community organization: an ordinal continuum of greater inclusion between the nuclear family and the village.

13. CLANS: Number of clans per local community refers to the *complexity* of communities, ranging from no clans to many clans.

V. *Complexity of Settlement*

14. FARMING: Level of development and intensity of agriculture: an ordinal continuum between systems in which there is a total absence of any systematic agriculture and systems in which there is agricultural production based upon a high level of technology.

15. INHERITANCE: Distribution of inheritance among the members of surviving family: an ordinal continuum ranging from equal distribution to exclusive inheritance based on seniority.

VI. *Family Organization*

16. MODE OF MARRIAGE: An ordinal continuum extending between systems having a bride-price (in which the bride is viewed as an asset) and those having a dowry system (where the bride is viewed as a liability).

17. POLYGYNY: Degree to which polygyny is practised within a given society: an ordinal continuum ranging from no polygyny to its widespread practice within the society.

VII. *Authority Patterns*

18. AUTHORITY: Institutionalization of political authority: an ordinal continuum ranging from lesser to greater centralization and institutionalization of authority, in which political systems are classified as segmental, pyramidal, or hierarchical authority structures.

An example of the construction of these variables is the measure of *Patterns of Inheritance of Real Property* (See Table 2.21). George Peter Murdock in his *Ethnographic Atlas* has seven classifications regarding inheritance of real property. They are listed in Figure 2.5 in alphabetical order.

Figure 2.5   Murdock Classification of Real-Property Inheritance

Murdock Symbol	Variable Name
C	Inheritance by children of either sex or both.
D	Inheritance by children but daughter receives less than sons.
M	Matrilineal inheritance by sister's son or sons.
N	Inheritance by matrilineal heirs who take precedence over sister's sons.
O	Absence of individual property rights in land or any rule of inheritance governing the transmission of such rights.
P	Patrilineal inheritance by a son or sons.
Q	Inheritance by patrilineal heirs who take precedence over sons.

These classifications were then reordered on the basis of a scale measuring an ordinal progression of rules for the transmission of land and material goods ranging from relatives other than children to inheritance by a son or sons. This was accomplished by assigning numbers to each of the above categories such that the numeric designation reflects a ranking on the scale continuum defined above. The correspondence is as follows:

Murdock Code	O	N Q	C	D	M	P
Assigned Number	1	2	3	4	5	6
No Inheritance						Patrilineal Inheritance by son or sons

Once ethnic units had been decided upon and coded on these variables, factor analysis was used to refine and differentiate these measures for dimensionality. Some of the results of this factor analytic work are included in Figure 2.6. Six dimensions emerge which closely approximate our original guidelines. These dimensions are all relevant to community formation and there is no significance to the order of listing since there were no predominant factors. Six variables representative of these dimensions were used to construct measures of cultural pluralism which are given in this chapter's tables.

The data in this chapter are intended to indicate *within-country* variance with respect to traditional cultural patterns across each country's ethnic units. Codings were made on the aforementioned variables for each ethnic unit through the use of a representative group for that ethnic unit. For instance, codings were made using the Makonde as representative of Tanzania's Central Bantu cluster. Standard deviations across ethnic units were calculated for each country. The assumption behind this relatively crude procedure is that the greater the standard deviation the greater the cultural pluralism within a country.[54] Countries with only one ethnic unit will have no variance of course. But it is also possible that a country with several ethnic units would have no variance since all ethnic units might have the same codings on a particular variable. This is the case for Ghana on the *Agricultural Development* measure where all four units have the same patterns of shifting cultivation.

Each table also includes the mean or average score on the index for each country. The mean reflects the national average for that variable, and for this reason may be of interest in cross-national comparisons. It must be noted here that neither the mean nor the standard deviation take into account the *size* of the groups involved, however. Thus the "predominant level" must be interpreted in terms of units, not individuals. If one group comprising 80 percent of the population of a country ranks high on a particular index while the remaining four groups (20 percent of the population) have low values, the mean will not reflect the fact that four-fifths of the people coded have the high value.[55]

Reliability

The definition of ethnic units is treated at length in Sect. A of this book and will not be discussed further here. Once the units have been defined, there remains the difficulty of coding our variables, and the accompanying source and coder reliability problems. The primary data and coding sources were Murdock's *Ethnographic Atlas*,[56] *Cultural Summaries*,[57] and the periodical *Ethnology*.[58] Coder error, therefore, is restricted almost exclusively to the errors that may have occurred in the coding of ethnographies into the classification used by Murdock in his works cited above. We have no assessment of this error, although periodically issues of *Ethnology* update and correct codings that originally appeared in the *Ethnographic Atlas* or previous issues of *Ethnology*. A new version of the Atlas entitled *Atlas of World Cultures* (University of Pittsburgh Press, 1981) was published recently which incorporates these corrections and drops groups for which data is sparse or of low reliability.

The major reliability problem appears to be with the

Figure 2.6   Culture Dimensionality: Factor Loadings for Each Variable on Its Principal Factor*

(Varimax Rotation)

Factor	Variable	Loading
I. *Descent*		
	1. Matrilineal kinship	−.899
	2. Patrilineal kinship	.805
	3. Marital residence	.888
	4. Descent principles	.913
II. *Economic Structure*		
	5. Dependence on animal husbandry	−.895
	6. Dependence on agriculture	.809
	7. Settlement complexity	.764
III. *Social Stratification*		
	8. Hierarchy above family (social structure)	−.699
	9. Class stratification	−.842
	10. Caste stratification	−.606
IV. *Social*		
	11. Scale of domestic or family organization	−.739
	12. Levels of organization above family	−.815
	13. Number of clans per community	−.602
V. *Complexity of Settlement*		
	14. Complexity of agricultural systems	.549
	15. Land inheritance	.696
VI. *Family Organization*		
	16. Mode of marriage	−.743
	17. Degree of polygyny	.651

*Variable 18, AUTHORITY, was added after the factor analysis was run.

data sources, that is the ethnographies themselves. Many of the sources are not written by modern professional anthropologists and the time period in which the works were written shows considerable variance. Furthermore, even the professional ethnographers vary widely in their intentions and fieldwork methods,[59] and their descriptions can be expected to vary depending on how adequate their sampling of the population in a particular ethnic group has been. Finally, given the timing of ethnographic fieldwork, and given the knowledge that the structure of ethnic groups is not static, but varies in time with the incorporation of new populations and the assimilation of new values,[60] these data are, at best, a reliable picture of ethnic pluralism in Black Africa only for a period approximately twenty to forty years *before* independence. It is our hope, therefore, that these data will stimulate, and be superseded by, measures of cultural pluralism based on more systematic survey research, replicated at different time periods in the Black African nations.

Notes

[1]Like many other widely used concepts in social science, cultural pluralism enjoys no universally accepted definition. The term was introduced in J. S. Furnivall, *Colonial Policy and Practice* (Cambridge: Cambridge University Press, 1948) to describe the peculiarities of tropical colonies in which historically and culturally segregated races, societies or tribes were brought into limited contact by the extension of the colonial economic market, but retained separate identities and organization for all but economic activity. In subsequent usage, definitions of cultural pluralism have attempted to distinguish the term from the more general notion of cultural heterogeneity by stressing the rigidity and institutional incompatibility of cultural cleavages in the populations of culturally plural societies. See the somewhat different discussion in M. G. Smith, "Social and Cultural Pluralism," *Annals of the New York Academy of Sciences*, 83 (January, 1960), 763—777; Leo A. Despres, *Cultural Pluralism and Nationalist Politics in British Guinea* (Chicago: Rand McNally, 1967); and Pierre van den Berghe, "Towards a Sociology for Africa," *Social Forces*, 43 (October 1964), 11—18. Another specification of the meaning of cultural pluralism, which we think too limiting and which we do not make use of, is the suggestion that cul-

tural pluralism is distinctively different from cultural heterogeneity because of the political subjugation of one cultural group by another that is a condition of cultural pluralism. See the articles by the editors in Leo Kuper and M. G. Smith, eds. *Pluralism in Africa* (Berkeley: University of California Press, 1969). For a major review of theories relating to cultural pluralism see Levine, R. and D. T. Campbell, *Ethnocentrism: Theories of Conflict, Ethnic Attitudes, and Group Behavior* (New York: Wiley, 1972) and for an empirical analysis see M. Brewer and D. T. Campbell *Ethnocentrism and Intergroup Attitudes* (New York: Halsted Press, 1976).

[2]Notable examples of this argument are contained in Karl W. Deutsch, "Social Mobilization and Political Development," *American Political Science Review*, 55 (September 1961), 493—514; and S. N. Eisenstadt, *Modernization: Protest and Change* (Englewood Cliffs, New Jersey: Prentice-Hall, 1966). See also Robert Melson and Howard Wolpe, "Modernization and the Politics of Communalism: A Theoretical Perspective," *American Political Science Review*, 64 (December 1970); 1112—1130; R. H. Bates, "Ethnic Competition and Modernization in Contemporary Africa," *Comparative Political Studies*, 6, 4 (January 1974): 457—484 and the general discussion of ethnic stratification in Tamotsu Shibutani and Kian M. Kwan, *Ethnic Stratification: A Comparative Approach* (New York: Macmillan, 1965). Preliminary research using a cross-national analysis of data in the first edition of this book, however, indicates that cultural pluralism is a partial but by no means sufficient indicator of sources of conflict in these nations, that such conflict is associated with the extent of political instability in these nations, but that social mobilization and economic development may mitigate, not accentuate, this relationship. D. G. Morrison and H. M. Stevenson, "Cultural Pluralism, Modernization and Conflict: An Empirical Analysis of Sources of Political Instability in African Nations," *Canadian Journal of Political Science*, V (March 1972): 82—103. See Mawlana and Robinson in Said and Simmons (1976) for an attempt to incorporate ethnicity into the Deutschian view of social mobilization.

[3]Jan Knappert, "Language Problems of the New Nations of Africa," *Africa Quarterly*, 5 (1965): 95—105.

[4]See Diedrich Westermann and Margaret Bryan, *Languages of West Africa, Handbook of African Languages* (London: Oxford University Press, 1952).

[5]Malcolm Guthrie, *The Classification of the Bantu Languages* (London: Oxford University Press, 1948); also, "Bantu Origins: A Tentative New Hypothesis," *Journal of African Languages*, 1 (1962): 9—21.

[6]Joseph H. Greenberg, *The Languages of Africa* (Bloomington: Indiana University Press, 1966); also, *Studies in African Linguistic Classification* (New Haven, Conn.: Compass Publishing Company, 1955), and J. Berry and J. Greenberg (eds.) *Linguistics in Sub-Saharan Africa* (Paris: Mouton, 1971). C. F. and F. M. Voegelin, "Languages of the World: African Fascicle One," *Anthropological Linguistics*, 6 (May 1964): 1—339.

[8]See, F. D. D. Winston, "Greenberg's Classification of African Languages," *African Language Studies*, 7 (1966): 160—170; David Dalby, "Levels of Relationship in the Comparative Study of African Languages," *African Language Studies*, 7 (1966): 171—179; Diedrich Westermann, "African Linguistic Classifications," *Africa*, 22 (1952): 250—256; Istvan Fodor, "La classification des langues negro-africaines et la theorie de J. H. Greenberg," *Cahiers d'etudes Africaine*, 7 (1968): 617—631; Istvan Fodor, *The Problems in the Classification of the African Languages: Methodological and Theoretical Conclusions Concerning the Classification System of Joseph H. Greenberg* (Budapest: Cen-

ter for Afro-Asian Research of the Hungarian Academy of Sciences, 1966); J. H. Kwabena Nketia, "The Language Problem and the African Personality," *Presence Africaine*, no. 67 (1968): 157—171; Jean Mfoulou, "Science et pseudo-science des langues Africaines," *Presence Africaine*, no. 70 (1969): 147—161; "Table ronde sur les langues Africaines," *Presence Africaine*, no. 67 (1968): 53—156; Jack Berry, "Language Systems and Literature" in *The African Experience*, Vol. 1, eds. John Paden and Edward Soja (Evanston, Ill.: Northwestern University Press, 1970). Other additions to the literature are W. E. Welmers, *African Language Structures* (Berkeley: University of California Press, 1973) and P. Alexandre, *An Introduction to Languages and Language in Africa* (London: Heinemann 1972).

[9]Guthrie, *Classification of the Bantu Languages* and D. Dalby *Language Map of Africa (London: International African Institute, 1977)*.

[10]See Joshua A. Fishman, Charles A. Ferguson, and Jyotirindra Das Gupta, eds., *Language Problems of Developing Nations* (New York: John Wiley, 1968). Within this anthology, see in particular, Jyotirindra Das Gupta, "Language Diversity and National Development," pp. 17—26; Joshua A. Fishman, "Nationality-Nationalism and Nation-Nationism," pp. 39—52; Joshua A. Fishman, "Some Contrasts between Linguistically Homogenous and Linguistically Heterogenous Polities," pp. 53—68; Heinz Kloss, "Notes Concerning a Language-Nation Typology," pp. 69—86; Dankwart Rustow, "Language, Modernization and Nationhood—An Attempt at Typology," pp. 87—106; Pierre Alexandre, "Some Linguistic Problems of Nation-Building in Negro-Africa," pp. 119—128; John N. Paden, "Language Problems of National Integration in Nigeria: The Special Position of Hausa," pp. 199—214; Joshua Fishman, "Language Problems and Types of Political and Sociocultural Integration," pp. 491—498. See also J. H. Greenberg, *Language, Culture, and Communication* (Stanford: Stanford University Press, 1971) and D. G. Morrison and H. M. Stevenson, "Cultural Pluralism, Modernization, and Conflict: An Empirical Analysis of Sources of Political Instability in African Nations" *Canadian Journal of Political Science* V. 1 (1972), pp. 82—103.

[11]Arthur S. Banks and Robert B. Textor, *A Cross- Polity Survey* (Cambridge: Massachusetts Institute of Technology Press, 1963).

[12]Irma Adelman and Cynthia Taft Morris, *Society, Politics and Economic Development: A Quantitative Approach* (Baltimore, Md.: Johns Hopkins University Press, 1967), p. 54—56.

[13]Charles Anderson, Fred von der Mehden and Crawford Young, *Issues of Political Development* (Englewood Cliffs, N.J.: Prentice-Hall, 1967).

[14]Kloss, "Notes Concerning a Language-Nation Typlogy," p. 75.

[15] *Ibid.*

[16]See, for example, Obafemi Awolowo, *The People's Republic* (Ibadan: Oxford University Press, 1968); also *Thoughts on Nigerian Constitution* (Ibadan: Oxford University Press, 1966).

[17]See Joshua A. Fishman, "National Languages and Languages of Wider Communication in the Developing Nations," *Anthropological Linguistics*, 11 (April 1969): 11—135.

[18]*The Nationalist*, December 20, 1968 (quoted in ibid., p. 118).

[19]For a discussion of multilingualism, see Scientific Council for Africa, *Symposium on Multilingualism: Brazzaville, 1962*, Publication no. 87 (London: 1962). For a summary of a pilot research project on multilingualism, see Jack Berry, "The Madina Project; Sociolinguistic Research in Ghana" in *Expanding Horizons in African Studies*, eds. Gwendolen M. Carter and Ann Paden (Evanston, Ill.: Northwestern University Press, 1969), pp. 303—314. See W. H. Whiteley, ed., *Lan-*

guage Use and Social Change: Problems of Multilingualism with Special Reference to Eastern Africa (London: Oxford University Press, 1971). Also see D. Dalby (ed.), *Language and History in Africa* (New York: Africana, 1971); B. Heine *Status and Use of African Lingua Francas* (Munich: Weltforum Verlag, 1970) and ILO "Towns and Lingua Francas in West Africa", *International Migration Review* (Summer) 1971; and M. A. Adekunle, "Multilingualism and Language Function in Nigeria", *African Studies Review*, XV, 2 (Sept. 1972), pp. 185—208.

[20]See John Spencer, Ed., *Language in Africa* (Cambridge, Cambridge University Press, 1963); also Istvan Fodor, "Lingusitic Problems and 'Language Planning' in Africa," *Linguistics*, 25 (September, 1966): 18—33.

[21]David Barrett, *Schism and Renewal in Africa: An Analysis of Six Thousand Contemporary Religious Movements* (Nairobi: Oxford University Press, 1968).

[22]Duncan MacDougald, Jr., *The Languages and Press of Africa*, (Philadelphia: University of Pennsylvania Press, 1944).

[23]*Ibid.*

[24]Knappert, "Language Problems of the New Nations of Africa."

[25]Dankwart Rustow, "Language, Modernization and Nationhood—An Attempt at Typology" in *Language Problems of Developing Nations*, eds. Fishman et. al., pp. 87—106. Rustow codes "Mother Tongue of Largest Group" as "Per Cent of Population." Although he codes all the countries in the world, most of his coding for the African states is based on "Source C," which is S.I. Bruk, ed. *Chislennost'i Rasselenie Naradox Mira* (Moscow: Izdatel'stvo Akademii Nauk S.S.S.R., Institut Ethnografii, 1962).

[26]Kloss, "Notes Concerning a Language-Nation Typology," p. 81.

[27]The survey is being conducted at the International Center for Research on Bilingualism, Cite Universitaire, Quebec, Canada. It is administering mail questionaires to assess linguistic aspects of "language corpus," demographic distribution of languages, and literary uses of language.

[28]Daryll Forde, ed., *African Worlds: Studies in the Cosmological Ideas and Social Values of African Peoples* (London: Oxford University Press, 1954); John S. Mbiti, *African Religions and Philosophy* (New York: Praeger, 1969); John V. Taylor, *The Primal Vision: Christian Presence and African Religion* (London: SCM Press, 1968); Fr. Piacide Tempels, *La Philosophie Bantoue* (Elizabethville: Editions Louvania, 1945). Also see N. S. Book, *African Religions: A Symposium* (New York: NOK 1977) and H.W. Turner *Bibliography of New Religious Movements in Primal Societies vol 1: Black Africa.* (Boston: G. K. Hall, 1977).

[29] Jean C. Froelich, *Les Musulmans d'Afrique Noire* (Paris: Editions de l'Orane, 1962): I.M. Lewis, ed., *Islam in Tropical Africa* (London: Oxford University Press, 1966); Vincent Nonteil, *L'Islam Noire* (Paris: Editions de Seuil, 1964); J. Spencer Trimingham, *The Influence of Islam upon Africa* (London: Longmans, 1968); J. Kritzeck and W. I. Lewis, eds., *Islam in Africa* (Cincinnati, Ohio: Van Nostrand-Reinhold) and J.M. Cuoq *Les Musulmans en Afrique* (Paris: Maisonneuve et Larouse, 1975) and R.V. Weekes *Muslim Peoples* (Westport: Greeenwood Press, 1978). For a review of available literature see A. Oded "A Bibliographic Essay on the History of Islam in Africa" in *A Current Bibliography on African Affairs* 8, 1 (1975). Also see P.E. Ofori, *Islam in Africa South of the Sahara* (Nendeln, Lichtenstein: KTO Press, 1977) and S.M. Zoghby *Islam in sub-Saharan Africa: A partially annotated guide,* (Washington D.C., Library of Congress, 1978).

[30]C.G. Baeta, ed., *Christianity in Tropical Africa* (London: Oxford University Press, 1968); T.A. Beetham, *Christianity and the New Africa* (London: Pall Mall, 1967). See also the *Journal of Religion in Africa* (Leiden, the Netherlands: E.O. Brill) and C.P. Groves, *The Planning of Christianity in Africa*, 4 vols. (London: Lutterworth Press, 1948—1958).

[31]R.P. Beaver, ed., *Christianity and African Education* (Grand Rapids, Mich.: Erdmans, 1966). Many African countries have nationalized the educational system in recent years and missionary based education is rapidly disappearing.

[32]Raymond F. Hopkins, "Christianity and Sociopolitical Change in Sub-Saharan Africa," *Social Forces*, 44 (1966): 555—562.

[33]Robert Cameron Mitchell and Donald George Morrison, "On Christianity and Sociopolitical Change," *Social Forces*, 48 (1970): 397—408.

[34]H.J. Fisher, *Ahmadiyyah: A Study in Contemporary Islam on the West African Coast* (London: Oxford University Press, 1963).

[35]David B. Barrett, *Schism and Renewal in Africa: An Analysis of Six Thousand Contemporary Religious Movements* (Nairobi: Oxford University Press, 1968); Robert Cameron Mitchell and Harold W. Turner, eds., *A Comprehensive Bibliography of Modern African Religious Movements* (Evanston, Ill.: Northwestern University Press, 1967). Also see B. R. Wilson *Magic and the Millenium* (London: Heineman, 1974).

[36] H. Wakelin Coxill and Kenneth Grubb, eds., *World Christian Handbook 1968* (London: Lutterworth Press, 1968). Previous editions of this work appeared in 1949, 1952, 1957 and 1962. This source does not date its information, but it is presumed that it generally is for the year preceding each edition, so in using the 1968 Handbook we refer to 1967 data. The Handbook is probably the most commonly used source for Protestant data in Africa, and is used widely as authoritative despite its various faults.

[37]These two groupings are not exactly comparable as the Protestant "Christian community" category is somewhat broader. The official definition for the Christian community category given in the *World Christian Handbook* states that the category includes all communicants and full members and in addition "all participants in the life of your church, such as regular worshipers, children of Christian parents, catechumens, and members of functional groups, etc.." Of course the Roman Catholic data always includes baptized children as members, but even the Catholic catechumen category would not necessarily include "regular worshipers."

[38]For the 1968 data we used the Mission Information Centre, *Ready Information about Africa* (London: Mission Information Centre, 1965). Previous editions appeared in 1956 and 1962. It presents the *Propaganda Fide* data for 1963.

[39]Eglise Vivant, *Bilan du Monde* (Paris: Casterman, 1964). A previous edition appeared in 1958—1959.

[40]Regrettably, the 1968 *Handbook* presented the Catholic data only for "Roman Catholics" omitting the "catechumen" category which it had included in the 1962 *Handbook*. The *Handbook* gets its data from official Roman Catholic sources.

[41]It should be noted that each edition of the Handbook points out the problems of unreliability and urges caution in the use of the data, especially over time. The editors mention missing information, the varying quality of the information supplied, the duplication of churches, and the respondents' differing interpretations of the categories they are asked to use, as the major sources of error in the *Handbook*.

[42]Rycroft and Clemmer, in a useful compilation of religious and non-religious data on Africa, present a table giving Protestant totals for na-

tions which edits the 1962 *Handbook* data to eliminate these duplica-
tions. W. Stanley Rycroft and Myrtle M. Clemmer, *A Factual Study of
Sub-Saharan Africa* (New York: Commission on Ecumenical Mission
and Relations, the United Presbyterian Church in the U.S.A., 1962), p.
110.

[43]Two of the most important of these sources are: Harlan P. Beach
and Charles H. Fahs, eds., *World Missionary Atlas* (New York: Institute of Social and Religious Research, 1925); and Joseph I. Parker, *In-
terpretative Statistical Survey of the World Mission of the Christian
Church* (New York: International Missionary Council, 1938).

[44]Hildegard Binder Johnson, "Christian Mission Stations in Africa
in the 1920's" *The Geographical Review*, 57, no. 2 (1961), Plate 1.

[45]Hildegard Binder Johnson, "The Location of Christian Missions in
Africa," *The Geographical Review*, 57, no. 2 (1961): 168.

[46]It would seem that the data in the *Handbook*, when given, are
relatively reliable. A fairly precise change measure could be developed
for a limited number of Protestant denominations by calculating the
growth of only those denominations whose data could be traced
through the different editions of the *World Christian Handbook*. This
would eliminate missing data. It would of course be biased towards the
bigger, more main-line denominations, and also towards those with the
more reliable data-gathering procedures. It should be noted that data
cited in a later *Handbook* as coming from the previous *Handbook* are
sometimes from an even earlier *Handbook*, thereby vastly complicating
the calculation of Protestant growth rates.

[47]The Christian religion data in the first edition of this work were
drawn from the *World Christian Handbook* and therefore represent in-
dicators of adherence. The data for the second edition was supplied by
David Barrett and includes the African Independent Churches in the
Christian category—the Christian variables are of identifiers. Bruce M.
Russett, ed., *World Handbook of Political and Social Indicators* (New
Haven, Conn.: Yale University Press, 1964) and C.L. Taylor and M.
Hudson *World Handbook of Political and Social Indicators* (New Ha-
ven: Yale University Press, 1972).

[48]The second edition of the *World Handbook of Political and Social
Indicators*, C.L. Taylor and M. Hudson (eds.) presents a "total Christian" variable, but Roman Catholic data used in this variable only includes "Roman Catholics" (baptized only), thus leaving out Roman
Catholic catechumens, while the corresponding Protestant data includes catechumens. This results in an underestimate of adherence,
particularly in the heavily Roman Catholic countries. We attempt to
compensate here for the lack of catechumen data for 1966 by calculating
for each nation a ratio of catechumens to Roman Catholics for 1963. We
then multiply the ratio by the 1966 Roman Catholic data. The result is
an estimate of the 1966 catechumens for each country. We add this estimate to the 1966 Roman Catholic figure and then add the result, estimated Roman Catholic adherents 1966, to the Protestant, African Independent Churches, and Ethiopian Orthodox data to obtain "total
Christian affiliators" for 1966.

[49]For two succinct discussions of the problems of ethnic unit classification or identification, see Raoul Naroll, "On Ethnic Unit Classification," *Current Anthropology*, 5 (1964): 282—312, and Alan Merriam,
"The Concept of Culture Clusters Applied to the Belgian Congo,"
Southeastern Journal of Anthropology, 15 (1959): 373—395.

[50]For a discussion of concepts, see Jack Goody, *Comparative Studies in Kinship* (Stanford: Stanford University Press, 1960); George Peter
Murdock, *Social Structure* (New York: Free Press, 1949).

[51]For a discussion of ethnic political authority patterns, see Ronald

Cohen and A. Schlegel, "The Tribe as a Socio-Political Unit—A Cross-
Cultural Examination," in *Essays on the Problem of Tribe*, ed. June
Helm (Seattle: University of Washington Press, 1968), pp. 120—149;
Ronald Cohen and John Middleton, eds., *Comparative Political Sys-
tems* (Garden City, N.Y.: The Natural History Press, 1967); John Mid-
dleton and David Tait, eds., *Tribes Without Rulers* (London: Rout-
ledge and Kegan Paul, 1958); Marc J. Swartz, Victor W. Turner, Arthur
Tuden, eds., *Political Anthropology* (Chicago: Aldine, 1966); Max
Gluckman, *Politics, Law and Ritual in Tribal Society* (Oxford:
Blackwell, 1965); Michael Banton, ed., *Political Systems and the Distribution of Power* (Edinburgh: Tavistock Publications, 1963).

[52]For a discussion of economic factors in ethnic society, see George
Dalton, "Traditional Economic Systems," in *The African Experience*,
Vol. I, eds. John N. Paden and Edward W. Soja (Evanston, Ill.: Northwestern University Press, 1970); George Dalton, ed., *Tribal and Peasant Economies: Readings in Economic Anthropology* (New York: Doubleday, 1967).

[53]These scales were constructed for the most part from the nominal
classifications used in George P. Murdock, *Ethnographic Atlas* (Pittsburgh: University of Pittsburgh Press, 1967). Complete operational
definitions of the ordinal scales used in the measures of cultural pluralism given in this chapter are provided in the tables. The full definitions
of the other variables summarized in Figure 2.4 are contained in a machine-readable codebook which can be consulted upon request to be
author.

[54]Because the data is ordinal, this is, at best, only an approximation
of an ideal measure of pluralism. It is offered here to encourage other
measures that might be more accurate indicators.

[55]The choice of weighting depends on the view of the researcher as
to the main interacting units in his own research (i.e., individuals or
groups of individuals).

[56]George Peter Murdock, *Ethnographic Atlas* (Pittsburgh: University of Pittsburgh Press, 1967).

[57]George Peter Murdock, *Cultural Summaries: Africa*, 6 volumes,
unpublished. Available at Africana Library, Northwestern University

[58]Additional sources that were consulted where necessary were the
Human Relations Area Files (HRAF), computer indexed at Northwestern University (see Donald G. Morrison, "An Index to the Human Relations Area Files," *American Behavioral Scientist*, 10 (February 1967):
27—30; George Peter Murdock, *Outline of Cultural Materials* (New
Haven, Conn.: HRAF Press, 1962), and *Outline of World Cultures* 3rd
ed. (New Haven, Conn.: HRAF Press, 1965); and Robert B. Textor, *A
Cross-Cultural Summary* (New Haven, Conn.: HRAF Press, 1967).
For a discussion of the above, see Robert B. Textor "Computer Summarization of Coded Cross-Cultural Literature," in *Comparative Research across Cultures and Nations*, ed. Stein Rokkan (The Hague:
Mouton, 1968), pp. 54—63.

[59]For a discussion of cross-cultural reliability, see Robert M. Marsh,
Comparative Sociology (New York: Harcourt, Brace and World, 1967);
Frank W. Moore, ed., *Readings in Cross-Cultural Methodology* (New
Haven, Conn.: HRAF Press, 1961), pp. 261—279; and Raoul Naroll,
Data Quality Control (New York: Free Press, 1962).

[60]For a discussion of incorporation and integration in ethnic groups
over time, see Ronald Cohen and John Middleton, *From Tribe to Nation in Africa: Studies in Incorporation Processes* (Scranton, Pa.: Chandler Publishing Company, 1970). An example of the reverse process
whereby a new group is created is J.T. Gallagher "The Emergence of
an African Ethnic Group: the Case of the Ndendeli" *International Jour-*

nal of African Studies, 7, 1 (1974) pp. 1—26.

TABLE 2.1 Percent Speaking Dominant Vernacular Language, ca. 1977.

Definition: Percent of the total population who speak the dominant vernacular language as a first or second language.

```
Range =            76.00
Mean =             61.80
Standard Deviation =            22.84
```

Population Percent Cum.	Country	Rank	Country Name	A	Range Decile
2.48	2.48	1.0	Madagascar	100	1
2.86	.38	2.0	Lesotho	99	
3.09	.23	3.5	Botswana	98	
4.45	1.36	3.5	Rwanda	98	
5.48	1.03	5.0	Somalia	97	
5.64	.16	6.5	Swaziland	95	
10.80	5.16	6.5	Tanzania	95	
12.08	1.28	8.5	Burundi	90	2
12.54	.46	8.5	Mauritania	90	
12.64	.10	10.5	Equatorial Guinea	85	
17.24	4.60	10.5	Kenya	85	
18.57	1.33	12.0	Niger	81	3
20.83	2.26	13.0	Zimbabwe	78	
22.47	1.64	14.0	Senegal	67	5
22.57	.10	15.5	Djibouti	65	
28.81	6.24	15.5	Sudan	65	
29.81	1.00	19.0	Benin	60	6
31.15	1.34	19.0	Chad	60	
31.32	.17	19.0	Gambia	60	
32.98	1.66	19.0	Malawi	60	
34.95	1.97	19.0	Upper Volta	60	
55.95	21.00	22.0	Nigeria	55	
56.40	.45	23.0	Congo	52	7
66.11	9.71	26.0	Ethiopia	50	
66.27	.16	26.0	Gabon	50	
68.14	1.87	26.0	Mali	50	
68.43	.29	26.0	Namibia	50	
69.18	.75	26.0	Togo	50	
70.75	1.57	29.0	Guinea	48	
71.74	.99	30.0	Sierra Leone	45	8
75.25	3.51	31.5	Ghana	44	
75.78	.53	31.5	Liberia	44	
79.73	3.95	33.0	Uganda	41	
81.68	1.95	35.0	Angola	40	
84.67	2.99	35.0	Mozambique	40	
92.96	8.29	35.0	Zaire	40	
94.61	1.65	37.0	Zambia	35	9
95.19	.58	38.0	Central African R	31	10
95.38	.19	39.0	Guinea-Bissau	30	
97.60	2.22	40.0	Ivory Coast	27	
100.00	2.41	41.0	Cameroon	24	

TABLE 2.2 Primacy of First Language, ca. 1977.

Definition: Primacy ratio based on percent speakers of the first (most widely spoken) language divided by the percent speakers of the second language. The higher the ratio, the greater the primacy.

```
Range =            97.90
Mean =             8.55
Standard Deviation =            20.95
```

Population Percent Cum.	Country	Rank	Country Name	A	Range Decile
.38	.38	1.0	Lesotho	99.0	1
.61	.23	2.0	Botswana	98.0	
1.64	1.03	3.0	Somalia	32.3	7
1.74	.10	4.0	Equatorial Guinea	8.5	10
6.90	5.16	5.0	Tanzania	7.9	
7.36	.46	6.0	Mauritania	6.9	
8.72	1.36	7.0	Rwanda	6.7	
8.88	.16	8.0	Swaziland	6.3	
10.16	1.28	9.0	Burundi	6.0	
12.42	2.26	10.0	Zimbabwe	5.2	
12.71	.29	11.0	Namibia	5.0	
13.71	1.00	12.0	Benin	4.3	
13.88	.17	13.5	Gambia	3.8	
16.36	2.48	13.5	Madagascar	3.8	
22.60	6.24	15.0	Sudan	3.6	
27.20	4.60	16.5	Kenya	3.4	
28.53	1.33	16.5	Niger	3.4	
30.19	1.66	18.0	Malawi	3.2	
32.06	1.87	19.0	Mali	3.1	
33.70	1.64	20.0	Senegal	3.0	
35.67	1.97	21.0	Upper Volta	2.9	
39.18	3.51	22.0	Ghana	2.8	
39.63	.45	23.0	Congo	2.6	
39.79	.16	24.5	Gabon	2.5	
40.54	.75	24.5	Togo	2.5	
41.88	1.34	26.0	Chad	2.1	
62.88	21.00	27.5	Nigeria	2.0	
64.53	1.65	27.5	Zambia	2.0	
67.52	2.99	29.0	Mozambique	1.7	
69.47	1.95	30.0	Angola	1.6	
71.04	1.57	32.0	Guinea	1.5	
71.23	.19	32.0	Guinea-Bissau	1.5	
73.45	2.22	32.0	Ivory Coast	1.5	
73.55	.10	34.5	Djibouti	1.4	
77.50	3.95	34.5	Uganda	1.4	
79.91	2.41	37.0	Cameroon	1.3	
89.62	9.71	37.0	Ethiopia	1.3	
90.61	.99	37.0	Sierra Leone	1.3	
91.14	.53	39.0	Liberia	1.2	
91.72	.58	40.5	Central African R	1.1	
100.00	8.29	40.5	Zaire	1.1	

SOURCES: Estimates based on data by Jan Knappert, "Language Problems of the New Nations of Africa," *African Quarterly*, 5 (1965): 95—105; Dankwart Rustow, "Language, Modernization and Nationhood-An Attempt at Typology," in *Language Problems of Developing Nations*, eds. Joshua A. Fishman et al. (New York: John Wiley, 1968); Duncan MacDougald, *The Languages and Press of Africa* (Philadelphia: University of Pennsylvania Press, 1944). For discussions of estimations and languages for each country see Part II of this Handbook.

SOURCES: Estimates for percent speakers of second and first languages are detailed by country in Part II.

Notes: Madagascar has only one vernacular language. The ratio is formed by taking the ratio of Malagasy to French speakers.

TABLE 2.3 **Estimated Number of Languages per Million Population (A) and Total Number of Indigenous Languages Spoken, ca. 1972 (B).**

Definition and Comments: This is the number of individual indigenous languages. The source gives a figure of 1014 such languages for thirty-eight countries, but many experts regard this as an under-estimate. The major problem is in deciding whether a language is a dialect of another language or a language in its own right. The number of languages is divided by the country's 1972 population in millions. Since rank order is maintained over the years no recalculation for 1977 was necessary.

```
Range =         27.60
Mean =           6.53
Standard Deviation =        6.90
```

Population Percent Cum.	Country	Rank	Country Name	A	Range Decile	B
.75	.75	1.0	Togo	27.7	1	56
1.33	.58	2.0	Central African R	24.3	2	41
1.49	.16	3.0	Gabon	21.4	3	15
2.02	.53	4.0	Liberia	18.3	4	29
2.12	.10	5.0	Equatorial Guinea	17.0		5
3.77	1.65	6.0	Zambia	15.2	5	69
3.94	.17	7.5	Gambia	12.6	6	6
6.16	2.22	7.5	Ivory Coast	12.6		57
6.35	.19	9.5	Guinea-Bissau	12.0		6
12.59	6.24	9.5	Sudan	12.0		171
15.00	2.41	11.0	Cameroon	8.3	8	50
15.16	.16	12.0	Swaziland	7.0		3
16.50	1.34	13.0	Chad	5.9		22
16.95	.45	14.0	Congo	5.8		7
17.05	.10	15.0	Djibouti	5.5	9	6
18.62	1.57	16.0	Guinea	5.4		22
19.62	1.00	17.0	Benin	5.3		15
21.59	1.97	18.0	Upper Volta	4.8		27
23.54	1.95	19.0	Angola	4.2		25
27.05	3.51	20.0	Ghana	4.1		37
32.21	5.16	21.0	Tanzania	4.0		56
33.54	1.33	22.0	Niger	3.3		14
33.77	.23	23.0	Botswana	3.1		2
34.76	.99	24.0	Sierra Leone	2.9		8
36.63	1.87	25.0	Mali	2.8	10	15
44.92	8.29	26.0	Zaire	2.7		61
54.63	9.71	27.0	Ethiopia	2.4		63
58.58	3.95	28.0	Uganda	2.3		24
79.58	21.00	29.0	Nigeria	2.2		125
81.22	1.64	30.0	Senegal	2.0		8
81.60	.38	31.0	Lesotho	1.9		2
86.20	4.60	32.0	Kenya	1.8		22
86.66	.46	33.0	Mauritania	1.6		2
89.65	2.99	34.0	Mozambique	1.3		11
91.31	1.66	35.0	Malawi	1.1		5
91.60	.29	36.0	Namibia	.8		10
92.63	1.03	37.0	Somalia	.7		2
93.91	1.28	38.0	Burundi	.6		2
95.27	1.36	39.0	Rwanda	.5		2
97.53	2.26	40.0	Zimbabwe	.4		3
100.00	2.48	41.0	Madagascar	.1		1

SOURCE: Based on data in Knappert, "Language Problems of the New Nations of Africa." Angola and Equatorial Guinea data provided by Dr. David Barrett and the *World Christian Handbook*.

Note: Counts of the number of languages spoken in a country are somewhat variable, particularly for the large plural states. Hence, care should be taken in the uncritical use of data in this table.

TABLE 2.4 **Language Classification: Corpus Distance Index 1977.**

Definition: The following categories are an ordinal scale on the degree of linguistic similarity between the vernacular languages of a country's ethnic units.

(1) One category, no internal sub-categories (all indigenous languages are in the same linguistic classification category).
(2) One category, two or three internal sub-categories.
(3) One category, more than three sub-categories.
(4) Two major categories, no internal sub-categories.
(5) Two major categories, two or three internal sub-catagories.
(6) Two major categories, more than three internal sub-categories.
(7) Three major categories, no internal sub-categories.
(8) Three major categories, two or three internal sub-categories.

The higher the number on the scale, the more linguistically heterogeneous are the country's ethnic units.

```
Range =         7.00
Mean =          2.76
Standard Deviation =        2.27
```

Population Percent Cum.	Country	Rank	Country Name	A	Range Decile
1.87	1.87	2.5	Mali	8	1
3.20	1.33	2.5	Niger	8	
24.20	21.00	2.5	Nigeria	8	
30.44	6.24	2.5	Sudan	8	
30.73	.29	5.0	Namibia	7	2
33.14	2.41	6.0	Cameroon	6	3
34.48	1.34	7.5	Chad	5	5
38.43	3.95	7.5	Uganda	5	
39.71	1.28	10.5	Burundi	4	6
44.31	4.60	10.5	Kenya	4	
44.77	.46	10.5	Mauritania	4	
46.13	1.36	10.5	Rwanda	4	
47.13	1.00	19.0	Benin	2	9
56.84	9.71	19.0	Ethiopia	2	
57.01	.17	19.0	Gambia	2	
60.52	3.51	19.0	Ghana	2	
62.09	1.57	19.0	Guinea	2	
62.28	.19	19.0	Guinea-Bissau	2	
64.50	2.22	19.0	Ivory Coast	2	
65.03	.53	19.0	Liberia	2	
66.67	1.64	19.0	Senegal	2	
67.66	.99	19.0	Sierra Leone	2	
68.41	.75	19.0	Togo	2	
70.38	1.97	19.0	Upper Volta	2	
78.67	8.29	19.0	Zaire	2	
80.62	1.95	33.5	Angola	1	
80.85	.23	33.5	Botswana	1	
81.43	.58	33.5	Central African R	1	
81.88	.45	33.5	Congo	1	
81.98	.10	33.5	Djibouti	1	
82.08	.10	33.5	Equatorial Guinea	1	
82.24	.16	33.5	Gabon	1	
82.62	.38	33.5	Lesotho	1	
85.10	2.48	33.5	Madagascar	1	
86.76	1.66	33.5	Malawi	1	
89.75	2.99	33.5	Mozambique	1	
90.78	1.03	33.5	Somalia	1	
90.94	.16	33.5	Swaziland	1	
96.10	5.16	33.5	Tanzania	1	
97.75	1.65	33.5	Zambia	1	
100.00	2.26	33.5	Zimbabwe	1	

SOURCE: Calculated on the basis of the classifications in J. Greenberg, *The Languages of Africa* (Bloomington: Indiana University, 1966). See Part II, Country Profiles, for the individual ethnic unit language classifications. See Part II language sections for alternative codings using David Dalby's procedure.

TABLE 2.5 Vernacular Lingua Franca, ca. 1980.

Definition: Lingua franca refers to a vernacular language which is spoken by 5 percent or more of the total population as a "second" language. This ordinally scaled variable is coded as follows.
(1) No vernacular lingua franca in the country.
(2) Existence of a lingua franca in the country which is neither the largest nor the second largest language.
(3) Second largest language serves as a lingua franca.
(4) Largest language serves as a lingua franca.
(5) Largest and second largest languages both serve as lingua francas. In most African states, the language of their ex-metropole is the effective *lingua franca* but we exclude those languages in this measure.

```
Range =              4.00
Mean =               3.68
Standard Deviation =         1.11
```

Population Percent Cum.	Country	Rank	Country Name	A	Range Decile
1.28	1.28	4.5	Burundi	5	1
1.38	.10	4.5	Equatorial Guinea	5	
11.09	9.71	4.5	Ethiopia	5	
12.66	1.57	4.5	Guinea	5	
14.02	1.36	4.5	Rwanda	5	
17.97	3.95	4.5	Uganda	5	
19.94	1.97	4.5	Upper Volta	5	
28.23	8.29	4.5	Zaire	5	
30.18	1.95	20.0	Angola	4	3
31.18	1.00	20.0	Benin	4	
31.41	.23	20.0	Botswana	4	
32.75	1.34	20.0	Chad	4	
33.20	.45	20.0	Congo	4	
33.36	.16	20.0	Gabon	4	
33.53	.17	20.0	Gambia	4	
33.72	.19	20.0	Guinea-Bissau	4	
38.32	4.60	20.0	Kenya	4	
38.70	.38	20.0	Lesotho	4	
41.18	2.48	20.0	Madagascar	4	
42.84	1.66	20.0	Malawi	4	
44.71	1.87	20.0	Mali	4	
45.17	.46	20.0	Mauritania	4	
46.50	1.33	20.0	Niger	4	
67.50	21.00	20.0	Nigeria	4	
69.14	1.64	20.0	Senegal	4	
70.17	1.03	20.0	Somalia	4	
76.41	6.24	20.0	Sudan	4	
76.57	.16	20.0	Swaziland	4	
81.73	5.16	20.0	Tanzania	4	
82.48	.75	20.0	Togo	4	
84.74	2.26	20.0	Zimbabwe	4	
85.73	.99	32.0	Sierra Leone	3	5
88.14	2.41	36.0	Cameroon	2	8
88.72	.58	36.0	Central African R	2	
88.82	.10	36.0	Djibouti	2	
92.33	3.51	36.0	Ghana	2	
94.55	2.22	36.0	Ivory Coast	2	
95.08	.53	36.0	Liberia	2	
95.37	.29	36.0	Namibia	2	
98.36	2.99	40.5	Mozambique	1	10
100.00	1.65	40.5	Zambia	1	

SOURCE: See Part II for a discussion of this coding for each country.

TABLE 2.6 Primary Language Standardization, ca. 1977.

Definition: The first or second largest vernacular language (depending on which is most standardized) is judged on its degree of standardization (i.e., orthography and literary tradition). The four-fold ordinal scale is coded as follows:
(1) Pre-literate language.
(2) Unstandardized alphabetized language.
(3) Young standardized language.
(4) Mature standardized language.

```
Range =              3.00
Mean =               2.80
Standard Deviation =         .94
```

Population Percent Cum.	Country	Rank	Country Name	A	Range Decile
1.28	1.28	7.5	Burundi	4	1
2.62	1.34	7.5	Chad	4	
12.33	9.71	7.5	Ethiopia	4	
16.93	4.60	7.5	Kenya	4	
17.39	.46	7.5	Mauritania	4	
17.68	.29	7.5	Namibia	4	
19.01	1.33	7.5	Niger	4	
40.01	21.00	7.5	Nigeria	4	
41.37	1.36	7.5	Rwanda	4	
47.61	6.24	7.5	Sudan	4	
52.77	5.16	7.5	Tanzania	4	
56.72	3.95	7.5	Uganda	4	
65.01	8.29	7.5	Zaire	4	
67.27	2.26	7.5	Zimbabwe	4	
67.44	.17	17.5	Gambia	3	4
69.01	1.57	17.5	Guinea	3	
69.20	.19	17.5	Guinea-Bissau	3	
71.68	2.48	17.5	Madagascar	3	
73.55	1.87	17.5	Mali	3	
75.19	1.64	17.5	Senegal	3	
77.14	1.95	30.5	Angola	2	7
78.14	1.00	30.5	Benin	2	
78.37	.23	30.5	Botswana	2	
80.78	2.41	30.5	Cameroon	2	
81.36	.58	30.5	Central African R	2	
81.81	.45	30.5	Congo	2	
81.91	.10	30.5	Djibouti	2	
82.01	.10	30.5	Equatorial Guinea	2	
82.17	.16	30.5	Gabon	2	
85.68	3.51	30.5	Ghana	2	
87.90	2.22	30.5	Ivory Coast	2	
88.28	.38	30.5	Lesotho	2	
88.81	.53	30.5	Liberia	2	
90.47	1.66	30.5	Malawi	2	
91.46	.99	30.5	Sierra Leone	2	
92.49	1.03	30.5	Somalia	2	
92.65	.16	30.5	Swaziland	2	
93.40	.75	30.5	Togo	2	
95.37	1.97	30.5	Upper Volta	2	
97.02	1.65	30.5	Zambia	2	
100.00	2.99	41.0	Mozambique	1	10

SOURCE: Scale adapted from Heinz Kloss, "Notes Concerning a Language-Nation Typology," in *Language Problems of Developing Nations*, eds. Fishman et al., pp. 77—83. *Burundi, Zaire, Gambia, Guinea, Guinea, Mali, Senegal, Uganda*: Standardization calculated on second largest language rather than first.

TABLE 2.7   Vernacular Language Policy, ca. 1977.

Definition: An ordinal scale based on the degree of official government encouragement of the use of vernacular language, ranging from the complete lack of utilization to complete utilization.

(1) Non-indigenous (exoglossic) language primacy as government policy (e.g., French or English).
(2) Use of the vernacular in public communications *media* (e.g., radio).
(3) Use of vernacular in *educational* institutions (any level, but excluding adult literacy campaigns).
(4) Existence of one or more official *regional* vernacular languages.
(5) Existence of an official national vernacular language, which is *symbolic* but not used in government operations.
(6) Existence of an official national vernacular language (usually co-equal with an exoglossic language in which the government conducts a significant number of operations).
(7) Existence of an official national vernacular language (which is clearly dominant over any exoglossic language) which constitutes the major *working* language of the government.

```
Range =           6.00
Mean =            3.51
Standard Deviation =          2.07
```

Population Percent Cum.	Country	Rank	Country Name	A	Range Decile
9.71	9.71	2.0	Ethiopia	7	1
15.95	6.24	2.0	Sudan	7	
21.11	5.16	2.0	Tanzania	7	
21.34	.23	8.5	Botswana	6	2
22.62	1.28	8.5	Burundi	6	
27.22	4.60	8.5	Kenya	6	
27.60	.38	8.5	Lesotho	6	
30.08	2.48	8.5	Madagascar	6	
30.54	.46	8.5	Mauritania	6	
31.90	1.36	8.5	Rwanda	6	
32.93	1.03	8.5	Somalia	6	
33.09	.16	8.5	Swaziland	6	
41.38	8.29	8.5	Zaire	6	
41.96	.58	14.5	Central African R	5	4
42.71	.75	14.5	Togo	5	
63.71	21.00	16.5	Nigeria	4	6
67.66	3.95	16.5	Uganda	4	
67.76	.10	19.0	Equatorial Guinea	3	7
67.93	.17	19.0	Gambia	3	
68.92	.99	19.0	Sierra Leone	3	
69.92	1.00	28.0	Benin	2	9
72.33	2.41	28.0	Cameroon	2	
73.67	1.34	28.0	Chad	2	
74.12	.45	28.0	Congo	2	
74.28	.16	28.0	Gabon	2	
77.79	3.51	28.0	Ghana	2	
79.36	1.57	28.0	Guinea	2	
81.58	2.22	28.0	Ivory Coast	2	
82.11	.53	28.0	Liberia	2	
83.77	1.66	28.0	Malawi	2	
85.64	1.87	28.0	Mali	2	
86.97	1.33	28.0	Niger	2	
88.61	1.64	28.0	Senegal	2	
90.58	1.97	28.0	Upper Volta	2	
92.23	1.65	28.0	Zambia	2	
94.18	1.95	38.5	Angola	1	
94.28	.10	38.5	Djibouti	1	
94.47	.19	38.5	Guinea-Bissau	1	
97.46	2.99	38.5	Mozambique	1	
97.75	.29	38.5	Namibia	1	
100.00	2.26	38.5	Zimbabwe	1	

SOURCE: Scale developed by Kloss, "Notes Concerning a Language-Nation Typology" pp. 79—81. See Part II for discussion of each nation's language policy.

TABLE 2.8   Estimated Percent Identifiers with Islam, ca. 1980 (A), 1970 (B) and 1966 (C).

Definition: Identifiers refers to those who would identify with a particular religion when asked their religion by someone such as a census taker. Since no official roles exist for Islamic religious membership this is the only way to identify Muslims.

```
Range =      100.00
Mean =        29.90
Standard Deviation =          33.08
```

Population Percent Cum.	Country	Rank	Country Name	A	Range Decile	B	C
1.03	1.03	1.0	Somalia	100	1	100	99
1.49	.46	2.0	Mauritania	99		99	96
1.59	.10	3.5	Djibouti	91		87	90
3.23	1.64	3.5	Senegal	91		90	82
4.56	1.33	5.0	Niger	88	2	86	85
4.73	.17	6.0	Gambia	85		84	80
6.60	1.87	7.0	Mali	80	3	78	65
12.84	6.24	8.0	Sudan	73		71	60
14.41	1.57	9.0	Guinea	69	4	68	65
35.41	21.00	10.0	Nigeria	45	6	44	50
36.75	1.34	11.0	Chad	44		42	50
38.72	1.97	12.0	Upper Volta	43		35	22
39.71	.99	13.0	Sierra Leone	39	7	38	30
39.90	.19	14.0	Guinea-Bissau	38		35	33
45.06	5.16	15.0	Tanzania	33		31	23
54.77	9.71	16.0	Ethiopia	31		31	40
56.99	2.22	17.0	Ivory Coast	24	8	23	23
59.40	2.41	18.0	Cameroon	22		20	15
59.93	.53	19.0	Liberia	21		19	15
60.68	.75	20.0	Togo	17	9	13	8
64.19	3.51	21.5	Ghana	16		14	19
65.85	1.66	21.5	Malawi	16		16	12
66.85	1.00	23.0	Benin	15		14	15
69.84	2.99	24.0	Mozambique	13		12	12
71.20	1.36	25.0	Rwanda	9	10	8	1
75.15	3.95	26.0	Uganda	7		6	6
79.75	4.60	27.0	Kenya	6		6	4
80.33	.58	28.0	Central African R	3		3	5
82.81	2.48	29.0	Madagascar	2		2	1
84.09	1.28	32.5	Burundi	1		1	1
84.54	.45	32.5	Congo	1		0	0
84.64	.10	32.5	Equatorial Guinea	1		1	0
84.80	.16	32.5	Gabon	1		1	1
93.09	8.29	32.5	Zaire	1		2	1
95.35	2.26	32.5	Zimbabwe	1		1	0
97.30	1.95	38.5	Angola	0		0	0
97.53	.23	38.5	Botswana	0		0	0
97.91	.38	38.5	Lesotho	0		0	0
98.20	.29	38.5	Namibia	0		0	0
98.36	.16	38.5	Swaziland	0		0	0
100.00	1.65	38.5	Zambia	0		0	0

SOURCES: (1966) Unless otherwise noted, the estimates are based on J.S. Trimingham, *The Influence of Islam upon Africa* (London: Longmans, 1968), pp. 113—114 and the *Statesman's Yearbook 1967—68*. Official government census or sample survey data were available on religion and used to make the estimates for: *Ghana, Benin, Kenya, Lesotho, Mali, Nigeria and Senegal. Cameroon: Islam en Afrique* (Brussels: Pro Mundi Vita, forthcoming); *Tanzania*: L.W. Swantz, "Church, Mission and State Relations in Pre- and Post-Independence Tanzania (1955—1964)," Occasional paper No. 19 (Syracuse: Program of East African Studies, 1966). (1970, 1980) D. B. Barrett ed. *World Christian Encyclopedia* (Nairobi: Oxford University Press), 1982).

TABLE 2.9   Estimated Percent Identifiers with Christianity, ca. 1980 (A), 1970 (B) and 1966 (C).

Definition: Identifiers refers to those who would identify with a particular religion when asked their religion by someone such as a census taker. Includes the African Independent Churches, the Orthodox Churches as well as the Protestant and Roman Catholic Churches.

```
Range =        96.00
Mean =         47.59
Standard Deviation =      33.13
```

Population Percent			Country		Range		
Cum.	Country	Rank	Name	A	Decile	B	C
.16	.16	1.5	Gabon	96	1	96	75
.45	.29	1.5	Namibia	96		95	89
8.74	8.29	3.0	Zaire	95		90	65
9.19	.45	4.5	Congo	93		92	64
9.57	.38	4.5	Lesotho	93		86	81
11.52	1.95	6.0	Angola	90		83	55
11.62	.10	7.0	Equatorial Guinea	89		88	89
12.90	1.28	8.0	Burundi	86	2	74	64
13.48	.58	9.0	Central African R	84		77	47
17.43	3.95	10.0	Uganda	78		69	60
17.59	.16	11.0	Swaziland	77		70	60
22.19	4.60	12.5	Kenya	73	3	64	58
23.55	1.36	12.5	Rwanda	73		62	42
25.20	1.65	14.0	Zambia	72		65	30
26.86	1.66	15.0	Malawi	65	4	59	42
30.37	3.51	16.0	Ghana	63		53	46
32.63	2.26	17.0	Zimbabwe	58		52	45
42.34	9.71	18.0	Ethiopia	57	5	55	37
44.75	2.41	19.0	Cameroon	56		47	49
47.23	2.48	20.0	Madagascar	51		49	38
47.46	.23	21.0	Botswana	50		43	29
68.46	21.00	22.0	Nigeria	49		45	35
73.62	5.16	23.0	Tanzania	44	6	36	40
76.61	2.99	24.0	Mozambique	40		30	21
77.36	.75	25.0	Togo	37	7	30	28
77.89	.53	26.0	Liberia	35		31	25
79.23	1.34	27.0	Chad	33		31	10
81.45	2.22	28.0	Ivory Coast	32		28	18
82.45	1.00	29.0	Benin	23	8	19	18
84.42	1.97	30.0	Upper Volta	12	9	10	6
84.61	.19	31.0	Guinea-Bissau	10		13	9
84.71	.10	33.0	Djibouti	9	10	13	10
85.70	.99	33.0	Sierra Leone	9		8	7
91.94	6.24	33.0	Sudan	9		7	4
93.58	1.64	35.0	Senegal	6		6	4
93.75	.17	36.0	Gambia	3		3	4
95.62	1.87	37.0	Mali	2		2	1
97.19	1.57	39.0	Guinea	1		1	1
97.65	.46	39.0	Mauritania	1		1	0
98.98	1.33	39.0	Niger	1		1	1
100.00	1.03	41.0	Somalia	0		0	0

SOURCES: (1966) These estimates were made by Robert Cameron Mitchell. They are based on the following assumptions: (1) Islam and Christianity are growing rapidly in Black Africa today, (2) Christianity is growing most rapidly where it is already the religion of a strong minority, (3) national census data or sample survey data for 1966 represent the most satisfactory estimate possible, (4) the reported data for affiliators (members and adherents) given by Protestant churches in the *World Christian Handbook* considerably underestimates the Protestant identifiers, especially where Protestants constitute a strong minority (see Figure 2.3), and (5) official Roman Catholic affiliator data also underestimates Roman Catholic identifiers, but to a lesser extent than the Protestant data. The following notes attempt to specify the process of estimation as fully as possible. The principal source upon which the estimate is based is given along with any change in the data. Five or six different estimates of identifiers were consulted in the process of making these estimates.

Botswana: Beetham, *Christianity and the New Africa*, plus 2 percent; *Burundi*: *Handbook* plus 2 percent, *Cameroon*: *Handbook* plus 18 percent. *C.A.R.*:*AID Economic Data Book*; *Chad*: *Handbook* plus 4 percent; *Congo*: *Handbook* plus 10 percent; *Zaire*: *Handbook* plus 10 percent; *Benin*: 1961 sample survey plus extrapolation; *Ethiopia*: George Lipsky, *Ethiopia* (New Haven, Conn.: HRAF Press, 1962) (a conservative estimate of 7,600,000 Ethiopian Orthodox identifiers was used); *Gabon*: *Handbook* plus 8 percent; *Gambia*: *Handbook*; *Ghana*: census plus 3 percent; *Guinea*: *Handbook*; *Ivory Coast*: *Handbook* plus 8 percent; *Kenya*: Census 1964; *Lesotho*: census 1956 plus 10 percent; *Liberia*: *Handbook* plus 13 percent; *Malawi*: *Handbook* plus 16 percent or lower end of *Statesman's yearbook 1968—69* estimate; *Mali*: sample survey 1964—1965; *Mauritania, Niger*: *Handbook*; *Nigeria*: census 1963; *Rwanda*: *Handbook* plus 12 percent; *Senegal*: census 1960—1961; *Sierra Leone*: *Handbook* plus 3 percent; *Somalia*: *Handbook*; *Sudan*: *Europa Yearbook 1967*; *Tanzania*: Swartz, "Church, Mission and State Relations"; *Togo*: *Statesman's Yearbook 1967—68* plus 3 percent; *Uganda*: *Area Handbook for Uganda*, pp. 161—162; *Upper Volta*: *Handbook* plus 1 percent; *Zambia*: *Area Handbook for Zambia*, p. 185. (1970, 1980) D. B. Barrett, *World Christian Encyclopedia* op. cit.

TABLE 2.10 Estimated Percent Identifiers with Protestantism, ca. 1980(A), 1970 (B) and ca. 1966 (C).

Definition: Identifiers refers to those who would identify with a particular religion when asked their religion by someone such as a census taker. Protestantism includes the African independent churches but not the Orthodox Churches.

Range = 77.00
Mean = 21.59
Standard Deviation = 20.64

Population Percent Cum. Country	Percent Country	Rank	Country Name	A	Range Decile	B	C
.29	.29	1.0	Namibia	77	1	76	75
.45	.16	2.0	Swaziland	66	2	60	50
1.03	.58	3.0	Central African R	51	4	47	19
1.41	.38	4.0	Lesotho	49		46	39
9.70	8.29	5.0	Zaire	46	5	44	20
13.21	3.51	6.5	Ghana	44		37	23
17.81	4.60	6.5	Kenya	44		37	36
19.46	1.65	8.0	Zambia	43		38	9
21.72	2.26	9.0	Zimbabwe	42		38	32
21.95	.23	10.0	Botswana	41		36	26
42.95	21.00	11.0	Nigeria	40		34	18
43.40	.45	12.0	Congo	39		39	22
45.06	1.66	13.0	Malawi	37	6	34	22
45.59	.53	14.0	Liberia	33		29	24
45.75	.16	15.0	Gabon	31		31	19
49.70	3.95	16.0	Uganda	29	7	25	25
52.18	2.48	17.0	Madagascar	25		24	17
54.13	1.95	18.0	Angola	21	8	21	11
56.54	2.41	19.0	Cameroon	20		17	18
57.90	1.36	20.0	Rwanda	17		15	7
63.06	5.16	21.0	Tanzania	16		13	14
65.28	2.22	22.0	Ivory Coast	13	9	11	5
66.62	1.34	23.0	Chad	12		11	5
67.37	.75	24.0	Togo	8		7	7
68.65	1.28	26.0	Burundi	7	10	6	9
71.64	2.99	26.0	Mozambique	7		6	4
72.63	.99	26.0	Sierra Leone	7		6	5
73.63	1.00	28.5	Benin	5		4	3
73.73	.10	28.5	Equatorial Guinea	5		5	4
83.44	9.71	30.0	Ethiopia	4		4	1
89.68	6.24	31.5	Sudan	2		2	1
91.65	1.97	31.5	Upper Volta	2		2	1
91.82	.17	33.5	Gambia	1		1	2
92.01	.19	33.5	Guinea-Bissau	1		1	4
92.11	.10	38.0	Djibouti	0		0	0
93.68	1.57	38.0	Guinea	0		0	0
95.55	1.87	38.0	Mali	0		0	0
96.01	.46	38.0	Mauritania	0		0	0
97.34	1.33	38.0	Niger	0		0	0
98.98	1.64	38.0	Senegal	0		0	0
100.00	1.03	38.0	Somalia	0		0	0

TABLE 2.11 Estimated Percent Identifiers with Roman Catholicism, ca. 1980 (A), 1970 (B) and ca. 1966 (C).

Definition: Identifiers refers to those who would identify with a particular religion when asked their religion by someone such as a census taker.

Range = 78.00
Mean = 23.98
Standard Deviation = 21.92

Population Percent Cum. Country	Percent Country	Rank	Country Name	A	Range Decile	B	C
1.28	1.28	1.0	Burundi	78	1	68	55
1.38	.10	2.0	Equatorial Guinea	71		71	85
3.33	1.95	3.0	Angola	69	2	62	43
3.49	.16	4.0	Gabon	65		65	56
4.85	1.36	5.0	Rwanda	56	3	47	35
5.30	.45	6.0	Congo	54	4	53	42
9.25	3.95	7.0	Uganda	50		44	35
17.54	8.29	8.0	Zaire	48		46	45
17.92	.38	9.0	Lesotho	44	5	40	42
20.33	2.41	10.0	Cameroon	35	6	30	31
20.91	.58	11.0	Central African R	33		30	28
23.90	2.99	12.0	Mozambique	31	7	24	16
24.65	.75	13.0	Togo	29		24	21
26.31	1.66	14.5	Malawi	28		25	20
31.47	5.16	14.5	Tanzania	28		23	26
36.07	4.60	17.0	Kenya	26		24	22
38.55	2.48	17.0	Madagascar	26		25	21
40.20	1.65	17.0	Zambia	26		24	21
41.54	1.34	19.0	Chad	21	8	20	25
45.05	3.51	20.5	Ghana	19		16	23
45.34	.29	20.5	Namibia	19		18	14
46.34	1.00	22.5	Benin	18		15	15
48.56	2.22	22.5	Ivory Coast	18		16	13
50.82	2.26	24.0	Zimbabwe	14	9	13	10
71.82	21.00	25.0	Nigeria	12		11	17
71.98	.16	26.0	Swaziland	11		10	10
72.17	.19	27.0	Guinea-Bissau	10		12	8
72.40	.23	28.5	Botswana	9		7	3
74.37	1.97	28.5	Upper Volta	9		7	5
74.47	.10	30.0	Djibouti	7	10	10	8
76.11	1.64	31.0	Senegal	6		6	4
82.35	6.24	32.0	Sudan	4		4	3
82.52	.17	34.0	Gambia	2		2	2
83.05	.53	34.0	Liberia	2		2	1
84.04	.99	34.0	Sierra Leone	2		2	2
93.75	9.71	37.0	Ethiopia	1		1	1
95.32	1.57	37.0	Guinea	1		1	1
97.19	1.87	37.0	Mali	1		1	1
97.65	.46	40.0	Mauritania	0		0	0
98.98	1.33	40.0	Niger	0		0	1
100.00	1.03	40.0	Somalia	0		0	0

SOURCES: See sources for Table 2.9. *Equatorial Guinea and Swaziland: Estimates.*

SOURCES: See sources for Table 2.9.

TABLE 2.12 Estimated Percent Identifiers with Traditional African Religions, ca. 1980 (A), 1970 (B) and ca. 1966 (C).

Definition: Identifiers refers to those who would identify with a particular religion when asked their religion by someone such as a census taker.

Range = 61.00
Mean = 21.90
Standard Deviation = 17.62

Population Percent Cum.	Country	Rank	Country Name	A	Range Decile	B	C
1.00	1.00	1.0	Benin	61	1	67	67
1.99	.99	2.0	Sierra Leone	52	2	54	63
2.18	.19	3.0	Guinea-Bissau	51		52	58
2.41	.23	4.0	Botswana	49		56	71
5.40	2.99	5.0	Mozambique	48	3	58	67
7.88	2.48	6.0	Madagascar	47		49	61
8.63	.75	7.0	Togo	46		56	64
10.60	1.97	8.0	Upper Volta	45		55	72
12.82	2.22	9.5	Ivory Coast	44		49	59
13.35	.53	9.5	Liberia	44		50	60
15.61	2.26	11.0	Zimbabwe	40	4	46	48
17.18	1.57	12.0	Guinea	30	6	31	34
18.83	1.65	13.0	Zambia	27		34	70
20.17	1.34	14.5	Chad	23	7	27	40
25.33	5.16	14.5	Tanzania	23		32	37
27.74	2.41	16.0	Cameroon	22		32	36
31.25	3.51	17.5	Ghana	21		33	35
31.41	.16	17.5	Swaziland	21		28	40
36.01	4.60	19.5	Kenya	19		28	36
37.67	1.66	19.5	Malawi	19		25	46
39.54	1.87	21.5	Mali	18	8	20	34
40.90	1.36	21.5	Rwanda	18		29	57
47.14	6.24	23.0	Sudan	17		21	36
48.42	1.28	24.0	Burundi	14		25	35
52.37	3.95	25.0	Uganda	13		22	34
52.95	.58	26.5	Central African R	12	9	20	48
54.28	1.33	26.5	Niger	12		14	15
63.99	9.71	28.5	Ethiopia	11		14	23
64.16	.17	28.5	Gambia	11		12	16
66.11	1.95	30.0	Angola	10		17	45
66.49	.38	31.5	Lesotho	6	10	13	19
87.49	21.00	31.5	Nigeria	6		11	15
87.59	.10	33.0	Equatorial Guinea	5		7	11
87.88	.29	34.0	Namibia	4		5	11
88.04	.16	36.0	Gabon	3		3	24
89.68	1.64	36.0	Senegal	3		4	14
97.97	8.29	36.0	Zaire	3		8	34
98.42	.45	39.5	Congo	0		1	36
98.52	.10	39.5	Djibouti	0		0	0
98.98	.46	39.5	Mauritania	0		0	1
100.00	1.03	39.5	Somalia	0		0	0

SOURCES: See sources for Table 2.9. In the cases where official census or sample survey data were not available, the traditionalists represent the *residual* after percentages of Muslims and Christian had been estimated. *Kenya*: The 2 percent classified as having "no religion" in the census are not included in any of these tables, hence Christians, Muslims and Traditionalists do not add up to 100 percent in this case.

TABLE 2.13 Total Christian Mission Stations per Million Population ca. 1925 (A), Protestant Mission Stations per Million Population ca. 1925 (B) and Roman Catholic Mission Stations per Million Population(C).

Definition: Total is the sum of Protestant and Roman Catholic Stations, each divided by 1925 country population.

Range = 635.00
Mean = 150.51
Standard Deviation = 161.47

Population Percent Cum.	Country	Rank	Country Name	A	Range Decile	B	C
.38	.38	1.0	Lesotho	635	1	431	204
.54	.16	2.0	Gabon	629		126	503
2.19	1.65	3.0	Zambia	498	3	406	92
2.72	.53	4.0	Liberia	407	4	363	44
11.01	8.29	5.0	Zaire	378	5	223	155
11.46	.45	6.0	Congo	349		141	228
16.62	5.16	7.0	Tanzania	291	6	159	132
17.61	.99	8.0	Sierra Leone	289		178	111
17.84	.23	9.0	Botswana	245	7	214	33
18.13	.29	10.0	Namibia	240		163	77
19.79	1.66	11.0	Malawi	185	8	139	46
24.39	4.60	12.0	Kenya	159		132	27
26.80	2.41	13.0	Cameroon	138		109	29
28.16	1.36	14.0	Rwanda	137		57	80
28.91	.75	15.0	Togo	136		34	102
29.08	.17	16.0	Gambia	131		44	87
33.03	3.95	17.0	Uganda	125	9	45	80
33.13	.10	18.0	Equatorial Guinea	105		38	65
33.29	.16	19.0	Swaziland	100		95	5
34.93	1.64	20.0	Senegal	96		1	96
35.51	.58	21.0	Central African R	93		35	58
39.02	3.51	22.0	Ghana	90		54	36
40.59	1.57	23.0	Guinea	88		39	49
42.81	2.22	24.0	Ivory Coast	67		0	67
43.84	1.03	25.0	Somalia	64		32	32
46.10	2.26	26.0	Zimbabwe	62	10	50	12
47.38	1.28	27.0	Burundi	60		34	27
48.38	1.00	28.0	Benin	57		7	50
48.84	.46	29.5	Mauritania	51		17	34
55.08	6.24	29.5	Sudan	51		30	21
56.95	1.87	31.0	Mali	44		11	33
77.95	21.00	32.0	Nigeria	40		33	10
80.43	2.48	33.0	Madagascar	36		23	13
90.14	9.71	34.0	Ethiopia	27		10	17
92.09	1.95	35.0	Angola	26		15	11
94.06	1.97	36.0	Upper Volta	24		6	18
97.05	2.99	37.0	Mozambique	10		4	6
98.39	1.34	38.5	Chad	4		4	0
98.58	.19	38.5	Guinea-Bissau	4		0	4
98.68	.10	40.5	Djibouti	0		0	0
100.00	1.33	40.5	Niger	0		0	0

SOURCES: Foldout map with Hildegard B. Johnson, "The Location of Christian Missions in Africa," *The Geographical Review*, 57 (April 1961): 168—202. Population data for 1925 from Appendix 2 in this Handbook.

TABLE 2.14 Percent Christian Affiliators, 1980 (A) and 1970 (B).

Definition: Adherents and full members claimed by the Churches themselves.

```
Range =        96.00
Mean =         39.44
Standard Deviation =        29.22
```

Population Percent Cum.	Country	Rank	Name	A	Range Decile	B
.29	.29	1.0	Namibia	96	1	95
.45	.16	2.0	Gabon	95		95
8.74	8.29	3.0	Zaire	91		90
8.84	.10	4.0	Equatorial Guinea	89		88
9.22	.38	5.0	Lesotho	81	2	78
10.50	1.28	6.0	Burundi	80		74
11.86	1.36	7.0	Rwanda	70	3	65
13.81	1.95	8.0	Angola	66	4	50
18.41	4.60	9.0	Kenya	62		58
18.86	.45	10.0	Congo	59		59
20.52	1.66	11.5	Malawi	57	5	55
24.47	3.95	11.5	Uganda	57		54
26.12	1.65	13.0	Zambia	56		53
35.83	9.71	14.5	Ethiopia	54		53
35.99	.16	14.5	Swaziland	54		52
36.57	.58	16.0	Central African R	53		48
38.98	2.41	17.0	Cameroon	48	6	45
41.46	2.48	18.0	Madagascar	47		46
43.72	2.26	19.0	Zimbabwe	45		42
47.23	3.51	20.0	Ghana	44		41
52.39	5.16	21.0	Tanzania	40		36
55.38	2.99	22.0	Mozambique	34	7	30
56.13	.75	23.0	Togo	33		30
56.36	.23	24.5	Botswana	29		27
58.58	2.22	24.5	Ivory Coast	29		27
79.58	21.00	26.0	Nigeria	28	8	26
80.58	1.00	27.0	Benin	22		20
81.11	.53	28.0	Liberia	21		20
82.45	1.34	29.0	Chad	18	9	15
84.42	1.97	30.0	Upper Volta	12		11
84.52	.10	32.0	Djibouti	9	10	11
84.71	.19	32.0	Guinea-Bissau	9		9
90.95	6.24	32.0	Sudan	9		8
91.94	.99	34.0	Sierra Leone	8		8
93.58	1.64	35.0	Senegal	5		5
93.75	.17	36.0	Gambia	3		3
95.62	1.87	37.0	Mali	2		2
97.19	1.57	38.5	Guinea	1		1
98.52	1.33	38.5	Niger	1		1
98.98	.46	40.5	Mauritania	0		1
100.00	1.03	40.5	Somalia	0		0

SOURCES: D.B. Barrett, *World Christian Encyclopedia* op. cit.

TABLE 2.15 Number of Estimated Affiliators of African Independent Churches per Thousand Population, 1980 (A) and 1970 (B.)

Definition: Barrett defines independency as "the formation and existence within a tribe or tribal unit, temporarily or permanently, of any organized religious movement with a distinct name and membership, even as small as a single organized congregation, which claims the title Christian in that it acknowledges Jesus Christ as Lord, and which has either separated by secession from a mission church or an existing African independent church, or has been founded outside the mission churches as a new kind of religious entity under African initiative and leadership." (p. 50). His data include both members and adherents claimed by the churches. Children are presumably included in these figures.

```
Range =        230.00
Mean =         43.78
Standard Deviation =        61.98
```

Population Percent Cum.	Country	Rank	Name	A	Range Decile	B
.16	.16	1.0	Swaziland	230	1	220
8.45	8.29	2.0	Zaire	201	2	198
13.05	4.60	3.0	Kenya	171	3	158
16.56	3.51	4.0	Ghana	158	4	129
18.82	2.26	5.0	Zimbabwe	136	5	123
19.35	.53	6.0	Liberia	133		127
19.51	.16	7.0	Gabon	121		121
19.80	.29	8.0	Namibia	88	7	86
22.02	2.22	9.0	Ivory Coast	82		76
23.67	1.65	10.0	Zambia	78		68
23.90	.23	11.0	Botswana	72		62
24.28	.38	12.0	Lesotho	69	8	64
45.28	21.00	13.0	Nigeria	60		55
45.73	.45	14.0	Congo	30	9	30
47.39	1.66	15.0	Malawi	27		25
49.80	2.41	16.5	Cameroon	22	10	20
52.28	2.48	16.5	Madagascar	22		20
53.28	1.00	18.0	Benin	18		16
55.23	1.95	19.0	Angola	13		12
55.33	.10	20.5	Equatorial Guinea	12		12
56.08	.75	20.5	Togo	12		9
60.03	3.95	22.0	Uganda	9		8
61.02	.99	23.0	Sierra Leone	8		7
61.60	.58	24.0	Central African R	7		6
64.59	2.99	25.0	Mozambique	6		5
69.75	5.16	26.0	Tanzania	5		4
71.09	1.34	27.0	Chad	4		3
73.06	1.97	28.0	Upper Volta	1		1
74.34	1.28	35.0	Burundi	0		0
74.44	.10	35.0	Djibouti	0		0
84.15	9.71	35.0	Ethiopia	0		0
84.32	.17	35.0	Gambia	0		0
85.89	1.57	35.0	Guinea	0		0
86.08	.19	35.0	Guinea-Bissau	0		0
87.95	1.87	35.0	Mali	0		0
88.41	.46	35.0	Mauritania	0		0
89.74	1.33	35.0	Niger	0		0
91.10	1.36	35.0	Rwanda	0		0
92.74	1.64	35.0	Senegal	0		0
93.77	1.03	35.0	Somalia	0		0
100.00	6.24	35.0	Sudan	0		0

SOURCES: Barrett *World Christian Encyclopedia* op. cit.

TABLE 2.16 Average Annual Change in Percent Population Who Identify as Muslim (A), Christian (B), Protestant (C), Roman Catholic (D) and Traditional African Religionist (E), During the Period 1970 to 1980.

```
Range =              5.38
Mean =               2.76
Standard Deviation =        .97
```

Population Percent Cum.	Country	Rank	Name	A	Range Decile	B	C	D	E
.75	.75	1.0	Togo	5.4	1	4.8	5.5	5.1	.8
2.72	1.97	2.0	Upper Volta	4.4	2	4.7	3.7	4.8	.2
6.23	3.51	3.0	Ghana	4.1	3	4.6	4.5	4.6	-1.5
10.18	3.95	4.0	Uganda	4.0		4.3	5.0	4.2	-2.5
11.18	1.00	5.0	Benin	3.6	4	4.7	5.5	4.9	1.9
13.66	2.48	6.0	Madagascar	3.6		3.4	3.8	3.3	2.5
14.19	.53	7.0	Liberia	3.5		3.7	3.6	3.5	1.1
20.43	6.24	8.0	Sudan	3.4		5.1	4.2	4.5	.9
25.59	5.16	9.0	Tanzania	3.4		5.1	6.1	5.1	-.3
27.85	2.26	10.0	Zimbabwe	3.4		4.6	5.1	4.5	2.1
30.07	2.22	11.0	Ivory Coast	3.1	5	4.0	4.4	3.8	1.5
51.07	21.00	12.0	Nigeria	3.0		3.7	3.5	3.7	-3.7
52.43	1.36	13.0	Rwanda	3.0		4.4	4.1	4.4	-2.0
55.42	2.99	14.5	Mozambique	3.0		4.9	4.3	4.9	.4
56.75	1.33	14.5	Niger	3.0		1.3	.9	1.1	1.2
56.91	.16	16.0	Swaziland	2.9		3.8	4.2	3.9	-.2
57.49	.58	17.0	Central African R	2.9		3.2	4.8	3.2	-3.0
59.90	2.41	18.0	Cameroon	2.9		3.5	3.5	3.5	-2.0
60.89	.99	19.0	Sierra Leone	2.9		3.5	3.7	3.5	2.1
62.76	1.87	20.0	Mali	2.8		3.9	2.5	4.4	1.3
64.04	1.28	21.0	Burundi	2.8		3.9	3.5	4.0	-3.6
65.07	1.03	22.0	Somalia	2.7		-7.1	0	2.2	0
65.17	.10	23.5	Djibouti	2.7		-1.4	0	-2.2	0
69.77	4.60	23.5	Kenya	2.7		4.2	4.9	4.2	-.6
71.42	1.65	25.0	Zambia	2.7	6	4.2	4.3	4.0	.8
72.99	1.57	26.0	Guinea	2.6		1.6	1.8	1.9	2.2
73.22	.23	27.5	Botswana	2.6		4.1	4.4	5.6	1.2
81.51	8.29	27.5	Zaire	2.6		3.0	3.0	3.0	-5.1
83.17	1.66	29.0	Malawi	2.6		3.4	3.5	3.3	-.2
84.51	1.34	30.0	Chad	2.5		2.7	5.6	2.6	.4
84.96	.45	31.0	Congo	2.5		2.7	2.8	2.7	-.8
86.60	1.64	32.0	Senegal	2.5		2.4	2.6	2.4	-.4
96.31	9.71	33.0	Ethiopia	2.5		2.8	2.5	2.6	.2
96.50	.19	34.0	Guinea-Bissau	2.1	7	-1.2	1.8	-1.4	1.0
96.96	.46	35.0	Mauritania	2.1		-.2	0	-.9	-2.2
97.13	.17	36.0	Gambia	2.0		3.4	2.3	1.9	1.1
97.51	.38	37.0	Lesotho	1.9		2.8	3.0	2.8	-5.7
97.61	.10	38.0	Equatorial Guinea	1.8		1.8	1.7	1.8	-1.9
97.77	.16	39.0	Gabon	.9	9	.9	.9	.9	-.7
99.72	1.95	40.5	Angola	0	10	3.5	3.3	3.5	-4.7
100.00	.29	40.5	Namibia	0		2.5	3.3	2.6	-1.9

SOURCE: Barrett, *World Christian Encyclopedia* op. cit.

TABLE 2.17　Principles of Reckoning Descent: Standard Deviation (A) and Mean (B).

Definition: Scaling assumes an ordinal continuum ranging from matrilineality, through double descent, to exclusive patrilineality.

(1) *Matrilineal exclusive* (individuals affiliate within groups exclusively on the basis of relationship through the female line of descent).

(2) *Matrilineal mixed* (individuals affiliate with kin groups bilaterally, though the female line predominates).

(3) *Ambilineal* (individuals affiliate optionally with either matrilineal or patrilineal kin groups).

(4) *Double Descent* (individuals affiliate with specified kin groups through matrilineal descent and specified kin groups through patrilineal descent).

(5) *Patrilineal mixed* (individuals affiliate with kin groups bilaterally, though the male line predominates).

(6) *Patrilineal exclusive* (individuals affilate with kin groups exclusively on basis of relationship through the male line of descent).

Coding is on each nation's ethnic units (not tribes). The greater the standard deviation, the greater the cultural pluralism on this variable.

```
Range =            2.36
Mean =              .98
Standard Deviation =          .73
```

Population Percent Cum.	Country	Rank	Country Name	A	Range Decile	B
8.29	8.29	1.0	Zaire	2.36	1	3.42
13.45	5.16	2.0	Tanzania	2.15		3.78
13.90	.45	3.5	Congo	1.96	2	2.60
14.06	.16	3.5	Gabon	1.96		2.60
16.28	2.22	5.0	Ivory Coast	1.81	3	3.86
17.03	.75	6.0	Togo	1.77		4.83
19.00	1.97	7.0	Upper Volta	1.73		4.38
25.24	6.24	8.0	Sudan	1.61	4	4.50
26.90	1.66	9.0	Malawi	1.60		2.20
28.77	1.87	10.0	Mali	1.53		4.00
30.10	1.33	11.0	Niger	1.50		3.40
31.75	1.65	12.0	Zambia	1.46		2.17
52.75	21.00	13.0	Nigeria	1.30	5	3.75
53.74	.99	14.0	Sierra Leone	1.09	6	4.75
57.25	3.51	15.5	Ghana	1.00		4.00
58.89	1.64	15.5	Senegal	1.00	♥	4.00
59.06	.17	17.0	Gambia	.98		4.20
59.52	.46	18.0	Mauritania	.94	7	4.33
60.86	1.34	19.0	Chad	.90		4.83
70.57	9.71	20.0	Ethiopia	.83		4.86
71.10	.53	21.0	Liberia	.80		4.60
73.51	2.41	22.0	Cameroon	.75		4.67
78.11	4.60	23.5	Kenya	.69	8	5.17
82.06	3.95	23.5	Uganda	.69		5.17
83.06	1.00	29.0	Benin	0		5.00
83.29	.23	29.0	Botswana	0		3.00
84.57	1.28	29.0	Burundi	0		5.00
85.15	.58	29.0	Central African R	0		5.00
86.72	1.57	29.0	Guinea	0		5.00
86.91	.19	29.0	Guinea-Bissau	0		5.00
87.29	.38	29.0	Lesotho	0		5.00
88.65	1.36	29.0	Rwanda	0		5.00
89.68	1.03	29.0	Somalia	0		5.00

```
DATA NOT AVAILABLE OR NOT APPLICABLE
FOR THE FOLLOWING COUNTRIES

Angola      Djibouti    Equatorial Guinea  Madagascar
Mozambique  Namibia     Swaziland          Zimbabwe
```

SOURCE: Murdock, *Ethnographic Atlas* and specific ethnographies.

TABLE 2.18   Settlement Patterns: Standard Deviation (A) and Mean (B).

Definition: Refers to the permanence and complexity of community settlements. Scaling assumes an ordinal continuum extending from migratory bands with small non-complex settlement patterns to systems with permanent and complex bases.

(1) *Fully migratory* or nomadic bands.

(2) *Seminomadic* (communities whose members wander in bands for at least half the year, but occupy fixed settlement for some seasons).

(3) *Semisedentary* (communities whose members shift from one to another fixed settlement at different seasons, or who occupy a relatively permanent single settlement as a base from which shifting camps are set up).

(4) *Compact but impermanent settlements* (villages whose location is shifted every few years).

(5) *Neighborhoods* of dispersed family homesteads.

(6) *Separated hamlets* which form a relatively permanent single community.

(7) *Compact and relatively permanent settlements* (e.g. nucleated towns).

(8) *Complex settlements* (consisting of nucleated villages or towns with outlying homesteads).

Coding is on each nation's ethnic units (not tribes). The greater the standard deviation, the greater the cultural pluralism on this variable.

```
Range =           2.53
Mean =            1.03
Standard Deviation =        .83
```

Population Percent Cum.	Country	Rank	Country Name	A	Range Decile	B
1.33	1.33	1.0	Niger	2.53	1	5.00
11.04	9.71	2.0	Ethiopia	2.50		4.43
12.38	1.34	3.0	Chad	2.49		4.67
14.25	1.87	4.0	Mali	2.43		5.33
20.49	6.24	5.0	Sudan	2.27	2	3.83
20.95	.46	6.0	Mauritania	2.16		4.00
25.55	4.60	7.0	Kenya	2.13		5.33
25.72	.17	8.0	Gambia	1.74	4	5.60
28.20	2.48	9.0	Madagascar	1.65		5.71
29.84	1.64	10.0	Senegal	1.61		5.50
31.49	1.65	11.0	Zambia	1.60		5.67
33.90	2.41	12.0	Cameroon	1.49	5	5.67
54.90	21.00	13.5	Nigeria	1.32.		6.00
56.87	1.97	13.5	Upper Volta	1.32		5.50
57.06	.19	15.0	Guinea-Bissau	1.25	6	6.67
65.35	8.29	16.0	Zaire	1.14		6.17
65.93	.58	17.0	Central African R	1.00	7	6.00
66.93	1.00	18.5	Benin	.94		6.33
72.09	5.16	18.5	Tanzania	.94		6.00
73.75	1.66	20.0	Malawi	.80		6.40
77.70	3.95	21.0	Uganda	.75	8	5.33
79.92	2.22	22.0	Ivory Coast	.70		6.71
80.67	.75	23.0	Togo	.69		6.83
84.18	3.51	24.5	Ghana	.50	9	7.50
87.17	2.99	24.5	Mozambique	.50		6.50
87.70	.53	26.0	Liberia	.49		7.40
89.27	1.57	27.5	Guinea	.43		7.25
90.26	.99	27.5	Sierra Leone	.43		7.75
92.21	1.95	29.0	Angola	.37		6.83
92.44	.23	33.5	Botswana	0	10	8.00
93.72	1.28	33.5	Burundi	0		5.00
94.17	.45	33.5	Congo	0		7.00
94.33	.16	33.5	Gabon	0		7.00
94.71	.38	33.5	Lesotho	0		6.00
96.07	1.36	33.5	Rwanda	0		5.00
97.10	1.03	33.5	Somalia	0		1.00
97.26	.16	33.5	Swaziland	0		6.00

```
DATA NOT AVAILABLE OR NOT APPLICABLE
FOR THE FOLLOWING COUNTRIES

Djibouti     Equatorial Guinea  Namibia      Zimbabwe
```

SOURCE: Murdock, *Ethnographic Atlas* and specific ethnographies.

TABLE 2.19   Hierarchy above Family: Standard Deviation (A) and Mean (B).

Definition: Refers to the number of levels of community structure above the family. Scaling assumes an ordinal continuum of increasing structural inclusion above the family.
(1) Stateless or segmentary societies.
(2) Petty and paramount chiefdoms.
(3) Tribal chiefdoms.
Coding is on each nation's ethnic units (not tribes). The greater the standard deviation, the greater the cultural pluralism on this variable.

```
Range =        1.49
Mean =          .50
Standard Deviation =        .38
```

Population Percent			Country			Range	
Cum.	Country	Rank	Name		A	Decile	B
.45	.45	1.0	Congo		1.49	1	1.40
1.44	.99	2.0	Sierra Leone		1.09	3	2.25
3.92	2.48	3.0	Madagascar		1.00	4	2.00
5.89	1.97	4.0	Upper Volta		.97		1.25
14.18	8.29	5.0	Zaire		.93		1.71
18.13	3.95	6.0	Uganda		.90		1.83
27.84	9.71	7.0	Ethiopia		.83	5	1.86
29.18	1.34	8.5	Chad		.82		2.00
34.34	5.16	8.5	Tanzania		.82		1.67
34.87	.53	10.0	Liberia		.80		2.40
37.28	2.41	11.0	Cameroon		.76		1.50
38.61	1.33	12.0	Niger		.75		2.20
42.12	3.51	13.0	Ghana		.71	6	2.00
46.72	4.60	14.0	Kenya		.69		1.83
67.72	21.00	15.0	Nigeria		.66		2.25
69.59	1.87	17.0	Mali		.58	7	2.00
75.83	6.24	17.0	Sudan		.58		2.00
77.48	1.65	17.0	Zambia		.58		2.00
77.65	.17	19.0	Gambia		.49		1.60
78.65	1.00	22.5	Benin		.47		2.67
79.23	.58	22.5	Central African R		.47		1.33
79.42	.19	22.5	Guinea-Bissau		.47		.67
79.88	.46	22.5	Mauritania		.47		1.67
81.52	1.64	22.5	Senegal		.47		1.67
82.27	.75	22.5	Togo		.47		1.33
84.49	2.22	26.0	Ivory Coast		.45		1.71
86.15	1.66	27.0	Malawi		.40	8	1.80
88.10	1.95	33.0	Angola		0	10	1.00
88.33	.23	33.0	Botswana		0		2.00
89.61	1.28	33.0	Burundi		0		3.00
89.71	.10	33.0	Equatorial Guinea		0		1.00
89.87	.16	33.0	Gabon		0		1.00
91.44	1.57	33.0	Guinea		0		2.00
91.82	.38	33.0	Lesotho		0		3.00
94.81	2.99	33.0	Mozambique		0		1.00
96.17	1.36	33.0	Rwanda		0		3.00
97.20	1.03	33.0	Somalia		0		2.00
97.36	.16	33.0	Swaziland		0		3.00

```
DATA NOT AVAILABLE OR NOT APPLICABLE
FOR THE FOLLOWING COUNTRIES

Djibouti    Namibia    Zimbabwe
```

SOURCE: Murdock, *Ethnographic Atlas* and specific ethnographies.

TABLE 2.20   Number of Levels of Hierarchy in Local Community Organization: Standard Deviation (A) and Mean (B).

Definition: Refers to the levels of relationship between family units and local community organization. Scaling assumes an ordinal continuum ranging from situations in which the nuclear family itself is the highest level of authority, to situations in which the village is the significant level of authority.
(1) *Nuclear family* Highest level of authority.
(2) *Extended family* highest level of authority.
(3) *Clan barrio* highest level of authority.
(4) *Village* highest level of authority.
Coding is on each nation's ethnic units (not tribes). The greater the standard deviation, the greater the cultural pluralism on this variable.

```
Range =         .75
Mean =          .44
Standard Deviation =        .22
```

Population Percent			Country			Range	
Cum.	Country	Rank	Name		A	Decile	B
1.34	1.34	1.5	Chad		.75	1	2.67
1.87	.53	1.5	Liberia		.75		3.20
4.35	2.48	3.5	Madagascar		.71		3.00
25.35	21.00	3.5	Nigeria		.71		3.50
27.22	1.87	5.5	Mali		.69		3.17
27.97	.75	5.5	Togo		.69		2.83
29.63	1.66	7.0	Malawi		.63	2	3.00
31.60	1.97	8.0	Upper Volta		.60	3	3.13
39.89	8.29	9.0	Zaire		.54		2.71
41.84	1.95	10.0	Angola		.52	4	2.67
45.35	3.51	13.0	Ghana		.50		3.50
46.92	1.57	13.0	Guinea		.50		3.50
49.91	2.99	13.0	Mozambique		.50		2.50
50.90	.99	13.0	Sierra Leone		.50		3.50
56.06	5.16	13.0	Tanzania		.50		2.56
56.51	.45	17.5	Congo		.49		3.40
66.22	9.71	17.5	Ethiopia		.49		2.57
66.38	.16	17.5	Gabon		.49		3.60
68.60	2.22	17.5	Ivory Coast		.49		3.43
69.60	1.00	22.5	Benin		.47		3.67
70.18	.58	22.5	Central African R		.47		2.67
70.37	.19	22.5	Guinea-Bissau		.47		3.33
70.83	.46	22.5	Mauritania		.47		2.67
74.78	3.95	22.5	Uganda		.47		2.67
76.43	1.65	22.5	Zambia		.47		2.67
76.60	.17	26.5	Gambia		.40	5	2.80
77.93	1.33	26.5	Niger		.40		2.80
80.34	2.41	29.5	Cameroon		.37	6	2.83
84.94	4.60	29.5	Kenya		.37		2.83
86.58	1.64	29.5	Senegal		.37		2.83
92.82	6.24	29.5	Sudan		.37		3.17
93.05	.23	34.5	Botswana		0	10	3.00
94.33	1.28	34.5	Burundi		0		3.00
94.71	.38	34.5	Lesotho		0		3.00
96.07	1.36	34.5	Rwanda		0		3.00
97.10	1.03	34.5	Somalia		0		3.00
97.26	.16	34.5	Swaziland		0		3.00

```
DATA NOT AVAILABLE OR NOT APPLICABLE
FOR THE FOLLOWING COUNTRIES

Djibouti    Equatorial Guinea    Namibia    Zimbabwe
```

SOURCE: Murdock, *Ethnograophic Atlas* and specific ethnographies.

TABLE 2.21   Inheritance of Real Property: Standard Deviation (A) and Mean (B).

Definition: Refers to the rules for the transmission and disposition of real property (especially land), ranging from relatives other than children to inheritance by a son or sons.

(1) *Absence of individual property rights*, i.e. systems lacking any consistent rules of inheritance.
(2) *Inheritance by matrilineal heirs takes precedence over sisters' sons*; or, *inheritance by patrilineal heirs takes precedence over sons.*
(3) *Inheritance by children of either sex.*
(4) *Inheritance by children with daughter receiving less than sons.*
(5) *Matrilineal inheritance by sisters' sons or son.*
(6) *Patrilineal inheritance by a son or sons*

Coding is on each nation's ethnic units (not tribes). The greater the standard deviation, the greater the cultural pluralism on this variable.

```
Range =            2.36
Mean =             1.39
Standard Deviation =        .85
```

Population Percent						
Cum.	Country	Rank	Country Name	A	Range Decile	B
2.41	2.41	2.0	Cameroon	2.36	1	4.33
2.87	.46	2.0	Mauritania	2.36		4.33
9.11	6.24	2.0	Sudan	2.36		3.67
12.10	2.99	4.0	Mozambique	2.28		3.75
33.10	21.00	5.0	Nigeria	2.18		4.00
33.63	.53	6.0	Liberia	2.06	2	3.60
38.79	5.16	7.0	Tanzania	2.05		4.00
42.30	3.51	9.5	Ghana	2.00		4.00
43.87	1.57	9.5	Guinea	2.00		4.00
44.62	.75	9.5	Togo	2.00		4.00
46.59	1.97	9.5	Upper Volta	2.00		3.50
56.30	9.71	12.0	Ethiopia	1.99		4.43
56.75	.45	13.0	Congo	1.96		4.40
56.94	.19	14.0	Guinea-Bissau	1.89		3.33
65.23	8.29	15.0	Zaire	1.88	3	3.25
65.39	.16	16.0	Gabon	1.85		2.40
67.05	1.66	17.0	Malawi	1.83		4.20
68.92	1.87	18.0	Mali	1.80		3.33
69.09	.17	19.0	Gambia	1.79		3.00
70.42	1.33	20.5	Niger	1.67		4.00
72.06	1.64	20.5	Senegal	1.67		2.83
73.05	.99	22.0	Sierra Leone	1.64	4	3.25
74.39	1.34	23.0	Chad	1.61		3.50
76.34	1.95	24.0	Angola	1.56		4.83
80.94	4.60	25.5	Kenya	1.49		5.33
82.59	1.65	25.5	Zambia	1.49		2.67
85.07	2.48	27.0	Madagascar	1.30	5	5.25
87.29	2.22	28.0	Ivory Coast	.53	8	2.00
88.29	1.00	33.0	Benin	0		6.00
88.52	.23	33.0	Botswana	0		6.00
89.80	1.28	33.0	Burundi	0		6.00
90.38	.58	33.0	Central African R	0		6.00
90.76	.38	33.0	Lesotho	0		1.00
92.12	1.36	33.0	Rwanda	0		6.00
93.15	1.03	33.0	Somalia	0		4.00
93.31	.16	33.0	Swaziland	0		6.00
97.26	3.95	33.0	Uganda	0		6.00

DATA NOT AVAILABLE OR NOT APPLICABLE
FOR THE FOLLOWING COUNTRIES

Djibouti   Equatorial Guinea Namibia   Zimbabwe

SOURCE: Murdock, *Ethnographic Atlas* and specific ethnographies.

TABLE 2.22   Mode of Marriage: Standard Deviation (A) and Mean
(B).

Definition: Assume an ordinal continuum extending between systems having a system of brideprice or bridewealth in which the woman is regarded as an asset which is being lost by her lineage, and the systems of the opposite type in which dowry payment represents a compensation by the bride's kin group in exchange for the less productive female role.

(1) *Brideprice or bridewealth* is prevailing pattern, i.e. societies in which money, livestock, or other goods are transferred from the groom or his kin group to the relatives of the bride.

(2) *Brideservice*, e.g. systems in which labor or other services are rendered by the groom to the bride's kinsmen.

(3) *Token brideprice*, e.g. systems in which a small or symbolic payment is required.

(4) *Reciprocal gift exchange*, e.g. systems in which gifts of substantial value are exchanged between the family of the groom and the family of the bride.

(5) *Exchange of siblings*, e.g. systems in which there is a transfer of a female relative of the groom in exchange for the bride.

(6) *Absence* of any significant exchange or consideration.

(7) *Dowry*, e.g. systems in which there is institutionalized transfer of property from the bride's relatives to the married couple or kinsmen of the groom.

Coding is on each nation's ethnic units (not tribes). The greater the standard deviation, the greater the cultural pluralism on this variable.

```
Range =            2.24
Mean =              .56
Standard Deviation =         .77
```

Population Percent			Country		Range	
Cum.	Country	Rank	Name	A	Decile	B
4.60	4.60	1.0	Kenya	2.24	1	2.00
5.59	.99	2.0	Sierra Leone	2.17		2.25
15.30	9.71	3.0	Ethiopia	2.05		2.29
15.83	.53	4.0	Liberia	2.00	2	2.00
18.31	2.48	5.0	Madagascar	1.78	3	3.25
19.97	1.66	6.0	Malawi	1.72		2.80
20.55	.58	7.0	Central African R	1.49	4	1.67
21.30	.75	8.0	Togo	1.46		2.17
42.30	21.00	9.0	Nigeria	1.32	5	1.63
45.29	2.99	10.0	Mozambique	.87	7	1.25
46.94	1.65	11.0	Zambia	.82		2.00
49.16	2.22	12.0	Ivory Coast	.73		1.43
51.13	1.97	13.0	Upper Volta	.71		1.50
59.42	8.29	14.0	Zaire	.61	8	1.29
59.61	.19	15.0	Guinea-Bissau	.47		1.33
64.77	5.16	16.0	Tanzania	.31	9	1.11
66.72	1.95	27.0	Angola	0		1.00
67.72	1.00	27.0	Benin	0		1.00
67.95	.23	27.0	Botswana	0		1.00
69.23	1.28	27.0	Burundi	0		3.00
71.64	2.41	27.0	Cameroon	0		1.00
72.98	1.34	27.0	Chad	0		1.00
73.43	.45	27.0	Congo	0		1.00
73.59	.16	27.0	Gabon	0		1.00
73.76	.17	27.0	Gambia	0		1.00
77.27	3.51	27.0	Ghana	0		1.00
78.84	1.57	27.0	Guinea	0		1.00
79.22	.38	27.0	Lesotho	0		1.00
81.09	1.87	27.0	Mali	0		1.00
81.55	.46	27.0	Mauritania	0		1.00
82.88	1.33	27.0	Niger	0		1.00
84.24	1.36	27.0	Rwanda	0		1.00
85.88	1.64	27.0	Senegal	0		1.00
86.91	1.03	27.0	Somalia	0		1.00
93.15	6.24	27.0	Sudan	0		1.00
93.31	.16	27.0	Swaziland	0		1.00
97.26	3.95	27.0	Uganda	0		1.00

DATA NOT AVAILABLE OR NOT APPLICABLE
FOR THE FOLLOWING COUNTRIES

Djibouti   Equatorial Guinea Namibia   Zimbabwe

SOURCE: Murdock, *Ethnographic Atlas* and specific ethnographies.

TABLE 2.23   **Type of Authority System: Standard Deviation (A) and Mean (B).**

Definition: Refers to the locus of decision-making authority within the total community. Scaling assumes ordinal continuum ranging from lesser to greater centralization and institutionalization of authority.

(1) *Segmental authority*, e.g. acephalous, kinship-based societies lacking governmental organs, legal institutions, and centralized leadership. Decisions made by the group as a whole or on an ad hoc basis.

(2) *Pyramidal authority*, e.g. that of segmentary societies in which there is a vertical distribution of power which is largely upward. The powers exercised in this way are approximately of the same type at the several different levels of the pyramidal segmentary structure.

At highest level, frequently a council of paramount chiefs who make joint decisions.

(3) *Hierarchical authority*, e.g. that of centralized societies. This system is patterned along bureaucratic or military lines. At the top is a central command figure—a ruler, chief, king, commander, etc. He combines in his role symbolic, integrational, ethnic, and sanctioned functions. Power by subordinates devolves from the central leader.

Coding is on each nation's ethnic units (not tribes). The greater the standard deviation, the greater the cultural pluralism on this variable.

```
Range =            1.30
Mean =              .65
Standard Deviation =          .43
```

Population Percent Cum.	Country	Rank	Country Name	A	Range Decile	B
.99	.99	1.0	Sierra Leone	1.30	1	2.25
2.63	1.64	2.0	Senegal	1.21		2.17
3.97	1.34	3.0	Chad	1.15	2	2.00
5.84	1.87	4.0	Mali	1.11		2.33
7.17	1.33	5.0	Niger	1.10		2.00
15.46	8.29	6.0	Zaire	1.04		.46
19.41	3.95	7.0	Uganda	1.00	3	2.00
19.86	.45	8.0	Congo	.98		1.80
20.86	1.00	10.5	Benin	.94		1.33
23.27	2.41	10.5	Cameroon	.94		1.67
23.85	.58	10.5	Central African R	.94		1.67
24.04	.19	10.5	Guinea-Bissau	.94		1.67
26.01	1.97	13.0	Upper Volta	.93		1.88
28.23	2.22	14.0	Ivory Coast	.90	4	2.43
29.80	1.57	15.5	Guinea	.87		2.50
50.80	21.00	15.5	Nigeria	.87		2.00
50.97	.17	18.0	Gambia	.80		2.60
51.50	.53	18.0	Liberia	.80		2.60
53.16	1.66	18.0	Malawi	.80		2.40
59.40	6.24	20.0	Sudan	.76	5	2.50
61.05	1.65	21.0	Zambia	.75		2.33
61.80	.75	22.0	Togo	.69		2.17
66.96	5.16	23.0	Tanzania	.67		2.67
70.47	3.51	24.5	Ghana	.50	7	2.50
75.07	4.60	24.5	Kenya	.50		1.50
84.78	9.71	26.0	Ethiopia	.35	8	2.14
85.01	.23	31.0	Botswana	0	10	3.00
86.29	1.28	31.0	Burundi	0		3.00
86.39	.10	31.0	Equatorial Guinea	0		1.00
86.55	.16	31.0	Gabon	0		1.00
86.93	.38	31.0	Lesotho	0		2.00
87.39	.46	31.0	Mauritania	0		3.00
88.75	1.36	31.0	Rwanda	0		3.00
89.78	1.03	31.0	Somalia	0		2.00
89.94	.16	31.0	Swaziland	0		3.00

DATA NOT AVAILABLE OR NOT APPLICABLE FOR THE FOLLOWING COUNTRIES

Angola	Djibouti	Madagascar	Mozambique
Namibia	Zimbabwe		

SOURCES: (variable definition) David Apter, *The Politics of Modernization*, (data) Murdock, *Ethnographic Atlas*; and specific ethnographies.

3. Economic Development

Africa is a continent rich in raw materials, cultivatable land, and potential energy resources, but African countries are in many respects the poorest economies in the world. The average per capita income of African countries is less than ⅛ that of Middle Eastern countries, ½ that of Latin American countries, and one-fifth that of Southern European countries, and slightly lower than that of South Asian countries. This relative poverty is even more marked when one considers the list of nineteen countries classified as the least developed of ninety less developed countries analyzed by UNESCO in 1970. In this list based on indices of per capita income, energy consumption, education, and health care, 16 of the nineteen poorest countries in the world were located in black Africa.[1] The gap between economic potential and performance, and the absolute poverty facing so many Africans, is a matter that demands human concern, political judgement, and an intellectual understanding that can suggest rational means to the achievement of the goals of economic development in black Africa.

The purpose of this chapter is to provide basic data for an evaluation of levels and rates of economic development in black Africa, and to suggest some of the conceptual and theoretical perspectives which should be kept in mind when considering such data. The specification of a complete theory and empirical explanation of economic development in Africa is not a task we can undertake here, but we hope to indicate some of the concepts and data relevant to such a task. In this Chapter we shall focus on aggregate measures of national income, labor and capital. In Chapter 1, we have discussed measures of land area, cultivation, and raw material resources, which should be referred to as indicators of the first of the traditional factors of production—land, labor and capital. In Chapter 4, we discuss measures of education, transportation and communication facilities, which are important indicators of the infra-structural requirements for the mobilization and distribution of the factors and output of production. In Chapter 5, we discuss measures of political instability, governmental organization and military/security developments, which can be seen as important factors modifying the social and economic conditions for economic development. In Chapter 6, finally, we discuss measures of international relations which indicate dimensions of economic dependency and political autonomy that have a potentially critical effect on domestic economic development within black African countries. In these other Chapters, we have discussed important historical considerations for the understanding of the data on social mobilization, political development and international relations in the post-independence period in these states. These historical considerations apply as well to the interpretation of data presented in this Chapter, since they indicate the origins of patterns of international economic dependency, political centralization and instability, and ethnic or regional inequalities, which limit the opportunities for effective national economic development initiatives and at the same time accentuate the social and political necessity of overcoming such limits.[3]

An increase in agricultural production, industrialization, and economic welfare are primary objectives in virtually all countries, rich and poor alike. These objectives are at the heart of the theory and planning of economic development which emphasize the creation and augmentation of productive capabilities. However, while there may be unanimity as to the goal of economic development, the means of such growth and the appropriate response to economic gain are questions that are not amenable to purely "technical" answers. The determination of what constitutes economic development involves the selection of both ends and means, but human values are involved in the identification of both ends and means, and ethical and political conflict surrounds both the theoretical and practical approaches to economic development.[4] There are no strictly logical or empirical resolutions to problems of growth without development, efficiency without equity, consumption without waste, work without dignity and creativity, and the host of other problems that arise in considering the economic activity of men and societies. Economic policy, therefore, is as much political as economic, and the very complex issues involved in decisions about appropriate investment, savings, and distribution patterns cannot be adequately discussed with the aggregate data we present in this Chapter. Aggregate data analysis can serve only as an introduction to the detailed and critical historical and political analysis that is required in order to understand and evaluate differences in economic policy in countries like Liberia, Gabon, and Ivory Coast, where the emphasis has been on foreign investment as the "engine of growth"; countries like Guinea and Tanzania where emphasis is on indigenous public development and ownership, and countries like Kenya, Nigeria and Zaire where attempts have been made to legislate protections and incentives for foreign and domestic private entrepreneurship in more explicitly "mixed" economies.

Income and Welfare

Economic development refers to the process by which societies generate a capacity to achieve preferred distributions and rates of growth of the production of goods and services. Conceptually, therefore, economic development depends critically on the values of the observer which define what goods and what services should be produced; in what quantities they should be produced, and how they should be allocated among individuals, institutions and other groupings in society. The conventional simplification of these issues is to define economic development in terms of the growth and distribution of national income, measured in terms of currencies that are comparable when adjusted by international exchange rates to a common standard of value. Such operational simplification obscures differences in the real purchasing power of income within domestic markets as opposed to international markets; it masks the "value" of human production which is not distributed and priced by market institutions and which can be only very arbitrarily estimated, and it disregards important differences of taste and ideology within and between societies which give different weight to the production and distribution and, therefore, to the associated price measures, of different goods and services which are exchanged. Measures of the level and rate of change of aggregate national income and its sectoral distribution, nevertheless, provide an important preliminary approach to the evaluation of economic development.[5]

Tables 3.1, 3.2 and 3.3 give data on Gross Domestic Product (GDP). Gross National Product is a measure of the value to the final consumer of all goods and services consumed in a country, and GDP is equal to GNP adjusted for the value of net foreign investment. Data on national income in the period prior to Independence are generally unreliable and in many cases not available, but estimates indicate that average annual growth rates of national income in black Africa in the period following the Second World War were about 4%, although with considerable inter-country variation, and that they have remained at this level in the post-independence period. This average rate of growth has to be related, of course, to the rate of growth of population if we are to obtain any measure of the human impact of economic development. The average rate of growth of *per capita* national income in the post-independence period is certainly less that 4%

and is estimated at about 1%, although population estimates are themselves unreliable. Still, if one assumes a very low population growth rate of only 2% annually in black Africa as a whole, it is estimated that the average per capita income in this region would quadruple to the level of $400 (that is about the level for Latin America in the 1960's in constant dollars) by 2000 A.D. *if* the average rate of GNP growth all but doubles to 7%.[6]

The variation illustrated in Tables 3.1 to 3.3 indicates that some black African countries have considerably better chances of attaining this minimum threshold of economic development than others. But for all black African states the problems of achieving a sustained rate of growth of per capita income are formidable, especially in this era of high energy prices. Of critical importance to the kinds of forecasting summarized in the last paragraph is the assumption that inflation will not seriously increase the price of a given "basket of goods" in the future, thereby limiting the purchasing power of the per-capita income set as a goal for future development. The causes of inflation constitute a major area of debate and uncertainty in contemporary economics, but are generally related to an imbalance between excess demand for, and inadequate supplies of, goods and services. This imbalance relates to declining or insufficiently expanding productivity, to rising expectations, changing tastes, to an increase in the money supply with higher propensities for consumption than savings, and to changes in terms of trade which make imported intermediate and finished goods more expensive with particularly serious results in economies where the price elasticity of demand for such goods is low. Whatever the causes of inflation, increases in national income will be poorly related to increases in national welfare as inflation increases. Measures of national income, adjusted for inflation, like those in Table 3.3 are preferable, therefore, to measures not so adjusted, and measures of inflation like the estimates given in Table 3.4 should be used to qualify measures of national income unadjusted for inflation.

Whether black African countries can maintain or increase their real (that is inflation adjusted) rates of growth or national income in the future will depend critically on the full impact of direct and spill-over effects of the very marked inflationary changes in international markets, particularly those for non-renewable energy resources such as oil. Real growth in national income in black African states will depend, therefore, on their ability to decrease vulnerability to such "imported" inflation and to increase domestic productivity. In these countries with a heavy dependence on international trade for the generation of national income, and with serious balance of trade problems affecting their ability to import capital goods, as discussed in Chapter 6, the stimulation of future growth in real income must involve industrial and agricultural development which allow for import substitution and reductions in balance of trade and terms of trade disadvantages.

National income statistics fortunately can be disaggregated to indicate the growth of economic activity outside of the primary production sectors in agriculture and raw material extraction and outside of public sector employment. The data in Table 3.5 indicate the percentage of gross domestic product derived from sectors other than agriculture, mining and government. But while these data give some preliminary indication of economic diversification, they are unfortunately not sufficiently disaggregated to review the extent to which foreign controlled operations dominate the secondary and tertiary economic sectors, possibly affecting the real level of employment, income and potential new investment within the host economy. Still, such data suggest the far reaching changes that will still have to be made in black African nations before most of these economies are characterized by the shift from a dominance of economic activity in the primary sector to activity in secondary and tertiary sectors, and the shift within the secondary sector itself from raw material processing to the production of intermediate products for further processing like chemicals, metals, and building materials, to the production of durable consumer goods, and finally to the production of capital goods.[7]

These structural and sectoral shifts are themselves likely to depend, however, on the stimulation of agricultural productivity, without which industrialization is constrained by inadequate effective demand for manufactured products, by the rising price of food which results in pressure on wages and a tendency to reduce employment in favor of capital intensive technologies, and by the absence of agriculturally generated surpluses for internally controlled investment in industrialization.[8] Data in Table 3.6 give a preliminary indication of agricultural productivity in these nations. Unfortunately these data do not discriminate between the generally very large proportion of agricultural produce traded in international markets and that proportion which is related to domestic food consumption. While the value of agricultural production for exports has risen, a weighted average of indices of net agricultural output per active male working in agriculture tended to decrease in African countries from 7.8 in the period 1934—38 to 7.26 in 1946—50, to 5.19 in 1953—57 and 4.71 in 1960—64, and the per capita output of food in black Africa is reported to have decreased by 0.4% per year over the years 1952—55 and 1962—65.[9] In the period 1960—65, estimates developed by the Economic Commission for Africa show that indices of agricultural production based on the period

1952—56 equals 100 have increased from 121 to 128 for the per capita production of non-food products, but decreased from 105 to 103 for the per capita production of food products. Correspondingly, the balance of trade deficits in meat, dairy products and cereals for African countries deteriorated in that period with the difference between exports and imports of cereals, for example, being minus 18,828 metric tons in 1960 and minus 40,289 metric tons in 1965.[10] These processes have been exacerbated in the 1970s. Despite problems in the reliability of estimates of agricultural productivity in these nations,[11] such information at least provokes a sense of caution in treating aggregate data on national income as direct indicators of the welfare expectations of individuals in these societies.

Welfare, as well as growth, is a time dependent phenomenon and we expect that a country's savings rate will reflect its ability to produce resources in the future. Table 3.7 presents data on savings rates.

The relationship between national income and human welfare in these societies is obscure because the aggregation underlying the measures provides no indication of the distribution of goods and services. Unless we assume, therefore, that all goods and services are equally valued and distributed across all individuals and groups within a society, the interpretation of such measures as differences in welfare among black African states leaves much to be desired. The conceptual and mathematical complexity of welfare economics as a specialized field of inquiry, and the difficulties involved in the operationalization of concepts like individual and social utility, are such that development economists themselves often pay little attention to the major theoretical questions of welfare economics, and very few other social scientists in welfare issues understand and apply such thinking.[12] Even the growing field of social indicator research has little grounding in such theoretical issues.[13] We certainly are in no position to clarify such matters in relation to African states, where data on income distributions are generally limited or unavailable, let alone data on the values and perceptions of the quality of life held by individuals in these societies.

It is possible when dealing with theories of economic develoment, social modernization, political development and similar concepts grounded in normative assumptions to supplement measures of national income with measures on the distribution of public goods, like the education data presented in the next Chapter and the data on the distribution of health care capabilities provided in Table 3.8 in this Chapter. Also one may refer to data on dietary adequacy such as those in Table 3.9. Comparable data on social welfare expenditures by black African governments which supplement earned income in these countries are not available to us, and there are only very incomplete data on standard measures of the equality of income distribution for these countries.[14] Imaginative estimates of income inequalities have been suggested which make use of job advertisements for selected occupations in daily newspapers, obtaining thereby an average salary that can be expressed as a ratio of per capita GNP. A preliminary illlustration of such data shows, for example, that between 1960 and 1970 salaries advertised for senior civil servants rose from 29 to 37 times per capita GNP in Ghana, from 58 to 65 times per capita GNP in Nigeria, and decreased from 93 to 88 times per capita GNP in Tanzania.[15] Table 3.10 presents data for the limited subset of Black African states for which patterns of individual income distribution have been estimated recently. We can only hope that in the future academic case study research and improvements in the statistical data collected by black African government agencies will provide more comprehensive indications of the pattern of income distribution in these countries.[16]

Only with such data will agencies like the World Bank be able to pursue their stated concerns with the redistribution of income as a priority goal of international capital loans and assistance to less developed countries. Social scientists will require such data in order to examine questions about changes in income inequality as a result of, or precondition for, changes in economic and political development.[17]

TABLE 3.1 Gross Domestic Product in Millions of U.S. Dollars, 1977 (A), 1972 (B), 1967 (C) and 1960 (D) at constant 1975 market prices.

```
Range =      25870.00
Mean =        1769.05
Standard Deviation =         4035.82
```

Population Percent Cum.	Country	Rank	Country Name	A	Range Decile	B	C	D
21.00	21.00	1.0	Nigeria	25960	1	19006	9431	9160
23.22	2.22	2.0	Ivory Coast	6441	8	4450	3126	1863
29.46	6.24	3.0	Sudan	4673	9	3565	3047	2909
29.62	.16	4.0	Gabon	2809		580	401	298
32.61	2.99	5.0	Mozambique	2722		2185	1251	1118
34.56	1.95	6.0	Angola	2701		2067	1093	1006
39.16	4.60	7.0	Kenya	2225	10	2020	1402	1070
41.57	2.41	8.0	Cameroon	2197		1710	1354	1077
51.28	9.71	9.0	Ethiopia	2175		1762	1323	944
54.79	3.51	10.0	Ghana	1741		1494	1954	2064
57.05	2.26	11.0	Zimbabwe	1731		1758	1141	870
59.53	2.48	12.0	Madagascar	1564		1527	1357	1179
64.69	5.16	13.0	Tanzania	1481		1329	1035	702
64.98	.29	14.0	Namibia	1270				263
66.63	1.65	15.0	Zambia	1241		1267	1083	783
74.92	8.29	16.0	Zaire	1198		2070	1648	1392
76.56	1.64	17.0	Senegal	1184		1043	930	764
80.51	3.95	18.0	Uganda	1086		1170	973	676
82.08	1.57	19.0	Guinea	1075		752	600	462
82.53	.45	20.0	Congo	613		535	430	356
83.53	1.00	21.0	Benin	527		414	379	309
84.86	1.33	22.0	Niger	503		431	436	322
86.52	1.66	23.0	Malawi	482		397	352	236
87.05	.53	24.0	Liberia	473		421	323	240
87.51	.46	25.0	Mauritania	444		343	317	173
88.50	.99	26.0	Sierra Leone	422		567	507	400
90.37	1.87	27.0	Mali	414		313	305	431
91.12	.75	28.0	Togo	396		333	249	141
93.09	1.97	29.0	Upper Volta	356		345	330	260
94.45	1.36	30.0	Rwanda	328		246	170	330
95.79	1.34	31.0	Chad	311		279	266	261
96.02	.23	32.0	Botswana	303		192	95	70
97.30	1.28	33.0	Burundi	290		244	198	282
97.88	.58	34.0	Central African R	227		183	163	149
98.91	1.03	35.0	Somalia	221		207	167	154
99.10	.19	36.0	Guinea-Bissau	177		128	71	34
99.26	.16	37.0	Swaziland	146		129	93	43
99.36	.10	38.5	Equatorial Guinea	112		78	73	65
99.53	.17	38.5	Gambia	112		89	80	50
99.91	.38	40.0	Lesotho	110		81	68	47
100.00	.10	41.0	Djibouti	90		84	55	24

SOURCE: *World Tables: The Second Edition 1980* figures converted at the current official exchange rate. *Namibia: World Bank Atlas 1981*, 1979 data.

**TABLE 3.2   Per Capita GDP in U.S. Dollars, 1977 (A), 1972 (B),
1967 (C) and 1960 (D) at constant 1975 prices.**

```
Range     =      5254.00
Mean      =       377.49
Standard Deviation =        814.58
```

Population Percent			Country			Range			
Cum.	Country	Rank	Name	A	Decile	B	C	D
.16	.16	1.0	Gabon	5301	1	1142	818	631
.45	.29	2.0	Namibia	1290	8			
2.67	2.22	3.0	Ivory Coast	863	9	788	698	538
2.77	.10	4.0	Djibouti	809		840	605	294
4.72	1.95	5.0	Angola	432	10	349	209	65
5.17	.45	6.0	Congo	431		426	384	367
5.40	.23	7.0	Botswana	416		159	158	134
5.50	.10	8.0	Equatorial Guinea	349		264	261	
5.69	.19	9.0	Guinea-Bissau	335		252		
26.69	21.00	10.0	Nigeria	329		273	153	178
29.68	2.99	11.0	Mozambique	296		253	164	59
30.14	.46	12.0	Mauritania	295		261	275	178
30.30	.16	13.0	Swaziland	286		287	230	125
30.83	.53	14.0	Liberia	281		295	266	246
33.24	2.41	15.0	Cameroon	277		242	211	189
39.48	6.24	16.0	Sudan	276		180	232	258
41.13	1.65	17.0	Zambia	242		288	284	249
43.39	2.26	18.0	Zimbabwe	241		240	310	259
45.03	1.64	19.0	Senegal	226		226	229	222
46.60	1.57	20.0	Guinea	216		174	161	151
46.77	.17	21.0	Gambia	202		175	196	153
49.25	2.48	22.0	Madagascar	193		214	213	216
50.00	.75	23.0	Togo	169		162	138	94
53.51	3.51	24.0	Ghana	164		163	242	303
54.51	1.00	25.0	Benin	163		149	155	151
59.11	4.60	26.0	Kenya	152		167	138	134
60.10	.99	27.0	Sierra Leone	132		200	202	185
60.68	.58	28.0	Central African R	122		109	109	116
62.01	1.33	29.0	Niger	103		102	118	112
67.17	5.16	30.0	Tanzania	91		94	84	69
71.12	3.95	31.0	Uganda	90		113	54	99
71.50	.38	32.0	Lesotho	88		73	68	54
73.16	1.66	33.0	Malawi	86		83	85	69
74.52	1.36	34.0	Rwanda	75		65	52	119
75.86	1.34	35.0	Chad	74		73	78	86
85.57	9.71	36.0	Ethiopia	72		65	56	47
86.85	1.28	37.0	Burundi	70		65	59	98
88.72	1.87	38.0	Mali	68		58	64	106
90.69	1.97	39.0	Upper Volta	65		68	71	62
91.72	1.03	40.0	Somalia	60		63	58	63
100.00	8.29	41.0	Zaire	47		92	82	80

SOURCE: *World Tables 1980* Table 3.1 normed by population in each country. *Namibia*: *World Bank Atlas 1981*, 1979 data.

TABLE 3.3 Average Annual Real Growth Rate of GDP Per Capita, 1970—77 (A), 1965—70 (B), 1960—65 (C) and 1950—60 (D).

Definition and Comment: The average annual growth rates given are the compounded rates of growth between the relevant years. Over an extended period, and except where marked cyclical or irregular factors are present, this method may generally be taken to yield a fair approximation of the trend according to the World Bank. These figures are adjusted for inflation.

```
Range =          25.00
Mean =             .69
Standard Deviation =        3.82
```

Population Percent			Country		Range			
Cum.	Country	Rank	Name	A	Decile	B	C	D
.23	.23	1.0	Botswana	13.5	1	7.8	2.2	1.2
.61	.38	2.0	Lesotho	5.5	4	-.1	6.7	2.8
.71	.10	4.0	Djibouti	4.9				
.87	.16	4.0	Gabon	4.9		1.1	1.9	-.7
1.04	.17	4.0	Gambia	4.9		1.1	1.9	-.7
1.23	.19	6.0	Guinea-Bissau	4.7				
1.39	.16	7.0	Swaziland	3.7		4.1	11.0	6.3
22.39	21.00	8.0	Nigeria	3.3	5	1.9	2.7	1.6
24.05	1.66	9.0	Malawi	3.1		1.5	.6	6.5
30.29	6.24	10.0	Sudan	2.7		-1.0	-.7	3.5
31.86	1.57	11.0	Guinea	2.4		0	1.2	
33.22	1.36	12.0	Rwanda	2.2		5.6	-5.3	-1.2
35.09	1.87	13.5	Mali	2.1		.5	.7	1.0
40.25	5.16	13.5	Tanzania	2.1		3.1	2.6	3.7
40.70	.45	15.5	Congo	1.4		1.2	.6	-.5
41.45	.75	15.5	Togo	1.4		3.9	5.6	-.9
43.86	2.41	17.0	Cameroon	1.2		5.3	1.2	.3
48.46	4.60	18.0	Kenya	1.0	6	4.9	.2	.7
49.04	.58	19.0	Central African R	.9		1.3	-1.7	1.1
51.26	2.22	20.0	Ivory Coast	.5		3.5	6.1	1.5
52.54	1.28	21.0	Burundi	.4		3.3	.5	-3.2
54.18	1.64	22.0	Senegal	.2		-1.2	1.1	
63.89	9.71	23.0	Ethiopia	.1		1.2	2.7	1.7
64.89	1.00	24.5	Benin	-.1		0	.6	
67.15	2.26	24.5	Zimbabwe	-.1		2.4	-.9	
68.80	1.65	26.0	Zambia	-.2		-.1	2.6	3.1
69.26	.46	27.0	Mauritania	-.5		2.0	7.2	
69.79	.53	28.0	Liberia	-.6		3.1	6.1	7.4
71.13	1.34	29.0	Chad	-.9		-.3	-1.3	
72.12	.99	30.5	Sierra Leone	-1.0		1.6	2.1	1.8
74.09	1.97	30.5	Upper Volta	-1.0		1.6	1.0	-.3
75.12	1.03	32.0	Somalia	-1.1		.9	-2.8	10.6
76.45	1.33	33.0	Niger	-1.5	7	-2.9	2.5	
84.74	8.29	34.0	Zaire	-1.7		2.2	1.7	1.1
88.69	3.95	35.0	Uganda	-2.4		2.2	1.8	.5
92.20	3.51	36.0	Ghana	-2.5		.4	.6	-.4
94.68	2.48	37.0	Madagascar	-3.2		2.5	-.7	.5
94.78	.10	38.0	Equatorial Guinea	-5.0	8	.1	11.8	
97.77	2.99	39.0	Mozambique	-6.1		5.9	.2	1.7
99.72	1.95	40.0	Angola	-11.5	10	1.6	4.3	

DATA NOT AVAILABLE OR NOT APPLICABLE
FOR THE FOLLOWING COUNTRIES

Namibia

SOURCE: *World Tables 1980* Comparative Economic. Data-Table 1, p 372-373. *Djibouti and Guinea-Bissau*: *World Bank Atlas 1981*.

TABLE 3.4   Consumer Price Index 1977 (A), 1972 (B), 1967 (C) and 1960 (D).

Definition: Ratio of prices in the given years to prices in 1970 times 100.

Note: There are considerable variations in the population base used and the inclusion of goods in the calculation of this index and reference to the source would be appropriate for users of this data.

```
Range =        583.90
Mean =         230.19
Standard Deviation =        116.99
```

Population Percent Cum.	Country	Rank	Country Name	A	Range Decile	B	C	D
8.29	8.29	1.0	Zaire	714.7	1	122.5	56.9	82.0
11.80	3.51	2.0	Ghana	633.9	2	114.8	83.6	48.4
15.75	3.95	3.0	Uganda	434.0	5	112.3	84.3	65.0
36.75	21.00	4.0	Nigeria	281.6	8	120.1	80.2	66.4
38.70	1.95	5.0	Angola	251.2		14.1	10.5	9.9
44.94	6.24	6.0	Sudan	246.0	9	115.0	94.9	71.7
46.81	1.87	7.0	Mali	245.2		130.0		
48.17	1.36	8.0	Rwanda	236.7		103.6	95.7	
48.33	.16	9.0	Gabon	224.6		107.5	91.4	104.0
53.49	5.16	10.0	Tanzania	224.0		112.8	92.7	81.9
58.09	4.60	11.5	Kenya	219.6		109.8	98.1	82.7
59.42	1.33	11.5	Niger	219.6		114.4	92.0	75.8
60.17	.75	13.0	Togo	216.5		114.9	90.5	-0
61.81	1.64	14.0	Senegal	211.7		110.0	93.7	77.9
64.03	2.22	15.0	Ivory Coast	206.5		95.5	83.7	69.1
65.68	1.65	16.0	Zambia	201.7		111.7	85.8	65.8
66.14	.46	17.0	Mauritania	199.2		116.3	87.9	65.8
66.31	.17	18.0	Gambia	198.6		106.0	91.8	83.0
68.72	2.41	19.0	Cameroon	197.7		110.1	93.9	86.0
69.30	.58	20.0	Central Afri. R	193.0		116.7	91.5	62.2
69.53	.23	21.5	Botswana	192.9		112.5	91.2	76.2
69.91	.38	21.5	Lesotho	192.9		112.5	91.2	76.1
70.90	.99	23.0	Sierra Leone	191.0		103.8	88.8	66.7
71.43	.53	24.0	Liberia	189.1	10	103.6	87.3	92.0
72.46	1.03	25.0	Somalia	183.1		96.5	90.2	65.3
72.91	.45	26.0	Congo	179.0		114.3	95.8	66.9
82.62	9.71	27.0	Ethiopia	178.4		79.7	89.4	66.0
82.78	.16	28.0	Swaziland	175.8		103.5	91.9	
84.06	1.28	29.0	Burundi	174.6		107.8	90.8	
87.05	2.99	30.0	Mozambique	172.0		124.0	111.0	100.0
88.71	1.66	31.0	Malawi	170.7		112.1	82.2	68.3
91.19	2.48	32.0	Madagascar	168.8		111.4	92.8	88.0
92.53	1.34	33.0	Chad	167.6		109.3	88.0	62.3
94.50	1.97	34.0	Upper Volta	167.5		99.2	89.9	71.3
95.50	1.00	35.0	Benin	166.6		106.8	87.9	
97.76	2.26	36.0	Zimbabwe	160.1		106.0	95.7	96.0
97.86	.10	37.0	Equatorial Guinea	130.8				10.8

```
DATA NOT AVAILABLE OR NOT APPLICABLE
FOR THE FOLLOWING COUNTRIES

Djibouti    Guinea     Guinea-Bissau  Namibia
```

SOURCE: *World Tables 1980* Economic Data Sheet 1.

Angola: *Accelerated Development South of the Sahara* (Washington, D.C.: World Bank, 1981).

TABLE 3.5   Per Cent GDP in Secondary and Tertiary Sectors 1977 (A), 1971 (B), 1965 (C) and 1960 (D).

Definition: % GDP at current factor cost, in manufacturing and electrical, construction, communications, transportation, and other services—i.e. not including product originating in agriculture, mining, and public administration.

```
Range =          55.00
Mean =           47.53
Standard Deviation =        12.06
```

Population Percent Cum.	Country	Rank	Country Name	A	Range Decile	B	C	D
1.65	1.65	1.0	Zambia	74	1	55	41	28
3.87	2.22	2.0	Ivory Coast	68	2	63	54	49
4.90	1.03	4.0	Somalia	63	3	47	39	38
13.19	8.29	4.0	Zaire	63		69	58	48
15.45	2.26	4.0	Zimbabwe	63		70	70	70
15.90	.45	6.5	Congo	59		67	66	65
16.65	.75	6.5	Togo	59		54	43	33
18.29	1.64	8.0	Senegal	58		66	61	63
20.24	1.95	9.5	Angola	57	4	56	58	58
22.65	2.41	9.5	Cameroon	57		56	49	47
25.64	2.99	11.0	Mozambique	56		60	60	56
31.88	6.24	12.0	Sudan	54		43	42	35
32.04	.16	13.0	Swaziland	53		51	41	41
33.04	1.00	14.0	Benin	51	5	42	35	35
36.55	3.51	15.5	Ghana	50		46	48	33
39.03	2.48	15.5	Madagascar	50		57	48	47
39.19	.16	18.0	Gabon	49		41	43	41
40.85	1.66	18.0	Malawi	49		42	35	38
42.72	1.87	18.0	Mali	49		76	41	36
42.95	.23	21.0	Botswana	48		45	66	43
47.55	4.60	21.0	Kenya	48		52	51	50
49.52	1.97	21.0	Upper Volta	48		46	34	29
49.90	.38	23.0	Lesotho	47		42	33	28
50.48	.58	24.0	Central African R	46	6	47	34	33
51.47	.99	25.0	Sierra Leone	43		45	39	
52.83	1.36	26.0	Rwanda	42		19	14	11
62.54	9.71	28.0	Ethiopia	41	7	40	37	32
63.07	.53	28.0	Liberia	41		34	30	45
64.40	1.33	28.0	Niger	41		36	32	35
69.56	5.16	30.0	Tanzania	39		48	40	46
71.13	1.57	31.0	Guinea	36		36	21	33
72.47	1.34	32.0	Chad	35	8	31	39	36
72.93	.46	33.0	Mauritania	34		31	20	28
73.10	.17	34.0	Gambia	33		33	33	26
94.10	21.00	35.0	Nigeria	32		34	38	33
94.29	.19	36.0	Guinea-Bissau	26	9			
95.57	1.28	37.0	Burundi	25		24	23	22
99.52	3.95	38.0	Uganda	19	10	33	36	39

DATA NOT AVAILABLE OR NOT APPLICABLE FOR THE FOLLOWING COUNTRIES

Djibouti   Equatorial Guinea   Namibia

SOURCES: Economic Commission for Africa, *Survey of Economic Conditions in Africa*, 1970, Part II, Table 1, Chapter 5, Apendix B. (1977) *World Tables 1980* Economic Data Sheet I. *Angola, Burundi, Gambia, Guinea-Bissau, Mozambique, Swaziland, Togo: Accelerated Development South of the Sahara* (Washington, D.C.: World Bank, 1981). Sierra Leone—staff estimate.

TABLE 3.6   Index of Total Agricultural Production, 1972 (A), 1966 (B) and 1960 (C).

Definition: Ratio of a given year's production to the average of the period 1960 to 1965, times 100.

```
Range =        152.00
Mean =         119.07
Standard Deviation =       28.28
```

Population Percent Cum.	Country	Rank	Country Name	A	Range Decile	B	C
.16	.16	1.0	Swaziland	199	1	136	85
1.82	1.66	2.0	Malawi	171	2	127	95
3.47	1.65	3.0	Zambia	164	3	122	82
5.69	2.22	4.0	Ivory Coast	153	4	105	88
7.05	1.36	5.0	Rwanda	152		109	101
7.34	.29	6.0	Namibia	149		93	94
9.75	2.41	7.5	Cameroon	136	5	112	92
10.28	.53	7.5	Liberia	136		109	101
11.27	.99	9.0	Sierra Leone	132		100	94
11.43	.16	10.0	Gabon	131		110	92
13.91	2.48	11.5	Madagascar	130		111	90
20.15	6.24	11.5	Sudan	130		106	82
28.44	8.29	13.0	Zaire	128		113	114
33.04	4.60	14.5	Kenya	127		115	90
36.03	2.99	14.5	Mozambique	127		106	97
37.60	1.57	16.0	Guinea	126		97	97
37.83	.23	17.5	Botswana	125		92	97
39.11	1.28	17.5	Burundi	125		112	102
39.86	.75	19.0	Togo	124		104	106
43.81	3.95	20.0	Uganda	123	6	114	90
44.81	1.00	21.0	Benin	122		105	100
45.84	1.03	22.0	Somalia	120		106	94
55.55	9.71	23.5	Ethiopia	119		104	92
76.55	21.00	23.5	Nigeria	119		109	93
81.71	5.16	25.0	Tanzania	117		118	90
82.29	.58	26.0	Central African R	116		102	106
84.24	1.95	27.5	Angola	113		108	81
84.70	.46	27.5	Mauritania	113		105	94
88.21	3.51	29.0	Ghana	111		108	90
88.38	.17	30.0	Gambia	108		135	95
90.64	2.26	31.0	Zimbabwe	100	7		
92.51	1.87	32.5	Mali	92	8	102	97
94.48	1.97	32.5	Upper Volta	92		92	93
95.81	1.33	34.0	Niger	91		102	76
96.00	.19	35.0	Guinea-Bissau	86		102	100
96.38	.38	36.0	Lesotho	84		95	100
96.83	.45	37.0	Congo	77	9	87	104
98.17	1.34	38.0	Chad	76		104	97
99.81	1.64	39.0	Senegal	72		94	88
99.91	.10	40.0	Equatorial Guinea	47		121	78

DATA NOT AVAILABLE OR NOT APPLICABLE
FOR THE FOLLOWING COUNTRIES

Djibouti

SOURCES: *AID Economic Data Book 1973; UNECA Statistical Yearbook* 1972, 1973, 1974 editions; *Equatorial Guinea:* Cocoa only; *Guinea-Bissau:* Groundnuts only. Data for 1961 for *Central African Republic, Gabon, Gambia, Mauritania, Mozambique, Somalia, and Swaziland.*

Note: Countries in the Sahelian region including Senegal, Mauritania, Mali, Upper Volta, Niger, Nigeria, Chad and parts of other countries were severely affected by extensive drought in 1972 and had severe drops in agricultural production. *Zimbabwe: Accelerated Development South of the Sahara* (Washington, D.C.: World Bank, 1981).

TABLE 3.7 Thousands of Inhabitants per Physician, ca. 1977 (A), 1970 (B), 1960 (C).

```
Range =        80145.00
Mean =         22488.74
Standard Deviation =        17351.97
```

Population Percent Cum.	Population Percent Country	Rank	Country Name	A	Range Decile	B	C
9.71	9.71	1.0	Ethiopia	84850	1	74550	91000
11.68	1.97	2.0	Upper Volta	61798	3	92760	100000
13.34	1.66	3.0	Malawi	48500	5	38250	35000
14.62	1.28	4.0	Burundi	45430		59000	63000
17.61	2.99	5.5	Mozambique	42970	6	58260	21000
18.94	1.33	5.5	Niger	42970		58260	71000
20.28	1.34	7.0	Chad	41160		62880	62000
21.64	1.36	8.0	Rwanda	39350		57900	144000
22.64	1.00	9.0	Benin	34280	7	28920	47000
24.51	1.87	10.0	Mali	32459		41490	39000
25.09	.58	11.0	Central Afri. R	29410		38330	37000
29.04	3.95	12.0	Uganda	28330	8	9210	13000
34.20	5.16	13.0	Tanzania	18490	9	20677	21000
34.95	.75	14.0	Togo	18360		27940	35130
35.33	.38	15.0	Lesotho	17800		26290	
36.97	1.64	16.0	Senegal	16450		16640	35000
38.00	1.03	17.0	Somalia	15560		21140	30000
46.29	8.29	18.0	Zaire	15530		30040	63000
47.86	1.57	19.0	Guinea	15500		31090	48000
50.08	2.22	20.0	Ivory Coast	15220		15320	25480
52.03	1.95	21.0	Angola	15000		8460	14000
73.03	21.00	22.0	Nigeria	14810		20530	32000
74.02	.99	23.0	Sierra Leone	14500		17110	26000
74.48	.46	24.0	Mauritania	14140		17210	30000
76.89	2.41	25.0	Cameroon	13980		25960	34000
77.06	.17	26.0	Gambia	13120		18950	
79.54	2.48	27.0	Madagascar	10780	10	11390	8800
81.19	1.65	28.0	Zambia	10370		13520	12860
84.70	3.51	29.0	Ghana	10200		12950	21000
85.23	.53	30.0	Liberia	10050		11590	12000
91.47	6.24	31.0	Sudan	9760		13660	31000
91.70	.23	32.0	Botswana	9600		15460	20870
91.86	.16	33.0	Swaziland	9200		8270	10000
96.46	4.60	34.0	Kenya	8840		7830	10000
96.91	.45	35.0	Congo	7320		9160	13000
99.17	2.26	36.0	Zimbabwe	7030		6370	
99.36	.19	37.0	Guinea-Bissau	6750			
99.52	.16	38.0	Gabon	4705		5210	6120

DATA NOT AVAILABLE OR NOT APPLICABLE
FOR THE FOLLOWING COUNTRIES

Djibouti   Equatorial Guinea   Namibia

SOURCE: U.N. Statistical Yearbook 1973; UNECA Statistical Yearbook (1972, 1973 and 1974). *World Tables 1980* Part IV Table 3.
Angola, Sierra Leone, Zaire, and Zimbabwe: Accelerated Development South of the Sahara (Washington, D.C.: World Bank, 1981.

TABLE 3.8   Average National Savings Rate as a Percent of GDP, 1977 (A), 1970 (B), 1965 (C) and 1960 (D).

```
Range =          83.10
Mean =           10.25
Standard Deviation =           13.00
```

Population Percent Cum.	Country	Rank	Country Name	A	Range Decile	B	C	D
.16	.16	1.0	Gabon	63.1	1	32.8	30.5	44.7
21.16	21.00	2.0	Nigeria	27.2	5	10.1	12.2	7.0
21.39	.23	3.0	Botswana	24.5		-.5	-16.7	-6.2
23.61	2.22	4.0	Ivory Coast	23.2		18.2	14.5	11.3
25.87	2.26	5.0	Zimbabwe	21.9		20.8	20.3	19.3
30.47	4.60	6.0	Kenya	21.7		20.7	12.8	14.3
32.42	1.95	7.0	Angola	18.9	6	18.5	12.0	13.7
34.07	1.65	8.0	Zambia	18.7		42.4	35.6	32.1
34.82	.75	9.0	Togo	17.7		9.9	12.6	2.1
36.39	1.57	10.0	Guinea	16.5		8.4	9.6	4.6
38.80	2.41	11.0	Cameroon	15.9		13.7	12.9	9.3
42.75	3.95	12.0	Uganda	14.8		15.5	13.7	15.8
44.41	1.66	13.0	Malawi	14.1		11.3	-.3	-5.2
49.57	5.16	14.0	Tanzania	13.3		17.9	14.5	17.4
50.85	1.28	15.5	Burundi	11.4	7	2.5	2.5	4.3
53.33	2.48	15.5	Madagascar	11.4		10.8	-.3	.4
54.36	1.03	17.5	Somalia	10.0		8.2	1.6	7.2
62.65	8.29	17.5	Zaire	10.0		22.3	36.6	15.6
63.23	.58	19.5	Central African R	9.5		.8	6.5	-2.4
64.56	1.33	19.5	Niger	9.5		5.8	8.1	12.1
65.09	.53	21.0	Liberia	9.2		11.4	-3.3	8.5
66.73	1.64	22.0	Senegal	9.1		8.9	6.1	12.1
66.83	.10	23.0	Equatorial Guinea	8.2		11.2	27.7	
68.19	1.36	24.0	Rwanda	7.3		2.9	4.5	7.8
71.18	2.99	25.0	Mozambique	7.2		10.7	7.3	8.0
72.17	.99	26.0	Sierra Leone	7.0		16.0	6.8	
81.88	9.71	27.0	Ethiopia	5.7		10.8	11.8	10.3
85.39	3.51	28.0	Ghana	5.0		11.0	7.1	16.2
86.39	1.00	29.0	Benin	4.3	8	6.3	2.6	7.6
88.26	1.87	30.0	Mali	3.9		6.3	11.4	6.7
90.23	1.97	31.0	Upper Volta	3.8		3.0	4.5	.9
90.40	.17	32.0	Gambia	1.9		8.5	.2	4.2
96.64	6.24	33.0	Sudan	1.6		10.9	6.8	8.8
97.10	.46	34.0	Mauritania	.1		12.8	3.8	-7.5
97.26	.16	35.0	Swaziland	-4.7	9	6.2	31.2	15.8
98.60	1.34	36.0	Chad	-6.7		3.3	-.5	3.0
99.05	.45	37.0	Congo	-7.6		-.6	-.8	-23.5
99.43	.38	38.0	Lesotho	-8.7		-2.8	-14.1	-13.2
99.62	.19	39.0	Guinea-Bissau	-20.0	10			

```
DATA NOT AVAILABLE OR NOT APPLICABLE
FOR THE FOLLOWING COUNTRIES

Djibouti    Namibia
```

SOURCE: *World Tables 1980.* Table 9 Part III.
Guinea-Bissau: Accelerated Development South of the Sahara (Washington, D.C.: World Bank, 1981).

TABLE 3.9   Average Daily Per Capita Food Consumption (calories per person per day) 1977 (A), 1970 (B), 1966 (C) and 1960 (D).

```
Range =          822.00
Mean =          2192.05
Standard Deviation =       194.36
```

Population Percent Cum.	Population Percent Country	Rank	Country Name	A	Range Decile	B	C	D
2.26	2.26	1.0	Zimbabwe	2576	1	2300	2420	2120
4.48	2.22	2.0	Ivory Coast	2573		2384	2151	2078
6.96	2.48	3.0	Madagascar	2486	2	2460	2402	2460
9.37	2.41	4.5	Cameroon	2428		2411	2244	2411
9.53	.16	4.5	Gabon	2428		2207	2169	2177
10.06	.53	6.0	Liberia	2404	3	2234	2168	2179
10.22	.16	7.0	Swaziland	2357		2087	1941	
10.41	.19	8.0	Guinea-Bissau	2326	4	2099	1958	
10.58	.17	9.0	Gambia	2318		2346	2227	2207
31.58	21.00	10.0	Nigeria	2308		2327	2261	2479
39.87	8.29	11.0	Zaire	2304		2249	2227	2249
40.32	.45	12.0	Congo	2284		2165	2035	2165
46.56	6.24	13.0	Sudan	2282		2189	1824	1953
47.92	1.36	14.0	Rwanda	2264		2227	1967	2093
49.56	1.64	15.0	Senegal	2261		2263	2282	2263
50.84	1.28	16.0	Burundi	2254		2293	2296	1880
51.84	1.00	17.0	Benin	2249		2214	2189	2165
52.22	.38	18.0	Lesotho	2245	5	2079	2102	
52.80	.58	19.0	Central African R	2242		2223	1969	2230
54.46	1.66	20.0	Malawi	2235		2353	2033	2189
55.49	1.03	21.0	Somalia	2221		2187	2179	2187
55.72	.23	22.0	Botswana	2186		2020	1998	1970
56.01	.29	23.0	Namibia	2182		2256	2287	
57.00	.99	24.0	Sierra Leone	2150	6	2204	2153	2207
58.33	1.33	25.0	Niger	2139		2090	2151	2090
60.28	1.95	26.0	Angola	2133		2008	1936	2008
62.15	1.87	27.0	Mali	2117		2200	2079	2149
66.10	3.95	28.0	Uganda	2110		2274	2069	2213
70.70	4.60	29.0	Kenya	2095		2287	2189	2316
71.45	.75	30.0	Togo	2069	7	2178	2209	2057
76.61	5.16	31.0	Tanzania	2063		2116	2134	1991
78.26	1.65	32.0	Zambia	2002		1934	1941	1896
81.77	3.51	33.0	Ghana	1983	8	2239	2072	2086
82.23	.46	34.0	Mauritania	1976		1921	1934	1837
83.80	1.57	35.0	Guinea	1943		2070	1970	2060
86.79	2.99	36.0	Mozambique	1906	9	2055	1963	1999
88.76	1.97	37.0	Upper Volta	1875		1992	2041	2064
90.10	1.34	38.0	Chad	1762	10	2130	2288	2306
99.81	9.71	39.0	Ethiopia	1754		1939	1905	2060

DATA NOT AVAILABLE OR NOT APPLICABLE FOR THE FOLLOWING COUNTRIES

Djibouti   Equatorial Guinea

SOURCE: Part III Table 9 *World Tables 1980.*

TABLE 3.10 Distribution of Personal Income before Taxes ca. 1965.

Definition: The data in this table are values for the Gini concentration ratio, which describes the area above a Lorenz curve, which links the percentage of total income received by the equivalent percentage of income recipients, in relation to a line of perfect equality. The Gini index is 0 for complete income equality and 1 for maximum income inequality, and the higher the value of the index the greater the inequality in income distribution.

```
Range =          .30
Mean =           .50
Standard Deviation =           .09


 Population
   Percent              Country              Range
                 Rank  Name           A     Decile
Cum. Country

    .16    .16   1.5  Gabon          .64      1
   4.76   4.60   1.5  Kenya          .64
   5.75    .99   3.0  Sierra Leone   .61      2
   5.98    .23   4.0  Botswana       .57      3
   7.62   1.64   5.0  Senegal        .56
  12.78   5.16   6.0  Tanzania       .54      4
  15.00   2.22   7.5  Ivory Coast    .53
  17.48   2.48   7.5  Madagascar     .53
  38.48  21.00   9.0  Nigeria        .51      5
  40.13   1.65  10.0  Zambia         .48      6
  41.79   1.66  11.0  Malawi         .47
  42.79   1.00  12.0  Benin          .42      8
  49.03   6.24  13.5  Sudan          .40
  52.98   3.95  13.5  Uganda         .40
  54.32   1.34  15.0  Chad           .35     10
  55.65   1.33  16.0  Niger          .34


DATA NOT AVAILABLE OR NOT APPLICABLE
FOR THE FOLLOWING COUNTRIES

Angola       Burundi      Cameroon      Central Afri. R
Congo        Djibouti     Equ. Guinea   Ethiopia
Gambia       Ghana        Guinea        Guinea-Bissau
Lesotho      Liberia      Mali          Mauritania
Mozambique   Namibia      Rwanda        Somalia
Swaziland    Togo         Upper Volta   Zaire
Zimbabwe
```

SOURCE: Felix Paukert, "Income Distribution at Different Levels of Development: A Survey of Evidence," *International Labour Review* August-September 1973 108, 2—3: 97—126, Table 6. See the appendix, in this source, for a discussion of the data quality and computations as well as citations to the original sources of data. *Botswana, Ivory Coast, Kenya, Malawi, Sierra Leone, Uganda: Size Distribution of Income: A Compilation of Data* Washington, D.C.: World Bank, 1975.

Labor and Capital

In order to understand ways in which black African countries may transcend the relative poverty described by data on national income, it is necessary to understand the conditions which produce economic growth, and to plan for the stimulation of such growth-producing conditions. Economic theory and planning suffer alike, however, from ambiguous identification of the means to economic growth. Economic growth requires the transformation by labor and technology of the raw materials of the environment into goods and services, and the distribution of such goods on a larger scale, and at a faster rate for given expenditures of labor time. But what kinds and sequencing of production are most efficient for the stimulation of sustained economic growth; what composition of technology and capital are most desirable for such purposes; what psychological and institutional factors stimulate labor productivity and savings; and what distribution of income stimulates greater investment and effective demand for production, and what social and political arrangements promote economic growth are questions of great complexity. We cannot here summarize or clarify theories of economic development, but refer simply to certain fundamental features of the distribution of labor and capital which need to be taken into account in explaining differences in economic development and in planning for future economic growth.

The data in Table 3.11 indicate the generally substantial concentration in agricultural employment of the labor force in black African countries. Such concentrations of labor in agriculture, with concommitantly high subsistence sectors, low per-capita money incomes, and low productivity generally means that these countries lack the managerial and technical skills and the effective demand necessary to stimulate domestic markets for industrial production, and that the generation of savings and revenue necessary to create the infrastructure for such development is heavily dependent on, and very much restricted by, agricultural activity. For the forseeable future, agriculture will remain the dominant sector of employment and the major potential source of savings in these economies, and growth in national income and savings will depend on stimulating agricultural productivity in general, and, more particularly, on shifting human labor resources from low productivity subsistence farming to higher productivity employment in the urban and cash crop sectors. Such a shift will, furthermore, have to be so controlled that it allows for the generation of new employment, without which the necessary demand for agricultural produce and the growth of new varieties of domestic manufacturing production will be restricted.

The rate of expansion of new employment opportunities in the cash economies of these countries is indicated by data such as that presented on wage employment in Tables 3.12 and 3.13. Because these figures include wage earners in the agricultural sector they do not simply reflect the inverse of the proportion of the labor force employed in agriculture. Data in Table 3.14 provide a more precise indication of the expansion of employment in non-agricultural activities—in the case of these data, the rate of employment in manufacturing activity. These data on wage employment generally, and employment in manufacturing in particular, emphasize the still narrow base of the cash market. And the low level of development of industrialization, in these countries. Even where relatively high rates of growth of national income have been achieved in black African countries, this growth has to a large extent been based on capital-intensive investments with very restrictive employment expansion.[18] Despite high capital investment and the rapid growth of public sector employment in these countries in the late colonial period and the early post-independence period, the average annual percentage change in total industrial employment for the period 1960 to 1977 (or for approximately that period) varied somewhat across different countries: the rate of growth in Ghana was 5.0%; in Kenya 9.2%; in Malawi 8.8%; in Nigeria 9.5%; Zaire 5.2%; in Uganda 9.5% and in Tanzania 7.3%.[19]

Situations like this lead to widespread unemployment; in 1964, it was reported that 200,000 persons were registered as unemployed in Kenya, 40,000 of whom were registered in Nairobi.[20] Lagos, in 1965, is said to have had 34% of its laboring population out of work.[21] In Brazzaville and Pointe Noire, 40% of the working age population have been reported as unemployed, and more than 40% of the population of the Congo live in these cities.[22] Unemployment in Contonou and Porto Novo in 1963 was estimated at 30,000 and was thought to have been increasing at a rate of 5,000 a year.[23] In Ghana in 1968, it was estimated that there were no less than 80,000 people out of work and that 40,000 of 52,000 middle school leavers from 1967 were unemployed. In Nigeria, the number of those leaving primary school and failing to find employment rose from 221,000 in 1961 to an estimated 366,000 in 1965; unemployed secondary grammar school leavers rose from 5,000 to 11,000 between those years, and unemployed secondary modern school leavers rose from 24,000 to 39,000 in that period.[25] In summary, the percentage of the population in African cities between the ages of 15 and 55 that was unemployed—although a very small percentage of these would be formally registered as such at employment offices—was projected to reach as high as 35% by the late 1970's, and unemployed in these cities were estimated to constitute between 12 and 22% of the urban population in 1967.[26]

In order to break the cycle of agricultural poverty, rapid rural-urban migration and unemployment, black African countries face the enormously complex task of stimulating and channeling investment into infra-structural developments, manpower training, technological development, energy production, and employment-generating industrialization. How to optimize the growth of income and welfare by allocating investment capital among these diverse activities, and how to generate the required capital, are major problems of economic theory and planning in these countries. Although a central ingredient in all economic development theory and planning is capital – that is, resources which are not immediately consumed and which can be used for future production – it is unfortunately no easy matter to specify the optimum composition and deployment of capital resources for faster rates of economic growth. Conventional theories of economic development were dominated by the ideas of Harrod and Domar in which investment in physical capital was seen as the primary motive force behind economic growth. Capital-output ratios, relating the amount of capital investment associated with each unit of income growth, were observed to be relatively constant among industrial economies in the Western world. The rapid regeneration of European economies after the Second World War following the massive infusion of capital aid under the Marshall Plan encouraged the view that investment capital was the major obstacle to economic growth elsewhere. Typical of such a perspective was Chenery's two-gap model of blockages to development which emphasized the ability of an economy (1) to generate internal savings for investment, and (2) to generate foreign exchange in sufficient quantities to import physical capital.[27]

Capital clearly is a vital ingredient in economic development, but it is not the sole factor which stimulates or inhibits economic growth. The capacity of an economy to absorb capital and to "take-off" into self-sustaining growth, is related to social structural and psychological conditions of human experience, as work by McClelland and Hagen suggests;[28] to economies of scale, balanced institutional and sectoral growth, and to the development of integrating linkages between social, economic and political sectors, as the work of Hirschman, Rustow, Adelman and Morris and others suggest;[29] and to the structure of interdependency in the world economy of capitalism in which the balance of political control over economic development and the new flow of capital tends to favor the metropolitan rather than the peripheral countries like those in Black Africa, as recent "dependency theory" suggests.[30] And planning, especially "planning without facts" in countries with very poor statistical information on economic activities, requires careful feasibility and evaluation studies of the productivity of specific projects rather than a simple faith in abstract capital-output ratios, since it requires the coordination of government's capital budgets, recurrent budgets for activities like agricultural extension, and the formulation of institutional arrangements for the expansion of markets, credit facilities, cooperatives, etc.[31]

These comments caution against any mechanical or deterministic assumptions about the relationship between capital and economic growth. It is nevertheless important for macro-analytic generalizations about the potentialities for economic development, to get some understanding of the process of capital accumulation in these countries. Table 3.15 provides data on Gross Domestic Investment—i.e., the total fixed invesment in buildings, equipment, communication facilities and inventories in a given year, without adjustment for depreciation in the value of the initial capital stock. The average percentage of GDP made up by Gross Domestic Capital Formation in these countries in 1963 was 13%, which was just lower than the equivalent figure for Mexico in 1950, the date at which that country generally is thought to have entered its take-off period.[32] But these highly aggregated data on Gross Domestic Investment cannot in and of themselves suggest the probabilities of future economic growth in these countries. Critical questions have to be asked about the disaggregated distribution of investment in these countries. Such questions deal, for example, with inter-sectoral allocations of investment. Should agriculture receive priority as in the recent experience of Ivory Coast where economic growth has been more pronounced than in most black African countries? Should investments in infra-structural and manpower development receive priority over investment in capital intensive technology in these countries where imported physical capital, though it may stimulate productivity, tends to be ill-adapted to the "spill-over" developments of internal capital and intermediate-goods production and to the generation of employment within the domestic economy, and, therefore, ineffective in dealing with problems of underdevelopment and unemployment? Should energy resource development be a high priority, and what magnitude of such investment is required for given levels of investment in industrial technology? Should capital accumulation be encouraged through foreign aid and foreign private investment, and what concentration of public, centralized investment, as opposed to private, decentralized investment should be encouraged?[33]

While questions such as these cannot be resolved definitively by aggregate data, we do have access to data on foreign aid and foreign private investment in Chapter 6, and to data on the proportional volume of imports of machinery and equipment also in that Chapter. The concentration of public sector investment can be investigated by analysis of the data in Tables 3.16 and 3.17 on government consumption and capital budgets. Additional discussion of the role of government in economic development—the concentration of public sector employment, fiscal policies, and government expenditures—is given in Chapter 5.

The extent to which capital investment activity has stimulated productive capacity and potential increases in the productivity of labor can be assessed in part by reference to the data in Tables 3.18 and 3.19 on energy consumption and saving rate in these countries. Such measures of energy consumption, however, are only indicative of potential growth in energy-output-per-capita. The distribution of energy resources and consumption may be so concentrated in single, capital-intensive industries, that productivity per man *in those industries* increases while per capita productivity in the economy as a whole remains unchanged or decreases if there is no increasing demand for labor in those industries and if they do not generate forward or backward linkages to other industrial developments within the economy. In Ghana and Zambia, for example, large percentages of power consumption go to producing, for export, alumina and copper respectively, and it may not be true to say that the typical productivity per worker in Ghana and Zambia is proportionally higher than that in countries where such industries do not exist on the same scale. Finally, in the absence of a complete specification of the sources, composition and distribution of capital and of associated factors of production, and of the capital-output ratios for different types of capital investment, we present data in Tables 3.20 and 3.21 which summarize judgements by expert commentators on African development as to the difficulty of achieving economic growth because of inadequate economic resources, and the number of types of industry that it is possible to develop in the 1980s in these countries.

Reliability

The measurement of factors of production and the income derived from production in modern economies requires methodological sophistication and considerable expenditures on manpower and facilities for the collection, storage and analysis of statistical data. Such data are generally, therefore, more accurate and comprehensive for the wealthier, more industrialized countries than for poorer countries. This is so not only because of the relative lack of experience and facilities required for sophisticated national accounting, but also because the conceptual and methodological approaches to national accounts developed in the advanced industrial economies may often be inapplicable, or applied only with very great difficulty, in less developed countries. We are unable to give any quantitative estimate of the reliability of data presented in this Chapter, and they should be used, therefore, with caution. Although the correlations between conceptually related indicators collected or published by different agencies for the same countries are generally high for the kinds of data that we have discussed in this Chapter, there are frequently substantial differences between estimates for the value of a given variable for individual countries. We have relied heavily on data published by agencies such as the World Bank and the Economic Commission for Africa, whose statistical publications are based on detailed examination of government sources and of the time series available for individual countries on given indicators. Nevertheless, neither we nor such agencies can claim that these data are highly reliable, and it will be well for users of these data to keep in mind the following basic threats to their reliability.

First, the countries discussed here have large subsistence sectors where exchanges of goods and services are not recorded in the market, but must be imputed in income calculations. Because of the confines of the operational definition of GNP and GDP, "it is only exceptionally thought appropriate to impute economic values to activities that do not enter the market, as for instance the rental value of owner-occupied housing or the unsold part of the product of ones "own trade," as the UN system puts it. [But] in underdeveloped countries where the market plays a smaller part, imputation becomes necessary on a very large scale if income and product are to have any meaning at all."[34] Such imputations, though conceptually necessary, are probably seriously unreliable, especially when one considers the unreliability of basic demographic data required for such imputation.

Second, there are problems of reliability of aggregate economic indices standardized by exchange rates, price indices and population data. The standardization of national income measures by conversion to international trading currencies at official exchange rates, for example, probably understates the value of goods in domestic markets, and accentuates the appearance of productivity differences between rich and poor nations, since the price of foreign exchange is primarily related to those goods and services which do or might enter foreign trade. Products and services which by their nature are produced and consumed locally are at best indirectly affected by prices of foreign goods. Furthermore, the exchange rates used are often non-equilibrium rates which are periodically devalued and hence an inaccurate measure of value even for internationally traded goods and services. Ideally, for cross-national, comparative purposes, national income statistics should compare purchasing prices for the range of items used in income calculation. The effects of such a procedure are illustrated in a study cited by the *World Bank Atlas*, in which the per capita product in the U.S. compared to that of India was in ratio 30:1, whereas calculations based on purchasing power parities yielded a ratio of 12:1.[35] Additional sources of unreliability pertain to the standardization of national income data by inflation rates, which are measured with only limited degrees of geographical comprehensiveness within these countries. Income measures standardized by population statistics suffer, obviously, from the errors attributable to estimates of population in all these countries. Third, there are problems of validity attributable to the non-comparability of conceptual and operational definitions of aggregate economic measures, and such invalidity necessarily constrains the reliability of these measures. For example, the measurement of capital formation in these countries, where much activity that is formally defined as capital investment, as in residential construction, may bear little relation to similar forms of activity in advanced industrial countries.[36] The data presented in this Chapter are generally published in a form consistent with standardized UN procedures, but inconsistencies in the interpretation of accounting definitions may well limit the comparability of data collected in different countries. Definitions of the public and private sector, of wage employment, and of inflation are typically subject to variable definition in different countries.

Notes

[1]Andrew M. Kamarck, *The Economics of African Development*, (New York: Praeger, 1971, revised edition), p. 21. This list does change over time but its general relevance to the African situation is still valid.

[2]For an introduction to the current views of economists with respect to issues of development see H.B. Chenery *Structural Change and Development Policy* (New York: Oxford University Press, 1979); C.R. Frank et al. *Income Distribution and Growth in the Less Developed Countries* (Washington D.C.: Brookings Instituions, 1977) and D. Colman and F. Nixson *Economics of Change in Less Developed Countries* (N.Y.: Wiley, 1978). Literature specifically concerned with dependence on foreign influences in Africa includes T.J. Biersteker *Distortion or Development?* (Cambridge: M.I.T. Press, 1978).

[3]For a provocative introduction to the historical background to contemporary problems of economic development in Africa, see Walter Rodney, *How Europe Underdeveloped Africa* (Dar es Salaam: Tanzania Publishing House, 1972). Sources on particular countries are given in part II, and there are numerous comparative historical studies such as

A. Pim, *The Financial and Economic History of the African Tropical Territories* (New York: Argosy-Antiquarian, 1970—originally published in 1940); A.G. Hopkins, *An Economic History of West Africa* (New York: Columbia University Press, 1973), and E.A. Brett, *Colonialism and Underdevelopment in East Africa* (London: Heinemann, 1973) For a sophisticated statistical analysis see T. I. Birnberg and S.A. Resnick *Colonial Development: An Econometric Study* (New Haven: Yale University Press, 1974). See J.P. Powelson *A Select Bibliography on Economic Development: With Annotations* (Boulder, Colo.: Westview Press, 1979) for a review of current literature.

[4]"The desire for or commitment to economic development as an end does not necessarily include desire for or commitment to economic development as a means. The fact that these two aspects of development can vary somewhat independently means that even though the desire for development as a goal may exist and be physically achievable, commitment to development as a process of change may not exist." Wilbert E. Moore and Arnold S. Feldman, eds., *Labor Commitment and Social Change in Developing Areas* (New York: Social Science Research Council, 1960), p. 6. Note that the conventional neo-classical theory of growth is being challenged in economics today. See J.L. Yellin "On Keynesian Economics and the Economics of the Post-Keynesians" *American Economic Review* 70, 2 May 1980 15—19, and J.R. Crotty "Post Keynesian Economic Theory: An Overview and Evaluation" *American Economic Review* 70, 2 May 1980, pp. 20—25. For an empirical evaluation see E.F. Dennison in "The Contribution of Capital to Economic Growth" *American Economic Review* 70, 2 May 1980, pp. 220—224.

[5]For information on the details of national income calculation in Africa, see Peter Ady and Michel Courcier, *Systems of National Accounts in Africa* (Paris: Organization for European Economic Cooperation, 1960); and D.A. Lury, "National Accounts in Africa," *Journal of Modern African Studies*, 2 (1964): 94—110. See also, Goran Ohlin, "Aggregate Comparisons: Problems and Prospects of Quantitative Analysis Based on National Accounts,' in *Comparative Research across Cultures and Nations*, ed. S. Rokkan (Paris: Mouton, 1968) and D.W. Blades *Non-Monetary (Subsistence) Activities in the National Accounts of Developing Countries* (Washington: OECD, 1952). Robert Eisner and his colleagues have been concerned with measures of income, output, productivity and investment that are less sensitive to the general procedures for income calculation that ignore much production (such as home clothes washing) that does not enter the market place. For a review of this work see R. Eisner "Total Income, Total Investment, and Growth" American Economic Review 70, 2 May 1980, p. 225.

[6]Kamarck, *op. cit.*, pp. 296—298. These statistics are in constant 1960 dollars.

[7]See the summary discussion of such issues in G.J. Ligthart and B. Abbai, "Economic Development in Africa: Aims and Possibilities," in E.A.G. Robinson, ed., *Economic Development for Africa South of the Sahara* (New York: St. Martin's Press, 1967): 3—47.

[8]For an introduction to problems of agricultural development, see W. Allen, *The African Husbandman* (New York: Barnes and Noble, 1965); John de Wilde, *et al.*, *Experiences With African Agricultural Development* (Baltimore: Johns Hopkins University Press, 1967); B.F. Johnston and J.W. Mellor, "The Nature of Agriculture's Contribution to Economic Development," *Food Research Institute Studies*, II, no. 1 (Feburary, 1961): and R. Dumont, *African Agricultural Development* (Addis Ababa: Economic Commission for Africa, 1966); B.F. Johnston *Agriculture and Structural Transformation: Economic Strategies for*

Late-Developing Countries (New York: Oxford University Press, 1975); and U. Lele *The Design of Rural Development: Lessons from Africa* (Baltimore: Johns Hopkins University Press, 1975) See G. De Lusignan, *French Speaking Africa Since Independence* (New York: Praeger, 1968) p. 322.

9See G. De Lusignan, *French Speaking African Since Independence* (New York: Praeger, 1968) p. 322.

10Economic Commission for Africa, *A Survey of Economic Conditions in Africa: 1967* (New York: United Nations, 1969), p. 29 and p. 53.

11See the discussion of evidence for somewhat more favorable estimates of agricultural productivity in Africa in John H. Dalton, "Shifting Perspectives of African Agriculture," in R.K.A. Gardner et al., ed., *Africa and the World* (Addis Ababa: Oxford University Press, 1970), pp. 95—109.

12Useful reviews of the scope of welfare economics are J.R. Hicks, "The Foundation of Welfare Economics," *Econometrica*, 7 (1939): 215—228; I.M.D. Little, *A Critique of Welfare Economics* (London: Oxford University Press, 1950); Kenneth Arrow, *Social Choice and Individual Values* 2nd edition (New York: John Wiley, 1963); T.C. Koopmans, *Three Essays on the State of Economic Science* (New York: McGraw-Hill, 1957); E.J. Mishan, "A Survey of Welfare Economics, 1939—1959," *Economic Journal*, 70 (1960): 197—265; Paul Samuelson, *Foundations of Economic Analysis* (Cambridge: Harvard University Press, 1947); Tibor Scitovsky, "A Note on Welfare Propositions in Economics," *Review of Economic Studies*, 9 (November 1941): 77—88; K. Arrow and T. Scitovsky, eds., *A.E.A. Readings in Welfare Economics* (Homewood, Ill.: Irwin, 1970); James S. Coleman, "The Possibility of a Social Welfare Function," *American Economic Review*, 56 (December 1966): 1105—1122. Examples of the use of the theory of welfare economics outside of economics are Herbert A. Simon, *Administrative Behavior* (New York: Macmillan, 1974); Robert A. Dahl and Charles E. Lindblom, *Politics, Economics, and Welfare* (New York: Harper and Row, 1953); and Anthony Downs, *An Economic Theory of Democracy* (New York: Harper and Row, 1957).

13Cf. Frank Andrews and B. Stephen, "Developing Measures of Perceived Quality of Life: Results from Several National Surveys," *Social Indicators Research*, 1 (1974): 1—26; K.A. Fox, *Social Indicators and Social Theory: Elements of an Operational System* (New York: Wiley, 1974); E. Allardt, "A Welfare Model for Selecting Indicators of National Development," *Policy Sciences* 4 (1973): 63—74.

14For discussions and data on the Gini index, see Bruce M. Russett, ed., *The World Handbook of Political and Social Indicators* (New Haven: Yale University Press, 1964); and Hayward R. Alker, Jr., and B. Russett, "Indices for Comparing Inequality," in *Comparing Nations*, eds. R. Merritt and S. Rokkan (New Haven, Conn.: Yale University Press, 1966), pp. 337—348. A more recent evaluation is R. Taagepera "Inequality, Concentration, Imbalance" *Political Methodology* 6,3 1979, 275-292.

15William T. Levine, "Political Change? Some Indicators on Enduring Stability in Unstable Political Systems," a paper prepared for delivery at the Annual Meeting of the American Political Science Association, Chicago, August 29—September 2, 1974.

16See H. Bienen and V.P. Diejomaoh, eds., *The Political Economy of Income Distribution in Nigeria* (New York: Barnes and Noble, 1981) for an attempt to review the data for Nigeria.

17For an introduction to these concerns of social scientists, see A.O. Hirschman, "The Changing Tolerance for Income Inequality in the Course of Economic Development," *Quarterly Journal of Economics*, LXXXVII, (November 1973): 544—566; I. Adelman and C. T. Morris, *Economic Growth and Social Equity in Developing Countries* (Stanford: Stanford University Press, 1973); Felix Paukert, "Income Distribution at Different Levels of Development: A Survey of Evidence," *International Labour Review*, 108, 2—3 August/September 1973, 97—126; Bruce M. Russett, "Inequality and Instability: The Relation of Land Tenure to Politics," *World Politics*, 16 (April 1964): 442—54; Robert W. Jackman, *Politics and Social Equality: A Comparative Analysis* (New York: John Wiley, 1975).

18For a review of this general problem see G. Arrighi, "International Corporations, Labor Aristocracies, and Economic Development in Tropical Africa," in R. Rhodes, ed., *Imperialism and Underdevelopment* (New York: Monthly Review Press, 1970); F. Stewart, "Technology and Employment in LDC's," *World Development*, 2 (March 1974): 17—46; D. Morawetz, "Employment Implications of Industrialization in Developing Countries: A Survey," *Economic Journal*, 84 (September 1974): 491—542, and J.P. Powelson, *Employment in Africa: Some Critical Issues* (Geneva: I.L.O. 1973), R. Clignet *The Africanization of the Labor Market: Educational and Occupational Segmentation in the Cameroons* (Berkeley: Univerisity of California Press, 1976); K. Hincliffe "Labor Aristocracy: A Northern Nigerian Case Study" *Journal of Modern African Studies* (March) 1974 p. 57—67; and J.B. Knight "Wages in Africa: What Should a Foreign Firm Do?" *Oxford Bulletin of Economics and Statistics* 37, 2 (May).

19*World Tables 1980* op. cit. p460-61.

20I. L. O. op. cit.

21I. L. O. op. cit.

22I. L. O. op. cit.

23I. L. O. op. cit.

24I. L. O. op. cit.

25I. L. O. op. cit.

26For a review of the literature on employment see D. Byerlee et al. *Rural Development in Tropical Africa: Summary of Findings* East Lansing MI: Department of Agricultural Economics, Michigan State University, 1977. Also see P. C. W. Gutkind *Bibliography on Unemployment with Special Reference to Africa* (Montreal: McGill Centre for Developing Area Studies, 1977; G. R. Martens *African Trade Unionism: A Bibliography* (Boston: G. K. Hall, 1977); and J. L. Stanley *Bibliography on Labour Force Participation in Nigeria 1970-1976* (Montreal: McGill Centre for Developing Area Studies, 1978).

27For a review of Chenery's thinking see Chenery (1979).

28See D. M. McClelland *The Achieving Sociewty*, and E. Hagen *Theory of Social Change* op. cit.

29see Adelman and Morris op. cit. and and A. O. Hirschmann op. cit.

30See the discussion in Chapter Six.

31For more extended commentary along these lines, see W.F. Stolper, "The Contribution of Economic Research to African Development" in E.A.G. Robinson, ed., *Economic Development for Africa South of the Sahara* (New York: St. Martin's Press, 1964), pp. 712—729; W. Stolper, *Planning Without Facts* (Cambridge: Harvard University Press, 1966), Herbert Frankel, "Capital and Capital Supply in Relation to the Development of Africa," and Robinson, *ed., op. cit.*, pp. 407—435. The latter comments on p. 434, "The belief in the miracles wrought by 'capital investment' *per se* is an illusion. In particular, it overlooks the fact that the essence of capital itself is that it wears out rapidly unless continually renewed, replaced or maintained. The poorer a country in skilled labor and in natural resources the less capital it is likely to have, and the less *it can afford to have until the whole social and economic complex of its activities has gradually evolved patterns of economic behaviour suited to its use, reproduction and further accumulation.*"

[32]See Ligthart and Abbai, *op. cit.*

[33]For analysis of such questions see D. Demery and L. Demery, "Cross-Section Evidence for Balanced and Unbalanced Growth," *Review of Economics and Statistics*, 55, (November 1973): 459—64; P.J. Drake, "Natural Resources versus Foreign Borrowing in Economic Development," *Economic Journal*, 82 (September 1972): 951—62; Frederick Harbison and Charles A. Meyers, *Education, Manpower, and Economic Growth* (New York: McGraw-Hill, 1964); R. Solow, "Technical Progress, Capital Formation and Economic Growth," *American Economic Review*, 52 (May 1962): 76—86; G.F. Papanek, "The Effect of Aid and Other Resource Transfers on Savings and Growth in Less Developed Countries," *Economic Journal*, 82 (September 1972): 934—1950; Elliot J. Berg, "Socialism and Economic Development in Tropical Africa," *Quarterly Journal of Economics*, 78 (November 1964): 549—573; G. Helleiner, "Development Policies for Africa in the 1970's," *Canadian Journal of African Studies*, 4 (Fall 1970): 285—304; M. Todaro, *Development Planning: Models and Methods* (Nairobi: Oxford University Press, 1971); H.B. Chenery et al. *Redistribution with Growth* (New York: Oxford University Press, 1974); A. Weintraub, E. Schwartz, and J.R. Aronson, eds., *The Economic Growth Controversy* (London: MacMillan, 1974); H.G. Jones *An Introduction to Modern Theories of Economic Growth* (New York: McGraw Hill, 1976); and G.M. Meier *Problems of Cooperation for Development* (New York: Oxford University Press, 1974) and the recent H.B. Chenery *Structural Change and Development Policy* (Oxford University Press, 1979).

[34]Goran Ohlin, *op. cit.*

[35]*World Bank Atlas* (Washington, D.C.: International Bank for Reconstruction and Development, 1969), and for a report on a major study of purchasing power comparability see B. Kravis, *A System of International Comparison of Gross Product and Purchasing Power* (Washington, D.C.: World Bank, 1975).

[36]See Stolper, "The Contribution of Economic Research to African Development," p. 718.

TABLE 3.11 Percent Labor Force in Agriculture and Animal Husbandry ca. 1977 (A), 1970 (B), and 1960 (C).

```
Range =          56.00
Mean =           75.54
Standard Deviation =        13.70
```

Population Percent Cum.	Country	Rank	Country Name	A	Range Decile	B	C
1.33	1.33	1.5	Niger	92.0	1	92.3	95.2
2.69	1.36	1.5	Rwanda	92.0		93.2	95.4
2.79	.10	3.0	Equatorial Guinea	90.0		79.9	83.7
3.37	.58	4.0	Central Afri. R	89.0		91.3	94.1
5.24	1.87	5.0	Mali	88.7		91.0	94.0
5.62	.38	6.0	Lesotho	88.0		89.7	93.4
6.96	1.34	7.5	Chad	87.0		90.1	94.4
8.62	1.66	7.5	Malawi	87.0		89.1	92.5
9.90	1.28	9.0	Burundi	85.0	2	87.2	90.0
10.36	.46	10.0	Mauritania	84.3		87.5	91.2
12.84	2.48	12.5	Madagascar	84.0		89.4	92.8
18.00	5.16	12.5	Tanzania	84.0		86.0	89.3
21.95	3.95	12.5	Uganda	84.0		85.9	89.4
23.92	1.97	12.5	Upper Volta	84.0		86.8	91.5
24.11	.19	15.0	Guinea-Bissau	83.8		87.0	90.9
24.34	.23	17.0	Botswana	83.0		86.7	92.0
25.91	1.57	17.0	Guinea	83.0		84.7	88.2
26.94	1.03	17.0	Somalia	83.0		84.7	87.9
29.16	2.22	19.0	Ivory Coast	82.0		84.5	88.8
38.87	9.71	20.0	Ethiopia	81.0		84.1	88.1
39.04	.17	21.0	Gambia	79.2	3	81.9	85.3
43.64	4.60	22.5	Kenya	79.0		82.1	85.8
49.88	6.24	22.5	Sudan	79.0		82.0	85.7
50.04	.16	24.0	Gabon	77.9		81.4	84.8
51.68	1.64	25.0	Senegal	77.0		79.7	83.6
59.97	8.29	26.0	Zaire	76.0		79.3	83.4
60.13	.16	27.0	Swaziland	75.4		81.1	89.1
62.54	2.41	28.0	Cameroon	73.8	4	75.9	78.5
63.07	.53	29.0	Liberia	73.0		75.6	80.7
63.36	.29	30.0	Namibia	70.0			
64.11	.75	31.5	Togo	69.0	5	73.3	79.5
65.76	1.65	31.5	Zambia	69.0		72.8	78.7
66.75	.99	33.0	Sierra Leone	68.0		71.5	77.7
69.74	2.99	34.0	Mozambique	67.0		73.0	81.1
71.69	1.95	35.0	Angola	60.0	6	63.7	69.4
92.69	21.00	36.5	Nigeria	56.0	7	62.1	70.8
94.95	2.26	36.5	Zimbabwe	56.0		62.1	70.8
98.46	3.51	38.0	Ghana	54.0		58.4	63.8
99.46	1.00	39.0	Benin	47.0	9	49.7	54.5
99.56	.10	40.0	Djibouti	40.0	10		
100.00	.45	41.0	Congo	36.0		41.8	51.7

SOURCES: A.I.D. *Economic Data Book 1970, Lesotho: Europa Yearbook 1967; Angola, Equatorial Guinea, Guinea-Bissau, Swaziland:* author's estimates. World Bank *World Tables* second edition, 1980 Series IV, TABLE 5. *Angola and Mozambique: Accelerated Development South of the Sahara* 1979 data; *Djibouti, Equatorial Guinea, and Namibia* staff estimates.

TABLE 3.12 Number of Wage Earners, 1970 (A), 1963 (B) and 1957 (C) in thousands.

```
Range =        1795.00
Mean =          304.68
Standard Deviation =        400.33
```

Population Percent Cum.	Country	Rank	Country Name	A	Range Decile	B	C
1.95	1.95	1.0	Angola	1800.0	1	1400.0	800.0
10.24	8.29	2.0	Zaire	1300.0		1200.0	1200.0
12.50	2.26	3.0	Zimbabwe	1023.0	5		51.0
15.49	2.99	4.5	Mozambique	1000.0		500.0	300.0
36.49	21.00	4.5	Nigeria	1000.0		423.0	465.0
41.09	4.60	6.0	Kenya	680.0	7	535.0	593.0
47.33	6.24	7.0	Sudan	600.0		350.0	470.0
49.74	2.41	8.0	Cameroon	560.0		160.0	139.7
59.45	9.71	9.0	Ethiopia	500.0	8		
61.11	1.66	10.0	Malawi	415.0		135.0	167.0
66.27	5.16	11.0	Tanzania	390.0		340.0	370.0
69.78	3.51	12.0	Ghana	380.0		350.0	253.0
71.43	1.65	13.0	Zambia	363.0	9	266.4	267.0
75.38	3.95	14.0	Uganda	313.0		221.0	300.0
77.86	2.48	15.0	Madagascar	300.0		255.0	243.2
80.08	2.22	16.0	Ivory Coast	270.0		209.0	171.0
80.53	.45	17.0	Congo	170.0	10	70.0	63.4
80.91	.38	18.5	Lesotho	150.0		70.0	60.0
81.44	.53	18.5	Liberia	150.0		100.0	75.0
83.08	1.64	20.0	Senegal	130.0		120.0	100.0
84.36	1.28	21.5	Burundi	100.0		90.0	60.0
85.72	1.36	21.5	Rwanda	100.0		100.0	60.0
87.29	1.57	23.0	Guinea	76.0		65.0	109.4
87.52	.23	24.0	Botswana	73.5		25.0	22.0
87.81	.29	25.0	Namibia	70.0			
89.15	1.34	26.0	Chad	69.0		32.0	34.8
90.14	.99	27.0	Sierra Leone	65.0		80.0	80.0
90.72	.58	28.0	Central Afri. R	64.0		55.0	48.6
90.82	.10	29.0	Equatorial Guinea	50.0		30.0	25.0
90.98	.16	30.0	Swaziland	44.0		35.0	23.0
91.14	.16	31.5	Gabon	40.0		35.0	41.6
92.17	1.03	31.5	Somalia	40.0		35.0	
94.14	1.97	33.0	Upper Volta	34.0		27.5	24.6
95.14	1.00	34.5	Benin	30.0		25.0	22.0
95.89	.75	34.5	Togo	30.0		11.6	12.0
97.76	1.87	36.5	Mali	25.0		18.8	41.8
99.09	1.33	36.5	Niger	25.0		18.5	13.6
99.55	.46	38.0	Mauritania	23.0		18.5	4.8
99.65	.10	39.0	Djibouti	20.0			1.4
99.82	.17	40.0	Gambia	14.4		10.0	6.0
100.00	.19	41.0	Guinea-Bissau	5.0		3.0	2.5

TABLE 3.13 Number of Wage Earners as a Percent of the Working Population, 1970 (A), 1963 (B) and 1957 (C).

Definition: Number of wage earners divided by the total population aged 15 through 59.

```
Range =          73.90
Mean =           13.50
Standard Deviation =          14.36
```

Population Percent Cum.	Country	Rank	Country Name	A	Range Decile	B	C
2.26	2.26	1.0	Zimbabwe	75.0	1		
4.21	1.95	2.0	Angola	51.7	4	46.6	28.9
4.59	.38	3.0	Lesotho	32.0	6	14.8	17.9
5.04	.45	4.0	Congo	31.1		18.7	18.4
5.14	.10	5.0	Equatorial Guinea	27.7	7	22.4	18.1
5.37	.23	6.0	Botswana	25.3		9.5	9.9
7.02	1.65	7.0	Zambia	21.7	8	19.1	22.0
7.18	.16	8.0	Swaziland	20.5		17.0	15.1
7.28	.10	9.0	Djibouti	20.0			
10.27	2.99	10.0	Mozambique	19.6		14.7	7.9
11.93	1.66	11.0	Malawi	18.7		7.2	8.6
12.46	.53	12.0	Liberia	18.6		18.3	13.2
12.75	.29	13.0	Namibia	18.0			
15.16	2.41	14.0	Cameroon	17.1		5.7	5.5
19.76	4.60	15.0	Kenya	13.1	9	13.1	16.8
19.92	.16	16.0	Gabon	12.3		11.8	15.2
28.21	8.29	17.0	Zaire	12.2		16.3	18.2
30.43	2.22	18.0	Ivory Coast	11.6		10.6	10.2
32.91	2.48	19.0	Madagascar	9.3		7.6	9.9
36.42	3.51	20.0	Ghana	8.6		9.3	7.7
42.66	6.24	21.0	Sudan	8.4	10	6.4	9.3
43.24	.58	22.0	Central African R	7.4		7.8	7.7
47.19	3.95	23.0	Uganda	6.6		6.4	9.8
47.36	.17	24.5	Gambia	6.4		6.5	4.2
49.00	1.64	24.5	Senegal	6.4		6.9	6.5
50.28	1.28	26.0	Burundi	6.0		6.2	4.7
55.44	5.16	27.0	Tanzania	5.5		5.9	7.4
56.80	1.36	28.0	Rwanda	5.3		6.7	4.7
57.79	.99	29.0	Sierra Leone	4.6		6.2	6.5
59.36	1.57	30.0	Guinea	4.1		3.8	8.0
69.07	9.71	31.0	Ethiopia	4.0			
69.53	.46	32.0	Mauritania	3.8		3.5	1.0
70.87	1.34	33.0	Chad	3.7		2.0	2.3
91.87	21.00	34.0	Nigeria	3.5		1.8	1.2
92.62	.75	35.0	Togo	3.3		1.6	1.9
93.65	1.03	36.0	Somalia	2.8		2.9	
94.65	1.00	37.0	Benin	2.3		2.3	2.4
94.84	.19	38.0	Guinea-Bissau	1.7		.9	.8
96.17	1.33	39.5	Niger	1.2		1.1	1.0
98.14	1.97	39.5	Upper Volta	1.2		1.1	1.1
100.00	1.87	41.0	Mali	1.1		.9	2.3

SOURCES: (1957) V. I. Junod ed. *The Handbook of Africa* (New York, New York University Press, 1963); *Ethiopia*: Addis Ababa only; *Botswana, Lesotho, and Swaziland*: includes workers in the Republic of South Africa; 1956 data: *Sudan; 1958 data: Botswana, Kenya, Tanzania;* 1959 data: *Ghana; Nigeria*: in establishments employing one hundred or more workers. *Ethiopia*, 1961 data.

(1963) *Étude Monographique*, p. 15. *Botswana*: estimate based on "a low level of wage employment in the country" according to *Europa Yearbook* 1967, p. 104; *Ethiopia, Sudan*: A.I.D. *Economic Data Book*; *Malawi, Somalia, Zambia*: *Overseas Business Reports 1966*; 1964 data; *Ivory Coast*; *Equatorial Guinea*: most of the labor force are Nigerians under contract in the cocoa plantations.

(1970) Estimates derived from data in International Monetary Fund *Surveys of African Economies* Vols. 1-6; A.I.D. *Economic Data Book 1973*; UNECA *Statistical Yearbook* 1972. Zimbabwe, 1973 data.

Note: There is considerable variation in the definition of wage earners and rarely can it be established if the values are comparable.

SOURCES: See Table 3.12 for wage earners data. Percent population in age group 15-59 from UNECA *Statistical Yearbook 1972* - Table 2; *Somalia, Sudan*: Estimate of 51% of total population in (15-59) age group. This is equal to the Ethiopian figure which is an adjoining country. *Zimbabwe*: 1958 data.

TABLE 3.14   Percent of the Labor Force in Industrial Employment 1977 (A), 1970 (B) and 1960 (C).

```
Range =           25.00
Mean =             9.37
Standard Deviation =        5.87
```

Population Percent Cum. Country	Country	Rank	Name	A	Range Decile	B	C
.45	.45	1.0	Congo	26.0	1	21.5	16.8
.74	.29	2.0	Namibia	20.0	3	15.0	10.0
4.25	3.51	3.0	Ghana	19.0		16.7	14.1
25.25	21.00	4.5	Nigeria	18.0	4	13.8	10.4
26.24	.99	4.5	Sierra Leone	18.0		14.8	11.7
29.23	2.99	6.0	Mozambique	17.0		12.7	7.5
31.18	1.95	7.0	Angola	16.0	5	14.2	11.8
32.18	1.00	8.5	Benin	15.0		11.8	8.9
34.44	2.26	8.5	Zimbabwe	15.0		13.4	11.3
34.97	.53	10.0	Liberia	14.6		11.6	9.7
35.72	.75	11.0	Togo	14.0		10.9	8.1
44.01	8.29	12.0	Zaire	13.0	6	10.8	8.8
45.98	1.97	13.5	Upper Volta	11.0	7	8.5	5.4
47.63	1.65	13.5	Zambia	11.0		8.8	7.0
47.79	.16	16.5	Gabon	10.0		8.4	7.2
47.96	.17	16.5	Gambia	10.0		8.2	6.6
49.53	1.57	16.5	Guinea	10.0		8.5	6.1
55.77	6.24	16.5	Sudan	10.0		7.8	6.2
60.37	4.60	20.0	Kenya	9.0		7.1	5.1
62.01	1.64	20.0	Senegal	9.0		6.6	5.4
62.17	.16	20.0	Swaziland	9.0		6.3	3.8
71.88	9.71	22.5	Ethiopia	7.0	8	5.8	4.5
72.91	1.03	22.5	Somalia	7.0		5.9	4.4
75.32	2.41	24.0	Cameroon	6.3		6.0	4.6
76.66	1.34	26.0	Chad	6.0	9	3.9	2.4
81.82	5.16	26.0	Tanzania	6.0		5.0	3.8
85.77	3.95	26.0	Uganda	6.0		4.6	3.6
88.25	2.48	28.0	Madagascar	5.3		3.4	2.5
88.48	.23	31.0	Botswana	5.0		3.7	2.7
89.76	1.28	31.0	Burundi	5.0		3.9	3.0
91.42	1.66	31.0	Malawi	5.0		3.7	2.7
93.29	1.87	31.0	Mali	5.0		4.1	2.7
93.75	.46	31.0	Mauritania	5.0		3.9	2.9
94.33	.58	35.0	Central African R	4.0		2.5	1.8
96.55	2.22	35.0	Ivory Coast	4.0		2.6	2.1
96.93	.38	35.0	Lesotho	4.0		3.2	2.2
98.26	1.33	37.5	Niger	,3.0	10	2.2	1.4
99.62	1.36	37.5	Rwanda	3.0		1.6	1.1
99.72	.10	40.0	Djibouti	1.0			
99.82	.10	40.0	Equatorial Guinea	1.0		7.5	5.9
100.00	.19	40.0	Guinea-Bissau	1.0		4.8	3.6

SOURCE: *World Tables* second edition, 1980 Part IV, Table 5 p. 461. *Angola, Botswana, Gabon, Gambia, Guinea-Bissau, Mozambique, Swaziland, and Zimbabwe: Accelerated Development South of the Sahara* (Washington, D.C.: World Bank, 1981). *Djibouti, Equatorial Guinea, and Namibia* staff estimates.

TABLE 3.15   **Gross Domestic Investment as a Percent of GDP 1977 (A), 1970 (B), 1965 (C) and 1960 (D), and Gross Domestic Investment at 1975 prices in Millions of U.S. Dollars in 1977 (E).**

Definition: Gross Domestic Investment is the value at the official exchange rate of all buildings, equipment, inventories and all other increments to the economy's physical capital.

```
Range =          62.50
Mean =           21.88
Standard Deviation =        11.78
```

Population Percent		Country			Range				
Cum.	Country	Rank	Name	A	Decile	B	C	D	E
.16	.16	1.0	Gabon	67.8	1	34.6	30.8	50.1	1877.0
.62	.46	2.0	Mauritania	51.8	3	20.5	16.3	37.4	230.0
.85	.23	3.0	Botswana	37.6	5	42.2	6.1	8.4	113.9
1.88	1.03	4.0	Somalia	35.4	6	18.1	17.3	15.0	78.2
2.63	.75	5.0	Togo	32.1		14.4	22.4	10.8	127.0
2.82	.19	6.0	Guinea-Bissau	32.0					
23.82	21.00	7.0	Nigeria	31.1		14.9	18.3	13.2	9003.1
24.20	.38	8.0	Lesotho	29.9	7	10.2	11.5	2.0	32.9
26.42	2.22	9.0	Ivory Coast	27.3		22.1	19.0	14.6	1758.9
28.07	1.65	10.0	Zambia	25.9		27.1	24.7	23.9	208.4
30.04	1.97	11.0	Upper Volta	25.1		11.4	9.7	9.5	57.0
30.57	.53	12.0	Liberia	24.9		14.5	12.7	20.9	115.1
31.90	1.33	13.0	Niger	23.3	8	18.0	15.2	12.5	126.2
32.48	.58	14.0	Central Afri. R	22.5		18.9	21.4	19.6	48.8
34.89	2.41	15.0	Cameroon	21.7		14.9	15.1	10.6	460.9
39.49	4.60	16.0	Kenya	21.2		24.4	14.4	19.7	430.4
41.15	1.66	17.0	Malawi	21.0		26.1	14.2	10.4	101.3
42.72	1.57	18.0	Guinea	20.3		19.8	20.0	4.5	217.9
43.72	1.00	19.0	Benin	20.2		15.2	11.5	15.0	89.9
45.98	2.26	20.0	Zimbabwe	19.0		21.4	15.4	23.3	261.0
54.27	8.29	21.0	Zaire	18.6		25.3	27.8	12.3	246.6
54.44	.17	22.0	Gambia	18.2		8.1	11.7	10.4	20.4
54.89	.45	23.0	Congo	18.1		25.4	18.9	44.9	108.7
55.05	.16	24.0	Swaziland	17.8	9	16.4	33.8	12.9	26.0
60.21	5.16	25.0	Tanzania	17.1		22.5	14.6	14.4	266.7
61.85	1.64	26.0	Senegal	16.9		15.7	11.9	15.5	175.0
63.19	1.34	27.0	Chad	16.6		13.4	9.2	11.3	48.4
65.67	2.48	28.0	Madagascar	15.7		15.6	10.2	11.0	196.6
71.91	6.24	29.0	Sudan	15.3		10.3	9.1	8.6	707.8
73.27	1.36	30.0	Rwanda	14.9		7.0	9.8	6.1	78.0
75.14	1.87	31.0	Mali	14.7		15.2	22.6	13.6	47.4
75.24	.10	32.0	Equatorial Guinea	13.5		19.9	18.6		10.1
78.23	2.99	33.5	Mozambique	13.3		13.2	9.3		339.2
79.22	.99	33.5	Sierra Leone	13.3		15.8	11.8	15.5	56.1
80.50	1.28	35.0	Burundi	12.3		6.3	5.8	6.3	33.5
90.21	9.71	36.0	Ethiopia	8.9	10	11.5	13.3	11.5	193.0
92.16	1.95	37.0	Angola	7.4		13.1	9.6	11.6	229.8
95.67	3.51	38.0	Ghana	5.5		14.2	17.9	24.4	95.0
99.62	3.95	39.0	Uganda	5.3		13.3	14.0	11.2	57.8

```
DATA NOT AVAILABLE OR NOT APPLICABLE
FOR THE FOLLOWING COUNTRIES

Djibouti    Namibia
```

SOURCE: *World Tables* second edition, 1980 Series III, Table 3, and Economic Data Sheet.

TABLE 3.16   Government Consumption as a Percent of GDP 1977 (A), 1970 (B), 1965 (C) and 1960 (D).

```
Range =          40.10
Mean =           17.75
Standard Deviation =          7.83
```

Population Percent Cum.	Country	Rank	Country Name	A	Range Decile	B	C	D
1.03	1.03	1.0	Somalia	48.0	1	24.1	19.4	19.6
1.49	.46	2.0	Mauritania	37.5	3	17.4	15.3	24.4
1.94	.45	3.0	Congo	33.7	4	24.3	21.4	22.9
3.59	1.65	4.0	Zambia	30.6	5	15.5	25.3	11.1
3.69	.10	5.0	Equatorial Guinea	28.9		22.2	13.5	
5.64	1.95	6.0	Angola	25.6	6	14.1	11.3	9.4
5.81	.17	7.0	Gambia	21.1	7	15.6	20.6	18.4
14.10	8.29	8.0	Zaire	20.9		27.0	18.0	18.4
14.29	.19	9.5	Guinea-Bissau	20.0				
14.58	.29	9.5	Namibia	20.0				
15.16	.58	11.0	Central Afri. R	19.4	8	21.1	22.2	19.3
19.76	4.60	12.0	Kenya	18.0		16.3	14.8	11.0
21.10	1.34	13.0	Chad	17.7		19.4	14.2	13.1
21.26	.16	14.5	Swaziland	17.1		14.3	13.8	18.0
26.42	5.16	14.5	Tanzania	17.1		13.2	10.5	8.9
26.80	.38	16.0	Lesotho	17.0		12.6	17.6	16.6
28.67	1.87	17.0	Mali	16.5		15.6	17.0	12.0
28.90	.23	18.5	Botswana	16.3		20.4	24.1	14.8
31.38	2.48	18.5	Madagascar	16.3		18.5	22.6	20.1
33.02	1.64	20.0	Senegal	15.6	9	14.9	17.4	17.3
34.01	.99	21.0	Sierra Leone	15.1		7.0	8.0	
34.11	.10	23.0	Djibouti	15.0				
35.68	1.57	23.0	Guinea	15.0		18.0	17.6	13.6
56.68	21.00	23.0	Nigeria	15.0		9.8	6.6	5.9
59.09	2.41	25.0	Cameroon	14.1		14.5	17.2	14.1
59.84	.75	26.0	Togo	14.0		7.1	7.6	8.1
62.83	2.99	27.0	Mozambique	13.8		14.0	12.4	11.2
64.16	1.33	28.0	Niger	13.3		9.8	7.6	9.3
66.38	2.22	29.5	Ivory Coast	13.2		14.5	10.6	9.6
68.64	2.26	29.5	Zimbabwe	13.2		11.3	11.5	10.8
78.35	9.71	31.0	Ethiopia	13.1		9.9	10.6	7.8
81.86	3.51	32.0	Ghana	12.7		12.8	14.5	10.0
82.86	1.00	33.5	Benin	12.6		15.5	14.1	16.2
84.14	1.28	33.5	Burundi	12.6		9.5	6.9	2.7
84.30	.16	35.0	Gabon	12.5		13.7	11.4	9.9
90.54	6.24	36.0	Sudan	12.2		15.9	9.2	5.7
92.51	1.97	37.0	Upper Volta	11.8	10	9.5	6.7	9.9
93.04	.53	38.0	Liberia	11.4		10.7	11.9	7.1
94.70	1.66	39.5	Malawi	10.9		17.0	14.8	16.2
98.65	3.95	39.5	Uganda	10.9		10.4	10.1	9.4
100.00	1.36	41.0	Rwanda	7.9		8.0	14.1	10.1

SOURCE: *World Tables* second edition, 1980 Series III, Table 3.
Djibouti, Guinea-Bissau, and Namibia staff estimates.

**TABLE 3.17   Government Capital Budget as a Percent of GDP
1977(A), 1972(B), 1967 (C) and 1960 (D).**

```
Range =          37.40
Mean =            7.05
Standard Deviation =        6.63
```

Population Percent Cum.	Country	Rank	Country Name	A	Range Decile	B	C	D
.23	.23	1.0	Botswana	38.2	1	38.2	7.9	
1.80	1.57	2.0	Guinea	22.6	5	22.6	20.3	13.4
2.18	.38	3.0	Lesotho	12.9	7	12.9	6.1	
2.34	.16	4.0	Gabon	12.8		12.8	6.7	19.5
2.44	.10	5.0	Equatorial Guinea	12.2		12.2	8.1	
4.09	1.65	6.0	Zambia	10.5	8	10.5	13.2	8.5
5.12	1.03	7.0	Somalia	10.3		10.3	8.3	10.0
5.28	.16	8.0	Swaziland	9.1		9.1	2.9	
26.28	21.00	9.0	Nigeria	8.7		8.7	.7	3.2
27.94	1.66	10.0	Malawi	8.6		8.6	6.2	12.9
30.16	2.22	11.0	Ivory Coast	8.3		8.3	5.7	6.2
34.76	4.60	12.0	Kenya	8.0	9	8.0	3.1	7.0
34.93	.17	13.0	Gambia	7.9		7.9	9.8	9.3
43.22	8.29	14.0	Zaire	7.6		7.6	3.1	1.0
48.38	5.16	15.0	Tanzania	7.5		7.5	3.3	4.3
50.86	2.48	16.0	Madagascar	7.0		7.0	2.5	
53.27	2.41	17.0	Cameroon	6.4		6.4	1.7	4.7
53.46	.19	18.0	Guinea-Bissau	5.9		5.9	8.2	
57.41	3.95	19.0	Uganda	5.7		5.7	4.4	8.2
59.36	1.95	20.0	Angola	4.6		4.6	3.0	
62.35	2.99	21.0	Mozambique	4.5	10	4.5	1.7	
63.69	1.34	22.0	Chad	4.4		4.4	1.0	4.3
73.40	9.71	23.5	Ethiopia	4.0		4.0	2.9	7.0
79.64	6.24	23.5	Sudan	4.0		4.0	7.1	10.0
83.15	3.51	25.0	Ghana	3.9		3.9	3.1	5.3
83.60	.45	26.0	Congo	3.7		3.7	3.1	7.5
84.60	1.00	27.5	Benin	3.4		3.4	.8	6.6
85.96	1.36	27.5	Rwanda	3.4		3.4	.5	
86.49	.53	29.5	Liberia	2.9		2.9	5.2	6.5
87.48	.99	29.5	Sierra Leone	2.9		2.9	2.9	6.5
88.06	.58	31.5	Central African R	2.5		2.5	1.1	3.3
88.81	.75	31.5	Togo	2.5		2.5	2.1	3.2
90.68	1.87	33.5	Mali	2.4		2.4	8.2	4.8
91.14	.46	33.5	Mauritania	2.4		2.4	1.6	19.5
92.78	1.64	35.0	Senegal	2.2		2.2	2.4	5.0
94.11	1.33	36.0	Niger	2.1		2.1	.8	4.3
96.08	1.97	37.0	Upper Volta	1.2		1.2	1.5	4.2
97.36	1.28	38.0	Burundi	.8		.8	.6	

```
DATA NOT AVAILABLE OR NOT APPLICABLE
FOR THE FOLLOWING COUNTRIES

Djibouti    Namibia    Zimbabwe
```

SOURCES: A.I.D. *Economic Data Book* various years, UNECA *Statistical Yearbook* various years, *World Tables* second edition, 1980. (1967) *Swaziland*: 1968 data. (1972) *Guinea*: 1970 data. *Upper Volta*: 1973 data. (1977) *Chad, Ethiopia, Swaziland, Ghana, Tanzania*: 1976 data. *Lesotho*: 1974 data. *Senegal*: 1975 data. *Guinea-Bissau, Ivory Coast, Upper Volta: Accelerated Development in Sub-Saharan Africa* (Washington, D.C.: World Bank, 1981).

TABLE 3.18 **Per Capita Energy Consumption in Kilograms of Coal Equivalent 1977 (A), 1970 (B), 1965 (C) and 1960 (D).**

```
Range =        1695.00
Mean =          190.81
Standard Deviation =        300.47
```

Population Percent Cum.	Country	Rank	Country Name	A	Range Decile	B	C	D
.16	.16	1.0	Gabon	1707	1	897	248	187
.26	.10	2.0	Djibouti	748	6	441	716	292
2.52	2.26	3.0	Zimbabwe	598	7	692	581	
4.17	1.65	4.0	Zambia	483	8	495	493	
4.70	.53	5.0	Liberia	402		454	202	86
6.92	2.22	6.0	Ivory Coast	356		228	153	76
7.38	.46	7.0	Mauritania	198	9	144	75	18
9.33	1.95	8.0	Angola	185		155	104	86
10.97	1.64	9.0	Senegal	175	10	139	134	121
14.48	3.51	10.0	Ghana	167		173	105	106
20.72	6.24	11.0	Sudan	165		130	81	52
25.32	4.60	12.0	Kenya	141		135	126	143
25.77	.45	13.0	Congo	140		118	118	119
28.76	2.99	14.0	Mozambique	138		138	101	114
31.17	2.41	15.0	Cameroon	122		91	59	55
52.17	21.00	16.0	Nigeria	107		52	53	34
53.16	.99	17.0	Sierra Leone	103		134	64	31
53.33	.17	18.0	Gambia	102		51	33	24
54.36	1.03	19.0	Somalia	96		39	26	19
55.11	.75	20.0	Togo	95		67	39	23
55.21	.10	21.5	Equatorial Guinea	92		65	149	123
56.78	1.57	21.5	Guinea	92		98	100	65
59.26	2.48	23.0	Madagascar	76		71	46	38
59.45	.19	24.5	Guinea-Bissau	71		63	54	19
67.74	8.29	24.5	Zaire	71		81	75	87
72.90	5.16	26.0	Tanzania	65		62	52	41
76.85	3.95	27.0	Uganda	56		74	39	30
77.85	1.00	28.0	Benin	55		42	32	39
79.51	1.66	29.0	Malawi	51		46	38	
80.09	.58	30.0	Central African R	41		63	34	37
81.42	1.33	31.0	Niger	37		25	13	5
83.29	1.87	32.0	Mali	30		21	23	15
84.63	1.34	33.5	Chad	23		25	18	10
86.60	1.97	33.5	Upper Volta	23		13	11	5
96.31	9.71	35.0	Ethiopia	19		33	14	8
97.67	1.36	36.0	Rwanda	18		11	9	11
98.95	1.28	37.0	Burundi	12		15	15	11

DATA NOT AVAILABLE OR NOT APPLICABLE
FOR THE FOLLOWING COUNTRIES

Botswana   Lesotho   Namibia   Swaziland

SOURCE: *World Tables* second edition, 1980 Table 9, Series III.

TABLE 3.19   Gross National Savings as a Percent of Gross Domestic Investment 1977 (A), 1972 (B), 1966 (C) and 1960 (D).

```
Range =        323.20
Mean =          58.63
Standard Deviation =        60.77
```

Population Percent Cum.	Country	Rank	Country Name	A	Range Decile	B	C	D
3.95	3.95	1.0	Uganda	277.6	1	112.8	87.0	139.8
5.90	1.95	2.0	Angola	255.0		141.0	125.0	11.8
8.16	2.26	3.0	Zimbabwe	113.0	6	101.1	99.8	80.0
12.76	4.60	4.0	Kenya	98.6		76.3	92.4	70.0
16.27	3.51	5.0	Ghana	92.1		158.7	53.9	65.6
17.55	1.28	6.0	Burundi	90.8		43.9	-16.7	68.5
17.71	.16	7.0	Gabon	87.6		76.1	80.8	80.3
38.71	21.00	8.0	Nigeria	86.9		80.0	63.7	52.4
40.93	2.22	9.0	Ivory Coast	77.8	7	62.7	66.9	72.7
46.09	5.16	10.0	Tanzania	77.7		74.3	97.5	118.6
49.08	2.99	11.0	Mozambique	77.0		81.0	78.0	84.0
50.65	1.57	12.0	Guinea	76.1		-16.7	58.9	100.0
53.13	2.48	13.0	Madagascar	71.5		53.6	31.1	3.4
55.54	2.41	14.0	Cameroon	70.9		59.7	60.9	82.8
57.19	1.65	15.0	Zambia	69.2		88.4	123.8	119.8
57.42	.23	16.0	Botswana	67.2		24.3	-37.3	-71.4
59.08	1.66	17.0	Malawi	65.1		45.3	6.4	-2.3
68.79	9.71	18.0	Ethiopia	64.6		79.3	73.0	89.0
68.89	.10	19.0	Equatorial Guinea	61.0		56.0	67.0	
69.64	.75	20.0	Togo	54.3		44.9	69.0	18.7
71.28	1.64	21.0	Senegal	52.9		66.0	81.4	76.0
79.57	8.29	22.0	Zaire	52.6		47.8	69.1	118.7
80.56	.99	23.0	Sierra Leone	51.6		69.7	53.0	56.6
81.92	1.36	24.0	Rwanda	48.5	8	-9.7	21.4	128.9
82.50	.58	25.0	Central Afri. R	41.0		8.4	9.8	-11.1
83.84	1.34	26.0	Chad	40.1		45.0	16.4	26.0
85.17	1.33	27.0	Niger	39.1		42.9	60.1	97.4
85.70	.53	28.0	Liberia	32.2		64.1	13.9	32.1
86.73	1.03	29.0	Somalia	28.2		49.4	24.5	48.3
88.60	1.87	30.0	Mali	26.0		13.1	43.6	47.8
89.60	1.00	31.0	Benin	21.7		4.5	1.5	50.0
91.57	1.97	32.0	Upper Volta	16.1	9	35.3	53.0	9.6
91.74	.17	33.5	Gambia	10.2		44.9	25.0	39.0
97.98	6.24	33.5	Sudan	10.2		80.5	73.2	101.5
90.44	.46	35.0	Mauritania	.2		56.6	33.4	-19.3
98.63	.19	36.0	Guinea-Bissau	-6.3				
98.79	.16	37.0	Swaziland	-26.2	10	53.1	93.0	103.6
99.24	.45	38.0	Congo	-39.9		-22.2	-7.2	-51.0
99.62	.38	39.0	Lesotho	-45.6		-173.9	-87.8	-720.0

```
DATA NOT AVAILABLE OR NOT APPLICABLE
FOR THE FOLLOWING COUNTRIES

Djibouti    Namibia
```

SOURCE: *World Tables* second edition, 1980 Economic Data Sheet. *Guinea-Bissau*: *Accelerated Development South of the Sahara* (Washington, D.C.: World Bank, 1981).

TABLE 3.20 Number of Industrial Types Possible in the 1980's

Definition: Ewing estimated the number of different types of industries which normally require a market of two or three countries that could be established in each country by the 1980's. The totals are presented here.

```
Range =          28.00
Mean =            8.56
Standard Deviation =        7.26
```

Population Percent Cum.	Country	Rank	Country Name	A	Range Decile
21.00	21.00	1.0	Nigeria	29	1
25.60	4.60	2.0	Kenya	27	
27.86	2.26	3.0	Zimbabwe	20	4
31.37	3.51	4.0	Ghana	19	
33.02	1.65	5.0	Zambia	18	
34.66	1.64	6.0	Senegal	17	5
36.61	1.95	7.5	Angola	16	
44.90	8.29	7.5	Zaire	16	
47.31	2.41	9.5	Cameroon	15	6
47.76	.45	9.5	Congo	15	
49.98	2.22	11.0	Ivory Coast	13	
52.97	2.99	13.0	Mozambique	12	7
58.13	5.16	13.0	Tanzania	12	
62.08	3.95	13.0	Uganda	12	
63.95	1.87	15.0	Mali	11	
65.52	1.57	16.0	Guinea	9	8
71.76	6.24	17.0	Sudan	8	
81.47	9.71	19.0	Ethiopia	7	
81.63	.16	19.0	Gabon	7	
82.62	.99	19.0	Sierra Leone	7	
83.96	1.34	21.0	Chad	6	9
84.96	1.00	24.5	Benin	5	
85.49	.53	24.5	Liberia	5	
87.97	2.48	24.5	Madagascar	5	
88.43	.46	24.5	Mauritania	5	
88.59	.16	24.5	Swaziland	5	
90.56	1.97	24.5	Upper Volta	5	
91.89	1.33	28.0	Niger	4	
92.47	.58	29.5	Central African R	3	10
93.22	.75	29.5	Togo	3	
93.45	.23	32.5	Botswana	2	
93.55	.10	32.5	Djibouti	2	
94.91	1.36	32.5	Rwanda	2	
95.94	1.03	32.5	Somalia	2	
97.22	1.28	38.0	Burundi	1	
97.32	.10	38.0	Equatorial Guinea	1	
97.49	.17	38.0	Gambia	1	
97.68	.19	38.0	Guinea-Bissau	1	
98.06	.38	38.0	Lesotho	1	
99.72	1.66	38.0	Malawi	1	
100.00	.29	38.0	Namibia	1	

SOURCES: A. F. Ewing *Industry in Africa* (New York: Oxford University Press, 1968). *Angola, Botswana, Djibouti, Equatorial Guinea, Guinea-Bissau, Lesotho, Mozambique, Swaziland, Zimbabwe* coded by author using Ewing's categories.

TABLE 3.21 Difficulty in Achieving Long-Run Economic Growth ca. 1977 (A), ca. 1972 (B) and 1967 (C).

Definition:
1. Growth not difficult.
2. Growth not very difficult.
3. Growth difficult.
4. Growth very difficult.

```
Range =          3.00
Mean =           2.83
Standard Deviation =        .91
```

Population Percent Cum.	Country	Rank	Country Name	A	Range Decile	B	C
1.28	1.28	5.5	Burundi	4	1	4	4
1.86	.58	5.5	Central African R	4		4	4
3.20	1.34	5.5	Chad	4		4	4
3.30	.10	5.5	Djibouti	4		3	3
3.40	.10	5.5	Equatorial Guinea	4		3	3
3.59	.19	5.5	Guinea-Bissau	4		4	4
4.95	1.36	5.5	Rwanda	4		4	4
5.98	1.03	5.5	Somalia	4		4	4
9.93	3.95	5.5	Uganda	4		3	1
11.90	1.97	5.5	Upper Volta	4		4	4
12.90	1.00	19.5	Benin	3	4	4	4
13.35	.45	19.5	Congo	3		3	3
23.06	9.71	19.5	Ethiopia	3		3	2
23.23	.17	19.5	Gambia	3		3	4
26.74	3.51	19.5	Ghana	3		2	2
28.31	1.57	19.5	Guinea	3		2	1
28.69	.38	19.5	Lesotho	3		4	4
29.22	.53	19.5	Liberia	3		2	2
31.70	2.48	19.5	Madagascar	3		3	3
33.57	1.87	19.5	Mali	3		4	4
34.03	.46	19.5	Mauritania	3		2	3
37.02	2.99	19.5	Mozambique	3		2	2
38.35	1.33	19.5	Niger	3		4	4
39.99	1.64	19.5	Senegal	3		3	2
40.98	.99	19.5	Sierra Leone	3		3	3
47.22	6.24	19.5	Sudan	3		2	2
52.38	5.16	19.5	Tanzania	3		3	3
60.67	8.29	19.5	Zaire	3		2	2
62.62	1.95	33.0	Angola	2	7	1	2
65.03	2.41	33.0	Cameroon	2		2	2
69.63	4.60	33.0	Kenya	2		2	2
71.29	1.66	33.0	Malawi	2		2	3
71.58	.29	33.0	Namibia	2		1	1
71.74	.16	33.0	Swaziland	2		2	2
72.49	.75	33.0	Togo	2		3	4
74.14	1.65	33.0	Zambia	2		1	2
76.40	2.26	33.0	Zimbabwe	2		2	3
76.63	.23	39.5	Botswana	1	10	2	3
76.79	.16	39.5	Gabon	1		1	1
79.01	2.22	39.5	Ivory Coast	1		1	1
100.00	21.00	39.5	Nigeria	1		1	2

SOURCES: (1967) William Hance *African Economic Development* second edition (New York: Praeger, 1967), Table 13, pp 290-291. *Botswana, Djibouti, Equatorial Guinea, Guinea-Bissau, Lesotho, Madagascar, Namibia, Swaziland, and Zimbabwe* have been coded by the author using Hance's categories.

(1972 and 1977) All countries were coded by the author using Hance's categories.

4. Social Mobilization

All changes in society, whether they be social, economic, or political in nature, involve changes in the values, attitudes, or behaviors of at least some of the individuals who comprise that society. Post World War II history has seen fundamental and pervasive changes in social, political, and economic relations both between and within nations. Africa has been no exception to this phenomenon. In particular, as African nations have shed their colonial ties, leaders of these nations have established two fundamental goals: (1) the development of their economies, usually on the model of an industrial state, and (2) the development of the political capabilities of the new nation-states and the socialization of its citizens to view the new nation as the primary political and social grouping to which they owe their allegiance and with which they identify.

This process of change is reflected in massive changes in statuses, roles, role-sets, physical locations and life styles imposed by the structure of such changes. Traditional leaders have fallen into the background in the face of new forms of political and economic mobilization. Large migrations, principally rural to urban, introduce a country's citizens to new life styles as well as to previously unknown mechanisms for achieving these new values. The pervasive transistor radio communicates to most of a country's population the awareness of worlds other than their own.

Many of the changes that occur in such a process are unpredictable, particularly from the point of view of the affected persons. For most new urban dwellers the living conditions are abysmal, the opportunities limited, and the future bleak. Income differentials in this 'modern' sector of the society are generally much greater than in the traditional rural society and the growth of an urban lumpen-proletariat may be a major factor for the future in terms of political change and instability in these nations. However, for the few, there is a success and reward far beyond anything that could be achieved in a rural village, and for others, the variety and excitement of the city may outweigh all the real disadvantages.

While much change is not directly controlled or even understood, these societies do have major commitments towards directing the character of change through the medium of formal education, through the use of mass communications devices such as radio and cinema, and through a process of increasing physical mobility for movement and trade via the construction of roads and railroads. In this chapter we present data on aspects of education, communications, and transport which can be viewed both as important causes and effects of economic development and socio-political change.

Educational Systems

Education can be conceptually characterized as the more or less consciously pursued, or programmatic, phase of acculturation present in all societies. It involves the cognition and internalization of social norms, values, ideas, and substantive information necessary for the full participation and survival of the individual in his social and ecological setting. From the perspective of structural-functionalist theory,[1] educational institutions are often viewed as essentially conservative forces insuring the transmission and perpetuation of existing cultural patterns, value orientations, and behavioral norms. This perspective is, however, not applicable to the formal educational systems in Africa, which have been dominated by the values, concepts and content of European models of education, and which have been key instruments of transition and potential conflict during the colonial period and after.[2] The growth of formal education in Africa over recent decades has been phenomenal by any standard and rates of school attendance have often increased by several hundred percent.

Four Approaches

The impact of education in Africa and other developing areas of the world has been examined from varying points of view. One approach, adopted by economic planners, has been to view educational systems as the developers and mobilizers of human capital for the modern sector of the economy.[3] Those who take this approach see human capital formation as one of several key factors determining increased national production and consumption.

A second approach emphasizes the "mass mobilizing" aspect of education. Political scientists and sociologists who are particularly associated with this point of view treat education as an important transformer of traditional social values and norms and a stimulant to participation in modern institutions. In this sense, education is one of six major categories of indicators in the "auditing of modernization,"[4] suggested by Daniel Lerner. He compared elementary, vocational, teacher training, and university enrollment per capita for several Middle Eastern countries and observed that an important requisite for non-erratic social change and political stability is balanced growth among major categories of indicators and among indicators within each category (e.g., within the education category, teacher training must keep pace with elementary enrollment).[5] S. N. Eisenstadt has expressed similar views by describing development in education as a basic characteristic of modernization.[6] A more direct, empirical study of the influence of early educational experience on the political system in terms of adult political participation was conducted by Gabriel Almond and Sidney Verba.[7] They found a positive relationship between participation in decision-making in the home and classroom and later political participation in adulthood.[8]

In contrast to this, a third approach is the "elite formation" emphasis of scholars such as C. Arnold Anderson, Remi Clignet, and Philip Foster. They examine the impact of education on the social structure of African countries and argue that while education has in fact accelerated individual social mobility along new paths, certain groups or categories of people in the population have greater opportunity for education than others. Most particularly, the educated elite's children enjoy an advantage in pursuing educational qualifications. These scholars question whether schooling has had much ameliorative effect on the intensity of ethnic identification and inequalities based on such identification.[9] The importance of modern education in Africa is seen by this approach in terms of its "elite" effects rather than as a mass mobilizing process in which general psychological commitments are reformed.[10]

A fourth view concentrates on a particular aspect of modernization, the developing of a sense of national identification which transcends ethnic loyalties,[11] and assesses the contribution made to this process by the modern educational system. While positive attitudes toward the national political system may be internalized in the early stages of the formal educational process,[12] the effective transmission of such attitudes increases as education itself becomes accepted as a social value.[13] This process is not, however, without difficulties. Although education at the mass level continues to inculcate the national loyalties and participatory values necessary for the perpetuation of modern political systems, the danger remains that the somewhat less than universal access to modern education in new nations will accentuate a growing rift between traditional and modern sectors of the population.[14] And, as Coleman argues, inequalities in the distribution of education "may intensify divisions among different ethnic, regional, and parochial groups out of

which nation-builders, partly through education, must forge a larger sense of national identity."[15]

As this review of some of the theoretical relationships between education, and economic and political development suggest, there are numerous hypotheses which can be tested if adequate data is forthcoming. Although quantitative information pertaining to education in Africa has been produced in abundance first by colonial administrators and, since the First World War, by governmental and international organizations, literature on this subject, until recently, has been largely descriptive and country-specific rather than quantitative or broadly comparative. [16]

Data Sources

A precursor to comparative research in African education was the publication of the widely acclaimed Phelps-Stokes reports in 1922 and 1925 under the editorship of T.J. Jones. These reports included a comprehensive evaluation of the various colonial educational systems together with enrollment estimates and recommendations for reform.[17] More recently several works, including those by Donald G. Burns on education in Commonwealth nations and Abdou Moumouni on the former French African territories,[18] have been produced which are broadly comparative in their approach and offer a liberal selection of cross-national data.

The availability of what might be classed as original data sources, particularly for the colonial period official government publications, colonial reports on education, and statistical periodicals emanating from official sources is somewhat limited, at least in the United States, to several larger institutions.[19] British colonial governments characteristically issued yearly reports often with detailed data on enrollment and expenditures in all administrative subdivisions. During the Second World War, however, statistical reporting was negligible due to the lack of funds and personnel. Comprehensive data on the French areas, published in Paris, are available for approximately the final eight years of colonial rule.[20]

By far the largest and most useful single body of statistical information on enrollment and expenditure for education at various levels in the 1950's is available in *A World Survey of Education*, published by UNESCO in four volumes between the years 1955 and 1966.[21] The above publications, together with material from the *UN Statistical Yearbook* for the later periods, represent major sources of data on enrollment and expenditures for the tables which follow in this chapter. Four broad categories which can be used to characterize sets of indicators of the state of educational development are:
(1) student enrollment

Figure 4.1 Correlations between Literacy and Primary Enrollment per Capita for 32 African Countries.

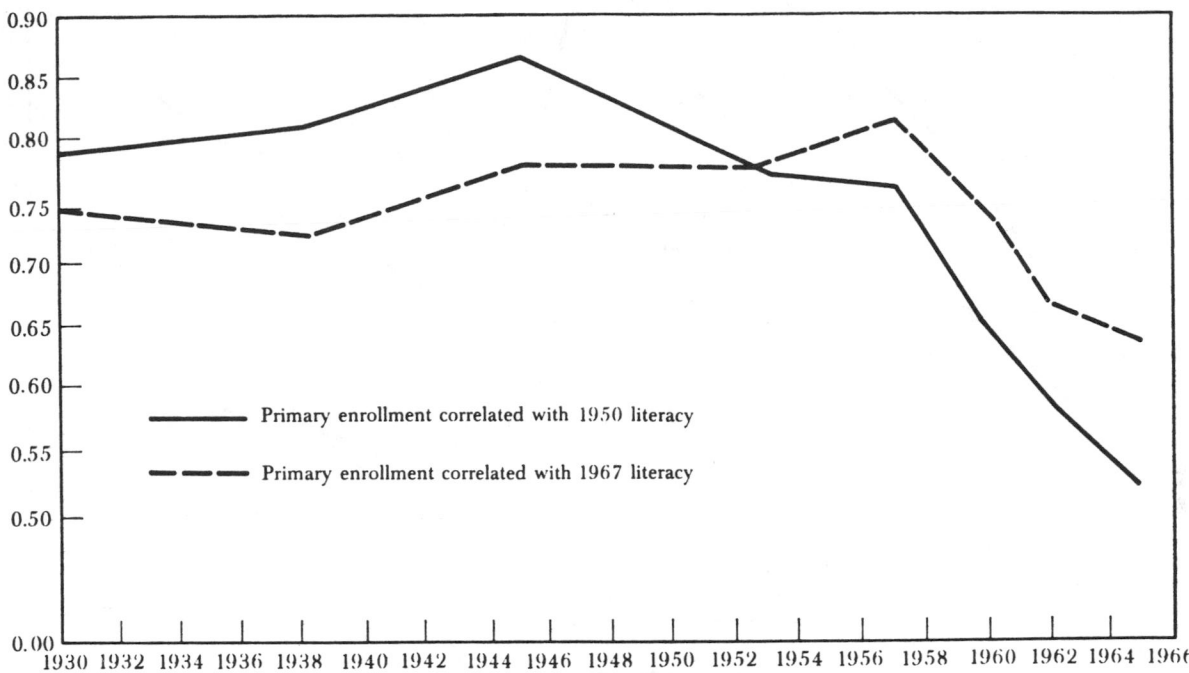

(2) literacy

(3) expenditures

(4) staffing or teaching personnel

(1) Data on student enrollment are given in Tables 4.1-4.10. These data are reported in terms of the numbers of persons enrolled in different levels of education—primary, secondary, and higher education. In addition to aggregate enrollments, enrollment data standardized by population, rates of change over periods extending from 1930 onwards, and indicators relating to female enrollment are provided.[22] One of the problems confronting educational planners has been to determine the appropriate 'mix' of primary and secondary school places. Table 4.9 presents data on the ratio of secondary to primary pupils.

It should be noted here that student enrollment *per se* is not as sensitive a measure of a nation's education level as it might appear. Census reports for certain nations contain information on the percentages of the population which have attained various levels of education, but complete information on this subject is not generally available.[23] Some countries have only recently increased enrollment levels, so their stock of educated persons is

often much lower than other countries which have had higher enrollments for longer periods of time. For many contexts, it is more useful to know the ratio of enrollment to the population of the appropriate age group from which the students are drawn. However, reliable data which pertain to age cohort groups are not systematically available for these countries.[24] For some purposes, enrollment figures may require adjustment according to attendance rates, which vary across countries and also radically within territorial units, as well as according to season of the year.[25] Systematic data on attendance rates were unavailable to us. Finally, these figures do not include secondary students who are studying in other countries.

(2) Tables 4.11 and 4.12 relate to current literacy estimates and increased literacy rates from 1950 to 1967, and from 1967 to 1972. Data in this category are admittedly less reliable than enrollment figures and countries may use different definitions of literacy. However, individual values should not be in error more than plus or minus 10 percent. Figure 4.1 shows that for all units the correlation between literacy and per capita primary enrollment is quite high.

Figure 4.2 Trends in Public and Private Enrollment in French Togo, 1921-1937.

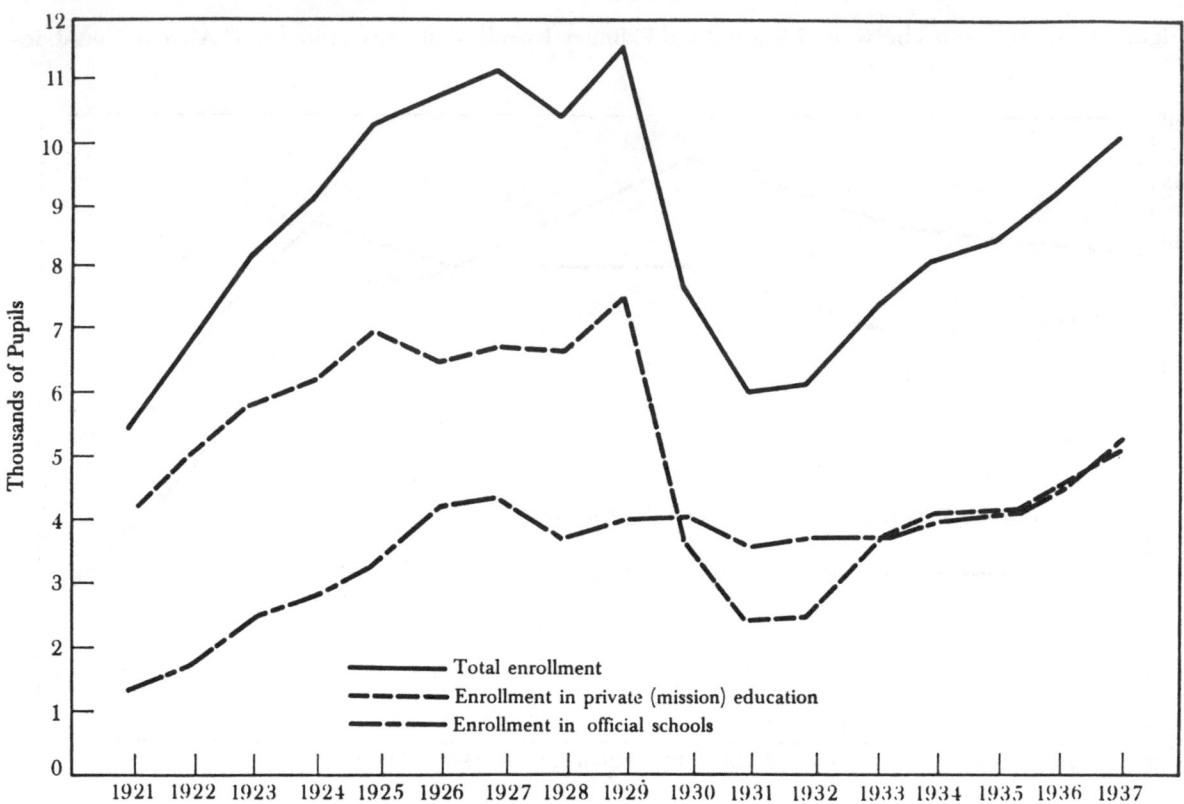

(3) A number of economic indicators which relate to educational expenditure have been employed in quantitative analyses. Two types are included in this chapter: total educational expenditure, as a percent of gross domestic production (Table 4.13); and as a percent of total government expenditures (Table 4.14). Thus we present a measure of level of schooling emphasizing a control for economic development, and lastly a measure with relative emphasis on educational development as opposed to other government priorities. Variables which are not included here but which are of interest include: educational expenditure per capita[26] and expenditure per pupil enrolled (possibly an indicator of instructional quality).[27]

(4) Data on the number of teachers at the various levels of the educational system and the number of students enrolled in teacher training are available in the African National Integration Project Data Bank, but are not presented here.

Dimensionality and Reliability

A factor analysis of 74 indicators of educational development confirmed the utility of focusing on enrollment, expenditures, and staffing as independent dimensions. In addition, the factor solution shows well defined and independent dimensions of size (absolute enrollment figures),

and change in enrollment. Furthermore, primary and secondary enrollment figures fall on separate dimensions, showing the importance of examining educational development at different levels.

The relatively low level of abstraction involved in the measures discussed here should not produce a false sense of security in regard to their reliability. Unfortunately, educational figures on Africa, especially for the earlier colonial period, are sometimes merely estimates, and poor ones at that. In the collection of the present data and in our continuing attempt to discover additional sources to fill in missing data, a number of problems have come to the surface which are the result of both random and systematic errors in existing published, quantitative information on African education.

Errors which specifically relate to educational variables are often the result of definitional ambiguity relating to and stemming from structural differences in school systems. These differences include: varying lengths in the duration of primary and secondary programs, the categorizing of pre-primary grades or middle-level grades (where they exist) as primary-level education, and defining vocational and teacher-training enrollments as secondary-level or parallel-level education.[28] The variety of school systems within one national unit is itself a continual source of error. For example, separate systems within British territories during the colonial era have included: official government schools (usually only a small percentage of the total), native authority schools, assisted (usually mission) schools and unassisted institutions, and inspected and uninspected schools. The accuracy of reporting, the chance of inclusion in official published figures, and consistency in standards maintained can be presumed to decrease with the distance from control by the central administration.[29]

Techniques to Assess Reliability

Other than careful discrimination among reporting agencies in the actual choice of data using the criteria of reputation and professional accountability, the number of available strategies open to the researcher for insuring against unreliable aggregate data are few. Certain reliability checks, of course, can be applied. These are based on several simple assumptions about the variation of the data across time and in relation to other indicators. These assumptions are:

(1) That indicators such as enrollment are relatively stable and, with few exceptions, increase with geometric regularity (as with population). Unusual fluctuations from one time period to another thus signal possible significant changes in accounting procedures, a redefinition of categories by reporters, or generally unreliable reporting methods. The fact that indicators of enrollment across different time periods fall unambiguously on the same factors in the factor analysis of the data facilitates reasonably accurate interpolation for unreported years, and helps establish the reliability of the individual measures.

(2) That variation is affected by external factors and temporal conditions. For example, the trend on all indices from the introduction of Western education to the present has been generally upward; however, events such as the world wars and, in particular, the great depression, had a generally negative effect on enrollment in colonies which relied on mission support for a large part of the education program. The trend of public and private enrollment for the French mandate territory of Togo demonstrates this effect (see Figure 4.2).[30] Questionable data must therefore be assessed in terms of over-all trends within the total time continuum and in consideration of the unique systemic characteristics of the territorial units studied.

(3) Certain testable propositions as to the relationship among variables across time can be hypothesized. While the finding of no relationship is by no means prima-facie evidence of unreliability, those in support of the hypothesized relationship offer a degree of credibility. This sort of test was applied to the two available sets of literacy estimates included in the tables for which we had a much

lesser degree of confidence than for the various indices of enrollment. Literacy is presumably a strong correlate of primary education.[31] Using factor analysis, we found that these literacy measures loaded highly on the same factor as the per capita measures of primary enrollment. This suggests co-variation but does not permit us to make a very strong conclusion as to the reliability of the literacy data. We can further hypothesize that there will be an increasingly stronger relationship between literacy (as a percentage of the population above 15 years of age) at specific points of time with aggregate indicators of educational experience which precede the literacy estimates in time. As the impact of changing early primary enrollment patterns will not be felt in terms of adult literacy for several years, evidence of a time-lag should be apparent in the correlational measures. It can be argued that correlations between literacy and subsequent enrollment patterns in the 1960s *following* the date of the literacy estimate should fall sharply, not only due to the absence of direct causality but as a result of the implementation of comprehensive policy changes brought about by independence. These bivariate correlations were inspected and appear in Figure 4.1.

The expectations in this case are essentially realized. Comparing literacy estimates for 1950 and 1967 with nine measures of per capita primary enrollment from 1930 to 1965, literacy in 1950 correlates highest with enrollment in 1945 (.88) and literacy in 1967 with enrollment in 1957 (.82).

TABLE 4.1   Primary School Enrollment per 1000 Population 1960 (A), 1953 (B) and 1930 (C).

Definition: Total enrollment in primary or first-level education (typically including the first six to eight years of education) in all schools, public and private, divided by the national population estimate for the appropriate year.

```
Range =          181.00
Mean =            61.24
Standard Deviation =        40.94
```

Population Percent Cum.	Country	Rank	Country Name	A	Range Decile	B	C
.38	.38	1.0	Lesotho	189	1	151	147
.83	.45	2.0	Congo	150	3	80	6
3.09	2.26	3.0	Zimbabwe	128	4	89	
3.25	.16	4.0	Gabon	123		68	9
11.54	8.29	5.0	Zaire	105	5	79	15
11.83	.29	6.0	Namibia	103		86	
11.99	.16	7.0	Swaziland	101		79	32
16.59	4.60	8.0	Kenya	97	6	48	17
19.00	2.41	9.0	Cameroon	92		50	2
20.65	1.65	10.0	Zambia	88		63	42
23.13	2.48	11.0	Madagascar	85		61	50
24.79	1.66	12.0	Malawi	82		71	46
24.89	.10	13.0	Equatorial Guinea	81		75	
28.84	3.95	14.0	Uganda	80	7	50	54
32.35	3.51	15.0	Ghana	72		80	11
32.58	.23	16.0	Botswana	70		44	27
34.80	2.22	17.0	Ivory Coast	65		16	2
37.79	2.99	18.0	Mozambique	64		29	
38.54	.75	19.0	Togo	63		43	7
39.07	.53	20.0	Liberia	56	8	45	14
39.65	.58	21.0	Central African R	55		28	2
60.65	21.00	22.0	Nigeria	54		24	5
61.93	1.28	24.0	Burundi	47		25	7
63.29	1.36	24.0	Rwanda	47		25	7
68.45	5.16	24.0	Tanzania	47		30	21
69.45	1.00	26.0	Benin	44	9	35	6
71.09	1.64	27.0	Senegal	37		18	4
71.19	.10	28.5	Djibouti	36		23	
72.18	.99	28.5	Sierra Leone	36		21	7
73.75	1.57	30.0	Guinea	31		9	2
79.99	6.24	31.0	Sudan	26	10	16	5
81.33	1.34	32.5	Chad	23		5	1
81.50	.17	32.5	Gambia	23		15	6
83.45	1.95	34.0	Angola	22		4	
83.64	.19	35.0	Guinea-Bissau	21		6	
85.51	1.87	36.0	Mali	16		9	3
87.48	1.97	37.0	Upper Volta	13		6	1
87.94	.46	38.0	Mauritania	12		5	1
88.97	1.03	39.0	Somalia	11		6	1
98.68	9.71	40.5	Ethiopia	8		4	1
100.00	1.33	40.5	Niger	8		3	1

SOURCES: (1930) Population estimates for this and the following tables are from Appendix B. Otto Martens and O. Karstedt, *The African Handbook and Travelers Guide* (London: Allen and Unwin, 1932). *Botswana, Gambia, Guinea, Lesotho, Mali, Mauritania, Niger, Senegal, Upper Volta*: Estimates for 1930 based on reported figures from 1934 or 1935; *Ghana, Kenya, Malawi, Nigeria, Sierra Leone, Tanzania, Uganda, Zambia*: Reports from individual colonial departments of education for 1930; *Tanazania*: total for Tanzania is the officially reported enrollment for Tanganyika and Zanzibar combined; *Zaire, Ethiopia, Sudan*: UNESCO *World Survey of Education*, Vol. 2, "Primary Education" (Paris: 1958), see separate country reports; *Central African Republic, Chad, Congo, Gabon*: Historique et Organization General de l'Enseignement en A.E.F. (Brazzaville: Gouvernement Generale de l'Afrique Equatoriale Française, 1931); *Burundi, Rwanda*: Enrollment for Burundi and Rwanda calculated by applying the estimated total population ratio for these units in 1930 to the total enrollment given by UNESCO for Ruanda-Urundi; *Togo*: L. Pechoux, *Le Mandat Français sur le Togo* (Paris: A. Peddone, 1939); *Benin*: "Rapports et Compte-Rendu du Congres Intercolonial de l'Enseignement dans les Colonies et les Pays d'Outre-mer," *L'Adaptation de l'Enseignement dans les Colonies* (Paris: Henri Didier, 1932); *Cameroon*: This figure is for British Cameroons only; enrollment in the French mandate is probably somewhat larger; *Ivory Coast*: The enrollment given by Martens and Karstedt for the Ivory Coast is assumed to include Upper Volta which was part of the Ivory Coast from 1932 to 1947. The ratio of total enrollment between the two units in 1948 was applied to obtain an estimate for each in 1930; *Ethiopia*: For Eritrea only, and may include children of Italian personnel. Enrollment in Ethiopia proper (except for traditional Coptic schools) at this time was negligible; *Somalia*: I.M. Lewis, *The Modern History of Somaliland* (New York: Praeger, 1965), p. 97. Lewis states that non-traditional schools were not begun in British Somaliland until after World War II; therefore this figure represents enrollment in the Italian mandate only. *Madagascar and Swaziland*: Statesman's Yearbook 1934.

(1953) *Enseignement Outre-mer*: Bulletin de l'inspection général de l'enseignement et de la jeunesse du ministere de France d'outre-mer (Paris: Ministere de la France d'Outre-mer, December 1954). *Botswana, Burundi, Zaire, Ethiopia, Ghana, Kenya, Lesotho, Liberia, Malawi, Nigeria, Rwanda, Sierra Leone, Somalia, Tanzania, Uganda, Zambia*: Reports from individual colonial departments on education, 1953; *Cameroon, Gambia, Sudan: U.N. Statistical Yearbook 1955—1960*); *Cameroon*: Combined figures for French and British areas; *Tanzania*: Calculated as for 1930; *Nigeria*: Includes the British Cameroons; *Somalia*: Combined figures for British and Italian areas. *Angola and Mozambique*: 1952 figures; *Guinea-Bissau*: 1950 figure; *Swaziland*: Statesman's Yearbook 1954.

(1960) *UN Statistical Yearbook 1962—1964*. *Burundi, Chad, Gabon, Ghana, Guinea, Ivory Coast, Mauritania, Niger, Rwanda, Senegal, Sierra Leone, Tanzania, Togo, Zambia*: Estimates of 1960 enrollment based on 1959, 1961, and 1962 data given in the same source; *Burundi, Rwanda*: Enrollment for Burundi and Rwanda calculated by applying the estimated total population ratio for these units in 1960 to the total enrollment given for Ruanda-Urundi. *Angola, Mozambique, Guinea-Bissau*: Statesman's Yearbook.

TABLE 4.2 Primary School Enrollment per 1000 Population, 1976 (A), 1972 (B), 1966 (C) and Total Primary Enrollment, 1976 (D) and 1972 (E).

Definition: Total enrollment in primary or first-level education (typically including the first six to eight years of education) in all schools public and private, divided by the national population estimate for the appropriate year.

```
Range =          224.00
Mean =           108.24
Standard Deviation =        55.01
```

Population Percent Cum.	Country	Rank	Name	A	Range Decile	B	C	D	E
.16	.16	1.0	Gabon	248	1	203	169	130398	105600
4.76	4.60	2.0	Kenya	210	2	144	105	2894617	1676000
5.05	.29	3.0	Namibia	206		186	122	181616	155036
5.21	.16	4.0	Swaziland	187	3	176	152	92721	76343
5.59	.38	5.0	Lesotho	182		181	195	222004	176404
7.24	1.65	6.0	Zambia	178	4	176	124	872392	777873
7.47	.23	7.0	Botswana	177		119	124	125588	81662
8.22	.75	8.0	Togo	170		123	94	395381	257877
16.51	8.29	9.0	Zaire	150	5	141	130	3429076	3219554
18.92	2.41	10.5	Cameroon	149		158	133	1146437	968000
21.40	2.48	10.5	Madagascar	149		137	108	1133013	1004447
21.59	.19	12.0	Guinea-Bissau	140		100	23	83781	48007
23.85	2.26	13.0	Zimbabwe	130	6	134	128	863059	798046
25.51	1.66	14.0	Malawi	128		104	71	663940	484676
26.09	.58	15.0	Central African R	124		109	105	221412	177924
31.25	5.16	16.0	Tanzania	123		72	63	1956320	1004000
34.76	3.51	17.0	Ghana	122		159	163	1213291	1447195
34.86	.10	18.0	Equatorial Guinea	120		109	107	35977	31600
36.22	1.36	19.0	Rwanda	104	7	108	57	434150	400000
38.44	2.22	20.5	Ivory Coast	100		119	98	672707	527615
38.97	.53	20.5	Liberia	100		112	101	157821	135000
39.97	1.00	22.5	Benin	92		65	55	293648	186000
40.07	.10	22.5	Djibouti	92		78	47	9764	7746
42.02	1.95	24.0	Angola	88	8	89	42	516131	516131
45.97	3.95	25.0	Uganda	87		75	73	1036920	786227
46.42	.45	26.0	Congo	83		267	221	319101	262000
67.42	21.00	27.0	Nigeria	82		68	51	4889857	3854539
68.41	.99	28.0	Sierra Leone	73		64	52	205910	174000
69.44	1.03	29.0	Somalia	71		21	11	229030	61000
72.43	2.99	30.0	Mozambique	68	9	63	66	577997	526962
74.00	1.57	31.0	Guinea	65		49	46	324165	191287
80.24	6.24	32.0	Sudan	64		60	35	1217510	961411
81.88	1.64	33.0	Senegal	63		66	61	311800	266383
83.22	1.34	34.0	Chad	50		49	51	210882	184020
83.68	.46	35.0	Mauritania	49		32	19	72932	38900
83.85	.17	36.0	Gambia	47		51	42	25513	19421
85.72	1.87	37.0	Mali	43	10	45	35	252393	229879
87.05	1.33	38.0	Niger	34		24	21	159515	100892
88.33	1.28	39.5	Burundi	33		50	57	130739	180000
98.04	9.71	39.5	Ethiopia	33		28	16	959272	716729
100.00	1.97	41.0	Upper Volta	24		19	22	149270	108000

SOURCES:(1966) *UNESCO Statistical Yearbook 1968*, Table 2.7. *Rwanda*: 1963 data; *Gambia, Guinea, Mauritania, Senegal, Sudan, Upper Volta*: 1965; *Botswana, Malawi*: 1967; *Angola, Guinea-Bissau, Madagascar, Mozambique, Swaziland*: UNECA Statistical Yearbook 1972. (1972) *UNESCO Statistical Yearbook* 1973 and 1974; *Africa South of the Sahara 1975*: UNECA Statistical Yearbook 1973. *Namibia*: 1973 data.
(1976) *U.N. Statistical Yearbook, 1978*. From the same source but for different years are: (1977) Benin, Mauritania, Cameroon, Guinea. (1975) Central African Republic, Congo, Ivory Coast, Liberia, Madagascar, Mali, Senegal, Sierra Leone, Zimbabwe. (1974) Ethiopia, Zaire. (1973) Equatorial Guinea, Nigeria. (1972) Mozambique, Angola.

TABLE 4.3   Average Annual Percent Change in Primary School Enrollment per Capita, 1972—1976 (A), 1960—1972 (B) and 1953—1960 (C).

Range =   68.00
Mean =   5.63
Standard Deviation =   10.41

Population Percent Cum.	Country	Rank	Country Name	A	Range Decile	B	C
1.03	1.03	1.0	Somalia	59.3	1	7.6	11.9
22.03	21.00	2.0	Nigeria	20.7	6	2.2	17.9
27.19	5.16	3.0	Tanzania	17.7	7	4.4	8.1
27.42	.23	4.0	Botswana	12.3		5.8	8.4
30.93	3.51	5.0	Ghana	11.8		9.5	-1.4
35.53	4.60	6.0	Kenya	11.4	8	4.0	14.5
35.99	.46	7.0	Mauritania	10.9		13.9	20.0
37.32	1.33	8.0	Niger	10.2		16.7	23.8
37.42	.10	9.0	Equatorial Guinea	10.1		2.9	1.1
37.61	.19	10.0	Guinea-Bissau	10.0		31.3	35.7
38.36	.75	11.0	Togo	9.6		7.9	6.6
48.07	9.71	12.0	Ethiopia	9.5		20.1	14.3
49.07	1.00	13.0	Benin	8.3		4.0	3.7
50.64	1.57	14.0	Guinea	8.2		4.8	34.9
52.61	1.97	15.0	Upper Volta	6.6		3.8	16.7
54.27	1.66	16.0	Malawi	5.8		2.2	2.2
54.43	.16	17.0	Gabon	5.6		5.4	11.6
54.72	.29	18.0	Namibia	5.3		6.7	2.8
54.82	.10	19.0	Djibouti	4.5	9	9.7	8.0
58.77	3.95	20.0	Uganda	4.0		-.5	8.6
59.35	.58	21.0	Central African R	3.4		8.2	13.8
61.83	2.48	22.0	Madagascar	3.0		5.2	5.6
62.00	.17	23.0	Gambia	1.8		10.1	4.8
68.24	6.24	24.0	Sudan	1.7		10.9	8.9
68.40	.16	25.0	Swaziland	1.5		6.2	4.0
69.74	1.34	26.0	Chad	.5		5.8	30.0
71.39	1.65	27.0	Zambia	.3		5.0	5.7
71.77	.38	28.0	Lesotho	.1		-.4	3.6
73.72	1.95	31.0	Angola	0		25.4	64.3
74.17	.45	31.0	Congo	0		6.5	12.5
77.16	2.99	31.0	Mozambique	0		-.1	17.2
78.15	.99	31.0	Sierra Leone	0		6.5	10.2
86.44	8.29	31.0	Zaire	0		2.8	4.7
88.70	2.26	34.0	Zimbabwe	-.7		.4	6.2
91.11	2.41	35.0	Cameroon	-.9		6.0	12.0
92.47	1.36	36.0	Rwanda	-1.0		10.8	12.6
94.34	1.87	37.0	Mali	-1.4		15.1	11.1
95.98	1.64	38.0	Senegal	-1.7		6.5	15.1
96.51	.53	39.0	Liberia	-3.5	10	8.3	3.5
98.73	2.22	40.0	Ivory Coast	-5.2		6.9	43.8
100.00	1.28	41.0	Burundi	-8.7		.5	12.6

SOURCE: See Tables 4.1 and 4.2.

TABLE 4.4   Average Annual Percent Change in Primary School Enrollment per Capita, 1966—1972 (A) and 1960—66 (B).

Definition: Values are shown in whole percentiles in the table below.

Range =   58.30
Mean =   5.93
Standard Deviation =   9.48

Population Percent Cum.	Country	Rank	Country Name	A	Range Decile	B
.19	.19	1.0	Guinea-Bissau	55.8	1	1.7
2.14	1.95	2.0	Angola	18.7	7	15.2
3.17	1.03	3.0	Somalia	18.1		1.0
4.53	1.36	4.0	Rwanda	14.9	8	3.5
10.77	6.24	5.0	Sudan	14.3		5.8
20.48	9.71	6.0	Ethiopia	12.5		16.7
20.94	.46	7.0	Mauritania	11.4		9.7
21.04	.10	8.0	Djibouti	11.0		5.1
21.33	.29	9.0	Namibia	8.7	9	3.1
22.99	1.66	10.0	Malawi	7.7		-2.2
27.59	4.60	11.0	Kenya	7.4		2.0
29.24	1.65	12.0	Zambia	7.0		6.0
50.24	21.00	13.0	Nigeria	6.7		-1.0
52.11	1.87	14.0	Mali	5.7		19.8
52.86	.75	15.0	Togo	5.1		8.2
55.34	2.48	16.0	Madagascar	4.5		5.0
57.56	2.22	17.0	Ivory Coast	4.3		8.5
59.97	2.41	18.5	Cameroon	3.8		7.5
60.96	.99	18.5	Sierra Leone	3.8		7.3
61.13	.17	20.0	Gambia	3.6		13.8
61.58	.45	21.0	Congo	3.5		7.8
61.74	.16	22.0	Gabon	3.4		6.2
62.74	1.00	23.0	Benin	3.0	10	4.2
62.90	.16	24.0	Swaziland	2.6		8.4
64.23	1.33	25.5	Niger	2.4		27.2
69.39	5.16	25.5	Tanzania	2.4		5.7
69.92	.53	27.0	Liberia	1.8		13.3
71.49	1.57	28.5	Guinea	1.6		8.0
73.13	1.64	28.5	Senegal	1.6		10.8
81.42	8.29	30.0	Zaire	1.4		4.0
82.00	.58	31.5	Central African R	.8		15.2
84.26	2.26	31.5	Zimbabwe	.8		.1
84.36	.10	33.5	Equatorial Guinea	.5		5.3
88.31	3.95	33.5	Uganda	.5		-1.5
91.82	3.51	35.0	Ghana	.4		21.0
92.05	.23	36.0	Botswana	-.6		12.8
93.39	1.34	37.0	Chad	-.8		20.3
96.38	2.99	38.0	Mozambique	-1.1		.5
96.76	.38	39.0	Lesotho	-1.2		.5
98.73	1.97	40.0	Upper Volta	-2.3		11.5
100.00	1.28	41.0	Burundi	-2.5		3.5

SOURCES: See Tables 4.1 and 4.2.

TABLE 4.5 Percent Females Enrolled in Primary Education per Total Primary School Students, 1976 (A), 1972 (B) and 1960 (C).

Range = 34.00
Mean = 39.85
Standard Deviation = 7.01

Population Percent Cum. Country		Rank	Country Name	A	Range Decile	B	C
.38	.38	1.0	Lesotho	59	1	60	62
.61	.23	2.0	Botswana	55	2	54	59
.77	.16	3.5	Gabon	49	3	48	38
.93	.16	3.5	Swaziland	49		48	50
1.38	.45	6.0	Congo	47	4	45	34
3.86	2.48	6.0	Madagascar	47		46	44
5.22	1.36	6.0	Rwanda	47		44	24
7.17	1.95	9.0	Angola	46		36	33
11.77	4.60	9.0	Kenya	46		42	32
14.03	2.26	9.0	Zimbabwe	46			
14.13	.10	11.5	Equatorial Guinea	45	5	44	44
15.78	1.65	11.5	Zambia	45		45	40
19.29	3.51	13.5	Ghana	43		43	34
24.45	5.16	13.5	Tanzania	43		39	34
28.40	3.95	15.0	Uganda	41	6	40	32
30.81	2.41	18.0	Cameroon	40		43	30
32.47	1.66	18.0	Malawi	40		28	36
53.47	21.00	18.0	Nigeria	40		39	37
55.11	1.64	18.0	Senegal	40		39	33
56.10	.99	18.0	Sierra Leone	40		40	34
57.38	1.28	21.5	Burundi	39		33	24
65.67	8.29	21.5	Zaire	39		38	29
67.89	2.22	23.0	Ivory Coast	38	7	37	26
74.13	6.24	24.5	Sudan	37		34	27
76.10	1.97	24.5	Upper Volta	37		37	29
76.68	.58	27.5	Central African R	36		33	19
77.21	.53	27.5	Liberia	36		33	23
79.08	1.87	27.5	Mali	36		34	28
79.83	.75	27.5	Togo	36		32	28
79.93	.10	30.5	Djibouti	35	8	23	
80.96	1.03	30.5	Somalia	35		26	26
82.53	1.57	32.5	Guinea	34		32	26
85.52	2.99	32.5	Mozambique	34		34	38
85.71	.19	34.5	Guinea-Bissau	33		30	31
86.17	.46	34.5	Mauritania	33		28	18
87.17	1.00	37.0	Benin	32		31	27
96.88	9.71	37.0	Ethiopia	32		32	23
97.05	.17	37.0	Gambia	32		31	31
98.39	1.34	39.0	Chad	27	10	25	11
99.72	1.33	40.0	Niger	25		35	29

DATA NOT AVAILABLE OR NOT APPLICABLE
FOR THE FOLLOWING COUNTRIES

Namibia

SOURCES: (1960) *UNESCO Statistical Yearbook 1968*, Table 2.7. *Burundi*: Data for 1961; *Zaire, Senegal*: UN Compendium of Social Statistics (New York: United Nations, 1963). *Angola, Madagascar, Mozambique, Swaziland*: UN Statistical Yearbook 1963; 1965 data for *Guinea-Bissau and Equatorial Guinea*: UN Statistical Yearbook 1967.
(1972) *UN Statistical Yearbook 1973*. 1968 data for *Malawi and Mauritania*; 1970 data for *Angola, Burundi, Benin, Equatorial Guinea, Guinea, Guinea-Bissau, Lesotho, Liberia, Rwanda, and Sierra Leone*; 1967 data for *Mozambique*.
(1976) *UN Statistical Yearbook 1978*. *Cameroon*: 1974 data, *Central African Republic*: 1975 data. See also Table 4.1.
Angola, Guinea, Mauritania, Senegal and Tanzania : *UNESCO Statistical Yearbook 1981*. Angola, 1960 data.

TABLE 4.6 Secondary School Enrollment per 10,000 Population, 1976 (A), 1972 (B), 1966 (C), 1962 (D)

Defintion: Enrollment in general secondary education, excluding teacher training and vocational enrollment, in all schools public and private, divided by national population estimated for the appropriate year.

Range = 734.00
Mean = 172.65
Standard Deviation = 155.53

Population Percent Cum. Country		Rank	Country Name	A	Range Decile	B	C	D
.45	.45	1.0	Congo	756	1	296	151	21
3.96	3.51	2.0	Ghana	578	3	640	213	281
4.15	.19	3.0	Guinea-Bissau	464	4	86	19	29
4.31	.16	4.0	Gabon	447	5	184	101	84
5.06	.75	5.0	Togo	350	6	123	75	53
5.22	.16	6.0	Swaziland	300	7	253	104	64
6.79	1.57	7.0	Guinea	250		153	46	12
7.02	.23	8.0	Botswana	230	8	114	32	17
7.55	.53	9.0	Liberia	217		132	104	61
12.15	4.60	10.0	Kenya	209		134	51	35
12.25	.10	11.0	Djibouti	188		191	97	42
20.54	8.29	12.0	Zaire	185		99	33	51
22.76	2.22	13.0	Ivory Coast	178		171	83	57
23.76	1.00	14.5	Benin	172		65	43	29
30.00	6.24	14.5	Sudan	172		106	66	56
32.41	2.41	16.5	Cameroon	166	9	124	53	60
33.40	.99	16.5	Sierra Leone	166		127	57	51
35.05	1.65	18.0	Zambia	156		133	63	23
36.69	1.64	19.0	Senegal	150		150	72	60
37.07	.38	20.0	Lesotho	147		91	33	15
37.17	.10	21.0	Equatorial Guinea	146		179	79	16
37.34	.17	22.0	Gambia	139		110	110	89
39.29	1.95	23.5	Angola	134		89	29	17
39.87	.58	23.5	Central African R	134		116	33	24
42.13	2.26	25.0	Zimbabwe	118		115	52	16
44.00	1.87	26.5	Mali	95	10	70	20	12
65.00	21.00	26.5	Nigeria	95		61	39	43
65.46	.46	28.0	Mauritania	75		48	14	1
75.17	9.71	29.0	Ethiopia	68		54	22	7
78.16	2.99	30.0	Mozambique	64		23	12	6
82.11	3.95	31.0	Uganda	56		42	118	56
83.45	1.34	32.0	Chad	46		27	24	10
88.61	5.16	33.0	Tanzania	41		31	20	19
89.64	1.03	34.0	Somalia	38		93	28	24
90.92	1.28	35.0	Burundi	34		18	12	13
92.58	1.66	36.0	Malawi	33		29	17	12
93.94	1.36	37.0	Rwanda	30		19	9	12
95.91	1.97	38.0	Upper Volta	29		19	11	7
97.24	1.33	39.0	Niger	28		20	9	8
99.72	2.48	40.0	Madagascar	22		23	89	80

DATA NOT AVAILABLE OR NOT APPLICABLE
FOR THE FOLLOWING COUNTRIES

Namibia

SOURCES: (1962,1966) *UN Statistical Yearbook 1968*; *Equatorial Guinea*: *Africa South of the Sahara 1974*; *Swaziland*: 1967 figure, *UNECA Statistical Yearbook 1973*. 1961 data for *Guinea-Bissau*, and 1960 data for Angola.
(1972) *UN Statistical Yearbook 1973*, *UNECA Statistical Yearbook 1973* and 1974. *UNESCO Statistical Yearbook 1973*. *Africa South of the Sahara 1973*; 1969 data for *Mozambique*; 1970 data for *Burundi, Equatorial Guinea, Guinea, and Senegal*; 1971 data for *Angola, Chad, Benin, Ghana, Ivory Coast, Mali, Nigeria, and Somalia*; 1973 data for *Central African Republic and Niger*.
(1976) *UN Statistical Yearbook 1978*. 1975 data for *Central African Republic, Malawi, and Tanzania*. See Table 4.1 also.

TABLE 4.7 Average Annual Percent Change in Secondary School Enrollment per Capita 1972—76 (A), 1966—72 (B) and 1962—66 (C).

Range = 84.10
Mean = 4.97
Standard Deviation = 14.30

Population Percent Cum.	Country	Rank	Country Name	A	Range Decile	B	C
.19	.19	1.0	Guinea-Bissau	82.6	1	5.9	-.7
2.06	1.87	2.0	Mali	41.9	5	5.0	-2.1
5.57	3.51	3.0	Ghana	20.1	8	-1.4	-.7
26.57	21.00	4.0	Nigeria	5.6	10	1.1	.2
27.02	.45	5.0	Congo	5.2		1.6	15.0
27.77	.75	6.0	Togo	4.6		1.1	1.1
36.06	8.29	7.5	Zaire	4.3		3.3	-.9
37.71	1.65	7.5	Zambia	4.3		1.9	4.3
38.71	1.00	9.0	Benin	3.3		1.0	1.2
38.94	.23	10.5	Botswana	2.6		2.9	2.2
48.65	9.71	10.5	Ethiopia	2.6		2.4	5.4
49.98	1.33	12.0	Niger	2.2		1.7	.3
50.51	.53	13.0	Liberia	2.1		.5	1.8
51.85	1.34	14.0	Chad	1.8		.3	3.5
53.42	1.57	15.5	Guinea	1.6		5.8	7.1
59.66	6.24	15.5	Sudan	1.6		1.0	.5
62.07	2.41	17.5	Cameroon	1.5		2.2	-.3
62.45	.38	17.5	Lesotho	1.5		2.9	3.0
67.05	4.60	20.5	Kenya	1.4		2.7	1.2
67.51	.46	20.5	Mauritania	1.4		4.1	32.5
68.87	1.36	20.5	Rwanda	1.4		1.9	-.6
74.03	5.16	20.5	Tanzania	1.4		.9	.1
76.00	1.97	23.0	Upper Volta	1.3		1.2	1.4
76.58	.58	24.0	Central African R	1.2		3.6	1.0
76.74	.16	25.0	Swaziland	1.1		2.4	1.6
77.73	.99	26.0	Sierra Leone	1.0		2.1	.3
77.89	.16	27.0	Gabon	.9		1.4	.5
81.84	3.95	28.0	Uganda	.8		-1.1	2.8
82.01	.17	29.0	Gambia	.7		0	.6
82.11	.10	30.0	Equatorial Guinea	.6		3.2	9.8
84.33	2.22	32.0	Ivory Coast	.1		2.1	1.2
85.99	1.66	32.0	Malawi	.1		1.2	1.1
88.25	2.26	32.0	Zimbabwe	.1		.2	4.4
90.20	1.95	35.0	Angola	0		4.1	1.8
93.19	2.99	35.0	Mozambique	0		1.5	2.5
94.83	1.64	35.0	Senegal	0		2.7	.5
94.93	.10	37.0	Djibouti	-.1			
97.41	2.48	38.0	Madagascar	-1.0		2.8	.3
98.69	1.28	39.5	Burundi	-1.5		-.2	-.2
99.72	1.03	39.5	Somalia	-1.5		4.6	.4

DATA NOT AVAILABLE OR NOT APPLICABLE FOR THE FOLLOWING COUNTRIES

Namibia

SOURCE: See Table 4.6.

TABLE 4.8 Females Enrolled per 100 Secondary School Students 1976 (A), 1972 (B) and 1960 (C).

Definition: Enrollment in general secondary education, excluding teacher training and vocational enrollment, in all schools public and private.

Range = 43.00
Mean = 31.41
Standard Deviation = 8.97

Population Percent Cum.	Country	Rank	Country Name	A	Range Decile	B	C
.38	.38	1.0	Lesotho	56	1	55	43
.61	.23	2.0	Botswana	53		47	45
.77	.16	3.0	Swaziland	46	3	43	44
2.72	1.95	4.0	Angola	44		42	41
5.20	2.48	5.0	Madagascar	43	4	42	37
8.71	3.51	6.0	Ghana	39		27	24
9.16	.45	7.5	Congo	37	5	32	29
9.32	.16	7.5	Gabon	37		30	21
19.03	9.71	10.0	Ethiopia	36		25	10
20.60	1.57	10.0	Guinea	36		21	13
25.20	4.60	10.0	Kenya	36		30	36
26.85	1.65	12.0	Zambia	34	6	34	15
47.85	21.00	13.5	Nigeria	33		33	21
56.14	8.29	13.5	Zaire	33		22	10
58.55	2.41	17.0	Cameroon	32		30	18
58.65	.10	17.0	Djibouti	32		48	
61.64	2.99	17.0	Mozambique	32		38	38
62.63	.99	17.0	Sierra Leone	32		28	28
68.87	6.24	17.0	Sudan	32		27	17
70.23	1.36	21.0	Rwanda	31		33	19
75.39	5.16	21.0	Tanzania	31		29	32
77.36	1.97	21.0	Upper Volta	31		27	19.
77.53	.17	23.5	Gambia	30	7	25	26
79.19	1.66	23.5	Malawi	30		28	17
80.19	1.00	25.5	Benin	29		29	28
81.52	1.33	25.5	Niger	29		24	16
83.16	1.64	27.0	Senegal	28		29	28
84.44	1.28	29.0	Burundi	27		27	19
86.31	1.87	29.0	Mali	27		16	20
90.26	3.95	29.0	Uganda	27		24	21
90.45	.19	32.0	Guinea-Bissau	25	8	36	43
92.67	2.22	32.0	Ivory Coast	25		22	12
93.20	.53	32.0	Liberia	25		23	20
93.95	.75	34.0	Togo	23		25	21
94.53	.58	36.0	Central African R	18	9	19	14
94.63	.10	36.0	Equatorial Guinea	18		26	38
95.66	1.03	36.0	Somalia	18		19	8
96.12	.46	38.0	Mauritania	17	10	10	5
97.46	1.34	39.0	Chad	13		7	7

DATA NOT AVAILABLE OR NOT APPLICABLE FOR THE FOLLOWING COUNTRIES

Namibia   Zimbabwe

SOURCES: (1960) *UNESCO Statistical Yearbook* 1968, Table 2.8. *Burundi, Rwanda*: Data refer to the former Trust Territory of Ruanda-Urundi, as a unit. *Madagascar, Mozambique, Swaziland*: *UN Statistical Yearbook 1963*; *Angola* (1964 data: *UN Statistical Yearbook 1967*; *Equatorial Guinea*: 1966 data *UN Statistical Yearbook 1968*.
(1972) *UN Statistical Yearbook* 1973; *Sierra Leone and Swaziland*: *UN Statistical Yearbook* 1974: *Malawi* (1968 data) and *Mozambique* (1967 data): *UN Statistical Yearbook* 1972.
(1976) *UN Statistical Yearbook* 1978. See also Table 4.1.

TABLE 4.9   Average Annual Change in Ratio of Secondary to Primary School Enrollment, 1972—1976 (A), 1966—1972 (B), 1952—1966 (C),

```
Range =            19.30
Mean =              1.99
Standard Deviation =        3.57
```

Population Percent		Rank	Country Name	A	Range Decile	B	C
Cum.	Country						
3.51	3.51	1.0	Ghana	16.2	1	-1.1	-3.7
4.79	1.28	2.0	Burundi	14.0	2	.3	-3.7
6.66	1.87	3.0	Mali	7.3	5	3.0	-4.9
14.95	8.29	4.0	Zaire	4.7	6	2.6	-3.0
15.05	.10	5.0	Djibouti	4.2	7		
15.50	.45	6.0	Congo	4.0		1.8	-1.4
17.07	1.57	7.0	Guinea	3.9		3.4	-1.9
19.33	2.26	8.0	Zimbabwe	3.5			
20.08	.75	9.0	Togo	2.9		.3	-.2
20.54	.46	10.0	Mauritania	2.7		.7	-1.8
20.70	.16	11.0	Gabon	2.6	8	.8	-2.3
23.11	2.41	12.0	Cameroon	2.3		1.4	-2.1
23.34	.23	13.0	Botswana	2.2		2.8	-.5
24.34	1.00	14.0	Benin	1.9		.5	-.9
25.68	1.34	15.5	Chad	1.8		.4	1.1
31.92	6.24	15.5	Sudan	1.8		-.3	-.5
33.87	1.95	17.5	Angola	1.6		.7	3.4
36.35	2.48	17.5	Madagascar	1.6		1.9	6.7
36.73	.38	19.0	Lesotho	1.5		3.2	-2.1
38.09	1.36	20.0	Rwanda	1.3		2.3	-4.5
39.42	1.33	22.0	Niger	.9		1.6	.2
60.42	21.00	22.0	Nigeria	.9		.7	-1.4
61.41	.99	22.0	Sierra Leone	.9		1.3	-2.3
61.94	.53	24.0	Liberia	.8		.9	-.5
62.10	.16	25.5	Swaziland	.7	9	1.8	8.8
64.07	1.97	25.5	Upper Volta	.7		1.5	-2.2
66.29	2.22	28.0	Ivory Coast	.5		1.4	2.8
70.24	3.95	28.0	Uganda	.5		-1.1	1.4
71.89	1.65	28.0	Zambia	.5		1.2	1.1
81.60	9.71	30.0	Ethiopia	.2		.8	-.7
86.20	4.60	31.5	Kenya	.1		1.6	-.7
89.19	2.99	31.5	Mozambique	.1		3.0	29.2
89.77	.58	33.0	Central African R	-.1		4.1	-1.0
91.43	1.66	34.0	Malawi	-.2		.4	-1.8
96.59	5.16	35.0	Tanzania	-.5		.6	-.8
96.69	.10	36.5	Equatorial Guinea	-.8		3.0	9.4
96.86	.17	36.5	Gambia	-.8		.1	-.7
97.05	.19	38.0	Guinea-Bissau	-1.4	10	.1	23.1
98.08	1.03	39.0	Somalia	-2.2		1.6	-2.1
99.72	1.64	40.0	Senegal	-3.1		2.2	-1.2

DATA NOT AVAILABLE OR NOT APPLICABLE
FOR THE FOLLOWING COUNTRIES

Namibia

SOURCES: (1952) *UNESCO World Survey of Education*, Vols. 2, 3 and 4; *UN Statistical Yearbook* 1955—1960; *Enseignement Outre-mer* (December 1953); *Education in the United Kingdom Dependencies*.
(1965—66 ratio) *UN Statistical Yearbook* 1968.
(1972) *UN Statistical Yearbook* 1973.
(1976) *UN Statistical Yearbook* 1978. See also Table 4.1.

TABLE 4.10 Students in Post-Secondary Education (third level) per 100,000 population, 1975 (A), 1972 (B), 1966 (C) and 1961 (D).

Definition: Includes all post-secondary technical training as well as university attendance which requires completion of secondary education for admission.

```
Range    =    304.00
Mean     =     86.35
Standard Deviation =      76.14
```

Population Percent Cum.	Country	Rank	Country Name	A	Range Decile	B	C	D
1.57	1.57	1.0	Guinea	314	1	50	16	
2.02	.45	2.0	Congo	273	2	115	92	6
2.18	.16	3.0	Gabon	236	3	60	5	
2.34	.16	4.0	Swaziland	206	4	18		
3.99	1.65	5.0	Zambia	177	5	52	8	
5.63	1.64	6.0	Senegal	174		117	84	5
6.16	.53	7.0	Liberia	159	6	73	71	4
12.40	6.24	8.0	Sudan	131	7	121	67	3
14.62	2.22	9.0	Ivory Coast	125		104	51	1
15.37	.75	10.0	Togo	116		73	5	
15.75	.38	11.0	Lesotho	112		40		2
18.16	2.41	12.0	Cameroon	105		74	36	1
26.45	8.29	13.0	Zaire	101	8	70	22	11
31.05	4.60	14.5	Kenya	87		29	10	
52.05	21.00	14.5	Nigeria	87		34	22	
53.05	1.00	16.0	Benin	80		21	13	
54.08	1.03	17.0	Somalia	74		34	22	
54.31	.23	18.0	Botswana	72		42	13	
56.18	1.87	19.0	Mali	60	9	14	5	
57.17	.99	20.0	Sierra Leone	51		76	30	1
59.65	2.48	21.0	Madagascar	49		81	65	2
63.60	3.95	22.0	Uganda	44		29	14	9
67.11	3.51	23.0	Ghana	38	10	66	9	3
67.57	.46	24.0	Mauritania	32		9		
68.85	1.28	25.5	Burundi	30		10	7	
69.43	.58	25.5	Central African R	30		6	6	
69.60	.17	27.0	Gambia	29				
79.31	9.71	28.0	Ethiopia	28		24	13	
79.41	.10	29.0	Djibouti	27				
80.77	1.36	30.0	Rwanda	26		14	4	
82.43	1.66	31.0	Malawi	22		21	12	
87.59	5.16	32.0	Tanzania	20		12	13	
89.56	1.97	33.0	Upper Volta	19		6	1	
90.90	1.34	34.0	Chad	18		1		
91.00	.10	35.0	Equatorial Guinea	17				
92.33	1.33	36.0	Niger	16		7		
95.32	2.99	37.0	Mozambique	10		31	14	1

DATA NOT AVAILABLE OR NOT APPLICABLE FOR THE FOLLOWING COUNTRIES

Angola   Guinea-Bissau Namibia   Zimbabwe

SOURCES: (1961) UNESCO, *Development of Higher Education in Africa*, Report of the Conference on the Development of Higher Education in Africa (Paris: UNESCO, 1962), p. 226. *Burundi, Rwanda*: separate estimates were made from the 270 enrollment total given for Ruanda-Urundi by assigning a proportion of the total value to each country in the same ratio as their secondary school enrollments; *Malawi, Zambia*: Estimates were made from the combined figure given for the *Federation of Rhodesia and Nyasaland*, on the basis of their other school enrollments. *UNECA Statistical Yearbook* 1967.

(1966) *UN Statistical Yearbook* 1969 and *UNECA Statistical Yearbook* 1974.

(1972) *UN Statistical Yearbook* 1974: *Africa South of the Sahara* 1975: and *UNECA Statistical Yearbook* 1975.

(1975) *UN Statistical Yearbook* 1978. From the same source but for different years are: 1976: *Ivory Coast, Mozambique, Niger, Somalia.* 1974: *Kenya, Lesotho, Zaire.*

TABLE 4.11 Estimated Percent of Population Literate, ca. 1975 (A), ca. 1972 (B), 1965 (C) and 1955 (D).

Definitions and Comments: The United Nations definition of literacy is the ability both to read and write. A literate person must be able to read with understanding, and to write a short statement on everyday life, in any one language. We assume that the A.I.D. definition of literacy is similar to that of the UN.

```
Range =        61.00
Mean =         25.10
Standard Deviation =        16.29
```

Population Percent Cum.	Country	Rank	Country Name	A	Range Decile	B	C	D
5.16	5.16	1.0	Tanzania	66	1	18	15	8
5.32	.16	2.0	Swaziland	65		36	30	22
6.35	1.03	3.0	Somalia	60		5	5	1
6.73	.38	4.0	Lesotho	52	3	70	60	50
7.18	.45	5.5	Congo	50		30	23	3
9.66	2.48	5.5	Madagascar	50		40	40	35
14.26	4.60	7.0	Kenya	40	5	25	25	23
15.91	1.65	8.0	Zambia	39		40	40	23
16.14	.23	9.5	Botswana	35	6	33	30	23
18.55	2.41	9.5	Cameroon	35		15	10	7
26.84	8.29	11.0	Zaire	31		50	40	37
30.35	3.51	13.5	Ghana	30		30	30	23
30.88	.53	13.5	Liberia	30		12	10	8
34.83	3.95	13.5	Uganda	30		30	30	25
37.09	2.26	13.5	Zimbabwe	30		28	25	
38.37	1.28	17.0	Burundi	25	7	10	10	8
40.03	1.66	17.0	Malawi	25		15	10	8
61.03	21.00	17.0	Nigeria	25		25	20	12
62.39	1.36	19.0	Rwanda	23	8	10	10	8
63.96	1.57	21.5	Guinea	20		10	10	3
66.18	2.22	21.5	Ivory Coast	20		21	20	3
66.47	.29	21.5	Namibia	20		18	15	
72.71	6.24	21.5	Sudan	20		13	13	12
73.46	.75	24.0	Togo	18		10	10	8
73.92	.46	25.0	Mauritania	17	9	5	5	3
75.26	1.34	28.0	Chad	15		8	5	3
75.36	.10	28.0	Equatorial Guinea	15		30	25	20
85.07	9.71	28.0	Ethiopia	15		5	5	3
88.06	2.99	28.0	Mozambique	15		7	3	2
89.05	.99	28.0	Sierra Leone	15		10	10	8
89.21	.16	31.0	Gabon	13		15	13	3
91.16	1.95	32.0	Angola	12		13	8	5
92.16	1.00	33.0	Benin	11	10	15	5	3
92.33	.17	35.0	Gambia	10		10	10	7
94.20	1.87	35.0	Mali	10		5	5	3
95.84	1.64	35.0	Senegal	10		10	7	3
97.17	1.33	37.0	Niger	8		5	3	1
97.75	.58	38.5	Central African R	7		8	5	3
97.94	.19	38.5	Guinea-Bissau	7		5	3	1
98.04	.10	40.5	Djibouti	5		5	5	
100.00	1.97	40.5	Upper Volta	5		7	7	3

SOURCES: (1955) see Table 4.12.

(1965) *AID Economic Data Book* 1967. p. 5. Data are assumed to represent percent of total adult population who are literate. *Botswana, Ghana, Lesotho, Uganda*; AID estimate considered unreliable in these instances; an estimate has been made on the basis of earlier census reports included in: *UN Report on the World Social Situation* (New York: 1957), *UN Compendium of Social Statistics, 1957*, and UNESCO, *Basic Facts and Figures* (Paris: 1952); *Burundi, Zaire, Kenya, Malawi, Mauritania, Rwanda, Togo*: Cases for which a range is given and, due to consideration of earlier data, the highest value of the range has been taken; *Congo, Gabon, Mali, Senegal, Sudan, Upper Volta*: Cases for which a range is given and the mid-point has been taken. Additional sources were *UNECA Statistical Yearbook 1967* and *Africa South of the Sahara.*

(1972) Estimates were derived from the following sources: *Africa: Economic Growth* (U.S.A.I.D. Washington, October 1974 p 13); David Barrett, ed., *World Christian Handbook*: *A.I.D. Economic Data Book* (Washington, D.C.: December 1973).

(1975) *World Development Report* 1980 pp. 110—111.

Note: The most recent literacy figures are given as percentages of the adult population aged 15 and over. The estimates for the following countries are for unspecified years usually within three years of 1975: *Benin, Ethiopia, Kenya, Upper Volta* and *Zambia*. 1978 figures are given for *Botswana* and *Swaziland*. The figure for the Gambia is from 1976. *Gabon, Botswana, Guinea-Bissau, Swaziland and Upper Volta, Accelerated Development South of the Sahara. Angola, Cameroon, CAR, Djibouti, Equatorial Guinea, Gambia, Mozambique, Namibia, Nigeria, Uganda, and Zimbabwe The World Factbook* April 1981 U.S. Government. For 1972, Zimbabwe, Namibia, and Djibouti are staff estimates.

TABLE 4.12 Percent Change in Literacy Rate. 1965—1975 (A) and 1955—65 (B).

Definition and Comments: Date for 1955 are given by the source as "percent literate in the 1950's." Where the sources provide a range (e.g. 35—40 percent), a midpoint value has been chosen, often with the aid of additional sources. It should be noted that all the former French West African and French Equatorial African countries were estimated at between 5 and 10 percent literate for 1955.

```
Range =        1163.00
Mean =          105.51
Standard Deviation =        187.26
```

Population Percent Cum.	Country	Rank	Country Name	A	Range Decile	B
1.03	1.03	1.0	Somalia	1100	1	400
4.02	2.99	2.0	Mozambique	400	7	50
9.18	5.16	3.0	Tanzania	340		88
11.59	2.41	4.0	Cameroon	250	8	43
12.05	.46	5.0	Mauritania	240		67
13.39	1.34	6.5	Chad	200		67
13.92	.53	6.5	Liberia	200		25
15.25	1.33	8.0	Niger	167	9	200
16.53	1.28	9.5	Burundi	150		25
18.19	1.66	9.5	Malawi	150		25
18.38	.19	11.0	Guinea-Bissau	133		200
19.74	1.36	12.0	Rwanda	130		25
20.74	1.00	13.0	Benin	120		67
21.19	.45	14.5	Congo	117		667
21.35	.16	14.5	Swaziland	117		36
31.06	9.71	17.0	Ethiopia	100		67
32.63	1.57	17.0	Guinea	100		233
34.50	1.87	17.0	Mali	100		67
35.25	.75	19.0	Togo	80		25
39.85	4.60	20.0	Kenya	60		9
41.80	1.95	21.5	Angola	50	10	60
42.79	.99	21.5	Sierra Leone	50		25
44.43	1.64	23.0	Senegal	43		133
44.72	.29	24.0	Namibia	33		
47.20	2.48	25.5	Madagascar	25		14
68.20	21.00	25.5	Nigeria	25		67
70.46	2.26	27.0	Zimbabwe	20		
70.69	.23	28.0	Botswana	17		30
72.34	1.65	29.0	Zambia	3		74
72.44	.10	33.0	Djibouti	0		0
72.60	.16	33.0	Gabon	0		333
72.77	.17	33.0	Gambia	0		43
76.28	3.51	33.0	Ghana	0		30
78.50	2.22	33.0	Ivory Coast	0		567
84.74	6.24	33.0	Sudan	0		8
88.69	3.95	33.0	Uganda	0		20
89.07	.38	37.0	Lesotho	-8		20
91.04	1.97	38.0	Upper Volta	-30		133
91.14	.10	39.0	Equatorial Guinea	-40		25
91.72	.58	40.0	Central African R	-53		400
100.00	8.29	41.0	Zaire	-63		8

SOURCES: See previous table for 1965 and 1975. For ca. 1955: *UN Report on the World Social Situation. Cameroon, Zaire, Nigeria, Somalia*: UNESCO, *Basic Facts and Figures*; *Botswana, Gabon, Lesotho, Niger, Senegal, Sudan, Uganda, Zambia*: Census reports from *UN Compendium of Social Statistics, 1967. Note*: This data represents, in many instances, very tentative estimates of literacy based on fragmentary evidence and generally before a modern census was completed.

TABLE 4.13 Educational Expenditure as a Percent of Gross Domestic Product, 1976 (A), 1972 (B) and 1965 (C).

```
Range =           6.90
Mean =            3.79
Standard Deviation =        1.39
```

Population Percent Cum.	Country	Rank	Country Name	A	Range Decile	B	C
.45	.45	1.0	Congo	8.5	1	7.5	4.3
.64	.19	2.0	Guinea-Bissau	6.8	3		
5.24	4.60	3.0	Kenya	5.4	5	4.7	4.0
7.46	2.22	4.0	Ivory Coast	5.3		6.7	3.2
9.11	1.65	5.0	Zambia	5.2		5.2	2.8
9.86	.75	6.0	Togo	5.1		2.2	1.9
10.86	1.00	7.5	Benin	4.8	6	5.2	3.8
12.73	1.87	7.5	Mali	4.8		2.4	1.7
21.02	8.29	9.0	Zaire	4.6		4.1	4.6
21.48	.46	10.0	Mauritania	4.5		3.8	2.1
21.71	.23	11.0	Botswana	4.4		2.3	4.0
22.29	.58	12.0	Central African R	4.3	7	3.8	2.8
24.77	2.48	13.0	Madagascar	4.1		3.1	3.2
24.87	.10	15.5	Djibouti	4.0		4.9	
31.11	6.24	15.5	Sudan	4.0		1.8	2.8
36.27	5.16	15.5	Tanzania	4.0		3.8	3.7
38.53	2.26	15.5	Zimbabwe	4.0		3.5	
42.04	3.51	18.5	Ghana	3.9		3.6	4.8
43.61	1.57	18.5	Guinea	3.9		7.0	3.9
44.64	1.03	20.0	Somalia	3.6	8	1.4	1.4
44.81	.17	21.5	Gambia	3.5		2.5	3.2
46.45	1.64	21.5	Senegal	3.5		2.8	2.1
48.86	2.41	23.0	Cameroon	3.3		1.0	2.1
49.02	.16	24.0	Swaziland	3.2		4.5	4.1
50.35	1.33	25.0	Niger	3.1		1.4	1.6
50.73	.38	26.5	Lesotho	3.0		4.9	3.2
51.72	.99	26.5	Sierra Leone	3.0		2.7	2.6
72.72	21.00	28.0	Nigeria	2.8	9	2.5	1.6
76.67	3.95	29.0	Uganda	2.6		3.3	1.5
78.64	1.97	30.0	Upper Volta	2.5		1.7	2.6
79.92	1.28	31.5	Burundi	2.3		3.4	5.0
81.26	1.34	31.5	Chad	2.3		2.6	2.9
81.79	.53	33.0	Liberia	2.2	10	2.4	2.0
91.50	9.71	34.5	Ethiopia	2.1		3.0	1.3
93.16	1.66	34.5	Malawi	2.1		3.0	3.8
94.52	1.36	36.0	Rwanda	2.0		3.2	2.1
94.68	.16	37.0	Gabon	1.6		3.7	3.1

DATA NOT AVAILABLE OR NOT APPLICABLE
FOR THE FOLLOWING COUNTRIES

Angola   Equatorial Guinea Mozambique Namibia

SOURCES:(1965) For cases in which data pertain to years other than 1965, computation of percent of GDP has been made using GDP figures for the corresponding year, thus providing an estimate of the 1965 value. Gross Domestic Product data from *UN Statistical Yearbook 1968*, pp. 184 and 190. *Ivory Coast*: Hallak and Poignant, *Les aspects financiers d'education en Cote-d'Ivoire*, p. 13; *UN Statistical Yearbook 1967—1968*. Percentages computed from absolute figures given in local currencies for all levels. *Rwanda*: Data for 1963; *Lesotho, Nigeria, Togo*: Data for 1966; *Ivory Coast, Mauritania*: Data for 1964; *Uganda*: Data for 1960; *Ivory Coast*: Jacques Hallak and Raymond Poignant, *Les aspects financiers d'education en Cote-d'Ivoire* (Paris: UNESCO, Institut international de planification de l'education, 1966), p. 33. *Equatorial Guinea and Mozambique*: UNECA Statistical Yearbook 1973.
(1972) Educational Expenditures—*AID Economic Data Book 1973*;

UNESCO Statistical Yearbook 1973, UNECA Statistical Yearbook 1973 and 1974; Africa South of the Sahara 1975; IMF Surveys of African Economies; GDP—*UN First Biennial Review of African Performance* (New York: United Nations, 1973). 1969 data—*Gabon, Guinea, Zaire*; 1970 data *Benin, Central African Republic, Congo, Madagascar, Niger, Togo*: 1971 data *Botswana, Burundi, Gambia, Lesotho, Sierra Leone, Sudan, Tanzania, Uganda, Upper Volta*.
(1976) *UN Statistical Yearbook 1978* pp. 928—32. 1975 figures are given for *Benin, Botswana, Congo, Ethiopia, Ivory Coast, Liberia, Madagascar, Malawi, Mali, Swaziland, and Uganda*. 1974 figures are given for: *Kenya, Nigeria and Sudan*. 1973 figures are given for: *Central African Republic, Lesotho and Zimbabwe*. 1972 figures are given for: *Angola, Guinea, Guinea-Bissau and Mauritania*.

TABLE 4.14 Educational Expenditure as a Percent of Total Government Expenditure, 1977 (A), 1972 (B), 1965 (C) and 1958 (D).

Definition: For cases in which educational expenditure data pertain to a year other than 1965, computation of percent of total government expenditure has been made using budget figures for the corresponding year, thus providing an estimate of the 1965 allocation.

```
Range            =    31.90
Mean             =    19.89
Standard Deviation =          7.15
```

Population Percent Cum.	Country	Rank	Country Name	A	Range Decile	B	C	D
1.00	1.00	1.0	Benin	40.0	1	28.3	16.5	24.6
3.22	2.22	2.0	Ivory Coast	37.0		23.5	16.7	19.0
5.09	1.87	3.0	Mali	30.6	3	19.0	12.9	24.6
6.08	.99	4.0	Sierra Leone	28.8	4	22.2	19.4	24.2
6.53	.45	5.0	Congo	28.0		25.3	20.3	26.2
27.53	21.00	6.0	Nigeria	27.3		14.8	16.0	38.8
32.13	4.60	7.0	Kenya	26.6	5	18.7	11.9	23.4
40.42	8.29	8.0	Zaire	26.5		14.8	21.4	17.3
41.78	1.36	9.0	Rwanda	24.0	6	25.7	20.5	21.7
44.26	2.48	10.5	Madagascar	23.0		9.5	5.5	9.7
46.23	1.97	10.5	Upper Volta	23.0		21.5	16.1	16.4
48.64	2.41	12.0	Cameroon	22.5		19.7	16.4	14.0
49.39	.75	13.0	Togo	22.0		19.9	17.9	16.6
49.77	.38	14.0	Lesotho	21.2		19.3	27.9	18.8
51.05	1.28	15.0	Burundi	20.8	7	23.5	23.0	21.7
56.21	5.16	16.0	Tanzania	20.2		14.4	17.8	33.8
57.85	1.64	17.0	Senegal	19.8		13.9	8.7	12.5
61.36	3.51	18.0	Ghana	19.4		25.5	20.9	21.9
61.52	.16	19.0	Swaziland	18.7		15.3	15.8	9.7
63.18	1.66	20.0	Malawi	18.3		13.4	15.0	20.4
64.52	1.34	21.0	Chad	17.2	8	14.5	18.5	11.5
64.68	.16	22.5	Gabon	17.1		16.0	12.1	19.6
66.01	1.33	22.5	Niger	17.1		12.9	12.2	12.3
66.59	.58	24.5	Central Afri. R	17.0		15.6	13.6	19.3
68.16	1.57	24.5	Guinea	17.0		20.8	30.1	15.6
68.39	.23	26.0	Botswana	16.8		6.9	16.2	15.1
68.58	.19	27.0	Guinea-Bissau	15.6		7.9		
69.04	.46	28.0	Mauritania	15.4		26.6	14.3	15.0
75.28	6.24	29.0	Sudan	14.7		5.7	20.1	9.7
76.31	1.03	30.5	Somalia	13.0	9	6.3	7.0	6.1
77.96	1.65	30.5	Zambia	13.0		12.8	10.6	13.1
87.67	9.71	32.0	Ethiopia	12.8		16.7	10.2	11.3
91.62	3.95	33.0	Uganda	12.6		18.6	10.8	21.4
93.88	2.26	34.0	Zimbabwe	12.0		21.1	14.5	
93.98	.10	35.0	Djibouti	9.6	10			
94.51	.53	36.0	Liberia	9.1		13.1	13.5	10.7
94.68	.17	37.0	Gambia	8.1		9.8	12.6	10.6

DATA NOT AVAILABLE OR NOT APPLICABLE FOR THE FOLLOWING COUNTRIES

Angola   Equatorial Guinea   Mozambique   Namibia

SOURCES: (1965) For educational expenditures see notes to Table 5.18 in *Black Africa* (first edition). Total government expenditure based on *Europa Yearbook 1967* and *UN Statistical Yearbook 1967*. *Ivory Coast*: Hallak and Poignant, *Les aspects financiers d'education en Cote-d'Ivoire*, p. 13. Also see Table 4.13.

(1972) *AID Economic Data book 1973*; *UNECA Statistical Yearbook 1973 and 1974*; *UN Statistical Yearbook 1973*; *UNESCO Statistical Yearbook 1973*; *Africa South of the Sahara 1975*.

(1958) Sources for Table 4.13 and Junod, *Handbook for Africa*; *Swaziland and Somalia*: *UNECA Statistical Yearbook 1973*.

(1977) *World Tables 1980* and *UN Statistical Yearbook 1978*. See Table 4.13 for additional information. 1976 figures are given for: *Zambia, Tanzania, Swaziland*. 1975 figures are given for: *Uganda, Senegal*. 1973 figures are given for: *Zimbabwe, Upper Volta*.

TABLE 4.15 Average Annual Percent Change in Educational Expenditure as a Proportion of Total Government Expenditure 1972—1977 (A), 1965—72 (B) and 1958—65 (C).

Comment: The higher the number the greater the increase in the percent of the total government budget which is devoted to education.

```
Range =          39.10
Mean =            1.36
Standard Deviation =         8.30
```

Population Percent Cum.	Country	Rank	Country Name	A	Range Decile	B	C
.19	.19	1.0	Guinea-Bissau	30.9	1		
1.22	1.03	2.0	Somalia	24.4	2	-1.4	2.1
2.55	1.33	3.0	Niger	16.0	4	.8	-.1
4.19	1.64	4.0	Senegal	10.3	6	7.5	-4.3
5.84	1.65	5.0	Zambia	7.2	7	3.5	-2.7
7.71	1.87	6.0	Mali	6.3		6.8	-6.8
7.87	.16	7.0	Swaziland	5.6		-.5	12.6
8.25	.38	8.0	Lesotho	4.9		-4.4	6.9
16.54	8.29	9.0	Zaire	3.7		-4.4	3.4
19.02	2.48	10.0	Madagascar	3.5	8	10.4	-6.2
23.62	4.60	11.5	Kenya	3.3		8.2	-7.0
24.08	.46	11.5	Mauritania	3.3		17.2	-.7
25.08	1.00	13.5	Benin	2.6		11.9	-4.7
25.61	.53	13.5	Liberia	2.6		-.4	.3
26.06	.45	15.0	Congo	1.6		3.5	-3.2
28.28	2.22	16.0	Ivory Coast	1.0		5.8	-1.7
28.86	.58	17.0	Central African R	.9		2.1	-4.2
29.03	.17	18.0	Gambia	.4		-3.2	3.5
34.19	5.16	19.0	Tanzania	-.5	9	-2.7	-6.8
35.53	1.34	20.0	Chad	-1.7		-5.4	8.7
36.81	1.28	21.5	Burundi	-2.5		3.1	.9
43.05	6.24	21.5	Sudan	-2.5		-10.2	15.3
45.46	2.41	23.0	Cameroon	-2.9		-5.8	2.4
47.43	1.97	24.0	Upper Volta	-3.1		5.6	-.1
49.69	2.26	25.0	Zimbabwe	-3.2		6.5	
51.35	1.66	26.0	Malawi	-3.4		-1.5	-3.8
51.58	.23	27.0	Botswana	-4.5	10	-8.2	1.0
55.09	3.51	28.5	Ghana	-4.8		3.1	-.6
56.66	1.57	28.5	Guinea	-4.8		-7.7	13.3
66.37	9.71	30.0	Ethiopia	-5.8		9.1	-1.4
70.32	3.95	31.0	Uganda	-5.9		10.3	-7.1
70.48	.16	32.5	Gabon	-6.1		5.4	-5.5
71.23	.75	32.5	Togo	-6.1		2.2	1.1
72.22	.99	34.0	Sierra Leone	-6.4		1.8	-2.8
93.22	21.00	35.0	Nigeria	-7.0		-.8	-8.4
94.58	1.36	36.0	Rwanda	-8.2		3.6	-.8

DATA NOT AVAILABLE OR NOT APPLICABLE
FOR THE FOLLOWING COUNTRIES

Angola   Djibouti   Equatorial Guinea   Mozambique
Namibia

SOURCES: Data for educational and total government expenditure for 1958 are from: *Enseignement Outre-mer* (December 1958) (individual unit reports give percent of total government expenditure allocated for education); *Europa Yearbook 1961*, Vol. 2; *UN Statistical Yearbook 1968*, Table 185; UNESCO, *World Survey of Education*, Vol. 3; *United Nations Trusteeship Report on Ruanda-Urundi* (New York: 1960), p. 68. For 1965 and 1972 and 1977 refer to Table 4.14.

Communication and Transportation

The circulation and flow of information (communications), and the movement of physical goods and populations (transportation) has been emphasized in theories of both economic and political development.[32] In this chapter we present data on mass communication and transportation systems—i.e. the facilities available for communication and transport—but it is useful to introduce these data in the context of theories which concern the effects of actual flows of information, goods and people on economic and political development.[33]

Theoretical Importance of Communication

In terms of *economic development* communications play a critical role in (1) the creation of demands for the goods and benefits of an industrial society and the associated "revolution of rising expectations," and (2) the transmission of values and norms compatible with an integrated and industrialized economic system.[34] The growth of communications and transport systems have additional economic ramifications since they represent a major aspect of the development of social overhead capital.[35] Once constructed, facilities for mass communication and transportation may effect considerable economies of scale in the movement of goods and information, providing increasingly large pay-offs as usage increases without concomitant increases in the investment in infra-structure. Extensions of communication and transportation systems, therefore, can enlarge existing markets, diminishing the size and isolation of subsistence sectors, and satisfy some minimum conditions for the establishment of manufacturing industries.

One should, nevertheless, be wary of any simplistic equation of the growth of communication and transporation infrastructure with growth in national income. Relatively easy though it has been to persuade foreign aid agencies of the utility of infra-structure development, and satisfying though it may be for government officials to have themselves associated with the visible facilities of progress, "the role of infra-structure facilities in development is coordinate with that of many other pieces of capital equipment and change in management practices and in institutions. Increasingly large infra-structure facilities have their place in the course of development, but they deserve no special niche as absolute or near-absolute prerequisites to growth."

In theories of *political development*, the growth of communication and transportation systems is linked to the shift from traditional to modern society, the development of democratic decision-making structures, and the integration of national political communities. A unifying explanatory concept related to these hypothesized developments is Daniel Lerner's notion of empathy or the capacity of the individual to place himself in the role of others. Lerner views modernization as a progressive diffusion of empathy which is characteristic of people who display relatively higher levels of physical, social and psychic mobility, and he argues that empathy is a consequence of the sequential effects of urbanization and literacy and is 'multiplied' by exposure to mass media.

Lerner's emphasis on the role of communications in changing the traditional habits and world-view of individuals and thus effecting a transition to modern society, is clearly reflected in the work of political scientists who see the growth of modern society as the result of a multidimensional process of social mobilization. Karl Deutsch has described social mobilization as the overall process of change involving large segments of the population, "in which major clusters of social, economic and psychological commitments are eroded or broken and people become available for new patterns of socialization and behavior."[37] Deutsch emphasizes the role of radio and newsprint in mobilizing populations into an awareness of new styles of life[38] and Gabriel Almond and G.B. Powell argue that social mobilization is "in large part a communication phenomenon" that must occur before the development of political and economic capabilities.[39]

The consequences of social mobilization in terms of the political systems that result from the growth of communication and transportation are not well understood, although there is a considerable body of social research that emphasizes the linkage between increasing communications and increasingly democratic political organization. Both Lerner and Deutsch remark on the association between mass political participation and increasing social mobilization. In this connection, a notable empirical-analysis by Phillips Cutwright describes a strong association between political development, operationalized as the presence and persistence of aspects of democratic institutionalization, and the extent of mass communication. Comparing seventy-one countries on these two variables Cutwright reported a correlation of .80[40].

In addition to the development of empathy, rationality,[41] and democratic behavior as hypothesized consequences of an increasing experience of mass communication and transportation, theories of political development emphasize the disruptive political consequences implied in the conceptualization of social mobilization as a breakdown of traditional patterns of thought and behavior, and a mechanism for the development of new and potentially unsatisfiable demands. Depending, therefore, on the ratio of demand arousal to demand satisfaction, communication development may result in political instability in new nations.[42] But as social mobilization dislocates people from their habitual environment and provides for the intensification of formerly unexpressed demands and inter-group conflicts, so the development of communications and transportation may facilitate the integration of political communities. Integration is the increasing linkage, interdependence, cohesion, unification and consensus characteristic of social groupings   (see Sect. A Chapter One), and the use of communication facilities for increasing transactions between spatially and socially disparate political actors is a crucial aspect of political integration.[43]

The measurement of integration with data on communication and transportation facilities of the kind presented in this chapter is, it must be emphasized, subject to some reservation. Communication potential as measured by the number and type of mass media and transportation facilities in each national unit is neither indicative of the intensity of communications and transactions nor is it specific as to the geographical and social location of the source and receivers of goods and messages.[44] Empirical analysis of national integration must eventually incorporate measures of within-nation transaction flows, since the theoretical linkage between communication development and national integration is based on the argument that, aside from official boundaries, the composition of functional political communities can be determined by the identification of discontinuities in the flow of mutually rewarding transactions between members of a given nation. The model of this kind of analysis is to be found in studies of international or regional integration, an example of which is a study by Edward Soja, in which the salience of telephonic communications between urban centers in Kenya, Uganda, and Tanzania between 1961 and 1965 was reduced and a pattern of intra-national clustering became more clearly evident.[45]

Measuring Communication

The data presented in the tables which follow have been chosen to cover a broad range of communications and transport phenomena within the limits of aggregate measurement. Information concerning radios (Table 4.16 and 4.17), newspapers (Tables 4.18 and 4.19), telephones (Tables 4.20 and 4.21), cinemas (Table 4.22), roads (Table 4.23), passenger cars (Table 4.26), commercial vehicles (Table 4.24 and 4.25), and miles of railroad track (Table 4.27) are included. Per capita figures are usually presented for four time points, and the road and railroad mileage measures have been standardized on the basis of area of the country. Percentage changes are given to

show relative rates of growth.

These data are directly applicable to the operationalization of measures of social mobilization and social overhead capital as conceptual explanations of political and economic development. There are serious difficulties, however, in justifying these aggregate explanations of the mechanisms linking communications development to the growth of democracy, political instability, or economic development in ways which are by no means obvious. Summary indicators of the scale of communication and transportation facilities in a given country obscure the details of who uses such facilities, how often people use them and how mutually rewarding the transactions are, who controls them, and what consequences are entailed by patterns of usage and control for the content and effectiveness of communications.

In interpreting the data in this chapter, therefore, one must have in mind the unidentified variation between African nations in the concentration of communications in particular sectors of the population. Deutsch has specified several levels of social communication which are differentiated both by the actors involved and the media employed.[46] If one distinguishes broadly between the elite, opinion leaders, and the mass public, it is necessary, from the point of view of a satisfying explanation of political and economic development, to know (1) how great is the concentration of ownership[47], control[48], and usage[49] of communications by the elite; (2) how clearly communications from the elite to the mass public are transmitted in the two-step flow[50] of messages from opinion leaders to the average citizen; and (3) to what extent reactive media like telephones, transportation, and face-to-face communications differ in their effects on individual perception and feeling from nonreactive media like radios, television, newspapers, and cinemas.

Reliability

Most communications data are generated in accordance with the maintenance and accounting requirements of the various operating systems and can be expected to have high reliability. Accurate measures of communications volume within nations are often readily available to the researcher, although not in disaggregated form. Nevertheless, each of the variables included in this chapter has certain specific reliability problems.

The most serious reliability problems are two which are associated with the measurement of radios. The first is occasioned by the procedure in some countries in which radios must be licensed, while the number of radios is only estimated in those countries without licensing requirements. Furthermore, since the licensing process is usually a taxing device, understatement is to be expected in those countries where radio licenses are the basis of measurement. Whenever available, the numbers reported in Table 4.16 and 4.17 are estimates of the total number of receivers in a given country. A second measurement problem occurs when estimates of radio receivers obtained from available sources show considerable variance for the same or adjacent year.[51]

Daily newspapers (Tables 4.18 and 4.19) are a major source of information for the literate population, and are capable of presenting a variety of positions that government-owned or regulated radio stations may not present—this, of course, provided that newspapers are not owned or censored by government. The difficulty with measures of newspaper circulation, however, is that the definition of daily newspapers is not always consistently adhered to by the reporting countries. The figures given in this chapter are intended to include the circulation of all indigenous newspapers issued regularly, either daily or at least three to four times a week.

We expect telephones (Tables 4.20 and 4.21), passenger cars (Table 4.26), and commercial vehicles (Tables 4.24 and 4.25) to be reported with reasonable accuracy in original sources, since telephonic technology requires accurate measures of usage, and, unlike radios, the licensing of vehicles is generally enforceable. Conversely, the measures of improved roads (Table 4.23) are plagued by a lack of a clear cut definition of "improved".[52] Nevertheless, this latter figure should provide a rudimentary ranking of the countries with respect to road density. Railroad mileage is, in principle, a well-defined measure, but secondary track and side spurs are sometimes included with figures for primary track mileage.[53] The variable reported in Table 4.27 is intended to represent primary track mileage only.

In addition to lending general support to the reliability of the data in this chapter by showing high intercorrelations between different measures of the same variable, a factor analysis of seventy-four communications and transport variables showed the following pattern of dimensionality. Four factors, accounting for 85 percent of the total variance, may be characterized as follows:

1. Radios, newspapers, cinemas (mass or non-reactive communications).
2. Telephones, passenger cars, railroad mileage (personal or reactive communications).
3. Commercial transport.
4. Air transport

The data in this chapter have been selected to provide coverage of these dimensions and to indicate temporal aspects of communications development.[54]

Notes

[1]Structural- functionalism involves the basic proposition that social systems can be compared in terms of functions which are performed by structures which vary. This is described for political systems in developing nations by Gabriel Almond and G.B. Powell, *Comparative Politics, A Developmental Approach* (Boston: Little, Brown and Co, 1966) Chapter 2, pp. 16—41.

[2]Clignet and Foster in a work on secondary education in the Ivory Coast, state: "The school in Africa is inevitably an agent of change…Schools in Africa can never become agencies of simple culture transmission facilitating consensus and stability whether the content of instruction is African or European." Remi Clignet and Philip Foster, *The Fortunate Few, A Study of Secondary Schools and Students in the Ivory Coast* (Evanston, Ill.: Northwestern University Press, 1966), p. 201.

[3]A composite index of human resource development is employed in Frederick Harbison and Charles A. Myers, *Education, Manpower and Economic Growth* (New York: McGraw-Hill, 1964). This is calculated as the sum of the second level enrollment ratio and five times the third level enrollment ratio. In another report of quantitative analysis, Irma Adelman and C.T. Morris, *Society, Politics and Economic Development* (Baltimore, Md.: Johns Hopkins University Press, 1967), the Harbison and Myers Index is used in addition to a number of other social and political measures. Also see on this issue, R. de L. Loken, *Manpower Development in Africa* (New York: Praeger, 1969); F. Harbison, *A Human Resource Approach to the Development of African Nations* (Washington, D.C.: American Council on Education, 1971); and F.B. Waisanen and H. Kumata, "Education, Functional Literacy and Participation in Development," *International Journal of Comparative Sociology*, XIII, 1 (1972), pp. 21—35. It is not surprising that while economists such as Harbison stress secondary and higher education as important factors in development, theorists concerned with development in other spheres focus more often on primary education, the source of literacy skills, and modern political value orientations.

[4]Others include literacy, voting, media consumption, and media production. Daniel Lerner, *The Passing of Traditional Society*. (Glencoe, Ill.: The Free Press, 1958), p. 86. Also see A. Peshkin, "Limitations of Schooling for Planned Political Socialization: Reflections on Nigeria," *Comparative Education* (Sept. 1972), pp. 63—73; D.R. Evans, *Teachers as Agents of National Development* (New York: Praeger, 1972); and K. Prewitt, *Education and Political Values* (Nairobi: East African Pub. House, 1973).

[5]Daniel Lerner, *The Passing of Traditional Society*, pp. 87—89. The mass media, as well as educational systems, work to create what Lerner terms "mobile personalities," who have "high capacity for identification with new aspects of [their] environment," p. 49.

[6] S.N. Eisenstadt, *Modernization: Protest and Change* (Englewood Cliffs, N.J.: Prentice-Hall, 1966), pp. 16—18. For a later view that is more discouraging on the modernizing role of education see L. Aran, S.N. Eisenstadt, C. Adler, "The Effectiveness of Educational Systems in the Process of Modernization," *Comparative Education Review*, 16, 1, (Feb. 1972), pp. 30—43.

[7]Gabriel A. Almond and Sidney Verba, *The Civic Culture* (Boston: Little, Brown and Co., 1963), Chapter 9, "Political Socialization and Civic Competence," pp. 208—243.

[8]Also see Lucian W. Pye, *Politics, Personality, and Nation Building;*

Burma's Search for Identity (New Haven, Conn.: Yale University Press, 1962) and Robert E. Schott, "Mexico, The Established Revolution," in *Political Culture and Political Development*, eds. L.W. Pye and Sydney Verba (Princeton, N.J.: Princeton University Press, 1965), pp. 330—395. In Mexico, according to Scott, the educational system's relationship to change is ambivalent; many institutions tend to reinforce traditional attitudes. Also see M. Armer and R. Youtz, "Formal Education and Individual Modernity in an African Society," *American Journal of Sociology* (Jan. 1972), pp. 604—626.

[9]C. Arnold Anderson, "Patterns and Variability in the Distribution and Diffusion of Schooling," in *Education and Economic Development*, eds. C. Arnold Anderson and Mary Jean Bowman (Chicago: Aldine Co., 1965); Remi Clignet, "Ethnicity, Social Differentiation and Secondary Schooling in West Africa," *Cahiers d'Etudes Africaines*, 7 (1967): 360—378; Philip Foster, "Secondary Schooling and Social Mobility in a West African Nation," *Sociology of Education*, 37 (1963): 159; Philip Foster, *Education and Social Change in Ghana* (Chicago: University of Chicago Press, 1965); M. Peil, "The Influence of Formal Education on Occupational Choice," *Canadian Journal of African Studies*, VII, 2 (1973), pp. 199—214; and the special issue on educational problems in Africa in the *Canadian Journal of African Studies*, 8, 3 (1974), edited by R. Santerre.

[10]Clignet goes on to state that his findings suggest "ethnic differentials in attitudes do not seem to be deeply eroded by education," thus challenging the assertion that educational systems operate as powerful agents for resocialization to modern commitments. Clignet, "Ethnicity, Social Differentiation and Secondary Schooling..." p. 378.

[11]For works on political socialization relating to the early acquisition of national identification, the first resulting from case studies, the second from the quantitative analysis of data from a large sample, see Erik H. Erikson, *Childhood and Society*, 2nd printing rev. (New York: W.W. Norton & Co., 1963); and Robert D. Hess and Judith V. Torney, *The Development of Political Attitudes in Children* (New York: Doubleday & Co., 1968).

[12]Robert A. LeVine, "Political Socialization and Culture Change," in *Old Societies and New States*, ed. Clifford Geertz (New York: The Free Press, 1963), pp. 280—303.

[13]Penelope Roach, *Political Socialization in the New Nations of Africa* (New York: Teachers College Press, Columbia University, 1967).

[14]Primary enrollment ratios as late as 1957 did not exceed 40 percent in most African territories and were considerably smaller in many.

[15]James S. Coleman, ed., *Education and Political Development* (Princeton, N.J.: Princeton University Press, 1965), p. 30. In his introduction (pp. 3—22) Coleman offers a discussion of education and political socialization, recruitment, and integration. He points out that on the whole both political scientists and educators have failed to recognize the importance of the "education-polity nexus"; the efforts of educators themselves in cross-national research has been largely limited to intra-system analysis as if education were an autonomous sector of activity.

Jerry B. Bolibaugh described how in former French Africa the educated elite was developed as a controlling link between the metropole and the masses: Jerry B. Bolibaugh and Paul R. Hanna, *Education as an Instrument of National Policy in Selected Newly Developing Nations* (Stanford Calif.: Comparative Education Center, School of Education; Stanford University, 1964), p. 96.

[16]However, much of the descriptive material is especially useful for general familiarization with the variety of educational systems and their unique problems. Important works of this type are L. Gray Cowan, James O'Connell, and David G. Scanlon, eds., *Education and Nation Building in Africa* (New York: Praeger, 1965); John W. Hanson and Cole S. Brembeds, eds., *Education and the Development of Nations* (New York: Holt, Rinehart and Winston, 1966); David G. Scanlon, ed., *Church, State and Education in Africa* (New York: Teachers College Press, Columbia University, 1966); David G. Scanlon, ed., *Traditions of African Education* (New York: Teachers College Press, Columbia University 1964); John Wilson, *Education and Changing West African Culture* (New York: Teachers College Press, Columbia University, 1963); D. Abernethy, *The Political Dilemma of Popular Education—An African Case* (Palo Alto: Stanford University Press, 1969); Pierre L. Van Den Berghe, *Power and Privilege at An African University*, (London: Routledge & Kegan Paul, 1973); G. Williams, "Education and Government in Northern Nigeria," *Presence Africaine* 3e Trim (1973), pp. 156—178.

[17]Thomas Jesse Jones, *Education in Africa* (New York: The Phelps-Stokes Fund, 1922); and Thomas Jesse Jones, ed., *Education in East Africa* (London: Edinburgh House Press, 1925). Also see L.J. Lewis, ed., *Phelps-Stokes Reports on Education in Africa* (London: Oxford University Press, 1962).

[18]Donald G. Burns, *African Education, An Introductory Survey of Education in Commonwealth Countries* (London: Oxford University Press, 1965). For former French territories, Abdou Moumouni, *Education in Africa* trans. by Phyllis N. Ott (New York: Praeger, 1968), originally published under the title *L'Education en Afrique* (Paris: Francois Maspero, 1964). While this volume has been unfavorably reviewed by both Clignet and Foster, it offers broad cross-national comparisons with a strong quantitative orientation. Also, Elliot Berg, "French Educational Policy in Senegal, Guinea, and the Ivory Coast," in Harbison and Myers, *Manpower and Education*, pp. 232—267. For an excellent overview of the continent, see Guy Hunter, "Education in Africa," *African Affairs*, 66 (April 1967): 127—139.

[19]Extensive holdings of education reports, primarily for British territories exist at the following locations: The Library of Congress, Washington, D.C.; Teachers College Library (Columbia University); The Cubberly Library (Stanford University); and the Library of the Department of Health, Education, and Welfare, Washington, D.C.

[20]Enseignement Outre-mer: *Bulletin de l'inspection general de l'enseignement et de la jeunesse du ministere de la France d'outre-mer* (Paris: Ministere de la France d'Outre-mer, issued yearly from approximately 1950 through 1958). These issues are available for reference at the Teachers College Library, Columbia University.

[21]UNESCO, *World Survey of Education* (Paris: UNESCO); Vol. 1 (General), 1955; Vol. 2 (Primary Education), 1953; Vol. 3 (Secondary Education), 1961; Vol. 4 (Higher Education), 1966.

[23]There are ways, other than those we use, of calculating changes in enrollment. The following formula is provided for calculating rates of increase from given enrollment ratios for the beginning and end date of a span of years:

$p_n = p_o (1 \pm r)^t$

p_o = ratio at the beginning of period

p_n = ratio at the end of period

r = rate of increase or decrease per year

t = number of years $(n - o)$

[23]For a discussion of this need see Harbison and Myers, *Education*,

Manpower and Economic Growth, pp. 24—25.

[24]Enrollment by class, age, or number of years of education completed is available in certain of the more detailed reports from Commonwealth nations and territories. A general discussion of measuring enrollment is found (in addition to the *World Survey* volumes), in *Manual of Education Statistics* (Paris: UNESCO, 1961); and W.L. Kendall, *Statistics of Education in Developing Countries, an Introduction to their Collection and Presentation* (Paris: UNESCO, 1968).

[25]For example, comparing attendance rates for seven districts in Tanzania in 1964 and 1965, Jane King reports a range of variation between 11 percent and 79 percent. Jane King, *Planning Non-Formal Education in Tanzania*, African Research Monography 16 (Paris: UNESCO International Institute for Educational Planning, 1967), p. 23. These research monographs are useful data sources for educational planning in Africa; each deals with a particular national unit.

[26]Daniel Blot and Michel Debeauvais, "Educational Expenditure in Developing Areas: Some Statistical Aspects," in *Financing of Education for Economic Growth*, ed. Lucille Reifman (Paris: Organization for Economic Co-operation and Development, 1964).

[27]For a use of this measure see UNESCO *World Survey of Education, Vol. 3, Secondary Education* (individual country reports).

[28]A detailed outline and comparison of African educational structures is found in Mawtena Sasnett and Inez Sepmeyer, *Educational Systems of Africa* (Berkeley: University of California Press, 1966). This information corresponds to earlier descriptions found in individual national unit sections of the UNESCO, *World Survey of Education* series.

[29]For a discussion of the problems of cross-national comparisons see Kendall, *Statistics of Education in Developing Countries*, pp. 74—78.

[30]Data used to construct this figure were taken from L. Pechoux, *Le Mandat Francais sur le Togo* (Paris: A. Pedone, 1939), pp. 344—347.

[31]Statistical relationship between expenditures and other educational measures in order to test reliability are also plausible. Blot and Debeauvais, for example, investigate the predictive relationship between educational expenditure and GDP which correlates at .94, Blot and Debeauvais, "Educational Expenditure in Developing Areas."

[32]See, for example: Lucian Pye, ed., *Communications and Political Development* (Princeton: Princeton University Press, 1962); Karl W. Deutsch, *Nationalism and Social Communications: An Inquiry into the Foundations of Nationalism* (New York: The Technology Press of M.I.T. and John Wiley, 1953); Philip Jacob and James V. Toscano, eds., *The Integration of Political Communities* (New York: J.B. Lippincott Co., 1964); Daniel Lerner, *The Passing of Traditional Society* (Glencoe, Ill.: The Free Press, 1958); Everett Rogers, *Modernization Among Peasants: The Impact of Communication* (New York: Holt, Rinehart and Winston, 1969).

[33]The emphasis in this section is on 'stock' data (i.e. data which refers to the numbers of communications devices or their capacity) as contrasted with 'flow' data which measures actual usage of communications devices. The newspaper circulation data are the single example of flow data in this section.

[34]For a discussion of the importance of communications in the development of labor commitment in developing countries see Peter B. Hammond, "Management in Economic Transition," in Wilbert E. Moore and Arnold S. Feldman, eds., *Labor Commitment and Social Change in Developing Areas* (New York: Social Science Research Council, 1960), pp. 109-122; and for an anlysis of the positive effects of mass media exposure on individual innovation, see Rogers, *Moderniza-*

tion Among Peasants, Chapter 5.

[35]For a discussion of social overhead capital, see Stephen Enke, *Economics for Development* (London: Dennis Dobson, 1963).

[36]Everett E. Hagen, *The Economics of Development* (Homewood, Illinois: Irwin, 1968), 129.

[37]Daniel Lerner, *The Passing of Traditional Society*, pp. 47-65.

[38]Karl W. Deutsch, "Social Mobilization and Political Development," *American Political Science Review*, 55 (September 1961): 494.

[39]Gabriel A. Almond and G. B. Powell, Jr., *Comparative Politics: A Developmental Approach* (Boston: Little, Brown, 1966), p. 177.

[40]Philips Cutwright, "National Political Development: Measurement and Analysis," *American Sociological Review*, 28 (1963): 253-264. For related discussions of these concepts see Deane N. Neubauer, "Some Conditions of Democracy," *American Political Science Review*, 61 (1967): 1002-1009; Marvin E. Olsen, "Multivariate Analysis of National Political Development," *American Sociological Review*, 33 (1968): 699-712; and Arthur K. Smith Jr., "Socio-Economic Development and Political Democracy: A Causal Analysis," *Midwest Journal of Political Science*, (1969): 96-125.

[41]For the importance of communications in the development of political rationality, see, for example, Lucian Pye, *Aspects of Political Development* (Boston: Little, Brown, 1966), Chapter 8.

[42]See the clear-cut formulation of this problem in Deutsch, "Social Mobilization and Political Development."

[43]See Karl W. Deutsch, "Communication Theory and Political Integration," and "Transaction Flows as indicators of Political Cohesion," in *The Integration of Political Communities*, Jacob and Toscano, eds., pp. 46-74 and 75-97.

[44]See the discussion and analysis in Donald G. Morrison *Conflict and Violence in Black Africa: A Comparative Analysis of a Theory of Political Learning* (Forthcoming).

[45]See Edward W. Soja, "Communication and Territorial Integration in East Africa: An Introduction to Transaction Flow Analysis," in *The Structure of Political Geography*, eds. Roger E. Kasperson and Julain V. Menghi (Chicago: Aldine, 1969), p. 231—242. The salience of communications is determined by the value of the relative acceptance index, first introduced by I.R. Savage and Karl W. Deutsch, "A Statistical Model of the Gross Analysis of Transaction Flows," *Econometrica*, 28 (1960): 551—572. This index is a measure of the signficance of the actual or observed flow of communications as a proportion of the flow expected by a chance or "null" model. For related aspects of spatial analysis of communication see B. Riddell, *The Spatial Dynamics of Modernization in Sierra Leone* (Evanston: Northwestern University Press, 1970).

[46]See Karl W. Deutsch, *The Analysis of International Relations* (Englewood Cliffs, N.J.: Prentice-Hall, 1968), pp, 101—110.

[47]Annual compendia such as *Europa Yearbook*, *Africa South of the Sahara*, and the *Statesman's Yearbook* contain detailed information on radio and the press in African countries. See also *The Commercial Radio in Africa* (German African Society, October 1969); Fritz Feuereisen and Ernst Schmacke, eds., *Africa: A Guide to Newspapers and Magazines* (New York: Africana, 1970); W.A. Hatchon, *Muffled Drums: The News Media in Africa* (Ames: Iowa State University Press, 1971); S. Olav, ed., *Reporting Africa in African and International Mass Media* (Upsala: Scandanavian Institute of African Studies, 1971); and D.L. Wilcox *Mass Media in Black Africa: Philosophy and Control* (New York: Praeger, 1975); S.W. Head, ed., *Broadcasting in Africa: A Continental Survey of Radio and Televison* (Philadelphia: Temple University

Press, 1974); A. Ogunbi "A Current Bibliography on African Communication in Africa" *A Current Bibliography on Africa Affairs* 8, 1 (1975): 2—43; and A.E. Opubor and M.K. Hobbs "Development Communication: A Selected Annotated Bibliography" *Rural Africana* 27 Spring 1975: 127—56.

[48]Reports on press censorship covering some of the black African countries are available from the University of Missouri and Indiana University.

[49]The concentration of facilities and usage in government offices and capital cities may be illustrated by the fact that of the 25,513 telephones in Senegal in 1967, 20,373 were in Dakar. *Statesman's Yearbook, 1968—1969.*

[50]For the "two-step flow" hypothesis that "ideas often flow from radio and print to opinion leaders and from them to the less active sections of the population" see Paul F. Lazarsfeld, et al., *The People's Choice* (New York: Meredith Press, 1944); and Elihu Katz, "The Two-Step Flow of Communication: An Up-To-Date Report on an Hypothesis," *Public Opinion Quarterly*, 21 (1957): 61—78.

[51]For example, the *UN Statistical Yearbook 1967* reports 58,000 radio receivers in Ivory Coast in 1964. Another report for the same year, in *Africa Report*, 9 (February 1964): p. 32, gives a figure of 100,000 receivers. A third source *Africa 1968*, reports 300,000 radio receivers in Ivory Coast in 1965.

[52]This can be observed by comparing the figures on improved roads in *AID Economic Data Book: Africa 1970* with more detailed descriptions of road surface in *Statesman's Yearbook 1968—69.*

[53]It should be noted that Sierra Leone's uneconomical railway was phased out in 1972 and replaced with increased use of the road system.

[54]Air transport data were not included because data were lacking for a third of the countries.

TABLE 4.16   Radios per 1,000 Population 1978 (A), 1970 (B), 1965 (C), 1960 (D) and Total Number of Radios (in 1,000's), 1976 (E).

Definition: Involves estimates of total radio ownership and not the number actually licensed except where noted.

```
Range =          224.00
Mean =            67.17
Standard Deviation =       55.32
```

Population Percent Cum.	Country	Rank	Country Name	A	Range Decile	B	C	D	E
.10	.10	1.0	Equatorial Guinea	231	1	244	222		80
.63	.53	2.0	Liberia	221		115	100	78	265
.79	.16	3.0	Gabon	178	3	124	78	48	96
.95	.16	4.0	Swaziland	147	4	71	21	6	80
1.05	.10	5.5	Djibouti	133	5	74	94	62	15
2.71	1.66	5.5	Malawi	133		80	24	9	1100
4.93	2.22	7.0	Ivory Coast	118	6	14	15	17	900
5.10	.17	8.0	Gambia	111		108	115	9	63
13.39	8.29	9.0	Zaire	101		60	3	3	2582
16.90	3.51	10.5	Ghana	100		82	71	22	100
17.19	.29	10.5	Namibia	100		80		35	100
18.18	.99	12.0	Sierra Leone	99		76	44	4	325
18.41	.23	13.0	Botswana	85	7	35	8	4	62
39.41	21.00	14.0	Nigeria	76		23	7	4	5500
45.65	6.24	15.0	Sudan	74	8	35	23	1	1325
46.11	.46	16.0	Mauritania	65		44	29	12	100
48.52	2.41	17.5	Cameroon	62		31	19	3	500
48.97	.45	17.5	Congo	62		54	44	14	92
49.55	.58	19.5	Central African R	56		29	21	10	105
51.19	1.64	19.5	Senegal	56		63	64	48	268
52.19	1.00	21.0	Benin	53		31	15	3	180
54.67	2.48	22.0	Madagascar	47	9	43	31	15	130
56.93	2.26	23.0	Zimbabwe	42		27	26	16	90
61.53	4.60	24.5	Kenya	36		37	39	9	530
62.86	1.33	24.5	Niger	36		36	13	1	180
63.05	.19	26.0	Guinea-Bissau	29	10	8	7	4	16
64.33	1.28	27.0	Burundi	26		18	10	6	110
65.90	1.57	28.5	Guinea	25		23	21	13	121
68.89	2.99	28.5	Mozambique	25		11	9	6	250
69.27	.38	31.0	Lesotho	23		5	5	5	30
70.30	1.03	31.0	Somalia	23		18	14	12	80
71.05	.75	31.0	Togo	23		20	18	4	50
72.70	1.65	33.0	Zambia	22		18	12	5	120
74.04	1.34	35.0	Chad	20		16	8	3	85
79.20	5.16	35.0	Tanzania	20		11	10	4	325
83.15	3.95	35.0	Uganda	20		22	24	15	250
85.10	1.95	37.5	Angola	19		17	15	11	125
86.46	1.36	37.5	Rwanda	19		8	5	3	85
88.43	1.97	39.0	Upper Volta	17		16	10	1	110
90.30	1.87	40.0	Mali	14		12	6	2	90
100.00	9.71	41.0	Ethiopia	7		6	6	5	215

SOURCES: (1960) *UNESCO Statistical Yearbook 1972* and *UNESCO World Communications*(New York: UNESCO, 1963); *Guinea-Bissau*: *UN Statistical Yearbook 1969*. *Djibouti*: 1959 data, *Namibia*: 1958 data. (1966) *UN Statistical Yearbook 1969*; *Cameroon, Congo, Lesotho*: *UNESCO Statistical Yearbook 1968*; *Burundi, Rwanda*: "Press and Radio in Africa," *Africa Report*, 9 (1964): 32; *Zaire, Ethiopia, Mauritania, Nigeria, Sierra Leone, Sudan*: *UN Statistical Yearbook 1967* (1964); *Swaziland*: *UNECA Yearbook 1972*;
(1965, 1970, 1978) *UNESCO Statistical Yearbook 1981* Liberia, Malawi, Namibia, and Nigeria Staff estimates. *Niger*: 1978 data estimated from 1981 figure of 101,000 radios. from *Europa Yearbook 1982*.

TABLE 4.17   Percent Increase in Radios per 1,000 Population, 1972—1976 (A), 1966—72 (B) and 1960—66 (C).

```
Range =          94.00
Mean =           10.29
Standard Deviation =        16.19
```

Population Percent		Rank	Country Name	A	Range Decile	B	C
Cum.	Country						
2.22	2.22	1.0	Ivory Coast	93	1		-3
2.60	.38	2.0	Lesotho	45	6		
2.79	.19	3.0	Guinea-Bissau	33	7	2	13
23.79	21.00	4.0	Nigeria	29		38	13
24.02	.23	5.0	Botswana	18	8	56	17
25.38	1.36	6.0	Rwanda	17	9	10	11
28.37	2.99	7.0	Mozambique	16		4	85
34.61	6.24	8.0	Sudan	14		8	10
37.02	2.41	10.0	Cameroon	13		11	89
38.05	1.03	10.0	Somalia	13		5	3
38.21	.16	10.0	Swaziland	13		60	42
38.79	.58	12.5	Central African R	12		6	18
39.32	.53	12.5	Liberia	12		4	5
39.42	.10	14.5	Djibouti	10		-4	9
44.58	5.16	14.5	Tanzania	10		2	25
45.58	1.00	16.0	Benin	9		18	67
47.24	1.66	17.5	Malawi	8	10	39	28
55.53	8.29	17.5	Zaire	8			
57.79	2.26	19.0	Zimbabwe	7		6	4
59.07	1.28	20.5	Burundi	6		13	11
59.53	.46	20.5	Mauritania	6		3	18
59.69	.16	22.0	Gabon	5		11	10
60.68	.99	23.0	Sierra Leone	4		-5	200
62.02	1.34	25.5	Chad	3		17	28
65.53	3.51	25.5	Ghana	3		3	37
65.82	.29	25.5	Namibia	3			
67.47	1.65	25.5	Zambia	3		8	23
67.92	.45	29.5	Congo	2		4	36
77.63	9.71	29.5	Ethiopia	2			3
79.50	1.87	29.5	Mali	2			17
80.25	.75	29.5	Togo	2		2	58
82.20	1.95	33.5	Angola	1		2	6
83.77	1.57	33.5	Guinea	1		2	10
86.25	2.48	33.5	Madagascar	1		6	18
88.22	1.97	33.5	Upper Volta	1		10	150
88.39	.17	37.0	Gambia	0		-1	235
92.99	4.60	37.0	Kenya	0			52
94.32	1.33	37.0	Niger	0			
94.42	.10	40.0	Equatorial Guinea	-1		3	
96.06	1.64	40.0	Senegal	-1			6
100.00	3.95	40.0	Uganda	-1		-1	10

SOURCE: See Table 4.16.

TABLE 4.18 Daily Newspaper Circulation per 10,000 Population, 1978 (A), 1972 (B), 1966 (C), 1960 (D) and Total Daily Circulation (in hundreds), 1976 (E).

Definition: Total daily circulation is given in hundreds. Includes all regular newspapers published at least three times a week. Only newspapers published in the country are included. In some cases, readership of foreign papers was significant before the beginning of indigenous dailies.

```
Range =        349.00
Mean =          78.78
Standard Deviation =        90.82
```

Population Percent Cum.	Country	Rank	Country Name	A	Range Decile	B	C	D	E
.45	.45	1.0	Congo	349	1	8	16	12	500
3.96	3.51	2.0	Ghana	310	2	300	291	300	3450
4.12	.16	3.0	Gabon	283		39	11	0	150
4.35	.23	4.0	Botswana	230	4	222	0	0	170
4.64	.29	5.0	Namibia	191	5			120	180
6.59	1.95	6.0	Angola	180		150	87	91	1200
8.24	1.65	7.0	Zambia	178		130	68	48	930
9.23	.99	8.0	Sierra Leone	170	6	176	63	68	500
11.49	2.26	9.0	Zimbabwe	160		150	150	320	1090
11.68	.19	10.0	Guinea-Bissau	110	7	10	41	23	60
16.28	4.60	11.0	Kenya	100	8	138	72	115	1560
16.44	.16	12.0	Swaziland	98					50
37.44	21.00	13.5	Nigeria	97		41	66	69	5270
42.60	5.16	13.5	Tanzania	97		39	29	25	1580
45.08	2.48	15.0	Madagascar	90		80	87	81	590
45.61	.53	16.0	Liberia	80		45	51	9	80
47.83	2.22	17.0	Ivory Coast	72		97	81	24	530
49.49	1.66	18.0	Malawi	60	9	30			310
49.66	.17	19.0	Gambia	55		41	45	63	30
51.30	1.64	20.0	Senegal	50		61	57	67	250
52.87	1.57	21.5	Guinea	40		12	7	2	200
55.86	2.99	21.5	Mozambique	40		59	74	35	420
58.27	2.41	23.0	Cameroon	39		23	34	14	280
59.02	.75	24.0	Togo	32	10	62	59	13	70
68.73	9.71	25.0	Ethiopia	21		18	15	20	520
72.68	3.95	26.0	Uganda	20		75	73	73	23
80.97	8.29	27.0	Zaire	17		92	31	15	450
81.35	.38	28.0	Lesotho	12		16	0	0	13
82.38	1.03	29.5	Somalia	10		14	22	9	40
88.62	6.24	29.5	Sudan	10		9	5	5	190
89.95	1.33	31.0	Niger	6		5	4	3	30
91.23	1.28	32.5	Burundi	5		1	0	0	2
93.10	1.87	32.5	Mali	5		6	7	2	30
94.44	1.34	34.0	Chad	4		2	5	2	15
95.44	1.00	35.5	Benin	3		7	8	15	10
97.41	1.97	35.5	Upper Volta	3		4	3	0	15
97.87	.46	37.0	Mauritania	2		4	0	0	30
99.23	1.36	38.0	Rwanda	1		0	0	0	2
99.81	.58	40.0	Central African R	0		3	3	4	0
99.91	.10	40.0	Djibouti	0		0	0	0	0
100.00	.10	40.0	Equatorial Guinea	0		33	40	32	0

SOURCES: (1960) *UN Statistical Yearbook* Various years.

(1966) *UN Statistical Yearbook 1968: UNESCO Statistical Yearbook*, 1973.

(1972) *UN Statistical Yearbook 1974: Africa South of the Sahara 1975;* and *Europa Yearbook* Vol. II 1973; *Nigeria, Ethiopia*: Includes the eight major dailies only; *Uganda, Ghana*: six dailies only: *Congo* 1973 data from *UN Statistical Yearbook* 1975.

(1978) *UNESCO Statistical Yearbook 1982. Burundi, Central African Republic, Congo, Djibouti, Equatorial Guinea, Gabon, Gambia, Namibia, Niger, Sudan, Swaziland: Accelerated Development in Sub-Saharan Africa* and *Europa Yearbook 1982*. (1976)*Tanzania, Malawi, and Guinea: UN Statistical Yearbook 1979-80. Niger, Namibia, Sudan: UN Statistical Yearbook 1979-80, Congo: Europa Yearbook 1982. Gambia and Burundi* Staff estimates.

TABLE 4.19   Average Annual Percent Change in Newspaper Circulation per Capita, 1972— 75 (A), 1965—72 (B) and
1960—65 (C).

Note: In countries where the beginning circulation rate was zero and
the final rate was non-zero, the figure of 100 percent increase over the
period was arbitrarily taken.

```
Range =         726.70
Mean =           27.80
Standard Deviation =        112.73
```

Population Percent Cum.	Country	Rank	Country Name	A	Range Decile	B	C
.45	.45	1.0	Congo	710.0	1	251.9	6.7
.64	.19	2.0	Guinea-Bissau	166.7	8	-12.6	15.7
.80	.16	3.0	Gabon	104.2	9	42.4	99.9
2.08	1.28	4.0	Burundi	66.7		99.9	
3.65	1.57	5.0	Guinea	38.9	10	11.9	50.0
8.81	5.16	6.0	Tanzania	24.8		5.7	3.2
29.81	21.00	7.0	Nigeria	22.8		-6.3	-.9
30.39	.58	9.5	Central Afri. R	16.7		0	-5.0
31.73	1.34	9.5	Chad	16.7		-10.0	30.0
33.39	1.66	9.5	Malawi	16.7		99.9	
34.75	1.36	9.5	Rwanda	16.7			
35.28	.53	12.0	Liberia	12.9		-2.0	93.0
37.69	2.41	13.0	Cameroon	11.6		-5.4	28.6
39.34	1.65	14.0	Zambia	6.2		26.0	8.3
39.51	.17	15.5	Gambia	5.7		-1.5	-5.7
39.67	.16	15.5	Swaziland	5.7			
41.62	1.95	17.5	Angola	3.3		12.1	-.9
42.95	1.33	17.5	Niger	3.3		4.2	6.7
52.66	9.71	19.0	Ethiopia	2.8		3.3	-5.0
55.14	2.48	20.0	Madagascar	2.1		12.1	14.8
61.38	6.24	21.0	Sudan	1.9		11.4	4.0
63.64	2.26	22.0	Zimbabwe	1.1			-53.0
63.87	.23	23.0	Botswana	.6		99.9	
67.38	3.51	24.0	Ghana	.5		10.9	-.6
67.48	.10	25.0	Djibouti	0			
68.47	.99	26.0	Sierra Leone	-.6		29.9	-1.5
70.34	1.87	27.0	Mali	-2.8		-2.4	50.0
71.98	1.64	28.0	Senegal	-3.0		1.2	-3.0
72.36	.38	29.5	Lesotho	-4.2		99.9	
74.33	1.97	29.5	Upper Volta	-4.2		5.6	99.9
76.55	2.22	31.0	Ivory Coast	-4.3		3.3	47.5
81.15	4.60	32.0	Kenya	-4.6		22.9	-7.5
82.18	1.03	33.0	Somalia	-4.8		-6.1	28.9
85.17	2.99	34.0	Mozambique	-5.4		-3.4	22.3
85.92	.75	35.0	Togo	-8.1		8.5	10.8
86.38	.46	36.0	Mauritania	-8.3		99.9	
87.38	1.00	37.0	Benin	-9.5		-2.1	-9.3
91.33	3.95	38.0	Uganda	-12.2		.5	
99.62	8.29	39.0	Zaire	-13.6		32.8	21.3
99.72	.10	40.5	Equatorial Guinea	-16.7		-3.5	5.0
100.00	.29	40.5	Namibia	-16.7			

SOURCES: See Table 4.18.
(1965) *UN Statistical Yearbook* 1968.
(1972) *UN Statistical Yearbook* 1973.
(1975) *UN Statistical Yearbook* 1977.

TABLE 4.20   Telephones per 10,000 Population 1977 (A), 1972 (B), 1967 (C), 1963 (D) and Total Number of Telephones in Thousands, 1977 (E).

```
Range =          610.00
Mean =            84.73
Standard Deviation =        130.33
```

Population Percent Cum.	Country	Rank	Country Name	A	Range Decile	B	C	D	E
.29	.29	1.0	Namibia	620	1	432	390	374	46
.45	.16	2.0	Gabon	600		216	86	62	15
2.71	2.26	3.0	Zimbabwe	290	6	254	224	215	198
2.87	.16	4.0	Swaziland	170	8	138	103	88	9
5.09	2.22	5.0	Ivory Coast	130	9	91	59	35	67
5.32	.23	6.5	Botswana	120		73	50	27	8
5.42	.10	6.5	Equatorial Guinea	120					3
5.52	.10	8.5	Djibouti	110		171			3
7.17	1.65	8.5	Zambia	110		131	114	89	53
11.77	4.60	10.0	Kenya	100		78	61	58	144
12.22	.45	11.5	Congo	90		700	103	92	12
13.86	1.64	11.5	Senegal	90		102	67	26	39
17.37	3.51	13.0	Ghana	70	10	56	42	45	67
17.54	.17	14.5	Gambia	60		53	38	20	3
20.53	2.99	14.5	Mozambique	60		58	29	26	52
20.72	.19	16.0	Guinea-Bissau	53		63	28	18	4
22.67	1.95	17.5	Angola	50		55	40	25	32
23.66	.99	17.5	Sierra Leone	50		42	28	25	15
26.14	2.48	21.0	Madagascar	40		37	135	30	32
27.80	1.66	21.0	Malawi	40		32	23	18	22
32.96	5.16	21.0	Tanzania	40		31	23	19	64
33.71	.75	21.0	Togo	40		29	16	18	10
37.66	3.95	21.0	Uganda	40		33	31	24	46
40.07	2.41	24.0	Cameroon	37		34	9	8	30
41.07	1.00	27.0	Benin	30		28	19	14	10
50.78	9.71	27.0	Ethiopia	30		21	15	9	79
51.16	.38	27.0	Lesotho	30		31	20	8	4
51.69	.53	27.0	Liberia	30		41	30	28	7
57.93	6.24	27.0	Sudan	30		32	30	27	62
58.51	.58	30.0	Central African R	26		28	19	17	5
60.08	1.57	33.0	Guinea	20		19	17	13	10
60.54	.46	33.0	Mauritania	20		12	25	8	1
61.87	1.33	33.0	Niger	20		9	8	6	8
82.87	21.00	33.0	Nigeria	20		17	14	12	121
91.16	8.29	33.0	Zaire	20		18	14	21	48
92.19	1.03	36.0	Somalia	18		20	17	12	6
93.47	1.28	39.0	Burundi	10		12	9	8	4
94.81	1.34	39.0	Chad	10		13	11	8	7
96.68	1.87	39.0	Mali	10		10	16	10	6
98.04	1.36	39.0	Rwanda	10		7	4	3	4
100.00	1.97	39.0	Upper Volta	10		9	6	4	6

SOURCES: (1963) *UN Statistical Yearbook* 1968.

(1967) *UN Statistical Yearbook* 1969; *Gambia, Mauritania*: *Statesman's Yearbook* 1968—69.

(1972) *UN Statistical Yearbook* 1974; *Uganda*: *Statesman's Yearbook* 1973—74.

(1977) *UN Statistical Yearbook* 1979; 1976 figures are given for: *Angola, Burundi, Gambia, Madagascar, Mozambique, Niger, Nigeria, Senegal, Sierra Leone, Uganda, Tanzania, Zaire and Zimbabwe.* 1975 figures are given for: *Botswana, Namibia and Upper Volta.*

Cameroon, Central African Republic, Equatorial Guinea, Gabon, Guinea-Bissau, Mali, Mauritania, and Somalia: Staff estimates from data for other years.

TABLE 4.21   Percent Change in the Number of Telephones per Capita, 1970—77 (A), 1967—1972 (B) and 1963—1967 (C).

```
Range =          194.00
Mean =           14.20
Standard Deviation =        32.14
```

Population Percent Cum.	Country	Rank	Country Name	A	Range Decile	B	C
.16	.16	1.0	Gabon	178	1	151	41
.69	.53	2.0	Liberia	73	6	37	11
1.15	.46	3.0	Mauritania	67		-52	213
6.31	5.16	4.0	Tanzania	59	7	35	35
6.41	.10	5.0	Djibouti	32	8		
7.74	1.33	6.0	Niger	31		13	60
7.97	.23	7.5	Botswana	21	9	58	92
8.26	.29	7.5	Namibia	21			4
10.52	2.26	9.0	Zimbabwe	17			4
11.27	.75	10.0	Togo	14		81	-6
13.68	2.41	12.5	Cameroon	9		278	13
23.39	9.71	12.5	Ethiopia	9		40	88
25.61	2.22	12.5	Ivory Coast	9		54	79
26.97	1.36	12.5	Rwanda	9		75	100
27.55	.58	15.0	Central African R	8		47	19
32.15	4.60	16.0	Kenya	6		28	13
35.66	3.51	19.0	Ghana	5		33	-2
37.32	1.66	19.0	Malawi	5		39	35
38.31	.99	19.0	Sierra Leone	5		50	17
38.47	.16	19.0	Swaziland	5		34	17
42.42	3.95	19.0	Uganda	5		7	41
63.42	21.00	22.5	Nigeria	4		21	27
65.39	1.97	22.5	Upper Volta	4		50	50
65.56	.17	25.0	Gambia	3	10	40	100
67.20	1.64	25.0	Senegal	3		52	-7
75.49	8.29	25.0	Zaire	3		29	-30
76.49	1.00	27.5	Benin	2		47	36
78.97	2.48	27.5	Madagascar	2		6	17
80.92	1.95	30.0	Angola	1		38	60
82.49	1.57	30.0	Guinea	1		12	31
85.48	2.99	30.0	Mozambique	1		100	16
87.35	1.87	32.0	Mali	0		-38	78
93.59	6.24	33.0	Sudan	-1		7	173
94.04	.45	34.5	Congo	-2		9	16
94.42	.38	34.5	Lesotho	-2		55	150
96.07	1.65	36.0	Zambia	-3		15	37
97.35	1.28	37.0	Burundi	-4		33	13
98.69	1.34	38.0	Chad	-5		18	38
99.72	1.03	39.0	Somalia	-11		18	-35
99.91	.19	40.0	Guinea-Bissau	-16		54	128

DATA NOT AVAILABLE OR NOT APPLICABLE FOR THE FOLLOWING COUNTRIES

Equatorial Guinea

SOURCES: (1967) *UN Statistical Yearbook* 1969. *Gambia, Mauritania: Statesmen's Yearbook 1968—69.*
(1972) *UN Statistical Yearbook* 1973.
(1977) *UN Statistical Yearbook* 1979. See also Table 4.20.

TABLE 4.22   Number of Movie Houses, ca. 1977 (A), 1972 (B) and 1966 (C).

Definition: Includes both 16 mm. and 35 mm. cinemas.

```
Range =          119.00
Mean =           27.14
Standard Deviation =        28.40
```

Population Percent Cum.	Country	Rank	Country Name	A	Range Decile	B	C
21.00	21.00	1.0	Nigeria	120	1	67	27
29.29	8.29	2.0	Zaire	91	3	34	25
31.51	2.22	3.0	Ivory Coast	78	4	80	48
33.77	2.26	4.0	Zimbabwe	72	5	72	26
35.41	1.64	5.0	Senegal	60	6	77	77
41.65	6.24	6.0	Sudan	58		52	23
43.60	1.95	7.5	Angola	48	7	40	30
48.20	4.60	7.5	Kenya	48		32	84
50.61	2.41	9.0	Cameroon	43		41	23
60.32	9.71	11.0	Ethiopia	31	8	30	29
62.80	2.48	11.0	Madagascar	31		43	40
67.96	5.16	11.0	Tanzania	31		29	41
70.95	2.99	13.5	Mozambique	28		28	25
74.90	3.95	13.5	Uganda	28		16	21
75.43	.53	15.0	Liberia	19	9	26	10
75.60	.17	16.5	Gambia	18		8	7
75.89	.29	16.5	Namibia	18		18	
77.23	1.34	18.0	Chad	16		9	8
78.88	1.65	19.0	Zambia	13		28	17
79.34	.46	20.0	Mauritania	12	10	10	7
81.31	1.97	21.0	Upper Volta	11		6	7
81.41	.10	22.0	Equatorial Guinea	10		11	11
84.92	3.51	23.0	Ghana	9		57	99
85.50	.58	24.0	Central African R	8		8	7
85.95	.45	25.5	Congo	7		10	12
86.14	.19	25.5	Guinea-Bissau	7		8	1
87.14	1.00	27.5	Benin	6		6	3
87.30	.16	27.5	Gabon	6		2	3
88.58	1.28	29.0	Burundi	5		4	7
88.68	.10	31.0	Djibouti	4		2	
90.34	1.66	31.0	Malawi	4		13	7
90.50	.16	31.0	Swaziland	4		4	2
91.86	1.36	33.0	Rwanda	3		4	8
92.24	.38	34.0	Lesotho	2		2	3
92.47	.23	35.0	Botswana	1		11	7

DATA NOT AVAILABLE OR NOT APPLICABLE FOR THE FOLLOWING COUNTRIES

| Guinea | Mali | Niger | Sierra Leone |
| Somalia | Togo | | |

SOURCES: (1966) *UN Statistical Yearbook* 1967.
(1972) *UN Statistical Yearbook* 1974.
(1977) *UNESCO Statistical Yearbook* 1981 and *UN Statistical Yearbook* 1979-80. *Central African Republic, Chad, Gabon, Lesotho, Mozambique, Namibia, Upper Volta, and Zimbabwe: 1972 data.*

TABLE 4.23 Miles of Improved Roads per 1,000 Square Miles of Surface Area 1979 (A) and Miles of Improved Roads 1979 (B).

```
Range =        324.00
Mean =          88.49
Standard Deviation =        75.34
```

Population Percent			Country		Range	
Cum.	Country	Rank	Name	A	Decile	B
1.28	1.28	1.0	Burundi	326	1	31
1.44	.16	2.0	Swaziland	258	3	119
4.95	3.51	3.0	Ghana	216	4	87
6.31	1.36	4.0	Rwanda	187	5	202
27.31	21.00	5.0	Nigeria	185		126
29.53	2.22	6.0	Ivory Coast	170		125
31.79	2.26	7.0	Zimbabwe	167		
31.96	.17	8.0	Gambia	166		248
32.95	.99	9.0	Sierra Leone	164	6	70
34.61	1.66	10.0	Malawi	143		106
34.80	.19	11.0	Guinea-Bissau	142		140
39.40	4.60	12.5	Kenya	119	7	106
39.78	.38	12.5	Lesotho	119		39
41.42	1.64	14.0	Senegal	113		68
41.95	.53	15.0	Liberia	106		58
50.24	8.29	16.0	Zaire	98	8	14
52.65	2.41	17.0	Cameroon	97		21
52.94	.29	18.0	Namibia	72		
53.69	.75	19.0	Togo	71		51
53.79	.10	20.0	Equatorial Guinea	67		77
55.44	1.65	21.0	Zambia	63	9	22
56.02	.58	22.0	Central African R	56		16
56.12	.10	23.0	Djibouti	53		
58.60	2.48	24.0	Madagascar	52		33
59.63	1.03	25.0	Somalia	49		16
61.58	1.95	26.0	Angola	48		60
62.58	1.00	27.5	Benin	46		97
66.53	3.95	27.5	Uganda	46		72
68.50	1.97	29.0	Upper Volta	38		26
70.07	1.57	30.0	Guinea	32	10	26
75.23	5.16	31.0	Tanzania	30		12
75.39	.16	32.0	Gabon	27		10
75.62	.23	33.5	Botswana	21		21
81.86	6.24	33.5	Sudan	21		2
91.57	9.71	35.0	Ethiopia	15		12
92.02	.45	36.0	Congo	14		52
95.01	2.99	37.0	Mozambique	10		23
96.88	1.87	38.0	Mali	7		10
98.22	1.34	39.5	Chad	6		8
99.55	1.33	39.5	Niger	6		9
100.00	.46	41.0	Mauritania	2		2

SOURCES: *AID Economic Data Book 1973* and *Africa South of the Sahara 1975.*

Note: Definitions are highly variable for road mileage and great variance is noted in many countries over time, therefore, no temporal change data is presented for this variable.

National Basic Intelligence Factbook 1979,(Washington, D.C., January 1980).

Equatorial Guinea, Gabon, Madagascar, Namibia, Somalia, Tanzania, and Zambia: Europa Yearbook. Sudan: Staff estimate.

TABLE 4.24 Commercial Vehicles per 100,000 Population 1976 (A), 1972 (B), 1966 (C), 1958 (D) and Number of Commerical Vehicles, in hundreds 1976 (E).

Definitions: Includes all buses, taxis, trucks used for commercial purposes but excludes, tractors, jeeps, and motor-cycles.

```
Range =        2827.00
Mean =          536.76
Standard Deviation =      574.38
```

Population Percent Cum.	Country	Rank	Name	A	Range Decile	B	C	D	E
.10	.10	1.0	Djibouti	2870	1	2222	1147	493	31
.39	.29	2.0	Namibia	1648	5				
2.04	1.65	3.0	Zambia	1548		1030	390	366	784
2.20	.16	4.0	Swaziland	1429	6	778	838		71
2.36	.16	5.0	Gabon	1420		1184	448	682	73
2.59	.23	6.0	Botswana	1299		778	346	132	92
4.85	2.26	7.0	Zimbabwe	1099	7	1027	579	890	700
5.30	.45	8.0	Congo	937		700	556	493	130
7.71	2.41	9.0	Cameroon	665	8	616	400	398	512
8.24	.53	10.0	Liberia	657		840	625	250	100
10.72	2.48	11.0	Madagascar	645		560	461	335	501
12.94	2.22	12.0	Ivory Coast	632		1268	800	307	435
13.11	.17	13.0	Gambia	620		510	536	241	31
15.06	1.95	14.0	Angola	589	9	583	317	216	357
19.66	4.60	15.0	Kenya	538		172	196	141	743
21.30	1.64	16.0	Senegal	515		578	526	494	250
24.81	3.51	17.0	Ghana	431		341	235	238	459
25.56	.75	18.0	Togo	319	10	306	226	147	70
33.85	8.29	19.0	Zaire	316		260	180	171	764
33.95	.10	20.0	Equatorial Guinea	310					
34.95	1.00	21.0	Benin	305		275	206	103	95
40.11	5.16	22.0	Tanzania	280		269	200	97	418
40.49	.38	23.0	Lesotho	268		279	58	59	32
41.82	1.33	24.0	Niger	250		200	128	90	118
42.01	.19	25.0	Guinea-Bissau	220		229			11
42.59	.58	26.0	Central African R	213		168	183	171	39
44.25	1.66	27.0	Malawi	205		174	170	126	106
45.24	.99	28.0	Sierra Leone	202		426	324	112	63
46.81	1.57	29.0	Guinea	190		263	230	269	95
47.84	1.03	30.0	Somalia	176		272	240	152	60
49.81	1.97	31.0	Upper Volta	166		144	103	76	101
51.15	1.34	32.0	Chad	159		162	160	114	63
72.15	21.00	33.0	Nigeria	136		119	65	44	952
74.02	1.87	34.0	Mali	133		169	119	84	76
80.26	6.24	35.0	Sudan	132		139	128	131	270
81.62	1.36	36.0	Rwanda	118		80	31	24	48
84.61	2.99	37.0	Mozambique	106		238	186	110	
85.07	.46	38.0	Mauritania	83		456	251	149	43
89.02	3.95	39.0	Uganda	80		78	77	88	89
90.30	1.28	40.0	Burundi	55		67	4	18	22
100.00	9.71	41.0	Ethiopia	43		49	31	39	131

SOURCES: (1958) *UN Statistical Yearbook* 1964, 1967.

(1966) *UN Statistical Yearbook* 1967; *UNECA Statistical Yearbook* 1972: *Swaziland*: *UNECA Statistical Yearbook* 1973

(1972) *UN Statistical Yearbook* 1973; *UN Statistical Yearbook* 1973 and 1974; *UNECA Statistical Yearbooks* 1972, 1973 and 1974; Data for 1968 for *Somalia*; 1969 for *Central African Republic, Guinea, Niger*; 1970 for *Benin, Cameroon, Gabon, Ghana, Madagascar, Sierra Leone*; 1971 for *Ethiopia, Mali, Sudan, Upper Volta, Zaire*.

(1976) *UN Statistical Yearbook* 1978. 1977 figures are given for: *Botswana, Ghana, Kenya, Madagascar and Tanzania*. 1975 figures are given for: *Lesotho, Rwanda and Upper Volta*. 1974 figures are given for: *Central African Republic, Gabon, Liberia, Mali, Senegal, Togo, Uganda, Zaire and Zimbabwe*. 1973 figures are given for: *Angola, Chad, Gambia and Nigeria*.

Gambia, Guinea, Guinea-Bissau, Mauritania, Nigeria, Somalia, and Sudan: *Europa Yearbook* 1982. *Equatorial Guinea, Mozambique, Namibia*: Staff estimates.

**TABLE 4.25   Percent Change in Commercial Vehicles per Capita,
1972—1976 (A), 1966—1972 (B), and 1958—1966 (C).**

```
Range =          135.00
Mean =             3.97
Standard Deviation =        20.39
```

Population Percent Cum.	Country	Rank	Country Name	A	Range Decile	B	C
4.60	4.60	1.0	Kenya	53	1	18	4
4.70	.10	2.0	Djibouti	29	2	93	133
6.27	1.57	3.0	Guinea	28		14	-12
6.85	.58	4.0	Central African R	27		-8	8
7.02	.17	5.0	Gambia	22	3	-5	122
7.18	.16	6.0	Swaziland	21		-6	
7.41	.23	7.0	Botswana	17		125	57
8.77	1.36	8.0	Rwanda	16		158	10
11.25	2.48	9.0	Madagascar	15		21	38
32.25	21.00	10.0	Nigeria	14		83	87
33.90	1.65	11.0	Zambia	13		164	5
42.19	8.29	12.0	Zaire	11	4	44	5
42.35	.16	13.0	Gabon	10		162	-34
44.76	2.41	14.5	Cameroon	8		54	150
45.21	.45	14.5	Congo	8		28	13
48.72	3.51	16.5	Ghana	7		45	-1
50.98	2.26	16.5	Zimbabwe	7		77	-35
52.31	1.33	18.0	Niger	6		56	44
54.28	1.97	19.0	Upper Volta	5		40	37
54.47	.19	21.0	Guinea-Bissau	4			
56.13	1.66	21.0	Malawi	4		2	36
61.29	5.16	21.0	Tanzania	4		35	108
62.29	1.00	23.0	Benin	3		33	104
63.04	.75	24.0	Togo	2		34	54
64.99	1.95	25.5	Angola	1		54	75
68.94	3.95	25.5	Uganda	1		1	-1
69.32	.38	27.0	Lesotho	-1	5	381	-2
70.66	1.34	28.0	Chad	-2		1	40
80.37	9.71	29.0	Ethiopia	-3		26	0
81.65	1.28	30.0	Burundi	-4		46	64
83.29	1.64	31.5	Senegal	-5		10	18
89.53	6.24	31.5	Sudan	-5		9	9
90.06	.53	33.5	Liberia	-11		34	146
91.93	1.87	33.5	Mali	-11		42	30
94.15	2.22	35.5	Ivory Coast	-13		59	173
95.14	.99	35.5	Sierra Leone	-13		31	120
96.17	1.03	37.0	Somalia	-35	7	13	58
96.63	.46	38.0	Mauritania	-82	10	82	68

DATA NOT AVAILABLE OR NOT APPLICABLE
FOR THE FOLLOWING COUNTRIES

Equatorial Guinea   Mozambique   Namibia

SOURCES: See Table 4.24.

TABLE 4.26 Passenger Cars per 10,000 Population 1976 (A), 1972 (B), 1966 (C) and Number of Passenger Cars in Hundreds 1976 (D).

```
Range    =      1043.00
Mean     =       104.88
Standard Deviation =        174.37
```

Population Percent Cum.	Country	Rank	Country Name	A	Range Decile	B	C	D
.10	.10	1.0	Djibouti	1056	1		540	114
.39	.29	2.0	Namibia	499	6			
2.65	2.26	3.0	Zimbabwe	264	8	216	221	1800
4.60	1.95	4.0	Angola	210	9	199	92	1273
4.76	.16	5.0	Gabon	196		196	85	101
6.41	1.65	6.0	Zambia	185		149	110	935
6.57	.16	7.0	Swaziland	159		111	105	79
7.02	.45	8.0	Congo	144		179	88	200
9.24	2.22	9.0	Ivory Coast	123		200	100	849
10.88	1.64	10.0	Senegal	92	10	104	80	448
13.87	2.99	11.0	Mozambique	84		99	79	800
14.40	.53	12.0	Liberia	79		73	70	121
16.81	2.41	13.0	Cameroon	77		58	40	595
21.41	4.60	14.0	Kenya	75		93	76	104
23.89	2.48	15.0	Madagascar	72		68	57	561
25.86	1.97	16.0	Upper Volta	70		13	9	420
26.05	.19	17.0	Guinea-Bissau	66		68		33
29.56	3.51	18.0	Ghana	64		44	33	681
29.66	.10	19.0	Equatorial Guinea	62				
30.65	.99	20.0	Sierra Leone	61		163	60	189
30.82	.17	21.0	Gambia	60		61	41	30
31.57	.75	22.0	Togo	59		53	20	130
31.80	.23	23.0	Botswana	58		43	40	41
32.80	1.00	24.0	Benin	55		49	32	170
33.38	.58	25.0	Central African R	52		36	28	91
33.84	.46	26.0	Mauritania	45		36	10	
34.22	.38	27.0	Lesotho	39		20	35	46
42.51	8.29	28.0	Zaire	35		36	22	848
43.54	1.03	29.0	Somalia	29		25	21	100
48.70	5.16	30.0	Tanzania	27		25	30	420
52.65	3.95	31.0	Uganda	24		24	32	270
54.52	1.87	33.0	Mali	21		14	10	119
55.85	1.33	33.0	Niger	21		17	8	99
76.85	21.00	33.0	Nigeria	21		21	14	1538
78.51	1.66	35.0	Malawi	20		22	21	102
80.08	1.57	36.0	Guinea	19		25	24	100
89.79	9.71	37.0	Ethiopia	17		15	12	525
91.15	1.36	38.5	Rwanda	16		12	5	65
97.39	6.24	38.5	Sudan	16		19	21	320
98.73	1.34	40.0	Chad	15		14	11	58
100.00	1.28	41.0	Burundi	13		12	8	51

SOURCES:

(1966) *UN Statistical Yearbook* 1967.

(1972) *UN Statistical Yearbooks* 1974 and 1973; *Africa South of the Sahara*: Burundi, Ghana: *UNECA Statistical Yearbook* 1972; Congo: *UNECA Statistical Yearbook* 1974.

(1976) *UN Statistical Yearbook* 1978. See also table 4.24.

Equatorial Guinea, Mauritania, Namibia: Staff estimates. *Gambia, Guinea, Guinea-Bissau, Mozambique, Nigeria, Somalia, Sudan*: *Europa Yearbook 1982.*

TABLE 4.27 Number of Miles of Primary Railroad Track per 100,000 Square Miles Surface Area (A) and Miles of Primary Railroad Track 1979 (B).

```
Range =      2074.00
Mean =        421.63
Standard Deviation =        453.35
```

Population Percent Cum.	Population Percent Country	Rank	Country Name	A	Range Decile	B
.16	.16	1.0	Swaziland	2074	1	139
2.42	2.26	2.0	Zimbabwe	1481	3	2082
3.17	.75	3.0	Togo	1411	4	305
4.17	1.00	4.0	Benin	908	6	395
5.81	1.64	5.0	Senegal	855		650
9.76	3.95	6.0	Uganda	831		760
9.86	.10	7.0	Djibouti	816	7	64
11.52	1.66	8.0	Malawi	770		352
14.51	2.99	9.0	Mozambique	765		2314
18.02	3.51	10.0	Ghana	641		590
39.02	21.00	11.0	Nigeria	611	8	2178
39.55	.53	12.0	Liberia	581		250
41.12	1.57	13.0	Guinea	538		511
45.72	4.60	14.0	Kenya	481		1081
46.01	.29	15.0	Namibia	473		1404
51.17	5.16	16.0	Tanzania	441		1600
53.12	1.95	17.0	Angola	425		2044
55.53	2.41	18.0	Cameroon	410	9	703
63.82	8.29	19.0	Zaire	354		3207
65.47	1.65	20.0	Zambia	344		1000
67.44	1.97	21.0	Upper Volta	322		341
73.68	6.24	22.0	Sudan	305		2953
75.90	2.22	23.0	Ivory Coast	301		375
76.35	.45	24.0	Congo	242		320
78.83	2.48	25.0	Madagascar	232		532
79.06	.23	26.0	Botswana	170	10	393
88.77	9.71	27.0	Ethiopia	149		680
88.93	.16	28.0	Gabon	125		120
89.39	.46	29.0	Mauritania	105		419
91.26	1.87	30.0	Mali	84		400
91.64	.38	31.0	Lesotho	42		5
92.92	1.28	36.5	Burundi	0		0
93.50	.58	36.5	Central African R	0		0
94.84	1.34	36.5	Chad	0		0
94.94	.10	36.5	Equatorial Guinea	0		0
95.11	.17	36.5	Gambia	0		0
95.30	.19	36.5	Guinea-Bissau	0		0
96.63	1.33	36.5	Niger	0		0
97.99	1.36	36.5	Rwanda	0		0
98.98	.99	36.5	Sierra Leone	0		0
100.00	1.03	36.5	Somalia	0		0

SOURCES: *National Basic Intelligence Factbook*, January 1980.

Note: The existing railroad network in Sierra Leone has been abandoned so the country is coded as having zero miles of railroad per 100,000 square miles area. The figure for the existing but unused track in 1318 miles per 100,000 square miles area. Earlier data for railroad mileage is not presented since very little variance would be observed. Only a few countries have had changes in mileage throughout the last fifteen years. *Cameroon, Djibouti, Namibia, Zimbabwe: The World Factbook 1981* (Washington, D.C.: Government Printing Office, 1981)

5. Political Development

Political developments in Black African states in the post-independence period have prompted confusion, despair and insecurity among those interested in the area. The well-justified approval of the "liberation" of African peoples from colonial regimes gave rise to optimism about the unity and legitimacy of victorious nationalist leaders and movements, and obscured the profound obstacles to subsequent development in these new states. In the euphoria of anti-colonial nationalism, the ideological and institutional superstructures of the new nations—the vaunted aspirations for self-determination, neutralism, positive action, African unity and African socialism, the new elites, political parties, and elections—attracted attention and admiration. But 'the tradition of all the dead generations weighs like a nightmare on the brain of the living," and names, battle cries and costumes borrowed from the spirits of the past[1] quickly distorted the promise of the new political kingdom.

Values, identities and interests associated with ethnic, religious and class-based institutions that were older than the state itself, undermined the fragile unity of nationalist movements. The colonial inheritance of autocratic administration and sometimes illegal political opposition was poor socialization for the competitive democratic constitutions of newly independent governments. Restricted educational development, uneven economic development based on export cash crops and extractive industries, and extreme inequalities in income between colonist and colonized, government and the general public, management and worker, meant that new development initiatives and policies in the post-colonial era were constrained by inadequate manpower resources and capital absorptive capacity, vulnerability to fluctuations in single-market and single commodity economies, by inadequate effective demand for local manufactures, distorted elite consumption of luxury imports, and accelerated demands and frustrations arising from economic inequalities between regions, ethnic groups, and different sectors of the labor force. The very late indigenization of the officer corps in African armies, and the use of African armed forces to put down anti-colonial protest and rebellion, hardly assured a spirit of loyalty to civilian powers after the revolution, or loyalty and cohesiveness within the command structure of the armies themselves. And the new civilian governors, practised in the art of opposition but not government, had often to forsake the parties which brought them to power and bound together what support they had, in order to devote their energies to the business of government.

Theories of political development abstracted from the long historical experience of Europe could scarcely be expected, in these circumstances, to apply in the new nations of Africa. Problems or crises involving the establishment of a unified sense of national identity, the legitimation of constitutional and political arrangements, the integration of culturally diverse populations and their incorporation in meaningful political participation, and the development of welfare policies for the re-distribution of wealth and resources came "not in single spies but battalions." The sequential and centuries-long process of political development along these lines in the Anglo-American tradition had to be quickly and simultaneously resolved in newly independent African nations.[2] That failure has been more obvious than success in this confrontation, that uneven or imbalanced development, stagnation and recession, confusion and instability has characterized political change since independence, is not, therefore, surprising. It is too easy, however, with the advantage of hindsight, to view the succession of African coups d'etat or civil wars, the all but universal demise of competitive parties and elections, the corruption and inefficiency of bureaucracy, the intensified gaps between rich and poor, and the shift from idealism to cynicism and self-interest in domestic and foreign policy, as a necessary consequence of the colonial experience. And it is too easy to side-step the real confusion and the very great dilemmas in practical politics and in the intellectual understanding of politics by settling for generalizations about the inevitability of instability,[3] or by calling for a new public morality,[4] or by choosing sides in the peripatetic shift in academic arguments over the locus of the true explanation for political change—whether it be national elites and political parties or local politics and patron-client relations, foreign imperialism or domestic collaboration and political incapacity, ethnic pluralism or class conflict, indigenous political culture or emerging ideological and material interests, etc.

The variation and complexity of contemporary African politics is too great for any single methodology or causal explanation and any single body of data to be expected to answer all the questions that bear on contemporary African political development. It is the purpose of this chapter to suggest that comparative cross-national research can clarify some of these questions, and to provide data on some significant dimensions of variation in the political experience of Black African nations. In Section A of this book some more systematic analytic interpretations of such data are suggested, but the focus here is on their conceptual and descriptive significance. We shall discuss, in sequence, comparative data on political instability, parties and elections, national governmental institutions, and military and security systems.

Political Instability

From 1958 through December 1981, there have been more than fifty successful coups in twenty- five sub-Saharan states. In addition, there have been at least fifty major, attempted, but unsuccessful, coups during this period. Many of these coups occurred during the period 1963 to 1969, i.e., during the first decade of independence (see Figures 5.1—5.3). By the end of 1981 eighteen countries were still under the leadership of a military officer who took control of the country in a coup d'etat. Two other countries, without formal armies at the time of the coup have also had coups and were still under the coup leader (Lesotho, Swaziland). A considerable number of military regimes have been "civilianized" to varying degrees, including Sudan, Upper Volta, Mali, Togo, Benin and Zaire. Ghana, Nigeria, C.A.R., and Sierra Leone, by the end of 1979, had reverted from a military government to a fully civilian regime not led by a former army officer but Ghana and C.A.R. fell under military control again.

In almost every case, the military assumed control in a relatively bloodless manner. In contrast, considerable violence has characterized threats to the governments of Black African nations by disaffected communal or ethnic groups. The most widely publicized attempts at secession have been in Zaire (Katanga) and Nigeria (Biafra), but other instances have also occurred in Sudan (in the three southern provinces) and in Ethiopia (with the disaffection of Eritrea and the Ogaden). The Tiv in Nigeria were in a state of armed rebellion from 1961 through 1965. The Baganda of Uganda strongly resisted the efforts of the central government to limit the powers of the Kabaka. Members of the Lumpa Church of Zambia rebelled against the demand for the supremacy of national loyalties over religious loyalties. Finally, there have been significant instances of irredentism, in which ethnic groups have sought re-unification across arbitrarily imposed boundaries. This has often led to communal violence or strong political pressure as with the Ewé (in Ghana and Togo), the Kongo (in Congo, Zaire, and An-

gola), and the Somali (in Ethiopia, Somalia and Kenya).

Although there is no lack of commentary on events like those just referred to, the analysis of such historical experience is encumbered by differences of value and conceptual terminology. In this chapter, we refer to these kinds of events as "political instability," which we mean to define in ways which assume no *a priori* evaluation of stability as a normal or preferable condition of political systems, and which we attempt to measure in theoretically useful ways.

Conceptualizations of Political Instability

In the long historical tradition of political theory, the analysis of the basis of order is closely tied to the central issues of clarifying the nature of the "good" society. Order, stability, and political development are often assumed to be identical in political research, and in common wisdom the identity is all but a hallowed truth. It is important, however, to distinguish between *development* and *stability* in political analysis.

Political development has meaning as a concept only in the sense of a political process that approximates a normative preference of some kind.[5] In this sense, most of the analysis of political development in contemporary political science is deficient because of a failure to specify the normative justification for the characteristics of political systems that are identified as "developed."[6] From our point of view, *political development* is a *process* of continuous change in the adaptation of political systems to conflicting demands for justice, which we conceptualize as the capacity of political systems to maximize the opportunity of individuals to live their lives in the way they wish. *Political instability*, in contrast, is defined as a condition in political systems in which the institutionalized patterns of authority break down, and the expected compliance to political authorities is replaced by violence intended to change the personnel, policies or sovereignty of the authorities through injury to persons or property. While it is clear that violence obstructs the opportunity of people to live their lives in the way they wish, it is also clear that established and stable patterns of political authority are no guarantee of justice, and that violence may well promote the opportunites for justice for some or even most actors in the political system.

Leaving aside the critical, but difficult, evaluations of the relationship between political instability and political development in concrete historical situations, political scientists have been interested in the no less relevant questions of the conditions under which the likelihood of political instability is increased or reduced. The terminology varies, but whether the subject matter is defined as political instability,[8] political violence,[9] conflict behavior,[10] internal war,[11] or civil strife,[12] the phenomena under investigation have included revolutions, rebellions, civil and guerrilla wars, coups d'etat and riots. This agreement on the richness of ordinary language in describing different kinds of events has, however, created one of the issues to which most attention has been given by political scientists: namely, how to systematically categorize and measure what we have chosen to refer to generically as political instability.

It has been assumed, perhaps too naively, that there is relatively little difficulty in recording the incidence of events in which political violence occurs, but there is little agreement as to how these events shall be classified or weighted as types or intensities of political instability. Factor analysis has been widely used as an inductive approach to typologies of political instability, and factor solutions of variables measuring the frequency in nations of revolts, civil wars, coups d'etat, and so on, have been interpreted as revealing either two or three dimensions of political instability. These dimensions have been labelled variously as revolution, subversion and turmoil;[13] internal war and turmoil;[14] or organized and anomic violence;[15] and, on the basis of these results, more recent research is based on the direct coding of raw data as incidents of internal war, conspiracy and anomic violence.[16] In response to this linguistic and empirical confusion, other political scientists have criticized the attempt to categorize types of political instability as being dependent more on statistical explanation than analytic needs,[17] and they have chosen to treat events described by different words in ordinary language as instances of a single behavioral phenomenon, which they define broadly as internal war, revolution,[18] or mass violence.[19] Similarly, it has been suggested that a simple index of the number of persons killed in domestic group violence is the most satisfactory indication of political instability in nations.[20]

It is clear that it *is* important to distinguish between types of political instability. In accordance with what we have said in defining political development and political instability, we suggest that political instability is the result of conflict between different groups over the values according to which justice is defined, and according to which rewards are allocated in the political system. Theoretically, therefore, it is anticipated that the nature of political instability will vary according to the nature of the groups involved in political conflict, and that the processes that inhibit or intensify the likelihood of political instability will be different for the various types of conflict observed in African nations. In what follows, therefore, political instability is categorized and measured in terms of the organizational basis of the insurgent groups involved in political violence, and the structural alterations they intend to realize in the political system.

We distinguish between three different kinds of social grouping or organization as distinctive actors in events involving political violence: elites, communal groups and mass movements. Depending on which of these three actors are the insurgents in an event involving political violence, we distinguish between elite, communal and mass instability. *Elites* are those relatively small groups who hold the command positions in social institutions, and elite instability is violent action by members of either the political elite, or some alternative elite which is intended to remove persons from their positions of authority in the government. *Communal groups* are large social groups in which membership is based on ascribed characteristics of ethnicity, language, religion or territory; communal instability is violent action by members of one or more communal groups who aim to restructure the distribution of authority or rewards among communal groups, or between communal groups and the national government. *Mass movements* are large social groups organized for the attainment of relatively specific political goals; membership in mass movements is based on the associational or voluntary commitment of individuals to these goals. Mass instability is violent action by mass movements intended to reorganize the structure and policy of the national government. This typology[21] is elaborated in terms of the kinds of events we have coded and represented in quantitative indices of political instability. *Elite instability* involves limited violence and structural reorganization. The characteristic behaviors involving elites in conflict are (1) the replacement or reorganization of elite personnel by dismissal, resignation, and reallocation of persons in elite office; and (2) coups d'etat organized from within a single elite, or by an alternative functional elite, usually the military. Table 5.1 gives data on the extent of elite instability as measured by the frequency of dismissals and resignations of cabinet officials. Table 5.2 gives a composite index of the frequency of coups, attempted coups and alleged plots for coups d'état.

Communal instability involves much more extensive violence than elite instability, and threatens more extensive change in the structure of the political system. The events coded as communal instability are: (1) civil wars, in which one or more communities engage in violence to alter their authority relationships within the national unit, mostly by attempted secession; (2) rebellions, in which a community seeks to gain a significant measure of autonomy from the elite controlling the wider political system of which it is a part; and (3) irredentism, in which a community seeks to change its political allegiance from one national political elite to another or to a new political system, in which the members of the new polity have closer communal ties with the community involved than with their fellow citizens in the established political system. We have also coded instances of inter-ethnic violence which are not aimed at secession, autonomy, or political realignment, but which nevertheless represent a breakdown of authority relationships within the political system. Table 5.3 gives a weighted measure of communal instability. The specific events incorporated in this measure, as in the elite instability measures, are given by country in Part II of this Handbook.

Mass instability involves revolts or revolutions in which agents and supporters of the established political authority are attacked by insurgents whose primary source of common identity is their associational membership in a political movement, rather than any ascriptive communal identity. Mass instability, in these terms, is very difficult to isolate in contemporary African nations[22]—the revolt in Zaire coordinated by the *Comité Nationale de Liberation*, the revolt in Malawi in support of Chipembere, the sporadic revolt in Niger led by the Sawaba party, the revolt against the Sudanese military government in 1964, and opposition to the Dergue through various peasant uprisings and support for secessionist movements in Ethiopia are instances of significant political violence in the post-independence period in which associational rather than communal organization may have been a predominant characteristic of the insurgents. In a number of countries mass instability before independence was a significant political factor. Examples of this are the *Union de Population de Cameroons* in the Cameroons and the independence movements in Zimbabwe and Mozambique.

Finally we are generally unable to distinguish from available sources whether events such as riots, demonstrations, and strikes are based on communal rather than associational organization, and whether the intention of such activity is political reorganization or more restricted social change. We are reluctant therefore, to classify such phenomena as a form of political instability, and certainly disagree with the classification of such events as anomic or unorganized. Since there is no doubt a connection between such activity and forms of instability, however, and since measures of this kind are so frequently used in the study of political instability, we give a composite measure of turmoil in Table 5.4.

All forms of instability involve violence,[23] and in the most extreme cases, death. Table 5.5 gives figures on the number of persons killed in domestic violence, giving credence to our reasoning that communal instability involves more violence than elite instability, because the correlations between the number of persons killed in do-

mestic violence and measures of communal instabilty are uniformly higher than the comparable relationship with measures of elite instability.[24] Finally, Table 5.6 gives a measure of the durability of regimes in these Black African countries.

The intelligibility of this classification and measurement of political instability in Black African nations is indicated by the empirical tendency for measures of the frequency of different events classified together to covary and cluster as independent dimensions describing the political instability of these nations. We have reported elsewhere on the evidence for this dimensionality of political instability,[25] and the data in the following table provide more up to date and more incisive evidence of this pattern underlying the frequency counts of the various political instability indicators.

Useful though these factor analytic results are to the evaluation of our classification of types of political instability, it is important to bear in mind that the orthogonal rotation necessarily manufactures a statistical independence between different types of political instability, and thereby obscures relationships between them particularly those relationships having to do with the temporal sequencing of events. As we have shown before,[26] from corelations between measures of different types of political instability aggregated for the periods 1960—64 and 1965—69 in these nations, types of instability covary across these nations. Elite instability is more likely to be followed than preceded by communal instability, and turmoil is more likely to follow than precede communal and elite instability. These results suggest the hypothesis that communal instability in these nations is often a response on the part of communal groupings in national populations to elite instability which either fails to bring about a reapportionment of ethnic representation in government or a redistribution of other goods, or which effects a too radical reapportionment and redistributiion, and that turmoil is a localized response to such failures in countries which have experienced elite and communal instability.

It will be important in future research to look more closely at such sequencing in processes of political instability, particularly that within individual countries over time. As a prelude to such research, we present in Figures 5.1, 5.2, and 5.3, graphs representing the frequency over time of different types of political instability within the region as a whole. Whether or not the patterns of declining numbers of coups d'etat and civil wars, of the tendency for the number of civil wars to increase, and fall off, somewhat after the number of coups, and of the trend of plots and attempted but unsuccessful coups to rise over time, will be further evidence *within* these na-

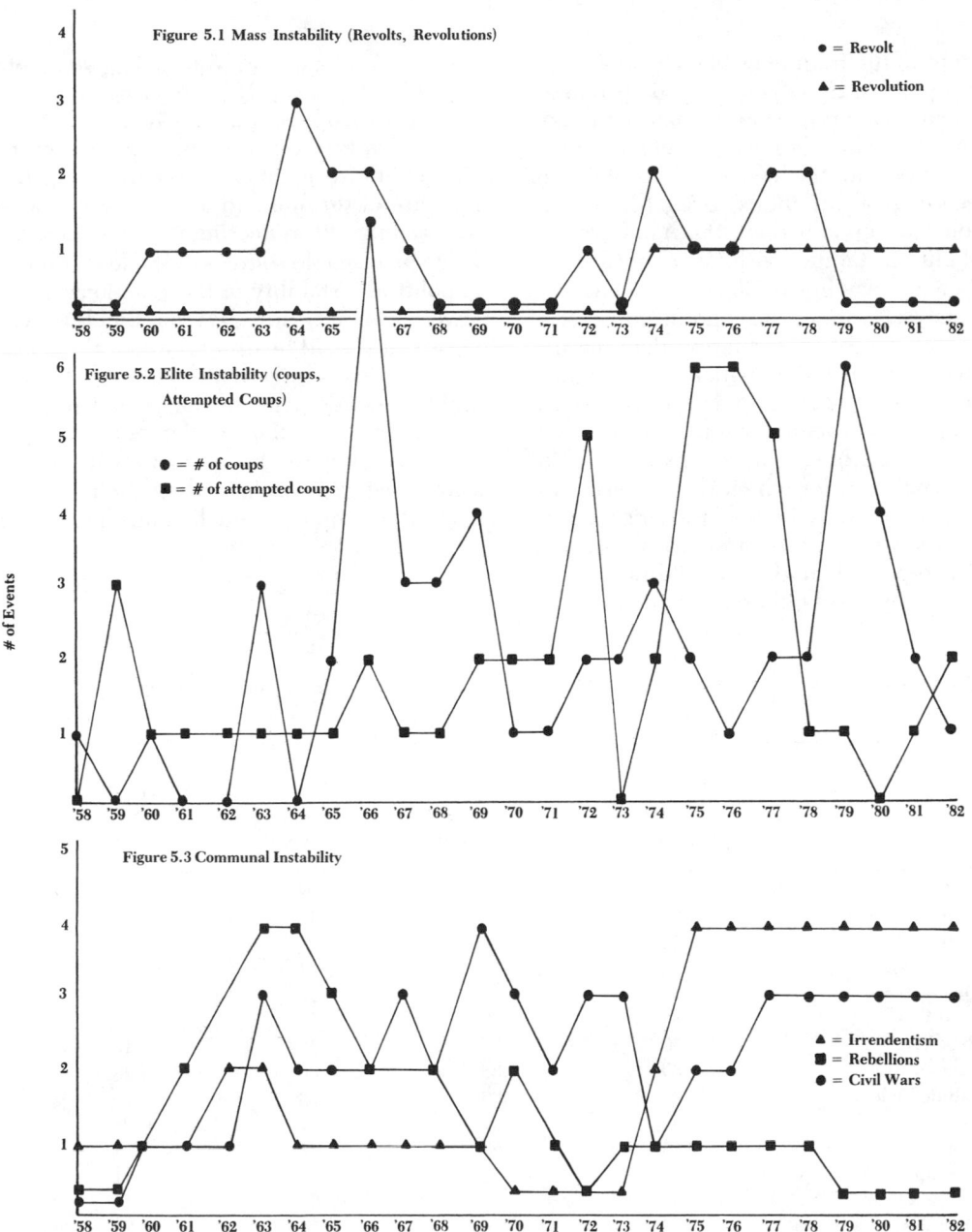

Figure 5.1 Mass Instability (Revolts, Revolutions)

● = Revolt
▲ = Revolution

Figure 5.2 Elite Instability (coups, Attempted Coups)

● = # of coups
■ = # of attempted coups

# of Events

Figure 5.3 Communal Instability

▲ = Irrendentism
■ = Rebellions
● = Civil Wars

tions, and whether such patterns reflect any greater institutional capacity to contain political instability in these nations in the near future, are questions of some interest. Annual data for individual countries are provided in Part II.

Reliability of Political Instability Data

The stability of factor analytic solutions of our measures of political instability in Black African nations in different periods gives credibility to the reliability and validity of these measures. It is clear, nevertheless, that errors in the measurement of political instability may result from definitional ambiguity in the operationalization of individual measures, and from lack of comparability in the coverage of different events in different sources. We are satisfied that there is high agreement between different members of our own research project who have coded political instability events for the same countries using the same sources, but independent research has also supported the reliability of these political instability measures.

The measurement of the frequency of coups d'etat, attempted coups and plots in these countries by two independent authors using different source material differs very little from our own. Correlations between our measure of elite instability and the coup activity index of Wells[27] and a recoding of our index using the data in work by Thompson[28] are greater than .90. A comparison of our measure of elite instability with Gurr's measure of the magnitude of conspiracy in the Black African nations included in his analysis[29] shows no significant correlations, but Gurr includes other information than the frequency of coups d'état in his index, which, furthermore, he standardizes by meures of the population size in each country. A more meaningful comparison with the Gurr data involves our measure of communal instability with his measure of internal war, for which the correlation is .72. In addition, the correlation between Gurr's composite measure of civil strife and the summary measure of political instability reported in the first edition of our data is .82, and the measure of political instability developed by Adelman and Morris[30] for some of these nations during the period 1957 to 1962 is highly correlated (r = .81) with our comparable data.

Data on turmoil and violence are very much less reliable for these nations. The correlation between Gurr's measure of turmoil and a comparable measure from our data is only .40, reflecting the much less systematic coverage in available sources of the less "dramatic" instances of political instability in these nations. In addition to this lower reliability for data on the less widely reported events, it should be observed that the quantity and quality of original source material available to us was considerably less adequate in the period prior to rather than after 1964 when the regular publication of the *Africa Research Bulletin* began, and within that period the source material was less adequate for the smaller, particularly the formerly French-controlled, territories.

Figure 5.4   Rotated Factor Matrix of Instability Measures for 30 Black African Nations, Independence to 1972.

VARIABLES*	FACTORS			
	I. Communal Instability	II. Elite Instability	III. Mass Instability	IV. Turmoil
Riots	.50	−.26	.02	−.61
Demonstrations	.56	−.27	−.16	−.47
Strikes	.20	−.03	−.09	−.82
Terrorism	.32	−.02	−.01	−.15
Declarations	.56	−.34	−.11	−.52
Civil War	.85	−.10	−.28	−.18
Rebellion	.50	−.28	−.18	−.10
Irredentism	.50	.38	.06	−.24
Ethnic Violence	.03	−.03	−.23	−.76
Revolts	−.03	.01	−.91	−.08
Plots	.12	−.83	−.13	−.13
Attempted Coups	.32	−.72	−.09	.11
Coups d'État	−.01	−.78	.01	−.47
Mutinies	.17	−.25	−.71	−.32
Percent of Variance accounted for—	17.9	17.0	11.2	16.5
Percent Total Variance accounted for by 4 factors—65%				

*All variables transformed to the form $\log_{10} (x + 1)$ to eliminate skew in their distributions. Each variable is the measure of the number of events reported, or the number of years in which an event was reported, in each nation in the period from its independence through 1972. The countries compared in this analysis do not include Botswana, Lesotho, Angola, Mozambique, Guinea-Bissau, or Equatorial Guinea, where independence was relatively more delayed than in most Black African states.

TABLE 5.1   Cabinet Resignations and Dismissals as a Proportion of Cabinet Size, Average Annual Rate: Independence to 1972 (A); Independence to 1967 (B); and 1968 to 1972 (C).

Definition: The number of resignations or dismissals has been coded for each year in the period from independence to December 31, 1972 and this number is standardized as a proportion of the largest size of the cabinet in the relevant year. Changes in cabinet personnel as an immediate result of coups d'etat or elections are *not* taken into account in these calculations. The index in this table is the *average* ratio of resignations and dismissals to cabinet size per annum for each period.

```
Range =            .64
Mean =             .18
Standard Deviation =          .13
```

Population Percent Cum.	Country	Rank	Country Name	A	Range Decile	B	C
8.29	8.29	1.0	Zaire	.64	1	.80	.38
9.29	1.00	2.5	Benin	.40	4	.22	.65
10.32	1.03	2.5	Somalia	.40		.38	.43
11.60	1.28	4.5	Burundi	.34	5	.38	.29
17.84	6.24	4.5	Sudan	.34		.33	.38
18.29	.45	6.0	Congo	.31	6	.18	.48
18.75	.46	7.0	Mauritania	.28		.35	.17
18.91	.16	8.0	Gabon	.26		.34	.15
20.57	1.66	9.0	Malawi	.25	7	.37	.17
21.91	1.34	10.0	Chad	.22		.25	.18
24.32	2.41	11.5	Cameroon	.19	8	.19	.18
25.07	.75	11.5	Togo	.19		.25	.09
28.58	3.51	13.0	Ghana	.18		.18	.18
30.15	1.57	15.0	Guinea	.16		.10	.27
31.79	1.64	15.0	Senegal	.16		.16	.16
36.95	5.16	15.0	Tanzania	.16		.14	.20
37.53	.58	17.5	Central African R	.15		.07	.27
38.06	.53	17.5	Liberia	.15		.13	.13
40.28	2.22	20.5	Ivory Coast	.14		.21	.03
42.15	1.87	20.5	Mali	.14		.12	.16
42.31	.16	20.5	Swaziland	.14		0	.16
44.28	1.97	20.5	Upper Volta	.14		.23	.01
44.45	.17	23.5	Gambia	.12	9	.07	.14
46.10	1.65	23.5	Zambia	.12		.07	.15
47.09	.99	25.0	Sierra Leone	.11		.09	.15
47.47	.38	26.5	Lesotho	.10		0	.12
48.83	1.36	26.5	Rwanda	.10		.12	.07
50.16	1.33	28.0	Niger	.08		.03	.06
71.16	21.00	29.0	Nigeria	.07		.08	.05
75.11	3.95	30.0	Uganda	.03	10	.05	.01
79.71	4.60	31.0	Kenya	.02		.05	0
79.94	.23	32.5	Botswana	0		0	0
80.04	.10	32.5	Equatorial Guinea	0		0	0

DATA NOT AVAILABLE OR NOT APPLICABLE
FOR THE FOLLOWING COUNTRIES

Angola	Djibouti	Ethiopia	Guinea-Bissau
Madagascar	Mozambique	Namibia	Zimbabwe

SOURCES: *Africa Digest, Africa Report, Africa Diary, African Research Bulletin, Europa Yearbook* and *Middle East Journal*. A compilation from French language newspapers prepared by George Martens at Northwestern University and Crawford Young's *Politics in the Congo* (Princeton, N.J.: Princeton University Press, 1966), was used both to supplement the general reference works and for the early post-independence period.

TABLE 5.2   Average Annual Elite Instability, Independence to 1979 (A); Independence to 1975 (B); Independence to 1969 (C), and 1970—1975 (D).

Definition: A numerical weight was given to coups d'etat (5), attempted coups (3), and plots (1).* The indexes given here are the sum of the scores for all such events coded for a given country during the period indicated, divided by the number of years in the period.

Range = 2.82
Mean = .79
Standard Deviation = .69

Population Percent Cum.	Country	Rank	Country Name	A	Range Decile	B	C	D
3.95	3.95	1.0	Uganda	2.82	1	2.05	1.11	3.17
4.95	1.00	2.0	Benin	2.26	2	2.55	2.80	2.17
5.40	.45	3.0	Congo	2.16	3	2.09	2.47	1.50
11.64	6.24	4.0	Sudan	2.04		1.70	1.57	2.00
15.15	3.51	5.0	Ghana	1.68	5	1.28	1.02	1.83
16.43	1.28	6.0	Burundi	1.47		1.48	2.13	.67
16.53	.10	7.0	Equatorial Guinea	1.36	6	1.25	6.67	.17
16.91	.38	8.0	Lesotho	1.30		1.20	.31	1.67
17.66	.75	9.0	Togo	1.21		1.72	2.16	.17
25.95	8.29	10.0	Zaire	1.16		1.42	2.11	3.67
26.53	.58	11.0	Central African R	1.11	7	.72	.86	.50
28.10	1.57	12.5	Guinea	.95		1.10	.63	2.00
49.10	21.00	12.5	Nigeria	.95		1.18	1.29	1.00
50.09	.99	14.0	Sierra Leone	.94		1.16	1.26	1.00
51.43	1.34	15.5	Chad	.79	8	.78	.54	1.17
53.40	1.97	15.5	Upper Volta	.79		.78	.75	.83
55.35	1.95	17.0	Angola	.75				
56.38	1.03	18.0	Somalia	.68		.65	.84	.33
56.84	.46	19.0	Mauritania	.58		.07		.17
66.55	9.71	20.0	Ethiopia	.54	9	.43	.27	.83
69.03	2.48	21.5	Madagascar	.53		.39	.63	
70.90	1.87	21.5	Mali	.53		.53	.76	.17
72.23	1.33	23.0	Niger	.52		.46	.11	1.00
72.39	.16	24.0	Swaziland	.45		.69		.83
72.58	.19	25.0	Guinea-Bissau	.40				
74.22	1.64	26.0	Senegal	.32		.39	.65	
75.58	1.36	27.0	Rwanda	.29		.37	0	.83
80.18	4.60	28.5	Kenya	.25	10	.25	.17	.33
83.17	2.99	28.5	Mozambique	.25				
88.33	5.16	30.0	Tanzania	.22				
88.49	.16	31.5	Gabon	.16		.20	.32	
90.71	2.22	31.5	Ivory Coast	.16		.20	.22	.17
91.24	.53	33.0	Liberia	.14		.38	.40	.33
93.65	2.41	34.0	Cameroon	.11		.06	.10	
95.30	1.65	35.0	Zambia	.07		.09	0	.17
95.53	.23	37.0	Botswana	0		0	0	0
95.70	.17	37.0	Gambia	0		0	0	0
97.36	1.66	37.0	Malawi	0		0	0	0

DATA NOT AVAILABLE OR NOT APPLICABLE FOR THE FOLLOWING COUNTRIES

Djibouti   Namibia   Zimbabwe

SOURCES: The same as Table 5.1. In addition, reference was made to *Deadline Data* and *The New York Times Index*.

* A *coup d'etat* is defined as an event in which the existing political regime is suddenly and illegally displaced by the action of relatively small elite groups without an overt mass participation in the event. The scope of change in the regime resulting from coups d'etat may vary from the wholesale replacement of political decision-makers by instigators of the coup and their followers, to a dissolution of the constitutional relationships between different groups of decision-makers (e.g., the dissolution of legislatures) without any substantial replacement of decision-makers. The coup may be organized by members of the governing elite (palace revolution), or by members of an alternate elite (notably the military). The stated aims of the insurgent elite may vary from reaction to reform, and the degree of physical injury resulting from a coup may be negligible or pronounced.

Attempted coups are unsuccessful coups d'etat, in which an insurgent elite fails to effect any lasting displacement of the political regime, but is known to have succeeded in some combination of the following: (a) the assassination, attempted assassination, or arrest of some members of the political elite; (b) the temporary (for less than a week) disruption, interruption, or takeover of government facilities; and (c) the sudden mutiny, mobilization of, or action by armed forces *explicitly* aimed at the takeover of government.

Plots are events in which an announcement or admission is made by the elite group in power that a plot to overthrow the government by violence has been discovered. Reported plots may take various forms ranging from a simple statement that a plot has been thwarted, without further elaboration, to the arrest, identification, and trial of alleged plotters. Plots may in fact be manufactured by the government as a pretext for the elimination of competing elites or for the imposition of extreme or coercive policies. Although there is no reliable means by which the researcher can clearly distinguish between bona fide plots and manufactured allegations, the "reported plot" may in any case be viewed as a political datum, indicative of elite instability.

TABLE 5.3   Average Annual Communal Instability, Independence
to 1979 (A), Independence to 1975 (B); Independence to
1969 (C); and 1970—1975 (D).

Definition: A numerical weight was given to civil wars (5), rebellions
(4), irredentism (3), and ethnic violence (1).* The index was computed
by multiplying the score for each event by the number of years in which
it was reported in any country, and by summing the resultant scores.
The scores presented are the total score divided by the number of years
in the period.

Range =   6.25
Mean =   .72
Standard Deviation =   1.36

Population Percent		Country			Range			
Cum.	Country	Rank	Name	A	Decile	B	C	D
1.95	1.95	1.0	Angola	6.25	1	5.00	0	5.00
11.66	9.71	2.0	Ethiopia	4.37	4	3.48	2.87	5.00
13.00	1.34	3.0	Chad	3.63	5	3.20	2.26	4.67
19.24	6.24	4.0	Sudan	2.52	6	2.90	2.79	3.17
27.53	8.29	5.0	Zaire	1.42	8	1.74	2.84	0
32.13	4.60	6.0	Kenya	1.37		1.83	3.67	0
53.13	21.00	7.0	Nigeria	1.26		1.57	2.58	0
54.49	1.36	8.5	Rwanda	1.18	9	1.48	2.00	.83
58.44	3.95	8.5	Uganda	1.18		1.52	2.64	.17
59.72	1.28	10.0	Burundi	.88		1.11	.67	1.67
61.94	2.22	11.0	Ivory Coast	.47	10	.59	.54	.67
63.81	1.87	12.0	Mali	.42		.53	.87	0
65.46	1.65	13.0	Zambia	.27		.36	.77	0
65.91	.45	14.5	Congo	.26		.33	.54	0
68.39	2.48	14.5	Madagascar	.26		.26	0	.67
69.42	1.03	16.0	Somalia	.21		.26	.42	0
72.93	3.51	17.0	Ghana	.18		.21	.31	0
73.93	1.00	19.0	Benin	.10		.13	.11	.17
76.34	2.41	19.0	Cameroon	.10		.06	.10	0
76.80	.46	19.0	Mauritania	.10		.13	.22	0
77.79	.99	21.0	Sierra Leone	.05		.07	.11	0
78.02	.23	29.5	Botswana	0		0	0	0
78.60	.58	29.5	Central African R	0		0	0	0
78.70	.10	29.5	Equatorial Guinea	0		0	0	0
78.86	.16	29.5	Gabon	0		0	0	0
79.03	.17	29.5	Gambia	0		0	0	0
80.60	1.57	29.5	Guinea	0		0	0	0
80.79	.19	29.5	Guinea-Bissau	0		0	0	0
81.17	.38	29.5	Lesotho	0		0	0	0
81.70	.53	29.5	Liberia	0		0	0	0
83.36	1.66	29.5	Malawi	0		0	0	0
84.69	1.33	29.5	Niger	0		0	0	0
86.33	1.64	29.5	Senegal	0		0	0	0
86.49	.16	29.5	Swaziland	0		0	0	0
91.65	5.16	29.5	Tanzania	0		0	0	0
92.40	.75	29.5	Togo	0		0	0	0
94.37	1.97	29.5	Upper Volta	0		0	0	0

DATA NOT AVAILABLE OR NOT APPLICABLE
FOR THE FOLLOWING COUNTRIES

Djibouti   Mozambique   Namibia   Zimbabwe

SOURCES: The same as Table 5.2. In addition, reference was made to Young, *Politics in the Congo*, and Jules Gerard-Libois, *Katanga Secession* (Madison: University of Wisconsin Press, 1966) for details of early events in Zaire; and to John P. MacKintosh, *Nigerian Government and Politics* (Evanston, Ill.: Northwestern University Press, 1966), for details of the Tiv rebellion in Nigeria.

* *Civil war* is defined as an event in which an identifiable communal group (in which membership is based on ascribed characteristics of ethnicity, or combinations of common language, and/or religion, and/or territory) seeks by violence to form a new political system based on boundaries of ethnic community, or attempts by violence to monopolize political power for the communal group within the existing political system.

Rebellion is defined as an event in which an identifiable communal group seeks by violence to gain increased autonomy from the national political authorities, or attacks supporters or agents of the national government without aiming to secede from or monopolize power within the existing political system.

Irredentism is defined as an event in which an identifiable communal group seeks to change its political allegiance from the government of the territorial unit in which it resides to a political system, either existing or to be created, in which the authorities share the communal identification of the irredentist group concerned. Successful irredentism, therefore, involves the establishment of new political units transcending (rather than coinciding with or incorporated within) existing national boundaries.

Ethnic violence is defined as an event of short duration (no more than a few days) in which two identifiable communal groups are antagonists in violence to secure some short-term goal, but are not designed to secure independence, autonomy, or political realignment for the groups concerned.

**TABLE 5.4   Average Annual Turmoil: Independence to 1974 (A), In-
dependence to 1969 (B), and 1970—1974 (C).**

Definition: This index is calculated as the sum of all reported riots,
demonstrations, strikes, terrorist events, and declarations of emergency* in the period from independence through December, 1974, divided by the number of years in the period.

```
Range =            2.61
Mean =              .70
Standard Deviation =          .60
```

Population Percent		Rank	Country Name	A	Range Decile	B	C
Cum.	Country						
1.00	1.00	1.0	Benin	2.61	1	3.44	1.60
9.29	8.29	2.0	Zaire	1.74	4	2.63	.40
10.94	1.65	3.0	Zambia	1.59		3.40	1.00
17.18	6.24	4.0	Sudan	1.55	5	1.86	0
20.69	3.51	5.0	Ghana	1.50		1.50	1.80
22.03	1.34	6.0	Chad	1.31		1.72	.80
31.74	9.71	7.0	Ethiopia	1.29	6	1.00	2.40
36.34	4.60	8.0	Kenya	1.25		2.33	.20
36.79	.45	9.0	Congo	1.05		1.29	.80
39.20	2.41	10.0	Cameroon	1.00	7	1.20	.80
40.19	.99	11.0	Sierra Leone	.95		1.03	1.00
40.57	.38	12.0	Lesotho	.86		1.25	.80
44.52	3.95	13.0	Uganda	.68	8	1.25	.80
44.98	.46	14.0	Mauritania	.66		1.09	0
46.31	1.33	15.0	Niger	.65		.43	1.20
47.59	1.28	16.5	Burundi	.52	9	.93	0
49.56	1.97	16.5	Upper Volta	.52		.65	.40
50.09	.53	18.0	Liberia	.48		.67	0
52.31	2.22	19.0	Ivory Coast	.46		.65	.20
52.47	.16	20.0	Gabon	.39		.43	.40
53.22	.75	21.0	Togo	.38		.52	.20
54.88	1.66	22.0	Malawi	.35		.55	.20
60.04	5.16	23.0	Tanzania	.33		.33	.40
60.27	.23	24.5	Botswana	.32		.91	0
61.30	1.03	24.5	Somalia	.32		.53	0
61.88	.58	26.0	Central African R	.26	10	0	.60
63.45	1.57	27.0	Guinea	.23		.35	0
64.81	1.36	28.5	Rwanda	.15		.27	0
66.45	1.64	28.5	Senegal	.15		.27	0
68.32	1.87	30.0	Mali	.13		.22	0
68.49	.17	31.5	Gambia	0		0	0
68.65	.16	31.5	Swaziland	0		0	0

DATA NOT AVAILABLE OR NOT APPLICABLE
FOR THE FOLLOWING COUNTRIES

```
Djibouti    Equatorial Guinea  Guinea-Bissau Madagascar
Namibia     Nigeria      Zimbabwe Angola  Mozambique
```

SOURCES: The same as Tables 5.2 and 5.3.

* *Riots* are defined as events involving relatively spontaneous, un-
planned, but violent activity, in which the generalized aim of the activity, or objects of aggression, are not coherently specified, but which
is responded to by political authorities and their supporters as subversive of "law and order."

Demonstrations are defined as events involving relatively organized
and nonviolent activity, in which the aim of the activity is to protest
some specific action on the part of domestic political authorities. When
demonstrations are counteracted by violence on the part of others (notably police), they become riots.

Strikes are defined as events involving organized disruptions of the
economy by groups who refuse to work at their regular employment in
order to react against, or bring pressure to bear on political or economic
authorities. A strike event is identified in terms of the organizational
unity of the strikers, not the economic or geographical differentiation of
work locations. A strike of mine workers which begins at one mine on
Monday and another mine on Wednesday is counted as one event not
two, which accounts for disparities between our coding and figures reported for strikes by other sources, in Zambia particularly.

Terrorism is defined as events involving organized and planned activity, on the part of small but cohesive groups, in which the aim of the
activity is to damage, injure, or eliminate government property or personnel. These activities include bomb plants, sabotage of electrical and
transportation facilities, assassinations (attempted and successful), and
isolated guerrilla activities.

Declaration of emergency is defined as a formal declaration of emergency by the national government in response to real or presumed
threats to public order.

TABLE 5.5   Average Annual Intensity of Violence in Political Instability Events, Independence through 1969.

Definition: This index is calculated as the average annual number of deaths per million population reported in instability events of all kinds in the period from independence through December, 1969.* In cases of conflicting reports, we have used the highest figure given, since we had no independent means of assessing the reliability of different reports.

Range =   8.30
Mean =   1.62
Standard Deviation =   2.13

Population Percent Cum.	Country	Rank	Country Name	A	Range Decile
21.00	21.00	1.0	Nigeria	8.3	1
22.36	1.36	2.0	Rwanda	6.5	3
30.65	8.29	3.0	Zaire	6.0	
31.93	1.28	4.0	Burundi	5.4	4
33.27	1.34	5.0	Chad	4.3	5
33.72	.45	6.0	Congo	3.7	6
38.32	4.60	7.0	Kenya	3.2	7
44.56	6.24	8.0	Sudan	2.5	
46.21	1.65	9.0	Zambia	2.1	8
48.62	2.41	10.5	Cameroon	2.0	
52.57	3.95	10.5	Uganda	2.0	
62.28	9.71	12.0	Ethiopia	1.8	
62.66	.38	13.5	Lesotho	1.6	9
63.12	.46	13.5	Mauritania	1.6	
63.28	.16	15.0	Gabon	1.5	
64.28	1.00	16.0	Benin	1.2	
65.03	.75	17.0	Togo	.6	10
66.02	.99	18.0	Sierra Leone	.5	
69.53	3.51	20.0	Ghana	.4	
71.19	1.66	20.0	Malawi	.4	
72.22	1.03	20.0	Somalia	.4	
74.44	2.22	22.5	Ivory Coast	.2	
79.60	5.16	22.5	Tanzania	.2	
80.18	.58	25.5	Central African R	.1	
80.71	.53	25.5	Liberia	.1	
82.04	1.33	25.5	Niger	.1	
83.68	1.64	25.5	Senegal	.1	
83.91	.23	30.0	Botswana	0	
84.08	.17	30.0	Gambia	0	
85.95	1.87	30.0	Mali	0	
86.11	.16	30.0	Swaziland	0	
88.08	1.97	30.0	Upper Volta	0	

DATA NOT AVAILABLE OR NOT APPLICABLE
FOR THE FOLLOWING COUNTRIES

Djibouti	Equatorial Guinea	Guinea	Madagascar
Namibia	Zimbabwe	Angola Guinea-Bissau	Mozambique

SOURCES: See Tables 5.2 and 5.3.

* This method has been used because it reduces the distortions in raw and often unreliable reports of death, and gives greater emphasis to the symbolic intensity of violence rather than the actual incidence of death. Angola, Djibouti, Guinea-Bissau, Mozambique, Namibia and Zimbabwe were not independent until after 1969 and therefore were not included in this table.

TABLE 5.6   Average Durability (in years) of Regimes from Independence through 1979.

Definition: Number of years from independence to 1979 divided by the number of regimes in the country during the period. A change of regime occurs whenever a new government comes to power.

Range =   20.20
Mean =   8.44
Standard Deviation =   5.87

Population Percent Cum.	Country	Rank	Country Name	A	Range Decile
1.57	1.57	1.0	Guinea	21.0	1
3.98	2.41	3.0	Cameroon	19.0	
6.20	2.22	3.0	Ivory Coast	19.0	
7.84	1.64	3.0	Senegal	19.0	
13.00	5.16	5.0	Tanzania	18.0	2
13.53	.53	6.0	Liberia	17.5	
15.19	1.66	7.5	Malawi	15.0	3
16.84	1.65	7.5	Zambia	15.0	
17.01	.17	9.0	Gambia	14.0	4
17.24	.23	10.5	Botswana	13.0	
17.62	.38	10.5	Lesotho	13.0	
17.78	.16	12.0	Swaziland	11.0	5
17.94	.16	14.5	Gabon	9.5	6
19.81	1.87	14.5	Mali	9.5	
21.14	1.33	14.5	Niger	9.5	
23.11	1.97	14.5	Upper Volta	9.5	
32.82	9.71	17.0	Ethiopia	8.8	7
34.18	1.36	18.0	Rwanda	8.5	
34.76	.58	20.0	Central African R	6.3	8
36.10	1.34	20.0	Chad	6.3	
37.13	1.03	20.0	Somalia	6.3	
37.23	.10	22.0	Equatorial Guinea	5.5	
37.42	.19	23.0	Guinea-Bissau	5.0	
37.88	.46	24.5	Mauritania	4.8	9
38.63	.75	24.5	Togo	4.8	
39.62	.99	26.0	Sierra Leone	4.5	
43.57	3.51	27.0	Uganda	4.3	
46.56	2.99	28.0	Mozambique	4.0	
49.04	2.48	29.0	Madagascar	3.8	
49.49	.45	31.0	Congo	3.2	
70.49	21.00	31.0	Nigeria	3.2	
78.78	8.29	31.0	Zaire	3.2	
82.29	3.51	33.0	Ghana	2.8	10
88.53	6.24	34.0	Sudan	2.6	
89.81	1.28	35.0	Burundi	2.1	
91.76	1.95	36.5	Angola	2.0	
91.86	.10	36.5	Djibouti	2.0	
92.86	1.00	38.0	Benin	1.7	
97.46	4.60	39.0	Kenya	.8	

DATA NOT AVAILABLE OR NOT APPLICABLE
FOR THE FOLLOWING COUNTRIES

Namibia	Zimbabwe

SOURCES: Table 5 in each of the country sections in Part II of this *Handbook*. Zimbabwe and Namibia are excluded from this calculation because they became independent after 1979.

Political Participation

It is a fundamental tenet of much contemporary political analysis that political development involves the progressive differentiation and autonomy of plural institutions with functionally specific interests in different modes of political activity, and that political order is a result of the longevity, adaptability and mutually congruent values characteristic of these different institutions, and of the checks and balances, and the need for compromise and accommodation, constraining different interests in a complex structure of relatively autonomous organizations.[31] The organization of political activity, following Almond and Coleman,[32] involves the development of institutional structures to deal with the basic functions of the socialization to political values, the communication of political information, the articulation and aggregation of political interests, rule making or legislation, rule implementation or the administration and enforcement of law, and rule adjudication or judicial arbitration.

Political institutionalization, which involves the process by which the organization of political activity acquires value and stability,[33] is marked in the new states of Africa more in the breach than the observance. Recent political history is characterized by the emergence of unitary and authoritarian political structures rather than by differentiated and competitive ones, and by the fragility rather than the longevity and adaptability of whatever national political institutions have emerged. Nowhere is this more obvious than in the history of political parties and elections in Black African states. Up until recent years there had been a widespread tendency towards the abolition of opposition political parties and competitive elections and a shift towards the diffuse one-party state, receptive to public opinion, if at all, through referenda as the only institutionalized means of the public expression of support and opposition. Recently, however, a number of states have converted from military regimes to multi-party civilian governments, these include Ghana, Nigeria, and Upper Volta. Senegal has changed from a single party civilian government to a multi-party system. Table 5.7 gives data on the number of years before independence that the first political party was established in these nations. Table 5.8 gives data on the number of years prior to the date of independence in which the first territory-wide election based on universal suffrage was held. It will be observed from these data that political parties were organized earlier, in general, in formerly British colonial territories than in the former French colonies, but that the experience of territory-wide elections with universal suffrage was somewhat more in advance of independence in French than in British colonies. It is

also the case that there were considerably *more* direct elections in French than in British colonies in the pre-independence period. Nevertheless, the transfer of the institutional structure for democratic politics was very much delayed throughout Africa, and the institutionalization of parties and elections was low as measured in terms of longevity. One should not however gloss over the variation in Tables 5.7 and 5.8, since correlations between these measures and measures of elite and communal instability are consistent with the hypothesis that the incidence of political instability has been lower where parties and elections were institutionalzied earlier.

The data in Table 5.9 give the voting turnout rate in elections closest but prior to the date of independence in these nations. As with the earlier and more frequent experience of elections in French as opposed to British colonies, higher rates of voting turnout were achieved earlier, and there was a generally higher rate of electoral participation in the elections leading to independence in French as compared to British colonies. That this greater scope of electoral participation is significant is indicated by correlations between data in Table 5.9 and measures of elite and communal instability which show that greater institutionalization of electoral practices measured in this way has been associated with less political instability. The data in Tables 5.10, 5.11 and 5.12 give some indication of the complexity and coherence of the political institutionalization of party and electoral systems. The data in Table 5.10 show the number of legal political parties that existed in the period from independence to 1979 and Table 5.11 indicates changes in the number of parties during the period. The correlations between these data and our measures of elite and communal instability indicate that countries with more numerous political parties were likely to experience greater political instability than countries with fewer political parties. More direct measures of the coherence or consolidation of political parties than the sheer numbers of political parties organized is given in Tables 5.12 and 5.13 where the data refer to the percentage of the vote given to ruling parties, and the fractionalization of party representation in legislatures, following the pre-independence elections in these countries. These latter measures show an even more pronounced association with measures of political instability—countries with greater legislative fractionalization being more likely to experience greater elite and communal instability than those less fractionalized, and countries with a greater percentage of the popular vote in support of ruling parties are less likely to experience these kinds of political instability in general.

Some indication of the autonomy of political party organizations is indicated by the data in Tables 5.14 and

5.15. The first of these tables shows organizational discontinuity in the party system—the extent to which party organization was characterized by splits and mergers rather than by the autonomous and stable development of individual parties. The data in Table 5.15 indicate more directly the limitations of the autonomy of political parties introduced by the banning or proscription of such organizations. These data do not distinguish between party discontinuity and proscription prior to the experience of political instability and that which resulted from political instability, so that one cannot meaningfully account for political instability by reference to them. With careful attention, however, to the sources of such data, and to the diagrammatic representation of party systems over time in Part II of this book, these data on party stability and autonomy can be recoded to explore the effects of party splits, mergers, proscriptions, and combinations of these in the past, on the subsequent stability of national regimes. Finally, it will be important to look in the future at one-party states in Black African nations for variation in the extent of participation, debate and opposition within the party framework, and for variation in the kinds of decisions and policy that emerge from party activity.[34]

Reliability of Party and Election Data

The collection of data on parties and elections in Black Africa requires searching numerous country-specific sources, and raises severe problems of inter-coder and inter-source reliability. The problem is magnified by the difficulty of precisely defining a *party*. The data presented here are based on information on all organizations that call themselves political parties. On this basis, we get fairly high reliabilty between coders using similar sources—we found that the average inter-coder reliability for coding the number of parties in each year after independence is $r = .91$. The critical problem in assessing the reliability of this information is the difficulty of assuring access to the relevant sources of information. Our data are based on an intensive search of case study materials for each country, and a systematic search of new sources and yearbooks. From these sources we diagrammed the historical development of political parties, as shown in Part II of this Handbook, and had these diagrams checked by 'experts' for many of the countries. The reliability of data gathered in this way is contingent not only on coder error, but more critically on the expectation that researchers can be expected to reference the same sources. The reliability of election data is less affected by the difficulty of assuring comprehensive coverage in the source material, although there are no easily available single sources of information on the elections

and referenda in these countries, especially not for the pre-independence period. Errors in the reporting of voting turnout no doubt exist, but we have no reasonable estimate of their distribution.

TABLE 5.7 Number of Years from the Establishment of the First Political Party to Independence.

Note: Since Namibia is still not independent as of mid-1983, it has not been included in this table.

Definition: Any organization open to African membership and either calling itself a political party, or having a specific program for changing the structure of territorial government, is considered to be a political party.

```
Range =          95.00
Mean =           18.25
Standard Deviation =          15.27
```

Population Percent Cum.	Country	Rank	Country Name	A	Range Decile
.53	.53	1.0	Liberia	95	1
5.13	4.60	2.0	Kenya	43	6
5.29	.16	3.0	Gabon	40	
26.29	21.00	4.0	Nigeria	37	7
31.45	5.16	5.0	Tanzania	31	
35.40	3.95	6.0	Uganda	27	8
35.57	.17	7.5	Gambia	24	
37.21	1.64	7.5	Senegal	24	
39.16	1.95	9.0	Angola	22	
40.82	1.66	10.0	Malawi	20	
41.01	.19	11.5	Guinea-Bissau	19	9
43.27	2.26	11.5	Zimbabwe	19	
44.92	1.65	13.0	Zambia	18	
45.95	1.03	14.0	Somalia	17	
48.94	2.99	15.5	Mozambique	15	
50.91	1.97	15.5	Upper Volta	15	
51.91	1.00	22.5	Benin	14	
52.49	.58	22.5	Central African R	14	
53.83	1.34	22.5	Chad	14	
54.28	.45	22.5	Congo	14	
54.38	.10	22.5	Djibouti	14	
56.60	2.22	22.5	Ivory Coast	14	
56.98	.38	22.5	Lesotho	14	
59.46	2.48	22.5	Madagascar	14	
61.33	1.87	22.5	Mali	14	
61.79	.46	22.5	Mauritania	14	
63.12	1.33	22.5	Niger	14	
63.87	.75	22.5	Togo	14	
66.28	2.41	30.0	Cameroon	12	
67.85	1.57	30.0	Guinea	12	
74.09	6.24	30.0	Sudan	12	
75.08	.99	32.0	Sierra Leone	11	
78.59	3.51	33.5	Ghana	10	
86.88	8.29	33.5	Zaire	10	
86.98	.10	35.5	Equatorial Guinea	8	10
87.14	.16	35.5	Swaziland	8	
87.37	.23	37.0	Botswana	7	
88.65	1.28	38.5	Burundi	3	
90.01	1.36	38.5	Rwanda	3	
99.72	9.71	40.0	Ethiopia	0	

DATA NOT AVAILABLE OR NOT APPLICABLE
FOR THE FOLLOWING COUNTRIES

Namibia

SOURCES: Ruth Schachter Morgenthau, *Political Parties in French-Speaking West Africa* (London: Oxford University Press, 1964). *Burundi, Congo, Zaire, Liberia, Rwanda, Togo*: Ronald Segal, *Political Africa: A Who's Who of Personalities and Parties* (New York: Praeger, 1961); *CAR, Chad, Gabon*: Virginia Thompson and Richard Adloff, *The Emerging States of French Equatorial Africa* (London: Oxford University Press, 1960). (For Gabon, the actual date of the founding of *Jeune Gabonaise* is not given. Thompson and Adloff say it was founded in the post-World War I depression.) *Kenya, Malawi, Tanzania, Uganda, Zambia*: Stanley Diamond and Fred G. Burke, eds., *The Transformation of East Africa* (New York: Basic Books, 1966); *Nigeria*: Richard L. Sklar, *Nigerian Political Parties* (Princeton, N.J.: Princeton University Press, 1963); *Gambia*: Harry A. Gailey, *A History of the Gambia* (New York: Praeger, 1965); *Somalia*: I.M. Lewis, *The Modern History of Somaliland* (New York: Praeger, 1965); *Sudan*: P.M. Holt, *A Modern History of the Sudan* (New York: Grove Press, 1961); *Botswana, Ghana*: Colin Legum, ed., *Africa: A Handbook to the Continent* (London: Anthony Blond, 1961); *Cameroon*: Victor LeVine, *Cameroon: From Mandate to Independence* (Berkeley: University of California Press, 1964); *Sierra Leone*: James S. Coleman and Carl G. Rosberg, Jr., eds., *Political Parties and National Integration in Tropical Africa* (Berkeley: University of California Press, 1966); *Lesotho*: J.E. Spence, *Lesotho: The Politics of Dependence* (London: Oxford University Press, 1966); *Ethiopia*: No parties.

TABLE 5.8 Number of Years before Independence to Date of First Territory-Wide, General Election to Central Legislature.

Note: Since Namibia is not independent, it has not been included in this table.

```
Range =          10.00
Mean =            3.40
Standard Deviation =          2.19
```

Population Percent		Rank	Country Name	A	Range Decile
Cum.	Country				
.99	.99	1.0	Sierra Leone	10	1
21.99	21.00	2.0	Nigeria	9	2
25.50	3.51	3.0	Ghana	7	3
25.88	.38	4.0	Lesotho	6	4
26.05	.17	5.0	Gambia	5	5
27.05	1.00	13.0	Benin	4	6
29.46	2.41	13.0	Cameroon	4	7
30.04	.58	13.0	Central African R	4	
31.38	1.34	13.0	Chad	4	
31.83	.45	13.0	Congo	4	
31.99	.16	13.0	Gabon	4	
34.21	2.22	13.0	Ivory Coast	4	
36.69	2.48	13.0	Madagascar	4	
38.56	1.87	13.0	Mali	4	
39.02	.46	13.0	Mauritania	4	
40.35	1.33	13.0	Niger	4	
41.99	1.64	13.0	Senegal	4	
42.15	.16	13.0	Swaziland	4	
42.90	.75	13.0	Togo	4	
44.87	1.97	13.0	Upper Volta	4	
46.53	1.66	21.5	Malawi	3	8
52.77	6.24	21.5	Sudan	3	
54.34	1.57	24.5	Guinea	2	9
58.94	4.60	24.5	Kenya	2	
64.10	5.16	24.5	Tanzania	2	
65.75	1.65	24.5	Zambia	2	
65.98	.23	30.5	Botswana	1	10
67.26	1.28	30.5	Burundi	1	
67.36	.10	30.5	Djibouti	1	
68.72	1.36	30.5	Rwanda	1	
69.75	1.03	30.5	Somalia	1	
73.70	3.95	30.5	Uganda	1	
81.99	8.29	30.5	Zaire	1	
84.25	2.26	30.5	Zimbabwe	1	
84.35	.10	35.0	Equatorial Guinea	0	

```
DATA NOT AVAILABLE OR NOT APPLICABLE
FOR THE FOLLOWING COUNTRIES

Angola       Ethiopia    Guinea-Bissau
Mozambique   Namibia     Liberia
```

SOURCES: Figures in Part II on Parties and Elections *Ethiopia* and *Liberia* were not colonies. *Angola, Guinea-Bissau* and *Mozambique* did not have pre-independence territory-wide general elections.

TABLE 5.9 Voting Turnout at Independence.

Definition: Number of persons voting in the national legislative election closest to, but before, the date of independence, as a percentage of the total population in that year.

```
Range =        61.00
Mean =         24.94
Standard Deviation =          13.71
```

Population Percent			Country			
Cum.	Country	Rank	Name		A	Range Decile
.16	.16	1.0	Swaziland		62	1
.54	.38	2.0	Lesotho		52	2
1.90	1.36	3.0	Rwanda		46	3
4.12	2.22	4.0	Ivory Coast		45	
4.58	.46	5.5	Mauritania		38	4
6.84	2.26	5.5	Zimbabwe		38	
7.01	.17	7.5	Gambia		37	5
8.66	1.65	7.5	Zambia		37	
9.11	.45	9.5	Congo		34	
9.27	.16	9.5	Gabon		34	
9.37	.10	11.0	Equatorial Guinea		33	
11.78	2.41	12.0	Cameroon		30	6
13.42	1.64	13.0	Senegal		28	
13.95	.53	14.0	Liberia		27	
15.23	1.28	15.0	Burundi		26	
15.46	.23	16.5	Botswana		23	7
16.21	.75	16.5	Togo		23	
17.78	1.57	19.0	Guinea		22	
22.38	4.60	19.0	Kenya		22	
24.35	1.97	19.0	Upper Volta		22	
25.35	1.00	22.0	Benin		20	
26.38	1.03	22.0	Somalia		20	
34.67	8.29	22.0	Zaire		20	
36.01	1.34	24.0	Chad		19	8
37.88	1.87	25.0	Mali		18	
58.88	21.00	26.0	Nigeria		16	
62.83	3.95	27.0	Uganda		15	
72.54	9.71	28.0	Ethiopia		13	9
73.87	1.33	29.0	Niger		12	
77.38	3.51	30.0	Ghana		11	
83.62	6.24	31.0	Sudan		10	
84.20	.58	32.5	Central African R		8	
85.19	.99	32.5	Sierra Leone		8	
86.85	1.66	34.0	Malawi		3	10
92.01	5.16	35.0	Tanzania		1	

```
DATA NOT AVAILABLE OR NOT APPLICABLE
FOR THE FOLLOWING COUNTRIES

Angola      Djibouti    Guinea-Bissau Madagascar
Mozambique  Namibia
```

SOURCES: Same as those listed in Table 5.12 with the following additions: *Cameroon*: The first federal elections for President were held in 1965, and the data are based on that election. Members of the National Assembly are chosen by state legislators; *Congo*: Le Monde, June 16, 1959, p. 1; *Ethiopia*: *A Review of Elections 1961 and 1962* (London 1964), p. 77 for election in 1957, the first election ever held in Ethiopia; *Gambia*: Gambia Echo, June 4, 1962, p. 2; *Liberia*: In Liberia, election results for 1959 seem less than credible; Tubman received 537,472 votes with 55 votes for his opponent. Data for the 1955 election is used here. See G. Carter, *African One-Party States*; *Malawi*: In Malawi the April 1964 elections were not held because the candidates of the M.C.P. were unopposed. The estimate of voters is based on the fact that 1,871,170 people were registered to vote; *Niger, Upper Volta*: These data are taken from the unpublished dissertation research files of George Martens, Northwestern University, who spent 1968—1969 doing field work in Niger and Upper Volta; *Somalia*: Touval, *Somali Nationalism*, gives 313,760 voting in the Trust Territory of Somalia but no data for British Somaliland. We estimate 400,000 voting in both Somali territories: *Sudan*: Data for the 1958 election from *Electoral Commission Final Report, Parliamentary Elections 1957/8.* (Khartoum: 1958), p. 59; *Tanzania*: In Tanzania the low turnout is partially explained by a April 18, 1962. *Zimbabwe: Africa South of the Sahara,* 1982—1983. Zimbabwe election figures are for the February 1980 elections. Turnout figures were obtained from the *New York Times.* Angola, Mozambique, and Guinea-Bissau did not have national elections with a universal franchise before independence. Namibia has still not gained independence. Equatorial Guinea for the September 20, 1968 election. For Liberia 1955 is taken as the year of independence.

TABLE 5.10   Number of Political Parties, Independence to 1979 (A)
and 1969—1975 (B).

Definition: All political parties that were legal for any part of this period
are counted, whether or not they resulted from mergers or splits.

Range =   27.00
Mean =   6.72
Standard Deviation =   5.54

Population Percent		Rank	Country Name	A	Range Decile	B
Cum. Country						
3.51	3.51	1.0	Ghana	27	1	11
24.51	21.00	2.0	Nigeria	19	3	0
32.80	8.29	3.0	Zaire	17	4	1
35.21	2.41	5.0	Cameroon	13	6	1
41.45	6.24	5.0	Sudan	13		12
43.42	1.97	5.0	Upper Volta	13		9
44.42	1.00	7.5	Benin	11		1
46.90	2.48	7.5	Madagascar	11		6
47.93	1.03	9.0	Somalia	10	7	7
48.31	.38	11.0	Lesotho	8	8	5
49.30	.99	11.0	Sierra Leone	8		4
50.95	1.65	11.0	Zambia	8		5
51.12	.17	13.5	Gambia	7		4
56.28	5.16	13.5	Tanzania	7		1
56.51	.23	18.0	Botswana	6		6
57.79	1.28	18.0	Burundi	6		1
58.37	.58	18.0	Central African R	6		1
58.82	.45	18.0	Congo	6		1
58.98	.16	18.0	Gabon	6		1
59.14	.16	18.0	Swaziland	6		5
59.89	.75	18.0	Togo	6		1
59.99	.10	24.0	Djibouti	5	9	0
60.09	.10	24.0	Equatorial Guinea	5		5
60.55	.46	24.0	Mauritania	5		1
61.91	1.36	24.0	Rwanda	5		2
65.86	3.95	24.0	Uganda	5		2
67.20	1.34	27.5	Chad	4		2
71.80	4.60	27.5	Kenya	4		2
72.33	.53	29.5	Liberia	3		1
73.99	1.66	29.5	Malawi	3		1
75.86	1.87	31.0	Mali	2	10	0
77.81	1.95	35.0	Angola	1		3
79.38	1.57	35.0	Guinea	1		1
79.57	.19	35.0	Guinea-Bissau	1		2
81.79	2.22	35.0	Ivory Coast	1		1
84.78	2.99	35.0	Mozambique	1		4
86.11	1.33	35.0	Niger	1		1
87.75	1.64	35.0	Senegal	1		3
97.46	9.71	39.0	Ethiopia	0		0

DATA NOT AVAILABLE OR NOT APPLICABLE
FOR THE FOLLOWING COUNTRIES

Namibia   Zimbabwe

SOURCES: *Europa Yearbook* and *Africa Research Bulletin* were consulted for all countries. The major sources for each individual country were: *Zaire*: Crawford Young, *Politics in the Congo* (Princeton, N.J.: Princeton University Press, 1964) and *Congo: Les dosiers du C.R.I.S.P.*, Vol. 1 and *Congo*, 1965 (Princeton: Princeton University Press, 1967). The 49 parties regrouped as CONACO for the 1965 election are counted as one; *Nigeria*: Sklar, *Nigerian Political Parties*, pp. 35—37. This figure represents parties which fought in elections from 1936 onwards and gained seats, or a proportion of the vote in sufficient number to be recorded by Sklar; *Cameroon*: V. LeVine, *Cameroon: From Mandate to Independence*; *Sudan*: U.S. Department of the Army, *Area Handbook for the Sudan*, 2nd ed. (Washington, D.C.: Government Printing Office, 1964); *Ghana*: Dennis Austin, *Politics in Ghana, 1946—61* (London: Oxford University Press, 1964); *Somalia*: Lewis, *Modern History of Somaliland*, and Saadia Touval, *Somali Nationalism* (Cambridge, Mass.: Harvard University Press, 1963); *CAR, Chad, Congo, Gabon*: Thompson and Adloff; *Emerging States of French Equatorial Africa*; Gwendolen M. Carter, ed., *National Unity and Regionalism in Eight African States* (Ithaca, N.Y.: Cornell University Press, 1966); and unpublsihed research files of George Martens, Northwestern University; *Dahomey*: Segal, *Political Africa*, and Martens' unpublished files. *Guinea, Mali, Senegal, Sierra Leone*: Coleman and Rosberg, *Political Parties and National Integration in Tropical Africa*; *Botswana*: Helen Kitchen, ed., *A Handbook of African Affairs* (New York: Praeger, 1964); *Lesotho*: Spence, *Lesotho*; *Mauritania*: Segal, *Political Africa*, and Martens' unpublished files; *Burundi, Rwanda*: Segal, *Political Africa* and Legum, *Africa*; *Togo*: Segal, *Political Africa*, and M.H. Dorsinville, "Report of the UN Commissioner for Supervision of Elections in Togoland under French Administration," UN Document T/1392, June 30, 1958; *Gambia, Zambia*: Richard Hall, *Zambia* (New York: Praeger, 1965); *Kenya, Tanzania*: Diamond and Burke, *Transformation of East Africa* (for Tanzania, Zanzibar's four parties are not included); *Uganda*: Carter, *National Unity in Eight African States*; *Malawi*: Lucy Mair, *The Nyasaland Elections of 1961* (London: Athlone Press, 1962); and John G. Pike, *Malawi: A Political and Economic History* (New York: Praeger, 1968); *Ivory Coast*: Aristide R. Zolberg, *One-Party Government in the Ivory Coast* (Princeton, N.J.: Princeton University Press, 1964), and Gwendolen M. Carter, ed., *African One-Party States* (Ithaca, N.Y.: Cornell University Press, 1962); *Liberia*: Carter, *African One-Party States*; *Niger, Upper Volta*: Information gathered by George Martens in Niger and Upper Volta for dissertation research, 1968—69; *Ethiopia*: Richard Greenfield, *Ethiopia: A New Political History* (New York: Praeger, 1965).

TABLE 5.11   Change in the Number of Parties, Independence to 1979 (A) and 1969 to 1975 (B).

Definition: Number of parties with legislative representation at the end of 1979 minus the number of parties with legislative representation at independence (or December 1969). Independents were counted as one party.

```
Range =            18.00
Mean =             -2.02
Standard Deviation =        2.86
```

Population Percent			Country		Range	
Cum.	Country	Rank	Name	A	Decile	B
1.97	1.97	1.0	Upper Volta	4	1	-3
2.20	.23	2.0	Botswana	2	2	-1
3.84	1.64	3.0	Senegal	1		0
13.55	9.71	8.5	Ethiopia	0	3	0
15.12	1.57	8.5	Guinea	0		0
15.31	.19	8.5	Guinea-Bissau	0		0
17.53	2.22	8.5	Ivory Coast	0		0
17.91	.38	8.5	Lesotho	0		0
18.44	.53	8.5	Liberia	0		0
20.31	1.87	8.5	Mali	0		0
23.30	2.99	8.5	Mozambique	0		0
28.46	5.16	8.5	Tanzania	0		0
30.72	2.26	8.5	Zimbabwe	0		0
33.13	2.41	16.5	Cameroon	-1		0
33.29	.16	16.5	Gabon	-1		0
33.46	.17	16.5	Gambia	-1		0
35.12	1.66	16.5	Malawi	-1		0
35.58	.46	16.5	Mauritania	-1		0
36.91	1.33	16.5	Niger	-1		0
38.19	1.28	22.5	Burundi	-2	4	0
38.77	.58	22.5	Central African R	-2		0
39.22	.45	22.5	Congo	-2		0
39.32	.10	22.5	Equatorial Guinea	-2		-2
43.92	4.60	22.5	Kenya	-2		0
45.57	1.65	22.5	Zambia	-2		-2
47.52	1.95	28.5	Angola	-3		0
48.52	1.00	28.5	Benin	-3		0
49.86	1.34	28.5	Chad	-3		-1
56.10	6.24	28.5	Sudan	-3		1
56.85	.75	28.5	Togo	-3		0
60.80	3.95	28.5	Uganda	-3		-1
60.90	.10	34.0	Djibouti	-4	5	0
63.38	2.48	34.0	Madagascar	-4		-2
64.74	1.36	34.0	Rwanda	-4		-1
65.73	.99	34.0	Sierra Leone	-4		-1
65.89	.16	34.0	Swaziland	-4		-2
86.89	21.00	37.0	Nigeria	-5		0
87.92	1.03	38.0	Somalia	-6	6	-7
91.43	3.51	39.0	Ghana	-7	7	-4
99.72	8.29	40.0	Zaire	-14	10	0

```
DATA NOT AVAILABLE OR NOT APPLICABLE
FOR THE FOLLOWING COUNTRIES

Namibia
```

SOURCES: See Table 5.10.

TABLE 5.12   Percentage of the Vote Cast for the Winning Party in
the Election Closest to, but before, the Date of Independence.

Definition: The winning party is the party from which the government
executive (Cabinet), or head of government in a coalition is chosen.

```
Range =          92.00
Mean =           64.77
Standard Deviation =         23.27
```

Population Percent Cum.	Country	Rank	Country Name	A	Range Decile
2.22	2.22	1.5	Ivory Coast	100	1
2.68	.46	1.5	Mauritania	100	
3.21	.53	3.5	Liberia	99	
4.87	1.66	3.5	Malawi	99	
5.45	.58	5.0	Central African R	89	2
5.68	.23	6.0	Botswana	87	
7.32	1.64	7.5	Senegal	83	
12.48	5.16	7.5	Tanzania	83	
13.76	1.28	9.0	Burundi	81	3
13.92	.16	10.0	Swaziland	80	
15.28	1.36	11.0	Rwanda	78	
15.38	.10	13.0	Djibouti	77	
16.95	1.57	13.0	Guinea	77	
18.28	1.33	13.0	Niger	77	
20.15	1.87	15.5	Mali	76	
21.18	1.03	15.5	Somalia	76	
22.83	1.65	17.0	Zambia	70	4
24.17	1.34	18.0	Chad	68	
26.43	2.26	19.0	Zimbabwe	62	5
26.60	.17	21.0	Gambia	60	
27.35	.75	21.0	Togo	60	
29.32	1.97	21.0	Upper Volta	60	
29.77	.45	23.0	Congo	58	
33.28	3.51	24.0	Ghana	57	
37.88	4.60	25.0	Kenya	54	6
41.83	3.95	26.0	Uganda	52	
44.24	2.41	27.5	Cameroon	50	
44.40	.16	27.5	Gabon	50	
45.39	.99	29.0	Sierra Leone	46	
45.77	.38	30.0	Lesotho	42	7
45.87	.10	31.0	Equatorial Guinea	39	
66.87	21.00	32.0	Nigeria	28	8
75.16	8.29	33.0	Zaire	25	9
76.16	1.00	34.0	Benin	16	10
82.40	6.24	35.0	Sudan	8	

DATA NOT AVAILABLE OR NOT APPLICABLE
FOR THE FOLLOWING COUNTRIES

Angola   Ethiopia   Guinea-Bissau Madagascar
Mozambique   Namibia

SOURCES: The same as for Table 5.9 with the following additions: *Cameroon*: This figure is an estimate for the ruling coalition of Ahidjo and Foncha after federation. Ahidjo's party got 45 percent of the vote in the 1960 election in East Cameroon and Foncha's party got 55 percent of the vote in the 1961 West Cameroon election; *Zaire*: *Congo: Les dossiers du C.R.I.S.P.* (1960), Vol. 1, pp. 257—266. This includes the alliance of MNC-L, MNC-K, COAKA, UNC. Alone, the MNC-L got 592,456 votes. *Ethiopia*: There are no political parties in Ethiopia. *Gambia*: This estimate is based on the fact that the ruling PPP got 64.5 percent of the Protectorate vote but, in alliance with the Democratic Congress, won only 46.5 percent of the Colony vote: *Somalia*: This figure is for the ruling SYL vote in the Trust Territory of Somalia 1959 election; *Sudan*: The ruling National Unionist Party won nearly 60 percent of the seats. Angola, as of August 1982 has still not yet held national elections. Mozambique held indirect elections from September to December 1977, but under a one party state. *Guinea-Bissau* held regional council elections in December 1976, but no information on party outcomes was found. Namibia held elections in 1978 for the National Assembly. The Democratic Turnhalle Alliance won 82% of the vote. It should be noted, however, that as of mid-1983 Namibia is not an independent state. See V. Bloomfield *Commonwealth Elections 1945—1970: A Bibliography* (Westport, Conn.: Greenwood Press, 1976) for more detailed source information on elections.

TABLE 5.13   Legislative Fractionalization at Independence (A) and December 1972 (B).

Definition: The index is computed on the basis of seats won in the election closest to, but before, the date of independence by the various parties and for 1972 by the last election before December 31, 1972. The values of this index range from 0 to 1; the higher the value of the index,[1] the higher the party fractionalization of the legislature.

[1] $1 - \Sigma PR_i^2$ where PR_i equals proportion of seats in the lower house held by the ith political party. Independents are treated as belonging to a single party.

Range = .86
Mean = .35
Standard Deviation = .26

Population Percent						
Cum.	Country	Rank	Country Name	A	Range Decile	B
8.29	8.29	1.0	Zaire	.86	1	0
12.24	3.95	2.0	Uganda	.71	2	0
14.65	2.41	3.5	Cameroon	.68	3	0
14.81	.16	3.5	Swaziland	.68		.23
35.81	21.00	5.0	Nigeria	.66		0
35.97	.16	6.5	Gabon	.60	4	0
42.21	6.24	6.5	Sudan	.60		0
43.21	1.00	8.0	Benin	.59		0
47.81	4.60	9.0	Kenya	.57		0
48.19	.38	10.0	Lesotho	.56		.64
49.22	1.03	11.0	Somalia	.53		0
49.39	.17	12.5	Gambia	.52		.22
50.38	.99	12.5	Sierra Leone	.52		
51.72	1.34	14.5	Chad	.50	5	0
55.23	3.51	14.5	Ghana	.50		0
55.98	.75	16.0	Togo	.45		0
58.24	2.26	17.0	Zimbabwe	.43	6	
59.60	1.36	18.0	Rwanda	.34	7	0
60.05	.45	20.0	Congo	.26		0
62.02	1.97	20.0	Upper Volta	.26		.50
63.67	1.65	20.0	Zambia	.26		.36
63.90	.23	22.5	Botswana	.18	8	.37
65.23	1.33	22.5	Niger	.18		0
66.51	1.28	24.0	Burundi	.17	9	0
71.67	5.16	25.0	Tanzania	.15		0
72.25	.58	26.5	Central African R	.14		0
73.82	1.57	26.5	Guinea	.14		0
75.48	1.66	28.0	Malawi	.12		0
75.58	.10	32.0	Djibouti	0		
85.29	9.71	32.0	Ethiopia	0		0
87.51	2.22	32.0	Ivory Coast	0		0
88.04	.53	32.0	Liberia	0		0
89.91	1.87	32.0	Mali	0		0
90.37	.46	32.0	Mauritania	0		0
92.01	1.64	32.0	Senegal	0		0

DATA NOT AVAILABLE OR NOT APPLICABLE FOR THE FOLLOWING COUNTRIES

Angola   Equatorial Guinea Guinea-Bissau Madagascar
Mozambique Namibia

SOURCES: (Independence) *Botswana*: *Africa Research Bulletin* (March 1965), p. 1079; *Burundi, Rwanda*: *Europa Yearbook 1962; Cameroon*: Willard R. Johnson, *The Cameroon Federation* (Princeton: Princeton University Press, 1970), appendix; *C.A.R.*; Thompson and Adloff, *Emerging States of French Equatorial Africa*, p. 396 and a clipping file from French newspapers collected by George Martens; *Chad*: Michel Saint-Louis, "Le parti progressiste tchadien dans la vie politique de Tchad (PPT-RDA)," unpublished doctoral dissertation, University of Paris; *Congo*. Jean M. Magret, "l'assumption politique de l'UDDIA (Congo) et sa prise du pouvoir (1956—1959)," *Revue juridique et politique d'outre-mer* (April-June, 1963); *Zaire*: Young, *Politics in the Congo*, and *C.R.I.S.P.*; *Benin*: Thomas Hodgkin, *African Political Parties* and *Keesings Contemporary Archives*, 1957, p. 15587; *Ethiopia*: Greenfield, *Ethiopia; Gabon*: Thompson and Adloff, *Emerging States of French Equatorial Africa, Keesings Contemporary Archives, 1969—60*, p. 15587; *Gambia*: *The Gambia Echo*, and Gailey, *History of the Gambia; Ghana*: Austin, *Politics in Ghana, 1946— 61; Guinea, Ivory Coast, Mali, Senegal; Sierra Leone*: Coleman and Rosberg, *Political Parties and National Integration in Tropical Africa; Kenya*: Clyde Sange and John Nottingham, "The Kenya General Election of 1963," *Journal of Modern African Studies*, 2 (1964): 342; *Lesotho*: Spencer *Lesotho; Liberia*: Carter, *African One-Party States*, p. 342 for May 1955 election; *Malawi*: Lucy Mair, *The Nyasaland Elections of 1961* (London: The Athlone Press, 1962), pp. 80—81; *Niger, Mauritania*: Martens' French newspaper clipping file; *Nigeria*: K.W.J. Post, *The Nigerian Federal Election of 1959* (London: Oxford University Press, 1963); *Somalia*: Touval, *Somali Nationalism; Sudan*: Egyptian Gazette, December 11, 1953, p. 1; *Tanzania*: Henry Bienen, *Tanzania: Party Transformation and Economic Development* (Princeton, N.J.: Princeton University Press, 1967); *Togo*: UN Report, June 30, 1958; *Uganda*: *Africa Diary*, May 11—18, 1962, p. 551; *Upper Volta*: Thomas Hodgkin, *African Political Parties* (Baltimore, Md.: Penguin Books, 1961); *Zambia*: David C. Mulford, "Some Observations on the Elections," *Africa Report* (February 1964): 14.

(1972): *Africa South of the Sahara 1973*; Countries without legislatures are given a value of zero; Note: Angola, and Mozambique did not have elections either before 1972, or before independence. *Ethiopia* has never had any political parties.

TABLE 5.14 Organizational Discontinuity in the Party System, 1957—1979 (A) and 1969—1975 (B).

Definition: Number of splits and mergers in the parties. *Mergers* are calculated as the number of times there is either a formation of a new political party by two or more existing parties, or the joining of one existing party by another. *Splits* are calculated as the number of times a new party, formed by a breakaway faction of an existing party, continues in existence after the break.

```
Range =           7.00
Mean =            2.71
Standard Deviation =          2.43
```

Population Percent Cum.	Country	Rank	Country Name	A	Range Decile	B
2.41	2.41	3.0	Cameroon	7	1	0
4.05	1.64	3.0	Senegal	7		0
5.04	.99	3.0	Sierra Leone	7		2
7.01	1.97	3.0	Upper Volta	7		1
8.66	1.65	3.0	Zambia	7		2
29.66	21.00	7.0	Nigeria	6	2	0
30.69	1.03	7.0	Somalia	6		0
30.85	.16	7.0	Swaziland	6		1
31.02	.17	9.5	Gambia	5	3	1
33.50	2.48	9.5	Madagascar	5		1
38.10	4.60	12.0	Kenya	4	5	0
42.05	3.95	12.0	Uganda	4		0
50.34	8.29	12.0	Zaire	4		0
50.72	.38	14.5	Lesotho	3	6	0
51.47	.75	14.5	Togo	3		0
52.81	1.34	18.5	Chad	2	8	0
52.97	.16	18.5	Gabon	2		0
56.48	3.51	18.5	Ghana	2		1
56.94	.46	18.5	Mauritania	2		0
59.93	2.99	18.5	Mozambique	2		0
65.09	5.16	18.5	Tanzania	2		0
67.04	1.95	26.5	Angola	1	9	0
68.04	1.00	26.5	Benin	1		0
69.32	1.28	26.5	Burundi	1		0
69.90	.58	26.5	Central African R	1		0
70.00	.10	26.5	Equatorial Guinea	1		1
71.57	1.57	26.5	Guinea	1		0
73.79	2.22	26.5	Ivory Coast	1		0
75.66	1.87	26.5	Mali	1		0
76.99	1.33	26.5	Niger	1		0
78.35	1.36	26.5	Rwanda	1		0
78.58	.23	35.0	Botswana	0		0
79.03	.45	35.0	Congo	0		0
88.74	9.71	35.0	Ethiopia	0		0
88.93	.19	35.0	Guinea-Bissau	0		0
89.46	.53	35.0	Liberia	0		0
91.12	1.66	35.0	Malawi	0		0
97.36	6.24	35.0	Sudan	0		0

DATA NOT AVAILABLE OR NOT APPLICABLE
FOR THE FOLLOWING COUNTRIES

Djibouti   Namibia   Zimbabwe

SOURCES: These data are taken from the diagrammatic representations of party development in Part II. The data in those diagrams are based primarily on the sources given for Table 5.10.

TABLE 5.15   Number of Illegal Parties, 1957—1979 (A) and 1969—1975 (B).

Definition: Number of parties banned or proscribed during any part of the period 1957 through 1979 or for any part of the period 1969 through 1975.

```
Range =            15.00
Mean =              4.02
Standard Deviation =          3.83
```

Population Percent Cum.	Country	Rank	Country Name	A	Range Decile	B
1.97	1.97	1.0	Upper Volta	15	1	8
22.97	21.00	2.0	Nigeria	14		0
31.26	8.29	3.0	Zaire	13	2	0
34.77	3.51	4.5	Ghana	10	4	8
41.01	6.24	4.5	Sudan	10		10
42.01	1.00	6.5	Benin	7	6	0
43.04	1.03	6.5	Somalia	7		7
45.52	2.48	9.5	Madagascar	6	7	6
48.51	2.99	9.5	Mozambique	6		1
49.26	.75	9.5	Togo	6		0
50.91	1.65	9.5	Zambia	6		4
51.90	.99	13.0	Sierra Leone	5		1
52.06	.16	13.0	Swaziland	5		5
56.01	3.95	13.0	Uganda	5		5
57.29	1.28	17.5	Burundi	4	8	0
57.87	.58	17.5	Central African R	4		0
59.21	1.34	17.5	Chad	4		2
59.66	.45	17.5	Congo	4		0
60.12	.46	17.5	Mauritania	4		0
61.48	1.36	17.5	Rwanda	4		4
63.43	1.95	22.5	Angola	3	9	3
65.84	2.41	22.5	Cameroon	3		0
65.94	.10	22.5	Equatorial Guinea	3		3
68.20	2.26	22.5	Zimbabwe	3		0
68.39	.19	27.5	Guinea-Bissau	2		2
70.26	1.87	27.5	Mali	2		0
70.55	.29	27.5	Namibia	2		0
71.88	1.33	27.5	Niger	2		1
73.52	1.64	27.5	Senegal	2		0
78.68	5.16	27.5	Tanzania	2		0
83.28	4.60	31.5	Kenya	1	10	1
84.94	1.66	31.5	Malawi	1		0
85.17	.23	37.0	Botswana	0		0
85.27	.10	37.0	Djibouti	0		0
94.98	9.71	37.0	Ethiopia	0		0
95.14	.16	37.0	Gabon	0		0
95.31	.17	37.0	Gambia	0		0
96.88	1.57	37.0	Guinea	0		0
99.10	2.22	37.0	Ivory Coast	0		0
99.48	.38	37.0	Lesotho	0		0
100.00	.53	37.0	Liberia	0		0

SOURCES: *Europa Yearbook* and *Africa Research Bulletin* were consulted for all countries. The data in this table are based on the party charts given in Part II, and sources correspond to those for Table 5.14; *Nigeria*: This figure is based on the data in Table 5.14. *Africa Research Bulletin* reports a statement to the effect that 81 political parties and alliances were banned by the 1966 coup; *Sierra Leone*: Coleman and Rosberg, *Political Parties and National Integration in Tropical Africa*. *Africa Research Bulletin* lists four Sierra Leone parties in 1967—SLPP, APC, National Council of Sierra Leone, and Sierra Leone Labor Party. The latter two have not been mentioned elsewhere, and it is unclear if they are new parties or continuations of others. In any case, the abso-lute number of bannings remains the same; *Liberia, Upper Volta, Zambia*: Segal, *Political Africa*. In Liberia there was "no 'legal' ban on the formation of parties before the army coup"; *Cameroon*: Levine, *Cameroon: From Mandate to Independence*, and *Africa Diary*. The UPC became moribund when its leaders were arrested, and is coded as proscribed; *Chad*: Martens' unpublished data from French newspapers; *Ghana*: Austin, *Politics in Ghana, 1946—61*; *Senegal*: Morgenthau, *Political Parties in French-Speaking West Africa*; *Tanzania*: Diamond and Burke, eds., *The Transformation of East Africa*; *Gabon*: In Gabon, the PDID, though not banned, can hardly be said to have enjoyed an autonomous existence; *Lesotho*: Spence, *Lesotho*.

Governmental Institutions

The importance of the institutionalization of political parties and elections relates primarily to the need for organization and representation of individual interests in the population. In addition, political systems must institutionalize organizations for making, administering, adjudicating, and enforcing policy and laws which distinguish those interests that are to be supported and enforced with the resources at the disposal of governments, and which specify the procedures for such support and enforcement.

Table 5.16 gives data on the size of central government legislatures in African states and indicates which nations have had federal or quasi-federal rather than unitary constitutions, and which have had bicameral rather than unicameral legislatures. Changes in the size of legislative bodies may bear some relation to more effective representation of diverse political interest groups, but the development of personalist, highly centralized executive power at the expense of autonomous legislative initiative and review powers has been nearly universal in this region. There is more significant variation, therefore, in the degree to which recruitment to national executive bodies is representative of population characteristics, and in the relative size and organization of the bureaucracy in these nations. Table 5.17 provides information on the proportionate representation of ethnic units in the national cabinets of Black African governments; Table 5.18 shows the percentage of wage and salary earners employed in the public sector, and Table 5.19 gives a rough categorization of differences in the organization of local government institutions.

The dominance of centralized bureaucracy in the political life of these nations indicated by generally high concentrations of public sector employment coupled with the declining importance of party and electoral institutions is reinforced by the increasing weight of government influence in the economic life of these nations. Tables 5.20 through 5.27 provide data on the budgets, revenues and expenditures of governments in these nations. All contemporary governments, of course, can play a critical economic role stimulating and attracting private investment, investing public revenues in support of the development of public goods, stimulating production in regions underdeveloped by private markets, and redistributing national wealth.[35] The rise of government influence in the economy indicated by data in this Chapter is not *ipso facto* undesirable, therefore, but the evaluation of data on government spending and revenues presented here should be undertaken with a cautious eye to the disfunctional consequences of highly centralized government.

The effects of growth in government revenues and spending have to be carefully evaluated in relation to sustained growth in the national tax base, the incidence across population strata of effective tax rates, and the income redistributive effects of taxation, as well as in relation to the effective investment of government revenues. High rates of growth in government revenue from direct taxes, coupled with low rates of growth of income, may stimulate opposition and tax avoidance in the mass public. High rates of indirect taxation may stimulate opposition from elites whose tastes for imported goods are frustrated in this way. High rates of government spending, furthermore, may have little relation to shifts from consumption to productive investment or to equitable income redistribution.

The number and experience of skilled bureaucrats is limited in these countries, and bureaucratic recruitment tends to be based more on the qualities of a general rather than a technical educational experience, so that the bureaucracy's capacity for efficient economic decision-making is limited. Also, bureaucratic organization may obscure communications by loss of information through complex hierarchical decision claims. Centralized decision-making within bureaucracies may, therefore, promote inefficiency, inertia and unwillingness to take responsibility or initiative.[36] Finally, the redistributive motives of governments may emphasize the enrichment of the government elite and the buying of political support from alternative elites rather than the reduction of economic inequality in the society at large.[37]

For these reasons, the institutional imbalance between rapid bureaucritization, and the centralization of government influence relative to the lack of development of political representation and democratic conflict resolution, and the generally slow rates of economic development, has been a major impediment to orderly political change in the region. The colonial pattern of centralized, unrepresentative and paternalistic bureaucratic administration, and of great gaps in income and privilege between employees in government and other employment sectors, has been accentuated by such imbalance. Corruption and inefficiency within bureaucracies have likewise been accentuated by the relative lack of non-bureaucratic avenues for political control and career mobility, by the very late devolution of administrative responsibility to Africans, and by the disproportionate recruitment to administrative office from population groups with superior access to the educational skills required for such employment. It is not surprising, therefore, that there are high correlations between measures of political instability and measures of the concentration of public sector employment. The measures of central government revenues and spending tend, however, to show a more complex relationship to measures of political instability. They tend to be positively associated with measures of communal instability and negatively associated with measures of elite instability, illustrating a dilemma for the political leadership of these countries—increased economic influence on the part of the central government may allow for the flexible co-optation of dissident elites and for the moderation of inter-elite conflict over scarce resources, but, used for such purposes, government spending intensifies conflict involving the mass public. Subtleties such as this need careful exploration in future research.[38]

Because of the weaknesses of legislative and bureaucratic organization, the relative importance of judicial and law-enforcement institutions in these countries is correspondingly great, but so is the difficulty of developing adequate institutional capabilities in this area. The capacity of legal systems to generate conformity to political and administrative decisions is threatened by the plurality of legal traditions in African countries, which include: (1) laws of European origin, applied in many countries as the dominant legal code during the colonial and post-independence periods; (2) Islamic law; and (3) systems of customary law developed within the different indigenous societies that make up the colonial and post-independence populations.[39] Structural adaptations of national legal systems in response to the existence of these multiple systems of law have been grouped into three basic categories. One approach to the development of post-independence legal systems adopted in many of the Francophone countries was to abolish the parallel hierarchies of customary or Islamic law in favor of a single legal code based upon adaptations of common law or continental codified law. Another group of nations have maintained customary or Islamic legal structures at the lower levels of the system in the form of criminal and family law courts. In nations fitting this pattern, Islamic and customary law have been subordinated to general law courts at the higher appellate levels of the system. The third group of nations has fully institutionalized the basic dualism in their set of legal norms by establishing a structurally parallel hierarchy of courts for the application of customary or Islamic law. Data on the variation in these forms of legal institutionalization is given in Table 5.28. It should be noted, however, that this measure reflects formal constitutional requirements, and may be a very inadequate measure of the extent of variation in legal norms and practices at the local level in highly pluralistic nations.[40]

Apart from the problems of the pluralism of laws, the institutionalization of African legal systems is affected by the level of professional experience in legal practice. Systematic legal education is important to the inculcation of a regularized approach to political decision-making.[41] The number of trained lawyers is, therefore, important, particularly in relation to the extent of bureaucratic decision-making. Where legal training lags behind bureaucratic development, administrative efficiency may be impaired, and where legal training outstrips the development of the political sector it may contribute to the formation of a relatively powerful political opposition. Unfortunately, there are no adequate means of assessing whether the academic requirements for admission to higher education in law are equivalent in these nations, or whether the levels of professional certification are comparable across nations. Furthermore, the basic indicators of the size of the pool of qualified lawyers within any nation are extremely time-bound. Many African nations have large numbers of law students who, when certified, will substantially increase the size of the country's legal profession. For example, in 1962, Senegal is listed as having only 53 lawyers officially admitted to the Bar, but it is also listed as having 764 students studying law within the country itself.[42] Similarly, in 1965, in Cameroon, there were only 15 certified members of the Bar, while at the same time there were 328 students preparing for *La Capacité Endroit*. This situation should be kept in mind when reviewing the data in Table 5.29 on the legal profession.

The extent to which legal institutions moderate arbitrary political power, develop conformity to national policy, and legitimate political authority, is, finally, affected by the autonomy of the judiciary in relation to legislative and executive institutions. Unfortunately, most cross-nationally valid measures of the relative level of judicial control over legislative decision-making processes are based upon formal constitutional requirements. Without going into the actual decision records of the high courts, it is impossible to determine whether constitutional provisions for judicial review have actually been utilized. As Table 5.30 indicates, however, the majority of the African nations in our sample have no provision for judicial review of legislation.

Reliability of Data on Governmental Institutions

Measures of the size of legislatures should be highly reliable, but the measures of cabinet ethnic representation, local government organization, and characteristics of the legal system are clearly vulnerable to coding error and should be treated with caution in the absence of any independent evidence of their reliability. Measures of the size of public sector employment should be more accurate, but systematic coverage of such data is not available from independent sources, and there may be errors in our data due to variation among reporting agencies in the precise definition of the public sector or because of attempts to disguise employment in certain areas. Data derived from government budgets are probably reliable, although over-reporting of government expenditures may result from the failure to fully implement development projects for which expenditures are budgeted, and underestimates of expenditure may occur because of the failure to report systematically, if at all, expenditures of publicly-owned or quasi-public corporations and socially 'undesirable' expenditures on military and para-military projects.

TABLE 5.16   Size of the Legislature, 1978.

Definition: The number of members in the central government legislature.

```
Range =          544.00
Mean =            84.27
Standard Deviation =        106.20
```

Population Percent			Country		Range
Cum.	Country	Rank	Name	A	Decile
21.00	21.00	1.0	Nigeria	544	1
22.00	1.00	2.0	Benin	336	4
30.29	8.29	3.0	Zaire	268	6
31.86	1.57	4.0	Guinea	210	7
36.46	4.60	5.0	Kenya	158	8
36.91	.45	6.0	Congo	153	
39.13	2.22	7.0	Ivory Coast	147	
41.61	2.48	8.0	Madagascar	137	
45.56	3.95	9.0	Uganda	126	
47.21	1.65	10.0	Zambia	125	
48.24	1.03	11.0	Somalia	121	
50.65	2.41	12.0	Cameroon	120	
55.81	5.16	13.0	Tanzania	111	
57.45	1.64	14.0	Senegal	100	9
59.11	1.66	15.0	Malawi	87	
60.10	.99	16.0	Sierra Leone	85	
60.26	.16	17.0	Gabon	84	
62.13	1.87	18.0	Mali	82	
64.39	2.26	19.0	Zimbabwe	80	
70.63	6.24	20.0	Sudan	68	
71.38	.75	21.0	Togo	67	
71.48	.10	22.0	Djibouti	65	
72.84	1.36	23.0	Rwanda	64	
73.13	.29	24.0	Namibia	50	10
73.30	.17	25.0	Gambia	35	
73.53	.23	26.0	Botswana	32	
75.48	1.95	34.0	Angola	0	
76.76	1.28	34.0	Burundi	0	
77.34	.58	34.0	Central African R	0	
78.68	1.34	34.0	Chad	0	
78.78	.10	34.0	Equatorial Guinea	0	
88.49	9.71	34.0	Ethiopia	0	
92.00	3.51	34.0	Ghana	0	
92.19	.19	34.0	Guinea-Bissau	0	
92.57	.38	34.0	Lesotho	0	
93.10	.53	34.0	Liberia	0	
93.56	.46	34.0	Mauritania	0	
96.55	2.99	34.0	Mozambique	0	
97.88	1.33	34.0	Niger	0	
98.04	.16	34.0	Swaziland	0	
100.00	1.97	34.0	Upper Volta	0	

SOURCE: *Africa South of the Sahara.*

TABLE 5.17 Cabinet Ethnic Representativeness at Independence (A) and December 1972 (B).

Definition: This index is a *C* coefficient,[1] measuring the extent to which ethnic proportions in cabinet membership *deviate* from proportions 'expected' from the national ethnic population distributions. A high value on this index means the cabinet is unrepresentative of the ethnic composition of the population.

[1]The coefficient is calculated according to this formula:

$$C = \sqrt{(\chi^2/(\chi^2 + N))}$$

Range = .84
Mean = .22
Standard Deviation = .26

Population Percent Cum.	Country	Rank	Country Name	A	Range Decile	B
.53	.53	1.0	Liberia	.84	1	.82
1.87	1.34	2.0	Chad	.79		.79
5.38	3.51	3.0	Ghana	.77		.77
5.96	.58	4.0	Central African R	.72	2	.69
8.37	2.41	5.0	Cameroon	.58	4	.59
8.54	.17	6.0	Gambia	.55		.54
9.53	.99	7.0	Sierra Leone	.54		.36
9.69	.16	8.0	Gabon	.51		.14
10.97	1.28	9.0	Burundi	.37	6	.21
16.13	5.16	10.0	Tanzania	.25	7	.08
16.23	.10	11.0	Equatorial Guinea	.23	8	
18.45	2.22	12.0	Ivory Coast	.17		.07
28.16	9.71	13.0	Ethiopia	.17	9	.18
28.26	.10	14.0	Djibouti	.16		
29.59	1.33	15.0	Niger	.16		.03
31.24	1.65	16.0	Zambia	.11		.07
32.60	1.36	17.0	Rwanda	.09		.09
36.55	3.95	18.0	Uganda	.09		.17
37.00	.45	19.0	Congo	.08	10	.17
38.66	1.66	20.0	Malawi	.08		.09
44.90	6.24	21.0	Sudan	.08		.04
46.77	1.87	22.0	Mali	.08		.24
47.52	.75	23.0	Togo	.06		.06
49.16	1.64	24.0	Senegal	.06		.03
57.45	8.29	25.0	Zaire	.05		.11
57.91	.46	26.0	Mauritania	.05		.05
62.51	4.60	27.0	Kenya	.05		.02
83.51	21.00	28.5	Nigeria	.03		.07
85.48	1.97	28.5	Upper Volta	.03		.05
87.05	1.57	30.0	Guinea	.03		.04
88.05	1.00	31.0	Benin	.03		.04
89.08	1.03	32.0	Somalia	.03		.03
89.31	.23	33.0	Botswana	.00		.01
89.69	.38	34.5	Lesotho	0		0
89.85	.16	34.5	Swaziland	0		

DATA NOT AVAILABLE OR NOT APPLICABLE FOR THE FOLLOWING COUNTRIES

Angola   Guinea-Bissau Madagascar   Mozambique
Namibia   Zimbabwe

$$\chi^2 = \Sigma[(P_i - E_i)^2 / E_i]$$

Where k is the number of ethnic groups in a national population, Pi is the proportion of the cabinet membership belonging to the ith ethnic group. Ei is the proportion of the national population belonging to the ith ethnic group.

SOURCE: The sources and coding of ethnic units in national populations are detailed by country in Part II. The ethnicity of cabinet members was obtained from identifications made by country experts, nationals of particular countries, and various published reference works. Detailed information can be obtained by direct inquiry to the authors of this Handbook. Angola, Guinea-Bissau, Mozambique, Swaziland, Djibouti, Zimbabwe, and Namibia were not independent in 1972.

TABLE 5.18   Percentage of the Wage and Salary Earners Employed in the Public Sector, ca. 1965

Definition: Definitions of wage and salary earners, and of the 'public sector' vary from country to country. The measure given here is reported directly from government economic statistics, and we have no means of comparing their operationalizations.

```
Range =           64.00
Mean =            32.50
Standard Deviation =        14.86
```

Population Percent Cum.	Country	Rank	Country Name	A	Range Decile
.17	.17	1.0	Gambia	70	1
1.20	1.03	2.0	Somalia	60	2
7.44	6.24	3.0	Sudan	57	3
8.43	.99	4.0	Sierra Leone	54	
18.14	9.71	5.0	Ethiopia	53	
18.89	.75	6.0	Togo	48	4
19.89	1.00	7.0	Benin	46	
20.12	.23	8.0	Botswana	43	5
41.12	21.00	9.0	Nigeria	41	
41.58	.46	10.0	Mauritania	36	6
45.09	3.51	12.5	Ghana	35	
45.47	.38	12.5	Lesotho	35	
47.11	1.64	12.5	Senegal	35	
55.40	8.29	12.5	Zaire	35	
58.39	2.99	15.5	Mozambique	33	
60.36	1.97	15.5	Upper Volta	33	
65.52	5.16	17.0	Tanzania	32	
69.47	3.95	18.0	Uganda	31	7
70.81	1.34	19.5	Chad	30	
72.68	1.87	19.5	Mali	30	
77.28	4.60	21.5	Kenya	29	
78.61	1.33	21.5	Niger	29	
81.02	2.41	23.0	Cameroon	28	
81.47	.45	24.5	Congo	23	8
81.63	.16	24.5	Gabon	23	
82.21	.58	26.5	Central African R	21	
82.37	.16	26.5	Swaziland	21	
84.03	1.66	28.0	Malawi	19	
85.68	1.65	29.0	Zambia	18	9
87.25	1.57	30.0	Guinea	16	
87.78	.53	31.0	Liberia	15	
90.00	2.22	32.0	Ivory Coast	14	
91.28	1.28	33.5	Burundi	6	10
92.64	1.36	33.5	Rwanda	6	

```
DATA NOT AVAILABLE OR NOT APPLICABLE
FOR THE FOLLOWING COUNTRIES
```

Angola	Djibouti	Equatorial Guinea	Guinea-Bissau
Madagascar	Namibia	Zimbabwe	

SOURCES: *Directory of Labor Organizations, Africa*, Vols. I and II (Washington: D.C.: United States Department of Labor, May 1966). *Burundi, Rwanda, Somalia*: Estimate based on the figures given in *Directory of Labor Organizations*; *Sudan*: Estimate based on the figures given in *Directory of Labor Organizations*, and in *AID Economic Data Handbook*; *Gabon, Liberia*: Unpublished data collected by George Martens, Northwestern University; *Botswana*: In Basutoland in 1956 'the public sector, particularly the government, is the largest employer,' *Directory of Labor Organizations*; *Ghana, Tanzania*: Giovani Arrighi, 'International Corporations, Labor Aristocracies and Economic Development in Tropical Africa,' in *Imperialism and Underdevelopment*, ed. Robert I. Rhodes (New York: Monthly Review Press, 1970), p. 232.

TABLE 5.19   Centralization of Local Government Administration 1968

Definition: Local government is here defined as the set of formally recognized decision-makers having specified competences (granted by the central government) within the administrative unit next in size to the national unit itself. In federal systems, local government is subordinate to state or regional governments, and for all nations this definition excludes municipalities as local government agencies. The data for this variable are applicable to 1968, or to the period preceding a coup d'etat in countries which had coups before 1968, and it is coded as follows:

1. Administrative officials salaried and appointed by the national government, but no provision for representative institutions at the local level.
2. Administrative officials salaried and appointed by the national government with local councils having elected membership.
3. Administrative officials salaried and appointed by the national government with local councils composed of some mixture of traditional and elected membership.

```
Range =          2.00
Mean =           1.83
Standard Deviation =        .82
```

Population Percent Cum.	Country	Rank	Country Name	A	Range Decile
.23	.23	6.0	Botswana	3	1
1.51	1.28	6.0	Burundi	3	
1.68	.17	6.0	Gambia	3	
4.16	2.48	6.0	Madagascar	3	
4.45	.29	6.0	Namibia	3	
25.45	21.00	6.0	Nigeria	3	
26.81	1.36	6.0	Rwanda	3	
27.80	.99	6.0	Sierra Leone	3	
34.04	6.24	6.0	Sudan	3	
34.20	.16	6.0	Swaziland	3	
35.85	1.65	6.0	Zambia	3	
36.85	1.00	17.5	Benin	2	5
37.30	.45	17.5	Congo	2	
38.87	1.57	17.5	Guinea	2	
41.09	2.22	17.5	Ivory Coast	2	
45.69	4.60	17.5	Kenya	2	
47.35	1.66	17.5	Malawi	2	
48.68	1.33	17.5	Niger	2	
50.32	1.64	17.5	Senegal	2	
51.35	1.03	17.5	Somalia	2	
52.10	.75	17.5	Togo	2	
56.05	3.95	17.5	Uganda	2	
58.02	1.97	17.5	Upper Volta	2	
59.97	1.95	32.5	Angola	1	10
62.38	2.41	32.5	Cameroon	1	
62.96	.58	32.5	Central African R	1	
64.30	1.34	32.5	Chad	1	
64.40	.10	32.5	Djibouti	1	
64.50	.10	32.5	Equatorial Guinea	1	
74.21	9.71	32.5	Ethiopia	1	
74.37	.16	32.5	Gabon	1	
77.88	3.51	32.5	Ghana	1	
78.07	.19	32.5	Guinea-Bissau	1	
78.45	.38	32.5	Lesotho	1	
78.98	.53	32.5	Liberia	1	
80.85	1.87	32.5	Mali	1	
81.31	.46	32.5	Mauritania	1	
84.30	2.99	32.5	Mozambique	1	
89.46	5.16	32.5	Tanzania	1	
97.75	8.29	32.5	Zaire	1	
100.00	2.26	32.5	Zimbabwe	1	

SOURCES: Gwendolen M. Carter, ed., *National Unity and Regionalism in Eight African States* (Ithaca, N.Y.: Cornell University Press, 1966). *Botswana: Bechuanaland: Report for the Year 1965* (London: Her Majesty's Stationery Office, 1966); *Gambia*: Harry A. Gailey, *A History of the Gambia* (New York: Praeger, 1965); *Sierra Leone*: Martin Kilson, *Political Change in a West African State* (Cambridge, Mass.: Harvard University Press, 1966); *Sudan*: U.S. Department of the Army, *Handbook for the Sudan*; *Zambia:Zambia* (London: British Information Services, 1964); *Benin, Senegal, Mauritania*: M.J. Campbell, T.G. Brierly, and L.F. Blitz, *The Structure of Local Government in West Africa* (The Hague, Netherlands: Martinus Nijhoff, 1965); *Ghana, Guinea, Ivory Coast*: Aristide R. Zolberg, *Creating Political Order* (Chicago, Ill.: Rand McNally, 1966); *Kenya*: S. Nyagah, *The Politicalization of Administration in East Africa*, Kenya Institute of Administration, Occasional Paper No. 1 (1968); *Malawi:Malawi* (London: British Information Services, April, 1964); *Somalia*: I.M. Lewis, *The Modern History of Somaliland* (New York: Praeger, 1965); *Cameroon*: Information from unpublished field research by Gene Larimore; *Zaire*: Crawford Young, *Politics in the Congo* (Princeton, N.J.: Princeton University Press, 1965); *Lesotho*: Statesman's Yearbook, 1968-1969; *Liberia*: Gwendolen Carter, ed., *African One-Party States* (Ithaca, N.Y.: Cornell University Press, 1962); *Mali*: James S. Coleman and Carl G. Rosberg, Jr., eds., *Political Parties and National Integration in Tropical Africa* (Berkeley: University of California Press, 1966); *Tanzania*: Henry Bienen, *Tanzania: Party Transformation and Economic Development* (Princeton, N.J.: Princeton University Press, 1967).

TABLE 5.20 Per Capita Central Government Budget in U.S. Dollars, 1977 (A), 1972 (B), 1966 (C), 1961 (D), and 1951 (E).

```
Range =         2467.00
Mean =           145.95
Standard Deviation =      383.67
```

Population Percent Cum.	Country Percent	Rank	Country Name	A	Range Decile	B	C	D	E
.16	.16	1.0	Gabon	2475	1	239	112	6	16
.26	.10	2.0	Djibouti	531	8	0	0	0	0
2.48	2.22	3.0	Ivory Coast	217	10	93	39	33	5
2.93	.45	4.0	Congo	182		89	41	33	12
3.09	.16	5.0	Swaziland	180		82	36	26	10
6.60	3.51	6.0	Ghana	169		53	67	63	23
7.06	.46	7.5	Mauritania	156		24	17	26	9
28.06	21.00	7.5	Nigeria	156		41	3	8	4
28.29	.23	9.0	Botswana	155		106	7	2	4
30.55	2.26	10.0	Zimbabwe	123		0	0	0	0
32.50	1.95	11.0	Angola	122		85	37	19	9
34.15	1.65	12.0	Zambia	120		125	25	23	22
34.68	.53	13.0	Liberia	98		41	44	33	11
35.43	.75	14.0	Togo	90		23	13	12	4
35.60	.17	15.0	Gambia	81		33	24	20	11
41.84	6.24	16.5	Sudan	76		33	6	12	6
45.79	3.95	16.5	Uganda	76		31	7	8	6
47.36	1.57	18.0	Guinea	73		37	13	11	9
49.77	2.41	19.0	Cameroon	72		44	24	23	12
51.41	1.64	20.5	Senegal	58		42	53	41	9
59.70	8.29	20.5	Zaire	58		32	4	12	3
64.30	4.60	22.0	Kenya	57		40	22	17	7
64.68	.38	23.0	Lesotho	56		26	10	5	60
65.67	.99	24.0	Sierra Leone	52		31	21	16	5
66.70	1.03	25.0	Somalia	45		26	10	10	8
71.86	5.16	26.0	Tanzania	42		26	16	8	5
72.44	.58	27.0	Central African R	40		32	25	16	8
75.43	2.99	28.0	Mozambique	35		54	29	25	10
77.09	1.66	29.0	Malawi	32		21	12	10	4
79.57	2.48	30.0	Madagascar	29		29	19	13	13
80.90	1.33	31.0	Niger	26		13	10	10	5
82.24	1.34	33.0	Chad	22		16	13	8	4
84.11	1.87	33.0	Mali	22		10	9	12	3
85.47	1.36	33.0	Rwanda	22		8	6	4	2
85.66	.19	35.0	Guinea-Bissau	20		0	0	11	0
86.94	1.28	36.0	Burundi	19		8	6	6	2
96.65	9.71	37.0	Ethiopia	18		11	8	4	1
97.65	1.00	38.0	Benin	16		16	14	13	4
97.75	.10	39.0	Equatorial Guinea	9		33	39	30	0
99.72	1.97	40.0	Upper Volta	8		8	8	6	2

DATA NOT AVAILABLE OR NOT APPLICABLE
FOR THE FOLLOWING COUNTRIES

Namibia

SOURCES: (1951) *ECA Statistical Bulletin I. Cameroon:* French Cameroon only; *Botswana: Basutoland, Bechuanaland Protectorate, and Swaziland, Report of an Economic Survey Mission* (London: Her Majesty's Stationery Office, 1960); *Angola, Mozambique*(1952),*Madagascar*(1953), *Zambia, Swaziland, Lesotho, Gambia, Mauritania*(1959),*Gabon* (1953),*Congo* (1953):*Statesman's Yearbook 1954.*

(1961) *ECA Statistical Bulletin I*, Table 71, pp. 366-367. *Lesotho:* Estimated; similar to Botswana; *Somalia:* International Monetary Fund, *Surveys of African Economies*, Vol. 2.

(1966) *Africa Contemporary Record 1968-69. Botswana, Ivory Coast, Malawi, Somalia:* data for 1967; *Congo, Liberia:* data for 1969.

(1972) *AID Economic Data Book 1973.* UNECA Statistical Yearbook 1972, 1973, 1974 editions, *Equatorial Guinea:* 1970 data.

(1977) *World Tables* (2nd Edition 1980) (World Bank; Washington D.C.)

TABLE 5.21   Average Annual Growth of the Per Capita Central
Government Budget 1972-1977 (A), 1961-1972 (B) and
1951-1961 (C)

```
Range =         205.00
Mean =           24.08
Standard Deviation =        34.68
```

Population Percent							
Cum.	Country	Rank	Country Name	A	Range Decile	B	C
.16	.16	1.0	Gabon	187	1	353	−6
.62	.46	2.0	Mauritania	110	4	−1	17
1.37	.75	3.0	Togo	58	7	8	18
22.37	21.00	4.0	Nigeria	56		38	5
25.88	3.51	5.0	Ghana	44		−1	16
27.24	1.36	6.0	Rwanda	35	8	9	9
27.41	.17	7.5	Gambia	29		6	7
31.36	3.95	7.5	Uganda	29		26	3
31.74	.38	9.5	Lesotho	28		38	−2
32.27	.53	9.5	Liberia	28		2	18
33.55	1.28	11.0	Burundi	27		3	18
39.79	6.24	12.0	Sudan	26		16	6
41.66	1.87	13.5	Mali	24		−2	27
41.82	.16	13.5	Swaziland	24		20	15
44.04	2.22	15.0	Ivory Coast	22	9	17	41
45.37	1.33	16.0	Niger	20		3	9
45.82	.45	17.0	Congo	17		15	18
47.39	1.57	18.0	Guinea	16		21	2
48.42	1.03	19.0	Somalia	15		15	2
50.37	1.95	20.0	Angola	14		32	11
51.36	.99	21.0	Sierra Leone	13		9	20
53.77	2.41	22.0	Cameroon	13		8	8
63.48	9.71	23.0	Ethiopia	12		16	9
68.64	5.16	24.0	Tanzania	12		21	3
70.30	1.66	25.0	Malawi	10		10	10
70.53	.23	26.0	Botswana	9		473	−5
75.13	4.60	27.0	Kenya	8		12	13
76.77	1.64	28.5	Senegal	8			28
85.06	8.29	28.5	Zaire	8		15	27
86.40	1.34	30.0	Chad	7		8	9
86.98	.58	31.0	Central African R	4		9	9
87.98	1.00	33.0	Benin	0	10	2	20
90.46	2.48	33.0	Madagascar	0		11	
92.43	1.97	33.0	Upper Volta	0		3	18
94.08	1.65	35.0	Zambia	−1		40	
97.07	2.99	36.0	Mozambique	−7		11	14
97.17	.10	37.0	Equatorial Guinea	−18		1	

DATA NOT AVAILABLE OR NOT APPLICABLE
FOR THE FOLLOWING COUNTRIES

Djibouti   Guinea-Bissau Namibia   Zimbabwe

SOURCE: See Table 5.20.

TABLE 5.22 Central Government Expenditures as a Percent of
GDP 1977 (A), and as percent of GNP 1972 (B), 1968
(C), 1963 (D), and 1961 (E).

```
Range =         57.00
Mean =          19.78
Standard Deviation =        11.87
```

Population Percent		Country			Range				
Cum.	Country	Rank	Name	A	Decile	B	C	D	E
.10	.10	1.0	Djibouti	65.0	1				
.29	.19	2.0	Guinea-Bissau	50.3	3			8	20
1.32	1.03	3.0	Somalia	48.0		32	29	19	19
1.78	.46	4.0	Mauritania	37.5	5	14	16	23	20
2.23	.45	5.0	Congo	34.0	6	33	41	26	23
3.88	1.65	6.0	Zambia	31.0		32	42	14	14
3.98	.10	7.0	Equatorial Guinea	29.0	7	11	18	16	17
5.93	1.95	8.0	Angola	26.0		22	27	18	14
6.10	.17	9.0	Gambia	21.1	8	32	21	27	23
14.39	8.29	10.0	Zaire	21.0		38	22	14	12
14.97	.58	11.0	Central African R	19.4		21	21	16	11
16.31	1.34	12.5	Chad	18.0	9	18	19	11	13
20.91	4.60	12.5	Kenya	18.0		24	22	19	17
21.07	.16	14.5	Swaziland	17.1		31	28	19	17
26.23	5.16	14.5	Tanzania	17.1		23	20	16	18
26.61	.38	16.0	Lesotho	17.0		33	11	13	8
28.48	1.87	17.0	Mali	16.5		13	12	14	19
28.71	.23	18.5	Botswana	16.3		45	59	11	8
31.19	2.48	18.5	Madagascar	16.3		20	27	15	15
32.83	1.64	20.0	Senegal	16.0		17	25	25	24
33.82	.99	21.0	Sierra Leone	15.1		16	13	15	19
35.39	1.57	22.5	Guinea	15.0		35	42	31	31
56.39	21.00	22.5	Nigeria	15.0		25	8	10	11
58.80	2.41	24.0	Cameroon	14.1		22	19	10	8
61.79	2.99	25.5	Mozambique	14.0		19	18	17	16
62.54	.75	25.5	Togo	14.0		15	12	16	13
63.87	1.33	27.0	Niger	13.3	10	14	12	12	13
66.09	2.22	28.5	Ivory Coast	13.2		23	25	19	26
68.35	2.26	28.5	Zimbabwe	13.2					
78.06	9.71	30.0	Ethiopia	13.1		14	12	11	10
79.06	1.00	31.5	Benin	13.0		15	18	19	16
82.57	3.51	31.5	Ghana	13.0		18	24	24	26
83.85	1.28	33.0	Burundi	12.6		12	12	12	11
84.01	.16	34.0	Gabon	12.5		28	24	16	14
90.25	6.24	35.0	Sudan	12.2		26	23	20	16
92.22	1.97	36.0	Upper Volta	12.0		11	13	20	14
92.75	.53	37.0	Liberia	11.4		16	31	28	21
94.41	1.66	38.5	Malawi	11.0		20	33	22	23
98.36	3.95	38.5	Uganda	11.0		21	24	17	16
99.72	1.36	40.0	Rwanda	8.0		13	11	11	10

DATA NOT AVAILABLE OR NOT APPLICABLE
FOR THE FOLLOWING COUNTRIES

Namibia

SOURCES: (1961) *AID Economic Data Book* 1970, *ECA Statistical Bulletin* (1968), and *AID Economic Data Book* 1967,
(1963, 1968) *AID Economic Data Book* 1970. *Zaire, Senegal: Europa Yearbook* 1961; *C.A.R., Cameroon, Congo, Chad, Gabon*: International Monetary Fund, *Surveys of African Economies*, Vol. 1; *Kenya*: International Monetary Fund, *Surveys of African Economies*, Vol. 2; *Botswana: Bechuanaland Report* 1965 (London: Her Majesty's Stationery Office; 1966); *Lesotho*: Estimated; similar to Botswana.
(1972) *AID Economic Data Book* 1973 and *World Bank Atlas* 1974.
(1977) *World Tables* (second edition, 1980); *Guinea- Bissau: Accelerated Development in Sub-Saharan Africa*, data as a percent of GDP. *Djibouti: Africa Research Bulletin.*

153

Table 5.23 Ratio of Central Government Expenditures to GDP: Average Rate of Growth 1970-1977 (A), 1961-1972 (B) and 1963-1968 (C)

Range = 21.66
Mean = 3.00
Standard Deviation = 5.89

Population Percent Cum.	Country	Rank	Country Name	A	Range Decile	B	C
.99	.99	1.0	Sierra Leone	16.5	1	-2	-3
1.45	.46	2.0	Mauritania	16.5		-3	-6
2.48	1.03	3.0	Somalia	14.2	2	6	11
4.13	1.65	4.0	Zambia	13.9		16	40
4.88	.75	5.0	Togo	13.9		1	-5
6.83	1.95	6.0	Angola	11.6	3	5	10
27.83	21.00	7.0	Nigeria	7.6	5	12	-4
32.99	5.16	8.0	Tanzania	5.9		2	5
33.44	.45	9.0	Congo	5.5	6	4	12
34.77	1.33	10.0	Niger	5.1		1	
34.94	.17	11.0	Gambia	5.0		4	-4
35.32	.38	12.0	Lesotho	5.0		28	-3
36.60	1.28	13.0	Burundi	4.7		1	
46.31	9.71	14.0	Ethiopia	4.6		4	2
46.41	.10	15.0	Equatorial Guinea	4.3		-3	3
48.38	1.97	16.0	Upper Volta	3.5	7	-2	-7
48.54	.16	17.0	Swaziland	2.8		7	9
50.80	2.26	18.0	Zimbabwe	2.4			
51.33	.53	19.0	Liberia	.9	8	-2	2
53.20	1.87	20.0	Mali	.8		-3	-3
57.15	3.95	21.0	Uganda	.7		3	8
58.79	1.64	22.0	Senegal	.7		-3	
62.30	3.51	23.0	Ghana	-.1		-3	
63.66	1.36	24.0	Rwanda	-.2		3	
66.65	2.99	25.0	Mozambique	-.2		2	1
69.06	2.41	26.0	Cameroon	-.4		16	18
69.64	.58	27.0	Central African R	-1.1	9	8	6
70.98	1.34	28.5	Chad	-1.3		3	15
71.14	.16	28.5	Gabon	-1.3		9	10
73.36	2.22	30.0	Ivory Coast	-1.3		-1	6
75.84	2.48	31.0	Madagascar	-1.7		3	16
77.41	1.57	32.0	Guinea	-2.4		1	7
78.41	1.00	33.0	Benin	-2.7		-1	-1
78.64	.23	34.0	Botswana	-3.0	10	42	87
86.93	8.29	35.0	Zaire	-3.2		20	11
93.17	6.24	36.0	Sudan	-3.3		6	3
97.77	4.60	37.0	Kenya	-5.0		4	3
99.43	1.66	38.0	Malawi	-5.1		-1	10

DATA NOT AVAILABLE OR NOT APPLICABLE FOR THE FOLLOWING COUNTRIES

Djibouti   Guinea-Bissau   Namibia

SOURCES: See Table 5.22

TABLE 5.24 Central Government Revenue as a Percent of GNP 1977 (A), 1972 (B) and 1966 (C).

Range = 32.07
Mean = 20.25
Standard Deviation = 7.14

Population Percent Cum.	Country	Rank	Country Name	A	Range Decile	B	C
.16	.16	1.0	Gabon	35.1	1	28	26
.62	.46	2.0	Mauritania	30.8	2	15	17
1.07	.45	3.0	Congo	30.6		26	33
1.23	.16	4.0	Swaziland	30.5		31	16
2.26	1.03	5.0	Somalia	30.4		23	22
3.01	.75	6.0	Togo	28.7		15	13
3.24	.23	7.0	Botswana	28.4	3	30	21
11.53	8.29	8.0	Zaire	27.0		44	31
13.18	1.65	9.0	Zambia	27.0		37	38
34.18	21.00	10.0	Nigeria	25.9		27	9
34.35	.17	11.0	Gambia	25.3	4	24	26
36.61	2.26	12.0	Zimbabwe	25.0			
38.18	1.57	13.0	Guinea	24.0		27	32
38.71	.53	14.0	Liberia	22.0	5	27	22
39.29	.58	15.0	Central African R	21.0		21	27
40.93	1.64	16.0	Senegal	20.6		19	18
41.31	.38	17.0	Lesotho	20.4		22	13
45.26	3.95	18.0	Uganda	20.0		13	17
47.67	2.41	19.0	Cameroon	19.4		19	13
49.54	1.87	20.0	Mali	19.2		11	18
52.02	2.48	21.0	Madagascar	18.2	6	21	20
56.62	4.60	22.0	Kenya	17.4		24	17
57.95	1.33	23.0	Niger	17.0		13	15
63.11	5.16	24.0	Tanzania	17.0		24	17
69.35	6.24	25.0	Sudan	16.9		33	18
70.34	.99	26.0	Sierra Leone	16.4		13	14
72.31	1.97	27.0	Upper Volta	15.6	7	11	14
72.50	.19	28.0	Guinea-Bissau	15.3			
74.16	1.66	29.0	Malawi	14.6		22	19
75.44	1.28	30.0	Burundi	14.1		13	11
77.66	2.22	31.0	Ivory Coast	14.0		23	22
78.66	1.00	32.0	Benin	13.2		14	16
88.37	9.71	33.0	Ethiopia	12.9		15	11
89.71	1.34	34.0	Chad	12.8		16	16
91.07	1.36	35.0	Rwanda	12.3	8	8	7
94.58	3.51	36.0	Ghana	6.9	9	18	16
94.68	.10	37.0	Djibouti	3.0	10		

DATA NOT AVAILABLE OR NOT APPLICABLE FOR THE FOLLOWING COUNTRIES

Angola   Equatorial Guinea   Mozambique   Namibia

SOURCES: (1966) *AID Economic Data Book* 1970. *Congo*: International Monetary Fund, *Surveys of African Economies*, Vol. 1. (1972) *AID Economic Data Book* 1973 and *World Bank Atlas* 1974. (1977) *World Tables* (2nd edition, 1980).

TABLE 5.25 Central Government Revenue, Average Annual Percent Rate of Growth, 1972-1977 (A), 1966-1972 (B), and 1963-1966 (C).

```
Range =            113.40
Mean =              24.91
Standard Deviation =         25.28
```

Population Percent		Rank	Country Name	A	Range Decile	B	C
Cum.	Country						
.46	.46	1.0	Mauritania	105.4	1	40	6
.62	.16	2.0	Gabon	78.2	3	139	30
2.49	1.87	3.0	Mali	74.7		97	20
23.49	21.00	4.0	Nigeria	52.8	5	359	12
23.72	.23	5.0	Botswana	51.7		107	25
25.08	1.36	6.0	Rwanda	51.5		74	75
25.24	.16	7.0	Swaziland	37.5	6	119	0
28.75	3.51	8.0	Ghana	34.5	7	29	14
30.03	1.28	9.0	Burundi	31.2		77	0
30.41	.38	10.0	Lesotho	30.9		13	10
30.58	.17	11.0	Gambia	28.0		-8	13
31.03	.45	12.0	Congo	27.9		46	27
35.63	4.60	13.0	Kenya	26.7		129	21
37.60	1.97	14.0	Upper Volta	25.9	8	24	-7
42.76	5.16	15.0	Tanzania	24.5		138	31
49.00	6.24	16.0	Sudan	24.3		115	12
50.66	1.66	17.0	Malawi	23.8		94	26
51.69	1.03	18.0	Somalia	21.5		82	57
59.98	8.29	19.0	Zaire	13.7	9	535	41
60.51	.53	20.0	Liberia	11.6		33	4
70.22	9.71	21.0	Ethiopia	11.5		65	37
74.17	3.95	22.0	Uganda	11.0		76	13
75.17	1.00	23.0	Benin	10.0		57	23
77.58	2.41	24.0	Cameroon	9.9		83	30
78.92	1.34	25.0	Chad	6.8		44	33
79.91	.99	26.0	Sierra Leone	6.0		40	-12
82.17	2.26	27.0	Zimbabwe	3.0	10	0	0
84.65	2.48	28.0	Madagascar	2.3		0	0
84.94	.29	29.0	Namibia	.2		0	0
85.52	.58	30.0	Central African R	0		39	92
87.09	1.57	31.0	Guinea	-2.0		18	7
88.74	1.65	32.0	Zambia	-5.0		54	18
90.96	2.22	33.0	Ivory Coast	-8.0		79	10

DATA NOT AVAILABLE OR NOT APPLICABLE
FOR THE FOLLOWING COUNTRIES

Angola	Djibouti	Equatorial Guinea	Guinea-Bissau
Mozambique	Niger	Senegal	Togo

SOURCES:(1963)*AID Economic Data Book* 1970. *Botswana*: E.S. Munger, *Bechuanaland*, p. 115; *Lesotho*: Estimate for 1964. (1966) *AID Economic Data Book* 1970 and *ECA Statistical Bulletin II*. Edwin S. Munger, *Bechuanaland* (London: Oxford University Press, 1965); *Lesotho*: Estimate. (1972) *AID Economic Data Book 1973*, and *World Tables* (2nd edition, 1980)
(1977) *World Tables* (second edition, 1980), *Africa Research Bulletin*, and *Accelerated Development in Sub-Saharan Africa*.

TABLE 5.26 Direct Taxes as a Percent of Total Central Government Revenue. 1977 (A), 1972 (B), 1966 (C), and 1960 (D).

Definition: Direct taxes include income and profits taxes and all other taxes paid directly by the ultimate taxpayer to the government without passing though any intermediary collector.

```
Range =          58.40
Mean =           24.39
Standard Deviation =         12.32
```

Population Percent Cum.	Population Percent Country	Rank	Country Name	A	Range Decile	B	C	D
21.00	21.00	1.0	Nigeria	66.4	1	39	6	6
23.26	2.26	2.0	Zimbabwe	52.0	3	0	0	0
24.91	1.65	3.0	Zambia	49.7		26	29	34
29.51	4.60	4.0	Kenya	35.6	6	28	22	27
29.67	.16	5.0	Swaziland	34.9		18	20	49
31.33	1.66	6.0	Malawi	32.5		19	14	46
31.86	.53	7.0	Liberia	32.0		15	11	0
37.02	5.16	8.0	Tanzania	29.9	7	20	20	21
37.47	.45	9.0	Congo	27.1		16	15	19
38.22	.75	10.0	Togo	26.0		17	9	8
39.55	1.33	11.0	Niger	25.3	8	29	28	25
40.13	.58	12.5	Central African R	25.0		29	20	22
41.77	1.64	12.5	Senegal	25.0		20	23	22
41.93	.16	14.0	Gabon	24.2		20	25	17
51.64	9.71	15.0	Ethiopia	23.0		18	13	20
53.00	1.36	16.0	Rwanda	22.6		29	27	0
54.87	1.87	17.0	Mali	20.8		18	19	34
63.16	8.29	18.0	Zaire	20.6		18	14	31
65.64	2.48	19.0	Madagascar	20.2		14	14	11
66.63	.99	20.0	Sierra Leone	19.8		18	15	20
67.91	1.28	21.5	Burundi	19.3	9	31	32	25
68.37	.46	21.5	Mauritania	19.3		23	17	7
68.60	.23	23.0	Botswana	18.9		10	9	16
72.11	3.51	24.0	Ghana	18.2		12	14	7
74.08	1.97	25.0	Upper Volta	16.8		25	23	21
75.42	1.34	26.0	Chad	16.7		22	24	19
76.42	1.00	27.0	Benin	14.6		15	9	14
78.83	2.41	28.0	Cameroon	14.4		16	29	0
79.21	.38	29.0	Lesotho	13.1	10	19	10	19
85.45	6.24	30.0	Sudan	11.3		10	4	3
85.62	.17	31.0	Gambia	11.0		6	4	6
86.65	1.03	32.0	Somalia	10.7		8	7	5
88.87	2.22	33.0	Ivory Coast	8.0		14	11	6

DATA NOT AVAILABLE OR NOT APPLICABLE
FOR THE FOLLOWING COUNTRIES

```
Angola        Djibouti     Equatorial Guinea  Guinea
Guinea-Bissau Mozambique   Namibia       Uganda
```

SOURCES: *World Tables* (second edition, 1980); *Accelerated Development in Sub-Saharan Africa*.

TABLE 5.27   Percent Growth of the Ratio of Direct Taxes to Total
Central Government Revenue, 1972-1977 (A), 1966-
1972 (B) and 1960-1966 (C).


```
Range =          37.96
Mean =            1.98
Standard Deviation =        8.27
```

Population Percent Cum.	Country	Rank	Country Name	A	Range Decile	B	C
.16	.16	1.0	Gabon	27.3	1	-20	47
8.45	8.29	2.0	Zaire	24.3		29	-55
8.62	.17	3.0	Gambia	17.0	3	50	-33
9.37	.75	4.0	Togo	12.0	5	89	13
9.60	.23	5.0	Botswana	8.8		11	-44
10.05	.45	6.0	Congo	6.8	6	7	-21
11.71	1.66	7.0	Malawi	4.4	7	36	-70
13.58	1.87	8.0	Mali	3.0		-5	-44
34.58	21.00	9.0	Nigeria	2.9		550	
35.92	1.34	10.0	Chad	2.7		-8	26
36.91	.99	11.0	Sierra Leone	2.0		20	-25
40.42	3.51	12.0	Ghana	1.6		-14	100
46.66	6.24	13.0	Sudan	1.2		150	33
47.19	.53	14.5	Liberia	1.0		36	
48.83	1.64	14.5	Senegal	1.0		-13	5
48.99	.16	16.0	Swaziland	.9		-10	-59
53.59	4.60	17.0	Kenya	-.3	8	27	-19
54.59	1.00	18.0	Benin	-1.0		67	-36
57.00	2.41	19.0	Cameroon	-2.0		-45	
62.16	5.16	20.0	Tanzania	-2.2			-5
71.87	9.71	21.0	Ethiopia	-2.5		38	-35
72.45	.58	23.0	Central African R	-3.0		45	-9
72.91	.46	23.0	Mauritania	-3.0		35	143
74.24	1.33	23.0	Niger	-3.0		4	12
75.52	1.28	25.0	Burundi	-3.1	9	-3	28
77.74	2.22	26.0	Ivory Coast	-4.0		27	83
79.10	1.36	27.0	Rwanda	-4.4		7	
81.07	1.97	28.0	Upper Volta	-4.6		9	10
82.72	1.65	29.0	Zambia	-5.1		-10	-15
83.75	1.03	30.0	Somalia	-6.7		14	40
84.13	.38	31.0	Lesotho	-10.7	10	90	-47

```
DATA NOT AVAILABLE OR NOT APPLICABLE
FOR THE FOLLOWING COUNTRIES

Angola        Djibouti      Equatorial Guinea  Guinea
Guinea-Bissau Madagascar    Mozambique   Namibia
Uganda        Zimbabwe
```

SOURCES: See Table 5.26.

TABLE 5.28   Structural Dualism of the National Legal System, 1968.

Definition: The structural heterogeneity of the national legal system is operationalized in terms of the existence of parallel hierarchies of Islamic or customary law. The three prototypes of legal systems include:

1. Unitary systems—i.e., national legal systems in which a separate and parallel hierarchy of courts for the administrators of Islamic or customary law is not present.

2. Unitary systems of higher courts with differentiated lower courts—

i.e., nations maintaining Islamic and/or customary courts at lower levels, and integrating them with general law courts at the high court or appellate level.

3. Separate parallel hierarchy—i.e., national legal systems maintaining a separate hierarchy of courts for the application of Islamic or customary law.

```
Range =            2.00
Mean =             1.73
Standard Deviation =      .70
```

Population Percent Cum.	Country	Rank	Country Name	A	Range Decile
.53	.53	3.5	Liberia	3	1
.99	.46	3.5	Mauritania	3	
2.02	1.03	3.5	Somalia	3	
8.26	6.24	3.5	Sudan	3	
9.01	.75	3.5	Togo	3	
10.98	1.97	3.5	Upper Volta	3	
11.21	.23	15.5	Botswana	2	5
12.49	1.28	15.5	Burundi	2	
14.90	2.41	15.5	Cameroon	2	
16.24	1.34	15.5	Chad	2	
16.69	.45	15.5	Congo	2	
16.79	.10	15.5	Djibouti	2	
16.96	.17	15.5	Gambia	2	
20.47	3.51	15.5	Ghana	2	
20.66	.19	15.5	Guinea-Bissau	2	
25.26	4.60	15.5	Kenya	2	
25.64	.38	15.5	Lesotho	2	
27.30	1.66	15.5	Malawi	2	
27.59	.29	15.5	Namibia	2	
48.59	21.00	15.5	Nigeria	2	
49.58	.99	15.5	Sierra Leone	2	
57.87	8.29	15.5	Zaire	2	
59.52	1.65	15.5	Zambia	2	
61.78	2.26	15.5	Zimbabwe	2	
63.73	1.95	33.0	Angola	1	10
64.73	1.00	33.0	Benin	1	
65.31	.58	33.0	Central African R	1	
65.41	.10	33.0	Equatorial Guinea	1	
75.12	9.71	33.0	Ethiopia	1	
75.28	.16	33.0	Gabon	1	
76.85	1.57	33.0	Guinea	1	
79.07	2.22	33.0	Ivory Coast	1	
81.55	2.48	33.0	Madagascar	1	
83.42	1.87	33.0	Mali	1	
86.41	2.99	33.0	Mozambique	1	
87.74	1.33	33.0	Niger	1	
89.10	1.36	33.0	Rwanda	1	
90.74	1.64	33.0	Senegal	1	
90.90	.16	33.0	Swaziland	1	
96.06	5.16	33.0	Tanzania	1	
100.00	3.95	33.0	Uganda	1	

SOURCES: Thomas Lee Roberts, *Judicial Organization and Institutions of Contemporary West Africa: A Profile* (New York: Institute of Public Administration, 1966). *Burundi, Cameroon, Congo, Zaire, Benin, Ethiopia, Gabon, Malawi, Mauritania, Somalia, Sudan, Togo*: *Law and the Judicial Systems of Nations* (Washington, D.C.: World Peace through Law Fund, 1965); *Botswana*: *Bechuanaland* 1965 (London: Her Majesty's Stationery Office, 1965); *Central African Republic, Chad*: Amos Peaslee, *Constitutions of Nations* (New York: Justice House, 1965); *Gambia*: Gailey, *History of the Gambia*; *Kenya*: *Statesman's Yearbook 1967-1968*; *Lesotho*: J.E. Spence, *Lesotho: The Problems of Independence* (London: Oxford University Press, 1968); *Guinea* L.G. Cowan, 'Guinea' in *African One-Party States*, ed. G. Carter; *Tanzania*. Personal communication, Professor Roland Young, Northwestern University. *Uganda*: Donald Rothchild and Michael Rogan, 'Uganda' in *National Unity and Regionalism in Eight African States*, ed. G. Carter.

**TABLE 5.29   Number of Practicing Lawyers (A) and Form of Legal
Training Requirement, ca. 1965 (B).**

Definition: Number of lawyers are those officially admitted to the Bar as qualified members of a regulated legal profession. Unofficial advisors and counsellors on legal matters are not included. The types of training required to qualify as an accredited, full member of the national legal profession are coded as follows:
0. Data unavailable.

1. Those requiring apprenticeship only.
2. Those having only requirements for formal schooling.
3. Those requiring both formal schooling and apprenticeship. 'Formal schooling' is defined as a specified number of years in a law school, and 'apprenticeship' is defined as a specified number of years in a local law office or other form of practical local experience.

```
Range =        1965.00
Mean =          226.71
Standard Deviation =          486.41


   Population
     Percent                Country                 Range
                    Rank    Name             A      Decile
   Cum. Country

    9.71   9.71    1.0  Ethiopia         1967        1
   30.71  21.00    2.0  Nigeria          1600        2
   34.22   3.51    3.0  Ghana             400        8
   38.82   4.60    4.0  Kenya             380        9
   39.35    .53    5.0  Liberia           315
   45.59   6.24    6.0  Sudan             176       10
   50.75   5.16    7.0  Tanzania          173
   54.70   3.95    8.0  Uganda             75
   56.36   1.66    9.5  Malawi             53
   58.00   1.64    9.5  Senegal            53
   58.45    .45   11.0  Congo              40
   59.44    .99   12.0  Sierra Leone       38
   60.72   1.28   14.0  Burundi            30
   62.94   2.22   14.0  Ivory Coast        30
   71.23   8.29   14.0  Zaire              30
   72.57   1.34   16.0  Chad               27
   74.98   2.41   17.0  Cameroon           15
   76.34   1.36   18.0  Rwanda              8
   77.34   1.00   19.0  Benin               7
   79.21   1.87   20.5  Mali                6
   79.96    .75   20.5  Togo                6
   80.12    .16   22.5  Gabon               5
   81.69   1.57   22.5  Guinea              5
   83.66   1.97   24.0  Upper Volta         2
```

DATA NOT AVAILABLE OR NOT APPLICABLE
FOR THE FOLLOWING COUNTRIES

Angola	Botswana	C A R	Djibouti
Equatorial Guinea	Gambia		Guinea-Bissau Lesotho
Madagascar	Mauritania	Mozambique	Namibia
Niger	Somalia	Swaziland	Zambia
Zimbabwe			

SOURCES: *Law and the Judicial Systems of Nations* (Washington, D.C.: World Peace through Law Fund, 1965). *Ghana, Ivory Coast, Mali, Senegal, Sierra Leone, Togo, Upper Volta*: Thomas Lee Roberts, *Judicial Organization and Institutions of Contemporary West Africa: A Profile* (New York: Institute of Public Administration, 1966): *Guinea*: U.S. Department of the Army, *Area Handbook for Guinea* (Washington, D.C.: U. S. Government Printing Office, 1961).

TABLE 5.30 The Presence of Institutional Provisions for Judicial Review of Legislation ca. 1969.

Definition: Structural approaches to judicial review of legislation in the constitution are coded:

1. Systems in which judicial review of legislation exists in full.
2. Systems in which partial judicial review exists either because it applies to legislation or because the review process can only be started by certain bodies.
3. Systems in which there is no constitutional provision for judicial review of legislation.

```
Range =           2.00
Mean =            2.63
Standard Deviation =          .70
```

Population Percent Cum.	Country	Rank	Country Name	A	Range Decile
1.00	1.00	12.5	Benin	3	1
1.23	.23	12.5	Botswana	3	
2.51	1.28	12.5	Burundi	3	
3.09	.58	12.5	Central African R	3	
3.54	.45	12.5	Congo	3	
13.25	9.71	12.5	Ethiopia	3	
13.41	.16	12.5	Gabon	3	
13.58	.17	12.5	Gambia	3	
17.09	3.51	12.5	Ghana	3	
18.66	1.57	12.5	Guinea	3	
23.26	4.60	12.5	Kenya	3	
23.64	.38	12.5	Lesotho	3	
25.30	1.66	12.5	Malawi	3	
46.30	21.00	12.5	Nigeria	3	
47.66	1.36	12.5	Rwanda	3	
48.65	.99	12.5	Sierra Leone	3	
49.68	1.03	12.5	Somalia	3	
55.92	6.24	12.5	Sudan	3	
61.08	5.16	12.5	Tanzania	3	
61.83	.75	12.5	Togo	3	
65.78	3.95	12.5	Uganda	3	
67.75	1.97	12.5	Upper Volta	3	
76.04	8.29	12.5	Zaire	3	
77.69	1.65	12.5	Zambia	3	
79.91	2.22	26.5	Ivory Coast	2	5
81.78	1.87	26.5	Mali	2	
82.24	.46	26.5	Mauritania	2	
83.57	1.33	26.5	Niger	2	
85.98	2.41	30.5	Cameroon	1	10
87.32	1.34	30.5	Chad	1	
87.85	.53	30.5	Liberia	1	
89.49	1.64	30.5	Senegal	1	

```
DATA NOT AVAILABLE OR NOT APPLICABLE
FOR THE FOLLOWING COUNTRIES

Angola        Djibouti     Equatorial Guinea  Guinea-Bissau
Madagascar    Mozambique   Namibia            Swaziland
Zimbabwe
```

SOURCE: Jean Blondel, *An Introduction to the Study of Comparative Government* (New York: Praeger, 1970).

Military and Security Systems

Hierarchical and unrepresentative bureaucracies, coupled with weak, fictional or non-existent party and electoral systems, and with little constraint on political power by autonomous legal institutions, have stimulated the rise to political prominence of military and security organizations in African states. In this chapter we have already discussed the incidence of military intervention, and some of the political antecedents of a shift from conciliation to force in the practice of African politics.[43] But military intervention is stimulated by military reasons as well as by reasons of the general state of the nation, and information on these organizations is, therefore, vital to an understanding of the recent political history of Black Africa.

Armed forces that were inherited from colonial governments in new African states were, if they existed at all, generally small in number, limited in experience, and unrepresentative of the variation in socio-cultural characteristics of the national population. As such they were ill-suited to play the modernizing and reformist role in developing countries that has been argued to stem from the presumed rationality and efficiency of the military's bureaucratic organization, technological infrastructure, national identification, and detachment from civilian and traditional power structures.[44] Rather, it may be argued that the use and maintenance, as opposed to the manufacture and the development, of technically advanced equipment has been insufficient to imbue the African military with a passion and expertise for development, and that hierarchical organization and socialization limit their ability to adapt to the political skills of compromise and bargaining.[45]

Analysis of the predisposition of African military men towards modernization, national rather than sub-national identification, and political intervention requires reference to detailed information on the organizational structure, cohesion, skill distribution, recruitment policy, and ideological orientation of the armed forces.[46] Aggregate data presented in this Chapter cannot provide sufficient information of this kind, but may yet indicate interesting relationships between variation in military and security systems and other aspects of development. The size of Black African armed forces and internal security forces (see Tables 5.30, 5.31 and 5.32) is generally low in comparison to countries in other regions of the world. By 1978 all but fourteen Black African states——Angola, Nigeria, Zaire, Ethiopia, Kenya, Sudan, Uganda, Tanzania, Somalia, Madagascar, Mozambique, Zambia, Zimbabwe and Ghana had less than 10,000 men in their armed forces. Such a generalization masks significant variation

among these nations, however, and scholars who optimistically concluded that the small size of these armies reduced the possibility of military intervention after independence[47] were seriously wide of the mark for this continent in which an army only 300 strong has carried out a successful coup d'etat.

The small numbers in the armed forces of these countries at independence relative to the demands placed upon them accounts in part for their rapid growth thereafter (see Table 5.33 and 5.34). Levels of expenditures on armed forces are also, as indicated in Tables 5.35 and 5.36, generally low: the average of 3.5% of G.N.P. spent on defense in 22 of these states in 1977 is still somewhat lower than the mean of 3.7% for 82 states in 1959 or thereabouts as reported by Russett *et al.*[48] Again however, the average rate of increase in defense expenditures (see Table 5.37) is high for these countries with limited economic resources.

The relationship between such data as these and other aspects of the political experience of these nations requires very careful exploration, but some preliminary observations can be suggested. First, with respect to the colonial inheritance, the French used proportionately more of the population of their African colonies as recruits to the armed forces during the First World War than was the case for the British. Although the British recruited over 370,000 throughout Africa, slightly under half of whom gained military experience outside of their home territories, they recruited only 30,000 in West Africa.[49] In the Second World War, after the end of the Vichy administration in French West Africa, over 100,000 African soldiers fought with the Allied armies between 1943 and 1945, along with a considerable number of troops from British African colonies. Black African soldiers from French territories also saw action on the side of the French government in the wars for colonial liberation in Southeast Asia and Algeria. Black African troops in French territories were commanded by Black African officers sooner, and in greater numbers, than was the case in British ruled territories. While, therefore, army and police forces in all Black African territories had to make the difficult transition from agencies of colonial reaction against nationalist movements to agencies of support for such movements after independence,[51] the experience of African troops and commanders in the field was somewhat greater in French than in British territories.

The lower degree of institutionalization of the armed forces in British colonies is reflected by data such as that in Table 5.31, which show that of the eleven Black African countries which had one tenth of 1% or more of their populations in the armed forces by 1967, only Ghana and the Sudan were former British colonies. Furthermore, French colonial troops were often stationed outside of their home territories and were, therefore, less directly involved in the suppression of what were to become their future civilian governors. This, along with the observation that French metropolitan forces directly assisted in putting down insurgency in Chad, Cameroon, Niger, Mauritania, Congo and Gabon between 1960 and 1963, and that French metropolitan troops were stationed in large numbers to support their 'colleagues' in African armies in the maintenance of the new civilian regimes—the number of French troops garrisoned in Africa being reduced as late as 1964 from 35,000 to 16,000, and remaining as large as 6-7,000 in 1968[52]—helps to account for marginally lower or less immediate rates of military intervention in former French territories as compared to the former British colonies.

The differences in colonial experience, notwithstanding, the generally small size of the armed forces and the late indigenization of the officer corps in these nations intensified competition for recruitment and promotion with the advent of independence. This competition was further intensified by the colonial governments' preference for recruitment to the army rank and file from what were perceived to be the more 'bellicose' ethnic groups,[53] and for recruiting officers when they finally chose to do so from groups with greater exposure to education. Added to this lack of cohesion within the armed forces were potential conflicts between African military men, trained at metropolitan military schools in the fear of Communist nations and in the use and appreciation of the arms and equipment of Western nations, and the African politicians concerned to balance the preponderance of Western neo-colonial influence by receiving economic and military aid from non-Western nations. Civilian involvements in the 'business' of the military, as in the acceptance of non-Western weaponry and training facilities in many countries; the direction by Nkrumah of the Ghanaian army in opposition to the United Nation's command in Zaire. The 'retiring' of senior officers in the Ghanaian army; the concerted effort to recruit and promote an ethnically representative officer corps in Nigeria, and the development of special presidential guards independent of regular army control in Ghana and Mali, have further undermined already fragile civil-military relations.

Such conflict within the military and between civilian governments and the military, and the wider social conflicts over ethnic and ideological differences that they in part reflect, have, if anything, been intensified by the growth of armed forces in these nations. There are consistently positive correlations between measures of the size, growth and financing of armed forces and indices of

political instability rather than *vice versa*. Detailed analysis of the data for military expenditures in constant 1960 prices and exchange rates given in the SIPRI yearbook 1972[55] indicates the analytic complexity involved. By calculating the average annual percentage change in these expenditures in the periods 1960-1965 and 1965-1969, we can analyze the cross-lagged correlation of these variables against the measures of political instability aggregated for the periods Independence to 1965, and 1965 to 1972. The data shown in Figure 5.5 indicates that increasing military expenditures within these 5-year periods were slightly associated with increasing communal instability in the same periods, that there is some faint evidence of a lagged effect in which increasing military expenditures in the earlier period were associated with less instability in the later period, and that the rate of increase in military expenditures was not affected by prior political instability.

A more detailed investigation of the correlations for the average annual increase in military expenditures in each year from 1960 to 1970 with measures of political instability for each year through 1972 shows a preponderance of positive signs in the correlations for the military expenditure variables lagged one year behind the political instability variables, and generally negative signs for the reverse lag. The only significant correlations in these series, however, are those between the increase in military expenditures in 1965 to 1966 and elite instability in 1967 (-.38) and between elite instability in 1966 and increasing military expenditures in 1965 to 1967 (.43). Except for this period in which Black Africa experienced a spate of coups d'état, therefore, there is very little clear-cut evidence that increasing coercive potential decreased the likelihood of political instability, and there is no solid evidence that increasing coercive potential *increased* the likelihood of political instability in these nations.

There is, however, one striking observation that can be made from a close inspection of the time series of military expenditures for individual countries which have experienced coups d'état. In these cases, a pattern emerges in which coups take place immediately after downward shifts in an upward secular trend in the growth of military expenditures. Without getting into a complex time series analysis, or presenting the graphed data for all individual countries, the following summary will illustrate the pattern. The 1968 coup d'état in Congo took place following a 1.6% decline in military expenditures after an 25% average annual increase in the two years before that. The 1965 Benin coup followed a 6% decrease in military expenditures after a 15% average annual increase in the three preceding years. The attempted coup in Gabon in 1964 followed a 23% decrease after a 3-year period in which the average annual increase in military expendi-

Figure 5.5

**Correlations Between Indicators of Change in Military
Expenditure and Political Instability in Black African Countries***

MILITARY EXPENDITURE	POLITICAL INSTABILITY			
	Communal		*Elite*	
	Independence to 1965	*1965—72*	*Independence to 1965*	*1965—72*
Percent average annual change in military expenditure 1960—65	.14	−.20	−.06	−.10
Percent average annual change in military expenditure 1965—69	−.01	.34	−.15	−.12

*Calculations for Black African countries independent before 1965.

tures had been 50%. The Nigerian coup in 1966 followed an 11% decrease after an average 24% increase in military expenditures for the 3 years preceding the drop. The coup in Uganda in 1969 followed a 12% decrease after an average annual increase of 24% in military expenditures for the three previous years. The coup in Ghana in 1966 followed a 5-year period in which military expenditures declined by an average of 17% a year. These are the most dramatic examples, but all other coups d'état in these nations in the period 1960-1970, except that in Zaire, followed a declining rate of growth in military expenditures. Inspection of the series in countries which have not had coups d'état reveals either that military expenditures had generally been consistently rising or that, where there have been decreases, they were followed quickly by a compensating increase.

Reliability of Data on the Military

The size of the armed forces would appear, in principle, to be well defined. However, multiple sources provide different information on this variable, even when reported for identical years. One analytic device which can be utilized to increase confidence in the figures is a comparison of a country's defense expenditures with the size of its armed forces. The value of this procedure is limited, however, unless detailed data can be obtained for a series of points in time. Where possible, we have followed this procedure to choose between conflicting sources.

Figures for the size of internal security forces suffer from similar problems of inter-source reliability. "Internal security forces are all those personnel whose primary function is the maintenance of internal order in the society," but sources disagree on whether or not to include military and para-military personnel in their figures for this indicator. Since the available compendia of information on internal security forces do not cite the sources of *their* information, it is impossible to speculate on reasons for differences in the original reporting of the data.

The figures for defense expenditures are taken from the national government budgets. Problems of reliability in these data arise because of the lack of comparability in the definition of fiscal years from country to country, and because of the possibliity that certain military and paramilitary expenditures may not be reported as such in the budgets.

Notes

[1]K. Marx, *The 18th Brumaire of Louis Bonaparte* (New York: International, 1964).

[2]See the discussion of sequential processes of political development in Lucian Pye, *Aspects of Political Development* (Boston: Little, Brown, 1966); L. Binder, ed., *Crises of Political Development* (Princeton, N.J.: Princeton University Press, 1971); Michael F. Lofchie, "Representative Government, Bureaucracy and Political Development: The African Case," *Journal of Developing Areas*, 2 (October 1967): 37— 55.

[3]See, for example, James O'Connell, "The Inevitability of Instability," *Journal of Modern African Studies*, V (March 1967): 181—91; Edward Feit, "Military Coups and Political Development: Some Lessons from Ghana and Nigeria," *World Politics*, XX (January 1963): 173—93; Aristide Zolberg, "The Structure of Political Conflict in the New States of Tropical Africa," *American Political Science Review*, LXII (March 1968): 70—87 and Zolberg, "Military Intervention in the New States of Tropical Africa: Elements of a Comparative Analysis," in Henry Bienen, ed., *The Military Intervenes* (New York: Russell Sage, 1968): pp. 71—98.

[4]See, for example, Peter P. Ekeh, "Citizenship and Political Conflict: A Sociological Interpretation of the Nigerian Crisis," op. cit.

[5]See the comparison of the concepts "change," "movement," and "development" in Adam Schaff's contribution to Raymond Aron, ed., *Symposium on Social Development* (Paris: UNESCO, 1961).

[6]Contemporary students of political development define their subject matter in terms of any, or all, of the following characteristics of nations: (1) structural differentiation, institutionalization, and autonomy within the political system; (2) the integration of formerly diverse cultural elements and the collective acquisition of national loyalties; (3) higher magnitudes of popular participation and equality of opportunity in political life; (4) greater centralization and distributive capacity in the political system; and (5) stability in the exercise of political authority. Details and variations in the definition of political development along these lines can be seen in the publications issued under the auspices of the Committee on Comparative Politics of the Social Science Research Council. For a useful summary of conceptualization and data collection in studies of political development, see Raymond F. Hopkins, "Aggregate Data and the Study of Political Development," *Journal of Politics*, 31 (1969), 71—94. For a work referring specifically to Africa see J. Scarritt, *Political Development and Cultural Change Theory: A Propositional Synthesis with Applications to Africa* (Beverly Hills, Ca.: Sage, 1972).

[7]Ivo K. Feierabend, Rosalind L. Feierabend, and Betty A. Nesvold, "Social Change and Political Violence: Cross-National Patterns" in *The History of Violence in America*, eds. Hugh Davis Graham and Ted Robert Gurr (New York: Bantam Books, 1969), pp. 632—37.

[8]Ted Gurr, "Psychological Factors in Civil Violence," *World Politics*, 20 (1968): 245—278.

[9]R.J. Rummel, "Dimensions of Conflict Behavior Within Nations, 1946—59," *Journal of Conflict Resolution*, 10 (1966): 65—73.

[10]Harry Eckstein, ed., *Internal War: Problems and Approaches* (New York: The Free Press of Glencoe, 1964).

[11]Ted Gurr, "A Causal Model of Civil Strife: A Comparative Analysis Using New Indices," *American Political Science Review*, 68 (1968): 1104—1124 and Ted Gurr, *Why Men Rebel* (Princeton: Princeton University Press, 1970).

[12]R.J. Rummel, "Dimensions of Conflict Behavior Within Nations." op. cit.

[13]Raymond Tanter, "Dimensions of Conflict Behavior Within and Between Nations, 1957—60," *Journal of Conflict Resolution*, 10 (1966): 41—64.

[14]D.P. Bwy, "Political Instability in Latin America: The Cross-Cultural Test of a Causal Model," *Latin American Research Review*, 3 (1968); 17—66.

[15]Gurr, "A Causal Model of Civil Strife."

[16]See the discussion in Harry Eckstein, "On the Etiology of Internal War," *History and Theory*, 4 (1965), especially p. 135.

[17]Eckstein, "On the Etiology of Internal War."

[18]P.A.R. Calvert, "Revolution: The Politics of Violence," *Political Studies*, 15 (1967): 1—11.

[19]Douglas A. Hibbs, Jr., *Mass Political Violence: A Cross-National Causal Analysis* (New York: Wiley-Interscience, 1973).

[20]Bruce M. Russett, et al., *World Handbook of Political and Social Indicators* (New Haven: Yale University Press, 1964), 97—98. Also see C. L. Taylor and M. Hudson, *World Handbook of Political and Social Indicators 2nd edition* (New Haven: Yale University Press, 1972).

[21]A comparable typology is sketched in James N. Rosenau, "Internal War as an International Event," in James Rosenau, ed., *International Aspects of Civil Strife* (Princeton, N.J.: Princeton University Press, 1964), pp. 45—91. Rosenau speaks of personal authority and structural wars as types of internal war (pp. 63—64). See D. G. Morrison and H. M. Stevenson, "Political Instability in Independent Black Africa: More Dimensions of Conflict Behavior Within Nations," *Journal of Conflict Resolution*, XV, 3 (Sept. 1971): 347—368.

[22]Interestingly, colonial revolts such as those in Kenya and Cameroon were events in which the organizational basis of insurgency was a mass movement, involving associational rather than communal ties as the sources of primary identification. This has, of course, also been true of most liberation movements in Southern Africa.

[23]Violence, like instability, is variously defined, but includes behaviors ranging from activity intended to injure physically, to actions that flout institutionalized expectations of "proper" behavior. See Chalmers Johnson, *Revolution* (Stanford: Hoover Institution, Stanford University, 1964), p. 8, and H. L. Nieburg, *Political Violence* (New York: St. Martin's Press, 1969), p. 13.

[24]The correlations are low, however, probably reflecting the lack of reliability in estimates of death in civil violence, as well as the wide variation in destruction during periods of political instability.

[25]See D. G. Morrison and H. M. Stevenson, "Political Instability in Independent Black Africa: More Dimensions of Conflict Behavior Within Nations," *Journal of Conflict Resolution*, XV (September 1971): 347—368.

[26]Ibid.

[27]See A. Wells, "The Coup D'Etat in Theory and Practice: Independent Black Africa in the 1960's," *American Journal of Sociology*, 79 (January 1974): 871—87.

[28]See William R. Thompson, *The Grievances of Military Coup-Makers* (Beverly Hills: Sage Publications, 1973), Appendix A.

[29]Gurr, "A Causal Model of Civil Strife," the data for which were kindly made available by Professor Gurr.

[30]Irma Adelman and Cynthia Taft Morris, *Society, Politics and Economic Development* (Baltimore: Johns Hopkins University Press, 1967).

[31]Cf. Samuel P. Huntington, *Political Order in Changing Societies* (New Haven: Yale University Press, 1968); Brunner and Brewer, *Organized Complexity: Empirical Theories of Political Development* (New York: Free Press, 1971); H. Eckstein and T.R. Gurr, *Authority Pat-*

terns (New York: Wiley, 1975).

[32]Gabriel A. Almond and James A. Coleman, eds. *The Politics of the Developing Areas* (Princeton, N.J., Princeton University Press, 1960).

[33]Huntington, *op. cit.*, p. 12.

[34]The importance of these variable characteristics of individual parties rather than the general structure of the party system has long been argued in the study of African politics. Cf. Ruth Schachter Morgenthau, "Single-Party Systems in West Africa," *American Political Science Review*, 55 (1961): 304—305; Thomas Hodgkin, *African Political Parties* (London: Penguin Books, 1961), pp. 155—159; Aristide Zolberg, *One-Party Government in the Ivory Coast* (Princeton, N.J.: Princeton University Press, 1964), p. 9, and Martin Kilson, "Authoritarian and Single-Party Tendencies in African Politics," *World Politics*, 15 (1963): p. 292. A good study of grassroots involvement and mobilization within an African party organization is Peter Harries-Jones, *Freedom and Labour: Mobilization and Political Control on the Zambian Copperbelt* (Oxford:Basil Blackwell, 1975). Analytically insightful studies of the dynamics of single-party organization are also available in Zolberg, *ibid.*, and Henry Bienen, *Tanzania: Party Transformation and Economic Development* (Princeton: Princeton University Press, 1970) and *Kenya: The Politics of Participation and Control* (Princeton: Princeton University Press, 1974).

[35]This is obviously a restrictive statement of the economic role of government. The concern with fiscal policy and the neglect of monetary policy is, however, appropriate in the African context, where the ability of governments to control the value and availability of money is restricted by the absence of developed financial institutions, and by the external controls over African currency exercised by the governments of foreign countries, whose central banks control the international standards of exchange used in Africa. For a discussion of the role of government in economic development see Ursula Hicks, *Development Finance: Planning and Control* (New York: Oxford University Press, 1965); Otto Eckstein, "A Summary of the Theory of Public Expenditures," in *Public Finances: Needs, Sources, and Utilization* (Princeton, N.J.: National Bureau and Princeton University Press, 1961); and A.R. Prest, *Public Finance in Underdeveloped Countries* (London: Weidenfeld and Nicholson, 1962).

[36]See Joseph J. Spengler, "Bureaucracy and Economic Development." in Joseph LaPalombara, ed., *Bureaucracy and Political Development* (Princeton, N.J.: Princeton University Press, 1963), especially pp. 223—232, and the discussion contained in Albert Waterson, *Development Planning: Lessons of Experience* (Baltimore, Md.: Johns Hopkins University Press, 1966), and Martin Stanisland, "Colonial Government and Populist Reform: The Case of the Ivory Coast—I and II," *Journal of Administration Overseas*, X (January, April 1971): 33—42 and 113—126.

[37]Rimmer, D, "The Abstraction from Politics: A Critique of Economic Theory and Design with Reference to West Africa," *Journal of Development Studies*, 5 (April), 190—204. For a review of the contemporary political economy of African states see M. J. Grieve and T. M. Shaw "The Political Economy of Africa: Internal and International Inequalities," *Cultures et Developpement*, 10 (1978): 609—48.

[38]See a preliminary analysis of the integrative and disintegrative effects of patterns of political centralization in D. G. Morrison and H. M. Stevenson, "Integration and Instability: Patterns of African Political Development," *American Political Science Review*, LXVI (September 1972): 902—927.

[39]See Thomas Lee Roberts, *Judicial Organization and Institutions*

of Contemporary West Africa: A Profile (New York: Institute of Public Administration, 1966), for the discussion on which this paragraph is based.

[40]"Any human society...does not possess a single consistent legal system, but as many such systems as there are functioning subgroups. Conversely, every functioning subgroup of a society regulates the relations of its members by its own legal system, which is of necessity different, at least in some respects, from those of the other groups." Leopold Popisil, "Legal Levels and Multiplicity of Legal Systems in Human Societies," *Journal of Conflict Resolution*, 11 (March 1967): 3.

[41]Peter C. Lloyd, ed., *The New Elites of Tropical Africa* (New York: Oxford University Press, 1966), p. 8.

[42]UNESCO, *The Development of Higher Education in Africa* (New York, 1962), p. 230.

[43]The best general statement of this shift is Aristide Zolberg, "The Structure of Political Conflict in the New States of Tropical Africa," *American Political Science Review*, LXII (March 1968): pp. 70—87.

[44]For details of these arguments, see Chalmers Johnson, ed., *The Role of the Military in Underdeveloped Countries* (Princeton, N.J.: Princeton University Press, 1962), especially the articles by Pye and Shils, and Samuel P. Huntington, ed. *Changing Patterns of Military Politics* (New York: The Free Press, 1962). Also see the application of this argument to African politics in Harvey Glickman, "The Military in African Politics: A Bibliographic Essay," *African Forum*, 2 (Summer 1966): 73; and H. Bienen, ed., *The Military and Modernization* (Chicago: Aldine, 1971).

[45]See Morris Janowitz, *The Military in the Development of New Nations* (Chicago: The University of Chicago Press, 1964). Also, Kenneth Grundy, *Conflicting Images of the Army in Africa* (Nairobi: East Africa Publishing House, 1968); Henry Bienen, ed., *The Military Intervenes: Case Studies in Political Development* (New York: Russell Sage Foundation, 1968); and Ernest W. Lefever, *Spear and Scepter: Army, Police and Politics in Tropical Africa* (Washington, D.C.: The Brookings Institution, 1970), J. M. Lee, *African Armies and Civil Order* (London: Chatto and Windus, 1969), and A. B. Bozeman *Conflict in Africa: Concepts and Realities* (Princeton: Princeton University Press, 1975.)

[46]See Janowitz, *op. cit.*, and the excellent case study by Robin Luckham, *The Nigerian Military* (New York: Cambridge University Press, 1972).

[47]Cf. W.F. Gutteridge, *Military Institutions and Power in the New States* (London, 1964); and James Coleman and Belmont Brice, Jr., "The Role of the Military in Sub-Saharan Africa," in *The Role of the Military in Underdeveloped Countries*, Johnson, ed., (Princeton, N.J.: Princeton University Press, 1962). For more contemporary views see W. F. Gutteridge *Military Regimes in Africa* (London: Methuen, 1975); and G. Kennedy *The Military in the Third World* (London: Duckworth, 1974).

[48]Russett, *et. al. World Handbook of Social and Political Indicators* (New Haven: Yale University Press, 1964).

[49]See Roger Murray, "Militarism in Africa," *New Left Review*, 38 (July-August 1966): 36—59.

[50]Lee, *op. cit.*

[51]Cf. Ali A. Mazrui and Donald Rothchild, "The Soldier and the State in East Africa: Some Theoretical Conclusions on the Army Mutinies of 1964," *Western Political Quarterly*, 20 (March 1967): especially p. 38.

[52]Chester A. Crocker, "France's Changing Military Interests," *Africa Report*, June 1968, and Ruth First, *The Barrel of a Gun* (Balti-

more: Penguin Books, 1970), p. 422.

[53]Cf. Samuel C. Ukpabi, "Military Recruitment and Social Mobility in Nineteenth Century British West Africa," *Journal of Modern African Studies*, 2 (Spring 1975): 87—107.

[54]Cf. Morrison and Stevenson, "Integration and Instability: Patterns of African Political Development," and A. Wells, "The Coup D'Etat in Theory and Practice: Independent Black Africa in the 1960's," *American Journal of Sociology*, 79 (January 1974): 871—887.

[55]*SIPRI Yearbook 1972* (Stockholm: International Peace Research Institute: Almquist and Wicksell, 1972).

TABLE 5.31   Total Manpower in the Armed Forces, in Thousands, 1977 (A), 1972 (B), 1967 (C), and 1963 (D).

Definition: All members of the regular army, navy and air force and reservists on active duty. Inactive reserves, gendarmerie para-military units, and national police excluded.

```
Range =          156.00
Mean =            18.00
Standard Deviation =        29.18
```

Population Percent Cum.	Country	Rank	Country Name	A	Range Decile	B	C	D
21.00	21.00	1.0	Nigeria	156.0	1	274.0	50.0	8.5
30.71	9.71	2.0	Ethiopia	80.0	5	45.0	35.0	31.0
36.95	6.24	3.0	Sudan	71.0	6	36.3	18.5	12.0
37.98	1.03	4.0	Somalia	62.6		15.0	9.5	5.2
43.14	5.16	5.0	Tanzania	44.9	8	11.6	5.0	4.5
45.40	2.26	6.0	Zimbabwe	34.0				
47.35	1.95	7.0	Angola	33.0				
50.34	2.99	8.0	Mozambique	26.7	9			
58.63	8.29	9.0	Zaire	22.1		50.0	35.4	32.0
61.11	2.48	10.0	Madagascar	19.6		4.1	4.1	2.7
62.76	1.65	11.0	Zambia	15.5	10	5.7	3.0	3.2
66.27	3.51	12.0	Ghana	15.3		18.6	16.0	8.7
70.87	4.60	13.0	Kenya	14.8		7.2	4.8	2.8
72.44	1.57	14.0	Guinea	9.9		6.1	5.0	5.2
74.08	1.64	15.0	Senegal	9.6		5.9	5.5	2.7
74.53	.45	16.0	Congo	9.5		2.2	1.8	.8
74.99	.46	17.0	Mauritania	8.0		1.1	1.0	.5
78.94	3.95	18.0	Uganda	7.5		12.6	6.0	2.2
81.35	2.41	19.0	Cameroon	7.3		4.4	3.5	2.9
83.57	2.22	20.0	Ivory Coast	6.6		4.5	4.5	4.3
83.76	.19	21.0	Guinea-Bissau	6.3				
85.04	1.28	22.0	Burundi	6.0		3.0	1.0	.9
85.57	.53	23.0	Liberia	5.4		4.2	4.1	3.8
86.93	1.36	24.0	Rwanda	5.2		2.8	2.5	1.0
88.59	1.66	25.5	Malawi	5.0		1.1	.9	1.6
90.46	1.87	25.5	Mali	5.0		3.7	3.5	3.3
92.43	1.97	27.0	Upper Volta	3.8		1.8	1.5	1.1
93.18	.75	28.0	Togo	3.6		1.3	1.5	.3
94.52	1.34	29.0	Chad	3.2		3.7	.9	.8
95.52	1.00	30.0	Benin	3.1		2.3	1.8	1.1
96.51	.99	31.0	Sierra Leone	2.7		1.4	1.9	1.9
96.67	.16	32.0	Swaziland	2.6		0	0	0
96.77	.10	33.0	Djibouti	2.4				
98.10	1.33	34.0	Niger	2.2		2.1	1.3	1.3
98.33	.23	36.0	Botswana	2.0		0	0	0
98.43	.10	36.0	Equatorial Guinea	2.0		1.0		
98.59	.16	36.0	Gabon	2.0		1.2	.8	.6
99.17	.58	38.0	Central African R	1.9		3.0	.6	.6
99.55	.38	39.0	Lesotho	1.5		0	0	0
99.72	.17	40.0	Gambia	0		0	0	0

```
DATA NOT AVAILABLE OR NOT APPLICABLE
FOR THE FOLLOWING COUNTRIES

Namibia
```

SOURCES: (1963,1967) D. Wood, *The Armed Forces of African States,* Adelphi Papers, no. 27 (London: Institute for Strategic Studies, 1966). Robert C. Sellers, *Reference Handbook of the Armed Forces of the World,* 2nd ed. (Garden City, N.Y.: Robert C. Sellers and Assoc., 1968). *Nigeria:* Estimated—Nigerian armed forces were officially given as 12,500 in Sellers, but rapid expansion due to the civil war escalated this figure to as much as 100,000 in 1968 and, some observers report, to 300,000 in 1970.
(1972) *Africa South of the Sahara 1973* and *World Military Expendi-tures and Arms Transfers 1965-1974* (Washington D.C.: U.S. Arms Control and Disarmament Agency, 1976).
(1977) *The Military Balance*; *Equatorial Guinea*; Staff estimate.

Note: Angola, Guinea-Bissau and Mozambique are not coded until independence, since the size of the Portuguese army would not be a meaningful indicator of the independent country's military and coercive capabilities.

TABLE 5.32   Armed Forces Manpower Per 100,000 Population,
1977 (A), 1972 (B), 1967 (C), and 1963 (D).

```
Range =        1590.00
Mean =          352.98
Standard Deviation =        322.16
```

Population Percent Cum.	Country	Rank	Country Name	A	Range Decile	B	C	D
1.03	1.03	1.0	Somalia	1590	1	510	357	221
1.22	.19	2.0	Guinea-Bissau	1000	4			
1.68	.46	3.0	Mauritania	860	5	90	91	52
11.39	9.71	4.0	Ethiopia	750	6	174	149	142
11.84	.45	5.0	Congo	730		176	209	92
11.94	.10	6.0	Djibouti	727				
13.89	1.95	7.0	Angola	720				
14.05	.16	8.0	Gabon	670		237	169	132
14.15	.10	9.0	Equatorial Guinea	606	7	333		
15.72	1.57	10.0	Guinea	507		148	135	155
15.88	.16	11.0	Swaziland	433	8	0	0	0
16.11	.23	12.0	Botswana	430		0	0	0
16.64	.53	13.0	Liberia	410		261	369	364
22.88	6.24	14.0	Sudan	400		240	129	102
28.04	5.16	15.0	Tanzania	380		83	16	41
29.69	1.65	16.0	Zambia	360		129	76	92
31.95	2.26	17.0	Zimbabwe	340				
52.95	21.00	18.0	Nigeria	280	9	472	81	15
55.43	2.48	19.0	Madagascar	250		58	64	48
57.07	1.64	20.0	Senegal	240		143	150	81
58.41	1.34	21.0	Chad	210		98	26	25
59.69	1.28	22.5	Burundi	200		85	30	28
60.44	.75	22.5	Togo	200		60	87	16
68.73	8.29	24.0	Zaire	190		218	216	213
69.31	.58	25.0	Central African R	180		177	41	42
72.82	3.51	26.0	Ghana	170		204	196	119
73.20	.38	27.0	Lesotho	146	10	0	0	0
75.61	2.41	28.0	Cameroon	140		73	64	58
77.48	1.87	29.5	Mali	130		69	74	75
80.47	2.99	29.5	Mozambique	130				
81.47	1.00	31.0	Benin	120		78	72	49
83.69	2.22	32.0	Ivory Coast	110		99	112	117
88.29	4.60	34.0	Kenya	90		59	48	32
89.95	1.66	34.0	Malawi	90		25	22	43
91.92	1.97	34.0	Upper Volta	90		31	30	22
93.25	1.33	36.5	Niger	80		50	37	41
94.61	1.36	36.5	Rwanda	80		71	76	34
98.56	3.95	38.0	Uganda	50		121	76	31
99.55	.99	39.0	Sierra Leone	30		53	78	82
99.72	.17	40.0	Gambia	0		0	0	0

DATA NOT AVAILABLE OR NOT APPLICABLE
FOR THE FOLLOWING COUNTRIES

Namibia

SOURCES: See Table 5.31.

TABLE 5.33   Size of Internal Security Forces per 100,000 Population, 1977 (A), 1971 (B), 1967 (C), and 1964 (D).

Definition: Includes all police forces, gendarmarie and para-military units.

```
Range =           781.00
Mean =            126.56
Standard Deviation =          144.58
```

Population Percent Cum.	Country	Rank	Country Name	A	Range Decile	B	C	D
2.26	2.26	1.0	Zimbabwe	790	1			
2.36	.10	2.0	Djibouti	400	5			
23.36	21.00	3.0	Nigeria	301	7	69	37	41
23.81	.45	4.0	Congo	260		120	174	182
24.00	.19	5.0	Guinea-Bissau	250				
25.03	1.03	6.0	Somalia	239	8	221	180	198
25.26	.23	7.0	Botswana	164	9	79	118	129
27.67	2.41	8.0	Cameroon	138		116	103	116
29.01	1.34	9.0	Chad	128		106	59	59
29.17	.16	10.0	Gabon	118		343	190	196
30.83	1.66	11.0	Malawi	117		126	143	153
31.82	.99	12.0	Sierra Leone	108		89	82	86
32.28	.46	13.0	Mauritania	100		33	73	39
32.86	.58	14.0	Central African R	92		118	103	105
42.57	9.71	15.5	Ethiopia	88		79	128	135
43.10	.53	15.5	Liberia	88		44	63	67
43.48	.38	17.0	Lesotho	87	10	106	56	61
48.08	4.60	18.0	Kenya	86		95	116	126
49.36	1.28	19.0	Burundi	82		24	27	25
51.84	2.48	20.0	Madagascar	81		83	107	107
53.41	1.57	21.0	Guinea	73		80	89	96
54.16	.75	22.0	Togo	65		62	75	81
56.38	2.22	23.0	Ivory Coast	64		39	57	61
64.67	8.29	24.0	Zaire	56		65	92	98
69.83	5.16	25.0	Tanzania	55		36	41	45
70.83	1.00	26.0	Benin	53		59	68	74
74.34	3.51	27.0	Ghana	41		99	111	119
75.98	1.64	28.0	Senegal	39		39	82	88
77.31	1.33	29.0	Niger	36		40	42	46
79.28	1.97	30.0	Upper Volta	30		33	36	38
85.52	6.24	31.0	Sudan	29		33	70	83
87.39	1.87	32.0	Mali	21		11	34	36
88.75	1.36	33.0	Rwanda	15		17	24	20
92.70	3.95	34.0	Uganda	9		10	69	75

DATA NOT AVAILABLE OR NOT APPLICABLE
FOR THE FOLLOWING COUNTRIES

Angola	Equatorial Guinea	Gambia	Mozambique
Namibia	Swaziland	Zambia	

SOURCES: See Table 5.31.

Angola, Guinea-Bissau, Mozambique were not independent during the period before 1972 and Portuguese force levels would be misleading as a characteristic of these countries. An additional source for 1971 data was R. C. Sellers, *Armed Forces of the World: A Reference Handbook*, 3rd ed. (New York: Praeger, 1971).

TABLE 5.34   Average Annual Percent Change in Total Armed Forces Manpower 1972-1977 (A) 1967-1972 (B), and 1963-1967 (C).

```
Range =        68.30
Mean =         11.04
Standard Deviation =        13.28
```

Population Percent Cum. Country	Percent Country	Rank	Country Name	A	Range Decile	B	C
.46	.46	1.0	Mauritania	62.7	1	2.0	22.5
2.94	2.48	2.0	Madagascar	37.8	4	0	92.5
4.60	1.66	3.0	Malawi	33.5	5	5.6	-11.0
5.05	.45	4.0	Congo	33.2		4.4	35.8
6.08	1.03	5.0	Somalia	31.7		11.6	21.3
11.24	5.16	6.0	Tanzania	28.7		26.4	2.8
11.99	.75	7.0	Togo	18.8	7	-3.4	142.3
13.64	1.65	8.0	Zambia	17.2		18.0	1.5
15.61	1.97	9.0	Upper Volta	11.7	8	3.4	10.8
20.21	4.60	10.0	Kenya	10.6		9.8	17.8
22.16	1.95	15.5	Angola	10.0			
22.39	.23	15.5	Botswana	10.0		0	
23.67	1.28	15.5	Burundi	10.0		40.0	3.8
23.77	.10	15.5	Djibouti	10.0		-0	
23.87	.10	15.5	Equatorial Guinea	10.0		20.0	
24.06	.19	15.5	Guinea-Bissau	10.0			
24.44	.38	15.5	Lesotho	10.0		0	
27.43	2.99	15.5	Mozambique	10.0			
27.59	.16	15.5	Swaziland	10.0		0	
29.85	2.26	15.5	Zimbabwe	10.0			
36.09	6.24	21.0	Sudan	9.6		19.2	13.5
37.08	.99	22.0	Sierra Leone	9.3		-5.2	.3
38.44	1.36	23.0	Rwanda	8.9		2.0	38.3
48.15	9.71	24.0	Ethiopia	7.8	9	5.8	3.5
48.31	.16	25.0	Gabon	6.5		10.2	7.5
50.72	2.41	26.0	Cameroon	6.4		5.4	5.3
52.36	1.64	27.0	Senegal	6.3		1.4	25.8
53.93	1.57	28.0	Guinea	6.2		4.4	-1.0
56.15	2.22	29.0	Ivory Coast	4.7		0	1.0
57.15	1.00	30.0	Benin	3.8		5.0	16.0
59.02	1.87	31.0	Mali	3.7		.8	1.5
59.55	.53	32.0	Liberia	3.0		.2	2.5
60.88	1.33	33.0	Niger	.5	10	12.4	0
61.05	.17	34.0	Gambia	0		0	0
62.39	1.34	35.0	Chad	-1.4		62.2	29.3
65.90	3.51	36.0	Ghana	-1.8		3.2	20.8
66.48	.58	37.0	Central African R	-3.7		80.0	2.8
70.43	3.95	38.0	Uganda	-4.0		22.0	45.5
91.43	21.00	39.0	Nigeria	-4.3		89.6	119.8
99.72	8.29	40.0	Zaire	-5.6		8.2	2.5

```
DATA NOT AVAILABLE OR NOT APPLICABLE
FOR THE FOLLOWING COUNTRIES

Namibia
```

SOURCES: See Table 5.31. *Equatorial Guinea* which had no army in 1967 is arbitrarily coded 100 percent for the period.

TABLE 5.35   Average Annual Percent Change in Internal Security Forces per 100,000 Population, 1972-1977 (A), 1967-1972 (B) and 1964-1967 (C).

```
Range =     123.30
Mean =        7.71
Standard Deviation =        21.86
```

Population Percent Cum. Country	Percent Country	Rank	Country Name	A	Range Decile	B	C
.45	.45	1.0	Congo	116.7	1	-3.1	18.5
21.45	21.00	2.0	Nigeria	33.6	7	8.6	-.8
22.73	1.28	3.0	Burundi	24.2	8	-1.1	6.9
24.07	1.34	4.0	Chad	20.8		8.0	
24.53	.46	5.0	Mauritania	20.3		-5.5	8.7
24.76	.23	6.0	Botswana	10.8	9	-3.3	-.7
25.29	.53	7.0	Liberia	10.0		-3.0	-.6
27.16	1.87	8.0	Mali	9.1		-6.8	2.6
29.38	2.22	9.0	Ivory Coast	6.4		-3.2	-.3
34.54	5.16	10.0	Tanzania	5.3	10	-1.2	-.9
35.53	.99	11.0	Sierra Leone	2.1		.9	-.5
37.94	2.41	12.0	Cameroon	1.9		1.3	-1.0
39.30	1.36	13.0	Rwanda	1.2		-2.9	2.0
49.01	9.71	14.0	Ethiopia	1.1		-3.8	-.5
50.04	1.03	15.0	Somalia	.8		2.3	-1.1
50.79	.75	16.0	Togo	.5		-1.7	-.1
52.43	1.64	17.0	Senegal	0		-5.2	-3.1
54.91	2.48	18.0	Madagascar	-.2		-2.2	.7
56.57	1.66	19.0	Malawi	-.7		-1.2	8.3
58.14	1.57	21.0	Guinea	-.9		-1.0	-.8
62.74	4.60	21.0	Kenya	-.9		-1.8	-.9
64.71	1.97	21.0	Upper Volta	-.9		-.8	2.9
65.71	1.00	24.0	Benin	-1.0		-1.3	-.8
67.04	1.33	24.0	Niger	-1.0		-.5	-1.1
70.99	3.95	24.0	Uganda	-1.0		-4.8	-.8
77.23	6.24	26.0	Sudan	-1.2		-5.3	-.8
85.52	8.29	27.0	Zaire	-1.4		-2.9	-.7
85.90	.38	28.0	Lesotho	-1.8		8.9	-1.0
86.48	.58	29.0	Central African R	-2.2		1.5	-9.6
89.99	3.51	30.0	Ghana	-5.9		-1.1	-.8
90.15	.16	31.0	Gabon	-6.6		8.1	-.3

```
DATA NOT AVAILABLE OR NOT APPLICABLE
FOR THE FOLLOWING COUNTRIES

Angola        Djibouti      Equatorial Guinea  Gambia
Guinea-Bissau Mozambique    Namibia       Swaziland
Zambia        Zimbabwe
```

SOURCES: See Table 5.31. In addition, see R.C. Sellers *Armed Forces of the World: A Reference Handbook* 3rd edition (New York: Praeger, 1971).

Note: The large number of countries with negative values on this variable is generally caused by little or no increase in the size of the internal security forces (numerator) along with normal population growth (denominator). In general, expansion in force capability has been in the armed forces in African states.

TABLE 5.36   Defense Budget as a Percent of GNP 1977 (A), 1972 (B), 1967 (C) and 1963 (D).

```
Range =            13.80
Mean =              3.09
Standard Deviation =           2.53
```

Population Percent Cum.	Country	Rank	Country Name	A	Range Decile	B	C	D
1.03	1.03	1.0	Somalia	13.8	1	6.2	4.6	3.5
1.22	.19	2.5	Guinea-Bissau	7.1	5			
1.68	.46	2.5	Mauritania	7.1		2.0	1.4	4.3
3.94	2.26	4.0	Zimbabwe	6.8	6			
4.39	.45	5.0	Congo	5.2	7	4.7	3.3	2.0
4.55	.16	6.0	Swaziland	4.3		0	0	0
6.12	1.57	8.0	Guinea	4.2		4.0	4.3	2.6
27.12	21.00	8.0	Nigeria	4.2		4.4	2.8	1.1
32.28	5.16	8.0	Tanzania	4.2		2.4	.9	.2
38.52	6.24	10.0	Sudan	4.0	8	5.2	3.3	1.9
38.75	.23	11.0	Botswana	3.8		0	0	0
40.62	1.87	12.0	Mali	3.5		2.4	2.4	2.7
41.96	1.34	13.5	Chad	3.4		5.2	3.9	.5
43.93	1.97	13.5	Upper Volta	3.4		1.3	1.2	1.1
47.88	3.95	15.5	Uganda	3.1		5.4	1.5	.2
49.53	1.65	15.5	Zambia	3.1		5.2	1.4	2.0
59.24	9.71	18.0	Ethiopia	2.8		2.6	2.3	1.9
61.72	2.48	18.0	Madagascar	2.8		1.4	1.6	1.5
62.47	.75	18.0	Togo	2.8		1.4	1.8	.7
65.46	2.99	20.0	Mozambique	2.4	9			
66.74	1.28	22.5	Burundi	2.2		2.1	1.5	.9
67.32	.58	22.5	Central African R	2.2		2.1	2.0	.7
69.54	2.22	22.5	Ivory Coast	2.2		1.3	1.4	.1
71.18	1.64	22.5	Senegal	2.2		1.9	2.1	1.1
72.84	1.66	25.0	Malawi	2.1		.4	.5	.5
73.84	1.00	26.0	Benin	2.0		1.7	1.9	.6
76.25	2.41	28.0	Cameroon	1.6		1.9	2.2	2.6
80.85	4.60	28.0	Kenya	1.6		1.3	1.2	.7
82.21	1.36	28.0	Rwanda	1.6		1.7	1.8	2.2
82.74	.53	30.0	Liberia	1.1	10	1.1	1.3	1.9
83.73	.99	31.0	Sierra Leone	1.0		.8	.6	.7
85.06	1.33	32.0	Niger	.8		.7	.8	1.0
93.35	8.29	33.0	Zaire	.7		3.8	4.1	1.8
93.51	.16	34.0	Gabon	.5		1.6	1.1	1.3
97.02	3.51	35.0	Ghana	.4		1.5	3.0	2.0
97.40	.38	36.0	Lesotho	.1		0	0	0
97.57	.17	37.0	Gambia	0		0	0	0

```
DATA NOT AVAILABLE OR NOT APPLICABLE
FOR THE FOLLOWING COUNTRIES

Angola      Djibouti    Equatorial Guinea  Namibia
```

SOURCES: *World Tables 1980. National Basic Intelligence Factbook 1980. World Military Expenditures and Arms Transfers 1965-1974* (and 1975 edition for 1963-73 data). (Washington D.C.: U.S. Arms Control and Disarmament Agency, 1976).

TABLE 5.37   Defense Budget as Percent of Government Expenditures, 1979 (A), 1972 (B), 1967 (C), and 1963 (D).

```
Range =          39.00
Mean =           14.09
Standard Deviation =        9.21
```

Population Percent			Country			Range			
Cum.	Country	Rank	Name	A	Decile	B	C	D	
.46	.46	1.0	Mauritania	39.0	1	13.5	17.9	18.8	
10.17	9.71	2.0	Ethiopia	32.9	2	16.7	17.0	17.4	
10.27	.10	3.0	Djibouti	27.9	3				
13.26	2.99	4.0	Mozambique	27.8					
14.60	1.34	5.0	Chad	25.8	4	29.0	13.5	4.6	
16.86	2.26	6.0	Zimbabwe	25.0					
18.81	1.95	7.0	Angola	24.8					
19.00	.19	8.0	Guinea-Bissau	24.0					
20.65	1.65	9.0	Zambia	22.5	5	20.0	5.7	0	
20.75	.10	10.0	Equatorial Guinea	21.0		0	0	0	
21.78	1.03	11.0	Somalia	20.1		30.5	18.1	18.4	
23.65	1.87	12.0	Mali	18.6	6	23.8	21.2	19.4	
44.65	21.00	13.0	Nigeria	17.9		37.1	9.9	11.1	
49.25	4.60	14.0	Kenya	16.0		5.3	6.9	3.7	
53.20	3.95	15.0	Uganda	15.1	7	35.6	10.2	1.0	
53.65	.45	16.0	Congo	14.0		19.6	8.9	7.8	
59.89	6.24	17.0	Sudan	13.6		17.5	17.7	9.4	
61.25	1.36	18.0	Rwanda	12.4		13.7	3.0	20.4	
62.91	1.66	19.0	Malawi	11.3	8	2.1	3.3	0	
64.19	1.28	20.0	Burundi	11.2		18.7	6.9	7.1	
66.16	1.97	21.0	Upper Volta	11.0		14.2	14.1	5.7	
74.45	8.29	22.0	Zaire	10.8		15.1	14.5	12.6	
76.09	1.64	23.0	Senegal	10.7		10.9	11.6	4.2	
81.25	5.16	24.0	Tanzania	10.5		9.1	3.8	1.4	
82.25	1.00	25.0	Benin	9.7		13.0	12.0	3.2	
83.00	.75	26.0	Togo	9.6		10.4	13.5	4.1	
83.58	.58	27.0	Central African R	8.6		11.1	7.9	4.3	
85.99	2.41	28.0	Cameroon	8.3		10.6	19.5	13.8	
86.15	.16	29.0	Swaziland	8.1		0		0	
86.31	.16	30.0	Gabon	8.0		6.6	7.6	8.1	
87.30	.99	31.0	Sierra Leone	7.8		4.2	4.9	4.7	
89.52	2.22	32.0	Ivory Coast	7.2	9	6.5	6.9	.7	
90.85	1.33	33.0	Niger	6.1		7.4	10.8	8.2	
94.36	3.51	34.0	Ghana	5.3		9.0	7.4	8.1	
96.84	2.48	35.0	Madagascar	4.1		8.3	9.6	10.0	
97.37	.53	36.0	Liberia	2.7	10	4.4	6.7	6.9	
97.60	.23	38.0	Botswana	0		0	0	0	
97.77	.17	38.0	Gambia	0		0	0	0	
98.15	.38	38.0	Lesotho	0		0	0	0	

```
DATA NOT AVAILABLE OR NOT APPLICABLE
FOR THE FOLLOWING COUNTRIES

Guinea      Namibia
```

SOURCE: R.C. Sellers, *Reference Handbook to the Armed Forces of the World* 1st, 2nd eds. *AID Economic Data Book* 1970 and 1975 editions; Institute for Strategic Studies, *The Military Balance* various years; *Africa South of the Sahara* 1974 and 1975; and *World Military Expenditures and Arms Transfers 1965-1974* (and 1963-1973 editions) (Washington D.C.: U.S. Arms Control and Disarmament Agency); *National Basic Intelligence Factbook 1980, World Factbook*, 1981, and *Africa South of the Sahara*, 1982—83.

TABLE 5.38   Average Annual Percent Change in Defense Budget, 1972-79 (A), 1967 to 1972 (B), and 1963 to 1967 (C).

Range =   44.90
Mean =   6.14
Standard Deviation =   10.08

Population Percent							
Cum.	Country	Rank	Country Name	A	Range Decile	B	C
.46	.46	1.0	Mauritania	37.0	1	-3	-11
5.62	5.16	2.0	Tanzania	33.3		59	104
7.28	1.66	3.0	Malawi	29.1	2	6	18
8.31	1.03	4.0	Somalia	18.2	5	16	16
10.28	1.97	5.0	Upper Volta	16.7		7	6
11.93	1.65	6.0	Zambia	11.0	6	84	3
15.88	3.95	7.0	Uganda	9.7	7	92	184
16.11	.23	9.5	Botswana	9.1		0	0
16.49	.38	9.5	Lesotho	9.1		0	0
16.65	.16	9.5	Swaziland	9.1		0	0
18.91	2.26	9.5	Zimbabwe	9.1			
21.39	2.48	12.0	Madagascar	6.8		4	9
22.38	.99	13.0	Sierra Leone	6.1		12	
22.83	.45	14.5	Congo	5.2	8	18	13
25.05	2.22	14.5	Ivory Coast	5.2		9	10
25.80	.75	16.0	Togo	5.1		13	46
46.80	21.00	17.0	Nigeria	4.5		56	58
48.08	1.28	18.5	Burundi	4.2		10	5
49.95	1.87	18.5	Mali	4.2		9	-9
54.55	4.60	20.0	Kenya	3.0		14	38
64.26	9.71	21.0	Ethiopia	2.0		15	16
70.50	6.24	22.0	Sudan	1.9		23	26
71.08	.58	23.0	Central African R	.9	9	9	71
72.08	1.00	24.0	Benin	.5		10	75
73.72	1.64	25.0	Senegal	.4		4	26
73.89	.17	26.5	Gambia	0		0	0
75.22	1.33	26.5	Niger	0		15	3
76.79	1.57	28.0	Guinea	-.2		7	32
78.15	1.36	29.0	Rwanda	-1.0		19	3
79.49	1.34	30.0	Chad	-1.2		19	175
80.02	.53	31.0	Liberia	-1.4		3	7
82.43	2.41	32.0	Cameroon	-2.4		7	7
82.59	.16	33.0	Gabon	-5.0	10	24	13
90.88	8.29	34.0	Zaire	-7.5		16	45
94.39	3.51	35.0	Ghana	-7.9		-7	20

DATA NOT AVAILABLE OR NOT APPLICABLE
FOR THE FOLLOWING COUNTRIES

Angola   Djibouti   Equatorial Guinea   Guinea-Bissau
Mozambique   Namibia

SOURCES: See Table 5.37.

6. International Relations

The greatest proportion of this book is devoted to descriptions of the geographical, social, cultural, economic and political characteristics of individual Black African states, and to discussions of the potential relevance of such aggregate attributes of national political systems to the explanation of variable patterns of development within them. It is clear, however, that national political systems, especially those Black African countries conceived in the historical process of colonialism, are parts of the wider international environment, and that their development is affected to a considerable extent by support, opposition, controls and shocks that emanate from this international environment.[1] A considerable proportion of the energy of the leaders of political, economic and cultural institutions within these countries is devoted to activity in international governmental and nongovernmental organizations and in formal or informal diplomatic relations. Such activity affects changing patterns of international integration and regionalization, changing patterns of international conflict and influences, and changing constraints on the autonomous development of individual nations.[2]

The historic commitments of African nationalists to the freedom and unity of African peoples were nurtured first in international, pan-African organizations, and these symbolic commitments continue. The post-independence era, however, has involved a tendency more towards a diversity than unity in the ideological orientation and foreign policy of Black African states. The unifying themes of anti-colonialism and anti-racism have lost much of their practical importance as these countries divide over issues such as support to partisans in the struggle for post-colonial sovereignty in Angola and the former Spanish Sahara, and as the resilience and economic power of the regime in the Republic of South Africa stimulates accommodation and dialogue on the part of some (although still a minority) of the Black African countries. Similarly, the ideals of the "Pax Africana" and "Neutralism" or "Non-Alignment" have lost some of their gloss in a decade when foreign mercenaries or foreign armies have played critical roles in support of parties to civil wars in Zaire, Chad, Ethiopia and Angola, or in support of established governments threatened by coups d'état in many other Black African states. The achievement of African unity was perhaps as much set back as advanced by the establishment of the Organization of African Unity,

committed as it has been to the principles of national sovereignty which protect and reinforce differences associated with national boundaries. Certainly the record of regional integration in the Mali Federation, the East African Common Market, and the various Central and West African international organizations or common markets, has not so far been encouraging.

Nevertheless, if African unity is not reality, the potential international influence of these nations, making up as they do the largest regional block of voting strength in the United Nations, and having increasing representation in the executive offices of international organizations, is a matter of considerable significance. If it is correct to suggest "that the influence in international affairs of the African states seems in direct ratio to both their cohesiveness and their internal stability,"[3] it is important to understand factors in the international system that influence their cohesiveness and internal stability. Three characteristics of the international environment threaten this cohesiveness and internal stability: (1) the historic ties of African states to different European metropolitan powers; (2) ideological and economic divisions between the super-power parties to the 20th century cold war; and (3) the stark divisions between industrial and Third World nations, the gap between which is preserved by the economic dependency of the latter on the former. It is the purpose of this Chapter to review, with reference to illustrative aggregate data, generalizations about these variable features of Black Africa's situation in the international system.

The Colonial Background

The incorporation of African societies into the world economic system predates the international "partition" of Africa and the establishment of formal colonial rule.[4] The reluctance of the European powers to undertake the financial and administrative burden of colonial government in Africa did not, however, extend to financial support for economically motivated exploration or for the establishment of trading monopolies with official protection. Whatever the political and strategic reasons for the eventual colonization of Africa, international economic interests were clearly involved. And while it has been argued by intellectuals in and out of government, throughout the period of colonial rule and after, that African colonies were not profitable,[5] the fact did not diminish the attempts to make real the self-fulfilling prophecy: if Africa had been partitioned for European occupation and exploitation, it must have been because Europe could derive value from that effort. The stimulation of production in Africa for export to Europe was required to mobilize Africa into a cash economy from which revenue might be extracted to pay the cost of colonial administration and to increase the wealth of the industrial and commercial enterprises of the European metropoles. In general, therefore, infra-structure and investment was concentrated in those areas where the greatest payoff to Europe might be secured, and the African territories were developed to be, and have remained, critically dependent on foreign trade and foreign financial support for trade.

It has been estimated that the total investment in Sub-Saharan Africa between 1870 and 1936 was about 1,222,000,000 pounds made up in approximately equal proportions of loans or grants to governments, and private capital.[6] But of this total, less that ⅛ was invested in African countries where mineral exploitation is not a principal basis of trade, and because of the geography of colonization and mineral location, only 5.6% of this pre-World War II investment was in French territories, where the majority of the investment was controlled by the government—54.15% in French West Africa, 60.71% in Togo and the Cameroon, and 71.72% in Equatorial Africa. Investment in South Africa, Rhodesia, and the Belgian Congo, where the opportunities for mineral exploitation were great, was more than 10 times the investment in other areas of Africa.

Investments in areas where mineral exploitation was not possible were highly concentrated in government controlled developments of transportation for the extraction of African agricultural produce to Europe. Profits accruing to the early charter and concessionaire companies were limited because these organizations succeeded by 1910 in bleeding the readily accessible wealth of the tropical forest without reinvesting the substantial capital required to prevent their exports from declining.[7] And, because of the ravages of tropical disease, it was only in Eastern and Southern Africa that large-scale commercialization of agriculture on lands expropriated from Africans by English colonists took place with supporting levels of foreign investment. In other areas, Europeans were not given land, and European companies could not compete with African agricultural producers, who adapted quickly to the production of cocoa, palm oil, palm kernels, peanuts, and cotton for export to foreign markets.[8]

The dependence of the African territories on the political economy of Europe was made starkly obvious during the Second World War, which brought disruptions of trade and investment and reorganization of the institutional controls over the African worker and entrepreneur. Particularly in French territories, after the Vichy administration took over and the British blockade took effect, there was a very marked fall in the production and export of cash crops, and in both British and French West Africa there were pressures on the African producer to move from previously lucrative cash crops to the production of different crops and secondary goods not demanded by the allied war effort.[9] All major exports from British West Africa came under government control in 1942, and licenses for the export trade were given to a limited number of the largest foreign companies making it more difficult than ever for Africans to break into the export markets.[10]

In French West Africa, also, the colonial government took direct control of agriculture, intensifying compulsory labor and solidifying the competitive position of the European-owned plantations.[11] While these developments brought a certain amount of economic diversification and even some growth in the monetary value of exports in a few territories between 1938 and 1946, there were definite drops in the export of Africa's major cash crops,[12] and there was a serious decline in the real incomes earned by Africans.[13] The period after the Second World War, furthermore, involved a substantial intensification of foreign control of the African economies.

Motivated by the need to rebuild the war-ravaged European economies, by the allies' indebtedness to their African territories for contributions to the war effort, and the acceptance, in the U.N. charter, of the responsibility of colonial powers to develop the territories under their control and to prepare for their administration by the indigenous inhabitants, the influx of colonial investment to Black African territories in the period following World War II greatly exceeded that of the pre-war period. The British Colonial Development and Welfare Act set aside five million pounds a year for development projects and 500,000 pounds for research, and, in contrast to the minimal capital investment in French West Africa before the war, the French government provided perhaps as much as 400 million pounds to this area in the fifteen years following the Second World War.[14] As a partial consequence of this stimulation, the value of exports from Tropical Africa rose by about 70% from 1950 to 1960,[15] and, in contrast to the late 1940's, the real incomes of Africans rose in the decade of the 1950's.[16] The net benefits, however, of these new developments in trade and investment should not be assumed to have been consistently favorable to the Black African economies. The growth in the value of exports from Black Africa has been critically dependent on fluctuations in the demand and price for tropical commodities, and in the decade before independence the value of exports rose by 55% between 1950 and 1955, but by only 15% between 1955 and 1960.[17] Furthermore, the surplus capital generated from investments in Black Africa has been removed from the control of those most directly responsible for its generation. The most clear cut example of this phenomenon in the colonial era was the establishment of marketing boards throughout the British African colonies after the Second World War which led to government-controlled trading monopolies which set commodity prices below the world market price. The surplus so generated was then held at minimal rates of interest in London banks, and the sterling balances of the British colonies increased in this way from 670 million pounds to 1,301,000,000 pounds between 1945 and 1956.[18]

International Trade in Independent Black Africa

International relations between Black African countries, their former colonial metropolises, and other industrial states in the independence period have to be related to changing patterns of international trade and investment. With respect to trade, the value of exports from Black Africa has continued to reflect the upward trend in the post Second World War period, rising by close to 100% between 1960 and 1969.[19] The value of this trend to individual Black African nations, however, is modified by corresponding increases in the values of imports. The data in Table 6.1 indicate that two-thirds of these Black African states had a negative cumulative balance of trade expressed as a percentage of Gross National Product in the period 1973 to 1978. Adverse balances of trade can be accommodated by imported capital funds or by deflationary fiscal and monetary policy, neither of which is desirable. Economic and political policy designed to balance future trade accounts is, furthermore, critically constrained in these nations by their relative dependence on international trade for the generation of national income, and by their dependence on the production for a limited number of foreign markets.[20]

The data in Table 6.2 indicate the dependence on foreign trade in these nations as measured by the value of trade as a percentage of Gross National Product. In industrial countries such figures range from as low as 4 or 5% to 50% and more, but the average figure for Black African nations is at least 10 percentage points higher than the comparable figure for all nations in the world during the 1960's. The significance of this observation is indicated by the substantial relationship between higher rates of foreign trade dependency and lower levels of economic development reported for the data in the *World Handbook of Social and Political Indicators*.[21] General constraints on economic development resulting

from foreign trade dependency are magnified by a country's dependency on a limited range of export commodities. Data in Table 6.3 and 6.4 show the concentration of the three primary export items in the country's total exports, and the percentage of total exports made up by the value of trade in a country's principle export commodity. This latter measure ranges from over 90 down to 15 percent in these African states, but one or two specific products generally constitute a much higher percentage of total trade than is common in the industrial countries.

The relatively great trade and commodity dependence of these countries increases their vulnerability to fluctuating terms of trade which may lower their expected export incomes and increase the price of imports of intermediate capital goods required for domestic economic development.[22] Data such as those in Table 6.5 on the concentration of machinery, vehicles and mechanical equipment in the stock of imported commodities indicate the vulnerability of these economies to adverse terms of trade, although they may also indicate the extent to which Black African countries are able to initiate import substitution activities and, in the long run, decrease their trade dependency. In the short run, however, commodity dependencies are not likely to be conducive to national economic development, and the concentration of primary commodities in Black Africa's exports and of manufactured goods in imports increased in the early post-independence period. Exports of twenty leading primary commodities acccounted for 65.7% in 1960 and 70.1% in 1965 of all exports from Africa (excluding South Africa), while at the same time the imports of industrial manufactured goods accounted for 70.6% of all imports in 1960 and 71.8% in 1965.[23] Over this same period, estimates made by Belassa of the expected 1975 prices of Africa's main export commodities and of imported manufactured goods implied a decline in Africa's overall barter terms of trade of about 5%, with indices based on 1960 prices remaining relatively stable for manufactures between 1960 and 1975, but declining for all export commodities except coffee, which also remained stable.[24] Independent evidence of this trade disadvantage for countries with substantial dependency on primary commodity exports is shown by the prices of tropical commodities sold to the European Economic Community in 1958 and 1965. Between those dates the price of cocoa decreased by 55%, the price of cotton decreased by 24%, the price of vanilla by 23%, groundnuts by 22% and coffee by 20%.[25]

Another aspect of the international trading relationships is the relative dependency of African countries on single markets or products. The relatively great importance of the former colonial powers as trading partners to these African states is illustrated by figures for 1965 which show that 35% of exports from Africa went to France and the United Kingdom and 34% to the rest of Western Europe, while 30% of all imports came from France and the United Kingdom with an additional 24% from the rest of Western Europe.[26] Despite these figures, and suggestions that there has been little change in the trading relationships between Black African states and foreign countries,[27] the data in Table 6.7 show widespread decline in the concentration of trade between these states and their former colonial powers. There are, as indicated in Table 6.8 through 6.10, corresponding changes in the diversification of international trading relationships between these African countries, the United States, and Eastern-bloc countries. While this diversification is somewhat encouraging, it remains true that Black African countries are critically dependent on relations with non-African industrial nations, and that the low rates of inter-African trade severely limit the scope of regional integration among these countries.

Analysis of the relationships between variable patterns of foreign trade dependency and other aspects of development will require very great care. The effects of foreign trade are ambiguous to the extent that trade patterns reflect comparative advantages between trading partners, to the extent that imports are necessary for the acquisition of capital for initiating new economic development, and to the extent that exports are required to generate foreign exchange for the purchase of imports.[28] Without careful examination of the commodities exchanged and the inequalities in market power, the conceptualization of economic dependency will be gross.[29] From a preliminary inspection of correlational patterns in data like those presented in this book, it appears, for example, that increasing growth in the absolute value of exports and imports, or of the proportion of Gross Domestic Product (GDP) made up by exports and imports, is associated with increasing rates of growth in the GDP and Gross Domestic Capital Formation, and with *less* political instability. Such beneficial effects need to be qualified, however, by the evidence that deteriorating terms of trade, higher proportions of exports in a small number of commodities, negative trade balances, and higher volumes of bilateral foreign aid are associated with *lower* growth rates of national income and capital formation and a *higher* incidence of political instability.[30] The direct and indirect effects of foreign trade on economic and political developments require, therefore, very careful examination in future research.

Reliability

Generally, figures are estimated for all unregistered trade and these are added to the registered trade to get a total figure. While the reliability of trade statistics is generally high, two problems in particular affect the accounting of several countries in this Handbook. (1) Countries such as Sierra Leone that export small high-value items such as gold or diamonds often have considerable amounts smuggled out of the country to avoid export taxes and control. Smuggling is also a problem, however, with any commodity for which the structure of the market imposes substantial economic penalties for legal transactions within it, as for example in the cocoa market in Ghana and the coffee market in Guinea. (2) Another phenomenon affects coastal countries where goods are imported for re-export to land-locked interior countries. As a result, the trade figures for such countries are inflated and do not reflect the actual conditions of internal consumption. This does not necessarily diminish the relevance of the data, however, since importation for re-export allows for an increase in value-added for the economy. Nevertheless, the trade figures given here should be considered in the light of these data problems.

TABLE 6.1 Cumulative Balance of Trade, 1973—1978 (A), 1969—1972 (B), and 1963—1968 (C) as Percent of GNP.

Definition: The sum of the balance of trade (Exports minus Imports) for the years 1963 through 1968 divided by GNP in 1967, for the years 1969 through 1972 divided by GNP in 1972, and for the years 1973 through 1978 divided by GNP in 1977.

TABLE 6.2 Trade as Percent of GNP, ca. 1977 (A), 1972 (B) and 1968 (C).

Definition: Sum of Exports and Imports divided by Gross National Product.

```
Range =        220.00
Mean =         -22.06
Standard Deviation =        47.34
```

Population Percent Cum.	Country	Rank	Country Name	A	Range Decile	B	C
1.95	1.95	1.0	Angola	67	1	6	1
2.48	.53	2.0	Liberia	51		94	70
3.47	.99	3.0	Sierra Leone	42	2	-7	25
3.57	.10	4.0	Equatorial Guinea	34			46
3.73	.16	5.0	Gabon	31		67	130
3.89	.16	6.0	Swaziland	25		41	37
24.89	21.00	7.0	Nigeria	17	3	14	11
26.46	1.57	8.5	Guinea	14		-22	12
28.11	1.65	8.5	Zambia	14		70	98
30.33	2.22	10.0	Ivory Coast	8		19	36
34.28	3.95	11.0	Uganda	3		19	29
37.79	3.51	12.0	Ghana	-2	4	2	-19
39.07	1.28	13.0	Burundi	-4		-10	-16
41.48	2.41	15.0	Cameroon	-7		-8	-4
51.19	9.71	15.0	Ethiopia	-7		-8	-16
51.94	.75	15.0	Togo	-7		-23	19
56.54	4.60	17.0	Kenya	-8		-31	21
62.78	6.24	18.0	Sudan	-14		2	16
65.26	2.48	19.0	Madagascar	-18		-19	-43
66.62	1.36	20.0	Rwanda	-22	5	-16	11
68.26	1.64	21.0	Senegal	-23		-26	19
76.55	8.29	22.0	Zaire	-24		24	47
81.71	5.16	23.0	Tanzania	-28		-15	28
81.88	.17	24.0	Gambia	-30		-40	-53
83.54	1.66	25.0	Malawi	-40		-37	22
86.53	2.99	26.5	Mozambique	-42		-26	-32
87.86	1.33	26.5	Niger	-42		-20	7
88.44	.58	28.0	Central Afri. R	-53	6	-2	-15
89.44	1.00	29.0	Benin	-55		-59	-77
89.90	.46	30.0	Mauritania	-68	7	71	44
91.77	1.87	31.0	Mali	-73		-20	3
93.74	1.97	32.0	Upper Volta	-74		-34	-56
95.08	1.34	33.0	Chad	-84		-36	-18
95.53	.45	34.0	Congo	-99	8	-47	-129
96.56	1.03	35.0	Somalia	-123	9	-10	21
96.75	.19	36.0	Guinea-Bissau	-153	10	-71	-42

DATA NOT AVAILABLE OR NOT APPLICABLE
FOR THE FOLLOWING COUNTRIES

Botswana	Djibouti	Lesotho	Namibia
Zimbabwe			

```
Range =        156.00
Mean =          66.93
Standard Deviation =        39.08
```

Population Percent Cum.	Country	Rank	Country Name	A	Range Decile	B	C
.16	.16	1.0	Swaziland	166	1	128	84
.54	.38	2.0	Lesotho	146	2	81	52
1.07	.53	3.0	Liberia	133	3	110	120
1.24	.17	4.0	Gambia	131		88	95
1.70	.46	5.0	Mauritania	126		83	65
2.15	.45	6.5	Congo	122		43	73
2.31	.16	6.5	Gabon	122		58	96
2.54	.23	8.0	Botswana	119	4	111	69
2.83	.29	9.0	Namibia	101	5		
5.05	2.22	10.0	Ivory Coast	87	6	55	69
6.70	1.65	11.0	Zambia	83		81	109
9.11	2.41	12.5	Cameroon	81		43	49
10.75	1.64	12.5	Senegal	81		47	29
11.78	1.03	14.0	Somalia	80		48	55
13.12	1.34	15.0	Chad	76		31	24
13.87	.75	16.0	Togo	67	7	41	42
34.87	21.00	17.0	Nigeria	65		39	21
35.87	1.00	18.5	Benin	61		48	71
40.47	4.60	18.5	Kenya	61		44	51
41.46	.99	20.0	Sierra Leone	60		46	49
42.04	.58	21.5	Central Afri. R	57		27	39
43.37	1.33	21.5	Niger	57		30	21
51.66	8.29	23.0	Zaire	53	8	65	63
53.32	1.66	24.5	Malawi	52		45	59
55.19	1.87	24.5	Mali	52		29	19
57.67	2.48	26.0	Madagascar	49		36	43
59.93	2.26	27.0	Zimbabwe	48			
61.90	1.97	28.0	Upper Volta	47		20	25
67.06	5.16	29.0	Tanzania	44		46	58
67.25	.19	30.0	Guinea-Bissau	43		25	9
68.61	1.36	31.0	Rwanda	42		22	26
70.18	1.57	32.0	Guinea	31	9	33	27
71.46	1.28	33.5	Burundi	30		25	22
81.17	9.71	33.5	Ethiopia	30		17	18
87.41	6.24	35.0	Sudan	28		33	22
91.36	3.95	36.0	Uganda	25	10	29	51
91.46	.10	37.5	Djibouti	23			
91.56	.10	37.5	Equatorial Guinea	23		67	66
94.55	2.99	39.0	Mozambique	17		21	30
98.06	3.51	40.0	Ghana	15		25	37
100.00	1.95	41.0	Angola	10		41	58

SOURCES: (1963—68) *AID Economic Data Book 1970*; *World Bank Atlas 1969*; *Botswana, Lesotho, Guinea-Bissau, Swaziland, Equatorial Guinea, Swaziland*: Estimated from partial data for the period.
(1969—72) *Africa: Economic Growth Trends* (Washington D.C.: A.I.D. *Statistics and Reports* Division, October 1974); *Guinea-Bissau* estimated from partial data. *World Bank Atlas 1975*.
(1973—1978) *World Tables 1980*.

SOURCE: *Trade data*: U.S. A.I.D. *Africa: Economic Growth Trends*; *Europa Yearbook*, various years. GNP data: *World Bank Atlas* various years.
(1977) *World Tables 1980*.

TABLE 6.3   Commodity Concentration 1977 (A), 1970 (B), 1965 (C) and 1961 (D).

Definition: Percentage contribution of three major commodities in total merchandise exports.

```
Range =          74.80
Mean =           77.89
Standard Deviation =      17.88
```

Population Percent Cum.	Country	Rank	Country Name	A	Range Decile	B	C	D
1.28	1.28	1.5	Burundi	99.9	1	95.7	89.6	99.1
1.38	.10	1.5	Djibouti	99.9				
1.61	.23	3.0	Botswana	99.6		96.5	60.3	20.0
1.99	.38	4.0	Lesotho	98.5		48.1	88.8	72.6
2.45	.46	5.0	Mauritania	97.1		87.8	93.9	28.5
5.96	3.51	6.0	Ghana	96.8		77.9	81.9	84.5
7.61	1.65	7.0	Zambia	95.8		98.3	93.9	93.9
7.71	.10	8.0	Equatorial Guinea	95.6		97.5	97.8	99.7
11.66	3.95	9.0	Uganda	94.8		85.4	86.3	69.8
11.82	.16	10.0	Swaziland	93.7		49.0	42.0	22.3
12.01	.19	11.0	Guinea-Bissau	93.4		75.0	58.0	78.9
12.17	.16	12.0	Gabon	93.3		98.2	80.7	69.8
13.20	1.03	13.0	Somalia	90.6	2	35.6	69.0	60.3
13.73	.53	14.0	Liberia	89.4		91.0	93.0	84.3
13.90	.17	15.0	Gambia	87.7		75.9	61.7	95.7
22.19	8.29	16.0	Zaire	87.1		73.0	59.1	52.0
24.06	1.87	17.0	Mali	86.4		35.0	33.9	60.5
45.06	21.00	18.5	Nigeria	84.3	3	77.5	44.6	45.6
45.81	.75	18.5	Togo	84.3		83.4	85.6	60.6
47.14	1.33	20.0	Niger	84.1		64.7	58.7	77.2
56.85	9.71	21.0	Ethiopia	83.9		69.1	78.3	63.8
58.19	1.34	22.0	Chad	82.1		79.8	86.5	90.5
58.64	.45	23.0	Congo	81.8		93.0	41.7	76.4
60.21	1.57	24.0	Guinea	78.8		24.9	20.4	27.6
61.87	1.66	25.0	Malawi	77.4	4	70.3	73.6	93.8
63.23	1.36	26.0	Rwanda	77.2		59.5	54.1	91.9
69.47	6.24	27.0	Sudan	71.8		70.2	60.3	60.3
71.69	2.22	28.0	Ivory Coast	71.6		75.1	80.2	81.2
72.27	.58	29.0	Central African R	65.3	5	49.1	37.0	74.8
74.75	2.48	30.0	Madagascar	65.1		36.2	42.4	43.3
77.16	2.41	31.0	Cameroon	62.6		54.1	50.7	59.5
77.45	.29	32.5	Namibia	60.0	6			
79.71	2.26	32.5	Zimbabwe	60.0				
80.71	1.00	34.0	Benin	59.0		42.0	29.1	36.4
85.87	5.16	35.0	Tanzania	58.5		43.4	52.5	49.2
90.47	4.60	36.0	Kenya	56.4		49.7	50.5	34.2
92.42	1.95	37.0	Angola	54.5	7	55.1	56.3	50.0
94.06	1.64	38.0	Senegal	50.9		46.1	79.1	79.9
95.05	.99	39.0	Sierra Leone	50.4		21.6	20.7	19.6
97.02	1.97	40.0	Upper Volta	48.9		35.6	13.7	14.3
100.00	2.99	41.0	Mozambique	25.1	10	34.2	33.9	46.9

Accelerated Development in Sub-Saharan Africa: p. 156. *Namibia, Zimbabwe*: Staff estimates. Note: *World Tables* and *Accelerated Development in Sub-Saharan Africa* have quite different figures for this variable even though the same source. We have modified *World Tables* data for *Chad, Somalia, Niger* and *Mali* since they did not appear to be correct in the original source.

TABLE 6.4 Principal Export as Percent of Total Exports, 1975—1977 (A), 1970—1972 (B) and 1966—68 (C)..

Comment: This is an average over the three-year time span.

```
Range =        75.00
Mean =         57.05
Standard Deviation =        21.44
```

Population Percent Cum.	Country	Rank	Country Name	A	Range Decile	B	C
.10	.10	1.0	Djibouti	100	1		
21.10	21.00	2.0	Nigeria	94		73	27
22.38	1.28	3.5	Burundi	91	2	83	84
24.03	1.65	3.5	Zambia	91		93	94
24.20	.17	5.0	Gambia	88		94	95
28.15	3.95	6.0	Uganda	87		53	53
30.10	1.95	7.0	Angola	85	3	28	48
30.56	.46	8.0	Mauritania	83		78	85
30.66	.10	9.5	Equatorial Guinea	80		58	55
30.82	.16	9.5	Gabon	80		42	35
32.18	1.36	11.0	Rwanda	72	4	51	57
32.71	.53	12.5	Liberia	69	5	66	73
34.04	1.33	12.5	Niger	69		51	65
34.49	.45	14.0	Congo	68		58	48
35.52	1.03	15.0	Somalia	63		53	47
37.09	1.57	16.5	Guinea	61	6	66	64
37.28	.19	16.5	Guinea-Bissau	61		83	90
40.79	3.51	18.5	Ghana	58		64	55
41.17	.38	18.5	Lesotho	58		32	60
50.88	9.71	20.0	Ethiopia	56		54	56
51.63	.75	21.0	Togo	54	7	33	37
57.87	6.24	22.0	Sudan	53		61	55
59.21	1.34	24.0	Chad	51		67	80
61.08	1.87	24.0	Mali	51		35	18
62.07	.99	24.0	Sierra Leone	51		61	57
62.65	.58	26.5	Central African R	44	8	40	51
64.31	1.66	26.5	Malawi	44		37	25
72.60	8.29	28.0	Zaire	43		63	61
74.57	1.97	29.0	Upper Volta	41		35	51
74.86	.29	30.5	Namibia	40	9		
76.50	1.64	30.5	Senegal	40		47	75
76.66	.16	32.0	Swaziland	37		24	26
79.07	2.41	33.0	Cameroon	34		25	28
81.29	2.22	34.5	Ivory Coast	33		31	35
83.77	2.48	34.5	Madagascar	33		27	31
84.00	.23	36.5	Botswana	32	10	84	96
89.16	5.16	36.5	Tanzania	32		15	19
90.16	1.00	38.5	Benin	31		32	49
94.76	4.60	38.5	Kenya	31		20	26
97.75	2.99	40.5	Mozambique	25		20	16
100.00	2.26	40.5	Zimbabwe	25			

SOURCE:(1966—68) *AID Economic Data Book 1970. Equatorial Guinea: IMF Surveys of African Economies* Volume 5; *Guinea-Bissau: Europa Yearbook* various years.
(1970-1972) *A.I.D. Africa: Economic Growth Trends*; *Guinea-Bissau*: Humbaraci A. and Muchnik N., *Portugal's African Wars* (London: Macmillan, 1974).
(1975—1977) *International Financial Statistics* Washington D.C. *Angola, Namibia, Zimbabwe*: Staff estimates. *Djibouti, Guinea, Equatorial Guinea: Africa Research Bulletin*. Note: There are data inconsistencies between this table and Table 6.3. We cannot resolve these inconsistencies.

TABLE 6.5   Percent of Total Imports Composed of Equipment, 1977 (A), 1970 (B), 1965 (C) and 1960 (D).

Definition: All imports composed of machinery, vehicles, and other capital equipment.

```
Range =         57.00
Mean =          33.06
Standard Deviation =         10.18
```

Population Percent Cum.	Country	Rank	Country Name	A	Range Decile	B	C	D
1.65	1.65	1.0	Zambia	71	1	39	33	
22.65	21.00	2.0	Nigeria	44	5	22	22	21
24.62	1.97	3.0	Upper Volta	43		27	19	22
29.22	4.60	4.0	Kenya	41	6	20	8	77
31.17	1.95	5.0	Angola	40		36		
33.58	2.41	7.0	Cameroon	39		10	21	13
33.74	.16	7.0	Gabon	39		39	11	33
35.96	2.22	7.0	Ivory Coast	39		18	11	27
36.54	.58	9.5	Central African R	38		8	13	9
44.83	8.29	9.5	Zaire	38		34	33	22
45.58	.75	11.0	Togo	37		22	32	20
51.82	6.24	12.0	Sudan	36	7	27	21	30
61.53	9.71	13.0	Ethiopia	35		9	10	8
63.79	2.26	14.0	Zimbabwe	34				
65.12	1.33	15.5	Niger	33		37	34	24
70.28	5.16	15.5	Tanzania	33		40	30	26
70.73	.45	17.5	Congo	32		7	34	10
71.26	.53	17.5	Liberia	32		34	33	41
73.74	2.48	19.0	Madagascar	31	8	30	25	7
75.61	1.87	20.0	Mali	30		21	23	37
75.80	.19	21.0	Guinea-Bissau	29				
77.14	1.34	22.5	Chad	28		23	21	23
78.17	1.03	22.5	Somalia	28		17	24	16
79.45	1.28	24.5	Burundi	27			29	
83.40	3.95	24.5	Uganda	27		10	15	42
86.91	3.51	26.0	Ghana	26		16	18	16
87.90	.99	27.0	Sierra Leone	24	9	26	30	19
88.90	1.00	28.0	Benin	22		21	17	20
90.54	1.64	29.0	Senegal	18	10	25	15	17
92.20	1.66	30.0	Malawi	17		11	14	
92.37	.17	31.0	Gambia	14		15		16

```
DATA NOT AVAILABLE OR NOT APPLICABLE
FOR THE FOLLOWING COUNTRIES

Botswana    Djibouti     Equatorial Guinea  Guinea
Lesotho     Mauritania   Mozambique         Namibia
Rwanda      Swaziland
```

SOURCE: *World Tables* second edition, 1980.
Accelerated Development in Sub-Saharan Africa.

TABLE 6.6 Exports to Colonial Power or Ex-Colonial Power as Percent of Total Exports, 1955 (A), and 1925 (B).

See Part II for identification of ex-colonial power.

```
Range =          98.00
Mean =           52.83
Standard Deviation =        27.61
```

Population Percent Cum. Country		Rank	Country Name	A	Range Decile	B
.29	.29	1.0	Namibia	100	1	
.48	.19	2.0	Guinea-Bissau	94		95
1.48	1.00	3.0	Benin	93		38
1.58	.10	4.5	Djibouti	90	2	
1.68	.10	4.5	Equatorial Guinea	90		95
3.01	1.33	6.5	Niger	85		45
3.76	.75	6.5	Togo	85		40
4.34	.58	8.0	Central African R	83		8
6.21	1.87	9.0	Mali	81		59
7.85	1.64	10.0	Senegal	80	3	74
9.19	1.34	11.5	Chad	73		3
10.18	.99	11.5	Sierra Leone	73		76
12.66	2.48	13.0	Madagascar	69	4	82
14.23	1.57	14.0	Guinea	63		52
35.23	21.00	15.0	Nigeria	62		56
36.89	1.66	16.5	Malawi	60	5	96
38.54	1.65	16.5	Zambia	60		39
40.76	2.22	18.0	Ivory Coast	58		52
40.93	.17	19.5	Gambia	55		47
41.39	.46	19.5	Mauritania	55		45
43.80	2.41	21.5	Cameroon	53		28
52.09	8.29	21.5	Zaire	53		62
52.25	.16	23.0	Gabon	51		44
52.78	.53	24.0	Liberia	48	6	
62.49	9.71	25.5	Ethiopia	44		
65.48	2.99	25.5	Mozambique	44		70
71.72	6.24	27.0	Sudan	43		47
73.00	1.28	28.5	Burundi	37	7	50
74.36	1.36	28.5	Rwanda	37		50
77.87	3.51	30.0	Ghana	36		35
78.32	.45	31.0	Congo	34		23
83.48	5.16	32.0	Tanzania	33		69
88.08	4.60	33.0	Kenya	27	8	84
90.03	1.95	34.0	Angola	22		70
93.98	3.95	35.0	Uganda	21	9	84
95.95	1.97	36.0	Upper Volta	6	10	6
96.18	.23	37.5	Botswana	5		3
96.34	.16	37.5	Swaziland	5		3
96.72	.38	39.0	Lesotho	3		3
97.75	1.03	40.0	Somalia	2		40

```
DATA NOT AVAILABLE OR NOT APPLICABLE
FOR THE FOLLOWING COUNTRIES

Zimbabwe
```

SOURCES: (1955) Service des Statistiques d'Outre-mer, *Outre-mer, 1958* (Paris: Ministere de la France d'Outre-mer, 1960). *C.A.R.*: 1958 figure, *AID Economic Data Book*; *Mali*: 1958 figure, *Europa Yearbook 1961*, p. 787; *Malawi*: Estimate based on 1964 data on Malawi of 48 percent and Zambia in 1958 value of 60 percent. Expect 1955 figure to be higher than 1964 and of same order as Zambia's; *Chad*: 1959 figure, *Europa Yearbook 1961*, p.376; *Zambia: Annual Statement of the Trade of Northern Rhodesia* (Lusaka: 1953); *Gambia, Mauritania*: 1962 figure; *Gabon*: International Monetary Fund, *Survey of African Economies*, Vol. 1, p. 330; *Cameroon*: 1959 figure, East Cameroon only, *Europa Yearbook 1961*, p. 307; *Sudan*: 1954 figure, *Sudan Almanac, 1956*, p. 91; *Burundi, Rwanda*: 1958 figure, *Europa Yearbook 1961*, p. 1012, Burundi and Rwanda combined figure. *Ghana*: 1958 figure, *Europa Yearbook 1961*, p. 535; *Congo*. 1959 figure, *Europa Yearbook 1961*, p. 376; *Tanzania*: Tanganyika only; *Lesotho*: Estimate, vast majority of trade with South Africa. *Ethiopia, Liberia*: Trade with major trading partner (United States) since they were not colonial countries. (1925) Buell *The Native Problem in Africa*. *Sudan*: 1938 figure, *Sudan Almanac 1956* (Khartoum: National Guidance Office, 1956), p. 91. *Mauritania, Niger*: Total figure for French West Africa; *Botswana, Lesotho*: Estimate assuming most trade to be with the *Republic of South Africa; Liberia*: 1932 data; *Statesman's Yearbook 1954* for *Malawi, Gambia and Zaire* (1951). For the following countries estimates were made based on partial information: *Equatorial Guinea, Rwanda, Burundi, Angola, Guinea-Bissau, Upper Volta, Somalia, Swaziland*. These estimates are only rough approximations but may be more useful than missing data. *Namibia, Djibouti*, Staff estimates.

TABLE 6.7 Trade with Ex-Colonial Power as Percent of Total Trade, 1977 (A), 1972 (B), 1968 (C) and 1962 (D).

Definition: Total Trade is the sum of exports and imports of goods and services. See Part II for identification of ex-colonial power.

```
Range =        100.00
Mean =          29.76
Standard Deviation =         20.59
```

Population Percent Cum.	Country	Rank	Country Name	A	Range Decile	B	C	D
.29	.29	1.0	Namibia	100	1			
.39	.10	2.0	Djibouti	90	2			
.97	.58	3.0	Central Afri. R	60	4	52	50	59
2.30	1.33	4.0	Niger	49	6	42	56	54
10.59	8.29	5.0	Zaire	48		35	37	32
10.78	.19	6.5	Guinea-Bissau	45		60	90	90
11.24	.46	6.5	Mauritania	45		34	29	55
11.40	.16	8.0	Gabon	44		45	42	61
11.50	.10	9.5	Equatorial Guinea	42		94	81	85
13.14	1.64	9.5	Senegal	42		53	77	74
15.01	1.87	11.0	Mali	41		35	27	15
17.42	2.41	12.0	Cameroon	38	7	43	46	57
18.76	1.34	13.5	Chad	37		31	51	64
20.73	1.97	13.5	Upper Volta	37		40	34	47
23.21	2.48	15.5	Madagascar	33		48	51	65
24.24	1.03	15.5	Somalia	33		29	40	38
26.46	2.22	17.0	Ivory Coast	32		37	41	54
27.45	.99	18.0	Sierra Leone	31		44	48	46
29.11	1.66	19.0	Malawi	30	8	33	33	34
29.86	.75	20.0	Togo	29		33	35	41
30.03	.17	21.0	Gambia	28		34	47	55
30.48	.45	22.0	Congo	26		48	37	51
30.71	.23	23.0	Botswana	25		23	30	35
31.24	.53	24.0	Liberia	24		21	29	43
32.24	1.00	25.0	Benin	23		39	38	69
33.89	1.65	26.0	Zambia	19	9	22	26	30
37.40	3.51	27.5	Ghana	17		17	27	33
38.97	1.57	27.5	Guinea	17		17	13	17
43.57	4.60	29.0	Kenya	16		22	24	30
64.57	21.00	32.5	Nigeria	15		24	30	39
65.93	1.36	32.5	Rwanda	15		20	22	31
72.17	6.24	32.5	Sudan	15		11	15	21
72.33	.16	32.5	Swaziland	15		20	17	20
77.49	5.16	32.5	Tanzania	15		14	23	45
81.44	3.95	32.5	Uganda	15		20	22	20
84.43	2.99	36.0	Mozambique	12		29	46	33
85.71	1.28	37.0	Burundi	9	10	14	21	20
87.66	1.95	38.0	Angola	5		25	45	30
97.37	9.71	39.0	Ethiopia	3		23	34	39
97.75	.38	40.5	Lesotho	0		5	5	10
100.00	2.26	40.5	Zimbabwe	0		0	0	

SOURCES:(1962 and 1968) *AID Economic Data Book 1970; Europa Year-book* various editions.
(1972 and 1977) A.I.D. *Africa: Economic Growth Trends* October 1974; IMF *Directions of Trade*; IMF *Surveys of African Economies*.
Botswana, Djibouti, Lesotho, Namibia, Swaziland and Zimbabwe: Staff estimates.

**TABLE 6.8 Percent of Total Trade with Eastern-bloc Countries,
1977 (A), 1972 (B), 1968 (C) and 1961 (D).**

Definition: 'Eastern bloc' includes *Bulgaria, China, Czechoslovakia,
East Germany, Hungary, Poland, Romania, Soviet Union and Cuba.*
Total trade is the sum of exports and imports.

```
Range =          40.00
Mean =            4.63
Standard Deviation =          6.96
```

Population Percent Cum.	Country	Rank	Country Name	A	Range Decile	B	C	D
1.95	1.95	1.0	Angola	40	1	0	0	1
2.98	1.03	2.0	Somalia	17	6	9	6	1
12.69	9.71	3.5	Ethiopia	12	7	8	4	3
12.86	.17	3.5	Gambia	12	8	11		5
16.37	3.51	6.0	Ghana	10		11	6	4
22.61	6.24	6.0	Sudan	10		17	20	10
23.36	.75	6.0	Togo	10		6	5	1
24.35	.99	8.0	Sierra Leone	9		2	5	2
26.83	2.48	9.0	Madagascar	8	9	0	0	0
27.02	.19	10.5	Guinea-Bissau	7		0	0	0
28.89	1.87	10.5	Mali	7			2	7
29.89	1.00	14.5	Benin	4	10		3	0
31.17	1.28	14.5	Burundi	4		0	0	0
33.58	2.41	14.5	Cameroon	4		2	3	1
35.15	1.57	14.5	Guinea	4		15	36	22
36.51	1.36	14.5	Rwanda	4			2	0
41.67	5.16	14.5	Tanzania	4		10	6	0
42.20	.53	18.5	Liberia	3			1	0
43.85	1.65	18.5	Zambia	3		3	1	0
45.19	1.34	22.5	Chad	2		0	0	1
45.64	.45	22.5	Congo	2		3	9	0
47.86	2.22	22.5	Ivory Coast	2		2	1	0
49.19	1.33	22.5	Niger	2		3	4	0
70.19	21.00	22.5	Nigeria	2		3	5	1
72.16	1.97	22.5	Upper Volta	2		2	0	0
76.76	4.60	28.5	Kenya	1		3	2	0
77.22	.46	28.5	Mauritania	1			2	0
80.21	2.99	28.5	Mozambique	1		0	0	0
81.85	1.64	28.5	Senegal	1		2	2	1
85.80	3.95	28.5	Uganda	1		7	4	4
94.09	8.29	28.5	Zaire	1		0	0	0
94.32	.23	36.5	Botswana	0		0	0	0
94.90	.58	36.5	Central African R	0		0	0	0
95.00	.10	36.5	Djibouti	0		0	0	0
95.10	.10	36.5	Equatorial Guinea	0		0	0	0
95.26	.16	36.5	Gabon	0		5	0	0
95.64	.38	36.5	Lesotho	0		0	0	0
97.30	1.66	36.5	Malawi	0		0	0	0
97.59	.29	36.5	Namibia	0		0	0	0
97.75	.16	36.5	Swaziland	0		0	0	0
100.00	2.26	36.5	Zimbabwe	0		0	0	0

SOURCES:(1961 and 1968) *A.I.D. Africa: Economic Growth Trends* October.
(1972) AID *Africa: Economic Growth Trends* October 1974.
(1977) *IMF Direction of Trade*.
Angola, Botswana: Staff estimates.

TABLE 6.9   Trade with the United States as Percent of Total Trade, 1977 (A), 1972 (B), 1968 (C) and 1962 (D).

Definition: Total trade is the sum of exports and imports.

```
Range     =      36.00
Mean      =       9.56
Standard Deviation =        8.64
```

Population Percent Cum.	Country	Rank	Country Name	A	Range Decile	B	C	D
1.95	1.95	1.0	Angola	36	1	13	19	18
5.90	3.95	2.0	Uganda	27	3	12	15	13
26.90	21.00	3.0	Nigeria	26		11	8	9
27.43	.53	4.0	Liberia	24	4	21	29	43
28.71	1.28	5.5	Burundi	23		32	34	70
30.07	1.36	5.5	Rwanda	23		25	4	20
30.23	.16	7.0	Swaziland	20	5	5	1	
38.52	8.29	8.0	Zaire	18	6	6	11	24
42.03	3.51	9.0	Ghana	14	7	18	21	12
44.51	2.48	10.5	Madagascar	13		13	15	9
45.50	.99	10.5	Sierra Leone	13		13	8	3
45.73	.23	13.0	Botswana	12		1	1	
45.89	.16	13.0	Gabon	12		7	10	6
47.46	1.57	13.0	Guinea	12		9	13	11
50.45	2.99	15.5	Mozambique	11		8	9	6
52.10	1.65	15.5	Zambia	11		3	5	3
54.32	2.22	17.0	Ivory Coast	9	8	11	12	10
59.48	5.16	18.0	Tanzania	8		5	8	7
61.14	1.66	19.5	Malawi	7	9	2	4	2
63.11	1.97	19.5	Upper Volta	7		3	3	3
65.52	2.41	21.5	Cameroon	6		12	9	6
70.12	4.60	21.5	Kenya	6		6	7	8
71.12	1.00	25.5	Benin	5		7	5	1
71.57	.45	25.5	Congo	5		6	4	5
72.03	.46	25.5	Mauritania	5		3	5	6
73.67	1.64	25.5	Senegal	5		3	3	2
79.91	6.24	25.5	Sudan	5		4	4	4
80.66	.75	25.5	Togo	5		3	2	5
80.83	.17	29.0	Gambia	4		2	2	6
81.41	.58	32.5	Central African R	3	10	11	18	8
82.75	1.34	32.5	Chad	3		1	5	3
92.46	9.71	32.5	Ethiopia	3		23	34	39
92.65	.19	32.5	Guinea-Bissau	3				
94.52	1.87	32.5	Mali	3		1	4	1
95.85	1.33	32.5	Niger	3		2	4	3
96.88	1.03	36.0	Somalia	1		5	6	5
96.98	.10	37.0	Equatorial Guinea	0		9	0	0
97.08	.10	39.5	Djibouti	0		0	0	0
97.46	.38	39.5	Lesotho	0		3	1	0
97.75	.29	39.5	Namibia	0		0	0	0
100.00	2.26	39.5	Zimbabwe	0		0	0	0

SOURCES:(1962) *AID Economic Data Book 1970*, and *Europe-France Outre-mer*; *Zaire*: Economist Intelligence Unit, *Annual Supplement 1962*, (London: The Economist, 1962). *Congo*, 1961 data; *Botswana, Lesotho, Swaziland*: Average for the total figures for these three countries from *IMF Surveys of African Economies* Volume 5, 1973.
(1968) AID *Economic Data Book* 1970.
(1972) A.I.D. *Africa Economic Growth Trends* October 1974.
(1977) *IMF Direction of Trade*.
Data for *Angola, Mozambique, Guinea-Bissau* from Abshire and Samuels, *Portuguese Africa: A Handbook* for all years.
Swaziland, Lesotho and Namibia: Staff estimates.

TABLE 6.10   Percent of Export Trade with African States, 1977 (A), 1972 (B), 1968 (C), and 1960 (D).

Definition: Includes all trade with states in Black Africa (excluding South Africa).

```
Range =          34.00
Mean =            7.67
Standard Deviation =          7.74
```

Population Percent Cum.	Country	Rank	Country Name	A	Range Decile	B	C	D
1.87	1.87	1.0	Mali	34	1	25	54	53
3.53	1.66	2.0	Malawi	31		12	19	24
5.50	1.97	3.5	Upper Volta	21	4	59	71	84
13.79	8.29	3.5	Zaire	21		2	1	9
17.74	3.95	5.0	Uganda	19	5	9	18	18
20.73	2.99	6.0	Mozambique	17	6	3	7	5
22.37	1.64	7.0	Senegal	12	7	21	12	
26.97	4.60	8.5	Kenya	11		37	39	30
27.43	.46	8.5	Mauritania	11		0	3	55
27.53	.10	10.0	Djibouti	10	8	1		
28.89	1.36	11.0	Rwanda	9		59	67	4
30.84	1.95	12.5	Angola	8		4	5	7
33.25	2.41	12.5	Cameroon	8		10	9	5
33.48	.23	14.0	Botswana	7		5	5	3
34.82	1.34	16.0	Chad	7		23	10	27
37.04	2.22	16.0	Ivory Coast	7		11	8	12
38.37	1.33	16.0	Niger	7		10	30	26
38.95	.58	19.5	Central African R	6	9	6	1	9
39.12	.17	19.5	Gambia	6		1	1	3
40.15	1.03	19.5	Somalia	6		2	1	4
41.80	1.65	19.5	Zambia	6		2	1	5
42.80	1.00	22.5	Benin	5		10	17	18
44.08	1.28	22.5	Burundi	5		3	1	7
44.53	.45	25.5	Congo	4		14	4	11
54.24	9.71	25.5	Ethiopia	4		8	5	3
54.43	.19	25.5	Guinea-Bissau	4		5	5	5
59.59	5.16	25.5	Tanzania	4		21	18	8
59.75	.16	30.0	Gabon	3	10	15	7	6
63.26	3.51	30.0	Ghana	3		1	1	4
64.83	1.57	30.0	Guinea	3		16	9	10
67.31	2.48	30.0	Madagascar	3		23	21	18
68.06	.75	30.0	Togo	3		1	5	8
68.16	.10	34.5	Equatorial Guinea	2		0	0	0
68.69	.53	34.5	Liberia	2		2	2	0
89.69	21.00	34.5	Nigeria	2		3	2	1
90.68	.99	34.5	Sierra Leone	2		1	0	1
96.92	6.24	37.0	Sudan	1		7	0	1
97.30	.38	39.5	Lesotho	0		0	5	0
97.59	.29	39.5	Namibia	0		0	0	0
97.75	.16	39.5	Swaziland	0		3	2	2
100.00	2.26	39.5	Zimbabwe	0		0	0	0

SOURCES: AID *Economic Data Book* 1973; IMF *World Trade*; and AID *Africa: Economic Growth Trends* (October 1974). *Direction of Trade* IMF, Washington D.C.
Djibouti, Namibia: Staff estimates.

International Aid and Investment

Policies dealing with the solicitation and control of foreign aid and investment are fundamentally important to the international relations of these African states where, during the 1960's the average value of foreign trade was equivalent to more than half the value of gross domestic product; where more than half their export trade was dependent on the sale of a single commodity, and where their balance of trade was in deficit to the value of 10% of their Gross National Product in the period 1969 to 1978. In such circumstances, these countries negotiated in the late 1960's more than 1 billion dollars in foreign financial aid a year, which amounted to an average of 5% of each nation's Gross National Product. In addition to foreign public financial assistance—foreign aid—foreign private investment has been an important source of capital accumulation for economic development in these nations. Black African states depend more on foreign capital in the form of foreign aid and private investment than other less developed countries—about 30% of gross investment in Africa in the late 1960's was financed by foreign capital compared to an average of less than 20% for all under-developed countries.[30] It is important, therefore, to evaluate patterns of international capital flows between Black Africa and the industrial world.

The rising trend in the value of public financial assistance from colonial powers to their Black African colonies in the decades before independence continued as the net flow of such assistance from the major industrial areas of the capitalist world rose consistently by over 30% from 1960 to 1969 as indicated in Figure 6.1 below. Tables 6.11 through 6.16 provide comparative data on the distribution of foreign aid from various sources to these countries. Intensive analysis of the relationship between patterns of foreign aid distribution and other aspects of the development of Black African states will have to distinguish between several components in the total aggregate figures presented here.

In particular, the distinction between grants and loans requires attention. Grants involve an outright gift of money or resources, often for projects that are unlikely to have direct or immediate financial return. These grants may be "tied" to the country giving the aid, in the sense that they must be used for the purchase of goods and services from the donor country. French foreign aid has been most concentrated in the form of grants. British and American aid has increasingly been in the form of loans, and Eastern-bloc aid has involved a complex mixture of grants, loans, and subsidized trade. In addition to grants and loans, foreign aid to Black African countries has been given under the United States Food for Peace Program.

Figure 6.1   Net Flow of Financial Resources to Developing Countries

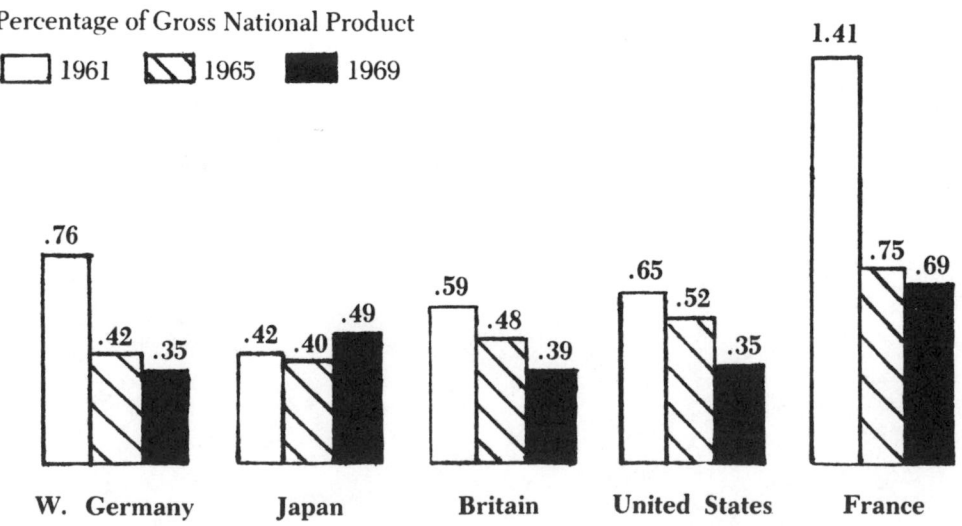

SOURCE: *New York Times*, January 29, 1971.

Under this program, American grain surpluses have been sold to developing nations in exchange for local currencies which can be used only in the recipient country with the governments' mutual consent. Foreign aid has also been received through technical aid and co-operation programs involving grants payable to "experts" for work in developing countries dealing with the implementation and evaluation of development programs and policies or the training of indigenous personnel for various technical occupations. Foreign aid is also distributed in the form of financial assistance from multilateral, intergovernmental agencies. Finally, foreign aid may involve financial and material assistance to the military in developing countries. Data on foreign military aid are given in Table 6.17.

Foreign aid is given ostensibly to encourage economic development in the recipient countries. It is questionable, however, to what extent foreign aid serves such purposes. Whether, for example, military aid releases domestic resources for economic rather than military investments, is a question that needs serious examination. [32] Furthermore, there are indications that the distribution of foreign aid is associated with the political and economic interests of the donor countries rather than with the economic needs of particular developing countries who receive such aid. To begin with, it should be noted that the proportion of national income devoted to foreign aid in the major industrial countries has rarely even approached in some countries the widely advertised goal of 1 percent, and, as illustrated in Figure 6.1 the proportional commitments to foreign aid have in fact been declining. The actual distribution of foreign aid tends, furthermore, to follow the flow of direct private investment from donor countries to Black African nations; to flow to countries with deteriorating balance of payments positions which limit the importation of capital goods from the donors' countries or the repatriation of profits and capital to them, [33] and to follow domestic political changes which increase the opportunities for political influence in the recipient country.

Some partial illustrations of these points are given by data which indicate that the volume of United States foreign aid distributed to Black African countries by 1968 was very closely tied to the extent of U.S. private investment in these countries (r = .67); that U.S. aid was substantially linked to the proportion of a country's trade with the United States and with the number of subsidiaries of multinational corporations established in the recipient country (the correlations with both these latter measures being .44); that there was a zero correlation between the measure of total U.S. foreign aid and the percentage of change in G.N.P. over the same period in these countries, [34] and that U.S. aid distribution fluctuated substantially over time following coups d'état in these countries. The Sudan, which received $400,000 in U.S. aid in 1958, received $30,900,000 in 1959, the year after the first coup in that country. Ethiopia, which received $4,800,000 from the U.S. government in 1960, the year of the attempted coup in that country, received $38,400,000 the following year. Congo was given $2,900,000 in 1964 after receiving only $400,000 in 1963, the year of the first coup d'état in that country. Ghana, having received appropriations of $1,000,000 and $1,700,000 in 1965 and 1966 (the year of the first coup d'etat in Ghana), received $30,100,000 the following year.

Information on the flow of foreign private investment, as opposed to foreign public financial assistance, to Black African nations is more difficult to obtain. Gross private foreign investment in Tropical Africa appears to have reached a peak between 1950 and 1957, when it is estimated that some 800 million dollars per year flowed to this area. [35] Subsequently, the volume of foreign private investment in these nations has declined, although trends are somewhat variable. Total private direct investments from the United Kingdom and the United States to African countries, *not* including investments in oil developments, declined from $173,000,000 in 1959 to only $50,000,000 in 1964. [36] After the initial political uncertainties of the early independence period, this trend has been somewhat reversed. The annual flow of private investment from all major capitalist economies—the so-called development assistance countries—rose from $486,000,000 in 1967—68 to $768,000,000 in 1971—72. This increase, however, was only a little better than half the rate of increase of total private foreign investment to all the developing countries of the world in this period. [37] Table 6.18 gives data on the total stock of private direct investment from development assistance countries to Black Africa for the years 1967 and 1972 and Table 6.19 relates the stock of private foreign investment to GNP.

When considering these data, it will be important to bear in mind that the total stock of private direct investment in these countries amounts to only 12% of the comparable investment in all Third World countries. Further, it is important to note that the colonial pattern of concentration of investment in extractive industries has continued, so that while the annual flow of investment into manufacturing has doubled between 1967 and 1972, investments in extractive industries remains three times as great as those in manufacturing. [38] Finally, it is important to analyze the institutional control of foreign investment in Black African states, particularly the increasingly important role of the multinational corporation. Data in Table 6.20 give a preliminary indication of the distribution of multinational corporations and their subsidiaries within Black African countries.

The growing importance of oligopolistic, multinational corporations in Black Africa is illustrated by the evidence for 187 large manufacturing corporations in the United States, of which there were only 4 established in Black Africa in 1945, but 24 in 1960, and 62 in 1967.[39] The increasing importance of such corporate involvement in Black Africa can be expected to continue in the future, given estimates that 75% of the world's productive capacity will be controlled in this decade by a group of only 300 multinational corporations, and that profits on direct investment in developing countries as a percentage of the book value for total investments are more than twice as great as comparable profits on investment in developed countries, and that the earnings from the foreign subsidiaries and branches of U.S. corporations were already 20% of the net profits of those organizations in 1969.[40]

The relationship between the concentration of foreign private investment and foreign multinational corporate activity in Black African nations and patterns of economic and political development in these nations is exceedingly complex, and much more extensive data than can be presented in this Chapter will be required to explore such relationships. It is important, nevertheless, to indicate the range of questions that need to be addressed.[41] In the first place, it will be important to examine to what extent capital formation by foreign firms constitutes a net addition to the domestic stock of capital in these nations. In this connection, it is important to examine the extent to which foreign firms generate the financial capital they invest from local banks and other sources *within* the domestic economy of the host Black African states. Further, it is important to examine the outflow of profits as compared to the inflow of capital, and to consider especially the difficulties surrounding the measurement of profit repatriation that result from such practices as transfer pricing, in which foreign corporations over-invoice purchases and under-invoice sales from and to their subsidiaries so that lower profit rates are calculated than actually apply. With respect to non-financial capital, it is important to investigate the extent to which technological investment by increasingly capital-intensive productive organizations is appropriate to the local economic conditions in Black Africa. Imported technologies may replace important local technologies with greater domestic economic benefits; they may stimulate imported tastes that are inappropriate to the local economic and political requirements of welfare and productivity; they may retard the expansion of the wage labor force, and they may simply substitute foreign entrepreneurship and capital for local resources of these kinds without mobilizing new resources and net economic development.

Certainly it is possible that Black African states can derive benefit from the transfer of technology, and the training of effective indigenous managerial capability offered by foreign corporations, but the costs of technological dependence need to be very carefully weighed.[42] Payments for the right to use patents, licenses, process "know-how," trademarks, and technical services needed at all levels, are very substantial, and provisional estimates by the UNCTAD secretariat indicate that in 1968 the developing countries paid out about $1,500,000,00 in foreign exchange on such direct costs, which were forecasted to rise by about 20% per year, or to increase to close to $10 billion by the end of the 1970's.[43] Furthermore, the political rather than economic impact of foreign multinational investment activity needs to be evaluated. The creation of a "favorable climate for investment" leads foreign investors to negotiate special exemptions from tax and trade legislation, and to establish client relations with local politicians to advance such interests. The scale of such direct political influence is very difficult to estimate, but the disclosures of information on the bribes and kick-backs made by U.S. corporations to foreigners in high places makes it clear that such practices are routine. The $410,000 paid to two officials in Gabon and the $430,000 paid to a Nigerian consultant by Ashland Oil Corporation are substantial even when compared to the $1,000,000 reportedly paid Prince Bernhard of the Netherlands by Lockheed, and they are significant evidence for a pervasive set of practices.[44] Less direct political influence results from the impact of foreign investment on the political organization of labor, the introduction of multinational labor union activity, the very high wages paid indigenous management personnel, and, possibly, the development of a labor aristocracy with greater job security, relatively higher wages and benefits offered by foreign as opposed to domestic employers.[45] Finally, the visibility of foreign personnel with extraordinarily high incomes and consumption privileges and too often with racist or patronizing attitudes, creates resentment and hostility on the part of local citizens against the domestic government which sanctions the foreign presence.[46]

TABLE 6.11   Total United States Economic Aid 1976—79(A),
through 1972 (B), through 1968 (C), and 1969 to
1972 (D), in Millions of U.S. Dollars.

Definition: Includes grants, loans, Food for Peace, and all other forms
of U.S. economic aid. The time period covers all years in which the
U.S. Government was distributing economic aid.

```
Range =          180.00
Mean =            40.39
Standard Deviation =          50.10
```

Population Percent Cum.	Country	Rank	Country Name	A	Range Decile	B	C	D
21.00	21.00	1.0	Nigeria	180	1	422	229	192
30.71	9.71	2.0	Ethiopia	179		298	229	69
34.22	3.51	3.0	Ghana	166		300	240	60
39.38	5.16	4.0	Tanzania	152	2	78	62	16
47.67	8.29	5.0	Zaire	122	4	452	405	47
48.20	.53	6.0	Liberia	97	5	296	252	44
52.80	4.60	7.0	Kenya	77	6	97	63	34
54.13	1.33	8.0	Niger	63	7	21	15	6
56.00	1.87	9.0	Mali	55		28	19	11
57.97	1.97	10.0	Upper Volta	52	8	22	11	11
59.61	1.64	11.0	Senegal	48		43	32	14
61.18	1.57	12.0	Guinea	43		109	74	36
63.59	2.41	13.0	Cameroon	36	9	47	27	15
64.62	1.03	14.0	Somalia	35		77	73	7
64.85	.23	15.0	Botswana	34		30	16	16
65.84	.99	16.0	Sierra Leone	30		53	39	15
67.50	1.66	17.0	Malawi	29		29	23	7
68.84	1.34	18.5	Chad	28		10	8	3
69.22	.38	18.5	Lesotho	28		13	4	3
70.87	1.65	20.0	Zambia	24		68	41	28
71.33	.46	21.0	Mauritania	23		6	3	3
72.33	1.00	22.0	Benin	22		14	11	3
78.57	6.24	23.5	Sudan	20		106	107	16
82.52	3.95	23.5	Uganda	20		48	30	16
84.74	2.22	25.5	Ivory Coast	17	10	110	67	49
87.73	2.99	25.5	Mozambique	17		0	0	0
88.48	.75	27.0	Togo	15		18	14	6
89.84	1.36	28.0	Rwanda	13		8	7	2
92.32	2.48	29.0	Madagascar	11		15	13	3
92.48	.16	30.0	Swaziland	9		6	5	5
92.65	.17	31.0	Gambia	7		4	1	3
93.93	1.28	32.0	Burundi	4		10	7	3
95.88	1.95	37.0	Angola	0		0	0	0
96.46	.58	37.0	Central African R	0		8	5	3
96.91	.45	37.0	Congo	0		5	2	3
97.01	.10	37.0	Djibouti	0		0	0	0
97.11	.10	37.0	Equatorial Guinea	0		0	0	0
97.27	.16	37.0	Gabon	0		7	8	0
97.46	.19	37.0	Guinea-Bissau	0		0	0	0
97.75	.29	37.0	Namibia	0		0	0	0
100.00	2.26	37.0	Zimbabwe	0		0	0	0

SOURCES: AID *Economic Data Book* various years.
(1976—1979) *Geographical Distribution of Financial Flows to Developing Countries, 1976/79*, (Paris: OECD, 1981)

TABLE 6.12   **United States Economic Aid Per Capita in U.S. Dollars, 1977 (A), 1972 (B), 1967 (C) and 1962 (D).**

Definition: Loans and grants from the United States government in fiscal years 1977, 1972, 1967 and 1962.

```
Range =          7.06
Mean =           1.17
Standard Deviation =        1.39
```

Population Percent Cum.	Country	Rank	Country Name	A	Range Decile	B	C	D
.53	.53	1.0	Liberia	7.06	1	7.82	10.69	10.48
.76	.23	2.0	Botswana	4.29	4	6.36	12.72	
2.41	1.65	3.0	Zambia	3.14	6	`	1.56	.09
2.79	.38	4.0	Lesotho	3.08		2.63	1.26	.07
4.76	1.97	5.0	Upper Volta	2.55	7	.89	.57	.22
5.76	1.00	6.0	Benin	2.50		.35	.52	.97
7.10	1.34	7.0	Chad	2.14		.26	.61	.09
7.26	.16	8.0	Swaziland	2.00	8	4.45	.13	
8.90	1.64	9.0	Senegal	1.92		.65	1.80	1.05
14.06	5.16	10.0	Tanzania	1.89		.51	.52	1.14
17.57	3.51	11.0	Ghana	1.70		2.64	4.44	18.20
17.74	.17	12.0	Gambia	1.67		2.08	1.10	.16
19.07	1.33	13.0	Niger	1.43		.47	.62	.39
19.53	.46	14.0	Mauritania	1.33	9	.82	.28	.10
20.52	.99	15.5	Sierra Leone	1.25		1.09	1.60	1.10
21.27	.75	15.5	Togo	1.25		.48	.83	.50
29.56	8.29	17.0	Zaire	1.13		.53	2.17	4.61
31.43	1.87	18.0	Mali	.98		.38	.65	.59
36.03	4.60	19.0	Kenya	.89		.41	.40	1.13
39.02	2.99	20.0	Mozambique	.82		0	0	0
40.05	1.03	21.0	Somalia	.81		1.01	6.72	6.58
41.62	1.57	22.0	Guinea	.80		.19	.35	3.19
44.03	2.41	23.0	Cameroon	.76		.44	.29	2.55
45.69	1.66	24.0	Malawi	.71		.64	.63	.49
47.05	1.36	25.0	Rwanda	.68	10	.26	.21	.28
56.76	9.71	26.0	Ethiopia	.36		.66	.80	.29
63.00	6.24	27.0	Sudan	.30		.14	1.63	1.04
65.48	2.48	28.0	Madagascar	.25			.44	.11
66.76	1.28	29.0	Burundi	.24			.06	.96
68.98	2.22	30.0	Ivory Coast	.13		.34	.34	.74
89.98	21.00	31.0	Nigeria	.01		.40	.36	.43
91.93	1.95	36.5	Angola	0		0	0	0
92.51	.58	36.5	Central Afri. R	0		1.20	.60	.18
92.96	.45	36.5	Congo	0		0	0	1.50
93.06	.10	36.5	Djibouti	0		0	0	0
93.16	.10	36.5	Equatorial Guinea	0		0	0	0
93.32	.16	36.5	Gabon	0		0	2.55	.88
93.51	.19	36.5	Guinea-Bissau	0		0	0	0
93.80	.29	36.5	Namibia	0		0	0	0
97.75	3.95	36.5	Uganda	0		.29	.77	.60
100.00	2.26	36.5	Zimbabwe	0		0	0	

SOURCES: AID *Economic Data Book* various years.

TABLE 6.13 Percent Change in U.S. Economic Aid Per Capita,
1972 to 1977 (A), 1967 to 1972 (B), and 1962 to 1967 (C).

```
Range =           165.00
Mean =             15.50
Standard Deviation =           34.52
```

Population Percent Cum.	Country	Rank	Country Name	A	Range Decile	B	C
1.34	1.34	1.0	Chad	145	1	-16	116
2.34	1.00	2.0	Benin	123	2	-11	-9
3.91	1.57	3.0	Guinea	64	5	-10	-18
9.07	5.16	4.0	Tanzania	54	6	-12	-11
10.40	1.33	5.0	Niger	41	7	-8	12
12.04	1.64	6.0	Senegal	39		-11	14
14.01	1.97	7.0	Upper Volta	37		1	32
15.88	1.87	9.0	Mali	32		-10	2
17.24	1.36	9.0	Rwanda	32		-8	-5
17.99	.75	9.0	Togo	32		-8	13
22.59	4.60	12.0	Kenya	23	8	2	-13
28.83	6.24	12.0	Sudan	23		-13	11
37.12	8.29	12.0	Zaire	23		-18	-11
39.53	2.41	14.0	Cameroon	15		110	-18
39.99	.46	15.0	Mauritania	12	9	62	36
40.37	.38	16.5	Lesotho	3		3	340
41.36	.99	16.5	Sierra Leone	3		-3	9
43.02	1.66	18.0	Malawi	2		5	6
44.97	1.95	23.0	Angola	0			
45.42	.45	23.0	Congo	0		999	-100
45.52	.10	23.0	Djibouti	0		0	
45.62	.10	23.0	Equatorial Guinea	0		0	
45.78	.16	23.0	Gabon	0		-18	38
45.97	.19	23.0	Guinea-Bissau	0			
48.96	2.99	23.0	Mozambique	0			
49.25	.29	23.0	Namibia	0			
51.51	2.26	23.0	Zimbabwe	0			
52.04	.53	28.0	Liberia	-2		0	
52.21	.17	29.5	Gambia	-4	10	-3	128
53.24	1.03	29.5	Somalia	-4		-100	
53.47	.23	31.0	Botswana	-6		6	999
56.98	3.51	32.0	Ghana	-7		-13	-15
66.69	9.71	33.0	Ethiopia	-9		12	35
66.85	.16	34.0	Swaziland	-11		185	999
69.07	2.22	35.0	Ivory Coast	-12		261	-11
90.07	21.00	36.0	Nigeria	-19		18	-3
90.65	.58	37.5	Central African R	-20		28	47
94.60	3.95	37.5	Uganda	-20		-6	6

DATA NOT AVAILABLE OR NOT APPLICABLE
FOR THE FOLLOWING COUNTRIES

Burundi   Madagascar   Zambia

SOURCES: AID *Economic Data Book* various years.

TABLE 6.14 **Average Annual Per Capita Net Official Aid from De-velopment Assistance Countries (DAC) in U.S. Dollars 1976-78 (A), 1971-73 (B), and 1967-69 (C).**

Definition: DAC countries include the advanced industrial nations of the Western world.

```
Range =        299.94
Mean =          28.83
Standard Deviation =       47.18
```

Population Percent Cum.	Country	Rank	Country Name	A	Range Decile	B	C
.10	.10	1.0	Djibouti	300.55	1		
.33	.23	2.0	Botswana	75.35	8	44.49	27.12
.49	.16	3.0	Gabon	65.55		55.45	21.00
.68	.19	4.0	Guinea-Bissau	63.46		14.00	
.84	.16	5.0	Swaziland	60.14	9	5.91	20.81
1.30	.46	6.0	Mauritania	48.78		11.97	7.31
1.75	.45	7.0	Congo	42.59		23.07	31.18
1.92	.17	8.0	Gambia	33.40		9.98	8.91
2.30	.38	9.0	Lesotho	31.26		14.62	15.47
3.05	.75	10.0	Togo	29.49	10	10.77	6.77
4.69	1.64	11.0	Senegal	28.43		14.47	11.41
6.02	1.33	12.0	Niger	24.26		11.93	5.94
7.38	1.36	13.0	Rwanda	22.35		7.94	4.36
9.03	1.65	14.0	Zambia	22.15		6.68	10.56
14.19	5.16	15.0	Tanzania	21.20		5.11	2.84
14.72	.53	16.0	Liberia	21.15		7.40	21.53
15.75	1.03	17.0	Somalia	20.54		10.15	8.78
17.09	1.34	18.0	Chad	20.48		9.02	5.16
19.50	2.41	19.0	Cameroon	20.22		9.53	27.00
21.37	1.87	20.0	Mali	18.34		8.68	3.41
23.34	1.97	21.0	Upper Volta	18.13		7.17	3.48
23.92	.58	22.0	Central African R	18.08		13.28	10.19
24.92	1.00	23.0	Benin	16.19		8.80	5.50
27.14	2.22	24.0	Ivory Coast	15.92		11.92	8.96
28.80	1.66	25.0	Malawi	14.58		6.88	6.41
33.40	4.60	26.0	Kenya	13.20		6.48	5.57
34.68	1.28	27.0	Burundi	13.12		7.19	3.17
40.92	6.24	28.0	Sudan	10.00		1.88	1.35
49.21	8.29	29.0	Zaire	9.64		5.37	4.50
51.69	2.48	30.0	Madagascar	8.83		7.08	4.49
54.68	2.99	31.0	Mozambique	8.46		4.38	1.84
55.67	.99	32.0	Sierra Leone	8.40		4.40	3.42
59.18	3.51	33.0	Ghana	7.86		5.70	8.66
61.13	1.95	34.0	Angola	6.30		5.24	2.76
62.70	1.57	35.0	Guinea	5.68		4.62	2.73
72.41	9.71	36.0	Ethiopia	4.42		2.06	1.72
72.51	.10	37.0	Equatorial Guinea	1.68			
76.46	3.95	38.0	Uganda	1.45		2.37	2.58
78.72	2.26	39.0	Zimbabwe	1.10			
99.72	21.00	40.0	Nigeria	.61		1.51	1.62

DATA NOT AVAILABLE OR NOT APPLICABLE
FOR THE FOLLOWING COUNTRIES

Namibia

SOURCES: (1967-69) *Development Assistance: 1970 Review* (Paris: OECD, December 1970), pp. 194-196, *Angola, Madagascar, Mozambique, Swaziland*: 1967 through 1968 the average from UNECA *Statistical Yearbook 1972*. (1971-73) *UN Statistical Yearbook 1974*. (1976-1978) *United Nations Statistical Yearbook 1979*.

TABLE 6.15 Total Aid from Ex-Metropole per Capita in U.S. Dollars, 1977 (A), 1971 (B), 1967 (C) and 1964 (D).

Definition: Includes all forms of intergovernmental economic aid. Figures for Liberia and Ethiopia are for aid from their principal donor over time which is in both cases, the United States. However, this pattern has changed in Ethiopia since the overthrow of Haile Selassie.

```
Range =          293.64
Mean =            13.55
Standard Deviation =        45.83
```

Population Percent Cum.	Population Percent Country	Rank	Country Name	A	Range Decile	B	C	D
.10	.10	1.0	Djibouti	293.64	1			
.26	.16	2.0	Gabon	50.80	9	32.25	16.10	17.22
.42	.16	3.0	Swaziland	31.40		5.69	22.80	38.43
.87	.45	4.0	Congo	21.86	10		10.20	13.26
1.45	.58	5.0	Central African R	14.89		4.00	10.60	7.02
1.68	.23	6.0	Botswana	11.43		16.51	27.00	16.80
3.32	1.64	7.0	Senegal	11.13		3.76	8.50	12.93
3.49	.17	8.0	Gambia	9.07		.66	7.30	8.04
3.95	.46	9.0	Mauritania	8.60		3.44	7.30	9.11
6.17	2.22	10.0	Ivory Coast	8.55		3.49	6.40	7.27
7.51	1.34	11.0	Chad	7.62		3.75	3.10	3.52
8.04	.53	12.0	Liberia	7.06		6.92	33.70	11.87
9.40	1.36	13.0	Rwanda	6.50		3.23	2.50	1.67
11.81	2.41	14.0	Cameroon	6.14		3.32	3.30	3.50
12.56	.75	15.0	Togo	5.87		2.09	2.70	2.16
14.53	1.97	16.0	Upper Volta	5.42		1.76	2.70	2.16
15.86	1.33	17.0	Niger	5.00		3.78	3.40	3.68
17.73	1.87	18.0	Mali	4.25		2.26	1.70	1.39
26.02	8.29	19.0	Zaire	4.23		2.48	3.10	4.55
27.30	1.28	20.0	Burundi	3.93		2.88	2.10	1.90
28.96	1.66	21.0	Malawi	3.84		2.89	5.90	8.27
30.61	1.65	22.0	Zambia	3.80		2.85	10.90	6.14
31.61	1.00	23.0	Benin	3.50		5.23	3.40	5.52
34.09	2.48	24.0	Madagascar	2.99		3.88	4.60	5.95
34.47	.38	25.0	Lesotho	2.92		7.63	13.30	7.11
35.50	1.03	26.0	Somalia	1.97		4.25	.90	3.36
40.10	4.60	27.0	Kenya	1.55		1.58	2.20	5.65
41.09	.99	28.0	Sierra Leone	.97		.15	.90	2.42
46.25	5.16	29.0	Tanzania	.71		.28	.20	2.35
48.51	2.26	30.0	Zimbabwe	.67				
54.75	6.24	31.0	Sudan	.52		.02	.10	.27
58.26	3.51	32.0	Ghana	.46		1.76	.10	.93
67.97	9.71	33.0	Ethiopia	.36		.90	.50	.42
88.97	21.00	34.0	Nigeria	.14		.17	2.60	3.38
92.92	3.95	35.0	Uganda	.07		.76	1.80	2.41
94.49	1.57	36.0	Guinea	.04		0	-.40	0
96.44	1.95	38.5	Angola	0		2.19	3.40	1.41
96.54	.10	38.5	Equatorial Guinea	0			8.90	
96.73	.19	38.5	Guinea-Bissau	0		13.33		
99.72	2.99	38.5	Mozambique	0		6.73	2.50	.40

```
DATA NOT AVAILABLE OR NOT APPLICABLE
FOR THE FOLLOWING COUNTRIES

Namibia
```

SOURCES: Ministere de la Cooperation, *1959-64, Cinq ans de fonds d'aide et de Cooperation* (Paris: 1965), pp. 49-53; *Special Commonwealth African Assistance Plan Report* (London: 1964). *Malawi: AID Economic Data Book*, 1962 figures; *Botswana*: Edwin S. Munger, *Bechuanaland* (London: Oxford University Press, 1965); *Gabon*: International Monetary Fund, *Surveys of African Economies*; *Angola, Madagascar, Mozambique, Swaziland*: 1965 data from UNECA *Statistical Yearbook* 1973 and 1974 editions.
(1967) *Geographical Distribution of Financial Flows to Less Developed Countries 1966-1967* (Paris: OECD, 1969). *Equatorial Guinea*: excludes cocoa subsidies; *Angola, Equatorial Guinea, Mozambique,* (1977) *Geographical Distribution of Financial Flows to Developing Countries, 1976/79* (Paris: OECD, 1981).

Swaziland: UNECA *Statistical Yearbook* 1973 and 1974 editions.
(1971) OECD *Flow of Resources to Developing Countries* (Paris: OECD, 1973). Data for 1968 for *Benin, Ivory Coast*; 1969 for *Madagascar, Mauritania, Niger, Togo*; 1970 for *Sierra Leone, Sudan*; 1972 for *Central African Republic, Chad*; data for *Cameroon, Central African Republic, Chad, Gabon, Mali, Senegal, Upper Volta* for aid from the European Economic Community (EEC) (for French grants, information was not available). This data is from A.I.D. *Economic Data Book 1973*; data from I.M.F. *Surveys of African Economies: Madagascar* (Vol. 4), *Niger* (Vol. 3), *Swaziland* (Vol. 5). For Somalia, data is for Italian aid only. Aid from U.K. is virtually zero. (B)

TABLE 6.16   Total Eastern-Bloc Economic Aid, 1974-77 (A), 1965-73 (B), and 1958-65 (C) in Millions of U.S. Dollars.

Definition: Includes aid from Bulgaria, China, Czechoslovakia, East Germany, Hungary, Poland, Romania, and the Soviet Union.

```
Range =        156.00
Mean =          26.61
Standard Deviation =        37.15
```

Population Percent Cum.	Population Percent Country	Rank	Country Name	A	Range Decile	B	C
21.00	21.00	1.0	Nigeria	156	1	133	14
27.24	6.24	2.0	Sudan	115		303	22
28.81	1.57	3.0	Guinea	84	5	215	119
30.46	1.65	4.0	Zambia	79		263	0
32.87	2.41	5.0	Cameroon	75	6	71	0
35.35	2.48	6.0	Madagascar	69		11	0
38.86	3.51	7.0	Ghana	66		166	164
39.89	1.03	8.0	Somalia	63		212	96
41.86	1.97	9.0	Upper Volta	60	7	51	0
44.85	2.99	10.0	Mozambique	59			
46.18	1.33	11.0	Niger	54		2	0
51.34	5.16	12.0	Tanzania	47		280	51
51.80	.46	13.0	Mauritania	37	8	22	0
61.51	9.71	14.0	Ethiopia	28	9	203	114
61.67	.16	15.0	Gabon	25		0	0
61.86	.19	16.0	Guinea-Bissau	19			
62.03	.17	17.0	Gambia	17		0	0
63.90	1.87	18.0	Mali	14	10	115	2
64.43	.53	19.0	Liberia	11		0	0
65.77	1.34	20.0	Chad	9		57	0
67.72	1.95	21.0	Angola	2			
69.36	1.64	22.5	Senegal	1		9	7
70.11	.75	22.5	Togo	1		45	0
71.11	1.00	32.5	Benin	0		44	0
71.34	.23	32.5	Botswana	0		0	0
72.62	1.28	32.5	Burundi	0		20	0
73.20	.58	32.5	Central African R	0		6	4
73.65	.45	32.5	Congo	0		66	62
73.75	.10	32.5	Djibouti	0		0	0
73.85	.10	32.5	Equatorial Guinea	0		0	0
76.07	2.22	32.5	Ivory Coast	0		0	0
80.67	4.60	32.5	Kenya	0		71	55
81.05	.38	32.5	Lesotho	0		0	0
82.71	1.66	32.5	Malawi	0		0	0
83.00	.29	32.5	Namibia	0			
84.36	1.36	32.5	Rwanda	0		23	0
85.35	.99	32.5	Sierra Leone	0		28	28
85.51	.16	32.5	Swaziland	0		0	
89.46	3.95	32.5	Uganda	0		30	30
97.75	8.29	32.5	Zaire	0		100	0
100.00	2.26	32.5	Zimbabwe	0			

SOURCE: (1958-65) Ralph Meagher, *Bilateral Aid to Africa*, unpublished paper, (Evanston, Ill.: Africana Library, Northwestern University). (1965-73) *UN Statistical Yearbook 1974*. (1974-77) *U.N. Statistical Yearbook*.

TABLE 6.17   Number of Countries from which Military Aid was Received, ca. 1970 (A) and 1964 (B), and Index of Total Military Aid, 1964 (C).

Definition: Various forms of aid were weighted as follows and summed: (1) training, minor facilities, (2) training, extensive facilities, experts; (1) equipment up to fitting out units, (2) equipment basic for all or most of armed services, (3) lavish equipment beyond need of internal security. High values are the result of more than one country giving military aid, since each country's contribution was scored and summed to get a total score.

```
Range =        17.00
Mean =          2.59
Standard Deviation =        3.09
```

Population Percent Cum.	Population Percent Country	Rank	Country Name	A	Range Decile	B	C
.45	.45	1.0	Congo	17	1	2	2
3.96	3.51	2.0	Ghana	10	5	14	8
24.96	21.00	4.0	Nigeria	6	7	15	8
28.91	3.95	4.0	Uganda	6		7	4
37.20	8.29	4.0	Zaire	6		15	5
43.44	6.24	6.0	Sudan	5	8	12	5
53.15	9.71	8.0	Ethiopia	4		12	5
54.18	1.03	8.0	Somalia	4		11	4
54.93	.75	8.0	Togo	4		4	1
55.93	1.00	13.0	Benin	3	9	5	2
56.51	.58	13.0	Central Afri. R	3		5	2
58.08	1.57	13.0	Guinea	3		8	2
60.30	2.22	13.0	Ivory Coast	3		7	3
62.17	1.87	13.0	Mali	3		6	2
67.33	5.16	13.0	Tanzania	3		18	8
69.30	1.97	13.0	Upper Volta	3		5	2
71.71	2.41	19.0	Cameroon	2		5	2
73.04	1.33	19.0	Niger	2		7	2
74.68	1.64	19.0	Senegal	2		7	2
75.67	.99	19.0	Sierra Leone	2		5	2
77.32	1.65	19.0	Zambia	2		5	2
79.27	1.95	28.0	Angola	1	10	3	1
80.55	1.28	28.0	Burundi	1		4	1
81.89	1.34	28.0	Chad	1		4	1
82.05	.16	28.0	Gabon	1		4	1
82.22	.17	28.0	Gambia	1		0	0
82.41	.19	28.0	Guinea-Bissau	1		3	1
87.01	4.60	28.0	Kenya	1		8	5
87.54	.53	28.0	Liberia	1		4	1
90.02	2.48	28.0	Madagascar	1		4	1
91.68	1.66	28.0	Malawi	1		4	1
92.14	.46	28.0	Mauritania	1		4	1
95.13	2.99	28.0	Mozambique	1		4	1
96.49	1.36	28.0	Rwanda	1		4	1
96.72	.23	38.0	Botswana	0		0	0
96.82	.10	38.0	Djibouti	0		0	0
96.92	.10	38.0	Equatorial Guinea	0		0	0
97.30	.38	38.0	Lesotho	0		0	0
97.59	.29	38.0	Namibia	0		0	0
97.75	.16	38.0	Swaziland	0		0	0
100.00	2.26	38.0	Zimbabwe	0		0	0

SOURCES: (1964) M.J.V. Bell, *Military Assistance to Independent African States* Adelphi Paper no. 15 (London: Institute for Strategic Studies, 1964): Congo, Kenya, Tanzania: Uncertain whether Communist China actually gave aid.
(1970) Institute for Strategic Studies *The Military Balance 1973/74* (London: Institute for Strategic Studies, 1974.)

TABLE 6.18 Total Stock of Private Direct Investment from Development Assistance Countries 1972 (A) and 1967 (B) in Millions of U.S. dollars.

Definition: The current market value of all privately owned investment which is wholly owned or controlled by foreign firms or individuals.

```
Range    =   2098.00
Mean     =    185.53
Standard Deviation =    351.89
```

Population Percent Cum.	Country Percent	Rank	Country Name	A	Range Decile	B
21.00	21.00	1.0	Nigeria	2100	1	1109
29.29	8.29	2.0	Zaire	578	8	481
29.45	.16	3.0	Gabon	375	9	265
32.96	3.51	4.5	Ghana	360		260
33.49	.53	4.5	Liberia	360		300
35.71	2.22	6.0	Ivory Coast	340		202
37.36	1.65	7.0	Zambia	300		421
39.31	1.95	8.0	Angola	290		193
43.91	4.60	9.0	Kenya	235		172
46.32	2.41	10.5	Cameroon	210	10	150
47.96	1.64	10.5	Senegal	210		154
49.53	1.57	12.0	Guinea	175		93
49.99	.46	13.0	Mauritania	150		101
52.98	2.99	14.0	Mozambique	123		102
53.43	.45	15.0	Congo	100		90
55.91	2.48	16.0	Madagascar	95		72
56.90	.99	17.0	Sierra Leone	75		68
66.61	9.71	18.0	Ethiopia	70		50
71.77	5.16	19.5	Tanzania	65		60
72.52	.75	19.5	Togo	65		42
74.18	1.66	21.0	Malawi	55		30
74.76	.58	22.0	Central Afri. R	50		37
74.99	.23	24.5	Botswana	35		3
76.32	1.33	24.5	Niger	35		23
82.56	6.24	24.5	Sudan	35		37
82.72	.16	24.5	Swaziland	35		29
86.67	3.95	27.0	Uganda	30		48
87.67	1.00	28.0	Benin	25		18
89.01	1.34	29.0	Chad	20		18
90.29	1.28	30.5	Burundi	18		14
92.26	1.97	30.5	Upper Volta	18		16
93.62	1.36	32.0	Rwanda	17		15
94.65	1.03	33.0	Somalia	15		13
96.52	1.87	34.0	Mali	8		7
96.69	.17	35.0	Gambia	5		2
97.07	.38	36.0	Lesotho	2		1

DATA NOT AVAILABLE OR NOT APPLICABLE FOR THE FOLLOWING COUNTRIES

Djibouti   Equatorial Guinea   Guinea-Bissau   Namibia   Zimbabwe

TABLE 6.19 Ratio of the Stock of Private Foreign Direct Investment to GNP times 100, 1971 (A) and 1967 (C).

```
Range    =    101.00
Mean     =     19.83
Standard Deviation =     24.36
```

Population Percent Cum.	Country Percent	Rank	Country Name	A	Range Decile	B
.16	.16	1.0	Gabon	103	1	147
.69	.53	2.0	Liberia	100		125
1.15	.46	3.0	Mauritania	73	3	65
1.31	.16	4.0	Swaziland	44	6	39
2.88	1.57	5.0	Guinea	39	7	30
3.33	.45	6.0	Congo	33		72
11.62	8.29	7.0	Zaire	32	8	36
32.62	21.00	8.0	Nigeria	22	9	21
33.37	.75	9.0	Togo	21		21
35.01	1.64	10.0	Senegal	20		19
35.59	.58	11.5	Central Afri. R	19		19
37.24	1.65	11.5	Zambia	19		36
39.65	2.41	13.5	Cameroon	17		19
41.87	2.22	13.5	Ivory Coast	17		19
45.38	3.51	15.0	Ghana	15		15
47.33	1.95	16.5	Angola	13		19
48.32	.99	16.5	Sierra Leone	13		18
52.92	4.60	18.0	Kenya	11	10	15
53.15	.23	19.0	Botswana	10		4
55.63	2.48	20.5	Madagascar	9		10
57.29	1.66	20.5	Malawi	9		14
58.29	1.00	22.5	Benin	8		10
59.57	1.28	22.5	Burundi	8		10
60.93	1.36	24.5	Rwanda	7		16
61.96	1.03	24.5	Somalia	7		10
63.30	1.34	27.0	Chad	6		7
63.47	.17	27.0	Gambia	6		10
64.80	1.33	27.0	Niger	6		8
67.79	2.99	29.5	Mozambique	5		7
69.76	1.97	29.5	Upper Volta	5		6
74.92	5.16	31.5	Tanzania	4		7
78.87	3.95	31.5	Uganda	4		7
88.58	9.71	33.0	Ethiopia	3		3
88.96	.38	35.0	Lesotho	2		1
90.83	1.87	35.0	Mali	2		2
97.07	6.24	35.0	Sudan	2		2

DATA NOT AVAILABLE OR NOT APPLICABLE FOR THE FOLLOWING COUNTRIES

Djibouti   Equatorial Guinea   Guinea-Bissau   Namibia   Zimbabwe

SOURCE: H. Hveem *The Extent and Type of Direct Foreign Investment in Africa* (Dakar: UN Africa Institute for Economic Development and Planning, September 1974) CS/2562—15.

SOURCE: See Table 6.18.

TABLE 6.20 Number of Multinational Corporations with Subsidiaries in Each Country, ca. 1968

Definition and Comments: Multinational corporations in this context are corporations headquartered in Austria, Belgium, Denmark, France, German Federal Republic, Italy, Luxembourg, Netherlands, Norway, Portugal, Spain, Sweden, Switzerland, United Kingdom and the United States (data on Canada and Japan were unavailable) which have one or more subsidiaries in each country. The European data is for 1968 while the American data is for 1966. The American data available to the source did not distinguish between subsidiaries, associates and branches, which may result in slight overestimates.

```
Range     =    212.00
Mean      =     54.25
Standard Deviation =        53.52
```

Population Percent Cum.	Country	Rank	Country Name	A	Range Decile
21.00	21.00	1.0	Nigeria	222	1
25.60	4.60	2.0	Kenya	160	3
33.89	8.29	3.0	Zaire	138	4
35.54	1.65	4.0	Zambia	128	5
39.05	3.51	5.5	Ghana	66	8
41.27	2.22	5.5	Ivory Coast	66	
46.43	5.16	7.0	Tanzania	59	
46.96	.53	8.0	Liberia	56	
48.60	1.64	9.0	Senegal	52	9
52.55	3.95	10.0	Uganda	51	
54.96	2.41	11.0	Cameroon	47	
56.62	1.66	12.0	Malawi	38	
59.10	2.48	13.0	Madagascar	33	
68.81	9.71	14.0	Ethiopia	31	10
69.80	.99	15.0	Sierra Leone	28	
76.04	6.24	16.0	Sudan	23	
77.61	1.57	17.0	Guinea	19	
79.56	1.95	18.0	Angola	16	
82.55	2.99	19.0	Mozambique	14	
83.83	1.28	20.0	Burundi	12	
84.41	.58	22.0	Central Afri. R	11	
84.86	.45	22.0	Congo	11	
85.02	.16	22.0	Gabon	11	
85.77	.75	24.0	Togo	10	

DATA NOT AVAILABLE OR NOT APPLICABLE
FOR THE FOLLOWING COUNTRIES

Benin	Botswana	Chad	Djibouti
Equatorial Guinea	Gambia		Guinea-Bissau Lesotho
Mali	Mauritania	Namibia	Niger
Rwanda	Somalia	Swaziland	Upper Volta
Zimbabwe			

SOURCE: E. S. Tew, ed., *Yearbook of International Organizations 1968-1969* (Brussels: Union of International Associations, 1969), p. 1200.

TABLE 6.21 Service Payments on External Public Debt as a Percentage of Exports of Goods and Services 1979 (A), 1972 (B) and 1968 (C).

Definition: Includes all debt service payments actually made and excludes non-payments.

```
Range     =    58.90
Mean      =    11.14
Standard Deviation =        12.00
```

Population Percent Cum.	Country	Rank	Country Name	A	Range Decile	B	C
.19	.19	1.0	Guinea-Bissau	59.0	1		
6.43	6.24	2.0	Sudan	33.0	5	11.1	6.8
6.89	.46	3.0	Mauritania	32.4		2.1	1.3
7.64	.75	4.0	Togo	24.4	6	4.7	4.0
9.21	1.57	5.5	Guinea	22.2	7		
10.20	.99	5.5	Sierra Leone	22.2		8.4	5.7
11.85	1.65	7.0	Zambia	19.7		28.0	2.7
12.01	.16	8.0	Gabon	17.0	8	7.0	6.0
14.23	2.22	9.0	Ivory Coast	15.2		6.3	5.7
15.57	1.34	10.0	Chad	14.4		1.7	4.7
16.10	.53	11.0	Liberia	13.8		6.3	6.3
17.74	1.64	12.0	Senegal	13.7		8.1	1.9
20.15	2.41	13.0	Cameroon	9.5	9	5.4	3.0
21.81	1.66	14.0	Malawi	9.4		9.0	7.6
30.10	8.29	15.0	Zaire	9.1		7.0	2.9
31.97	1.87	16.0	Mali	8.5		1.6	8.9
36.57	4.60	17.0	Kenya	7.5		5.2	7.5
41.73	5.16	18.5	Tanzania	7.4		6.7	7.3
45.68	3.95	18.5	Uganda	7.4		5.6	8.2
46.13	.45	20.0	Congo	7.3		10.7	6.4
47.13	1.00	21.0	Benin	5.1	10	3.1	5.1
56.84	9.71	22.0	Ethiopia	5.0		6.4	9.4
60.35	3.51	23.0	Ghana	4.2		2.3	10.6
62.83	2.48	24.0	Madagascar	4.0		5.0	5.1
64.80	1.97	25.0	Upper Volta	3.8		8.3	4.5
66.13	1.33	26.0	Niger	3.6		2.9	3.7
67.41	1.28	27.0	Burundi	3.1		3.0	3.2
67.57	.16	28.0	Swaziland	2.0		10.5	4.3
67.80	.23	29.0	Botswana	1.6		2.5	4.8
88.80	21.00	30.0	Nigeria	1.5		2.1	6.0
89.83	1.03	31.0	Somalia	1.1		3.6	1.9
90.21	.38	32.5	Lesotho	.6		3.2	3.4
91.57	1.36	32.5	Rwanda	.6		1.3	2.6
91.74	.17	34.0	Gambia	.4			
92.32	.58	35.0	Central African R	.1		4.0	2.2

DATA NOT AVAILABLE OR NOT APPLICABLE
FOR THE FOLLOWING COUNTRIES

Angola	Djibouti	Equatorial Guinea	Mozambique
Namibia	Zimbabwe		

SOURCES: World Bank, *Annual Report* (Washington, D.C.: World Bank, 1981): *Benin, Chad, and Niger*, 1972 data.

Foreign Policy

The preceding discussion of international trade, aid, and investment in Black African countries has clearly suggested the political significance of such dimensions of international relations. The constraints on domestic economic policy imposed by foreign dependency are most obvious, and, since economic development is a key factor in a government's ability to generate legitimacy and to distribute goods and services, an indirect relationship between greater economic dependency and increased domestic political instability is a plausible expectation. It is important, however, to examine the foreign policy and international political relations of these countries as sources of additional constraint or opportunity in the adjustment to situations of economic dependency. The following discussion, therefore suggests attention to data which may give some preliminary indication of the extent to which the foreign policy of these countries leads to greater independence from neo-colonial or cold war pressures, and to greater pan-African solidarity.

In Table 6.22 we provide data on diplomatic relations between Black African nations and other nations of the world. The scope of foreign diplomatic activity within any Black African country indicates the extent of outside interest in that country and may, in conjunction with additional information on the size of the domestic elite in the country in which foreign representatives are stationed, indicate the potential range of foreign influence on domestic decision-making. The data on the size of an African country's diplomatic corps indicate the amount of attention given by that country to international affairs, and although this measure is probably closely related to a country's financial capacity to finance overseas missions, it may be worthwhile treating the extent of imbalance between diplomatic representation received and reciprocated as an indicator of the relative 'openness' of a country to foreign manipulation.[47] More detailed breakdowns of diplomatic representation in and from particular nations, or groups of nations, is necessary, however, for the examination of questions dealing with the influence of former metropolitan powers, cold-war political interests, and inter-African relations. In Table 6.23 and 6.24 we provide data on the extent of diplomatic representation from Communist countries and from other Black African countries.

In addition to bilateral diplomatic relations, it is important to consider foreign policy conducted in multilateral exchanges through membership in international organizations. In Tables 6.25 and 6.26, we present information on the extent of Black African governments' memberships in regional and international organizations.

Multiple memberships in international organizations provide an opportunity for the development of a cross-cutting system of alliances and loyalties, through which nations can relate to each other in a number of alternative roles, thereby modifying the intensity of international conflict between nations on any single issue.[48] In addition to the potential conflict-resolution effects of multilateral forms of international political interaction, international organizations offer a variety of financial, technical and manpower assistance to developing nations. Table 6.27 gives information on the extent of the involvement of international nonprofit organizations in Black African countries, which may be interpreted as a potential counterweight to the influence of bilateral trade and aid relations.

Finally, we refer to data which more directly indicate variation in the behavior of individual Black African nations within the international system. The preceding data on diplomatic exchange and involvement in international organizations suggest only limits or facilities for international integration, conflict-regulation, and independence. The study of international relations must, however, deal with more specific data on the political actions of nations in the international context. One relevant source of such information is of course the voting records of Black African nations within international organizations.[49] Another is the record and content of communication and behavior between nations. As illustrations of these types of data, we present in Table 6.28 information on financial and other commitments to votes in the Organization of African Unity supporting liberation movements in South Africa, Zimbabwe, and the former Portuguese territories, and in Table 6.29 we present data on the extent of aggressive communication and behavior characteristic of the international relations of these individual Black African countries.

The data on contributions by Black African states to liberation movements and on the frequency of their involvement in conflictive interaction with other Black African nations are only very preliminary indications of the ways in which international political relations in this region are becoming more complex. Such complexity reflects growing ideological divisions within the region, but also differences of economic growth and other development experiences. The connection between domestic and international affairs—between differences *within* nations and their interaction—is, for example, indicated by correlations showing fairly marked association between measures of civil war in Black African states and the extent to which they have been involved in conflictive international relations as measured in Table 6.29.[50] The absolute frequency of these latter measures of conflictive interaction between states rose in the period 1964-66 and subsequently declined in the period 1966-69, which also suggests a relationship to the graphic rise and decline in the frequency of domestic political instability in these states during this period, as discussed in Chapter Five. Whatever the reasons for such connections between domestic and international politics, one continuing international problem resulting from domestic instability is the growing number of refugees in Africa. The data in Table 6.30 on the origin and location of refugees indicate the magnitude of the problem.

The data on foreign policy issues discussed here do not provide more than very preliminary approaches to the problems of international relations affecting Black African states. Patterns of regional and global political alignment involving these nations have not been thoroughly researched, and we must look forward to new initiatives in this area[51]. The linkages between domestic and international political activity need to be more thoroughly conceptualized. We know a good deal about relatively straight-forward links like the distribution of ethnic groups across national boundaries,[52] but we know very little about domestic economic and political determinants of foreign policies dealing with special matters like foreign trade agreements, nationalization and partial control of foreign corporations, debt and currency negotiations, regional economic agreements, and diverse international issues involving Southern Africa, the Middle East, oil and other resources policies, etc. It may well be that in these highly centralized political systems, divergences in foreign policy reflect more the random peculiarities of personal leadership than underlying structural characteristics of government, society and economy. That, however, cannot be assumed. Finally, it should be noted that many of the questions that bear on the explanation of international relations implicitly refer to the characteristics of interaction *between* states, and that analysis of these questions should concentrate on data that measure dyadic or even more complex interactions or comparisons. Such additional transformation of aggregate data is, however, potentially unlimited and we must leave to others with specific research interests decisions about appropriate recombination of information like that presented in this and other chapters.

Notes

[1]For a theoretical introduction to the relationship between national and international activity, see the work in James N. Rosenau, *ed.*, *Linkage Politics: Essays on the Convergence of National and International Systems* (New York: The Free Press, 1969), and Rosenau, *ed.*, *International Aspects of Civil Strife* (Princeton, N.J.: Princeton University Press, 1964). The literature on African states' international relations is reviewed in M. W. De Lancey, *Bibliography on African International Relations*, (Boulder, Colo.: Westview Press, 1979); M. W. De Lancey "The Study of African International Relations" in *Aspects of International Relations in Africa* ed. by M. W. De Lancey (Bloomington, Ind.: Indiana University African Studies Program, 1979); and J. A. Kreslins, *Foreign Affairs Bibliography: A Selected and Annotated List of Books on International Relations, 1962—1972*. (New York: Bowkes, 1976).

[2]For interesting approaches to the changing structure of international systems, see Karl W. Deutsch, *et al.*, *Political Community in the North Atlantic Area* (Princeton, N.J.: Princeton University Press, 1957); Bruce M. Russett, "Delineating International Regions," in *Quantitative International Politics: Insights and Evidence*, ed., J. David Singer (New York: Free Press, 1968): 287—352; Leon Lindberg and Stuart Scheingold, *eds.*, *Regional Integration: Theory and Research* (Cambridge, Mass.: Harvard University Press, 1971).

[3]G. Carter, "The Impact of the African States in the United Nations," in R. K. A. Gardiner, M. J. Anstee and C. L. Patterson, *eds.*, *Africa and the World* (Addis Ababa: Oxford University Press, 1970), p. 26.

[4]Cf. Immanuel Wallerstein, *The Modern World System* (New York: Academic Press, 1974).

[5]Cf. Hobson, *Imperialism* (London: Allen and Union, 1930); (New York: St. Martin's 1930); J. Strachey, *The End of Empire* (London: Gollanz, 1959); Robinson and Gallagher, *Africa and the Victorians*.

[6]These figures, and those in the rest of this paragraph, came from S. H. Frankel, *Capital Investment in Africa* (London: Oxford University Press, 1930).

[7]W. J. Barber, "The Movement into the World Economy" in *Economic Transition in Africa*, M. J. Herskovits and M. Harwitz, *eds.* (London: Routledge and Kegan Paul, 1964).

[8]Bob Fitch and Mary Oppenheimer, *Ghana: The End of an Illusion* (New York: Monthly Review Press, 1966), p. 38.

[9]M. Crowder, *West African Under Colonial Rule* (Evanston: Northwestern University Press, 1968), pp. 295—7.

[10]Crowder, *op. cit.*, p. 493.

[11]Crowder, *op. cit.*, p. 497.

[12]Crowder, *op. cit.*, p. 495; and C. Johnson, *Revolutionary Change* (Boston: Little Brown, 1966), pp. 157—60.

[13]Elliot Berg, "Real Income Trends in West Africa, 1934—60," M. J. Herskovits and M. Harwitz, eds., *op. cit.* (1964), p. 203.

[14]Crowder, *op. cit.*, pp. 501—4.

[15]W. A. Chudson, "Trends in African Exports and Capital Inflows," Herskovits and Harwitz, *eds.*, *op. cit.* (1964), p. 337.

[16]Berg, *op. cit.*, pp. 218H.

[18]Fitch and Oppenheimer, *op. cit.*, pp. 42—47.

[19]*New York Times*, (January 29, 1971).

[20]See O. H. Abdel-Alam, "Balance of Payments Problems of African Countries," *Journal of Modern African Studies*, 4 (1966): 155—176.

[21]See Russett, *et al.*, *The World Handbook of Political and Social Indicators* (New Haven: Yale, 1963), pp. 164 and 276.

[22]See the emphasis on the adverse terms of trade for primary commodity exports from less developed nations in Gunner Myrdal, *Economic Theory and Underdeveloped Regions* (Mystic, Conn.: Lawrence Verry, 1957); and R. Prebisch, *Towards a Dynamic Development Policy for Latin America* (New York: U.N., 1963). Also see C. F. Bergsten and L. B. Krause, eds., *World Politics and International Economics* (Washington: Brookings, 1975).

[23]United Nations Document, E/CN/14/UNCTAD II/1.

[24]Robson, *op. cit.*, p. 57.

[25]De Lusignan, *op. cit.*, p. 341.

[26]Robson, *op. cit.*, pp. 53—54.

[27]Cf. B. Stallings, *Economic Dependency in Africa and Latin America* (Beverly Hills: Sage Publications, 1972), p. 27.

[28]For an introduction to the complexity of conventional international trade theory, see Jacob Viner, *International Trade and Economic Development* (Oxford: Clarendon Press, 1953); James Meade, *Trade and Welfare* (New York: Oxford University Press, 1955); Richard Caves, *Trade and Economic Structure* (Cambridge: Harvard University Press, 1963); Murray Kemp, *The Pure Theory of International Trade* (Englewood Cliffs, N.J.: Prentice-Hall, Inc., 1964); John Chipman, "A Survey of the Theory of International Trade, Part I, Classical Theory; Part II, Neo-Classical Theory," *Econometrica*, 33, nos. 3 and 4 (1965): 477—519; 685—760. See also the various contributions to I. G. Stewart and H. W. Ord, eds., *African Primary Products and International Trade* (Edinburgh: University of Edinburgh Press, 1965). For a complex argument against the conventional theories of trade see Arrighi Emmanuel, *Unequal Exchange: A Study of the Imperialism of Trade* (New York: Monthly Review Press, 1972).

[29]The "theory of dependency" is fragmented and multi-faceted, but useful introductory materials are: Andre Gunnar Frank, "The Development of Underdevelopment," in Robert Rhodes, ed., *Imperialism and Underdevelopment* (New York: Monthly Review Press, 1970), pp. 4—17; Green, (1970); Fernando Henrique Cardoso, "Dependency and Development in Latin America," *New Left Review*, 74 (July-August 1972): 83—95; Immanuel Wallerstein, "Dependence in an Interdependent World: The Limited Possibilities of Capital Formation within the Capitalist World Economy," *African Studies Review*, 17 (1974): 1—26; Christopher Chase-Dunn, "The Effects of International Economic Dependence on Development and Inequality: A Cross-National Study," *American Sociological Review*, 40 (December 1975): 720—738; Samir Amin, "Underdevelopment and Dependence in Black Africa," *Journal of Modern African Studies*, 10 (1972): 503—24; and J. Esseks, "Economic Dependency and Political Development in the New States of Africa," *Journal of Politics*, 33 (1971): 1052—75.

[30]These generalizations are documented in H. M. Stevenson and D. G. Morrison, "External Dependency and National Political Instability in Black African Nations," a paper presented to the *World Congress of African Studies*, (Addis Ababa, December 1973).

[31]See Arnold Rivkin, "Economic Systems Development," in John N. Paden and Edward W. Soja, eds., *The African Experience*. Vol. 1: Essays (Evanston: Northwestern University Press, 1970), p. 508.

[32]For an example of the kind of analysis required, see Phillipe C. Schmitter, "Foreign Military Assistance, National Military Spending and Military Rule in Latin America,"

[33]See G. Arrighi, "International Corporations, Labor Aristocracies, and Economic Development in Tropical Africa," p. 249, in *Imperialism and Underdevelopment*, R. Rhodes, ed., (New York: Monthly Review Press, 1970).

[34]These correlations are taken from *Black Africa: A Comparative Handbook*, first edition, 1972.

[35]See S. H. Frankel, "Capital and Capital Supply in Relation to the Development of Africa," in *Economic Development for Africa South of the Sahara*, E. A. G. Robinson, ed., (New York: St. Martin's Press, 1964), p. 428.

[36]Arrighi, *op. cit.*, p. 265.

[37]Leslie L. Rood, "Foreign Investment in African Manufacturing," *Journal of Modern African Studies*, 13 (March: 1975), pp. 21—22.

[38]*Ibid.*

[39]James Vaupel and Joan Curhan, *The Making of Multi-National Enterprise* (Boston: Harvard University, Graduate School of Business Administration, 1969), p. 11.

[40]Peter B. Evans, "National Autonomy and Economic Development: Critical Perspectives on Multi-National Corporations in Poor Countries," in Robert O. Keohane and Joseph Nye, eds., *Transnational Relations in World Politics* (Cambridge: Harvard University Press, 1972): 325—342.

[41]For an introduction to issues involved in the analysis of multi-national corporations see Sayre Schatz, "Crude Private Neo-Imperialism: A New Pattern in Africa," *Journal of Modern African Studies*, (December 1969): 677—88; James O'Connor, "The International Corporation and Economic Underdevelopment," *Science and Society*, 34 (Spring 1970): 42—6; Stephen Hymer, "The Multi-national Corporation and the Law of Uneven Development," J. N. Bhagwati, ed., *Economics and World Order* (New York: Macmillan, 1972); the review essay by Robert O. Keohane and Van Dorn Ooms, "The Multi-National Enterprise and World Political Economy," *International Organization*, 26 (Winter 1972): 84—120; and the entire issue of the *Review of African Political Economy*, 2 (1975). Also see D. Lal *Appraising Foreign Investment in Developing Countries* (London: Heinemann, 1975); and P. J. Drake, "Natural Resources versus Foreign Borrowing in Economic Development," *Economic Journal* 82, 3 (Sept 1972) pp. 951—962.

[42]Cf. Donald Rothchild and Robert L. Curry, Jr., "On Economic Bargaining between African Governments and Multi-National Companies," *Journal of Modern African Studies*, 12 (1974): 173—89.

[43]Surendra J. Patel, "The Technological Dependence of Developing Countries," *Journal of Modern African Studies*, 12 (1974): 1—18.

[44]See Ann Crittenden, "Closing in on Corporate Payoffs Overseas," *New York Times*, (Sunday, February 15, 1976).

[45]Cf. Robert Cox's contribution to Keohane and Nye, eds., *op. cit.*

[46]Cf. Raymond Tanter and Manus Midlarsky, "Toward a Theory of Political Instability in Latin America," *Journal of Peace Research*, 3 (1967): 209—27.

[47]For an indication of the kind of use to which data such as that discussed in this paragraph may be put, see Chadwick F. Alger and Stephen S. Brams, "Patterns of Representation in National Capitals and Intergovernmental Organizations," *World Politics*, 19 (July 1967): 646—663.

[48]See Chadwick F. Alger, "Comparison of Intranational and International Politics," *American Political Science Review*, 57 (1963): 406—419.

[49]We do not have available data on voting in international organizations, but see Richard Vengroff, "Neo-colonialism and Policy Outputs in Africa," *Comparative Political Studies*, 8 (July 1975); 234 for reference to the analysis of such data and for evidence that the extent of foreign aid received is strongly related to the extent of U.N. voting agreement with the ex-colonial power in formerly British African terri-

tories. This relationship is somewhat less pronounced for formerly French African territories, where, however, the extent of trade with France is strongly related to voting agreement with France.

[50]See Raymond W. Copson, "Foreign Policy Conflict Among African States; 1964—1969," in P. J. McGowan, ed., *Sage International Yearbook of Foreign Studies*, Vol. I, (Beverly Hills: Sage Publications, 1973); and compare John N. Collins, *Foreign Conflict Behavior and Domestic Disorder in Africa* (Syracuse: Program of Eastern African Studies Monograph IV, 1971).

[51]For an introduction to the application of cross-national research procedures to such issues, see Patrick J. McGowan, "Africa and Non-Alignment," *International Studies Quarterly*, XII (September 1968): 262—95; "The Pattern of African Diplomacy," *Journal of Asian and African Studies*, IV (July 1969): 202—21; and "Dimensions of African Foreign Policy Behaviour: In Search of Dependence," Research Report No. 3 of the African Foreign Relations and International Conflict Analysis Project of the Inter-University Comparative Foreign Policy Project, (Syracuse University, October 1972), pp. 1—45.

[52]I. William Zartman, "The Politics of Boundaries in North and West Africa," *Journal of Modern African Studies*, III (1965): 155—74; Saadia Touval, "Africa's Frontiers: Reaction to a Colonial Legacy," *International Affairs*, LXII (1966): 641—54; Ravi L. Kapil, "On the Conflict Potential of Inherited Boundaries in Africa," *World Politics*, 18 (1966): 656—73.

TABLE 6.22   Number of Foreign Diplomats Sent to, 1963—1964 (A) and Number Received from Foreign Countries 1963—1964 (B).

```
Range =          210.00
Mean =            43.04
Standard Deviation =        46.56
```

Population Percent Cum.	Country	Rank	Country Name	A	Range Decile	B
3.51	3.51	1.0	Ghana	212	1	242
24.51	21.00	2.0	Nigeria	151	3	223
30.75	6.24	3.0	Sudan	93	6	153
40.46	9.71	4.0	Ethiopia	81	7	129
42.10	1.64	5.0	Senegal	72		163
43.67	1.57	6.0	Guinea	63	8	158
45.54	1.87	7.0	Mali	55		115
46.07	.53	8.0	Liberia	54		99
48.48	2.41	9.0	Cameroon	41	9	80
50.70	2.22	10.5	Ivory Coast	39		98
51.73	1.03	10.5	Somalia	39		92
52.72	.99	12.0	Sierra Leone	35		50
54.69	1.97	13.5	Upper Volta	33		82
62.98	8.29	13.5	Zaire	33		158
63.43	.45	15.0	Congo	22	10	60
64.43	1.00	16.0	Benin	19		50
65.01	.58	18.0	Central African R	16		29
66.35	1.34	18.0	Chad	16		40
67.10	.75	18.0	Togo	16		45
68.43	1.33	20.0	Niger	15		38
69.71	1.28	21.5	Burundi	11		0
70.17	.46	21.5	Mauritania	11		26
70.33	.16	23.0	Gabon	10		23
75.49	5.16	24.0	Tanzania	9		104
76.85	1.36	25.0	Rwanda	8		0
80.80	3.95	26.0	Uganda	6		52
85.40	4.60	27.0	Kenya	2		75

DATA NOT AVAILABLE OR NOT APPLICABLE
FOR THE FOLLOWING COUNTRIES

Angola	Botswana	Djibouti	Equatorial Guinea
Gambia	Guinea-Bissau	Lesotho	Madagascar
Malawi	Mozambique	Namibia	Swaziland
Zambia	Zimbabwe		

SOURCE: Stephen Brams, *Flow and Form in the International System,* unpublished Ph.D. dissertation, Department of Political Science, Northwestern University, 1966. *Angola, Botswana, Djibouti, Guinea-Bissau, Equatorial Guinea, Gambia, Lesotho, Mozambique, Swaziland, Zambia, and Zimbabwe* were not independent states when this data was collected.

TABLE 6.23   Extent of Eastern Bloc Diplomatic Representation 1977 (A), 1972 (B) and 1967 (C).

Definition: Countries included in the Eastern bloc are Bulgaria, People's Republic of China, Czechoslovakia, Hungary, North Korea, North Vietnam, Poland, Rumania, Soviet Union, and Yugoslavia. Each country's representation is weighted as follows: 3 = Embassy; 2 = Consulate; 1 = Diplomatic representation without 3 or 2; 0 = No representation. The index gives the total for all Eastern bloc countries in each African state.

```
Range =           30.00
Mean =            13.34
Standard Deviation =         8.45
```

Population Percent Cum.	Country	Rank	Country Name	A	Range Decile	B	C
21.00	21.00	2.0	Nigeria	30	1	20	18
22.64	1.64	2.0	Senegal	30		12	9
27.80	5.16	2.0	Tanzania	30		24	30
37.51	9.71	4.0	Ethiopia	27	2	15	18
42.11	4.60	5.5	Kenya	24	3	19	18
50.40	8.29	5.5	Zaire	24		16	13
50.85	.45	8.0	Congo	21	4	13	23
52.42	1.57	8.0	Guinea	21		24	29
58.66	6.24	8.0	Sudan	21		6	16
60.61	1.95	12.0	Angola	18	5	0	
60.77	.16	12.0	Gabon	18		0	0
64.28	3.51	12.0	Ghana	18		21	21
65.31	1.03	12.0	Somalia	18		18	11
66.96	1.65	12.0	Zambia	18		18	12
70.91	3.95	15.0	Uganda	15	6	18	18
72.19	1.28	19.0	Burundi	12	7	12	3
74.60	2.41	19.0	Cameroon	12		6	4
76.82	2.22	19.0	Ivory Coast	12		3	0
77.35	.53	19.0	Liberia	12		6	6
79.83	2.48	19.0	Madagascar	12		2	
80.82	.99	19.0	Sierra Leone	12		10	7
82.79	1.97	19.0	Upper Volta	12		11	0
83.79	1.00	26.5	Benin	9	8	19	18
84.37	.58	26.5	Central African R	9		9	6
84.56	.19	26.5	Guinea-Bissau	9		0	
86.43	1.87	26.5	Mali	9		18	30
86.89	.46	26.5	Mauritania	9		19	16
88.22	1.33	26.5	Niger	9		3	0
89.58	1.36	26.5	Rwanda	9		3	3
90.33	.75	26.5	Togo	9		6	9
91.67	1.34	31.0	Chad	6	9	7	3
91.90	.23	33.5	Botswana	3	10	11	0
92.00	.10	33.5	Equatorial Guinea	3		4	0
92.17	.17	33.5	Gambia	3		2	2
93.83	1.66	33.5	Malawi	3		0	0
93.93	.10	37.0	Djibouti	0		0	
94.31	.38	37.0	Lesotho	0		0	0
94.47	.16	37.0	Swaziland	0		0	0

DATA NOT AVAILABLE OR NOT APPLICABLE
FOR THE FOLLOWING COUNTRIES

Mozambique   Namibia   Zimbabwe

SOURCES: *Europa Yearbook, Statesman's Yearbook, Africa South of the Sahara,* various years.

TABLE 6.24   Extent of Diplomatic Representation from Other Black African States, 1977 (A), 1972 (B) and 1966 (C) and 1962 (D).

Definition: The countries included are all those in this Handbook. The countries are weighted as follows: 0 = No diplomatic representation; 1 = Diplomatic representation with representatives resident in a third country; 2 = Diplomatic representation but no interchange of ambassadors; 3 = Full diplomatic relations with exchange of ambassadors.

```
Range =          57.00
Mean =           17.34
Standard Deviation =           14.06
```

Population Percent Cum.	Country Rank	Country Name	A	Range Decile	B	C	D
8.29 8.29	1.0	Zaire	57	1	52	3	119
18.00 9.71	2.5	Ethiopia	54		63	15	108
39.00 21.00	2.5	Nigeria	54		40	24	26
39.53 .53	4.0	Liberia	37	4	37	21	
45.77 6.24	5.0	Sudan	32	5	45	18	57
48.18 2.41	6.5	Cameroon	27	6	30	3	
48.34 .16	6.5	Gabon	27		17		
49.91 1.57	8.0	Guinea	26		24	24	69
51.55 1.64	9.0	Senegal	25		35	15	9
53.42 1.87	10.0	Mali	24		16	3	12
54.00 .58	11.5	Central African R	21	7	19	3	18
54.45 .45	11.5	Congo	21		31		37
59.05 4.60	13.5	Kenya	18		44		169
64.21 5.16	13.5	Tanzania	18		28		63
65.86 1.65	15.0	Zambia	17	8	15		108
69.37 3.51	16.5	Ghana	16		35	18	87
72.36 2.99	16.5	Mozambique	16				
73.64 1.28	19.5	Burundi	15		10		34
74.98 1.34	19.5	Chad	15		17	6	26
75.44 .46	19.5	Mauritania	15		13	3	8
76.19 .75	19.5	Togo	15		9		9
80.14 3.95	22.0	Uganda	12		23		37
82.36 2.22	23.5	Ivory Coast	11	9	26	9	39
83.39 1.03	23.5	Somalia	11		8	3	253
84.39 1.00	25.5	Benin	10		19	9	16
84.55 .16	25.5	Swaziland	10		2		
85.88 1.33	27.5	Niger	7		13	6	20
87.24 1.36	27.5	Rwanda	7		12		36
89.19 1.95	30.5	Angola	6				
89.29 .10	30.5	Equatorial Guinea	6		10		
89.46 .17	30.5	Gambia	6		13		
91.43 1.97	30.5	Upper Volta	6		14	3	9
91.62 .19	33.5	Guinea-Bissau	5	10			
92.00 .38	33.5	Lesotho	5				
92.99 .99	35.0	Sierra Leone	4		18	12	2
94.65 1.66	36.0	Malawi	2		7		66
97.13 2.48	37.0	Madagascar	1				
97.36 .23	38.0	Botswana			8		

DATA NOT AVAILABLE OR NOT APPLICABLE FOR THE FOLLOWING COUNTRIES

Djibouti   Namibia   Zimbabwe

SOURCE: See Table 6.23.

TABLE 6.25 Total Number of Memberships in Principal Regional and International Organizations and Conferences, ca. 1967.

Definition: The eighteen organizations listed by the source include the United Nations, Organization of African Unity, the Commonwealth and French Community, the Monrovia and Brazzaville Groups, the Belgrade and Bandung Conferences, Casablanca Powers and the East African Common Services Organization.

```
Range =            7.00
Mean =             6.59
Standard Deviation =            2.26
```

Population Percent	Cum. Country	Rank	Country Name	A	Range Decile
.45	.45	2.5	Congo	10	1
2.67	2.22	2.5	Ivory Coast	10	
4.00	1.33	2.5	Niger	10	
5.64	1.64	2.5	Senegal	10	
6.64	1.00	7.5	Benin	9	2
9.05	2.41	7.5	Cameroon	9	
9.63	.58	7.5	Central African R	9	
10.97	1.34	7.5	Chad	9	
11.13	.16	7.5	Gabon	9	
13.10	1.97	7.5	Upper Volta	9	
14.97	1.87	11.5	Mali	8	3
15.72	.75	11.5	Togo	8	
19.23	3.51	13.5	Ghana	7	5
25.47	6.24	13.5	Sudan	7	
35.18	9.71	18.0	Ethiopia	6	6
39.78	4.60	18.0	Kenya	6	
60.78	21.00	18.0	Nigeria	6	
62.14	1.36	18.0	Rwanda	6	
63.13	.99	18.0	Sierra Leone	6	
64.16	1.03	18.0	Somalia	6	
72.45	8.29	18.0	Zaire	6	
72.62	.17	23.5	Gambia	5	8
74.19	1.57	23.5	Guinea	5	
74.72	.53	23.5	Liberia	5	
78.67	3.95	23.5	Uganda	5	
80.33	1.66	27.5	Malawi	4	9
80.79	.46	27.5	Mauritania	4	
85.95	5.16	27.5	Tanzania	4	
87.60	1.65	27.5	Zambia	4	
87.83	.23	31.0	Botswana	3	
89.11	1.28	31.0	Burundi	3	
89.49	.38	31.0	Lesotho	3	

DATA NOT AVAILABLE OR NOT APPLICABLE FOR THE FOLLOWING COUNTRIES

Angola   Djibouti   Equatorial Guinea   Guinea-Bissau
Madagascar   Mozambique   Namibia   Swaziland
Zimbabwe

SOURCE: Abdul O. Said, *The African Phenomenon* (London: Allyn and Bacon, 1968), pp. 164-67.

TABLE 6.26 Total Number of Memberships in Major African Multilateral Economic Organizations, 1967.

Definition: These include all-African organizations such as the UN Economic Commission for Africa, regional organizations such as the Economic Community of West Africa and the Chad Basin Commission, and limited purpose organizations such as Air Afrique, an airline supported by most of the former-French colonies. The source lists a total of 25 organizations.

```
Range =            14.00
Mean =              7.44
Standard Deviation =            4.22
```

Population Percent	Cum. Country	Rank	Country Name	A	Range Decile
2.22	2.22	1.0	Ivory Coast	15	1
3.22	1.00	3.0	Benin	14	
5.63	2.41	3.0	Cameroon	14	
6.96	1.33	3.0	Niger	14	
7.41	.45	6.5	Congo	12	3
9.05	1.64	6.5	Senegal	12	
9.80	.75	6.5	Togo	12	
11.77	1.97	6.5	Upper Volta	12	
12.35	.58	9.5	Central African R	11	
13.69	1.34	9.5	Chad	11	
13.85	.16	11.5	Gabon	10	4
34.85	21.00	11.5	Nigeria	10	
35.31	.46	13.0	Mauritania	9	5
37.18	1.87	14.5	Mali	8	6
42.34	5.16	14.5	Tanzania	8	
46.94	4.60	17.0	Kenya	6	7
48.30	1.36	17.0	Rwanda	6	
56.59	8.29	17.0	Zaire	6	
66.30	9.71	20.5	Ethiopia	5	8
69.81	3.51	20.5	Ghana	5	
70.80	.99	20.5	Sierra Leone	5	
74.75	3.95	20.5	Uganda	5	
76.03	1.28	24.5	Burundi	4	
77.60	1.57	24.5	Guinea	4	
78.13	.53	24.5	Liberia	4	
79.16	1.03	24.5	Somalia	4	
80.82	1.66	27.5	Malawi	3	9
82.47	1.65	27.5	Zambia	3	
82.64	.17	29.5	Gambia	2	10
88.88	6.24	29.5	Sudan	2	
89.11	.23	31.5	Botswana	1	
89.49	.38	31.5	Lesotho	1	

DATA NOT AVAILABLE OR NOT APPLICABLE FOR THE FOLLOWING COUNTRIES

Angola   Djibouti   Equatorial Guinea   Guinea-Bissau
Madagascar   Mozambique   Namibia   Swaziland
Zimbabwe

SOURCE: *Africa Report*, 12 (June 1967): 24.

TABLE 6.27 **Total Number of International Non-profit Organizations with Representatives in Each Country, 1968.**

Definition: These include intergovernmental and international non-governmental, non-profit organizations.

```
Range =          226.00
Mean =           120.21
Standard Deviation =        55.22
```

Population Percent					
Cum.	Country	Rank	Country Name	A	Range Decile
21.00	21.00	1.0	Nigeria	263	1
24.51	3.51	2.0	Ghana	217	3
29.11	4.60	3.0	Kenya	185	4
31.59	2.48	4.0	Madagascar	176	
33.23	1.64	5.0	Senegal	168	5
41.52	8.29	6.0	Zaire	160	
45.47	3.95	7.0	Uganda	157	
47.88	2.41	8.0	Cameroon	141	6
53.04	5.16	9.0	Tanzania	140	
59.28	6.24	10.0	Sudan	131	
61.50	2.22	11.0	Ivory Coast	123	7
71.21	9.71	12.0	Ethiopia	109	
72.86	1.65	13.0	Zambia	107	
73.85	.99	14.0	Sierra Leone	105	
74.38	.53	15.0	Liberia	96	8
74.54	.16	16.0	Gabon	90	
74.99	.45	17.0	Congo	89	
76.65	1.66	18.0	Malawi	85	
77.40	.75	19.0	Togo	83	
77.98	.58	20.0	Central Afri. R	79	9
79.26	1.28	21.5	Burundi	51	10
80.83	1.57	21.5	Guinea	51	
82.78	1.95	23.0	Angola	42	
85.77	2.99	24.0	Mozambique	37	

DATA NOT AVAILABLE OR NOT APPLICABLE
FOR THE FOLLOWING COUNTRIES

Benin	Botswana	Chad	Djibouti
Equatorial Guinea	Gambia	Guinea-Bissau	Lesotho
Mali	Mauritania	Namibia	Niger
Rwanda	Somalia	Swaziland	Upper Volta
Zimbabwe			

SOURCE: Eyvind S. Tew, ed., *Yearbook of International Organizations 1968—69* (Brussels: Union of International Associations, 1969), p. 1200.

TABLE 6.28   Support for Liberation Movements 1966—1971.

Definition: The following types of support were each coded 1 if provided by a state and 0 if not:

(1) Regular payment of dues to OAU Liberation Committee.
(2) Establishment of military camps, bases, training facilities for Liberation Movements.
(3) Extra aid (financial, medical) from heads of state to Liberation Movements or OAU Liberation Committee.
(4) Establishment of field officers of Liberation Movements.
(5) Attempt to effect conciliation or unity between rival Liberation Movements.

(6) Administration of refugees from country in which Liberation Movements are active.
(7) Opposition to dialogue with authorities in target areas.
(8) Granting of asylum to political exiles who escape or are expelled.
(9) Occasional payment of OAU Liberation Committee dues.

These dichotomous items as coded for forty-one independent African states in 1971 constitute a Guttman scale. This table represents the total scores over the items for each country.

```
Range =            9.00
Mean =             3.51
Standard Deviation =           2.84
```

Population Percent		Rank	Country Name	A	Range Decile
Cum.	Country				
5.16	5.16	1.5	Tanzania	9	1
6.81	1.65	1.5	Zambia	9	
7.26	.45	5.0	Congo	8	2
16.97	9.71	5.0	Ethiopia	8	
20.48	3.51	5.0	Ghana	8	
22.05	1.57	5.0	Guinea	8	
30.34	8.29	5.0	Zaire	8	
31.98	1.64	8.5	Senegal	7	3
35.93	3.95	8.5	Uganda	7	
40.53	4.60	10.0	Kenya	6	4
61.53	21.00	11.0	Nigeria	5	5
62.81	1.28	16.0	Burundi	4	6
65.22	2.41	16.0	Cameroon	4	
65.39	.17	16.0	Gambia	4	
65.92	.53	16.0	Liberia	4	
67.58	1.66	16.0	Malawi	4	
68.04	.46	16.0	Mauritania	4	
69.03	.99	16.0	Sierra Leone	4	
70.06	1.03	16.0	Somalia	4	
76.30	6.24	16.0	Sudan	4	
76.53	.23	22.0	Botswana	3	7
78.40	1.87	22.0	Mali	3	
78.56	.16	22.0	Swaziland	3	
79.14	.58	25.5	Central Afri. R	2	8
80.48	1.34	25.5	Chad	2	
80.58	.10	25.5	Equatorial Guinea	2	
80.96	.38	25.5	Lesotho	2	
81.96	1.00	31.5	Benin	1	9
82.12	.16	31.5	Gabon	1	
84.34	2.22	31.5	Ivory Coast	1	
86.82	2.48	31.5	Madagascar	1	
88.15	1.33	31.5	Niger	1	
89.51	1.36	31.5	Rwanda	1	
90.26	.75	31.5	Togo	1	
92.23	1.97	31.5	Upper Volta	1	
94.18	1.95	38.5	Angola	0	
94.28	.10	38.5	Djibouti	0	
94.47	.19	38.5	Guinea-Bissau	0	
97.46	2.99	38.5	Mozambique	0	
97.75	.29	38.5	Namibia	0	
100.00	2.26	38.5	Zimbabwe	0	

SOURCE: Vincent B. Khapoya, *The Politics of Division: A Comparative Survey of African Policy Toward the Liberation Movements* (Denver, Colorado: University of Denver Monograph Series in World Affairs, 1975). Table 3.1, page 31.

TABLE 6.29   **Number of Conflictive Interactions with Other Black African States 1964—69.**

Definition: See source.

```
Range =          253.00
Mean =            47.90
Standard Deviation =            56.16
```

Population Percent		Rank	Country Name	A	Range Decile
Cum.	Country				
1.03	1.03	1.0	Somalia	253	1
5.63	4.60	2.0	Kenya	169	4
13.92	8.29	3.0	Zaire	119	6
23.63	9.71	4.5	Ethiopia	108	
25.28	1.65	4.5	Zambia	108	
28.79	3.51	6.0	Ghana	87	7
30.36	1.57	7.0	Guinea	69	8
32.02	1.66	8.0	Malawi	66	
37.18	5.16	9.0	Tanzania	63	
43.42	6.24	10.0	Sudan	57	
45.64	2.22	11.0	Ivory Coast	39	9
46.09	.45	12.5	Congo	37	
50.04	3.95	12.5	Uganda	37	
51.40	1.36	14.0	Rwanda	36	
52.68	1.28	15.0	Burundi	34	
54.02	1.34	16.5	Chad	26	
75.02	21.00	16.5	Nigeria	26	
76.35	1.33	18.0	Niger	20	10
76.93	.58	19.0	Central Afri. R	18	
77.93	1.00	20.0	Benin	16	
79.80	1.87	21.0	Mali	12	
81.44	1.64	23.0	Senegal	9	
82.19	.75	23.0	Togo	9	
84.16	1.97	23.0	Upper Volta	9	
84.62	.46	25.0	Mauritania	8	
85.61	.99	26.0	Sierra Leone	2	
88.02	2.41	28.5	Cameroon	0	
88.18	.16	28.5	Gabon	0	
88.71	.53	28.5	Liberia	0	
91.19	2.48	28.5	Madagascar	0	

```
DATA NOT AVAILABLE OR NOT APPLICABLE
FOR THE FOLLOWING COUNTRIES

Angola       Botswana       Djibouti       Equatorial Guinea
Gambia       Guinea-Bissau  Lesotho        Mozambique
Namibia      Swaziland      Zimbabwe
```

SOURCE: Raymond W. Copson, 'Foreign Policy Conflict Among African States: 1964—1969,' in P. J. McGowan, ed., *Sage International Yearbook of Foreign Policy Studies*, vol. I (Beverly Hills, Sage Publications, 1973).

TABLE 6.30   Number of Refugees Resident in each Black African State 1980 (A) and 1972 (B) and number coming from each Black African State and Resident in other Countries ca. 1980(C), in thousands of persons.

```
Range =        1540.00
Mean =           71.13
Standard Deviation =        247.36
```

Population Percent Cum.	Country	Rank	Country Name	A	Range Decile	B	C
1.03	1.03	1.0	Somalia	1540.0	1	0	0
7.27	6.24	2.0	Sudan	441.0	8	59.0	65.0
15.56	8.29	3.0	Zaire	301.8	9	489.0	40.0
20.72	5.16	4.0	Tanzania	155.7		82.5	0
24.67	3.95	5.0	Uganda	112.8	10	180.0	50.0
27.08	2.41	6.0	Cameroon	100.0		0	0
30.07	2.99	7.0	Mozambique	60.0		40.0	51.0
32.02	1.95	8.0	Angola	54.9		0	416.0
33.67	1.65	9.0	Zambia	51.0		17.0	5.0
34.95	1.28	10.0	Burundi	50.0		40.0	47.0
44.66	9.71	11.0	Ethiopia	11.0		17.5	55.0
65.66	21.00	12.0	Nigeria	8.0		0	0
66.24	.58	13.0	Central Afri. R	7.0		30.0	0
67.60	1.36	14.5	Rwanda	5.0		3.0	142.0
67.76	.16	14.5	Swaziland	5.0		0	
67.86	.10	16.0	Djibouti	4.2			
72.46	4.60	17.0	Kenya	3.5		1.5	0
72.69	.23	18.0	Botswana	3.4		3.8	0
73.07	.38	19.0	Lesotho	2.0		0	0
74.07	1.00	30.5	Benin	0		0	0
75.41	1.34	30.5	Chad	0		0	15.0
75.86	.45	30.5	Congo	0		0	0
75.96	.10	30.5	Equatorial Guinea	0		0	50.0
76.12	.16	30.5	Gabon	0		20.0	0
76.29	.17	30.5	Gambia	0		0	0
79.80	3.51	30.5	Ghana	0		0	0
81.37	1.57	30.5	Guinea	0		0	400.0
81.56	.19	30.5	Guinea-Bissau	0		0	81.0
83.78	2.22	30.5	Ivory Coast	0		0	0
84.31	.53	30.5	Liberia	0		0	0
86.79	2.48	30.5	Madagascar	0		0	0
88.45	1.66	30.5	Malawi	0		0	40.0
90.32	1.87	30.5	Mali	0		0	0
90.78	.46	30.5	Mauritania	0		0	0
91.07	.29	30.5	Namibia	0			
92.40	1.33	30.5	Niger	0		0	0
94.04	1.64	30.5	Senegal	0		481.0	0
95.03	.99	30.5	Sierra Leone	0		0	
95.78	.75	30.5	Togo	0		1.5	0
97.75	1.97	30.5	Upper Volta	0		0	0
100.00	2.26	30.5	Zimbabwe	0			

SOURCE: L. Rubin, 'Africa and Refugees,' *African Affairs*, 292 (July 1974): 290—31; *Statesman's Yearbook; Africa Contemporary Record* 1974—75.

(1980) Unpublished U.S. government sources.

Cross-National Research on Africa: Issues and Context

1. Comparative Analysis of African Nations: On the Uses and Limitations of Cross-National Data

A detailed account of comparative methodology or cross-national research in the social sciences is not possible here, although such a work is needed.[1] It is important, however, to indicate the purposes of cross-national research and the possibilities and limitations of such research in Africa. The discussion here is designed primarily to speak to professional social scientists and "Africanists," some of whom may be either dubious of the value of comparative research using aggregate data on macro-social entities such as countries, or skeptical of the validity of quantitative, comparative analysis.

This chapter discusses the following questions: (1) Are countries comparable? (2) Why focus on Black African countries, and what are the limitations of such a focus? (3) What kinds of approaches can be adopted to investigate questions about social life by comparing nations? (4) How accurately can one describe nations, and how much confidence can one have in the accuracy of generalizations based on such comparisons, and (5) How does one interpret such generalizations?

Nations as Units of Analysis in Comparative Research

Social science aims to establish generalizations about human behavior. All generalizations involve the comparison of two or more similar entities, and comparison is as basic to art as it is to science. A metaphor and a proposition both demand the comparison of entities which are not identical, but whose common properties may give us a richer knowledge of the individul entities. The need for comparison in the social sciences is well-illustrated by David McClelland:

> It is perhaps because I have spent time analyzing particular cases that I feel the need for generalizations and a comparative frame of reference. It is so easy to be mistaken if you analyze only a particular case. The clinical psychologist may decide, for example, that George is neurotic because his mother mistreated him. The detailed case record makes the point very clear. Yet might not the clinician's view of the case be quite different if he knew that mothers from George's social background generally mistreated their sons and that most of those sons did not become neurotic?[2]

Our concern with cross-national analysis is based on a similar argument. It may well be argued that a *coup d'état* in Ghana, for example, was the result of a highly personalistic regime,[3] or the result of the inhibiting consequences of neo-colonialist manipulation of the Ghanaian economy,[4] but if we discover that other African countries that have similar personalistic regimes and suffer equally from foreign economic domination—for example, the Ivory Coast—do not have coups d'état, we may be less satisfied with such explanations, and search for factors other than personalism and neo-colonialism as explanations of all, or most, cases of coups d'état.

But this argument begs too many questons, the most important of which is: are nations comparable in the same sense as McClelland's individuals? What do Gambia and Zaire, for example, have in common? While this is a question for empirical analysis, it is also a question which must be answered prior to the inclusion of these two countries in a sample of units for cross-national analysis. According to Przeworski and Teune:

> To study something 'comparatively' often means that at some stage countries become units of analysis. However, the very choice of countries as units of analysis threatens the validity of the findings. Accumulated experience leads to the expectation that most of the third, or intervening, variables that alter the character of examined relationships are to be found at the level of the nation-state. Concepts are expected to have different meanings in different countries. Relationships are expected to differ more between countries than within a single country. The critical problem in cross-national research is that of identifying "equivalent" phenomena and analyzing the relationships between them in an "equivalent" fashion.[5]

The initial problem is to determine how much alike phenomena must be in order to be used as a basis for comparative generalization. This is as much a problem of unit equivalence as it is a problem of the equivalence of indicators (which Przeworski and Teune discuss). The common dictum that you cannot compare apples and oranges is frequently the point of arguments made against cross-national research, and it needs to be considered.

The Problem of Unit Equivalence

That apples and oranges are different entities is accepted by most people, but it is also accepted that both apples and oranges are fruits, and that certain generalizations for fruits will describe some aspects of both varieties. In set theoretic terms, the sets (a, b, c, d) and (x, b, y, d) have the subset (b, d) in common, and if we can make generalizations about the behavior of (b, d) we can say something about both sets, even though the interaction of the unique elements in each set may be such as to drastically limit the power of generalizations about (b, d). This then is the essential problem of unit equivalence in cross-national research: what number of characteristics do two or more nations have in common, and what are the limits of comparison and generalization imposed on cross-national research by the range of this commonality?

There is no clear-cut answer to this problem and perhaps it should be recognized as an unanswerable problem. The limits of unit equivalence are set by the goals of the researcher, and different levels of analysis are suitable modes of comparison for different problems and differences in data availability. There seems to be no *a priori* way to compare the range of non-equivalence in a set of individuals or in a set of national units. The conceptual equivalence of the units of analysis is a first-order assumption of any scientific investigation, and the fruitfulness of that assumption is determined by the degree to which generalizations based on a set of units provide satisfying results. Individuals have no more intrinsic "comparative" utility than nations. According to Kaplan:

> A scientist *may* use whatever concepts he *can* use, whatever ones he finds useful in fact. The restriction to which he is subject is only that what he says be capable of being checked by experience, or alternatively, capable of providing some guidance to action...The choice of locus (the selection of units of analysis) is subject to the demand of empirical anchorage, but not necessarily to that of physicalistic reduction. The behavior in behavioral science does not serve to limit the science's choice of conceptual base but only to emphasize its ultimate empiricism.[6]

If we take this open-ended and pragmatic approach to what Kaplan calls "the autonomy of inquiry" and "the autonomy of the conceptual base," it is nevertheless important to explain the selection of a particular set of units of analysis. For this Handbook, it is necessary to justify the concentration of national units in general, and African national units in particular.

Units as System: The Equivalence of Nations

Nations as social entities are the subject of a very considerable conceptual and theoretical analysis.[7] For our purposes nations are geographically-bounded entities in which legal sovereignty is recognized to be the perogative of indigenous authorities. These parameters in the definition of nations change, of course, over time, but at any one time it is possible to establish the boundaries of a nation in these terms: what are the geographical frontiers of the national entity; who lives within those frontiers, and what proportion of them have the rights and obligations accruing to citizens; what institutions and officers are recognized as having the right to make rules for the behavior of citizens, and the right to enforce these rules in the event that citizens do not comply with them? These questions make clear the exclusively political character of nations—the laws which define them and the human relationships which sustain them are products of political action, and the importance of nations as subjects of academic study relates directly to the assumed importance of the impact of political decisions made by national authorities on the lives of people.

Our own evaluation of the importance of nations relates to the general historical development of nation-states as political entities, and, more particularly, to the development of nations in twentieth-century Africa. The growth of nationalism since the French Revolution has been a paradoxical conflict between an increasing institutionalization of the demands for individual liberty, fraternity, and equality, and an increasing alienation of individual and primary group autonomy to the more encompassing authority and coercive power of national governments. As men have expanded their conceptions of the scope of individual freedom, so they have expanded the institutional means for the limitation of freedom, and nations born in revolution have all too easily given birth to totalitarianism.

The prospect of a resolution of this inherent conflict in the growth of nationalism has been the greatest stimulation to social scientists, who have heralded either the withering away of the state or the emergence of supranational government. But as the dialectic continues, national citizenship becomes an increasingly unavoidable experience and the range of activities in which the life of the citizen is affected by national governments increases. The maintenance of territory, citizenship, and government as established in contemporary nations becomes increasingly a matter of life and death as the continuing history of struggles for national liberation or secession attests, and attempts at supra-national organization are founded on the fundamental assumption of the legitimacy of the principles of territorial integrity and the internal sovereignty of nations.

The Development of African Nations

The recency of the African experience as independent nation-states has not made for any less concern with the centrality of nationalism in the political culture of Africa as compared to other places. Of the 41 countries considered in this Handbook, only Ethiopia and Liberia were independent prior to 1955. Sudan became independent in 1956, and in 1957 Ghana became the first all-black African state to emerge from the colonial era. By 1960, most of the French-speaking states and Nigeria had opted for complete independence. In the early 1960s, the British East and Central African colonies followed the West African example of independence and in the mid-1970s the Portuguese colonies achieved independence. Zimbabwe became independent in 1980 and Namibia is expected to follow this example in the near future.

In the 1950s and early 1960s, there was considerable controversy among African statesmen as to the appropriate boundaries for the independent African nations.[8] The boundaries inherited from the colonial era were regarded as artificial and, in fact, as a continuing symbol of colonialism. Proposals were made for larger groupings of states, ranging from regional units of neighboring states, to continent-wide pan-Africanism. In July 1960, however, a series of events began to occur which polarized the African states: the Zairese army revolted against their Belgian officers, a coup d'état occurred, Katanga province attempted secession, and the Zairese civil war began, involving not only the world powers but other African states as well. During the period of the Katanga secession (1960-1963), African states were divided into two ideological groupings, centered at Monrovia and Casablanca, respectively.[9] Yet by 1963, it was clear to most African statesmen that such ideological division (which to some extent included disagreement about the means of Pan-African unification) was detrimental to their own goals as well as to Pan-Africanism. The Organization of African Unity (OAU), which was established in Addis Ababa in May, 1963, was a compromise between the Monrovia and Casablanca groups. It was agreed that the territorial boundaries of the African states should be regarded as inviolate, and boundary disputes were to be handled by a special commission of the OAU.[10] In return, the more radical states were assured that the continuing colonial situation in white-dominated southern Africa would receive priority attention by the OAU. In 1965, the African states refused to hold the OAU meeting in Ghana until the government had expelled the various "revolutionary" African governments-in-exile. By the time the OAU meeting was held in Accra (late 1965), it was clear that the principle of territorial integrity and non-subversion of fellow states was well-established. This was frequently tested but generally held until the early 1980's where border conflicts especially in North Africa or its borders with black Africa raised serious questions about the Organization's future. The dispute over the control of the former Spanish Sahara prevented the OAU from holding their meeting in Libya in 1982.

Since 1963, as political, social, and economic sectors within the national systems of the new independent states became established so too did a sense of national self-interest. Often neighboring countries were in direct competition for sales of primary products on the world market, or were in competition for scarce capital investment resources. While some efforts at regional cooperation developed (notably the Entente[11] between Ivory Coast, Upper Volta, Niger, and Benin), there was a strong counter-trend in the direction of weakening earlier ties between states (as in the East African Common Service Organization). The beginning of a West African common market system, ECOWAS, is promising but the problem of having a dominant partner exists since the Nigerian economy is larger than the total of all the other partners combined. With the growth and development of the OAU, there has been a clear re-affirmation of the goals of Pan-Africanism, but the goal of a united continent was premised primarily on the voluntary participation of existing national units. Thus far, the position of the OAU participant states on every major issue of attempted secession, irredentism, or border dispute in Africa has been overwhelmingly to affirm the existing state boundaries despite the fact that several states recognized Biafra during her secession attempt. The exception of the current crisis in the Organization over the former Spanish Sahara makes clear how serious an issue this is.

African and Cross-National Comparisons

Having argued that nations are comparable, why do we focus upon only a particular sub-set of nations in this Handbook? Zaire and Gambia may be less comparable than either nation and Denmark. One pressing reason for the focus upon Africa is the frequent lack of aggregate data on Africa which makes it difficult to generalize about the universe of nations, since about one-third of all nations in the world are in Africa. Thus, in addition to our own concerns with regard to the study of African nations, this Handbook attempts to make some contribution to the missing-data problems in cross-national research.

A focus upon a particular region of the world makes sense in a more general way, however. Regions of the world, such as Africa, share certain uniformities in historical development which render their constituent countries especially comparable.[12] These uniformities may also present problems relatively unique to the region, such as tribal ethnicity in Africa, that require the attention of specialists. Thus a regional focus permits a more sophisticated use of regional and national data sources and findings. The regional focus also permits consideration of special factors which differentiate the nations in the region, such as the colonial legacy. The relevance of these factors in the comparison of nations is an empirical question which bears careful analysis, an analysis which is more likely to be successful in an enterprise of limited geographical scope such as this Handbook than in a data collection which makes no such distinctions.[13]

Five Approaches to Cross-National Analysis

If it is accepted that nations are social entities of vital significance, and that they are conceptually equivalent as units of scientific and comparative analysis, there remains the question of what different procedures exist to compare nations, and what limitations are placed on our knowledge of national development by the selection of a particular research strategy.

Consider the following question which has attracted some attention in the social sciences: *Do nations tend to become more democratic as they become economically more developed?* More simply stated, is there a relationship between democracy and wealth? In order to discuss possible answers to this question, we are going to ignore the problem of valid operationalization (measurement) of the concepts of wealth and democracy. If we assume that it is meaningful to quantify the concepts in many different ways, what quantitative evidence might provide an answer to our question? At least five possibilities suggest themselves.[14]

Method 1

We might argue that it is reasonable to suppose that democratic institutions will develop in nations in which individuals hold democratic values and support the existence of such institutions. The answer to the question of whether or not there is a relationship between democracy and wealth in nations may be approached, therefore, in the following way: if in a number of nations people who are wealthier tend to support democratic practices more than people who are poorer, we might have some confidence in stating that nations tend to become more democratic as they become economically more developed.[15] In technical terms, we might present data as in Figure 1.1, in the form of regression lines for each nation.

In each nation the regression line is based on the plot of measures of income and democratic values for a sample of individuals in that nation. If we then discover that the form of the relationships (the slope of the regression line) in these countries are not significantly different,[16] or that they are all at least positive, we may argue that we have support for our hypothesis. If not, we might hypothesize that national characteristics, or national political culture, is a significant intervening factor in the relationship between wealth and democracy,[17] and that we cannot generalize that nations tend to become more democratic as they become more economically developed.[18]

Figure 1.1

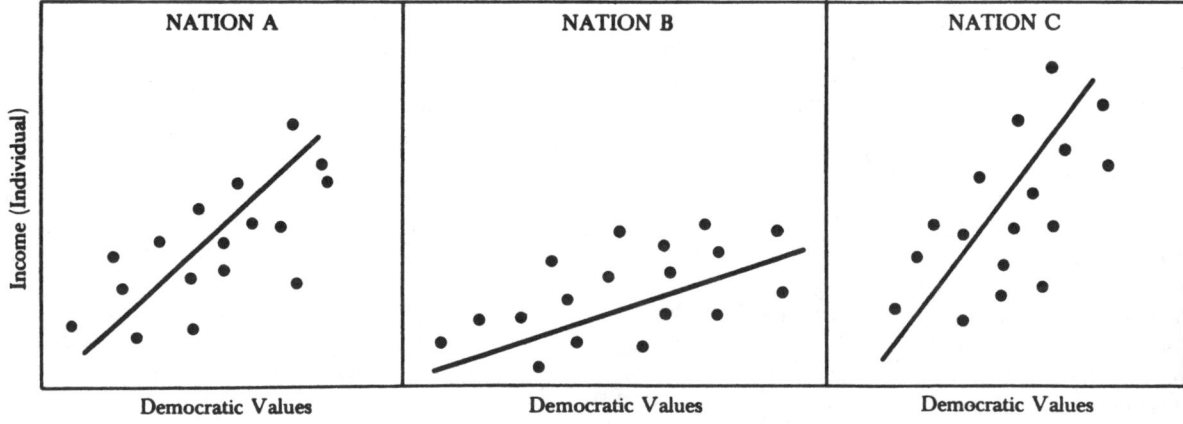

Method 2

In contrast to method 1, we might reason that although individual attitudes are critical to the support of democratic institutions, the presence or absence of such institutions in different nations can be observed, and that an answer to our question can be given if we observe that those nations which have more democratic institutions also tend to have greater degrees of economic development.[19] The evidence for such an answer would be presented in a form such as that suggested by Figure 1.2.

In this figure, the regression line represents a relationship between aggregate income and democracy based on a plot of the levels of income and democracy in each of a sample of nations at a given point in time. The statistical association summarizing this relationship might be used as evidence for a positive answer to the question whether or not there is a relationship between wealth and democracy. The nature of this answer, as compared to that provided by method 1 is, however, very different.[20]

Figure 1.2

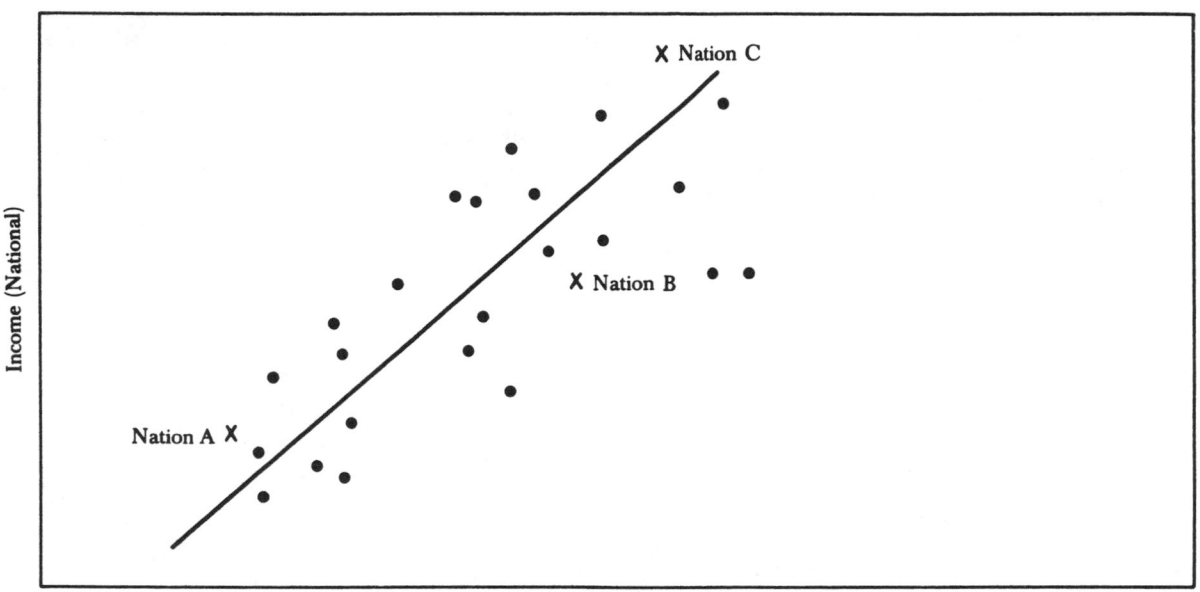

Method 3

In both methods 1 and 2, we have failed to take temporal relationships into consideration and we have failed to take strict notice of the meaning of *become* in our question—do nations become more democratic as they become more wealthy? A slight but significant modification of method 1 would be to suggest that, if there is evidence in a number of nations that people tend increasingly to support democratic practices as they become wealthier, we should be relatively confident of a positive reply to our question. The evidence for such an answer would be in the form suggested in Figure 1.3.

Here the plot is based on observations of individuals at two different points in time, and each point on the graph indicates the amount of the increase in income, and in the degree of democratic orientation of individuals from time 1 to time 2. The interpretation of these data, and the decisions about the confidence in making a generalization from such data are the same as in Figure 1.1.[21]

Figure 1.3

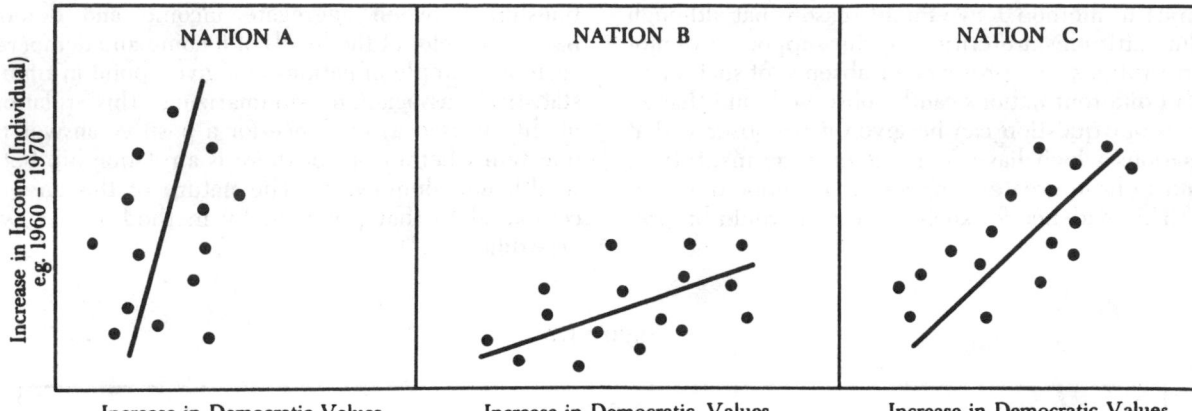

Method 4

An adaptation of method 2 is similar to the procedure outlined in method 3. We may argue that if nations are observed to increase the democratic nature of their institutions as they become more wealthy in the same period of time, then we have reason to give a positive answer to our question.[22]

Figure 1.4

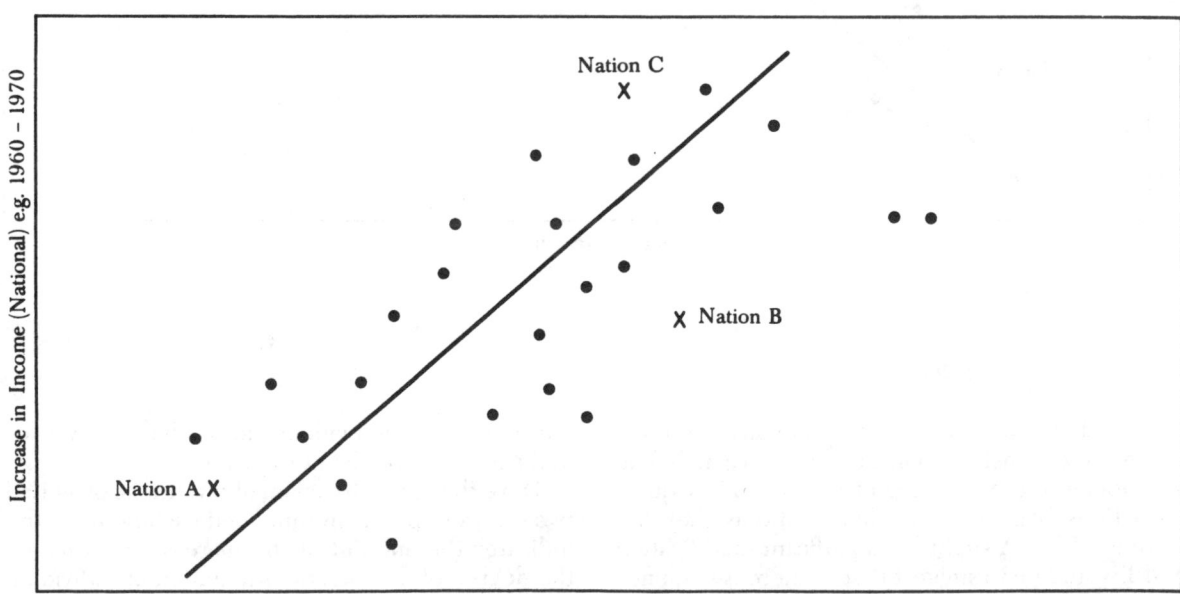

Method 5

The argument in method 4, as illustrated in Figure 1.4, is based on a very broad time period, and we may require more sensitive, detailed evidence of the process by which nations change on the two variables, wealth and democracy. We might therefore consider evidence for each country in the form suggested by Figure 1.5.[23]

In this example the statistical generalization is based on a plot in which each point represents a country's score on two variables in a particular year. The interpretation of such relationships is complicated by problems of the influence of temporal trend and autocorrelation, but the general logic of the argument is, hopefully, clear.

Figure 1.5

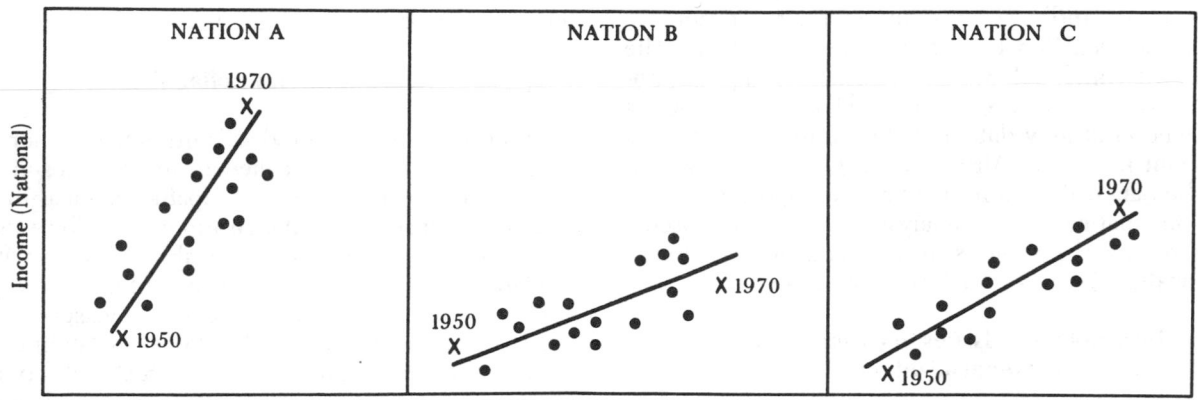

Multi-Method Approach

Each of the five methods is a reasonable basis for making a generalization about nations. If the basic hypothesis was supported by all five methods, we would have reason to be confident in making the generalization that nations tend to become more democratic as they become more economically developed. If only one of the methods was used, positive results would provide some corroboration for the generalization. Positive results for methods 3, 4, and 5 would be more satisfying than positive results from methods 1 and 2, because the former would take into account the contaminating, but omnipresent, influence of time. Positive results from methods 3 and 5 provide the strongest corroboration because they compare both the strength and form of the relationship. Nations may become more democratic as they become wealthier, but some nations may do so more rapidly than others, and it is the form of the statistical relationship, or the slope of the regression lines in Figures 1.3 and 1.5 which gives this additional dimension to our evidence.

One argument that does not seem tenable is that results from methods 1 and 3 are more satisfying than results from methods 2, 4, and 5. We cannot say on an *a priori* basis that inference from observations of individuals is necessarily preferable to inference from observations of nations as aggregate social entities. What is certain is that both levels of information are desirable, and that using only one level begs questions that cannot be resolved without reference to the other level. Unless we have results from both methods 1 and 2, we are in danger of committing ecological or composition fallacies in assuming that the results of the test indicated for method 1 will be similar to the tests for methods 2. Individuals may tend to support democratic practices in proportion to their personal wealth, but in nations with large numbers of wealthy and democratically-oriented people, there may be a relative absence of democratic institutions.

Likewise, nations which are wealthy and democratic may have citizens who are more likely to be democratic the less wealthy they are. Our approach, therefore, is to call for a *multi-method* approach to questions of national development, to recommend the use of various methods for which data are available, and to recommend the systematic collection of data which are presently not available but which are relevant to different methods of solving problems about social and political reality. Empirical social science does not *prove* anything: it seeks only to provide cumulative evidence for generalizations, and to subject generalizations to empirical tests which may refute them.[24] This Handbook aims, therefore, to provide the best data we can find to test such generalizations. The utility of the Handbook will be demonstrated by its application in cross-national research, and by its stimulation of the collection of new data and the posing of new questions about nations in Africa and throughout the world. Since the data collected in this book are appropriate primarily for national-level analysis, we should discuss briefly the major problems in assessing the meaning of generalizations based on such comparisons.[25]

Methodological Issues in Cross-National Generalization

In the most general ordinary-language sense, science attempts to provide accurate empirical descriptions of phenomena, and to make generalizations on the basis of such descriptions to future conditions of the phenomena.[26] The questions we ask in this section, therefore, relate to the possibility of accuracy in comparing nations with the data we have collected, and the intelligibility of interpreting statistical relationships between our measures of national characteristics as predictive either to future conditions of nations in Africa or to nations outside Africa.

Cross-national research seeks to evaluate hypothesized relationships by comparing characteristics of nations. Such relationships are normally based on the assumed, or empirically demonstrated, statistical associations between measures on a series of variables for a set of nations. Cross-national research typically follows the analytic paradigm suggested in Figure 1.4. We will confine the discussion of methodological problems to this basic model, shown again in Figure 1.6 representing a hypothesized relationship between economic development and political instability.

In this model, the nature of the relationship between change in national income and political instability in African nations is indicated by the regression line giving the best linear fit to the observations from which levels of instability can be predicted from a knowledge of levels of

national standard of living. As illustrated here, the empirical relationships between these two variables is such that increasing levels of instability are associated with increasing standards of living for a set of nations A, B,...N.[27]

A generalization of this kind is subject to several limitations: (1) the validity and reliability of the aggregate data on which the empirical relationship is based, (2) the threat of "ecological" fallacies in inference across different levels of aggregation,[28] (3) the limits of generalization from the set of nations used in the analysis to the universe of nations or to another time period, and (4) the difficulty of making causal inferences.

Validity and Reliability

If nations are to be accepted as legitimate units for social science research, related concepts and theories of interest to social science must be capable of measurement with valid and reliable data. In Figure 1.6, for example, we illustrate a theoretical relationship between national standard of living and political instability, and the problem is whether or not we can develop measures for national standards of living and political instability which will be valid and reliable. In this context, validity is the approximation of an indicator to the conceptual reality it is said to indicate: is it measuring what we want it to measure? Reliability is the amount of congruence between measures of the same indicator taken by different observers of the same conceptual reality: is the measure stable and repeatable? We begin with a discussion of the problem of reliability and follow that with a discussion of the problem of validity in cross-national measurement.

The Nature of Reliability

Each of the chapters in Part I contains a brief evaluation of the reliability of the data in that chapter. Here we discuss reliability in more general terms by examining the nature of the concept, the various types of threats to reliability, and some methods for reliability evaluation and control. Our focus is on the kinds of data presented in this book: comparative data at the national unit level.

Kerlinger suggests three ways to approach the concept of reliability.[29] The first approach, focused on accuracy, is summed up by the question: Are the measures obtained accurate representations of the property measured? For example, we may question the accuracy of reported national income, given the potential error resulting from imputing the "product" of subsistence agriculture. In a second approach, reliability is determined from the stability of results from the repeated measuring of a prop-

Figure 1.6

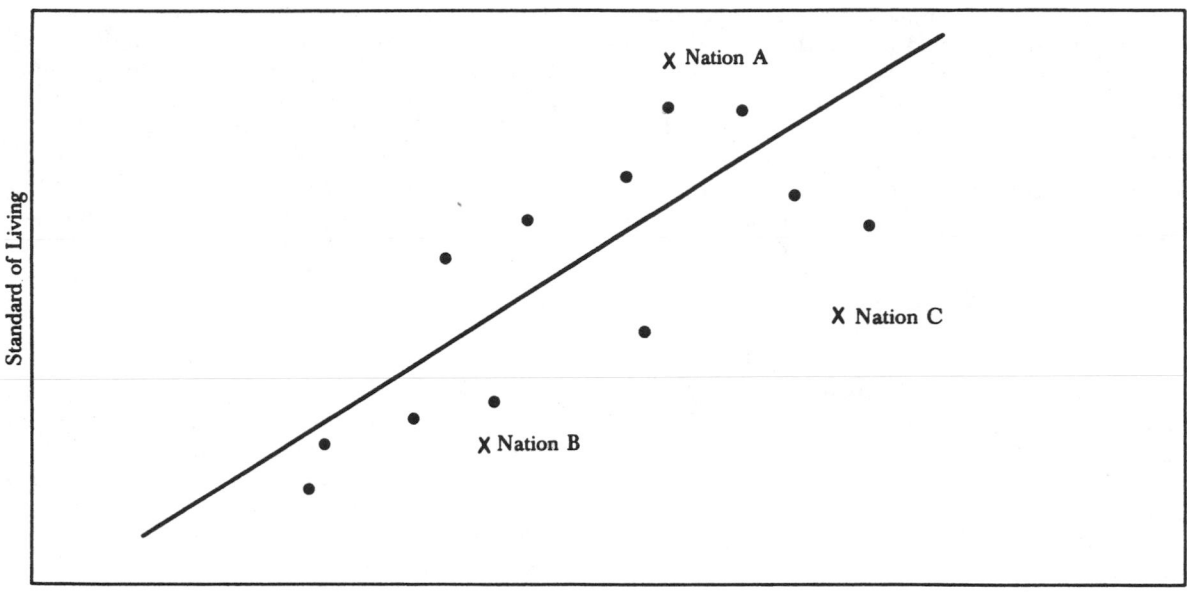

erty using the same method or instruments. Here the concern is with the magnitude of agreement among independent measurements of reality. In a third approach, more relevant to psychological testing, an attempt is made to determine a possible error of measurement present in a set of data which has been obtained through the use of a single instrument.

We are principally concerned with the first type of reliability here because much of our data (in Part I) are *aggregate* (aggregated at the national unit level) originating, at least in raw form, in published documents and reports. However, the second aspect of reliability is clearly involved in the presentation of what may be termed *typological* data in this book. This type of data are generally measures of the number, frequency, or duration of similar events, persons, or objects which have been classified by some conceptual framework of mutually exclusive categories.[30] The latter type can be said to be "secondary data" in that quantitative measures come about through a judgemental process (i.e., coding) using descriptive information of diverse origins. It is apparent that in this work two types of data can be distinguished: those which must be judged in terms of (a) *source reliability*, largely, but not exclusively related to aggregate data sources, and (b) *coder reliability*, which is a major consideration in the formulation of variables such as elite

instability and those indicators which relate to other characteristics of the political system.

Relationship of Reliability and Validity

Prior to a discussion of the practical evaluation of reliability, a related problem, that of *validity*, must be mentioned. Validity involves the question, "is the measure devised a satisfactory indicator of the property intended for measurement?" At first glance this appears to be a restatement of the question posed regarding accuracy as the prime concern of reliability, but there is an important distinction between the questions.

In a methodological article by Campbell and Fiske, who offer a schema for testing both validity and reliability, the following statement is made:

> Both reliability and validity concepts require that agreement between measures be demonstrated. A common denominator which most validity concepts share in contra-distinction to reliability is that this agreement represents the convergence of independent approaches.[31]

Therefore, while reliability concerns the stability and accuracy of a method of data collection and the corresponding accuracy of the quantitative results, irrespective of whether they are satisfactory measures of the theoretical concept or not, validity (or more precisely, construct validity) concerns the power or success of methodologies in measuring specified concepts through the convergent results of differing methods.[32]

In this Handbook the problem of validity is most clearly apparent in the construction of indices or summary variables to measure complex theoretical concepts such as instability for which no available single indicator is adequate. These indices often consist of a composite of two or more aggregate or typological variables which are sometimes weighted according to the analyst's criteria. The several "political instability" measures offered in this Handbook are of this type.[33] Political instability by any definition is a multi-faceted phenomenon involving events and behaviors of considerable variety. We found it necessary to specify three basic types of instability: elite, mass and communal. The validity of our measure of elite instability in terms of coups d'état, may be partially ascertained through comparisons with other independent measures of the same phenomenon—measures of administrative discontinuity, elite turnover, or possibly electoral patterns. In our own use of factor analytic techniques, the fact that these similiar indicators, chosen as measures of elite instability, loaded highly together on a factor which is orthogonal to that on which measures of mass or communal instability appeared, was reassuring in terms of the construct validity of these indices.[34]

In this Handbook we generally avoid labeling variables in terms of abstract concepts. "Total Christian Missions Stations per Million Population. ca. 1925" is used as a title for Table 2.13 instead of "Missionary Impact, 1920's." The use of the latter title would involve a number of assumptions about the ability of data on mission stations to measure missionary impact. For missionary impact the number of converts per 1000 population would seem to be a more valid measure since it would be possible to have many mission stations but few converts and hence little "impact." One could further argue, however, that converts are only one aspect of the impact of the missionaries and that the number of children in missionary schools per million population is equally or more valid a measure (or operationalization) of the concept.

Source Reliability

Considering first the quality of quantitative and descriptive sources from which the bulk of our data are gathered and often directly transcribed, the apparent threats to reliability are many while the strategies open to the researcher for assessing the accuracy of his data are few.

Often the fact that aggregate data are measured in seemingly unambiguous units—currencies, numbers of people, radios, etc.—tends in the mind of the user to give to the data an unwarranted degree of authority. A host of threats may in fact be present; unfortunately inaccuracies in "official" sources are neither all random nor, when systematic, totally unintentional. In addition, while international bodies such as those related to the United Nations may represent a higher degree of objectivity in the reporting of economic, educational, or demographic information, these organizations are to a large extent dependent upon the various national govenments and trusteeship authorities for the supply of original data.

One of the frustrating aspects of gathering data on Africa is the fact that so many of the non-governmental data sources for comparative data such as *Africa, AID Economic Data Book, Europa Yearbook, Statesman's Yearbook*, and Colin Legum's *Africa: A Handbook to the Continent*, present data without reference to the original source or to the date of the data. In the case of *Africa 69/70*, for instance, some of the urban data are quite up to date while the data for other cities are for 1960 or earlier.

When we have had to rely upon these sources for data, as in the case of acres of agricultural land per capita (Table 1.2), and where the sources differ, the procedure we have followed is to use the source which seems the most reliable on the basis of its recency, thoroughness, or its auspices. Where there seems to be a consensus on the part of the sources we sometimes took that consensus into account in assessing which figure to use. The difficulty with the latter procedure is that we have no way of knowing whether that consensus is the result of independent estimates or whether the sources have all used the same secondary source or whether the sources are all drawing upon each other in some incestuous way.

A few of the major threats to data reliability which relate to the original sources we have consulted are listed below:

(a) *Definitional non-equivalence and ambiguity.* From our experience in multiple source comparisons, especially for educational, economic, and military variable categories, wide divergencies in the definitional understanding of these measures is often the cause of otherwise irreconcilable differences in published figures. For education data these differences largely stem from structural variations. The difficulty of comparing enrollment levels for both primary and secondary education due to definitional differences is cited in Part I, Chapter 4. In another sphere, while gross national product per capita appears to be a straightforward index of economic development, it would be important to know the extent to which a portion of the total represents an imputed value for activities in the traditional sector—bartering, subsistence farming, etc.—and how this estimate has been made.

(b) *Sampling error and collection techniques.* The problem of the use and representativeness of sampling techniques is magnified in developing nations. A common malady in data collection is a systematic bias (overrepresentation) for the modern sector of the national system, characterized by urbanism, greater control under the central political authority, and the exchange economy, as opposed to the rural, traditional non-monetized sector. Frequently the latter is merely estimated. Prior to independence, for example, in many territories uncertain estimates of enrollment in "bush schools" or uncontrolled facilities were added to actual counts of students in official and government-inspected schools. In the same era, hindrances to cross-national comparability arose from contrasting methods of census-taking in French and British areas. In the former, authorities employed various sampling techniques rather than attempting to survey the entire population.

(c) *Cyclical phenomena and seasonal variations.* Throughout this volume one finds variables explictly identified by year. Except in instances where yearly values represent cumulative totals for the entire twelve month period, the reliability of year by year comparisons is somewhat attentuated by within-year or seasonal fluctuations unless, in the case of regular variation, the date of measurement is approximately the same from year to year. (While time series comparability for one unit would then be strengthened, cross-national comparability is still open to question.) Most vulnerable to seasonal variation in terms of reliability are indices of change from one time period to another several years later since minor changes, which may reflect only the time of year at which the measure was taken, become magnified. Population figures are frequently affected by seasonal migration of traditional peoples who respect no artificial borders and also by participants in the modern sector who follow seasonal labor markets. One case in point exists in the Horn of Africa where large nomadic groups observe a regular schedule of migration from Somalia to Ethiopia to find fresh pastureland.

No less problematic than seasonal variation are cyclical phenomena influencing yearly measurements which may represent the high or low point in the cycle regardless of the long-term trend. Economic indices such as balance of trade measures and gross national product tend to reflect such cyclical patterns. One control for this phenomenon is offered in the use of cumulative figures covering several years, average annual rates, or at least the total of one cycle (e.g., cumulative balance of trade. 1969-1972 Table 6.1).

(d) *Differences in systematic development.* Should cross-national comparisons be made for particular years regardless of the degree of autonomy enjoyed by the political and economic systems involved? Only with trepidation are independent states such as Ethiopia and Liberia included in pre-1960 comparisons with colonial territories.[35] It may be argued (and here the threat may be more correctly interpreted as one aimed toward validity) that independent, colonial, and semi-autonomous units are noncomparable systems and that rankings which include the same are of questionable value. Should the theoretical implications of this kind of noncomparability impair the utility of these data in the present form for his purposes, the user has a partial solution in using year of independence as a comparative benchmark instead of "real" years. For example, a number of political measures such as legislative fractionalization (Table 5.13) are given for the time of independence.

(e) *Intentional falsification.* Though difficult to document, there is every reason to suspect that on occasion both colonial administrators and, in recent years, public officials have been moved by political expediency to make adjustments in quantitative reports. Census figures, while crucial for social planning, are also used to determine political representation and thus are vulnerable to distorting influences. The Nigerian case, where the 1962 census was completely abrogated and the subsequent 1963 re-census widely criticized as a considerable overcount, is a dramatic case in point.[36]

Reliability Assessment

What follows are several guide-lines or strategies for reliability control which have been employed where applicable in the preparation of this volume. As suggested earlier, the careful discrimination among original data sources where more than one is available is of paramount importance. Selectivity may be based both on the reputed standards of the reporting organization and on the basis of agreement among acceptable sources. However, this would not preclude the necessity of further statistical testing to ascertain reliability.

In Part I we have followed the procedure of data evaluation utilizing factor analytic techniques and the inspection of cross-variable correlations. One may expect to find as an initial assurance of reliability, similar measures loading in a factor analysis on the same dimensions as well as high positive correlations among pairs of related variables. However, while negative or low product-moment correlations among like measures may be strong evidence of low reliability, the presence of high positive correlations may be seen only as a test of the absence of *random* error. The presence of systematic error in both measures may, of course, produce correlations as high as those between indicators having nearly identical values. For example, two measures of the same variable may correlate highly despite their different values when both of them are *consistently* exaggerated. The use of correlation as a test of reliabiltiy applies both to the question of source reliability and to coder reliability.

A more complex application of the correlational technique to establish reliability is one in which plausible bivariate relationships among dissimilar variables are tested. Such a comparison, made between indicators of aggregate educational attainment and literacy rates, was discussed in Part I. In this particular test, relationships across time demonstrated a predictable pattern of change in addition to close association. A related procedure, for cross-sectional as opposed to time-series data, is the use of scatter diagrams or the plotting of residuals from a best-fit linear regression. An example of residual plotting is the plot of newspapers per 1,000 and radios per 1,000 population which correlate at .87, in the *World Handbook of Political and Social Indicators*, by Bruce M. Russett et al.[37] Cases which show unusual deviation from their predicted values (the regression line) are not necessarily the product of unreliable data, but require additional verification through other sources.

The presence of time-series data in absolute values for individual units or nations facilitates additional reliability evaluation. These measures, which include population totals, school enrollments and economic indices, tend to change with geometric or incremental regularity, but they are also affected by historical events and trends in other spheres of activity. The marked relationship between world financial conditions and educational enrollment, for example, is discussed in Part I, Chapter 4. These data must therefore be assessed not only as they relate to other measures in cross-sectional analysis but, when possible, in the context of the total historical time continuum.

An important inter-coder variable which can affect the reliability of some data is conservatism in coding which introduces a degree of systematic difference, in addition to random disagreement between coders. With increased conservatism on the part of a coder, a greater number of "borderline cases" are excluded from the sample; as the difference between coders in terms of conservatism grows, the reliability coefficient diminishes. That the upward limits of reliability are in fact dependent upon the magnitude of difference in coder conservatism would imply that especially low coefficients may be explained in terms of this inter-coder variable.

At a relatively early stage in our data collection efforts,

an attempt was made to establish acceptable coder reliability for several quantitative measures relating to political conflict which had been collected for a separate study some months previously. We had hoped to use the same methods to supply data for years and political units not included in the original study. Our attempt to replicate the values for five indicators on five national units met with minimal success; the resulting coefficient was .58.[38] On this basis the attempt to supply the new data was discontinued and our efforts applied elsewhere. Upon later investigation and consultation with the author of the original study, several problems were isolated as explanations for the lack of agreement. Although conservatism on the part of the second coder was a strong factor, the major problem was lack of definitional precision for each category. Another unanticipated cause was the non-coincident favoring of one descriptive source over others among the four or five listed as original sources for coding.

Other results of a reliability check made for political parties' data are cited in Part I, Chapter 5. In this instance the measure of reliability was a product-moment correlation. (Earlier remarks as to the limitations of the Pearson product-moment correlation as a coefficient of reliability—that it is not sensitive to positive systematic error—also apply here.) In this study of a random sample of six countries out of 32, all variables were re-coded by a person other than the original coder. A correlational analysis was performed doubling the number of variables: the number of original variables being N, variable number 1 coded by a second coder becomes $N + 1$, in the cross-correlation matrix. Corre;ations between variables 1 and $N + 1 \ldots N$ and $N + N$ were then used as an initial indicator of inter-coder reliability.

Summary

The enumeration of these various threats to reliability should warn the researcher that data of this kind may pose severe reliability problems. Special attention should be paid to the information regarding the reliability of specific sets of data that is provided in the various chapter introductions in Part I and in the introduction to Part II. Where analysis requires highly accurate data the researcher is advised to re-collect the data as a double check.[39]

The Nature of Validity

The operational definition of a theoretical concept is a method of measurement for the concept. It is equivalent to the concept only in the vocabulary of operationalism.[40] Finding appropriate ways to measure theoretical concepts is one of the basic problems of social science. The problem of correspondence in cross-national research between aggregate data indicators and macro-theory concepts can be especially difficult.

Nations themselves are not directly observable, and the conceptual dimensions on which they vary are seldom easily equated with measures of some immediately observable characteristics. Macro theory is concerned with the properties of aggregates – groups of people of varying size and complexity. Commonly, the measures of these properties are aggregations from observations on individuals. The validity of such indices, based on aggregated data in the composition of a set of nations, is impaired by at least four possible sources of non-comparability in their measurement of concepts. These are: (1) differences in the way government agencies and researchers operationally define the same concepts; (2) differences in the coverage of the same concepts for different countries (the thoroughness, synchronization, and personnel involved in measurement); (3) error in the observations of different phenomena, even when the observations are made with similar thoroughness and operational definition; and (4) differences in the meaning and importance of similar phenomena in different countries.

The first of these difficulties concerns the lack of standardization in operational procedures used by agencies that collect aggregate data on nations. For example, in computing per capita national income, government agencies in different nations vary in the procedures they use to impute monetary values to goods and services that are not sold in the markets of countries with semi-subsistence economies.[41] The second difficulty relates to the availability and thoroughness of coverage of quantitative data that may be relevant to theoretically important concepts. Measures of health facilities and mortality, for example, may be considered fundamental to the measurement of standards of living, but data of this kind are not available for many African countries. When such data do exist, they are often very inadequate estimates. Thirdly, there is the related problem of error in available measurements, due to factors ranging from the political demand for growth on particular variables--especially those relating to standard of living--to the incapacity to collect data from anything but very unrepresentative samples of the national population.[42] Finally, there is the problem of the same indicators being very different in terms of their conceptual importance in different national contexts. The standard of living in a nation which has an almost entirely subsistence economy may be very inadequately measured by per capita income, but the same measure may be very descriptive of the standard of living in a more developed economy.[43]

These are serious difficulties, and some researchers regard them as so serious that they recommend not using most available aggregate data on nations, and imply that most cross-national research is futile if such data have to be used.[44] But validity problems plague all social measurement, and it seems useful to ask what procedures regarded as important in other styles of social research can be adopted to increase validity in cross-national research.

If it is accepted that no single indicator is a completely valid measure of a concept – i.e., that any indicator is only a partial representation of a conceptual phenomenon – there are nevertheless procedures which can be adopted to lend increased confidence to the validity of operationalized variables. Taken in isolation, a concept may be said to have a given meaning, and a number of alternative, equally valid, operationalizations. In cross-national analysis, the validity of a single indicator as a measure of some concept may vary for each nation being studied, and the validity of generalizations made about Africa with respect to that measure would be impossible to assess. One way out of this dilemma is to assess the equivalence of several indicators of the same concept, or to devise a composite index for measures of varying validity, which will minimize the invalidity of the single measures for particular countries. Thus:

> The problem of whether a concept can be measured cross-nationally by a set of identical indicators is empirical. Although complete equivalence is probably never possible, attempts can be made to measure equivalence if they are based on a set of comparable indicators.[45]

This argument can be illustrated with reference to the concept of standard of living. Standard of living might be measured by GNP per capita, GDP per capita, agricultural productivity, price indices, the distribution of educational and medical facilities, the number of telephones, radios, automobiles and other consumer goods, or energy consumption. The validity of these measures of the single concept "standard of living" may be determined by the functional equivalence, or unidimensionality of this set of indicators for a sample of nations. Factor analytic tests for unidimensionality provide a means of testing the equivalence of the indicators in terms of their covariation. Those indicators which do not fall on a single factor have unique variance unexplained by the phenomenon being measured by that factor, which is to say that they appear to measure a dimension that is empirically unassociated with the concept in question. On the basis of such tests for unidimensionality, one may select either a single representative variable from the loading pattern for the factor, or use a composite index such as a factor score based on all the information about the factor structure. [46]

A related approach to the assessment of the validity of aggregate data as measures of social science concepts is derived from multi-method, multi-trait procedures of concept validation. [47] Concepts may be measured by different indicators, and conceptually similar indicators may be measured by different methods. The validity of different indicators can be assessed by the inter-corelation between the values for a particular indicator (trait) as obtained by different methods of observation: the greater the corelation, the greater the validity of the respective measures, or of their methods of operationalization. The assessment of the validity of aggregate data in these terms may be based on the intercorelation between values of the same conceptual variable based on different sources of information, and on different methods of aggregation. The interrelationship between reliability and validity in these terms is underlined by Campbell and Fiske:

> Reliability is the agreement between two efforts to measure the same trait through maximally similar methods. Validity is represented in the agreement between two attempts to measure the same trait through maximally different methods. [48]

In view of the above considerations, the data in Part I of this Handbook attempt to provide multiple operationalizations of similar concepts, and to provide data gathered by different observers and different aggregation procedures for conceptually similar variables.

To summarize: all measures of social phenomena are partially accurate in that they invariably involve a margin of error. This does not mean, however, that generalizations based on errorful data are necessarily erroneous; in fact, one can often take advantage of error in order to improve the data quality. [49] Unless one assumes that errors are more likely to be random in survey research data than in aggregate data, the methods of index construction and scaling developed from psychometric research [50] are amenable to cross-national research. Such indices may be used to partially neutralize the effects of error and increase construct validity, even when the actual error distribution is not known. Generalizations based on aggregate data descriptions of nations are, therefore, not necessarily less valid or reliable than generalizations based on any other unit of analysis. Instead of holding to a belief in what someone had called the doctrine of the "immaculate perception", we should utilize all available data on our environment in order to find cumulative support for social theory, rather than search in vain for error-free and conceptually "pure" measures of social phenomena.

Ecological Fallacies

The ecological fallacy is commonly regarded as being the most clear-cut threat to research based on aggregate data. Ecological fallacies result from imputing the characteristics of a macro-system to its lower level components, and the logical problem is normally illustrated by the improper conclusion that relationships between two ecological variables (i.e. aggregate measures of a group, region, nation, etc.) are also characteristic of the same variables in their disaggregate form (i.e., measures of the component units of the macro-entity, commonly individuals). The most telling demonstration of the ecological fallacy was pointed out by William Robinson, [51] who showed in a dramatic example from the 1930 United States census that, the statistical relationship between color and literacy was .95 when aggregate descriptions of race and literacy for nine census regions were used, but that the same relationship was only .20 when the units of analysis were individuals and the variables used were measures of individual literacy and racial background. Any suggestion from the generalization based on aggregate data that individuals who were black were nearly certain to be relatively illiterate is fallacious. It is, however, proper to generalize that census regions with higher percentages of black residents are likely to have a higher percentage of illiteracy. This last observation is not usually stressed by critics of aggregate data analysis, but it should be emphasized as indicating that the ecological fallacy is not logically necessary to the use of aggregate data. [52]

If the ecological fallacy is not a *sine qua non* of aggregate data analysis, it is, nevertheless, a problem in most research of this kind because many relationships between aggregate entities, properly generalized only to aggregate entities at the same level, are in fact generalized to the component entities. Unless the generalization is treated as an hypothesis to be tested in the data on the component entities, or as the basis for a social reform which may be treated as an experiment to be evaluated with aggregate data, the ecological fallacy is likely to result.

Take, for example, the relationship between national standard of living and political instability. Theoretical explanations of political instability frequently deal with concepts such as systemic frustration or relative deprivation, which are operationalized in terms of levels or changes in the national standard of living.[53] Based on the assumption that individuals who are frustrated or relatively deprived will act out aggressive behavior, theories of national political instability frequently hypothesize that the lower the level of positive change in national standards of living, the greater the likelihood of political instability. To conclude from this kind of evidence alone that *individuals* whose standard of living is relatively low are most likely to engage in organized subversions of the political system is incorrect although it is often an attractive form of reasoning to those who hope that small-scale adjustments in income distribution can maintain faltering political systems. Without data on the individual level, what can be concluded is only that there is a relationship between standard of living and political instability *in nations*.

With proper caution, ecological fallacies can be avoided in cross-national research. The theoretical advantage of macro-theoretical generalizations based on aggregate data has been most clearly established in economics and it is inadvisable to conclude that similar advantage will not be realized in other areas of social inquiry.

The Limits of Cross-National Generalization

If it is accepted that aggregate data descriptive of nations is not inherently less reliable or valid than survey data for operationalizing concepts in social theory, there are further restrictions on the kinds of generalizations that can be made in cross-national research using aggregate data. Looking again at Figure 1.6, we observe a relationship between national standard of living and political instability, the form of which is such that we would generalize that the greater the standard of living in African nations, the greater the likelihood that they will experience some form of political instability. It is the purpose of this section to ask just what we can interpret such a generalization to mean.

The first question to be raised is *what relationship does the observation based on Figure 1.6, describing the experience of African nations, have to the experience of other, non-African nations?* The difficulties involved in answering such a question can be illustrated with reference to Figure 1.7.

In this figure we illustrate observations on the two

Figure 1.7

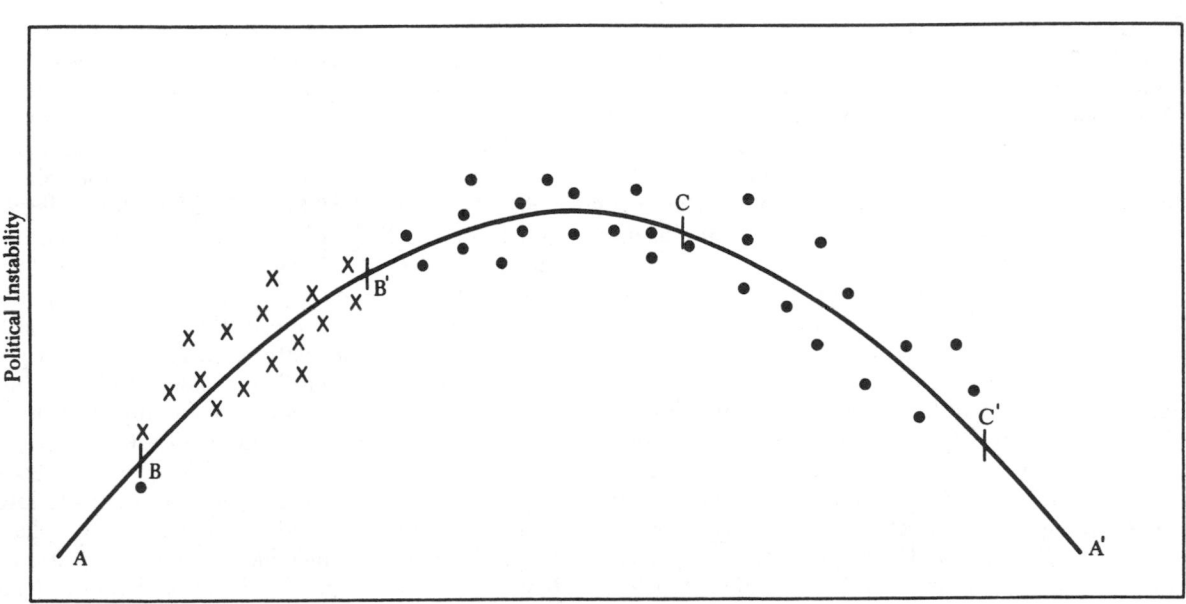

Political Instability

Standard of Living

variables under consideration for a hypothetical universe of nations. The observations marked "o" are for non-African nations; those marked "x" are for African nations. All these points represent observations which contain both a "true" score and measurement error,[54] so that the line AA' is the locus of all "true" scores on these variables for the universe of nations. The line BB' is the locus of the "true" scores for the sub-group of African nations in this illustration, and corresponds to the line drawn in Figure 1.6. Looking at these lines, we would generalize that there is a curvilinear relationship (AA') between the standard of living and political instability in the universe of nations, such that at extreme levels of national standard of living there is a likelihood of relatively low political instability, but between these extremes the likelihood increases. The former generalization from Figure 1.6--that the likelihood of political instability for African nations increases with standard of living--is still true (BB'), but it is apparent that this relationship is not true for the universe of nations since the African nations do not represent a random sample of the world's nations.

The illustration in Figure 1.7 is intentional, although hypothetical. In the first place, curvilinear relationships are frequently hypothesized to exist for the universe of nations, and the illustrated relationship is theoretically intelligible.[55] Second, it is important to make this likelihood apparent to users of this Handbook, and to users of any other set of cross-national data, since inasmuch as data for African nations are available, they are often reported in the tail of the distributions for "all" the nations of the world.[56] Furthermore, most handbooks have omitted data for many of the nations of Black Africa. There is a problem that generalizations for the universe of nations might take the form of the line CC' in Figure 1.7, which is as unrepresentative of the true relationship between standard of living and stability, as is the generalization based only on observations from Africa.[57]

This illustration suggests a number of qualifications that have to be made when cross-national generalizations are proposed from data on a set of nations that is less than the universe of nations, and which therefore may not represent fully the historical, ecological, and developmental differences in the universe. The initial qualification is this: that if the set of nations used is taken from a theoretically homogeneous "region," any generalization of the relationship for that region to other nations may be seriously misleading. Second, if the selection of nations is not based on some regional definition of historical, ecological or developmental homogeneity, statistical generalizations are likely to be misleading if applied to nations not included in the analysis. The way out of this latter problem is to take a random sample of the nations

in the universe. This procedure is not adopted in the present state of the art of cross-national analysis, primarily because of the lack of adequate data on all nations likely to be randomly selected. In the absence of probability sampling, it is not appropriate to make generalizations from cross-national research to individual nations not included in the analysis,[58] and for the user of this Handbook, it is important to realize that any statistical relationship discovered in our data applies only to these forty-one African nations, and that it should be regarded as having no known relationship to the general development of the nations of the world. Of course, it is the goal of social science to develop generalizations that apply to the universe of entities under consideration; in cross-national analysis we hope to make statements that apply to all nations. But, until available data permit either the analysis of the universe, or of strict probability samples of the nations of the universe, cross-national generalizations should be made with considerable caution.

The second question to asked about the generalization illustrated in Figure 1.6 is *what relationship does the observation that political instability increases with national standard of living have to the experience the same nations may have in future time?* If the generalization for Africa to the effect that increasing political instability varies with increased standards of living is true *ex post facto*, can we predict that the relationship will be true in the future?[59]

An extrapolation of a generalization based on a particular cross-sectional observation of African nations is based on the assumption that although the values of the two variables will change, the relationship between them will not. This assumption, and/or empirical observation, is illustrated in Figure 1.8, where the observations marked "o" are data for a decade after independence, and those marked "x" are data for the immediate post-independence period. As illustrated here, the form of the relationship between standard of living and political instability remains the same in the two decades after independence for African nations: throughout this period increasing political instability is associated with increasing levels in the national standard of living. But this illustration is entirely hypothetical. While many relations will not drastically change in the future, we can confidently expect some to be altered, since the decade after independence can be viewed as a "shaking out" phase of national development in which various institutions, which have not so far regularized national political behavior, develop this capability. It is important therefore to qualify all relationships found in data from this Handbook as holding for the time period on which the data is based, and holding in years ahead with less and less confidence.

Figure 1.8

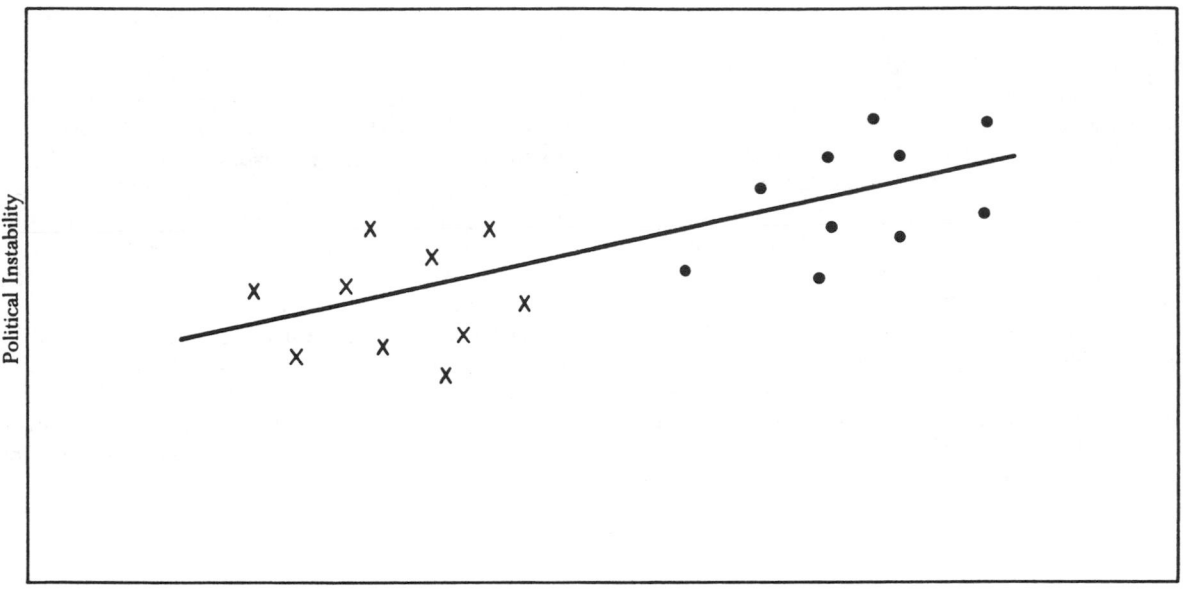

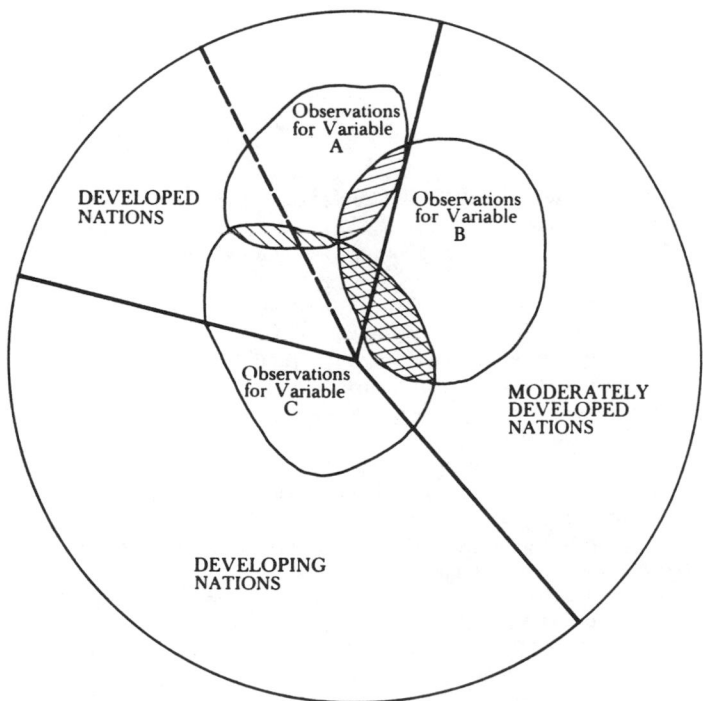

This of course is no more than common sense, and it applies to all predictions of human behavior, but it is a qualification that is particularly important for African nations at the present time.

The social scientist, and the student of national development, is not entirely at the mercy of time. There are many situations for which we can formulate and test theoretical expectations about intertemporal change in the relationship between two variables.[60] These changes may be hypothesized in some cases as the result of the definition of a particular variable. For example, one aspect of an operational definition of standard of living can be the distribution of educational opportunity, and we can expect that when education (at the primary level, at least) reaches a saturation point for the relevant age group in the national population, the effects of changes in this variable are not likely to be as great, if they are noticeable at all, as were the effects of changes fron a lower base level in time past. Considerations of the base value have, in fact, to be considered in any extrapolation of a relationship based on change variables. In the case of variables that do not have such clearly defined optimal distributions as education, the threshold levels at which relationships between two variables are likely to change in the future, as African political development progresses, can be hypothesized from empirical work on the universe of nations.[61]

The Difficulty of Making Casual Inferences

We cannot go into the statistical techniques for analyzing questions like those we have discussed in this chapter. But it is clear that the inspection of corelation matrices, such as that given in an Appendix to this book, cannot serve as anything more than an heuristic guide to the explanation of dependent variables in the study of nations,[62] and as a basis for employing multivariate techniques which break down the relationships between pairs in a set of interrelated variables into the direct and indirect effects of each variable, taking intervening and exogenous effects into account. Whether one uses stepwise regression analysis,[63] predictions from simultaneous equations,[64] or path analysis,[65] the ultimate decisions about the causal relationships between variables measured in *ex post facto* research must be based on the theoretical reasons for the primacy of one variable over another in a hypothesized causal sequence. As in all matters of scientific analysis, statistical or methodological procedures of causal inference can only invalidate or lend convergent validation to theoretical statements of causal relationships.

Generalization from cross-national analysis based on the statistical relationship between aggregate measures of the characteristics of nations is, therefore, a difficult business. Theoretical coherence and durability in the form of tests based on data from different samples, different time periods, and different units of aggregation, and using multiple methods and multiple indicators, is the basis of scientific generalization. Quantitative data do not provide certainty, and statistical relationships do not imply deterministic relationships between variables. No single piece of aggregate data is completely accurate as a measure of a theoretical concept, and nations are not bound by the sins of aggregate data-gathers or by the most confidently stated extrapolations from their past experience.

Notes

[1]A general review of comparative methodology is Robert M. Marsh, *Comparative Sociology* (New York: Harcourt, Brace and World, 1967), but a comprehensive analysis of cross-national research in political science would be a valuable complement to Marsh's broader focus on societies and the sociological and social anthropological literature. Adam Przeworski and Henry Teune, *The Logic of Comparative Social Inquiry* (New York: Wiley-Interscience, 1970), does much to meet this need on the level of theory and measurement. Some valuable discussions of methodology in cross-national research are contained in Richard L. Merritt and Stein Rokkan, eds., *Comparing Nations* (New Haven: Yale University Press, 1966), and in Stein Rokkan, ed., *Comparative Research Across Cultures and Nations* (Paris: Mouton, 1968); R. D. Brunner and G. D. Brewer, *Organized Complexity: Empirical Theories of Political Development* (New York: Free Press, 1971); T. R. Gurr, *Politimetrics* (Englewood Cliffs: Prentice Hall, 1972); G. Almond, ed., *Crisis, Choice and Change: Historical Studies of Political Development* (Boston: Little Brown, 1973); R. Naroll and R. Cohen, *A Handbook of Method in Cultural Anthropology* (Garden City: Natural History Press, 1970); E. R. Tufte, *Data Analysis for Politics and Policy* (Englewood Cliffs: Prentice Hall, 1974); R. Brislin, W. Lonner, R. Thorndike, *Cross-Cultural Research Methods* (New York: Wiley-Interscience, 1973).

[2]David C. McClelland, *The Achieving Society* (New York: Van Nostrand, 1961), p. viii.

[3]See Henry C. Bretton, *The Rise and Fall of Kwame Nkrumah* (New York: Praeger, 1966).

[4]See Bob Fitch and Mary Oppenheimer, "Ghana: The End of an Illusion," *Monthly Review*, 18 (July-August, 1966).

[5]Adam Przeworski and Henry Teune, "Equivalence in Cross-National Research," *Public Opinion Quarterly* 30 (1966—67): 552.

[6]Abraham Kaplan, *The Conduct of Inquiry* (San Francisco: Chandler, 1964), p. 79.

[7]See the excellent discussion in Karl W. Deutsch, *Nationalism and Social Communication* 2nd ed. (Cambridge: Massachusetts Institute of Technology Press, 1966).

[8]See John N. Paden, "African Concepts of Nationhood," in *The African Experience*, eds., John N. Paden and Edward W. Soja, Vol. I (Evanston, Ill: Northwestern University Press, 1970); Colin Legum, *Pan-Africanism: A Short Political Guide*, Revised edition (New York: Praeger, 1965); and Vincent Bakpetu Thompson, *Africa and Unity: The Evolution of Pan-Africanism* (London: Longmans, 1969).

[9]See William Zartman. *International Relations in the New African States* (Englewood Cliffs: Prentice-Hall, 1966).

[10]*Ibid*

[11]See V. Thompson's book *West Africa's Council of the Entente* (Ithaca: Cornell University Press, 1972).

[12]For a consideration of the problems of regional variation in the universe of nation-states, see the chapter on "Regionalism versus Universalism in Comparing Nations," in *World Handbook of Political and Social Indicators*, Bruce M. Russett, et al. (New Haven: Yale University Press, 1964), 322—340; and the empirical analysis in P. Coulter, *Social Mobilization and Liberal Democracy* (Lexington: Heath, 1975). For an argument for the collection of comprehensive data on another region, see Phillipe C. Schmitter, "New Strategies for the Comparative Analysis of Latin American Politics," *Latin American Research Review*, 4 (1969), 83—110.

[13]A data bank similar to this one for Africa has been compiled for Latin America by Phillipe Schmitter of the University of Chicago. It is hoped that an eventual consortium of regional data banks would contribute much to cross-national analysis. See Schmitter, *op. cit.*

[14]See Marsh, *Comparative Sociology*, and other citations in footnote 1, for a review of the approaches to comparative analysis.

This set of possibilities is intended to be neither exhaustive nor strictly comparable, but rather to suggest how a general problem related to the development of nations might be operationalized at different levels of analysis and to indicate certain communalities between the analyses. In all of the following discussion, we make the basic assumption that there are linear relationships between wealth and democracy, and that the best linear fit (regression line) for observations on these variables can be calculated. It should be clear in considering all the possibilities we outline, however, that given other equally plausible assumptions—e.g., that the relationship between these variables is nonlinear—the interpretation of the same evidence could be radically different. Not only may there be curvilinear relationships between wealth and democracy, but the relationships between these variables may shift markedly over time, either in terms of great change in the form of the relationship, or in terms of step-jumps in the historical norm (or intercept) on which the relationship, whose form does not itself change much, is based. This should emphasize the crucial role of theory in the determination of the statistical model to which data is fitted.

[15]This argument has been clearly stated in the very influential work on the general question of the relationship between economic development and democracy by Seymour M. Lipset, *Political Man* (Garden City: Doubleday, Anchor Books, 1960). See especially the chapter on "Working Class Authoritarianism" as a special test of the general proposition.

[16]Tests of this kind can be made using Bartlett's X^2 test.

[17]The kind of argument we have in mind here is best exemplified in Gabriel Almond and Sidney Verba, *The Civic Culture* (Boston: Little, Brown, 1962). For a review of this work by the authors and their colleagues see G. Almond and S. Verba eds. *The Civic Culture Revisited* (Boston: Little, Brown, 1980).

[18]We might also argue that the assumption behind this method is based on a composition fallacy since the existence of democratic values among certain parts of the national population may be only marginally related to the construction and maintenance of democratic institutions.

[19]This is the form of the argument made most often in the literature, from Lipset's *Political Man* to an exploration of this question in Marvin E. Olsen, "Multivariate Analysis of National Political Development," *American Sociological Review*, 33 (1968): 699—712.

[20]Cross-national comparisons such as these do have certain critical comparability assumptions built into them which should be accepted before the hypothesis is evaluated. Most important is the neo-evolutionary view of the development of social and political systems whereby the temporal development of political and economic systems is reflected in the distribution of properties across states at a given point in time.

[21]In this model, ignoring any lag effects, the diagram examines changes in income and its relation to changes in democratic values. Assumptions as to the independence of the starting point for individual scores on each variable are important since end points of the distributions of the variables may be where many individuals are coded. Hence, changes in one direction may be more likely than in another direction. This is commonly known as the "regression to the mean effect."

[22]We ignore for the purposes of this outline the critical question of time-lags in theoretical relationships. In addition to the analysis of two change measures, one could suggest relationships between state descriptions of an entity (democratic institutions) and rates of change in a characteristic of the entity at time 2 (income from time 1 to time 2).

[23]As illustrated, the chronological time for which the data in nations A, B, and C gathered is the same, but these periods may not represent comparable periods of institutional development for different nations.

[24]See the discussion in Robert F. Winch and Donald T. Campbell, "Proof? No. Evidence? Yes. The Significance of Tests of Significance," *The American Sociologist*, 4 (1969): 140—43.

[25]This discussion is necessarily condensed, for details on different points the reader should consult Merritt and Rokkan, eds., *Comparing Nations*,; Rokkan, ed. *Comparative Research across Cultures and Nations*; Charles Louis Taylor, ed., *Aggregate Data Analysis: Political and Social Indicators in Cross-National Research* (The Hague: Mouton, 1968); and for a critical point of view see Oran Young, "Professor Russett: Industrious Tailor to a Naked Emperor," *World Politics* 21 (April, 1969): 486—511.

[26]Of course, in some cases theoretical predictions precede any observation of the phenomenon itself as in the prediction of the existence of Pluto before that planet was sighted.

[27]The theoretical interest in these variables in the literature on cross-national research is considerable, although the empirical nature of the relationships between changes in the standard of living and political instability is by no means unambiguous. For a discussion of this and related hypotheses, see Donald G. Morrison *Political Learning: Conflict and Violence in Black Africa*, forthcoming.

[28]For a discussion of this issue see H. R. Alker, Jr., "A Typology of Ecological Fallacies," in *Quantitative Ecological Analysis in the Social Sciences* M. Dogan and S. Rokkan, eds. (Cambridge: Massachusetts Institute of Technology Press, 1969).

[29]Fred N. Kerlinger, *Foundations of Behavioral Research* 2nd edition (New York: Holt, Rinehart and Winston, 1975).

[30]Part II contains other types of data which pertain to national subsystems and elite group members as units of analysis. Remarks on reliability are, or course, applicable to this latter group.

[31]Donald T. Campbell and Donald W. Fiske, "Convergent and Discriminant Validation by the Multitrait-Multimethod Matrix," *Psychological Bulletin*, 50 (1959): 81—105.

[32]Campbell and Fiske, *op. cit.* admit to this point, stating that correlations between similar tests (methodologies) are somewhere between measures of reliability and validity.

[33]An example of the difficulties involved in assessing the validity of

complex indices of typological concepts is given in Part I, Chapter 5, where measures of "conspiracy" and "internal war" are compared with our measures of elite instability and communal instability. From the standpoint of face validity, these pairs of concepts should be closely related and the measures based on them should be closely related. The fact that the relevant intercorrelations are low, or in the wrong direction, does not reflect on the reliability of the measures involved, which may be error-free given different coding conventions, but does reflect seriously on the validity of alternative measures of political instability in Africa.

[34]Examples of empirical studies which rely on constructed indices from several indicators include Irma Adelman and C. T. Morris, *Society, Politics and Economic Development* (Baltimore: Johns Hopkins University Press, 1967); Arthur S. Banks and Robert B. Textor, *A Cross-Polity Survey* (Cambridge: Massachusetts Institute of Technology Press, 1963); and Raymond F. Bauer, *Social Indicators* (Cambridge: Massachusetts Institute of Technology Press, 1966.

[35]While 1960 marks the year of independence for 19 of these 41 units, four were independent prior to 1958, while nine did not achieve independence until after 1963.

[37]Bruce M. Russett, et al., *World Handbook of Political and Social Indicators* (New Haven: Yale University Press, 1964), 118.

[38]See Ole Holsti, "The Quantitative Analysis of Content," in *Content Analysis*, ed., Robert C. North, et al. (Evanston: Northwestern University Press, 1963), 49—50, for a description of the procedures we followed. See Chapter 3, Section A for more evidence on reliability.

[39]Corrections should be sent to Donald G. Morrison, Office for Information Technology, Harvard University, 1730 Cambridge St., Cambridge, MA 02138.

[40]The classic statement of philosophical operationalism is in Percy W. Bridgeman, *The Logic of Modern Physics* (New York: Macmillan, 1927). For a recent discussion of the issue see H. M. Blalock, Jr., "The Measurement Problem: A Gap Between the Languages of Theory and Research," *Methodology in Social Research* eds., H. Blalock, Jr., and A. Blalock (New York: McGraw-Hill, 1968), 5—27.

[41]In general, national income accounts are calculated on the basis of categories recommended by the United Nations. For particular problems and references, see the discussion of income data in Chapter 3, Part I.

[42]See the discussion of these problems in Donald V. McGrenchan, "Comparative Social Research in the United Nations," *Comparing Nations*, eds., Merritt and Rokkan, 525—544.

[43]A more specific example of this problem relates to the use of measures of vehicles per capita as an operationalization of horizontal integration, or communications potential in African nations. The difficulty is illustrated by Weinstein:
"Even though there is supposed to be one passenger vehicle for every 127 inhabitants (in Gabon), compared with one vehicle for every 180 in the four states of the former federation (AEF), only 6% of all vehicles are used for interior road transportation (in Gabon), compared with 25% in Chad.'
Brian Weinstein, *Gabon: Nation Building on the Ogoowe* (Cambridge: Massachusetts Institute of Technology Press, 1966), 76.

[44]A particularly blunt critique was given by Arnold S. Feldman in a review of cross-national research in Latin America. See "The New Comparative Politics in Latin America: A Comment," commentary delivered to Latin American Studies Association, New York City, 8 November, 1968. See also the commentary on D. P. Bwy, "Political Insta-

bility in Latin America: The Cross-Cultrual Test of a Causal Model," *Latin American Research Review*, 3 (1963): 17—66.

[45]Przeworski and Teune, "Equivalence in Cross-National Research," 556.

[46]For a detailed discussion, and for examples of this mode of index construction, see D. G. Morrison *Political Learning: Conflict and Violence in Black Africa*, forthcoming, and for a technical discussion of the approach see D. F. Alwin, "The Use of Factor Analysis in the Construction of Linear Composites in Social Research," *Sociological Methods and Research* 2,2 (November), 1973, 191-214, and K. W. Smith, "On Estimating the Reliability of Composite Indices Through Factor Analysis," *Sociological Methods and Research*, 2,4 (May, 1974), 485-510.

[47]See Donald T. Campbell and Donald W. Fiske, "Convergent and Discriminant Validation by the Multi-trait—Mulit-method Matrix," *Psychological Bulletin*, 56 (1959): 82—105; and J. Caparoso and L. Roos, eds., *Quasi-Experimental Approaches: Testing Theory and Evaluating Policy* (Evanston: Northwestern University Press, 1973).

[48]*Ibid.*, 83.

[49]For a review of this argument, and its particular application to anthropological data, see Raoul Naroll, *Data Quality Control* (New York: Free Press, 1962).

[50]For a thorough review of this field, see J. Nunnaly, *Psychometric Theory* (New York: McGraw-Hill, 1980).

[51]William S. Robinson, "Ecological Correlations and the Behavior of Individuals," *American Sociological Review*, 15 (1950): 351—357. Przeworski and Teune have an excellent discussion of this in *The Logic of Comparative Social Inquiry*, 57—73.

[52]For an excellent summary of logical and data problems in cross-national research, see Erwin K. Scheuch, "Cross-National Comparisons Using Aggregate Data: Some Substantive and Methodological Problems," in *Comparing Nations*, eds., Merritt and Rokkan, 131—167.

[53]See Chapter 5 Part I for references.

[54]This "true" score is defined as the observed score minus error due to measurement in that observation. For a discussion of this model see F. M. Lord and M. R. Novick *Statistical Theories of Mental Test Scores* (Reading: Addison-Wesley, 1968).

[55]See, for example, Ivo K. Feierabend, Rosalind L. Feierabend, and Betty A. Nesvold, "Social Change and Political Violence: Cross-National Patterns," in *The History of Violence in America*, eds., Hugh Davis Graham and Ted Robert Gurr (New York: Bantam Books, 1969), 632—687.

[56]See the data reported in Russett, et al., *World Handbook*; Arthur S. Banks and Robert Textor, *A Cross-Polity Survey* (Cambridge: Massachusetts Institute of Technology Press, 1963); and C. L. Taylor and M. Hudson, *World Handbook* 2nd edition. (New Haven: Yale University Press, 1972).

[57]Of the principal cross-national research, Gurr includes 23 "non-Islamic" African countries in his analysis, the Feierabends include four of our countries, and Rummel includes only one. See Graham and Gurr, eds., *A History of Violence in America*; and Rudolph J. Rummel, "Indicators of Cross-National and International Patterns," *American Political Science Review*, 73 (September, 1967): 145—72.

[58]This is particularly important when one considers the presentation of correlations, and factor analytic manipulations of these correlations, for sets of nations for which there are extensive missing data. Unless the missing data are distributed randomly, factor analytic models which require correlations to be comparable in terms of their being based on

samples of the same universe are inappropriate, and generalizations from the individual correlations apply to different sets of nations, and cannot be considered to hold for countries not included in the calculations. Consider the set of nations for analysis in the following diagram, and the variables A, B, and C. As illustrated the sets of nations used in the calculations of r_{AB}, r_{BC}, r_{AC} are mutually exclusive.

Only the set of nations with observations for C has any possibility of being a random sample of the universe of nations and therefore, statistical generalizations based on the mutually exclusive, non-random samples illustrated are not in any way comparable. While this is an extreme example, most correlations based on missing data are likely to have problems like those illustrated here, even if the sets of nations used in each correlation are not mutually exclusive.

[59]See the discussion in Chapter 3, Section A for an example of low intertemporal correlation of political variables.

[60]For a discussion of the very complex issues involved in the treatment of time in behavioral sciences, see C. W. Harris, ed., *Problems in Measuring Change* (Madison: University of Wisconsin Press, 1967); and D. Hibbs, Jr., "Problems of Statistical Estimation and Causal Inference in Time-Series Regression Models," in *Sociological Methodology, 1973—1974*, H. Costner ed. (San Francisco: Jossey-Bass, 1974).

[61]See the arguments for the differences in relationships between social, political and economic variables in sub-groups of the less-developed countries in Irma Adelman and Cynthia Taft Morris, *Society, Politics and Economic Development* (Baltimore: Johns Hopkins University Press, 1967); and the discussion of their data in Chapter 3, Part III in this Handbook.

[62]An elaboration of this point is Edward R. Tufte, "Improving Data Analysis in Political Science," *World Politics*, 21 (1969): 640—654.

[63]A discussion of this and other techniques is contained in Hayward R. Alker, Jr., "Statistics and Politics: The Need for Causal Data Analysis," in *Politics and the Social Sciences*, ed. Seymour Martin Lipset (New York: Oxford University Press, 1969), 244—313.

[64]Basic reviews of simultaneous equation methods are A. S. Goldberger, *Econometric Theory* (New York: John Wiley, 1965); J. Johnston, *Econometric Methods* (New York: McGraw-Hill, 1963); and H. Theil, *Principles of Econometrics* (New York: Wiley, 1971). These techniques have been introduced to non-econometricians by Herbert Simon and Hubert Blalock. See Hubert Blalock, Jr., *Causal Inference in Non-Experimental Research* (Chapel Hill: North Carolina University Press, 1964).

[65]See Sewall Wright, "Path Coefficients and Path Regressions: Alternative or Complimentary Concepts?" *Biometrics*, 16 (1960): 189—202; Otis Dudley Duncan, Jr., "Path Analysis: Sociological Examples," *American Journal of Sociology*, 72 (1966): 1—16; Kenneth Land, "Principles of Path Analysis," in *Sociological Methodology 1969* ed. Edgar Borgatta (San Francisco: Jossey Bass, 1969); and Richard P. Boyle, "Path Analysis and Ordinal Data," *American Journal of Sociology*, 75 (1970): 461—480.

2. Conflict and Political Violence in Black African States

Introduction

In the previous chapter we have presented an introductory discussion of the methodology of cross-national research, which gave some indication of the limits and objectives of the systematic comparative analysis of aggregate data describing countries. The discussion focused on the variety of competing and complementary formulations of empirical tests of generalizations about political life in countries. Although we emphasized the importance of theory as the basis of meaningful generalization and explanation in cross-national research, we gave little indication of the difficulty involved in constructing such theory.

This chapter is intended, therefore, as an illustration of ways in which a problem of national politics—the problem of explaining the incidence of political instability in African countries—can be theoretically formulated and empirically evaluated. The emphasis in this chapter will be on the development of a coherent theoretical explanation, and the empirical testing of the theoretical argument will be intentionally limited to a consideration of only a small sub-set of the data published in the first edition of this Handbook. The reader should bear in mind, therefore, that the generalizations made in this chapter are tentative and invite replication and re-examination using more extensive sets of data. In particular, it should be noted that we pay little attention to the issues of the validity and reliability of data used in this analysis. These issues are taken up in chapter three, which should serve as a guide to the critique and improvement of the analysis given in this chapter.

Whether or not it is ever likely that clear-cut paradigms will structure cumulative, "normal" research in political science (cf. Kuhn, 1970; Almond and Powell, 1978; Holt and Turner, 1970), it is clear that no such pattern characterizes research on political instability at present. The most sustained attempt at axiomatic theory in this area is Professor Gurr's elaboration of frustration-aggression theory (1970), but the difficulty of specifying the composition rules by which psychic motivations of individuals are translated into the interaction of large groups, and the historical experience of states, limits the operational validity of the aggregate cross-national tests of his theoretical argument (cf. Gurr, 1970; Muller, 1972, 1979). There remains a large number of alternative theories—relating political instability to economic development (following Lipset, 1960); participation, social mobilization and institutionalization (Huntington, 1968); the structure of military organization and civil-military relations (Janowitz, 1964); cultural pluralism (Kuper and Smith, 1969); political culture and socialization (Eckstein, 1961; Pye and Verba, 1965), economic dependency and the peculiarities of class formation in developing countries; rank-disequilibrium or imbalanced structural change (Galtung, 1964); or coalition structures and the system of political bargaining (Dudley, 1973). All these formulations can claim logical plausibility, but there are empirical data from case studies of single countries, or comparative analyses of many countries, that both support and cast doubt on elements of each theoretical argument. Political scientists appear to gain more from the invention of "new" theory than from sorting out the puzzles in existing theory, and there are no clear methodological criteria on which they are likely to agree in order to support or reject competing theories.[1] We are left with an embarrassment of theoretical riches, and a bewildering confusion of empirical information.

In the face of this confusion, there is an understandable tendency to reject the claims of social science to offer an explanation of political instability. With respect to events in Africa, some scholars who have made bold and ambitious predictions subsequently denied by history have left the field for other geographical areas where more regularity may be found or for the abstract realm of theory where empirical ambiguity may be less discomforting. Others like First (1970) confidently deride the misguided efforts of social scientists and offer historical commentary on coups d'état in particular countries which provides a mode of understanding, but not explanation of a kind acceptable to scientific methodology. And others, whose identity as social scientists is perhaps not affected by anxiety over the epistemological profession of the discipline, expound the difficulties of arriving at any rigorous explanation for African political instability, which is seen either as inevitable (Zolberg, 1968a; O'Connell, 1967) and, therefore, a constant which cannot be statistically explained, or as a phenomenon impervious to statistical explanation, because data on Africa are so poor as to free us from the incursions of statisticans in the evaluation of arguments about the explanation of political instability (Dowse, 1969).

There is, nevertheless, a growing body of research that has been concerned with the empirical examination of generalizations about the relationships structuring political change in sub-Saharan Africa. This research ranges from the rather bland, inductive assertion that there are statistical relationships between some measures of social, economic or political characteristics of nations and the incidence of coups d'état (Thomas, 1974; Wells, 1974), to more theoretically precise arguments about the effects of different party systems on national political development (Finer, 1967); the relationship between socio-political characteristics and economic development (Adelman and Morris, 1969); the relationship between different patterns of cultural pluralism, social mobilization, and integration, and different types of political instability (Morrison and Stevenson, 1973); the stage-sequencing of urbanization, economic development, literacy, communications, governmental capacity, and political stability (Sigelman, 1974); and the relationships between characteristics of nations and their international relations (McGowan and Shapiro, 1973).

This literature has, however, received little attention from most commentators on contemporary African politics. Zolberg, for example, reviewing the literature on military involvement in African politics (1973), comments that it is likely that interesting conclusions will emerge from "sophisticated multivariate analysis," but he refers to no such work.

Similarly, Decalo (1975) argues that "…the basic contention that coups occur as a result of systemic deficiencies … grossly lacks in explanatory value or utility …" and concludes that "cross-national multivariate analysis has …been unable to account for the relative frequency of the military's role-expansion activities in some political systems as opposed to others," but he cites no references in support of this conclusion.

This benign or not so benign neglect no doubt reflects justified scepticism about the reliability of data available for quantitative analysis, and about the theoretical "depth" of much apparently inductive searching for statistical relations. It also, probably, reflects the generally inchoate conclusions of research which is based on complicated statistical methodology, large numbers of measures for relatively few concepts and units of analysis, and which produces generally weak statistical relationships with often ambiguous directionality.

The purpose of this section is to show, mostly by use of elementary techniques of analysis, and by using a small body of data abstracted from the data archives of the African National Integration Project, that a coherent model of political instability in sub-Saharan Africa *can* be developed—that meaningful generalizations adequately confirmed by empirical tests *can* give a macro-analytic explanation of political stability in sub-Saharan Africa. This demonstration, hopefully, will encourage the development not only of more extensive macro-analytic investigation, but of systematic micro-analytic research designed to investigate the processes underlying aggregate relationships of the kind here produced. No pretense is made to offer a new theory, let alone a paradigm, for research on political instability. There is merit, however, in showing that models built from existing theory can justify much greater confidence in the social scientists' particular mode of explanation than seems to exist in the community of scholarship concerned with modern African studies. And there is merit in any attempt to bring a greater measure of coherence and generality to the confusion and case-study detail which presently governs our understanding of political instability in Africa.

A Model of Political Instability in Sub-Saharan Africa

A model is a concrete representation of abstract theory, in which the components of the model and the structure of relations between them are isomorphic to concepts and relations in the theory (Brodbeck, 1966). This architectonic correspondence between theory and model presumes, of course, the specification of a coherent theory, with unambiguous concepts linked by logically consistent hypotheses. Such theoretical resources are not available to the political scientist, who suffers from Abraham Kaplan's (1964) "Paradox of Conceptualization," that good theory requires good concepts and good concepts require good theory. In the absence of good theory or good concepts, a model of political instability must be more an intimation than an imitation of theory. In what follows, key concepts are isolated and interrelated with reference to the partial theories available, and the model is an operational representation of this conceptual system constructed by the assignment of concrete empirical measures to the conceptual variables and by the specification of mathematical relations defining the theoretical argument.

The model discussed in this section can be diagrammatically represented as in Figure 2.1. As diagrammed, the model represents political instability as a simplified "input-output" process. "Inputs" in the form of demands for political change arise from the structure of cultural pluralism and economic inequality in a political system, and they are "converted" by the conflict-regulation system into "outputs" of political instability. Conflict-regulation in the model is represented by the interrelationship of processes of economic development, social

Figure 2.1   Diagrammatic Illustration of the Model of Political Instability in Black African States.

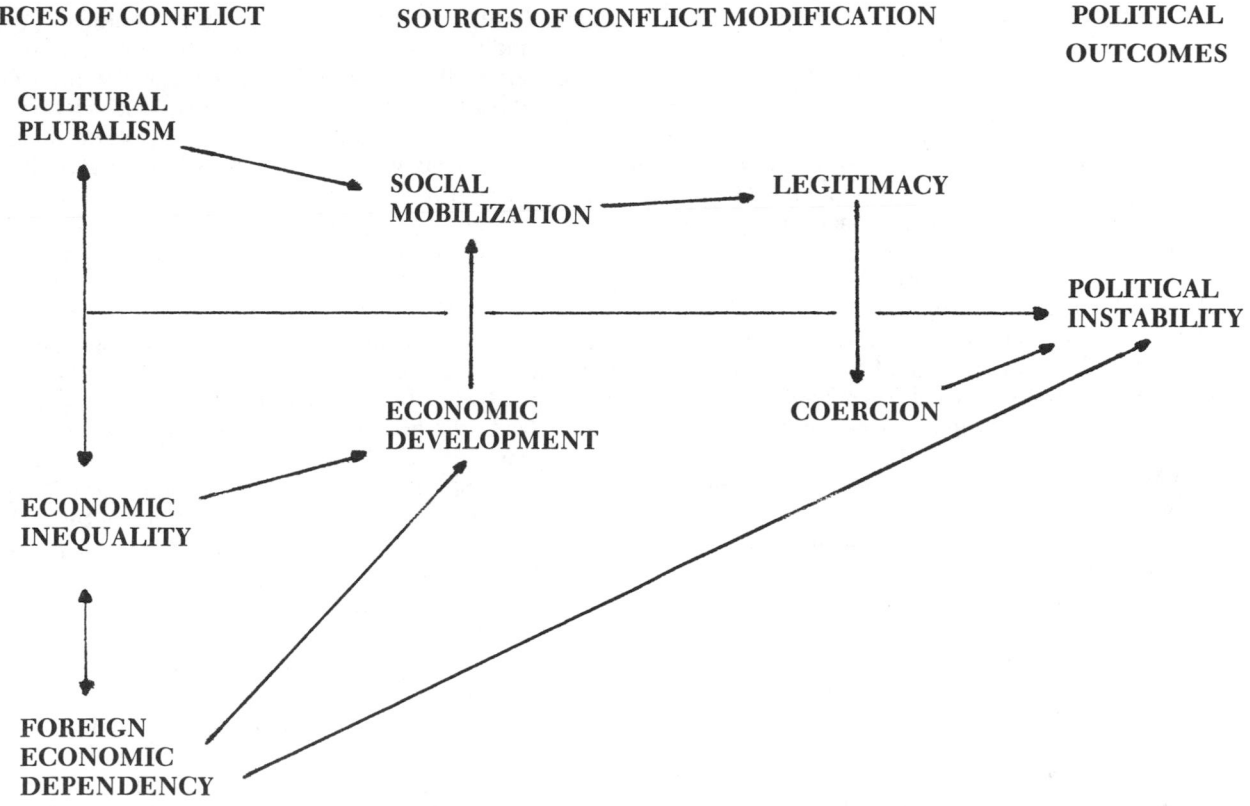

mobilization, legitimacy and coercion. Each of these independent components of the system are viewed as directly manipulable by government policy, and as having a potentially moderating impact on the intensity of conflict generated within the socio-economic structure. One further element of the model is the inclusion of external dependency, conceived as an exogenous influence (i.e., an influence determined from outside the boundaries of the political system) on political instability.

This model refers, obviously, to a theoretical understanding of the explanation of political instability in terms of factors effecting conflict and its modification. We have discussed at length elsewhere (Morrison and Stevenson, 1971) our notion of the proper conceptualization of political instability in terms of differences in inter-group conflict having to do with different types of political actors and different goals of political action which define conflict relations. In the following discussion of the model presented in Figure 2.1, we shall outline the relations iden-

tifying the model in terms of a series of interrelated hypotheses linking the concepts embedded in the model, and these hypotheses will be rationalized with respect to arguments derived from existing theory. In all cases, we shall be concerned to emphasize the logic of conflict and conflict regulation underlying the theoretical argument

1.1   The greater the cultural pluralism, the greater the likelihood, ceteris paribus, of political instability in political systems.

1.2   The greater the economic inequality, the greater the likelihood, ceteris paribus, of political instability in political systems.

1.3   The greater the interaction between cultural pluralism and economic inequality, the greater the likelihood, ceteris paribus, of political instability in political systems.

The first hypothesis gives a crude summary of the argument in the theoretical tradition dating from Furnivall (1938, 1948). Such arguments concentrate on the historical character of colonialism and decolonization, and emphasize the stimulation of conflict between distinct cultures and societies brought into a coercively-imposed colonial market and administrative structure. This conflict is, initially, regulated and controlled by the foreign monopoly of coercion, wealth, and political power in the colonial "order," but decolonization stimulates intense inter-societal conflict over the "spoils" of independence in the succession to the evacuated structures of colonial hegemony. Elaborations of this general argument have been concerned with greater specification of the structure and process of conflict implied in the general formulation. The theoretical problems turn, that is, on the identification of the groups in conflict (the plural societies or cultures within the political system), and the specification of the characteristics of inter-group relationships which govern the magnitude of conflict.

The most stringent specification of the theory of cultural pluralism makes it applicable only to political systems in which, like the typical colonial system, there are multiple segments in the population with culturally and institutionally distinctive structures, and in which one such (minority) population-group monopolizes political power. This political super-ordination and exploitation is seen to provide the motivational stimulus to political revolt, and to the only adequate specification of the relationship between cultural pluralism and political instability (see Kuper and Smith, 1969). Since the number of contemporary political systems to which this stringent "parameterization" of the theory of cultural pluralism applies is small,[2] other elaborations of the theory have sought more general applicability.

One such elaboration has been to conceptualize cultural pluralism in terms of the magnitude of heterogeneity or variation in the cultural and institutional values of the multiple population segments in any political system, and to see political instability as a function of this continuous range of variation (see van den Berghe, 1963, 1964). The difficulty with this alternative formulation is the inherent difficulty of measuring cultural pluralism defined this way,[3] and the lack of clarity as to

the motivational or causal basis for the relationship between cultural pluralism and political instability. Is variation or incongruity on any cultural or institutional attribute likely to motivate political conflict? Does the size and the distribution of the culturally separate groups not affect the relationship? Are there not intervening variables which moderate or intensify the relationship?

A third variant of the cultural pluralism thesis deals specifically with this last question. In this alternative argument, political instability is seen as the consequence of an interaction between differences of culture and institutionalization among a population's component groups, and inequalities in a distribution of wealth and power among them. Such an interaction produces ethnic stratification, and the differences between groups are "politicized" as conflict over the core values of economic[4] and political power. This argument is, obviously, not dissimilar to the first discussed here. In both cases the motivational or causal explanation for the linkage between cultural pluralism and political instability is sought not in the differences of identity or values between plural segments in the population, but in the overlapping inequalities of power or wealth typical of the relationships between such population segments. The central difficulty with this argument, however, relates to the "inevitability" of the development of ethnic stratification in the process of decolonization, economic development and social mobilization. What separates this third variant from the first is simply the proposition that in all culturally plural developing societies, these latter processes necessarily produce ethnic stratification on the additional dimensions of wealth and power. This necessary relationship between cultural pluralism and stratification on non-cultural values has been regularly assumed in the analysis of contemporary African politics, and the consequences of such a necessary development have been seen in terms of the inevitability of political instability (cf. Zolberg, 1968a, 1968b; O'Connell, 1967; Melson and Wolpe, 1970). It is, however, unclear why necessarily the scarcity of resources and the mutual distinctiveness of sub-national communities should combine to produce overlapping cleavages of ethnicity and inequality, and so intensify communalism and political instability. The probability of such a pattern of development should rather be seen as contingent on a number of factors—the extent of residential segregation and the division of labor of cultural sub-groups in the population; the development of integrating institutions with multiple group affiliation such as political parties, labor unions and voluntary associations, the distribution of income and positions, and the rate of mobility and recruitment to higher income and position—all of which are independently variable within political systems. Seen in this larger perspective, the apparently conflicting conclusions derived from scholarly analyses of different cases studies can be reconciled as the predictable result of different values on these kinds of intervening variables in the different situations studied.[5]

None of the formulations of the "theory" of cultural pluralism discussed so far can be dismissed as simply mystified or sophisticated versions of the naive argument that "tribalism" is the root cause of problems of political development in Africa. It is true, however, that such lines of theory construction give special significance to the ethnic group as a unit of analysis, and that such emphasis easily falls prey to the pitfalls of reification and of a static colonial bias. It is abundantly clear, that is, that the description of population groups in the ethnographic literature are at best time-bound descriptions of small, localized samples of populations which are larger and more heterogeneous than the observations suggest, and which are dynamically changing into more or less inclusive social systems (cf. Cohen and Middleton, 1970). At worst, they are descriptions of populations whose identity is a fiction of colonial administrative demography (cf. Apthorpe:1970). This is, of course, not to say that ethnicity is irrelevant to the dynamics of African political systems, but great care has to be taken in emphasizing the theoretical status of ethnicity as an independent variable affecting politics, when it is often a dependent variable effected by political processes and other situational determinants, and great caution must be exercised in assuming the homogeneity and salience of ethnic identity and values in large population groupings.

The second hypothesis given above is an even cruder summarization of a significantly more diverse and complex theoretical tradition, including, at least, the work of Aristotle, de Tocqueville and Marx as major progenitors of the theory of revolution. As with the theory of cultural pluralism, theoretical arguments in this tradition turn on the identification of the structure and process of conflict determined by the economic system. It is far beyond the scope of this chapter to give a formal, axiomatic account of the different theoretical arguments linking economic inequality to political instability. It will be sufficient to focus briefly on the Marxist tradition in order to emphasize the fundamentally different specification of the basic units of analysis, and of the significant variables defining the structure and process of conflict in political systems in this tradition, as compared to the lines of enquiry outlined for the theory of cultural pluralism. The importance of dealing with this separate theoretical tradition is not simply that it constitutes a distinctive and historically more important tradition than that we have labeled the theory of cultural pluralism, but that it is from this tradition, or variants of it, that the apparently obvious causal

force of economic and political inequality referred to in the discussion of the cultural pluralism tradition often derives.

Three central assumptions distinguish the Marxist tradition from that we have summarized as the theory of cultural pluralism. First, Marxist theory assumes the primacy of materialist as opposed to idealist factors in determining the character of social development. From this perspective, the phenomena of ethnicity and political organization are strictly a superstructural matrix of ideas, values and behavior incorporated into institutions and justified in ideology, whose character and stability are themselves determined by the underlying material-economic structure of a society. Second, the dynamics and directionality of change is assumed to be governed by the contradictions inherent in any economy where control over the products of human labor is not vested in the producers themselves. These contradictions arise from the fundamental assumption that men work to remake their environment into a more liberating and pleasurable world, and that the alienation of control over the products of work produces a basic motivation for change. The specific nature of contradiction and conflicts is a function of differences in the mode and relations of production, that is the technological character of productive processes and the socio-political organization of control over the surplus resources generated by production. This kind of argument, it should be noted, is much different from a simple-minded view of the universal quest for greater economic or political resources that seems to underly the logic of argument in the ethnic stratification variety of the cultural pluralism theory. Third, with specific reference to political systems formerly colonized by European powers, the Marxist tradition assumes that the dynamics of change and development have to be understood in the context of the over-riding determination by the structure of relations within which neo-colonial systems are incorporated, and dependent on, the world capitalist economic system. That is, the dynamics and directionality of change within the periphery is constrained by the interests and influences of relationships external to the neo-colonial political system.

The development of a macro-analytic theory of political instability based on the integration of concepts derived from theories of cultural pluralism and historical materialism may well be impossible, and would, otherwise, certainly require a very major volume of theoretical analysis. The fundamental problem would be one of the resolution of the opposing identification of the basic units of analysis, that is cultural sub-systems and social classes. In the extreme case, where these may be the same, the task of theoretical integration is simplified to the explanation of the dominance of cultural or economic factors in the motivation of conflict and its resolution. Where they are not the same, and we shall assume that they are in all probability not the same in the inchoate social structure of African states, the theoretical problems are considerable. The only partial solution which we adopt here, is to argue *a priori*, that dimensions of conflict based on culture and class are macro-attributes of countries, that they are independent but potentially interactive variables, and that a general macro-analytic model of a general systems variety can be formulated relating these variable attributes in hypotheses like those given above. The general utility of this approach will be determined by the empirical results produced by such a model. If by these pragmatic criteria the model is useful, its full explanation must, however, be left to subsequent theoretical investigation. This is so, particularly, because the macro-analytic model we are proposing allows simply for the independent and equally efficacious explanation of political instability by reference to the structure of relations between units defined by reference to culture or to class, and no resolution of the conflicting rationales for these alternative explanations is to be made. Rather, we avoid the issue, and simply define for comparative cross-national evaluation measures of cultural variation and economic inequality as macro-attributes of any political system which, for the reasons given in alternative theoretical traditions, are hypothesized to result in varying levels of political instability. The behavioral dynamics of that relationship are, however, not a problem at this level of analysis.

The preceding discussion elaborates an argument about the structure of conflict as summarized by the first three hypotheses specifying our model of political instability. The remainder of the theoretical discussion deals with the specification of processes of *conflict modification* and their intervening effects in moderating or accentuating the initial probabilities of conflict-producing political system breakdown. We begin with two components of the conflict modification process, economic development and social mobilization. The relevant hypotheses are:

II.1   **The greater the economic development in countries, the less their experience of political instability.**

II.2   **The greater the social mobilization in countries, the less their experience of political instability.**

II.3   **The greater the ratio between economic development and social mobilization in countries, the less their experience of political instability.**

Each of these hypotheses more properly refers to the probable impacts of economic development, social mo-

bilization, and their interaction, reducing the probability that higher levels of conflict, as discussed earlier, will lead to greater political instability. The hypotheses are stated, however, in the form of more simple bivariate relationships to avoid cumbersome expression. The hypotheses as such, nevertheless run counter to a good deal of the common-wisdom about patterns of political development, and they require more detailed elaboration.

A variety of conclusions opposite to those indicated by the first two hypotheses are frequently drawn. Following Deutsch (1966), it is often asserted that the experience of socio-economic development, modernization or social mobilization is an inherently destructive process in which individuals suffer a wrenching experience as they are pulled out of the solidarity of their traditional society into the differentiated and culturally alien institutional structure of modern society. In such a process, confusion and anomie result, and they are easily translated into political violence. A second variant of the argument for the politically destabilizing effects of socio-economic development implies (cf. Olsen:1963) that rapid growth fosters a "revolution of rising expectations," that is vulnerable to the frustrations imposed by inadequate capabilities for meeting such expectations. Such frustration breeds political unrest. In a similar vein, it is argued that processes of socio-economic change in developing countries are in all likelihood unstable, and that imbalanced progress in different sectors, or temporal recessions in a particular developmental sector, creates frustration with the attendant likelihood of political instability (cf. Davies: 1970, and Feierabend, et. al.: 1972). The third variant of the argument linking socio-economic change to political instability, suggests that changes along these lines produce new inequalities in the distribution of the "goods" of modernization, which are themselves sources of frustration and unrest, and which tend to overlap and reinforce existing lines of cleavage producing, in particular, the patterns of ethnic stratification already referred to.

Taken together, such arguments make for a theory of modernization that supercedes the economics of Malthus as *the* dismal science. In Huntington's expressive formulation (1968, 1971), modernity produces political development, but modernization produces political decay, and the passage from modernization to modernity must be one of long-run political restraint on the rate of development in which "it is not the form of government but the degree of government" is critical. There is, of course, a less dismal perspective from which, in dialectical terms, the seeds of progress are sown by decaying political systems – all conflicts are progressive in their consequences – and accelerated instability produces accelerated development.

From our point of view, neither of these perspectives

is sufficiently illuminating. They suffer equally from a vulgar biological metaphor (cf. Nisbet:1969), and they assume social systems that are more deterministic and closed than historical variety suggests. In our own view, the relationship between economic development, social mobilization and political instability can better be viewed in the terms summarized by our hypotheses. The third of these state a generalization agreed on by all the theorists of the 'dismal' school, and needs little further amplification. Where expectations produced by the experience of social mobilization (increased education, media exposure, and new opportunities for participation and communication) exceed the capacity for economic development which provides the techniques, products and generalized income resources for consumption and investment to satisfy such expectations, political conflict and instability are made more rather than less likely. Such 'gaps' should not, however, be assumed as necessary consequences of socio-economic development. Further, the empirical determination of the separate effects of such gaps, disequilibria or inconsistencies as opposed to the effects of the independent processes which produce them, is made difficult by the technical problems of 'determination' in simultaneous equation models of the combined system of variables.

In the same way that we do not assume a necessary relationship between economic development, social mobilization and greater gaps between economic development and social mobilization, we do not assume that economic development or social mobilization necessarily produce greater inequality in the economic structure and a greater intensity of ethnic stratification in developing countries. The reasons for these assumptions are in part empirical and in part axiomatic. From an empirical point of view, there is evidence from Africa that individuals (the core reference in the assumptions of the 'dismal' school) are in general not increasingly confused or anomic as a result of migration and mobility induced by modernization (cf. Peil:1972, 1976); that mobilized individuals tend to tailor their expectations to a rational perception of their real opportunities (Oberschall:1973); that individuals have highly flexible situational identities which reflect the generation of new ethnic and organizational identities in the process of social change, and which make a simple, let alone static, reference to ethnicity implied by the argument for ethnic stratification at least doubtful (Paden:1973, 1980; Cohen:1969; Epstein:1958, 1973, 1981).

From an axiomatic perspective, the formulation of macro-theory such as that proposed herein has either to formulate assumptions about micro-level activity which includes statements about the correspondence rules by which that activity produces system-level properties, or

else it requires assumptions stated at the level of systems properties as such. This is a complex epistemological point, but unless it can be shown how much economic development corresponds to how many frustrated individuals, and how many frustrated individuals correspond to the emergence of events and movements of the kind we designate as political instability, the theoretical rationale for a macro-relationship between the properties of aggregates such as national political systems is incomplete.

From this vantage point, therefore, we justify our hypotheses in terms of axiomatic assumptions about the nature of political systems, which our model purports to represent. Political systems, following Deutsch (1966) are viewed as cybernetic systems – i.e., they are systems of goal-oriented activity with developed self-steering capabilities through which evaluations of the relative success of attaining given goals are used to adjust or reinforce activities that retard or promote the achievement of given goals. The determination of which goal or goals should be achieved in society is made within the political structure of the social system. Political structures are made up of relations of power and authority, in which some actors in the society have a greater probability of influencing the activity of other actors without the reciprocal relation holding between them – that is, some have power and/or authority over others. From a macro-analytic view, the actual distribution of power and authority, and the actual structure (the hierarchy and salience) of the different values pursued by those with power and authority, are not of importance. Rather, we assume axiomatically, that the central goal of political systems is the stability of these political structures; that the primary indication of deviation from this goal is the experience of political instability; that the tendencies toward this deviation or entropy originate in the structure of conflict relations in the society where different groups hold mutually exclusive values, interests or goals; and that the self-steering capability of the system is evidenced in the adjustment of different parameters of the structure of social activity, so as to reduce the underlying 'drift' from conflict to instability.

Therefore, change in the parameters of economic development and social mobilization reflects in part a concious adaptation of these components to the system to counteract tendencies towards political instability. The extent to which this political manipulation or 'steerage' of the system is successful is not only a function of the quality of political life, but also of the extent to which change in these parameters of the system is exogenously determined by environmental influences outside of the system itself. In highly 'open' systems like the neo-colonial countries of much of Africa, this exogenous constraint on political self-determination is obviously great. Nevertheless, we argue that, in general, changes in the aggregate parameters of economic development and social mobilization represent adaptive responses to generic deviations from the goal of political instability. Policies which allow for greater economic development and social mobilization increase a government's capacity for conflict regulation. They directly satisfy the interests of some citizens in the acquisition of material and symbolic 'goods', and thereby increase the demonstration effect by which individuals come to perceive a more favorable opportunity structure for goods and services. They generate material and symbolic resources which governments can deploy for investment in further goal-directed activity. Finally, these processes indirectly diffuse the intensity of conflict in society by stimulating greater complexity in the structure of activity. Economic development and social mobilization, that is, extend and complicate the division and specialization of labor; the concentration and variety of residential locations; the variety and rapidity of information diffusion, and the scope of political participation and association. In general, this differentiation and complication increases the likelihood of cross-cutting cleavages in the structure of social action so that parties in conflict over one issue may find themselves in co-operation in conflicts over other issues.

While the general argument for the preceding hypotheses is adequate, the theoretical elaboration of our model of conflict-regulation requires the further inclusion of two additional components: legitimacy and coercion. The summary hypotheses relating characteristics in our model of political instability are:

III.1   The greater the legitimacy of national political systems, the less the likelihood of political instability.

III.2   The greater the coercion characteristic of national political systems, the less the likelihood of political instability.

III.3   The greater the ratio of coercion to legitimacy or social mobilization, the greater the likelihood of political instability.

The justification for these additional hypotheses relates not only to the logical and empirical content of the relations governing legitimacy, coercion and political instability, but also to the identification of these two new components in the argument already developed for the model as a whole. The identification of legitimacy and coercion as supplementary components to economic development and social mobilization in the structure of the conflict-regulation system is derived from the general theory of the integration of social and political systems. Integration involves the generation of greater independence between the interacting entities in any system, so that there is a high degree of covariance and mutual predictability in the behavior of any pair of interacting entities (Deutsch:1966). From this perspective, the process of economic development and social mobilization already referred to, increases the scale of interaction and interdependency between actors in the social system. Greater differentiation and complexity in the structure of social activity also produce, however, a tendency towards strain and anomie, which mitigates the extent to which interdependent actors interact in mutually predictable or mutually agreeable ways. That is, while the general effects of economic development and social mobilization increase the capacity for integration and conflict regulation (as our preceding argument indicated), this capacity is limited by the greater variability of information, opportunity and value with which independent actors may define their situation in society. These greater 'degrees of freedom' may lead to greater randomness rather than mutual predictability in behavior, at least with respect to political responses to changing social situations, and constrain, therefore, the collective goal-attainment of the system. Political integration requires, therefore, an independent control over social and economic differentiation. In our analysis, these independent controls involve the generation of consensus about the superordinate goals of political collaboration, and the concommitant development of efficient regulatory responses to deviance from such goals. These two 'integrative' processes define the extent of legitimacy and coercion characteristic of the political system.

Legitimacy has been generally defined (Lipset:1960) as "the capacity of the system to engender and maintain the belief that the existing political institutions are the most appropriate ones for the society." Such a belief system relates to the positive evaluation of the policies, personnel and institutional structure of particular regimes, although the underlying roots of such positive evaluations are based on more diffuse support (Easton:1965, 1981) for the structure of political relationships. This diffuse support is based on common values relating to the definition of the political community and to the structure of authority within it. Superordinate goals, that is, need to be developed so that members of political systems share what Deutsch (1966) describes as a sense of "we-feeling," mutual sympathy and loyalty, trust and mutual consideration, and of partial identification in terms of self-images and interests. More critical even than superordinate goals about the limits of political community, are superordinate goals about the nature of authority, so that, following Ekstein (1961, 1979) patterns of authority within government are congruent with other authority patterns in the society of which it is a part. Where legitimacy based on such superordinate goals is wide-spread within political systems, we expect a reduction in the relationship between conflict and instability, following the experimental evidence that:

1. When groups in a state of conflict are brought into contact under conditions embodying superordinate goals, which are compelling but cannot be achieved by the efforts of one group alone, they will tend to co-operate toward the common goal.

2. Co-operation between groups, necessitated by a series of situations embodying superordinate goals, will have a cumulative effect in the direction of reducing existing conflict between groups. (Sherif:1967)

Coercion is often viewed as conceptually opposed to the process of integration. It seems more appropriate to us, however, to see coercion, or the effective control over the means of violence (Etzioni:1973), as a critical feature of the integration of political systems. The actual employment of coercion by governments tends to vary inversely with levels of legitimacy, but no political systems have such high levels of legitimacy that coercion can be entirely foregone, and minimal integration may be enforced in the short-run by naked power in the form of government coercion.

Our hypotheses about the relationship between coercion and political instability indicate a reduction in the probability that conflict will lead to political instability as levels of coercion increase. This hypothesis must be modified, however, by the qualification that the relationship between coercion and compliance to political authorities is curvilinear, such that at very low or very intensive (totalitarian) applications of coercion, compliance and stability is most probable, but that at levels below or above some threshold values, increased coercion increases the probability of political instability. While we cannot state the threshold points at which the increasing marginal utility of coercion begins to operate, we expect that African countries will in general fall within intermediate values of coerciveness where political instability is more rather than less likely as a result. The curvilinear relationship suggested here has been indicated by Etzioni (1965), in his study of the development of international unions, and by Bwy (1968), Gurr (1968), and Feierabend, et. al. (1972) in their examination of the relationship between coercion and political instability in compar-

ative studies of different countries. While, therefore, this curvilinearity in the relation between coercion and political instability must be borne in mind, it is useful to emphasize the general theoretical understanding that coercion is the cutting edge of political integration and is the last resource of political authorities in the regulation of conflict.

This understanding of the independent effects of coercion on political instability needs modification, as in Hypothesis III.3 which specifies the balance or interaction between coercion, legitimacy and social mobilization. From a psychological point of view, negative and positive reinforcement effectively condition behavior, but positive reinforcement is a more reliable form of behavior modification. In these terms, legitimacy has a greater independent weight than coercion in the reduction of underlying processes of conflict and instability in political systems, and the likelihood of political instability will be reduced by a positive balance of legitimacy over coercion, and may correspondingly be increased when there is a net balance of coercion over legitimacy.

Empirical Analysis

In order to evaluate the model outlined in the preceding discussion, we shall use data published in the first edition of *Black Africa* to operationalize each of the conceptual components of the model, and then to investigate the statistical relationships between these variables. Because our aim is to give as parsimonious an explanation as possible, we shall depart from our previous practice of analyzing extensive sets of multiple indicators for each theoretical concept, and instead investigate no more than two alternative operationalizations for any concept in the model. The selection of these indicators has been governed by inspection of convergent patterns of relationship between large numbers of separate indicators already analyzed in Morrison and Stevenson, 1971; 1972a; 1972b; 1973; 1974a; and 1974b, and Stevenson 1971. The indicators chosen are representative of a larger set of complimentary operationalizations of the same concept.

We operationalize political instability as a weighted sum of the counts for each country, in the period from their independence to 1970, of the following events: Civil wars, rebellions, irredentism, inter-ethnic violence, coups d'état, attempted coups and reported plots. We have shown elsewhere (Morrison and Stevenson:1971) how measures of the frequency of these events in Black African states tend to cluster into two distinct dimensions that correspond to our conceptual distinctions between communal and elite instability. We have also shown that these dimensions of political instability are mutually interrelated, and while we have spent a good deal of effort exploring the differences in the explanation of these two types of political instability, it makes sense in the present context to consider the variance in a weighted sum of all these measures as an index of political instability, and to investigate the extent to which such variation is accounted for by variation in the operationalizations of other elements in our model. The index of political instability is calculated by the formula:

$$Y = X_1 + .5X_2$$

where

Y = The political instability score
X_1 = The communal instability index (see Table 11.3 first edition.
X_2 = The elite instability index (see Table 11.2 first edition)

We operationalize economic development in terms of two measures: the average annual growth rate in GNP per capita from 1961 to 1968, and Gross Domestic Capital Formation as a percentage of GDP in 1963. These measures index the realization of higher levels of average individual income and the extent to which savings from national income are devoted to new capital investments which have, theoretically, a lagged relationship to the capacity to generate new growth in income. We operationalize social mobilization by measures of the distribution of educational enrollment and information media in these countries. The measures used are the average annual percentage change in primary school enrollment from 1960 to 1966, and the percentage increase in radio ownership per capita for the same period. We operationalize legitimacy by a measure of the proportion of the popular vote won by the political party whose leadership dominated the executive of the government which came to power at independence. Coercion is operationalized as the rates of growth of manpower in the armed forces in the period 1963 to 1967. Finally, we operationalize the extent of economic dependency in terms of measures of the volume of foreign aid received from each country's ex-colonial power per capita in 1967 and the percentage of total trade with that ex-colonial power in 1962. The operationalization of the concepts of economic inequality and cultural pluralism are defined in terms of two measures — the percentage of wage and salary earners in the public sector, and a measure of linguistic heterogeneity. The latter measure combines the scores for each country on the number of languages spoken and the corpus distance index for the extent of structural dissimilarity be-

tween major language groupings.

The validity of any of these measures as operationalizations of the conceptual structure of our model can be questioned. The conflict regulation effects of economic development and domestic capital formation are indirect because the aggregate measures do not reflect real purchasing power, the increasing availability of real goods and services for mass consumption, or the generation of new employment opportunities. The measures of social mobilization do not indicate the effectiveness or content of exposure to education and the mass media. The measure of legitimacy is especially problematic assuming as it does that voting opportunities encompassed the full range of political preferences in a population at the time of independence, and that votes for a ruling party directly expressed public opinion as to the legitimacy of that party's program and policies as well as of the constitutional order as a whole. We do not have relevant information on public opinion, and there are no doubt voters whose support was coerced, bought or a reflection of the best alternative in a system to which voters generally ascribed little or no legitimacy. The measure of coercion is a satisfactory measure of potential but not actual governmental coercion in the political process — increasingly large armed forces may reflect as much the predictable rate of growth in states with minimal armies at independence which saw the increasing utilization of the armed forces in the coercive manipulation of politics. The measure of cultural pluralism in terms of the linguistic heterogeneity of national populations does not reflect differences in the institutional and cultural structure of ethnic groups within a population although differences in language are likely to be correlated with differences in these latter dimensions. The measure of economic inequality in terms of the preponderance of employment in the public sector does not provide a measure of the distributive characteristics of income in the population, although we would argue that because of the very small wage earning class within each country's total population and the inherited salary structure of public service employment from the colonial era which makes public service employment disproportionately enticing compared to most other sectors of employment, that this measure will, in the short run, be substantially correlated with other measures of distributive inequality in income. Finally, the measures of economic dependency are only crude indicators of the extent to which these countries have predominantly neo-colonial economic relationships with the rest of the world, and they do not indicate directly the extent to which these relationships are exploitative or dependent. With these kinds of cautions in mind, however, the aggregative relationships in the model are nevertheless of interest.

The indicators chosen as operationalizations of our model are in most cases so distributed that a meaningful range of variation is observed across the countries that we wish to compare, and although there are problems of skew in the distribution of some measures – particularly in the measure of political instability – it is clear that we are not dealing with constants or with such homogeneity and reduced variance that statistical analysis is not useful. It is, of course, necessary to question the extent to which the distributions of these measures are affected by other variables not incorporated as operationalizations of the model. Such a question is, however, too open-ended to admit of any final answer. All models or theories inevitably fail to account for a complete and consistent set of terms for the explanation of any phenomenon. However, two obvious sources of possible interference, or specification error, in the explanation of national political instability relate to the historical experience and to the scale of political systems. In the case of these African political systems, one may well question whether or not the distinctive colonial experience of countries ruled by different colonial powers may have determined substantially different patterns of political development in the post-colonial period, or whether or not the differences in size from the micro-states like Djibouti, Equatorial Guinea, and Gambia to the large states like Nigeria, Sudan and Zaire may not have determined different patterns of development.

Preliminary answers to these latter questions can be derived from a relatively simple statistical test of the differences in the distribution of the variables used to operationalize the model for countries under one system of colonial rule versus countries under another system, or for countries that are large as opposed to those that are small in population or area. Table 2.1 shows the results of a t-test of the significance of differences in the means of the distributions of these variables in comparisons of the sub-Saharan countries grouped into French or other colonial experience, and large versus small population states. The grouping by colonial experience is a matter of unambiguous historical record, but the choice of comparing the formally French colonies to those under any other type of colonial rule is justified less ambiguously by the assumption that there was a greater emphasis on direct rule and assimilation into the European metropolitan community in the French colonial system than in others. This emphasis may have produced a greater measure of elite integration and of public legitimacy for central national political institutions, than might be the case for other countries under different systems of colonial rule, and may have resulted in differences in their political instability patterns. Similarly, these differences in the style of colonial rule may have affected the emergence of dif-

ferent patterns of socio-economic development and economic dependency. The grouping by size is somewhat ambiguous, since it involves an arbitrary determination that eight countries in the upper nine deciles of the range in the skewed distribution of population size are large, and all others are small. Whether the lower bound of a population size greater than 5,991,300 for large countries is an appropriate indicator of large scale political systems is arguable. This parameter is probably too low to demarcate large from small political systems in the universe of nations, but it is an obvious line of demarcation for the countries we are considering here.

The results in Table 2.1 show that the mean levels of political instability in countries with a non-French colonial history and in the group of large countries are significantly higher than those in former French colonies and in small countries. The mean distribution of ex-metropolitan aid per capita is significantly greater in small countries than in large ones. The mean percentage of total trade with ex-metropolitan powers is significantly greater in former French colonies and in small countries than in countries with other colonial histories or large countries. The mean percentage of the vote for the ruling party at the time of independence is significantly greater in small than in large countries, and the percentage rate of growth in primary school enrollment is greater in French than in other ex-colonial territories. Finally, the average linguistic heterogeneity is greater in the larger than in the smaller countries. These results indicate that we must be cautious about conclusions which do not take into account the possible effects of colonial inheritance and size in considering the explanation of political instability in these countries. This cautionary note should be observed as we deal with the individual hypotheses which structure our model of political instability and which do not control for these latter factors. We shall refer again to these factors at the end of our analysis and their general significance for a complete multivariate analysis of the model.

With these precautions in mind, we can proceed directly to the evaluation of our model of political instability in sub-Saharan African states, by examining the hypotheses describing the relations between different variables in the model. It is useful to initially consider elementary cross-tabulations of the measures relevant to these hypotheses, reducing the continuous measures to simple dichotomous measures of high or low values for each of these national characteristics. This simplification is a conservative response to the problem of error in the continuous measures, and the cross-tabulation procedure gives an appealing visual summary of the underlying pattern of relationships. We shall therefore dichotomize each continuous measure either at the median value of

Table 2.1   T-tests for Differences in Means between Black African Nations Grouped by Colonial Inheritance and Population Size.

VARIABLES	Colonial Inheritance		Population Size	
	French (N=14)	Others (N=16)	Large (N=8)	Small (N=22)
	i ii			
Political Instability index	64 (56)	150 (145)	241 (151)	63 (54)
	t=2.21**		t=3.27**	
Aid from ex-metropolitan power per capita	57 (43)	50 (80)	19 (16)	65 (71)
	t=.31		t=2.85**	
Trade with ex-metropolitan power as percent of total trade.	51 (17)	35 (10)	32 (8)	46 (16)
	t=3.32**		t=3.25**	
Percent change in armed forces	86 (141)	73 (118)	113 (148)	66 (120)
	t=.27		t=.80	
Percent vote for ruling party, pre-independence election	69 (22)	59 (27)	40 (24)	72 (19)
	t=1.13		t=3.38**	
GDCF as percent GDP	135 (81)	122 (50)	121 (27)	130 (76)
	t=.53		t=.51	
Average annual growth of GDP per capita	1.5 (3.2)	.9 (1.2)	.6 (10)	1.3 (26)
	t=.65		t=1.17	
Average annual growth of primary school enrollment	71 (38)	38 (39)	40 (46)	57 (40)
	t=2.30**		t=.98	
Percent increase in radios per capita	293 (326)	324 (339)	199 (121)	304 (352)
	t=.26		t=1.21	
Percent wage earners in public sector	29 (10)	33 (15)	37 (8)	28 (14)
	t=.85		t=2.22**	
Linguistic heterogeneity	78 (75)	179 (313)	322 (390)	57 (67)
	t=1.25		t=1.91	

i = Mean
ii = variance
** = p<.01, otherwise not significant, for one-tailed test.

Table 2.2   Cross-Tabulation of Dichotomous Measures of Linguistic Heterogeneity: Wage Earners in the Public Sector, and Political Instability in Black African States.

POLITICAL INSTABILITY

	Low	High
Low	10	5
High	5	10

LINGUISTIC HETEROGENEITY

$\chi^2 = 2.13$ $p = .14$
gamma $= .60$ $p = .01$ (one tailed test)

POLITICAL INSTABILITY

	Low	High
Low	10	5
High	6	9

% WAGE EARNERS IN PUBLIC SECTOR

$\chi^2 = 1.21$ $p = .27$
gamma $= .50$ $p = .01$ (one tailed test)

the distribution, or at that value closest to the median which gives the most meaningful discontinuity in the split-half distribution of the measure.

Consider, first, the relationship between cultural pluralism, income inequality and political instability as discussed in the first two hypotheses above. As shown in Tables 2.2 and 2.3, there is a strong positive association between high and low levels of linguistic heterogeneity and correspondingly high or low levels of political instability. The association between the concentration of wage earners in the public sector and the extent of political instability is similarly positive, but less pronounced — 75% of these countries with low linguistic heterogeneity experienced low political instability and 71% of those with high linguistic heterogeneity experienced high political instability. Sixty-three percent with a low concentration of wage earners in the public sector and 57% with a high concentration had, respectively, low and high political instability. This evidence tends to support both hypotheses I.1 and I.2 of our model, although the less significant relationship for the public sector concentration of

wage earners may be taken as an indication of the relatively poor validity of this measure as an operationalization of income inequality. We cannot show that better measures would produce stronger relationships, but we assume this to be so on the basis of this partial evidence.

The effects of an interaction between cultural pluralism and income inequality, as summarized in hypothesis I.3, can be assessed from Table 2.3. With the small number of cases that we have, a three-way cross-tabulation produces very small cell frequencies, so that the evidence derived from them must be considered of only heuristic value. Nevertheless, the evidence for the hypothesized interaction is dramatic. Sixty-seven percent of the countries having a high concentration of wage earners in the public sector and low linguistic heterogeneity have low political instability, but 100% of the countries with high public sector concentrations and high linguistic heterogeneity have high political instability. Despite the ambiguous validity of this labor force characteristic as a measure of income inequality, this finding tends to support the generalization in hypothesis I.3.

Table 2.3 Cross-Tabulation Between Dichotomous Measures of the Percent Wage Earners in the Public Sector and Political Instability, Controlling for a Dichotomous Measure of Linguistic Heterogeneity.

	LINGUISTIC HETEROGENEITY			
	Low		**High**	
	Political Instability		**Political Instability**	
	Low	**High**	**Low**	**High**
Low	6	3	4	3
High	6	1	0	7

% WAGE EARNERS IN PUBLIC SECTOR

$$\chi^2 = 49.2 \qquad p > .01$$

Looking next at the pattern of association between measures of economic development and political instability, the results reported in Table 2.4 show no association between the dichotomous measure of average annual growth rates in GNP and the index of political instability. There is, however, a tendency for a disproportionate number of countries with high levels of domestic capital formation relative to national income to have low political instability, and for somewhat more than 60% of those with low levels of domestic capital formation to have high political instability.

These results for the GDCF measure confirm the hypothesis that increasing economic development decreases the likelihood of political instability. The absence of any relationship for the more direct measure of increasing per capita income, however, cautions against any firm conclusions about the validity of this hypothesis on the basis of these simple tests. The problem of the effects of economic development on political instability is clearly more complex than the cross-tabulations of these data can explicate.

The results in Table 2.5 for the dichotomous measures of social mobilization are similarly ambiguous. There is a slight, but statistically insignificant, tendency towards a negative relationship between increasing primary school enrollment and political instability – that is, high enrollment rates are somewhat more likely to be associated with low rather than high political instability, and vice-versa. Such a result supports our hypothesis II.2, but the results for the measure of increasing availability of radio receivers per capita – a positive, and statistically more significant relationship – contradict the hypothesis. We have, therefore, to await more detailed examination of the relationship between social mobilization and political instability, before deciding on the validity of hypothesis II.2.

One possibility, in this connection, is that the direct relationships specified in hypotheses II.1 and II.2 are insignificant, and that the importance of these variables, seen in the context of the whole model, is only in their intervening effects or interaction in relation to other variables. Our model clearly implies that the positive relationships between cultural pluralism and income inequality with political instability will be *reduced* by the intervening effects of higher levels of economic development and social mobilization. This additional hypothesis can be evaluated by looking at the relationships between linguistic heterogeneity and political instability controlling for levels of economic development or social mobilization. Table 2.6, for example, shows that the dichotomous measure of average annual GNP growth, which was not at all associated by itself with the measure of political instability, *does* have the hypothesized effect of re-

ducing the relationship between linguistic heterogeneity and political instability. That is, the positive relationship between linguistic heterogeneity and political instability is much less marked or significant for countries with high rates of GNP growth than for countries with low rates of growth. The results for the relationship between linguistic heterogeneity and political instability controlled for levels of educational enrollment or radios per capita do not, however, show any meaningful interaction. The results in Table 2.6, nevertheless, suggest the importance of economic development as a process which has, as our model suggests, intervening, conflict-regulating effects on the relationship between socio-economic conflict and political instability in these countries.

The effects on political instability of an interaction between economic development and social mobilization, as in hypothesis II.3, have also to be considered. We have shown elsewhere (Morrison and Stevenson:1974a) that the often discussed 'gap' between high rates of social mobilization (education, information exposure and urbanization) and low rates of economic development (per capita income and capital formation) *is* systematically related to the incidence of political instability in these countries. The demonstration of this relationship was based on product-moment correlations of our measures of elite and communal instability with indices measuring the differences in standard scores for variables relating to social mobilization and economic development. For the sake of completeness in this analysis, it is useful to investigate whether similar results obtain in cross-tabulation procedures for the dichotomous measures described here.

Table 2.7 shows, as expected by hypothesis II.3, that in countries where economic development levels are proportionately greater than social mobilization levels, low political instability is a much more likely experience than high political instability, and in countries where economic development levels are proportionately less than social mobilization levels there is a tendency for higher rather than low political instability. The interaction effect of relatively high economic development and relatively low social mobilization is particularly marked. One hundred per cent of the countries with high domestic capital formation and low rates of radios per capita growth have low political instability, and eighty-six per cent of countries with high rates of growth of GNP per capita and low radios per capita growth have low political instability. These results lend support, therefore, to hypothesis II.3.

The relationship between political instability, legitimacy and coercion as measured by the dichotomous variables is given in Table 2.8. As predicted by our hypothesis III.1, greater legitimacy is clearly associated with less political instability. The hypothesized (III.2) conflict-

Table 2.4   Cross-Tabulation of Dichotomous Measures of Economic Development and Political Instability in Black African States.

POLITICAL INSTABILITY

	Low	High
Low	7	8
High	8	7

AVERAGE ANNUAL
GROWTH RATE OF GNP
Per Capita

$\chi^2 = 0.0$ $p = 1.0$
gamma $= -.13$ $p =$ n.s. (one tailed test)

POLITICAL INSTABILITY

	Low	High
Low	5	10
High	11	4

GROSS DOMESTIC CAPITAL
FORMATION AS % GDP

$\chi^2 = 3.35$ $p =$ $.07$
gamma $= -.69$ $p = .01$ (one tailed test)

Table 2.5 Cross-Tabulation of Dichotomous Measures of Social Mobillization and Political Instability in Black African Countries.

% INCREASE IN PRIMARY SCHOOL ENROLLMENT Per Capita	POLITICAL INSTABILITY Low	POLITICAL INSTABILITY High
Low	6	9
High	9	6

χ^2 = .53 p = .47
gamma = −.39 p = .01 (one tailed test)

% INCREASE IN RADIO RECEIVERS Per Capita	POLITICAL INSTABILITY Low	POLITICAL INSTABILITY High
Low	10	5
High	5	10

χ^2 = 2.13 p = .14
gamma = .60 p = .01 (one tailed test)

Table 2.6   Cross-Tabulation of Dichotomous Measures of Linguistic Heterogeneity and Political Instability, Controlling for a Dichotomous Measure of Economic Development in Black African States.

AVERAGE ANNUAL GROWTH IN GNP

		Low Political Instability		High Political Instability	
		Low	High	Low	High
LINGUISTIC HETEROGENEITY	Low	7	1	5	3
	High	1	6	3	4

$\chi^2 = 8.04$ $p = .001$
gamma = .95

$\chi^2 = .579$ n.s.
gamma = .38

Table 2.7   Cross-Tabulations of Dichotomous Measures of Social Mobilization and Political Instability Controlling for Dichotomous Measures of Economic Development.

GDCF as Percent of GNP

	Low		High	
	Political Instability		Political Instability	
	Low	High	Low	High
% INCREASE IN RADIOS Per Capita — Low	3	5	8	0
% INCREASE IN RADIOS Per Capita — High	3	6	2	3

$\chi^2 = 40.97$ $p > .01$

AVG. ANNUAL GROWTH IN GDP
Per Capita

	Low		High	
	Political Instability		Political Instability	
	Low	High	Low	High
% INCREASE IN RADIOS Per Capita — Low	5	4	6	1
% INCREASE IN RADIOS Per Capita — High	4	2	2	6

$\chi^2 = 50.2$ $p > .01$

Table 2.8   Cross-Tabulation of Dichotomous Measures of Political Instability, Legitimacy and Coercion in Black African Countries.

POLITICAL INSTABILITY

	Low	High
Low	5	10
High	10	5

PERCENT CHANGE IN ARMED FORCES

$\chi^2 = 2.13$ $p = .14$
gamma $= -.60$ $p = .01$ (one tailed test)

POLITICAL INSTABILITY

	Low	High
Low	11	4
High	4	11

PERCENT VOTE FOR RULING PARTY IN PRE-INDEPENDENCE ELECTION

$\chi^2 = 4.80$ $p = .03$
gamma $= .77$ $p = .01$ (two tailed test)

modifying effects of coercion are, however, contradicted by these data. The data show greater political instability associated with greater growth of the armed forces. There is, however, a clear problem of interpreting this result. We do not know, because of the temporal simultaneity of the observations, whether political instability increased despite a growing coercive threat, or whether coercive capabilities were increased in response to the threat of political instability. While this kind of problem relates to all these cross-sectional relationships, it is particularly problematic for the measures of coercion, since other measures may more easily be interpreted as having some lagged relationship to the observation of political instability. The strength of this positive relationship, however, warns against any assumption that political instability is deterred by increasing the coercive capability available to governments in Black African states.

Another way of reinforcing this conclusion that increasing the potential coercive capability of governments in these countries failed to reduce the incidence of political instability that they experienced is to look at the interaction between coercion and other conflict-regulating variables in our model. The style of presenting three-way cross-tabulations in which the relationship between two dichotomous measures is controlled by a third will now be sufficiently familiar for us to simply give a verbal summary of relationships involving political instability and linguistic heterogeneity when increase in the size of the armed forces is controlled. In fairly dramatic fashion, the relationship between low and high linguistic heterogeneity and low and high political instability jumps from an insignificant but positive relationship (C = .32) to a highly significant positive relationship (C = .55), when we move from countries with low rates of armed forces growth to those with high rates. All the seven countries with high linguistic heterogeneity *and* high rates of growth of armed forces personnel experienced high political instability, whereas only three of the other seven nations with high linguistic heterogeneity but low rates of armed forces growth experienced high political instability.

Corresponding to this evidence that increasing coercion increases the likelihood that linguistic heterogeneity leads to political instability, is the equally persuasive evidence that legitimacy *reduces* the likelihood that linguistic heterogeneity leads to political instability. The positive relationship between linguistic heterogeneity and political instability drops from C = .88 in countries with low percentages of the vote for the ruling party to C = .45 in countries where the percentage vote for ruling party was high.

The effect on political instability of the interaction between coercion, legitimacy and social mobilization as given in hypothesis III.3 can be summarized in the same way. There is no meaningful interaction between primary school enrollment and armed forces growth rates, but the hypothesis *is* confirmed by the evidence for interactions between armed forces and radio receivers per capita growth rates, and for armed forces growth and the percentage vote for the ruling party. In the former case, the apparently positive relationship between radio receivers growth and political instability is magnified by growth in the armed forces. Where armed forces growth is low, 57% of the countries with high radio receivers growth have *low* political instability, but where armed forces growth is high, 86% of the countries with high radio receivers have *high* political instability. In the case of the interaction between coercion and legitimacy, ten of the fifteen countries with low armed forces growth had high levels of legitimacy, and eight of these countries had low political instability. In contrast, ten of the fifteen countries with high armed forces had low levels of legitimacy, and eight of these countries had high political instability. This evidence supports the argument that where coercion outgrows communication and commitment in the relations between regimes and citizens, the likelihood of political instability is intensified.

Finally, we consider the exogenous influences of external economic dependency on the relationships governing domestic political instability in our model. The data in Table 2.9 show a relationship between greater trade or aid dependency on the former metropolitan power and a lower incidence of political instability. This relationship contradicts our hypothesis IV.1. The clarity of these empirical distributions in Table 2.9 notwithstanding, we should be cautious in the interpretation of such negative relationships. We have elsewhere (Stevenson and Morrison:1973) shown that there is convergent evidence over a large number of measures of the total volume of imports and exports, of the proportion of trade to GNP, or of the concentrations of aid or trade relationships with the ex-colonial powers, that external dependency measured in these ways *is* associated with lower magnitudes of political instability. While, therefore, we are inclined to accept the argument that at this stage of the development of African countries there is a clear dependence on external markets for development resources and that without substantial involvement in these markets the ability to regulate domestic conflict is decreased, we should nevertheless emphasize the need for caution in interpreting this generalization. We have observed that the dependency relationship is a two-edged sword. Trade and aid dependency can allow for greater economic resources in these countries, but they also allow for greater vulnerability to commodity price fluctuations (which were at a 30 year low in 1982), deter-

Table 2.9   **Cross-Tabulations of Dichotomous Measures of External Dependence and Political Instability in Black African Countries.**

POLITICAL INSTABILITY

	Low	High
Low	4	11
High	10	5

% NET FOREIGN AID FROM EX-COLONIAL POWER Per Capita

$\chi^2 = 3.35$ $p = .07$
$gamma = -.69$ $p = .01$

POLITICAL INSTABILITY

	Low	High
Low	3	12
High	12	3

% TOTAL TRADE WITH EX-COLONIAL POWER

$\chi^2 = 8.53$ $p = .003$
$gamma = -.88$ $p = .01$

iorating terms of trade, and single commodity concentrations rather than import diversification, and these factors are associated with *increased* political instability (Stevenson and Morrison:1973). Furthermore, greater measures of trade and aid dependency are positively associated with a greater measure of external public debt and more onerous service payments on external debt. And the correlation of World Bank measures of total public debt outstanding in 1969, and total service payments on external debt as a percentage of the value of exports in the period 1965-69, with our measure of political instability are .38 and .24 respectively. That is to say, dependency increases indebtedness which in turn increases the likelihood of political instability in these countries. Attention must therefore be focused on this complex system of external relations in which beneficial and debilitating direct and indirect effects counteract one another, in order to get an adequate account of the exogenous effects of external dependency on domestic political instability in Black Africa.

It will be clear, hopefully, from the preceding discussion of the contingencies relating elementary dichotomous measures, that there are meaningful generalizations to be made about aggregate differences in the experience of political systems in sub-Saharan Africa. In order to get a more general summary of the explanation of political instability in these countries, it will be useful to proceed through an analysis of the original variables treated as continuous measures in regression analysis. Table 2.10 shows the zero-order correlation coefficients for the bivariate relationships between any pair of the indicators we have used in this analysis. It will be observed from these data that the signs of the coefficients indicate that the likelihood of political instability is decreased by increased aid and trade dependency, by increased economic development, by increased social mobilization and legitimacy, but that increased political instability is associated with increased linguistic heterogeneity and increased military expenditures.

TABLE 2.10 Zero-order Pearson Product-moment Correlation Coefficients for Measures of Characteristics of Black African Countries.

	1	2	3	4	5	6	7	8	9	10
1. Aid from ex-metro power per capita										
2. Trade with ex-metro power as percent of total trade	.32									
3. Linguistic heterogeneity	−.20	−.22								
4. Percent wage earners in the public sector	−.37	.10	.36							
5. GDCF as Percent GDP	.53	.07	−.13	−.23						
6. Average annual growth of GDP per capita	.09	−.04	−.19	−.14	.61					
7. Average annual growth primary school enrollment	.13	.26	−.18	−.05	.10	−.19				
8. Percent increase in radios per capita	.19	.21	−.15	.39	−.30	−.17	.10			
9. Percent vote for ruling party	.32	.11	−.53	−.54	.40	.30	.14	−.12		
10. Percent change in armed forces	−.16	−.02	.39	.29	−.14	−.10	−.24	−.22	−.21	
11. Political instability index	−.28	−.36	.69	.38	−.24	−.21	−.17	−.18	−.74	.27

The possibility of non-linear relationships between any of these independent variables and our index of political instability was investigated by inspection of the scattergrams of the bivariate distributions of nations on these pairs of measures. Only in the case of the trade dependency measure is there a curvilinear tendency, such that political instability decreases as trade dependency increases to about 50% of total trade with the ex-metropole power, beyond which point political instability tends to increase with additional trade dependency. There is, however, only a marginal increase in variance accounted for by the curvilinear regression model as compared to the simple linear model. The only other non-linear modification of the results in Table 2.10 affects the relationship between military expenditures and political instability. When this relationship is estimated by a log-linear regression model, with both variables transformed to logarithms, the correlation coefficient is considerably increased to .56, indicating that political instability increases as a power function of the magnitude of military expenditures — i.e. that increases in military expenditures are associated with exponential not linear increases in political instability. This latter observation further reinforces our early conclusions about the impotence of coercion as a means to the management of conflict and the reduction of political instability in these African countries during the post-independence period.

Multiple regression analysis allows for a summary interpretation of the additive explanation of variance in a dependent variable by a number of independent variables in combination. Considering the small number of cases we are dealing with here, and the problems of significant but unknown distributions of error in the measurement of the independent variables, there is a need for parsimony in the number of independent variables used to specify our model as a multiple regression equation. Inspection of the data in Table 2.10 indicate that there are no serious problems of multi-colinearity — i.e. pronounced inter-correlations between the independent variables — which would make spurious the identification of the unique contribution of different variables to the accounting of variance in the dependent variable. Although we can account for 85% of the variance in political instability using all ten independent variables, the values of many regression coefficients are small and statistically insignificant, and it is advisable to reduce the number of independent variables as we have done in Table 2.11. Because of the theoretical importance, already discussed, of the interaction between income inequality and linguistic heterogeneity, we have constructed a single independent variable as the product of the public sector employment concentration and the linguistic heterogeneity measures. The remaining five independent variables represent a single measure for each of the economic development, social mobilization, legitimacy, coercion and foreign dependency components of our model.

As indicated in Table 2.11, this specification of our model using six independent variables accounts for 75% of the total variation in the political instability index. Using alternate indicators for the different components of the model, we obtained fractionally less variance accounted for, and no change in the signs of the coefficients. These standardized partial regression coefficients, it is important to observe, retain the same signs as given for the zero-order correlation coefficients, and indicate that the direct effect of a given component of the model

TABLE 2.11   Multiple Regression Equation for Variables Measuring Components of the Political Instability Model

Dependent Variable

Political Instability Index

Independent Variables	*Regression Coefficient*	*Multiple R*
1. Linguistic heterogeneity x% wage earners in public sector	.344	.72
2. Trade with ex-metro power as % total trade	−.184	.74
3. Average annual military expenditures	.004	.75
4. Percent vote for ruling party	−.546	.85
5. Average annual increase in GDP per capita	−.013	.86
6. Percent increase in radios per capita	−.149	.87
		$R^2 = .75$

on the explanation of political instability has the form suggested by our hypotheses. It is interesting, here, to note that the ambiguous directionality of the relationship between social mobilization measures revealed in our earlier analysis is resolved by multiple regression analysis in which both the school enrollment and the radio receiver measures have inverse relationships to the index of political instability.

Although the summary explanation given in Table 2.11 here is theoretically coherent and accounts for a very substantial proportion of the variance in the political instability index, the small size of some coefficients, particularly those for the economic development and military appropriations measures, indicates that the contribution of some variables to a linear additive explanation of the phenomenon of political instability in Black Africa is somewhat tenuous. The economic development measures – i.e. measures of GNP and GDCF – are themselves inter-correlated, and the capital formation measure is strongly associated with the measure of foreign aid, as we would expect, but otherwise these measures of economic development are only very weakly connected with other elements in our model. The correlations that do exist are theoretically valid, and we can have some confidence that the measures of economic development are therefore themselves tolerably reliable. It has, nevertheless, to be said that at this stage in the development of Black African countries, economic development remains a euphemism for economies still substantially below any threshold at which sustained economic growth is observable and effectively related to growth in social mobilization and to the regulation of political conflict. There is, nevertheless, a slight tendency, which should not be completely discounted, for measures of economic development to be inversely related to measures of political instability.

The weak link between the measure of military expenditures and political instability reviewed in Table 2.11 is intelligible for reasons discussed previously in this chapter. Of particular importance, in this connection, is the previous evidence for non-linear relationships between military appropriations and political instability. It is predictable, that is, that were we to include in the equation summarized in Table 2.11, the military appropriations measure raised to the power given by the coefficient in the log-linear regression of that measure against the political instability index, we would obtain a significant increase in the value of the regression coefficient for that transformed variable and in the total variance accounted for. In the same connection, the behavior of the military appropriations measure in a log-linear specification of the model summarized in Table 2.11 is instructive.

The data in Table 2.12 shows the comparable results for the multiple regression equation discussed in Table 2.11 when all variables are transformed to logarithms. The theoretical interest in this transformation is that it treats the explanation of political instability as a multiplicative not additive function of the independent variables – i.e. as a function of the interaction of all the independent variables. Such an explanation has plausibility not simply because of our earlier indication that interaction effects involving some pair-wise combinations of independent variables are discernable in relation to the political instability index, but also because of persuasive evidence in support of Steven's Law that the magnitude of a psychological sensation always increases as a power function of the magnitude of a related physical stimulus, and of the application of this law to the relationship between aggregate behavioral phenomenon (such as voting, or in this case political instability) and social-structural contexts to which such phenomena may be said to 'react.' (See Stevens, 1968 and 1975). The results in Table 2.12 do *not* indicate that the multiplicative model is a better explanation of political instability in Black African countries than the corresponding linear model, but they emphasize dramatically the importance of the military appropriations measure in the multiplicative as opposed to the additive model. The military appropriations measure has the lowest weight in the additive explanation, and the highest weight in the multiplicative model, indicating the fundamental importance to the explanation of political instability of the interaction of coercion with other components in our model.

Finally, it is important to ask a further question about the adequacy of the explanation of political instability discussed so far – namely, to what extent are the errors of estimates given by a multiple regression specification of the model associated with some underlying pattern of variation not included in the measurements we have used to describe the model. This question can be addressed by analysis of the distribution of residuals from the multiple regression equation given in Table 2.11. The relevant information is given in Table 2.13, which shows that in the case of Zaire and Chad we have considerably under-estimated the extent of political instability, and that in the case of Zambia, Upper Volta, Guinea, Gabon and Cameroon we have over-estimated the extent of instability, when using the multiple regression model. In all other cases, the fit of the predicted and actual values of the political instability index is relatively good. The outlying cases in this analysis of residuals do not easily suggest an underlying pattern of explanation for their departures from the model's prediction. Only three of these

TABLE 2.12   Multiple Regression Equation for Variables Measuring Components of the Political Instability Model Where All Variables are Expressed as Logarithms.

Dependent Variable

Political Instability Index (Log)

Independent Variables	Regression Coefficient	Multiple R
1. Trade with ex-metropolitan power as percent total trade (Log)	− .29	.33
2. Average annual military expenditures (Log)	.54	.68
3. Percent vote for ruling party (Log)	− .42	.76
4. Average annual increase in GNP per capita (Log)	− .04	.77
5. Percent increase in radios per capita (Log)	.05	.77
6. Percent wage earners in the public sector (Log)	− .22	.78
7. Linguistic heterogeneity (Log)	.09	.78
		$R^2 = .61$

TABLE 2.13   Residuals from Multiple Regression Model Summarized in Table 2.11.

Political Instability

	Observed	Predicted	Residual
Benin	140.00	169.05	− 29.05
Burundi	130.00	95.20	34.80
Cameroon	15.00	94.97	− 79.97
CAR	40.00	1.03	38.97
Chad	195.00	68.48	126.52
Congo	125.00	86.22	38.78
Ethiopia	320.00	249.14	− 70.86
Gabon	15.00	114.36	− 99.36
Gambia	0.00	90.52	− 90.52
Ghana	115.00	136.40	− 21.40
Guinea	20.00	106.75	− 86.75
Ivory Coast	60.00	− .37	60.37
Kenya	115.00	140.31	4.69
Liberia	30.00	10.71	19.29
Malawi	5.00	17.75	− 12.75
Mali	95.00	115.16	− 20.16
Mauritania	20.00	− 14.91	34.91
Niger	5.00	12.25	− 7.25
Nigeria	330.00	349.03	− 19.03
Rwanda	150.00	86.97	63.03
Senegal	30.00	13.62	16.38
Sierra Leone	65.00	68.16	− 3.16
Somalia	70.00	25.84	44.16
Sudan	490.00	478.30	11.70
Tanzania	0.00	51.20	− 51.20
Togo	100.00	136.57	− 36.57
Uganda	160.00	165.77	− 5.77
Upper Volta	35.00	115.38	− 80.38
Zambia	30.00	101.12	− 71.12
Zaire	370.00	220.03	150.00

cases for which the model gives poor predictions are nations that were not formerly French colonies, so that there is a sense in which colonial inheritance may be seen as an additional underlying factor accounting for political instability in these countries, which needs to be taken into account in more adequate specifications of the model. In addition, the inadequate fit of the model predictions for the small states—Gabon, Guinea, Gambia—suggests that size may still be an important additional independent source of variation in political instability, but there are the same number of larger states for which the model over-estimates the extent of political instability, and the predictions for two of the larger states under-estimate the extent of political instability. We must leave to further research the question of a more exact specification of the model by inclusion of yet other conceptually relevant variables or the possible improvement of the pattern of explanation by movement towards more exact measurement of the variables that we have discussed.

Conclusions

This analysis of a macro-analytic model of political instability in Black African states is a preliminary attempt to suggest the most general form of an explanation of patterns of political change in this region. Preliminary though the analysis is, there are a number of quite positive conclusions to be drawn from it.

First, it seems clear that meaningful statistical generalizations *can* be made about the determinants of political instability in Black African states. At least, it should be clear that it is incumbent on those who dispute such a conclusion to indicate clearly and with reference to specific statistical analysis why statistical patterns are spurious, what theoretical errors or ambiguities invalidate the logic of conclusions derived from such statistical patterns, what threats to the validity of the statistical measures as operationalizations of the theoretical process examined invalidate the conclusion, and what distributions of error in the measurement of such variables are the cause of spurious generalization.

Second, it is clear that an explanation such as that given in this Chapter by no means exhausts the domain of meaningful explanatory statements about the incidence of political instability in these countries. Complimentary, and no doubt rival theories to the model investigated here may prove to have equal or greater explanatory power. What such alternative explanations may be is essentially a matter for empirical demonstration, however. Whether the essential form of the relationship between political instability and the other processes described in our model are significantly modified by the inclusion of yet other empirically defined processes must await such demonstration. For the moment, however, we are confident that the results of this analysis indicate that our general hypotheses about the basic underlying relationships affecting these variables are empirically supportable, and that together they provide a coherent and well generalized explanation of political instability in these states.

Third, the analysis presented here suggests certain strategies for future research. The fundamental strategy would be to treat each component of our model as a block of interrelated components of sub-systems of the larger political system and to reformulate the model as a block recursive system with more complex patterns of inter-relationship between these components within any sub-system, but with the same simplified linkages between the block components of the overall model. The summary, "umbrella" concepts that describe the components of our model cannot, without excess simplification, be operationalized by single variables, and we need to investigate more intricate, multi-variate processes underlying foreign dependency, economic development, social mobilization and legitimation. Particularly important, from the point of view of the argument we have outlined here, will be the detailed investigation of public policy in these countries as it affects economic development, social mobilization, income inequality, coercion and legitimation. Two other strategies for future research are, however, equally desirable. One is to move from the cross-sectional analysis presented here to temporal analysis in which the model is operationalized for individual countries at different points in time. Such analysis will not be possible before substantially better time-series for most of these measures becomes available. The data in this edition of the Handbook is an attempt to move in that direction, however. The other strategy is to explore the underlying dynamics of the model at different "levels of analysis," by focusing on the political behavior of individuals in relation to their differing ethnic and class positions, their exposure to social mobilization and their experience of economic mobility, their involvement in different social and political networks of associations and formal organizations, and their perceptions of the benefits and beneficiaries of public policy.

Notes

[1]See the witty and tough-minded critique of the 'Leisure of the Theory Class' in Dudley, 1973.

[2]In Africa, the obvious cases to which this argument applies or applied are Rwanda, Burundi, Zanzibar, Zimbabwe, the Republic of South Africa, and the former Portuguese colonies, as well as some pre-colonial African states.

[3]The measurement difficulties relate both to the identification of the sub-national societies into which the population is grouped, and to the measurement of variation between such groups on indicators of cultural and institutional values. See the discussion in Morrison and Stevenson, 1972.

[4]See, for example, the work of Michael Hechter, *Internal Colonialism: The Celtic Fringe in British National Development 1536-1966*, Berkeley, CA.: University of California Press, 1975.

[5]Compare especially the work of Epstein, 1958, 1981 and Cohen, 1969 and the interesting evaluation of the relative importance of different intervening variables in Bates, 1976.

References.

Adelman, I. and C. T. Morris.
1969   "Society, Politics and Economic Development in Africa." In *Expanding Horizons in African Studies*, eds., G. Carter and A. Paden. Evanston, Ill.: Northwestern University Press.

Almond, G. A. and B. Powell
1978   *Comparative Politics* 2nd. ed. Little Brown.

Apthorpe, R. J.
1970   in *Co-operatives and Rural Development in East Africa*, C. G. Widstrand ed. Uppsala: Scandanavian Institute of African Studies, New York: Africana.

Bates, R. H.
1976   *Rural Responses to Industrialization*, New Haven: Yale University Press.
1981   *Markets and States in Tropical Africa*, Berkeley: University of California Press.

Brodbeck, May.
1968   *Readings in the Philosophy of Science*, New York: Macmillan.

Bwy, D. P.
1968   "Political Instability in Latin America," *Latin American Research Review* v. 3, 17-66.

Cohen, A.
1969   *Custom and Politics in Urban Africa: A Study of Hausa Migration in Yoruba Towns*, Berkeley: University of California Press.

Cohen, Ronald and John Middleton.
1970   *From Tribe to Nation*, eds., Scranton, Penn.: Chandler Publishing Co.

Davies, J. C.
1970   *When Men Revolt and Why*, New York: Free Press.

De Calo, S.
1975   *Coups and Army Rule in Africa*. New Haven: Yale University Press.

Deutsch, Karl W.
1966   *Nationalism and Social Communication*. Cambridge, Mass.: MIT Press, 2nd. Edition.

Dowse, Robert E.
1969   "The Military and Political Development." In Colin Leys, ed., *Politics and Change in Developing Countries: Studies in the Theory and Practice of Development*. London: Cambridge University Press, 213—246.

Dudley, B. J.
1973   *Instability and Political Order: Politics and Crisis in Nigeria*. Ibadan: Ibadan University Press.

Easton, D.
1965   *A Systems Analysis of Political Life*, New York: Wiley.
1981   *The Political System*, 2nd ed. reprinted, New York: Knopf.

Eckstein, H.
1961   *A Theory of Stable Democracy*, Woodrow Wilson School, Princeton University.
1979   *Support for Regimes: Theories and Tests*, Princeton: Woodrow Wilson School.

Eckstein, H. and T. R. Gurr
1975   *Patterns of Authority*, New York: Wiley.

Epstein, A. L.
1958   *Politics in an Urban African Community*. Manchester: Manchester University Press.
1978   *Ethos and Identity*, Chicago: Aldine.
1981   *Urbanization and Kinship*, New York: Academic Press.

Etzioni, A.
1965   *Political Unification*, New York: Holt, Rinehart and Winston.
1973   *Social Change* 2nd ed. New York: Basic Books.

Feierabend, I.R., R.L. Feierabend, and T. R. Gurr.
1972   *Anger, Violence and Politics*, New York.

Finer, S. E.
1967   "The One Party Regimes in Africa: Reconsiderations." *Government and Opposition*, 2 (July/October), 491—508.

First, Ruth.
1970   *The Barrel of a Gun: Political Power in Africa and the Coup d'État*. London: The Penguin Press.

Furnivall, J. S.
1938   *Netherlands India: A Study of Plural Economy*. Cambridge, Cambridge University Press.
1948   *Colonial Polity and Practice*. Cambridge: Cambridge University Press.

Galtung, Johan.
1964   "A Structural Theory of Aggression." *Journal of Peace Research*, 2, 95—115.

Gurr, Ted R.
1968   "A Causal Model of Civil Strife," *American Political Science Review* 63 1104-1124.
1970   *Why Men Rebel*. Princeton, N.J.: Princeton University Press.

Holt and, R. T. and J. E. Turner.
1970   *The Methodology of Comparative Research.* N.Y.: Free Press.

Huntington, Samuel P.
1968   *Political Order in Changing Societies.* New Haven: Yale University Press.
1971   "The Change to Change," *Comparative Politics,* 3,3 283-322.

Janowitz, M.
1964   *The Military in the Political Development of New Nations.* Chicago: University of Chicago Press.

Kaplan, A.
1964   *The Conduct of Inquiry.* San Francisco: Chandler.

Kuhn, Thomas S.
1970   *The Structure of Scientific Revolutions.* 2nd edition.

Kuper, Leo and M. G. Smith.
1969   *Pluralism in Africa,* eds., Berkeley: University of California Press.

Lipset, S. M.
1960   *Political Man.* Garden City, N.Y.: Doubleday Anchor Books.

McGowan, P. and H. Shapiro.
1973   *The Comparative Study of Foreign Policy.* Beverly Hills, Ca.: Sage.

Melson, Robert and Howard Wolpe.
1970   "Modernization and the Politics of Communalism: A Theoretical Persepctive." *American Political Science Review,* LXIV (December), 1112—1130.

Morrison, D. G. and H. M. Stevenson.
1971   "Political Instability in Independent Black Africa: Continuities and Extensions in the Quantitative Study of Dimensions of Conflict Behavior Within Nations." *Journal of Conflict Resolution* (September).
1972a   "Cultural Pluralism, Modernization and Conflict: an Empirical Analysis of Sources of Political Instability in African Nations." *Canadian Journal of Political Science,* 82-103.
1972b   "Inegration and Instability: Patterns of African Political Development." *American Political Science Review* 66 p.902-927.
1973   *Conflict and Violence in Black Africa.* Toronto: York University, mimeo.
1974a   "Measuring Social and Political Requirements for System Stability: Empirical Validation of an Index Using Latin American and African Data." *Comparative Political Studies* July 7,2 252-263.

1974b   "Social Complexity, Economic Development and Military Coups d'Etat: Convergence and Divergence of Empirical Tests of Theory in Latin America, Asia and Africa." *Journal of Peace Research* 345-347.

Muller, E. N.
1972   "A Test of a Partial Theory of Potential for Political Violence." *American Political Science Review,* 66, 3 (September), 928—959.
1979   *Aggressive Political Participation,* Princeton: Princeton University Press.

Nisbet, R. A.
1969   *Social Change and History,* New York: Oxford University Press.

Oberschall, A.
1973   *Social Conflict and Social Movements,* Englewood Cliffs, N.J.: Prentice Hall.

O'Connell, I.
1967   "The Inevitability of Instability." *Journal of Modern African Studies,* V. 181—191.

Olsen, Mancur, Jr.
1963   "Rapid Growth as a Destabilizing Force." *Journal of Economic History.* 23 (December), 529—552.

Paden, J.
1973   *Religion and Political Culture in Kano,* Berkeley: University of California Press.
1980   *Values, Identity and National Integration,* Evanston: Northwestern University Press.

Peil, M.
1972   *The Ghanaian Factory Worker,* New York: Cambridge University Press.
1976   *Nigerian Politics,* London: Cassell.

Pye, L. W. and Sidney Verba (eds.)
1965   *Political Culture and Political Development.* Princeton, N.J.: Princeton University Press.

Rogers, E.
1969   *Modernization Among Peasants,* New York: Holt, Rinehart Winston.
1981   *Communications Networks,* New York, Free Press.

Sherif, M. A.
1967   *Social Interaction, Process and Products: Selected Essays,* Chicago, Aldine.

Sigelman, Lee.
1974   "Lerner's Model of Modernization," in *Journal of the Developing Areas* 8,3 375-394.

Stevens, S. S.
1968   "Measurement, Statistics aand the Schemapiric View," *Science* 30 August, 849-856.
1975   *Psychophysics,* New York: Wiley.

Stevenson, H. M. and D. G. Morrison.
1973   *External Dependency and National Political Instability in Black Africa*, paper presented to the World Congress of Africanists in Addis Ababa.

Thomas, D. B.
1974   "Political Development Theory and Africa: Toward a Conceptual Clarification and Comparative Analysis." *Journal of the Developing Areas*, 8, 3, 375-94.

Van den Berghe, Pierre.
1963   "Dialectic and Functionalism: Toward a Theoretic Synthesis." *American Sociological Review*, 28 695—705.
1964   "Towards a Sociology for Africa." *Social Forces*, 43 (October), 11—18.

Welfling, M.
1975   *Political Institutionalization*, Beverly Hills: Sage.

Wells, A.
1974   "The Coup d'État in Theory and Practice: Independent Black Africa in the 1960's." *American Journal of Sociology*, 79, 871—887.

Zolberg, Aristide.
1968   "The Structure of Political Conflict in the New States of Tropical Africa." *American Political Science Review*, LXII (March), 70—87.
1968   "Military Intervention in the New States of Tropical Africa: Elements of Comparative Analysis." in Henry Bienen, ed., *The Military Intervenes*. New York: Russell Sage Foundation, 1968, 71—98.
1973   *World Politics*.

3. Measures, Models and Meaning in Aggregate Data for African States

Introduction

In recent years there has been a considerable upsurge in the use of aggregate data for cross-national or holonational studies (Naroll, 1972). This work has been stimulated by, and has stimulated, a dramatic growth in the creation of computer accessible or machine-readable aggregate-data sets descriptive of regional samples or of the universe of nation-states (Russett, et al., 1964; Rummel, 1972; Feierabend and Feierabend, 1965; Gurr, 1966; Adelman and Morris,, 1967 and 1973; Schmitter, 1970; Banks and Textor, 1964; Morrison et. al., 1972; Taylor and Hudson, 1972; Singer, 1972; McGowan, 1974).

Research in the social sciences using such data has been oriented towards the empirical evaluation of theoretical models intended to explain various aspects of national systems development; and accepts the basic scientific assumption that "to the understanding of the world about us, neither the formal model nor the concrete measure is dispensable" (Stevens, 1968). Despite broad methodological and epistemological agreement, the growth of cross-national research, particularly that dealing with problems of political change and development, has been marked by a proliferation of conflicting empirical conclusions. In the face of this confusion it is becoming increasing clear that basic problems of measurement reliability and validity in the operationalization and use of different data sets need more attention than they have been given thus far.

In this chapter we discuss, with detailed reference to a number of recent publications that deal with comparative aggregate analysis of the development of African states, three central problems: (1) measurement error in single items; (2) index construction and the reduction of measurement error; and (3) measurement error and the evaluation of theoretical models. The first two of these problems concern issues of 'internal validity', while the last has to do with 'external validity' in generalizations about social phenomena (Campbell and Stanley, 1963). Our discussion of the first issue will concentrate on the evaluation of inter-coder reliability for measures involving identical operationalizations and observation sources, inter-source reliability for measures involving identical operationalizations but different sources of observation, inter-temporal reliability for measures involving identical operationalizations and sources of observation but different periods of observation, and problems of construct validity related to inadequate conceptualization and operationalization of measures[1]. With respect to the second problem, we shall deal with the evaluation of multi-item index construction, and with the evaluation of the utility of such procedures for the reduction of measurement error in the operationalization of critical theoretical concepts. In dealing with the last problem, we shall review and critically evaluate conflicting generalizations based on aggregate data descriptive of African states that purport to explain facets of the development of these nations.

The argument in this chapter will be critical of existing comparative cross-national research on African national development, but at the same time insistent on the great potential value of such research when based on appropriate methodological criteria for measurement adequacy. The professional credibility of cross-national aggregate data analysis is greatly jeopardized by the proliferation of research which minimized lack of attention to measurement issues by reference to the 'inductive' or exploratory nature of the inquiry. The threat is not simply that a professional community may be grossly misrepresenting reality, but that the 'reality' they purport to discover may be accepted as such by political authorities for public policy purposes. If cross-national research is to grow as a useful arm of empirical social science, it is vital that the primacy of measurement validity in the canon of scientific methodology be emphasised, especially in areas of investigation where these criteria are most difficult to meet--as in the measurement of the economic and political development of Black African states.

1. Measurement Models: Sources of Error

Scientific generalizations or 'explanations' are derived from the formulation of theory; the construction of models which represent the form of the relationships between concepts as defined in theory, and the testing of such models by reference to empirical data describing the relevant entities to which the theory applies. The meaning of explanations so arrived at is governed by the logical consistency of the theoretical argument; by the structural identity of the model used to represent the theoretical argument, and by the validity and reliability of the empirical data used as measures of the phenomena being explained.

Error in scientific generalizations arises, therefore, as a result of logical fallacies in the theoretical argument, or as a result of logically correct deductions based on incorrect assumptions; as a result of inappropriate or incomplete specifications of theoretical models (generally referred to as specification error), the results of which are to ignore phenomena which critically affect the structure of relationships between concepts included in the model; as a result of failures to observe sufficiently representative or large samples of the entities to which the empirical generalizations are applied (generally referred to as sampling error); as a result of assuming that a particular set of indicators constitute equivalent or sufficient operationalizations of concepts that have to be measured (generally referred to as the problem of validity); as a result of error in the observations coded on some measure to describe the conceptual attributes of the units of analysis (generally referred to as the problem of reliability); and as a result of errors of statistical inference, in which the analyst accepts or rejects the null hypothesis of no relationship of the kind specified by theory when the opposite conclusion is true, despite the low probability of its being so.

These abbreviated remarks emphasize the priority of theory in the construction of meaningful generalizations about African states or any other phenomena. Errors of logic, specification, sampling, measurement, or statistical inference can rarely be definitively resolved, and the plausibility of theoretical argument must be the ultimate guide to the meaning of generalizations about the external world. It is, nevertheless, the strength of scientific methodology, as a critical approach to meaning, that it attempts systematically to isolate and to evaluate sources of error in explanations that purport to be empirically valid. The *sine qua non* of such critical evaluations is the consideration of measurement error.

A useful point of departure for our consideration of measurement error in aggregate data describing African countries is an article entitled "Models, Measurement and Sources of Error: Civil Conflict in Black Africa" (Welfling, 1975). Measurement error is here referred to as "the problem of inaccuracy in concept scores," and is properly conceptualized in terms of "the twin issues of reliability and validity" (p. 876). Validity is defined as "the degree to which we are measuring," and is evaluated by reference to arguments for *face validity* — i.e., the degree of statistical relationship between the indicator and other measures (whose validity and reliability are assumed) to which it is theoretically related. Reliability is defined as a problem of "the consistency and accuracy of our measures, assuming their validity." Reliability, that is, refers to the extent of inter-subjective agreement on the part of independent observers as to the scores to be

assigned the same phenomena using the same indicators, or more generally, the agreement between observers, using equally valid but not identical indicators, as to the variation in the conceptual attributes measured by those indicators in application to the same set of units of observation.

Validity and reliability are, therefore, closely inter-related properties of measurement error. The upper limit of an estimate of the validity of any indicator is a direct function of the reliability of that indicator. Although it is possible to develop formal analytic models of the relationship between these twin properties of measurement error, operational procedures for identifying the validity components of single measures are not as easy to develop as estimates of reliability derived from the correlation of independent sets of observations. The nature of the errors of measurement identified by such procedures is not, however, easily described. Errors of observation, that is, may be random or systematic. If systematic, they may be related in a linear or non-linear fashion to the values of the attribute being measured, or to values of attributes not being measured. Finally, the errors of observation may be common to independent sets of observations or unequally distributed among them.

In her attempt to isolate and identify these various sources of measurement error in two independent sets of data on African nations, Welfling proposes the following general "model of measurement"

$$X' = X + f(X) + g(Z) + c + e$$

Where X' = observed score X = 'true' score
Z = Other variables C = Constant
e = random disturbances

The assumptions of this model are that errors of observation (i.e., variation in X' not accounted for by the 'true' variation in X) are attributable to (a) non-linear components of systematic bias in observation, since $f(X)$ can only be part of some function of X not accounted for by X alone (vis. a non-linear component) in order to be independently estimated in the model, and since $g(Z)$ can only include those variables which are not constant or random in their effects on X, or (b) to random errors of observation not correlated with any of the other terms in the right-hand side of the equation and not correlated in two or more independent sets of observations of the measure.

From these assumptions, Welfling attempts to derive certain decision rules "to estimate the nature and extent of measurement error from the correlation between two measures of a concept." She attempts, first, to make deductions from the model as to the likelihood of different components of error (random, systematic and linear, or

TABLE 3.1   Decision Rules for Type of Error as a Function of Observed Correlation Between Independent Measures of a Concept

Correlation	Possible Types of Error		
Value	*Random*	*Systematic-Linear*	*Systematic-Nonlinear*
High (close to 1.00)	Small, random	Systematic linear in at least one of the data sets	Nonlinear systematic but of the same form in both data sets
Medium (?)	?	?	?
Low (differ greatly from 1.00)	At least one score contains large random component	None	At least one score nonlinear systematic.

systematic and non-linear) from inspection of the correlations between observations of the same concept using equivalent indicators in two independent sets of data on a sample of African countries. These deductions are summarized in Table 3.1 which shows that few constraints on the possibilities of different types of error in independent sets of observations can be made from inspection of the correlations between them. This is especially true, as we indicate in the table, since no threshold values are given to distinguish low and high correlations. Welfling proceeds, however, to propose a means of distinguishing random from systematic error as the dominant source of error in correlated indicators of the same concept, and of determining the extent to which systematic error may be shared among two indicators or be unique to one of them.

This ambitious effort depends on an argument that if two measures of the same concept correlate very differently with a criterion measure of some other theoretically related concept, then systematic error is involved in at least one bias in observation, since f(X) has to be part of some function of X not accounted for by X alone in order to be independently estimated in the model, and since g(Z) can only include (a) those variables which are not constant or random in their effects on X, or (b) random errors of observation not correlated with any of the other terms in the right hand side of the equation and not correlated in two or more independent sets of observations for the measure whose error properties we are evaluating. This argument depends on the assumption that random error in each of the independent observations of the same concept will attenuate the correlation of each of those measures with the criterion third variable, and that the attenuation in correlation due to random error will be

similar in each case. This argument is false, since there is no basis for assuming that random error in the two independent sets of observations would act to attenuate their correlation with the criterion variable in the same amount. Since the extent to which random or systematic error affects the intercorrelation between two independent sets of observations of the same concept cannot be determined by inspection of the difference in correlation between these measures and a third criterion variable, Welfling's subsequent procedure for determining whether or not systematic error is shared or unique to one of two independent sets of observations of *related* concepts, by inspection of the difference in covariance between the related measures as scored in the two data sets, is likewise unacceptable.

While, therefore, Welfling's discussion usefully indicates the complexity involved in the identification of possible sources of error in measurement, she radically misrepresents the difficulty of operationally estimating the effects of different error terms in independent sets of observations of the same concepts. Were procedures like those she recommends acceptable, we would be close to the reconstruction of error-free data, and could for example move quickly to unbiased estimates of theoretical models of civil conflict and other phenomena in African states. We cannot, however, be so sanguine. Adequate formal analysis of the covariance of independent indicators of the same concepts has not yet been applied to measurement models as complex as the one Welfling describes. The investigation of 'simpler' models has been far advanced in the psychometric literature (see Nunnally, 1967), and the analytic demonstration of the reliability of factor-analytic indices of attributes measured by multiple indicators with random error is, for example, well understood (Cronbach, 1972). Similarly, it is possible to estimate 'true' correlations between concepts by adjusting for the estimated attenuation due to random error and the inflation due to correlated method effects in multiples of each of the terms. Both the latter error terms can be estimated as unmeasured variables in multivariate models[3]. Such estimation requires, however, progressively more stringent assumptions; more exacting demands for the extensive replication of data collection, and the use of multiple methods of observing the same concepts. Such demands are much more easily satisfied in survey research, for example, than in cross-national research using aggregate data.

In this latter area it would be wise not to rush in where angels fear to tread. In what follows, therefore, we attempt simply to underline the importance of systematically evaluating the reliability of aggregate data by the direct comparison of independent observations using the same indicators. We use correlation coefficients to estimate the magnitude of measurement error involved in such independent observations, but make no attempt to isolate the various sources of such error. We go on to show that multiple-item scaling procedures applied to aggregate data on African countries tend to show converging patterns of dimensionality in independently collected observations using indicators which are themselves of dubious reliability. We show, that is, that the dimensionality of these data sets is more reliably described than are the differences in national attributes using the original indicators. Finally, we show that the operationalization of models using homogeneous multiple item scales, rather that the original items on which they are based, increases the convergence of estimates of the structure of such models across independent sets of observations. We hope that such practical illustrations of the problems of reliability in aggregate data on African countries, and of the prospects for dealing intelligently with unreliable data, will justify some cautious optimism in the approach to data such as those given in this book. Such optimism cannot serve as an excuse, however, to evade the very pressing need to develop more and more sophisticated models of measurement, and the means with which to apply such models to the isolation and estimation of errors in aggregate data.

(2) Estimates of Error in Single Items.

As a basic reference for the analysis of measurement problems associated with studies of development in Black African countries, we shall refer to the data compiled and used by Professors Adelman and Morris (1967). This work is chosen not only because of its intrinsic substantive interest, related as it is to the analysis of the so-

cio-political determinants of economic development, but also because of its use by other authors dealing with problems of African political development (Thomas, 1974, and Sigelman, 1974). An initial evaluation of the utility of the measures reported by Adelman and Morris, and of the analysis based on these measures, referred to as recoding of their variables, and to an assessment of the intercoder reliability reflected in this recoding exercise follows.

Two coders each undertook an independent recoding of 22 of the original 24 variables described by Adelman and Morris. The two variables excluded from this exercise were those labelled 'degree of administrative efficiency' and 'extent of centralization of political power' for which the conceptualizations and operationalizations were not sufficiently well-defined to enable us to make use of them. In all other cases, the data sources for recoding these variables were derived from the holdings of the African National Integration Project (ANIP) data archives, which include the data reported in both editions of this Handbook. Recoding was carried out for 20 Black African countries, as described in the Appendix to this chapter. This set of African countries differs slightly from that analysed by Thomas and Sigelman who, in addition to dealing with these 20 countries, deal also with Zimbabwe (then Rhodesia), South Africa and Madagascar. We omit the latter because of inadequate information at our disposal at the time this review was undertaken, and we omit the former two countries because of their unique status as white minority-controlled regimes. The face validity of the indicators used to describe these two countries is questionable since the Adelman and Morris data (circa 1960) show only two of the other Black African countries having stronger democratic institutions, only five with greater freedom of the press and opposition, and none with a more competitive party system than South Africa and Rhodesia. The 20 nations in our recoded sample are all, except for Ghana, included in Adelman and Morris' (1969) sample of African countries, which, however, includes the North African countries, Rhodesia, South Africa and Malagasy. When, therefore, we have occasion later in this chapter to compare factor analytic results based on our recoded sample with results obtained from slightly different samples used by these other authors, some differences may be due to sample deviations.

In Table 3.2, squared Pearson product-moment coefficients are used as reliability indices for the 22 Adelman-Morris variables as coded by them and by one of the coders, for the original period of observaton. The value of these indices is surprisingly low (that is, they indicate less than 50% shared variance between the two independent codings for at least 70% of these measures). These indices provide a discouraging picture to those wishing to use such data to analyze the effects of socio-political characteristics on economic development in Black African countries, as Adelman and Morris do (1969), or the role of socio-economic factors in the political development of these nations as Thomas (1974) and Sigelman (1974) do. While we cannot assert that the recoded data are generally correct and the original data are generally in error, we can make some inferences about the reliability of these measures.

First, the heavy reliance on 'expert' judgement in the measurement of these variables means an equivalently great sensitivity of coding to the sources of information available to the experts. The recodings profit, we believe, from later, more accurate, evaluations of data for the period for which the variables are measured, and from more intensive data collection with respect to a number of key variables. This is particularly the case with respect to the socio-political measures as will be discussed later. Second, even with strict equivalence in the source information from which the codings were made, the conceptualization and operationalization of a large majority of these variables by Adelman and Morris inhibits inter-subjective agreement. This is the case because some of the variables are defined in terms of categories that are not mutually exclusive or collectively exhaustive of the empirical possibilities – for example, the 'mass communications' and 'basis of the political party system' measures. This latter difficulty seems to have been apparent from the initial returns from the experts consulted by Adelman and Morris, and their strategy of changing the coding conventions, or the definition, of the variable in response to ambiguous information received from experts did little, apparently to resolve the threats to the reliability in the original conceptualization of these variables. Third, we should point out that the reliability index used in Table 3.2 is sensitive to the extent of variance in the measures being compared, and that many of the very low reliability scores may be artifacts of the non-linear transformation procedure that Adelman and Morris use to map the original letter codes onto a set of numbers. In the case of a relatively homogeneous sample like the one we are dealing with, this procedure tends often to artifactually inflate the variance and skew the distribution of individual measures (cf. Mitchell and Morrison 1970)

Having found low reliability in the coding for the original period for which data are reported by Adelman and Morris, we investigated the reliability of these measures further by recoding the variables for the same sample, but for a later time period. Two coders, therefore, independently coded the sample on these measures for a time period ten years after that specified in the original Adel-

man-Morris coding, and from this exercise we evaluate the inter-coder reliability of the measures for the later time period. This recoding was based on information from identical source materials. We evaluate as well the inter-temporal variability of the codings by author for the two different periods, in order to assess possible deviations from expected temporal trends on these measures due to unreliability.

In Table 3.3, we present the results of the coder reliability study for the Adelman and Morris variables coded for our African sample in the period circa 1970. Specifically, the variables were recoded for a period ten years later than the original codings so that a variable originally coded for 1960 was coded for 1970, a variable for the period 1957 to 1962 was coded for 1967 to 1972, etc. The reliability indices in this table measure the extent of agreement between the independent codings by the two authors. The overall results can be summarized quickly. Overall reliabilities are somewhat higher than those derived from the comparison of our recoding with that of Adelman and Morris as given in Table 3.2 (.51 compared to .38), but the dramatic differences are in the reliabilities of different types of variables. Variables measured by reference to strictly quantitative and well defined data, e.g. per capita GNP, are, as expected, of a satisfactory reliability, but those variables measured in part or exclusively by reference to expert judgement have unsatisfactory reliability. Further the evidence in Table 3.3 is that there is relatively greater reliability in the strictly judgmental variables than in those variables where complex combinations of judgement and reference to quantitative data are required, in contrast to the higher reliability of the partly judgemental variables. The reliabilities of the judgmental and partly judgmental variables, judgmental variables found earlier in Table 3.2, however, are low and roughly in the same range as those reported in Table 3.2, and they are substantially lower than the reliabilities for the quantitative indices. The purpose of constructing judgmental indicators is, of course, to get some measure of crucial theoretical concepts for which adequate quantitative measures do not exist. The lesson, however, is clear - that the search for increase in validity is purchased at the cost of a generally unacceptable decline in reliability.

In Table 3.4, we present correlation coefficients for the measures of the Adelman-Morris variables coded by one of the coders in the two different time periods noted in Tables 3.2 and 3.3. The data in Table 3.4 show that some indicators are very highly correlated over·the ten year period and that some have virtually no inter-temporal correlation. On closer inspection, there appears to be a pattern in these differences: the social and economic variables have high correlations over time reflecting little

TABLE 3.2   Reliability Indices for 22 Adelman- Morris Variables (ca. 1960) versus Recoding of Same Variables for Same Period by Coder 1.

Type of Variable	Variable	Reliability Index r^2
J	1. Modernization of Outlook	29
Q	2. Per capita GNP	24
PJ	3. Extent of Economic Dualism	88
Q	4. Size of Traditional Agricultural Sector	52
Q	5. Extent of Urbanization	36
Q	6. Literacy Rate	72
Q	7. Social Mobility	12
Q	8. Mass Communications	14
PJ	9. Strength of Democratic Institutions	44
PJ	10. Strength of the Labor Movement	46
PJ	11. Degree of Freedom of Opposition and Press	58
Q	12. Degree of Competitiveness of Political Parties	64
PJ to Q	13. Extent of Political Stability	17
J	14. Political Strength of Traditional Elite	34
PJ	15. Leadership Commitment to Economic Development	59
Q	16. Cultural and Ethnic Homogeneity	40
J	17. National Integration and Sense of Unity	03
Q	18. Crude Fertility Rate	27
PJ	19. Predominant Basis of Political Party System	00
PJ	20. Importance of Indigenous Middle Class	36
J	21. Degree of Social Tension	41
J	22. Political Strength of the Military	49
	Table Average**	38

*Type refer to following categories

Q = quantitative
PJ = partly judgemental − partly quantitative
J = judgemental

**Variable 19 added to the average as a zero because of its negative correlation

Average reliability by type of variable

	r	r^2
Q (9)	59	38
PJ (8)	60	44
J (5)	53	31

*Number of variables of that type in parentheses

change in the rank order of economic development and basic social characteristics such as ethnic homogeneity, dualism, urbanization, etc. Conversely, the political variables are poorly intercorrelated over time. This pattern is intelligible in our view, and reflects no particular source of unreliability in the measures due to temporal insensitivity. With respect, however, to the utility of the original Adelman-Morris measures for the analysis of African national development, the periodicity of the measures of political factors is particularly unfortunate, reflecting, as it does to a considerable degree, colonial constitutional transfers that were flimsily related to the political realities of the new states, and which, it is apparent, have been highly transient, unstable features of the political characteristics of these states during the ensuing period of political independence. From the point of view, there-

TABLE 3.3   Reliability Indices for 22 Adelman- Morris Variables Between Two Alternates Coders for Circa. 1970.

Variable	Reliability index r^2
1. Modernization of Outlook	27
2. Per capita GNP	(100)
3. Extent of Economic Dualism	55
4. Size of Traditional Agricultural Sector	07
5. Extent of Urbanization	50
6. Literacy Rate	(98)
7. Social Mobility	(92)
8. Mass Communications	(88)
9. Strength of Democratic Institutions	22
10. Strength of the Labor Movement	00*
11. Degree of Freedom of Opposition and Press	01
12. Degree of Competitiveness of Political Parties	19
13. Extent of Political Stability	66
14. Political Strength of Traditional Elite	53
15. Leadership Commitment to Economic Development	48
16. Cultural and Ethnic Homogeneity	(76)
17. National Integration and Sense of Unity	16
18. Crude Fertility Rate	(100)
19. Predominant Basis of Political Party System	(71)
20. Importance of Indigenous Middle Class	03
21. Degree of Social Tension	60
22. Political Strength of the Military	(71)
Table Average**	51

Negative correlation taken to be a zero reliability
**Averages taken with variable 10 as a zero

All index scores above 70 are in parentheses

Average by type of variable*

	r	r^2
Q (9)	80	70
PJ (8)	47	33
J (5)	66	45

*Number of variables in each category in parentheses

Note: All decimal points omitted

fore, of cross-sectional comparative analysis, the original Adelman and Morris measures are very poorly related to the usual neo-evolutionary assumption that an equilibrium structure is being analyzed across nations.

It is clear from this analysis of the reliability of measurements for the single items coded by Adelman and Morris, and used subsequently by other authors, that these data are unsatisfactory. We believe that such problems of reliability and stability are generally typical, though not necessarily as pronounced, for all aggregate measures of development in African states. Careful analytic and methodological approaches have to be adopted

TABLE 3.4 Correlation Coefficients for 22 Adelman- Morris Variables ca. 1960 versus ca. 1970 Codings by Coder One.

Variable	Correlation
1. Modernization of Outlook	74
2. Per capita GNP	87
3. Extent of Economic Dualism	95
4. Size of Traditional Agricultural Sector	75
5. Extent of Urbanization	75
6. Literacy Rate	89
7. Social Mobility	84
8. Mass Communications	78
9. Strength of Democratic Institutions	16
10. Strength of the Labor Movement	40
11. Degree of Freedom of Opposition and Press	22
12. Degree of Competitiveness of Political Parties	20
13. Extent of Political Stability	42
14. Political Strength of Traditional Elite	58
15. Leadership Commitment to Economic Development	55
16. Cultural and Ethnic Homogeneity	90
17. National Integration and Sense of Unity	32
18. Crude Fertility Rate	42
19. Predominant Basis of Political Party System	15
20. Importance of Indigenous Middle Class	72
21. Degree of Social Tension	17
22. Political Strength of the Military	08

Average Correlation*

1. Social variables (11)—.74
2. Economic variables   (1)—.87
3. Political variables (10)—.31
4. Overall variables (22)—.55

*Number of variables in each category
in parentheses.

**All decimal points omitted.

for their use, therefore, if any sense is to be made out of them. Before moving to a discussion of methodological procedures by which such errorful measurements may be used with more confidence it is important to substantiate two points: (1) that problems of reliability are typical of single-item aggregate measures derived from authorities other than Adelman and Morris, and (2) that these problems notwithstanding, it is not necessarily the case that *all* single-item measures of development are *ipso facto* unreliable to the same extent.

With respect to the first point about the generality of problems of reliability in single-item measures of development in Black African states, it is useful to look at the data used by Wells (1974) in his attempt to examine the concommitants of variation in the experience of coups d'état in these countries. The independent variables in Wells' analysis are drawn largely from United Nation's statistical handbooks and from a study of the African military by Booth (1970). We have checked these data for reliability by comparing the data Wells reports to data on

TABLE 3.5 Reliability Indices* Between Alternate Codings of Socio-Economic and Military Structure Variables as Coded by Wells and, Morrison and Stevenson.

Indicator	Reliability*
Socio-economic Variables	
1. Population	1.00
2. Population growth rate	.76
3. Urbanization (100,000)	.75
4. Centrality	.74
5. Literacy	.25
6. Mass media	.74
7. Economic growth rate	.08
average	.62
Military Variables	
1. M P R	.74
2. Military size	.79
3. Police size	.86
4. Defense budget	.53
5. Military/Government Budget	.53
6. Military/GNP	.31
average	.63

*squared Pearson product—moment correlation coefficients are used as reliability indices.

the same variables independently collected and published in the first edition of this *Handbook*.

In Table 3.5, we present the reliability indices describing the percentage of shared variance in the data used by Wells and that given in Black Africa. Indices for the 'economic level' measure used by Wells are omitted since our own data are derived from the identical source, and the item measuring cumulated U.S. aid is omitted, since Wells gives no full citation for this item and the World Bank reports to which he refers do not seem to report data in the specific maner he indicates (see Morrison and Stevenson: 1976 for more detail).

The reliabilities for these variables range widely, and although the overall average reliability of these measures is somewhat greater than that indicated for the Adelman-Morris data referred to in Table 3.3, it is clear that these data must be evaluated with some care. While the results here do not indicate any reason to prefer our data to that used by Wells, there are, we believe, a number of points which can be made in support of such a preference and which clarify some of the problems of reliability reflected

in these indices. First, while our own data for these variables are based on sources which contain virtually no missing data, the sources cited by Wells reveal substantial missing data. In the case of the urbanization measure, 14 of the 30 countries analyzed by Wells are not referred to in the source he cites for the data. His analysis of urbanization, therefore, is based either on additional data which he does not reference, or on a sample drastically reduced because of missing data. Similar problems arise for other variables: the military size data are based on a source which does not give data for 9 of the countries in the sample; the population growth rate data comes from a source that has no data for 4 countries; the source for the radios per capita has no data for 4 countries, and data for a different year than the one reported for 3 other countries, and the literacy data has no figures for Ethiopia and Liberia in the source.

A second problem with Wells' data has to do with the definitional validity of some of his measures. Economic growth, for example, is measured over the abbreviated period 1963-1965. There is too much variance over time, and too little reliability in single measures of GNP for individual years, to expect valid and reliable measurement of economic growth over such a short period. Average annual growth rates for longer periods would be preferable. The definition of urbanization is another case in point. Wells' definition in terms of the percentage of a nation's population living in cities of greater than 100,000 population seriously restricts and skews the variance of the measure of urbanization. Seven of the thirty countries analyzed by Wells have *no* city with a population of over 100,000, and several others have just one city which only slightly exceeds that population size. Another case of problematic reliability arising from the definition of an item is Wells' military participation ratio: the percent of men of military age serving in the military. The size of the military age group is a very difficult figure to obtain for most African countries, and the total population is likely to be a more reliable denominator.

A third problem with Wells' data relates to an inadequate examination and documentation of sources. Wells reports the use of data on the military budget as a percentage of total budget for 1968 when the source cited gives data for 1969. He notes that he was unable to obtain data on the military for earlier dates than 1970, but the first page of the source he cites for this data, references an earlier work in the same series which *does* provide such data. We have already referred to the ambiguity of the reference to the source of his foreign aid data.

A final comment on the reliability of aggregate measures based on the coding of historical events, such as Wells' measures of coup activity, is in order. We have commented, with respect to the Adelman-Morris data, that the reliability of their data seems to increase as items are defined less in terms of the observers' judgments about complex institutional, behavioral, or historical patterns, and more in terms of precisely operationalized decisions based on the observation of established quantitative data. As one moves on this continuum, of course, the importance of the source reliability of the original data base used by the coder remains of vital importance, but the magnitude of error due to inter-coder reliability declines. With respect to event or interaction data, which is so important for political instability measures, it is necessary to establish that despite the clear threats of both source and coding error, reliable measurement is feasible.

Wells' study of coup activity is instructive in this connection. Although he does not define the phenomena, he presents data on 'coups', 'aborted coups', and 'plots'. These data, coded apparently from the New York Times for the period 1960-1969, are given in Table 3.6, along with our own data for the presumed identical variables, as reported and defined in chapter 11 of the first edition of this *Handbook*.

The most striking difference between the Wells data and the Handbook data lies in the consistently lower number of plots coded by Wells. We assume that the use of more specialized regional sources of information as opposed to Wells' use of international sources such as the New York Times explains the greater detail about events that are less "dramatic" from an international point of view than is found in regional and country sources (Cf. Doron, Pendley and Antunes, 1973). Alternatively, the explanation for this variation may lie in another difference between the two data sets — Wells' more frequent coding of aborted coups than our coding of unsuccessful coups. Wells may have coded as aborted coups a number of the events we code as plots. If this has occurred, it may again be due to less detailed information in the source he uses, or to differences in the definition of events.

There are, as expected, fewer differences in the coding of coups d'état, and this is important precisely because of the assumption that one would expect to find very little inter-coder disagreement over the identification of major events like coups. We, however, code only two coups in Nigeria (in January and July, 1966). The second of these is in fact a problematic case, and might better be coded as a rebellion (Cf. Dudley, 1973). In any event, we can find no support for Wells' coding of four coups in this country. In the Sudan we code only one coup as opposed to the two identified by Wells. The difference probably relates to the coding of the change of government in 1964, which we argue was the result of a mass revolt rather than a coup d'état. We code a coup d'état for Uganda at the time of Dr. Obote's assumption

of the constitutional powers of the King of Buganda, whom he ousted as President, suspending parliament at the same time, Wells does not code this coup. Wells has coded one more coup than we have in both Dahomey(Benin) and Zaire — differences for which we cannot account.

The effect of coding disagreements of the kind illustrated above on the reliability of measures of coup activity, or what we have called elite instability, can be assessed from Table 3.7. The reliability indices show reasonably high levels of reliability, although less than one might hope for, given the discrete and, in principle, easily classified nature of the events. Nevertheless, the strict replication of the Wells index using our data shares 86% of the variance with his own computation. From a more general perspective, it seems clear that it makes very little difference what weights one attaches to the component events aggregated into some index of frequency, or whether or not one standardizes by the length of the period since independence when dealing with elite instability in the Black African states of this sample.

In summary, our discussion here of the reliability of single-item aggregate measures of the characteristics of development in Black African countries suggests the following generalizations. First, the agreement between different sources of data for clearly defined measures of national accounts and other established statistical series is relatively high, but not sufficiently high to allow for the casual acceptance of individual sources. Second, the inter-coder reliability for measures defined in terms of counts of well-defined events, like coup events, is quite satisfactory, but very explicit operational definition is required, and there is clearly an unacceptable measure of source unreliability for such measures in African countries as one moves away from detailed regional sources — especially as less "dramatic" instances of political instability than the successful coup d'état are the subject of measurement. Third, the inter-coder reliability of complex, often ambiguously defined, measures requiring observer judgment and imprecise combinations of observations is inadequate. For all the kinds of data we have reviewed here, therefore, it is clear that careful methodological approaches to the examination of measurement error have to be conducted before useful analysis can be made of such data. The next sections of this chapter deal with methodological procedures by which one can move from data which are errorful, but for which the exact distribution of error is not known, to more reliable measurement and valid generalization.

TABLE 3.6   Wells[1] and Morrison/Stevenson.[2] Coup Event Data For Thirty African Countries 1960—1969[3]

	Wells Coups	M/S Coups	Wells Aborted	M/S Aborted	Wells Plots	M/S Plots	Years Independent	Coup Activity Index Wells	Coup Activity Index M/S	C.A.I.	M/S Weights C.A.I.	M/S Weights
1. Benin	5	4	0	0	0	6	10	5.1	46	4.7	26	2.7
2. Burundi	2	2	1	1	2	3	8	3.25	26	3.38	16	2.2
3. Cameroon	0	0	0	0	0	1	10	0.1	1	.2	1	.2
4. Central African Republic	1	1	0	0	2	3	10	1.30	13	1.4	8	.9
5. Chad	0	0	0	0	0	5	10	0.1	5	.6	5	.6
6. Congo	3	2	3	2	2	7	10	4.2	33	3.4	23	2.4
7. Ethiopia	0	0	2	1	1	1	10	.8	4	.5	4	.5
8. Gabon	0	0	1	1	0	0	10	.4	3	.4	3	.4
9. Gambia	0	0	0	0	0	0	5	.2	0	.2	0	.2
10. Ghana	1	1	1	1	1	4	10	1.5	17	1.8	12	1.3
11. Guinea	0	0	0	0	2	4	10	.3	4	.5	4	.5
12. Ivory Coast	0	0	0	0	2	4	10	.3	4	.5	4	.5
13. Kenya	0	0	1	0	0	1	7	.57	1	.28	1	.28
14. Liberia	0	0	0	0	2	3	10	.3	3	.4	3	.4
15. Malawi	0	0	0	0	0	0	6	.17	0	.17	0	.17
16. Mali	1	1	0	0	0	2	10	1.1	12	1.3	7	.8
17. Mauritania	0	0	1	0	0	0	10	.4	0	.1	0	.1
18. Niger	0	0	0	0	1	1	10	.2	1	.2	1	.2
19. Nigeria	4	2	0	0	2	2	10	4.3	22	2.3	12	1.3
20. Rwanda	0	0	0	0	0	0	8	.13	0	.17	0	.17
21. Senegal	0	0	1	1	0	3	10	.4	6	.7	6	.7
22. Sierra Leone	2	2	0	0	1	1	9	2.44	21	2.33	11	1.33
23. Somalia	1	1	1	1	0	0	10	1.4	13	1.4	8	.9
24. Sudan	2	1	0	3	2	3	10	2.3	22	2.3	17	1.8
25. Tanzania	0	0	1	0	2	0	9	.67	0	.11	0	.11
26. Togo	2	2	2	1	0	7	10	2.7	30	3.10	20	2.1
27. Uganda	0	1	1	0	3	3	8	.88	13	1.75	8	1.12
28. Upper Volta	1	1	0	0	0	2	10	1.10	12	1.30	7	.8
29. Zaire	2	2	4	1	5	7	10	3.8	30	3.1	20	2.1
30. Zambia	0	0	0	0	2	0	6	.50	0	.17	0	.1

(3) Multiple Item Scaling and Measurement Error

It is, or in our view should be, a basic tenet of social science research that many social phenomena are too complex to be measured with satisfactory validity by single item measures. The character of social phenomena, or the character of relationships between such phenomena, should, therefore, be evaluated using multiple-item indicators and multivariate analytic technique. Two general methodological strategies arise from this perspec-

TABLE 3.7   Reliability Indices* Between Alternate Indicators of African Coup Activity.

	1.	2.	3.	4.
1. Wells original coding				
2. Recoded data—Wells weights	.86			
3. M/S recoded data—M/S weights	.81	.98		
4. M/S recoded data—not standardized by years independent	.84	.96	.98	

*squared Pearson product—moment correlations are used as reliability indices in this table.

tive—multiple item scaling, and convergent—discriminant validation (Cf. Blalock: 1970, Campbell and Fiske: 1959). Both these strategies assume that any single item contains a measure of the true score of some phenomenon as well as error. Both strategies seek, therefore, to analyse phenomena by using a combination of multiple items in which the errors are assumed to be randomly distributed and the true scores are assumed to be mutually independent or cumulative, so that basic patterns of additivity and convergence as well as increased reliability and validity can be established in the interrelationship between such measures.

Factor analysis is a technique which can be used for scaling and convergent-discriminant analysis, as well as for purposes of multivariate explanation of variance. In this section, we shall explore the use of this technique as applied to questions about the measurement of development in Black African states.

In Table 3.8 we present the results of a rotated factor analysis of the original Adelman-Morris data for the twenty Black African states that we have sampled for purposes of reliability evaluations. This factor analysis matrix, as well as all others reported in this chapter, is a varimax rotation of a principal components analysis which employed initial communalities of unity (see Rummel, 1970). The boxed loadings in this table are the dimensions on which the enclosed variables were located in the factor analysis of the sample of 23 nations reported by Thomas (1974).

There is substantial congruence between our results and those of Thomas, although the differences are worth noting as possible evidence of the greater regional coherence of this sample of states as compared to Thomas. The

first factor, which Thomas labels "socio-economic modernization", is distinguished in our analysis by the addition to Thomas' eight high loading variables of the measures of "leadership commitment to economic development" and "importance of the indigenous middle class". Both of these additions make intuitive good sense, as does the location of the measure "degree of social tension", which was unassigned by Thomas but had its highest loading on this factor in his analysis. That variable, in our analysis, loads more appealingly on the factor measuring aspects of political stability—factor three—and only has a marginal loading on our first factor. This third factor is considerably different in Thomas' and our analyses, as opposed to the second factor which is identical in terms of high loadings for the same five variables, and which, following Thomas, we label 'democratic development.' In the third factor, we have high loadings on political stability and degree of social tension but not as Thomas does on the less direct aspects of stability such as leadership commitment to economic development and political strength of the military and traditional elites. The remaining two factors in Table 3.8 may be labelled 'cultural pluralism' and 'political integration,' both of which relate to what Thomas called "national integration."

The multiple item dimensions of development in Black African states reflected in Table 3.8 are of interest if it can be show that the factor structure on which they are based is relatively invariant as a function of observer coding of the input data. In order to investigate this question we present in Table 3.9 comparable factor analytic results to those in Table 3.8, but results which are based on the recoded data discussed with reference to Table 3.2 in the last section. A comparison of this and the

TABLE 3.8   Rotated Factor Analysis for Adelman-Morris Data for 20 African Nations

Variables	Rotated Factor Loadings					Communality
	1	2	3	4	5	
1. Degree of Modernization of Outlook	.819	−.124	−.099	.104	.029	.706
2. Per Captia GNP	.669	.259	.337	.177	−.029	.660
3. Extent of Economic Dualism	.752	−.320	−.098	.292	−.179	.796
4. Size of Traditional Agricultural Sector	−.736	.131	−.168	−.074	−.108	.605
5. Extent of Urbanization	.877	.053	−.006	.073	−.121	.791
6. Extent of Literacy	.591	−.320	.474	.062	−.157	.705
7. Extent of Social Mobility	.826	−.309	−.089	−.105	.078	.802
8. Extent of Mass Communications	.337	.001	.027	−.073	.089	.128
9. Strength of Democratic Institutions	.124	−.896	−.068	−.153	.012	.846
10. Strength of Labor Movement	.223	.555	.340	−.252	−.433	.725
11. Freedom of Opposition and Press	−.126	−.836	−.058	−.372	.048	.860
12. Competitiveness of Political Parties	.165	−.801	.306	−.345	−.078	.887
13. Political Stability	.190	.224	−.853	.013	.009	.314
14. Political Strength of Traditional Elite	−.273	−.060	−.115	.392	−.677	.703
15. Leadership Commitment to Economic Development	.613	.146	−.421	−.047	.452	.780
16. Cultural and Ethnic Homogeneity	−.230	−.019	−.103	.255	.803	.774
17. National Integration and Unity	.148	.032	.801	.067	−.061	.673
18. Crude Fertility Rate	.525	.222	.119	−.684	−.224	.857
19. Basis of Political Party System	−.119	−.381	.144	−.702	−.056	.675
20. Importance of Indigenous Middle Class	.533	−.399	−.366	.179	−.167	.637
21. Degree of Administrative Efficiency	.346	−.717	.216	.240	−.144	.759
22. Degree of Social Tension	.148	−.032	.801	.067	−.061	.673
23. Political Strength of the Military	.137	.262	.205	.780	−.081	.744
24. Centralization of Political Power	.124	.094	.077	.724	.086	.561
Variables in Factor	1—8, 15, 20	9—12, 21	13, 17, 22	18, 19, 23, 24	14, 16	
Sum Squares	5.22	3.12	3.61	2.50	2.62	17.07

Boxed loadings on the tables are the variables which were assigned to that factor by Thomas. 5 factors accounted for 77% of variance (32, 14, 12, 11, 8 percent variance for the five factors respectively).

preceding table show that *certain regularities appear despite the fact that the individual reliabilities for the measures used in the factor analyses are so low.* This is an important result since it promises a potential approach to dealing with measurement error, as we discuss shortly.

The five factor solution derived from the recoded data is compared to the results in Table 3.8 as follows: the democratic development factors (2 in Table 3.8 and 3 in Table 3.9) are identical; the socio-economic modernization factors (1 in both tables) are very similar except that the results for the recoded data in Table 3.9 show the measures of GNP per capita and the importance of the indigenous middle class loading on a fifth factor (a distinct dimension of economic development) with the crude fertility rate and the mass communications measure; the political stability and the social or political integration factors are somewhat less similar although the results in Table 3.9 show meaningful dimensions of political stability (factor 2) and social integration (factor 4).

It appears reasonable, on the basis of the evidence presented so far, to argue that, despite severe reliability problems in the measurement of single items, it is possible to measure, with substantial inter-subjective agreement, underlying 'dimensions' of socio-economic modernization, democratic development, political stability

TABLE 3.9   1970 Adelman-Morris Variables Recoded 1960—Coder 1

| Variable Description—Name | Rotated Factor Loadings | | | | | Communality |
	1	2	3	4	5	
1. Modernization of Outlook	0.822	−0.178	0.197	−0.120	−0.054	0.763
2. Per Capita GNP	0.207	−0.342	−0.054	−0.181	0.739	0.742
3. Extent of Economic Dualism	0.850	0.110	0.137	−0.172	0.276	0.925
4. Size of Traditional Agricultural Sector	−0.708	0.035	−0.314	0.150	−0.140	0.643
5. Extent of Urbanization	0.701	0.050	0.231	0.028	0.220	0.596
6. Literacy Rate	0.712	−0.040	0.310	−0.185	0.050	0.641
7. Social Mobility	0.425	−0.018	0.460	−0.437	0.169	0.612
8. Mass Communication	0.519	−0.091	0.124	−0.258	0.653	0.786
9. Strength of Democratic Institutions	0.068	−0.160	0.887	−0.068	−0.005	0.822
10. Stength of Labor Movement	0.273	−0.254	0.536	−0.308	0.162	0.548
11. Freedom of Opposition and Press	0.173	−0.180	0.859	0.302	0.043	0.893
12. Competitiveness of Political Parties	0.202	0.054	0.923	−0.096	−0.029	0.905
13. Political Stability	0.089	−0.915	−0.006	0.060	0.198	0.883
14. Political Strength of Traditional Elite	−0.313	0.641	0.081	0.266	0.157	0.611
15. Leadership Commitment to Economic Development	0.704	−0.256	−0.050	0.066	0.091	0.712
16. Cultural and Ethnic Homogeneity	−0.175	−0.003	0.067	0.917	−0.178	0.908
17. National Integration and Sense of Unity	0.038	0.029	−0.116	0.913	−0.097	0.859
18. Crude Fertility Rate	0.453	0.278	−0.087	−0.000	−0.701	0.782
19. Basis of Political Party System	0.710	−0.292	−0.423	0.185	−0.207	0.846
20. Middle Class Importance	0.432	0.151	0.033	−0.115	0.789	0.847
22. Social Tension	0.080	0.791	−0.245	−0.298	−0.315	0.881
23. Political Strength of Military	−0.065	0.835	−0.368	0.144	−0.041	0.859
Sum Squares	5.216	3.124	3.609	2.503	2.617	17.069

Percent of Variance accounted for

	32	14	12	11	8	77
Variables in Factor	1, 3-8, 15, 19	13, 14, 22, 23	9-12	16, 17	2, 8, 18, 20	
	same	same	same			

and national integration in Black African states. Which of the results are the best approximation to such measures, and which input data are therefore to be considered the most valid and reliable, canrnot be determined exactly from this analysis, and we shall need more extensive corroboration of these results in order to bolster the conclusion in the first sentence of this paragraph. Before moving to further corroboration, however, it should be noted that the communalities of the individual items used in the factor analyses so far are higher in Table 3.9 than in Table 3.8. That is to say, we seem to obtain a more coherent pattern in the five factor solution of the recoded data as well as increased variance accounted for by key variables such as the measure of GNP per capita. Such evidence suggests the possibility of greater accuracy in our recoded data as compared to the original Adelman-Morris data although this result could be influenced by the slight differences in countries and variables included in

the two analyses.

In Table 3.10 we present the results of a factor analysis of the Adelman-Morris variables measured by one of the authors for the period circa 1970, and in Table 3.11 we present the results for these variables measured for this later period by the one of our coders. It should be noted, that the communalities in both these tables are higher than those for the analysis of either the Adelman-Morris data or our recoded data for the original period of measurement. Furthermore, the explanation of the key variable in Adelman and Morris' analysis--GNP per capita--increases from 74% in the original Adelman-Morris analysis to 83% and 88% in these two sets of results. The explanatory power, therefore, of our data for this later period, seems to be generally superior to the original data. With respect to the dimensionality of these data, as compared to those for the earlier period, there are, however, some important divergences from the earlier results.

TABLE 3.10 1970 Adelman-Morris Variables Coded—Coder 1

Variable Description—Name	Rotated Factor Loadings					Communality
	1	2	3	4	5	
1. Modernization of Outlook	0.885	0.117	−0.030	0.103	−0.038	0.809
2. Per Capita GNP	0.389	0.448	0.581	−0.063	−0.367	0.828
3. Extent of Economic Dualism	0.902	0.170	0.080	0.022	−0.148	0.971
4. Size of Traditional Agricultural Sector	−0.789	0.117	−0.334	−0.018	0.093	0.756
5. Extent of Urbanization	0.441	0.043	0.607	0.020	−0.313	0.663
6. Literacy Rate	0.828	0.061	−0.073	0.437	−0.028	0.886
7. Social Mobility	0.531	0.351	0.139	0.115	−0.612	0.812
8. Mass Communication	0.796	0.061	0.296	0.133	−0.112	0.755
9. Strength of Democratic Institutions	0.064	0.260	0.684	0.539	−0.059	0.835
10. Stength of Labor Movement	0.725	−0.122	0.228	−0.185	0.321	0.750
11. Freedom of Opposition and Press	0.443	−0.001	0.713	0.159	0.143	0.751
12. Competitiveness of Political Parties	0.423	0.208	0.486	0.410	−0.110	0.638
13. Political Stability	−0.033	0.876	0.201	0.130	0.085	0.833
14. Political Strength of Traditional Elite	−0.026	0.170	−0.116	−0.887	0.084	0.837
15. Leadership Commitment to Economic Development	0.411	0.455	−0.103	0.506	−0.189	0.679
16. Cultural and Ethnic Homogeneity	−0.461	0.012	−0.404	0.355	−0.127	0.517
17. National Integration and Sense of Unity	0.192	0.100	−0.720	0.069	−0.021	0.571
18. Crude Fertility Rate	0.019	−0.059	−0.030	−0.067	0.916	0.849
19. Basis of Political Party System	−0.062	0.617	0.016	0.511	0.218	0.694
20. Middle Class Importance	0.646	−0.348	−0.114	−0.282	−0.176	0.662
22. Social Tension	−0.175	−0.847	−0.030	0.026	0.274	0.824
23. Political Strength of Military	0.130	−0.860	0.133	0.233	0.191	0.864
Sum Squares	5.960	3.491	2.980	2.346	1.889	16.667
Variables in Factor	1, 3, 4, 5, 7, 8, 10, 20	13, 15, 19, 22, 23	9, 11, 12, 16, 17	14, 15	18	

Original unrotated solutions accounted for 75.8% of total variance.

Table 3.12 summarizes the variables which load highly on different factors in the various analyses presented so far. It is apparent, first, that despite the higher reliability coefficients for the latter two recoded data sets these data show the most dissimilar factor structures. The measurement of dimensions of African national development for this later period is, therefore, a matter of some difficulty, and independent observations for these variables reveal substantially different patterns of development. It is, nevertheless, apparent that for *all* the recoded data, our analyses reveal much more complex patterns of political development than defined by the original Adelman-Morris measures.

What is interesting, further, is that these results indicate the likelihood that certain basic underlying measures or "dimensions" of development in Black African countries emerge from any factor analysis of these variables for this regional sample. All our results indicate a fairly stable structure to the measurement of socio-economic modernization as a dimension of the development of these nations. All the results derived from the recoded data indicate that this dimension is, however, analytically and empirically separate from a dimension of economic development *per se*. Furthermore, there is evidence that analytically and empirically distinct dimensions of political stability, national integration, and democratic devel-

TABLE 3.11   1970 Adelman-Morris Variables Coded by Coder 2

Variable Description—Name	Rotated Factor Loadings					Communality
	1	2	3	4	5	
1. Modernization of Outlook	0.014	*0.780*	−0.145	0.093	0.404	0.801
2. Per Capita GNP	0.366	0.051	−0.341	*0.770*	0.195	0.884
3. Extent of Economic Dualism	−0.074	*0.812*	−0.187	0.433	−0.135	0.906
4. Size of Traditional Agricultural Sector	−0.433	*−0.512*	−.323	−0.333	0.430	0.849
5. Extent of Urbanization	−0.066	0.085	0.033	*0.898*	−0.030	0.825
6. Literacy Rate	−0.078	*0.832*	−0.197	0.253	0.128	0.818
7. Social Mobility	0.207	0.267	−0.356	0.468	0.423	0.632
8. Mass Communication	−0.127	0.407	−0.149	*0.657*	0.007	0.636
9. Strength of Democratic Institutions	*0.586*	0.201	−0.026	0.371	0.532	0.806
10. Stength of Labor Movement	*0.690*	−0.078	0.195	0.107	0.546	0.829
11. Freedom of Opposition and Press	0.222	*0.458*	0.400	−0.119	0.334	0.545
12. Competitiveness of Political Parties	*0.893*	0.007	−0.040	−0.002	0.264	0.868
13. Political Stability	*0.952*	0.044	0.137	−0.007	0.031	0.928
14. Political Strength of Traditional Elite	−0.180	−0.417	0.067	0.016	*−0.706*	0.709
15. Leadership Commitment to Economic Development	0.273	*0.857*	0.129	−0.024	0.093	0.835
16. Cultural and Ethnic Homogeneity	−0.089	−0.136	*0.932*	−0.091	−0.132	0.922
17. National Integration and Sense of Unity	0.184	−0.042	*0.922*	−0.138	0.047	0.906
19. Basis of Political Party System	*0.746*	0.502	−0.054	−0.021	−0.128	0.829
20. Middle Class Importance	0.158	*0.500*	0.032	0.384	0.247	0.484
22. Social Tension	*−0.939*	−0.035	−0.077	−0.157	−0.076	0.919
23. Political Strength of Military	*−0.958*	−0.072	0.049	0.077	−0.057	0.935
Sum Squares	5.458	4.164	2.429	2.791	1.982	16.864
Variables in Factor	9, 10, 12, 13, 19, 22, 23	1, 3, 4, 6, 20, 15	16, 17	2, 5, 7, 8	14	

Original principal components—5 factors account for 80% of variance (34, 20, 11, 8, 6).

opment underlie these data, although the composition and measurement of these dimensions is somewhat less consistent as a function of the different data structures derived from different observers.

This evidence that underlying dimensions of development in Black African states, measured by a combination of single and errorful items, seem to recur, and to have relatively similar structure across different data sets derived from independent observations for the same variables, is important for the following reasons. First, it indicates that *patterns* or *dimensions* of development, and, by extension, regions or "stages" of development, can be analytically defined and empirically measured. Not only are these dimensions or properties of development relatively invariant across the different data sets for African states discussed so far, but they are given additional confirmation in other studies. Rummel's extensive analysis

of the "dimensions of nations" (1972), uses an all but universal sample of the world's countries as of 1955, when only two of the countries that we deal with were independent and included in the sample, confirms, for example, the distinctive appearance of a socio-economic modernization factor based on analagous aggregate measures to those we have discussed for Black Africa. It appears, therefore, that something akin to what Deutsch refers to as the process of social mobilization reveals itself in terms of unidimensional factors that discriminate between nations at different levels or stages of the process. Similarly, dimensions of political development and political instability appear in the Rummel work. Other similarities are restricted, however, by the rather different variables used by Rummel as compared to those we have been discussing.

Further confirmation of the dimensionality of devel-

TABLE 3.12 Factor Patterns in Four Factor Analyses.

	*Factor Identification**				
Data Base	Socio-economic Modernization	Democratic Development	Political Stability	National Integration	Economic Development
Adelman-Morris circa 1960	Factor 1 1—8, 15, 20	Factor 2 9—12, 21	Factor 3 13, 22	Factor 4/5 19, 23, 24/14, 16	—
Our Data recode, c. 1960	Factor 1 1—8, 15, 19 22, 23	Factor 3 9—12, 13, 14,	Factor 2 16, 17	Factor 4 2, 8, 18, 20	Factor 5
coder one recode, c. 1970	Factor 1 1, 3—8, 10, 20	Factor 3 2, 5, 9, 11, 17	Factor 2 13, 15, 22, 23	Factor 4 14, 15	Factor 5 7, 18
Coder two recode, c. 1970	Factor 2 1, 3, 4, 6, 15, 19, 20	Factor 1 9, 10, 12, 13, 22, 23	Factor 1 9, 10, 12, 13, 22, 23	Factor 3 16, 17	Factor 4 2, 5, 7, 8

*The numbers which appear below the factor 5 in the body of the table refer to the variables included in that factor. See the preceding tables for the identification of the variables corresponding to these numbers.

opment in Black African countries discussed here is, moreover, obtained from the various analyses conducted by Adelman and Morris of different samples using their original data. Two factor analyses of a sample of 74 "developing nations", and consisting of 27 African nations, and a second consisting of the 27 "least developed" nations of the 74 (Adelman and Morris, 1967, 1969, 1965) reveal relatively consistent dimensions of socio-economic modernization, political development, political instability, and national integration, although the last property is less well or consistently defined across the different samples. If there are such underlying dimensions as these, it is strategically important for the analysis of development that these dimensions be increasingly refined, and that they be incorporated into well defined and more parsimonious models.

The second point that we would make with respect to these dimensions of development is that they allow for potentially more reliable measurement than that based on the single items on which they are scaled. The general logic of the development from factor analysis of unidimensional scales, in which component items are so mutually intercorrelated that the scale accounts for about 80% of their total variance, and in which it is expected that the error in the component items is randomized in the scale score, is argued and illustrated in Morrison and Stevenson 1972a, 1972b, and 1974a and in Orbell and Rutherford, 1973. We will not repeat the argument here, but will give evidence for it in the following section.

There we will establish the extent to which regression models explaining aspects of the development of Black African states (using the same variables but with independently coded data) tend to give converging explanations when composited factor scores for multiple item factors in the original data structure are used as opposed to the use of representative single items. We shall show, further, that this convergence in explanation is further increased when the models are operationalized by strict unidimensional scales, rather than by the factor scores from a comprehensive factor analysis whose computation includes weightings for variables that have no apparent relation to the underlying dimension being measured. These illustrations of convergence in the tests of multivariate models are, strictly speaking, illustrations of external validity rather than internal validity or reliability. But there is a fundamental relation between the two concepts, and the convergence here is a product of the greater reliability—i.e. agreement—of the scales constructed from the independent codings as compared to the single-item component measures.

Although it is possible to show analytically, or by Monte-Carlo simulation analysis, that factor analytic scales *do* have reduced error properties, or that they *do* give a more robust and error-resistant estimation of the true score of some factor or property than other non-resistant estimation of the true score of some factor or property than other non-psychometric scaling devices (see Morrison and Campbell, forthcoming), our purpose here

TABLE 3.13   Factor Score Correlations Between Alternate Codings, c. 1960.

Morrison/Stevenson Data

		X_1	X_2	X_3	X_4
Adelman/Morris Data	X_1	.86	(.29)		
	X_2		.55	(.01)	
	X_3			.56	(.11)
	X_4				.57	(.19)

X_1 = factor score for socio-economic modernization
X_2 = factor score for democratic development
X_3 = factor score for political stability
X_4 = factor score for national integration

Factor scores for Adelman/Morris data from factor structure reported in Table 3.8, and those for Morrison/Stevenson data from Table 3.9.

TABLE 3.14   Factor Score Correlations From c. 1970 Data

Coder Two Data 1970

		X_1	X_2	X_3
Coder One Data	X_1	.68 (.77)		
1970	X_2		.57 (.23)	
	X_3			.85 (.74)

X_1 = *factor score for socio-economic modernization*
X_2 = *factor score for democratic development*
X_3 = *factor score for political stability*

Factor derived from Tables 3.9 and 3.10

is to add weight to these more abstract arguments by reference to the comparison of the data sets discussed in this chapter, in which it is known that error exists, but not in what distribution. Given that we can make the demonstrations outlined above, it seems clear that we can argue for a clear cut methodological procedure using factor analytic scales which will reduce errors in measurement and increase the validity of generalization (see Smith, 1974).

(4) Measurement Error and the Evaluation of Theoretical Models of African Development

The first demonstration that multiple item scales derived from the factor analysis of large data sets provide more reliable measures than the original single item component measures can be made with reference to Table 3.13. In this table we present the correlations between two sets of factor scores for dimensions of socio-economic modernization, democratic development, political instability and national integration. One set is generated from the Adelman-Morris coding and the other from our recoding of their data for circa 1960.

The correlations falling in the diagonal of Table 3.13 are followed in parentheses by the average correlation for the high loading variables on a given dimension in the Adelman/Morris factor structure with the same variables as measured in the Morrison/Stevenson recode data. Although the factor score correlations are not in themselves sufficiently pronounced to warrant great confidence in the reliability of these measures, the reliabilities of the factor scores *are*, nevertheless, more pronounced than for the component measures.

This general point is further established for the independent coding of these variables for the period 1970. As illustrated in Table 3.14, the factor score measures for two of the three dimensions common to the analyses of these data are more reliable then the component measures. (It should be noted, in line with our earlier argument in this chapter that the reliability over time of the multiple item scales as measured by independent observers is *not* guaranteed or spuriously inflated in comparison to the inter-temporal correlation of the component measures. The Adelman/Morris 1960 and our 1970 factor scores for socio-economic modernization and political instability, for example, have correlations of .31 and .05).

We can move now to the illustration of the greater reliability of multiple-item scales as indicated by convergent results in tests of multivariate models of national development in Black Africa, when the tests are based on independently coded data for variables in these models. In what follows, we adopt from the literature reviewed in this paper simple models describing relationships between variables in the general form and we seek to show that the empirical structure of these models is more reliably estimated, i.e., is more similar or convergent in tests derived from independently coded measures, when the original single-item candidate measures for X1, X2...Xn are replaced by increasingly refined multiple-item scales measuring these variables.

In pursuing this argument, it is important to note that the enterprise we call social science is concerned with establishing the structure of relations between variables measuring aspects of social systems or processes, but that the structure of such relations is principally deduced from *theory* not induced from statistical measures. The latter are used only to test the null hypothesis that there is no relationship of the kind given by theory, and, in situations where the null hypothesis can be rejected with high probability, to estimate the form of the theoretical relationship. In this connection the work discussed here by Adelman and Morris, Thomas, and Wells is flawed. All these authors tend to work by induction from data to theory, and their theoretical generalizations are of a primitive kind - i.e. that there is a relationship, as given by the data, between different characteristics of the development of African nations. The point of the present chapter is to emphasize, at the risk of stating the obvious, (a) that especially with errorful data of the kind we are discussing no relationship can be positively said to exist, (b) that it can be taken for granted that there will be *some* empirically defined relationships between different measures in even a completely random set of observations, and therefore, (c) that it is not useful simply to assert the existence of such relationships as in the work under discussion, but vital in the present state of our knowledge and information to clarify theoretical models that give reasonable explanations of development relationships, and to show which of these models withstand tests for convergent and discriminant validity based on independent observations of the variables.

Although all the authors whose work we are discussing here share the inductivist approach just mentioned, they opt for different methodological strategies by which to generalize about the structure of relationships between measures of development. Except for Sigelman, whose work we discuss at the end of this section, all of these authors use elaborations of the basic linear regression model. This model, depending as it does on assumptions about the error-free measurement of independent variables, must be cautiously employed when errorful data like those under discussion are used. We review, therefore, the comparative strengths of the different uses these authors make of regression models in generalizing about patterns of development.

The most elementary methodological procedure in the work under review is that adopted by Wells (1974). The author proceeds from an analysis of the bivariate correlations and multiple regression coefficients relating his measures of coup activity and other variables to the conclusion that there are relationships between socio-economic processes and military structures, and the extent of coup activity in Black African states; that the relationships for socio-economic variables are less important than those for military variables, and that there is theoretically some interaction between these variables and patterns of external political or economic constraint on African nations (a conclusion that might certainly be interesting if any theoretical specification could be given to the nature of such interaction, and if it were in any way related to the empirical analysis). Our interest here, however, is in showing that whatever the relationships between such variables as Wells uses they are unreliably estimated by

TABLE 3.15 Zero-Order Correlations Between Independent Variables and Measures of Coup Activity in Wells (1974) and Morrison et. al. (1972)

	Wells	Morrison et. al.
1. Population size	.04	.14
2. Population growth	.07	−.02
3. Urbanization	.11	−.44
4. Centrality	.09	.20
5. Literacy	.34	.16
6. Mass media consumption	−.20	−.14
7. Economic level	.10	−.12
8. Economic growth	.06	−.28
9. Military participation ratio	.25	.18
10. Military size	.36	.24
11. Police size	.24	.07
12. Defense budget	.37	.31
13. Military spending as % Government expenditure	.36	.21
14. Military spending as % GNP	.32	.19
15. U.S. Aid (total thru 1968)	.32	.32

the procedure he employs.

The zero-order correlations Wells interprets are variable both in size and sign when calculated for the independent measures of the same variables that we have discussed earlier in this chapter. As illustrated in Table 3.15, there are more non-zero correlations for the socio-economic variables measured with our data compared to the correlations for Well's data; there are differences in sign for the correlations involving some of the socio-economic variables; and our results for the military variables are generally less pronounced than Wells', albeit in the same consistently positive direction.

If we compare the results of the multiple regression of these independent variables against the coup activity measures, more pronounced divergences between our data and Wells' are revealed. Of the fifteen possible coefficients in the equations for each data set, there are seven for which the signs are *reversed* in the two solutions or which are included in the one and excluded in the other. It is simply not possible in the face of such failure to achieve convergent results to make any intelligible statements about the development of Black African states without modifying Wells' procedure.

Thomas (1974) adopts a potentially more fruitful procedure. After factor analyzing the Adelman-Morris data for his sample, he derives a composite measure for the dimension of democratic development that was obtained in the factor solution, and then treats this measure as a dependent variable to be accounted for by multiple regression analysis on other measures. This procedure has the advantage of dealing with dependent variables that have reduced error properties, although, as we shall dis-

TABLE 3.16 Regression Results (Standardized Partial Regression Coefficients and Coefficients of Determination) for Explanations of Three Dependent Variables Measured by Factor Scores.

Independent Variables	DEPENDENT VARIABLES							
	Democratic Political Development			Political Stability			National Integration	
	*A/M 1960	M/S 1960	M/S 1970**	A/M 1960	M/S 1960	M/S 1970	A/M 1960	M/S 1960
1. Basis of Political Party System	−.28	−.84				.48		.54
2. National Integration and Sense of Unity	.38					.30		
3. Per Capita GNP	.29			.36	−.44	.53	−.73	
4. Political Stability	.34	−.77					−.94	
5. Political Strength of Military	.24			.53				
6. Strength of Labor Movement						−.45	−.34	
7. Middle Class Importance			.33		.33	−.17	−.93	
8. Crude Fertility Rate		.33	.28		.32			.45
9. Freedom of Opposition and Press					−.70		−.50	.87
10. Extent of Urbanization			.45	−.27				.37
11. Literacy Rate			.01	.34			−.19	
12. Leadership Commitment to Economic Development				−.64			.60	
13. Modernization of Outlook		.55						
14. Social Tension		−.40						
15. Political Strength of Traditional Elite			−.50					
16. Cultural and Ethnic Homogeneity			−.41					
17. Mass Communication			.78				.31	
18. Social Mobility							.30	−.08
19. Strength of Democratic Institutions							.64	−.35
20. Size of Traditional Agricultural Sector							.88	−.63
21. Extent of Economic Dualism			−1.23		.52			−.69
R^2	.89	.84	.90	.91	.90	.89	.88	.89
Numbered variables in regression	5	5	8	8	5	5	10	7

*A/M = Adelman-Morris data
M/S = Morrison-Stevenson recode data
**The 1970 factor analysis gave a combined factor for democratic development and national integration.

cuss later, further refinements in the measurement of dependent variables could and should be obtained by constructing unidimensional scales. A disadvantage of this procedure is, that the results for these coefficients are highly sensitive to the errors in the single item measures. This latter point is illustrated in Table 3.16, where we show the regression results (allowing nine independent variables to enter the equations in a stepwise routine) for the original Adelman-Morris data, c. 1960, and for our recoded data for 1960 and 1970.

These results show the differences in the particular variables entered into the equations for the same dependent variables, and differences in the signs and magnitude of the coefficients for variables that are common to the equations for the two data sets. Conclusions from any one of these equations are, therefore, hazardous, and Thomas' procedure does not seem well adapted to indicating convergent validity for generalizations based on unreliable data.

Adelman-Morris (1969) adopt another variation of the use of factor analysis for generalizations about the structure of development relationships. Whereas Thomas constructs multiple-item scale scores for a factor and then regresses these scores against the single item measures used in the factor solution, Adelman and Morris proceed directly from the factor analysis results to generalizations about the relationships of a single-item dependent variable (GNP) to the independent dimensions of development measured by each factor in the solution. In this procedure, the variance explained in the dependent variable is given by the communality for that variable in the rotated factor solution and the contribution to variance explained (and the derived regression coefficients) for the independent variables are given by the squared factor loadings for that variable on each factor in the solution – each factor being in effect an independent multiple-item scale. This procedure *does*, therefore, make use of the central argument of this chapter that theoretical generalizations should be based on the variation explained in a given dependent variable by multiple-item scales. Given the apparent invariance of factor structures derived from independent codings of the same input variables for the same sample that we have established in the previous section of this chapter, this procedure does tend to give convergent, although not identical, results for a multiple regression model estimated by the different data sets.

The general procedure adopted by Adelman and Morris has significant advantages, therefore, but two problems relate to it. First, the extent to which results converge in this procedure is clearly strongly influenced by the reliability of the single-item measure of the dependent variable, which needs to be adequately established before using their procedure. Second, the procedure is affected by departures from simple structure and low communalities for any of the input variables in the factor solution. That is to say, the coefficients in the regression model for the independent factor-variables are influenced by the weighting of irrelevant component items on those factors.

Our preference, therefore, is for a procedure that establishes more reliable dependent *and* independent variables, both ideally being measured by strictly unidimensional scales. As discussed in Morrison and Stevenson, 1972a and 1972b, this involves an iterative procedure by which the variables loading coherently on any factor in a comprehensive factor solution are separately factor analyzed and a constraint imposed on the rotation of only two factors for those variables. Provided the first of the unrotated factors explains most of the total variance in the input variables, we call such a factor unidimensional and use the factor scores derived from it as a measure of the property being scaled. Using these unidimensional scales to estimate a multivariate regression model gives, we argue, a more reliable procedure and more convergent results when the model is operationalized by independent observations.

That this is so can be indicated by a comparison of the regression equations for the Adelman and Morris data and for our recoded data for our sample of 20 African countries in the period c. 1960, using first the regression interpretation of the composite factor analysis, and second a separate regression based on unidimensional scale measures of the dimensions indicated by the original factor structures. These results are given in Table 3.17.

In concluding this discussion of measurement error and generalizations about the development of Black African states, we turn to the work of Sigelman (1974). This writer uses the Adelman-Morris data for African states to evaluate Lerner's (1958) theory of the sequence of development in the "passing of traditional society."

The Lerner theory can be seen as one of a certain class of development theories that can be called 'stage theories.' As in the work of Marx, Comte or Durkheim in the

TABLE 3.17 Comparisons of Regression Equations (Standardized Partial Regression Coefficients) Based on Rotated Factor Structure and on Reconstructed Unidimensional Scale Scores for Independent Variables

	Data Set	
Procedure	Adelman-Morris, c. 1960	Morrison-Stevenson, c. 1960
1. Regression equation using rotated factor solution	a. $Y = -.16\,X_2 + .19\,X_3$	b. $Y = -.04\,X_1 + .18\,X_2 + .35\,X_3$
$R^2 =$	.05	.16
2. Regression equation using reconstructed unidimensional indices	a. $Y = .43\,X_1 - .41\,X_2 + .10\,X_3$	b. $Y = .65\,X_1 - .38\,X_2 + .18\,X_3$
$R^2 =$	.37	.62

Y = GNP per capita, 1961
X_1 = factor or unidimensional scale score measuring socio-economic modernization, c. 1960 (GNP per capita omitted in equations 2)
X_2 = factor or unidimensional scale score measuring political development, c. 1960
X_3 = factor or unidimensional scale score measuring political stability, c. 1960

nineteenth century, and in the work of Rostow and Lerner more recently, certain socio-economic processes are depicted as having, 'threshold points' with fundamental and generally irrevocable effects on changes in the political-economic system. While Lerner and most of those following up his work have used linear regression models to examine the sequential interaction of urbanization, education, mass-media consumption, political participation and political stability, Sigelman opts for the use of the Guttman scalogram technique to examine the stage sequencing of developments like these. In doing so, he overlooks the implications of procedures used in the Guttman technique and derives questionable generalizations from his analysis. We shall examine briefly these misunderstandings, and investigate the extent to which the technique properly used is affected by the poor reliability of data.

Like most scaling methodologies, Guttman's technique presupposes the existence of some underlying conceptual continuum which cannot or was not directly measured by a single measure. The Guttman model is concerned with deriving an ordering of items by level of difficulty so that it is possible to locate individuals (or other units of analysis) on the underlying continuum measured by the ordered items. The Guttman coefficient of reliability (CR) is intended to measure how well any given set of items can be so ordered - i.e. whether or not the ordered items form a scale. This scaling model differs from factor analytic procedures so far discussed inasmuch as the item components of the scale are measures of cumulative but independent gradations of the continuum, not of cumulative but overlapping aspects of the continuum. That is, items in a factor based scale are independent but intercorrelated, whereas items in a Guttman scale are interactive and related as a function of threshold values or 'level of difficulty.'

The use of this model for the evaluation of theories which imply staged processes of development is obvious and correct. Sigelman, however, makes two inappropriate uses of the model for such purposes. First, following the inductivist approach of which we have already spoken he uses the Guttman procedure to order his aggregate measures in a *best fit* scale, according to the values of the coefficient of reproducibility (CR) error criterion. This is no more egregious a problem than the similar inductive and iterative use of path analysis in other tests of the Lerner theory, but it is nevertheless possible and even likely that generalizations from best fit solutions are somewhat spurious artifacts of measurement error. The second problem has to do with the dichotomization or trichotomization in Sigelman's case of the variables subjected to Guttman scale analysis. The technique does not require information about the continuous range of any

variable, but about variation above and below threshold values which mark the point at which attainment of higher values on other more 'difficult' variables is probable. When one is working, as Sigelman is, from raw data which do not form obvious dichotomies or trichotomies, some rationalization has to be given for their transformation into such scales[4]. Sigelman offers no such discussion, and one must question whether or not the arbitrary transformations he uses provide valid generalizations.

However, we have followed exactly Sigelman's trichotomization of the Adelman-Morris variables which he uses to operationalize Lerner's model. Sigelman modifies this model by adding the term 'political capacity', and the perfect scale pattern following Lerner's theoretical ordering with Sigelman's addition is as given in Table 3.18. In Table 3.19, we show the results of the analysis as summarized by Guttman's coefficient of reproducibility for the sample of 20 African states using first the original Adelman-Morris data and then our independently-coded data for the same variables. The results show the CR values for different orderings of the model, and also for dichotomous transformations of the data.

TABLE 3.18   Ideal Scale Patterns for the Adelman- Morris Data on 74 Countries as Trichotomized by Sigelman.

Economic Development	Political Participation	Mass Communication	Literacy	Urbanization	Political Capacity	Scale Score
2	2	2	2	2	2	12
1	2	2	2	2	2	11
1	2	1	2	2	2	10
1	1	1	2	2	2	9
1	1	1	1	2	2	8
1	1	1	1	1	2	7
1	1	1	1	1	1	6
0	1	1	1	1	1	5
0	1	1	1	0	1	4
0	1	1	1	0	0	3
0	0	1	1	0	0	2
0	0	1	0	0	0	1
0	0	0	0	0	0	0

1. There would be no ideal pattern defined for nine according to the Guttman procedures since it does not occur in the data table (see Appendix A). We have assumed it to be as given above.

TABLE 3.19 Guttman CR Values For Scales Based on Different Model and Data Structures, Using Sigelman Transformations.

Models	Data	
	Adelman-Morris	Morrison-Stevenson
1. Pure Lerner (trichotomous data)	.89	.87
2. Lerner without Education (trichotomous)	.87	.85
3. Pure Lerner (dichotomous)	.82	.81
4. Lerner without Education and Political Capacity (dichotomous)	.73	.71
5. Best Fit*	.93	.97

*The best fit model for both data assets reflects the following ordering: political capacity, political participation, mass communications, literacy, urbanization, education (from least to most difficult stages). All other models reflect the Lerner order as augmented by Sigelman and shown in Table 3.18.

These results show, first, that the Guttman CR values are not influenced by the different error distributions in the data from the two independent sources. These convergent results must, however, be viewed with suspicion since it has been established in simulation studies (Rutherford, Morrison and Campbell:1971) that the Guttman coefficient of reliability is not robust with respect to error in data and tends to show scalability when none exists. Even if we suspend such doubt, it is apparent, that the best fit model for both data structures is radically different from the Lerner model. This would be a potentially interesting conclusion (the best fit model indicates something of the 'primacy of politics' in the development of Black African states) if we could be sure that the difference in CR values is sufficiently significant to reject the Lerner model. Finally, the results indicate that the trichotomous data give marginally greater CR values than the dichotomous data for tests of the Lerner model, but the best fit ordering of these variables is obtained using the dichotomous data. Whether or not decisions about when to order the original data into trichotomies or dichotomies makes a difference can be assessed from the data in Table 3.20.

These results were obtained using trichotomous or dichotomous data derived by coding the single lowest category of the original Adelman-Morris variables as cut-off points as contrasted with the higher threshold values generally used by Sigelman. The similarity in these results as compared to these in Table 3.19 indicates that

TABLE 3.20 Guttman CR Values for Scales Based on Different Model and Data Structures, Using Alternate Transformations.

Models	Data	
	Adelman-Morris	Stevenson-Morrison
1. Pure Lerner (trichotomous)	.85	.86
2. Pure Lerner (dichotomous)	.81	.83
3. Best Fit*	.94	.93

*The best fit model for both data sets reflects the folowing ordering of increasing difficulty: political participation, political capacity, mass communications, literacy, education, urbanization.

tests of the Lerner model with these variables are not in fact sensitive to the arbitrary threshold chosen to transform the original continuous variables. It should, however, be observed that the best fit model with the alternative transformations in Table 3.20 is different from that shown for the original Sigelman transformations.

While, therefore, the Guttman technique adopted by Sigelman appears to be relatively insensitive to different error distributions in these data for Black African states, the utility of the technique for specifying models of development is limited by the generally poor discrimination between the values of the CR coefficients for different models imposed on the data; by the lack of any clear decision rule to choose between the significance of these value; and by the apparent variability in the best-fit models derived from different transformations of raw data to threshold-type values. For these reasons it is our view that generalizations of the kind made by Sigelman must be viewed with caution.

Conclusions

This chapter makes the following very general points – (1) that aggregate data for Black African countries are generally unreliable; (2) that the extent to which they are unreliable varies with the degree to which they are dependent on expert judgements of macro-phenomena as opposed to clearly operationalized measurement and imputation; (3) that it jeopardizes meaningful analysis, in the face of these first two conclusions, to use such data without investigating basic estimates of their coding and source reliability, and (4) that even when such estimates are low, the use of multiple-item scaling, particularly the development of unidimensional indices, can provide for greater measurement reliability and for convergent validity in the empirical generalizations about the structure of relationships between variables.

These conclusions are not in any way contrary to the most basic epistemological arguments for the proper conduct of scientific inquiry. It is clear, however, from this survey of literature on cross-national aggregate data analysis of African nations that greater attention to such issues of measurement is required. We hope that the analysis here will be seen not as an attack on authors whose work has been used to demonstrate these points, but as documentation of the hazards of working in a field of interest we share with them. Furthermore, we hope that this analysis will dissuade their and our critics from the view that errors in cross-national generalizations are easily identifiable.

It would be misleading, in our view, to indicate that conventional estimates of reliability like inter-coder or inter-source correlations for individual measures adequately describe the utility of the data given in Part I of this book. Such estimates cannot, as we have suggested in this chapter, be used to isolate random, systematic, linear or non-linear components of error in these measures. The simplifying assumption that attenuation in correlations between two sets of observations of the same phenomena using equally valid measures indicates the extent of random error in those measures is a useful way to attack the problems of unreliability, but it is by no means a complete answer to such problems. The possibilities of linear or non-linear systematic errors of observation discussed at the beginning of this chapter cannot be willed away. While there are no simple technical procedures for estimating such components of error, the user of aggregate data on African nations has to pay meticulous attention to the scatter diagrams of these data plotted against indicators of possible contaminating sources of systematic bias, such as historical time, levels of economic development, and geographical contiguity or diffusion.

Finally, it cannot be assumed that even the most reliable measures *ipso facto* reveal meaningful generalizations. Data do not speak for themselves, nor do they prove theoretically plausible arguments. Valid empirical generalizations depend, that is, not only on reliable measures, but also on the avoidance of errors of logic and assumption in the theoretical argument supporting such generalization, and on the conservative and cautious examination of possible errors of statistical inference, sampling bias, and misspecification, and in the interpretation of patterns of relationship revealed in any given set of data. We have not done more than mention these latter problems, but they deserve as much attention as the issues of measurement we have explored[7].

Notes

1. This problem of construct validity is not extensively examined. We refer only to problems associated with select variables in the data sets discussed in this paper. General critiques of the validity of measures that are conceptually defined to indicate aspects of 'development' are contained in Seers (1972) and Baxter (1972). For another related view of types of validity error see Cook and Campbell (1973).

2. Welfling's analysis is based on the comparison of data collected by Gurr and Duvall with data published in the first edition of this handbook. Although she goes to considerable length to argue for the functional equivalence of different indicators drawn from these two sources — i.e., for the validity of these different indicators as measures of the same concepts — we cannot accept her conclusion that such equivalence and validity is established. Analysis of the sets of indicators drawn from the two data sets to operationalize concepts like 'strain', 'stress', and 'regime institutional support', shows that the face equivalence of the indicators is very far from obvious, and that the statistical covariation within each set of indicators is hardly sufficient to allow for the simple addition (without weighting) of scores on those indicators into single composite indices of the underlying concepts they are supposed to measure. Welfling's assertion that unshared variance in such indices represents estimates of their unreliability is, therefore, not compelling, and her indication of the relatively greater reliability of the *Black Africa* data as compared to those data derived from the work of Gurr and Duvall must be treated as inconclusive.

3. The methodology of unidimensional scaling is extensively covered in Torgerson, 1957; Magnusson, 1967; Mokken, 1971; and Maranell, 1974. For work on multidimensional scaling see Young, Takane and De Leeuw (1967), and Kruskal and Wish (1978).

4. Note that the Adelman-Morris data first is coded in categories which are assigned letter designations and then translated to numerical measures depending on the number of categories used for each variable.

5. It should be noted that Lerner himself specifically estimates threshold values for each variable in his theory.

7. Of these other problems, sampling bias and specification error are the most amenable to systematic evaluation. That they are not easily disposed of, however, can be seen from a critical reading of Welfling's (1973, pp. 880-877) discussion of these matters. Welfling compares two variable correlations in her two African data sets with the corresponding correlations in the data for an 86 nation sample analyzed by Gurr and Duvall. The latter sample did not include most of the African states. Welfling concludes that where such correlations were similar in the two sets of African data, but different from the equivalent correlations in the 86 countries data, sampling error threatens to invalidate the generalizations made by Gurr and Duvall. But this conclusion is not supportable. The African data are *a priori* a more biased 'sample' than the data for the larger set of states, even though the latter systematically underrepresent the poorest countries in the world. Unless the means and variances of measures in all three data sets are compared, and unless the inclusion of African data significantly affects the correlations in the 86 countries data, it is difficult to conclude that these latter data rather than the African data are biased. The problem of sampling bias is related to that of specification error, as Welfling indicates, to the extent that the inclusion of additional units of analysis involves the discovery of new variables which correlate with the independent and dependent variables in some model, and whose exclusion will bias

the estimates of parameters of that model. More generally, specification error is indicated whenever the addition of one or more independent variables to a model described by a system of equations results represents a significant alteration in the structural parameters of that system of equations — i.e., whenever the inclusion of new variables alters the estimates of the beta coefficients derived from analyais of the original model. It is not appropriate, as Welfling suggests, to use increases in explained variance (R^2) as a criterion for deciding that specification error exists in models omitting variables that account for such increases. Specification error is indicated only if the estimates of the form and significance of the relationships between independent and dependent variables change as the result of the inclusion of new independent variables in a model, irrespective of the change in the explanatory power of the model.

References.

Adelman, I. and C. T. Morris.
1965 "A Factor Analysis of the Interrelationship between Social and Political Variables and Per Capita Gross National Product." *Quarterly Journal of Economics*, 79 (November), 555—78.

Adelman I., M. Geier and C. T. Morris.
1969a "Instruments and Goals in Economic Development." *American Economic Review*, LIX, 2 (May 1969), 409—434.

Adelman, I., G. Dalton and C. T. Morris.
1969b "Society, Politics, and Economic Development in Africa." In *Expanding Horizons in African Studies*, eds. G. Carter and A. Paden Evanston, Ill.: Northwestern University Press, 209—42.

Adelman, I. and C. T. Morris.
1967 *Society, Politics and Economic Development.* Baltimore: Johns Hopkins Press.

Adelman, I. and C. T. Morris.
1973 *Economic Growth and Social Equity in Developing Countries.* Palo Alto: Stanford University Press.

Banks A. and R. Textor.
1964 *A Cross-Polity Survey.* Cambridge, Mass.: MIT Press.

Banks, A.
1971 *Cross-Polity Time Series.* Cambridge, Mass.: MIT Press.

Baxter, N. (ed.)
1972 "Measuring Development: Special Issue on Develop;ment Indicators." *Journal of Development Studies*, 8 (April).

Blalock, H.
1970 "A Causal Approach to Nonrandom Measurement Error." *American Political Science Review*, LXIV, 4, 1099—1112 (December).

Booth, R.
1970 *The Armed Forces of African States, 1970.* Adelphi Papers, London: International Institute for Strategic Studies, report number 67.

Campbell, D. T. and J. Stanley.
1963 *Experimental and Quasi-Experimental Designs for Research.* Chicago: Rand McNally.

Campbell, D. T. and D. Fiske.
1959 "Convergent and Discriminant Validation by the Multitrait-Multimethod Matrix." *Psychological Bulletin*, 56, 81—105.

Cook, D. T. and D. T. Campbell.
1979 *Quasi-Experimentation. Design and Analysis Issues for Field Settings.* Chicago: Rand McNally

Cronbach, L. et. al.
1972 *The Dependability of Behavioral Measurement: Theory of Generalizability for Scores and Profiles.* New York: Wiley.

Doron, C. F., R. E. Pendley and G. E. Antunes.
1973 "A Test of Cross-National Event Reliability: Global Versus Regional Data Sources." *International Studies Quarterly*, 12, 3 (June 1973) 175—204.

Dudley, B. J.
1973 *Instability and Political Order: Politics and Crisis in Nigeria.* Ibadan: Ibadan University Press.

Feierabend, I. and R. L. Feierabend.
1965 *Cross-National Data Bank of Political Instability Events, Code Index.* San Diego, Ca.: Public Affairs Research Institute, San Diego State College.

Gurr, T. R.
1966 *New Error-Compensated Measures for Comparing Nations: Some Correlates of Civil Violence.* Princeton, N.J.: Center of International Studies, Princeton University.

Kruskal, J. and M. Wish.
1978 *Multidimensional Scaling.* Beverly Hills, Ca.: Sage.

Lerner, D.
1958 *The Passing of Traditional Society.* New York: Free Press.

Maranell, G.
1974 *Scaling: A Sourcebook for Behavioral Scientists.* Chicago: Aldine.

Magnusson, D.
1967 *Test Theory.* Reading, Mass.: Addison-Wesley.

McGowan, P.
1973 *The Comparative Study of Foreign Policy.* Beverly Hills, Ca.: Sage Publications.

Mickiewicz, E. (ed.)
1973 *Handbook of Soviet Social Science Data.* New York: Free Press.

Morrison, D. G., and D. T. Campbell.
Measurement Models in the Social Sciences. forthcoming.

Morrison, D. G., R. C. Mitchell, J. N. Paden and H. M. Stevenson.
1972 *Black Africa: A Comparative Handbook.* New York: Free Press,

Morrison, D. G. and H. M. Stevenson.
1980 "Cultural Pluralism, Modernization, and Conflict: An Empirical Analysis of Sources of Political Instability in African Nations." In Paden (1980).

1971   "Political Instability in Independent Black Africa: Continuities and Extensions in the Quantitative Study of Dimensions of Conflict Behavior Within Nations." *Journal of Conflict Resolution*, September.

1972   "Integration and Instability: Patterns of African Political Development." *American Political Science Review*, LXVI, 3 (Sept.), 902—27.

1974a   "Measuring Social and Political Requirements for System Stability: Validation of an Index Using Latin American and African Data." *Comparative Political Studies*, 7, 2, 252—63.

1974b   "Social Complexity, Economic Development, and Military Coups d'État: Convergence and Divergence of Empirical Tests of Theory." *Journal of Peace Research*, (December), 345—47.

Naroll, R.
1972   "Holonational Bibliography." *Comparative Political Studies*, 5, 2 (July), 211-30.

Nunnally, J. C.
1967   *Psychometric Theory*. New York: McGraw Hill.

Orbell, J. and B. Rutherford.
1974   "Can Leviathan Make the Life of Man Less Solitary, Poor, Nasty, Brutish and Short?" *British Journal of Political Science*, 3, 383—407.

Paden, J.
1980   *Values, Identities and National Integration*. Evanston, Ill.: Northwestern University Press.

Rummel, R.
1970   *Applied Factor Analysis*. Evanston, Ill.: Northwestern University Press.

Rummel, R.
1972   *The Dimensions of Nations*. Beverly Hills: Sage Publications.

Russett, B. et. al.
1964   *World Handbook of Social and Political Indicators*. New Haven, Conn.: Yale University Press.

Schmitter, P.
1969   "New Strategies for the Comparative Analysis of Latin American Politics." *Latin American Research Review*, 4 (Summer), 83—110.

Seers, D.
1972   "What Are We Trying to Measure?" *Journal of Development Studies*, 8 (April), 21—36.

Singer, J. D. and M. Small.
1972   *The Wages of War, 1816—1965: A Statistical Handbook*. New York: J. Wiley.

Stevens, S. S.
1968   "Measurement, Statistics and the Schemapiric View." *Science*, 161, 30 (August), 849—56.

Smith, K. W.
1974   "Forming Composite Scales and Estimating Their Validity Through Factor Analysis." *Social Forces*, 53, 2 (December), 168—80.

Taylor, C. and M. Hudson.
1972   *World Handbook of Political and Social Indicators*. New Haven: Yale University Press.

Thomas, D. B.
1974   "Political Development Theory and Africa: Toward a Conceptual Clarification and Comparative Analysis." *Journal of Developing Areas*, 8, 3 (April), 375—94.

Torgerson, W.
1967   *Theory and Methods of Scaling*. New York: John Wiley.

Welfling, M.
1975   "Models, Measurement and Sources of Error: Civil Conflict in Africa." *American Political Science Review*. LXIX, 3 (Sept.), 871—88.

Wells, A.
1974   "The Coup d'État in Theory and Practice: Independent Black Africa in the 1960's." *American Journal of Sociology*, 79, 4 (January), 871—87.

Young, F. W., J. de Leeuw and Y. Takane.
1980   *Multidimensional Scaling: Theory and Method*. N.Y.: Erlbaum Associates.

Young, F. W., J. de Leeuw and Y. Takane.
1977   "Nonmetric Individual Differences Multidimensional Scaling: An Alternating Least Squares Methods with Optional Scaling Features." *Psychometrika*, 42, 1 (March).

Appendix A   Coder 1 Recoding for Adelman-Morris Data, c. 1960.

1. Modernization of Outlook	B	C	C	C	C	A-	B	B-	B	C	C	C	B+	B	B	C	C+	B+	B	B
2. Per Capita-Gross National Product	121	60	75	48	437	227	99	208	101	186	52	78	75	213	128	69	104	67	71	150
3. Extent of Economic Dualism	C+	D-	D-	D	C-	B	D	B-	B-	C-	D	D-	B-	B-	C-	D	C+	C-	C+	C
4. Size of Traditional Agricultural Sector	A	A+	B	A	A	C	A	B	B	A-	A-	A	C	C+	B	A	A-	A	B	B
5. Extent of Urbanization	D	E	D-	E	D+	C-	E+	D	+D-	E	E-	E-	C-	C	E	+D	D-	E	E-	C
6. Literacy Rate	D	D-	D-	D-	D	C	D	D+	C	D	D-	D-	C-	D	D	D-	D+	C-	C	C
7. Social Mobility	A-	C	C+	C-	A-	B	C	B-	B+	C-	C+	C	B-	C	C	C	C	C+	B-	A
8. Mass Communications	D	D-	D-	D-	C-	C+	D-	D+	C-	C-	D-	C-	D	+C-	D+	D-	D	D	C-	D
9. Strength of Democratic Institutions	B	C	B	D-	B	C	C-	C-	C+	C-	C	C-	B+	C-	B	B	D-	C-	B-	B
10. Strength of Labor Movement	B-	D+	B-	D	B-	C	C-	B-	B	B-	B-	B-	B	B	B-	D+	C-	B-	B-	B
11. Degree of Freedom of Opposition and Press	B	B	B	C-	B-	B-	C-	B	B	B-	B	C+	A	B	A	A	C-	A	A	A
12. Degree of Competitiveness of Political Parties	A	C	B-	D	B	B-	C	C	A-	C	B	C	A	B-	A	A	D	C	A	A
13. Extent of Political Stability	D	B	C	C-	A	B	A	A	C-	B	B	C	B	B	B	C	D	A	B	B
14. Political Strength of Traditional Elite	B	C	B-	A+	C	C	C-	B+	B	A-	B	B	B+	B-	B	A	B	A-	B-	C
15. Extent of Leadership Commitment to Economic Development	B	B-	B-	C+	B+	A	B	A+	B	C	C	B	A-	B-	B-	B-	B	B+	B-	B
16. Degree of Cultural and Ethnic Homogeneity	D	C	C-	D	D	D	D	D	D	D	C	C+	D	C	D	A+	C-	A	D	D
17. Degree of National Integration and Sense of Unity	D	C	C	D	C-	C	C-	D	D	D	+C	C	C-	B-	D	A	B	B+	D	D+
18. Crude Fertility Rate	A-	B.	A	B	C	A-	A	A	A	B	A-	B+	A-	B+	B-	A-	A	B	B-	A-
19. Predominant Basis of Political Party System	C	C	C	E	D	A-	A-	A-	C	D	D	D	C	B-	C	D	A	A-	C	D
20. Importance of Indigenous Middle Class	C	D	D	C	B	B	E	C	C	C	D	D	B-	C	C	D-	C	C	C	D
21. Degree of Administrative Efficiency																				
22. Degree of Social Tension	A+	B	B+	A	C	B+	B	C	A	B-	B-	B+	B	B-	C	B-	A	C+	B	B-
23. Political Strength of the Military	B	C+	C	B+	C	C	C	C	B-	C+	C	C+	C	C	C	B	A	C	C	C
24. Extent of Centralization of Political Power																				

Appendix B   Adelman-Morris Variables Coded for c. 1970-Codes 1.

Variable	1	2	3	4	5	6	7	8	9	10	11	12	13	14	15	16	17	18	19	20
1. Modernization of Outlook	B	C-	C	C	C	B+	C	B-	B	C	C-	C-	B+	C+	C	C-	C	C	C+	B-
2. Per Capita-Gross National Product	150	60	80	70	320	190	90	240	130	200	50	70	70	200	170	60	110	80	110	290
3. Extent of Economic Dualism	C	D-	D	D-	C	B	D	B	B	C	D	D-	B	C+	C-	D-	C-	D+	C	C
4. Size of Traditional Agricultural Sector	B+	A	A-	A	A-	C	A-	B+	B+	B+	B+	A+	B	B-	B+	A-	B	A	B+	B+
5. Extent of Urbanization	C-	D	D	D-	B-	B-	D-	B-	D	C-	C	D-	C+	B	B-	C	C-	D-	D-	B+
6. Literacy Rate	D+	D	D	D-	D+	C+	D	C-	C	D	D+	D-	C	D	D+	D-	D+	C-	C-	C-
7. Social Mobility	A+	C	C	C-	A+	A+	C	B-	B+	C+	C+	C-	C+	C+	C	C-	C	C+	C+	B
8. Mass Communications	B-	D	D+	C-	C+	A+	C-	B	A-	B-	D	D+	B-	B-	A-	C	B-	C+	B+	B
9. Strength of Democratic Institutions	C-	C-	D	D-	C-	C	C-	C-	C-	C-	C-	D+	D-	C-	C	C	C	C-	C	B
10. Strength of Labor Movement	C-	C-	D	D-	C	C	C-	C-	C-	C-	C-	D+	D-	C-	C	C	C	C-	C	B
11. Degree of Freedom of Opposition and Press	C-	C-	C-	C-	C-	A	C-	C-	C-	B-	C-	C-	C-	C-	B	C-	C-	C-	C-	A
12. Degree of Competitiveness of Political Parties	C	C	D	D	C	A	C	C	C	C	C	C	D	C	B-	D	D	C	C	B
13. Extent of Political Stability	B	D-	D	D	C+	D+	B	B	C+	A	C-	D+	D-	B-	C-	C	D-	A	D	B+
14. Political Strength of Traditional Elite	B	C+	B	A+	C	C-	C-	C+	B	A-	C	C	C	B	C	C	B	C-	C-	C-
15. Extent of Leadership Commitment to Economic Development	A	B-	B-	C	B	B	B	A	A	C	B-	C	B	B	B-	B	B-	A-	B-	A-
16. Degree of Cultural and Ethnic Homogeneity	D	C-	C	C-	C+	C	C	C	D	C	D	C	B	D	C+	D	A+	C-	A	D
17. Degree of National Integration and Sense of Unity	D	C-	C	C	C+	C+	C	D+	B-	D	C-	C+	C+	B-	D+	D	C	B+	D	D
18. Crude Fertility Rate	B-	B+	A-	B	C-	B	B+	B	B+	A-	B+	A	A-	B	B	B	B+	B+	B-	A-
19. Predominant Basis of Political Party System	B	D	E	E	D	E	A-	B-	B	D	B	B	E	B-	C	E	E	A-	A-	A-
20. Importance of Indigenous Middle Class	C	D	C	B	C	A	E	C+	D+	D	C	C	B	C	B-	E	B	C	C	B+
21. Degree of Administrative Efficiency																				
22. Degree of Social Tension	C	A	A	A	C	B	A	B-	B-	C	A-	B	A+	B	A	A	A+	C	A	B
23. Political Strength of the Military	C	B	A-	C	O	A-	B	C	C	C	C	B-	A+	C	A-	A	A	C	A-	B-
24. Extent of Centralization of Political Power																				

Appendix C   Coded Scores for 22 Adelman-Morris Variables-Coder 2, c. 1970.

Variable	Coded scores
1. Modernization of Outlook	B C B- B- B A A- A- B+ C B- C B+ B- B+ C B A+ B B+
2. Per Capita-Gross National Product	150 65 85 75 320 190 95 240 130 200 55 75 75 200 170 65 110 85 110 290
3. Extent of Economic Dualism	B C C C C B+ B- B+ B+ C+ D D B+ B- C C B- B B B+
4. Size of Traditional Agricultural Sector	B B+ B+ A A B B C- C- C B A A C A C+ A C+ B C
5. Extent of Urbanization	D+ D- C- D- C+ C D C D D+ E E+ C B D C D D- D B-
6. Literacy Rate	D+ D D D- D C D D- C D D+ D- C D D D- D+ C- D- D-
7. Social Mobility	A- C- C C- A- A- C B B+ C- B- C- C+ C C C- C C C+ B
8. Mass Communications	B- D C- C- C+ A C- B A- B- D C- B A- A- C B+ C+ B B
9. Strength of Democratic Institutions	C- D- D- D- C- C- C- C- C- D D C- D- C- C+ D- D- C+ D- C+
10. Strength of Labor Movement	C- C- C- D C D C- C C C D C- C D- C C- D D D C
11. Degree of Freedom of Opposition and Press	C+ C C C C C C C C+ C C C C D+ B- C C B+ C C+
12. Degree of Competitiveness of Political Parties	C C D D C D+ C C C C C C D C C C C D C D+ C
13. Extent of Political Stability	A- D D D- B- D A- B+ B+ A- A- A- D- B C C D- A- D- A-
14. Political Strength of Traditional Elite	C C + A C+ C C- C- B- A C+ B- B- B+ C+ B+ B+ C C+ C-
15. Extent of Leadership Commitment to Economic Development	B B- B- B- B- B B A B+ B- B- B- B B- B- B- B- A B+ B+
16. Degree of Cultural and Ethnic Homogeneity	D C+ C- D D D D D C- D C- C+ D C+ D A+ C- B D D
17. Degree of National Integration and Sense of Unity	D+ D+ C- D+ D D+ D+ D+ C- D C- C D- C D C+ D+ C+ D D+
18. Crude Fertility Rate	
19. Predominant Basis of Political Party System	A- D E E D E A B- B- B D D E B- D E E A B+ B+
20. Importance of Indigenous Middle Class	D+ D+ D+ E C- C+ E C- C D D D- E D+ E E C C+ C B-
21. Degree of Administrative Efficiency	
22. Degree of Social Tension	C- A+ A- A C A- C+ C C+ C C C A+ C A- A- A+ C A+ C
23. Political Strength of the Military	C B+ A+ B+ C+ A C C C C C C A+ B A- A A+ C A C-
24. Extent of Centralization of Political Power	

4. Ethnic Unit Classification and Analysis

Introduction

In Section B, Part I, Chapter 2 and in each of the country profiles in Part II we give information based on the ethnic composition of the populations of African states. This information is not given to perpetuate esoteric interests in *traditional* or *primitive* societies, nor are we interested per se in exotic statistics on the number of different languages and tribes in the African continent and the national boundaries of their constituents. Rather the collection and presentation of these data are intended to inform the analysis of sociological theories of pluralism, integration, and other approaches to the continuing, but not unique, problems of national unity in Africa.

The utility of this information is dependent on the theoretical meaning and explanatory power of our concepts relating to ethnicity[1], as well as the reliability, comparability, and reproducibility of the measures used to describe these concepts. The reader should note that our basic concept, the ethnic unit, is not the same thing as a tribe (or ethnic identity group), though ethnic units are made up of one or more tribes. This chapter, therefore, discusses: (1) the theoretical context of the ethnic data in this book, (2) the conceptualization of ethnicity and the theoretical equivalence of ethnic units used for the collection of this data, and (3) the operational procedures used for the classification and description of ethnic units listed here.

Ethnicity and National Integration

The theoretical relevance of our method of classifying the national ethnic units in Part II should be assessed in terms of the theory of: conflict, conflict regulation, and system breakdown in which framework we set, data priorities for this Handbook. (See Section A, Chapter 2) One major aspect of conflict regulation relates to the theory of integration. In the most abstract terms, integration has been defined as "a relationship among units in which they are mutually interdependent and jointly produce system properties which they would separately lack."[2] More loosely defined, integration is the degree of cohesion and consensus binding members of a social entity together, and as integration increases, there is a decrease in the salience of sub-unit boundaries or the lines of demarcation between members of the social entity. The theory of integration is the search for those behavioral relationships which increase or decrease the cohesion and consensus within social groupings, and the analysis of national integration is the search for those relationships which have an impact on the cohesion and consensus characteristic of the populations of nation-states.

By cohesion and consensus we refer principally to the degree to which members of a nation regard themselves as sharing a common identity and the degree to which they share common values. Whatever the relationship between values and indentities in the process of integration, a major threat to consensus and cohesion in contemporary states is thought to be the existence, within national boundaries, of ethnic groups (or "tribes") based on real or assumed blood ties, language, region, religion, or custom[3]. National integration in these terms means the shift in the principal locus of political identity and loyalty from the ethnic group to the national population as a whole and to the formulation of some minimal set of shared socio-political values.

Despite the apparent importance of the role of ethnicity in African national integration, the empirical problems of analyzing ethnic heterogeneity are formidable. The problem, which we shall spend the bulk of this chapter discussing, is the empirical identification and comparability of ethnic groups. In order to decide whether there is more ethnic heterogencity in one nation than another, it is necessary to answer such apparently simple questions as: What is an ethnic group, and what are the boundaries between one ethnic group and another? The attempt to provide answers to these questions is generally phrased in terms of populations sharing common values and common identity. These two aspects of national integration require some elaboration at this point.

The question of the communality of values held by populations and the operational problem of measuring this value congruence are important issues in the study of national integration[4]. In the simplest terms, values are the preferences individuals or groups have for particular social arrangements (e.g. polygyny vs. monogamy) or actions (e.g. negotiation vs. physical aggression in resolving marital conflicts). The fundamental hypothesis of structural-functional theories of the social systesm is that societies are distinguished from fluctuating aggregates of interacting individuals by the boundaries of value consensus to which members of the social system subscribe. Conflict theorists also presuppose some *rules of the game* which are accepted by the contending parties in an integrated society. The range of common values necessary for integration is not specified, but it seems that the range of minimal consensus for political integration is quite narrow. Two value dimensions are important in this context: (a) common values which define the purpose of community, and (b) common values that legitimate the exercise of power within the community—in particular, values that legitimate decision-making and conflict resolution procedures.

A second approach to the analysis of integration is one which focuses upon common identity. Identities are the recognition by individuals or groups that they are alike in some significant respect, and that this likeness distinguishes them from others. Individuals may hold multiple identities[5], the primacy of which varies with the situation of the individual, and completely new identities may be assumed in new situations[6].

In terms of identities, national integration is a process by which individuals recognize themselves to be members of the same nation. The movement "from tribe to nation"[7] is not, however, necessarily incompatible with the retention of sub-national ethnic identities. The identity shift is not an all or nothing phenomenon; the ethnic identities utilized by single individuals are not limited in number, nor should they be considered static. Thus, continued ethnic identity, under certain conditions, is not necessarily incompatible with national political integration; as Mercier argues:

> In the new states, ethnic identity does not always have a centrifugal effect. It can just as well be an integrative factor to the extent that the rules of a common game are explicitly or implicitly accepted. Ethnic diversity can, in many different ways, contribute to unification or be utilized toward that end."[8]

In considering the relationship between value congruence and common identity as aspects of national integration, it is important first to recapitulate the point made in the last paragraph that ethnic identities are not necessarily incompatible with a shared national identity. It may be supposed, however, that the growth of a shared national identity is contingent on the growth of a measure of value congruence between differently identified ethnic groups who, in Mazrui's words, assume increasingly "a capacity for constant discovery of areas of compatibility."[9] However, while national identity may be facilitated by the relative cultural homogeneity of the ethnic groups in any nation, it cannot be said that such identity is a necessary consequence of value congruence. As Deutsch points out:

> The population of different territories might easily profess verbal attachment to the same set of values without having a sense of political community that leads to political integration. The kind of sense of community that is relevant for integration…turns out to be rather a matter of mutual sympathy and loyalty; of 'we-feeling,' trust, and mutual consideration; of partial identification in terms of self-images and interests; of mutually successful predictions of behavior and of cooperative action in accordance with it…[10]

At this stage in the empirical study of national integration it is not possible to determine the relative importance of, or relationship between, common values and shared identities in national populations. The approach taken here is to devise a method of assessing degrees of value congruence in ethnically heterogeneous African states rather than to assess the growth of a national identity. We adopt this strategy for theoretical and practical reasons.

Theoretically, as we have implied above, value congruence may be argued to precede national identity in that some minimal agreement on political values is necessary to produce the cooperation and mutual confidence that develop a sense of identity. The underlying hypothesis guiding this approach is, therefore, that the greater the value congruence among the ethnic groups within a nation, the greater the potential for their development of a shared national identity.

In practical terms, the available information on African populations, while highly unsatisfactory for determining contemporary identity groups (as we shall discuss below), does permit the classification of the groups identified by anthropologists into *ethnic units* that are homogeneous in terms of shared traditional cultural characteristics. For example, in Nigerian politics it might be argued that the critical identity groups in Western Nigerian politics have been the Yoruba sub-tribes (Ekiti, Ijebu, Oyo, etc.) rather than the broader Yoruba, non-Yoruba identities. The breakup of the former Western State in 1976 may even accentuate such rivalries at the national level although there is other evidence that former local identities are being submerged in a wider Pan-Yoruba identity. But it is still relevant, in value congruence terms, to speak of a homogeneous Yoruba culture and the relative congruence between this and other traditional cultures in Nigeria may be thought of as an important factor influencing the development of Nigerian national integration. The 1979 elections seem to be consistent with this judgement.

In the remainder of this chapter, we will discuss an approach to classifying ethnic units in Black African nations on the basis of their internal cultural homogeneity. The development of this classification is the theoretical basis for our operationalizations of national ethnic pluralism given in Part I, Chapter 2. The composition of these ethnic units, their population and their geographic location is given for each country in Part II.

The Comparability of Ethnic Units

The most extensive data on the cultural values of African peoples are contained in the work of anthropologists who have studied populations, variously described as 'societies', 'people', 'ethnic groups' or 'tribes'. To the non-specialist there is hardly more difficulty in accepting the existence of 'tribes' than in accepting the existence of nations and both words serve to bolster deep-seated prejudices. In the language of social scientists, however, the concept of 'tribe', despite its apparent simplicity to the non-specialist, is a complex matter which has eluded satisfactory definition by anthropologists.[11] The conceptual confusion which bedevils the description of ethnic groups is particularly threatening to cross-national research which seeks to utilize ethnographic information. Aggregated data for cross-nation research must be based on the summary characteristics of groups of equivalent units, and aggregate ethnic data descriptive of nation-states is of little use if the unit of aggregation — the ethnic unit — is one thing in nation A and another in nation B. The aim of this section is, therefore, to investigate what James Fernandez has called "one of the most tangled areas in our taxonomies," in which "one man's tribe is another man's super-tribe and a third man's sub-tribe."[12]

The variety of analytic definitions of ethnic groups in the ethnographic literature is considerable, and the lack of correspondence in definition is, of course, a major threat to the comparability of the units about which we *know* something. Summarizing the literature, Naroll found at least ten different criteria proposed for the definition of ethnic units: (1) distribution of particular traits being studied; (2) territorial contiguity; (3) political organization; (4) language; (5) ecological adjustment; (6) local community structure; (7) widest relevant social unit; (8) native name; (9) common folklore or history and (10) ethnographer's units.[13]

Whichever of these criteria anthropologists use to define the boundaries of the populations they study, our assumption is that they base their field research on micro-societies that will in most cases correspond to functional identity groups. That is to say, the members of the population labelled X by the ethnographer will, with a high degree of probability, use the identity X in some situations, even if it is not their primary identity. It is impossible, however, to know whether ethnic groups studied by different anthropologists comprise populations for whom the identities given them by anthropologists have similar significance. It is not possible, therefore, to treat the groups named in ethnographies as equivalent identity groups, and to assess national integration in terms of the number of named-groups in a national population[14]. In addition, it is not clear, that the named-groups in the ethnographic literature correspond to culturally discrete populations. Apart from the situational and subjective relativity of ethnic identity, the effects of the diffusion of cultural traits from one named-group to another, further "fuzzes the discreteness of tribal units. Different tribes may in the process of historical diffusion turn out to be simple reiterations of the same entity and not truly discrete."[15]

In order to compare named-groups studied by anthropologists, social scientists interested in cross-cultural research have attempted, therefore, to establish criteria by which groups may be considered equivalent. Naroll, for example, specifies linguistic, political and interactional criteria to define comparable "culture-bearing units" as:

> People who are domestic speakers of a common distinct language and who belong either to the same state or the same contact group.[16]

This attempt relates directly to our problem: What conceptual approaches can be taken in order to abstract from the ethnographic literature a set of comparable units for cross-national research?

The requirements that were selected for the classification of ethnic units for the countries in Black Africa are as follows: (1) each unit should be made up of people whose basic cultural characteristics are similar; (2) each unit should be of significant population size: i.e., units which comprise either more than 5 percent of the national population or more than one million people (within the country); (3) the set of ethnic units in each country should be sufficiently inclusive to account for at least 80 percent of the total population; and (4) the set of ethnic units in each country should reflect all major cultural variations represented in its population. The demographic requirements (2 and 3) require no further discussion until we come to the problem of finding demographic data on ethnic groups. The major quesion at this stage is how to aggregate ethnic identity groups to obtain ethnic units meeting these criteria.

Three Approaches to Aggregating Ethnic Identity Groups[17]

Let us consider three alternative approaches: (1) a single classification rule in which all identified ethnic identity groups which are identical on a set of cultural variables may be aggregated into a single unit; (2) an analysis of variance model in which identified ethnic identity

Figure 4.1 Hypothetical Cultural Value Data on Ethnic Identity Groups for Two Countries

Ethnic Identity Groups	NATION A			Ethnic Identity Groups	NATION B		
	Authority	Hierarchy	Distribution		Authority	Hierarchy	Distribution
EIG₁	1	2	1	EIG₁	1	1	1
EIG₂	1	2	1	EIG₂	1	1	1
EIG₃	2	1	5	EIG₃	2	3	3
EIG₄	3	4	6	EIG₄	2	3	3
EIG₅	3	4	6	EIG₅	3	2	2
Variance	.80	1.44	5.36	Variance	.56	.80	.80
	Total Variance 7.60				Total Variance 2.16		

EIG = Ethnic identity group
Authority, hierarchy, and distribution are ordinalized variables

groups are aggregated into single units whenever the cultural variance within the aggregate is less than a given percentage of the total variance for all identified ethnic groups being considered; (3) a cross-national research model, which is adopted here, in which the principles of aggregation in either (1) or (2) are modified by a consideration of the range of variation across the identified ethnic identity groups located within a given national boundary.

In this third approach ethnic distinctiveness is assessed not simply in terms of the cultural differences between ethnic identity groups, but in terms of the range of those differences relative to the range of difference within the national boundaries in which the identity groups are located. This is a somewhat complicated procedure. Let us illustrate this procedure by taking two hypothetical countries and their constituent ethnic identity groups as shown in Figure 4.1

In these two national contexts, it is clear in qualitative terms that there is more cultural diversity (variance) in country A than in country B. There are, however, fundamental similarities in the cultural distribution of the two national populations. For each country there are two sets of two culturally identical ethnic identity groups, and a single ethnic group that is different from all the others on each dimension. The identical groups could be grouped into a common unit at a higher level of abstraction by the single classification rule as one way of classifying national ethnic units[18].

A modified approach, using the analysis of variance model, is to inspect the actual *distance* of the outlying identity groups from the other ethnic units. In country A, it will be observed, the outlying identity group (EIG₃) differs markedly and not uniformly from the two pairs of

identical groups. In country B, the outlying group (EIG₅) is 'closer' to one ethnic unit (EIG₃, EIG₄) than the other, and this is uniformly true.[19] Since we have already observed that the total variance in country B is less than that in country A, it may be more reflective of the country's cultural diversity to include EIG₅ in the ethnic cluster it most closely approximates, giving two ethnic units in country B.[20] In order to decide how to include identity groups into aggregate ethnic units in more complex cases than that illustrated here, one might decide on a decision-rule such as the following: Whenever the inclusion of an identity group in an ethnic unit means that the ratio of the variance in the ethnic unit to the total national variance is more than 15 percent, the identity group should not be included.

In countries with many more identity groups and greater cultural diversity than the hypothetical cases discussed here, the internal complexity of ethnic units may be much greater. For all countries, the classification of ethnic units may be viewed along two continua: scope of unit membership (ranging from exclusive to inclusive membership), and criteria of unit membership, both quantitative (from many to few definitional components) and qualitative (from concrete to abstract components). The three levels of inclusion on these continua that are relevant to the understanding of the ethnic units classified in this book are illustrated in Figure 4.2.

Figure 4.2 Ethnic Units: Model for the Definition of Levels of Inclusion for a Hypothetical Country.

Type of Ethnic Unit	Levels of Inclusion and Their Definitional Components		
	1. Common identity 2. Similar manifest culture 3. Similar value premises	1. Similar manifest culture 2. Similar value premises	1. Similar value premises
Ethnic Identity Group (EIG)	EIG_1 ⟶		
Ethnic Type (ET)	EIG_2 EIG_3 EIG_4 ⟶	ET_1 ⟶	
Ethnic Cluster (EC)	EIG_5 EIG_6 EIG_7 EIG_8 EIG_9 EIG_{10} ⟶	ET_2 ET_3 ⟶	EC_1 ⟶
Analytical Continuum of Inclusion	Exclusive membership Multiple definitional components Concrete definitional criteria		Inclusive membership Few definitional components Abstract criteria

Group, Type, Cluster: Three Levels of Inclusion

The clustering of identity groups discussed above with reference to Figure 4.1 did not proceed beyond the first two levels of inclusion illustrated in Figure 4.2. This latter figure presents a hypothetical example of a national population from which ten named identity groups (EIG_1-EIG_{10}) have been selected for classification. Ideally, one's minimal units should be even more exclusive than those which operational limitations have obliged us to employ. Instead of starting with groups (tribes), the best starting point would be at the level of primary identity groups (i.e., sub-tribes, village clusters, etc.). Be this as it may, the identity groups which we do use out of necessity (such as Kikuyu and Kamba in Kenya) are assumed to be definable by three components: shared identity (and language), similar institutions, and similar value premises.

We define our second level (Ethnic Type) by dropping the identity and language criteria, which leaves us with combinations of identity groups which are manifestly similar with respect to institutional organization as well as to the sharing of basic value premises. Our final level of inclusion (ethnic cluster) aggregates those types

which, although somewhat variant in specific aspects of institutional organization, still are relatively culturally similar. The various groups which make up a cluster share similar metaphysical and social assumptions or value orientations.[21]

In the example shown in Figure 4.2, we present a classification which yields three basic ethnic units (EIG_1, ET_1 and EC_1). It happens that each unit has been established at a *different level of inclusion*. EIG_1 shares neither manifest cultural traits nor more abstract cultural premises with any other such population in the country. It, therefore, stands alone as a distinct unit. EIG_2, EIG_3, and EIG_4 all have similar institutions which are likewise premised on similar assumptions and values, although this similarity has never been recognized and symbolized by a notion of common identity. There are, however, no other groups within the country which share similar value premises with these three groups. They have thus been grouped as a single type, ET_1. Finally EC_1 has been established from two types which share similar value premises, although their institutions differ from each other in certain significant respects.

Each ethnic unit in this country, then, although established at different levels of inclusion, represents a population sharing a set of similar value premises which is significantly different from that of any other unit within the country. The major ambiguity arising from this discussion of Figure 4.2 is what is meant by 'significant' similarity or difference. How similar must the institutions of two identity groups be to consider that they constitute a type? How similar must the value premises of two types be to consider them as one cluster? Given the quality and quantity of data we had to deal with in classifying the populations of 41 countries, it was impossible to set up rigid criteria to guide our judgments. Our decisions were more or less subjective, depending on the ethnic situation presented by each country, and the quality of its description in the ethnographic literature. An example which illustrates Figure 4.2 and the discussion of levels of inclusion is our classification of ethnic units in Benin.

Example of Benin

In this Handbook we have defined three major ethnic units in Benin and each of these units represents a different level of inclusion. The Yoruba correspond to our identity group level. Such groups as the various branches of the Egba Yoruba (the Holli, Dassa, Ketu, Manigri, Itsha, Chabe, and Anago) all speak closely related dialects of Yoruba. Their cultures are all highly similar at the institutional level, being characterized by a social organization including such features as large villages comprised of large extended patrilineal kin groups. These villages are organized into paramount chiefdoms in which authority is hierarchical and passed hereditarily to a patrilineal heir rather than a son. These societies recognize an hereditary aristocracy which rules over a class of freemen. As is common with most groups at this level of abstraction, the members of the group have a common sense of Egba Yoruba identity.

The peoples we have classified within the Fon type also manifest a high degree of cultural similarity, but they do not share a common identity. Historically the kingdoms of the Gun, the Adja and Wachi, the Aizo, and the Popo have been in relationships of varying degrees of autonomy with the Kingdom of Dahomey (Fon), but they have never considered themselves to be one people. The Gun have always been relatively isolated from the Dahomeans due to their marsh environment. In many respects these groups are quite similar to our description of the Yoruba groups. They are different in that the family unit is restricted to independent polygynous families. What is more, political succession among the Fon type is guided by principles of patrilineality and primogeniture.

Our third group, which represents a cluster, is comprised of the Bargu, the Kilinga, and the Somba. These peoples all speak languages of the Bargu division

of the Mossi-Grunshi branch of the Niger-Congo linguistic stock. They do not, however, share a common identity. They manifest a fair degree of similarity in numerous aspects of local community structure, e.g., neighborhoods of dispersed homesteads, each of which is comprised of a patrilineage. There are, however, marked differences in form at the higher levels of political organization. While the Bargu are organized as a centralized state and the Kilinga into paramount chiefdoms, the Somba have no political organization above the local community level. Be this as it may, we have grouped these people into a cluster because government at the Somba local level and government at the Bargu state level appear to be premised on similar assumptions. Among the Somba, local authority is centered in a *chef-de-terre* with ritual powers who administers the distribution and use of communally owned land. He is the eldest member of the founding lineage. Within the family, land and other property is held by the family head. Property transfer and political succession follow principles of patrilineality, with transferences moving from elder brother to younger brother. Such patterns are indicators of a notion of hierarchy in status relationships. These patterns and principles are also those of the other groups within the cluster. Although the level of political development varies within the Bargu cluster, the three major groups within it premise their political relationships on the same basic assumption.

What this means, therefore, is that for our purposes ethnic units are equivalent in terms of their cultural similarity in their national context, but that they differ greatly in terms of their salience and intelligibility to the individual citizen. Identity groups, types, and clusters may by classified as ethnic units in a given country, and they are equivalent or comparable because the values shared within their constituent populations are sufficiently distinctive to distinguish them from other groups in the national population.

Therefore, an ethnic unit, as we define it for any African country, is a culturally distinctive and numerically significant segment of the national population, in which individuals have similar values, the national distribution of which is such that (a) the rest of the population, or any other subset of it, has a different set of values in common, and (b) the degree of cultural diversity within the ethnic unit is substantially less than that within the total national population, and not substantially more than that in any other ethnic unit classified for the same nation.

Thus defined, ethnic units may be:

1. *Ethnic identity groups*, in which individuals have values, institutions and identity in common;
2. *Ethnic types*, in which individuals have values and institutions in common; or
3. *Ethnic clusters*, in which individuals have values in common.

The preceding discussion is greatly simplified, and exceedingly abstract, in order to present the logic of equivalence between ethnic units as we conceptualize them for cross-national research purposes. The empirical problems involved in our application of this conceptual framework to the data on African ethnicity are discussed in the next section, which also includes a list of the units (identity groups, types, and clusters) we coded for the 41 black African states.

Selection of Ethnic Units in African States

In attempting to implement the conceptual and methodological framework for the ethnic unit classification outlined in the previous section, we used the following general procedures:
a. Search out and compare all existing classifications of ethnic units by country to determine all major cultural distinctions within each national population.
b. Evaluate and revise existing classifications in terms of the cultural homogeneity and demographic significance of the ethnic units in their national context.
c. Provide quantitative data on the cultural characteristics of each unit finally selected. (These data are the basis for the measures of cultural variance for each nation given in Part I, Chapter 2)

Location of Information

Available ethnic classifications of African populations tend to be based on either (i) maximal identity groups,[22] (ii) linguistic criteria,[23] (iii) geographic proximity or historical relatedness,[24] (iv) similarity with respect to multiple criteria.[25] The last of these is closest to our own interest, but even those classifications which purport to be based on a consideration of multiple criteria tend to be biased in favor of a single variable such as language, historical relatedness, political organization, ecological adaptation, or geographic proximity. Our task, at any rate, was to search the literature for ethnic classifications of all kinds, and to establish on what criteria they were based, and how significantly they diverged from our interest in

ethnic units that are culturally and demographically distinctive in the national context.

The bibliographic references in Part II of this book indicate the sources which we found particularly helpful in locating ethnic classifications for each of the 41 countries. Three sources of information can be characterized. First, we had recourse to the extensive case-study literature on individual African countries, and monographs such as Weinstein's book on Gabon,[26] or one of the Area Handbooks[27] that provide ethnic classification on national populations. This literature is not directly written by or for anthropologists, but the focus on nations as entities agrees with our own, as does the concern for politically relevant categories.

Second, we had access to official reports and censuses containing statistical information in varying detail on the ethnic composition of national populations. Because we needed to couple our own ethnic unit classifications with reliable demographic data, we tended to be biased towards the use of official census categories if it was at all possible to find a correspondence between these and the categories used in culturally defined classifications. Where the census categories correspond to identity groups described in ethnographic sources, there is of course no problem. But some census classifications reflect the ascriptive categories employed by European administrators rather than indigenous categories or categories formulated by professional anthropologists.[28] In other cases, census categories are aggregate clusters of identity groups, which are not individually specified, and are aggregated according to criteria which are not fully explained in the census documentation.[29] Another difficulty posed by census classifications occurs when the populations of only the major identity groups in the country are reported,[30] which may inhibit the production of classifications that cover more than 80 percent of the population.

Finally, there are ethnic classifications which are the work of professional anthropologists. Based on individual case studies of identity groups, these classifications range from detailed maps of the geographical location of identity groups,[31] to typological classifications in which identity groups are clustered according to some well defined principles. Although the former are useful for interpreting the national location of many classifications, the latter work is of most use to us. Of particular importance is the work of George Peter Murdock, whose comprehensive book, *Africa: Its Peoples and Their Culture History*,[32] is something of a *tour de force*. Based on a thorough review of the existing African ethnographic literature of the time, Murdock developed a full classification system of African ethnic groups, relying especially on the criteria of historical and linguistic relatedness as a basis for combining identity groups into composite ethnic units. Although this work is idiosyncratic in some of its classifications, and is badly in need of updating in the light of recent anthropological field work and more recent linguistic classifications,[33] it is an invaluable aid for any work in ethnic unit clustering for Africa.

The search of the literature on ethnic unit classification produced a list for our countries of over 600 ethnic groups which are included in categories of varying inclusiveness and analytic definition. Because of the great variation in the detail of the classifications we found for different countries, this figure is in itself not particularly helpful. The list of identified groups does not mean that we have a comparable set of identity groups, defined at the same level of inclusion, for each country. If it had been possible to obtain such a list – say of N groups all defined as primary identity groups, and if there were comparably detailed ethnographic case studies on each identified unit, it would have been possible to code each unit on a number of variables, and then follow our methodological outline for ethnic unit classification very precisely. Faced with the great variation in ethnic unit definition and case study information, however, we were bound to follow a far less precise procedure.

Dealing with each country separately, we sought to evaluate the cultural content and demographic significance of each unit specified in available ethnic classifications. The ethnographic descriptions of each named group in a country's population were searched, and, wherever possible, we made initial judgments about the coding for each group on our variables. These variables, operationalized as ordinal scales, are based to a large extent on the coding categories used by Murdock in his *Ethnographic Atlas*[34]. A significant proportion of this coding was, in fact, already available in Murdock's works,[35] and our own task was simplified in many cases to checking Murdock's judgments. In other cases, where Murdock has not published codings, or where more recent ethnographic material is available, we made our own judgments.

On the basis of this qualitative investigation of the cultural characteristics of each identified ethnic group within the national population, we proceeded to cluster groups that we judged to be culturally similar. The classification of ethnic types – the aggregation of culturally similar ethnic groups – was not, however, to rely on judgments as to the overriding importance of linguistic, historical and geographical relationships, or the documentation on a widely perceived sense of communal identity said to be characteristic of a set of identified groups, whose cultural characteristics were not otherwise clearly defined. These judgments concerning the degree of cultural similarity between groups, and the significance of single variables in predicting to multivariate cultural congruity are briefly summarized in Part II, but the results of the classification may be detailed here and exemplified by a discussion of the classification for a single country.

For most countries, our threefold schema of identity groups, types, and clusters adequately describes the ethnic units which we classified from our comparisons of the cultural characteristics of ethnic groups identified in available ethnic unit classifications. In five countries, however, we utilized an additional conceptual category – the residual, or 'shatter-belt' cluster – to describe a set of geographically contiguous ethnic groups, whose cultural experience varies in homogeneity, but who have received a common, out-group ascription or identity. The ethnic units we have classified for African states are summarized in Figure 4.3, which shows the levels of inclusion, and the criteria for inclusion, characteristic of each unit. The classification may be further elaborated by an account of the selection of ethnic units for Cameroon.

Cameroon Example

Our starting point in developing the Cameroon classification was Victor T. LeVine's book, *The Cameroons: From Mandate to Independence*[36] LeVine defines eleven ethnic groups in Cameroon. Several of LeVine's categories are based on Murdock:[37] Southern Nigerians, Northwestern and Coastal Bantu, Cameroon Highlanders, Plateau Nigerians, Eastern Nigritic, Fulani, and Pygmies.

Reviewing the ethnographic material on each of the identified groups within the clusters identified by Murdock and LeVine, we selected six culturally distinctive units, five of which correspond to Murdock's units, although we have labeled them differently to identify the ethnic group that we judge to be most typical of the cultural unit. Of the six units we have selected, the Fulani are a clear-cut identity group. The Beti-Pahouin (Equatorial Bantu), the Bassa-Bakoko (Northwestern and Coastal Bantu), and the Baya-Mbum (Eastern Nigritic) are types, in our formulation. Each of these three units is made up of different identity groups which share a common culture. All of these three types are quite similar to each other with respect to principles of social and political organization. With few exceptions, the political level goes no higher than the local level. The local grouping is invariably a localized kin group residing in a compact village or hamlet. Principles of descent, inheritance, and succession are patrilineal. Our reasons for not carrying the classification of these types to the cluster level are primarily linguistic. The Baya-Mbum type speak languages of the Eastern or Adamawa-Eastern subfamily of the Niger-Congo family, while the Beti-Pahouin and

Figure 4.3   African Ethnic Units: Levels of Inclusion for Forty-One Countries

Country	Percent Country Population Classified	Relationship to Census Categories	Identity Group	Type	Cluster	Residual or "Shatter-Belt" Cluster
1. Angola	96	1		Ovimbundu Mbundu Central Bantu (Kongo) Lunda Chokwe (Chokwe) Nganguela* (Nyemba) Nyaneka-Humbe (Nyaneka)		
2. Benin	93	2	Yoruba (Egba)	Fon	Bargu	
3. Botswana	90	1	Tswana			
4. Burundi	98	1		Rundi		
5. Cameroon	81	3	Fulani (Bororo)	Beti-Pahaouin Fang Bassa-Bakoko Douala Baya-Mbum Baya	Highland Bantu	Kirdi (Masa)
6. Central African Republic (CAR)	90	1	Banda Baya Mandjia (Mandja) Mbum Mbaka (Bwaka)	Riverine		
7. Chad	91	4	Arab		Sudanic (Sara) Nilotic (Maba)* Saharan (Teda)	
8. Congo	90	1	Kongo Téké M'Bété* Sanga	M'Bochi*		
9. Djibouti	99	1	Afars Arabs Issas			
10. Equatorial Guinea	95	2	Bubi	Fang		
11. Ethiopia	96	4	Galla Amhara Somali Afar	Kafa-Sidamo	Nilotic	

Figure 4.3   (continued)

Country	Percent Country Population Classified	Relationship to Census Categories	Identity Group	Type	Cluster	Residual or "Shatter-Belt" Cluster
12. Gabon	83	3	Fang	Eshira* M'Bété* Kota Omyènè (Mpongwe)		
13. Gambia	81	1	Mandingo (Malinké) Fulani (Bororo) Wolof Diola Serahuli (Soninké)			
14. Ghana	82	1	Ewé Ga-Adangbe (Ga)		Akan (Ashanti) Mole-Dagbani (Gurensi)	
15. Guinea	97	2	Fulani (Foula Djallon)	Mandé-Fu (Kpellé)	Mandé (Malinké) West Atlantic (Kissi)	
16. Guinea-Bissau	93	1	Manding (Malinké) Peul (Fulani)	Senegambian (Bangum)		
17. Ivory Coast	95	1		Kru (Bété) Senufo Lagoon (Attie) Lobi	Akan (Baule) Mandé (Malinké) Peripheral Mandé (Gouro)	
18. Kenya	85	1	Luo		Western Bantu (Luhya) Coastal Bantu (Digo) Kalenjin (Nandi) Central Bantu (Kikuyu)	Other Eastern Nilotic (Masai)
19. Lesotho	95	1	Sotho			
20. Liberia	94	4	Vai	Mandé-Fu (Kpellé) Kru-Bassa (Kru)	Gola-Kissi (Gola)	

Figure 4.3 (continued)

Country	Percent Country Population Classified	Relationship to Census Categories	Identity Group	Type	Cluster	Residual or "Shatter-Belt" Cluster
21. Madagascar	95	1		Central Plateau (Merina) East Coast (Betsimisaraka*) Escarpment (Tamala) Plains (Antandroy)		
22. Malawi	94	3	Lomwe* Yao Ngoni	Tumbuka	Chewa	
23. Mali	98	4	Fulani (Bororo) Tuareg (Asben) Songhai	Mandé (Bambara) Senufo Sarakolé (Soninké)		
24. Mauritania	95	2	Moors (Zenaga)	Tukulor-Fulani (Tukulor)		
25. Mozambique	95	2		Makua-Lomwe (Yao) Maravi (Chewa) Thonga Shona*		
26. Namibia	91	1	Herero Ovambo Kavango Damara Khoisan Coloureds	Europeans		
27. Niger	93	1	Hausa Djerma-Songhai (Sunghai) Fulani (Bororo) Tuareg (Asben) Kanuri			
28. Nigeria	86	3	Yoruba Ibo Nupe Ijaw Bororo	Hausa-Fulani (Hausa) Ibibio and Semi-Bantu (Ibibio) Kanuri and Kanuri-dominated peoples (Kanuri) Edo (Bini) Idoma, Igala, Igbirva (Igala)		Tiv and Planteau (Tiv)

Figure 4.3   (continued)

Country	Percent Country Population Classified	Relationship to Census Categories	Identity Group	Type	Cluster	Residual or "Shatter-Belt" Cluster
29. Rwanda	100	1		Rwanda		
30. Senegal	94	2	Serer	Wolof Fulani-Tukulor (Bororo) Diola Mandé (Malinké)		
31. Sierra Leone	89	2		Temne Mendé Nuclear Mandé (Koranko)		
32. Somalia	95	4	Somali			
33. Sudan	95	3	Beja Arab (Kababish)	Darfur (Fur) Nuba (Mesakin)	Southern Nile (Dinka) Southwestern (Azandé)	
34. Swaziland	90	1	Swazi			
35. Tanzania	90	3		Nyamwesi (Sukuma) Interlacustrine Bantu (Haya) Northeast Coastal Bantu (Hadimu)	Central Bantu (Makonde) Rift (Gogo) Rufiji (Hehe) Nyakyusa (Nyakusa) Rukwa Cluster (Fipa) Kenya Highland Bantu (Chagga)	
36. Togo	91	4	Gurma	Ewé Kabré Moba Kotocoli*		Central Togo (Buem)
37. Uganda	94	3		Nilote (Lango) Lugbara	Eastern Lacustrine (Ganda) Western Lacustrine (Nyankole) Karamajong (Teso) Gisu	

Figure 4.3 (continued)

Country	Percent Country Population Classified	Relationship to Census Categories	Identity Group	Type	Cluster	Residual or "Shatter-Belt" Cluster
38. Upper Volta	100	1	Mossi Fulani (Bororo) Gurma Busansi (Bisa)	Western Mandé (Bobo) Senufo Grunshi (Nankanse) Lobi		
39. Zaire	84	4		Central Bantu (Kongo) Luba (Songye) Mongo Ngbandi-Ngbaka-Mbandja	Azandé-Mangbetu (Azandé) Kivu (Shi)	
40. Zambia	98	3		Tonga (Plateau Tonga) Nyanja (Chewa) Lunda-Kaonde (Luvale) Barotze (Lozi)	Mambwe Bemba	
41. Zimbabwe	92	1	Nyanja	Shona Ndebele Nguni Europeans		

KEY:

* = ethnic units not contained in Murdock, *Ethnographic Atlas*; coded by Handbook staff

( ) = Murdock name of ethnic identity group on which we based our cultural variable coding

Relationship to official or census categories:
1 = based on census categories
2 = modified from census categories
3 = dissimilar from census categories
4 = census or ethnic codings in census not available

Bassa-Bakoko groups speak languages of the Bantu sub-family of the same stock. The Beti-Pahouin and Bassa-Bakoko types have not been clustered together because the latter type still maintain elements of their former matrilineality in their principles of social organization.

We have classified the peoples Murdock identifies as the Cameroon Highlanders as the Highland Bantu cluster. The distinct identity groups included in this cluster share similar basic value patterns and assumptions, while varying fairly widely in their more specific cultural forms as well as language forms. Specifically, there is rather wide variation in the level of political development. In all cases, villages are governed by an hereditary headman who is advised by a council of lineage heads. Some of the Highlander groups have no political organization above this level (Fia, Nen, Widekum), while the others are organized into states with paramount chiefs. These states tend to be small although the Mum, Nsaw, and some Bamiléké states attain substantial size. Regardless of size, all such states are characterized by divine kings, territorial courts, specialized officials, dual class stratification and prestigious queen-mothers.[38] With respect to community organization, the Highlanders all segment themselves into localized kin groups of varying degrees of inclusion. Principles of descent, inheritance, and succession are in all cases patrilineal.

Finally, we have classified an ethnic *shatter-belt* cluster – the Kirdi – in which numerically small and culturally and linguistically distinct peoples have for social and administrative reasons come into increasingly direct association and received a common out-group ascription. Because of these out-group pressures and because of the generally low level of socio-political organization of the constituent units, these peoples are coming to share a more or less common culture.

It should be clear that the procedures for ethnic unit selection just described fall far short of the mathematical precision which our methodological discussion given above might indicate. In order to follow that conceptual and methodological framework in empirical work, we require complete data on the variable characteristics of each identified ethnic group within any given country. As we have indicated, this is not possible, but the heuristic utility of the model may be illustrated by a highly quantitative experiment in ethnic cluster analysis that we applied to Zaire, a country for which relatively detailed information on ethnic identity groups is available.

The human mind is probably incapable of assessing simultaneously all of the multiple dimensions and degrees of variation found among populations, and accurately judging consistent thresholds of inclusion or exclusion for units defined in terms of cultural similarity. We have used the statistical techniques of Q-factor analysis which can be employed to establish clusterings of units at different levels of similarity on the basis of patterns of variation across a range of variables. Such techniques have been used experimentally by others in culture trait analysis, and as an approach to a number of different ethnological problems.[39] We have applied this technique to the classification of the populations of Zaire.

Jan Vansina, in his *Introduction a l'Ethnographie du Congo* (1965),[40] has looked at 250 Zairese ethnic groups, providing one of the most valuable attempts at a comprehensive ethnic classification of an African state. In considering this diversity of possible identity groups, Vansina is struck by the cultural unity of the Zairese population:

> This all too brief glance at the different cultures of the Congo has certainly given to the reader, as to the author, a growing sense of deja vu. Institutions, beliefs, and even other traits, have become familiar to us by dint of their re-appearing so often. The reason for this is that the cultural unity of the Congo around 1900 was far greater than most specialized ethnological studies would allow one to suppose. Such works, by their very nature, emphasize differences more than resemblances. Certainly, there existed 250 cultures, but all of them and in particular those of the Kivu and the Northwest, belonged to one single type. The Congo knows a single fundamental way of life, and rather than making these cultures mutually unintelligible, the diversities enriched the cultural heritage.[41]

The cultural unity of Zaire suggests the utility of clustering the 250 ethnic groups into a more parsimonious set of ethnic units, and Vansina has described a classification of 15 major ethnic types, or regions. The distribution of cultural regions classified by Vansina is shown in Figure 4.4 along with a much less detailed map of cultural clusters given earlier by Merriam.

Such classifications cannot help but suffer from the limitations inherent in any grouping derived from the individual researcher's attempt to perceive and interrelate multiple patterns of variation. Vansina himself recognizes the problems:

> ...We have tried to group those peoples whose cultures seemed, objectively, to resemble each other the most. We have, thus, defined groups of peoples and culture regions which incorporate numerous groups. In more than one instance it was necessary to make comprises.... The absence of data and the fact that the author was only familiar with a portion of the Congolese cultures, constituted a major obstacle. Consequently, it was necessary to resolve certain cases through intuition or employing the most practical arrangement rather than following vigorously established criteria.[42]

Figure 4.4 Geographic Description of Ethnic Regions or Clusters in Zaire (Congo K.), as suggested by Merriam and Vansina.

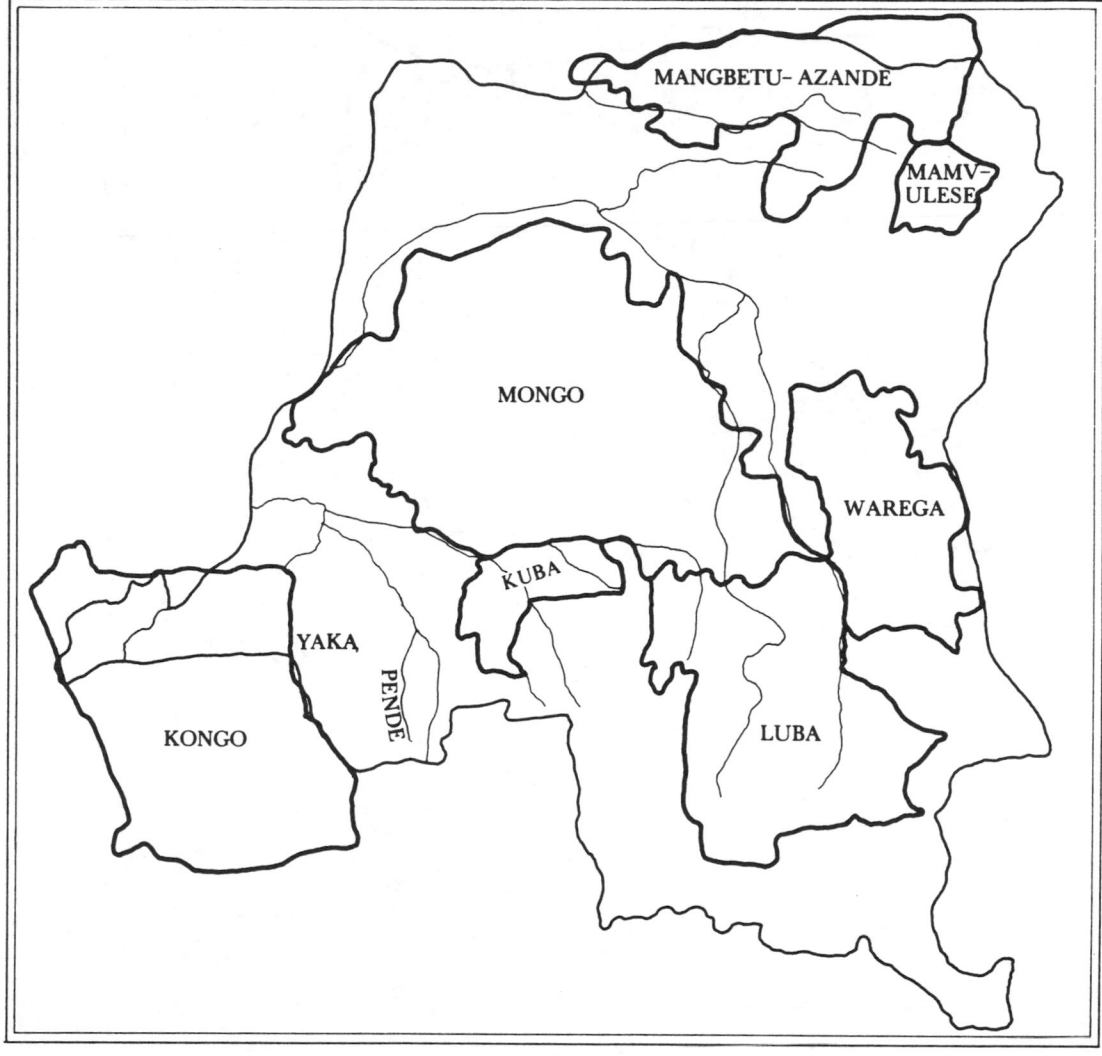

Alan P. Merriam, "The Concept of Culture Clusters Applied to the Belgian Congo," *Southwestern Journal of Anthropology*, 15 (Winter 1959), p. 347. Jan Vansina, *Introduction à l'Ethnographie du Congo* (Brussels: CRISP, Editions Universitaires du Congo, 1965).

Whatever the variability of Vansina's knowledge, intuition, and compromise, his outline of the cultural types in Zaire seems as good as the data will permit. What he has done may be considered a very well-informed, but not mathematically precise classification of 250 identity groups into 15 types, to use the vocabulary of this chapter.

Where Vansina groups peoples on the basis of historical, geographic, or linguistic grounds, we have tried to adapt his work so as to present a less aggregated classification of 23 units which are more culturally coherent than the 15 already illustrated. Our adaptation is shown in Figure 4.5. Working on our adapted classification of 23 types, we selected the most prominent identity group in each type for which there was complete information on the 17 variables defined in Part I, Chapter 2. These codings were then assumed to be the modal characteristes of the types, and using the data on 17 variables for 23 ethnic types we employed a Q-factor analysis routine to identify the most inclusive cultural clustering of these types. The

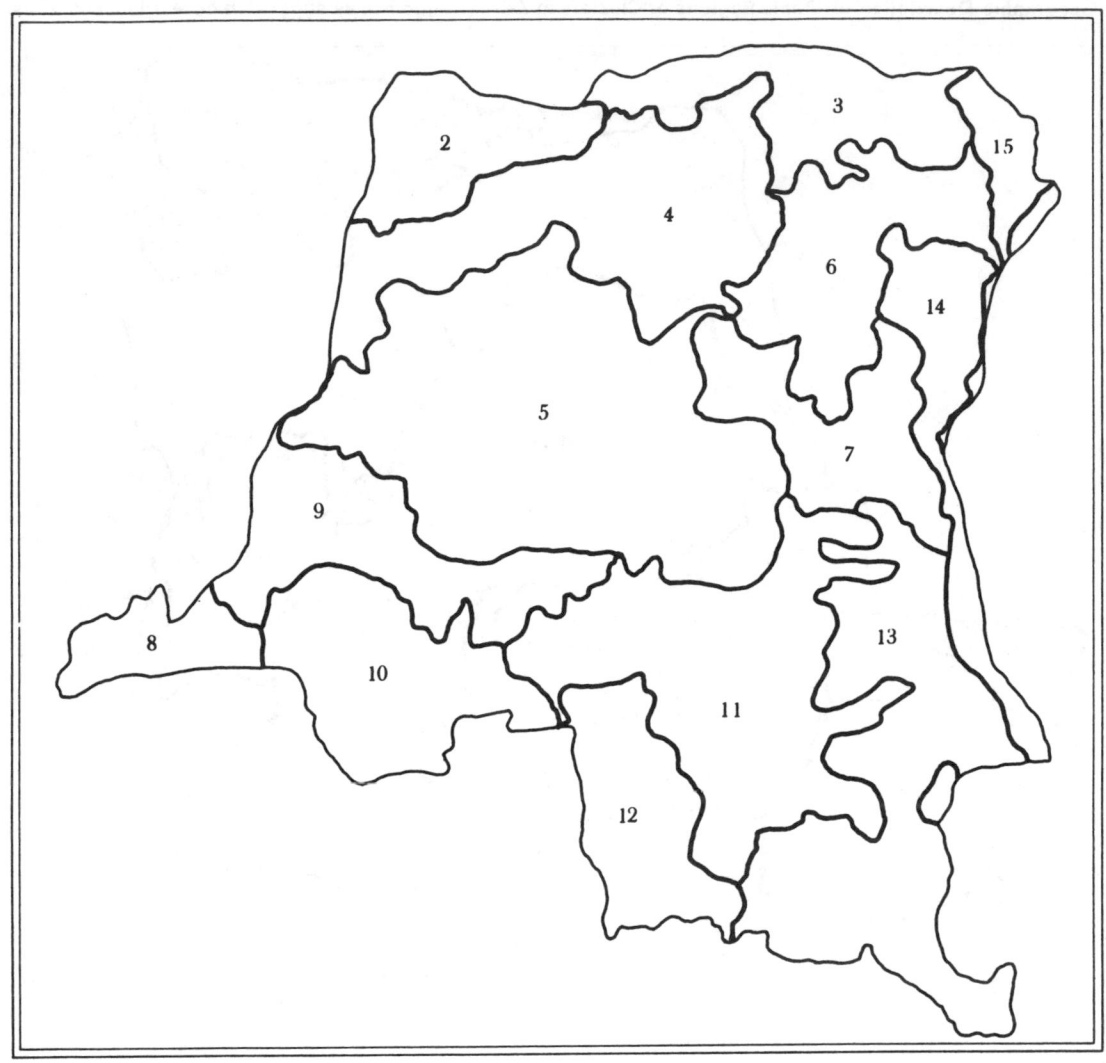

2	Région de l'Ubangi	9	Région du Bas Kasai
3	Région de l'Uele	10	Région de l'entre Kwango-Kasai
4	Région de l'Itimbiri-Ngiri	11	Région du Kasai-Katanga
5	Région de la Cuvette Centrale	12	Région Lunda
6	Région Balese-Komo	13	Région Tanganyika-Haut Katanga
7	Région du Maniema	14	Région du Kivu
8	Région Kongo	15	Région du Nord-Est

aim of this experiment was to derive a set of ethnic units, more inclusive than Vansina's, and, in terms of cultural homogeneity, somewhere between the 23 distinctive types and the unitary culture zone Vansina referred to earlier.

The clusters and factor loadings obtained from a four-factor solution are illustrated in Figure 4.5. The factor loadings indicated for each of the 23 ethnic types the degree to which it is similar to other types in the cluster. The higher the loading—from 0 to 1.0—the greater the correspondence. The Q-factor analysis technique was used to generate a variety of different solutions by vary-

Figure 4.5 Ethnic Culture Clusters with Factor Analytic Loadings: The Example of Zaire (Congo K.).

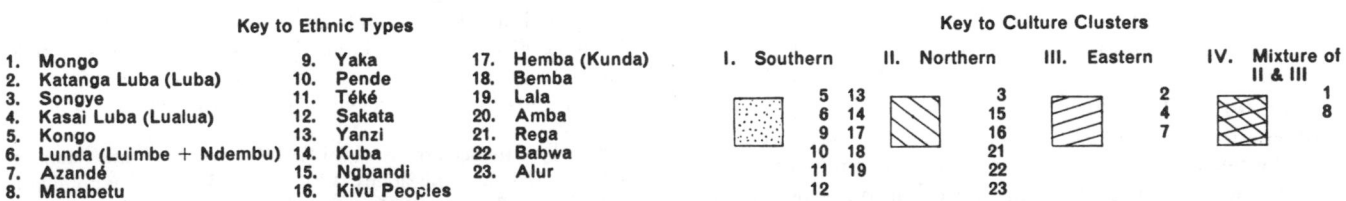

Ethnic Type Units (adapted from Vansina*)	Ethnic Culture Clusters with Factor Analytic Loading

Key to Ethnic Types

1.	Mongo	9.	Yaka	17.	Hemba (Kunda)
2.	Katanga Luba (Luba)	10.	Pende	18.	Bemba
3.	Songye	11.	Téké	19.	Lala
4.	Kasai Luba (Lualua)	12.	Sakata	20.	Amba
5.	Kongo	13.	Yanzi	21.	Rega
6.	Lunda (Luimbe + Ndembu)	14.	Kuba	22.	Babwa
7.	Azandé	15.	Ngbandi	23.	Alur
8.	Manabetu	16.	Kivu Peoples		

Key to Culture Clusters

I. Southern	II. Northern	III. Eastern	IV. Mixture of II & III
5 13	3	2	1
6 14	15	4	8
9 17	16	7	
10 18	21		
11 19	22		
12	23		

* Jan Vansina, *Introduction à l'Ethnographie du Congo* (Brussels: CRISP, Editions Universitaires du Congo, 1965).

ing the number of variables used in the computation of the factor matrix. Results of the kind illustrated here might well lend precision to the final selection of ethnic units for cross-national research, although we will have to wait for more comprehensive numerical data on identified ethnic groups, and for means of comparing typological solutions based on statistical relationships found in different national samples of ethnic groups. In the meantime, the example discussed here may clarify our approach to cluster analysis, and, hopefully, stimulate further research.

Conclusion

We have described so far the process by which we selected ethnic units for African states. We believe that the units we have listed in Figure 4.3, and in Part II, are comparable in that they each represent demographically and culturally distinctive populations within the national boundaries in which they are located. If we are correct in this belief, this data on ethnic unit classification provides a basis for the measurement of national integration in terms of the degree of ethnic pluralism, value congruence, or cultural variation characteristic of each of the 41 countries we have been concerned with in this Handbook.

In order to develop aggregate data for concepts like these,[43] we had to ascribe to each ethnic unit selected a coding representative of the modal characteristic of the culture cluster for any of our cultural variables. Where an ethnic unit is isomorphic with an identity group, we assign, of course, the coding of the identity group to the national ethnic unit. In cases where the ethnic unit is a type, cluster, or shatter-belt aggregate, we have assigned the coded characteristics of the largest identity group within the aggregate to the unit itself, or, in cases where we have evidence that the largest group in the aggregate is not the 'most typical,' we assign the variable scores of an identified group that is more typical of the ethnic unit. Furthermore, for some aggregates we were forced to use the only group for which complete data were available in order to generate unit codings.[44] In these ways, we have ascribed to each of our national ethnic units quantitative measures of their cultural characteristics, and utilizing this information we are able to develop aggregate indices of national variance of the kind discussed in Part I, Chapter.

Without the means for more precise quantitative evaluation of our ethnic unit classification, the comparability of the units we have selected in each nation is suspect, and the validity of our aggregate data on ethnic pluralism or cultural variance may be questioned. The most obvious difficulty relates to the selection of single units as 'typical' of an aggregate ethnic unit. The judgments we have made fall short of a precise selection of the most typical group, and, at any rate, it would be preferable to give the aggregate entity a unique score reflective of some measure of central tendency for all the constituent groups on all the variables used for classification. Another rather obvious difficulty is that the data we have used, whether for description of ethnic units or in the process of clustering units, are based on non-comparable temporal observations. Furthermore, whatever the reliability of the observations of the ethnographer we have consulted, there is the additional problem of the reliability of our own second-hand coding and judgment, which has not been systematically tested. Even more important as a threat to the validity of our data, is the fact that we have no precise indication that our units are equivalent in terms of their cultural distinctiveness in each ethnic unit share a range of values in common, and that the values they share are different from those shared by other groups in the population. But we have no precise method of evaluating the correspondence of our selections in each country to this intention. Finally, the ethnic units we have selected are appropriate for comparing variance between African countries but not necessarily for making statements about cultural variance in Black Africa as a whole, since our unit selection is based on within-country criteria.

Whatever the limitations of the data, or the con-

ceptual and methodological approaches to it that we have discussed in this chapter, we believe that it is important to consider the complexity of African ethnicity in any research in that continent, and that it is imperative that cross-national research develop ethnic data for Africa that is comparable and theoretically relevant.[45] If the attempt discussed in this book is considerably less than ideal, we hope, at least, that it will stimulate future research along similar lines.

Notes

[1]The word *ethnicity* is used here only to indicate the general focus of this chapter. It is in itself a concept that is more confusing than enlightening since it involves connotations of both ethnic identity and common culture, two subjects we feel it necessary to distinguish between in what follows. For a detailed review of their concepts of ethnicity and associated theories see R. A. Levine and D. T. Campbell *Ethnocentrism* (Wiley: N.Y., 1972) and for East African data (Kenya, Uganda, and Tanzania) see M. Brewer and D. T. Campbell *Ethnocentrism: East African Evidence* (Beverly Hills, Ca.: Sage, 1977) and J. A. Kenny "Statistical Classification of African Ethnic Units," *Journal of Asian and African Studies*, XI, 3—4 (July/October), 1976, pp. 180—93. Also see D. G. Morrison *The Adaptive Culture: Social Change in a Plural Society*, (forthcoming).

[2]Karl W. Deutsch, *The Analysis of International Relations*. (Englewood Cliffs, N.J.: Prentice-Hall, 1968), p. 159.

[3]A very clear statement of this argument is found in Clifford Geertz, "The Integrative Revolution: Primordial Sentiments and Civic Politics in the New States," in *Old Societies and New States: The Quest for Modernity in Asia and Africa*, ed. Clifford Geertz (New York: The Free Press, 1963).

[4]See the extended arguments in Karl W. Deutsch, "Integration and the Social System: Implications of Functional Analysis," and Philip E. Jacob, "The Influence of Values in Political Integration," in *The Integration of Political Communities*, eds. Jacob and James V. Toscano (New York: J. B. Lippincott Co., 1964), pp. 179—246. Also see Levine and Campbell, op. cit.

[5]For a very clear theoretical argument for this statement, based on an analysis of international relations, see Harold Guetzkow, *Multiple Loyalties: A Theoretical Approach to a Problem in International Organization* (Princeton, N.J.: Center for Research on World Political Institutions, Princeton University, 1955).

[6]The evidence for situational ethnicity is primarily based on studies of urban ethnicity, of which two brilliant but contrasting examples are Arnold L. Epstein, *Politics in an Urban African Community* (Manchester, England: University of Manchester Press, 1958), and Abner Cohen, *Custom and Politics in Urban Africa: A Study of Hausa Emmigrants in Yoruba Towns* (Berkeley: University of California Press, 1969). Also see J. Paden (ed.) *Values, Identities and National Integration* (Evanston, Ill.: Northwestern University Press, 1980).

[7]See Ronald Cohen and John Middleton, eds., *From Tribe to Nation: Studies in Incorporation Process* (Scranton, Pa.: Chandler Publishing Co., 1970) and P. H. Gulliver, ed., *Tradition and Transition in East Africa: Studies of the Tribal Element in the Modern Era* (Berkeley: University of California Press, 1969).

[8]Paul Mercier, "On the Meaning of 'Tribalism' in Black Africa," in *Africa: Social Problems of Change and Conflict*, ed. P. L. van den Berghe (San Franciso: Chandler Publishing Co., 1965), p. 486.

[9]See the argument in Ali Mazrui, "Pluralism and National Integration," in *Pluralism in Africa*, eds. Leo Kuper and M. G. Smith, (Berkeley: University of California Press, 1969). The quotation is from p. 334.

[10]Karl W. Deutsch, et. al., "Political Community in the North Atlantic Area," in *International Political Communities—An Anthology* (New York: Doubleday Anchor Book, 1966). p. 17.

[11]The following is the conclusion of a contemporary student of anthropology: "If I had to select one word in the vocabulary of anthropology as the single most egregious case of meaninglessness, I would have to pass over 'tribe' in favor of 'race.' I am sure, however, that 'tribe' figures prominently on the list of putative technical terms ranked in order of degree of ambiguity." Morton H. Fried, *The Evolution of Political Society*. New York: Random House, 1967, p. 154. For further discussion, see other essays in *Essays on the Problem of Tribe*, ed. June Helm (Seattle: University of Washington Press, 1968), and Raoul Naroll. "The Culture-Bearing Unit in Cross-Cultural Surveys," in *Handbook of Method in Cultural Anthropology*, eds. Raoul Naroll and Ronald Cohen (New York: Natural History Press, 1970). For a review of the boundary problems in ethnic group definition see R. A. Levine and D. T. Campbell *Ethnocentrism*, op. cit., chapter 7.

[12]James W. Fernandez, "Contemporary African Religion: Confluents of Inquiry," in *Expanding Horizons in African Studies*, eds. Gwendolen M. Carter and Ann Paden (Evanston, Ill.: Northwestern University Press, 1969), p. 38.

[13]Naroll, "Culture-Bearing Unit," p. 726. For an earlier version of this, see Raoul Naroll, "On Ethnic Unit Classification." *Current Anthropology*, 5 (1964): 283—312. In this work Naroll elaborates six criteria: (1) distribution of particular traits being studied; (2) territorial contiguity; (3) political organization; (4) language; (5) ecological adjustment; and (6) local community structure.

[14]For arguments in favor of using "named-groups" as identity groups see Michael Moerman. "Ethnic Identification in a Complex Civilization: Who are the Luo?" *American Anthropologist*, 67 (1967): 1215—1230.

[15]This is referred to as Galton's problem in the literature on cross-cultural analysis. See Raoul Naroll, "Two Solutions to Galton's Problem." *Philosophy of Science*, 28 (January 1961): 15—39, and R. Naroll and Roy G. D'Andrade, "Two Further Solutions to Galton's Problem. *American Anthropologist*, 65 (1963): 1053—1067.

[16]Naroll, "Culture-Bearing Unit," p. 731.p [17]The term "ethnic identity group" will hereafter refer to a "named-group," from ethnographic case studies.

[18]Giving the three units for country A: [EIG$_1$, EIG$_2$], [EIG$_3$], and [EIG$_4$, EIG$_5$] and for country B: [EIG$_1$, EIG$_2$], [EIG$_3$, EIG$_4$], and [EIG$_5$].

[19]That is, in nation A, when [EIG$_4$, EIG$_5$] is greater than [EIG$_1$, EIG$_2$] then [EIG$_3$] is not necessarily greater than [EIG$_1$, EIG$_2$], but in nation B, when [EIG$_3$, EIG$_4$] is greater than [EIG$_1$, EIG$_2$] then [EIG$_5$] is always greater than [EIG$_1$, EIG$_2$].

[20]These two units being [EIG$_1$, EIG$_2$] and [EIG$_3$, EIG$_4$, EIG$_5$].

[21]A cluster being defined as a set of similar and aggregated ethnic types. It should be noticed that our use of the word "cluster" may be closer to the conventional meaning of culture *area* than culture *cluster* in the anthropological literature. "....While the dividing point between the two is probably not always precise, two characteristics of the cluster tend to disinguish it from the area. The first of these is size; while it is conceivable that a culture cluster encompasses as large a geographic distribution as an area, this would seldom be the case, for the cluster pertains most directly to smaller groups of peoples whose culture shows a degree of unity rather than simple similarity as in a culture area. This is emphasized in the second difference between the two: The culture cluster involves a real commonality among the people concerned, with recognition of this commonality by the various groups. Thus the concept of the culture area is imposed upon the data by the ethnologist, while the concept of the culture cluster is both imposed by the ethnologist and recognized to varying degrees by the people concerned." Alan P. Merrmam, "The Concept of Culture Clusters Applied to the Belgian Congo.' *South-Western Journal of Anthropology*, 15 (Winter, 1959): 374. We have used the word cluster rather than area becuse we do not wish to attach any suggestion of geographic coherence to our ethnic units.

[22]The 1962 Kenya census is an example of a list based on this criterion.

[23]The classification of ethnic groups for Liberia given in Colin Legum, ed., *Africa* (New York: Praeger, 1966), pp. 231—232, is of this kind.

[24]The classification for the ethnic groups of Tanganyika in J. P. Moffett, ed., *Handbook of Tanganyika*, 2nd. ed. (Dar es Salaam: Government Printer, 1958), pp. 283—297, is largely based on geographical criteria.

[25]See the *Population Census of Ghana*. Special Report E-1, "Tribes in Ghana," (Accra: Census Office, 1964), pp. 1—5, for an example.

[26]Brian Weinstein, *Nation-Building on the Ogooué* (Cambridge: Massachusetts Institute of Technology Press, 1966), pp. 30—33.

[27]For example, U.S. Department of the Army, *Area Handbook for the Republic of the Sudan* (Washington, D.C.: Government Printing Office, 1960), pp. 51—74. At present these handbooks are available for a number of African countries including Angola, Burundi, Zaire, Ethiopia, Guinea, Ivory Coast, Kenya, Chad, Zimbabwe, Liberia, Nigeria, Rwanda, Senegal, Sudan, Tanzania, Uganda, Zambia and others. Despite their curious auspices, these handbooks, which are written by scholars at American University, are generally comprehensive and relatively authoritative. They are publicly available from the U.S. Supt. of Documents, Washington, D.C.

[28]See, for example, the censuses for Nyasaland and Northern Rhodesia which tended to classifiy populations into three categories—"European," "Asian," and "African."

[29]*Enquête demographique de la République du Congo* (Brazzaville, 1960), is an example.

[30]See *Étude Démographique par Sondage en Guinée*, 1954—1955 (Administration Générale des services de la France d'Outre-Mer, Services des Statistiques).

[31]For example, Clyde Mitchell, *African Tribes and Languages of the Federation of Rhodesia and Nyasaland* (Map), (Salisbury: Federal Government Printer, 1964).

[32]George Peter Murdock, *Africa: Its People and Their Culture History* (New York: McGraw-Hill, 1959).

[33]See Jospeh Greenberg,*The Languages of Africa* (Bloomington: Indiana University Press, 1966), and Voegelin and Voegelin, "Languages of the World," in *Anthropological Linguistics*, March 1964 to April 1966. Apart from problems of linguistic classification, Murdock's classifications are eclectic in terms of the inclusiveness and criteria of selection, and his ethnographic sources range widely in historical time, and

do not always reflect contemporary data.

[34]George P. Murdock, *Ethnographic Atlas* (Pittsburgh, Pa.: University of Pittsburgh Press, 1967).

[35]In addition to the *Ethnographic Atlas*, Murdock has published additional, corrected or expanded codings in the journal *Ethnology*, in which the material in the *Atlas* first appeared. We should record further our indebtedness to Professor Murdock's *African Cultural Summaries* (New Haven, Conn.: 1958), unpublished manuscript.

[36]Victor T. LeVine, *The Cameroons: From Mandate to Independence* (Berkeley: University of California Press, 1964). See Chapter 1.

[37]Murdock, *Africa—Its Peoples and Their Culture History.*

[38]*Ibid.*, p. 241.

[39]See R. M. Needham, "Computer Methods for Classification and Grouping," in *The Use of Computers in Anthropology*, ed. D. Hymes (The Hague: Mouton, 1965), pp. 345—346, and H. E. Driver and K. F. Schuessler, "Factor Analysis of Ethnographic Data," *American Anthropologist*, 59 (1967), 655—663.

[40]Jan Vansina, *Introduction à l'Ethnographie du Congo* (Brussels: CRISP, Editions Universitaires du Congo, 1965).

[41]*Ibid.*, p. 223 (Our translation)

[42]*Ibid.*, p. 9 (Our translation)

[43]The reader should consult Part I, Chapter 2, for this data, and additional commentary.

[44]The groups selected for representative codings for each ethnic unit are given in brackets in the summary classification in Figure 4.3, when the unit does not have the same label as the group coded.

[45]For an attack on the use of "tribalism" as the major explanatory variable for Black African countries by some "expatriate and African middle-class ideologists," see Archie Mafeja, "The Ideology of 'Tribalism'." in *The Journal of Modern African Studies* 9 (1971): 253—261. The emphasis here on ethnicity is meant to avoid some of the excesses of the analysis of 'tribalism.'

5. The African Data Manager System (ADMS): Principles, Procedures and Future Developments

Introduction

The African National Integration Project (ANIP) was organized in 1967 at Northwestern University to generate, systematize, distribute and analyze quantitative information on African political systems. The project has been located at York University (1970-1975), MIT (1975-1981) and the University of Washington (1981-1983) where work has continued on the expansion of the ANIP data holdings. This chapter is a report on the storage and distribution system of the project and the design for its future development.

We have previously reported on the archiving activities of the ANIP project (Mitchell et al. 1969, Morrison et al. 1972, Morrison et al. 1974c) where we point out the advantages of storage and retrieval offered by a system oriented around computerized machine-readable storage systems. Such procedures can be designed to alter or add data, to accommodate different levels and units of analysis as well as to satisfy other criteria. However, it has become increasingly clear that the earlier structure of the files is not optimum for a rapidly growing volume of data, nor will it meet the need to handle increasingly varied levels of analysis (e.g. nations, ethnic groups, elites, individual surveys, events-codes such as coups d'etat etc.). While ever bigger data files and faster computers can be used to accommodate growth, this increases costs without gains in the efficiency of information return. Hence, two of the objectives of a new storage system must be: (a) to store data with high information content[2] and (b) to design an information retrieval system to minimize the cost of searching files for the required data.

The discussion about this system will be organized as follows: (1) a review of the concepts and rationale for a data archive; (2) a description of the structure of the present ANIP system; (3) a review of the problems that the current system presents in terms of maximally achieving the data bank objectives as set out in (1); and (4) the design for a new data storage and retrieval system to replace the current structure.

1. Information and the Data Archive: Concepts and Rationale.

In this section we discuss the goals that should direct the form and contents of data archives and their constituent data bases, the reasons for constructing ANIP in its current form, and the need for restructuring in order to continue to meet those goals as the storage system grows in terms of data collections and users and as new innovations in computer technology appear.

The popular image of a bank for describing collections of social science information is useful, but like all good metaphors, subject to various emphases in interpretation[3]. Banks, in the most limited sense, are places where valuables are kept, and in addition to facilitating the storage of valuables, they function to increase the productive utility of deposits by arrangements for loans, investments and interest. Data banks, similarly arrange for the storage or withdrawal, and stimulate the productive analysis of information. But there are limits to the analogy between money banks and data banks, or money and information, which may help elucidate the importance and goals of the ANIP archive.

Money is a store of value, unit of account, and a generalized medium of exchange[4]. We symbolize value by money, and exchange valued goods and services for equivalent monetary values. Information, too, is a medium of exchange by which we share experiences of the world in symbolically valued ways:

> Information is a name for the content of what is exchanged with the outer world as we adjust to it, and make our adjustment felt upon it. The process of receiving and of using information is the process of our adjusting to the contingencies of the outer environment, and of our living effectively within that environment. (Weiner:1954,18)

But we have to be careful in distinguishing certain nonequivalent properties of money and information as media of exchange.

In the first place, the value of money remains constant (If problems of inflation can be neglected for the moment) no matter for how long a time, or how much one may have of it. A dollar bill is a dollar bill is a dollar bill, even if a poor man aches for it and a rich man lights his cigar with it. Information, in contrast, has value only if a man wants it *and* does not have it, and its value declines over time as it becomes more probable that men either already have it or are no longer interested in it. Although money attracts dirt, it remains valuable over time and circulation, but information attracts noise and becomes progressively less valuable as it is circulated. "The idea that information can be stored in a changing world without an overwhelming depreciation in its value is false" (Weiner:1954,120). A money bank is important the greater its assets in terms of the sheer quantity of money in its possession, but data banks are important to the degree that they can service highly specific queries and ignorance. Data banking is therefore as complicated as money banking would be if requests for money had to be responded to with the provision of bills carrying specific serial numbers.

There is, nevertheless, a superficial similarity between inflation in the realm of money and noise in the realm of information. The value of money may decrease in situations of inflated money supply — i.e., when there is too much money in circulation its purchasing power may decrease. Similarly, unless very careful systems of control are exercised in the banking of information, there is reason to believe that the cost of, and noise-to-information ratio in data retrieval from massive data banks increases disproportionately with escalating deposits. This problem may be stated otherwise in terms of the neoclassical formulation of the declining marginal utility of money accompanying marginal increases of personal income. As applied to information, we may suggest that at high levels in the availability of data the ability of an individual to consume information tapers off as additional data increases the noise in the information supply.

These comments suggest a number of principles relevant to the construction and utility of data archives.

1) *The Scarcity Principle.* A data archive is useful to the degree that the information it contains is wanted and is not widely known or available in retrievable form.

2) *The Specificity Principle.* A data archive is useful to the degree that increases in its information supply do not increase noise — i.e., to the degree that the new information does not decrease the ease and cost with which wanted information can be found, and does not create ambiguity, redundancy or error in responses to requests for information.

3) *The Utility Principle.* A data archive is useful to the degree that its stored information is easily circulated or invested so as to maximize the intellectual 'profit' or interest accruing to members of the bank in the form of additional supplies of information that replace or add to the value of existing supplies.

Before detailing the contents and construction of the ANIP archive, it is useful briefly to elaborate these principles as they have influenced that project.

Scarcity. As political research has sought the status of social *science*, there has been a growth in the demand for political analysis based on the systematic and controlled comparison of different political units as a means of arriving at empirically verified propositions about variation in political experience and behavior. This intellectual orientation has meant a complementary, although not always mutually informed, growth in the energy devoted to the development of theory and data for comparative analysis (cf. Hopkins:1969, Gurr:1974).

Most obviously, and not surprisingly, in the field of comparative politics, this movement has led to an astonishing development of depositories of comparative information relating to national political systems (cf. Russett, et.al.:1964; Banks and Textor:1964; Feierabends:1965; Rummel:1966; Rokkan:1966; Janda:1980; Schmitter:1969; Flanigan and Fogelman:1970; Banks:1971; Singer and Small:1982; Taylor and Hudson:1972; Mickiewicz:1973). Similarly, there has been a considerable deployment of research energies in 'new nations,' where formerly only anthropologisits dared to venture. It is perhaps surprising, therefore, that, although there is no conspicuous lack of political research that has been carried out in Africa (some would argue quite the contrary), there has been a conspicuous scarcity of conveniently stored information on sub-Saharan African states in established data banks, until recently.

Where data have been collected for the comparative analysis of world samples including African countries, the quantitative data used has been almost exclusively based on 'expert'-coded ordinal variables of unestablished reliability, having little documented bases in the scholarly literature on Africa (cf. Adelman and Morris:1967 and Gurr:1966). It must be emphasized that there have been attempts, other than that of the African National Integation Project, to collect African research materials, but they have not as yet moved towards the systematic generation of data in a comparative format. The African Data Project at Columbia University, directed by Professors Hopkins and Wallerstein, with the cooperation of the U.N. Economic Commission for Africa, collected lists of African government holdings of country-specific surveys, censuses, and other studies which provide information on within-country distributions of data on demographic, economic and educational phenomena. The project was unable to actually collect the data holdings of most African governments, however, and the project was eventually abandoned (Hopkins and Wallerstein: 1971). Another important source of information on African countries was the work done by the International Data Library and Reference Service of the Survey Research Center at the University of California at Berkeley, where a number of surveys conducted on different subjects in various countries were deposited. Some of this collection has now been taken over by the ICPSR at the University of Michigan. Again, however, there is no systematic effort to provide comparable information on a wide sample of African countries. The Roper Center also maintains holdings on African surveys.

Because of this general scarcity in established data banks of comparative data on African countries – a situation partially reflecting the eclectic, case-study and non-quantitative orientation of a great number of social scientists who have worked in Africa – it was the purpose of ANIP to collect quantitative data for sub-Saharan nations in order to assist detailed comparative analysis of African socio-political development, and broaden the samples used in cross-national research that are not specifically focused on Africa.

Specificity: The ANIP data bank does not pretend, nor should it aim, we think, to contain information on Africa relevant to all possible interests. The intention is rather more specific: to bank, in an efficient storage and retrieval system, information that is relevant to a limited set of theoretical interests – those relating to the analysis of states of, changes in, and processes producing or decreasing, social and political integration in African countries. In these terms, noise is related not only to errors or redundancies in information, but also to theories of political and social change, and its utility depends on the user's ability to draw from it data that are specified by relevant conceptual descriptions.

This theoretical orientation towards the collection of data has been elaborated in Paden:1968; Staff:1968; Morrison:forthcoming and Morrison et.al.:1972. Very briefly, we have been concerned with processes of contact, cooperation and consensus-formation as linkages between ethnic groups, elites, regions, and mass publics in national political systems, and we have been concerned with the relationship of these processes to conflict, pluralism, social mobilization and political instability in nations. Inasmuch as pre-colonial, colonial and neo-colonial experiences in Africa have affected these aspects of national development we have also aimed to include data relevant to them. As we shall discuss later, the largest collection of data in the ANIP archive, as presently established, is that describing aggregate characteristics of nations, but this collection is supplemented by data describing individual ethnic groups and elite members, and we are hopeful that new approaches will involve the systematic archiving of survey data on individuals. (See the symposism on survey research data archiving in Hopkins and Mitchell, 1974)

Utility: The value of this information will ultimately be judged by whether or not it can be easily translated into theoretically intelligible and empirically reliable statements about the ways in which national political systems develop. In the absence of short-run answers to this question, however, the productivity of the archive can be assessed in terms of how well-designed it is for the circulation and analysis of information by social scientists.[7]

The rapid growth of information processing machinery and technique in the past twenty years has greatly facilitated the circulation and analysis of vast quantities of data (cf. Janda:1965, 1969; Bisco:1967; Klimbie and Koffeman:1974). But banks store data in ways which provide for archiving and retrieval with the aid of computing machinery. Information is archived in machine-readable files – on cards, magnetic tapes, or discs. These files are scanned by machines using information retrieval programs which are instructions to computers to search the files and report information relevant to the particular needs of individual users of the data bank. Machine-readable information has the advantage of being easily and cheaply circulated and expanded relative, that is, to the costs of collecting the information and the costs of alternative forms of circulating the information. But the costs are not negligible, and they relate particularly to the machine-time used to retrieve, and print or punch information that occurs with the use of any automated information retrieval system. Contemporary developments in low-cost micro computers and widely available data base management software packages is likely to decrease the cost of access although the cost of storage will remain more resistant to the rapid decreases in cost of the computer itself. With the typical user in mind, we turn to a description of the ANIP data archive.

2. Contents, Organization, and Use of the ANIP Archive

a. Contents of the ANIP Archive
The present holdings of the ANIP data bank include:
(1) A *national file*, containing information on over 3000 indices descriptive of demographic, social, economic, political, and cultural characteristics of 41 African countries at different points in time but primarily from the mid 1950's to the present.
(2) An *ethnic unit file* containing information for ethnic units as described in Chapter 4 of these essays, and based on ordinalized variables constructed and coded for the most part from the work of Professors Murdock (1967) and Barrett (1968).
(3) An *elite file* containing data descriptive of the background and careers of over 1000 members of African governments in the period from national independence to 1972.
(4) A *bibliographic file* containing citations to over 10,000 published and unpublished pieces of research on African nations completed before 1970.
(5) The *Black Africa II* file which contains over 300 variables originally from the national file which have been extensively edited and indexed for general distribution.

Unfortunately the bibliographic file is not a systematic and exhaustive summary of research on African nations.

However, this file may be searched automatically by author or by any word in the title of citations (see Larimore and Dillaman:1970), and it serves as a useful model for a bibliographic enterprise that should have considerable utility and ought, therefore, to receive funding. The elite file is also deficient and of limited use at the present time because of the erratic nature of published biographical material on African leaders. The utility of this file will ultimately depend on systematic research being carried out in African countries with the view to gathering comparable data on elites. The usefulness of the ethnic file is also limited inasmuch as the ethnic units it deals with have been defined in somewhat ambiguous terms. Members of ANIP are currently working on a revised classification of ethnic units, which should increase the utility of this data file.

Despite their deficiencies these files are mentioned because they involve categories of information of interest to the project and we expect to improve these files in the future. We further intend to create a file of sample surveys conducted in African countries, as well as an additional file on international relations between African states. The importance of banking sample surveys has been emphasized by Mitchell, one of the directors of the ANIP project (see Hopkins and Mitchell:1974). The creation of the international relations file is dependent on future research producing relevant data sets, such as the international events data made available by Azar; 1975. At the moment, however, it is the national file which has received most attention and to which we will refer most consistently in the following sections on the organization of the archive and the systems constructed for its use.

(b) Organization of the ANIP Data Archive

The ANIP data archive was established to collect and archive data referring to the characteristics of nations, urban areas, ethnic groups, and individuals. Data files were initially constructed, therefore, for each of these units of analysis. Each file contained a *data set* in which the information on variable characteristics was coded for each unit of analysis, and a *machine-readable codebook*, which indexes the variable characteristics by conceptual labels, operational coding procedures, location in the data set, and sources of original information. The machine-readable codebook was originally developed to be used by the information retrieval program TRIAL (see Borman and Dillaman:1968). The format of these codebooks is illustrated in the following reproduction of a section of the codebook which was written for the full ANIP data set.

Figure 5.1 ANIP Machine-readable Codebook Structure and Introduction

STUDY SERIES 300-AFRICAN DATA BANK FOR THE AFRICAN NATIONAL INTEGRATION PROJECT, IBADAN AND YORK UNIVERSITIES DIRECTORS ROBERT C. MITCHELL, (RESOURCES FOR THE FUTURE), DONALD G. MORRISON (M.I.T), JOHN PADEN (NORTHWESTERN), HUGH MICHAEL STEVENSON (YORK)

AFRICAN NATIONAL INTEGRATION PROJECT-
M.I.T. AND YORK UNIVERSITY
REPORT NUMBER 4

VERSION DECEMBER 1982

DISTRIBUTED BY THE INSTITUTE FOR BEHAVIORAL RESEARCH, YORK UNIVERSITY, TORONTO ONTARIO, CANADA

THIS STUDY CONTAINS OVER 3100 VARIABLES COLLECTED FOR THE AFRICAN NATIONAL NTEGRATION PROJECT AT YORK AND IBADAN UNIVERSITIES AND COVERS INDEPENDENT COUNTRIES OF SUB-SAHARAN AFRICA. THESE ARE NAMED IN TABLE 1, BELOW. SOURCES ARE INDICATED. CATEGORY NAMES AND NUMBER ARE GIVEN IN TABLE 2 BELOW.

THE VARIABLES HAVE BEEN GROUPED INTO 40 CATEGORIES EACH OF WHICH CONTAINS SEVERAL SUB-SECTIONS, AS DEFINED IN TABLE 2. FULL DEFINITIONS, PUNCHING LOCATIONS, MISSING DATA, CODING PROCEDURES ARE INDICATED.

TABLE 1. COUNTRY CODE NUMBERS * * * * * * * * *

01	ANGOLA	02	BENIN	03	BOTSWANA
04	BURUNDI	05	CAMERON	06	C. A. R.
07	CHAD	08	CONGO	09	DJBOUTI
10	EQUATORIAL GUINEA			11	ETHIOPIA
12	GABON	13	GAMBIA	14	GHANA
15	GUINEA	16	GUINEA-BISSAU	17	IVORY COAST
18	KENYA	19	LOSOTHO	20	LIBERIA
21	MADAGASCAR	22	MALAWI	23	MALI
24	MAURITANIA	25	MOZAMBIQUE	26	NAMIBIA
27	NIGER	28	NIGERIA	29	RWANDA
30	SENEGAL	31	SIERRA LEONE	32	SOMALIA
33	SUDAN	34	SWAZILAND	35	TANZANIA
36	TOGO	37	UGANDA	38	UPPER VOLTA
39	ZAIRE	41	ZAMBIA	42	ZIMBABWE

ALL THE RECORDS HAVE A COMMON FORMAT FOR THE IDENTIFYING INFORMATION. THIS IS AS FOLLOWS,

COL		
1- 6	COUNTRY NAME FIRST SIX LETTERS	
7-11	CATEGORY NAME (SHORT ACRONYM, SEE TABLE 5.2)	
12-75	CONTAINS DATA OR BLANKS AS SPECIFIED	
76-77	COUNTRY NUMBER (SEE TABLE 5.1)	
78-79	CATEGORY NUMBER (SEE TABLE 5.2)	
80	RECORD NUMBER WITHIN CATEGORY	

HENCE ALL REFERENCES TO COUNTRY, CATEGORY, AND RECORD NUMBERS BELOW ARE TO NUMBERS ACTUALLY ON THE DATA CARDS.

STRUCTURE OF MACHINE READABLE CODEBOOK RECORDS.

CATEGORY TITLE RECORDS (RECORD TYPE 1, COL 75)

COL		
1-3	CATEGORY NUMBER	
4-6	BLANK	
7-60	TITLE OF CATEGORY	
61-74	BLANK	
75	NUMBER 1	
76-77	BLANK	
78-80	STUDY NUNBER (SEE TABLE 5.2)	

VARIABLE NAME RECORDS (RECORD TYPE 7, COL 75)

COL		
1- 2	VARIABLE NUMBER IN THAT CATEGORY (ARBITRARILY ASSIGNED)	
3	BLANK	
4- 9	ABBREVIATED VARIABLE NAME (FOR COMPUTER ANALYSIS)	
10	BLANK	
11-60	SHORT DEFINITION (CONTINUE ON EXTRA RECORDS AS NEEDED). THESE RECORDS CONTAIN THE NUMBER WITHIN THE DATA CATEGORY ASSIGNED TO THAT VARIABLE, A SIX COLUMN ACRONYM FOR THE PURPOSE OF UNIFORM SHORT NAMES WHICH ARE REQUIRED IN MANY COMPUTER PROGRAMS, AND A TITLE OF THE VARIABLE. IF THE TITLE IS NOT SUFFICIENT TO OPERATIONALLY DEFINE THE VARIABLE, AN OPERATIONAL DEFINITION IS GIVEN ON A TYPE 8 RECORD.	
66-74	BLANK	
75	NUMBER 7	
76-77	BLANK	
78-80-	STUDY NUMBER (SEE TALBE 2)	

VARIABLE DESCRIPTION RECORDS-(RECORD TYPE 8, COL 75)

FORMAT FOR TYPE 8 RECORDS

COL 1-2   BLANK

RECORDS:

1- DATA RECORD COLUMN LOCATIONS AND TABLE NUMBER IN BOOK.

THE FIRST RECORD OF THE TYPE 8 RECORDS GIVES THE RECORD COLS. FOR THE DATA AND RECORD. THE NUMBER WITHIN THE DATA SET FOR THAT CATEGORY OF DATA (E.G. RECORD 2 IN THE LANGUAGE AND RELIGION DATA). THE FORMAT IS AS FOLLOWS, COLUMN NUMBERS/RECORD NUMBER WITHIN CATEGORY. (SEE DESCRIPTION OF DATA RECORD FORMAT ABOVE) THE CATEGORY NUMBER APPEARS IN COL 78-80 OF THE CODEBOOK RECORD.

2-OPERATIONAL DEFINITION

IF THE TITLE FOR THE VARIABLE (SEE RECORD TYPE 7) DOES NOT MAKE CLEAR THE DEFINITION OF THE VARIABLE, ONE OR MORE RECORDS OF THE TYPE 8 ARE ADDED BEGINNING WITH THE LETTERS DEF; THESE RECORDS GIVE A FULL OPERATIONAL DEFINITION OF THE VARIABLES.

3-MISSING DATA

WHEN THERE IS NO MISSING DATA, THIS RECORD MERELY STATES THIS DIRECTLY. IF THERE IS MISSING DATA THEN THE COUNTRY NUMBERS (SEE TABLE 1) OF THE COUNTRIES WITHOUT DATA ARE GIVEN ON A RECORD BEGINNING WITH THE WORDS—MISSING DATA.

DATA SOURCE RECORDS (RECORD TYPE 9, IN COL 75)

THE SOURCES OF THE DATA ARE GIVEN ON RECORD TYPE NUMBER 9.

COL 1-2 BLANK
3-60 INFORMATION AS DETAILED BELOW
61-74 BLANK
75 NUMBER 9
76-77 BLANK
78-80 DATA CATEGORY NUMBER (SEE TABLE 2).

THE DATA SOURCES ARE GIVEN ON RECORD TYPE 9. IF THE DATA COMES FROM SEVERAL SOURCES, COUNTRY NUMBERS ARE ATTACHED TO EACH SOURCE WHEN DATA CORRESPONDING TO THAT COUNTRY NUMBER COMES FROM THE SOURCE GIVEN. (SEE TABLE 1 FOR CORRESPONDENCE BETWEEN COUNTRY NUMBERS AND COUNTRY NAMES).

By instructing a computer to read and print a list of the records in the codebook in which the number 5 is contained in column 75, the user would get a list of categories and sub-sections by which the information in the codebook is grouped as well as detailed descriptions of the structure of the codebook and data sets. The list for the complete national file is as follows:

Figure 5.2   Data Categories and Sub-Categories in the ANIP Data Bank

TABLE 2. CATEGORY CODE NUMBERS

THE CATEGORY CODE NUMBERS APPEAR IN THE RIGHT-MOST THREE COLUMNS ON CODE BOOK ENTRIES THAT PERTAIN TO THAT CATEGORY

301-RELIGION   (RELIG.)
    01-CATHOLIC   02-PROTESTANT   03-TRADITIONAL
    04-MUSLIM   05-GENERAL
302-COMMUNICATIONS AND TRANSPORTATION   (COMMU.)
    01-RADIO   02-NEWSPAPERS   03-CINEMA
    04-TELEPHONES   05-BOOKS/PUBLISHING
    06-ROADS   07-CARS   08-RAILWAYS
    09-AIRLINES
303-ECONOMIC RESOURCES AND STANDARD OF LIVING (ECONO.)
    01-LABOR/MANWR   02-ENERGY/ELECTRICAL
    03-INVESTMENT AND INDUSTRIALIZATION
    04-INFLATION/COST OF LIVING   05-NATL INCOME CHAR
    06-CALORIC/FOOD CONS
    07-AGRICULTURAL PRODUCTION 08-MONETARY CHARAC-TERISTICS
304-EDUCATION   (EDUCA.)
    01-GENERAL/COMP.   02-PRIMARY
    03-SECONDARY   04-UNIV/HIGHER   05-LITERACY

305-DEMOGRAPHY AND ECOLOGY   (DEMOG.)
    01-SIZE-AREA, POP   02-LOCATIONAL CHARACTERISTICS
    03-PHYSICAL RESOURCE POTENTIAL
306-MILITARY   (MILIT.)
    01-SIZE, STRENGTH 02-DEFENSE EXPEND. 03-CIVIL/MIL RELTNS
    04-INTERNAL CHAR. 05-EXTERNAL LINKAGES AND EX-PERIENCE
307-NOT CURRENTLY IN USE
308-ECONOMIC AID   (AID.)
    01-US FOREIGN AID   02-FOREIGN AID-OTHER
309-NOT CURRENTLY IN USE
310-SOCIAL WELFARE   (SOCWE.)
    01-MEDICAL SERV.   02-DISEASES
311-INTERNATIONAL RELATIONS   (INREL.)
    01-DIPLOMATIC RELATIONS
    02-CONFLICT BEHAVIOUR   03-EXTERNAL CONNECTIVITY
312-TRADE AND COMMERCE   (TRCOM.)
    01-INTERNAL   02-EXTERNAL   03-MONETARY CHAR.
313-URBAN COMPOSITE VARIABLES   (URBAN.)
    01-URB/RUR RATIOS02-URBAN DESNITY   03-DIFFERNTIAL
314-GENRAL POLITICAL   (GEPOL.)
    01-POL MODELS   02-POL TIMING
    03-NATL INT GRPS, LABOR   04-NATL INT GRPS, STU-DENTS
    05-CONSTITUTIONAL   06-GENERAL
316-ADELMAN DATA   (ADELM.)
317-NATIONAL INSTABILITY   (NSTAB.)
    01-ELITE INSTABILITY
318-POLITICAL INSTABILITY   (PSTAB.)
    01-ELITE   02-REGIME   03-COMMUNITY
319-LANGUAGE   (LANGU.)
320-CABINET COMPOSITE FACTOR SCORE   (CABCO.)
321-NATL BUDGET CHARACTERISTICS   (NABUD.)
322-CABINET TURNOVER   (CABTU.)
323-COUPS D'ETAT NOT INCLUDED IN THIS CODE-BOOK
324-(SEE ETHNIC CODE BOOK REPORT NUMBER 39)
325-(SEE ETHNIC CODE BOOK REPORT NUMBER 39)
326-ETHNIC COMPOSITE VARIABLES   (ETHNI.)
327-POPULATION   (POPUL.)
328-ELECTIONS   (ELECT.)
329-INSTABILITY/INTEGRATION ANALYSIS   (INSIN.)
330-UNWEIGHTED ETHNIC VARIANCES
    01-PROPORTIONALITY   02-STRESS
331-WEIGHTED ETHNIC VARIANCES   (WETHN.)
    01-CULTURE-TRAIT CONGRUITY
332-CABINET REPRESENTATION SCORES   (CCOEF.)
333-GURR DATA   (GURR.)
334-CABINET ETHNIC DISTRIBUTIONS
335-CAB ETHNIC MEANS AND STANDARD DEVIATIONS   (CABVA.)
336-SOCIAL MOBILIZATION   (SOCMB.)
337-CABINET MEMBERSHIP   (CABME.)
338-STUDENT HANDBOOK DECK   (STHAN.)
339-EXTERNAL INFLUENCE   (EXINF.)
340-EXTERNAL CONFLICT   (EXTCO.)

From this list the user may decide that he has an interest defined by one of these broad categories, say *Standard of Living - national income characteristics*, and call for a list of all the variable titles in that category. Such a procedure would require the computer to read and print all the records having the numbers, 7 in column 75 (Variable Name record), 5 in column 74 (sub-category number), and 303 in columns 78-80 (category of data). This would produce a rather lengthy output, which we shall not reproduce here. For the sake of further illustration, we shall assume that the user wishes to compare the GNP of African nations in 1966.

In order to get this particular information, the user instructs the machine to ascertain whether or not that data exists in the data base by reading all the variable title records (7 in column 75) of the codebook in this category (303 in columns 78-80), and by printing out those cards which contain the key words *GNP 1966*, or *Gross National Product 1966*, or any other set of key words which might identify what he wants, in columns 11-60. In response to such a search, the user would get the following information:

Figure 5.3   Type Seven Records: Variable Name Records for ANIP Data Base

42	GNPIMS	GNP PER CAPITA, U.S. 4, 1966	4257	303
43	PCHGNC	PERCENT CHANGE GNP/CAPITA, 1958-1966 US DOLLARS	4357	303

Having ascertained that there are variables measuring what he wants, and that these variables are numbers 42 and 43 in sub-section 5 of the codebook, the user now needs to see the variable description records (see Table 5.1), and he therefore instructs the machine to print out all records with the numbers 42 or 43 in columns 72-73, 5 in columns 74, and 303 in columns 78-80. The information produced would be as follows:

Figure 5.4   Full Codebook Entries for Selected Variables in ANIP Data Base

42 GNPIMS GNP PER CAPITA, U.S. 4, 1966	4257	303
COL 18-20/12	4258	303
NO MISSING DATA	4258	303
FINANCE AND DEVELOPMENT, VOL 6, NO. 1, 1969, PP. 30-42	4259	303
43 PCHGNC PERCENT CHANGE GNP/CAPITA, 1958-1966 US	4357	303
DOLLARS	4358	303
COL 21-26/12	4358	303
FINANCE AND DEVELOPMENT, VOL 6, NO. 1, 1969, PP. 30-42	4359	303
AND ECONOMIC BULLETIN FOR AFRICA, JAN. 1964, P. 389	4359	303

At this point, the user may decide that the data described by variable 42, *GNP per Capita-U.S.$,1966* are all he requires. This information is in the economics data set, record category 03, in columns 18-20 of the twelfth record for each country and the data, complete for all countries, come from *Finance and Development*, Vol. 6, No. 1, 1969. Note that the record category numbers are not coterminous with the category numbers of the codebook. Usually the record category is the final two digits of the codebook category.

All records in the data set are stored according to the following format:

Columns 1-6   County Name or abbreviation

(e.g., MAURIT for Mauritania)

Columns 7-11 Category Name (e.g. ECONO for Economic Resources)

Columns 12-74 Data fields

Columns 75-76 Country Number (countries are numbered from 1-41 in alphabetic order, see Table 5.1).

Columns 77-78 Record Category Number (e.g. 03 for Economic Resources)

Columns 79-80 Record Number

As previously indicated in the codebook search, GNP per capita in 1966 is located in columns 18-20 of the twelfth record of the economic data set for each country. The relevant data record for Ghana, Mauritania and Zambia are illustrated below.

Figure 5.5   Sample Data Record for the ANIP Data Base

ZAMBIA	842180	48	132032
MAURITEECONO	127130	164	119032
GHANA ECONO	2207230	64	112032

The numbers in columns 18-20 of these records, given the fact (reported in the codebook) that the data is given in US dollars, means that in 1966 Ghana has a GNP per capita of $230, Mauritania had $130, and Zambia had $180, according to *Finance and Development*[9].

In order to get information in a convenient manner (generally one does not labor through the task of reading individual records as in the last paragraph), the user can instruct the computer to use the program RANKOR along with the data deck and print out the rank-ordered tabulation of GNP per capita for African countries in 1966. (The very simple instructions--control card-format--for the use of RANKOR are given with the program[10]). The result of such an operation would be a table in the form that appears in Part I of this Handbook.

Aside from tabulations of data such as this, which provide a visual basis for comparison, cross-tabulations, correlation matrices, or any other statistical analyses of variables in the data set can be carried out using other computer programs with the relevant parameters indicated by the variable descriptions in the codebook.

Bibliography: Besides the four data files listed in the beginning of this section, there is a fifth file held by ANIP which is a bibliography in machine-readable form of over 10,000 items of research (books, monographs, dissertations, articles) on African subjects. Each citation is coded in a format which records the standard bibliographic information and, when desired, annotations as well. The citations may be indexed alphabetically by author, or by any key word in the title, using features of the TRIAL program. Such procedures provide well-organized, printed bibliographies that can be used like any library catalogue. We shall not, however, illustrate possible printed outputs of such procedures since there is adequate discussion and illustration in Larimore and Dillaman: 1970 and Paden and Soja: 1970. In addition to obtaining a complete computer-printed bibliography, the user may simply have the machine search for and print out specific citations according to instructions specifying the desired author or subjects.

Planned Future Developments for the Data Bank:

While codebooks of the sort discussed here were well suited to the relatively limited collections of data archived in each file during the first years of ANIP's activity, it became clear that the sequential indexing of the original system was cumbersome and expensive as the contents of the files expanded. Therefore, we have moved towards the construction of a fully automated data base management system that will (1) search for and abstract information from any of these files more rapidly and less expensively; (2) provide sub-set data for particular units and variables in order to carry out specific studies using the data; and (3) integrate the information on different units of analysis so that we may aggregate data from smaller units of analysis into measures for larger ones.

In the next section, the problems in the use of the present system are detailed and the specifications that are necessary for a new system are derived. The system designed to meet these specifications is described in the following section of this chapter.

3. Weakness in the Current Organization of the ANIP Data Bank

The underlying reason for collecting information is to subject our *a priori* expectations in the form of theories, hypotheses, and propositions to empirical testing. In this context, there is a continuum of data needs which dictate, to some extent, the choices to make of the manner of storage, access and analysis. At one end of the continuum we have the simplest of data needs. Examples might be data which could be represented in a 2 x 2 table such as the presence or absence of some other property (e.g. political stability). Even simpler data requirements such as the distribution of a single indicator could be encountered. In cases of this type, where a small amount of data and little, if any, statistical analysis is to be performed, data need never be recorded in machine readable form, let alone be built into a full machine-readable system. As the number of variables and/or observations increases, it soon becomes necessary to codify the data in some machine readable form. If the data complexity continues to increase, it becomes useful and ultimately necessary to have machine-readable codebooks to replace the typed sheets giving the locations of the data on the records and to incorporate sources, definitions and other information into the system. At the opposite end of this continuum, the number of variables and observations becomes so large that it is no longer certain, even to the original collectors, what information is in the data set. A point is reached where the procedure will require a fully automated system of data retrieval and analysis because of this increasing complexity. Thus a data archive such as ANIP which is continually expanding its holdings faces the problem of adjusting its structure and accessibility to accommodate growing acquisitions.

While the current ANIP banking system can be manipulated to produce data sets as desired, there are a number of problems that arise as the bank holdings become very large. The system can now be used as discussed in the previous section to automatically search the machine readable codebooks and inform the user if the required data are available. The user must access his data separately from the codebook search, a process that introduces a very difficult problem in data bank usage. Since the data is not directly tied to the codebook and separate programs for reading the data are required, the user wanting a subset of the data has difficulty in getting a codebook to describe the data subset he desires.

Since the preceding paragraphs are abstractly framed, it will be useful to construct an example that will clarify how specific retrieval cases are currently handled and how a new system should be constructed so as to be a major improvement over the current system. For this discussion we extend the earlier example to one where we want to locate an annual time series for gross national product for each country in the ANIP data base for the period 1958 through 1972. To illustrate the problems in producing such a data set we follow the process from data acquisition to its eventual use in the time series required.

As discussed earlier, data are added to the bank by determining the category of data and defining a field on that category's data records where the new indicator is to be located. New GNP data would be added to the same category as our earlier example, number 303, sub-category 2. As each new year of GNP data is made available, the next available field on the economic data records is assigned to this use. The GNP data for adjacent years will, in general, not be in adjacent fields on the data records. This occurs since the process of accessing new data is such that other variables appropriate to the data category (economics, in our example) will be added to the data set as it expands along with the desired GNP data. Hence, the result is that the GNP data for various years will appear in data fields throughout the economics data set. Correspondingly, the machine readable codebook entries are numbered in order of data acquisition within each data sub-category.[13]

Given that data has been stored in the above manner, we can now review the process by which data is retrieved by a user. The process would start with a user inspecting the codebook either visually or by some automated information search system. After determining whether the desired GNP data is available, the user could then use the entire ANIP data set (over 10,000 records) reading only the data fields desired and skipping the unneeded fields. This is obviously a cumbersome procedure and in practice a 'working data set' would be constructed either using only those original entries with the desired data on them or by writing a computer program which would produce a new set of data containing only the required information. While the latter process is the most convenient for further statistical analysis, a new requirement arises as a result. This new data set will require a new codebook defining the location of the variables in the working data set. After this is completed, the new data set is available for input into statistical analysis programs; however, as should be clear, to construct some other data sub-set the process must be repeated again with the inevitable production of many sets of data representing different working files. Before we examine how this system can be altered to satisfy our goals, one other aspect of the current system should be noted.

As currently constructed, a new data file including a machine readable codebook, is created for each new unit of analysis (e.g. country, ethnic group, coup events, urban centers). When a measure is to be composited from one level of analysis to be used for testing hypotheses at another level, a computer program has to be written and the calculations performed.

An example of this situation would be the requirement that a variable be created at the country level as a weighted combination of sub-units of the country. Such a variable could be the population-weighted percent traditional dependence on agriculture. For each ethnic group in that file there is a measure from Murdock's *Ethnographic Atlas* (1967) which gives that group's percent dependence on agriculture (as opposed to cattle raising, fishing, etc.). A population-weighted measure for each country would be the product of each group's value on that variable by the group's proportion of the total population. By adding up these products we would get a measure for each country. Since the countries have varying numbers of ethnic groups of a wide range of relative sizes, computer programs would have to be written to calculate this composite or any analagous indicators. Then the resultant indicators will have to be added to the country level file.

At this point, we can now enquire into the problems in the current system. The first major difficulty centers around the sequential storage of data records which is characteristic of punched cards or their representations on tapes and disks. If data could be 'tagged' or indexed

according to their characteristics then the retrieval of sub-sets of data would be much easier. As we see in the next section, the proposed new design will adopt an indexed non-sequential file procedure where the storage system is no longer bound by the rigidities derived from the basic punched card structure of the current bank. Data sets will be added, deleted, or modified on a magnetic disk file and 'tagged' so they can be accessed by various descriptors such as country, level of analysis, variable number, etc. This new design centered around the TOTAL data base management system will considerably improve our ability to achieve the goal of a fully automated system and will end the separate files for each unit of analysis since the unit of analysis will be one of the descriptors (keys) in the new indexing system. While this will substantially improve the versatility of data manipulation, further improvements are needed in order that a codebook to describe a new data set will also be produced. This is the second major difficulty to deal with in the new design. The new system will receive keyword descriptors from the user (e.g. GNP 1958, 1959, etc., Kenya). The main codebook will be automatically searched, data locations determined, and a codebook for the data and the derived data set produced for input into statistical programs as the user may determine.[14]

We can summarize the requirements for the new design as follows. It should be able to:

1) easily add, delete, or modify the data contents;

2) handle large numbers of variables and be expandable;

3) produce 'working' sets of data for specific analyses including a machine-readable codebook for the subset of the data holdings being represented in such working sets and perform these tasks at maximally rapid access times with minimal supervision from the user;

4) merge sets of data from different levels and units of analysis (e.g. nations and ethnic units);

5) produce data sets to carry out reliability studies (e.g. alternative measures on the same variable for the same time period);

6) facilitate statistical analysis as required (e.g. prepare sets of data for input to large statistical packages such as those by Nie et al. (1970), and Armor and Crouch(1972);

7) carry out functions (1) through (6) on an interactive basis via remote access to a 'main frame' or on a substantial micro-computer with large mass storage devices.

In the last section of this chapter, we report on the design for a system which is almost entirely automated for managing and disseminating data sets such as those in the ANIP data bank. We will also discuss some substantive issues that are buried in this discussion of the technical structure and organization of the data bank in order to maximize the *information content* of the data bank.

4. New Directions for the ANIP Data Manager System (ADMS)

As we have noted, there are two major areas where improvement in the ANIP data bank is required. The first is concerned with the technical problems of organizing and fully automating the access to both the data files and to various statistical capabilities. The second deals with the substantive content of the data bank and its *information content*. We begin with a proposal for a design of a computerized system to deal with the first issue and problems associated with it as detailed in the previous section.

In the design of a new data base system, we start from certain premises regarding cost-benefit considerations and the character of the stored information. We want to build a computerized system that will involve a minimum monetary, human and temporal cost for its achievement. New programming can be prohibitively expensive. Therefore every attempt will be made in the design of the ADMS system to link together existing or modified existing computer programs and their associated proven concepts in terms of search algorithms, file structures, storage methods, etc. Given the current level of sophistication in data base software, we can see no substantial benefits that would accrue from the design of an entirely new system. Therefore the ADMS system will primarily represent the application and linkage interfacing of existing programs rather than new programming. Even this apparently limited effort will take up to two person-years of programming and considerable computer time.

The components for the ADMS system must be able to handle the vast and diversified set of data and documentation that ANIP will eventually possess. Hence we will require a data management system which employs completely different concepts in file structure and accessing procedures than are available with the common systems based on sequential data processing methods. Ultimately, the system would be capable of creating and outputing any user-specified sequential 'working data set' with accurate and complete documentation. Further, it should accomplish this without placing demands on a user to acquire a knowledge of the internal theory or technology which is reacting to his requests.

In Figure 5.6 we indicate a gross schematic for the design of the new data management system. Segment one (1) is comprised of the files and computer program to manage the documentation (codebooks, etc.) for the entire data bank. Segment two (2) is comprised of the files

and computer programs to retrieve and update data (variables) corresponding to the documentation found in (1).

The entries in the documentation file will include a complete textual description for each variable in the form of an 'abstract' including the sources of the data, the aggregation level, the coding scheme, where applicable, and notation of missing data fields. These abstract (codebook) files will be maintained entirely by the Social Science Information System (SSIS).[15]

SSIS stores textual information by first extracting all the main words (not including conjunctions, articles and other common delimiters) from input text and adds these 'keywords' with an abstract number to an alphabetic keyword file (dictionary). If the word already exists in the dictionary, a new entry is not created but the old entry is updated to include the additional abstract number. New texts or abstracts are added intact to the main abstract file.

The abstract numbers stored with each keyword are called *reference pointers* or *indexes* and function conceptually in a similar manner to a library catalogue of books. Each keyword is thereby linked directly via these pointers to all of the abstracts which contain that word. As more textual accounts (codebook entries) are added to the system, multiple entries begin to appear for many keywords, sometimes indexing hundreds of variable descriptions. The total number of keyword entries in the dictionary increases as well.

On retrieval from the files, SSIS matches a given keyword(s) against the alphabetic dictionary using a binary search technique to determine if there is a 'find'. If there has been, SSIS seeks out the corresponding abstract(s) from the codebook file using the reference pointers that have been stored with the 'found' word in the dictionary. The text describing the 'find' is then extracted and printed for the user. Figure 5.7 shows a basic schematic of the SSIS structure and search process.[16]

Abstract number '164' in Figure 5.7 is an example of the basic format that will be used for all variable descriptors. It is only a minor reformat of the entry as it exists in the original ANIP codebooks. (see Figure 5.4) The YPEE, AME, etc. have been added as key fields within the abstract itself in order to standardize segments of text and allow flexibility for additional kinds of entries other than ANIP codebook abstracts.[17]

Only minor modifications will be made to the SSIS system to adapt its use for the ADMS project. One will allow recognition of additional abstract keyfields such as MISSING DATA.

The data files will be stored in a data base to be managed by the TOTAL system[18]. The description of the TOTAL system given here is very brief. Reviews of the basic

Figure 5.6   Schematic for the SSIS Data System

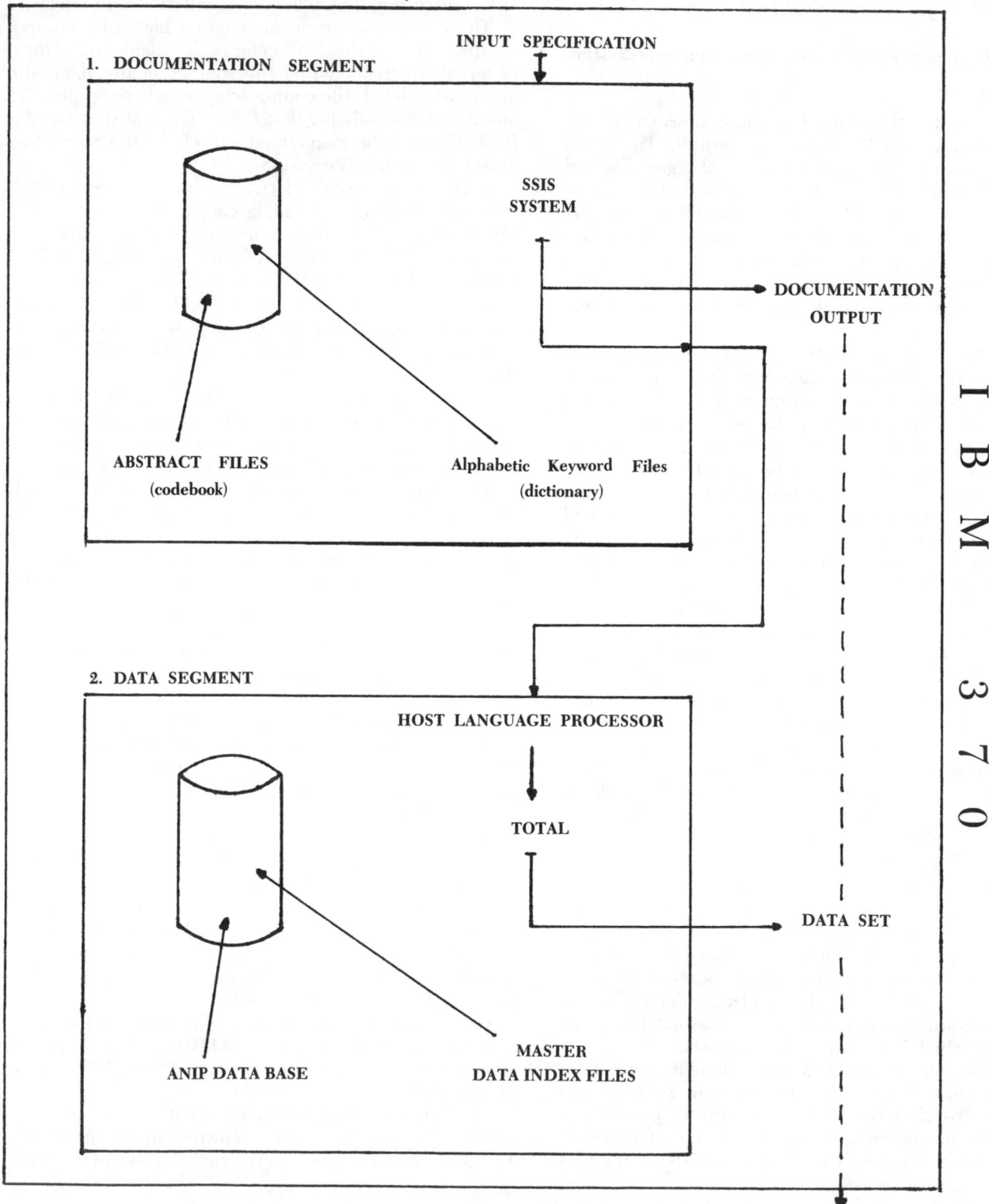

Figure 5.7   Social Science Information System (SSIS)

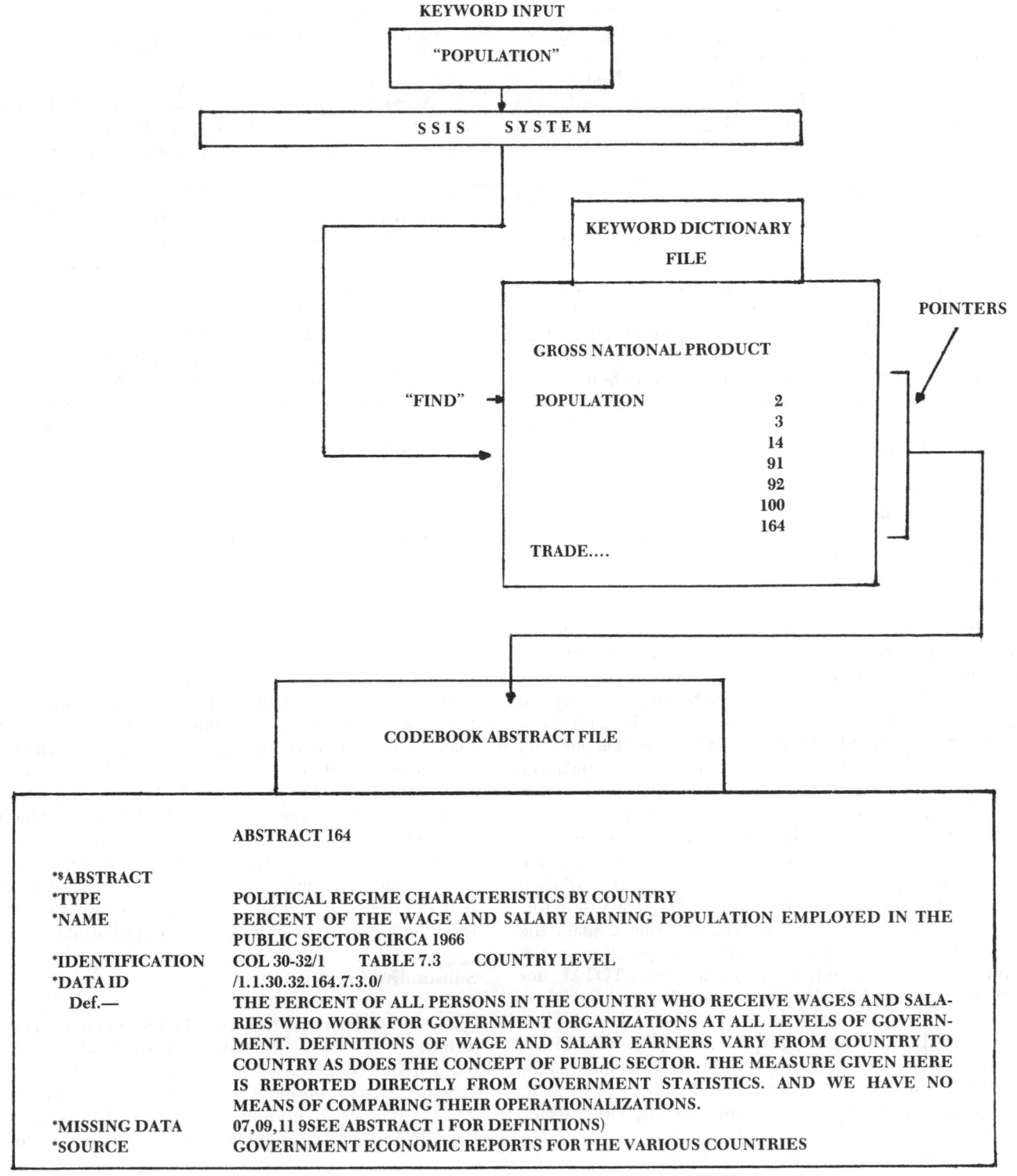

concepts involved can be found in Flores:1970, and details of this system can be found in the TOTAL user's manual. In the TOTAL environment, two functional types of data exist: Single entry (or master files) and variable entry. SINGLE ENTRY data set records are stored randomly and retrieved directly by identification of a unique control field (or logical key) of each record. Thus there is a one-to-one correspondence between keys and records in a SINGLE ENTRY data set. Each single entry data set record can 'own' records of many VARIABLE ENTRY (VE) data sets, the second type of data set under TOTAL.

Variable entry data records are also stored in randomly selected locations and accessed directly[19] but not by the identification of a unique control field. In variable entry data sets, a control field assumes the following meaning: the definitions of a control field directs TOTAL to 'relate' all variable entry records containing that control field to each other in what is called a *chain of records*, each record being a member of a logical linkage path (or series of addresses) that is entered by the defined control field. Each control field of a VE file must be defined as the key of an existing single entry record. Thus the single entry record 'owns' all VE records that contain that unique control field[20].

Figure 5.8 depicts a data base design under TOTAL. It consist of three MASTER Files and a VARIABLE ENTRY FILE. An abstract number key links up all the data fields corresponding to one codebook entry. Upon entering the VE file by a country number, for instance, all data fields for a single country will be accessed. Similarly, if one enters for a particular year, data will be passed back to the processor for all records where that year is coded and appropriate. We can now describe the process of data retrieval in ADMS terms. Suppose that abstract '164' is a find from step 1 (Figure 5.6) for a 'population' keyword. We see from the abstract file (Figure 5.7) that the data is for countries. We require a working data set of records that fits the variable description. Using the temporary output file created by SSIS, the contents of abstract 164 are passed to the data base where TOTAL then uses the information on the DATA ID record to determine the location of the data records that contain the 'percent of wage and salary earning population in the public sector' for countries in Black Africa. TOTAL, for each read in the VE file, will return a record linked on this particular path until the end of the linkage path is reached. The host language processor (e.g. FORTRAN or Pl/1 programs) will then use the DATA ID information to further subset each record in order to extract the actual positions (or columns) that correspond to its abstract.

While few of the technical considerations can be discussed here, it is important to point out the extensive conceptual advantages inherent in the use of these existing state-of-the art computer systems, TOTAL and SSIS. The single most important of these advantages is that the same data or text can be accessed from numerous points of entry (i.e., point of view) without the user having to consider the structure of the files. The user can access items of information via variable names, country names, record/column numbers, dates, subject matter, levels of aggregation and so on, since there exists the multiple linkage path notion in the case of TOTAL, or the dictionary file in the case of SSIS. This is not dissimilar to 'threading' ones way through a multidimensional maze while making decisions at each step as to the progress toward a specified 'finish.'

Secondly, updating under this system becomes a very simple task. No reorganization of any files is necessary when information (text or data) is added, deleted or changed. Both SSIS and TOTAL are responsible for maintaining the 'knowledge' of the locations of all records and all relationships between data files and records. The physical sequence or location of data records is unimportant both to the software using the files and to its user.

Another of the most significant ideas incorporated in this design is that documentation of data is tied to the actual data fields. This separation in the past has consistently been the single largest source of error in data management by researcher, programmer and system analyst alike.

Some preliminary testing has already been carried out using SSIS on a codebook from the ANIP, namely the Black Africa data set (referred to as file number 5 in section 2 of this chapter). The codebook was reformatted to make it acceptable to SSIS (see Figure I) and variable descriptions were segmented into individual units.

In summary these major features eliminate the manual search of massive sets of codebooks which in themselves are oriented only to a one way sequential search down a list of entries. This does not even consider the technical difficulty one would have of searching for data of interest that might be located on six or more different tape files with six or more different formats.

Substantive Improvements

The previous part of this section has been concerned with the problems of efficiently accessing and using large and disparate data files. In the remainder of this section we would like to comment on the more neglected aspects of data archives. We know that not all data is of equal value for various reasons. Data contains measurement er-

Figure.5.8   Data Base Design Using TOTAL.

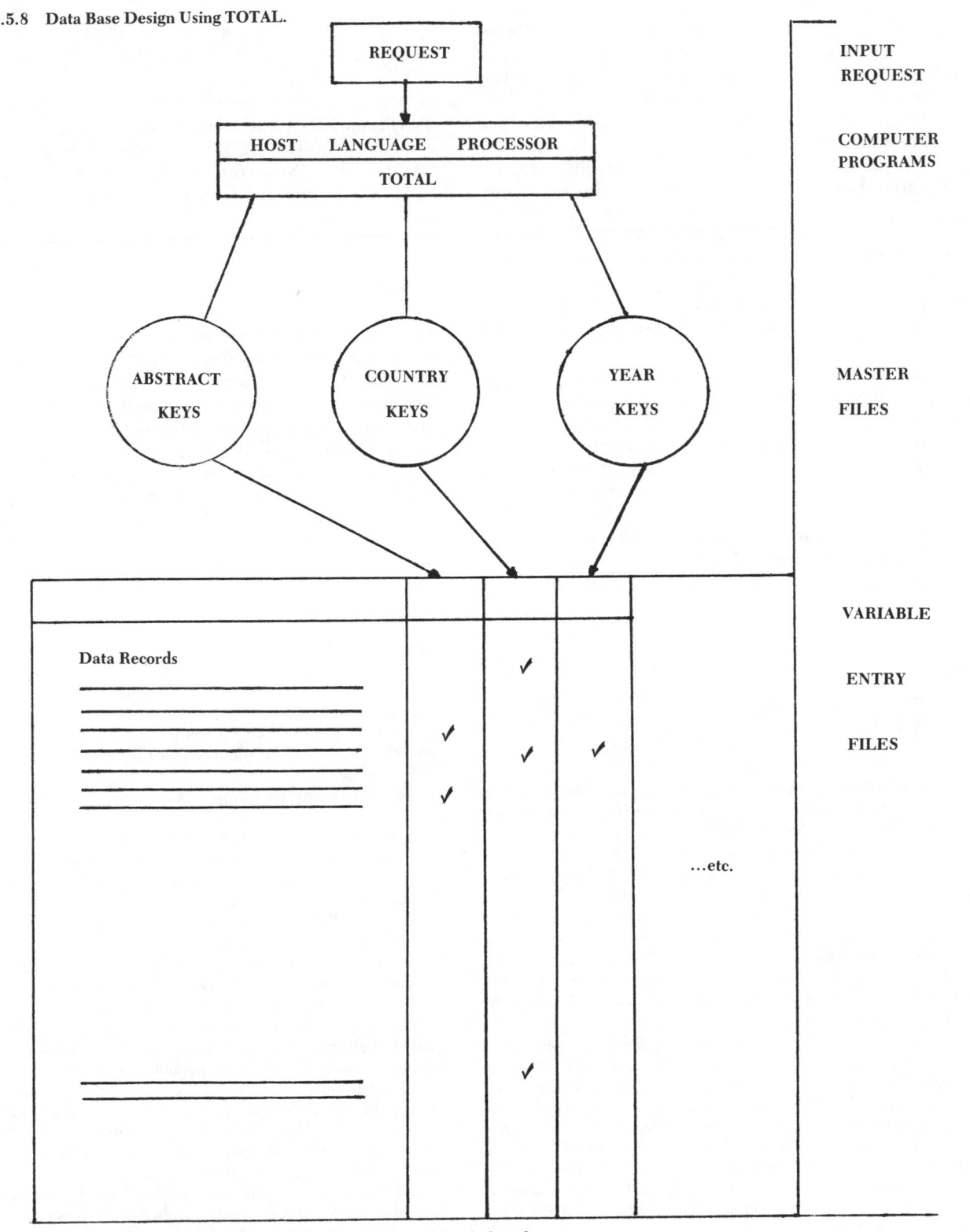

✔ indicates data record is member of that link path.

ror, is not specific to a particular interest, or may be redundant. All of these issues relate to the problems of maximizing information content, and we would like to offer a few suggestions on this set of issues.

First, with respect to reliability we would like to see each separate variable in the archive evaluated. Procedures to do this would include coder reliability studies, factor and other multivariate tests of indicator homogeneity, and tests of relationships with other variables[21]. Secondly, as we specified earlier in this chapter, the ANIP archive is constructed around certain theoretical interests, and we will continue to exercise discrimination in the incorporation of new data so that wasteful searching through data files irrelevant to these interests are avoided.

We have discovered as a result of factor analyses of the data that considerable redundancy exists in the data bank[22]. An instance of this is the very high intercorrelation of mass communications indicators over time as well as across indicator. Hence, it would not appear useful to measure such concepts every year or two nor to measure so many of them. Conversely, trade balances or economic growth indicators can radically change from year to year so that more frequent and detailed examination of these variables seems appropriate. Consequently, a long term objective of the ADMS and ANIP will be to constantly 'weed out' redundant measures, create conceptually relevant indices which satisfy reasonable requirements for index construction (see Morrison and Stevenson:1974), and to compact the data system wherever possible. The ADMS is expressly designed to facilitate this effort. Nevertheless, this will be a long term goal needing considerable feedback from theoretical models and empirical analysis.

Summary

This chapter has reported on the data banking acitvity of the African National Integration Project (ANIP) with its rationale, current structure, and the design of a new information processing data manager system. It is hoped that increasingly efficient means of storing the "wealth" of information available about Africa will lead to greater understanding of the processes of social change and political development that these countries are undergoing. It is our expectation that such an activity has relevance not only to the development of the social sciences, but also to the greater human and national autonomy that depends critically on the availability and utilization of information.

Notes

[1] This chapter, especially the last section on future developments, was written with Mr. John Tibert of the Institute for Behavioural Research, York University, Toronto, Canada.

We wish to acknowledge earlier support at Northwestern University for this project through the Program of African Studies directed by Professor Gwendolen Carter and the Council for Intersocietal Studies directed by Richard Schwartz. Additional funding has come from the National Institute of Mental Health, Rockefeller Foundation, the University of Ibadan and the Canada Council. Both the Institute for Behavioural Research and Bethune College at York University have provided facilities and support for this work as have M.I.T. and the University of Washington

[2] For a statement on the relation between information content and the probability of occurrence of the observation, see the pioneering work of Weiner:1948 and 1954. In this literature, information, as a concept, is clearly delineated from and related to facts or data. Briefly a fact or datum constitutes 'information' in *inverse proportion* to the *a priori* expectation of it being true. Hence, the statement that the sun came up this morning has very little information content while the statement that the sun will not rise tomorrow, if true, would have very high information content. Nevertheless, both statements are assumed, in this hypothetical example, to be true, and hence 'facts'.

[3] In this section we have chosen for the sake of completeness and readability to present the arguments that were earlier made in Morrison et.al.:1974c.

[4] See Newlyn:1962 for a compact discussion of the characteristics of money.

[5] If it is required to ascertain the truth of a certain proposition, then data which, while true, do not relate to the question, are 'noise' from the perspective of the user. A study of economic development in Ghana, for instance, would regard as 'noise' data on the level of production of steel in Brazil for that year even though this would be information with regard to a study of Brazilian economic development. Therefore, information must not only be relatively independent data from that already known but must also be salient to the questions being asked by the observer. See Weiner: 1948 and 1954.

[6] The original sample of nations for which ANIP collected data comprised all those Sub-Saharan African nations independent (in the full sense which excludes the Republic of South Africa) in 1967: Botswana, Burundi, Cameroon, Central African Republic, Chad, Congo, Dahomey, Ethiopia, Gabon, Gambia, Ghana, Guinea, Ivory Coast, Kenya, Lesotho, Liberia, Malawi, Mauritania, Mali, Niger, Nigeria, Rwanda, Senegal, Sierra Leone, Somalia, Sudan, Tanzania, Togo, Uganda, Upper Volta, Zaire, and Zambia. Current expansion added nine new nations: Equatorial Guinea, Namibia, Djibouti, Zimbabwe, Swaziland, Mozambique, Angola, Guinea-Bissau and Madagascar, making a total of 41 countries.

[7]The Black Africa data set has already been circulated to several hundred users by the IBR Data Bank. We do not know how many others have received it from Northwestern University, the ICPSR at Michigan, or other sources.

[8]The following discussion presumes the use of the retrieval program TRIAL in using the casebook. The user without the facilities of this program can simply list the contents of the codebook and read it himself along the lines indicated for the computer in the text. This program is now available for super-micro computers.

[9]As we consider elsewhere, there is often considerable difference between sources for a given variable. See Morrison and Stevenson:1974a, 1974b and Chapter Three on measurement in this Handbook.

[10]See Morrison, D.G. and Stevenson, H.M.; *RANKOR: A FORTRAN Program for Rank Ordering*; Institute for Behavioural Research, York University, 1971.

[11]In order to increase the availability of data through the ANIP data bank, the authors hope that scholars who have collected information on African countries will consider the possibility of having their information added to the existing ANIP data sets, and circulated by the project. The authors therefore invite interested readers to send data on national characteristics, ethnic group characteristics, elite biography or urban centres for inclusion in the ANIP data bank. In addition, titles of unpublished monographs or research reports on African subjects that are not usually referenced in established bibliographic guides will be welcomed for inclusion in the ANIP bibliography. Copies of codebooks and data sets from social surveys in Africa will be archived in machine-readable form, returned in that form, and distributed under conditions specified by the survey directors. It is the intention to make available year-end bibliographies, and summaries of items contained in the survey archive. Correspondence relating to the deposit of information in ANIP data bank can be addressed to Donald G. Morrison, Dept. of Sociology, University of Washington, Seattle, WA. 98195.

The ANIP data archive may be purchased at the present time from the following address, where specific requests for tapes, printed codebooks, or data processing will be attended to: Irvington Publishers, 551 Fifth Avenue, New York, N.Y. 10017.

[12]One exception is the system at Northwestern University with the Remote Information Query System (RIQS) which is for a CDC 6400 computer and cannot practically be put on other computer systems except those identical to Northwestern's. SIR (Scientific Information Retrieval) is a descendant of RIQS and is now available on a number of machines. The SPSS system (Nie et.al.:1970) has been expanded to an interactive form (SCSS) although this system is primarily a data analysis system rather than an integrated information retrieval system.

[13]This process can, of course, be reversed and data can be deleted by taking the entry out of the codebook and dropping the data fields from the record. Modification of data is analagously accomplished by correcting entries as apropriate.

[14]The eventual system would also be on a terminal interactive basis in the manner of Northwestern University's RIQS system but this will be a second stage of accomplishing a new design.

[15]SSIS is an acronym for the Social Science Information System developed at the Data Bank Section of the Institute for Behavioural Research, York University.

[16]For purposes of exposition the abstract numbers are substituted for the reference pointers although this is not the case internally.

[17]This form of the abstract was derived from that presently used at the Institute for Behavioural Research (IBR) for cataloguing more than 200,000 abstracts taken from Social Science journals since 1967. The IBR abstract file has the following format:
ABSTRACT
AUTHOR(S)
TITLE
DATA
SUMMARY
AFFILIATION
SOURCE

[18]TOTAL is a pure data-base manager offered by CINCOM Systems Inc. and is widely used in business and government for personnel and accounting purposes. TOTAL was used at IBR, York University to handle and disseminate data sets from the 1971 Canadian Census summary tapes. This system as it operates at York works on a data set which is 42000 enumeration areas by 1200 characteristics or a total of over 50 million data points! There is currently an explosion of inexpensive but very powerful data base management programs for micro-computers which are often able to input information directly into data analysis programs. This development will only make the ADMS task easier. For a general review of data base systems see Ullman (1982).

[19]See Borman and Hays:1974 for a discussion of RIQS applications.

[20]See Flores:1970 and CODASYL:1969 for a discussion of this literature.

[21]For example see our measurement chapter in this book and Morrison and Stevenson:1974b.

Adelman, Irma and Cynthia Taft Morris.
1967 *Society, Politics and Economic Development.* Baltimore: Johns Hopkins University Press.

Azar, E. E. and T. J. Sloan
1975 *Dimensions of Interaction.* Pittsburgh: International Studies Association.

Armor, David J. and Arthur S. Couch.
1972 *Data-Text Primer.* New York: Free Press.

Atkinson, T. and J. Tibert.
1973 "A Census Data Management System." In *Canadian Datasystems.* MacLean Hunter, 5, 8, 21—23.

Banks, A. S.
1971 *Cross-Polity Time-Series Data.* Cambridge, Mass.: The MIT Press.

Banks, Arthur and Robert Textor.
1964 *A Cross-Polity Survey.* Cambridge, Mass.: M.I.T. Press.

Barrett, David B.
1968 *Schism and Renewal in Africa: An Analysis of Six Thousand Religious Movements.* Nairobi: Oxford University Press.

Bisco, R. L.
1967 "Social Science Data Archives: Progress and Prospects." *Social Science Information*, VI, 39—74.

Borman, L. and D. Dillaman.
1968 *TRIAL: User's Manual.* Evanston, Ill.: Vogelback Computing Center, Northwestern University (December), Report NUCC118.

Borman, L. and R. Hay, Jr.
1974 *Data Resources for the Social Sciences.* Evanston, Ill.: Vogelback Computing Center, Northwestern University (January). Report IS 74—004.

Codasyl Systems Committee Technical Report.
1969 *A Survey of Generalized Data Base Management Systems* (May).

Deutsch, Karl W.
1963 *The Nerves of Government.* New York: The Free Press.

Feierabend, Ivo K. and Rosalind L.
1965 *Cross-National Data Bank of Political Instability Events, (Code Index).* San Diego: Public Affairs Research Institute, San Diego State College, California, USA.

Flanigan, William H. and Edwin Fogelman.
1970 "Patterns of Political Violence in Comparative Historical Perspective." *Comparative Politics*, 3 (October), 1—20.

Flores, Ivan.
1970 *Data Structure and Management.* Englewood Cliffs, N.J.: Prentice-Hall.

Gurr, T. R.
1966 *New Error-Compensated Measures for Comparing Nations: Some Correlates of Civil Violence.* Princeton, N.J.: Center of International Studies, Princeton University, Research Monograph no. 25.

Gurr, T. R.
1974 "The Neo-Alexandrians: A Review Essay on Data Handbooks in Political Science." *American Political Science Review*, LXVIII, 1 (March), 243—52.

Hopkins, Raymond F.
1969 "Aggregated Data and the Study of Political Development." *Journal of Politics.* 31, 71—94.

Hopkins, R. and R. C. Mitchell.
1974 "Survey Research in Africa: The Viability of Survey Research in Africa—Some Propositions." *African Studies Review*, XVII, 3 (December), 567—74.

Hopkins, T. K. and I. Wallerstein.
1971 "A Proposal for a Data Bank of African Materials." *Social Science Information*, 10 (2), 135—47.

Janda, Kenneth.
1965 *Data Processing: Applications to Political Research.* Evanston, Ill.: Northwestern University Press.

1969 *Information Retrieval: Applications to Political Science.* New York: Bobbs-Merrill

1980 *Political Parties: A Cross-National Survey.* New York: Free Press.

Larimore, Kenneth E. and Donald Dillaman.
1970 "Computers and Africana Bibliographies." In John N. Paden and Edward W. Soja (eds.), *The African Experience*, vol. IIIB (Guide to Resources). Evanston, Ill.: Northwestern University Press, 131—39.

Klimbie, J. W. and K. L. Koffeman (eds.)
1974 *Data Base Management.* New York: North Holland.

Laswell, Harold D.
1965 "The Policy Sciences of Development." *World Politics*, (January), 268—90.

Mickiewicz, Ellend (ed.)
1973 *Handbook of Soviet Social Science Data.* New York: Free Press.

Mitchell, R. C., D. G. Morrison and J. N. Paden.
1969   "National Integration and Stability in Africa." In Gwendolen M. Carter and Ann Paden (eds.), *Expanding Horizons in African Studies*. Evanston, Ill.: Northwestern University Press, 329—336.

Morrison, D. G., R. C. Mitchell, J. N. Paden and H. M. Stevenson.
1972   *Black Africa: A Handbook for Comparative Research*, 1st edition. New York: The Free Press.

Morrison, D. G., forthcoming.
    Conflict and Political Violence in Black Africa: Empirical Tests of a Theory of Political Learning in Africa.

Morrison, D. G., H. M. Stevenson, R. C. Mitchell, and J. N. Paden.
1974   "Information on African Political Systems: The African National Integration Project Data Bank." *Social Science Information*, XIII, 6 (December), 109—23.

Morrison D. G. and H. M. Stevenson.
1972   "Integration and Instability: Patterns of African Political Development." *American Political Science Review* (September), 902—28.

Morrison, D. G. and H. M. Stevenson.
1974a   "Measuring Social and Political Requirements for System Stability: Empirical Validation of an Index Using Latin American and African Data." *Comparative Political Studies*, 7, 2 (July), 252—63.

Morrison, D. G. and H. M. Stevenson.
1974b   "Social Complexity, Economic Development and Coups d'État in Africa, Latin America and Asia." *Journal of Peace Research*.

Murdock, George P.
1967   *Ethnographic Atlas*. Pittsburgh: University of Pittsburgh Press.

Nasater, D.
1973   *Data Archives for the Social Sciences: Purposes, Operations and Problems*. Reports and Papers in the Social Sciences, no. 26. Paris: UNESCO.

Newlyn, W. T.
1962   *Theory of Money*. London: Oxford University Press.

Nie, Norman H., Dale H. Bert and C. Hadlai Hull.
1970   *Statistical Package for the Social Sciences*. McGraw Hill, Inc.

Paden, J. and E. Soja.
1970   *The African Experience, Vol. IIIa Bibliography*. Evanston, Ill.: Northwestern University Press.

Rokkan, Stein (ed.)
1966   *Data Archives for the Social Sciences*. Paris: Mouton.

Rummel, R. J.
1966   "The Dimensionality of Nations Project." In Richard Merritt and Stein Rokkan (eds.), *Comparing Nations*. New Haven: Yale University Press.

Russett, Bruce M., *et. al.*
1964   *World Handbook of Political and Social Indicators*. New Haven: Yale University Press.

Schmitter, Phillipe C.
1969   "New Strategies for the Comparative Analysis of Latin American Politics." *Latin American Research Review*. 4 (Summer), 83—110.

Singer, J. D. and M. Small
1982   *Resort to Arms*, 2nd ed. Beverly Hills: Sage.

Staff.
1968.   *Propositional Inventory No. 1: National Integration*. African Natonal Integration Project, Institute for Behavioural Research, York University, Toronto, Canada.
    Propositional Inventory No. 2: Social Frustration and Conflict.
    Propositional Inventory No. 3: Pluralism.
    Propositional Inventory No. 4: Civil—Military Relations.
    Propositional Inventory No. 5: Nation—Building in Africa.

Taylor, C. L. and M. C. Hudson.
1972   *World Handbook of Political and Social Indicators*. 2nd. ed. New Haven: Yale University Press.

Ullman, J. D.
1982   *Database Systems* 2nd ed. Rockville, MD: Computer Sciences Press.

Weiner, N.
1948   *Cybernetics*. Cambridge, Mass.: The Technology Press.

Weiner, Norbert.
1954   *The Human Use of Human Beings: Cybernetics and Society*. Garden City, N.Y.: Doubleday Anchor Books.

```
            V1.1      V1.6      V1.2      V1.4      V1.5      V1.3      V1.7      V1.9      V1.10     V1.11     V1.13     V1.14     V1.15     V1.12     V1.8

V1.1      1.0000
          (    0)
          P=******

V1.6       .0024    1.0000
          (   41)  (    0)
          P= .494  P=******

V1.2       .2653     .0389    1.0000
          (   41)  (   41)  (    0)
          P= .047  P= .405  P=******

V1.4       .4517     .1067    -.0684    1.0000
          (   41)  (   41)  (   41)  (    0)
          P= .002  P= .253  P= .335  P=******

V1.5      -.3334     .0735    -.0561     .1255    1.0000
          (   41)  (   41)  (   41)  (   41)  (    0)
          P= .017  P= .324  P= .364  P= .217  P=******

V1.3       .1408     .3198     .0387     .2952    -.2555    1.0000
          (   41)  (   41)  (   41)  (   41)  (   41)  (    0)
          P= .190  P= .021  P= .405  P= .030  P= .053  P=******

V1.7      -.0187    -.0527    -.1824    -.1807    -.2699     .1588    1.0000
          (   41)  (   41)  (   41)  (   41)  (   41)  (   41)  (    0)
          P= .454  P= .372  P= .127  P= .129  P= .044  P= .161  P=******

V1.9      -.1133    -.0191    -.0115    -.0246    -.1552     .0995     .5464    1.0000
          (   41)  (   41)  (   41)  (   41)  (   41)  (   41)  (   41)  (    0)
          P= .240  P= .453  P= .472  P= .439  P= .166  P= .268  P= .001  P=******

V1.10     -.0844    -.0826     .1924    -.0279    -.2298     .2908     .2582     .7350    1.0000
          (   41)  (   41)  (   41)  (   41)  (   41)  (   41)  (   41)  (   41)  (    0)
          P= .300  P= .304  P= .114  P= .431  P= .074  P= .033  P= .052  P= .001  P=******

V1.11      .2252    -.0602     .1783    -.0731    -.0687    -.1230    -.2976    -.4533    -.2174    1.0000
          (   41)  (   41)  (   41)  (   41)  (   41)  (   41)  (   41)  (   41)  (   41)  (    0)
          P= .078  P= .354  P= .132  P= .325  P= .335  P= .222  P= .029  P= .086  P= .089  P=******

V1.13      .5481     .2953     .0537     .8436    -.0135     .4142    -.1714     .0589     .1415    -.1099    1.0000
          (   41)  (   41)  (   41)  (   41)  (   41)  (   41)  (   41)  (   41)  (   41)  (   41)  (    0)
          P= .001  P= .030  P= .369  P= .001  P= .467  P= .004  P= .142  P= .357  P= .189  P= .247  P=******

V1.14     -.0794     .0388    -.1331    -.1108     .1288    -.1938     .2801     .0482    -.1121    -.1272    -.1013    1.0000
          (   41)  (   41)  (   41)  (   41)  (   41)  (   41)  (   41)  (   41)  (   41)  (   41)  (   41)  (    0)
          P= .311  P= .405  P= .203  P= .245  P= .211  P= .112  P= .038  P= .382  P= .243  P= .214  P= .264  P=******

V1.15      .0522     .0606     .0187    -.1434     .0397    -.1214    -.2271    -.2768    -.0846     .6669    -.1446    -.2264    1.0000
          (   41)  (   41)  (   41)  (   41)  (   41)  (   41)  (   41)  (   41)  (   41)  (   41)  (   41)  (   41)  (    0)
          P= .373  P= .353  P= .454  P= .186  P= .403  P= .225  P= .077  P= .040  P= .300  P= .001  P= .184  P= .077  P=******

V1.12     -.1945    -.3680    -.0154    -.1979    -.2695    -.0123     .1507     .3520     .5621     .1119    -.2392    -.3180     .2733    1.0000
          (   41)  (   41)  (   41)  (   41)  (   41)  (   41)  (   41)  (   41)  (   41)  (   41)  (   41)  (   41)  (   41)  (    0)
          P= .111  P= .009  P= .462  P= .107  P= .044  P= .470  P= .174  P= .012  P= .001  P= .243  P= .066  P= .021  P= .042  P=******

V1.8      -.5184     .0729    -.2231    -.4607     .2786    -.3336     .2970     .0689    -.1612    -.1356    -.4661     .7541    -.0680    -.1544    1.0000
          (   41)  (   41)  (   41)  (   41)  (   41)  (   41)  (   41)  (   41)  (   41)  (   41)  (   41)  (   41)  (   41)  (   41)  (    0)
          P= .001  P= .325  P= .080  P= .001  P= .039  P= .017  P= .030  P= .334  P= .157  P= .199  P= .001  P= .001  P= .336  P= .168  P=******

V2.1      -.0944    -.1243    -.3335    -.1155     .2533    -.4078    -.0862    -.0768    -.2492     .1888    -.2879    -.0585     .2839     .1907     .0550
          (   41)  (   41)  (   41)  (   41)  (   41)  (   41)  (   41)  (   41)  (   41)  (   41)  (   41)  (   41)  (   41)  (   41)  (   41)
          P= .279  P= .219  P= .017  P= .236  P= .055  P= .004  P= .296  P= .317  P= .058  P= .119  P= .034  P= .358  P= .036  P= .116  P= .366

V2.2      -.1012    -.1558    -.1612    -.1604    -.0115    -.1828    -.0721    -.1749    -.1030     .2045    -.2165    -.0290     .3508     .3353     .0326
          (   41)  (   41)  (   41)  (   41)  (   41)  (   41)  (   41)  (   41)  (   41)  (   41)  (   41)  (   41)  (   41)  (   41)  (   41)
          P= .265  P= .165  P= .157  P= .158  P= .472  P= .126  P= .327  P= .137  P= .261  P= .100  P= .087  P= .429  P= .012  P= .016  P= .420

V2.3      -.1527    -.0868     .2907    -.2315    -.1912     .1357    -.1222     .0743     .3744    -.1319    -.1681     .0386    -.1285     .3606     .0642
          (   41)  (   41)  (   41)  (   41)  (   41)  (   41)  (   41)  (   41)  (   41)  (   41)  (   41)  (   41)  (   41)  (   41)  (   41)
          P= .170  P= .295  P= .033  P= .073  P= .116  P= .199  P= .223  P= .322  P= .008  P= .206  P= .147  P= .405  P= .212  P= .010  P= .345

V2.4       .4513     .0571     .1629     .3827     .0641    -.0059     .0141    -.1966    -.3147     .2474     .2051     .0986     .0348    -.2765    -.0845
          (   41)  (   41)  (   41)  (   41)  (   41)  (   41)  (   41)  (   41)  (   41)  (   41)  (   41)  (   41)  (   41)  (   41)  (   41)
          P= .002  P= .362  P= .154  P= .007  P= .345  P= .485  P= .465  P= .109  P= .023  P= .059  P= .099  P= .270  P= .415  P= .040  P= .300

V2.5       .0672    -.2564    -.3297     .1565     .1955    -.4170    -.3615    -.2651    -.3486     .1442     .0855    -.0277     .1842    -.0377    -.0102
          (   41)  (   41)  (   41)  (   41)  (   41)  (   41)  (   41)  (   41)  (   41)  (   41)  (   41)  (   41)  (   41)  (   41)  (   41)
          P= .338  P= .053  P= .018  P= .164  P= .110  P= .003  P= .010  P= .047  P= .013  P= .184  P= .298  P= .432  P= .124  P= .407  P= .475

V2.6       .4488     .1245    -.0456     .4231     .1982    -.1217    -.0593    -.1649    -.3812     .1385     .3280     .2580     .0898    -.3415    -.0053
          (   41)  (   41)  (   41)  (   41)  (   41)  (   41)  (   41)  (   41)  (   41)  (   41)  (   41)  (   41)  (   41)  (   41)  (   41)
          P= .002  P= .219  P= .389  P= .003  P= .107  P= .224  P= .356  P= .151  P= .007  P= .194  P= .018  P= .052  P= .288  P= .014  P= .487

V2.7       .2641    -.0254    -.1675     .2685     .2883    -.3022    -.3993    -.3239    -.3006     .2185     .1800     .0260     .1945     .0265    -.1308
          (   41)  (   41)  (   41)  (   41)  (   41)  (   41)  (   41)  (   41)  (   41)  (   41)  (   41)  (   41)  (   41)  (   41)  (   41)
          P= .048  P= .437  P= .148  P= .045  P= .034  P= .027  P= .005  P= .019  P= .028  P= .085  P= .130  P= .436  P= .112  P= .435  P= .208

V2.13     -.1020    -.0565     .1878    -.1417     .0035     .2717    -.0437    -.0677     .1795    -.0321    -.0675     .0760     .0681     .0759     .1695
          (   41)  (   41)  (   41)  (   41)  (   41)  (   41)  (   41)  (   41)  (   41)  (   41)  (   41)  (   41)  (   41)  (   41)  (   41)
          P= .263  P= .363  P= .120  P= .188  P= .491  P= .043  P= .393  P= .337  P= .131  P= .421  P= .338  P= .318  P= .336  P= .319  P= .145

V2.8       .1779     .0215     .0510     .0276    -.0999    -.3636    -.0426     .1820     .1550     .2554     .0229     .2277     .2123    -.0730     .0124
          (   41)  (   41)  (   41)  (   41)  (   41)  (   41)  (   41)  (   41)  (   41)  (   41)  (   41)  (   41)  (   41)  (   41)  (   41)
          P= .133  P= .447  P= .376  P= .432  P= .267  P= .010  P= .396  P= .127  P= .167  P= .054  P= .444  P= .076  P= .091  P= .325  P= .469

V2.9      -.0414    -.0963    -.0539     .0630     .1375     .3277     .1580    -.0273    -.0182    -.2399     .0700    -.1440    -.1715     .1383     .0034
          (   41)  (   41)  (   41)  (   41)  (   41)  (   41)  (   41)  (   41)  (   41)  (   41)  (   41)  (   41)  (   41)  (   41)  (   41)
          P= .399  P= .275  P= .369  P= .348  P= .196  P= .018  P= .162  P= .433  P= .455  P= .065  P= .332  P= .185  P= .142  P= .194  P= .492

V2.10     -.0115     .1194     .0694     .0955    -.0539     .4693     .2569    -.0527     .0216    -.1337     .1018    -.1337    -.0774     .1531    -.0687
          (   41)  (   41)  (   41)  (   41)  (   41)  (   41)  (   41)  (   41)  (   41)  (   41)  (   41)  (   41)  (   41)  (   41)  (   41)
          P= .472  P= .229  P= .333  P= .276  P= .369  P= .001  P= .052  P= .372  P= .447  P= .202  P= .263  P= .202  P= .315  P= .170  P= .335

V2.11     -.1181    -.2390    -.1318    -.0882     .2815     .1210     .0206     .0081    -.0076    -.2123    -.0640    -.0750    -.1566     .0788     .1177
          (   41)  (   41)  (   41)  (   41)  (   41)  (   41)  (   41)  (   41)  (   41)  (   41)  (   41)  (   41)  (   41)  (   41)  (   41)
          P= .231  P= .066  P= .206  P= .292  P= .037  P= .226  P= .449  P= .480  P= .481  P= .091  P= .345  P= .321  P= .164  P= .312  P= .232

V2.12     -.2476     .1437     .0098    -.1642    -.0573     .0674    -.2094    -.3088    -.2752    -.0195    -.1693    -.1334    -.0687    -.1553    -.0236
          (   41)  (   41)  (   41)  (   41)  (   41)  (   41)  (   41)  (   41)  (   41)  (   41)  (   41)  (   41)  (   41)  (   41)  (   41)
          P= .059  P= .185  P= .476  P= .152  P= .361  P= .338  P= .094  P= .025  P= .041  P= .452  P= .145  P= .203  P= .335  P= .166  P= .442

V2.14     -.0346    -.1159    -.0910     .0321     .1670     .2376     .2014    -.0347    -.0654    -.2479     .0576    -.0949    -.1732     .0728     .0957
          (   41)  (   41)  (   41)  (   41)  (   41)  (   41)  (   41)  (   41)  (   41)  (   41)  (   41)  (   41)  (   41)  (   41)  (   41)
          P= .415  P= .235  P= .286  P= .421  P= .148  P= .067  P= .103  P= .415  P= .342  P= .059  P= .360  P= .277  P= .139  P= .326  P= .276

V2.15      .0266     .2460    -.0022     .1099    -.1067     .5098     .1037    -.0307     .0866    -.1015     .2720    -.1587    -.1030     .0860    -.0865
          (   41)  (   41)  (   41)  (   41)  (   41)  (   41)  (   41)  (   41)  (   41)  (   41)  (   41)  (   41)  (   41)  (   41)  (   41)
          P= .434  P= .061  P= .494  P= .247  P= .253  P= .001  P= .259  P= .425  P= .295  P= .264  P= .043  P= .161  P= .261  P= .297  P= .295

V2.16     -.1285     .2065     .0558     .1518     .1998    -.1075    -.4862    -.0828    -.1619    -.0780     .0935    -.2210    -.1209    -.2057    -.2488
          (   41)  (   41)  (   41)  (   41)  (   41)  (   41)  (   41)  (   41)  (   41)  (   41)  (   41)  (   41)  (   41)  (   41)  (   41)
          P= .212  P= .098  P= .364  P= .172  P= .105  P= .252  P= .001  P= .303  P= .156  P= .314  P= .281  P= .082  P= .226  P= .098  P= .058

V2.22     -.0636    -.2056    -.0476     .2766    -.0483     .1146    -.1786    -.0049    -.0689    -.2026     .2136    -.0371    -.1836    -.2031     .0154
          (   37)  (   37)  (   37)  (   37)  (   37)  (   37)  (   37)  (   37)  (   37)  (   37)  (   37)  (   37)  (   37)  (   37)  (   37)
          P= .354  P= .111  P= .390  P= .049  P= .388  P= .250  P= .145  P= .488  P= .343  P= .115  P= .102  P= .414  P= .138  P= .114  P= .464

V2.18      .5396    -.0810     .3634     .2767    -.3115    -.1155    -.2866     .0511    -.1288     .2509     .2273    -.0725    -.0036    -.2431    -.3242
          (   37)  (   37)  (   37)  (   37)  (   37)  (   37)  (   37)  (   37)  (   37)  (   37)  (   37)  (   37)  (   37)  (   37)  (   37)
          P= .001  P= .317  P= .014  P= .049  P= .030  P= .248  P= .043  P= .382  P= .224  P= .067  P= .088  P= .335  P= .492  P= .074  P= .025
```

Appendix
Correlation Matrix

The following matrix presents Pearson product-moment correlation coefficients for each variable A in the tables of Part I. It is intended to provide a quick way to check bivariate relationships between variables. The coefficient varies between -1.00 and 1.00; the higher the coefficient the more the two variables covary. For example, the correlation coefficient between Gross Domestic Investment as a Percent of GDP (Table 3.15) and GNP per Capita 1977 (Table 3.2) is .68 indicating a moderately strong relationship.

The variables are labeled with a chapter designation followed by the table number in the chapter. Hence chapter three Table 8 is identified as V3.8; chapter 4 table 7 as F.7; chapter 5, table 3 as V.3 and chapter six, table 7 as S.7.

```
   1.0000
  (     0)
  P=******

    .4757   1.0000
  (    41) (     0)
  P=  .001  P=******

   -.4003   -.1753   1.0000
  (    41) (    41) (     0)
  P=  .005  P=  .137  P=******

   -.0728   -.1963   -.1914   1.0000
  (    41) (    41) (    41) (     0)
  P=  .325  P=  .109  P=  .115  P=******

    .4558    .1041   -.2525    .0755   1.0000
  (    41) (    41) (    41) (    41) (     0)
  P=  .001  P=  .259  P=  .056  P=  .320  P=******

    .2621   -.1918   -.3789    .5814    .4753   1.0000
  (    41) (    41) (    41) (    41) (    41) (     0)
  P=  .049  P=  .115  P=  .007  P=  .001  P=  .001  P=******

    .5707    .3384   -.1020    .0162    .4188    .3631   1.0000
  (    41) (    41) (    41) (    41) (    41) (    41) (     0)
  P=  .001  P=  .015  P=  .263  P=  .460  P=  .003  P=  .010  P=******

   -.0171    .3753    .2427   -.2813   -.1332   -.2128    .0855   1.0000
  (    41) (    41) (    41) (    41) (    41) (    41) (    41) (     0)
  P=  .458  P=  .008  P=  .063  P=  .037  P=  .203  P=  .091  P=  .298  P=******

    .0907   -.1330   -.1339    .3239    .0786    .1887   -.0537   -.4070   1.0000
  (    41) (    41) (    41) (    41) (    41) (    41) (    41) (    41) (     0)
  P=  .286  P=  .204  P=  .202  P=  .019  P=  .313  P=  .119  P=  .369  P=  .004  P=******

   -.0085    .1235    .0622   -.2000    .0097   -.0245    .1458    .4743   -.8620   1.0000
  (    41) (    41) (    41) (    41) (    41) (    41) (    41) (    41) (    41) (     0)
  P=  .479  P=  .221  P=  .350  P=  .105  P=  .476  P=  .440  P=  .181  P=  .001  P=  .001  P=******

   -.0116    .2173   -.0100   -.0865   -.2572   -.0255    .0751    .4807   -.6724    .7367   1.0000
  (    41) (    41) (    41) (    41) (    41) (    41) (    41) (    41) (    41) (    41) (     0)
  P=  .471  P=  .086  P=  .475  P=  .295  P=  .052  P=  .437  P=  .320  P=  .001  P=  .001  P=  .001  P=******

    .0117    .0071    .1162   -.1907    .1865   -.0734    .0566    .3122   -.6621    .7878    .2376   1.0000
  (    41) (    41) (    41) (    41) (    41) (    41) (    41) (    41) (    41) (    41) (    41) (     0)
  P=  .471  P=  .482  P=  .235  P=  .116  P=  .122  P=  .324  P=  .363  P=  .023  P=  .001  P=  .001  P=  .067  P=******

   -.1586    .0124    .1214   -.2151   -.1830   -.3007   -.1789   -.1425   -.2329   -.2908   -.1407   -.2604   1.0000
  (    41) (    41) (    41) (    41) (    41) (    41) (    41) (    41) (    41) (    41) (    41) (    41) (     0)
  P=  .161  P=  .469  P=  .225  P=  .088  P=  .126  P=  .028  P=  .132  P=  .187  P=  .071  P=  .033  P=  .190  P=  .050  P=******

    .0338    .0924    .0440   -.1748    .0665    .0297    .1589    .4870   -.8169    .9626    .6378    .8027   -.2997   1.0000
  (    41) (    41) (    41) (    41) (    41) (    41) (    41) (    41) (    41) (    41) (    41) (    41) (    41) (     0)
  P=  .417  P=  .283  P=  .392  P=  .137  P=  .340  P=  .427  P=  .160  P=  .001  P=  .001  P=  .001  P=  .001  P=  .001  P=  .028  P=******

    .0098    .0720    .0330   -.1587   -.1582   -.0337    .0650    .4080   -.4743    .4703    .7335    .0621   -.0059    .4307   1.0000
  (    41) (    41) (    41) (    41) (    41) (    41) (    41) (    41) (    41) (    41) (    41) (    41) (    41) (    41) (     0)
  P=  .476  P=  .327  P=  .419  P=  .161  P=  .162  P=  .417  P=  .343  P=  .004  P=  .001  P=  .001  P=  .001  P=  .350  P=  .485  P=  .002  P=******

    .0231   -.1245    .1258   -.0003    .0294   -.0432    .2131   -.2310    .0605   -.3150   -.1996   -.2623    .4853   -.3628   -.0271
  (    41) (    41) (    41) (    41) (    41) (    41) (    41) (    41) (    41) (    41) (    41) (    41) (    41) (    41) (    41)
  P=  .443  P=  .219  P=  .217  P=  .499  P=  .428  P=  .394  P=  .090  P=  .073  P=  .354  P=  .022  P=  .105  P=  .049  P=  .001  P=  .010  P=  .433

   -.1803   -.2241    .1596   -.1718   -.2188   -.0690    .1163    .0420   -.2450    .0711    .1787   -.1778    .3237    .0758    .1352
  (    37) (    37) (    37) (    37) (    37) (    37) (    37) (    37) (    37) (    37) (    37) (    37) (    37) (    37) (    37)
  P=  .143  P=  .091  P=  .173  P=  .155  P=  .097  P=  .343  P=  .246  P=  .403  P=  .072  P=  .338  P=  .145  P=  .146  P=  .025  P=  .328  P=  .213

   -.1005   -.3412   -.0560    .5670    .0412    .5294    .0017   -.3933    .4941   -.4328   -.3578   -.4734   -.0980   -.4039   -.2367
  (    37) (    37) (    37) (    37) (    37) (    37) (    37) (    37) (    37) (    37) (    37) (    37) (    37) (    37) (    37)
  P=  .277  P=  .019  P=  .371  P=  .001  P=  .404  P=  .001  P=  .496  P=  .008  P=  .001  P=  .004  P=  .015  P=  .002  P=  .282  P=  .007  P=  .079
```

	V2.1	V2.2	V2.3	V2.4	V2.5	V2.6	V2.7	V2.13	V2.8	V2.9	V2.10	V2.11	V2.12	V2.14	V2.15
	-.5663 (37) P=.001	-.5751 (37) P=.001	.2651 (37) P=.056	.1334 (37) P=.216	-.1840 (37) P=.138	.0162 (37) P=.462	-.4554 (37) P=.002	-.1233 (37) P=.234	.0777 (37) P=.324	-.1937 (37) P=.125	-.1405 (37) P=.203	-.1805 (37) P=.143	.2238 (37) P=.091	-.2180 (37) P=.097	-.1025 (37) P=.273
	-.3024 (38) P=.032	-.3770 (38) P=.010	-.0704 (38) P=.337	.2195 (38) P=.093	-.0665 (38) P=.346	.2452 (38) P=.069	-.0728 (38) P=.332	.0074 (38) P=.482	.0622 (38) P=.355	-.1154 (38) P=.245	.0359 (38) P=.415	-.2306 (38) P=.082	.0863 (38) P=.303	-.1798 (38) P=.140	-.0094 (38) P=.478
	-.3870 (37) P=.009	-.4590 (37) P=.002	.1084 (37) P=.262	.2166 (37) P=.099	-.1473 (37) P=.192	.0985 (37) P=.281	-.3256 (37) P=.025	-.0450 (37) P=.396	.3227 (37) P=.026	-.3007 (37) P=.035	-.2770 (37) P=.048	-.2657 (37) P=.056	-.0279 (37) P=.435	-.2703 (37) P=.053	-.0805 (37) P=.318
	-.6692 (35) P=.001	-.4764 (35) P=.002	.0443 (35) P=.400	.2934 (35) P=.044	-.2346 (35) P=.087	.0651 (35) P=.355	-.5526 (35) P=.001	-.1987 (35) P=.126	.2431 (35) P=.080	-.3767 (35) P=.013	-.1871 (35) P=.141	-.3299 (35) P=.026	.2813 (35) P=.051	-.4339 (35) P=.005	-.2122 (35) P=.111
	-.2667 (33) P=.067	-.3887 (33) P=.013	.1761 (33) P=.163	.0935 (33) P=.302	-.0680 (33) P=.353	.0439 (33) P=.404	-.1395 (33) P=.219	.2175 (33) P=.112	.0211 (33) P=.454	.0550 (33) P=.381	.0604 (33) P=.369	.0388 (33) P=.415	-.1511 (33) P=.201	.0917 (33) P=.306	.2484 (33) P=.082
	.2775 (41) P=.040	.2010 (41) P=.104	.0365 (41) P=.410	.1740 (41) P=.138	.3475 (41) P=.013	.2767 (41) P=.040	.4034 (41) P=.004	-.0163 (41) P=.460	.1106 (41) P=.246	-.0786 (41) P=.313	-.1724 (41) P=.141	.0069 (41) P=.483	-.0437 (41) P=.393	.0099 (41) P=.475	-.1981 (41) P=.107
	-.2762 (41) P=.040	-.2689 (41) P=.045	-.1914 (41) P=.115	.1681 (41) P=.147	-.1470 (41) P=.180	.1765 (41) P=.135	-.1213 (41) P=.225	.0116 (41) P=.471	-.1168 (41) P=.233	.1525 (41) P=.171	.2409 (41) P=.065	.0246 (41) P=.439	-.0738 (41) P=.323	.0599 (41) P=.355	.3781 (41) P=.007
	.1039 (39) P=.264	.2698 (39) P=.048	.3336 (39) P=.019	-.0922 (39) P=.288	-.0382 (39) P=.409	-.1463 (39) P=.187	.0389 (39) P=.407	.3941 (39) P=.007	.1416 (39) P=.195	-.0958 (39) P=.281	.0368 (39) P=.412	-.0909 (39) P=.291	-.0718 (39) P=.332	-.0553 (39) P=.369	.1204 (39) P=.233
	-.2348 (41) P=.070	-.1500 (41) P=.175	-.2487 (41) P=.058	.0015 (41) P=.496	-.0409 (41) P=.400	.1216 (41) P=.224	-.0317 (41) P=.422	-.0616 (41) P=.351	-.2933 (41) P=.031	.3338 (41) P=.016	.2226 (41) P=.081	.2689 (41) P=.045	-.0725 (41) P=.326	.2879 (41) P=.034	.2646 (41) P=.047
	.0643 (41) P=.345	.2176 (41) P=.086	-.0771 (41) P=.316	-.3501 (41) P=.012	-.1350 (41) P=.200	-.1864 (41) P=.122	-.2631 (41) P=.048	.2013 (41) P=.103	-.4483 (41) P=.002	.4514 (41) P=.002	.4175 (41) P=.003	.3015 (41) P=.028	-.0301 (41) P=.426	.3828 (41) P=.007	.3448 (41) P=.014
	-.3342 (41) P=.016	-.2172 (41) P=.086	-.0500 (41) P=.378	-.0212 (41) P=.448	-.2314 (41) P=.073	-.1497 (41) P=.175	-.2884 (41) P=.034	.1952 (41) P=.111	-.2417 (41) P=.064	.1822 (41) P=.127	.3390 (41) P=.015	.0044 (41) P=.489	.1006 (41) P=.266	.1031 (41) P=.261	.3005 (41) P=.028
	.1568 (41) P=.164	.1143 (41) P=.238	-.0037 (41) P=.491	-.2047 (41) P=.100	-.0226 (41) P=.444	-.1193 (41) P=.229	.1016 (41) P=.264	.0685 (41) P=.335	.2211 (41) P=.082	-.0249 (41) P=.439	-.0296 (41) P=.427	-.0024 (41) P=.494	-.3950 (41) P=.005	-.0592 (41) P=.356	-.0845 (41) P=.300
	.0912 (26) P=.329	.1442 (26) P=.241	.0487 (26) P=.407	-.4571 (26) P=.009	-.1960 (26) P=.169	-.3698 (26) P=.031	.0509 (26) P=.402	.1052 (26) P=.305	-.3439 (26) P=.043	.2890 (26) P=.076	.4163 (26) P=.017	.1190 (26) P=.281	.1248 (26) P=.272	.2394 (26) P=.119	.3209 (26) P=.055
	-.1170 (37) P=.245	-.0917 (37) P=.295	.3487 (37) P=.017	-.2602 (37) P=.060	-.2500 (37) P=.068	-.2368 (37) P=.079	-.3007 (37) P=.035	.5495 (37) P=.001	-.1084 (37) P=.262	.1892 (37) P=.131	.2019 (37) P=.115	.1524 (37) P=.184	-.1412 (37) P=.202	.2374 (37) P=.079	.3882 (37) P=.009
	-.2394 (39) P=.071	-.2152 (39) P=.094	-.1294 (39) P=.216	.0384 (39) P=.408	.0380 (39) P=.409	.1509 (39) P=.180	-.1543 (39) P=.174	-.1571 (39) P=.170	-.2803 (39) P=.042	.2969 (39) P=.033	.0675 (39) P=.342	.3727 (39) P=.010	-.0247 (39) P=.441	.2720 (39) P=.047	-.0147 (39) P=.465
	.1325 (41) P=.205	-.1471 (41) P=.179	-.1003 (41) P=.266	-.0320 (41) P=.421	.2358 (41) P=.069	.1320 (41) P=.205	.0853 (41) P=.298	-.3055 (41) P=.026	-.2796 (41) P=.038	-.2196 (41) P=.084	-.4333 (41) P=.002	.0464 (41) P=.387	-.1184 (41) P=.230	-.1893 (41) P=.118	-.4800 (41) P=.001
	-.3405 (37) P=.020	-.2716 (37) P=.052	-.1006 (37) P=.277	.1458 (37) P=.195	.0279 (37) P=.435	.2373 (37) P=.079	.0325 (37) P=.424	.0910 (37) P=.296	-.0637 (37) P=.354	.2220 (37) P=.093	.2378 (37) P=.078	.1554 (37) P=.179	-.2861 (37) P=.043	.2325 (37) P=.083	.3938 (37) P=.008
	.2095 (38) P=.103	.6556 (38) P=.001	-.0329 (38) P=.422	-.2175 (38) P=.095	-.0812 (38) P=.314	-.2709 (38) P=.050	.1361 (38) P=.208	.1482 (38) P=.187	-.1995 (38) P=.115	.0592 (38) P=.362	.2321 (38) P=.080	-.1014 (38) P=.272	.2525 (38) P=.063	-.0065 (38) P=.485	.1624 (38) P=.165
	-.1953 (40) P=.114	-.4644 (40) P=.001	.0460 (40) P=.389	.0275 (40) P=.433	-.2900 (40) P=.035	-.0097 (40) P=.476	.0684 (40) P=.337	.0840 (40) P=.303	-.1681 (40) P=.161	.1608 (40) P=.161	.2752 (40) P=.043	.0019 (40) P=.495	.0260 (40) P=.437	.1974 (40) P=.111	.3075 (40) P=.027
	.0248 (38) P=.441	-.0554 (38) P=.370	-.2639 (38) P=.055	.1252 (38) P=.227	.2670 (38) P=.053	.1398 (38) P=.201	.0799 (38) P=.317	-.3470 (38) P=.016	.0501 (38) P=.383	-.0577 (38) P=.365	-.3317 (38) P=.021	-.0224 (38) P=.447	.0314 (38) P=.426	-.0004 (38) P=.499	-.4203 (38) P=.004
	-.1411 (39) P=.196	-.1915 (39) P=.121	.2290 (39) P=.080	-.0242 (39) P=.442	-.0824 (39) P=.309	-.0289 (39) P=.431	-.1034 (39) P=.266	.2781 (39) P=.043	-.2004 (39) P=.111	.2669 (39) P=.050	.1540 (39) P=.175	.2774 (39) P=.044	-.1095 (39) P=.253	.3280 (39) P=.021	.2294 (39) P=.080
	.2596 (39) P=.055	.6757 (39) P=.001	-.0732 (39) P=.329	-.1316 (39) P=.212	.0446 (39) P=.394	-.1460 (39) P=.188	.1869 (39) P=.127	.0915 (39) P=.290	-.1498 (39) P=.181	.0148 (39) P=.464	.1483 (39) P=.184	-.1075 (39) P=.257	-.2428 (39) P=.068	-.0540 (39) P=.372	.0723 (39) P=.331
	-.2261 (16) P=.200	-.6253 (16) P=.005	.1817 (16) P=.250*	-.2692 (16) P=.157	-.1927 (16) P=.237	-.0910 (16) P=.369	-.0738 (16) P=.393	.3540 (16) P=.089	-.0936 (16) P=.365	.2297 (16) P=.196	.0627 (16) P=.409	.3171 (16) P=.116	-.1966 (16) P=.233	.3842 (16) P=.071	.3745 (16) P=.076
	-.2462 (41) P=.060	-.4139 (41) P=.004	-.0236 (41) P=.442	.3851 (41) P=.006	-.0563 (41) P=.363	-.2323 (41) P=.072	-.0709 (41) P=.330	-.1435 (41) P=.185	-.0959 (41) P=.275	.0168 (41) P=.458	.0425 (41) P=.396	-.0059 (41) P=.485	-.2029 (41) P=.102	.0016 (41) P=.496	.0433 (41) P=.394
	-.1006 (41) P=.266	.0491 (41) P=.380	.3263 (41) P=.019	-.1128 (41) P=.241	-.0852 (41) P=.298	-.1803 (41) P=.130	-.1924 (41) P=.114	-.4503 (41) P=.002	-.1711 (41) P=.142	.2499 (41) P=.058	.1669 (41) P=.149	.2470 (41) P=.060	-.1452 (41) P=.183	.3120 (41) P=.024	-.2330 (41) P=.071
	.2501 (40) P=.060	.6759 (40) P=.001	-.0818 (40) P=.308	-.1196 (40) P=.231	.0406 (40) P=.402	-.1320 (40) P=.208	.1894 (40) P=.121	.0967 (40) P=.276	-.1468 (40) P=.183	.0169 (40) P=.459	.1766 (40) P=.138	-.1106 (40) P=.248	-.2417 (40) P=.067	-.0521 (40) P=.375	-.0758 (40) P=.321
	.2427 (41) P=.063	.7342 (41) P=.001	-.0425 (41) P=.396	-.2478 (41) P=.059	-.0366 (41) P=.410	-.2166 (41) P=.087	.1615 (41) P=.156	.4489 (41) P=.002	-.4997 (41) P=.001	.4168 (41) P=.003	.5301 (41) P=.001	.1799 (41) P=.130	.1331 (41) P=.203	.3442 (41) P=.014	.3844 (41) P=.007
	-.1015 (41) P=.264	.0011 (41) P=.497	.0265 (41) P=.435	.0141 (41) P=.465	.0563 (41) P=.363	.0794 (41) P=.311	-.0284 (41) P=.430	-.2050 (41) P=.099	.1691 (41) P=.145	-.2124 (41) P=.091	-.1879 (41) P=.120	-.1673 (41) P=.148	.0819 (41) P=.305	-.1938 (41) P=.112	-.1879 (41) P=.120
	.0683 (41) P=.336	.3440 (41) P=.014	.2655 (41) P=.047	-.2677 (41) P=.045	-.2157 (41) P=.088	-.2092 (41) P=.095	.1004 (41) P=.266	.5803 (41) P=.001	-.6111 (41) P=.001	.5679 (41) P=.001	.6970 (41) P=.001	.2758 (41) P=.040	.0659 (41) P=.341	.5728 (41) P=.001	.6168 (41) P=.001
	.2619 (41) P=.049	.0897 (41) P=.289	-.1017 (41) P=.263	-.0312 (41) P=.423	.1411 (41) P=.189	.0137 (41) P=.466	.2327 (41) P=.072	-.1584 (41) P=.161	.3737 (41) P=.008	-.2594 (41) P=.051	-.1533 (41) P=.169	-.2651 (41) P=.047	-.2119 (41) P=.092	-.2422 (41) P=.064	-.1211 (41) P=.225
	.0347 (40) P=.416	-.2166 (40) P=.090	.0078 (40) P=.481	-.1696 (40) P=.148	.0107 (40) P=.474	-.0437 (40) P=.394	.0176 (40) P=.457	.3528 (40) P=.013	-.3402 (40) P=.016	.4919 (40) P=.001	.3389 (40) P=.016	.4645 (40) P=.001	-.2886 (40) P=.035	.5335 (40) P=.001	.2767 (40) P=.042
	.1802 (40) P=.133	.6481 (40) P=.001	-.0082 (40) P=.480	-.1670 (40) P=.152	.0079 (40) P=.481	-.1970 (40) P=.112	-.1329 (40) P=.207	.1547 (40) P=.170	-.1894 (40) P=.121	.0599 (40) P=.357	.2285 (40) P=.078	-.0826 (40) P=.306	-.2349 (40) P=.072	-.0231 (40) P=.444	.1449 (40) P=.186
	-.2949 (39) P=.034	-.0780 (39) P=.318	.0834 (39) P=.307	.1422 (39) P=.194	.0044 (39) P=.489	.0303 (39) P=.427	-.2511 (39) P=.062	-.1470 (39) P=.186	.1016 (39) P=.269	-.2221 (39) P=.087	-.1448 (39) P=.190	-.1825 (39) P=.133	.2270 (39) P=.082	-.2255 (39) P=.084	-.0613 (39) P=.356

	V1.1	V1.6	V1.2	V1.4	V1.5	V1.3	V1.7	V1.9	V1.10	V1.11	V1.13	V1.14	V1.15	V1.12	V1.8
V2.20	.2192 (37) P=.096	.1143 (37) P=.250	.2484 (37) P=.069	.2699 (37) P=.053	-.4373 (37) P=.003	.3447 (37) P=.018	-.0208 (37) P=.451	.2341 (37) P=.082	.1326 (37) P=.217	-.0053 (37) P=.488	.2933 (37) P=.039	-.0343 (37) P=.420	-.1957 (37) P=.123	-.2584 (37) P=.061	-.2073 (37) P=.109
V2.19	.2341 (38) P=.079	.1892 (38) P=.128	.1971 (38) P=.118	.2620 (38) P=.056	-.2468 (38) P=.068	.1505 (38) P=.183	-.3796 (38) P=.009	.2501 (38) P=.065	.0479 (38) P=.388	-.0875 (38) P=.301	.2736 (38) P=.048	-.0437 (38) P=.397	-.2576 (38) P=.059	-.3116 (38) P=.028	-.2187 (38) P=.094
V2.21	.3522 (37) P=.016	-.0805 (37) P=.318	.0710 (37) P=.338	.2898 (37) P=.041	-.3896 (37) P=.009	.2911 (37) P=.040	-.0005 (37) P=.499	.2293 (37) P=.086	.1155 (37) P=.248	.1053 (37) P=.267	.2986 (37) P=.036	.0041 (37) P=.490	-.0431 (37) P=.400	-.2656 (37) P=.056	-.2103 (37) P=.106
V2.23	.2132 (35) P=.109	.2369 (35) P=.085	.3893 (35) P=.010	.1625 (35) P=.176	-.3274 (35) P=.027	.2147 (35) P=.108	-.2093 (35) P=.114	.2266 (35) P=.095	.0685 (35) P=.348	-.2198 (35) P=.102	.2843 (35) P=.049	.0428 (35) P=.404	-.3311 (35) P=.026	-.3876 (35) P=.011	-.1711 (35) P=.163
V2.17	.4072 (33) P=.009	.1769 (33) P=.162	.1937 (33) P=.140	.2522 (33) P=.078	-.3258 (33) P=.032	.4140 (33) P=.008	.1700 (33) P=.172	.3480 (33) P=.024	.2426 (33) P=.087	-.0046 (33) P=.490	.3594 (33) P=.020	-.1856 (33) P=.151	-.1034 (33) P=.283	-.1523 (33) P=.199	-.2928 (33) P=.049
V3.11	.1099 (41) P=.247	-.0742 (41) P=.322	.1630 (41) P=.154	-.1371 (41) P=.196	.1202 (41) P=.227	-.4570 (41) P=.001	-.4381 (41) P=.002	-.5963 (41) P=.001	-.4788 (41) P=.001	.3476 (41) P=.013	-.1588 (41) P=.161	.0977 (41) P=.272	.3894 (41) P=.006	-.0842 (41) P=.300	.1246 (41) P=.219
V3.20	.2734 (41) P=.042	.3309 (41) P=.017	.1267 (41) P=.215	.5995 (41) P=.001	-.0499 (41) P=.378	.6627 (41) P=.001	-.0957 (41) P=.276	.1242 (41) P=.220	.1836 (41) P=.125	-.0650 (41) P=.343	.6656 (41) P=.001	-.2566 (41) P=.053	-.2353 (41) P=.069	-.2168 (41) P=.087	-.5040 (41) P=.001
V3.15	-.0858 (39) P=.302	-.2077 (39) P=.102	-.0335 (39) P=.420	-.1277 (39) P=.219	-.1601 (39) P=.165	.1215 (39) P=.231	.0156 (39) P=.462	-.1383 (39) P=.200	.4162 (39) P=.004	.4181 (39) P=.004	-.1500 (39) P=.181	-.0298 (39) P=.429	.4726 (39) P=.001	.4025 (39) P=.006	-.0048 (39) P=.488
V3.12	.4947 (41) P=.001	.1298 (41) P=.209	-.1085 (41) P=.250	.5323 (41) P=.001	-.0936 (41) P=.280	.5597 (41) P=.001	.1028 (41) P=.261	.0347 (41) P=.415	-.0660 (41) P=.341	-.1622 (41) P=.155	.6218 (41) P=.001	-.1553 (41) P=.166	-.2116 (41) P=.092	-.2849 (41) P=.035	-.3973 (41) P=.005
V3.13	-.0628 (41) P=.348	.0584 (41) P=.358	-.1410 (41) P=.190	-.1577 (41) P=.162	-.1955 (41) P=.110	.4674 (41) P=.001	.3578 (41) P=.011	.2944 (41) P=.031	.1268 (41) P=.215	-.1845 (41) P=.124	-.0802 (41) P=.309	-.1559 (41) P=.165	-.0710 (41) P=.329	.1727 (41) P=.140	-.0423 (41) P=.396
V3.14	.0786 (41) P=.313	.0977 (41) P=.272	-.0642 (41) P=.345	.2205 (41) P=.083	-.1011 (41) P=.265	.5091 (41) P=.001	.1851 (41) P=.123	.0366 (41) P=.410	.1155 (41) P=.236	-.1329 (41) P=.204	.2533 (41) P=.055	-.0614 (41) P=.352	-.3593 (41) P=.011	-.1934 (41) P=.113	-.1940 (41) P=.112
V3.16	.1365 (41) P=.197	-.0907 (41) P=.286	.1532 (41) P=.170	-.1632 (41) P=.154	-.1214 (41) P=.225	-.1389 (41) P=.193	-.0079 (41) P=.480	.1348 (41) P=.200	.3820 (41) P=.007	.2922 (41) P=.032	-.0582 (41) P=.359	-.1401 (41) P=.191	.1930 (41) P=.113	.2990 (41) P=.029	-.1489 (41) P=.176
V3.17	-.2362 (26) P=.123	.1994 (26) P=.164	-.3257 (26) P=.052	-.2578 (26) P=.102	-.0503 (26) P=.404	.1055 (26) P=.304	.2086 (26) P=.153	-.2777 (26) P=.085	-.1148 (26) P=.288	-.1330 (26) P=.259	-.2190 (26) P=.141	-.2172 (26) P=.143	.3271 (26) P=.051	.2096 (26) P=.152	.1020 (26) P=.310
V3.18	-.1490 (37) P=.189	-.1363 (37) P=.211	-.0469 (37) P=.391	-.1697 (37) P=.158	-.1904 (37) P=.129	.4688 (37) P=.002	.4931 (37) P=.001	.3519 (37) P=.016	.5737 (37) P=.001	-.1297 (37) P=.222	-.1114 (37) P=.256	.0915 (37) P=.295	-.0013 (37) P=.497	.3583 (37) P=.015	.1036 (37) P=.271
V3.19	.0597 (39) P=.359	.1162 (39) P=.241	-.1124 (39) P=.248	.2136 (39) P=.096	.0822 (39) P=.309	.3698 (39) P=.010	.4013 (39) P=.006	.0199 (39) P=.452	-.1244 (39) P=.225	-.2253 (39) P=.084	.2169 (39) P=.092	-.0237 (39) P=.443	-.1072 (39) P=.258	-.1834 (39) P=.132	-.1401 (39) P=.198
V3.21	-.0713 (41) P=.329	-.3014 (41) P=.028	.0282 (41) P=.431	-.2512 (41) P=.057	.1951 (41) P=.111	-.7433 (41) P=.001	-.1305 (41) P=.208	.1114 (41) P=.244	-.1439 (41) P=.185	-.1255 (41) P=.217	-.2795 (41) P=.038	.2688 (41) P=.045	-.1971 (41) P=.108	-.1477 (41) P=.178	.2796 (41) P=.038
V3.4	.3353 (37) P=.021	.1424 (37) P=.200	.0812 (37) P=.316	.3524 (37) P=.016	.0692 (37) P=.342	.1922 (37) P=.127	-.1110 (37) P=.257	.0773 (37) P=.325	.0204 (37) P=.452	-.1487 (37) P=.190	.5831 (37) P=.001	.0928 (37) P=.293	-.2301 (37) P=.085	-.3324 (37) P=.022	-.0981 (37) P=.282
V3.5	.0542 (38) P=.373	-.0835 (38) P=.309	-.0147 (38) P=.465	-.1374 (38) P=.205	-.2040 (38) P=.110	.1033 (38) P=.269	.1370 (38) P=.206	-.0179 (38) P=.457	.1751 (38) P=.147	.2232 (38) P=.089	-.0868 (38) P=.302	-.3915 (38) P=.008	-.4104 (38) P=.001	.6558 (38) P=.001	-.3143 (38) P=.027
V3.6	-.0324 (40) P=.421	.3715 (40) P=.009	.0707 (40) P=.332	.0970 (40) P=.276	.3169 (40) P=.023	.2686 (40) P=.047	.1461 (40) P=.184	-.2249 (40) P=.082	-.1406 (40) P=.193	-.2029 (40) P=.105	.1274 (40) P=.217	.0668 (40) P=.341	-.1204 (40) P=.230	-.4382 (40) P=.002	.1374 (40) P=.199
V3.7	.0822 (38) P=.312	-.1582 (38) P=.171	.0144 (38) P=.466	.1208 (38) P=.235	.1768 (38) P=.144	-.5090 (38) P=.001	-.1763 (38) P=.145	-.3897 (38) P=.008	-.4688 (38) P=.001	.0187 (38) P=.456	-.0517 (38) P=.379	-.0928 (38) P=.290	.0453 (38) P=.393	-.2707 (38) P=.050	-.0640 (38) P=.351
V3.8	-.0145 (39) P=.465	.0842 (39) P=.305	-.0095 (39) P=.477	.2148 (39) P=.095	.0273 (39) P=.435	.5696 (39) P=.001	.3182 (39) P=.024	.1513 (39) P=.179	.3552 (39) P=.013	-.1318 (39) P=.212	.2472 (39) P=.065	-.1327 (39) P=.210	.0266 (39) P=.436	.0545 (39) P=.371	-.1921 (39) P=.121
V3.9	-.0003 (39) P=.499	-.1632 (39) P=.160	-.0993 (39) P=.274	-.1039 (39) P=.264	-.1400 (39) P=.198	-.0079 (39) P=.481	.0041 (39) P=.490	-.1619 (39) P=.162	.0545 (39) P=.371	.2721 (39) P=.047	-.1388 (39) P=.200	-.2638 (39) P=.052	.4704 (39) P=.001	.6627 (39) P=.001	-.1999 (39) P=.111
V3.10	-.3557 (16) P=.088	.1595 (16) P=.278	-.1002 (16) P=.356	.1197 (16) P=.329	.2440 (16) P=.181	.4238 (16) P=.051	.2384 (16) P=.187	.4101 (16) P=.057	.3140 (16) P=.118	-.5592 (16) P=.012	.2693 (16) P=.157	.4469 (16) P=.041	-.5709 (16) P=.010	-.4175 (16) P=.054	.5178 (16) P=.020
V3.1	.1734 (41) P=.139	.1999 (41) P=.105	-.0531 (41) P=.371	.7739 (41) P=.001	.1667 (41) P=.149	.3985 (41) P=.005	-.0336 (41) P=.417	.0971 (41) P=.273	.1312 (41) P=.207	-.1615 (41) P=.157	.6294 (41) P=.001	.0407 (41) P=.400	-.2869 (41) P=.034	-.2505 (41) P=.057	-.1954 (41) P=.110
V3.2	-.0915 (41) P=.285	-.2750 (41) P=.041	-.1475 (41) P=.179	-.1464 (41) P=.181	-.2277 (41) P=.076	.3675 (41) P=.009	.3232 (41) P=.020	.0858 (41) P=.297	.4159 (41) P=.003	-.0005 (41) P=.499	-.1320 (41) P=.205	-.0547 (41) P=.367	.0824 (41) P=.304	.3607 (41) P=.010	.0765 (41) P=.317
V3.3	.0105 (40) P=.474	-.1545 (40) P=.171	-.0927 (40) P=.285	-.0992 (40) P=.271	-.1389 (40) P=.196	-.0041 (40) P=.490	.0066 (40) P=.484	-.1115 (40) P=.247	.0268 (40) P=.435	.2653 (40) P=.049	-.1359 (40) P=.202	-.2430 (40) P=.065	.4730 (40) P=.001	.5399 (40) P=.001	-.2013 (40) P=.106
V4.1	-.1130 (41) P=.241	-.0879 (41) P=.292	-.1264 (41) P=.216	-.1224 (41) P=.223	-.1388 (41) P=.193	.2429 (41) P=.063	.0616 (41) P=.351	-.0374 (41) P=.408	.0857 (41) P=.297	.0936 (41) P=.280	-.1162 (41) P=.235	-.2892 (41) P=.033	.3077 (41) P=.025	.5112 (41) P=.001	-.1378 (41) P=.195
V4.4	.0501 (41) P=.378	-.1699 (41) P=.144	-.1308 (41) P=.207	-.0246 (41) P=.439	-.0066 (41) P=.484	-.2050 (41) P=.099	.0904 (41) P=.287	-.0451 (41) P=.390	.0115 (41) P=.472	.0444 (41) P=.391	-.0595 (41) P=.356	.2081 (41) P=.096	.0796 (41) P=.310	.0358 (41) P=.412	.1848 (41) P=.124
V4.2	-.1648 (41) P=.152	-.0548 (41) P=.367	-.0207 (41) P=.449	-.1525 (41) P=.171	-.1473 (41) P=.179	.3746 (41) P=.008	.2327 (41) P=.072	-.0227 (41) P=.444	.1521 (41) P=.171	-.1251 (41) P=.218	-.1053 (41) P=.256	-.1658 (41) P=.150	.0181 (41) P=.455	.3519 (41) P=.012	.0142 (41) P=.465
F.3	.0539 (41) P=.369	-.0905 (41) P=.287	-.1577 (41) P=.162	.2044 (41) P=.100	.0094 (41) P=.477	-.2627 (41) P=.048	-.0977 (41) P=.272	-.0438 (41) P=.393	.1477 (41) P=.178	.0192 (41) P=.453	.1057 (41) P=.255	-.1613 (41) P=.157	.0605 (41) P=.354	.0905 (41) P=.287	-.2588 (41) P=.051
F.5	-.1970 (40) P=.112	.0858 (40) P=.299	-.0583 (40) P=.360	.0424 (40) P=.398	.2336 (40) P=.073	.2274 (40) P=.079	.0428 (40) P=.397	.1100 (40) P=.250	.0083 (40) P=.480	-.2828 (40) P=.039	.0659 (40) P=.343	.1101 (40) P=.249	-.4143 (40) P=.004	-.2966 (40) P=.032	.2130 (40) P=.093
F.6	-.0338 (40) P=.418	-.1644 (40) P=.155	-.1087 (40) P=.252	-.1320 (40) P=.208	-.1812 (40) P=.132	.0560 (40) P=.366	.0225 (40) P=.445	-.0713 (40) P=.331	.1085 (40) P=.253	-.2292 (40) P=.077	-.1399 (40) P=.195	-.2365 (40) P=.071	.4233 (40) P=.003	.5772 (40) P=.001	-.1826 (40) P=.130
F.7	-.0318 (39) P=.424	-.2128 (39) P=.097	.1567 (39) P=.170	-.0485 (39) P=.385	-.1118 (39) P=.249	-.2004 (39) P=.111	-.0989 (39) P=.275	-.1335 (39) P=.209	-.0582 (39) P=.362	.1684 (39) P=.153	-.0606 (39) P=.357	-.2123 (39) P=.097	-.1062 (39) P=.260	-.0332 (39) P=.420	.2172 (39) P=.092

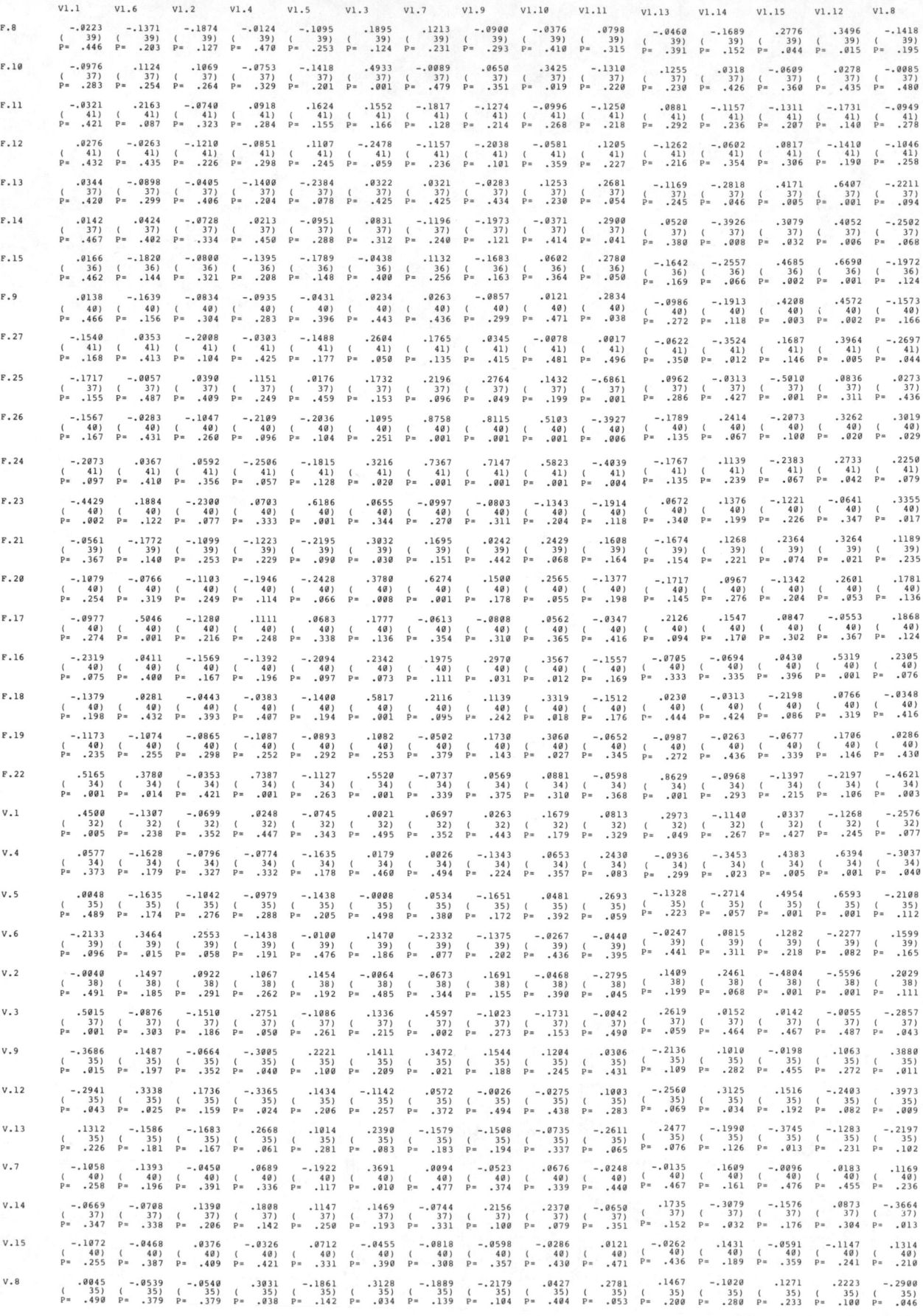

	V1.1	V1.6	V1.2	V1.4	V1.5	V1.3	V1.7	V1.9	V1.10	V1.11	V1.13	V1.14	V1.15	V1.12	V1.8
F.8	-.0223 (39) P= .446	-.1371 (39) P= .203	-.1874 (39) P= .127	-.0124 (39) P= .470	-.1095 (39) P= .253	.1895 (39) P= .124	.1213 (39) P= .231	-.0900 (39) P= .293	-.0376 (39) P= .410	.0798 (39) P= .315	-.0460 (39) P= .391	-.1689 (39) P= .152	.2776 (39) P= .044	.3496 (39) P= .015	-.1418 (39) P= .195
F.10	-.0976 (37) P= .283	.1124 (37) P= .254	.1069 (37) P= .264	-.0753 (37) P= .329	-.1418 (37) P= .201	.4933 (37) P= .001	-.0089 (37) P= .479	.0650 (37) P= .351	.3425 (37) P= .019	-.1310 (37) P= .220	.1255 (37) P= .230	.0318 (37) P= .426	-.0609 (37) P= .360	.0278 (37) P= .435	-.0085 (37) P= .480
F.11	-.0321 (41) P= .421	.2163 (41) P= .087	-.0740 (41) P= .323	.0918 (41) P= .284	.1624 (41) P= .155	.1552 (41) P= .166	-.1817 (41) P= .128	-.1274 (41) P= .214	-.0996 (41) P= .268	-.1250 (41) P= .218	.0881 (41) P= .292	-.1157 (41) P= .236	-.1311 (41) P= .207	-.1731 (41) P= .140	-.0949 (41) P= .278
F.12	.0276 (41) P= .432	-.0263 (41) P= .435	-.1210 (41) P= .226	-.0851 (41) P= .298	.1107 (41) P= .245	-.2478 (41) P= .059	-.1157 (41) P= .236	-.2038 (41) P= .101	-.0581 (41) P= .359	.1205 (41) P= .227	-.1262 (41) P= .216	-.0602 (41) P= .354	.0817 (41) P= .306	-.1410 (41) P= .190	-.1046 (41) P= .258
F.13	.0344 (37) P= .420	-.0898 (37) P= .299	-.0405 (37) P= .406	-.1400 (37) P= .204	-.2384 (37) P= .078	.0322 (37) P= .425	.0321 (37) P= .425	-.0283 (37) P= .434	.1253 (37) P= .230	.2681 (37) P= .054	-.1169 (37) P= .245	-.2818 (37) P= .046	.4171 (37) P= .005	.6407 (37) P= .001	-.2211 (37) P= .094
F.14	.0142 (37) P= .467	.0424 (37) P= .402	-.0728 (37) P= .334	.0213 (37) P= .450	-.0951 (37) P= .288	.0831 (37) P= .312	-.1196 (37) P= .240	-.1973 (37) P= .121	-.0371 (37) P= .414	.2900 (37) P= .041	.0520 (37) P= .380	-.3926 (37) P= .008	.3079 (37) P= .032	.4052 (37) P= .006	-.2502 (37) P= .068
F.15	.0166 (36) P= .462	-.1820 (36) P= .144	-.0800 (36) P= .321	-.1395 (36) P= .208	-.1789 (36) P= .148	-.0438 (36) P= .400	.1132 (36) P= .256	-.1683 (36) P= .163	.0602 (36) P= .364	.2780 (36) P= .050	-.1642 (36) P= .169	-.2557 (36) P= .066	.4685 (36) P= .002	.6690 (36) P= .001	-.1972 (36) P= .124
F.9	.0138 (40) P= .466	-.1639 (40) P= .156	-.0834 (40) P= .304	-.0935 (40) P= .283	-.0431 (40) P= .396	.0234 (40) P= .443	.0263 (40) P= .436	-.0857 (40) P= .299	.0121 (40) P= .471	.2834 (40) P= .038	-.0986 (40) P= .272	-.1913 (40) P= .118	.4208 (40) P= .003	.4572 (40) P= .002	-.1573 (40) P= .166
F.27	-.1540 (41) P= .168	.0353 (41) P= .413	-.2008 (41) P= .104	-.0303 (41) P= .425	-.1488 (41) P= .177	.2604 (41) P= .050	.1765 (41) P= .135	.0345 (41) P= .415	-.0078 (41) P= .481	.0017 (41) P= .496	-.0622 (41) P= .350	-.3524 (41) P= .012	.1687 (41) P= .146	.3964 (41) P= .005	-.2697 (41) P= .044
F.25	-.1717 (37) P= .155	-.0057 (37) P= .487	.0390 (37) P= .409	.1151 (37) P= .249	.0176 (37) P= .459	.1732 (37) P= .153	.2196 (37) P= .096	.2764 (37) P= .049	.1432 (37) P= .199	-.6861 (37) P= .001	.0962 (37) P= .286	-.0313 (37) P= .427	-.5010 (37) P= .001	.0836 (37) P= .311	.0273 (37) P= .436
F.26	-.1567 (40) P= .167	-.0283 (40) P= .431	-.1047 (40) P= .260	-.2109 (40) P= .096	-.2036 (40) P= .104	.1095 (40) P= .251	.8758 (40) P= .001	.8115 (40) P= .001	.5103 (40) P= .001	-.3927 (40) P= .006	-.1789 (40) P= .135	.2414 (40) P= .067	-.2073 (40) P= .100	.3262 (40) P= .020	.3019 (40) P= .029
F.24	-.2073 (41) P= .097	.0367 (41) P= .410	.0592 (41) P= .356	-.2506 (41) P= .057	-.1815 (41) P= .128	.3216 (41) P= .020	.7367 (41) P= .001	.7147 (41) P= .001	.5823 (41) P= .001	-.4039 (41) P= .004	-.1767 (41) P= .135	.1139 (41) P= .239	-.2383 (41) P= .067	.2733 (41) P= .042	.2250 (41) P= .079
F.23	-.4429 (40) P= .002	.1884 (40) P= .122	-.2300 (40) P= .077	.0703 (40) P= .333	.6186 (40) P= .001	.0655 (40) P= .344	-.0997 (40) P= .270	-.0803 (40) P= .311	-.1343 (40) P= .204	-.1914 (40) P= .118	.0672 (40) P= .340	.1376 (40) P= .199	-.1221 (40) P= .226	-.0641 (40) P= .347	.3355 (40) P= .017
F.21	-.0561 (39) P= .367	-.1772 (39) P= .140	-.1099 (39) P= .253	-.1223 (39) P= .229	-.2195 (39) P= .090	.3032 (39) P= .030	.1695 (39) P= .151	.0242 (39) P= .442	.2429 (39) P= .068	.1608 (39) P= .164	-.1674 (39) P= .154	.1268 (39) P= .221	.2364 (39) P= .074	.3264 (39) P= .021	.1189 (39) P= .235
F.20	-.1079 (40) P= .254	-.0766 (40) P= .319	-.1103 (40) P= .249	-.1946 (40) P= .114	-.2428 (40) P= .066	.3780 (40) P= .008	.6274 (40) P= .001	.1500 (40) P= .178	.2565 (40) P= .055	-.1377 (40) P= .198	-.1717 (40) P= .145	.0967 (40) P= .276	-.1342 (40) P= .204	.2601 (40) P= .053	.1781 (40) P= .136
F.17	-.0977 (40) P= .274	.5046 (40) P= .001	-.1280 (40) P= .216	.1111 (40) P= .248	.0683 (40) P= .338	.1777 (40) P= .136	-.0613 (40) P= .354	-.0808 (40) P= .310	.0562 (40) P= .365	-.0347 (40) P= .416	.2126 (40) P= .094	.1547 (40) P= .170	.0847 (40) P= .302	-.0553 (40) P= .367	.1868 (40) P= .124
F.16	-.2319 (40) P= .075	.0411 (40) P= .400	-.1569 (40) P= .167	-.1392 (40) P= .196	-.2094 (40) P= .097	.2342 (40) P= .073	.1975 (40) P= .111	.2970 (40) P= .031	.3567 (40) P= .012	-.1557 (40) P= .169	-.0705 (40) P= .333	-.0694 (40) P= .335	.0430 (40) P= .396	.5319 (40) P= .001	.2305 (40) P= .076
F.18	-.1379 (40) P= .198	.0281 (40) P= .432	-.0443 (40) P= .393	-.0383 (40) P= .407	-.1400 (40) P= .194	.5817 (40) P= .001	.2116 (40) P= .095	.1139 (40) P= .242	.3319 (40) P= .018	-.1512 (40) P= .176	.0230 (40) P= .444	-.0313 (40) P= .424	-.2198 (40) P= .086	.0766 (40) P= .319	-.0348 (40) P= .416
F.19	-.1173 (40) P= .235	-.1074 (40) P= .255	-.0865 (40) P= .298	-.1087 (40) P= .252	-.0893 (40) P= .292	.1082 (40) P= .253	-.0502 (40) P= .379	.1730 (40) P= .143	.3060 (40) P= .027	-.0652 (40) P= .345	-.0987 (40) P= .272	-.0263 (40) P= .436	-.0677 (40) P= .339	.1706 (40) P= .146	.0286 (40) P= .430
F.22	.5165 (34) P= .001	.3780 (34) P= .014	-.0353 (34) P= .421	.7387 (34) P= .001	-.1127 (34) P= .263	.5520 (34) P= .001	-.0737 (34) P= .339	.0569 (34) P= .375	.0881 (34) P= .310	-.0598 (34) P= .368	.8629 (34) P= .001	-.0968 (34) P= .293	-.1397 (34) P= .215	-.2197 (34) P= .106	-.4621 (34) P= .003
V.1	.4500 (32) P= .005	-.1307 (32) P= .238	-.0699 (32) P= .352	.0248 (32) P= .447	-.0745 (32) P= .343	.0021 (32) P= .495	.0697 (32) P= .352	.0263 (32) P= .443	.1679 (32) P= .179	.0813 (32) P= .329	.2973 (32) P= .049	-.1140 (32) P= .267	.0337 (32) P= .427	-.1268 (32) P= .245	-.2576 (32) P= .077
V.4	.0577 (34) P= .373	-.1628 (34) P= .179	-.0796 (34) P= .327	-.0774 (34) P= .332	-.1635 (34) P= .178	.0179 (34) P= .460	.0026 (34) P= .494	-.1343 (34) P= .224	.0653 (34) P= .357	.2430 (34) P= .083	-.0936 (34) P= .299	-.3453 (34) P= .023	.4383 (34) P= .005	.6394 (34) P= .001	-.3037 (34) P= .040
V.5	.0048 (35) P= .489	-.1635 (35) P= .174	-.1042 (35) P= .276	-.0979 (35) P= .288	-.1438 (35) P= .205	-.0008 (35) P= .498	.0534 (35) P= .380	-.1651 (35) P= .172	.0481 (35) P= .392	.2693 (35) P= .059	-.1328 (35) P= .223	-.2714 (35) P= .057	.4954 (35) P= .001	.6593 (35) P= .001	-.2108 (35) P= .112
V.6	-.2133 (39) P= .096	.3464 (39) P= .015	.2553 (39) P= .058	-.1438 (39) P= .191	-.0100 (39) P= .476	.1470 (39) P= .186	-.2332 (39) P= .077	-.1375 (39) P= .202	-.0267 (39) P= .436	-.0440 (39) P= .395	-.0247 (39) P= .441	.0815 (39) P= .311	.1282 (39) P= .218	-.2277 (39) P= .082	.1599 (39) P= .165
V.2	-.0040 (38) P= .491	.1497 (38) P= .185	.0922 (38) P= .291	.1067 (38) P= .262	.1454 (38) P= .192	-.0064 (38) P= .485	-.0673 (38) P= .344	.1691 (38) P= .155	-.0468 (38) P= .390	-.2795 (38) P= .045	.1409 (38) P= .199	.2461 (38) P= .068	-.4804 (38) P= .001	-.5596 (38) P= .001	.2029 (38) P= .111
V.3	.5015 (37) P= .001	-.0876 (37) P= .303	-.1510 (37) P= .186	.2751 (37) P= .050	-.1086 (37) P= .261	.1336 (37) P= .215	.4597 (37) P= .002	-.1023 (37) P= .273	-.1731 (37) P= .153	-.0042 (37) P= .490	.2619 (37) P= .059	.0152 (37) P= .464	.0142 (37) P= .467	-.0055 (37) P= .487	-.2857 (37) P= .043
V.9	-.3686 (35) P= .015	-.1487 (35) P= .197	-.0664 (35) P= .352	-.3005 (35) P= .040	.2221 (35) P= .100	.1411 (35) P= .209	.3472 (35) P= .021	.1544 (35) P= .188	.1204 (35) P= .245	-.0306 (35) P= .431	-.2136 (35) P= .109	.1010 (35) P= .282	-.0198 (35) P= .455	.1063 (35) P= .272	.3880 (35) P= .011
V.12	-.2941 (35) P= .043	.3338 (35) P= .025	.1736 (35) P= .159	-.3365 (35) P= .024	.1434 (35) P= .206	-.1142 (35) P= .257	.0572 (35) P= .372	-.0026 (35) P= .494	-.0275 (35) P= .438	.1003 (35) P= .283	-.2560 (35) P= .069	.3125 (35) P= .034	.1516 (35) P= .192	-.2403 (35) P= .082	.3973 (35) P= .009
V.13	.1312 (35) P= .226	-.1586 (35) P= .181	-.1683 (35) P= .167	.2668 (35) P= .061	.1014 (35) P= .281	.2390 (35) P= .083	-.1579 (35) P= .182	-.1508 (35) P= .194	-.0735 (35) P= .337	-.2611 (35) P= .065	.2477 (35) P= .076	-.1990 (35) P= .126	-.3745 (35) P= .013	-.1283 (35) P= .231	-.2197 (35) P= .102
V.7	-.1058 (40) P= .258	.1393 (40) P= .196	-.0450 (40) P= .391	.0689 (40) P= .336	-.1922 (40) P= .117	.3691 (40) P= .010	.0094 (40) P= .477	-.0523 (40) P= .374	.0676 (40) P= .339	-.0248 (40) P= .440	-.0135 (40) P= .467	.1609 (40) P= .161	-.0096 (40) P= .476	.0183 (40) P= .455	.1169 (40) P= .236
V.14	-.0669 (37) P= .347	-.0708 (37) P= .338	.1390 (37) P= .206	.1808 (37) P= .142	.1147 (37) P= .250	.1469 (37) P= .193	-.0744 (37) P= .331	.2156 (37) P= .100	.2370 (37) P= .079	-.0650 (37) P= .351	.1735 (37) P= .152	-.3079 (37) P= .032	-.1576 (37) P= .176	.0873 (37) P= .304	-.3664 (37) P= .013
V.15	-.1072 (40) P= .255	-.0468 (40) P= .387	.0376 (40) P= .409	-.0326 (40) P= .421	.0712 (40) P= .331	-.0455 (40) P= .390	-.0818 (40) P= .308	-.0598 (40) P= .357	-.0286 (40) P= .430	.0121 (40) P= .471	-.0262 (40) P= .436	.1431 (40) P= .189	-.0591 (40) P= .359	-.1147 (40) P= .241	.1314 (40) P= .210
V.8	.0045 (35) P= .490	-.0539 (35) P= .379	-.0540 (35) P= .379	.3031 (35) P= .038	-.1861 (35) P= .142	.3128 (35) P= .034	-.1889 (35) P= .139	-.2179 (35) P= .104	.0427 (35) P= .404	.2781 (35) P= .053	.1467 (35) P= .200	-.1020 (35) P= .280	.1271 (35) P= .233	.2223 (35) P= .100	-.2900 (35) P= .046

V2.1	V2.2	V2.3	V2.4	V2.5	V2.6	V2.7	V2.13	V2.8	V2.9	V2.10	V2.11	V2.12	V2.14	V2.15
.2823 (39) P=.041	.7210 (39) P=.001	-.2292 (39) P=.080	-.2149 (39) P=.094	.0441 (39) P=.395	-.1963 (39) P=.116	.2085 (39) P=.101	.2863 (39) P=.039	-.3276 (39) P=.021	.2258 (39) P=.084	.4052 (39) P=.005	-.0040 (39) P=.490	.1898 (39) P=.124	.1617 (39) P=.163	.2893 (39) P=.037
-.2382 (37) P=.078	-.0934 (37) P=.291	.2832 (37) P=.045	-.1432 (37) P=.199	-.0213 (37) P=.450	-.1923 (37) P=.127	-.1789 (37) P=.145	.4356 (37) P=.004	-.0828 (37) P=.313	.1198 (37) P=.240	.2394 (37) P=.077	.0313 (37) P=.427	-.0864 (37) P=.306	.0786 (37) P=.322	.3406 (37) P=.020
.3747 (41) P=.008	.1428 (41) P=.187	-.2076 (41) P=.096	-.1931 (41) P=.113	.0121 (41) P=.470	.0305 (41) P=.425	.4243 (41) P=.003	.3375 (41) P=.015	-.2542 (41) P=.054	.3249 (41) P=.019	.4135 (41) P=.004	.1427 (41) P=.187	-.1517 (41) P=.172	.2819 (41) P=.037	.3854 (41) P=.006
.2419 (41) P=.064	.0618 (41) P=.350	-.2255 (41) P=.078	-.0463 (41) P=.387	-.0473 (41) P=.385	-.0920 (41) P=.284	.1383 (41) P=.194	-.1623 (41) P=.155	.3553 (41) P=.011	-.3121 (41) P=.023	-.2832 (41) P=.036	-.1908 (41) P=.116	-.0637 (41) P=.346	-.2990 (41) P=.029	-.2285 (41) P=.075
.1773 (37) P=.147	.6177 (37) P=.001	-.0331 (37) P=.423	-.1710 (37) P=.156	-.0251 (37) P=.441	-.1968 (37) P=.117	.1329 (37) P=.217	.0737 (37) P=.332	-.1643 (37) P=.166	.0111 (37) P=.474	.1748 (37) P=.150	-.1127 (37) P=.253	.2790 (37) P=.047	-.0804 (37) P=.318	.0775 (37) P=.324
.1444 (37) P=.197	.5116 (37) P=.001	-.1697 (37) P=.158	-.0148 (37) P=.465	.0764 (37) P=.327	-.2044 (37) P=.113	.1344 (37) P=.214	.0579 (37) P=.367	-.2874 (37) P=.042	.0823 (37) P=.314	.1528 (37) P=.183	.0450 (37) P=.396	.3928 (37) P=.008	.0426 (37) P=.401	.1003 (37) P=.277
.2673 (36) P=.058	.6876 (36) P=.001	-.0901 (36) P=.301	-.1462 (36) P=.196	.0223 (36) P=.449	-.1759 (36) P=.152	.1692 (36) P=.162	.0709 (36) P=.341	-.1171 (36) P=.248	-.0175 (36) P=.460	.1466 (36) P=.197	-.1440 (36) P=.201	.2487 (36) P=.072	-.0895 (36) P=.302	.0593 (36) P=.366
.2189 (40) P=.087	.6106 (40) P=.001	-.1292 (40) P=.213	-.0573 (40) P=.363	.0279 (40) P=.432	-.0977 (40) P=.274	.1638 (40) P=.156	.0766 (40) P=.319	-.1923 (40) P=.117	.0857 (40) P=.299	.2040 (40) P=.103	-.0212 (40) P=.448	.2040 (40) P=.103	.0180 (40) P=.456	.1460 (40) P=.184
.1718 (41) P=.141	.3540 (41) P=.012	-.0433 (41) P=.394	-.2196 (41) P=.084	-.0436 (41) P=.393	-.2060 (41) P=.098	.0463 (41) P=.387	-.0257 (41) P=.437	-.2484 (41) P=.059	.0678 (41) P=.337	.3406 (41) P=.015	-.1728 (41) P=.140	.3348 (41) P=.016	-.0253 (41) P=.438	.3856 (41) P=.006
-.1079 (37) P=.263	-.1496 (37) P=.188	.1388 (37) P=.206	-.1114 (37) P=.256	-.0429 (37) P=.400	-.0449 (37) P=.396	-.1103 (37) P=.258	.0655 (37) P=.350	-.3840 (37) P=.009	.3458 (37) P=.018	.3859 (37) P=.009	.2073 (37) P=.109	.0677 (37) P=.345	.3272 (37) P=.024	.2834 (37) P=.045
-.0598 (40) P=.357	-.0891 (40) P=.292	-.0048 (40) P=.488	-.1429 (40) P=.190	-.3942 (40) P=.006	-.1615 (40) P=.160	-.3777 (40) P=.008	-.0087 (40) P=.479	.0692 (40) P=.336	.0330 (40) P=.420	.1378 (40) P=.198	-.0581 (40) P=.361	-.1950 (40) P=.114	.0553 (40) P=.367	.0939 (40) P=.282
-.0798 (41) P=.310	-.1505 (41) P=.174	.1521 (41) P=.171	-.2055 (41) P=.099	-.4462 (41) P=.002	-.2131 (41) P=.090	-.3673 (41) P=.009	.2280 (41) P=.076	-.0745 (41) P=.322	.1776 (41) P=.133	.3258 (41) P=.019	.0000 (41) P=.500	-.2014 (41) P=.103	.1868 (41) P=.121	.3420 (41) P=.014
.1442 (40) P=.187	.0574 (40) P=.362	-.1094 (40) P=.251	-.0806 (40) P=.311	.0171 (40) P=.458	.0302 (40) P=.427	.1105 (40) P=.249	.0036 (40) P=.491	-.2801 (40) P=.040	.2340 (40) P=.073	.2939 (40) P=.033	.1521 (40) P=.174	.0896 (40) P=.291	.2201 (40) P=.086	.4009 (40) P=.005
.0404 (39) P=.404	-.0969 (39) P=.279	.3460 (39) P=.015	-.0866 (39) P=.300	-.0630 (39) P=.351	-.0240 (39) P=.442	-.0485 (39) P=.385	.4566 (39) P=.002	-.0185 (39) P=.456	.1144 (39) P=.244	.0610 (39) P=.356	.1318 (39) P=.212	-.1727 (39) P=.146	.1840 (39) P=.131	.2064 (39) P=.104
-.0760 (40) P=.321	-.0682 (40) P=.338	.1469 (40) P=.183	-.0265 (40) P=.435	-.2114 (40) P=.095	-.0068 (40) P=.483	-.3061 (40) P=.027	.3679 (40) P=.010	-.2924 (40) P=.034	.3779 (40) P=.008	.4633 (40) P=.001	.1586 (40) P=.164	-.1759 (40) P=.139	.4558 (40) P=.002	.3940 (40) P=.006
-.1439 (40) P=.188	.3164 (40) P=.023	.0912 (40) P=.288	-.0450 (40) P=.391	-.2561 (40) P=.055	-.1703 (40) P=.147	.0083 (40) P=.480	.0579 (40) P=.361	-.0739 (40) P=.325	-.0234 (40) P=.443	.0496 (40) P=.381	-.0389 (40) P=.406	-.1958 (40) P=.113	-.0221 (40) P=.446	-.1180 (40) P=.234
-.0665 (40) P=.342	-.1410 (40) P=.193	.3838 (40) P=.007	-.1833 (40) P=.129	-.2010 (40) P=.107	-.3124 (40) P=.025	-.1941 (40) P=.115	.2835 (40) P=.038	-.1166 (40) P=.237	.1679 (40) P=.150	.2253 (40) P=.081	.0688 (40) P=.337	-.1217 (40) P=.227	.2024 (40) P=.105	.4134 (40) P=.004
-.2493 (40) P=.060	-.1557 (40) P=.169	.0629 (40) P=.350	-.2284 (40) P=.078	-.2817 (40) P=.039	-.2095 (40) P=.097	-.3413 (40) P=.016	.4093 (40) P=.004	-.3804 (40) P=.008	.3791 (40) P=.008	.4744 (40) P=.001	.1849 (40) P=.127	-.0264 (40) P=.436	.3010 (40) P=.030	.4174 (40) P=.004
-.1069 (40) P=.256	-.0671 (40) P=.340	.0493 (40) P=.381	-.1443 (40) P=.187	.0789 (40) P=.314	-.1214 (40) P=.228	-.1484 (40) P=.180	.2159 (40) P=.090	-.1523 (40) P=.174	.2057 (40) P=.101	.0989 (40) P=.272	.2461 (40) P=.063	-.1524 (40) P=.174	.1034 (40) P=.263	-.0532 (40) P=.372
-.2026 (34) P=.125	-.1890 (34) P=.142	-.1937 (34) P=.136	.3685 (34) P=.016	.0529 (34) P=.383	.3656 (34) P=.017	.0773 (34) P=.332	-.1617 (34) P=.180	.1044 (34) P=.278	-.0755 (34) P=.336	.0567 (34) P=.375	-.1560 (34) P=.189	-.0346 (34) P=.423	-.0924 (34) P=.302	-.2243 (34) P=.101
-.0556 (32) P=.381	-.0464 (32) P=.400	-.1156 (32) P=.264	-.1264 (32) P=.245	.1500 (32) P=.206	.0507 (32) P=.391	.2018 (32) P=.134	.0811 (32) P=.329	.0374 (32) P=.419	.0173 (32) P=.463	-.0430 (32) P=.408	.0829 (32) P=.326	-.1074 (32) P=.279	.0662 (32) P=.359	.1193 (32) P=.258
.2502 (34) P=.077	.6618 (34) P=.001	-.1018 (34) P=.283	-.1114 (34) P=.265	.0376 (34) P=.416	-.1039 (34) P=.279	.2029 (34) P=.125	.1039 (34) P=.279	-.1937 (34) P=.136	-.0350 (34) P=.422	.2068 (34) P=.120	-.1238 (34) P=.243	.3048 (34) P=.040	-.0341 (34) P=.424	.1137 (34) P=.261
.2830 (35) P=.050	.6737 (35) P=.001	-.0958 (35) P=.292	-.1334 (35) P=.222	.0557 (35) P=.375	-.1280 (35) P=.232	.1972 (35) P=.128	.0862 (35) P=.311	-.1657 (35) P=.171	.0226 (35) P=.449	.1836 (35) P=.146	-.1124 (35) P=.260	.2593 (35) P=.066	-.0485 (35) P=.391	.0780 (35) P=.328
-.1687 (39) P=.152	-.0903 (39) P=.292	.1622 (39) P=.162	-.0824 (39) P=.309	-.1654 (39) P=.157	-.1001 (39) P=.272	-.2100 (39) P=.100	.2467 (39) P=.065	.1869 (39) P=.127	-.1811 (39) P=.135	-.0656 (39) P=.346	-.2115 (39) P=.098	.0016 (39) P=.496	-.1389 (39) P=.200	-.0184 (39) P=.456
-.2555 (38) P=.061	-.6707 (38) P=.001	.0863 (38) P=.303	.1345 (38) P=.210	-.0233 (38) P=.445	.1388 (38) P=.203	-.1802 (38) P=.140	-.0932 (38) P=.289	.1449 (38) P=.193	-.0067 (38) P=.484	-.1800 (38) P=.140	.1262 (38) P=.225	-.2525 (38) P=.063	.0607 (38) P=.359	-.0857 (38) P=.304
-.0382 (37) P=.411	.1336 (37) P=.215	-.2235 (37) P=.092	.1051 (37) P=.268	.2173 (37) P=.098	.2525 (37) P=.066	.1481 (37) P=.191	-.2196 (37) P=.096	-.1526 (37) P=.184	.2012 (37) P=.116	.0114 (37) P=.473	.1398 (37) P=.205	-.0985 (37) P=.281	.1414 (37) P=.202	-.0611 (37) P=.360
.1883 (35) P=.139	.0843 (35) P=.315	.0990 (35) P=.286	-.2123 (35) P=.110	-.0344 (35) P=.422	-.1652 (35) P=.171	-.0617 (35) P=.362	.2277 (35) P=.094	-.1779 (35) P=.153	.2387 (35) P=.084	.1977 (35) P=.127	.2194 (35) P=.103	-.1387 (35) P=.213	.2622 (35) P=.064	.3295 (35) P=.027
-.0304 (35) P=.431	-.3664 (35) P=.015	.0429 (35) P=.403	-.1536 (35) P=.189	-.2441 (35) P=.079	-.0196 (35) P=.455	-.1965 (35) P=.129	-.1526 (35) P=.191	.2438 (35) P=.079	-.1648 (35) P=.172	-.1273 (35) P=.233	-.1246 (35) P=.238	-.1474 (35) P=.199	-.1701 (35) P=.164	-.1217 (35) P=.243
-.0572 (35) P=.372	-.0260 (35) P=.441	-.0008 (35) P=.498	.1509 (35) P=.194	.1701 (35) P=.164	.0845 (35) P=.315	.1567 (35) P=.184	.1871 (35) P=.141	-.2957 (35) P=.042	.3326 (35) P=.025	.3417 (35) P=.022	.3030 (35) P=.038	-.0624 (35) P=.361	.3451 (35) P=.021	.3810 (35) P=.012
-.0833 (40) P=.305	.0387 (40) P=.406	.2437 (40) P=.065	-.0236 (40) P=.443	-.2123 (40) P=.094	-.0683 (40) P=.338	-.1396 (40) P=.195	.3608 (40) P=.011	-.0515 (40) P=.376	-.0130 (40) P=.468	.2372 (40) P=.070	-.1325 (40) P=.208	.1254 (40) P=.220	-.0761 (40) P=.320	.3075 (40) P=.027
.1214 (37) P=.237	.0948 (37) P=.288	-.1070 (37) P=.264	-.0064 (37) P=.485	-.0694 (37) P=.342	-.0522 (37) P=.380	.0839 (37) P=.311	.0378 (37) P=.412	.0939 (37) P=.290	-.0181 (37) P=.458	.1998 (37) P=.118	-.1142 (37) P=.250	-.1351 (37) P=.213	-.0339 (37) P=.421	.2126 (37) P=.103
-.1163 (40) P=.237	-.0604 (40) P=.356	-.0933 (40) P=.283	-.0439 (40) P=.394	-.0881 (40) P=.294	-.1362 (40) P=.201	-.0225 (40) P=.445	.1262 (40) P=.219	.0365 (40) P=.412	-.1834 (40) P=.129	-.1034 (40) P=.263	-.1621 (40) P=.159	.2911 (40) P=.034	-.1742 (40) P=.141	-.0814 (40) P=.309
-.0858 (35) P=.312	.3689 (35) P=.015	.0298 (35) P=.433	.1722 (35) P=.161	-.2150 (35) P=.107	-.2132 (35) P=.109	-.0320 (35) P=.428	.0554 (35) P=.376	.0220 (35) P=.450	-.0936 (35) P=.296	.2526 (35) P=.072	-.3200 (35) P=.030	.1512 (35) P=.193	-.2204 (35) P=.102	.1131 (35) P=.259

	V2.1	V2.2	V2.3	V2.4	V2.5	V2.6	V2.7	V2.13	V2.8	V2.9	V2.10	V2.11	V2.12	V2.14	V2.15
	-.0327 (39) P=.422	-.0712 (39) P=.333	-.0449 (39) P=.393	.1491 (39) P=.183	-.0672 (39) P=.342	.0395 (39) P=.406	.1496 (39) P=.182	.0583 (39) P=.362	-.0947 (39) P=.283	.1650 (39) P=.158	.3055 (39) P=.029	.0613 (39) P=.355	-.1307 (39) P=.214	.1499 (39) P=.181	.3318 (39) P=.020
	.0084 (39) P=.480	.1211 (39) P=.231	.0941 (39) P=.284	-.0422 (39) P=.399	-.0597 (39) P=.359	-.1664 (39) P=.156	-.2806 (39) P=.042	-.0465 (39) P=.389	.1368 (39) P=.203	-.3043 (39) P=.030	-.3108 (39) P=.027	-.2266 (39) P=.083	.3144 (39) P=.026	-.3041 (39) P=.030	-.3922 (39) P=.007
	.2590 (35) P=.067	.6682 (35) P=.001	-.1051 (35) P=.274	-.1454 (35) P=.202	.0266 (35) P=.440	-.1611 (35) P=.178	.1859 (35) P=.142	.0918 (35) P=.300	-.1661 (35) P=.170	.0059 (35) P=.487	.1724 (35) P=.161	-.1231 (35) P=.240	.3265 (35) P=.028	-.0650 (35) P=.355	.0683 (35) P=.348
	.0348 (34) P=.423	-.0375 (34) P=.417	.0522 (34) P=.385	.1372 (34) P=.219	.1685 (34) P=.170	.1535 (34) P=.193	.1856 (34) P=.147	-.2599 (34) P=.069	.4683 (34) P=.003	-.3355 (34) P=.026	-.3108 (34) P=.037	-.3418 (34) P=.024	-.2685 (34) P=.062	-.3013 (34) P=.042	-.1828 (34) P=.150
	.1786 (41) P=.132	.3376 (41) P=.015	-.1562 (41) P=.165	.0027 (41) P=.493	.0107 (41) P=.473	-.0819 (41) P=.305	.1847 (41) P=.124	.1167 (41) P=.234	-.0590 (41) P=.357	-.1209 (41) P=.226	.0703 (41) P=.331	-.1993 (41) P=.106	.3401 (41) P=.015	-.1475 (41) P=.179	-.0222 (41) P=.445
	.1864 (41) P=.122	.6059 (41) P=.001	-.0695 (41) P=.333	-.0986 (41) P=.270	-.0189 (41) P=.453	-.1692 (41) P=.145	.1818 (41) P=.128	.1588 (41) P=.161	-.0443 (41) P=.392	-.1257 (41) P=.217	.0841 (41) P=.301	-.2324 (41) P=.072	.3197 (41) P=.021	-.1831 (41) P=.126	.0448 (41) P=.390
	-.3904 (25) P=.027	-.9892 (25) P=.001	.0989 (25) P=.319	.2160 (25) P=.150	.0056 (25) P=.489	-.2374 (25) P=.127	-.2082 (25) P=.159	-.1382 (25) P=.255	.2160 (25) P=.150	.0086 (25) P=.484	-.2421 (25) P=.122	-.1501 (25) P=.237	-.3390 (25) P=.049	.0981 (25) P=.320	-.0743 (25) P=.362
	.3444 (31) P=.029	.6296 (31) P=.001	-.0957 (31) P=.304	-.2878 (31) P=.058	.2022 (31) P=.138	-.1458 (31) P=.217	.3826 (31) P=.017	.1466 (31) P=.216	-.3209 (31) P=.039	.2057 (31) P=.134	.2995 (31) P=.051	.0533 (31) P=.388	.2355 (31) P=.101	.1548 (31) P=.203	.1176 (31) P=.264
	-.1358 (40) P=.202	-.1695 (40) P=.148	-.1551 (40) P=.170	.2172 (40) P=.089	.1100 (40) P=.250	.1817 (40) P=.131	.0218 (40) P=.447	.0337 (40) P=.418	.0136 (40) P=.467	-.0122 (40) P=.470	.0998 (40) P=.270	-.0416 (40) P=.399	-.0073 (40) P=.482	-.0257 (40) P=.437	.1224 (40) P=.226
	-.1120 (40) P=.246	-.0836 (40) P=.304	.3456 (40) P=.014	-.1464 (40) P=.184	-.0550 (40) P=.368	-.1707 (40) P=.146	-.1774 (40) P=.137	.4489 (40) P=.002	-.0935 (40) P=.283	.2230 (40) P=.083	.1110 (40) P=.248	.2587 (40) P=.054	-.2326 (40) P=.074	.2879 (40) P=.036	.2401 (40) P=.068
	-.0115 (37) P=.473	-.0701 (37) P=.340	.2675 (37) P=.055	.1129 (37) P=.253	.0799 (37) P=.319	.1003 (37) P=.277	.0313 (37) P=.427	.3303 (37) P=.023	.1023 (37) P=.273	.0659 (37) P=.349	.0367 (37) P=.415	.1115 (37) P=.256	-.3064 (37) P=.033	.1125 (37) P=.254	.1705 (37) P=.157
	-.0236 (40) P=.443	-.1229 (40) P=.225	.0477 (40) P=.385	-.2198 (40) P=.087	-.1629 (40) P=.158	-.1296 (40) P=.213	-.1759 (40) P=.139	-.1255 (40) P=.220	.3771 (40) P=.008	-.2113 (40) P=.095	-.2428 (40) P=.066	-.0902 (40) P=.290	-.3331 (40) P=.018	-.2069 (40) P=.100	-.1867 (40) P=.124
	.1572 (38) P=.173	.2500 (38) P=.065	.0377 (38) P=.411	-.1349 (38) P=.210	-.0469 (38) P=.390	-.1363 (38) P=.207	.1304 (38) P=.218	.0937 (38) P=.288	.1973 (38) P=.118	-.1740 (38) P=.148	-.1618 (38) P=.166	-.1236 (38) P=.230	-.0442 (38) P=.396	-.2178 (38) P=.095	-.2314 (38) P=.081
	-.0521 (37) P=.380	-.1754 (37) P=.150	.3002 (37) P=.035	-.0718 (37) P=.336	.1127 (37) P=.253	-.0217 (37) P=.449	.0715 (37) P=.337	.3625 (37) P=.014	.0003 (37) P=.499	.1595 (37) P=.173	.2021 (37) P=.115	.1284 (37) P=.224	-.3133 (37) P=.030	.1502 (37) P=.187	.2315 (37) P=.084
	-.0858 (33) P=.318	-.3673 (33) P=.018	.0073 (33) P=.484	.0828 (33) P=.323	-.1115 (33) P=.268	.2374 (33) P=.092	-.1767 (33) P=.163	.0712 (33) P=.347	-.2000 (33) P=.132	-.2676 (33) P=.066	.4214 (33) P=.007	.0237 (33) P=.448	-.1144 (33) P=.263	.1907 (33) P=.144	.3076 (33) P=.041
	.2609 (31) P=.078	.6591 (31) P=.001	-.0816 (31) P=.331	-.1569 (31) P=.200	.0619 (31) P=.370	-.1575 (31) P=.199	.1782 (31) P=.169	.0874 (31) P=.320	-.1834 (31) P=.162	.0318 (31) P=.433	.1826 (31) P=.163	-.1018 (31) P=.293	.2944 (31) P=.054	-.0422 (31) P=.411	.0805 (31) P=.333
	.3425 (32) P=.028	.0859 (32) P=.320	-.1011 (32) P=.291	.2545 (32) P=.080	.3074 (32) P=.043	.1408 (32) P=.221	.2091 (32) P=.125	.0479 (32) P=.397	.3448 (32) P=.027	-.0942 (32) P=.304	-.1691 (32) P=.177	.0688 (32) P=.354	-.4605 (32) P=.004	-.0639 (32) P=.364	-.0206 (32) P=.455
	.4550 (40) P=.002	.1676 (40) P=.151	-.1954 (40) P=.113	-.2729 (40) P=.044	.0711 (40) P=.331	-.0614 (40) P=.353	.2776 (40) P=.041	.0377 (40) P=.409	.1223 (40) P=.226	-.1111 (40) P=.248	-.1006 (40) P=.268	-.0664 (40) P=.342	-.0307 (40) P=.425	-.0978 (40) P=.274	-.2016 (40) P=.106
	.2147 (31) P=.123	.5208 (31) P=.001	-.1148 (31) P=.269	-.1236 (31) P=.254	.0473 (31) P=.400	-.1498 (31) P=.211	.0755 (31) P=.343	.1216 (31) P=.257	-.1995 (31) P=.141	.1322 (31) P=.239	.2559 (31) P=.082	.0208 (31) P=.456	.0927 (31) P=.310	-.0159 (31) P=.466	.0326 (31) P=.431
	.2743 (37) P=.050	.6750 (37) P=.001	-.0950 (37) P=.288	-.1380 (37) P=.208	.0541 (37) P=.375	-.1409 (37) P=.203	.1931 (37) P=.126	.0626 (37) P=.356	-.1295 (37) P=.222	.0005 (37) P=.499	.1555 (37) P=.179	-.1315 (37) P=.219	.2323 (37) P=.083	-.0758 (37) P=.328	.0534 (37) P=.377
	-.0929 (39) P=.287	-.3177 (39) P=.024	-.1957 (39) P=.116	.0621 (39) P=.354	.0125 (39) P=.470	.2335 (39) P=.076	-.1274 (39) P=.220	-.3978 (39) P=.006	.2426 (39) P=.068	-.1302 (39) P=.215	-.3190 (39) P=.024	-.0624 (39) P=.353	-.2168 (39) P=.092	-.1196 (39) P=.234	-.2589 (39) P=.056
	.3843 (35) P=.011	.0893 (35) P=.305	-.2531 (35) P=.071	-.1789 (35) P=.152	.1062 (35) P=.272	.0499 (35) P=.388	.2327 (35) P=.089	-.0472 (35) P=.394	.2026 (35) P=.122	-.1757 (35) P=.156	-.1045 (35) P=.275	-.1495 (35) P=.196	-.0587 (35) P=.369	-.1703 (35) P=.164	-.2560 (35) P=.069
	.0916 (40) P=.287	-.0398 (40) P=.404	.0517 (40) P=.376	-.2501 (40) P=.060	.0891 (40) P=.292	-.0670 (40) P=.341	.0387 (40) P=.406	-.0626 (40) P=.351	.2886 (40) P=.035	-.1162 (40) P=.238	-.2190 (40) P=.087	-.0646 (40) P=.346	-.3416 (40) P=.016	-.1055 (40) P=.258	-.1203 (40) P=.230
	.2430 (34) P=.083	.5070 (34) P=.001	-.1345 (34) P=.224	-.2509 (34) P=.076	-.0666 (34) P=.354	-.1120 (34) P=.264	-.0689 (34) P=.349	.0059 (34) P=.487	-.1469 (34) P=.204	.0389 (34) P=.413	.2803 (34) P=.054	-.1600 (34) P=.183	.1863 (34) P=.146	-.0582 (34) P=.372	-.1934 (34) P=.137
	.2414 (40) P=.067	.6039 (40) P=.001	-.1716 (40) P=.145	.0184 (40) P=.455	.0800 (40) P=.312	.0200 (40) P=.451	.2955 (40) P=.032	.0084 (40) P=.479	-.0777 (40) P=.317	-.0027 (40) P=.493	.1780 (40) P=.136	-.1778 (40) P=.136	-.1407 (40) P=.193	-.0770 (40) P=.318	.0611 (40) P=.354
	.1536 (40) P=.172	.3483 (40) P=.014	-.2066 (40) P=.100	-.0793 (40) P=.313	-.1261 (40) P=.219	-.1528 (40) P=.173	.0752 (40) P=.322	.5217 (40) P=.001	.0042 (40) P=.490	.0738 (40) P=.325	.3635 (40) P=.011	-.1512 (40) P=.176	-.1643 (40) P=.155	.0367 (40) P=.411	.3720 (40) P=.009
	.0087 (40) P=.479	.0110 (40) P=.473	.1546 (40) P=.170	.1003 (40) P=.269	.1308 (40) P=.211	.0740 (40) P=.325	-.0325 (40) P=.421	.1076 (40) P=.254	.2104 (40) P=.096	.0370 (40) P=.410	-.1763 (40) P=.138	.2212 (40) P=.085	-.4814 (40) P=.001	.0117 (40) P=.471	-.2342 (40) P=.073
	-.3099 (39) P=.027	-.3953 (39) P=.006	.2870 (39) P=.038	.2091 (39) P=.101	-.2239 (39) P=.085	.0635 (39) P=.351	-.4188 (39) P=.004	-.2068 (39) P=.103	.1713 (39) P=.149	-.2523 (39) P=.061	-.1951 (39) P=.117	-.1977 (39) P=.114	.1729 (39) P=.146	-.1859 (39) P=.129	-.2711 (39) P=.047
	-.0245 (41) P=.439	-.2468 (41) P=.060	.2219 (41) P=.082	.1057 (41) P=.255	.1460 (41) P=.181	.1727 (41) P=.140	.0542 (41) P=.368	.1265 (41) P=.215	.1682 (41) P=.147	.0803 (41) P=.309	-.0459 (41) P=.388	.1341 (41) P=.201	-.4773 (41) P=.001	.1131 (41) P=.241	.0761 (41) P=.318
	-.0751 (37) P=.329	-.0349 (37) P=.419	.1799 (37) P=.143	-.0759 (37) P=.328	-.1181 (37) P=.243	-.1120 (37) P=.255	.0370 (37) P=.414	.3276 (37) P=.024	-.3918 (37) P=.008	.3863 (37) P=.009	.3123 (37) P=.030	.2615 (37) P=.059	.0107 (37) P=.475	.3953 (37) P=.008	.3660 (37) P=.013
	-.3428 (32) P=.027	-.3709 (32) P=.018	.3118 (32) P=.041	.0816 (32) P=.328	-.3587 (32) P=.022	-.0031 (32) P=.493	-.0371 (32) P=.420	.2608 (32) P=.075	-.2714 (32) P=.066	.3172 (32) P=.038	.2762 (32) P=.063	.2017 (32) P=.134	-.0896 (32) P=.313	.3193 (32) P=.037	.2443 (32) P=.089
	-.2233 (41) P=.080	-.3037 (41) P=.027	.1780 (41) P=.133	.1882 (41) P=.119	-.2920 (41) P=.032	-.0054 (41) P=.487	-.3398 (41) P=.015	-.0761 (41) P=.318	.2891 (41) P=.033	-.1360 (41) P=.198	-.0047 (41) P=.488	-.1393 (41) P=.192	-.2805 (41) P=.038	-.0495 (41) P=.379	-.1091 (41) P=.249
	-.1365 (41) P=.197	-.1039 (41) P=.259	-.0179 (41) P=.456	-.0736 (41) P=.324	.0921 (41) P=.284	-.1002 (41) P=.267	-.0073 (41) P=.482	-.2387 (41) P=.066	.1091 (41) P=.249	-.0923 (41) P=.283	-.2660 (41) P=.046	.0641 (41) P=.345	-.0198 (41) P=.451	-.1160 (41) P=.235	-.2431 (41) P=.063

	V1.1	V1.6	V1.2	V1.4	V1.5	V1.3	V1.7	V1.9	V1.10	V1.11	V1.13	V1.14	V1.15	V1.12	V1.8
V.10	.1713 (39) P=.149	-.0572 (39) P=.365	-.0326 (39) P=.422	.4234 (39) P=.004	.1609 (39) P=.164	.2077 (39) P=.102	-.1790 (39) P=.138	.0900 (39) P=.293	.1458 (39) P=.188	-.1179 (39) P=.237	.4210 (39) P=.004	-.2683 (39) P=.049	-.2544 (39) P=.059	-.0754 (39) P=.324	-.3639 (39) P=.011
V.11	-.3593 (39) P=.012	-.0315 (39) P=.425	-.0141 (39) P=.466	-.3145 (39) P=.026	-.1634 (39) P=.160	-.1209 (39) P=.232	-.0451 (39) P=.392	-.1719 (39) P=.148	-.1855 (39) P=.129	.1916 (39) P=.121	-.5017 (39) P=.001	.0928 (39) P=.287	.1592 (39) P=.166	-.0067 (39) P=.484	.1944 (39) P=.118
V.17	.0037 (35) P=.492	-.1729 (35) P=.160	-.1049 (35) P=.267	-.1089 (35) P=.267	-.1509 (35) P=.193	.0097 (35) P=.478	.0238 (35) P=.446	-.1189 (35) P=.248	.0151 (35) P=.466	.2599 (35) P=.066	-.1438 (35) P=.205	-.2341 (35) P=.088	.4683 (35) P=.002	.5297 (35) P=.001	-.1993 (35) P=.126
V.18	.3275 (34) P=.029	-.0573 (34) P=.374	-.1749 (34) P=.161	.2782 (34) P=.056	-.2107 (34) P=.116	-.1695 (34) P=.169	-.1156 (34) P=.258	.1681 (34) P=.171	.0494 (34) P=.391	-.0384 (34) P=.415	.2165 (34) P=.109	-.0238 (34) P=.447	-.2772 (34) P=.056	-.1024 (34) P=.282	-.2973 (34) P=.044
V.19	-.1181 (41) P=.231	-.0306 (41) P=.425	-.0308 (41) P=.424	-.0456 (41) P=.389	.1778 (41) P=.133	-.0527 (41) P=.372	-.0644 (41) P=.345	-.1474 (41) P=.179	-.0533 (41) P=.370	.1109 (41) P=.245	-.1123 (41) P=.242	-.0332 (41) P=.418	.2414 (41) P=.064	.2015 (41) P=.103	.0159 (41) P=.461
V.28	-.0164 (41) P=.460	-.1628 (41) P=.155	-.0892 (41) P=.289	-.1089 (41) P=.249	-.0784 (41) P=.313	-.0560 (41) P=.364	-.0534 (41) P=.370	-.1129 (41) P=.241	.0251 (41) P=.438	.2825 (41) P=.037	-.1457 (41) P=.182	-.1313 (41) P=.207	.4301 (41) P=.003	.4110 (41) P=.004	-.1077 (41) P=.251
V.29	.0243 (25) P=.454	.1971 (25) P=.173	.1297 (25) P=.268	.1990 (25) P=.170	.1713 (25) P=.206	.0376 (25) P=.429	-.1961 (25) P=.174	.2101 (25) P=.157	-.0675 (25) P=.374	-.4848 (25) P=.007	.2301 (25) P=.134	.2921 (25) P=.078	-.6577 (25) P=.001	-.7871 (25) P=.001	.2060 (25) P=.162
V.30	-.0274 (31) P=.442	-.2143 (31) P=.123	-.1944 (31) P=.147	.0036 (31) P=.492	.0248 (31) P=.447	-.1032 (31) P=.290	.1374 (31) P=.230	-.1667 (31) P=.185	.0389 (31) P=.418	.1171 (31) P=.265	-.0831 (31) P=.328	-.2551 (31) P=.083	.3674 (31) P=.021	.6000 (31) P=.001	-.1788 (31) P=.168
V.16	.1344 (40) P=.204	.2527 (40) P=.058	.0036 (40) P=.491	.6583 (40) P=.001	.1222 (40) P=.226	.3730 (40) P=.009	-.1078 (40) P=.254	.1339 (40) P=.205	.2432 (40) P=.065	-.1238 (40) P=.223	.6490 (40) P=.001	-.2564 (40) P=.055	-.0891 (40) P=.292	-.0880 (40) P=.295	-.3542 (40) P=.012
V.20	-.1086 (40) P=.252	-.2765 (40) P=.042	-.1192 (40) P=.232	-.0986 (40) P=.272	-.1522 (40) P=.174	.3571 (40) P=.012	.3274 (40) P=.020	.1602 (40) P=.162	.4660 (40) P=.001	-.0568 (40) P=.364	-.0825 (40) P=.306	.0875 (40) P=.296	.0029 (40) P=.493	.2613 (40) P=.052	.0780 (40) P=.316
V.21	-.0599 (37) P=.362	-.1858 (37) P=.135	-.1912 (37) P=.128	.0177 (37) P=.459	.0441 (37) P=.398	.2818 (37) P=.046	.1519 (37) P=.185	-.1605 (37) P=.171	.2304 (37) P=.085	.3352 (37) P=.021	-.0458 (37) P=.394	.2483 (37) P=.069	.2445 (37) P=.072	.1128 (37) P=.253	.1657 (37) P=.163
V.22	-.0614 (40) P=.353	-.1655 (40) P=.154	.0199 (40) P=.451	-.1902 (40) P=.120	-.1256 (40) P=.220	-.2582 (40) P=.054	.4683 (40) P=.001	.5964 (40) P=.001	.5388 (40) P=.001	-.1150 (40) P=.240	-.1246 (40) P=.222	.2046 (40) P=.103	-.0738 (40) P=.325	-.2349 (40) P=.072	-.2236 (40) P=.083
V.23	-.0697 (38) P=.339	-.1822 (38) P=.137	.1147 (38) P=.246	-.0738 (38) P=.330	.1396 (38) P=.202	-.1352 (38) P=.209	-.0057 (38) P=.486	.0024 (38) P=.494	.1546 (38) P=.177	.3480 (38) P=.016	-.1721 (38) P=.151	.0873 (38) P=.301	.2445 (38) P=.069	.2327 (38) P=.080	.0051 (38) P=.488
V.24	.0673 (37) P=.346	-.0631 (37) P=.355	.1564 (37) P=.178	.0369 (37) P=.414	-.0695 (37) P=.341	.3153 (37) P=.029	-.2243 (37) P=.091	-.1398 (37) P=.205	.2118 (37) P=.104	.2059 (37) P=.111	.1022 (37) P=.274	-.0504 (37) P=.383	.0086 (37) P=.480	.0402 (37) P=.407	-.1297 (37) P=.222
V.26	-.0313 (33) P=.431	.0828 (33) P=.323	.2189 (33) P=.111	.4965 (33) P=.002	.1634 (33) P=.182	.4556 (33) P=.004	.2224 (33) P=.107	.3809 (33) P=.014	.1648 (33) P=.180	-.1990 (33) P=.133	.3199 (33) P=.035	-.1463 (33) P=.208	-.1911 (33) P=.143	-.0757 (33) P=.338	-.2220 (33) P=.107
V.27	.0070 (31) P=.485	-.1917 (31) P=.151	-.1217 (31) P=.257	-.1081 (31) P=.281	-.1760 (31) P=.172	.0203 (31) P=.457	.1858 (31) P=.159	-.1689 (31) P=.182	.0545 (31) P=.385	.2599 (31) P=.079	-.1370 (31) P=.231	-.2691 (31) P=.072	.4896 (31) P=.003	.6759 (31) P=.001	-.2124 (31) P=.126
V.25	.0487 (32) P=.396	-.3499 (32) P=.025	-.1676 (32) P=.180	.0668 (32) P=.358	.1308 (32) P=.238	-.1412 (32) P=.220	-.1121 (32) P=.271	-.2533 (32) P=.081	-.0040 (32) P=.491	.7235 (32) P=.001	-.1156 (32) P=.264	.0457 (32) P=.402	.4494 (32) P=.005	.2962 (32) P=.050	.0697 (32) P=.352
V.34	-.0422 (40) P=.398	-.0358 (40) P=.413	-.1879 (40) P=.123	-.2509 (40) P=.059	-.0350 (40) P=.415	-.1539 (40) P=.171	-.0462 (40) P=.389	-.0539 (40) P=.370	-.0136 (40) P=.467	.4715 (40) P=.001	-.3038 (40) P=.028	-.1848 (40) P=.127	.5096 (40) P=.001	.1167 (40) P=.237	-.0524 (40) P=.374
V.35	-.0182 (31) P=.461	-.1491 (31) P=.212	-.1552 (31) P=.202	-.0670 (31) P=.360	-.1377 (31) P=.230	.0942 (31) P=.307	.1930 (31) P=.149	.1532 (31) P=.205	.2426 (31) P=.094	.2644 (31) P=.075	-.1335 (31) P=.237	-.2861 (31) P=.059	.3864 (31) P=.016	.7023 (31) P=.001	-.2100 (31) P=.128
V.36	.0167 (37) P=.461	-.1742 (37) P=.151	-.1093 (37) P=.260	-.1067 (37) P=.265	-.1531 (37) P=.183	-.0237 (37) P=.445	.0888 (37) P=.301	-.1594 (37) P=.173	.0601 (37) P=.362	.2897 (37) P=.041	-.1453 (37) P=.195	-.2742 (37) P=.050	.4832 (37) P=.001	.6696 (37) P=.001	-.2215 (37) P=.094
V.37	.2775 (39) P=.044	-.1303 (39) P=.215	.0264 (39) P=.437	.1635 (39) P=.160	-.0801 (39) P=.314	-.1064 (39) P=.260	.3190 (39) P=.024	.2377 (39) P=.073	.1032 (39) P=.266	.1995 (39) P=.112	.1024 (39) P=.267	-.0358 (39) P=.414	.0859 (39) P=.301	-.0119 (39) P=.471	-.1673 (39) P=.154
V.38	-.0508 (35) P=.386	.0686 (35) P=.348	-.1086 (35) P=.267	-.0723 (35) P=.340	.0212 (35) P=.452	-.2755 (35) P=.055	-.1433 (35) P=.206	-.2365 (35) P=.086	-.2098 (35) P=.113	.4258 (35) P=.005	-.2409 (35) P=.082	-.1449 (35) P=.203	.4526 (35) P=.003	-.0351 (35) P=.421	-.0273 (35) P=.438
V.32	.0613 (40) P=.354	-.2541 (40) P=.057	-.1702 (40) P=.147	-.0718 (40) P=.330	-.1454 (40) P=.185	-.1410 (40) P=.193	.2269 (40) P=.080	.2139 (40) P=.093	.3702 (40) P=.009	.0240 (40) P=.441	-.0352 (40) P=.415	.0998 (40) P=.270	.0449 (40) P=.392	.2153 (40) P=.091	.0041 (40) P=.490
V.33	-.0909 (34) P=.305	-.1387 (34) P=.217	-.2625 (34) P=.067	-.0437 (34) P=.403	-.1799 (34) P=.154	.2028 (34) P=.125	.3551 (34) P=.020	.2533 (34) P=.074	.2858 (34) P=.051	.0538 (34) P=.381	-.0950 (34) P=.295	-.2501 (34) P=.077	.2807 (34) P=.054	.6617 (34) P=.001	-.1993 (34) P=.129
V.31	.1987 (40) P=.110	-.1321 (40) P=.208	-.1531 (40) P=.173	.2783 (40) P=.041	-.0903 (40) P=.290	.0978 (40) P=.274	-.0242 (40) P=.441	-.0995 (40) P=.271	.0450 (40) P=.391	.2186 (40) P=.088	.1616 (40) P=.160	-.2567 (40) P=.055	.3812 (40) P=.008	.4564 (40) P=.002	-.3904 (40) P=.006
S.2	-.2171 (40) P=.089	.1091 (40) P=.251	.0515 (40) P=.376	-.2520 (40) P=.058	-.0947 (40) P=.281	.1684 (40) P=.150	-.0324 (40) P=.421	-.1375 (40) P=.199	.1399 (40) P=.195	.2631 (40) P=.050	-.2424 (40) P=.066	.0875 (40) P=.296	.1910 (40) P=.119	.2411 (40) P=.067	.2027 (40) P=.105
S.4	-.1086 (40) P=.252	-.2559 (40) P=.056	.0510 (40) P=.377	.0616 (40) P=.353	.3600 (40) P=.011	-.1185 (40) P=.233	.0552 (40) P=.367	.2936 (40) P=.033	.3147 (40) P=.024	.0245 (40) P=.440	-.0758 (40) P=.321	.2755 (40) P=.043	.2286 (40) P=.078	.2962 (40) P=.032	.2711 (40) P=.045
S.6	-.0032 (39) P=.492	-.0404 (39) P=.404	.3027 (39) P=.031	-.1016 (39) P=.269	-.2645 (39) P=.052	-.0261 (39) P=.437	.2611 (39) P=.054	.3056 (39) P=.029	.2392 (39) P=.071	-.0266 (39) P=.436	-.0542 (39) P=.371	.0523 (39) P=.376	-.0211 (39) P=.449	.2692 (39) P=.049	.0980 (39) P=.276
S.3	-.1013 (41) P=.264	-.0025 (41) P=.494	.1458 (41) P=.182	.0167 (41) P=.459	.2784 (41) P=.039	-.1670 (41) P=.148	-.1133 (41) P=.240	.1570 (41) P=.163	.1464 (41) P=.181	-.0649 (41) P=.344	.0238 (41) P=.441	.2580 (41) P=.052	-.0560 (41) P=.364	-.0810 (41) P=.307	.3201 (41) P=.021
S.1	-.0817 (37) P=.315	.1683 (37) P=.160	-.0483 (37) P=.388	.1648 (37) P=.165	.0971 (37) P=.25	.5324 (37) P=.001	.2977 (37) P=.037	.0949 (37) P=.288	-.0046 (37) P=.489	-.2287 (37) P=.087	.1874 (37) P=.133	.0230 (37) P=.446	-.0428 (37) P=.401	.0700 (37) P=.340	.0488 (37) P=.387
S.5	.2887 (32) P=.055	.0776 (32) P=.337	.5195 (32) P=.001	.2782 (32) P=.062	.0507 (32) P=.391	.3753 (32) P=.017	.0657 (32) P=.360	.2314 (32) P=.101	.3041 (32) P=.045	-.1653 (32) P=.183	.3145 (32) P=.040	-.1428 (32) P=.218	-.2175 (32) P=.116	-.1513 (32) P=.204	-.3086 (32) P=.043
S.7	.0276 (41) P=.432	-.1193 (41) P=.229	.1851 (41) P=.123	-.2525 (41) P=.056	-.3264 (41) P=.019	-.1641 (41) P=.153	.5626 (41) P=.001	.4426 (41) P=.001	.3864 (41) P=.006	-.0753 (41) P=.320	-.1508 (41) P=.174	.2007 (41) P=.104	-.0686 (41) P=.335	.2063 (41) P=.098	.2602 (41) P=.050
S.8	.2080 (41) P=.096	-.0538 (41) P=.369	-.1058 (41) P=.255	.0342 (41) P=.416	.0183 (41) P=.455	.0435 (41) P=.393	.0177 (41) P=.456	-.1019 (41) P=.263	-.0851 (41) P=.298	-.0427 (41) P=.395	.0975 (41) P=.272	.1750 (41) P=.137	-.2050 (41) P=.099	-.2389 (41) P=.066	-.0356 (41) P=.412

	V1.1	V1.6	V1.2	V1.4	V1.5	V1.3	V1.7	V1.9	V1.10	V1.11	V1.13	V1.14	V1.15	V1.12	V1.8
S.9	.0073 (41) P=.482	.0656 (41) P=.342	-.0988 (41) P=.269	.3198 (41) P=.021	.4183 (41) P=.003	.3467 (41) P=.013	-.1007 (41) P=.266	-.2067 (41) P=.097	-.1979 (41) P=.107	-.1094 (41) P=.248	.2964 (41) P=.030	.1269 (41) P=.215	-.1123 (41) P=.242	-.2821 (41) P=.037	.0540 (41) P=.369
S.10	.1717 (41) P=.141	.0374 (41) P=.408	.2285 (41) P=.075	.0313 (41) P=.423	-.0079 (41) P=.481	-.1957 (41) P=.110	-.0885 (41) P=.291	-.0521 (41) P=.373	-.1586 (41) P=.161	.2653 (41) P=.047	.0890 (41) P=.290	-.1745 (41) P=.138	.1349 (41) P=.200	-.3007 (41) P=.028	-.0704 (41) P=.331
S.18	.1636 (36) P=.170	.0812 (36) P=.319	-.0234 (36) P=.446	.8115 (36) P=.001	.0925 (36) P=.296	.5700 (36) P=.001	.0168 (36) P=.461	.3369 (36) P=.022	.3553 (36) P=.017	-.0741 (36) P=.334	.7185 (36) P=.001	-.0896 (36) P=.302	-.0755 (36) P=.331	.0949 (36) P=.291	-.3162 (36) P=.030
S.19	-.1395 (36) P=.209	-.0911 (36) P=.299	-.0303 (36) P=.430	-.1514 (36) P=.189	-.2023 (36) P=.118	.4317 (36) P=.004	.1880 (36) P=.136	.0549 (36) P=.375	.3757 (36) P=.012	.2179 (36) P=.101	-.0640 (36) P=.355	.1277 (36) P=.229	.2316 (36) P=.087	.3018 (36) P=.037	.1773 (36) P=.150
S.17	.1709 (41) P=.143	.1246 (41) P=.219	.0217 (41) P=.446	.3020 (41) P=.028	-.0210 (41) P=.448	.1738 (41) P=.139	-.2502 (41) P=.057	.0996 (41) P=.268	.2329 (41) P=.071	-.0779 (41) P=.314	.3742 (41) P=.008	-.1638 (41) P=.153	-.1877 (41) P=.120	-.1021 (41) P=.263	-.3151 (41) P=.022
S.11	.3222 (41) P=.020	.1517 (41) P=.172	.0315 (41) P=.423	.7235 (41) P=.001	.0261 (41) P=.436	.1199 (41) P=.228	-.2951 (41) P=.031	-.1463 (41) P=.220	-.1240 (41) P=.220	.0107 (41) P=.474	.6571 (41) P=.001	-.0635 (41) P=.347	-.0694 (41) P=.333	-.2509 (41) P=.057	-.3454 (41) P=.013
S.12	-.1172 (41) P=.233	.0622 (41) P=.350	.2250 (41) P=.079	-.1972 (41) P=.108	-.0361 (41) P=.411	-.0232 (41) P=.443	-.2510 (41) P=.057	-.2401 (41) P=.065	-.1459 (41) P=.181	.1730 (41) P=.140	-.2074 (41) P=.097	-.0438 (41) P=.393	-.1797 (41) P=.130	.0316 (41) P=.422	.0209 (41) P=.448
S.13	.1640 (38) P=.163	-.0424 (38) P=.400	.2529 (38) P=.063	-.1204 (38) P=.236	-.0706 (38) P=.337	-.2406 (38) P=.073	-.1633 (38) P=.164	-.1430 (38) P=.196	-.2066 (38) P=.107	.0526 (38) P=.377	-.0892 (38) P=.297	-.1430 (38) P=.196	-.0038 (38) P=.491	-.2146 (38) P=.098	-.1799 (38) P=.140
S.14	-.2157 (40) P=.091	-.1876 (40) P=.123	-.1382 (40) P=.197	-.2625 (40) P=.051	-.1405 (40) P=.194	-.1531 (40) P=.173	.7729 (40) P=.001	.7153 (40) P=.001	.5212 (40) P=.001	-.2065 (40) P=.101	-.2778 (40) P=.041	.2458 (40) P=.063	.0420 (40) P=.398	.4217 (40) P=.003	.3263 (40) P=.020
S.15	-.1785 (40) P=.135	-.2429 (40) P=.066	-.0137 (40) P=.467	-.2824 (40) P=.039	-.1613 (40) P=.160	.2642 (40) P=.050	.1144 (40) P=.241	-.0112 (40) P=.473	.3768 (40) P=.008	.0969 (40) P=.276	-.2447 (40) P=.064	-.0623 (40) P=.351	.0893 (40) P=.292	.4373 (40) P=.002	.0183 (40) P=.455
S.16	.3163 (41) P=.022	-.0977 (41) P=.272	.0774 (41) P=.315	.5504 (41) P=.001	.0145 (41) P=.464	.1779 (41) P=.133	-.0736 (41) P=.324	.1436 (41) P=.185	.2167 (41) P=.087	-.0478 (41) P=.383	.3949 (41) P=.005	-.1220 (41) P=.224	.0010 (41) P=.498	-.0842 (41) P=.300	-.4166 (41) P=.003
S.25	.0741 (32) P=.343	-.0386 (32) P=.417	.1360 (32) P=.229	-.0778 (32) P=.336	-.3973 (32) P=.012	.2168 (32) P=.117	.3956 (32) P=.013	.4108 (32) P=.010	.3582 (32) P=.022	-.1956 (32) P=.142	.5794 (24) P=.002	-.2853 (24) P=.088	-.2379 (24) P=.131	.0207 (24) P=.462	-.4618 (24) P=.012
S.27	.1569 (24) P=.232	.2027 (24) P=.171	-.0827 (24) P=.350	.6347 (24) P=.001	.0771 (24) P=.360	.2583 (24) P=.111	-.4029 (24) P=.025	.2720 (24) P=.099	.1038 (24) P=.315	-.2161 (24) P=.155	.0617 (32) P=.369	-.2826 (32) P=.059	-.1884 (32) P=.151	.0722 (32) P=.347	-.2763 (32) P=.063
S.26	-.0288 (32) P=.438	.0901 (32) P=.312	.0890 (32) P=.314	.0060 (32) P=.487	-.2884 (32) P=.055	.2376 (32) P=.095	.2912 (32) P=.053	.2489 (32) P=.085	.2377 (32) P=.095	-.0039 (32) P=.492	.5170 (27) P=.003	-.1119 (27) P=.289	-.2300 (27) P=.124	-.0437 (27) P=.414	-.3620 (27) P=.032
S.22	.1222 (27) P=.272	.0643 (27) P=.375	-.0853 (27) P=.336	.5172 (27) P=.003	.0106 (27) P=.479	.3195 (27) P=.052	-.1730 (27) P=.194	.2915 (27) P=.070	.1811 (27) P=.183	-.1142 (27) P=.285	.6919 (24) P=.001	-.3169 (24) P=.066	.0018 (24) P=.497	-.0269 (24) P=.450	-.4122 (24) P=.023
S.20	.2509 (24) P=.119	.3042 (24) P=.074	.2212 (24) P=.149	.7084 (24) P=.001	.2253 (24) P=.145	.3518 (24) P=.046	-.2698 (24) P=.101	.2363 (24) P=.133	.1784 (24) P=.202	.0401 (24) P=.426	.2962 (30) P=.056	-.1689 (30) P=.186	-.0283 (30) P=.441	-.1796 (30) P=.171	-.2477 (30) P=.094
S.29	.2346 (30) P=.106	.2018 (30) P=.142	-.0203 (30) P=.458	.1657 (30) P=.191	.1296 (30) P=.247	-.1946 (30) P=.151	-.2358 (30) P=.105	.0377 (30) P=.422	-.1143 (30) P=.274	-.1863 (30) P=.162	.4420 (41) P=.002	-.1322 (41) P=.205	.0757 (41) P=.319	-.1607 (41) P=.158	-.2965 (41) P=.030
S.28	.1895 (41) P=.118	.1852 (41) P=.123	.2296 (41) P=.074	.3591 (41) P=.011	.1362 (41) P=.198	.0891 (41) P=.290	-.4218 (41) P=.003	-.0527 (41) P=.372	.0678 (41) P=.337	.0302 (41) P=.426	.1329 (41) P=.204	-.0693 (41) P=.333	-.0270 (41) P=.433	-.0602 (41) P=.354	-.2172 (41) P=.086
S.30	.2586 (41) P=.051	-.0309 (41) P=.424	-.0720 (41) P=.327	.0510 (41) P=.376	.0839 (41) P=.301	-.2212 (41) P=.082	-.0900 (41) P=.288	-.0281 (41) P=.431	.1389 (41) P=.193	-.0427 (41) P=.395	-.0644 (35) P=.357	.2522 (35) P=.072	.1230 (35) P=.241	-.0024 (35) P=.319	.1701 (35) P=.164
S.21	.1000 (35) P=.284	-.0964 (35) P=.291	.0540 (35) P=.379	-.1485 (35) P=.197	-.2249 (35) P=.097	-.0198 (35) P=.455	-.0367 (35) P=.417	-.0973 (35) P=.289	.0463 (35) P=.396	.1704 (35) P=.164	.6889 (38) P=.001	-.0027 (38) P=.494	-.2497 (38) P=.065	-.3552 (38) P=.014	-.4404 (38) P=.003
S.23	.4168 (38) P=.005	.1445 (38) P=.193	.0257 (38) P=.439	.6242 (38) P=.001	.0011 (38) P=.497	.3642 (38) P=.012	-.2065 (38) P=.107	-.0399 (38) P=.406	.0926 (38) P=.290	-.1126 (38) P=.250	.7630 (38) P=.001	.0666 (38) P=.346	-.1961 (38) P=.119	-.1503 (38) P=.184	-.3332 (38) P=.020
S.24	.5099 (38) P=.001	.0355 (38) P=.416	-.1366 (38) P=.207	.7001 (38) P=.001	-.0914 (38) P=.293	.3538 (38) P=.015	-.1106 (38) P=.254	-.2189 (38) P=.093	.2166 (38) P=.096	-.0682 (38) P=.342	.0642 (32) P=.364	-.2198 (32) P=.113	-.3957 (32) P=.012	.0484 (32) P=.396	-.2885 (32) P=.055

	V2.16	V2.22	V2.18	V2.20	V2.19	V2.21	V2.23	V2.17	V3.11	V3.20	V3.15	V3.12	V3.13	V3.14	V3.16
V2.16	1.0000 (0) P=******														
V2.22	.2494 (37) P=.068	1.0000 (0) P=******													
V2.18	.0650 (37) P=.351	.1588 (37) P=.174	1.0000 (0) P=******												
V2.20	.2024 (37) P=.115	.4314 (37) P=.004	.4505 (37) P=.003	1.0000 (0) P=******											
V2.19	.3981 (38) P=.007	.3496 (37) P=.017	.4437 (37) P=.003	.5812 (37) P=.001	1.0000 (0) P=******										
V2.21	-.0061 (37) P=.486	.2110 (37) P=.105	.4695 (37) P=.002	.6659 (37) P=.001	.4272 (37) P=.004	1.0000 (0) P=******									
V2.23	.3096 (35) P=.035	.2074 (34) P=.120	.4380 (34) P=.005	.6958 (34) P=.001	.7061 (35) P=.001	.4110 (34) P=.008	1.0000 (0) P=******								
V2.17	.1469 (33) P=.207	.1262 (33) P=.242	.2519 (33) P=.079	.5683 (33) P=.001	.5450 (33) P=.001	.6096 (33) P=.001	.3591 (33) P=.020	1.0000 (0) P=******							
V3.11	-.0429 (41) P=.395	-.0118 (37) P=.472	.2519 (37) P=.066	-.2305 (37) P=.085	-.3039 (38) P=.032	-.2205 (37) P=.095	-.2395 (35) P=.083	-.2042 (33) P=.127	1.0000 (0) P=******						
V3.20	.1017 (41) P=.263	.1321 (37) P=.218	.1929 (37) P=.126	.3047 (37) P=.033	.3367 (38) P=.019	.3601 (37) P=.014	.3381 (35) P=.023	.3627 (33) P=.019	-.3992 (41) P=.005	1.0000 (0) P=******					
V3.15	-.2104 (39) P=.099	-.0832 (37) P=.312	-.1212 (37) P=.237	-.0665 (37) P=.348	-.2525 (38) P=.063	.0498 (37) P=.385	-.3562 (35) P=.018	.0668 (33) P=.356	.1194 (39) P=.235	-.1721 (39) P=.147	1.0000 (0) P=******				

	V2.1	V2.2	V2.3	V2.4	V2.5	V2.6	V2.7	V2.13	V2.8	V2.9	V2.10	V2.11	V2.12	V2.14	V2.15
r	-.1543	-.2776	-.0895	.0428	.1085	.0687	.0530	.0350	-.3096	.3196	.1633	.3989	-.0075	.2549	.2025
N	(41)	(41)	(41)	(41)	(41)	(41)	(41)	(41)	(41)	(41)	(41)	(41)	(41)	(41)	(41)
P	.168	.039	.289	.395	.250	.335	.371	.414	.024	.021	.154	.005	.482	.054	.102
r	-.2061	-.2346	-.2565	.1562	.1072	-.0003	-.1732	-.1704	.1921	-.1337	-.1956	.0097	-.0971	-.1011	-.1619
N	(41)	(41)	(41)	(41)	(41)	(41)	(41)	(41)	(41)	(41)	(41)	(41)	(41)	(41)	(41)
P	.098	.070	.053	.165	.252	.499	.139	.143	.114	.202	.110	.476	.273	.265	.156
r	-.2324	-.1498	-.0124	.2788	-.0881	.1570	-.0864	.0330	-.0296	.1293	.2787	-.0058	-.1837	.0758	.2811
N	(36)	(36)	(36)	(36)	(36)	(36)	(36)	(36)	(36)	(36)	(36)	(36)	(36)	(36)	(36)
P	.086	.192	.471	.050	.305	.180	.308	.424	.432	.226	.050	.487	.142	.330	.048
r	-.1349	-.1577	.4292	-.1839	-.1298	-.1547	-.1460	.4436	-.0530	.1140	.2169	.0335	-.1182	.1128	.4251
N	(36)	(36)	(36)	(36)	(36)	(36)	(36)	(36)	(36)	(36)	(36)	(36)	(36)	(36)	(36)
P	.216	.179	.005	.141	.225	.184	.198	.003	.380	.254	.102	.423	.246	.256	.005
r	-.2881	-.1927	-.0048	.0655	.0610	-.0110	.0179	.0573	-.0242	.1090	.0764	.0873	-.1919	-.0037	.0215
N	(41)	(41)	(41)	(41)	(41)	(41)	(41)	(41)	(41)	(41)	(41)	(41)	(41)	(41)	(41)
P	.034	.114	.488	.342	.352	.473	.456	.361	.440	.249	.317	.294	.115	.491	.447
r	-.0517	-.0569	-.2216	.1798	.0756	.2975	.2676	.0145	.1019	-.0464	.0628	-.2662	-.0918	-.0647	.2252
N	(41)	(41)	(41)	(41)	(41)	(41)	(41)	(41)	(41)	(41)	(41)	(41)	(41)	(41)	(41)
P	.374	.362	.082	.130	.319	.029	.045	.464	.263	.387	.348	.046	.284	.344	.078
r	.1298	.3874	.1161	-.1642	-.1799	-.2435	.0400	.3752	-.0057	-.1726	.1019	-.3124	.3446	-.2266	.2424
N	(41)	(41)	(41)	(41)	(41)	(41)	(41)	(41)	(41)	(41)	(41)	(41)	(41)	(41)	(41)
P	.209	.006	.235	.152	.130	.063	.402	.008	.486	.140	.263	.023	.014	.077	.063
r	.1188	-.1224	-.0969	.1753	.2518	.2214	-.0933	-.1677	.1968	-.3185	-.3522	-.1087	.2461	-.2723	-.2443
N	(38)	(38)	(38)	(38)	(38)	(38)	(38)	(38)	(38)	(38)	(38)	(38)	(38)	(38)	(38)
P	.239	.232	.281	.146	.064	.091	.289	.157	.118	.026	.015	.258	.068	.049	.070
r	.0931	.1018	.0674	-.1899	-.2294	-.2057	-.1582	-.0139	.2765	-.1819	-.1060	-.1466	-.1813	-.1774	-.0415
N	(40)	(40)	(40)	(40)	(40)	(40)	(40)	(40)	(40)	(40)	(40)	(40)	(40)	(40)	(40)
P	.284	.266	.340	.120	.077	.101	.165	.466	.042	.131	.257	.183	.131	.137	.400
r	.0196	.0093	.3792	-.1988	-.0068	-.2471	-.0211	.4267	-.1772	.2870	.3211	.1999	-.2106	.2670	.3453
N	(40)	(40)	(40)	(40)	(40)	(40)	(40)	(40)	(40)	(40)	(40)	(40)	(40)	(40)	(40)
P	.452	.477	.008	.109	.483	.062	.449	.003	.137	.036	.022	.108	.096	.048	.015
r	-.0677	-.1509	-.0669	.3317	-.1805	.0744	.0212	-.2039	.3923	-.3480	-.1965	-.3320	-.0616	-.3567	-.1711
N	(41)	(41)	(41)	(41)	(41)	(41)	(41)	(41)	(41)	(41)	(41)	(41)	(41)	(41)	(41)
P	.337	.173	.339	.017	.129	.322	.448	.100	.006	.013	.109	.017	.351	.011	.142
r	.2030	.0808	-.2778	.4826	.0729	-.1882	-.5092	-.2869	.1503	-.1788	-.2236	-.0676	.0478	-.1973	-.0970
N	(24)	(24)	(24)	(24)	(24)	(32)	(32)	(32)	(32)	(32)	(32)	(32)	(32)	(32)	(32)
P	.171	.354	.094	.008	.368	.151	.001	.056	.206	.164	.109	.357	.398	.140	.299
r	-.3125	-.4235	.2101	.1919	-.1262	.4569	.2687	-.0884	.1927	-.0536	-.3573	-.3051	-.2073	-.0871	.4082
N	(32)	(32)	(32)	(32)	(32)	(24)	(24)	(24)	(24)	(24)	(24)	(24)	(24)	(24)	(24)
P	.041	.008	.124	.146	.246	.012	.102	.341	.184	.402	.043	.074	.165	.343	.024
r	-.2655	-.0957	-.1228	.1662	-.2778	-.0819	-.4161	-.3116	.0810	-.1358	-.2226	.0287	.1100	-.1473	-.1566
N	(27)	(27)	(27)	(27)	(27)	(32)	(32)	(32)	(32)	(32)	(32)	(32)	(32)	(32)	(32)
P	.090	.317	.271	.204	.080	.328	.009	.041	.330	.229	.110	.438	.274	.211	.196
r	.0372	-.0587	-.2278	.3983	-.0272	-.0844	-.1513	-.2141	.1594	-.1164	.1678	-.3581	-.0696	-.1865	.2489
N	(24)	(24)	(24)	(24)	(24)	(27)	(27)	(27)	(27)	(27)	(27)	(27)	(27)	(27)	(27)
P	.431	.393	.142	.027	.450	.338	.226	.142	.214	.282	.201	.033	.365	.176	.105
r	.2133	-.6298	-.2611	-.2036	.0729	.4064	.1417	.1011	.0078	.1010	.4955	-.1936	-.1988	.0671	.5646
N	(30)	(30)	(30)	(30)	(30)	(24)	(24)	(24)	(24)	(24)	(24)	(24)	(24)	(24)	(24)
P	.129	.001	.082	.140	.351	.024	.254	.319	.486	.319	.007	.182	.176	.378	.002
r	-.0797	-.0810	-.1346	-.0222	.1208	.0989	.3725	.0222	.0849	.0816	.1435	-.0947	-.3294	.1019	.2857
N	(41)	(41)	(41)	(41)	(41)	(30)	(30)	(30)	(30)	(30)	(30)	(30)	(30)	(30)	(30)
P	.310	.307	.201	.445	.226	.301	.021	.454	.328	.334	.225	.309	.038	.296	.063
r	.1986	.1376	-.1257	-.0263	.0696	-.2288	.3077	.2669	.0626	.0780	.0990	-.0582	-.2828	.0214	.1455
N	(41)	(41)	(41)	(41)	(41)	(41)	(41)	(41)	(41)	(41)	(41)	(41)	(41)	(41)	(41)
P	.107	.195	.217	.435	.333	.075	.025	.046	.349	.314	.269	.359	.037	.447	.182
r	-.3588	-.2467	.3172	.0579	-.0891	-.0272	.3008	-.0616	.3333	-.2026	-.1702	-.1307	-.2400	-.1770	-.0907
N	(35)	(35)	(35)	(35)	(35)	(41)	(41)	(41)	(41)	(41)	(41)	(41)	(41)	(41)	(41)
P	.017	.077	.032	.371	.305	.433	.028	.351	.017	.102	.144	.208	.065	.134	.286
r	-.1985	-.3201	-.1672	.1493	.1141	.0627	-.2447	-.0549	.2302	-.3721	-.3610	-.2214	.2698	-.3260	-.1683
N	(38)	(38)	(38)	(38)	(38)	(35)	(35)	(35)	(35)	(35)	(35)	(35)	(35)	(35)	(35)
P	.116	.025	.158	.186	.248	.360	.078	.377	.092	.014	.017	.101	.058	.028	.167
r	-.3484	-.2893	.0666	.2988	.0208	.4036	.1565	.0543	.0607	.0444	-.0057	-.0067	-.2017	.0404	.0669
N	(38)	(38)	(38)	(38)	(38)	(38)	(38)	(38)	(38)	(38)	(38)	(38)	(38)	(38)	(38)
P	.016	.039	.346	.034	.451	.006	.174	.373	.359	.395	.486	.484	.112	.405	.345
r	-.4342	-.4361	.2920	.1948	-.1554	.3544	.1643	.1101	.0764	.1022	.1164	-.0920	-.3319	.1035	.2567
N	(32)	(32)	(32)	(32)	(32)	(38)	(38)	(38)	(38)	(38)	(38)	(38)	(38)	(38)	(38)
P	.007	.006	.052	.143	.198	.015	.162	.255	.324	.271	.243	.291	.021	.268	.060

V3.17 V3.18 V3.19 V3.21 V3.4

```
            V3.18      V3.19      V3.21      V3.4       V3.5       V3.6       V3.7       V3.8       V3.9       V3.10      V3.1       V3.2       V3.3       V4.1

          1.0000
          (    0)
          P=******

           .1122     1.0000
          (   36)    (    0)
          P=  .257   P=******

          -.4349     -.1550     1.0000
          (   37)    (   39)    (    0)
          P=  .004   P=  .173   P=******

          -.0473      .2682      .1104     1.0000
          (   34)    (   37)    (   37)    (    0)
          P=  .395   P=  .054   P=  .258   P=******

           .2433     -.0096     -.4326     -.2875     1.0000
          (   35)    (   38)    (   38)    (   36)    (    0)
          P=  .080   P=  .477   P=  .003   P=  .045   P=******

           .1728      .0815     -.2102      .1968     -.4753     1.0000
          (   36)    (   39)    (   40)    (   37)    (   38)    (    0)
          P=  .157   P=  .311   P=  .096   P=  .121   P=  .001   P=******

          -.3800      .0278      .3516     -.1703     -.0770     -.0602     1.0000
          (   35)    (   38)    (   38)    (   36)    (   38)    (   38)    (    0)
          P=  .012   P=  .434   P=  .015   P=  .160   P=  .323   P=  .360   P=******

           .7367      .5161     -.5776      .0599      .0361      .2616     -.1598     1.0000
          (   36)    (   39)    (   39)    (   37)    (   38)    (   39)    (   38)    (    0)
          P=  .001   P=  .001   P=  .001   P=  .362   P=  .415   P=  .054   P=  .169   P=******

           .3452      .0221     -.3270     -.3010      .9600     -.5436     -.0155     -.0204     1.0000
          (   35)    (   38)    (   39)    (   36)    (   38)    (   38)    (   38)    (   38)    (    0)
          P=  .021   P=  .448   P=  .021   P=  .037   P=  .001   P=  .001   P=  .463   P=  .452   P=******

           .4629      .0514     -.1596      .3073     -.5738      .5877     -.5586      .5399     -.6251     1.0000
          (   15)    (   16)    (   16)    (   16)    (   16)    (   16)    (   16)    (   16)    (   16)    (    0)
          P=  .041   P=  .425   P=  .277   P=  .123   P=  .010   P=  .008   P=  .014   P=  .015   P=  .005   P=******

           .0410      .1355     -.2377      .2355     -.5194      .3215     -.0984      .3032     -.5194      .4209     1.0000
          (   37)    (   39)    (   41)    (   37)    (   38)    (   40)    (   38)    (   39)    (   39)    (   16)    (    0)
          P=  .405   P=  .205   P=  .067   P=  .080   P=  .001   P=  .022   P=  .278   P=  .030   P=  .001   P=  .052   P=******

           .8981      .0888     -.4485     -.0859      .1819      .0171     -.2438      .6704      .1637      .2549     -.0118     1.0000
          (   37)    (   39)    (   41)    (   37)    (   38)    (   40)    (   38)    (   39)    (   39)    (   16)    (   41)    (    0)
          P=  .001   P=  .296   P=  .002   P=  .307   P=  .137   P=  .458   P=  .070   P=  .001   P=  .160   P=  .170   P=  .471   P=******

           .2556      .0197     -.3262     -.2949      .9588     -.5069     -.0085     -.0234      .9999     -.6271     -.5176      .1657     1.0000
          (   37)    (   39)    (   40)    (   37)    (   38)    (   40)    (   38)    (   39)    (   38)    (   16)    (   40)    (   40)    (    0)
          P=  .063   P=  .453   P=  .020   P=  .038   P=  .001   P=  .001   P=  .480   P=  .444   P=  .001   P=  .005   P=  .001   P=  .153   P=******

           .3980     -.0118     -.4632     -.1840      .8499     -.3590     -.2256      .0839      .8311     -.4609     -.4295      .2829      .8308     1.0000
          (   37)    (   39)    (   41)    (   37)    (   38)    (   40)    (   38)    (   39)    (   39)    (   16)    (   41)    (   41)    (   40)    (    0)
          P=  .007   P=  .472   P=  .001   P=  .138   P=  .001   P=  .011   P=  .087   P=  .306   P=  .001   P=  .036   P=  .003   P=  .037   P=  .001   P=******

          -.0407     -.0779      .0765     -.1330     -.0375     -.0481     -.1520     -.2776      .0815     -.1938     -.0333      .0176      .0820     -.1081
          (   37)    (   39)    (   41)    (   37)    (   38)    (   40)    (   38)    (   39)    (   39)    (   16)    (   41)    (   41)    (   40)    (   41)
          P=  .405   P=  .319   P=  .317   P=  .216   P=  .412   P=  .384   P=  .181   P=  .044   P=  .311   P=  .236   P=  .418   P=  .457   P=  .308   P=  .250

           .5222      .0272     -.5390      .0132      .4092      .1456     -.4988      .3524      .3188      .2015     -.1906      .4891      .3340      .6425
          (   37)    (   39)    (   41)    (   37)    (   38)    (   40)    (   38)    (   39)    (   39)    (   16)    (   41)    (   41)    (   40)    (   41)
          P=  .001   P=  .435   P=  .001   P=  .469   P=  .005   P=  .185   P=  .001   P=  .014   P=  .024   P=  .227   P=  .116   P=  .001   P=  .018   P=  .001

          -.0909     -.0570      .1254      .0239     -.0515     -.0406     -.0433      .0553     -.0570      .1203      .1694     -.0469     -.0560     -.1913
          (   37)    (   39)    (   41)    (   37)    (   38)    (   40)    (   38)    (   39)    (   39)    (   16)    (   41)    (   41)    (   40)    (   41)
          P=  .296   P=  .365   P=  .217   P=  .444   P=  .379   P=  .402   P=  .398   P=  .369   P=  .365   P=  .329   P=  .145   P=  .385   P=  .366   P=  .115

           .3449      .0552      .0117      .2394     -.6024      .4448     -.2919      .1758     -.6847      .8625      .3795      .0553     -.6835     -.2503
          (   37)    (   39)    (   40)    (   37)    (   38)    (   40)    (   38)    (   39)    (   38)    (   16)    (   40)    (   40)    (   40)    (   40)
          P=  .018   P=  .369   P=  .471   P=  .077   P=  .001   P=  .002   P= .038   P=  .142   P=  .001   P=  .001   P=  .008   P=  .367   P=  .001   P=  .060

           .3147     -.0237     -.3566     -.2410      .9495     -.5134     -.1067     -.0329      .9800     -.5869     -.5176      .2287      .9799     .8570
          (   37)    (   39)    (   40)    (   37)    (   38)    (   40)    (   38)    (   39)    (   38)    (   16)    (   40)    (   40)    (   40)    (   40)
          P=  .029   P=  .443   P=  .012   P=  .075   P=  .001   P=  .001   P=  .262   P=  .421   P=  .001   P=  .008   P=  .001   P=  .078   P=  .001   P=  .001

          -.1107     -.1992      .1635      .3125     -.2337     -.2419     -.1279     -.3880      .0164     -.2417     -.0415     -.0430      .2213     -.1817
          (   37)    (   39)    (   38)    (   36)    (   37)    (   38)    (   37)    (   38)    (   37)    (   15)    (   39)    (   39)    (   39)    (   39)
          P=  .257   P=  .115   P=  .160   P=  .032   P=  .082   P=  .072   P=  .225   P=  .008   P=  .462   P=  .193   P=  .401   P=  .397   P=  .088   P=  .134

           .2037      .0381     -.4706     -.1720      .8378     -.3063     -.1041      .0200      .8426     -.4636     -.3892      .2040      .8348     .8614
          (   36)    (   38)    (   39)    (   36)    (   37)    (   38)    (   37)    (   38)    (   37)    (   16)    (   39)    (   39)    (   39)    (   39)
          P=  .117   P=  .410   P=  .001   P=  .158   P=  .001   P=  .031   P=  .270   P=  .453   P=  .001   P=  .035   P=  .007   P=  .106   P=  .001   P=  .001

           .4120     -.1955     -.3581      .0290     -.0733      .2393     -.5374      .2459     -.1646      .5114      .1322      .3334     -.1558     .0850
          (   34)    (   36)    (   37)    (   35)    (   35)    (   36)    (   35)    (   36)    (   35)    (   16)    (   37)    (   37)    (   37)    (   37)
          P=  .008   P=  .127   P=  .015   P=  .434   P=  .338   P=  .080   P=  .001   P=  .074   P=  .172   P=  .021   P=  .218   P=  .022   P=  .179   P=  .308

          -.0864     -.1122     -.0710      .1098     -.1455      .3704     -.3534     -.0497     -.2124      .3975      .1020     -.1793     -.2042     .1104
          (   37)    (   39)    (   41)    (   37)    (   38)    (   40)    (   38)    (   39)    (   39)    (   16)    (   41)    (   41)    (   40)    (   41)
          P=  .306   P=  .248   P=  .330   P=  .259   P=  .192   P=  .009   P=  .015   P=  .382   P=  .097   P=  .064   P=  .263   P=  .131   P=  .103   P=  .246

          -.1566     -.1260      .2157     -.1846     -.0689      .0932      .0503     -.0986     -.0936     -.0685     -.0473     -.1502     -.0877     -.2273
          (   37)    (   39)    (   41)    (   37)    (   38)    (   40)    (   38)    (   39)    (   39)    (   16)    (   41)    (   41)    (   40)    (   41)
          P=  .177   P=  .222   P=  .088   P=  .137   P=  .341   P=  .284   P=  .382   P=  .275   P=  .285   P=  .401   P=  .385   P=  .174   P=  .295   P=  .076

          -.1365     -.0458     -.3326     -.2729      .9424     -.5805     -.1430     -.1158      .9514     -.5996     -.5153      .1027      .9510     .8214
          (   34)    (   36)    (   37)    (   34)    (   36)    (   36)    (   36)    (   36)    (   36)    (   16)    (   37)    (   37)    (   37)    (   37)
          P=  .221   P=  .395   P=  .022   P=  .059   P=  .001   P=  .001   P=  .203   P=  .251   P=  .001   P=  .007   P=  .001   P=  .273   P=  .001   P=  .001

          -.2261     -.0338     -.4245     -.2020      .7907     -.4143      .0074      .0069      .7786     -.4187     -.2715      .0945      .7694     .6935
          (   34)    (   36)    (   37)    (   34)    (   36)    (   36)    (   36)    (   36)    (   36)    (   16)    (   37)    (   37)    (   37)    (   37)
          P=  .099   P=  .422   P=  .004   P=  .126   P=  .001   P=  .006   P=  .483   P=  .484   P=  .001   P=  .053   P=  .052   P=  .289   P=  .001   P=  .001

          -.1274     -.0021     -.3031     -.3125      .9563     -.5716     -.0306     -.0715      .9923     -.6380     -.5414      .1486      .9922     .8148
          (   33)    (   36)    (   36)    (   34)    (   36)    (   36)    (   36)    (   36)    (   36)    (   16)    (   36)    (   36)    (   36)    (   36)
          P=  .240   P=  .495   P=  .036   P=  .036   P=  .001   P=  .001   P=  .430   P=  .339   P=  .001   P=  .004   P=  .001   P=  .193   P=  .001   P=  .001

           .0390      .0526     -.2853     -.1165      .8866     -.4737     -.0087     -.0143      .9331     -.6401     -.4989      .1579      .9320     .7944
          (   37)    (   39)    (   40)    (   37)    (   38)    (   39)    (   38)    (   39)    (   38)    (   16)    (   40)    (   40)    (   40)    (   40)
          P=  .409   P=  .375   P=  .037   P=  .246   P=  .001   P=  .001   P=  .479   P=  .465   P=  .001   P=  .004   P=  .001   P=  .165   P=  .001   P=  .001
```

	V2.16	V2.22	V2.18	V2.20	V2.19	V2.21	V2.23	V2.17	V3.11	V3.20	V3.15	V3.12	V3.13	V3.14	V3.16	V3.17
V3.12	-.1657 (41) P= .150	.1463 (37) P= .194	.0362 (37) P= .416	.2043 (37) P= .113	.0309 (38) P= .427	.2912 (37) P= .040	.1849 (35) P= .144	.3778 (33) P= .015	-.2878 (41) P= .034	.6408 (41) P= .001	-.2933 (39) P= .035	1.0000 (0) P=******				
V3.13	-.3038 (41) P= .027	-.0776 (37) P= .324	-.4143 (37) P= .005	-.1753 (37) P= .150	-.2520 (38) P= .063	-.0822 (37) P= .314	-.3311 (35) P= .026	.0472 (33) P= .397	-.3748 (41) P= .008	.2281 (41) P= .076	-.0942 (39) P= .284	.4996 (41) P= .001	1.0000 (0) P=******			
V3.14	.0006 (41) P= .499	.1348 (37) P= .213	-.2576 (37) P= .062	.3215 (37) P= .026	.3544 (38) P= .015	.3627 (37) P= .014	.3073 (35) P= .036	.3484 (33) P= .023	-.6914 (41) P= .001	.4504 (41) P= .002	-.1462 (39) P= .187	.3605 (41) P= .010	.2488 (41) P= .058	1.0000 (0) P=******		
V3.16	-.3472 (41) P= .013	-.1885 (37) P= .132	-.0254 (37) P= .441	-.1620 (37) P= .169	-.0563 (38) P= .369	-.0202 (37) P= .453	-.2459 (35) P= .077	-.0402 (33) P= .412	-.0620 (41) P= .350	-.0238 (41) P= .441	.2492 (39) P= .063	-.0292 (41) P= .428	.0994 (41) P= .268	.0580 (41) P= .359	1.0000 (0) P=******	
V3.17	-.0207 (26) P= .460	-.1132 (26) P= .291	-.4353 (26) P= .013	-.1874 (26) P= .180	-.3224 (26) P= .054	-.1827 (26) P= .186	-.3369 (26) P= .046	.0279 (25) P= .447	-.0393 (26) P= .424	-.2681 (26) P= .093	-.0594 (26) P= .387	-.0405 (26) P= .422	.4231 (26) P= .016	-.0931 (26) P= .325	-.0483 (26) P= .407	1.0000 (0) P=******
V3.18	-.3109 (37) P= .031	-.0779 (34) P= .331	-.2544 (34) P= .073	.0668 (34) P= .354	-.2308 (35) P= .091	.1321 (34) P= .228	-.2908 (32) P= .053	.2916 (31) P= .056	-.2555 (37) P= .063	.0741 (37) P= .331	.6535 (36) P= .001	-.0239 (37) P= .444	.3092 (37) P= .031	.0586 (37) P= .365	-.0609 (37) P= .360	.0977 (23) P= .329
V3.19	-.0824 (39) P= .309	.0483 (37) P= .388	-.0850 (37) P= .308	.1756 (37) P= .149	-.0642 (38) P= .351	-.0606 (37) P= .361	.1087 (35) P= .267	.0139 (33) P= .469	-.0690 (39) P= .338	.3909 (39) P= .007	-.2960 (39) P= .034	.5345 (39) P= .001	.2449 (39) P= .066	.0636 (39) P= .350	-.1938 (39) P= .119	-.0607 (26) P= .384
V3.21	.1748 (41) P= .137	-.1477 (37) P= .192	.1061 (37) P= .266	-.0851 (37) P= .308	.1163 (38) P= .244	-.1622 (37) P= .169	.0721 (35) P= .340	-.3659 (33) P= .018	.2149 (41) P= .089	-.4186 (41) P= .003	-.3929 (39) P= .007	-.3237 (41) P= .019	-.3136 (41) P= .023	-.3146 (41) P= .023	.1335 (41) P= .203	-.2195 (26) P= .141
V3.4	.1495 (37) P= .189	-.1033 (35) P= .277	.0171 (35) P= .461	.1971 (35) P= .128	.2780 (36) P= .050	.1781 (35) P= .153	.2264 (33) P= .103	.3201 (31) P= .040	-.1641 (37) P= .166	.3978 (37) P= .007	-.2480 (37) P= .069	.3736 (37) P= .011	-.1510 (37) P= .186	.2576 (37) P= .062	-.0843 (37) P= .310	.0758 (25) P= .359
V3.5	-.0365 (38) P= .414	-.1043 (37) P= .269	-.2292 (37) P= .086	-.3253 (37) P= .025	-.2252 (37) P= .090	-.2492 (37) P= .068	-.2579 (34) P= .070	-.1244 (33) P= .245	-.0155 (38) P= .463	-.0734 (38) P= .331	.2217 (38) P= .090	-.0133 (38) P= .468	.2532 (38) P= .063	-.0415 (38) P= .402	.0481 (38) P= .387	.1611 (26) P= .216
V3.6	.0717 (40) P= .330	.2892 (37) P= .041	-.1310 (37) P= .220	.0330 (37) P= .423	-.0277 (38) P= .434	-.0281 (37) P= .435	-.0079 (35) P= .482	.1969 (33) P= .136	-.0623 (40) P= .351	.0766 (40) P= .319	-.0610 (39) P= .356	.1351 (40) P= .203	-.1051 (40) P= .259	.1375 (40) P= .199	-.1626 (40) P= .158	.3076 (26) P= .063
V3.7	.1413 (38) P= .199	.1537 (37) P= .182	.2472 (37) P= .070	.0315 (37) P= .427	.0233 (37) P= .446	-.0759 (37) P= .328	.0130 (34) P= .471	-.0918 (33) P= .306	.3225 (38) P= .024	-.3196 (38) P= .025	-.2912 (38) P= .038	-.0916 (38) P= .292	-.2930 (38) P= .037	-.2573 (38) P= .059	-.3128 (38) P= .028	-.1891 (26) P= .177
V3.8	-.1146 (39) P= .244	.1585 (37) P= .174	-.1534 (37) P= .182	.1674 (37) P= .161	-.1820 (38) P= .137	.0871 (37) P= .304	-.1165 (35) P= .252	.3116 (33) P= .039	-.0684 (39) P= .339	.3541 (39) P= .013	.3831 (39) P= .008	.2560 (39) P= .058	.1276 (39) P= .220	.1096 (39) P= .253	-.1851 (39) P= .130	-.1626 (26) P= .214
V3.9	-.0300 (39) P= .428	-.1226 (37) P= .235	-.2117 (37) P= .104	-.3361 (37) P= .021	-.2284 (37) P= .087	-.2756 (37) P= .049	-.2802 (34) P= .054	-.2367 (33) P= .092	.0872 (39) P= .299	-.1544 (39) P= .174	.2177 (38) P= .095	-.0972 (39) P= .278	.1427 (39) P= .193	-.1373 (39) P= .202	-.0268 (39) P= .436	.1582 (26) P= .220
V3.10	-.2766 (16) P= .150	.5438 (16) P= .015	-.1047 (16) P= .350	.3765 (16) P= .075	.1976 (16) P= .232	.4246 (16) P= .051	.0651 (15) P= .409	.4588 (15) P= .043	-.2058 (16) P= .222	.4707 (16) P= .033	.1440 (16) P= .297	.2455 (16) P= .180	-.1687 (16) P= .266	.3709 (16) P= .079	.0616 (16) P= .410	-.1893 (12) P= .278
V3.1	.0321 (41) P= .421	.2060 (37) P= .111	.1748 (37) P= .150	.3671 (37) P= .013	.1609 (38) P= .167	.3100 (37) P= .031	.2211 (35) P= .101	.2709 (33) P= .064	-.2420 (41) P= .064	.5460 (41) P= .001	-.0035 (39) P= .492	.3884 (41) P= .006	-.1145 (41) P= .238	.2786 (41) P= .039	-.0875 (41) P= .293	-.2464 (26) P= .112
V3.2	-.4109 (41) P= .004	-.1486 (37) P= .190	-.2651 (37) P= .056	-.0029 (37) P= .493	-.2635 (38) P= .055	.0536 (37) P= .376	-.2945 (35) P= .043	.2161 (33) P= .114	-.0670 (41) P= .339	-.0654 (41) P= .342	.6764 (39) P= .001	-.1160 (41) P= .235	.0833 (41) P= .302	.0528 (41) P= .371	-.0810 (41) P= .307	.2350 (26) P= .124
V3.3	-.0393 (40) P= .405	-.1225 (37) P= .235	-.2076 (37) P= .109	-.3348 (37) P= .021	-.2161 (38) P= .096	-.2725 (37) P= .051	-.2625 (35) P= .064	-.2373 (33) P= .092	.0851 (40) P= .301	-.1503 (40) P= .177	.2186 (39) P= .091	-.0969 (40) P= .276	.1299 (40) P= .212	-.1170 (40) P= .236	-.0292 (40) P= .429	.1565 (26) P= .223
V4.1	-.0876 (41) P= .293	-.0898 (37) P= .299	-.4135 (37) P= .005	-.3760 (37) P= .011	-.1792 (38) P= .141	-.3297 (37) P= .023	-.3464 (35) P= .021	-.1261 (33) P= .242	-.0578 (41) P= .360	-.0037 (41) P= .491	.2471 (39) P= .065	.0060 (41) P= .485	.4124 (41) P= .004	.0478 (41) P= .383	-.0414 (41) P= .399	.2785 (26) P= .084
V4.4	-.2600 (41) P= .050	-.0152 (37) P= .464	.0659 (37) P= .349	-.0941 (37) P= .290	-.1265 (38) P= .225	.0683 (37) P= .344	-.0654 (35) P= .355	-.2637 (33) P= .069	.0429 (41) P= .395	-.1644 (41) P= .152	.1891 (39) P= .124	.0119 (41) P= .471	-.0796 (41) P= .310	-.2251 (41) P= .079	.2355 (41) P= .069	.0788 (26) P= .351
V4.2	-.1998 (41) P= .105	.1274 (37) P= .226	-.3554 (37) P= .015	-.1995 (37) P= .118	-.2293 (38) P= .083	-.1996 (37) P= .118	-.3622 (35) P= .016	.0186 (33) P= .459	-.0423 (41) P= .397	.0587 (41) P= .358	.4095 (39) P= .005	.0372 (41) P= .409	.3176 (41) P= .021	.0325 (41) P= .420	-.0260 (41) P= .436	.3833 (26) P= .027
F.3	.0583 (41) P= .359	-.0058 (37) P= .486	-.0279 (37) P= .435	-.1171 (37) P= .245	-.1037 (38) P= .268	-.0389 (37) P= .410	-.2377 (35) P= .085	-.1275 (33) P= .240	.0396 (41) P= .403	-.0210 (41) P= .448	.2610 (39) P= .054	-.0896 (41) P= .289	-.2648 (41) P= .047	-.0415 (41) P= .398	.5412 (41) P= .001	.0027 (26) P= .495
F.5	-.1201 (40) P= .230	.0752 (37) P= .329	-.2277 (37) P= .088	-.0111 (37) P= .474	.0194 (38) P= .454	-.0010 (37) P= .498	-.1360 (35) P= .218	.2086 (33) P= .122	-.1319 (40) P= .209	.2729 (40) P= .044	-.1280 (39) P= .219	.2187 (40) P= .088	.2882 (40) P= .036	.1761 (40) P= .139	.0312 (40) P= .424	.0458 (26) P= .412
F.6	-.0447 (40) P= .392	-.1450 (37) P= .196	-.2692 (37) P= .054	-.3139 (37) P= .029	-.1776 (38) P= .143	-.2265 (37) P= .089	-.2522 (35) P= .072	-.2002 (33) P= .132	-.0200 (40) P= .451	-.1125 (40) P= .245	.2459 (39) P= .066	-.1147 (40) P= .240	.1537 (40) P= .172	-.0182 (40) P= .456	-.0051 (40) P= .488	.2025 (26) P= .161
F.7	-.0466 (39) P= .389	-.0895 (36) P= .302	.1540 (36) P= .185	.1500 (36) P= .191	.0603 (37) P= .361	.1744 (36) P= .155	.1996 (34) P= .129	-.1298 (32) P= .240	.0641 (39) P= .349	-.0515 (39) P= .378	.0563 (38) P= .369	-.1451 (39) P= .189	-.1950 (39) P= .117	-.1506 (39) P= .180	.0109 (39) P= .474	.0367 (25) P= .431
F.8	-.1318 (39) P= .212	-.1104 (37) P= .258	-.3321 (37) P= .022	-.4079 (37) P= .006	-.2120 (38) P= .101	-.2485 (37) P= .069	-.3192 (35) P= .031	-.1728 (33) P= .168	-.0751 (39) P= .325	.0083 (39) P= .480	.1046 (38) P= .266	.1106 (39) P= .251	.4270 (39) P= .003	.0565 (39) P= .366	-.1551 (39) P= .173	.2434 (26) P= .115
F.10	-.1592 (37) P= .173	-.1553 (35) P= .187	-.2911 (35) P= .045	.0084 (35) P= .481	-.0310 (36) P= .429	.1288 (35) P= .230	.0711 (34) P= .345	.1553 (32) P= .198	-.2808 (37) P= .046	.2762 (37) P= .049	.2609 (36) P= .062	-.0419 (37) P= .403	.2484 (37) P= .069	.4026 (37) P= .007	.1120 (37) P= .255	-.0427 (25) P= .420
F.11	.1325 (41) P= .204	.0012 (37) P= .497	-.2883 (37) P= .042	-.2720 (37) P= .052	.1029 (38) P= .269	-.1770 (37) P= .147	-.2898 (35) P= .046	.1048 (33) P= .281	-.0357 (41) P= .412	.2113 (41) P= .092	-.0826 (39) P= .309	.1022 (41) P= .262	.1629 (41) P= .154	.1165 (41) P= .234	.2986 (41) P= .029	.3335 (26) P= .048
F.12	.0358 (41) P= .412	-.1333 (37) P= .216	-.1456 (37) P= .195	-.2505 (37) P= .067	-.1902 (38) P= .126	-.0800 (37) P= .319	-.2222 (35) P= .100	-.2264 (33) P= .103	.1032 (41) P= .260	-.1430 (41) P= .186	.1383 (39) P= .201	-.0829 (41) P= .303	-.1773 (41) P= .134	-.0544 (41) P= .368	.4995 (41) P= .001	.0232 (26) P= .455
F.13	-.0504 (37) P= .384	-.1337 (35) P= .222	-.1897 (35) P= .138	-.2778 (35) P= .053	-.1459 (35) P= .201	-.2184 (35) P= .104	-.1862 (34) P= .146	-.1819 (33) P= .155	-.0427 (37) P= .401	-.0676 (37) P= .345	.2034 (36) P= .117	-.0839 (37) P= .311	.2015 (37) P= .116	-.0344 (37) P= .420	.1198 (37) P= .240	.1582 (26) P= .220
F.14	.0469 (37) P= .391	-.0702 (35) P= .344	-.2386 (35) P= .084	-.2065 (35) P= .117	-.1044 (35) P= .275	-.3112 (35) P= .034	-.0767 (34) P= .333	-.0914 (33) P= .306	-.0301 (37) P= .430	.0496 (37) P= .385	.1177 (36) P= .247	-.0215 (37) P= .450	.0099 (37) P= .477	.0610 (37) P= .360	-.1135 (37) P= .252	.0326 (26) P= .437
F.15	-.1037 (36) P= .274	-.1469 (35) P= .200	-.2013 (35) P= .123	-.3557 (35) P= .018	-.2676 (35) P= .060	-.2837 (35) P= .049	-.2747 (34) P= .058	-.2619 (33) P= .070	.1032 (36) P= .275	-.1814 (36) P= .145	.2344 (36) P= .084	-.1320 (36) P= .221	.1577 (36) P= .179	-.1693 (36) P= .162	.0439 (36) P= .400	.1502 (26) P= .232
F.9	.0240 (40) P= .442	-.2014 (37) P= .116	-.2530 (37) P= .065	-.3237 (37) P= .025	-.1940 (38) P= .122	-.2478 (37) P= .070	-.2922 (35) P= .044	-.2209 (33) P= .108	-.0142 (40) P= .465	-.0993 (40) P= .271	.1335 (39) P= .209	-.0781 (40) P= .316	.1280 (40) P= .216	-.0300 (40) P= .427	-.0953 (40) P= .279	.2081 (26) P= .154

	V2.16	V2.22	V2.18	V2.20	V2.19	V2.21	V2.23	V2.17	V3.11	V3.20	V3.15	V3.12	V3.13	V3.14	V3.16
F.27	.2454 (41) P=.061	-.0487 (37) P=.387	-.3110 (37) P=.030	-.2128 (37) P=.103	-.2159 (38) P=.097	-.2228 (37) P=.092	-.1685 (35) P=.167	-.0697 (33) P=.350	-.2620 (41) P=.049	.0894 (41) P=.289	.0516 (39) P=.377	.0821 (41) P=.305	.3395 (41) P=.015	.1456 (41) P=.182	-.2231 (41) P=.080
F.25	.0569 (37) P=.369	.2066 (35) P=.117	-.0669 (35) P=.351	.0056 (35) P=.487	.0290 (35) P=.434	-.0855 (35) P=.313	.1847 (33) P=.152	-.0267 (32) P=.442	-.1659 (37) P=.163	.2367 (37) P=.079	-.3086 (36) P=.034	.1526 (37) P=.184	.1313 (37) P=.219	.0558 (37) P=.371	-.4231 (37) P=.005
F.26	-.2643 (40) P=.050	-.0602 (36) P=.364	-.3098 (36) P=.033	.0182 (36) P=.458	-.1157 (37) P=.248	.0368 (36) P=.416	-.0990 (34) P=.289	.3294 (32) P=.033	-.5298 (40) P=.001	-.0822 (40) P=.307	.1853 (38) P=.133	-.0290 (40) P=.430	.3352 (40) P=.017	.0262 (40) P=.436	.0132 (40) P=.468
F.24	-.2673 (41) P=.046	-.0473 (37) P=.390	-.1848 (37) P=.137	-.0122 (37) P=.471	.0046 (38) P=.489	.0289 (37) P=.432	-.0934 (35) P=.297	.3626 (33) P=.019	-.5192 (41) P=.001	-.0306 (41) P=.425	.2302 (39) P=.079	-.0595 (41) P=.356	.3763 (41) P=.008	.1174 (41) P=.232	.0606 (41) P=.353
F.23	.0892 (40) P=.292	.0508 (36) P=.384	-.4140 (36) P=.006	-.4407 (36) P=.004	-.2399 (37) P=.076	-.3584 (36) P=.016	-.2553 (34) P=.073	-.2668 (32) P=.070	-.0338 (40) P=.418	.0632 (40) P=.349	-.1733 (38) P=.149	.0151 (40) P=.463	.1055 (40) P=.259	.0204 (40) P=.450	-.2649 (40) P=.049
F.21	-.2077 (39) P=.102	-.0171 (36) P=.461	-.1157 (36) P=.251	.1531 (36) P=.186	-.0998 (36) P=.281	.2248 (36) P=.094	-.3062 (33) P=.042	.3189 (32) P=.038	.0263 (39) P=.437	-.0834 (39) P=.307	.6720 (37) P=.001	-.1516 (39) P=.178	.0083 (39) P=.480	-.0231 (39) P=.444	-.1036 (39) P=.265
F.20	-.5003 (40) P=.001	-.0975 (36) P=.286	-.2668 (36) P=.058	-.0319 (36) P=.427	-.2467 (37) P=.070	.0382 (36) P=.412	-.3074 (34) P=.039	.3009 (32) P=.047	-.1720 (40) P=.144	-.0160 (40) P=.461	.5193 (38) P=.001	-.0634 (40) P=.349	.3145 (40) P=.024	.2544 (40) P=.057	-.0274 (40) P=.433
F.17	.0172 (40) P=.458	-.0043 (36) P=.490	-.2220 (36) P=.097	-.1654 (36) P=.167	-.1885 (37) P=.132	-.2655 (36) P=.059	-.0564 (34) P=.376	-.0370 (32) P=.420	.0801 (40) P=.312	.0194 (40) P=.453	.2124 (38) P=.100	.0186 (40) P=.455	.0157 (40) P=.462	-.2107 (40) P=.096	-.1072 (40) P=.255
F.16	-.1911 (40) P=.119	.1830 (36) P=.143	-.2548 (36) P=.067	.1419 (36) P=.205	-.0867 (37) P=.305	.1248 (36) P=.234	-.1748 (34) P=.161	.2976 (32) P=.049	-.1227 (40) P=.225	-.1670 (40) P=.152	.2145 (38) P=.098	-.1501 (40) P=.178	.1483 (40) P=.181	.0440 (40) P=.394	-.0336 (40) P=.418
F.18	-.2501 (40) P=.060	.0142 (36) P=.467	-.3517 (36) P=.018	.1568 (36) P=.181	.2446 (37) P=.072	.2616 (36) P=.062	-.0257 (34) P=.443	.3410 (32) P=.028	-.5316 (40) P=.001	.3902 (40) P=.006	.1015 (38) P=.272	.1721 (40) P=.144	.3683 (40) P=.010	.6494 (40) P=.001	.1213 (40) P=.228
F.19	-.0935 (40) P=.283	-.1532 (36) P=.186	-.2586 (36) P=.064	.0194 (36) P=.455	.3553 (37) P=.015	.1261 (36) P=.232	.0994 (34) P=.288	.1699 (32) P=.176	-.3950 (40) P=.006	.0855 (40) P=.300	.0652 (38) P=.349	-.1026 (40) P=.264	-.1448 (40) P=.186	.3655 (40) P=.010	.2751 (40) P=.043
F.22	.0876 (34) P=.311	.1988 (30) P=.146	.3018 (30) P=.053	.3049 (30) P=.051	.2286 (31) P=.108	.3012 (30) P=.053	.4078 (28) P=.016	.4084 (26) P=.019	-.1374 (34) P=.219	.7110 (34) P=.001	-.0708 (32) P=.350	.6711 (34) P=.001	.1302 (34) P=.231	.2467 (34) P=.080	-.1072 (34) P=.273
V.1	-.0444 (32) P=.405	-.2450 (31) P=.092	-.1243 (31) P=.253	-.0538 (31) P=.387	.0565 (32) P=.379	.0323 (31) P=.431	-.0081 (32) P=.482	.1529 (30) P=.210	-.2455 (32) P=.088	-.1057 (32) P=.282	.1619 (32) P=.188	.2850 (32) P=.057	-.0933 (32) P=.306	.2418 (32) P=.091	.2476 (32) P=.086
V.4	-.0073 (34) P=.484	-.1023 (34) P=.282	-.1496 (34) P=.199	-.3071 (34) P=.039	-.1430 (34) P=.210	-.2583 (34) P=.070	-.2393 (32) P=.094	-.2416 (31) P=.095	.0093 (34) P=.479	-.1274 (34) P=.236	.2023 (34) P=.126	-.0785 (34) P=.329	.1951 (34) P=.134	-.0979 (34) P=.291	-.0289 (34) P=.436
V.5	-.0423 (35) P=.405	-.1238 (35) P=.239	-.2108 (35) P=.112	-.3362 (35) P=.024	-.2377 (35) P=.085	-.2726 (35) P=.057	-.2805 (33) P=.057	-.2523 (32) P=.082	.0869 (35) P=.310	-.1577 (35) P=.183	.2113 (35) P=.112	-.0960 (35) P=.292	.2175 (35) P=.105	-.1346 (35) P=.220	-.0301 (35) P=.432
V.6	-.0130 (39) P=.469	-.0488 (37) P=.387	.0327 (37) P=.424	.0722 (37) P=.336	-.0438 (38) P=.397	.1666 (37) P=.162	.1955 (35) P=.130	.1440 (33) P=.212	.3122 (39) P=.026	-.0092 (39) P=.478	.0617 (38) P=.356	-.2017 (39) P=.109	-.0742 (39) P=.327	-.1871 (39) P=.127	-.1369 (39) P=.203
V.2	.0496 (38) P=.384	.1113 (37) P=.256	.2003 (37) P=.117	.3314 (37) P=.023	.2240 (37) P=.088	.2609 (37) P=.059	.2648 (35) P=.062	.2318 (33) P=.097	-.0919 (38) P=.292	.1533 (38) P=.179	-.2278 (38) P=.084	.0933 (38) P=.289	-.2076 (38) P=.106	.1339 (38) P=.211	.0320 (38) P=.424
V.3	-.3605 (37) P=.014	.0241 (36) P=.445	.1440 (36) P=.201	-.0126 (36) P=.471	-.0873 (37) P=.304	-.0108 (36) P=.475	-.0992 (35) P=.285	-.0973 (33) P=.295	-.0590 (37) P=.364	.1654 (37) P=.164	-.2571 (37) P=.062	.5953 (37) P=.001	.3645 (37) P=.013	.0609 (37) P=.360	-.0228 (37) P=.447
V.9	-.2718 (35) P=.057	-.2984 (33) P=.046	-.2608 (33) P=.071	-.3816 (33) P=.014	-.3596 (34) P=.018	-.2570 (33) P=.074	-.4005 (34) P=.009	-.1017 (32) P=.290	-.0479 (35) P=.392	-.0522 (35) P=.383	.2048 (35) P=.119	-.1414 (35) P=.209	.3657 (35) P=.015	-.0548 (35) P=.377	.1619 (35) P=.176
V.12	-.0118 (35) P=.473	.1393 (32) P=.223	.0188 (32) P=.459	.1202 (32) P=.256	-.0421 (33) P=.408	.0277 (32) P=.440	.0265 (33) P=.442	.0299 (31) P=.437	.2391 (35) P=.083	-.1593 (35) P=.180	.0091 (34) P=.480	-.3238 (35) P=.029	-.1044 (35) P=.275	-.2846 (35) P=.049	.0980 (35) P=.288
V.13	.0738 (35) P=.337	-.1301 (33) P=.235	-.1287 (33) P=.238	-.1042 (33) P=.282	.0572 (33) P=.376	-.0760 (33) P=.337	.0006 (33) P=.499	.0570 (32) P=.378	-.1553 (35) P=.187	.2639 (35) P=.063	-.0441 (34) P=.402	.4054 (35) P=.008	.0461 (35) P=.396	.3405 (35) P=.023	-.0057 (35) P=.487
V.7	-.0012 (40) P=.497	.2964 (37) P=.037	-.0829 (37) P=.313	.2793 (37) P=.047	.1031 (38) P=.269	.1720 (37) P=.154	.0780 (35) P=.328	.0639 (33) P=.362	-.0656 (40) P=.344	.1913 (40) P=.119	.2888 (39) P=.037	.0579 (40) P=.361	.0944 (40) P=.281	.1872 (40) P=.124	-.0949 (40) P=.280
V.14	.1635 (37) P=.167	-.1045 (36) P=.272	.0858 (36) P=.309	-.1456 (36) P=.198	.0337 (37) P=.422	-.0514 (36) P=.383	-.0104 (34) P=.477	.0771 (32) P=.337	-.0151 (37) P=.465	.3288 (37) P=.023	.1186 (37) P=.242	.0695 (37) P=.341	-.0577 (37) P=.367	.0186 (37) P=.456	.1847 (37) P=.137
V.15	.0460 (40) P=.389	.3475 (36) P=.019	-.1280 (36) P=.229	.0502 (36) P=.386	.2686 (37) P=.054	.0481 (36) P=.390	.2697 (34) P=.061	.0348 (32) P=.425	-.0978 (40) P=.274	-.0181 (40) P=.456	-.1213 (38) P=.234	-.0775 (40) P=.317	-.1082 (40) P=.253	.2551 (40) P=.056	-.0508 (40) P=.378
V.8	.0465 (35) P=.395	-.0132 (32) P=.471	.0363 (32) P=.422	.1350 (32) P=.231	.0768 (33) P=.336	.1408 (32) P=.221	.0645 (32) P=.363	-.0065 (30) P=.486	-.1443 (35) P=.204	.1552 (35) P=.187	.2695 (34) P=.062	-.0383 (35) P=.413	-.1410 (35) P=.210	.2852 (35) P=.048	-.1615 (35) P=.177
V.10	.3468 (39) P=.015	-.1054 (37) P=.267	-.0190 (37) P=.456	.0780 (37) P=.323	.2488 (38) P=.066	.1215 (37) P=.237	-.0112 (35) P=.475	.1871 (33) P=.149	-.3098 (39) P=.027	.3365 (39) P=.018	-.0532 (38) P=.376	.2093 (39) P=.100	-.1433 (39) P=.192	.3421 (39) P=.017	.0110 (39) P=.473
V.11	-.0302 (39) P=.428	.0403 (36) P=.408	.1154 (36) P=.251	.0384 (36) P=.412	-.0866 (37) P=.305	.1133 (36) P=.255	.0478 (34) P=.394	-.1229 (32) P=.251	.2298 (39) P=.080	-.1873 (39) P=.127	.1513 (38) P=.182	-.3375 (39) P=.018	.0616 (39) P=.355	-.1924 (39) P=.120	-.2028 (39) P=.108
V.17	-.0615 (35) P=.363	-.0920 (33) P=.305	-.2250 (33) P=.104	-.3275 (33) P=.031	-.2189 (34) P=.107	-.2650 (33) P=.068	-.2389 (34) P=.087	-.2501 (32) P=.084	.0720 (35) P=.341	-.1557 (35) P=.186	.2061 (34) P=.121	-.1033 (35) P=.278	.2710 (35) P=.058	-.0967 (35) P=.290	-.0328 (35) P=.426
V.18	.1046 (34) P=.278	-.1307 (34) P=.231	.4153 (34) P=.007	.1188 (34) P=.252	.0838 (34) P=.319	.2406 (34) P=.085	.0255 (33) P=.444	.1106 (32) P=.273	-.1202 (34) P=.249	.0202 (34) P=.455	.0047 (34) P=.490	.1582 (34) P=.186	-.2875 (34) P=.050	.0966 (34) P=.293	.2733 (34) P=.059
V.19	.0401 (41) P=.402	.1667 (37) P=.162	-.2311 (37) P=.084	-.2826 (37) P=.045	.0308 (38) P=.427	-.2427 (37) P=.074	-.0028 (35) P=.494	-.1461 (33) P=.209	.0076 (41) P=.481	-.1284 (41) P=.212	.0050 (39) P=.488	-.1902 (41) P=.117	-.0830 (41) P=.303	.1426 (41) P=.187	-.0764 (41) P=.318
V.28	.0498 (41) P=.378	.0590 (37) P=.364	-.2148 (37) P=.101	-.2643 (37) P=.057	-.0383 (38) P=.410	-.1461 (37) P=.194	-.1493 (35) P=.196	-.1800 (33) P=.158	.0061 (41) P=.485	-.1625 (41) P=.155	.2281 (39) P=.081	-.1374 (41) P=.196	.0696 (41) P=.333	.0418 (41) P=.398	.0316 (41) P=.423
V.29	.1112 (25) P=.298	.1415 (25) P=.250	.2853 (25) P=.083	.4685 (25) P=.009	.3068 (25) P=.068	.3805 (25) P=.030	.3509 (25) P=.043	.3086 (25) P=.067	-.1117 (25) P=.297	.2535 (25) P=.111	-.2687 (25) P=.097	.1810 (25) P=.193	-.4257 (25) P=.017	.1690 (25) P=.210	-.0677 (25) P=.374

V3.17	V3.18	V3.19	V3.21	V3.4	V3.5	V3.6	V3.7	V3.8	V3.9	V3.10	V3.1	V3.2	V3.3	V4.1
.3479	.1351	.1270	-.4709	-.1581	.6975	-.0824	-.1385	.0652	.6689	-.5716	-.2966	.0572	.6604	.6553
(26)	(37)	(39)	(41)	(37)	(38)	(40)	(38)	(39)	(39)	(16)	(41)	(41)	(40)	(41)
P= .041	P= .213	P= .221	P= .001	P= .175	P= .001	P= .307	P= .204	P= .347	P= .001	P= .010	P= .030	P= .361	P= .001	P= .001
.0597	.0748	.1403	-.1081	.0939	.0405	.1532	-.0549	.1912	.1157	.3252	.0779	.0556	.2203	.3014
(25)	(35)	(36)	(37)	(34)	(36)	(36)	(36)	(36)	(36)	(15)	(37)	(37)	(37)	(37)
P= .388	P= .335	P= .207	P= .262	P= .299	P= .407	P= .186	P= .375	P= .132	P= .251	P= .118	P= .323	P= .372	P= .095	P= .035
.1568	.5038	.1975	-.0479	-.1504	.5428	.2097	-.4428	.3590	.2420	.5434	-.0795	.2787	.1428	.1177
(25)	(37)	(38)	(40)	(36)	(37)	(39)	(37)	(38)	(38)	(15)	(40)	(40)	(39)	(40)
P= .227	P= .001	P= .117	P= .384	P= .191	P= .001	P= .100	P= .003	P= .013	P= .072	P= .018	P= .313	P= .041	P= .193	P= .235
.2163	.6909	-.0309	-.2232	-.0603	.0148	.3738	-.5178	.3596	-.1262	.4616	-.0209	.4008	-.1105	.0938
(26)	(37)	(39)	(41)	(37)	(38)	(40)	(38)	(39)	(39)	(16)	(41)	(41)	(40)	(41)
P= .144	P= .001	P= .426	P= .080	P= .361	P= .465	P= .009	P= .001	P= .012	P= .222	P= .036	P= .448	P= .005	P= .249	P= .280
.4483	-.0763	-.0088	-.1448	.1326	-.1161	.3332	-.1685	-.0214	.4251	.5035	.1688	-.1293	.2281	.2024
(25)	(37)	(38)	(40)	(36)	(37)	(39)	(37)	(38)	(38)	(15)	(40)	(40)	(39)	(40)
P= .012	P= .327	P= .479	P= .186	P= .220	P= .247	P= .019	P= .159	P= .449	P= .004	P= .028	P= .149	P= .213	P= .081	P= .105
.0384	.7895	.0486	-.3202	-.0489	-.0765	.1034	-.1814	.6189	.1610	.4072	-.0075	.8104	.1899	.1371
(25)	(36)	(37)	(39)	(35)	(37)	(38)	(37)	(37)	(38)	(15)	(39)	(39)	(38)	(39)
P= .428	P= .001	P= .388	P= .023	P= .390	P= .326	P= .268	P= .141	P= .001	P= .167	P= .066	P= .482	P= .001	P= .127	P= .203
.3829	.9171	.1095	-.4637	-.0819	.2445	.1868	-.3473	.6477	.2797	.5291	-.0040	.7719	.1966	.4328
(25)	(37)	(38)	(40)	(36)	(37)	(39)	(37)	(38)	(38)	(15)	(40)	(40)	(39)	(40)
P= .029	P= .001	P= .257	P= .001	P= .318	P= .072	P= .127	P= .018	P= .001	P= .045	P= .021	P= .490	P= .001	P= .115	P= .003
.2094	.0718	-.1681	-.2817	-.0551	.1604	.1803	-.1461	-.0203	.4127	.0850	.3298	.0463	.2487	.1603
(25)	(37)	(38)	(40)	(36)	(37)	(39)	(37)	(38)	(38)	(15)	(40)	(40)	(39)	(40)
P= .158	P= .336	P= .157	P= .039	P= .375	P= .171	P= .136	P= .194	P= .452	P= .005	P= .382	P= .019	P= .388	P= .063	P= .162
.4683	.4511	-.1435	-.2156	.0360	.0864	.1499	-.3730	.2256	.4974	.4478	.0342	.4060	.1113	.2372
(25)	(37)	(38)	(40)	(36)	(37)	(39)	(37)	(38)	(38)	(15)	(40)	(40)	(39)	(40)
P= .009	P= .003	P= .195	P= .091	P= .417	P= .305	P= .181	P= .011	P= .087	P= .001	P= .047	P= .417	P= .005	P= .250	P= .070
.3926	.4474	.1169	-.4573	.1833	.2594	.0902	-.4926	.2665	.1777	.7556	.1026	.4438	-.0534	.4432
(25)	(37)	(38)	(40)	(36)	(37)	(39)	(37)	(38)	(38)	(15)	(40)	(40)	(39)	(40)
P= .026	P= .003	P= .242	P= .002	P= .142	P= .061	P= .293	P= .001	P= .053	P= .143	P= .001	P= .264	P= .002	P= .373	P= .002
.1554	.0620	-.2776	.0320	-.0999	.0366	-.2404	-.1833	-.1949	.1262	.3598	-.0344	.1292	.1603	.3091
(25)	(37)	(38)	(40)	(36)	(37)	(39)	(37)	(38)	(38)	(15)	(40)	(40)	(39)	(40)
P= .229	P= .358	P= .046	P= .422	P= .281	P= .415	P= .070	P= .139	P= .121	P= .225	P= .094	P= .417	P= .213	P= .165	P= .026
-.3990	-.0647	.3044	-.4834	.3112	.2487	.0052	-.2281	.3316	.2798	.1688	.7015	-.1042	-.1512	-.0144
(20)	(31)	(32)	(34)	(31)	(31)	(33)	(31)	(32)	(32)	(13)	(34)	(34)	(33)	(34)
P= .041	P= .365	P= .045	P= .002	P= .044	P= .089	P= .489	P= .109	P= .032	P= .060	P= .291	P= .001	P= .279	P= .200	P= .468
.1498	.0447	-.2516	.0790	.3396	.3113	.1105	-.0292	-.0675	.1468	-.2289	-.1424	.0702	-.0350	.0008
(23)	(30)	(32)	(32)	(31)	(31)	(32)	(31)	(32)	(31)	(14)	(32)	(32)	(32)	(32)
P= .248	P= .407	P= .082	P= .334	P= .031	P= .044	P= .274	P= .438	P= .357	P= .215	P= .216	P= .218	P= .351	P= .425	P= .498
.1407	-.0614	.0048	-.3611	-.2485	.9574	-.5670	-.0212	-.0534	.9830	-.6520	-.8606	.1429	.9834	.8477
(24)	(31)	(34)	(34)	(33)	(34)	(34)	(34)	(34)	(34)	(14)	(34)	(34)	(34)	(34)
P= .256	P= .371	P= .489	P= .018	P= .082	P= .001	P= .001	P= .453	P= .382	P= .001	P= .006	P= .001	P= .210	P= .001	P= .001
.1501	-.0819	.0309	-.3360	-.3037	.9607	-.5528	-.0171	-.0146	.9998	-.6264	-.5147	.1646	.9998	.8471
(26)	(32)	(35)	(35)	(34)	(35)	(35)	(35)	(35)	(35)	(15)	(35)	(35)	(35)	(35)
P= .232	P= .328	P= .430	P= .024	P= .040	P= .001	P= .001	P= .461	P= .467	P= .001	P= .006	P= .001	P= .172	P= .001	P= .001
.1075	.0905	-.1468	-.1537	-.1523	-.2086	.2827	-.0364	.1312	-.2537	.3168	.0457	-.0014	-.2434	-.1830
(26)	(36)	(38)	(39)	(36)	(37)	(38)	(37)	(38)	(37)	(16)	(39)	(39)	(39)	(39)
P= .301	P= .300	P= .190	P= .175	P= .188	P= .108	P= .043	P= .415	P= .216	P= .065	P= .116	P= .391	P= .497	P= .068	P= .132
-.1565	-.2414	-.0207	.3484	.3104	-.9622	.5008	.0119	.0101	-.9991	.6147	.5195	-.1739	-.9991	-.8368
(26)	(35)	(38)	(38)	(36)	(37)	(38)	(37)	(38)	(37)	(16)	(38)	(38)	(38)	(38)
P= .223	P= .081	P= .451	P= .016	P= .033	P= .001	P= .001	P= .472	P= .476	P= .001	P= .006	P= .001	P= .148	P= .001	P= .001
-.1434	-.1175	.4508	-.1411	-.0168	.3150	-.2087	.2765	.0023	.3291	-.6341	-.0421	-.0200	.3318	.1479
(26)	(34)	(37)	(37)	(35)	(36)	(37)	(36)	(37)	(36)	(16)	(37)	(37)	(37)	(37)
P= .242	P= .254	P= .003	P= .202	P= .462	P= .031	P= .108	P= .051	P= .494	P= .025	P= .004	P= .402	P= .453	P= .022	P= .191
-.0056	.3615	-.3279	-.1212	-.1446	-.1594	.2424	-.3100	-.0598	-.2294	.3705	.0357	.1373	-.2352	.0424
(25)	(32)	(35)	(35)	(34)	(34)	(35)	(34)	(35)	(34)	(15)	(35)	(35)	(35)	(35)
P= .489	P= .021	P= .027	P= .244	P= .207	P= .184	P= .080	P= .037	P= .367	P= .096	P= .087	P= .419	P= .216	P= .087	P= .405
.1447	.0052	-.0397	.1952	-.1267	-.4322	.3822	.1672	-.0039	-.4320	.3692	-.0098	-.1324	-.4218	-.4743
(24)	(32)	(34)	(35)	(33)	(33)	(34)	(33)	(34)	(33)	(15)	(35)	(35)	(35)	(35)
P= .250	P= .489	P= .412	P= .131	P= .241	P= .006	P= .013	P= .176	P= .491	P= .006	P= .088	P= .478	P= .224	P= .006	P= .002
.0293	.0301	.1291	-.0837	.4438	-.2052	.2444	-.3409	.1023	-.2231	.1941	.2810	.0677	-.2131	.0343
(25)	(32)	(34)	(35)	(33)	(34)	(34)	(34)	(34)	(34)	(15)	(35)	(35)	(35)	(35)
P= .445	P= .435	P= .233	P= .316	P= .005	P= .122	P= .082	P= .024	P= .282	P= .102	P= .244	P= .051	P= .350	P= .109	P= .422
-.0423	.3306	.1309	-.2777	-.0795	.0941	-.0140	-.3339	.2978	.1373	.2735	.0927	.2532	.1375	.1616
(26)	(37)	(39)	(40)	(37)	(38)	(39)	(38)	(39)	(38)	(16)	(40)	(40)	(40)	(40)
P= .419	P= .023	P= .213	P= .041	P= .320	P= .287	P= .466	P= .020	P= .033	P= .206	P= .153	P= .285	P= .057	P= .199	P= .160
-.2214	.0170	.0313	-.1679	.0749	.2593	.1202	-.1902	.1473	.0704	.2105	.1981	-.0612	.0480	.1372
(25)	(35)	(37)	(37)	(35)	(36)	(37)	(36)	(37)	(36)	(15)	(37)	(37)	(37)	(37)
P= .144	P= .461	P= .427	P= .160	P= .335	P= .063	P= .239	P= .133	P= .192	P= .342	P= .226	P= .120	P= .359	P= .389	P= .209
-.1328	-.0668	-.0188	.0283	-.0279	-.0518	.0749	-.0768	-.0414	-.0442	.3130	-.0276	-.0632	-.0838	-.1023
(25)	(37)	(38)	(40)	(36)	(37)	(39)	(37)	(38)	(38)	(15)	(40)	(40)	(39)	(40)
P= .263	P= .347	P= .455	P= .431	P= .436	P= .380	P= .325	P= .326	P= .402	P= .396	P= .128	P= .433	P= .349	P= .306	P= .265
.0870	-.0338	-.2624	-.4944	-.0638	.3699	-.2581	-.1028	-.0739	.4066	-.3349	.2126	.1312	.3949	.3539
(23)	(32)	(34)	(35)	(33)	(33)	(34)	(33)	(34)	(33)	(16)	(35)	(35)	(35)	(35)
P= .347	P= .427	P= .067	P= .001	P= .362	P= .017	P= .070	P= .285	P= .339	P= .009	P= .102	P= .110	P= .226	P= .009	P= .019
.1291	-.0368	-.0640	-.0047	.6088	-.1400	.1376	-.2227	.0470	-.1844	.1207	.3875	-.0791	-.1829	-.0367
(26)	(36)	(38)	(39)	(36)	(37)	(38)	(37)	(38)	(37)	(16)	(39)	(39)	(39)	(39)
P= .265	P= .416	P= .351	P= .489	P= .001	P= .204	P= .205	P= .093	P= .390	P= .137	P= .328	P= .007	P= .316	P= .132	P= .412
-.0970	.0744	-.1087	-.0607	-.7231	.0629	-.2435	.2541	-.0286	.1124	.0315	-.1816	.0951	.1172	.0156
(25)	(36)	(38)	(39)	(36)	(37)	(38)	(37)	(38)	(37)	(15)	(39)	(39)	(39)	(39)
P= .322	P= .333	P= .258	P= .357	P= .001	P= .356	P= .070	P= .065	P= .432	P= .254	P= .456	P= .134	P= .282	P= .239	P= .462
.1500	-.0482	.0487	-.3400	-.3081	.9609	-.5141	-.0253	-.0331	.9967	-.6026	-.5208	.1588	.9967	.8397
(25)	(32)	(34)	(35)	(33)	(33)	(34)	(33)	(34)	(33)	(15)	(35)	(35)	(35)	(35)
P= .237	P= .397	P= .392	P= .023	P= .041	P= .001	P= .001	P= .444	P= .426	P= .001	P= .009	P= .001	P= .181	P= .001	P= .001
-.0815	-.1439	-.1574	.1179	.1449	-.1928	-.1337	.0388	-.1569	-.2152	-.1092	.2152	-.1408	-.2130	-.3089
(25)	(31)	(34)	(34)	(33)	(34)	(34)	(34)	(34)	(34)	(15)	(34)	(34)	(34)	(34)
P= .349	P= .220	P= .187	P= .253	P= .211	P= .137	P= .225	P= .414	P= .188	P= .111	P= .349	P= .111	P= .213	P= .113	P= .038
.0089	-.1464	-.0330	-.2330	-.2740	.5537	-.0917	-.0820	-.0307	.5902	-.2108	-.2493	.0134	.5921	.4446
(26)	(37)	(39)	(41)	(37)	(38)	(40)	(38)	(39)	(39)	(16)	(41)	(41)	(40)	(41)
P= .483	P= .194	P= .421	P= .071	P= .050	P= .001	P= .287	P= .312	P= .427	P= .001	P= .217	P= .058	P= .467	P= .001	P= .002
.0904	-.0564	-.0770	-.2537	-.2724	.8403	-.4212	-.0852	-.0891	.8776	-.4799	-.4695	.0773	.8772	.6960
(26)	(37)	(39)	(41)	(37)	(38)	(40)	(38)	(39)	(39)	(16)	(41)	(41)	(40)	(41)
P= .330	P= .370	P= .321	P= .055	P= .051	P= .001	P= .003	P= .306	P= .295	P= .001	P= .030	P= .001	P= .315	P= .001	P= .001
-.1905	-.0146	-.0031	.3477	.3421	-.9713	.6599	.0649	.0715	-.9940	.6565	.5718	-.1548	-.9939	-.9066
(19)	(24)	(25)	(25)	(24)	(25)	(25)	(25)	(25)	(25)	(13)	(25)	(25)	(25)	(25)
P= .217	P= .473	P= .494	P= .044	P= .051	P= .001	P= .001	P= .379	P= .367	P= .001	P= .007	P= .001	P= .230	P= .001	P= .001

	V3.17	V3.18	V3.19	V3.21	V3.4	V3.5	V3.6	V3.7	V3.8	V3.9	V3.10	V3.1	V3.2	V3.3	V4.1
1	.2963 (23) P=.085	.0037 (29) P=.492	.0878 (31) P=.319	-.2909 (31) P=.056	-.1731 (30) P=.180	.8158 (31) P=.001	-.4171 (31) P=.010	.0153 (31) P=.467	.0398 (31) P=.416	.8494 (31) P=.001	-.5146 (14) P=.030	-.4100 (31) P=.011	.1718 (31) P=.178	.8506 (31) P=.001	.7820 (31) P=.001
2	-.2663 (25) P=.099	-.0218 (36) P=.450	.1056 (38) P=.264	-.3257 (40) P=.020	.2531 (36) P=.068	-.0914 (37) P=.295	.1784 (39) P=.139	-.2267 (37) P=.089	.3276 (38) P=.022	-.1140 (38) P=.248	.3078 (15) P=.132	.6449 (40) P=.001	-.0152 (40) P=.463	-.1129 (39) P=.247	-.0261 (40) P=.436
3	.3021 (26) P=.067	.9151 (37) P=.001	.0832 (39) P=.307	-.3466 (40) P=.014	.0352 (37) P=.418	-.0371 (39) P=.413	.1275 (39) P=.220	-.2485 (38) P=.066	.6886 (39) P=.001	-.0540 (38) P=.374	.3916 (16) P=.067	.0947 (40) P=.281	.9633 (40) P=.001	-.0577 (40) P=.362	.0991 (40) P=.271
4	.0200 (25) P=.462	.7499 (34) P=.001	.0065 (37) P=.485	-.3388 (37) P=.020	.1275 (36) P=.229	-.1683 (36) P=.163	.1597 (37) P=.173	-.2806 (36) P=.049	.5574 (37) P=.001	-.1194 (36) P=.244	.3692 (16) P=.080	.2116 (37) P=.104	.7442 (37) P=.001	-.1117 (37) P=.255	-.0295 (37) P=.431
5	-.0315 (26) P=.439	.1353 (37) P=.212	-.2426 (39) P=.068	.3671 (40) P=.010	.0124 (37) P=.471	-.2667 (38) P=.053	-.0787 (39) P=.317	-.3205 (38) P=.025	-.3261 (39) P=.021	-.2967 (38) P=.035	.4630 (16) P=.035	.0061 (40) P=.485	-.0429 (40) P=.396	-.2526 (40) P=.058	-.2901 (40) P=.035
6	-.2111 (25) P=.155	-.0427 (35) P=.404	-.0263 (38) P=.438	-.0706 (38) P=.337	-.2399 (37) P=.076	.2093 (37) P=.107	-.1773 (38) P=.143	-.1189 (37) P=.242	-.0889 (38) P=.298	.2039 (37) P=.113	-.1184 (16) P=.331	-.0827 (38) P=.311	-.0776 (38) P=.322	.2050 (38) P=.108	.0550 (38) P=.371
7	-.1900 (26) P=.176	.2941 (34) P=.046	-.1642 (36) P=.169	-.2297 (37) P=.086	.0506 (34) P=.388	-.3087 (36) P=.033	.2964 (36) P=.040	-.4547 (36) P=.003	.2918 (36) P=.042	-.3863 (36) P=.010	.6156 (16) P=.006	.2702 (37) P=.053	.2421 (37) P=.074	-.3511 (37) P=.017	-.1244 (37) P=.232
8	-.1703 (25) P=.208	.1829 (30) P=.167	.3086 (33) P=.040	-.3041 (33) P=.043	.0598 (33) P=.370	-.3079 (33) P=.041	.3255 (33) P=.032	-.1587 (33) P=.189	.3307 (33) P=.030	-.3233 (33) P=.033	.3922 (15) P=.074	.6020 (33) P=.001	-.0515 (33) P=.388	-.3240 (33) P=.033	-.1455 (33) P=.209
9	.1629 (25) P=.218	.5043 (28) P=.003	.1212 (31) P=.258	-.3628 (31) P=.022	-.2947 (31) P=.054	.9712 (31) P=.001	-.5650 (31) P=.001	-.0335 (31) P=.429	-.0037 (31) P=.492	.9988 (31) P=.001	-.6370 (14) P=.007	-.5217 (31) P=.001	.1913 (31) P=.151	.9987 (31) P=.001	.8548 (31) P=.001
10	-.1064 (21) P=.323	.2543 (29) P=.092	-.2267 (31) P=.110	-.0699 (32) P=.352	.0379 (30) P=.421	-.2754 (31) P=.067	-.1405 (32) P=.221	-.0568 (31) P=.381	.0922 (31) P=.311	-.0689 (32) P=.354	.3857 (13) P=.097	.1398 (32) P=.223	.3193 (32) P=.037	.3524 (32) P=.026	-.1070 (32) P=.280
11	.3916 (26) P=.024	-.0239 (37) P=.444	-.2291 (39) P=.080	-.0476 (40) P=.385	-.3678 (37) P=.013	.1559 (38) P=.175	.0063 (39) P=.485	-.1068 (38) P=.262	-.1173 (39) P=.239	.1272 (38) P=.223	.0694 (16) P=.399	-.2435 (40) P=.065	-.0223 (40) P=.446	.1284 (40) P=.215	.1156 (40) P=.239
12	.1272 (22) P=.286	-.0883 (29) P=.324	-.1432 (31) P=.221	-.3041 (31) P=.048	-.3493 (30) P=.029	.8050 (31) P=.001	-.6782 (31) P=.001	-.1000 (31) P=.296	-.1918 (31) P=.151	.8283 (31) P=.001	-.6436 (15) P=.005	-.3572 (31) P=.024	.1035 (31) P=.290	.8281 (31) P=.001	.7817 (31) P=.001
13	.1549 (26) P=.225	-.1052 (34) P=.277	-.0344 (37) P=.420	-.3209 (37) P=.026	-.3159 (35) P=.032	.9586 (37) P=.001	-.5554 (37) P=.001	-.0207 (37) P=.452	-.0352 (37) P=.418	.9968 (37) P=.001	-.6336 (16) P=.004	-.5174 (37) P=.001	.1552 (37) P=.179	.9969 (37) P=.001	.8209 (37) P=.001
14	-.3196 (26) P=.056	.0151 (36) P=.465	.1648 (38) P=.161	.2087 (39) P=.101	-.0641 (37) P=.353	-.2412 (37) P=.075	-.0277 (38) P=.434	.2348 (37) P=.081	-.0919 (38) P=.292	-.2459 (37) P=.071	.0759 (16) P=.390	.1768 (39) P=.141	-.1098 (39) P=.253	-.2414 (39) P=.069	-.3753 (39) P=.009
15	.3583 (25) P=.039	-.1484 (32) P=.209	-.0658 (35) P=.354	.0488 (35) P=.390	-.2993 (34) P=.043	-.0675 (35) P=.350	.1241 (35) P=.239	.0845 (35) P=.315	-.1280 (35) P=.232	-.0495 (35) P=.389	.0896 (16) P=.371	-.0387 (35) P=.413	-.1968 (35) P=.129	-.0470 (35) P=.394	-.0979 (35) P=.288
16	.0132 (26) P=.475	.2286 (37) P=.087	-.1214 (39) P=.231	.1886 (40) P=.122	-.1095 (37) P=.259	-.1225 (38) P=.232	-.0442 (39) P=.395	-.1920 (38) P=.124	-.0562 (39) P=.367	-.1494 (38) P=.185	.3675 (16) P=.081	.0301 (40) P=.427	.1729 (40) P=.143	-.1535 (40) P=.172	-.2243 (40) P=.082
17	.1790 (23) P=.207	.3303 (32) P=.032	.0440 (33) P=.404	-.3608 (34) P=.018	-.3649 (31) P=.022	.7814 (33) P=.001	-.5720 (33) P=.001	-.1927 (33) P=.141	.0404 (33) P=.412	.7786 (33) P=.001	-.5640 (15) P=.014	-.2939 (34) P=.046	.1623 (34) P=.179	.7549 (34) P=.001	.7249 (34) P=.001
18	.0643 (26) P=.378	-.0995 (37) P=.279	.0814 (39) P=.311	-.4030 (40) P=.005	-.2328 (37) P=.083	.8682 (38) P=.001	-.4450 (39) P=.002	.0117 (38) P=.472	.0531 (39) P=.374	.9078 (38) P=.001	-.5830 (16) P=.009	-.1808 (40) P=.132	.1121 (40) P=.245	.9072 (40) P=.001	.7160 (40) P=.001
19	.1247 (25) P=.276	.3237 (37) P=.025	-.5553 (38) P=.001	-.3285 (40) P=.019	-.2540 (36) P=.067	.1125 (37) P=.254	.1863 (39) P=.128	-.3762 (37) P=.011	-.0668 (38) P=.345	.3313 (38) P=.021	.4405 (15) P=.050	-.0556 (40) P=.367	.2642 (40) P=.050	.4516 (39) P=.002	.3887 (40) P=.007
20	-.2112 (25) P=.155	.2283 (37) P=.087	.1944 (38) P=.121	.1659 (40) P=.153	.0773 (36) P=.327	-.4149 (37) P=.005	-.1376 (39) P=.202	-.0681 (37) P=.344	-.1177 (38) P=.241	-.1027 (38) P=.270	-.1929 (15) P=.246	.1697 (40) P=.148	.1716 (40) P=.145	.0617 (39) P=.354	-.1819 (40) P=.131
21	-.2571 (25) P=.107	.0369 (36) P=.415	-.1148 (37) P=.249	-.0053 (39) P=.487	-.1161 (35) P=.253	-.0717 (36) P=.339	-.2008 (38) P=.113	-.0096 (36) P=.478	.0051 (37) P=.488	.0724 (37) P=.335	-.2476 (15) P=.187	.0078 (39) P=.481	.0809 (39) P=.312	.0859 (38) P=.304	-.2246 (39) P=.085
22	.0771 (26) P=.354	.1911 (37) P=.129	-.1556 (39) P=.172	.2965 (41) P=.030	.3602 (37) P=.014	-.6274 (38) P=.001	.2721 (40) P=.045	-.1115 (38) P=.253	-.0603 (39) P=.358	-.5779 (39) P=.001	.2873 (16) P=.140	-.2634 (41) P=.048	.0024 (41) P=.494	-.5752 (40) P=.001	-.4327 (41) P=.002
23	.0547 (25) P=.398	.3215 (35) P=.030	.5022 (37) P=.001	-.4795 (37) P=.001	.0843 (35) P=.315	.1052 (36) P=.271	.2769 (37) P=.049	-.1809 (37) P=.146	.5519 (37) P=.001	.0856 (36) P=.310	.4372 (16) P=.045	.1570 (37) P=.177	.2349 (37) P=.081	.0750 (37) P=.329	.1908 (37) P=.129
24	-.3566 (23) P=.047	.2745 (31) P=.068	.1153 (32) P=.265	-.2122 (32) P=.122	.1173 (31) P=.265	-.2238 (32) P=.109	.4390 (32) P=.006	-.1165 (32) P=.263	.3414 (32) P=.028	-.3449 (32) P=.027	.3225 (16) P=.112	-.4032 (32) P=.011	.0768 (32) P=.338	-.3441 (32) P=.027	-.1972 (32) P=.140
25	-.2604 (26) P=.099	.2142 (37) P=.102	-.2859 (39) P=.039	.1935 (41) P=.113	.1299 (37) P=.222	-.2505 (38) P=.065	.0477 (40) P=.385	-.0642 (38) P=.352	-.0083 (39) P=.480	-.2249 (39) P=.084	.3089 (16) P=.122	-.0325 (41) P=.420	-.2230 (41) P=.081	-.2356 (40) P=.072	-.2425 (41) P=.063
26	-.0425 (26) P=.418	-.1636 (37) P=.167	.3605 (39) P=.012	.0133 (41) P=.467	.0821 (37) P=.315	-.0813 (38) P=.314	.0255 (40) P=.438	-.0427 (38) P=.400	-.0131 (39) P=.469	-.1138 (39) P=.245	-.1307 (16) P=.315	.0476 (41) P=.384	-.1371 (41) P=.196	-.1114 (40) P=.247	-.3090 (41) P=.025
27	.0022 (26) P=.496	-.0188 (37) P=.456	.5650 (39) P=.001	-.0897 (41) P=.288	.3830 (37) P=.010	-.2385 (38) P=.075	.4135 (40) P=.004	-.0922 (38) P=.291	.2672 (39) P=.050	-.1791 (39) P=.138	.3077 (16) P=.123	.3587 (41) P=.011	-.0189 (41) P=.453	-.1762 (40) P=.138	-.1507 (41) P=.174
28	-.0542 (26) P=.396	-.2061 (37) P=.110	.1510 (39) P=.179	.1730 (41) P=.140	.2542 (37) P=.064	-.1487 (38) P=.187	.0828 (40) P=.306	.3922 (38) P=.007	-.0129 (39) P=.469	-.1571 (39) P=.170	.0476 (16) P=.431	-.0371 (41) P=.409	-.1861 (41) P=.122	-.1575 (40) P=.166	-.2335 (41) P=.071
29	-.2165 (25) P=.149	.1527 (33) P=.198	.1691 (36) P=.162	-.4670 (36) P=.002	.2907 (35) P=.045	-.0825 (36) P=.316	.0862 (36) P=.309	-.2467 (36) P=.073	.3989 (36) P=.008	-.0698 (36) P=.343	.2224 (16) P=.204	.8252 (36) P=.001	.1227 (36) P=.238	-.0720 (36) P=.338	-.0144 (36) P=.467
30	.0473 (25) P=.411	.7058 (33) P=.001	-.1196 (36) P=.244	-.2877 (36) P=.044	.0336 (35) P=.424	-.0682 (36) P=.346	.1999 (36) P=.121	-.4148 (36) P=.006	.4022 (36) P=.008	-.0647 (36) P=.354	.4446 (16) P=.042	.0442 (36) P=.399	.5887 (36) P=.001	-.0674 (36) P=.348	.0520 (36) P=.382
31	-.0063 (26) P=.488	-.1770 (37) P=.147	-.0519 (39) P=.377	.0617 (41) P=.351	.4555 (37) P=.002	-.1064 (38) P=.262	-.0849 (40) P=.301	-.0966 (38) P=.282	-.1185 (39) P=.236	-.1429 (39) P=.193	-.0028 (16) P=.496	-.2321 (41) P=.072	-.1265 (41) P=.215	-.1369 (40) P=.200	-.0299 (41) P=.426
32	-.1088 (26) P=.298	-.2073 (37) P=.109	.0581 (39) P=.363	-.1165 (41) P=.234	.4599 (37) P=.002	-.0660 (38) P=.347	-.0045 (40) P=.489	.2085 (38) P=.104	.0676 (39) P=.341	-.0315 (39) P=.424	.1326 (16) P=.312	.3893 (41) P=.006	-.2056 (41) P=.099	-.0236 (40) P=.443	-.1061 (41) P=.255
33	.0297 (26) P=.443	-.0372 (37) P=.413	-.2884 (39) P=.037	-.0576 (41) P=.360	-.1471 (37) P=.192	.3515 (38) P=.015	-.1242 (40) P=.222	-.0312 (38) P=.426	-.2085 (39) P=.101	.3526 (39) P=.014	-.5277 (16) P=.018	-.3501 (41) P=.012	-.1290 (41) P=.211	.3545 (40) P=.012	.2849 (41) P=.036

	V2.16	V2.22	V2.18	V2.20	V2.19	V2.21	V2.23	V2.17	V3.11	V3.20	V3.15	V3.12	V3.13	V3.14	V3.16
V.30	-.0196 (31) P=.458	-.0574 (31) P=.380	-.3801 (31) P=.017	-.4364 (31) P=.007	-.3230 (31) P=.038	-.3716 (31) P=.020	-.4410 (31) P=.007	-.2187 (31) P=.119	-.0104 (31) P=.478	-.1718 (31) P=.178	.1721 (31) P=.177	-.0119 (31) P=.475	.2918 (31) P=.056	-.0204 (31) P=.457	.0134 (31) P=.471
V.16	.1491 (40) P=.179	.1170 (36) P=.248	.0180 (36) P=.458	.2454 (36) P=.075	.2291 (37) P=.086	.0604 (36) P=.363	.3170 (34) P=.034	.1649 (32) P=.184	-.3583 (40) P=.012	.5409 (40) P=.001	.0705 (38) P=.337	.2784 (40) P=.041	-.1538 (40) P=.172	.3189 (40) P=.022	-.0176 (40) P=.457
V.20	-.3392 (40) P=.016	-.1334 (37) P=.216	-.2320 (37) P=.084	.0538 (37) P=.376	-.1954 (38) P=.120	.1072 (37) P=.264	-.2582 (35) P=.067	.2807 (32) P=.057	-.1202 (40) P=.230	.0027 (40) P=.493	.6393 (39) P=.001	-.0939 (40) P=.282	.0436 (40) P=.395	.0471 (40) P=.386	-.0846 (40) P=.302
V.21	-.1971 (37) P=.121	-.1818 (36) P=.144	-.1276 (36) P=.229	.0462 (36) P=.395	-.1627 (37) P=.168	.1811 (36) P=.145	-.3347 (34) P=.027	.2156 (32) P=.118	-.0262 (37) P=.439	-.0085 (37) P=.480	.7144 (37) P=.001	-.1475 (37) P=.192	-.1565 (37) P=.178	.0582 (37) P=.366	-.0222 (37) P=.448
V.22	-.2932 (40) P=.033	-.1307 (37) P=.220	.0557 (37) P=.372	-.0259 (37) P=.439	.0055 (38) P=.487	.1035 (37) P=.271	-.0678 (35) P=.349	-.0847 (33) P=.320	-.2869 (40) P=.036	-.1377 (40) P=.198	.2071 (39) P=.103	-.1145 (40) P=.241	.0340 (40) P=.418	-.1743 (40) P=.141	.6371 (40) P=.001
V.23	-.1051 (38) P=.265	-.0167 (36) P=.462	-.1413 (36) P=.206	-.1641 (36) P=.169	-.0576 (37) P=.368	-.0055 (36) P=.487	-.2326 (34) P=.093	-.0237 (32) P=.449	-.1289 (38) P=.220	-.1165 (38) P=.243	.2493 (38) P=.066	-.0870 (38) P=.302	.0669 (38) P=.345	.1456 (38) P=.192	.5521 (38) P=.001
V.24	-.1930 (37) P=.126	-.0678 (35) P=.349	-.1199 (35) P=.246	.0780 (35) P=.328	-.0459 (35) P=.397	.1840 (35) P=.145	-.1052 (34) P=.277	.3157 (33) P=.037	-.0175 (37) P=.459	.1784 (37) P=.145	.4619 (36) P=.002	.1070 (37) P=.264	.1192 (37) P=.241	.3484 (37) P=.017	.4921 (37) P=.001
V.26	.0731 (33) P=.343	.3963 (32) P=.012	.0996 (32) P=.294	.3275 (32) P=.034	.1796 (32) P=.163	.2806 (32) P=.060	.1425 (31) P=.222	.2730 (30) P=.072	-.3519 (33) P=.022	.5933 (33) P=.001	-.0155 (33) P=.466	.4774 (33) P=.002	.3226 (33) P=.034	.3528 (33) P=.022	-.0401 (33) P=.412
V.27	-.0796 (31) P=.335	-.1326 (31) P=.239	-.2259 (31) P=.111	-.3131 (31) P=.043	-.2651 (31) P=.075	-.2684 (31) P=.072	-.2678 (31) P=.073	-.2464 (30) P=.095	.0775 (31) P=.339	-.1616 (31) P=.192	.2269 (31) P=.110	-.0948 (31) P=.306	.3171 (31) P=.041	-.1297 (31) P=.243	-.0350 (31) P=.426
V.25	-.2003 (32) P=.136	-.3270 (30) P=.039	.0412 (30) P=.414	-.1131 (30) P=.276	-.2662 (30) P=.078	.1893 (30) P=.158	-.4968 (29) P=.003	.1353 (28) P=.246	.1166 (32) P=.263	-.0226 (32) P=.451	.5157 (31) P=.001	-.1650 (32) P=.183	-.2104 (32) P=.124	-.1272 (32) P=.244	.1531 (32) P=.201
V.34	-.0527 (40) P=.373	.0357 (37) P=.417	-.0538 (37) P=.376	-.0859 (37) P=.307	.0027 (38) P=.494	.1018 (37) P=.274	-.3889 (35) P=.010	.0714 (33) P=.347	.0377 (40) P=.409	-.2176 (40) P=.089	.3449 (39) P=.016	-.1565 (40) P=.167	.0684 (40) P=.337	-.0789 (40) P=.314	.5196 (40) P=.001
V.35	-.1504 (31) P=.210	-.1843 (31) P=.160	-.2673 (31) P=.073	-.2570 (31) P=.081	-.0013 (31) P=.497	-.1577 (31) P=.198	-.1926 (30) P=.154	-.0992 (30) P=.301	-.2461 (31) P=.091	-.0287 (31) P=.439	.1651 (31) P=.187	-.1016 (31) P=.293	.5065 (31) P=.002	.1731 (31) P=.176	.2151 (31) P=.123
V.36	-.0719 (37) P=.336	-.1401 (36) P=.208	-.2160 (36) P=.103	-.3440 (36) P=.020	-.2482 (36) P=.072	-.2764 (36) P=.051	-.2943 (35) P=.046	-.2502 (33) P=.080	.0804 (37) P=.318	-.1625 (37) P=.168	.2300 (37) P=.085	-.1102 (37) P=.258	.1732 (37) P=.153	-.1366 (37) P=.210	.0334 (37) P=.422
V.37	-.2492 (39) P=.063	.0211 (36) P=.451	.3711 (36) P=.013	.2016 (36) P=.119	-.0405 (37) P=.406	.3030 (36) P=.036	-.0809 (34) P=.325	-.0049 (32) P=.489	-.1508 (39) P=.180	.1595 (39) P=.166	-.0088 (38) P=.479	.2603 (39) P=.055	.1270 (39) P=.221	-.0567 (39) P=.366	.3718 (39) P=.010
V.38	.0274 (35) P=.438	.0528 (34) P=.383	.0156 (34) P=.465	-.0156 (34) P=.465	-.0112 (34) P=.475	.0397 (34) P=.412	-.2111 (33) P=.119	.1386 (32) P=.225	.1995 (35) P=.125	-.1652 (35) P=.171	.2066 (35) P=.117	-.1066 (35) P=.271	.0331 (35) P=.425	-.2362 (35) P=.086	.3868 (35) P=.011
V.32	-.3675 (40) P=.010	-.1443 (37) P=.197	-.1182 (37) P=.243	-.1219 (37) P=.236	-.1874 (38) P=.130	.0841 (37) P=.310	-.3594 (35) P=.017	-.1242 (33) P=.246	-.1327 (40) P=.207	-.1417 (40) P=.192	.3285 (39) P=.021	-.0326 (40) P=.421	.0754 (40) P=.322	-.0556 (40) P=.367	.6876 (40) P=.001
V.33	-.1341 (34) P=.225	-.0865 (32) P=.319	-.2766 (32) P=.063	-.3252 (32) P=.035	-.2271 (32) P=.106	-.2146 (32) P=.119	-.2932 (31) P=.055	-.2536 (31) P=.084	-.2690 (34) P=.062	.0264 (34) P=.441	.2451 (33) P=.085	.1338 (34) P=.225	.6255 (34) P=.001	.0339 (34) P=.425	.1083 (34) P=.271
V.31	-.0278 (40) P=.432	-.0352 (37) P=.418	-.1213 (37) P=.237	-.2628 (37) P=.058	-.1668 (38) P=.158	-.1558 (37) P=.179	-.2537 (35) P=.071	-.1722 (33) P=.169	-.0002 (40) P=.500	.0556 (40) P=.367	.1883 (39) P=.125	.1172 (40) P=.236	.1102 (40) P=.249	.0031 (40) P=.492	.0110 (40) P=.473
S.2	-.1970 (40) P=.111	-.1068 (36) P=.268	-.1513 (36) P=.189	-.2105 (36) P=.109	-.0023 (37) P=.495	-.1233 (36) P=.237	-.2193 (34) P=.106	.0826 (32) P=.327	.0184 (40) P=.455	-.1510 (40) P=.176	.5346 (38) P=.001	-.3604 (40) P=.011	.0415 (40) P=.400	.1176 (40) P=.235	.2558 (40) P=.056
S.4	-.2530 (40) P=.058	-.2484 (36) P=.072	-.1086 (36) P=.264	-.1009 (36) P=.279	-.1812 (37) P=.142	-.0256 (36) P=.441	-.3074 (34) P=.039	-.1244 (32) P=.249	-.0846 (40) P=.302	-.1273 (40) P=.217	.1822 (38) P=.137	-.1104 (40) P=.249	-.0602 (40) P=.356	-.1208 (40) P=.229	.2536 (40) P=.057
S.6	-.0932 (39) P=.286	.1823 (36) P=.144	.4208 (36) P=.005	.5150 (36) P=.001	.1306 (37) P=.221	.2574 (36) P=.065	.4745 (34) P=.002	.0320 (32) P=.431	-.0883 (39) P=.296	-.1820 (39) P=.134	.0610 (37) P=.360	-.2689 (39) P=.049	-.2487 (39) P=.063	-.0960 (39) P=.280	-.1299 (39) P=.215
S.3	-.0130 (41) P=.468	-.1435 (37) P=.198	.0650 (37) P=.351	.0366 (37) P=.415	.0182 (38) P=.457	.0079 (37) P=.482	-.1850 (35) P=.144	.0776 (33) P=.334	.0448 (41) P=.390	-.1352 (41) P=.200	-.0868 (39) P=.300	-.2412 (41) P=.064	-.1815 (41) P=.128	-.2113 (41) P=.092	.2027 (41) P=.102
S.1	-.1215 (37) P=.237	.2355 (36) P=.083	-.2447 (36) P=.075	.0220 (36) P=.449	-.1956 (37) P=.123	.0031 (36) P=.493	-.1686 (34) P=.170	.1466 (32) P=.212	-.1124 (37) P=.254	.2566 (37) P=.063	-.1401 (37) P=.204	.3290 (37) P=.023	.4241 (37) P=.004	.1931 (37) P=.126	-.3418 (37) P=.019
S.5	.0034 (32) P=.493	.2006 (31) P=.140	.1797 (31) P=.167	.2515 (31) P=.086	.1367 (31) P=.232	.2460 (31) P=.091	.0397 (29) P=.419	.3522 (29) P=.030	-.1171 (32) P=.262	.4565 (32) P=.004	.1551 (32) P=.198	.3344 (32) P=.031	.1312 (32) P=.237	.1293 (32) P=.240	.1841 (32) P=.157
S.7	-.2707 (41) P=.043	.0225 (37) P=.448	.3396 (37) P=.020	.3665 (37) P=.013	.2543 (38) P=.062	.2187 (37) P=.097	.3892 (35) P=.010	.2694 (33) P=.065	-.0407 (41) P=.400	-.3019 (41) P=.028	.3012 (39) P=.031	-.3511 (41) P=.012	-.2528 (41) P=.055	-.1227 (41) P=.222	.1533 (41) P=.169
S.8	-.2184 (41) P=.085	-.0561 (37) P=.371	-.0293 (37) P=.432	.0532 (37) P=.377	-.1058 (38) P=.264	.1030 (37) P=.272	.0201 (35) P=.454	-.0971 (33) P=.295	-.1231 (41) P=.222	.0524 (41) P=.372	-.2609 (39) P=.054	.4152 (41) P=.003	.1130 (41) P=.241	.1865 (41) P=.122	.2501 (41) P=.057
S.9	.0046 (41) P=.489	.0388 (37) P=.410	-.3624 (37) P=.014	.0660 (37) P=.349	-.0625 (38) P=.355	-.0792 (37) P=.321	-.0132 (35) P=.470	.0442 (33) P=.403	-.0864 (41) P=.295	-.3064 (41) P=.026	-.2574 (39) P=.057	.4573 (41) P=.001	.0285 (41) P=.430	.2471 (41) P=.060	-.2045 (41) P=.100
S.10	.1044 (41) P=.258	.0267 (37) P=.438	.2658 (37) P=.056	.2957 (37) P=.038	.1435 (38) P=.195	.1587 (37) P=.174	.3416 (35) P=.022	.3070 (33) P=.041	.2138 (41) P=.090	.0806 (41) P=.308	-.1585 (39) P=.168	.1274 (41) P=.214	-.2040 (41) P=.100	-.1786 (41) P=.132	-.0932 (41) P=.281
S.18	-.0585 (36) P=.367	.2017 (36) P=.119	.0240 (36) P=.445	.3065 (36) P=.035	.0955 (36) P=.290	.2782 (36) P=.050	.1222 (33) P=.249	.2168 (32) P=.117	-.3629 (36) P=.015	.6464 (36) P=.001	.1814 (36) P=.145	.4549 (36) P=.003	-.0079 (36) P=.482	.3652 (36) P=.014	-.0327 (36) P=.425
S.19	-.2171 (36) P=.102	.0484 (36) P=.390	-.2253 (36) P=.093	.1789 (36) P=.148	-.0733 (36) P=.336	.2343 (36) P=.084	-.2170 (33) P=.113	.1657 (32) P=.182	-.1304 (36) P=.224	-.0075 (36) P=.483	.6150 (36) P=.001	-.1310 (36) P=.223	.1062 (36) P=.269	.1979 (36) P=.124	.1030 (36) P=.275
S.17	.2909 (41) P=.032	-.1021 (37) P=.274	-.0918 (37) P=.295	.2136 (37) P=.102	.5693 (38) P=.001	.2067 (37) P=.110	.3032 (35) P=.038	.3581 (33) P=.020	-.4378 (41) P=.002	.3833 (41) P=.007	-.1986 (39) P=.113	.0985 (41) P=.270	-.1253 (41) P=.218	.5234 (41) P=.001	.1818 (41) P=.128
S.11	.2602 (41) P=.050	.2807 (37) P=.046	.2569 (37) P=.062	.2609 (37) P=.059	.3545 (38) P=.014	.3581 (37) P=.015	.1193 (35) P=.247	.2527 (33) P=.078	-.0370 (41) P=.409	.4622 (41) P=.001	-.1638 (39) P=.160	.2760 (41) P=.040	-.2897 (41) P=.033	.1747 (41) P=.137	-.1690 (41) P=.145
S.12	.2361 (41) P=.069	.0647 (37) P=.352	-.0796 (37) P=.320	-.0311 (37) P=.427	.0340 (38) P=.420	-.0474 (37) P=.390	-.0226 (35) P=.449	-.1088 (33) P=.273	.0766 (41) P=.317	-.1266 (41) P=.215	.1209 (39) P=.232	-.2245 (41) P=.079	-.0398 (41) P=.402	.0604 (41) P=.354	-.0828 (41) P=.303

Table 1

	V2.16	V2.22	V2.18	V2.20	V2.19	V2.21	V2.23	V2.17	V3.11	V3.20	V3.15	V3.12	V3.13	V3.14	V3.16
S.13	.1669 (38) P=.158	-.2516 (34) P=.076	.3341 (34) P=.027	.2244 (34) P=.101	.1153 (35) P=.255	.0656 (34) P=.356	.3117 (33) P=.039	-.0314 (31) P=.433	.0655 (38) P=.348	-.0676 (38) P=.343	-.0875 (36) P=.306	-.1817 (38) P=.137	-.2980 (38) P=.035	-.0516 (38) P=.379	-.1388 (38) P=.203
S.14	-.1138 (40) P=.242	-.3348 (37) P=.021	-.2302 (37) P=.085	-.3600 (37) P=.014	-.2283 (38) P=.084	-.1396 (37) P=.205	-.3501 (35) P=.020	-.0808 (33) P=.327	-.3449 (40) P=.015	-.2766 (40) P=.042	.6481 (39) P=.001	-.2813 (40) P=.039	.0450 (40) P=.391	-.2795 (40) P=.040	.0180 (40) P=.456
S.15	-.2602 (40) P=.052	-.2166 (37) P=.099	-.2935 (37) P=.039	-.1475 (37) P=.192	-.1465 (38) P=.190	-.1167 (37) P=.246	-.2649 (35) P=.062	.2466 (33) P=.083	-.0177 (40) P=.457	-.1312 (40) P=.210	.5619 (39) P=.001	-.2973 (40) P=.031	.0173 (40) P=.458	.0649 (40) P=.345	.0125 (40) P=.469
S.16	.2005 (41) P=.104	-.0186 (37) P=.456	.2749 (37) P=.050	.2036 (37) P=.113	.1087 (38) P=.258	.4500 (37) P=.003	.0988 (35) P=.286	.1416 (33) P=.216	-.1451 (41) P=.183	.3067 (41) P=.026	.0934 (39) P=.286	.1681 (41) P=.147	-.2480 (41) P=.059	.0788 (41) P=.312	.0312 (41) P=.423
S.25	.1570 (32) P=.195	-.1015 (32) P=.290	.2480 (32) P=.086	.3556 (32) P=.023	.3528 (32) P=.024	.1751 (32) P=.169	.5172 (32) P=.001	.3116 (32) P=.041	-.2482 (32) P=.085	.1737 (32) P=.171	.0028 (32) P=.494	-.1332 (32) P=.234	-.2479 (32) P=.086	.1987 (32) P=.138	-.1083 (32) P=.278
S.27	.3177 (24) P=.065	.0920 (24) P=.334	.4640 (24) P=.011	.2096 (24) P=.163	.4851 (24) P=.008	.1291 (24) P=.274	.1913 (21) P=.203	.1906 (21) P=.204	-.1351 (24) P=.265	.6359 (24) P=.001	-.0410 (24) P=.425	.1051 (24) P=.312	-.3781 (24) P=.034	.0391 (24) P=.428	-.1332 (24) P=.267
S.26	.2114 (32) P=.123	-.0783 (32) P=.335	.2173 (32) P=.116	-.3796 (32) P=.016	.3230 (32) P=.036	.1486 (32) P=.209	.4216 (32) P=.008	.3017 (32) P=.047	-.2266 (32) P=.106	.2003 (32) P=.136	.1462 (32) P=.212	-.1082 (32) P=.278	-.2964 (32) P=.050	.0869 (32) P=.318	-.0766 (32) P=.338
S.22	.1754 (27) P=.191	.0264 (27) P=.448	.0630 (27) P=.378	-.2099 (27) P=.147	.0746 (27) P=.356	.3611 (27) P=.032	.0763 (27) P=.353	.0455 (27) P=.411	-.3856 (27) P=.023	-.4661 (27) P=.007	-.2463 (27) P=.108	.3512 (27) P=.036	-.0471 (27) P=.408	.4172 (27) P=.015	-.1434 (27) P=.238
S.20	.0578 (24) P=.394	-.2329 (24) P=.137	.3909 (24) P=.029	.1899 (24) P=.187	.2335 (24) P=.136	.1275 (24) P=.276	.1329 (21) P=.283	.1759 (21) P=.223	-.1482 (24) P=.245	.7759 (24) P=.001	.0860 (24) P=.345	.3689 (24) P=.038	-.1284 (24) P=.275	.1039 (24) P=.314	.1342 (24) P=.266
S.29	-.1285 (30) P=.249	.0570 (30) P=.382	-.0522 (30) P=.392	-.4158 (30) P=.011	-.1881 (30) P=.160	-.1782 (30) P=.173	-.3453 (29) P=.033	-.1456 (29) P=.226	.0388 (30) P=.419	.2094 (30) P=.133	-.0725 (30) P=.352	.3316 (30) P=.037	.0664 (30) P=.364	-.0217 (30) P=.455	.5189 (30) P=.002
S.28	.1674 (41) P=.148	.0390 (37) P=.409	.0990 (37) P=.280	.0391 (37) P=.409	.3890 (38) P=.008	.2224 (37) P=.093	.1467 (35) P=.200	.2258 (33) P=.103	-.0334 (41) P=.418	.4445 (41) P=.002	-.2320 (39) P=.078	.0920 (41) P=.284	-.2139 (41) P=.090	.1883 (41) P=.119	.1694 (41) P=.145
S.30	.0299 (41) P=.426	-.1710 (37) P=.156	-.1378 (37) P=.208	-.3246 (37) P=.025	-.1540 (38) P=.178	-.1898 (37) P=.130	-.2027 (35) P=.121	-.1113 (33) P=.269	.0913 (41) P=.285	-.0818 (41) P=.306	.1087 (39) P=.255	.0422 (41) P=.397	-.1248 (41) P=.219	-.0540 (41) P=.369	.5570 (41) P=.001
S.21	-.0968 (35) P=.290	.0244 (35) P=.445	.1989 (35) P=.126	.2716 (35) P=.057	.0432 (35) P=.403	.4430 (35) P=.004	.2060 (34) P=.121	.0718 (33) P=.346	.0246 (35) P=.444	-.0724 (35) P=.340	.2789 (35) P=.052	-.1041 (35) P=.276	-.1994 (35) P=.125	-.0719 (35) P=.341	.1002 (35) P=.283
S.23	.0329 (38) P=.422	-.1478 (36) P=.195	.1692 (36) P=.162	.2489 (36) P=.072	.3411 (37) P=.019	.4169 (36) P=.006	.2494 (35) P=.074	.3424 (35) P=.022	-.1750 (38) P=.147	-.7184 (38) P=.001	-.1044 (37) P=.269	.4929 (38) P=.001	-.1807 (38) P=.139	.4359 (38) P=.003	.0586 (38) P=.363
S.24	.0304 (38) P=.428	.2002 (37) P=.117	.2623 (37) P=.058	.3038 (37) P=.034	.2697 (38) P=.051	.4099 (37) P=.006	.1858 (35) P=.143	.3053 (33) P=.042	-.2120 (38) P=.101	.4907 (38) P=.001	.0094 (38) P=.478	.3920 (38) P=.007	-.1746 (38) P=.147	-.2959 (38) P=.036	-.0907 (38) P=.294

Table 2

	V4.4	V4.2	F.3	F.5	F.6	F.7	F.8	F.10	F.11	F.12	F.13	F.14	F.15	F.9	F.27
V4.4	1.0000 (0) P=******														
V4.2	.0853 (41) P=.298	1.0000 (0) P=******													
F.3	.2667 (41) P=.046	-.0472 (41) P=.385	1.0000 (0) P=******												
F.5	-.1624 (40) P=.158	.2195 (40) P=.087	-.0846 (40) P=.302	1.0000 (0) P=******											
F.6	.1168 (40) P=.236	.3968 (40) P=.006	-.0696 (40) P=.335	-.6348 (40) P=.001	1.0000 (0) P=******										
F.7	.7161 (39) P=.001	.0411 (39) P=.402	.0300 (39) P=.428	-.1648 (39) P=.158	.3613 (39) P=.012	1.0000 (0) P=******									
F.8	.0152 (39) P=.463	.4786 (39) P=.001	-.1768 (39) P=.141	-.3063 (39) P=.029	.8432 (39) P=.001	-.0951 (38) P=.285	1.0000 (0) P=******								
F.10	-.0763 (37) P=.327	.2740 (37) P=.050	-.1077 (37) P=.263	-.3382 (37) P=.020	-.0365 (37) P=.415	-.0244 (36) P=.444	.0527 (37) P=.378	1.0000 (0) P=******							
F.11	-.1503 (41) P=.174	.2948 (41) P=.031	.2942 (41) P=.031	.5405 (40) P=.001	-.1819 (40) P=.131	-.2082 (39) P=.102	.0388 (39) P=.407	.2887 (37) P=.042	1.0000 (0) P=******						
F.12	.1870 (41) P=.121	-.2205 (41) P=.083	.7084 (41) P=.001	-.1244 (40) P=.222	-.1249 (40) P=.221	-.0362 (39) P=.413	-.2419 (39) P=.069	-.0819 (39) P=.315	.3836 (41) P=.007	1.0000 (0) P=******					
F.13	.1843 (37) P=.137	.3571 (37) P=.015	-.0507 (37) P=.383	-.6546 (37) P=.001	.9665 (37) P=.001	.4202 (36) P=.005	.8044 (36) P=.001	-.0671 (35) P=.351	-.1673 (37) P=.161	-.0976 (37) P=.283	1.0000 (0) P=******				
F.14	-.0398 (37) P=.408	.2882 (37) P=.042	-.1372 (37) P=.209	-.4679 (37) P=.002	.7665 (37) P=.001	.0452 (36) P=.397	.6975 (36) P=.001	-.0953 (35) P=.293	-.1609 (37) P=.171	-.1640 (37) P=.166	.7921 (37) P=.001	1.0000 (0) P=******			
F.15	.1602 (36) P=.175	.3298 (36) P=.025	-.0108 (36) P=.475	-.7093 (36) P=.001	.9737 (36) P=.001	.5355 (35) P=.001	.8336 (35) P=.001	-.1716 (34) P=.166	-.2118 (36) P=.107	-.0336 (36) P=.423	.9592 (36) P=.001	.7611 (36) P=.001	1.0000 (0) P=******		
F.9	-.0137 (40) P=.467	.2846 (40) P=.038	-.1365 (40) P=.201	-.6192 (40) P=.001	.9353 (40) P=.001	.1008 (40) P=.271	.8084 (39) P=.001	-.1534 (37) P=.182	-.1963 (40) P=.112	-.1495 (40) P=.179	.8892 (37) P=.001	.7477 (37) P=.001	.9128 (36) P=.001	1.0000 (0) P=******	
F.27	-.0925 (41) P=.283	.4095 (41) P=.004	-.1049 (41) P=.257	-.3568 (40) P=.012	.6704 (40) P=.001	-.1594 (39) P=.166	.6756 (39) P=.001	.0958 (39) P=.286	.0322 (41) P=.421	-.1293 (41) P=.210	.6400 (37) P=.001	.5019 (37) P=.001	.6489 (36) P=.001	.6190 (40) P=.001	1.0000 (0) P=******
F.25	-.1196 (37) P=.240	.3962 (37) P=.008	-.2094 (37) P=.107	-.2407 (37) P=.076	.1829 (37) P=.139	-.0291 (37) P=.432	.4077 (36) P=.007	.1665 (34) P=.173	.0418 (37) P=.403	-.4299 (37) P=.004	.0529 (36) P=.380	.0286 (36) P=.434	-.1860 (35) P=.142	-.0055 (37) P=.487	.2229 (37) P=.092
F.26	.0862 (40) P=.299	.2137 (40) P=.093	-.0960 (40) P=.278	.0604 (39) P=.357	.1439 (39) P=.191	-.0822 (39) P=.309	.1318 (38) P=.215	.0289 (36) P=.433	-.1512 (40) P=.176	-.1686 (40) P=.149	.1092 (36) P=.263	-.2516 (36) P=.069	.0134 (35) P=.470	.0729 (39) P=.329	.2544 (40) P=.057
F.24	-.0126 (41) P=.469	.3965 (41) P=.005	-.1481 (41) P=.178	.2670 (40) P=.048	-.0476 (40) P=.385	-.1251 (39) P=.224	.0612 (39) P=.356	.3382 (37) P=.023	.0993 (41) P=.268	-.1987 (41) P=.106	-.0653 (37) P=.350	-.2496 (37) P=.068	-.1319 (36) P=.222	-.0309 (40) P=.288	.1826 (41) P=.127

	V3.17	V3.18	V3.19	V3.21	V3.4	V3.5	V3.6	V3.7	V3.8	V3.9	V3.10	V3.1	V3.2	V3.3	V4.1
	-.3059	-.2132	-.1662	.2433	-.0914	-.1235	-.1451	.2233	-.1699	-.1121	-.2102	-.1249	-.1650	-.1048	-.2369
	(25)	(34)	(36)	(38)	(34)	(35)	(37)	(35)	(36)	(36)	(14)	(38)	(38)	(37)	(38)
	P= .069	P= .113	P= .166	P= .071	P= .304	P= .240	P= .196	P= .099	P= .161	P= .258	P= .235	P= .227	P= .161	P= .269	P= .076
	.2889	.4236	-.4458	.0995	-.3281	.4406	-.1931	-.2718	-.1292	.4751	-.2647	-.2098	.2632	.1601	.1075
	(26)	(37)	(39)	(40)	(37)	(38)	(39)	(38)	(39)	(38)	(16)	(40)	(40)	(40)	(40)
	P= .076	P= .004	P= .002	P= .271	P= .024	P= .003	P= .119	P= .049	P= .217	P= .001	P= .161	P= .097	P= .050	P= .162	P= .255
	.2503	.7108	-.2354	-.3316	-.1430	.1171	.1292	-.2247	.3521	.0878	.2335	-.1201	.7614	.0891	.2579
	(26)	(37)	(39)	(40)	(37)	(38)	(39)	(38)	(39)	(38)	(16)	(40)	(40)	(40)	(40)
	P= .109	P= .001	P= .075	P= .018	P= .199	P= .242	P= .217	P= .088	P= .014	P= .300	P= .192	P= .230	P= .001	P= .292	P= .054
	-.1595	.0340	-.0252	-.0768	.1026	-.1226	.1191	-.0845	.1519	-.1226	-.0054	.5541	-.0360	-.1227	-.2432
	(26)	(37)	(39)	(41)	(37)	(38)	(40)	(38)	(39)	(39)	(16)	(41)	(41)	(40)	(41)
	P= .218	P= .421	P= .440	P= .317	P= .273	P= .232	P= .232	P= .307	P= .178	P= .228	P= .492	P= .001	P= .412	P= .225	P= .063
	-.4237	.1406	-.1503	-.0066	.0200	-.1816	-.1024	-.0310	.0962	-.2835	.1678	.1687	.1797	-.2859	-.2930
	(24)	(30)	(32)	(32)	(31)	(32)	(32)	(32)	(32)	(32)	(15)	(32)	(32)	(32)	(32)
	P= .020	P= .229	P= .206	P= .486	P= .458	P= .160	P= .288	P= .300	P= .058	P= .058	P= .275	P= .178	P= .163	P= .056	P= .052
	-.1971	-.1117	.0162	-.1991	.4615	-.0917	-.1480	-.2970	.0361	.1969	-.0192	.5467	-.1223	.2090	.1476
	(15)	(24)	(24)	(24)	(23)	(24)	(24)	(24)	(24)	(24)	(12)	(24)	(24)	(24)	(24)
	P= .241	P= .302	P= .470	P= .175	P= .013	P= .335	P= .245	P= .079	P= .433	P= .178	P= .476	P= .003	P= .285	P= .164	P= .246
	-.3994	.0554	-.0657	-.1000	-.0677	-.2117	-.0455	.0729	.1591	-.2725	.1874	.2640	.1107	-.2746	-.2821
	(24)	(30)	(32)	(32)	(31)	(32)	(32)	(32)	(32)	(32)	(15)	(32)	(32)	(32)	(32)
	P= .027	P= .386	P= .360	P= .293	P= .359	P= .122	P= .402	P= .346	P= .192	P= .066	P= .252	P= .072	P= .273	P= .064	P= .059
	.3319	-.0676	.0152	-.2157	.4294	.0753	-.0582	-.1224	-.0560	-.0747	-.0184	.4989	-.1136	-.0461	-.0941
	(19)	(27)	(27)	(27)	(26)	(27)	(27)	(27)	(27)	(27)	(12)	(27)	(27)	(27)	(27)
	P= .083	P= .369	P= .470	P= .140	P= .014	P= .355	P= .387	P= .272	P= .391	P= .356	P= .477	P= .004	P= .286	P= .410	P= .320
	-.3170	-.0768	.0494	-.3950	.3520	.0341	.1513	-.2372	.1737	.0611	.0719	.6439	-.1634	-.1532	.1656
	(15)	(24)	(24)	(24)	(23)	(24)	(24)	(24)	(24)	(24)	(12)	(24)	(24)	(24)	(24)
	P= .125	P= .361	P= .409	P= .028	P= .050	P= .437	P= .240	P= .132	P= .208	P= .388	P= .412	P= .001	P= .223	P= .237	P= .220
	.1914	-.1245	.0652	.0823	.2339	.2906	.1845	-.0329	-.0107	-.2066	.1565	-.0502	-.1877	-.1170	-.0045
	(21)	(30)	(30)	(30)	(29)	(30)	(30)	(30)	(30)	(30)	(15)	(30)	(30)	(30)	(30)
	P= .203	P= .256	P= .366	P= .333	P= .111	P= .060	P= .165	P= .432	P= .478	P= .137	P= .289	P= .396	P= .160	P= .269	P= .491
	.0579	-.1956	.0651	.0055	.4371	-.0505	.0630	-.0743	-.0043	-.0406	.1966	.0818	-.2327	-.0336	.0054
	(26)	(37)	(39)	(41)	(37)	(38)	(40)	(39)	(39)	(39)	(16)	(41)	(41)	(40)	(41)
	P= .389	P= .123	P= .347	P= .486	P= .003	P= .382	P= .350	P= .329	P= .490	P= .403	P= .233	P= .306	P= .072	P= .418	P= .487
	.0011	-.0743	-.0458	.2199	.0902	.0244	.0664	-.1084	-.0058	-.0451	-.1524	-.0057	-.0946	-.0456	-.1432
	(26)	(37)	(39)	(41)	(37)	(38)	(40)	(38)	(39)	(39)	(16)	(41)	(41)	(40)	(41)
	P= .498	P= .331	P= .391	P= .084	P= .298	P= .442	P= .342	P= .259	P= .486	P= .393	P= .287	P= .486	P= .278	P= .390	P= .186
	.0081	.1603	-.1353	.0346	-.0004	-.1566	.0015	-.3214	-.1592	-.1367	.2347	-.0021	.1084	-.1357	-.2356
	(26)	(32)	(35)	(35)	(33)	(35)	(35)	(35)	(35)	(35)	(16)	(35)	(35)	(35)	(35)
	P= .484	P= .190	P= .219	P= .422	P= .499	P= .184	P= .497	P= .030	P= .180	P= .217	P= .191	P= .495	P= .268	P= .219	P= .087
	-.3685	.0061	.3016	-.1698	.3667	-.1843	.0702	-.0863	.3533	-.2291	.5569	.4690	.0226	-.2021	-.2099
	(26)	(35)	(37)	(38)	(35)	(36)	(37)	(36)	(37)	(36)	(16)	(38)	(38)	(38)	(38)
	P= .032	P= .486	P= .035	P= .154	P= .015	P= .141	P= .340	P= .308	P= .016	P= .089	P= .013	P= .001	P= .446	P= .112	P= .103
	-.3697	.1294	.0103	-.1593	.4236	-.1878	.1418	.0517	.2411	-.2089	.2793	.5071	-.0627	-.2021	-.1684
	(26)	(35)	(38)	(38)	(36)	(37)	(38)	(37)	(38)	(37)	(16)	(38)	(38)	(38)	(38)
	P= .032	P= .229	P= .476	P= .170	P= .005	P= .133	P= .198	P= .381	P= .072	P= .107	P= .147	P= .001	P= .354	P= .112	P= .156

F.25   F.26   F.24   F.23   F.21

```
   1.0000
 (    0)
 P=******

   .2392   1.0000
 (   37) (    0)
 P= .077  P=******

   .3417   .8868   1.0000
 (   37) (   40) (    0)
 P= .019  P= .001  P=******
```

F.25	F.26	F.24	F.23	F.21	F.20	F.17	F.16	F.18	F.19	F.22	V.1	V.4	V.5	V.6
.1899 (37) P= .130	-.0548 (40) P= .369	.0340 (40) P= .417	1.0000 (0) P=******											
-.1457 (37) P= .195	.1790 (39) P= .138	.2996 (39) P= .032	-.2143 (39) P= .095	1.0000 (0) P=******										
.1617 (37) P= .169	.4482 (40) P= .002	.5924 (40) P= .001	.0041 (40) P= .490	.5535 (39) P= .001	1.0000 (0) P=******									
-.1321 (37) P= .218	-.0161 (40) P= .461	-.0319 (40) P= .423	.2824 (40) P= .039	-.0807 (39) P= .313	-.0309 (40) P= .425	1.0000 (0) P=******								
.0327 (37) P= .424	.2648 (40) P= .049	.3870 (40) P= .007	.2155 (40) P= .091	.5186 (39) P= .001	.3775 (40) P= .008	.0836 (40) P= .304	1.0000 (0) P=******							
.1548 (37) P= .180	.1662 (40) P= .153	.3814 (40) P= .008	.1288 (40) P= .214	.2699 (39) P= .048	.5261 (40) P= .001	-.0858 (40) P= .299	.2023 (40) P= .105	1.0000 (0) P=******						
.0661 (37) P= .349	.0114 (40) P= .472	.1086 (40) P= .252	-.0980 (40) P= .274	-.0006 (39) P= .498	.0530 (40) P= .373	-.0353 (40) P= .415	-.0152 (40) P= .463	.5366 (40) P= .001	1.0000 (0) P=******					
.0318 (31) P= .433	-.1258 (34) P= .239	-.1506 (34) P= .198	.0826 (34) P= .321	-.1452 (33) P= .210	-.0650 (34) P= .357	.2778 (34) P= .056	-.0745 (34) P= .338	-.0276 (34) P= .438	-.1818 (34) P= .152	1.0000 (0) P=******				
-.2931 (31) P= .055	-.0739 (32) P= .344	-.0570 (32) P= .378	-.0907 (32) P= .311	.0085 (31) P= .482	-.0280 (32) P= .440	-.0437 (32) P= .406	-.0298 (32) P= .436	-.0181 (32) P= .461	.1798 (32) P= .162	.1198 (26) P= .280	1.0000 (0) P=******			
.0372 (32) P= .420	-.1140 (33) P= .264	-.1340 (34) P= .225	-.1268 (33) P= .241	-.1533 (33) P= .197	-.1064 (33) P= .278	-.0614 (33) P= .367	-.0516 (33) P= .388	.0869 (33) P= .315	.0545 (33) P= .382	.1198 (27) P= .276	.4170 (30) P= .011	1.0000 (0) P=******		
.1761 (33) P= .163	-.2734 (34) P= .059	-.1352 (35) P= .219	.2446 (34) P= .082	-.1070 (34) P= .273	-.1117 (34) P= .265	.0131 (34) P= .471	-.1216 (34) P= .247	-.0499 (34) P= .390	.1707 (34) P= .167	.3878 (29) P= .019	.2147 (30) P= .127	.9846 (33) P= .001	1.0000 (0) P=******	
-.0069 (36) P= .484	-.1443 (38) P= .194	.0753 (39) P= .324	.0299 (38) P= .429	.1596 (37) P= .173	.0700 (38) P= .338	.2495 (38) P= .065	.1216 (38) P= .234	-.0715 (38) P= .335	-.1249 (38) P= .227	.0115 (32) P= .475	-.2592 (32) P= .076	-.3305 (34) P= .028	-.2743 (35) P= .055	1.0000 (0) P=******
-.0436 (35) P= .402	-.2231 (37) P= .092	.1184 (38) P= .239	-.0787 (37) P= .322	-.2620 (36) P= .061	-.1992 (37) P= .119	-.1493 (37) P= .189	-.1184 (37) P= .243	.0200 (37) P= .453	.2571 (37) P= .062	-.0457 (31) P= .404	.2173 (32) P= .116	-.9791 (34) P= .001	-.9988 (35) P= .001	.2305 (38) P= .082
.0064 (35) P= .485	.0799 (36) P= .322	-.2031 (37) P= .114	-.1848 (36) P= .140	-.1778 (35) P= .153	-.1443 (36) P= .201	-.1002 (36) P= .280	-.2959 (36) P= .040	-.0184 (36) P= .458	-.0855 (36) P= .310	.2934 (30) P= .058	.1797 (32) P= .162	.3485 (33) P= .023	.3353 (34) P= .026	-.3897 (37) P= .009
-.0243 (33) P= .447	.5198 (34) P= .001	.5613 (35) P= .001	.3262 (34) P= .030	.0683 (33) P= .353	.3322 (34) P= .027	.3540 (34) P= .020	.1971 (34) P= .132	.0786 (34) P= .329	.1104 (34) P= .267	-.1524 (28) P= .219	-.1298 (32) P= .239	-.2705 (32) P= .067	-.2325 (32) P= .100	.2707 (34) P= .061
-.2319 (33) P= .097	.1076 (34) P= .272	.1485 (35) P= .197	.0897 (34) P= .307	.1488 (33) P= .204	-.0577 (34) P= .373	.1252 (34) P= .240	.0137 (34) P= .469	-.0728 (34) P= .341	-.0185 (34) P= .459	-.3034 (28) P= .058	-.2106 (32) P= .124	-.5510 (31) P= .001	-.4369 (31) P= .007	.5317 (34) P= .001
.2531 (34) P= .074	-.1994 (34) P= .129	-.0340 (35) P= .423	.1928 (34) P= .137	-.1044 (34) P= .278	.1582 (34) P= .186	-.0690 (34) P= .349	.0252 (34) P= .444	.1450 (34) P= .207	-.0692 (34) P= .349	.2450 (28) P= .104	.2071 (31) P= .132	-.1547 (32) P= .199	-.2255 (32) P= .107	-.2854 (34) P= .051
.0460 (37) P= .393	.0120 (39) P= .471	.1067 (40) P= .256	-.0386 (39) P= .408	.4716 (38) P= .001	.1901 (39) P= .123	-.0045 (39) P= .489	.3893 (39) P= .007	.1933 (39) P= .119	-.0114 (39) P= .473	.1370 (33) P= .224	-.1912 (32) P= .147	.1153 (34) P= .258	.1291 (35) P= .230	.1823 (39) P= .133
.1506 (35) P= .194	.1927 (37) P= .127	.3364 (37) P= .021	.1141 (37) P= .251	-.1376 (36) P= .212	.0352 (37) P= .418	-.1046 (37) P= .269	-.1352 (37) P= .212	-.0734 (37) P= .333	-.2451 (37) P= .072	.2833 (31) P= .061	-.0891 (32) P= .314	-.0627 (33) P= .365	.0795 (34) P= .327	.1898 (37) P= .130
-.1380 (37) P= .208	-.0563 (40) P= .365	-.1063 (40) P= .257	.1594 (40) P= .163	-.0643 (39) P= .349	-.0581 (40) P= .361	-.0666 (40) P= .342	.0812 (40) P= .309	.1690 (40) P= .149	-.0451 (40) P= .391	.3477 (34) P= .022	-.0889 (32) P= .314	.0931 (33) P= .303	-.0703 (34) P= .346	-.1358 (38) P= .208
-.0428 (33) P= .407	-.2149 (34) P= .111	-.1751 (35) P= .157	.0958 (34) P= .295	.0189 (33) P= .458	-.0522 (34) P= .385	.2413 (34) P= .085	-.0071 (34) P= .484	.2642 (34) P= .066	.0764 (34) P= .334	.1730 (28) P= .189	-.1720 (31) P= .177	.4983 (30) P= .003	.4120 (30) P= .012	-.0620 (34) P= .364
.0865 (36) P= .308	-.0773 (38) P= .322	.0122 (39) P= .471	.2239 (38) P= .088	-.0831 (37) P= .312	-.0673 (38) P= .344	-.0401 (38) P= .406	.0771 (38) P= .323	.2045 (38) P= .109	-.0623 (38) P= .355	.2443 (32) P= .089	.3192 (32) P= .037	-.1014 (34) P= .284	-.1844 (35) P= .145	-.2046 (39) P= .106
-.1020 (36) P= .277	-.0559 (38) P= .369	-.0836 (39) P= .306	-.1786 (38) P= .142	.1490 (37) P= .189	.1014 (38) P= .272	.0823 (38) P= .312	-.1360 (38) P= .208	-.0653 (38) P= .349	.0573 (38) P= .366	-.2837 (33) P= .055	-.5504 (31) P= .001	.0463 (33) P= .399	.1110 (34) P= .266	.4286 (38) P= .004
-.1326 (33) P= .231	-.0285 (34) P= .437	-.1194 (35) P= .247	.1605 (34) P= .182	-.0549 (33) P= .381	-.0273 (34) P= .439	-.0621 (34) P= .364	.0838 (34) P= .319	.2014 (34) P= .127	-.0428 (34) P= .405	-.2203 (28) P= .130	-.1118 (32) P= .271	.9824 (32) P= .001	.9965 (32) P= .001	-.2765 (35) P= .054
-.1253 (32) P= .247	-.2315 (33) P= .097	-.1558 (34) P= .189	-.3243 (33) P= .033	-.1330 (33) P= .230	-.1373 (33) P= .223	-.1464 (33) P= .208	-.1823 (33) P= .155	-.2255 (33) P= .104	-.1513 (33) P= .200	.2460 (27) P= .108	.2338 (31) P= .103	-.1782 (33) P= .161	-.2231 (33) P= .106	-.1216 (34) P= .247
-.0085 (37) P= .480	-.0727 (40) P= .328	-.0998 (41) P= .267	.3219 (40) P= .021	-.1883 (39) P= .125	-.0066 (40) P= .484	-.0597 (40) P= .357	.0399 (40) P= .403	.1495 (40) P= .179	-.0255 (40) P= .438	.0691 (34) P= .349	-.1402 (32) P= .222	.5979 (34) P= .001	.5980 (35) P= .001	-.2195 (39) P= .090
-.3112 (37) P= .030	-.0065 (40) P= .484	-.1334 (41) P= .203	.1512 (40) P= .176	-.0590 (39) P= .361	-.0971 (40) P= .276	-.0715 (40) P= .330	.1035 (40) P= .263	.1227 (40) P= .225	-.0066 (40) P= .484	.0111 (34) P= .475	.0795 (32) P= .333	.8788 (34) P= .001	.8797 (35) P= .001	-.2942 (39) P= .035
.2506 (24) P= .119	-.1364 (24) P= .263	.1572 (25) P= .227	-.1334 (24) P= .267	.0231 (24) P= .457	-.0330 (24) P= .439	.0770 (24) P= .360	-.1474 (24) P= .246	-.1561 (24) P= .233	.0075 (24) P= .486	.3764 (20) P= .051	.0318 (23) P= .443	-.9815 (24) P= .001	-.9933 (24) P= .001	.2895 (25) P= .080
.3185 (30) P= .043	-.0510 (30) P= .394	-.1487 (31) P= .212	.1236 (30) P= .258	-.0976 (30) P= .304	.0900 (30) P= .318	-.0733 (30) P= .350	-.2142 (30) P= .128	.1789 (30) P= .172	.1228 (30) P= .259	-.1321 (25) P= .265	.1247 (29) P= .260	.8500 (30) P= .001	.8534 (30) P= .001	-.4555 (31) P= .005
.2003 (36) P= .121	-.0779 (39) P= .319	-.0246 (40) P= .440	.0406 (39) P= .403	-.0969 (38) P= .281	-.0633 (39) P= .351	.1463 (39) P= .187	-.0413 (39) P= .401	.0524 (39) P= .376	.0744 (39) P= .326	.6265 (34) P= .001	.1998 (31) P= .141	-.0523 (33) P= .386	-.1044 (34) P= .278	-.0344 (38) P= .419
.0714 (37) P= .337	.2942 (39) P= .035	.4551 (40) P= .002	-.1107 (39) P= .251	.8316 (38) P= .001	.8748 (39) P= .001	-.0012 (39) P= .497	.3861 (39) P= .008	.4317 (39) P= .003	.1327 (39) P= .210	-.1193 (33) P= .254	.0915 (32) P= .309	-.0766 (34) P= .333	-.0598 (35) P= .367	.0260 (39) P= .438
-.2853 (34) P= .051	.2178 (36) P= .101	.2590 (37) P= .061	-.0040 (36) P= .491	.8152 (35) P= .001	.6691 (36) P= .001	.0337 (36) P= .423	.2376 (36) P= .081	.3227 (36) P= .027	.0771 (36) P= .327	-.0673 (30) P= .362	.0918 (32) P= .309	-.1489 (34) P= .200	-.1261 (34) P= .239	-.0155 (37) P= .464
-.1392 (37) P= .206	.6006 (39) P= .001	.4754 (40) P= .001	-.1870 (39) P= .127	-.0718 (38) P= .334	-.0195 (39) P= .453	.0146 (39) P= .465	.0574 (39) P= .364	.0203 (39) P= .451	.2378 (39) P= .072	-.2236 (33) P= .105	.2495 (32) P= .084	-.3344 (34) P= .027	-.3045 (35) P= .038	-.1751 (39) P= .143

	V4.4	V4.2	F.3	F.5	F.6	F.7	F.8	F.10	F.11	F.12	F.13	F.14	F.15	F.9	F.27
F.23	-.0103 (40) P= .475	.1549 (40) P= .170	-.2036 (40) P= .104	.3166 (39) P= .025	.0858 (39) P= .302	.0519 (39) P= .377	.1981 (38) P= .117	-.0218 (36) P= .450	.1859 (40) P= .125	-.1573 (40) P= .166	-.1757 (36) P= .153	.0995 (36) P= .282	-.1070 (35) P= .270	.3370 (39) P= .018	.2351 (40) P= .072
F.21	-.1374 (39) P= .202	.3268 (39) P= .021	-.0093 (39) P= .477	.1154 (38) P= .245	.1521 (38) P= .181	-.1740 (38) P= .148	-.0209 (37) P= .451	.1965 (35) P= .129	-.0711 (39) P= .334	-.0514 (39) P= .378	-.3001 (36) P= .038	-.1984 (36) P= .123	-.2067 (35) P= .117	-.0068 (38) P= .484	-.0339 (39) P= .419
F.20	-.0288 (40) P= .430	.5955 (40) P= .001	-.0715 (40) P= .330	.3898 (39) P= .007	.3658 (39) P= .011	-.0802 (39) P= .314	.1985 (38) P= .116	.4183 (36) P= .006	-.0309 (40) P= .425	-.1850 (40) P= .127	-.0866 (36) P= .308	-.1176 (36) P= .247	-.1263 (35) P= .235	-.0074 (39) P= .482	.1655 (40) P= .154
F.17	.1842 (40) P= .128	.1037 (40) P= .262	-.0728 (40) P= .328	.1154 (39) P= .242	.0219 (39) P= .447	.1418 (39) P= .195	.0533 (38) P= .375	.0733 (36) P= .335	.0862 (40) P= .298	.0014 (40) P= .496	.1453 (36) P= .199	.3457 (36) P= .019	.1406 (35) P= .210	-.1323 (39) P= .211	-.0675 (40) P= .340
F.16	-.1527 (40) P= .173	.2923 (40) P= .034	-.1248 (40) P= .222	.1414 (39) P= .195	.2663 (39) P= .051	-.1463 (39) P= .187	-.0629 (38) P= .354	.1659 (36) P= .167	-.0508 (40) P= .378	-.2227 (40) P= .084	-.1844 (36) P= .141	-.1191 (36) P= .244	-.1393 (35) P= .212	-.0279 (39) P= .433	.1217 (40) P= .227
F.18	.0499 (40) P= .380	.4158 (40) P= .004	-.0685 (40) P= .337	.4497 (39) P= .002	.7297 (39) P= .001	.1197 (39) P= .234	.4027 (38) P= .006	.4696 (36) P= .002	.2335 (40) P= .073	-.1636 (40) P= .157	.3221 (36) P= .028	.0561 (36) P= .373	-.1057 (35) P= .273	.2616 (39) P= .054	.1098 (40) P= .250
F.19	.1261 (40) P= .219	-.0190 (40) P= .454	-.0842 (40) P= .303	.1666 (39) P= .155	.6752 (39) P= .001	.1807 (39) P= .135	.1087 (38) P= .258	.4616 (36) P= .002	.1948 (40) P= .114	.0104 (40) P= .475	.5623 (36) P= .001	.1340 (36) P= .218	.0865 (35) P= .311	.1017 (39) P= .269	-.1288 (40) P= .214
F.22	-.0514 (34) P= .386	-.0717 (34) P= .344	.0904 (34) P= .306	-.0348 (33) P= .424	-.1823 (33) P= .155	-.1254 (33) P= .243	.0234 (32) P= .449	.1071 (30) P= .287	.0223 (34) P= .450	-.1762 (34) P= .159	.0663 (30) P= .364	.2651 (30) P= .078	-.1308 (29) P= .249	-.1307 (33) P= .234	.1678 (34) P= .171
V.1	.1687 (32) P= .178	-.0550 (32) P= .382	.1205 (32) P= .256	-.2005 (32) P= .136	.1337 (32) P= .233	-.0486 (32) P= .396	-.0943 (32) P= .304	.1328 (32) P= .234	.0921 (32) P= .308	.2766 (32) P= .063	.1910 (31) P= .152	.1350 (31) P= .234	.1920 (31) P= .150	.2635 (32) P= .073	-.0289 (32) P= .438
V.4	.1786 (34) P= .156	.3581 (34) P= .019	-.0523 (34) P= .385	-.7005 (34) P= .001	.9722 (34) P= .001	.0504 (33) P= .390	.8412 (34) P= .001	-.1697 (33) P= .172	-.2153 (34) P= .111	-.1352 (34) P= .223	.9565 (32) P= .001	.8106 (32) P= .001	.9790 (32) P= .001	.9336 (34) P= .001	.6831 (34) P= .001
V.5	.0752 (35) P= .334	.3416 (35) P= .022	-.0586 (35) P= .369	-.6984 (35) P= .001	.9798 (35) P= .001	-.1584 (34) P= .186	.8515 (35) P= .001	-.1801 (33) P= .158	-.2152 (35) P= .107	-.1021 (35) P= .280	.9504 (33) P= .001	.7853 (33) P= .001	.9915 (33) P= .001	.9357 (35) P= .001	.6978 (35) P= .001
V.6	-.1965 (39) P= .115	-.0407 (39) P= .403	-.1232 (39) P= .227	.1862 (39) P= .128	-.2641 (39) P= .052	-.1071 (38) P= .261	-.1824 (39) P= .133	.3755 (37) P= .011	.1858 (39) P= .129	.0729 (39) P= .330	-.3092 (36) P= .033	-.2898 (36) P= .043	-.2678 (35) P= .060	-.3316 (39) P= .020	-.1324 (39) P= .211
V.2	-.0887 (38) P= .298	-.3411 (38) P= .018	.0593 (38) P= .362	.6907 (38) P= .001	-.9767 (38) P= .001	-.0493 (37) P= .386	-.8337 (38) P= .001	.1637 (36) P= .170	.2123 (38) P= .100	.0839 (38) P= .308	-.9477 (35) P= .001	-.7763 (35) P= .001	-.9925 (35) P= .001	-.9270 (38) P= .001	-.6936 (38) P= .001
V.3	.1998 (37) P= .118	-.0963 (37) P= .285	-.1156 (37) P= .248	-.2823 (37) P= .045	.2907 (37) P= .040	-.1108 (36) P= .260	.3381 (37) P= .020	-.2621 (35) P= .064	-.2315 (37) P= .084	-.0966 (37) P= .285	.3678 (35) P= .015	.2933 (35) P= .044	.4197 (35) P= .006	.3141 (37) P= .029	.1617 (37) P= .169
V.9	-.0983 (35) P= .287	.2171 (35) P= .105	-.2600 (35) P= .066	.5029 (35) P= .001	-.1978 (35) P= .127	-.1652 (34) P= .175	-.0422 (34) P= .406	.4126 (34) P= .008	.2906 (35) P= .045	-.0864 (35) P= .311	-.1976 (34) P= .131	-.1769 (34) P= .159	-.2221 (34) P= .103	-.2459 (35) P= .077	-.0088 (35) P= .480
V.12	-.0561 (35) P= .374	-.2786 (35) P= .053	-.0122 (35) P= .472	.1886 (35) P= .139	-.4445 (35) P= .004	-.0311 (34) P= .431	-.4983 (34) P= .001	.0237 (34) P= .447	.1246 (35) P= .238	.2810 (35) P= .051	-.4373 (34) P= .005	-.4946 (34) P= .001	-.4093 (33) P= .009	-.4108 (35) P= .007	-.2758 (35) P= .054
V.13	-.1381 (35) P= .214	.3188 (35) P= .031	.1613 (35) P= .177	.3623 (35) P= .016	-.1797 (35) P= .151	-.1230 (34) P= .244	-.0384 (34) P= .415	.1139 (34) P= .261	.3438 (35) P= .022	-.0045 (35) P= .490	-.2228 (35) P= .099	-.0820 (35) P= .320	-.2368 (34) P= .089	-.1967 (35) P= .129	-.0082 (35) P= .481
V.7	-.0222 (40) P= .446	.2405 (40) P= .067	.0172 (40) P= .458	-.0623 (40) P= .351	.1501 (40) P= .178	-.0246 (39) P= .441	.0863 (39) P= .301	.1903 (37) P= .130	.0620 (40) P= .352	.0357 (40) P= .413	.0884 (37) P= .301	-.0351 (37) P= .418	.1373 (36) P= .212	.0467 (40) P= .387	.1617 (40) P= .159
V.14	-.2032 (37) P= .114	.1996 (37) P= .118	.2189 (37) P= .097	.1969 (37) P= .121	-.1870 (37) P= .134	-.2197 (37) P= .096	.1452 (37) P= .196	.0829 (35) P= .318	.3188 (37) P= .027	.0993 (37) P= .279	-.0942 (34) P= .298	-.0945 (34) P= .298	.1106 (34) P= .267	-.2093 (37) P= .107	.2895 (37) P= .041
V.15	-.0457 (40) P= .390	-.1077 (40) P= .254	-.0684 (40) P= .337	.0109 (39) P= .474	-.0077 (39) P= .482	-.0472 (39) P= .388	.0214 (38) P= .449	-.0878 (36) P= .305	-.0919 (40) P= .286	-.0497 (40) P= .380	-.0916 (36) P= .298	.2225 (36) P= .096	-.1699 (35) P= .165	-.0360 (39) P= .414	-.1418 (40) P= .191
V.8	-.0652 (35) P= .355	.1215 (35) P= .243	-.0365 (35) P= .418	-.2812 (35) P= .051	.4325 (35) P= .005	.2872 (34) P= .050	.4796 (34) P= .002	.0060 (34) P= .487	-.1500 (35) P= .195	-.2115 (35) P= .111	.3844 (34) P= .012	.4602 (34) P= .003	.3938 (33) P= .012	.4034 (35) P= .008	.2799 (35) P= .052
V.10	-.2000 (39) P= .111	.0948 (39) P= .283	.2412 (39) P= .070	.2669 (39) P= .050	-.1416 (39) P= .195	-.0503 (38) P= .382	-.0518 (39) P= .377	-.0363 (37) P= .416	.2925 (39) P= .035	-.0640 (39) P= .349	-.1909 (36) P= .132	-.0699 (36) P= .343	-.2231 (35) P= .099	-.0145 (39) P= .465	-.0638 (39) P= .350
V.11	-.0013 (39) P= .497	-.1704 (39) P= .150	-.2160 (39) P= .093	-.1359 (39) P= .205	.0879 (39) P= .297	.0759 (38) P= .325	.0705 (38) P= .337	.0166 (36) P= .462	-.2689 (39) P= .049	-.0507 (39) P= .380	.0883 (36) P= .304	.0248 (36) P= .443	.1160 (35) P= .254	.0019 (39) P= .495	.0262 (39) P= .437
V.17	.2092 (35) P= .114	.3362 (35) P= .024	-.0706 (35) P= .343	-.7012 (35) P= .001	.9788 (35) P= .001	-.0544 (34) P= .380	.8529 (35) P= .001	-.1734 (35) P= .160	-.2275 (35) P= .094	-.0920 (35) P= .300	.9524 (34) P= .001	.7836 (34) P= .001	.9904 (33) P= .001	.9292 (35) P= .001	.6867 (35) P= .001
V.18	.2445 (34) P= .082	-.2384 (34) P= .087	.4850 (34) P= .002	-.0625 (34) P= .363	-.2210 (34) P= .105	.0406 (33) P= .411	-.2211 (34) P= .104	-.1406 (34) P= .214	.0175 (34) P= .461	.2409 (34) P= .085	-.1773 (33) P= .162	-.3176 (33) P= .036	-.1882 (33) P= .147	-.2718 (34) P= .060	-.1213 (34) P= .247
V.19	.0037 (41) P= .491	.1215 (41) P= .225	-.0936 (41) P= .280	-.3705 (40) P= .009	.5677 (40) P= .001	-.1559 (39) P= .172	.5380 (39) P= .001	-.0817 (37) P= .315	-.1063 (41) P= .254	-.1123 (41) P= .242	.5388 (37) P= .001	.5760 (37) P= .001	.5708 (36) P= .001	.5306 (40) P= .001	.3454 (41) P= .013
V.28	.0945 (41) P= .278	.2268 (41) P= .077	-.0115 (41) P= .471	-.6247 (40) P= .001	.8646 (40) P= .001	-.0253 (39) P= .439	.7019 (39) P= .001	-.1719 (37) P= .155	-.1938 (41) P= .112	-.0314 (41) P= .423	.8327 (37) P= .001	.6804 (37) P= .001	.8682 (36) P= .001	.8210 (40) P= .001	.5323 (41) P= .001
V.29	-.2656 (25) P= .100	-.4064 (25) P= .022	.1075 (25) P= .304	.8271 (25) P= .001	-.9782 (25) P= .001	.0707 (24) P= .371	-.9353 (25) P= .001	.2063 (25) P= .161	.3116 (25) P= .065	.1807 (25) P= .194	-.9556 (25) P= .001	-.8233 (25) P= .001	-.9920 (25) P= .001	-.9330 (25) P= .001	-.8119 (25) P= .001
V.30	.2748 (31) P= .067	.4116 (31) P= .011	.0895 (31) P= .316	-.4902 (31) P= .003	.8490 (31) P= .001	-.0682 (30) P= .360	.8435 (31) P= .001	-.1667 (31) P= .185	-.1061 (31) P= .285	-.1409 (31) P= .225	.8344 (31) P= .001	.6878 (31) P= .001	.8346 (31) P= .001	.8212 (31) P= .001	.6945 (31) P= .001
V.16	-.0860 (40) P= .299	.0368 (40) P= .411	.2285 (40) P= .078	.1046 (39) P= .263	-.1089 (39) P= .255	-.0901 (38) P= .295	-.0505 (38) P= .382	.2841 (36) P= .047	.1677 (40) P= .150	-.0294 (40) P= .429	-.0684 (36) P= .346	.2201 (36) P= .099	-.1475 (35) P= .199	-.1297 (39) P= .216	.0390 (40) P= .405
V.20	-.0427 (40) P= .397	.4051 (40) P= .005	-.0098 (40) P= .476	.2187 (40) P= .088	.0118 (40) P= .471	-.0724 (39) P= .331	.0345 (39) P= .417	.3644 (37) P= .013	-.0965 (40) P= .277	-.1220 (40) P= .227	-.1228 (37) P= .234	-.1135 (37) P= .252	-.0801 (36) P= .321	-.0295 (40) P= .428	-.0570 (40) P= .363
V.21	.0998 (37) P= .278	.2341 (37) P= .082	.0680 (37) P= .345	.1763 (37) P= .148	-.0515 (37) P= .381	.0538 (36) P= .378	-.0788 (37) P= .321	.2707 (36) P= .055	-.0826 (37) P= .313	-.0477 (37) P= .390	-.1863 (34) P= .146	-.1981 (34) P= .131	-.1536 (34) P= .193	-.0362 (37) P= .416	-.1006 (37) P= .277
V.22	.5057 (40) P= .001	-.0869 (40) P= .297	.3788 (40) P= .008	.0863 (40) P= .298	-.2075 (40) P= .099	.3153 (39) P= .025	-.3136 (39) P= .026	.0281 (37) P= .434	.0534 (40) P= .372	.2935 (40) P= .033	-.1031 (37) P= .272	-.3800 (37) P= .010	-.2066 (36) P= .113	-.2788 (40) P= .041	-.2767 (40) P= .042

	V4.4	V4.2	F.3	F.5	F.6	F.7	F.8	F.10	F.11	F.12	F.13	F.14	F.15	F.9	F.27
V.23	.3426 (38) P=.018	-.0800 (38) P=.317	.3090 (38) P=.030	-.1514 (38) P=.182	.1961 (38) P=.119	-.0681 (37) P=.344	.1133 (37) P=.252	-.1029 (36) P=.275	.0380 (38) P=.410	.2651 (38) P=.054	.2397 (35) P=.083	.0639 (35) P=.358	.2364 (35) P=.086	.1598 (38) P=.169	.0600 (38) P=.360
V.24	-.1134 (37) P=.252	.1583 (37) P=.175	.2123 (37) P=.104	.4051 (37) P=.006	-.3030 (37) P=.034	-.1421 (36) P=.204	-.2874 (35) P=.045	.5859 (35) P=.001	.3741 (37) P=.011	.2118 (37) P=.104	-.2881 (37) P=.042	-.3410 (37) P=.019	-.3726 (36) P=.013	-.4097 (37) P=.006	-.1300 (37) P=.222
V.26	-.1005 (33) P=.289	.1338 (33) P=.229	.0411 (33) P=.410	.3942 (33) P=.012	-.3148 (33) P=.037	.0023 (32) P=.495	-.2193 (32) P=.114	.2696 (32) P=.068	.2359 (33) P=.093	-.1411 (33) P=.217	-.3053 (33) P=.042	-.3334 (33) P=.029	-.3369 (33) P=.028	-.3365 (33) P=.028	.0821 (33) P=.325
V.27	.2099 (31) P=.129	.3569 (31) P=.024	-.0693 (31) P=.356	-.7139 (31) P=.001	.9851 (31) P=.001	.0790 (30) P=.339	.8625 (31) P=.001	-.1788 (31) P=.168	-.2464 (31) P=.091	-.1150 (31) P=.269	.9573 (31) P=.001	.7867 (31) P=.001	.9927 (31) P=.001	.9365 (31) P=.001	.7172 (31) P=.001
V.25	.2313 (32) P=.101	-.0630 (32) P=.366	.1205 (32) P=.256	.1122 (32) P=.274	.0968 (31) P=.302	.3626 (31) P=.023	-.0162 (30) P=.466	-.0676 (30) P=.361	-.0930 (32) P=.306	.0825 (32) P=.327	-.1128 (31) P=.273	.0116 (31) P=.475	-.0207 (31) P=.456	.2112 (31) P=.127	-.1352 (32) P=.230
V.34	.1861 (40) P=.125	.0646 (40) P=.346	.2731 (40) P=.044	.0084 (40) P=.479	.1203 (40) P=.230	-.0996 (39) P=.273	.0781 (39) P=.318	-.0245 (37) P=.443	.3226 (40) P=.021	.3714 (40) P=.009	.1992 (37) P=.119	.0558 (37) P=.372	.1461 (36) P=.198	.0765 (40) P=.319	.0511 (40) P=.377
V.35	.1621 (31) P=.192	.1936 (31) P=.148	-.1128 (31) P=.273	-.5631 (31) P=.001	.8644 (31) P=.001	.0531 (30) P=.390	.7126 (31) P=.001	-.0372 (31) P=.421	-.0776 (31) P=.339	-.0589 (31) P=.376	.8811 (31) P=.001	.7250 (31) P=.001	.8234 (31) P=.001	.8014 (31) P=.001	.6304 (31) P=.001
V.36	.1248 (37) P=.231	.3180 (37) P=.028	-.0039 (37) P=.491	-.6979 (37) P=.001	.9760 (37) P=.001	.1956 (36) P=.126	.8333 (36) P=.001	-.1626 (35) P=.175	-.1993 (37) P=.118	-.0419 (37) P=.403	.9549 (36) P=.001	.7645 (36) P=.001	.9938 (36) P=.001	.9247 (37) P=.001	.6681 (37) P=.001
V.37	.3354 (39) P=.018	-.3262 (39) P=.021	.1944 (39) P=.118	-.0291 (39) P=.430	-.2660 (39) P=.051	.1520 (38) P=.181	-.3735 (38) P=.010	-.1992 (36) P=.122	-.1689 (39) P=.152	.2287 (39) P=.081	-.1827 (36) P=.143	-.3418 (36) P=.021	-.2230 (35) P=.099	-.2540 (39) P=.059	-.1711 (39) P=.149
V.38	.2175 (35) P=.105	-.1046 (35) P=.275	.3348 (35) P=.025	.0735 (35) P=.337	-.1137 (35) P=.258	-.1724 (34) P=.165	-.1234 (34) P=.243	-.2482 (34) P=.078	.3231 (35) P=.029	.3701 (35) P=.014	-.0336 (35) P=.424	-.1170 (35) P=.252	-.0318 (35) P=.428	-.1445 (35) P=.204	.0126 (35) P=.471
V.32	.5382 (40) P=.001	-.0596 (40) P=.357	.6071 (40) P=.001	.0695 (40) P=.335	-.1055 (40) P=.259	.2051 (39) P=.105	-.2089 (39) P=.101	.2546 (37) P=.064	.1998 (40) P=.108	.5502 (40) P=.001	-.0765 (37) P=.326	-.3525 (37) P=.016	-.0848 (36) P=.312	-.2003 (40) P=.108	-.1974 (40) P=.111
V.33	.1675 (34) P=.172	.3416 (34) P=.024	.0240 (34) P=.447	-.4812 (34) P=.002	.7548 (34) P=.001	.0501 (33) P=.391	.7617 (33) P=.001	-.1099 (32) P=.275	-.1206 (34) P=.248	-.0220 (34) P=.451	.7542 (34) P=.001	.4742 (34) P=.002	.7762 (33) P=.001	.7010 (34) P=.001	.7338 (34) P=.001
V.31	.1384 (40) P=.197	-.2342 (40) P=.073	.1348 (40) P=.204	-.6304 (40) P=.001	.8737 (40) P=.001	-.0652 (39) P=.347	.7769 (39) P=.001	-.1613 (37) P=.170	-.1173 (40) P=.235	.0035 (40) P=.492	.8500 (37) P=.001	.6926 (37) P=.001	.8965 (36) P=.001	.8283 (40) P=.001	.6073 (40) P=.001
S.2	-.1368 (40) P=.200	.3253 (40) P=.020	-.0530 (40) P=.373	.2324 (39) P=.077	.2462 (39) P=.065	-.1246 (39) P=.225	.1382 (39) P=.204	.4536 (38) P=.003	.3438 (36) P=.015	.0620 (40) P=.352	.0421 (36) P=.404	-.0379 (36) P=.413	.1678 (35) P=.168	-.2303 (39) P=.079	.0885 (40) P=.294
S.4	.1620 (40) P=.159	-.2006 (40) P=.107	.0712 (40) P=.331	-.0263 (39) P=.437	.0653 (39) P=.346	.0073 (39) P=.482	-.0789 (39) P=.319	.0156 (38) P=.464	-.2036 (36) P=.104	-.0858 (40) P=.299	-.1570 (36) P=.180	-.4353 (36) P=.004	-.0369 (35) P=.417	.1641 (39) P=.159	-.3044 (40) P=.028
S.6	.1555 (39) P=.172	.0031 (39) P=.493	-.1816 (39) P=.134	-.4845 (38) P=.001	.0339 (38) P=.420	.3055 (38) P=.031	-.4503 (38) P=.002	-.1121 (36) P=.257	-.5846 (39) P=.001	-.2887 (39) P=.037	.2337 (35) P=.088	.1287 (35) P=.231	.1171 (34) P=.255	-.0504 (38) P=.382	-.0905 (39) P=.292
S.3	.0753 (41) P=.320	-.1171 (41) P=.233	.1421 (41) P=.188	.4233 (40) P=.003	-.5255 (40) P=.001	.2137 (39) P=.096	-.5152 (39) P=.001	.1978 (37) P=.120	.2236 (41) P=.080	.0176 (41) P=.456	-.6310 (37) P=.001	-.7017 (37) P=.001	-.6376 (36) P=.001	-.4433 (40) P=.002	-.4600 (41) P=.001
S.1	-.3932 (37) P=.000	.2819 (37) P=.045	-.3574 (37) P=.015	.2476 (37) P=.070	.0644 (37) P=.352	-.4816 (36) P=.001	.2778 (37) P=.048	.2370 (35) P=.085	.0167 (37) P=.461	-.4297 (37) P=.004	-.0421 (34) P=.407	.0669 (34) P=.354	.0199 (34) P=.456	.1086 (37) P=.261	.2588 (37) P=.061
S.5	-.0135 (32) P=.471	.2101 (32) P=.124	-.0104 (32) P=.478	.4507 (32) P=.005	-.3333 (32) P=.031	-.0694 (31) P=.355	-.2236 (31) P=.113	.3617 (29) P=.027	.2278 (32) P=.105	-.1336 (32) P=.233	-.2751 (31) P=.067	-.2625 (31) P=.077	-.3455 (31) P=.028	-.3389 (32) P=.029	-.2718 (32) P=.066
S.7	.1079 (41) P=.251	.0537 (41) P=.369	.0636 (41) P=.346	-.1117 (40) P=.246	-.2201 (40) P=.086	.1613 (39) P=.163	-.4512 (39) P=.002	-.0980 (37) P=.282	-.3081 (41) P=.025	-.0557 (41) P=.365	-.1930 (37) P=.126	-.2336 (37) P=.082	-.2408 (36) P=.079	-.2542 (40) P=.057	-.2646 (41) P=.047
S.8	.3468 (41) P=.013	-.2425 (41) P=.063	.2070 (41) P=.097	.0459 (40) P=.389	-.1090 (40) P=.252	.0714 (39) P=.333	-.0052 (39) P=.487	-.1012 (37) P=.276	-.0360 (41) P=.411	.2171 (41) P=.086	-.1366 (37) P=.210	-.1975 (37) P=.121	-.1429 (36) P=.203	-.0900 (40) P=.290	-.1757 (41) P=.136
S.9	-.0697 (41) P=.332	-.0735 (41) P=.324	-.1986 (41) P=.107	.3001 (40) P=.030	-.1805 (40) P=.133	-.1463 (39) P=.187	-.0019 (39) P=.495	.1592 (37) P=.173	.1495 (41) P=.175	-.1046 (41) P=.258	-.2883 (37) P=.042	-.0945 (37) P=.289	-.2440 (36) P=.076	-.0919 (40) P=.286	.0010 (41) P=.498
S.10	-.0827 (41) P=.304	-.2904 (41) P=.033	-.0915 (41) P=.285	-.0375 (40) P=.409	-.2152 (40) P=.091	.1362 (39) P=.204	-.2335 (39) P=.076	-.2704 (37) P=.053	-.2027 (41) P=.102	.0341 (41) P=.416	-.1689 (37) P=.159	-.0178 (37) P=.458	-.1550 (36) P=.183	-.1406 (40) P=.193	-.1338 (41) P=.202
S.18	.0315 (36) P=.428	.0718 (36) P=.339	.1549 (36) P=.184	.1108 (36) P=.260	-.0565 (36) P=.372	.0575 (35) P=.372	-.0147 (36) P=.466	.1453 (35) P=.202	.0044 (36) P=.490	-.1586 (36) P=.178	-.0818 (34) P=.323	.0542 (34) P=.380	-.0911 (34) P=.304	-.0594 (36) P=.365	.0168 (36) P=.461
S.19	-.0680 (36) P=.347	.2896 (36) P=.043	-.0797 (36) P=.322	-.1249 (36) P=.234	.0110 (36) P=.475	-.0957 (35) P=.292	-.0834 (36) P=.314	.5343 (35) P=.001	.0174 (36) P=.460	-.0441 (36) P=.399	-.0923 (34) P=.302	-.1968 (34) P=.132	-.0789 (34) P=.329	-.0546 (36) P=.376	.0441 (36) P=.399
S.17	-.1009 (41) P=.265	-.2095 (41) P=.094	.1391 (41) P=.193	.1115 (40) P=.247	-.0180 (40) P=.456	.0634 (39) P=.351	-.0815 (39) P=.311	.3116 (37) P=.030	.2255 (41) P=.078	.0095 (41) P=.477	.0042 (37) P=.490	.0450 (37) P=.396	-.1683 (36) P=.163	-.0157 (40) P=.462	-.1110 (41) P=.245
S.11	-.1226 (41) P=.223	-.1452 (41) P=.183	.2721 (41) P=.043	-.0668 (40) P=.341	-.0319 (40) P=.422	.0260 (39) P=.438	.0476 (39) P=.387	-.1295 (37) P=.222	.1736 (41) P=.139	-.0409 (41) P=.400	-.0907 (37) P=.297	.0168 (37) P=.461	-.0590 (36) P=.366	.0378 (40) P=.408	-.0212 (41) P=.448
S.12	-.2118 (41) P=.092	.0863 (41) P=.296	-.1189 (41) P=.230	-.2770 (40) P=.042	.3379 (40) P=.016	-.0930 (39) P=.287	.3126 (39) P=.026	.0570 (37) P=.369	.0823 (41) P=.305	.0497 (41) P=.379	.2777 (37) P=.048	.1960 (37) P=.122	.3612 (36) P=.015	.3057 (40) P=.028	.3027 (41) P=.027
S.13	-.1715 (38) P=.152	-.2475 (38) P=.067	-.0422 (38) P=.401	-.1979 (37) P=.120	-.1384 (37) P=.207	-.0425 (36) P=.403	-.2200 (36) P=.099	-.0003 (34) P=.499	-.1193 (38) P=.238	.0880 (38) P=.300	-.1137 (34) P=.261	.0951 (34) P=.296	-.1170 (33) P=.258	-.0923 (37) P=.293	-.1040 (38) P=.267
S.14	.2102 (40) P=.096	.1292 (40) P=.213	-.0237 (40) P=.442	-.1592 (40) P=.163	.1897 (40) P=.121	.0680 (39) P=.341	.1499 (39) P=.181	-.0247 (37) P=.442	-.1813 (40) P=.131	-.0713 (40) P=.331	.1759 (37) P=.149	-.0537 (37) P=.376	.5170 (36) P=.001	.1625 (40) P=.158	.2021 (40) P=.106
S.15	-.1493 (40) P=.179	.4156 (40) P=.004	-.1504 (40) P=.177	.1299 (40) P=.212	.1707 (40) P=.146	-.1207 (39) P=.232	.1400 (39) P=.198	.4760 (37) P=.001	.0550 (40) P=.368	-.1113 (40) P=.247	.0524 (37) P=.379	.0592 (37) P=.364	.0687 (36) P=.345	.0704 (40) P=.333	.1414 (40) P=.192
S.16	.0566 (41) P=.363	-.2153 (41) P=.088	.3547 (41) P=.011	-.0433 (40) P=.395	-.1399 (40) P=.195	-.0182 (39) P=.456	-.0489 (39) P=.384	.0731 (37) P=.334	.0821 (41) P=.305	.1653 (41) P=.151	-.1456 (37) P=.195	-.2065 (37) P=.110	-.1297 (36) P=.225	-.0990 (40) P=.272	-.1256 (41) P=.217
S.25	-.1913 (32) P=.147	-.1729 (32) P=.172	-.0677 (32) P=.356	.0193 (32) P=.458	-.2235 (32) P=.109	.1394 (31) P=.227	-.3588 (32) P=.022	.2061 (32) P=.129	-.3257 (32) P=.034	-.0822 (32) P=.327	-.2004 (32) P=.136	.0099 (32) P=.479	-.2735 (32) P=.065	-.3036 (32) P=.046	-.1882 (32) P=.151

	F.25	F.26	F.24	F.23	F.21	F.20	F.17	F.16	F.18	F.19	F.22	V.1	V.4	V.5	V.6
	-.5174 (35) P=.001	.1373 (37) P=.209	-.0012 (38) P=.497	-.0387 (37) P=.410	-.0026 (36) P=.494	-.1164 (37) P=.246	-.1059 (37) P=.266	-.1676 (37) P=.161	.1202 (37) P=.239	.0368 (37) P=.414	-.0738 (31) P=.347	-.0876 (32) P=.317	.1790 (34) P=.156	.2003 (34) P=.128	-.1667 (37) P=.162
	-.1963 (36) P=.126	-.2451 (36) P=.075	.0747 (37) P=.330	-.1296 (36) P=.226	.3124 (36) P=.032	.3724 (36) P=.013	-.1260 (36) P=.232	.1318 (36) P=.222	.2539 (36) P=.068	.2520 (36) P=.069	.1655 (30) P=.191	.2008 (31) P=.139	-.4351 (32) P=.006	-.3892 (33) P=.013	.2064 (36) P=.114
	.3120 (33) P=.041	.3795 (32) P=.016	.3825 (33) P=.014	.1894 (32) P=.150	.0721 (32) P=.348	.2110 (32) P=.123	-.1478 (32) P=.210	.0514 (32) P=.390	.3076 (32) P=.043	.0594 (32) P=.373	.3582 (27) P=.033	-.3391 (29) P=.036	-.4163 (30) P=.011	-.3341 (31) P=.033	.0843 (32) P=.323
	.2163 (30) P=.125	.2590 (30) P=.083	-.1300 (31) P=.243	-.0513 (30) P=.394	.4380 (30) P=.008	.5347 (30) P=.001	-.2698 (30) P=.075	.4759 (30) P=.004	.3362 (30) P=.035	.1736 (30) P=.179	.1867 (25) P=.186	.3823 (29) P=.020	.9837 (30) P=.001	.9987 (31) P=.001	-.3029 (31) P=.049
	-.4020 (31) P=.012	-.1881 (32) P=.151	-.1444 (32) P=.215	-.0284 (32) P=.439	.4598 (32) P=.004	.0489 (32) P=.395	-.1150 (32) P=.265	.0910 (32) P=.310	.0156 (32) P=.466	.0786 (32) P=.335	-.1567 (28) P=.213	.0188 (28) P=.462	-.2845 (28) P=.071	.1320 (28) P=.252	-.2330 (30) P=.108
	-.5102 (37) P=.001	.0062 (39) P=.485	.0014 (40) P=.497	-.2233 (39) P=.086	.1273 (38) P=.223	-.0477 (39) P=.387	-.0972 (39) P=.278	-.0884 (39) P=.296	.0844 (39) P=.305	.2407 (39) P=.070	-.2723 (33) P=.063	.1874 (32) P=.152	.1147 (34) P=.259	-.1396 (35) P=.212	-.0558 (39) P=.368
	-.0862 (30) P=.325	.2494 (30) P=.092	-.0012 (31) P=.498	-.0533 (30) P=.390	-.1150 (30) P=.272	-.0585 (30) P=.379	-.0199 (30) P=.458	-.0143 (30) P=.470	.4461 (30) P=.007	.9075 (30) P=.001	-.0266 (24) P=.451	.1278 (28) P=.258	.8286 (29) P=.001	.8314 (29) P=.001	-.3341 (31) P=.033
	-.4302 (35) P=.005	.0618 (36) P=.360	-.1373 (37) P=.209	-.1802 (36) P=.146	-.1759 (36) P=.152	-.0758 (36) P=.330	.0185 (36) P=.457	-.3036 (36) P=.036	-.0569 (36) P=.371	.1668 (36) P=.165	.0916 (30) P=.315	.2571 (31) P=.081	.9796 (33) P=.001	.9969 (34) P=.001	-.2739 (36) P=.053
	-.3511 (36) P=.018	.2594 (38) P=.058	.0763 (39) P=.322	-.3626 (38) P=.013	-.0607 (37) P=.361	-.0312 (38) P=.426	-.1479 (38) P=.188	-.2603 (38) P=.057	-.1194 (38) P=.238	-.0018 (38) P=.496	.0552 (33) P=.380	.0923 (31) P=.311	-.2314 (33) P=.098	-.2455 (35) P=.078	-.2712 (36) P=.050
	-.4917 (34) P=.002	-.0622 (34) P=.363	-.1294 (35) P=.229	-.1564 (34) P=.189	.0588 (34) P=.370	-.1508 (34) P=.197	.0261 (34) P=.442	-.1703 (34) P=.168	-.1423 (34) P=.211	-.0424 (34) P=.406	-.1739 (28) P=.188	-.0404 (31) P=.415	-.0890 (32) P=.314	-.0530 (32) P=.387	.1300 (34) P=.232
	-.3680 (37) P=.013	.2300 (39) P=.079	.2033 (40) P=.104	-.2575 (39) P=.057	.1569 (38) P=.173	.1593 (39) P=.166	-.0261 (39) P=.437	.0481 (39) P=.386	.1386 (39) P=.200	-.2668 (39) P=.050	-.1613 (33) P=.185	.3305 (32) P=.032	-.1649 (34) P=.176	-.1501 (35) P=.195	-.0978 (39) P=.277
	.0835 (33) P=.322	.4999 (33) P=.002	.2508 (34) P=.076	.1614 (33) P=.185	-.0027 (33) P=.494	.3581 (33) P=.020	.0453 (33) P=.401	.0752 (33) P=.339	.2642 (33) P=.069	.1906 (33) P=.144	.2296 (27) P=.125	.1353 (28) P=.246	.9449 (29) P=.001	.9281 (30) P=.001	-.3372 (33) P=.027
	-.0523 (37) P=.379	-.1290 (39) P=.217	-.1833 (40) P=.129	-.0135 (39) P=.468	-.1119 (38) P=.252	-.1209 (39) P=.232	.1043 (39) P=.264	-.1695 (39) P=.151	.0242 (39) P=.442	-.0596 (39) P=.359	.6706 (33) P=.001	.0748 (32) P=.342	.9522 (34) P=.001	.9118 (35) P=.001	-.2970 (39) P=.033
	-.1957 (37) P=.123	-.0190 (40) P=.454	.2624 (40) P=.051	.1175 (40) P=.235	.3181 (39) P=.024	.2947 (40) P=.032	.1944 (40) P=.115	.3245 (40) P=.021	.1876 (40) P=.123	.2215 (40) P=.085	-.1681 (34) P=.171	.0114 (32) P=.475	-.1158 (33) P=.260	-.0943 (34) P=.298	.3601 (38) P=.013
	-.1192 (37) P=.241	.2060 (40) P=.101	.1641 (40) P=.156	.0484 (40) P=.383	.1856 (39) P=.129	-.0614 (40) P=.353	-.1512 (40) P=.176	.1532 (40) P=.173	.0386 (40) P=.407	.1330 (40) P=.207	-.1745 (34) P=.162	-.1621 (32) P=.188	-.1349 (33) P=.227	.3317 (34) P=.028	-.1937 (38) P=.122
	.0562 (36) P=.372	.2580 (39) P=.056	.1673 (39) P=.154	-.1813 (39) P=.135	.0407 (38) P=.404	.1797 (39) P=.137	-.0812 (39) P=.311	.1934 (39) P=.119	-.0932 (39) P=.286	-.0801 (39) P=.314	.0134 (33) P=.470	-.0377 (32) P=.419	.1786 (33) P=.160	-.0631 (34) P=.362	-.0286 (38) P=.432
	-.1699 (37) P=.157	.0624 (40) P=.351	.1879 (41) P=.120	.1887 (40) P=.122	.1546 (39) P=.174	-.0405 (40) P=.402	.0463 (40) P=.388	.2617 (40) P=.051	-.0297 (40) P=.428	.1090 (40) P=.252	-.2817 (34) P=.053	.0777 (32) P=.336	-.5753 (34) P=.001	-.5926 (35) P=.001	.1110 (39) P=.250
	.2335 (34) P=.092	.3381 (36) P=.022	.3158 (37) P=.028	.2734 (36) P=.053	.2893 (35) P=.046	.2905 (36) P=.043	-.0355 (36) P=.419	.4360 (36) P=.004	.1984 (36) P=.123	-.3312 (36) P=.024	.2783 (30) P=.068	-.3890 (31) P=.015	.0676 (33) P=.354	.0902 (34) P=.306	.1389 (37) P=.206
	.2515 (31) P=.086	.3851 (31) P=.016	.4744 (32) P=.003	-.2122 (31) P=.126	.1001 (31) P=.296	.1628 (31) P=.191	.1341 (31) P=.236	-.1795 (31) P=.167	.1628 (31) P=.191	-.0241 (31) P=.449	.2205 (26) P=.140	-.1300 (26) P=.263	-.3100 (28) P=.054	-.3402 (30) P=.033	-.1125 (31) P=.273
	-.0214 (37) P=.450	.5676 (40) P=.001	.4703 (41) P=.001	-.2578 (40) P=.054	.2028 (39) P=.108	.3887 (40) P=.007	-.0831 (40) P=.305	.3173 (40) P=.023	-.0596 (40) P=.357	-.0275 (40) P=.433	-.1685 (34) P=.170	.1851 (32) P=.155	-.2958 (34) P=.045	-.2921 (35) P=.044	-.0083 (39) P=.480
	-.1428 (37) P=.200	-.0900 (40) P=.290	-.1513 (41) P=.173	-.0751 (40) P=.323	-.2077 (39) P=.102	-.2176 (40) P=.089	-.1315 (40) P=.209	-.2593 (40) P=.053	.1373 (40) P=.199	-.0645 (40) P=.346	.1038 (34) P=.280	.1974 (34) P=.139	-.1412 (34) P=.213	-.1229 (35) P=.241	-.1715 (39) P=.148
	.0764 (37) P=.327	-.1814 (40) P=.131	-.1092 (41) P=.248	.3514 (40) P=.013	.0424 (39) P=.399	-.1537 (40) P=.171	-.0138 (40) P=.466	.0453 (40) P=.391	.1602 (40) P=.162	-.0569 (40) P=.364	.2289 (34) P=.096	-.0363 (32) P=.422	-.2348 (34) P=.091	-.1890 (35) P=.138	-.0707 (39) P=.334
	-.0845 (37) P=.309	-.1012 (40) P=.267	-.2016 (41) P=.103	-.2050 (40) P=.102	-.1364 (39) P=.204	-.2719 (40) P=.045	-.1333 (40) P=.206	-.1636 (40) P=.157	-.3124 (40) P=.025	-.1208 (40) P=.229	.0236 (34) P=.447	.1229 (32) P=.251	-.2049 (34) P=.123	-.1760 (35) P=.156	.0658 (39) P=.345
	.1131 (34) P=.262	.0502 (35) P=.387	.0577 (36) P=.369	.2166 (35) P=.106	.0851 (35) P=.313	.0796 (35) P=.325	.2321 (35) P=.090	.2268 (35) P=.095	.2025 (35) P=.110	-.0163 (35) P=.463	.7160 (29) P=.001	-.0611 (31) P=.372	-.0801 (34) P=.326	-.0643 (34) P=.359	-.0791 (36) P=.323
	-.2094 (34) P=.117	.4091 (35) P=.007	.4732 (36) P=.002	-.0366 (35) P=.417	.7706 (35) P=.001	.5755 (35) P=.001	-.0315 (35) P=.429	.6968 (35) P=.001	.3390 (35) P=.023	.1721 (35) P=.161	-.1013 (29) P=.300	.1345 (31) P=.235	-.0913 (34) P=.304	-.0679 (34) P=.351	.1922 (36) P=.131
	-.0060 (37) P=.486	-.1941 (40) P=.115	-.1398 (41) P=.192	-.1264 (40) P=.219	-.1764 (39) P=.141	-.1944 (40) P=.115	-.0604 (40) P=.356	-.1249 (40) P=.221	.4310 (40) P=.003	.6793 (40) P=.001	.1483 (34) P=.201	.2835 (32) P=.058	-.0960 (34) P=.295	-.1518 (35) P=.192	-.1846 (39) P=.130
	.0234 (37) P=.445	-.2765 (40) P=.042	-.2885 (41) P=.034	.0305 (40) P=.426	.0284 (39) P=.432	-.2673 (40) P=.048	-.0285 (40) P=.431	-.0666 (40) P=.341	.0385 (40) P=.407	-.1565 (40) P=.167	.4141 (34) P=.007	.0107 (32) P=.477	.0206 (34) P=.454	-.0346 (35) P=.422	.0848 (39) P=.304
	-.1408 (37) P=.203	-.1803 (40) P=.133	-.0763 (41) P=.318	.0138 (40) P=.466	.1251 (39) P=.224	-.2319 (40) P=.075	-.0381 (40) P=.408	.1748 (40) P=.140	-.0937 (40) P=.283	-.1750 (40) P=.140	-.2057 (34) P=.122	-.0542 (32) P=.384	.3711 (34) P=.015	.3487 (35) P=.020	.2740 (39) P=.046
	.0089 (34) P=.480	-.1853 (37) P=.136	-.2052 (38) P=.108	-.3585 (37) P=.015	-.0864 (36) P=.308	-.2158 (37) P=.100	-.2177 (37) P=.098	-.3229 (37) P=.026	-.2968 (37) P=.037	-.0844 (37) P=.310	-.1189 (31) P=.262	.2305 (30) P=.110	-.0509 (32) P=.391	-.1065 (33) P=.278	.0764 (36) P=.329
	.1416 (37) P=.198	.9048 (39) P=.001	.7317 (40) P=.001	-.0677 (39) P=.341	.2287 (38) P=.084	.1971 (39) P=.115	.0329 (39) P=.421	.2378 (39) P=.072	-.0443 (39) P=.394	.0865 (39) P=.300	-.2914 (33) P=.050	.1121 (32) P=.271	.4848 (34) P=.002	.4752 (35) P=.002	-.1513 (39) P=.179
	.0719 (37) P=.336	.0984 (39) P=.276	.3767 (40) P=.008	.0149 (39) P=.464	.6381 (38) P=.001	.7179 (39) P=.001	-.0117 (39) P=.472	.3900 (39) P=.007	.3855 (39) P=.007	.3414 (39) P=.017	-.2611 (33) P=.071	.1112 (32) P=.272	.0341 (34) P=.424	.0758 (35) P=.333	.1100 (39) P=.253
	.0299 (37) P=.430	.0225 (40) P=.445	.0184 (41) P=.454	-.1828 (40) P=.129	-.0187 (39) P=.455	-.1772 (40) P=.137	.0075 (40) P=.482	-.1264 (40) P=.218	-.0231 (40) P=.444	-.1048 (40) P=.260	.3409 (34) P=.024	-.0281 (32) P=.439	-.1082 (34) P=.271	-.1194 (35) P=.247	.0435 (39) P=.396
	.1205 (31) P=.259	.3116 (31) P=.044	.2109 (32) P=.123	-.3253 (31) P=.037	.0495 (31) P=.396	.2351 (31) P=.102	.0686 (31) P=.357	.0420 (31) P=.411	.1365 (31) P=.232	.2547 (31) P=.083	.1572 (25) P=.226	.0299 (30) P=.438	-.2707 (31) P=.070	-.2950 (31) P=.054	.0479 (32) P=.397

F.25	F.26	F.24	F.23	F.21	F.20	F.17	F.16	F.18	F.19	F.22	V.1	V.4	V.5	V.6
.1949 (23) P= .186	-.2509 (24) P= .119	-.0330 (24) P= .439	.2548 (24) P= .115	-.0956 (24) P= .328	-.0794 (24) P= .356	.0905 (24) P= .337	.0889 (24) P= .340	.0923 (24) P= .334	-.1654 (24) P= .220	.5572 (21) P= .004	-.2127 (20) P= .184	.5831 (22) P= .002	.4415 (22) P= .020	-.1332 (24) P= .267
-.0420 (31) P= .411	.2452 (31) P= .092	.1262 (32) P= .246	-.2630 (31) P= .076	.1429 (31) P= .222	.1307 (31) P= .242	.1656 (31) P= .187	-.0587 (31) P= .377	.0046 (31) P= .490	.1818 (31) P= .164	.2019 (25) P= .167	-.0096 (30) P= .480	-.2624 (31) P= .077	-.2832 (31) P= .061	.0936 (32) P= .305
.0348 (27) P= .432	-.1052 (27) P= .301	-.0795 (27) P= .347	.2900 (27) P= .071	-.2035 (27) P= .154	-.1053 (27) P= .301	.0819 (27) P= .342	.1976 (27) P= .162	.3215 (27) P= .051	-.1055 (27) P= .300	.3499 (21) P= .060	-.0626 (26) P= .381	.2238 (26) P= .136	.0611 (26) P= .383	-.0295 (27) P= .442
.3726 (23) P= .040	-.0932 (24) P= .332	.0808 (24) P= .354	.2776 (24) P= .095	-.1457 (24) P= .248	-.1156 (24) P= .295	.1778 (24) P= .203	.0480 (24) P= .412	-.0080 (24) P= .485	-.2053 (24) P= .168	.6566 (21) P= .001	-.1474 (20) P= .268	.5756 (22) P= .003	.6169 (22) P= .001	-.0743 (24) P= .365
.0888 (30) P= .320	-.1082 (30) P= .285	-.0284 (30) P= .441	.0160 (30) P= .466	-.2853 (30) P= .063	-.1024 (30) P= .295	-.0152 (30) P= .468	-.2242 (30) P= .117	.0049 (30) P= .490	-.0719 (30) P= .353	.1923 (24) P= .184	.2648 (28) P= .087	.1794 (28) P= .181	.0849 (28) P= .334	-.1299 (30) P= .247
.0349 (37) P= .419	-.3138 (40) P= .024	-.1718 (41) P= .141	.0067 (40) P= .484	-.0967 (39) P= .279	-.2675 (40) P= .048	-.2413 (40) P= .067	-.1015 (40) P= .267	.1890 (40) P= .121	.2056 (40) P= .102	.1784 (34) P= .156	.1234 (32) P= .251	-.0084 (34) P= .481	-.0459 (35) P= .397	.2444 (39) P= .067
-.3009 (37) P= .035	-.0925 (40) P= .285	-.1224 (41) P= .223	-.1355 (40) P= .202	-.1428 (39) P= .193	-.1266 (40) P= .218	.0246 (40) P= .440	-.1326 (40) P= .207	-.1709 (40) P= .146	-.0764 (40) P= .320	.3697 (34) P= .016	.4386 (32) P= .006	-.0519 (34) P= .385	-.0518 (35) P= .384	-.0888 (39) P= .295
-.2973 (34) P= .044	.1040 (34) P= .279	-.0077 (35) P= .482	-.1653 (34) P= .175	.0846 (34) P= .317	.0905 (34) P= .305	.1258 (34) P= .239	.0159 (34) P= .465	.0920 (34) P= .300	.0931 (34) P= .300	-.0107 (28) P= .478	.1414 (31) P= .224	-.1446 (32) P= .215	-.1403 (33) P= .218	.0131 (35) P= .470
.0428 (36) P= .402	-.2487 (37) P= .069	-.1815 (38) P= .138	-.1556 (37) P= .179	.0660 (36) P= .351	.0266 (37) P= .438	-.1224 (37) P= .235	-.2769 (37) P= .049	.3062 (37) P= .033	.1481 (37) P= .191	.6312 (31) P= .001	.1828 (32) P= .158	-.1986 (33) P= .134	-.2215 (34) P= .104	.0784 (38) P= .320
.0517 (35) P= .384	-.1444 (37) P= .197	-.0135 (38) P= .468	-.1107 (37) P= .257	.1671 (36) P= .165	.0229 (37) P= .446	-.0316 (37) P= .426	.0784 (37) P= .322	-.0040 (37) P= .491	.0305 (37) P= .429	.6114 (31) P= .001	.3721 (32) P= .018	-.1790 (34) P= .156	-.2080 (35) P= .115	.0729 (38) P= .332

| V.29 | V.30 | V.16 | V.20 | V.21 | V.22 | V.23 | V.24 | V.26 | V.27 | V.25 | V.34 | V.35 | V.36 | V.37 |

1.0000
(0)
P=******

-.8566   1.0000
(24)   (0)
P= .001 P=******

.1912   -.0078   1.0000
(24)   (31)   (0)
P= .185 P= .483 P=******

.0704   -.0019   .0238   1.0000
(25)   (31)   (39)   (0)
P= .369 P= .496 P= .443 P=******

.1568   -.0820   .0264   .8176   1.0000
(25)   (31)   (36)   (37)   (0)
P= .227 P= .331 P= .439 P= .001 P=******

.5167   -.2587   -.0527   .0400   .0094   1.0000
(25)   (31)   (39)   (40)   (37)   (0)
P= .004 P= .080 P= .375 P= .403 P= .478 P=******

-.3658   .2562   -.1447   -.1026   .1178   .4572   1.0000
(25)   (31)   (37)   (38)   (37)   (38)   (0)
P= .036 P= .082 P= .196 P= .270 P= .244 P= .002 P=******

.4219   -.2985   .2181   .3241   .4838   .1059   .2654   1.0000
(25)   (31)   (36)   (37)   (34)   (37)   (35)   (0)
P= .018 P= .051 P= .101 P= .025 P= .002 P= .266 P= .062 P=******

Table 1 — Correlations (r, (N), P=p)

	V4.4	V4.2	F.3	F.5	F.6	F.7	F.8	F.10	F.11	F.12	F.13	F.14	F.15	F.9	F.27
S.27	-.0280 (24) P=.448	.1792 (24) P=.201	.5006 (24) P=.006	.2579 (24) P=.112	.0199 (24) P=.463	.4533 (24) P=.013	.1538 (24) P=.237	-.1877 (23) P=.195	.3340 (24) P=.055	-.3361 (24) P=.054	.0105 (24) P=.482	.2597 (22) P=.122	.0757 (22) P=.369	.0349 (24) P=.436	.1289 (24) P=.274
S.26	-.2771 (32) P=.062	-.1482 (32) P=.209	-.0479 (32) P=.397	.0041 (32) P=.491	-.2460 (32) P=.087	.0137 (31) P=.471	-.3975 (32) P=.012	.0749 (32) P=.342	-.2314 (32) P=.101	-.0308 (32) P=.434	-.1898 (32) P=.149	.0946 (32) P=.303	-.2680 (32) P=.069	-.2960 (32) P=.050	-.1165 (32) P=.263
S.22	.0538 (27) P=.395	-.1385 (27) P=.245	.1389 (27) P=.245	.0385 (27) P=.424	.2805 (27) P=.078	.3806 (27) P=.025	.3756 (27) P=.027	.0549 (27) P=.393	-.0316 (27) P=.438	-.1431 (27) P=.238	-.0714 (27) P=.362	-.0561 (27) P=.391	-.1588 (27) P=.214	.3877 (27) P=.023	.2077 (27) P=.149
S.20	.0546 (24) P=.400	.2451 (24) P=.124	.4189 (24) P=.021	.1703 (24) P=.213	-.1371 (24) P=.261	.2578 (24) P=.112	.0932 (24) P=.332	-.0617 (24) P=.390	.2754 (24) P=.096	-.2413 (24) P=.128	.0794 (22) P=.363	.2642 (22) P=.117	.2014 (22) P=.184	-.1008 (24) P=.320	.0973 (24) P=.326
S.29	.4808 (30) P=.004	.1260 (30) P=.254	.6545 (30) P=.001	.0539 (30) P=.389	-.0342 (30) P=.429	-.0733 (30) P=.350	.0332 (30) P=.431	-.0027 (30) P=.494	.5160 (30) P=.002	.5378 (30) P=.001	.1530 (30) P=.210	-.1979 (30) P=.147	.4373 (30) P=.008	-.0793 (30) P=.339	-.0983 (30) P=.303
S.28	-.2025 (41) P=.102	-.0919 (41) P=.284	.1228 (41) P=.222	.0813 (40) P=.309	.0016 (40) P=.496	-.1068 (39) P=.259	.0272 (39) P=.435	.3179 (37) P=.028	.3966 (41) P=.005	-.0307 (41) P=.424	-.0111 (37) P=.474	-.0908 (37) P=.296	-.0763 (36) P=.329	.0196 (40) P=.452	-.0417 (41) P=.398
S.30	.1989 (41) P=.106	-.1175 (41) P=.232	.7553 (41) P=.001	-.0487 (40) P=.383	-.0768 (40) P=.319	-.1012 (39) P=.270	-.1603 (39) P=.165	-.0131 (37) P=.469	.3695 (41) P=.009	.7786 (41) P=.001	-.0468 (37) P=.392	-.1517 (37) P=.185	.0044 (36) P=.490	-.1010 (40) P=.268	-.1403 (41) P=.191
S.21	.6537 (35) P=.001	.0230 (35) P=.448	-.0642 (35) P=.357	-.0791 (35) P=.326	-.0736 (35) P=.337	.5822 (34) P=.001	-.2563 (35) P=.069	.3486 (34) P=.022	-.2680 (35) P=.060	-.0504 (35) P=.387	-.0167 (35) P=.462	-.1998 (35) P=.125	-.0974 (35) P=.289	-.1723 (35) P=.161	-.1423 (35) P=.207
S.23	-.0096 (38) P=.477	-.1204 (38) P=.236	.2367 (38) P=.076	.1650 (38) P=.161	-.1797 (38) P=.140	-.0724 (37) P=.335	-.1170 (38) P=.242	.3037 (38) P=.036	.2066 (38) P=.107	.1030 (38) P=.269	-.1646 (36) P=.169	-.0925 (36) P=.296	-.2367 (35) P=.085	-.1953 (38) P=.120	-.1656 (38) P=.160
S.24	-.1108 (38) P=.254	-.1057 (38) P=.264	.0193 (38) P=.454	.0361 (38) P=.415	-.1825 (38) P=.136	-.0509 (37) P=.382	-.1674 (38) P=.157	.2882 (36) P=.044	.0204 (38) P=.452	-.0763 (38) P=.324	-.2258 (35) P=.096	-.1945 (35) P=.131	-.2417 (35) P=.081	-.1512 (37) P=.182	-.1067 (38) P=.262

Table 2 — Correlations (r, (N), P=p)

	V.2	V.3	V.9	V.12	V.13	V.7	V.14	V.15	V.8	V.10	V.11	V.17	V.18	V.19	V.28
V.2	1.0000 (0) P=******														
V.3	-.3304 (37) P=.023	1.0000 (0) P=******													
V.9	.2264 (34) P=.099	-.2932 (34) P=.046	1.0000 (0) P=******												
V.12	.4005 (33) P=.010	-.4764 (33) P=.003	.2096 (34) P=.117	1.0000 (0) P=******											
V.13	.2385 (33) P=.091	-.0183 (33) P=.460	.1418 (34) P=.212	-.5856 (34) P=.001	1.0000 (0) P=******										
V.7	-.1463 (38) P=.190	-.0561 (37) P=.371	-.0957 (35) P=.292	.0828 (35) P=.318	-.0898 (35) P=.304	1.0000 (0) P=******									
V.14	-.2059 (37) P=.111	-.1987 (36) P=.123	.2868 (33) P=.053	-.1035 (32) P=.286	.3755 (32) P=.017	.0180 (37) P=.458	1.0000 (0) P=******								
V.15	.0577 (37) P=.367	-.0816 (36) P=.318	-.2270 (34) P=.098	-.1691 (34) P=.169	.1448 (34) P=.207	-.0916 (39) P=.290	-.1576 (37) P=.176	1.0000 (0) P=******							
V.8	-.4008 (33) P=.010	.1588 (33) P=.189	-.0977 (33) P=.294	-.2852 (34) P=.051	.0062 (33) P=.486	.2957 (35) P=.042	.1601 (32) P=.191	-.0095 (34) P=.479	1.0000 (0) P=******						
V.10	.1980 (38) P=.117	-.1862 (37) P=.135	-.0758 (34) P=.335	-.3904 (34) P=.011	.5819 (34) P=.001	-.0926 (39) P=.288	.3898 (37) P=.009	-.0826 (38) P=.311	.2765 (34) P=.057	1.0000 (0) P=******					
V.11	-.1306 (37) P=.221	-.1228 (36) P=.238	.0613 (34) P=.365	.2851 (34) P=.051	-.5647 (34) P=.001	.1793 (39) P=.137	-.1110 (36) P=.260	-.4568 (38) P=.002	.1349 (34) P=.224	-.5623 (38) P=.001	1.0000 (0) P=******				
V.17	-.9958 (34) P=.001	.4437 (34) P=.004	-.2504 (34) P=.077	-.4307 (34) P=.005	-.2022 (34) P=.126	.1294 (35) P=.229	-.1968 (33) P=.136	.9977 (33) P=.001	.3950 (33) P=.011	-.2135 (34) P=.109	.1255 (34) P=.240	1.0000 (0) P=******			
V.18	.2190 (34) P=.107	.1103 (33) P=.271	-.0904 (32) P=.308	-.2763 (32) P=.063	.3000 (33) P=.045	-.0866 (33) P=.313	.2762 (33) P=.060	-.3240 (33) P=.033	.1506 (31) P=.209	.3331 (34) P=.027	-.1623 (33) P=.183	-.2384 (33) P=.091	1.0000 (0) P=******		
V.19	-.5905 (38) P=.001	.0954 (37) P=.287	-.2131 (35) P=.110	-.3730 (35) P=.014	.0208 (35) P=.453	-.0249 (40) P=.439	.0074 (37) P=.483	.8587 (40) P=.001	.2432 (35) P=.080	-.1408 (39) P=.196	.0454 (39) P=.392	.6522 (39) P=.001	-.3599 (34) P=.018	1.0000 (0) P=******	
V.28	-.8751 (38) P=.001	-.2347 (37) P=.081	-.2985 (35) P=.041	-.4386 (35) P=.004	-.1139 (35) P=.257	.1534 (40) P=.171	-.0551 (37) P=.373	.8234 (40) P=.001	.3572 (35) P=.018	-.1165 (39) P=.240	.0885 (39) P=.296	.9886 (35) P=.001	-.2395 (34) P=.086	.7925 (41) P=.001	1.0000 (0) P=******
V.29	.9930 (25) P=.001	-.4039 (25) P=.023	.2885 (25) P=.081	.4462 (25) P=.014	.2324 (25) P=.132	-.1078 (25) P=.304	.1839 (24) P=.195	-.8628 (24) P=.001	-.4269 (23) P=.021	.2371 (25) P=.127	-.1306 (24) P=.272	-.9984 (25) P=.001	.2956 (25) P=.076	-.6756 (25) P=.001	-.9220 (25) P=.001
V.30	-.8419 (31) P=.001	.3730 (31) P=.019	-.2929 (31) P=.055	-.5374 (30) P=.001	-.0386 (31) P=.418	-.0471 (31) P=.401	-.0909 (30) P=.316	.2857 (30) P=.063	.2947 (29) P=.060	-.0356 (31) P=.425	-.0319 (31) P=.432	.8502 (31) P=.001	-.1149 (31) P=.269	.8283 (31) P=.001	.8121 (31) P=.001
V.16	.1226 (37) P=.235	-.1097 (36) P=.262	-.1256 (34) P=.239	-.3482 (34) P=.022	.3705 (34) P=.016	.1030 (39) P=.266	.2649 (36) P=.059	.3839 (39) P=.008	.1546 (34) P=.191	.3920 (38) P=.007	-.3724 (39) P=.010	-.1265 (34) P=.238	.1321 (33) P=.232	.0734 (40) P=.326	-.1268 (40) P=.218
V.20	.0496 (38) P=.384	-.1052 (37) P=.268	.1784 (35) P=.153	-.0335 (35) P=.424	-.1376 (35) P=.215	.2214 (40) P=.085	-.0245 (37) P=.443	-.0523 (39) P=.376	.0457 (35) P=.397	.0163 (39) P=.461	.0117 (39) P=.472	-.0674 (35) P=.350	-.0809 (34) P=.325	-.1287 (40) P=.214	-.1023 (40) P=.265
V.21	.1100 (37) P=.258	-.1464 (36) P=.197	.2190 (34) P=.107	.0825 (33) P=.324	.1226 (33) P=.248	.2033 (37) P=.114	-.0686 (36) P=.345	-.0604 (36) P=.363	.2047 (33) P=.127	.1012 (37) P=.276	-.0161 (36) P=.463	-.1300 (34) P=.232	.0363 (34) P=.419	-.1438 (37) P=.198	-.0825 (37) P=.314
V.22	.2973 (38) P=.035	-.1478 (37) P=.191	.2252 (35) P=.097	.2342 (35) P=.088	-.1146 (35) P=.256	-.1229 (40) P=.225	.0644 (37) P=.352	-.0720 (39) P=.331	-.3480 (35) P=.020	-.0388 (39) P=.407	-.1835 (39) P=.132	-.2748 (35) P=.055	.3246 (34) P=.031	-.2751 (40) P=.043	-.1778 (40) P=.136
V.23	-.2067 (37) P=.110	.0860 (36) P=.309	.0415 (35) P=.406	.0105 (34) P=.477	-.1373 (34) P=.219	-.0594 (38) P=.362	.1325 (36) P=.221	.3828 (36) P=.010	.1187 (34) P=.252	-.1233 (37) P=.234	.0640 (37) P=.353	.2444 (34) P=.082	.0501 (34) P=.389	.3953 (38) P=.007	.4124 (38) P=.005
V.24	.3852 (35) P=.011	-.4279 (35) P=.005	.4456 (34) P=.004	.1242 (34) P=.242	.3247 (35) P=.029	.1504 (37) P=.187	.3429 (34) P=.024	-.0800 (36) P=.321	-.0901 (34) P=.306	.0642 (36) P=.355	-.1183 (36) P=.246	-.3619 (36) P=.018	.2265 (33) P=.102	-.2204 (37) P=.095	-.2983 (37) P=.036

	V.2	V.3	V.9	V.12	V.13	V.7	V.14	V.15	V.8	V.10	V.11	V.17	V.18	V.19	V.28
V.26	.3314 (32) P=.032	-.1683 (32) P=.179	.0782 (31) P=.335	.1543 (32) P=.204	.1000 (32) P=.293	.2674 (33) P=.066	.2299 (31) P=.107	-.0594 (32) P=.373	-.0427 (31) P=.410	.1420 (32) P=.219	-.0567 (32) P=.379	-.3438 (31) P=.029	-.1176 (31) P=.264	-.1800 (33) P=.158	-.3194 (33) P=.035
V.27	-.9981 (31) P=.001	.4532 (31) P=.005	-.2408 (31) P=.096	-.4476 (30) P=.007	-.2117 (31) P=.126	.1415 (31) P=.224	-.0221 (30) P=.454	.0094 (30) P=.480	.4191 (29) P=.012	-.2108 (30) P=.128	.1068 (30) P=.287	.9955 (31) P=.001	-.2116 (31) P=.127	.5958 (31) P=.001	.8824 (31) P=.001
V.25	-.1062 (30) P=.288	-.1218 (30) P=.261	.1866 (30) P=.162	.0651 (29) P=.369	-.0575 (30) P=.381	.0382 (31) P=.419	-.0435 (30) P=.410	-.1251 (32) P=.248	.2737 (29) P=.075	.0672 (30) P=.362	.0237 (30) P=.451	-.1516 (29) P=.216	.1054 (29) P=.293	-.1745 (32) P=.170	-.0409 (32) P=.412
V.34	-.1342 (38) P=.211	-.1237 (37) P=.233	.0594 (35) P=.367	.2622 (35) P=.064	-.3391 (35) P=.023	-.0742 (40) P=.325	-.0083 (37) P=.481	-.0269 (39) P=.436	-.0717 (35) P=.341	-.1369 (39) P=.203	.1571 (39) P=.170	.1418 (35) P=.208	-.0004 (34) P=.499	.0856 (40) P=.300	.1881 (40) P=.123
V.35	-.8213 (31) P=.001	.3899 (30) P=.015	-.0968 (30) P=.305	-.3464 (29) P=.033	-.2516 (30) P=.090	.1096 (31) P=.279	-.1742 (30) P=.179	-.0435 (30) P=.410	.4258 (29) P=.011	-.1919 (31) P=.151	.1117 (30) P=.278	.8231 (30) P=.001	-.2612 (30) P=.082	.5083 (31) P=.002	.7411 (31) P=.001
V.36	-.9961 (36) P=.001	.4512 (35) P=.003	-.2332 (34) P=.092	-.4185 (33) P=.008	-.2300 (34) P=.095	.1265 (37) P=.228	.1255 (36) P=.236	-.1266 (35) P=.231	.3865 (33) P=.013	-.1954 (38) P=.127	.1115 (36) P=.259	.9933 (33) P=.001	-.1926 (34) P=.138	.5843 (37) P=.001	.8791 (37) P=.001
V.37	.2386 (37) P=.077	.3730 (36) P=.013	.0097 (34) P=.478	.2105 (34) P=.116	-.2081 (34) P=.119	-.2364 (39) P=.074	-.1287 (36) P=.227	-.1213 (38) P=.234	-.4027 (34) P=.009	-.2240 (38) P=.088	.0182 (38) P=.457	-.2564 (34) P=.072	-.1982 (33) P=.134	-.3492 (39) P=.015	-.2382 (39) P=.072
V.38	.0389 (34) P=.414	-.2249 (34) P=.101	-.0593 (34) P=.370	.3809 (33) P=.014	-.2923 (34) P=.047	-.0267 (35) P=.439	.0562 (33) P=.378	-.0013 (34) P=.497	-.1707 (33) P=.171	-.1579 (34) P=.186	.2901 (34) P=.048	-.0448 (33) P=.402	.0397 (33) P=.413	-.0325 (35) P=.426	.0228 (35) P=.448
V.32	.1495 (38) P=.185	.0829 (37) P=.313	.1230 (35) P=.241	.1905 (35) P=.137	-.1129 (35) P=.259	-.0057 (40) P=.486	-.0678 (37) P=.345	-.1663 (39) P=.156	-.2924 (35) P=.044	-.0802 (39) P=.314	-.1028 (39) P=.267	-.1681 (35) P=.167	.3037 (34) P=.040	-.2894 (40) P=.035	-.1330 (40) P=.207
V.33	-.9271 (32) P=.001	.4067 (32) P=.010	-.0586 (31) P=.377	-.3369 (31) P=.032	-.1319 (32) P=.236	.1289 (34) P=.234	.0845 (31) P=.326	-.0259 (33) P=.443	.2302 (31) P=.106	-.1617 (33) P=.184	.0988 (33) P=.292	.8972 (31) P=.001	-.1774 (30) P=.174	.4001 (34) P=.010	.6937 (34) P=.001
V.31	-.9066 (38) P=.001	.4526 (37) P=.002	-.3326 (35) P=.025	-.5128 (35) P=.001	-.1240 (35) P=.239	.1571 (40) P=.167	.1450 (37) P=.196	-.0580 (39) P=.363	.4727 (35) P=.002	-.0282 (39) P=.432	.0188 (39) P=.455	.9032 (35) P=.001	-.0280 (34) P=.438	.5435 (40) P=.001	.7959 (40) P=.001
S.2	-.2566 (37) P=.063	-.3795 (36) P=.011	.6498 (34) P=.001	.1905 (34) P=.140	.1066 (34) P=.274	.3167 (39) P=.025	.2618 (37) P=.059	-.0393 (40) P=.405	.3843 (34) P=.012	-.0501 (38) P=.383	.1174 (38) P=.241	-.0417 (34) P=.408	.0165 (33) P=.464	.0607 (40) P=.355	.1151 (40) P=.240
S.4	.1629 (37) P=.168	.1603 (36) P=.175	.1110 (34) P=.266	.0214 (34) P=.452	-.0928 (34) P=.301	.0980 (39) P=.276	-.0522 (37) P=.379	-.0540 (40) P=.370	-.0318 (34) P=.429	-.0084 (38) P=.480	-.1300 (38) P=.218	-.0761 (34) P=.334	.0071 (33) P=.484	.0231 (40) P=.444	.0401 (40) P=.403
S.6	-.0633 (37) P=.355	-.1930 (36) P=.130	-.2923 (33) P=.049	-.0046 (34) P=.490	-.3129 (33) P=.038	-.0694 (38) P=.339	-.2891 (37) P=.041	.1003 (39) P=.272	.0171 (33) P=.462	-.2133 (38) P=.099	.0300 (37) P=.430	-.1385 (34) P=.217	-.0635 (33) P=.363	.0622 (39) P=.353	-.0092 (39) P=.478
S.3	.5947 (38) P=.001	-.3260 (37) P=.024	.3764 (35) P=.013	.3445 (35) P=.021	.1538 (35) P=.189	-.0861 (40) P=.299	-.0614 (37) P=.359	-.2502 (40) P=.060	-.2685 (35) P=.059	.2285 (39) P=.081	-.3188 (39) P=.024	-.6882 (35) P=.001	.1704 (34) P=.168	-.4678 (41) P=.001	-.5307 (41) P=.001
S.1	-.0783 (37) P=.323	.2174 (36) P=.101	.1480 (33) P=.206	-.1470 (32) P=.211	.1069 (32) P=.280	.2665 (37) P=.055	.0114 (36) P=.474	.2203 (36) P=.098	.0297 (32) P=.436	-.0090 (37) P=.479	-.0708 (36) P=.341	.1060 (33) P=.279	-.3864 (33) P=.013	.2524 (37) P=.066	-.0863 (37) P=.306
S.5	.3367 (31) P=.032	.0198 (31) P=.458	.3238 (29) P=.043	.0682 (28) P=.365	.1270 (29) P=.256	.0073 (32) P=.484	.2952 (30) P=.057	-.1452 (31) P=.218	-.1866 (28) P=.171	.2012 (31) P=.139	-.0739 (31) P=.346	-.3565 (28) P=.031	-.0905 (28) P=.323	-.2925 (32) P=.052	-.3378 (32) P=.029
S.7	.2783 (38) P=.045	-.4620 (37) P=.002	-.1048 (35) P=.275	.2878 (35) P=.047	-.1868 (35) P=.141	-.0682 (40) P=.338	.0506 (37) P=.383	.0019 (40) P=.495	-.1960 (35) P=.130	-.0107 (39) P=.474	-.1387 (39) P=.200	-.2656 (35) P=.062	.0225 (34) P=.450	-.1502 (41) P=.174	-.1615 (41) P=.157
S.8	.1159 (38) P=.244	.5498 (37) P=.001	-.2395 (35) P=.083	-.0687 (35) P=.348	.1136 (35) P=.258	-.0791 (40) P=.314	-.1028 (37) P=.272	.0995 (40) P=.271	.0145 (35) P=.467	-.0070 (39) P=.483	-.1394 (39) P=.199	-.1371 (35) P=.216	.5524 (34) P=.001	-.0091 (41) P=.477	-.0490 (41) P=.380
S.9	.1932 (38) P=.123	.2663 (37) P=.056	.1006 (35) P=.283	.0791 (35) P=.326	.2799 (35) P=.052	.2306 (40) P=.069	.0362 (37) P=.416	.0814 (40) P=.309	-.0191 (35) P=.457	.1474 (39) P=.185	-.3205 (39) P=.023	-.1890 (35) P=.138	-.3787 (34) P=.014	.0356 (41) P=.413	-.1709 (41) P=.143
S.10	.1567 (38) P=.174	-.0544 (37) P=.375	-.2329 (35) P=.089	.2505 (35) P=.073	-.1514 (35) P=.192	-.0822 (40) P=.307	.0509 (37) P=.383	-.1074 (40) P=.254	-.1944 (35) P=.129	-.0867 (39) P=.296	.0021 (39) P=.495	-.1771 (35) P=.154	-.0106 (34) P=.476	-.2384 (41) P=.067	-.1936 (41) P=.113
S.18	.0704 (36) P=.342	.0554 (35) P=.375	-.0456 (33) P=.400	-.2129 (32) P=.121	.2365 (33) P=.093	.2963 (36) P=.039	.2464 (34) P=.077	-.0281 (35) P=.436	.4467 (32) P=.005	.4747 (36) P=.002	-.3119 (35) P=.034	-.0776 (33) P=.334	.0480 (34) P=.394	-.0362 (36) P=.417	-.0662 (36) P=.351
S.19	.0597 (36) P=.365	-.2425 (35) P=.080	.3149 (33) P=.037	.2373 (32) P=.095	-.0750 (33) P=.339	.5574 (36) P=.001	-.0898 (35) P=.304	-.0621 (35) P=.362	.0505 (32) P=.392	-.0496 (36) P=.387	.0004 (35) P=.499	-.0803 (33) P=.328	-.2276 (34) P=.098	-.1672 (36) P=.165	-.0325 (36) P=.425
S.17	.1702 (38) P=.154	-.0469 (37) P=.391	-.2094 (35) P=.114	-.1697 (35) P=.165	.1597 (35) P=.180	-.1098 (40) P=.250	-.0582 (37) P=.366	-.0066 (40) P=.484	.1742 (35) P=.158	.4316 (39) P=.003	-.3103 (39) P=.027	-.1586 (35) P=.181	.1694 (34) P=.169	-.0878 (41) P=.292	-.0961 (41) P=.275
S.11	.0285 (38) P=.432	.1316 (37) P=.219	-.4330 (35) P=.005	-.1075 (35) P=.269	.0119 (35) P=.473	.2004 (40) P=.098	.0720 (40) P=.329	-.0131 (40) P=.468	.3581 (35) P=.017	.4123 (39) P=.005	-.2221 (39) P=.087	-.0459 (35) P=.397	.2183 (34) P=.107	-.1055 (41) P=.256	-.0224 (41) P=.445
S.12	-.3617 (38) P=.013	-.0834 (37) P=.311	-.0331 (35) P=.425	.0607 (35) P=.498	-.1817 (35) P=.149	.5674 (40) P=.001	.1364 (40) P=.201	.0163 (40) P=.455	.3984 (35) P=.009	-.0223 (39) P=.447	.1901 (39) P=.123	.3516 (35) P=.019	-.1273 (34) P=.236	.1907 (41) P=.116	.3991 (41) P=.005
S.13	.1134 (35) P=.258	.0544 (34) P=.380	-.1436 (33) P=.213	-.0720 (33) P=.345	.0421 (33) P=.408	-.1309 (37) P=.220	-.0564 (34) P=.376	-.0581 (37) P=.366	-.1011 (32) P=.291	-.0240 (36) P=.445	.0333 (36) P=.423	-.1213 (33) P=.251	.0620 (32) P=.368	-.1163 (38) P=.243	-.1292 (38) P=.220
S.14	-.4828 (38) P=.001	-.1315 (37) P=.219	.3145 (35) P=.033	.0876 (35) P=.308	-.2550 (35) P=.070	.0067 (40) P=.484	.0511 (37) P=.382	-.0633 (39) P=.377	-.0073 (35) P=.361	-.1314 (39) P=.213	-.0274 (39) P=.434	.1494 (35) P=.196	-.1330 (34) P=.227	-.0135 (40) P=.467	.1405 (40) P=.194
S.15	-.0905 (38) P=.295	-.1818 (37) P=.141	.3907 (35) P=.012	.0805 (35) P=.323	.0045 (35) P=.314	.1462 (40) P=.184	.0789 (37) P=.321	-.0998 (39) P=.273	.1986 (35) P=.139	-.0857 (39) P=.302	.0582 (39) P=.362	.0673 (35) P=.350	-.1903 (34) P=.140	.0044 (40) P=.489	-.0015 (40) P=.496
S.16	.1227 (38) P=.232	-.0527 (37) P=.378	-.2280 (35) P=.094	-.1701 (35) P=.164	.1070 (35) P=.270	-.0064 (40) P=.499	.3207 (37) P=.026	-.0927 (40) P=.285	.7538 (35) P=.071	.4034 (39) P=.001	-.0766 (39) P=.321	-.1378 (35) P=.215	.3130 (34) P=.036	-.0670 (41) P=.339	-.0919 (41) P=.284
S.25	.2674 (32) P=.055	-.1379 (32) P=.226	.0449 (32) P=.404	.0304 (31) P=.422	.0494 (32) P=.394	-.1477 (32) P=.210	.0276 (31) P=.441	-.0520 (31) P=.390	.1055 (30) P=.290	.0379 (32) P=.418	.0648 (31) P=.365	-.2890 (32) P=.054	.1073 (32) P=.280	-.2644 (32) P=.072	-.3319 (32) P=.032
S.27	.1050 (24) P=.313	-.1356 (24) P=.269	-.1559 (21) P=.250	-.4562 (20) P=.022	.4791 (21) P=.015	.1305 (24) P=.272	.5474 (24) P=.003	-.0741 (24) P=.366	.5551 (20) P=.006	.6727 (24) P=.001	-.4151 (23) P=.025	-.0873 (21) P=.353	.3866 (22) P=.038	.0402 (24) P=.426	.0044 (24) P=.492
S.26	.2730 (32) P=.065	-.2490 (32) P=.085	.0943 (32) P=.304	.1732 (31) P=.176	-.0467 (32) P=.400	-.1217 (32) P=.253	.1611 (31) P=.194	-.1106 (31) P=.277	.1191 (30) P=.265	.0059 (32) P=.487	.1320 (31) P=.240	-.2821 (32) P=.059	-.0115 (32) P=.475	-.3139 (32) P=.040	-.3464 (32) P=.026

V.29	V.30	V.16	V.20	V.21	V.22	V.23	V.24	V.26	V.27	V.25	V.34	V.35	V.36	V.37
.4276 (23) P= .021	-.2261 (29) P= .119	.4383 (32) P= .006	.0512 (33) P= .389	.0977 (32) P= .297	.0664 (33) P= .357	.0536 (33) P= .384	.3835 (33) P= .014	1.0000 (0) P=******						
-.9933 (23) P= .001	.8560 (29) P= .001	-.1181 (30) P= .267	-.0348 (31) P= .426	-.1123 (31) P= .274	-.3528 (31) P= .026	.2012 (31) P= .139	-.3750 (31) P= .019	-.3383 (31) P= .031	1.0000 (0) P=******					
.1870 (22) P= .202	.0251 (27) P= .450	-.0593 (31) P= .376	.3969 (31) P= .014	.7321 (30) P= .001	.1610 (31) P= .193	.2188 (31) P= .118	.3152 (31) P= .042	.0266 (29) P= .446	.2205 (27) P= .135	1.0000 (0) P=******				
-.2615 (25) P= .103	.1641 (31) P= .189	-.1434 (39) P= .192	-.0479 (40) P= .385	.1342 (37) P= .214	.2917 (40) P= .034	.4167 (38) P= .005	.2023 (37) P= .115	-.0790 (33) P= .331	.1274 (31) P= .247	.3240 (31) P= .038	1.0000 (0) P=******			
-.8206 (25) P= .001	.7047 (29) P= .001	-.0217 (30) P= .455	-.0858 (31) P= .323	-.1190 (31) P= .262	-.0711 (31) P= .352	.3154 (31) P= .042	-.1760 (31) P= .172	-.1744 (29) P= .183	.8287 (28) P= .001	.1331 (27) P= .254	.2590 (31) P= .080	1.0000 (0) P=******		
-.9924 (25) P= .001	.8509 (31) P= .001	-.1185 (36) P= .246	-.0694 (37) P= .342	-.1249 (35) P= .237	-.2423 (37) P= .074	.2485 (36) P= .072	-.3640 (36) P= .015	-.3161 (33) P= .037	.9950 (31) P= .001	.0957 (31) P= .304	.1654 (37) P= .164	.8359 (31) P= .001	1.0000 (0) P=******	
.4011 (24) P= .026	-.2451 (30) P= .096	-.0551 (38) P= .371	-.0545 (39) P= .371	.0390 (36) P= .411	.5147 (39) P= .001	.2429 (37) P= .074	.0654 (36) P= .352	.3151 (33) P= .037	-.2565 (31) P= .082	.2609 (30) P= .082	.2601 (39) P= .055	-.1022 (30) P= .295	-.1957 (36) P= .126	1.0000 (0) P=******
.0174 (25) P= .467	.0373 (31) P= .421	-.0990 (34) P= .289	-.1786 (35) P= .152	.0207 (34) P= .454	.3765 (35) P= .013	.4027 (35) P= .008	.1527 (35) P= .191	.1250 (33) P= .244	-.0647 (31) P= .365	.2520 (31) P= .086	.7560 (35) P= .001	.0038 (31) P= .492	-.0086 (35) P= .480	.3744 (34) P= .015
.2539 (25) P= .110	-.0867 (31) P= .321	-.0784 (39) P= .318	.2106 (40) P= .096	.2386 (37) P= .078	.7204 (40) P= .001	.3814 (38) P= .009	.3429 (37) P= .019	.0289 (33) P= .436	-.1562 (31) P= .201	.2208 (31) P= .116	.4096 (40) P= .004	.0077 (31) P= .484	-.0839 (37) P= .311	.5320 (39) P= .001
-.9372 (25) P= .001	.8087 (29) P= .001	-.0224 (33) P= .451	.0096 (34) P= .479	-.0832 (31) P= .328	.0604 (34) P= .367	.2842 (32) P= .057	-.1817 (34) P= .152	.0735 (30) P= .350	.9396 (28) P= .001	-.1106 (28) P= .288	.1486 (34) P= .201	.8938 (31) P= .001	.7962 (33) P= .001	.0685 (33) P= .353
-.8896 (25) P= .001	.8247 (31) P= .001	.1189 (39) P= .235	-.0885 (40) P= .294	-.0927 (37) P= .293	-.2411 (40) P= .067	.2511 (38) P= .064	-.2771 (37) P= .048	-.1159 (33) P= .260	.9069 (31) P= .001	.0631 (31) P= .368	.1033 (40) P= .263	.7802 (31) P= .001	.9170 (37) P= .001	-.1027 (39) P= .267
-.0756 (24) P= .363	-.3033 (30) P= .052	-.0372 (39) P= .411	.2576 (39) P= .057	.3721 (36) P= .013	.0155 (39) P= .463	.1742 (37) P= .151	.6260 (36) P= .001	-.0069 (32) P= .485	.1440 (30) P= .224	.2525 (32) P= .082	.1983 (39) P= .113	.3373 (30) P= .034	-.0158 (36) P= .464	-.3291 (38) P= .022
.1667 (24) P= .218	.2003 (30) P= .144	-.0087 (39) P= .479	.2398 (39) P= .071	.3908 (36) P= .009	.3925 (39) P= .007	.4563 (37) P= .002	.1098 (36) P= .262	.1704 (32) P= .176	.1390 (30) P= .232	.4020 (32) P= .011	-.0171 (39) P= .459	.3009 (30) P= .053	.0230 (36) P= .447	.1992 (38) P= .115
-.2134 (24) P= .158	-.3473 (30) P= .030	.1213 (38) P= .234	-.0005 (38) P= .499	-.0504 (36) P= .385	.1595 (38) P= .169	-.0870 (36) P= .307	-.2242 (35) P= .098	.0828 (31) P= .329	.2458 (30) P= .095	-.1777 (31) P= .169	-.1423 (38) P= .197	-.0763 (30) P= .344	-.1940 (35) P= .132	.1106 (37) P= .257
.7390 (25) P= .001	-.5444 (31) P= .001	.0048 (40) P= .488	.1992 (40) P= .109	.3793 (37) P= .010	.4185 (40) P= .004	.0201 (38) P= .452	.3507 (37) P= .017	.2255 (33) P= .104	-.6769 (31) P= .001	.4073 (32) P= .010	-.0593 (40) P= .358	-.5030 (31) P= .002	-.5886 (37) P= .001	.1477 (39) P= .185
-.1057 (25) P= .308	.0953 (30) P= .308	.0694 (36) P= .344	.2230 (37) P= .092	.1349 (36) P= .216	-.5204 (37) P= .001	.0467 (36) P= .393	.0147 (34) P= .467	.2994 (31) P= .051	.1147 (30) P= .273	-.1599 (29) P= .204	-.2731 (37) P= .051	-.0926 (30) P= .313	.0540 (35) P= .379	-.2743 (36) P= .053
.5130 (23) P= .006	-.2328 (27) P= .121	.1963 (31) P= .145	.1534 (32) P= .201	.0898 (30) P= .319	.2078 (32) P= .127	.1419 (31) P= .223	.3940 (31) P= .014	.5110 (29) P= .002	-.3564 (27) P= .034	-.1189 (26) P= .281	-.0739 (32) P= .344	-.3791 (27) P= .026	-.3387 (31) P= .031	.3688 (32) P= .019
.3494 (25) P= .043	-.4644 (31) P= .004	-.0572 (40) P= .363	.2309 (40) P= .076	.1538 (37) P= .182	.5606 (40) P= .001	-.1072 (38) P= .261	-.0181 (37) P= .458	-.1675 (33) P= .176	-.3073 (31) P= .046	-.0017 (32) P= .496	-.0075 (40) P= .482	-.3028 (31) P= .049	-.2782 (37) P= .048	.1114 (39) P= .250
.2193 (25) P= .146	-.0444 (31) P= .406	-.1179 (40) P= .234	-.1163 (40) P= .237	-.0623 (37) P= .357	.1415 (40) P= .192	.3512 (38) P= .015	.0106 (37) P= .475	-.3014 (33) P= .044	-.1738 (31) P= .175	-.0562 (32) P= .380	.0293 (40) P= .429	-.2283 (31) P= .108	-.1367 (37) P= .210	.1414 (39) P= .195
.2753 (25) P= .091	-.1273 (31) P= .247	.2215 (40) P= .085	.0538 (40) P= .371	.1379 (37) P= .208	-.2480 (40) P= .061	-.0013 (38) P= .497	.1500 (37) P= .188	.3754 (33) P= .016	-.2112 (31) P= .127	.0978 (32) P= .297	-.2292 (40) P= .077	-.1705 (31) P= .180	-.2197 (37) P= .096	-.0816 (39) P= .311
.1988 (25) P= .170	-.1946 (31) P= .147	.0359 (40) P= .413	-.1191 (40) P= .232	-.1238 (37) P= .233	-.0210 (40) P= .449	-.2844 (38) P= .042	-.0796 (37) P= .320	-.0454 (33) P= .401	-.1666 (31) P= .185	.2446 (32) P= .089	.0071 (40) P= .483	-.2105 (31) P= .128	-.1652 (37) P= .164	.1790 (39) P= .138
.1297 (25) P= .268	-.0483 (31) P= .398	.7118 (35) P= .001	.1460 (36) P= .198	.2322 (36) P= .086	-.0086 (36) P= .480	.0418 (36) P= .404	.2169 (34) P= .109	.6610 (32) P= .001	-.0663 (31) P= .362	.1583 (30) P= .202	-.2476 (36) P= .073	.0299 (31) P= .437	-.0721 (35) P= .340	.0845 (35) P= .315
.0836 (25) P= .346	-.1914 (31) P= .151	-.0110 (35) P= .475	.6251 (36) P= .001	.6744 (36) P= .001	.1157 (36) P= .251	.0279 (36) P= .436	.5621 (34) P= .001	.2133 (32) P= .121	-.0553 (31) P= .384	.3671 (30) P= .023	.1356 (36) P= .215	.0041 (31) P= .491	-.0712 (35) P= .342	-.0104 (35) P= .476
.2209 (25) P= .144	-.0121 (31) P= .474	.3359 (40) P= .017	-.0517 (40) P= .376	.0125 (37) P= .471	.0341 (40) P= .417	-.0167 (38) P= .460	.1752 (37) P= .150	.0489 (33) P= .394	-.1570 (31) P= .199	.0050 (32) P= .489	-.0074 (40) P= .482	.2233 (31) P= .114	-.1417 (37) P= .201	-.0581 (39) P= .363
.1344 (25) P= .261	-.0295 (31) P= .437	.3369 (40) P= .017	-.1450 (40) P= .186	-.0231 (37) P= .446	-.2369 (40) P= .071	-.0492 (38) P= .385	-.1401 (37) P= .204	.2753 (33) P= .061	-.0571 (31) P= .380	.0714 (32) P= .349	-.2020 (40) P= .106	-.1046 (31) P= .288	-.0455 (37) P= .395	-.0143 (39) P= .466
-.3944 (25) P= .026	.1080 (31) P= .282	-.1712 (40) P= .145	-.1706 (40) P= .146	-.1386 (37) P= .207	-.2632 (40) P= .050	.1349 (38) P= .210	-.0893 (37) P= .300	-.1126 (33) P= .266	.3427 (31) P= .030	-.0664 (32) P= .359	-.0100 (40) P= .476	.2383 (31) P= .098	.3357 (37) P= .021	-.3791 (39) P= .009
.1465 (24) P= .247	-.2502 (29) P= .095	.1445 (37) P= .197	-.1399 (37) P= .205	-.1692 (34) P= .169	-.1381 (37) P= .207	-.2373 (35) P= .085	-.1751 (34) P= .161	-.1820 (30) P= .168	-.1291 (29) P= .252	-.1061 (29) P= .292	-.0718 (37) P= .336	-.1453 (29) P= .226	-.1171 (34) P= .255	.0488 (36) P= .389
-.6463 (25) P= .001	.4378 (31) P= .007	-.1393 (39) P= .199	.2971 (40) P= .031	.4534 (37) P= .002	.6099 (40) P= .001	.2386 (38) P= .075	-.2777 (37) P= .048	-.2846 (33) P= .054	.5504 (31) P= .001	.5451 (31) P= .001	.1015 (40) P= .267	.6042 (31) P= .001	.4810 (37) P= .001	.1570 (39) P= .170
-.0971 (25) P= .322	.0503 (31) P= .394	-.1084 (39) P= .256	.7590 (40) P= .001	.6195 (37) P= .001	-.0877 (40) P= .295	-.0898 (38) P= .296	.4537 (37) P= .002	-.0354 (33) P= .422	.0889 (31) P= .317	.3736 (31) P= .019	.0359 (40) P= .413	.1947 (31) P= .147	.0706 (37) P= .339	-.2590 (39) P= .056
.1713 (25) P= .206	-.0704 (31) P= .353	.3893 (40) P= .007	.0308 (40) P= .425	.0795 (37) P= .320	.1276 (40) P= .216	.0498 (38) P= .383	.0394 (37) P= .408	.2813 (33) P= .056	-.1382 (31) P= .229	.0814 (32) P= .329	.0243 (40) P= .441	-.1333 (31) P= .237	-.1119 (37) P= .255	.1567 (39) P= .170
.3557 (25) P= .040	-.4260 (31) P= .008	.0842 (31) P= .326	.2061 (32) P= .129	.0342 (32) P= .426	-.0067 (32) P= .485	-.3033 (32) P= .046	.0755 (32) P= .341	-.0920 (30) P= .314	-.2910 (30) P= .059	-.1075 (28) P= .293	-.3111 (32) P= .042	-.1736 (30) P= .179	-.2895 (32) P= .054	-.0455 (31) P= .404
.2869 (19) P= .117	-.0640 (20) P= .394	.5943 (23) P= .001	-.0859 (24) P= .345	.0410 (24) P= .425	-.1326 (24) P= .268	-.1651 (24) P= .220	-.1913 (22) P= .197	.3493 (20) P= .066	-.0263 (19) P= .457	.2487 (20) P= .145	-.2183 (24) P= .153	-.0884 (21) P= .352	-.0535 (23) P= .404	-.2339 (23) P= .141
.3459 (25) P= .045	-.4374 (31) P= .007	.2172 (31) P= .120	.1318 (32) P= .236	.0999 (32) P= .293	.0183 (32) P= .460	-.1221 (32) P= .253	.1164 (32) P= .263	.0697 (30) P= .357	-.2860 (30) P= .063	.0243 (28) P= .451	-.0926 (32) P= .307	-.1409 (30) P= .229	-.2744 (32) P= .064	.0820 (31) P= .331

	V.29	V.30	V.16	V.20	V.21	V.22	V.23	V.24	V.26	V.27	V.25	V.34	V.35	V.36	V.37
	.2909	.0371	.2121	-.0900	-.0084	-.1408	-.0716	-.2464	.2451	-.0387	.0262	-.2866	-.0510	-.0576	-.0585
	(23)	(26)	(26)	(27)	(27)	(27)	(27)	(27)	(25)	(25)	(24)	(27)	(27)	(27)	(26)
	P= .089	P= .429	P= .149	P= .328	P= .483	P= .242	P= .361	P= .108	P= .119	P= .427	P= .452	P= .074	P= .400	P= .388	P= .388
	.3151	.0584	.7489	-.1383	-.0752	.1326	-.0136	.0779	.6867	-.0222	.1329	-.2964	-.0098	-.0130	.0978
	(19)	(20)	(23)	(24)	(24)	(24)	(24)	(22)	(20)	(19)	(20)	(24)	(21)	(23)	(23)
	P= .094	P= .403	P= .001	P= .260	P= .363	P= .268	P= .475	P= .365	P= .001	P= .464	P= .288	P= .080	P= .483	P= .477	P= .329
	.3251	.4032	.1063	-.1590	-.2386	.5178	.0740	.0883	.0204	-.1302	-.1774	.0980	-.1064	.5071	.2873
	(24)	(28)	(29)	(30)	(30)	(30)	(30)	(30)	(28)	(27)	(27)	(30)	(29)	(30)	(29)
	P= .061	P= .017	P= .292	P= .201	P= .102	P= .002	P= .349	P= .321	P= .459	P= .259	P= .188	P= .303	P= .291	P= .002	P= .065
	.1323	.0084	.2856	-.1541	-.1022	-.0828	.0252	.1670	.2111	-.0725	-.0669	.0334	.0752	-.0513	-.0343
	(25)	(31)	(40)	(40)	(37)	(40)	(38)	(37)	(33)	(31)	(32)	(40)	(31)	(37)	(39)
	P= .264	P= .482	P= .037	P= .171	P= .274	P= .306	P= .440	P= .162	P= .119	P= .349	P= .358	P= .419	P= .344	P= .382	P= .418
	.0891	-.0311	.1001	-.0614	-.0697	.3390	.2123	.2326	-.2152	-.0596	-.0482	.1919	-.0990	.0051	.1032
	(25)	(31)	(40)	(40)	(37)	(40)	(38)	(37)	(33)	(31)	(32)	(40)	(31)	(37)	(39)
	P= .336	P= .434	P= .269	P= .353	P= .341	P= .016	P= .100	P= .083	P= .115	P= .375	P= .397	P= .118	P= .298	P= .488	P= .266
	.1900	-.2583	-.1206	.0941	.3310	.4526	.1797	.1131	-.0105	-.1541	.1133	.1841	-.1623	-.1163	.4188
	(25)	(31)	(34)	(35)	(34)	(35)	(34)	(35)	(32)	(31)	(30)	(35)	(31)	(35)	(34)
	P= .182	P= .080	P= .248	P= .295	P= .028	P= .003	P= .155	P= .259	P= .477	P= .204	P= .276	P= .145	P= .191	P= .253	P= .007
	.3603	-.1551	.4805	.0635	.0657	-.1170	-.0504	.2314	.4008	-.2229	-.0705	-.0676	-.1411	-.2145	.1661
	(25)	(31)	(37)	(38)	(36)	(38)	(36)	(36)	(32)	(31)	(30)	(38)	(31)	(35)	(37)
	P= .038	P= .202	P= .001	P= .353	P= .352	P= .242	P= .385	P= .087	P= .012	P= .114	P= .356	P= .343	P= .225	P= .108	P= .163
	.3364	-.2472	.4538	.1363	.1776	-.0912	-.1987	.2761	.3982	-.2192	.0507	-.3258	-.1331	-.2181	.2129
	(25)	(31)	(37)	(38)	(37)	(38)	(37)	(35)	(32)	(31)	(30)	(38)	(31)	(36)	(37)
	P= .050	P= .090	P= .002	P= .207	P= .146	P= .293	P= .119	P= .054	P= .012	P= .118	P= .395	P= .023	P= .238	P= .101	P= .103

	S.19	S.17	S.11	S.12	S.13	S.14	S.15	S.16	S.25	S.27	S.26	S.22	S.20	S.29	S.28

	S.19	S.17	S.11	S.12	S.13	S.14	S.15	S.16	S.25
S.19	1.0000 (0) P=******								
S.17	-.0388 (36) P= .411	1.0000 (0) P=******							
S.11	-.0349 (36) P= .420	.3240 (41) P= .019	1.0000 (0) P=******						
S.12	.2798 (36) P= .049	-.1697 (41) P= .144	.2234 (41) P= .080	1.0000 (0) P=******					
S.13	-.1691 (33) P= .173	-.0760 (38) P= .325	.0048 (38) P= .489	.2242 (38) P= .088	1.0000 (0) P=******				
S.14	.4470 (36) P= .003	-.1757 (40) P= .139	-.2375 (40) P= .070	-.0245 (40) P= .440	-.1021 (37) P= .274	1.0000 (0) P=******			
S.15	.6248 (36) P= .001	.0347 (40) P= .416	-.2751 (40) P= .043	.0232 (40) P= .257	-.1110 (37) P= .444	.2040 (40) P= .103	1.0000 (0) P=******		
S.16	-.0497 (36) P= .387	.1762 (41) P= .135	.3737 (41) P= .008	-.0922 (38) P= .283	-.0256 (38) P= .439	.0469 (40) P= .387	-.2293 (40) P= .077	1.0000 (0) P=******	
S.25	.0220 (32) P= .452	.3212 (32) P= .037	-.1402 (32) P= .222	-.2754 (32) P= .064	.2730 (30) P= .072	-.0145 (32) P= .469	.3604 (32) P= .021	-.0209 (32) P= .455	1.0000 (0) P=******
S.27	-.1449 (24) P= .250	.2602 (24) P= .110	.6045 (24) P= .001	-.0082 (24) P= .485	-.1213 (21) P= .300	-.2240 (24) P= .146	-.1761 (24) P= .205	.4010 (24) P= .026	.0918 (21) P= .346

	S.27
S.27	1.0000 (0) P=******

	V.2	V.3	V.4	V.12	V.13	V.7	V.14	V.15	V.9	V.10	V.11	V.17	V.18	V.19	V.28
S.22	.1241	.1185	-.2657	-.2485	.0736	-.0065	.0954	-.0006	.6589	.6045	-.2191	-.0338	.2806	-.0177	.0354
	(27)	(27)	(27)	(26)	(27)	(27)	(27)	(27)	(25)	(27)	(26)	(27)	(27)	(27)	(27)
	P= .269	P= .278	P= .090	P= .110	P= .363	P= .499	P= .310	P= .461	P= .001	P= .001	P= .141	P= .434	P= .078	P= .465	P= .430
S.20	-.1547	-.0069	.0512	-.3110	.3489	.2668	.5450	-.0763	.7143	.4413	-.4228	-.1249	.1429	.0130	.0014
	(24)	(23)	(21)	(20)	(21)	(24)	(24)	(24)	(20)	(24)	(23)	(21)	(22)	(24)	(24)
	P= .235	P= .489	P= .413	P= .091	P= .060	P= .102	P= .003	P= .361	P= .171	P= .015	P= .022	P= .295	P= .263	P= .476	P= .498
S.24	-.0507	.2337	-.1254	-.0504	.2069	-.0791	.0664	-.1458	-.6098	.1492	-.4067	-.1594	.3654	-.1113	-.0136
	(30)	(30)	(29)	(28)	(29)	(30)	(30)	(30)	(28)	(30)	(29)	(29)	(29)	(30)	(30)
	P= .395	P= .107	P= .258	P= .400	P= .141	P= .339	P= .162	P= .271	P= .015	P= .216	P= .014	P= .204	P= .026	P= .279	P= .471
S.28	.0531	-.0368	-.2734	-.0108	.0240	.0655	.1731	.0342	-.0410	.7472	-.2146	-.0699	.0578	.0277	-.0090
	(38)	(37)	(35)	(35)	(35)	(40)	(37)	(40)	(35)	(39)	(39)	(35)	(39)	(41)	(41)
	P= .370	P= .415	P= .056	P= .475	P= .446	P= .344	P= .153	P= .417	P= .408	P= .065	P= .095	P= .345	P= .373	P= .432	P= .478
S.30	.0499	.0118	-.1367	-.0487	.2174	-.0063	.2239	-.0303	-.2918	.2070	-.3547	-.0542	.4096	-.0312	.0385
	(38)	(37)	(35)	(35)	(35)	(40)	(37)	(40)	(35)	(39)	(39)	(35)	(34)	(41)	(41)
	P= .383	P= .472	P= .217	P= .391	P= .105	P= .485	P= .091	P= .426	P= .050	P= .103	P= .013	P= .379	P= .008	P= .423	P= .406
S.21	.1339	-.0840	-.0243	.0453	-.0998	.0274	-.2461	.1481	-.1435	-.2313	.1553	-.1443	-.0204	-.0483	.0167
	(35)	(35)	(33)	(32)	(33)	(35)	(34)	(34)	(32)	(35)	(34)	(33)	(33)	(35)	(35)
	P= .222	P= .316	P= .447	P= .394	P= .290	P= .438	P= .079	P= .201	P= .217	P= .091	P= .190	P= .212	P= .455	P= .391	P= .462
S.23	.2173	.1615	-.3316	-.0966	.0759	.1566	.1466	-.0134	-.0269	.2262	-.1448	-.2056	.1856	-.1243	-.2052
	(37)	(37)	(34)	(34)	(34)	(38)	(38)	(37)	(34)	(38)	(37)	(35)	(33)	(38)	(38)
	P= .098	P= .141	P= .028	P= .293	P= .335	P= .171	P= .147	P= .467	P= .440	P= .086	P= .196	P= .118	P= .151	P= .229	P= .108
S.24	.2041	.1709	-.1525	-.1601	.1140	.1885	.0454	-.1489	.0644	.2779	-.3297	-.2407	.2367	-.2936	-.2156
	(38)	(37)	(34)	(33)	(34)	(38)	(37)	(37)	(34)	(38)	(37)	(34)	(34)	(38)	(38)
	P= .110	P= .156	P= .195	P= .187	P= .264	P= .129	P= .395	P= .189	P= .361	P= .046	P= .023	P= .085	P= .089	P= .037	P= .097

	V.38	V.32	V.33	V.31	S.2	S.4	S.6	S.3	S.1	S.5	S.7	S.8	S.9	S.10	S.18
V.38	1.0000														
	(0)														
	P=******														
V.32	.3013	1.0000													
	(35)	(0)													
	P= .039	P=******													
V.33	.0261	.1036	1.0000												
	(32)	(34)	(0)												
	P= .444	P= .280	P=******												
V.31	-.0110	-.0315	.7525	1.0000											
	(35)	(40)	(34)	(0)											
	P= .475	P= .424	P= .001	P=******											
S.2	.0976	.0651	.0054	-.2073	1.0000										
	(34)	(39)	(33)	(39)	(0)										
	P= .292	P= .347	P= .488	P= .103	P=******										
S.4	-.0256	.3019	.0326	.1031	.0024	1.0000									
	(34)	(39)	(33)	(39)	(40)	(0)									
	P= .443	P= .031	P= .429	P= .266	P= .494	P=******									
S.6	-.2652	-.1228	.1543	-.1699	-.1689	-.0095	1.0000								
	(33)	(38)	(32)	(38)	(39)	(39)	(0)								
	P= .068	P= .231	P= .200	P= .154	P= .152	P= .477	P=******								
S.3	-.0011	.3497	-.4910	-.5459	.2579	.6627	-.0373	1.0000							
	(35)	(40)	(34)	(40)	(40)	(40)	(39)	(0)							
	P= .498	P= .013	P= .002	P= .001	P= .054	P= .001	P= .411	P=******							
S.1	-.3155	-.3044	-.0292	.1004	-.0256	.2098	-.1018	-.0627	1.0000						
	(33)	(37)	(31)	(37)	(36)	(36)	(36)	(37)	(0)						
	P= .037	P= .033	P= .438	P= .277	P= .441	P= .110	P= .277	P= .356	P=******						
S.5	.0077	.1380	-.3118	-.2206	-.0123	.1599	-.1517	.2597	.2094	1.0000					
	(30)	(32)	(29)	(32)	(31)	(31)	(30)	(32)	(31)	(0)					
	P= .484	P= .226	P= .050	P= .112	P= .474	P= .195	P= .212	P= .076	P= .129	P=******					
S.7	-.0437	.1807	-.1953	-.3536	.0914	.0488	.6211	.1682	-.4080	.0196	1.0000				
	(35)	(40)	(34)	(40)	(40)	(40)	(39)	(41)	(37)	(32)	(0)				
	P= .402	P= .132	P= .134	P= .013	P= .287	P= .382	P= .001	P= .147	P= .006	P= .458	P=******				
S.8	-.0762	.3301	-.2209	-.0042	-.2774	.1979	-.2152	-.0283	.1390	.0206	-.2475	1.0000			
	(35)	(40)	(34)	(40)	(40)	(40)	(39)	(41)	(37)	(32)	(41)	(0)			
	P= .332	P= .019	P= .105	P= .490	P= .042	P= .110	P= .094	P= .430	P= .206	P= .456	P= .059	P=******			
S.9	-.1662	-.1165	-.3204	-.0793	-.1366	.3219	-.3761	.1201	.5662	.2118	-.3548	.3504	1.0000		
	(35)	(40)	(34)	(40)	(40)	(40)	(39)	(41)	(37)	(32)	(41)	(41)	(0)		
	P= .170	P= .237	P= .032	P= .313	P= .200	P= .021	P= .009	P= .227	P= .001	P= .122	P= .011	P= .012	P=******		
S.10	.2308	-.2330	-.2988	-.2208	-.2507	-.1000	-.0263	-.0106	-.2902	-.0716	.1538	-.0697	.0567	1.0000	
	(35)	(40)	(34)	(40)	(40)	(40)	(39)	(41)	(37)	(32)	(41)	(41)	(41)	(0)	
	P= .091	P= .074	P= .043	P= .085	P= .059	P= .270	P= .437	P= .474	P= .041	P= .348	P= .168	P= .332	P= .362	P=******	
S.18	-.1490	.0186	.1130	.2251	-.0024	.2905	.0952	.1134	.3105	.3311	-.0419	-.0495	.4122	-.1124	1.0000
	(34)	(36)	(31)	(36)	(35)	(35)	(35)	(36)	(35)	(30)	(36)	(36)	(36)	(36)	(0)
	P= .200	P= .457	P= .273	P= .093	P= .494	P= .045	P= .293	P= .255	P= .035	P= .037	P= .404	P= .387	P= .006	P= .257	P=******
S.19	-.0510	.3321	-.0063	-.1251	.5400	.2518	.0337	.2900	.3138	.1646	.2662	-.2029	.2270	-.2034	.2197
	(34)	(36)	(31)	(36)	(35)	(35)	(35)	(36)	(35)	(30)	(36)	(36)	(36)	(36)	(36)
	P= .387	P= .024	P= .487	P= .234	P= .001	P= .072	P= .424	P= .043	P= .033	P= .192	P= .058	P= .118	P= .092	P= .117	P= .099
S.17	-.1512	.0988	-.1636	-.0247	-.0569	.0700	-.1875	.1650	-.2223	.0721	-.1125	.0712	.1053	.0406	.2073
	(35)	(40)	(34)	(40)	(40)	(40)	(40)	(39)	(41)	(37)	(32)	(41)	(41)	(41)	(36)
	P= .193	P= .272	P= .178	P= .440	P= .364	P= .334	P= .127	P= .151	P= .093	P= .348	P= .242	P= .329	P= .256	P= .400	P= .113
S.11	-.0542	-.0709	-.1486	.2211	-.1669	-.0622	-.1664	.0489	.1340	.1024	-.2413	.0235	.1717	.0447	.5177
	(35)	(40)	(34)	(40)	(40)	(40)	(39)	(41)	(37)	(32)	(41)	(41)	(41)	(41)	(36)
	P= .379	P= .332	P= .201	P= .085	P= .152	P= .352	P= .156	P= .381	P= .215	P= .289	P= .064	P= .442	P= .142	P= .391	P= .001
S.12	-.0137	-.2231	.1149	.2336	.4321	-.0545	-.1676	-.1456	.1527	-.0915	-.2328	-.1395	.0200	-.0951	-.1134
	(35)	(40)	(34)	(40)	(40)	(40)	(39)	(41)	(37)	(32)	(41)	(41)	(41)	(41)	(36)
	P= .469	P= .083	P= .259	P= .073	P= .003	P= .369	P= .154	P= .182	P= .183	P= .309	P= .072	P= .192	P= .451	P= .277	P= .255
S.13	-.0749	-.1854	-.2464	-.1801	-.0952	-.2767	.2486	-.0958	-.2642	-.1130	-.0192	-.0634	-.1813	.0800	-.2349
	(32)	(37)	(32)	(37)	(37)	(37)	(36)	(38)	(34)	(29)	(38)	(38)	(38)	(38)	(33)
	P= .342	P= .136	P= .087	P= .143	P= .288	P= .049	P= .072	P= .284	P= .066	P= .280	P= .454	P= .353	P= .138	P= .316	P= .094
S.14	.0898	.2544	.3157	.0573	.0681	.3344	.2137	.1523	-.2553	-.2272	.5639	-.1780	-.2563	-.0332	-.2196
	(35)	(40)	(34)	(40)	(39)	(39)	(38)	(40)	(37)	(32)	(40)	(40)	(40)	(40)	(36)
	P= .304	P= .057	P= .034	P= .363	P= .340	P= .019	P= .099	P= .099	P= .064	P= .106	P= .001	P= .136	P= .055	P= .419	P= .099
S.15	-.1611	.0926	.0474	-.0345	.6172	.0508	-.0991	.1003	.0874	.0109	.1859	-.2556	.0087	-.1436	-.0470
	(35)	(40)	(34)	(40)	(39)	(39)	(38)	(40)	(37)	(32)	(40)	(40)	(40)	(40)	(36)
	P= .178	P= .285	P= .395	P= .416	P= .001	P= .379	P= .277	P= .269	P= .303	P= .476	P= .125	P= .056	P= .479	P= .188	P= .393
S.16	.0408	.1720	-.0541	.1512	-.2189	.1916	-.0479	.0789	.0018	.4133	-.0276	.0649	.0639	-.1068	.5200
	(35)	(40)	(34)	(40)	(40)	(40)	(39)	(41)	(37)	(32)	(41)	(41)	(41)	(41)	(36)
	P= .408	P= .144	P= .381	P= .176	P= .087	P= .118	P= .386	P= .312	P= .496	P= .009	P= .432	P= .344	P= .346	P= .253	P= .001
S.25	-.3989	-.0440	-.2841	-.3196	.0087	-.4085	.4036	-.1033	-.2929	.1034	.6084	-.0308	-.2542	.0719	-.0053
	(32)	(32)	(30)	(32)	(31)	(31)	(31)	(32)	(28)	(31)	(32)	(32)	(32)	(32)	(32)
	P= .012	P= .405	P= .064	P= .037	P= .482	P= .011	P= .012	P= .287	P= .055	P= .300	P= .001	P= .434	P= .080	P= .348	P= .488
S.27	-.1233	-.3038	.1580	.4720	.0286	-.0604	-.0056	.1544	-.0099	.0028	.0645	-.2262	.0269	-.0645	.5809
	(22)	(24)	(21)	(24)	(24)	(24)	(24)	(24)	(24)	(22)	(24)	(24)	(24)	(24)	(24)
	P= .292	P= .074	P= .247	P= .010	P= .447	P= .390	P= .490	P= .236	P= .482	P= .495	P= .382	P= .144	P= .450	P= .382	P= .001

	V.38	V.32	V.33	V.31	S.2	S.4	S.6	S.3	S.1	S.5	S.7	S.8	S.9	S.10	S.18
S.26	-.0894 (32) P= .313	-.0759 (32) P= .340	-.2574 (30) P= .085	-.2975 (32) P= .049	.0631 (31) P= .368	-.3642 (31) P= .022	.4436 (31) P= .006	-.1034 (32) P= .287	-.2663 (31) P= .074	.1845 (28) P= .174	.5838 (32) P= .001	-.2531 (32) P= .081	-.1417 (32) P= .220	.0719 (32) P= .348	.1301 (32) P= .239
S.22	-.2965 (27) P= .067	.0154 (27) P= .470	.1483 (27) P= .230	.5219 (27) P= .003	-.2930 (27) P= .069	.0975 (27) P= .314	-.0217 (27) P= .457	.1587 (27) P= .215	.2390 (27) P= .115	-.0353 (24) P= .435	-.2880 (27) P= .073	.3547 (27) P= .035	.1592 (27) P= .214	-.1916 (27) P= .169	.5168 (27) P= .003
S.20	-.0288 (22) P= .449	-.2505 (24) P= .119	.3372 (21) P= .067	.5203 (24) P= .005	.0990 (24) P= .323	.1241 (24) P= .282	-.0567 (24) P= .396	.1545 (24) P= .235	.1364 (24) P= .263	.4345 (22) P= .022	-.0667 (24) P= .378	-.2441 (24) P= .125	.2048 (24) P= .168	.1013 (24) P= .319	.7593 (24) P= .001
S.29	.1120 (30) P= .278	.5122 (30) P= .002	.2272 (29) P= .118	.3135 (30) P= .046	-.1920 (30) P= .155	-.0216 (30) P= .455	-.5222 (30) P= .002	.1877 (30) P= .160	-.2412 (30) P= .100	.1532 (27) P= .223	-.2752 (30) P= .071	.4122 (30) P= .012	-.1604 (30) P= .199	.0236 (30) P= .451	-.0166 (30) P= .465
S.28	.0644 (35) P= .357	.0153 (40) P= .463	-.2122 (34) P= .114	.0704 (40) P= .333	.0011 (40) P= .497	.1040 (40) P= .262	-.2749 (39) P= .045	.1787 (41) P= .132	.1187 (37) P= .242	.1204 (32) P= .256	-.2911 (41) P= .032	-.0560 (41) P= .364	-.1517 (41) P= .172	.0689 (41) P= .334	.1676 (36) P= .164
S.30	.1794 (35) P= .151	.5738 (40) P= .001	.0103 (34) P= .477	.0972 (40) P= .275	-.0343 (40) P= .417	.0159 (40) P= .461	-.3557 (39) P= .013	.1044 (41) P= .258	-.3200 (37) P= .027	-.0120 (32) P= .474	.0027 (41) P= .493	.2996 (41) P= .029	-.0954 (41) P= .277	.0011 (41) P= .497	-.0704 (36) P= .342
S.21	.1582 (34) P= .186	.3534 (35) P= .019	-.0689 (32) P= .354	-.1629 (35) P= .175	-.0803 (34) P= .326	.0650 (34) P= .357	.4086 (34) P= .008	.1579 (34) P= .183	-.2127 (35) P= .114	.1429 (30) P= .226	.2687 (35) P= .059	.1113 (35) P= .262	-.1564 (35) P= .185	-.0860 (35) P= .312	-.0482 (34) P= .393
S.23	-.0672 (34) P= .353	.1644 (38) P= .162	-.2475 (33) P= .082	.0679 (37) P= .343	-.2513 (37) P= .067	-.1048 (37) P= .269	-.1661 (37) P= .163	-.1228 (38) P= .231	.1056 (36) P= .270	.3695 (31) P= .020	-.2418 (38) P= .072	.1832 (38) P= .135	.2640 (38) P= .055	-.0344 (38) P= .419	.4652 (35) P= .002
S.24	-.3247 (34) P= .030	.1165 (38) P= .243	-.1553 (32) P= .198	.0549 (38) P= .372	-.0199 (37) P= .454	.0514 (37) P= .381	.0348 (37) P= .419	.2006 (38) P= .114	.1591 (37) P= .173	.3337 (31) P= .033	.0142 (38) P= .466	-.0860 (38) P= .304	.1814 (38) P= .138	.0253 (38) P= .440	.5740 (36) P= .001

	S.30	S.21	S.23	S.24
S.30	1.0000 (0) P=******			
S.21	-.0710 (35) P= .343	1.0000 (0) P=******		
S.23	.1996 (38) P= .115	.0464 (35) P= .396	1.0000 (0) P=******	
S.24	.0646 (38) P= .350	-.0014 (35) P= .497	.6567 (37) P= .001	1.0000 (0) P=******

```
        S.14      S.17      S.11      S.12      S.13      S.14      S.15      S.16      S.25      S.27      S.26      S.22      S.20      S.29      S.28

        .0844     .1880    -.0713    -.2475     .3273     .0239     .2761    -.0232     .8338     .1223    1.0000
      (   32)   (   32)   (   32)   (   32)   (   30)   (   32)   (   32)   (   32)   (   32)   (   21)   (    0)
      P= .323   P= .151   P= .349   P= .086   P= .039   P= .448   P= .063   P= .450   P= .001   P= .299   P=******

       -.0675     .3734     .6191     .0336    -.2684    -.4021    -.2739     .5991    -.0166     .5860    -.2314    1.0000
      (   27)   (   27)   (   27)   (   27)   (   26)   (   27)   (   27)   (   27)   (   27)   (   19)   (   27)   (    0)
      P= .369   P= .028   P= .001   P= .434   P= .092   P= .019   P= .083   P= .001   P= .467   P= .004   P= .123   P=******

       -.0465     .0527     .5679     .1373    -.0870    -.2780    -.2562     .3637    -.2183     .7261    -.0432     .3141    1.0000
      (   24)   (   24)   (   24)   (   24)   (   21)   (   24)   (   24)   (   24)   (   21)   (   24)   (   21)   (   19)   (    0)
      P= .415   P= .403   P= .002   P= .261   P= .354   P= .094   P= .113   P= .040   P= .171   P= .001   P= .426   P= .095   P=******

       -.2464     .1401     .2717    -.1045    -.1454    -.2433    -.2933     .1081    -.3354     .1824    -.4909     .1049     .4748    1.0000
      (   30)   (   30)   (   30)   (   30)   (   27)   (   30)   (   30)   (   30)   (   29)   (   22)   (   29)   (   27)   (   22)   (    0)
      P= .095   P= .230   P= .073   P= .291   P= .235   P= .098   P= .058   P= .285   P= .038   P= .208   P= .003   P= .301   P= .013   P=******

        .0202     .5329     .5848     .1529    -.0140    -.2526    -.1037     .1909    -.3266     .3580    -.3403     .3513     .3716     .4433    1.0000
      (   36)   (   41)   (   41)   (   41)   (   38)   (   40)   (   40)   (   41)   (   32)   (   24)   (   32)   (   27)   (   24)   (   30)   (    0)
      P= .453   P= .001   P= .001   P= .170   P= .467   P= .058   P= .262   P= .116   P= .034   P= .043   P= .028   P= .036   P= .037   P= .007   P=******

       -.1330     .1363     .0318    -.0787    -.0769    -.0520    -.1313     .2411    -.0790     .0973    -.2156     .0060     .0695     .7074     .1186
      (   36)   (   41)   (   41)   (   41)   (   38)   (   40)   (   40)   (   41)   (   32)   (   24)   (   32)   (   27)   (   24)   (   30)   (   41)
      P= .220   P= .198   P= .422   P= .312   P= .323   P= .375   P= .210   P= .064   P= .334   P= .326   P= .118   P= .488   P= .373   P= .001   P= .230

        .3675    -.0832    -.2357    -.1214     .0693     .2564    -.0830     .0875     .0331    -.3437     .0289    -.0502    -.2524    -.1912    -.1014
      (   34)   (   35)   (   35)   (   35)   (   32)   (   35)   (   35)   (   35)   (   32)   (   22)   (   32)   (   27)   (   22)   (   30)   (   35)
      P= .016   P= .317   P= .086   P= .244   P= .353   P= .069   P= .318   P= .309   P= .059   P= .059   P= .438   P= .402   P= .129   P= .156   P= .281

        .0378     .4701     .6032    -.1749     .0174    -.3695    -.1166     .3674     .1158     .4569     .1005     .3864     .4632     .3747     .6510
      (   35)   (   38)   (   38)   (   38)   (   35)   (   38)   (   38)   (   38)   (   32)   (   23)   (   32)   (   27)   (   23)   (   30)   (   38)
      P= .415   P= .001   P= .001   P= .147   P= .460   P= .011   P= .243   P= .012   P= .264   P= .014   P= .292   P= .023   P= .013   P= .021   P= .001

        .2956     .3446     .6391    -.0399    -.0629    -.2659     .0209     .3442     .0860     .3123     .0533     .4006     .4446     .1354     .4895
      (   36)   (   38)   (   38)   (   38)   (   35)   (   38)   (   38)   (   38)   (   32)   (   24)   (   32)   (   27)   (   24)   (   30)   (   38)
      P= .040   P= .017   P= .001   P= .406   P= .360   P= .053   P= .450   P= .017   P= .320   P= .069   P= .386   P= .019   P= .015   P= .238   P= .001
```

Part II

Country Profiles

Introduction

The nature of the aggregate indicators on dimensions such as ethnic pluralism, language, urbanization, political patterns, and political instability in Part I is, in many cases, based on disaggregated information about individuals, events, populations groups, institutions or urban centers within each nation. Part II, therefore, consists of 41 chapters, one for each country, which give such disaggregated information. These data and the more extensive bibliographic references to each country can be used to evaluate the quality of aggregate date in Part I and, potentially, to construct alternative indicators. Each chapter contains eight parts: (1) country map; (2) summary of basic information; (3) ethnic patterns; (4) language patterns; (5) urban patterns; (6) political patterns; (7) national integration and stability; and (8) selected references.

It should be emphasized that the data presented in Part II do *not* provide a comprehensive profile of the countries included. There are sources which do this, such as Colin Legum's *Africa: A Handbook to the Continent* and his annual publication, *Africa Contemporary Record*. Also there are the annuals Arthur Banks, ed., *Political Handbook of the World, Africa South of the Sahara* and the Jenue Afrique Yearbooks, etc., and the reader is referred to these for further information. Our purpose is to give comparable, detailed data on the dimensions that are covered in Part I. The brief descriptions that follow discuss the nature of the data, our defintions and intentions, and the basic sources used. The reliabilities of these data are similar to those presented in the other parts of this book. Wherever possible we had these sections checked by country experts of our acquaintance. In general, less information was available to us for the former French and Portuguese colonies than for former British colonies.

Country Map

Each map has been drawn to show the location of the country's ethnic units, and cities with a population of 20,000 or over. These cities are called "major cities" on the map's legend and are indicated by a small circle. We also give the locations of a number of the smaller population centers, which are shown by black dots, but only rarely have we named these centers. The map also shows the country's major communication linkages in the form of roads, railroads, and major rivers. Special attention has been given to the places where these linkages cross the country's boundaries. The principal sources for urban locations, spelling, and major transport networks, were P. Ady, *Oxford Regional Economic Atlas: Africa* (Oxford: Clarendon Press, 1965), *Africa 69/70* and *Atlas Jeune Afrique* (New York, Free Press, 1973). The sources for the ethnic unit locations are the various works cited in the ethnic patterns sections and George Peter Murdock, *Africa: Its Peoples and Their Culture History* (New York: McGraw-Hill, 1959). The locations of the ethnic units should be considered as rough approximations. The reader should note that these units are not ususaly coterminous with ethnic identity groups or "tribes" (see II below).

I. Basic Information

The mid-1980 population data are based on information from the U.S. Bureau of the Census' publication, *World Population 1977* (Washington, D.C.: 1977). Size of country data are from the *United Nations Demographic Yearbook* and *Africa South of the Sahara*. The major exports are given for 1979, when available, or otherwise for the latest available year. The sources for the export data are the International Monetary Fund's *International Financial Statistics* and the annuals *Africa South of the Sahara* and *Africa Contemporary Record*.

II. Ethnic Patterns

The concept, "ethnic unit," is discussed at length in an essay in Cross-National Research, Chapter 4. Briefly, ethnic units are analytic constructions which are meant to represent culturally distinctive and numerically significant segments of national populations whose members have similar values and practices. We constructed these ethnic units for the special purpose of cross-national research on national development and do not claim that they represent the only way to group African populations into larger units. Sometimes an ethnic unit will be coterminous with a single identity group or "tribe," but generally the ethnic unit is made up of *two or more identity groups (tribes)* whose individuals have values, practices, and institutions in common (ethnic types), or only value and practices in common (ethnic clusters). The organization of identity groups or tribes into ethnic units has been done *separately* for each country using the criteria described in Cross-Nation Research. Thus ethnic groups which are found in more than one country may be placed in different kinds of ethnic units (a) *type* in one country and *cluster* in another) because of the differing range of cultural variance that appears in each country.

In this section we list every *ethnic unit* (not identity group or tribe) which has 5 percent or more of the total country population. An introductory paragraph discusses the country's ethnic patterns and Table 1 gives the following information: (a) name of the ethnic unit with alternative ethnic names in parentheses; (b) constituent groups (tribes) which are included in the ethnic unit; (c) estimated population of the ethnic unit in 1980 and, wherever possible, the size of all the important constituent identity groups; and (d) percentage of the total 1980 country population accounted for by each ethnic unit.

The sources used in the ethnic unit classifications are indicated in each country's Table 1, and further references to the comparative literature will be found in Cross-National Research, Chapter 4, on ethnic unit classification. The availability of recent data on the size of ethnic groups is variable; the 1980 estimates are often extrapolations from earlier figures. In making these extrapolations we have had to operate on the assumption that the ethnic units in each country have all grown at the same rate and that the earlier data remain valid through 1980.

III. Language Patterns

A brief descriptive statement discusses the language families found within the country following Joseph Greenberg's seminal work, *The Language of Africa* (Bloomington: Indiana University Press, 1966). We also consider the various estimates of which language is most widely spoken within the country by speakers using it as a first language or as a *lingua franca*, and indicate our own estimates. There are three works which provide estimates for most of these countries: Duncan MacDougald, Jr.'s *The Languages and Press of Africa* (Philadelphia: University of Pennsylvania Press, 1944); Jan Knappert's "Language Problems of the New Nations of Africa," *Africa Quarterly*, 5 (1965): 95—105; and Dankwart Rustow's chapter, "Language, Modernization and Nationhood—An Attempt at Typology," in *Language Problems of Developing Nations*, eds. Joshua A. Fishman, et al. (New York: Wiley, 1968). These authors' estimates frequently vary widely. Our own estiamtes are based on recent information in some cases, but often amount to "educated" guesses.

Table 2 summarizes the language pattern of the country in four dimensions: (1) Primacy of the percent of the population that speaks the first and second most widely used indigenous language; (2) Greenberg's classification for all ethnic units over 5 percent; (3) the names of the indigenous *lingua franca(s)* which are defined as languages spoken by 5 percent or more of the population as a second or third language, and (4) the official language(s) in the country, including languages which are used officially in particular regions of the country. A fuller discussion of the issues and definitions involved in language classification, including a summary table of Greenberg's African Language families, will be found in Part I, Chapter 2.

IV. Urban Patterns

This section presents the data on all cities of 20,000 or more population from which the urban variables presented in Part I, Chapter 1, were derived. Table 3 gives the population figures for the capital city by decade from approximately 1920, or earlier when available, and, in cases whre the capital city is not the largest city, for the largest city as well. "UA" after the population figure indicates that the datum is for the urban agglomeration and not just the central city. The data should be treated as having varying reliability but usually less than 15—20 percent error. In some cases these data are somewhat out of date, and recent population growth in the cities may have changed the situation. The dominant ethnicity and name of the major vernacular language is coded for the capital city and, when available, the population percentage for the major ethnic group in the capital is given.

Table 4 gives the names and populations of all cities of 20,000 and over (Nigeria's list is restricted to cities of 50,000 and over because of the large number of Nigerian cities). The target date for the urban figures is 1977 as this was the latest date for which comparable data were available for most of the countries. Most of the data are, in fact, for one of the years 1971—1977, but in certain cases older data were all that was available although most such data exceptions are for the year 1970. When available the latest census data are given. When data for a city were available for either the central city or the urban agglomeration, the later were used to more accurately represent the urban reality. For details of this procedure see Part I, Chapter 1. The sources of the urban data are given in the table footnotes.

V. Political Patterns

There are two segments in this section: (A) Political Parties and Elections; and (B) Political Leadership. In (A) there is a brief descriptive statement regarding the development of political parties and the result of national elections during the period 1957 through 1979. Where military coups have suspended the political party system, this is noted. Figure 1 shows party and election data in time sequence. Minor parties as well as major parties are diagrammed in most cases in order to reflect the complexity of African political life (even if "one-party" states). A time grid scaled by years allows for an assessment of changes in the party system at any point in time, and also for an overview of the emergence of the party system. There is clearly a difference among one-party systems which are based on an original unity, those resulting from the banning of all other parties, those which have come about through voluntary mergers, those which are the result of the military assuming power and becoming a party, those in which small minority parties may operate legally, coalition systems of "national" government, two-party competitive systems, multi-party competitive systems, and multi-party systems based on large numbers of minority parties. All these different patterns are represented in the Black African countries, and are illustrated in the diagrams.

A number of symbols and abbreviations used in Figure 1 are listed below:

1.	⟶	governing party or parties
2.	⟶	active opposition party
3.	·-·-▸	party whose exact date of origin is unknown
4.	—·-·▸	party whose existence is unascertainable
5.	⟹	coalition between parties
6.	⟹	merger of parties
7.	OPS	one-party state instituted officially
8.	coup	coup d'état against the governing party
9.	b	party banned
10.	d	Party has dissolved itself

The discipline of codifying these data and drawing them on the chart in an unambiguous way was enlightening since it revealed the relatively unsystematic character of many of the sources' coverage of these events and the not infrequent disagreements among the sources on dates and other matters. We used various country political sources which may be found in the selected references section at the end of each chapter, and several comparative works, the most important of which were *Africa*; Colin Legum, ed., *Africa: A Handbook to the Content* (New York: Praeger, 1966); Colin Legum and John Drysdale, eds., *Africa Contemporary Record* (London: Africa Research Ltd., 1969, through 1976—77); *Europa Yearbook* and *Africa Research Bulletin*. It should be noted that although we have tried to record all referenda and general elections, the election data are sometimes incomplete, particularly for the earlier periods.

The Political Leadership section (B) contains information about the head of government plus cabinet-level leadership. Table 5 lists all the *post-independence* heads of government or occasionally, where the head of state is especially politically relevant (e.g., formerly the Emperor in Ethiopia), the head of state. The cutoff date is December 31, 1982. The ethnic data on the political leadership is given by ethnic *unit* except for those heads of government whose identity groups are not a part of oNe of the country's major ethnic units. The age of the present head of government is from the *New York Times Encyclopedic Almanac* 1971 (New York: New York Times, 1970), *Africa South of the Sahara* 1971 (London:

Europa Publications, 1971) which contains a useful "Who's Who," a *Who's Who in Africa* (London; Pike, 1973), and *Africa Research Bulletin*.

Table 6 delineates the distribution of the cabinet membership by ethnic unit for several time periods: at independence, December 31, 1967, when possible at December 31, 1972 and—in countries which had experienced coups—immediately prior to the first coup. This information was gathered from published lists of cabinet members, published country materials, *Who's Who*, and, in certain cases, communication with scholars who were familiar with the particular countries.

VI. National Integration and Stability

A brief descriptive statement summarizes the major *post-independence* events we have coded as elite instability (coups d'état, attempted coups); communal instability (civil wars, rebellions, irredentism); and mass instability (revolts and revolutions). The cut-off date is December 13, 1981 for these events. The reader may consult Part I, Chapter 5, for the detailed conceptual definitions of these events, reliability studies, and for the general sources used. We explicitly exclude from consideration such events as strikes, riots, arrests, terrorist events, etc., because of the difficulty of ascertaining the identity of the participants (e.g., ethnic or class primacy identification) and of obtaining accurate information in three broad categories: (a) description of the event; (b) characteristics of the participants; and (c) apparent (and/or stated) causes of the event. The accuracy of these summaries and the reliability of the coding depends upon the availabillity of published information on each event. The "dramatic" cases of coups d'état and civil war are gener-

ally well-documented, but attempted coups, rebellions, irredentism, and particularly those events we have coded as revolts, are less well-documented, and therefore may be less reliably coded. We relied upon *Africa Research Bulletin*, *Africa Confidential*, *Africa Contemporary Record*, *Africa Report*, *Africa Diary* and *The New York Times*, as well as upon numerous articles or books on particular events; specific sources are listed below Tables 7, 8 and 9, although general souurces for the events are not given for each event.

In Table 10 we list the number of events of each type, by year, so that time series analysis can be performed. Sources are generally from the publications cited in Chapter 5 of Part I of this Handbook. Since each event has one or more sources it is impractical to note all sources. They are available from the the author at the Department of Sociology, University of Washington, Savery Hall, 206Q, Seattle, Washington DK-40, 98195.

VII. Selected References

An effort was made to include recent, English language reference which would give the reader access to the best available information on each country. The references are highly selective and preference was given to those which treat the entire country and which would provide coverage on bibliographical, general, political, economic, and social topics.

The U.S. Army series of handbooks are often very useful summaries of the literature on African countries. The Boston University bibliography series is extremely useful for the 1960's, as is the International Monetary Fund's economic series. The former French and Portuguese Af-

rican countries posed special bibliographic problems because of the relative unavailability of literature on them in English. We try to compensate for this by referencing the appropriate sections of the comprehensive books by Virginia Thompson and Richard Adloff, and the somewhat less satisfactory book by Guy de Lusignan, *French-Speaking Africa since Independence* (New York: Praeger, 1969). Recently, however, more literature on the French and Portuguese areas is becoming available in English. we have added sources in other languages when the English language sources were substantially deficient.

1. Angola

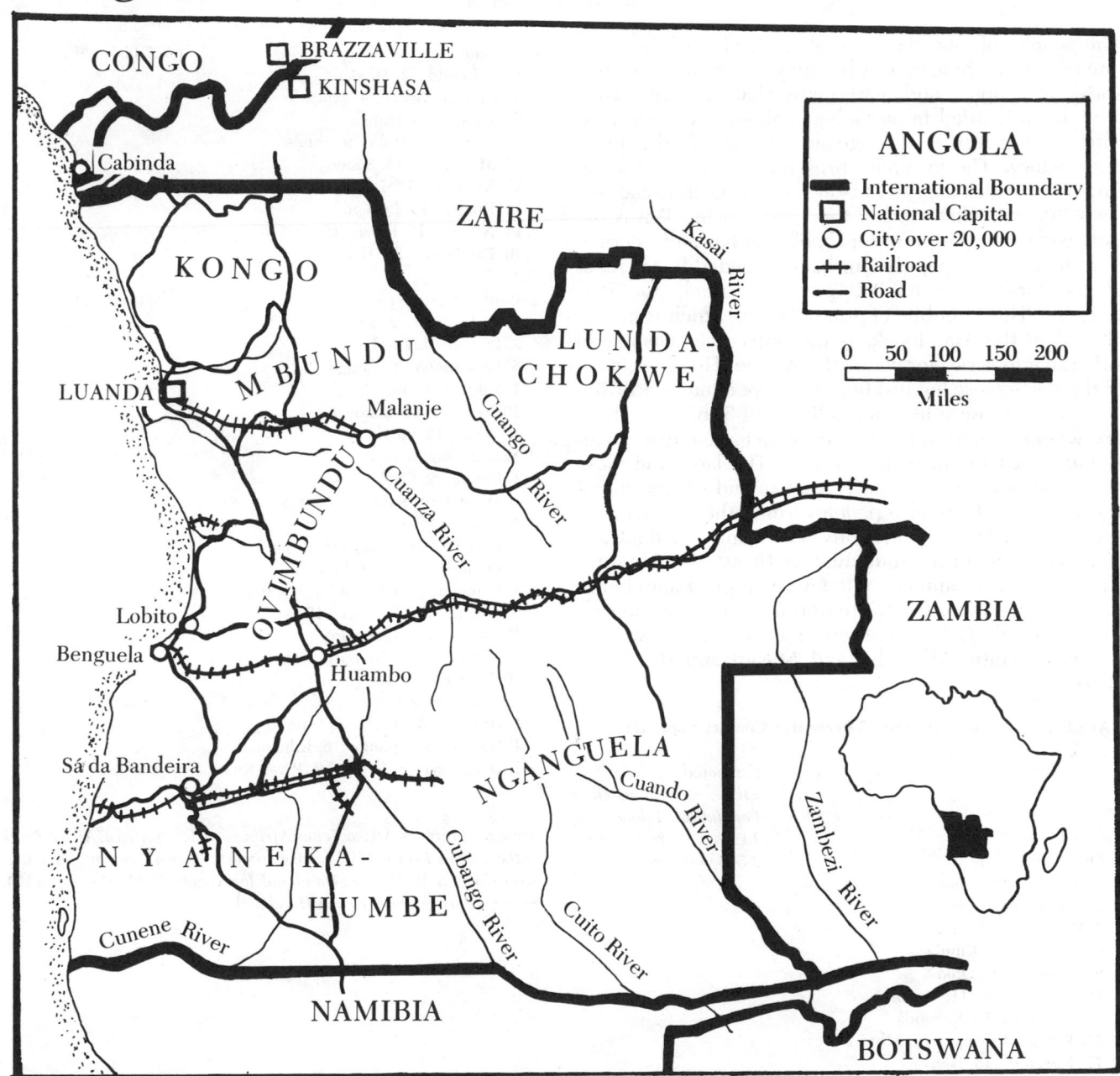

ANGOLA

- ▅▅ International Boundary
- ☐ National Capital
- ○ City over 20,000
- ┼┼ Railroad
- — Road

0 50 100 150 200
Miles

CONGO

BRAZZAVILLE
KINSHASA
Cabinda

ZAIRE

KONGO

Kasai River

LUNDA-CHOKWE

M B U N D U

LUANDA
Malanje

Cuango River

O V I M B U N D U

Cuanza River

Lobito
Benguela
Huambo

ZAMBIA

Sá da Bandeira

N G A N G U E L A

Cuando River

Zambezi River

N Y A N E K A-
HUMBE

Cubango River

Cuito River

Cunene River

NAMIBIA

BOTSWANA

1. Basic Information

Date of Independence: November 11, 1975
Former Colonial Ruler: Portugal
Estimated Population (1980): 6,759,000
Area Size (equivalent in U.S.): 481,354 sq. mi. (Texas, Oklahoma, New Mexico, Louisiana)

Date of Last Census: 1970
Major Exports 1973 as Percent of Total Exports: coffee—27 percent; crude petroleum—30 percent; diamonds—10 percent; iron ore—6 percent; fish and fish products—7 percent.

II. Ethnic Patterns

The peoples of Angola can be categorized into as many as one hundred ethnic groups but they are primarily Bantu-speaking peoples, and share many characteristics. They have been divided in our schema along lines that separate them in terms of language, ecological adaptation, and history. The grouping presented here is primarily linguistic, which follows Murdock's classification and corresponds with that used in the 1970 census. This is the only country reported in this book that has had a permanent non-African population that exceeeded five percent of the total (over 400,000 people), namely the Portuguese. The Republic of South Africa, which is not included in this Handbook, is the only other country in sub-Saharan Africa for which this is true. However, most of the Portuguese left just before independence in 1975.

Besides those ethnic units listed in Table 1.1, there are several groups in the country which are important although not large in relative terms. The largest of these are the mestizoes of mixed European and African ancestry (2%). There are also peoples from other former Portuguese territories, principally Sao Tome and the Cape Verde Islands. In the south and southeast of the country there are small numbers of the original pre-Bantu immigration population, the Hottentots and Bushmen (Koroca and Mukwe). Other southern Bantu peoples are the Zambezi Bantu (Mbukshu and Mashi) and the Ambo (1.5%).

TABLE 1.1   Ethnic Units Over 5 Percent of Country Population

Ethnic Units	Estimated Ethnic Population 1980	Estimated Ethnic Percentage
a. Ovimbundu type	2,568,000	38
1. Mbundu (Ovimbundu)		
2. Bailundu 3. Bié		
4. Wambo 5. Kiyaka		
6. Ngalangi 7. Kibula		
8. Ndulu 9. Kingolo		
10. Kalukembe 11. Sambu		
12. Ekekete 13. Kakonda		
14. Kitata 15. Sele 16. Mbui		
17. Kissanje 18. Hanya		
19. Ganda 20, Chicuma		
21. Dombe 22. Lumbo		
23. Sumbe 24. Sende		
b. Mbundu type	1,757,000	26
1. Ambundu 2. Mbaka		
3. Ndongo (Ngala) 4. Mbondo		
5. Dembos 6. Hungo		
7. Bangala 8. Holo 9. Shinje		
10. Munungo 11. Songo		
12. Kissama 13. Libolo		
14. Kibala 15. Luango		
16. Ntema 17. Puna 18. Cari		
19. Bambeiro 20. Haco		
21. Esela		
c. Central Bantu type	743,000	11
1. Bashikongo 2. Sosso		
3. Pombo 4. Zombo		
5. Bassorongo 6. Congo		
7. Yaka 8. Suku 9. Vili		
10. Yombe 11. Kakongo		
12. Oyo 13. Sundi		
d. Lunda-Chokwe type	608,000	9
1. Lunda 2. Chokwe (Kioko)		
3. Mataba 4. Kakongo 5. Mai		
e. Nganguela type	541,000	8
1. Luchazi 2. Nyemba (Nganguela)		
3. Luena (Luvale) 4. Luimbe		
5. Mbunda 6. Mbwela 7. Nyembe		
8. Mbane 9. Nkangala 10. Ngonyelo		
11. Avico 12. Ngongeiro		
13. Yahuma 14. Gengista 15. Nkoya		
16. Camochi		
f. Nyaneka—Humbe	338,000	5
1. Humbe 2. Mwila 3. Gambo		
4. Handa 5. Kipungu 6. Kilengi		
7. Donguena 8. Hinga 9. Kwan Kua		

SOURCES: Murdock *Africa; Jeune Afrique—Atlas of Africa; Africa South of the Sahara 1974* for 1970 census reports; *Africa Contemporary Record 1973/74* p. B521; *Area Handbook for Angola*; D.M. Abshire and M. Samuels *Portuguese Africa: A Handbook.*

III. Language Patterns

There is considerable linguistic diversity in Angola, but there are four main languages which together are spoken by over 70 percent of the population—Umbundu, Kimbundu, Kikongo, and Chokwe-Lunda. The fact that the Portuguese did not permit vernacular languages to be used in education at any level in their colonies limited the development of vernacular *lingua francas*. Umbundu, however, is reported to be used as a *lingua franca* in the central part of the country, especially in the urban areas of Huambo (Nova Lisboa) and Benguela-Lobito, and we estimate that 40 percent of the population speaks Umbundu. MacDougald estimates 39%. The Mbundu of the area around Luanda constitute the next largest group and we estimate that their language, Kimbundu, is spoken by 25 percent of the population. MacDougald estimates 22%. Portuguese, widely used in the urban areas, is spoken by at least 30 percent of the population.

TABLE 1.2   Language Patterns

1. Primacy			
1st language	Umbundu	(40%)	
2nd language	Kimbundu	(25%)	
2. Linguistic classification		Green-berg	Dalby
(all ethnic units in	Umbundu	IA5	R1
country over 5%)	Kimbundu	IA5	H2
	Kongo	IA5	H1
	Lunda-Chokwe	IA5	K1
3. *Lingua franca*	Umbundu		
4. Official Language	Portuguese		

SOURCES: Murdock *Africa*; Wheeler and Pelissier *Angola*; Marcum *The Angolan Revolution*; D. M. Abshire and M. Samuels *Portuguese Africa: A Handbook*.

IV. Urban Patterns

Capital and largest city: Luanda (founded 1575)
Dominant ethnicity/language of capital
　　Major vernacular: Kimbundu
　　Major ethnic group: Mbundu
　　Major ethnic group as percent of capital's population:

SOURCE: Wheeler and Pelissier, *Angola*.

TABLE 1.4   Cities of 20,000 and Over

City	Size	Date
Luanda[a]	600,000 UA	1974
Benguela/Lobito[a]	120,000 UA	1974
Huambo (Nova Lisboa)[a]	62,800	1974
Sa'da Bandeira[b]	31,674	1970
Malange[b]	31,599	1970
Cabinda[b]	21,124	1970

SOURCES: [a]*Africa South of the Sahara 1975*. [b]1970 census reports as published in *Africa: South of the Sahara 1974*.

TABLE 1.3   Growth of Capital/Largest City

Date	Luanda
1846	6,000
1866	15,000
1900	20,000
1930	50,000
1940	61,000
1950	141,000
1955	189,600
1960	224,000 UA
1970	475,238 UA
1974	600,000 UA

SOURCES: Wheeler and Pelissier *Angola*: Africa South of the Sahara 1975; *U.S. Army Area Handbook* p. 63.

Note: *The Political Handbook of the World 1979* gives figures for Luanda of 486,000 and Benguela of 102,700 for 1974. It is entirely likely that Luanda's population has decreased since independence given the large emigration of Portuguese.

V. Political Patterns

A. Political Parties and Elections

Until the first majority black government was appointed in February 1975, the history of indigenous political parties in Angola is one of illegal groups conducting guerrilla wars against the Portuguese and operating from bases outside of the country. The first party, founded by Holden Roberto in 1954, was the *Uniao des Populacoes de Norte Angola* (UPNA), which had as its main aim the reunification of the Kongo peoples which European colonization had spread over parts of three countries; Angola, Zaire, and Congo. This goal was modified in 1958 to a nationalist orientation, partly in response to the formation of the *Movimento Popular de Libertacao de Angola* (MPLA) in 1956 and its recognition by various outside groups such as the OAU. Nevertheless, the *Uniao des Populacoes de Angola*, the UPA (former UPNA) still had its base of power and operations in the Kongo areas of northern Angola while the MPLA headed by Dr. Antonio Agostino Neto, operated in the eastern areas and Luanda and was largely led by mestizo intellectuals. Roberto's group was headquartered in Kinshasa and supported by Mobutu as well as other interests including some American groups. Neto's group was headquartered in Lusaka, and later in Brazzaville; and received support from various Eastern-bloc countries, particularly the Soviet Union. In 1961, the UPA's name was changed again, to the *Frente Nacional de Libertaca de Angola* (FNLA). In 1966 a splinter group of the FNLA under the leadership of Dr. Jonas Savimbi was formed and named *Uniao Nacional para a Independencia Total de Angola* (UNITA). This group was composed largely of peoples from the center and south of the country, particularly the Ovimbundu, whose leaders had left the FNLA ostensibly reacting against the domination of the Kongo peoples in the FNLA. While several attempts were made to unify these groups under one banner, they were not successful. In late 1974, leaders of the three groups met to form a common front since the Portuguese initially refused to hand over power to an unrepresentative group. A new government appointed in February 1975 consisted of twelve members, three from each of the three guerilla groups and three Portuguese. This coalition was short-lived and the MPLA with major aid from the Soviet Union and Cuba took over Luanda and by the end of 1975 a large scale civil war was raging between the MPLA and an FNLA/UNITA coalition. The Portuguese instead of handing over power to one of these groups at independence, merely removed their troops from the country the day before independence. The MPLA with the aid of Cuban troops and Soviet equipment was able to hold back the FNLA/UNITA forces who were being supported by aid from the American and South African governments. The major fighting ended in February 1976 and the OAU recognized the MPLA as the legal government of Angola in mid-February of 1976. UNITA and the FNLA have continued to wage guerrilla war in the country since that time.

A group in Cabinda pressing for independence from Angola was called the *Frente de Libertacao do Enclave de Cabinda* (FLEC). By 1976, FLEC had split into two groups, the *Movement for the Liberation of Cabinda* (MOLICA) led by Joao da Costa and the *Provisional Government of Cabinda* led by N'Zita Henrique Tiago. They operated within the enclave and from bases in Zaire. Their previous bases in Congo are denied to them.

The first significant elections held in the Portuguese colonies were in March 1973. Only qualified voters were allowed to vote—the qualification was basically literacy in Portuguese—and none of the nationalist parties were allowed to participate. Nevertheless, 80 percent of the 600,000 persons eligible to vote were black Angolans. No elections have been held since that time nor has a legislative assembly been created. In 1975 a Constitution was promulgated and a one-party state was established. In November, 1980, a series of elections, within the MPLA were held for the People's National Assembly, which replaced the appointed Council of the Revolution. Later, lower level assemblies at urban and rural district levels are planned. The National Assembly will deliberate policy and make laws.

B. Political Leadership

The three pre-independence guerrilla movement were headed by Agostino Neto (MPLA), Holden Roberto (FNLA), and Jonas Savimbi (UNITA) and the conflict over the future direction of Angola centered around these men and their political organizations and ideologies. By independence, in November 1975, Neto's MPLA forces controlled the capital, Luanda, and by February 1976, Neto's government was recognized by the Organization for African Units as well as by most black African states as the legal government of Angola. Within the country, however, things were not so smooth for Neto. In May 1977, there was an attempted coup. And, throughout 1977, 1978 and 1979 there has been sporadic activity by UNITA which now claims it controls large areas of Angola. Within the MPLA there have been reports of divisions which led to the formation of the MPLA-PT (Marxist-Leninist Angola Worker's Party) in place of the MPLA. These divisions may also have prompted the December 1978 cabinet reshuffle in which the post of Prime Minister was abolished and several Council of Ministers members were dismissed. Since Neto's opponents promised a continued guerilla war, the future threats to MPLA control over the country may be considerable. President Neto died following an unsuccessful operation in Moscow on September 10, 1979. The MPLA chose José Eduardo dos Santos to succeed Neto.

FIGURE 1.1   Political Parties and Elections   ANGOLA

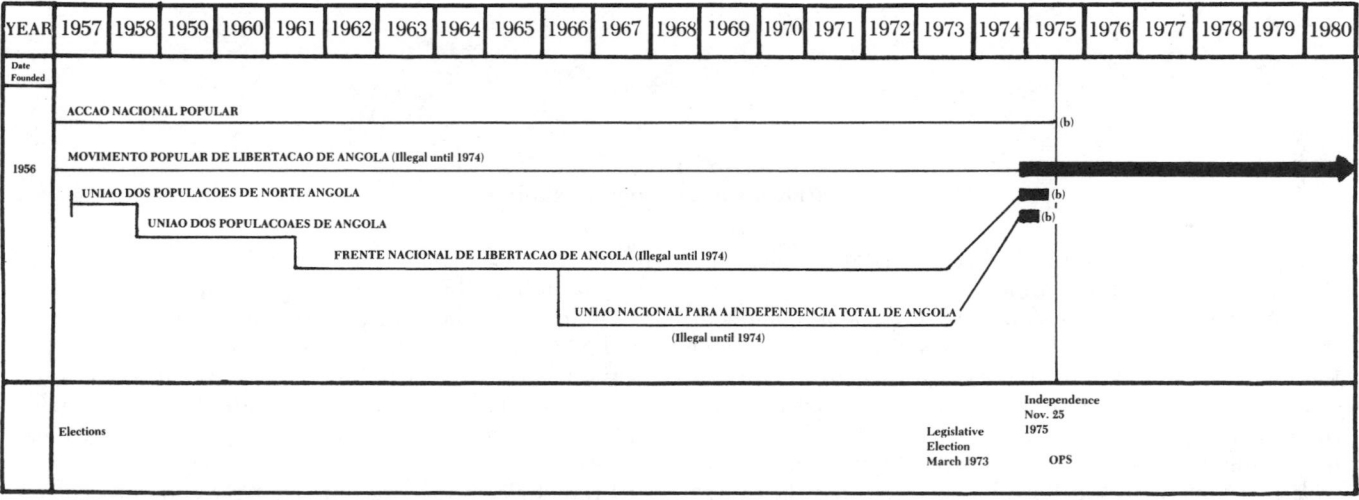

NOTE: A large number of organizations calling themselves parties (as many as 30 by some estimates) developed in the spring of 1974 but most had disappeared as independence approached.

TABLE 1.5   Head of Government (Post-Independence)

Name	Dates in Office	Age (1982)	Ethnicity	Education	Former Occupation
1. Antonio Agostinho Neto (President)	Nov. 1975— Sept. 1979	d. Sept. 1979, age 56	Mbundu	Medical (M.D.) Lisbon	Physician
2. José Eduardo dos Santos (President)	Sept. 1979—	40	Mbundu	Secondary School (Luanda) Petroleum Engineering (Moscow)	Former Deputy Prime Minister

VI. National Integration and Stability

Guerrilla activity began in February of 1961 against the Portuguese authorities under the sponsorship of the MPLA which was quickly followed by a major uprising in the North under the FNLA. Various other groups joined the fighting throughout the period 1961 to 1974, when a cease fire and negotiations for independence followed the military coup d'état in Portugal. The Angolan conflict had involved more than 40,000 Portuguese troops, as well as Angolans in the Portuguese army, but they were unable to defeat the liberation movements. This enormous drain on Portugal was responsible for the military coup in Portugal and brought groups to the fore in Portugal who were willing to disband the colonial empire.

It is too early to predict how the newly independent country will function although it can be pointed out that, unlike Guinea-Bissau and Mozambique, there has not been a unified liberation movement and, that, whatever the outcome of the civil war, political differences associated with the various liberation movments may continue in the future. This is particularly acute since the three major guerrilla groups were each identified with different ethnic groups and to a lesser extent competing ideologies.

From 1975 to the present, we have coded a civil war which began before independence and which continues to threaten the existence of the MPLA regime. The existence of large numbers of Cuban troops continues in the country and there is the possibility of a renewal of large-scale conflicts in the country.

TABLE 1.7   Elite Instability

Event and Date	Characteristics
1. Coup Attempt May 27, 1977	a. *Description*: Six days after the dismissal of Nito Alves and Jose van Dunem from the government and the MPLA Central Committee, forces under their control captured the Luanda radio station and the Luanda prison, freeing the political prisoners. By the end of the day, the government had restored its control and arrested hundreds of its opponents. Dunem was killed but Alves escaped.
	b. *Participants*: Alves and Dunem and MPLA forces loyal to the ousted leaders.
	c. *Apparent Causes*: Differences in political views between Neto and Alves as well as reported resentment of mestizo domination of the government and party.

TABLE 1.8   Communal Instability

Event and Date	Characteristics
1. Civil War Summer 1975— present	a. *Description*: After the breakdown of a pre-independence government shared by the three major liberation groups, the MPLA, UNITA, and FNLA, the MPLA took control of Luanda. Each group's membership was largely based on a particular area and ethnic group of the country and their forces took control of those areas: FNLA (North); UNITA (Center and South); MPLA (Luanda and East to the Zambian border), the war saw massive infusions of war materials to both sides and Cuban troops did a considerable part of the fighting for the MPLA while South Africans and mercenaries fought for the UNITA/FNLA coalition. b. *Participants*: Members of Angolan liberation groups as well as foreign troops from Cuba, South Africa and mercenaries. c. *Apparent Causes*: A complex of causes ranging from the three leaders' desires to lead the country, fears of one ethnic group's domination, ideological differences, and foreign competitions between African countries as well as between the United States and U.S.S.R.

TABLE 1.10   Annual Instability Events: Independence Through 1979—Angola

Year	'61	'62	'63	'64	'65	'66	'67	'68	'69	'70	'71	'72	'73	'74	'75	'76	'77	'78	'79
ELITE INSTABILITY																			
Assassinations																			
Plots																			
Attempted Coups d'État																	1		
Coups d'État																			
COMMUNAL INSTABILITY																			
Ethnic Violence																			
Irredentism																			
Rebellion																			
Civil War															1	1	1	1	1
MASS INSTABILITY																			
Revolt																			
Revolution																			

VII. Selected References

BIBLIOGRAPHY

Martin, Phyllis. *Historical Dictionary of Angola*. Metuchen, N.J.: Scarecrow Press, 1980.

Pélissier, René. "Contribution á la bibliographie de l'Angola." *Genève-Afrique* 15, 2 (1976): 136—152.

GENERAL

Abshire, David M and Michael Samuels (eds). *Portuguese Africa: A Handbook*. New York: Frederick A. Praeger, 1969.

Africa Report, Special Issue on Portuguese Africa. 12 (November 1967).

Birmingham, David. *The Portuguese Conquest of Angola.* London: Oxford University Press, 1965.

Chilcote, Ronald. *Portuguese Africa.* Englewood Cliffs, N.J.: Prentice-Hall, 1967.

Davidson, Basil. *In the Eye of the Storm, Angola's People.* Middlesex, England. Penguin Books, Ltd., 1974.

Davis, John A. and James K. Baker (eds). *Southern Africa in Transition.* New York: Praeger, 1966.

Duffy, James. *Portugal in Africa.* Cambridge: Harvard University Press, 1962.

Egero, B. *Mozambique and Angola.* Uppsala: Scandinavian Institute of African Studies, 1977.

Egerton, F. Clement C. *Angola in Perspective: Endeavour and Achievement in Portuguese West Africa.* London: Routledge and Kegan Paul, 1957.

U.S. Department of the Army. *Area Handbook for Angola.* Washington, D.C.: U.S. Government Printing Office, 1979.

Wheeler, Douglas and René Pélissier. *Angola.* New York: Praeger, 1971.

POLITICAL

Barnett, Don and Roy Garvey. *The Revolution in Angola,* Indianapolis, In: The Bobbs Merill Co., 1972.

Bender, Gerald J. *Angola under the Portuguese: The Myth and the Reality.* Berkeley: University of California Press, 1978.

Chilcote, Ronald. *Emerging Nationalism in Portuguese Africa.* Stanford: Hoover Institution Press, 1972.

Chilcote, R. H. (ed.) *Protest and Resistance in Angola and Brazil.* Berkeley: University of California Press, 1972.

Harsch, Ernest and Tony Thomas. *Angola, The Hidden History of Washington's War.* N.Y.: Pathfinder Press, Inc., 1976.

Henderson, Laurence W. *Angola: Five Centuries of Conflict.* Ithaca, N.Y.: Cornell University Press, 1979.

Humbaraci, A. and N. Muchnik. *Portugal's African Wars.* London: MacMillan, 1974.

Klinghoffer, A. J. *The Angolan War: A Study in Soviet Policy in the Third World.* Boulder, Colo.: Westview, 1980.

Legum, Colin and Tony Hodges. *After Angola.* New York: Africana Publishing Corp., 1976.

Serrans, Carlos Mireina Henriques. "Angola (1961—1976), Bibliografia." *Journal of Southern African Affairs,* 2 (1977): 295—32.

Marcum, John. *The Angolan Revolution, 1950—1962.* Cambridge, Mass.: Massachusetts Institute of Technology Press, 1969.

Marcum, J. A. *The Angolan Revolution: Volume II, Exile Politics and Guerrilla Warfare, 1962—1976.* Cambridge: MIT Press, 1978.

Okuma, Thomas. *Angola in Ferment: The Background and Prospects of Angolan Nationalism.* Boston: Beacon Press, 1962.

Stockwell, John. *In Search of Enemies: A CIA Story.* N.Y.: W. W. Norton and Company, Inc., 1978.

ECONOMIC

Hammond, Richard J. *Portugal's African Problem: Some Economic Facets.* New York: Carnegie Endowment for Peace, 1962. Occasonal Paper, No. 21.

Hance, William and I. S. Van Dongen. "The Port of Lobito and the Benguela Railway." *Geographical Review,* 46 (October 1956): 460-487.

SOCIAL

Davidson, Basil. *In the Eye of the Storm: Angola's People.* New York: Doubleday, 1972.

Edwards, A. C. *The Ovimbundu Under Two Sovereignties.* London: Oxford, 1962.

Estermann, Carlos. *The Ethnography of Southwestern Angola, Volume 1: The Non-Bantu Peoples: The Ambo Ethnic Group.* New York: Africana Publishing Company, 1976.

Heimer, F. W. (ed.). *Social Change in Angola.* Munich: Weltforum Verlag, 1974.

International Labour Organisation. *Official Bulletin,* 45 (April 1962), Supplement II: 1-253.

Samuels, Michael. *Education in Angola, 1873—1914.* New York: Columbia University Teachers College Press, 1970.

2. Benin

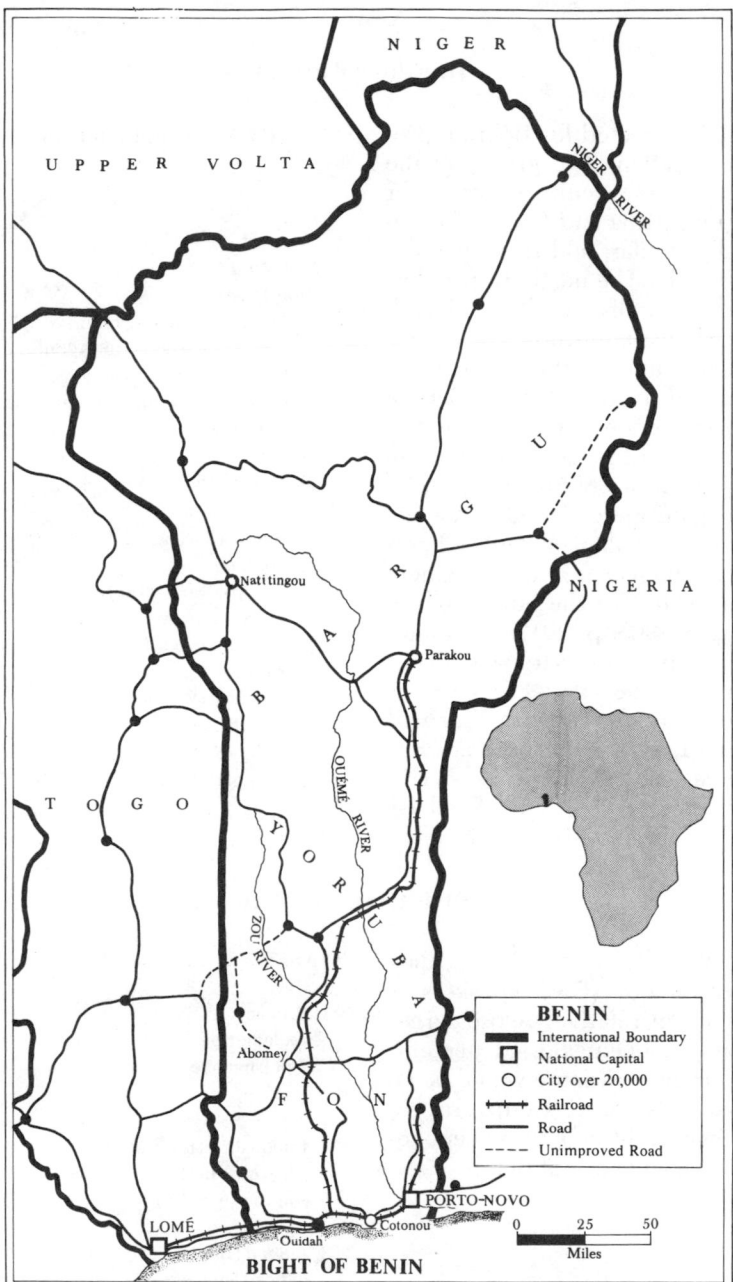

I. Basic Information

Date of Independence: August 1, 1960
Former Colonial Ruler: France
Change in Boundaries: Formerly part of the French West Africa Federation
Former Name: Dahomey (name change to Benin on December 1, 1975)

Estimated Population (1980): 3,464,000
Area Size (equivalent in U.S.): 43,484 sq. mi. (Tennessee)
Date of Last Census: 1979.
Major Exports 1977 as Percent of Total Exports: palm products—23 percent; cotton lint—21 percent; cocoa beans—11 percent.

II. Ethnic Patterns

The ethnic groupings we have selected for Benin represent a rather inclusive classification. The groups of the Fon-type generally share a common culture except for the coastal fishing groups (i.e., Mina and Gun). The Yoruba groups are linguistically similar, and these peoples also share a very similar life-style. The northern peoples, or Bargu cluster, are also culturally similar, although there is some justification for distinguishing the Kilinga and Somba from the Bariba inasmuch as they were indigenous people who acculturated to the intrusive Bariba. (Their general level of socio-economic development is also lower than that of the Bariba.) In addition to these peoples there are similar populations of Sudanic peoples such as the Dendi and Tienga (2 percent), Gurmanche, and Boko. Also significant are the Fulani or Peul (2.4 percent) who are migratory and who live as a social segment within the Bariba kingdom. Note that the ethnic figures given by Thompson (in Carter, 1963, p. 201) yield different percentages: i.e., Fon—51 percent, Bargu (Bariba)—13 percent, Yoruba—9 percent. Another set of figures of 1959 estimates is presented in *The Europa Yearbook 1979 World Survey* (Volume I, p. 1629). These are Fon Type—64% (Fon—47%, Adja—12.2%, and Aizo—5.1%); Bargu Cluster—14.7% (Bariba—9.7%, and Somba—5.0%); and Yoruba—8.8% (Yoruba and Mali—8.8%).

TABLE 2.1   Ethnic Units Over 5 Percent of Country Population

Ethnic Unit	Estimated Ethnic Population 1980	Estimated Ethnic Percentage
a. Fon Type	1,922,520	55.5
1. Fon (Dahomenas, Fonn)	(879,856)	(25.4)
i. Fon ii. Mahi iii. Agonlinu		
2. Gun	(415,680)	(12)
i. Gun ii. Guemenu iii. Tofinu		
3. Adja-Wachi	(374,000)	10.8
4. Aizo	(155,880)	(4.5)
5. Mina (Popo)	(96,992)	(2.8)
b. Bargu Cluster	779,400	22.5
1. Bariba (Bariba, Barba, Borgawa)	(426,074)	(12.3)
2. Somba	(197,448)	(5.7)
i. Berba ii. Natimba		
iii. Niendé iv. Woaba		
v. Soruba vi. Dye		
3. Kilinga	(155,880)	(4.5)
i. Dompago ii. Pila-Pila (Yowa)		
c. Yoruba (Egba)	471,104	13.6
1. Holli 2. Dassa 3. Ketu		
4. Manigri 5. Itsha 6. Chabe 7. Anago		

SOURCE: *Enquête Démographique au Dahomey*, 1961 (Paris: Ministère de la Coopération, 1964).

III. Language Patterns

The major language groups of Benin are Fon (Ewé), Bariba, and Yoruba. Estimates on Fon (Ewé) speakers as percent of total population are in relatively close agreement (Knappert, 50 percent; MacDougald, 51 percent; and Rustow, 58 percent). Our own estimate would be 60 percent. The Yoruba and Bariba language groups are second and third with approximately 14 and 12 percent respectively. French is the official language of Benin.

TABLE 2.2   Language Patterns

			Greenberg	Dalby
1. Primacy				
1st language	Fon-Ewé	(60%)		
2nd language	Yoruba	(14%)		
2. Linguistic classification (all ethnic units in country over 5%)	Fon-Ewé		IA4	45
	Bargu (Bariba)		IA3	48
	Yoruba		IA4	47
3. *Lingua franca*	Fon-Ewé			
4. Official language	French			

IV. Urban Patterns

Capital: Porto-Novo (founded early 18th century)
Largest City: Cotonou (founded 1868)
Dominant ethnicity/language of largest city (Cotonou)
   Major vernacular: Fon[1]
   Major ethnic group: Fon[2]
   Major ethnic group as percent of Cotonou's population: 49 percent (1955)

[1]Jan Knappert, "Language Problems of the New Nations of Africa," *African Quarterly*, 5 (1965), pp. 95-105. [2]Professor Dov Ronen suggests that contemporary Cotonou has a largely mixed population, ethnically, and that French is widely spoken in the city.

TABLE 2.3   Growth of Capital and Largest City

Date	Porto-Novo	Cotonou
1920	20,000	4,000
1930	26,000	9,000
1940	28,000	7,000
1950	29,000	20,000
1960	60,000	70,000
1964	71,000	111,000
1969	76,000	120,000
1973	97,000	175,000
1975	104,000	178,000

SOURCE: *Démographie Comparée, Europa Yearbook 1977 V. II,* and *Europa Yearbook 1979 V. I.*

TABLE 2.4   Cites of 20,000 and Over*

City	Size	Date
Cotonou	178,000	1975
Porto-Novo	104,000	1975
Natitingou	50,800	1975
Abomey	41,000	1975
Ouidah[a]	35,000	ca. 1975
Parakou	23,000	1975

SOURCE: *Africa South of Sahara 1980-81.* [a]*Europa Yearbook 1979 V. I.*

V. Political Patterns

FIGURE 2.1   Political Parties and Elections   BENIN

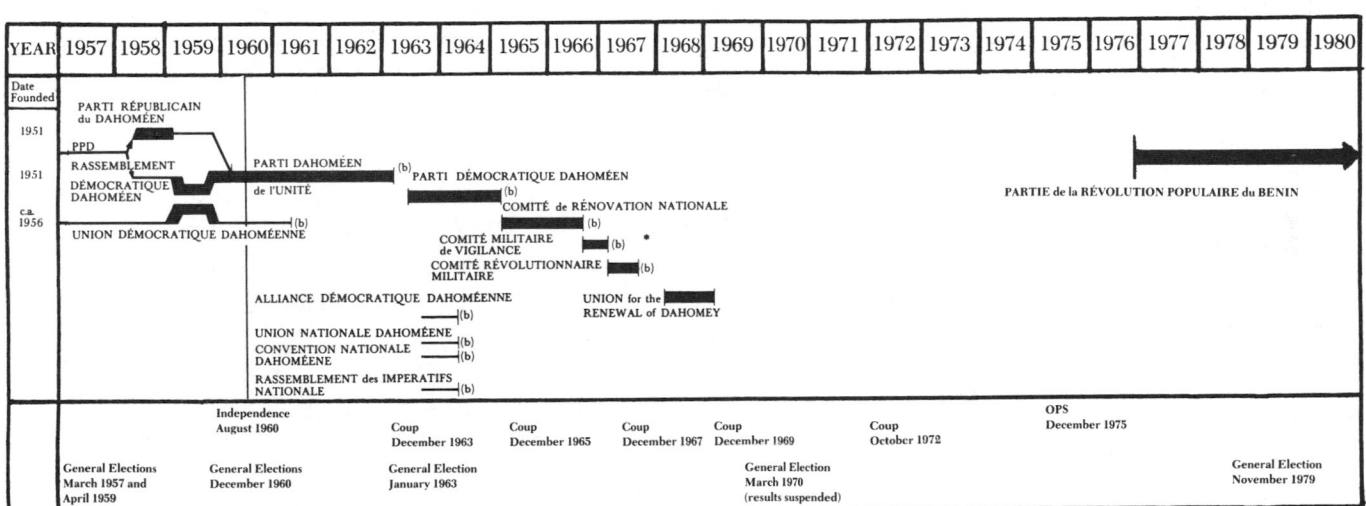

* The CRN, CMV and CRM were not political parties, but ruling military committees. They have been included to show shifts in the composition of military rule.

Note: An illegal party, the Front for the Liberation and Rehabilitation of Dahomey led by Dr. Emile Zinsou, operates outside of the country.

TABLE 2.5   Heads of Government (Post-Independence)

Name	Dates in Office	Age (1982)	Ethnicity	Education	Former Occupation
1. Hubert Maga (President)	1960— Oct. 1963	72	Bargu (Voltaic father Bariba mother)	Technical-Secondary Benin	Teacher, Civil Servant
2. Gen. Christophe Soglo (President)	Oct. 1963— Jan. 1964	73	Fon	In France	Soldier
3. Sourou Migan Apithy (President) and	Jan. 1964 Nov. 1965	69	Fon (Gun)	Diploma Paris Institute of Political Science	Accountant
Dr. Justin Ahomadegbe (Vice President)		65	Fon	Dental	Dentist
4. Tahirou Congacou (President)	Nov.— Dec. 1965				President of National Assembly
5. Gen. Christophe Soglo (President)	1965— Dec. 1967	73	Fon	In France	Soldier
6. Lt. Col. Alphonse Alley (President)	Dec. 1967— Aug. 1968	52	Other (Basila)	Secondary School (Senegal)	Soldier
and Col. Maurice Kouandété (Prime Minister)		43	"Northern"		Soldier
7. Dr. Émile-Derin Zinsou (President)	Aug. 1968 Dec. 1969	64	Fon (Mina) Paris	Graduate School	Doctor (M.D.)
8. Lt. Col. Paul Émile de Souza (Head of three-man directorate)	1969— May 1970				Soldier
9. Hubert Maga (President)	1970— 1972	72	Bargu (Voltaic father Bariba mother)	Technical Secondary	Teacher, Civil Servant
10. Dr. Justin Ahomadegbé (President)	May 1972— Oct. 1972	65	Fon	Dental	Dentist
11. Brig. Gen. Mathieu Kerekou (President)	Oct. 1972— present	49	Bargu (Somba)	Secondary School (Senegal) War College (Paris)	Teacher, Civil Servant, Soldier

A. Political Parties and Elections

Benin's complex early post-independence political history revolved around three dominant civilian figures: S. M. Apithy, Hubert Maga, and Justin Ahomadegbé, and a number of army officers. Sourou Migan Apithy supported by his *Parti Republicain du Dahoméen* (PRD) was vice-premier* from 1957 until 1959. Hubert Maga then served as the first prime minister from 1959 until 1960 at the head of a coalition of his party, the *Rassemblement Démocratique Dahoméen* (RDD), and the *Union Démocratique Dahoméenne* (UDD). After independence in 1960, he and Apithy formed a coalition party, the *Parti Dahoméen de l'Unité* (PDU), and he served as president until the military coup of October 1963. With the coup, General Christophe Soglo banned the PDU and called for elections in January 1964. The newly formed *Parti Démocratique Dahoméen* (PDD) came into power and, with Mr. Apithy as president and Justin Ahomadegbé (former leader of the UDD) as prime minister, governed until they were overthrown by General Soglo in November 1965. All political party activity was then banned. To replace the banned political parties, a committee— largely civilian—was then formed, the *Comité de Rénovation Nationale* (CRN) with Gen. Soglo at its head. In April 1967, the CRN was replaced, by Gen. Soglo, with the *Comité Militaire de Vigilance* (CMV), composed of younger generation soldiers. In December 1967, after another coup, General Soglo and the CMV were replaced by a ruling military committee, the *Comité Révolutionnaire Militaire* (CRM) under the direction of Lt. Col. Alley, who became president, and Col. Maurice Kouandété, who became prime minister. In June 1968, after a boycotted election, the military chose a civilian, Dr. Émile Derin Zinsou to become president and form a government. This government was removed by the military in December 1969. The presidential election held in March 1970 was suspended before its completion owing to violence. There were no political parties from 1965 until November 1975 when Kerekou created the *Parti de la Révolution Populaire du Bénin* (PRPB), which is intended to direct his projected program of "socialist development." In August 1977, an elected National Revolutionary Assembly was established to be the supreme authority of the state. Elections for this body were held in November 1979, 336 representatives were approved by a 97.5 percent favorable vote. The elections followed the first national congress of the PRPB where a 45-member central committee and 13- member political bureau were elected.

*As a colony, Benin was ruled by a French Governor who held the title Premier.

B. Political Leadership

The government of Benin has changed a great deal since independence. Several coups d'etat have introduced change from civilian to military rule, and vice versa. The civilian governments replaced by coups in 1963 and 1965 were characterized by fairly marked changes in the membership of cabinets, although patterns of recruitment to executive office appear to have remained similar throughout the post-independence period, with the continued predominance of the Fon. Twice the government included two leaders as "heads of government." In both instances the situations contributed to political instability. Shortly after the December 1969 coup, the establishment of a three-man military directorate was announced whose President was Paul Emile de Souza and whose other members were Col. Maurice Kouandété and Lt. Col. Benoit Sinzogan. The subsequent suspension of elections in March 1970, was followed in May 1970 with the re-establishment of civilian rule. President Maga initially headed a three-man presidential commission with the presidency rotating every two years amongst the three major political leaders. Ahomadegbe succeeded Maga in 1972 but was overthrown later that year. Cabinet membership stabilized after 1970 with only a minor reshuffle in 1971 until the military, under Major Kerekou, staged another coup in 1972. Kerekou has led the government ever since, although dissatisfaction in parts of the army has continued. In September 1973, the National Council of the Revolution (CNR) was established to carry out Kerekou's progressive policies. There were also cabinet reshuffles in 1973 (3) and 1974 (2). In November 1974, Lt. Col. Kerekou announced a program of "socialist development" for the country. In August 1977, the CNR set out guidelines for the organization of public authority. The supreme authority of the state is to be vested in an elected National Revolutionary Assembly. As of January 1980, however, the military was still in control of the government, although elections for the people's commissioners for the national assembly were held on November 20, 1979 and by February 1980 civilians held 15 of the 22 cabinet portfolios. On February 6, 1980 Kerekou was elected first president of the People's Republic of Benin by the members of the Assembly. He was the sole candidate.

TABLE 2.6   Cabinet Membership: Distribution by Ethnic Unit*

Ethnicity*	Independence Cabinet	Immediate Pre-Coup Cabinet	1967 Cabinet (Pre-Coup)
1. Fon (56%)	70%	92%	73%
2. Bargu (25)	20	8.3	18
3. Yoruba (14)	10		9.1
4. Others (8)			
N =	12	14	12

*Ethnic units arranged in rank order of size within country with the unit's percent of national population in parentheses.

VI. National Integration and Stability

The regionalism of Benin has contributed to political instability at the elite level; five successful coups have occurred since independence. The three significant regions in Benin are the north, the southeast, and the southwest. Within this framework, the three leading politicians came to represent each of the three regions respectively: Maga (from Parakou), Apithy (from Porto-Novo) and Ahomadegbé (from Abomey). The city of Cotonou stands apart from such regionalism, but has come to be identified with trade union and commercial interests. Military intervention under Soglo was undertaken as a stop-gap measure since in most cases, power was returned voluntarily to civilians. The army suffers from regional and generational differences, however. The assumption of power by Kerekou in October 1972 appears to break with

the tradition of rapid return to civilian rule. In January and October 1975, Kerekou announced the discovery of plots purportedly planned by former politicians and others. The plot was reportedly well directed by Émile Zinsou, the former President, according to the government. Serious unrest also followed the assassination of Captain Michel Aikpe in June 1975. In an apparent effort to dilute the power of the army, Kerekou formed a militia to 'help out' the army in 1977. Also, in 1977 and 1978, Gabon and Morocco purportedly aided the *Front de Libération et de Réhabilitation de Dahomey* in an air attack on Cotonou. In May of 1979, Kerekou sentenced to death nearly 100 people, including former President Zinsou, who were involved in the 1977 mercenary raid. Zinsou and most of these were in exile.

TABLE 2.7   Elite Instability

Event and Date	Characteristics
1. Coup d'État October 28, 1963	a. *Description*: Union and worker dissatisfaction with the government led to violent demonstrations in Parakou and Porto-Novo. Despite the presence of troops and a curfew, the demonstrations continued for several days. Various civilian factions failed to pacify the demonstrators and on October 28, Col. Christophe Soglo intervened. Popular approval and support for the military facilitated the takeover. On October 29, a provisional government was formed with Soglo as president, and the three major civilian leaders (Apithy, Ahomadegbé, and Maga) as the only members of his cabinet.
	b. *Participants*: Events preceding the coup were organized by labor unions and supported by many southerners, who accused President Maga (a northerner) of regional discrimination. The coup was carried out without violence by members of the military and their commander, Colonel Soglo.
	c. *Apparent Causes*: Worker dissatisfaction with government activity and southern antipathy for the government due to alleged discrimination by the former president seem to have been the major causes. The unions had been disturbed by the 10 percent cut in civil service wages. Soglo stated that the coup "preserved national unity and cohesion." Military spokesmen also cited other reasons for the coup: the high style of living of those in government (e.g., a 3.5 million dollar presidential palace; an unnecessary increase in the number of ministers; and various anti-democratic measures by the government). The military leaders returned power to civilians (Apithy and Ahomadegbé) through elections, January 1964.

Event and Date	Characteristics
2. Coup d'État December 22, 1965	a. *Description*: On the evening of November 27, 1965, there were violent demonstrations in Porto-Novo in support of President Apithy, whose resignation was demanded by "l'Assemble du Peuple," a group favoring Vice-President Ahomadegbe. On November 8, General Soglo obtained the resignation of both men, and in accordance with the constitution, Tahirou Congacou (president of the National Assembly) was appointed to head a civilian provisional government. A political impasse developed and Soglo once again stepped into the breach by dismissing the government, suspending the constitution, banning all political parties, and naming himself head of state. b. *Participants*: General Soglo, the army chief of staff, and military elements. c. *Apparent Causes*: According to official sources, "Before the spectacle of the struggling political leaders, and... after having seen that their replacements did not extinguish those passions, General Soglo decided to suspend the constitution, dissolve the National Assembly, and political parties." The conflicts between the head of state and the head of government were a big factor.
3. Coup d'État December 17, 1967	a. *Description*: Two commando units, led by Major Kerekou and Colonel Kouandété surrounded the residences of General Soglo, Colonel Alley, Lieutenant Colonel Aho, and Major Sinzogan. After four days, Army Chief of Staff Alley was asked to become head of state, apparently because he was satisfactory to the labor unions and to France, and had not been identified with any particular region. The cabinet eventually named consisted of an even number of northerners and southerners. b. *Participants*: Major Kerekou and Colonel Kouandété were northerners but they received support from many junior officers of southern origins. All the military men involved were younger than their predecessors. c. *Apparent Causes*: According to official sources, "Weakness and deficiency shown by an increasingly condemned leader"; the fact that decisions were made by a "family circle"; and the feeling that the army was threatened by internal cleavage from which "we could not retrace our steps." Northern elements in the army also complained that Soglo had given in too often to trade-union demands.
4. Coup de'État December 10, 1969	a. *Description*: President Émile-Derin Zinsou was seized by elements of the army and the military assumed control of the government. A three-man directorate was chosen to hold power, consisting of Lt. Col. Paul Émile de Souza, who was given the presidency of the directorate, Lt. Col. Benoit Sinzogan, and Col. Maurice Kouandété. b. *Participants*: The coup was engineered by Kouandété, a senior officer and army chief of staff, and by younger officers of the "third generation." c. *Apparent Cause*: Internal conflict in the army between the followers of Lt. Col. Alphonse Alley and Kouandété, following supposed attacks on Kouandété. Alley was sentenced to jail for one of these attacks. These attacks apparently led Kouandété to suspect President Zinsou of being involved in a plot to limit his power.
5. Coup Attempt February 23, 1972	a. *Description*: Units of the army apparently led by Lieutenant Colonel Kouandété try to take over strategic points and assassinate Army Chief of Staff de Souza. De Souza and his bodyguards kill the assassin and arrest the rebellious army men. b. *Participants*: Lieutenant-Colonel Kouandété, Captains Josue and Glele. c. *Apparent Causes*: It is not clear although some reports say that it was to prevent the handing over of the government from Maga to Ahomadegbe under the rules of the presidential commission of 1970 where each of three men were to take turns of two years at a time as Head of State.
6. Coup d'État October 26, 1972	a. *Description*: Army units under the paratroop commander, Major Kerekou, surround the presidential palace and take control of the national radio. The presidential commission is banned and its members are detained. b. *Participants*: Major Mathieu Kerekou and the paratroop unit from Ouidah. c. *Apparent Causes*: It is not clear but some suggestions are that Kerekou was upset by the death sentences placed on those military colleagues who participated in the Februrary 1972 coup attempt. Dissatisfaction with the presidential council's functioning also existed and is the more likely cause.

Event and Date	Characteristics
7. Coup Attempt January 21, 1975	a. *Description*: The armoured car unit from Ouidah led by Captain Assogba moves on Cotonou but is stopped by other army units. b. *Participants*: The armoured car unit led by Captain Assogba and reportedly backed by various deposed civilian politicians. c. *Apparent Causes*: Unclear but probably includes dissatisfaction with the Kerekou regime's stated intention to nationalize most foreign-owned businesses and take a Marxist political stance.
8. Coup Attempt January 16, 1977	a. *Description*: About one hundred mercenaries landed at the Cotonou airport and proceeded to attack the city: they were defeated by Benin's army that day and all of the invaders were captured or killed. b. *Participants*: A group of about one hundred mercenaries along with dissidents from Benin who supported one or another of the exiled former civilian politicians. The group was led by Gilbert Bourgeaud (Bob Denard), a French advisor to President Bongo of Gabon, and trained in Morocco. c. *Apparent Causes*: The group was backed by the *Front for the Liberation and Rehabilitation of Dahomey* which was organized in 1974 to oppose the socialist and nationalization policies of the Kerekou regime.

SOURCES: René Lemarchand, "Dahomey: Coup within a Coup," *Africa Report*, 13 (June 1968): 46—54. W. A. F. Skurnik, "Political Instability and Military Intervention in Dahomey and Upper Volta" in *Soldier and State in Africa* ed. Claude Welch (Evanston, Ill.: Northwestern University Press, 1970). Claude Garin, "Dahomey: Another Coup," *Africa Report*, 15 (January 1970): 3—4.

TABLE 2.8   Communal Instability

Event and Date	Characteristics
1. Ethnic Violence March 13, 1964	a. *Description*: In the town of Parakou, hometown of deposed President Maga, members of northern ethnic groups attacked resident southerners. Several persons were killed and homes were burned. The army put down the dissidents. b. *Participants*: Chabi Mama, secretary general of Maga's *Parti Dahoméen de l'Unité* was arrested and sentenced to prison. c. *Apparent Cause*: Northern resentment at southern treatment of their political leader.
2. Ethnic Violence March 1970	a. *Description*: In the town of Parakou six people were reported killed and 500 injured over electoral disputes between northerners and southerners and reported intimidation of voters. The army cancelled the rest of the elections. b. *Participants*: Supporters of Mr. Maga and supporters of political candidates from the south. c. *Apparent Causes*: An eruption of the continuing northern resentment of southerners' perceived advantages.

SOURCE: René Lemarchand, "Dahomey: Coup within a Coup," *Africa Report*, 13 (June 1968), pp. 46—54.

TABLE 2.10   Annual Instability Events: Independence Through 1979—Benin

Year	'61	'62	'63	'64	'65	'66	'67	'68	'69	'70	'71	'72	'73	'74	'75	'76	'77	'78	'79
ELITE INSTABILITY																			
Assassinations																			
Plots	1		1	1	1				2				1		1			1	
Attempted Coups d'État												1			1		1		
Coups d'État			1		1		1		1			1							
COMMUNAL INSTABILITY																			
Ethnic Violence				1						1									
Rebellion																			
Civil War																			
MASS INSTABILITY																			
Revolt																			
Revolution																			
TURMOIL																			
Demonstrations			1		1					1			1	1					
Strikes (no. days)			1	1	2	3	11		11			2			1				
Riots (no. days)			11	2	1		1			1									
Terrorism				2					2										
Declarations of Emergency	1		1							1									
CABINET INSTABILITY																			
Realloc. and new appts.	12	10	7	12	10	7	18	2	1										
New members	7	2	4	6		2	1	13	2	14	2	12							
Resig. and Dismissals	5	1	1	3	3	11	1		9	3	1								
No. of members (max.) (maximum in year)	13	13	16	10	11		12	10	3	14	15	12							

VII. Selected References

GENERAL

Cornevin, Robert. *Le Dahomey*. (2nd. ed.) Paris: Presse Universitaires de France, 1976

Decalo, S. *Historical Dictionary of Dahomey*. (People's Republic of Benin) Metuchen, N.J.: Scarecrow Press, 1976.

Morgan, W. B. and J. C. Pugh. *West Africa*. London: Methuen, 1969.

Pliya, Jean. *L'Histoire de mon pays*. Cotonou: Imprimerie Nationale du Dahomey, 1967.

Ronen, Dov. *Dahomey: Between Tradition and Modernity*. Ithaca, N.Y.: Cornell University Press, 1975.

Thompson, Virginia and Richard Adloff. *French West Africa*, pp. 139—145. Stanford, Ca.: Stanford University Press, 1957.

POLITICAL

Amir, Samin. *Neo-Colonialism in West Africa*. Harmondsworth, U.K.: Penguin, 1973.

Carter, Gwendolen M. (ed.) *Five African States*, N.Y.: Cornell University Press, 1963.

Decalo, S. *Coups and Army Rule in Africa*. New Haven: Yale University Press, 1976.

de Lusignan, Guy. *French-Speaking Africa since Independence*, pp. 159—169. London: Pall Mall Press, 1969.

Glélé, Maurice-A. *Naissance d'un État Noir*. Paris: Librairie Generale de Droit et de Jurisprudence, 1969.

La Republique de Dahomey. Paris: Berger Levrault, 1969.

Lemarchand, René. "Dahomey: Coup within a Coup." *Africa Report*, 13 (June 1968), pp. 46—54.

LeVine, Victor T. "The Coups in Upper Volta, Dahomey and the Central African Republic." In *Power and Protest in Black Africa*, eds. Robert I. Rotberg and Ali A. Mazrui, pp. 1035—1071. New York: Oxford University Press, 1970.

Terray, Emmanuel. "Les Revolutions Congolaise et Dahomeenne de 1963: Essai d'Interpretation." *Revue Française de Science Politique*, (October 1964), pp. 917—942.

Thompson, V. *West Africa's Council of Entente*. Ithaca, N.Y.: Cornell University Press, 1972.

ECONOMIC

International Monetary Fund. "Dahomey." In *Surveys of African Economics*, Vol. 3, Washington, D.C.: I.M.F., 1970.

Serreau, Jean. *Le Developpment a la base au Dahomey et au Senegal*. Paris: Librairie Generale de Droit et de Jurisprudence, 1966.

SOCIAL

Herskovitz, M. *Dahomey: An Ancient West African Kingdom*. Evanston, Ill.: Northwestern University Press, (1938), 1967.

Tardits, Claude. *Porto Novo: Les nouvelles generations africaines entre leur traditions et l'Occident*. The Hague: Mouton, 1958.

3. Botswana

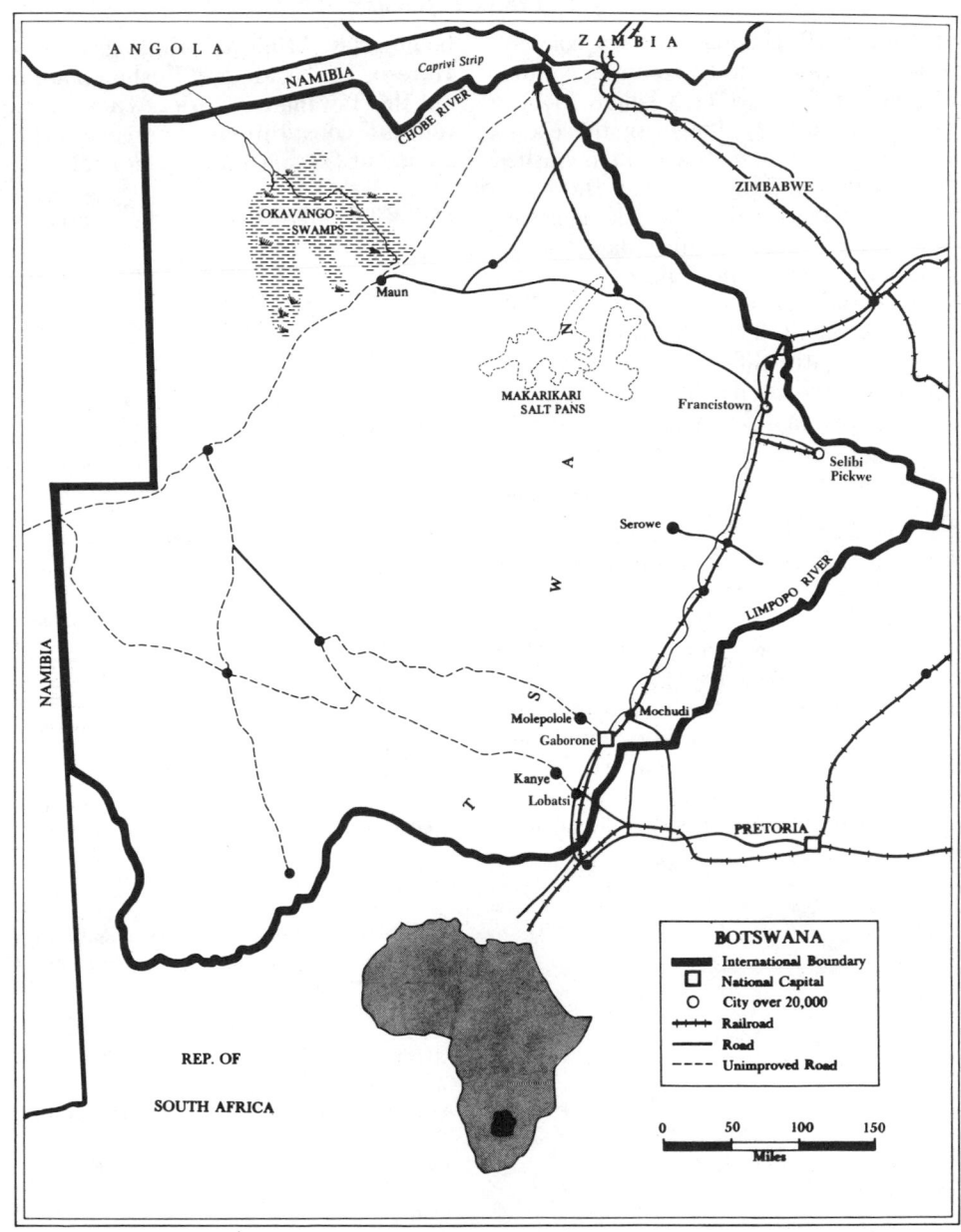

I. Basic Information

Date of Independence: September 30, 1966
Former Colonial Ruler: United Kingdom
Former Name: Bechuanaland
Estimated Population (1980): 787,000
Area Size (equivalent in U.S.): 231,805 sq. mi. (twice Arizona)

Date of Last Census: 1981
Major Exports 1977 as Percent of Total Exports: diamonds—31 percent; meat and meat products—27 percent; copper- nickel matte—26 percent

II. Ethnic Patterns

The Tswana (Batswana or Bechuana) share a common language (Sechuana or Setswana) and a common culture, and regard themselves to be part of a single identity group. Within this larger ethnicity, however, there are a number of distinct sub-groups which are distinguished primarily by lineage patterns. The largest of these, according to the 1964 census, are the Bamangwato (216,058), the Bakwena (65,251), the Bangwaketse (71,289), the Batawana (42,347), the Bakgatla (31,150), the Bamalete (13,861), the Barolong (10,662), the Batlokwa (3,711). It should be noted that Europa Yearbook 1979 (p. 1662) cites a slightly different distribution of these ethnic groups. Under colonial rule these sub-group identities were encapsulated by means of regional boundaries. Minority ethnic groups, such as the Koba, Herero, Kgalagadi, and Bushmen are dispersed throughout the Tswana territories. These, along with 8,000 Europeans, constitute the 3 percent of the population which are not of Tswana ethnicity in 1971.

TABLE 3.1   Ethnic Units Over 5 Percent of Country Population

Ethnic Units	Estimated Ethnic Population 1980	Estimated Ethnic Percentage
a. Tswana	763,390	97

SOURCE: *Report on the Population Census, 1971* (Gaborone: Central Statistics Office, 1972)

III. Language Patterns

Botswana is a state based primarily on a single language group: Tswana (Setswana, Sechuana). Approximately 97 percent of the population speak Tswana as a first language, and Denny (1963) suggests that it is a *lingua franca* throughout the country. Knappert estimates 100 percent of the population are Tswana-speaking. The estimate of Tswana speakers as 69 percent by Rustow (who suggests Shona is spoken by 9 percent of the population) is clearly too low. So as not to imply complete homogeneity, we have estimated that 98 percent of the population speak Setswana. English remains an official language.

TABLE 3.2   Language Patterns

1. Primacy			
1st language	Tswana	(98%)	
2nd language	Shona	(1%)	
		Green-berg	Dalby
2. Linguistic classification (all ethnic units in country over 5%)	Tswana	IA5	S3
3. *Lingua franca*	Tswana		
4. Official languages	English, Tswana		

SOURCE: Neville Denny, "Languages and Education in Africa" in *Language in Africa*, ed. John Spencer (London: Cambridge University Press, 1963), pp. 40-52.

IV. Urban Patterns

Capital: Gaborone
Largest city: Gaborone
Dominant ethnicity/language of capital
  Major vernacular: Setswana
  Major ethnic group: Tswana
  Major ethnic group as percent of capital's population:
    98%

SOURCE: 1971 Census.

TABLE 3.3   Growth of Capital and Largest City

Date	Gaborone*	Francistown
1950		
1960		
1964	4,000	9,500
1969	13,000	
1971	18,436	20,000
1972	23,000	22,000
1976	36,900	24,800
1980	55,000	

SOURCES: Various editions of the *Statesman's Yearbook*, *UN Demographic Yearbook 1969*, 1971 Census, and *Europa Yearbook 1979*.
*Gaborone is a new city.

TABLE 3.4 Cites of 20,000 or Over*

City	Size	Date
Gaborone	36,900	1976
Francistown	24,800	1976
Serowe	24,300	1976
Selibi-Pikwe*	23,000	1976
Kanye	21,600	1976
Molepolele	19,000	1976

SOURCE: Estimates from *Africa South of Sahara 1980-81*. p. 1662.

*Due to the large mining project at Selibi-Pickwe a new urban complex has developed. Its population in 1971 was about 5,000.

V. Political Patterns

A. Political Parties and Elections

A legislative council was established in Bechuanaland in June 1961, with an equal number of European and African members. The general election in March 1965 was the first direct election before independence. Two major African parties in competition were the *Bechuanaland People's Party* (BPP) formed in December 1960, and the *Bechuanaland Democratic Party* (BDP) founded in 1962. In 1962, a split occured in the BPP and a new party was formed by some former members of the BPP called the *Botswana Independence Party* (BIP). The BIP has had only a marginal influence on the country's politics, however. In 1966 a fourth party was created with an ethnic basis of the Bangwaketse clan, the *Botswana National Front*, BNF. The BNF and BPP remains the major opposition to the BDP. The BDP under the leadership of Seretse Khama, won a decisive victory (28 out of 31 seats) in the 1965 pre-independence elections and has continued to govern to the present time. In the October 1969 election, the BDP won re-election, with 68.6 percent of the vote, but lost four of its 28 seats. In October 1974, the BDP won again, taking 27 seats for an increase of 3 seats in the enlarged 32 seat assembly. While the number of seats going to the BDP is overwhelming, its plurality in the vote totals is somewhat smaller being about 70 percent in the 1969 elections. In the most recent election, October 20, 1979, Seretse Khama was re-elected for another five year term with the BDP winning 29 of the 32 seats. The leaders of the three opposition parties lost their seats to BDP members. The Botswana National Front (BNF) remains the principal opposition party with two seats in the assembly. The Botswana People's Party (BPP) maintains one seat and the Botswana Independence Party (BIP) has lost all of its seats. Voter turnout in the October 1979 election was greater than 50 percent which was a substantial increase over the previous electoral turnout.

B. Political Leadership

The Government was led by Sir Seretse Khama from independence until his death in July 1980 when vice president Quett Masire became president. No major policy changes were expected. Except for cabinet reshuffles in 1972 and after the 1974 elections most of the important ministers have continued in office since independence. The cabinet has been enlarged but, like the country, remains ethnically homogeneous with the exception of a single European member.

TABLE 3.5   Heads of Government (Post Independence)

Name	Dates in Office	Age (1982)	Ethnicity	Education	Former Occupation
1. Sir Seretse Khama (President)	1966— July 1980	died in 1980 aged 59	Tswana (Bamangwato)	Fort Hare, Univ. of Witwatersrand, Oxford	Read law
2. Quett Masire (President)	July 1980— present	56	Tswana (Banwaketse)	Tigerkloof	Journalist Vice-President

TABLE 3.6   Cabinet Membership: Distribution by Ethnic Unit*

Ethnicity*	Independence Cabinet	Immediate 1967 Cabinet	1972 Cabinet
1. Tswana (90%)	88%	86%	86%
2. Others (10)	12	14	14
N	8	7	7

Ethnic units arranged in rank order of size within country with the unit's percent of national population in parentheses.

FIGURE 3.1   Political Parties and Elections

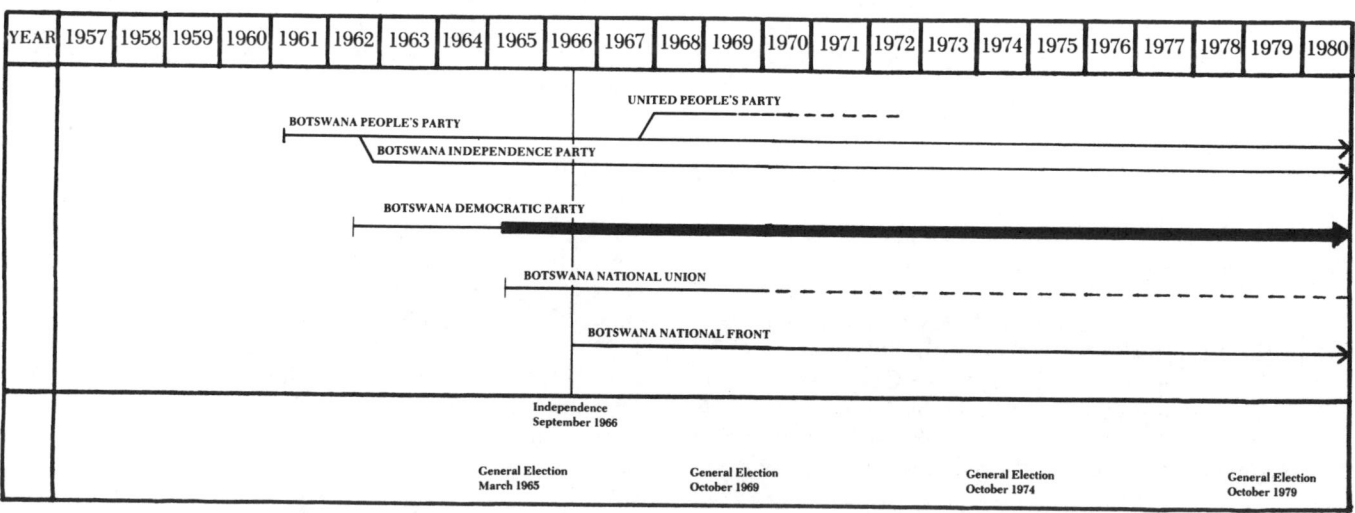

VI. National Integration and Stability

Botswana has been independent since 1966, preceded by a year and a half of self-rule. The apparent stability of the government since independence reflects the cultural, linguistic, and ecological homogeneity, in the country as a whole, although there is some inter-clan rivalry. As of 1980 we have coded no instances of political instability. Because of increasing incursions of Rhodesian troops into Botswana in search of guerillas, the country formed an army and airforce for the first time in October 1977. Botswana maintained three camps for Zimbabwe refugees. In October 1979 there was a minor confrontation between members of the Zimbabwe African Peoples' Union and the Botswana police over security arrangements in one of these camps.

TABLE 3.10   Annual Instability Events: Independence Through 1979—Botswana

Year	'61	'62	'63	'64	'65	'66	'67	'68	'69	'70	'71	'72	'73	'74	'75	'76	'77	'78	'79
ELITE INSTABILITY																			
Assasinations																			
Plots																			
Attempted Coups d'État																			
Coups d'État																			
COMMUNAL INSTABILITY																			
Ethnic Violence																			
Irredentism																			
Rebellion																			
Civil War																			
MASS INSTABILITY																			
Revolt																			
Revolution																			
TURMOIL																			
Demonstrations																			
Strikes (no. days)							3												
Riots (no. days)							1												
Terrorism							1												
Declarations of Emergency																			
CABINET INSTABILITY																			
Realloc. and new appts.																			
New members																			
Resig. and Dismissals							1												
No of members (max.) (maximum in year)							8	13	11	11	11	12							

VII. Selected References

BIBLIOGRAPHY

Mohome, Paulus, and John B. Webster. *A Bibliography of Bechuanaland*. Occasional Bibliography No. 5. Syracuse, N.Y.: Syracuse University Program of Eastern African Studies, 1966.

Mutter, Theo and Bernhard Weimer. *Botswana Research Directory 1976: A Compilation of Projects and Reports*. Gaborone: National Institute for Research in Development and African Studies, Documentation Unit, 1977.

Stevens, R. P. *Historical Dictionary of the Republic of Botswana*. Metuchen, N.J.: Scarecrow, 1975.

Webster, John B., et al. *A Supplement to a Bibliography on Bechuanaland*. Occasional Bibliography No. 12. Syracuse, N.Y.: Syracuse University Program of Eastern African Studies, 1968.

GENERAL

Alverson, Hoyt. *Mind in the Heart of Darkness: Value and Self-Identity Among the Tswana of Southern Africa*. New Haven, Conn.: Yale University Press, 1978.

Cervenka, Z. *Republic of Botswana: A Brief Outline of its Geographical Setting, History, Economy, and Politics*. Uppsala: Scandanavian Institute of African Studies, 1970.

Cervenka, Z., C. Donat, H. Lab and W. Lonski. *Botswana, Lesotho, and Swaziland*. Bern: Neue Reihe, 1974.

Chirenje, J. Mutero. *A History of Northern Botswana, 1850—1910*. Cranbury, N.J.: Fairleigh Dickinson University Press, 1977.

Dale, Richard. *Botswana and Its Southern Neighbor*. Athens, Ohio: Ohio University, 1970.

Griffiths, W.R. (Comp.) *Botswana: Some Basic Geographical Facts*. Gaborone: Government Printer, 1970.

Munger, Edwin S. *Bechuanaland, Pan-African Outpost or Bantu Homeland?* London: Oxford University Press, 1965.

Sillery, Anthony. *Botswana: A Short Political History*. London: Methuen, 1974.

Stevens, Richard. *Lesotho, Botswana and Swaziland*. London: Pall Mall Press, 1967.

Young, Bertram A. *Bechuanaland*. London: Her Majesty's Stationery Office, 1966.

POLITICAL

Conclough, C. and S. McCarthy. *The Political Economy of Botswana*. New York: Oxford University Press, 1979.

Halpern, J. *South Africa's Hostages*. Baltimore: Penguin Books. 1965.

Khama, Seretse. *Botswana: A Developing Democracy in Southern Africa*. Uppsala, Scandanavian Institute of African Studies, 1970.

Kuper, Adam. Kalahari Village Politics: An African Democracy. Cambridge: Cambridge University Press, 1970.

McCartney, W. A. J. "Botswana Goes to the Polls." *Africa Report* 14 (December 1969): 28—30.

Parson, Jack. "Political Culture in Rural Botswana: A Survey Result." In *Journal of Modern African Studies*, London, December 1977, pp. 639—650.

Picard, Louis A. "Bureaucrats, Cattle, and Public Policy: Land Tenure Changes in Botswana." *Comparative Political Studies* 13:313—56.

Schapera, Isaac. *Government and Politics in Tribal Societies*. New York: Schocken, 1970.

Vengsroff, R. *Bostswana: Rural Development in the Shadow of Apartheid*. Cranbury, N.J.: Fairleigh Dickinson University Press, 1977.

ECONOMIC

Colclough, Christopher. *Political Economy of Botswana*. New York: Oxford University Press, 1980.

Hartland-Thunberg, Penelope. *Botswana: An African Growth Economy*. Boulder, Col.: Westview Press, 1978

Hogblom, Goran. *Botswana*. Uppsala: Agricultural College of Sweden, 1973.

International Monetary Fund. "Botswana" in *Surveys of African Economies*. Vol. 5. Washington, D.C.: I.M.F., 1973.

Reynolds, Norman. *Rural Development in Botswana*. Capetown: University of Cape Town, School of Economics, 1977.

Selwyn, Percy. *Industries in the Southern African Periphery*. London: Croom Helm, Ltd., 1975.

Smit, P. *Botswana: Resources and Development*. Pretoria: African Institute, 1970.

SOCIAL

Alverson, Hoyt. *Mind in the Heart of Darkness.* New Haven: Yale University Press, 1979.

Rose, Brian. "Education in Botswana, Lesotho and Swaziland." In *Education in Southern Africa,* ed. B. Rose. London: Collier-Macmillan, 1970.

Russell, Margo and Martin. *Afrikaners of the Kalahari: White Minority in a Black State.* London: Cambridge University Press, 1979.

Schapera, Isaac. *The Tswana.* Ethnographic Survey of Africa. Southern Africa, Pt. 3. London: International African Institute, 1953.

Vivelo, Frank R. *The Herero of Western Botswana: Aspects of Change in a Group of Bantu-Speaking Cattle Herders.* St. Paul, Minn.: West Publishing Co., 1976.

4. Burundi

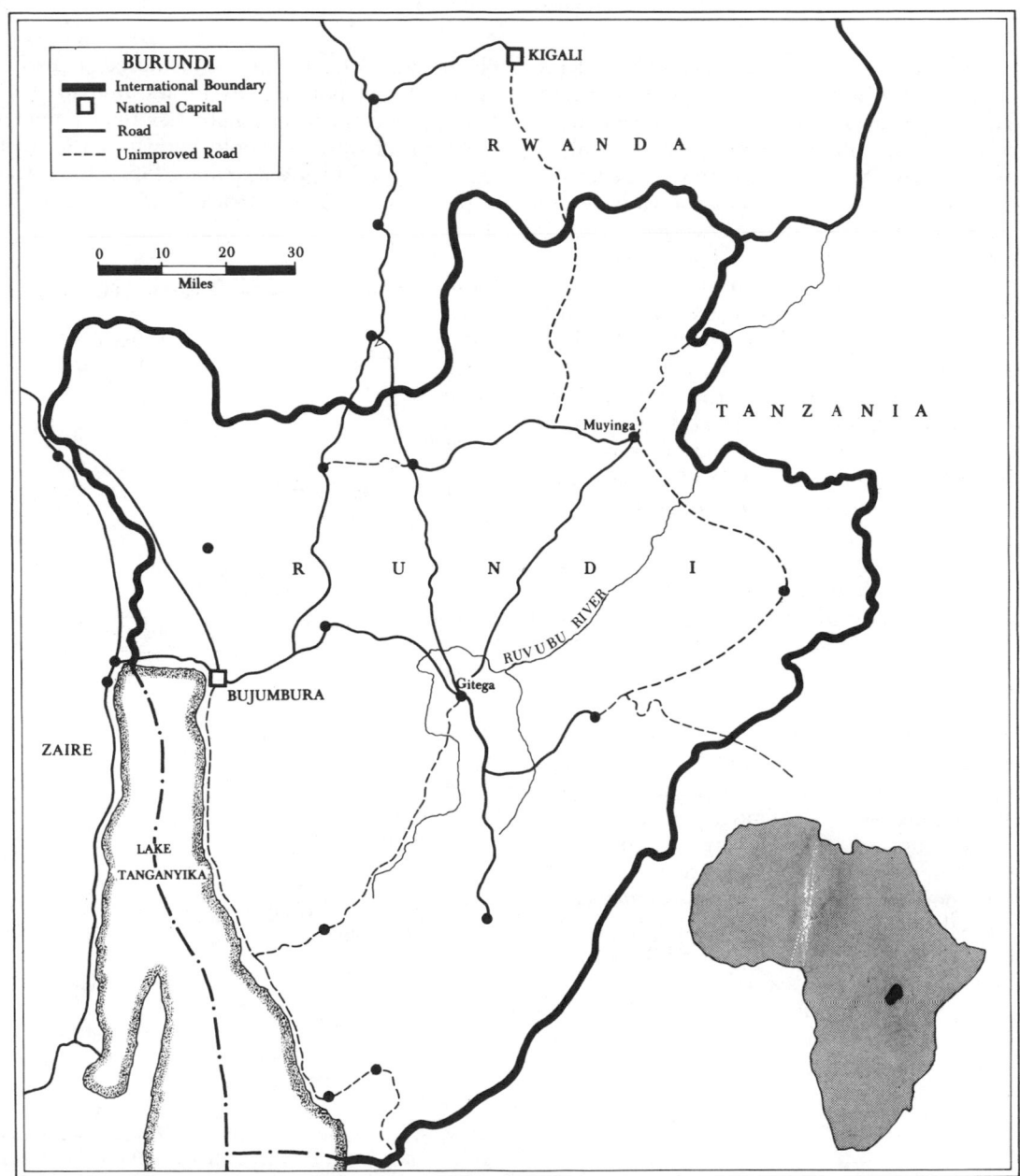

I. Basic Information

Date of Independence: July 1, 1962
Former Colonial Ruler: Belgium
Change in Boundaries: Split from pre-independence UN Trust territory of Ruanda-Urundi in 1962
Former Name: Urundi (in Ruanda-Urundi)
Estimated Population (1980): 4,429,000

Area Size (equivalent in U.S.): 10,747 sq. mi. (New Hampshire and Delaware)
Date of Last Census: 1970/71
Major Export 1978 as Percent of Total Exports: coffee— 85 percent.

II. Ethnic Patterns

Burundi is an ethnically stratified society in which the Tutsi have formed the nobility and the Hutu the common peasantry. These two groups originally represented divergent racial, cultural, and linguistic patterns (Nilotic and Bantu respectively), yet today they comprise a more or less unitary society. Considerable intermixing has taken place between the two groups. They have come to share a common language (Rundi) and social system in most areas. However, significant numbers of Hutu are geographically isolated from the mainstream of Burundi culture, and therefore retain a certain degree of distinctiveness. Estimates of Tutsi population previously ranged up to 17 percent. Because of the influx of Tutsi refugees from Rwanda (approximately 60,000 according to *Europa Yearbook 1967* and the fleeing of a number of Hutus from Burundi to Tanzania and Zaire after the 1972 and 1973 pogroms, an increase in the percent Tutsi population is likely. Estimates of the number of Hutu who were killed are as high as 200,000, including a large percentage of those with post-primary education. The Mwami and the *ganwa* (i.e. the king and princes of royal blood) are Tutsi but are considered a distinctive subgroup of that population. In addition to the Tutsi and Hutu, there is a very small (less than 1 percent) representation of pygmy people known as the Twa. In 1965 (according to *Europa Yearbook 1967*), there was a foreign population of 32,000 Africans, Europeans, Asians, and Arabs.

TABLE 4.1   Ethnic Units Over 5 Percent of Country Population

Ethnic Units	Estimated Ethnic Population (1980)	Estimated Ethnic Percentage
a. Rundi	4,340,000	98
1. Hutu (Bahutu, Wakhutu)	(3,543,000)	(80)
2. Tutsi (Tussi, Batusi, Watutsi)	(797,000)	(18)

SOURCES: "Burundi at Close Range" *Africa Report*, 10 (March 1965): 19—24; *Africa South of the Sahara 1974; Africa Contemporary Record 1973/74.*

III. Language Patterns

By ethnic identity, the population of Burundi is now about 80 percent Hutu and 18 percent Tutsi. However, they have come to share a common language—Rundi, the Hutu's Bantu language. MacDougald estimates that 84 percent of the people speak Rundi (or Kirundi); Knappert suggest 100 percent, and Rustow, peculiarly, estimates only 28 percent. Maquet (1960) suggests that Rundi is universal. We estimate at at least 90 percent of the population speak Rundi. The second language is Swahili, which Rustow estimates as understood by 17 percent of the population. Our estimate is 15 percent. French continues to be used in government and secondary schools. Rundi became an official language in Burundi after 1965.

TABLE 4.2   Language Patterns

1. Primacy			
1st language	Rundi	(90%)	
2nd language	Swahili	(15%)	
		Greenberg	Dalby
2. Linguistic classification (all ethnic units in country over 5%)	Hutu	IA5	E1
	Tutsi	IIE1	E1
3. *Lingua francas*	Rundi, Swahili		
4. Official languages	rundi, French		

SOURCES: J. J. Maquet, *The Premise of Inequality.* London: Oxford University Press, 1960. U.S. Department of the Army, *Area Handbook for Burundi.* Washington: Government Printing Office, 1969, pp. 43—44.

IV. Urban Patterns

Captial/largest city: Bujumbura (founded ca. 1892)
Dominant ethnicity/language of capital
   Major vernacular: Rundi

Major ethnic group: Rundi
Major ethnic group as percent of capital's population: Nearly 100 percent.

TABLE 4.3 Growth of Capital/Largest City

Date	Bujumbura
1930	6,000
1940	8,000a
1950	18,000b
1950	42,000c
1965	71,000c
1971	80,000d
1977	162,600e

SOURCES: aEstimated from 1935 and 1945 figures in Denis, *Le Phénoméne urbain.* bZaire, 10 (1956): 115-145. cUN Demographic Yearbook 1967. dAfrica South of the Sahara 1973. eEuropa Yearbook 1979, p. 1768.

TABLE 4.4 Cities of 20,000 and Over*

City	Size	Date
Bujumbura	162,000	1977

*The second largest town is the Mwamis' traditional headquarters, Gitega (formerly Kitega), with a population (1977) of 15,330. Buj

V. Political Patterns

A. Political Parties and Elections

The pre-independence struggle in Burundi centered largely around the Belgian backed *Parti Démocrate Chrétien* (PDC) and the more nationalistic *Unité et Progrés National* (UPRONA). PDC received a majority in the communal elections held in 1960 and governed until the legislative elections in September 1961 when UPRONA received an overwhelming majority. In the following month the UPRONA Prime Minister Prince Louis Rwagasore was assassinated, and the prime ministership passed to André Muhirwa who held office until June of 1963. In 1962 UPRONA split into two factions, the Muhirwa faction became known as the "Casablanca" group and the Mirerekano faction, the "Monrovia" group. In shifting coalitions of these factions, Muhirwa was succeeded as prime minister by Pierre Ngendandumwe, who was then followed in that office by Albin Nyamoya in April 1964, and a succession of three other prime ministers in 1965. In the July 1966 coup d'état Prince Ndizeye deposed the king (Mwambutsa IV), until that time the official head of state, and dismissed the UPRONA prime minister, Mr. Biha. Muhirwa and Biha are members of the *ganwa* clan. Michael Micombero was appointed to be the new UPRONA prime minister and Prince Charles Ndizeye was proclaimed King Mwami Ntare V. The following November, Captain Micombero ousted the newly enthroned king and proclaimed Burundi a republic. Micombero was elected President under a new constiution in 1974. The UPRONA party was proclaimed the only legal political party in 1966. After the 1976 coup, however, UPRONA was dissolved. The Supreme Revolutionary Council (formed November 2, 1976) was given the job of restructuring UPRONA.

In December 1979 UPRONA held its first national congress electing Col. Bagaza party president by a vote of 631 to 3. A 48-member central committee was also elected which included officers from the Supreme Revolutionary Council.

B. Political Leadership

The government of Burundi changed frequently from independence through 1966. Until 1972, six heads of government presided over ethnically balanced cabinets, in which Hutu and Tutsi ministers were carefully selected so as to maintain equal representativeness. After the second coup d'état in 1966, ethnic distinctions were officially proscribed, but membership in the new government initally remained ethnically balanced.

In January 1968, Micombero dissolved the National Council of the Revolution which had been established following the 1966 coup. In 1969, there were two shuffles of membership in it and the government, the second after a plot, purportedly led by Hutu army and government leaders was discovered. In late April 1972, Micombero's dissolution of the government was followed by an extremely violent repression of a Hutu uprising during the next two months. In July 1972, a new government was sworn in reflecting a break from the tradition of equal Hutu-Tutsi representation. Ten of the 14 ministers were Tutsi, five from the previous government, and of the four Hutus, none had been in the government before. In the ensuing period there has been a considerable movement in cabinet membership with the dismissal of the premier in July 1973, the periodic addition of army officers to the cabinet and other government posts, and a cabinet reshuffle in 1974. Micombero was overthrown in a coup on November 2, 1976 and is currently in prison.

The civil war of 1972 and 1973, eliminated most educated Hutus from the government and armed service as well as from private employment. They were either killed or they fled from the country. In October 1978, President Bagaza reorganized the cabinet and eliminated the post of Prime Minister.

FIGURE 4.1   Political Parties and Elections   BURUNDI

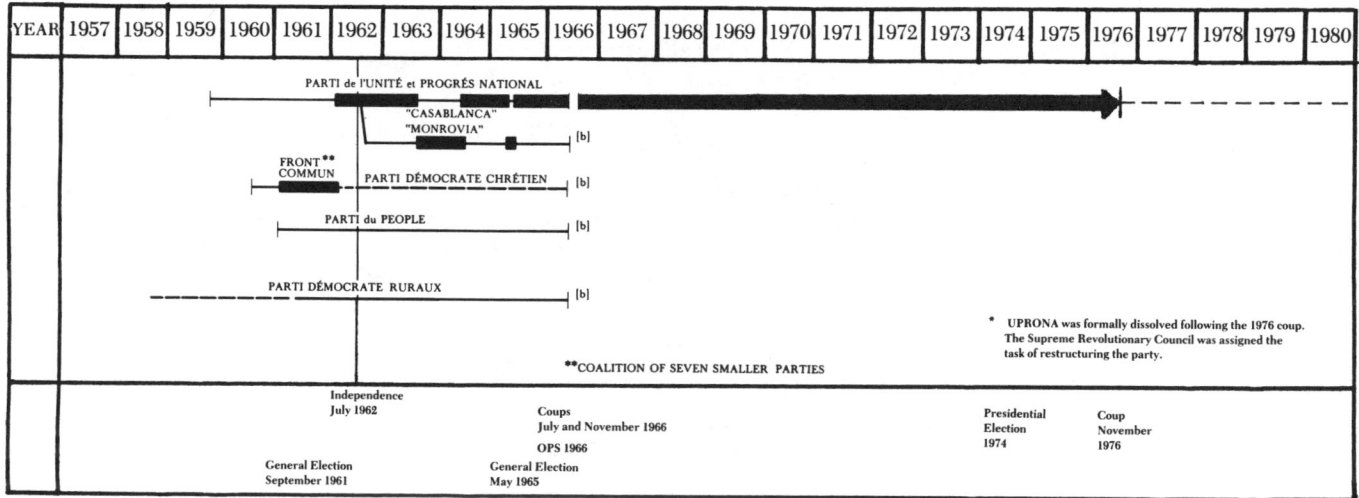

* On the eve of independence there were 24 political parties listed by *Europa Yearbook 1961*. However, according to the 1961 election results "other" parties won no seats and only 1.2 percent of the total vote.

TABLE 4.5   Heads of Government (Post-Independence)

Name	Dates in Office	Age (1982)	Ethnicity	Education	Former Occupation
1. André Muhirwa (Prime Minister)	1962—1963	about 60	Rundi (Tutsi)	Cercle Scholaire d'Astrida	Chief
2. Pierre Ngendandumwe (Prime Minister)	1963	Assassinated June 1965 Age 41	Rundi (Hutu)	Astrida	
3. Albin Nyamoya (Prime Minister)	1964—1965		Rundi (Tutsi)	Astrida	
4. Pierre Ngendandumwe (Prime Minister)	1965	Assassinated June, 1965 Age 41	Rundi (Hutu)	Astrida	
5. Joseph Bamina (Prime Minister)	1965		Rundi (Hutu)		
6. Leopold Bihumugani ('Biha') (Prime Minister)	1965—1966		Rundi (Tutsi)	Astrida	
7. General Michael Micombero (Prime Minister— President)	1966—1976	42	Mixed (Hutu— Tutsi)	Catholic College of St. Esprit (Burundi)	Military Officer
8. Lt. Col. Jean-Baptiste Bagaza (President)	1976— present	36	Rundi (Tutsi)	Belgian Military Academy (5 years)	Military Officer

TABLE 4.6   Cabinet Membership: Distribution by Ethnic Unit*

Ethnicity	Independence Cabinet	Immediate Pre-Coup Cabinet 1965	Dec. 31 1967 Cabinet	Dec. 31 1972 Cabinet
1. Rundi (Hutu) (80%)	50%	50%	56%	28%
2. Rundi (Tutsi) (18%)	50	50	44	72
3. Other (2%)				
N =	8	13	11	14

*Ethnic units arranged in rank order of size within country with the unit's percent of national population in parentheses.

VI. National Integration and Stability

Problems of national integration in Burundi centered initially on rivalry between the major *ganwa* (princely) clans and then on the unresolved cleavage between two ethnic groups: the Hutu (who, although a majority of the population, have not held political power until recently) and the Tutsi (who have dominated the political life of Burundi for 400 years). Regional splits, especially among the Tutsi, have also been an important influence in the political process. Initially Hutu partisans tried to achieve power through a violent, unsuccessful revolution. Later, when they had achieved political power through electoral means, they were resisted by the Tutsi monarchy, which was finally overthrown by military elements led by Colonel Micombero (of mixed Hutu-Tutsi parentage). This conflict has continued despite the official proscription of ethnic identification. Successive governments were kept strictly balanced between Hutu and Tutsi representatives until 1972, when the Tutsi became dominant. The civil war in 1972 and 1973 saw very large numbers of Hutus killed with estimates ranging up to 200,000 for the period. There were reported plots in 1969 and 1971. During 1979, tensions between the Catholic church and the government increased, particularly because the missionaries were reported to be urging young people to leave Burundi because of the threat of impending civil war.

TABLE 4.7   Elite Instability

Event and Date	Characteristics
1. Assassination January 15, 1965	a. *Description*: Prime Minister Pierre Ngendandumwe was killed in Bujumbura three days after he had been asked to form a national government by Mwami Mwambutsa IV. b. *Participants*: About a dozen men were eventually arrested for conspiracy against the security of the state, including: Albin Nyamoya, the outgoing prime minister; Augustin Ntamagara, president of the Fédération des Travailleurs du Burundi (FTB); Prim Nyongabo, president of Jeunesse Nationaliste Rwagasore (JNR), Zenon Nicayenzi and Pierre Ngunzu, former members of the Nyamoya government. The assassination was closely followed by the dismissal of gendarmerie commander Pascal Magenge, the banning of the FTB and JNR, and the severing of relations with mainland China. c. *Apparent Causes*: A few days before the assassination the Mwami had withdrawn support for the Nyamoya government after the persistent rumors of an impending coup d'état by pro-Chinese elements. Nyamoya had apparently sought Chinese support to offset "loss of domestic support." The connection between these events and the assassination is not clear.
2. Coup Attempt October 18, 1965	a. *Description*: Dissident Hutu members of the army and gendarmerie attacked the royal palace, but were eventually driven off by loyal troops under the command of Colonel Michael Micombero; Hutu troops also attacked the home of Prime Minister Biha who was seriously wounded. b. *Participants*: Members of the army and gendarmerie, mostly Hutu, led by Antoine Serukwavu, secretary of state for the gendarmerie. c. *Apparent Causes*: Continued attempts by Mwami Mwambutsa IV to transfer power from parliament to himself after Hutu members, for the first time since independence, had gained a parliamentary majority.
3. Coup d'État July 8, 1966	a. *Description*: Tutsi nationalists took over power. Prince Ndizeye (age 19) deposed his father, and transferred the premiership from Leopold Biha to Colonel Michael Micombero. On September 1, 1966, Ndizeye was proclaimed King (Mwami Ntare V), and the constitution was suspended. b. *Participants*: Prince Charles Ndizeye, Crown Prince of Burundi, supported by a number of young Tutsi politicians and army officers. c. *Apparent Causes*: Prince Charles said he took power in order to "safeguard the country's institutions and make the development of a national economy possible." Colonel Michael Micombero was named prime minister and the cabinet was staffed by young intellectuals.
4. Coup d'État November 28, 1966	a. *Description*: Prime Minister Micombero declared himself president while Ntare V was out of the country. b. *Participants*: Young Tutsi army officers led by Captain Micombero deposed Ntare V and abolished the monarchy c. *Apparent Causes*: Ntare V and those whose interests he represented had been vying for power with the military and government bureaucrats. Micombero accused Ntare of being influenced by criminals, practicing nepotism, and plotting to destroy the army.

Event and Date	Characteristics
5. Coup Attempt March 1972	a. *Description*: King Ntare V is killed shortly after his return to Burundi. The government states he led an attempted coup against Micombero. b. *Participants*: It is very unclear who was involved, but it probably involved traditional Tutsi clans as well as Hutus. c. *Apparent Causes*: Both royalist and Hutu elements were frustrated with the Micombero government and an uprising was apparently set off by Ntare V's return.
6. Coup d'État November 2, 1976	a. *Description*: General Micombero is overthrown by army units led by Lt. Col. Bagaza. UPRONA, the sole political party was banned and a Supreme Revolutionary Council was established to rule the country. b. *Participants*: Army units led by Lt. Col. Jean-Baptiste Bagaza. c. *Apparent Causes*: Army dissatisfaction with Micombero's rule. A statement after the coup said they acted to depose "self interested politicians" hungry for personal fame and wealth. An important component of the dissatisfaction was conflict between regionally associated Tutsi groups competing for power.

SOURCES: *New York Times* November 7, 1976, p. 6, section 4 and W. Weinstein, "The Burundi Coup," *Africa Report* (January/February 1977), pp. 52—56.

TABLE 4.8 Communal Instability

Event and Date	Characteristics
1. Civil War Oct. 20—Nov. 1965	a. *Description*: On October 19, 1965, a putsch by Hutu army and gendarmerie officers was thwarted by loyal army troops under Colonel Micombero. The king declared martial law. On October 20, Hutu peasants in Muramvya province and near the Rwanda border killed about 500 Tutsi. On October 23 Hutu began burning houses of Tutsi near the capital city. Shortly thereafter Tutsi reprisals took place. Almost all Hutu gendarmerie and army officers were executed and most of the Hutu political leaders were also killed. An estimated 5,000 Hutu were killed. Martial law was lifted in February 1966. b. *Participants*: It is difficult to specify leaders on either side for the duration of the war. The Hutu outburst seems to have been uncoordinated and the Tutsi retaliation was organized by the army. Antoine Serukwavu, secretary of state for the gendarmie, led the original coup attempt (October 18, 1965), and is alleged to have incited Hutu peasants to attack Tutsi during his escape to Rwanda. c. *Apparent Causes*: Precipitated by the Hutu putsch, the civil war gave vent to the Hutu-Tutsi animosity which had been developing since independence. The Hutu, influenced by events in Rwanda and aware of the advantages of democratic processes, were expecting to take advantage of the newly created opportunities in the social and political structures. The Tutsi saw democratic rule as a threat to their dominant position; by attempting to subvert further development of such institutions they incurred the hostility of the Hutu.
2. Civil War April to June 1972 May—Dec. 1973	a. *Description*: On 29 April 1972 a Hutu uprising throughout the southern part of the country took place. The army reacted with severe repression and the massacre of as many as 80,000 Hutu. Fighting broke out again in the summer of 1973. b. *Participants*: Hutu refugees from earlier fighting who were living in Zaire and Tanzania as well as internal groups, mainly from the South of the country. c. *Apparent Causes*: The continuing Hutu-Tutsi animosity was apparently touched off by, or coordinated with, the return of the deposed King Ntare V. who, while a Tutsi, was respected as a legitimate leader by many Hutu.

TABLE 4.10   Annual Instability Events: Independence Through 1979—Burundi

Year	'61	'62	'63	'64	'65	'66	'67	'68	'69	'70	'71	'72	'73	'74	'75	'76	'77	'78	'79
ELITE INSTABILITY																			
Assassinations																			
Plots			1			1			1		1								
Attempted Coups d'État				1									1						
Coups d'État						2											1		
COMMUNAL INSTABILITY																			
Ethnic Violence																			
Irredentism																			
Rebellion																			
Civil War					1							1	1						
MASS INSTABILITY																			
Revolt																			
Revolution																			
TURMOIL																			
Demonstrations																			
Strikes (no. days)																			
Riots (no. days)					2														
Terrorism					1														
Emergency	1			2	1														
CABINET INSTABILITY																			
Realloc. and new appts.			2	5	14	19	4	1	3		3	1							
New members			4	6	11	4	4	5	6	7	3	10							
Resig. and Dismissals			1	2	3	10	4	5	4		4	5							
No. of members (max.)																			
(maximum in year)			11	11	12	13	19	10	12	12	12	14							

VII. Selected References

BIBLIOGRAPHY

Nahayo, S. "Contribution à la bibliographie des ouvrage relatifs au Burundi (Afrique Central)" in 3 parts. *Geneve- Afrique*, 10, 1; 10, 2; 11, 1 (1971—72) pp. 92—99; 100—11; 94—104.

Nyambariza, Daniel. *Le Burundi: essai à une bibliographie* 1959—1973, Bujumbura Université du Burundi 1974

GENERAL

Lemarchand, René. *Rwanda and Burundi*. New York: Praeger, 1970.

Nsanze, T. *L'Edification de la Republique du Burundi*. Brussels: Remarques Africaines, 1970.

U.S. Department of the Army. *Area Handbook for Burundi*. Washington, D.C.: Government Printing Office, 1969.

Weinstein, W. *Historical Dictionary of Burundi*. Metuchen, N.J.: Scarecrow, 1976.

POLITICAL

Bowen, Michael, *Passing by: the United States and Genocide in Burundi, 1972*. Washington: Carnegie Endowment for International Peace, 1973.

Chronique de Politique Etrangère. *Decolonisation et Independence de Rwanda et du Burundi*. Brussels: Institut Royal des Relations Internationales, 1963.

Lemarchand, René. "Political Instability in Africa: *The Case of Rwanda and Burundi*." *Civilisations*, 16 (1966): 307—337.

Lemarchand, René. "Social Change and Political Modernisation in Burundi." *Journal of Modern African Studies*, 4 (1966): 401—433.

Melady, Thomas P. *Burundi: The Tragic Years*. Mary Knoll, N.Y.: Orbis, 1974.

Weinstein, Warren. *Political Conflict and Ethnic Strategies: A Case Study of Burundi*. Syracuse, N.Y.: Syracuse University, Maxwell School of Citizenship and Public Affairs, 1976.

ECONOMIC

International Monetary Fund. "Burundi" in *Surveys of African Economies*, Vol. 5. Washington, D.C.: I.M.F., 1973.

Leurquin, Philippe P. *Agricultural Change in Ruanda-Urundi 1945—1960*. Stanford, Calif.: Stanford University Food Research Institute, 1963.

SOCIAL

Baeck, L. *Étude socio-economique du centre extra-coutumier d'Usumbura*. Brussels: Academie Royale des Sciences Coloniales, 1957.

Liege Université. Foundation pour les recherches scientifiques au Congo Belge et au Ruanda-Urundi. *Le problème de l'enseignement dans le Ruanda-Urundi*. Elizabethville: C.E.P.S.I., 1958.

5. Cameroon

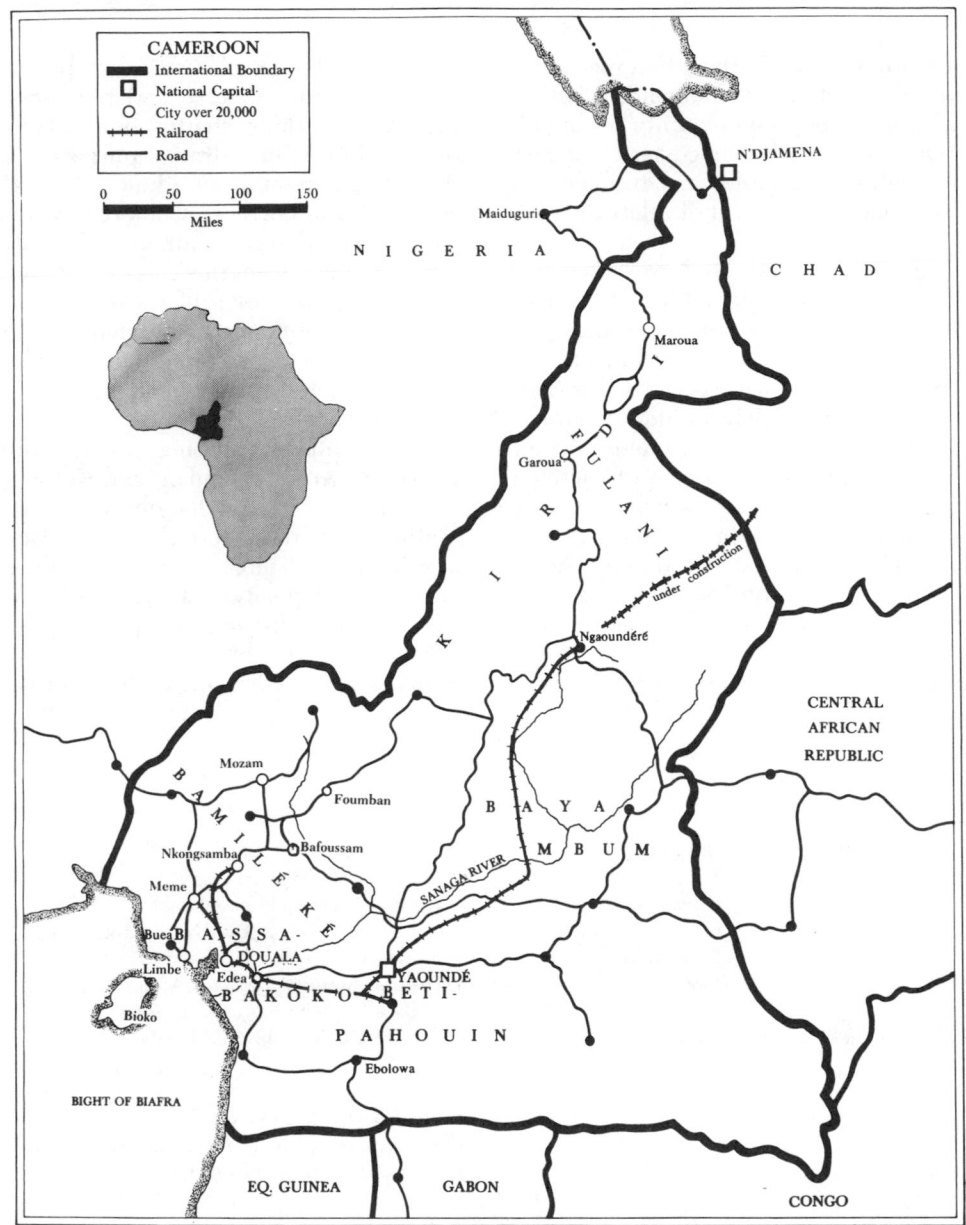

I. Basic Information

Date of Independence: January 1, 1960 (West Cameroon became independent in October, 1961)

Former Colonial Rulers: France and United Kingdom

Changes in Boundaries: The Southern Cameroons (British) voted to become part of the Cameroon Republic (French) on February 11, 1961

Former Names: Cameroun (Fr.), Kamerun (Ger.), Cameroon Federal Republic.

Estimated Population (1980): 8,332,000

Area Size (equivalent in U.S.): 183,569 sq. mi. (Oregon and Washington)

Date of Last Census: 1976

Major Exports 1978 as Percent of Total Exports: coffee—29 percent, cocoa and derivatives—34 percent, wood—12 percent, aluminum—4 percent, cotton products—4 percent.

II. Ethnic Patterns

The Cameroon is a country of great ethnic heterogeneity. Our categorization of this diversity demands a rather high level of abstraction. In judging greater or lesser cultural similarity between groups, it is necessary to ignore variation on specific cultural variables and to define an acceptable *range* of variation at a level of relatively high generalization.

The ethnic clusters we have selected are based primarily on cultural similarities, with additional weight given to linguistic criteria, common ecological adaptations, and historical relatedness. In most, but not all, cases these similarities are recognized locally as bases for group identity. The Fulani are clearly an identity group. The large majority of the Equatorial Bantu cluster (i.e., the Beti-Pahouin) recognize a vague sense of common identity. The Bamiléké are developing a sense of identity largely through outgroup ascription in the large cities of southern Cameroon. The other broad groupings (e.g., Bassa-Bakoko, Baya-Mbum) include peoples who have not necessarily translated their cultural similarity (and proximity) into an explicit notion of shared identity.

The Kirdi (the term is the Kanuri word for "pagan") raise particular problems. These peoples are in reality rather culturally diverse and represent what could be termed an "ethnic shatter belt." They are, however, identified for administrative purposes and by other peoples in Cameroon as an ethnic group. Historically, they are peoples in northern Cameroon who resisted the Fulani Jihad of the early nineteenth century. Their isolation, stemming from this early resistance, has resulted in a uniformly low level of socio-economic development. Some sense of common ethnicity and political identity appears to be developing among these peoples. (It should be noted that population estimates for the Kirdi range from 13—17 percent.)

Smaller ethnic groupings found within Cameroon are the Shuwa Arabs, Mandan, and Kotoko of the far north; once sizable, but now largely repatriated populations of Southern Nigerians (Ibo, Ibibio, etc.) and Plateau Nigerians (Mambila, Tigon, Jukun, etc.) in the western region; and a small population of Pygmies in the south. In addition to these indigenous peoples and Nigerian migrants, there are several hundred thousand other African migrants and refugees living in the country.

TABLE 5.1 Ethnic Units Over 5 Percent of Country Population

Ethnic Units	Estimated Ethnic Population 1980	Estimated Ethnic Percentage
a. Highland Bantu Cluster (Bamiléké)	2,249,600	27
1. Bamiléké 2. Tikar		
3. Widekum 4. Bamenda		
5. Bamoun 6. Banen		
7. Yanbasa 8. Meta		
b. Equatorial Bantu Type (Beti-Pahouin)	1,499, 800	18
1. Ewondo 2. Eton 3. Bane		
4. Fond 5. Bulu 6. Fang		
7. Maka 8. Djem		
c. Northern Animist Type (Kirdi)	1,249,800	15
1. Masa 2. Tupur 3. Matakam		
4. Musgum 5. Mofu 6. Gisiga		
7. Fali 8. Kapsigi 9. Daba		
10. Mundang		
d. Fulani (Peul)	791,500	9.5
e. Bassa-Bakoko Type	666,600	8
(Northwestern and Coastal Bantu)		
1. Bassa-Bakoko 2. Douala 3. Mbo		
4. Bakwiri-Mboko 5. Bakossi		
f. Eastern Nigritic Type (Baya- Mbum)	499,900	6
1. Baya 2. Mbum 3. Duru-Verre		
4. Vute 5. Namchi 6. Chamba		

SOURCE: Victor T. LeVine, *The Cameroons from Mandate to Independence* (Berkeley: University of California Press, 1964), pp. 12—14, extrapolated to 1980 population totals.

III. Language Patterns

Although Fulani (Fulfulde) is widely spoken throughout the north, even by Kirdi, the two major language groups are Bantu-speaking peoples in southern Cameroon: Bamiléké (27 percent) and Beti-Pahouin (Bulu) (18 percent). Rustow estimates that Fang (Bulu) is the major language (19 percent) and puts Bamiléké second with 18 percent. Since Bamiléké is an outgroup ascription of several different peoples, with at least seventeen dialects (some of which are mutually unintelligible), it is realistic to recognize its limitations as a language group. Beti-Pahouin (Pahouin is a European ascription of ethnicity) includes variations on Bulu and Ewondo which have come to be limited *lingua francas* in southern Cameroon. Pidgin English is also used as a *lingua franca* in southern Cameroon. French is widely spoken throughout the country.

In terms of official language policy, Cameroon requires governmental administration to be conducted in both French and English. Cameroon is the only state in Africa which is officially bilingual in French and English.

TABLE 5.2   Language Patterns

1. Primacy			
1st language	Beti-Pahouin	(24%)	
2nd language	Bamiléké	(18%)	
			Green- Dalby berg
2. Linguistic classification (all ethnic units in country over 5%)	Beti-Pahouin	IA5	A7
	Bamiléké	IA5	86
	Kirdi	IIIE	(05H,05J, 65N,65P)
	Fulani	IA1	201
	Bassa-Bakoko	IA4	A1-A2
	Baya-Mbum	IA6	(86,82, 65K,655)
3. *Lingua francas*	Beti-Pahouin (including Bulu des Cheffeurs and Ewondo Populaire); Fulfulde (Fulani); Pidgin English		
4. Official languages	French and English		

SOURCES: Pierre Alexandre, "Aperçu sommaire sur le pidgin A 70 du Cameroun," *Colloque sur le Multilinguisme* (1962): 251—56. Willard R. Johnson, "African-Speaking Africa: Lessons from the Cameroon," *African Forum*, 1 (1965): 65—77.

IV. Urban Patterns

Capital: Yaoundé (founded 1889)
Largest city: Douala (founded ca. 1600—1650)
Dominant ethnicity/language of capital
  Major vernacular: Ewondo[1]
  Major ethnic group: Ewondo
  Major ethnic group as percent of capital's population:
  14.42 percent (1957)

[1]Victor LeVine, *The Cameroons: From Mandate to Independence* (Berkeley and Los Angeles: University of California Press, 1964), p. 64.

TABLE 5.3   Growth of Capital and Largest City

Date	Yaoundé	Douala
1920		ca. 15,000
1930		26,000
1940		42,000
1950		102,000
1960	74,000	ca.140,000
1965	110,000	200,000 UA
1969	165,000	
1970	180,000 UA	250,000 UA
1973	230,000 UA	340,000 UA
1975	274,000 UA	486,000 UA

SOURCES: V. LeVine, *The Cameroons*, extrapolated to our time points and, for 1965 and 1969, sample survey data. It is not known whether the United Nation's urban agglomeration figure is comparable with the earlier data for Douala. 1970 figures from *UN Demographic Yearbook 1972*. 1973 data from *Africa South of the Sahara 1975*.

TABLE 5.4   Cities of 20,000 and Over

City	Size	Date
Douala	458,000 UA	1976
Yaoundé	313,000 UA	1976
N'Kongsamba	71,000	1976
Foumban	60,000	1976
Kumba	50,000	1976
Bafoussam	46,000	1976
Marousa	46,000	1976
Bamenda	40,000	1970
Garoua	37,000	1976
Victoria	31,000	1976
Edea[a]	23,000	1970

SOURCES: Africa South of Sahara 1980—81 (1976 census).
[a]UN Demographic Yearbook 1972.

V. Political Patterns

A. Political Parties and Elections

The Federal Republic of Cameroon formed in October 1961, was comprised of the former French U.N. trust territory and part of the former British U.N. trust territory. One of the informal arrangements of this federation was that the President (Ahidjo) would come from the French-speaking region and the Vice-President (Foncha) would come from the English-speaking region. This formula was continued until the country became a unitary state in 1972. The dominant party of the French-speaking area, the *Union Camerounaise* (UC) led by Ahidjo, and the dominant party of the English-speaking area, the *Kamerun National Democratic Party* (KNDP) led by Foncha, merged into a single national party, the *Union Nationale Camerounaise* (UNC) in 1966. This party continues to govern Cameroon as a one-party state. Although elections were due in 1969, the National Assembly extended its term by fifteen months and the elections were not held until June 1970. In May 1972, a referendum to convert from a federal to a unitary state was overwhelmingly accepted. Elections for the National As-

sembly were held in May 1973 and again in May 1978 when all seats were won by the UNC. In February 1980 the *Cameroon Action Movement* was formed as a protest over the unitary system of government. The group is calling for the return to a federal system of government, the immediate release of all political prisoners and the end of human rights violations. The CAM is an anglophone separatist movement and because of the recent discoveries of oil reserves in the anglophone-dominated western section of Cameroon, the government feels somewhat threatened by the movement as it might prevent the government from obtaining the potential source of wealth.

B. Political Leadership

From the birth of the Federation of former East and West Cameroons until 1982, the government was led by President Ahmadou Ahidjo. There have been many cabinet reshuffles, most recently in 1968 (twice), 1970, 1971 (twice) and 1973 (twice). Ahdijo was re-elected for five year terms in 1970 and 1975, and again (unopposed) in April 1980, with 99.9% of the vote. On November 4, 1982, Ahidjo unexpectedly resigned, perhaps for reasons of health, and was succeeded by his prime minister, Paul Biya.

TABLE 5.5   Heads of Government (Post-Independence)

Name	Dates in Office	Age (1982)	Ethnicity	Education	Former Occupation
1. Ahmadou Ahidjo (President)	1960— 1982	60	Fulani	Technical secondary Yaoundé	Radio technician
2. Paul Biya (President)	1982— present	50	'southerner'		Politician

TABLE 5.6   Cabinet Membership: Distribution by Ethnic Unit*

Ethnicity*	Independence Cabinet	1967 Cabinet
1. Bamiléké (27%)	40%	40%
2. Beti-Pahouin (18)	20	7
3. Kirdi (15)	0	0
4. Fulani (9.5)	20	20
5. Bassa-Bakoko (8)	10	27
6. Baya-Mbum (6)	10	7
7. Others (17)	0	0
N =	10	17

*Ethnic units arranged in rank order of size within country with the unit's percent of national population in parentheses.

FIGURE 5.1   Political Parties and Elections   CAMEROON

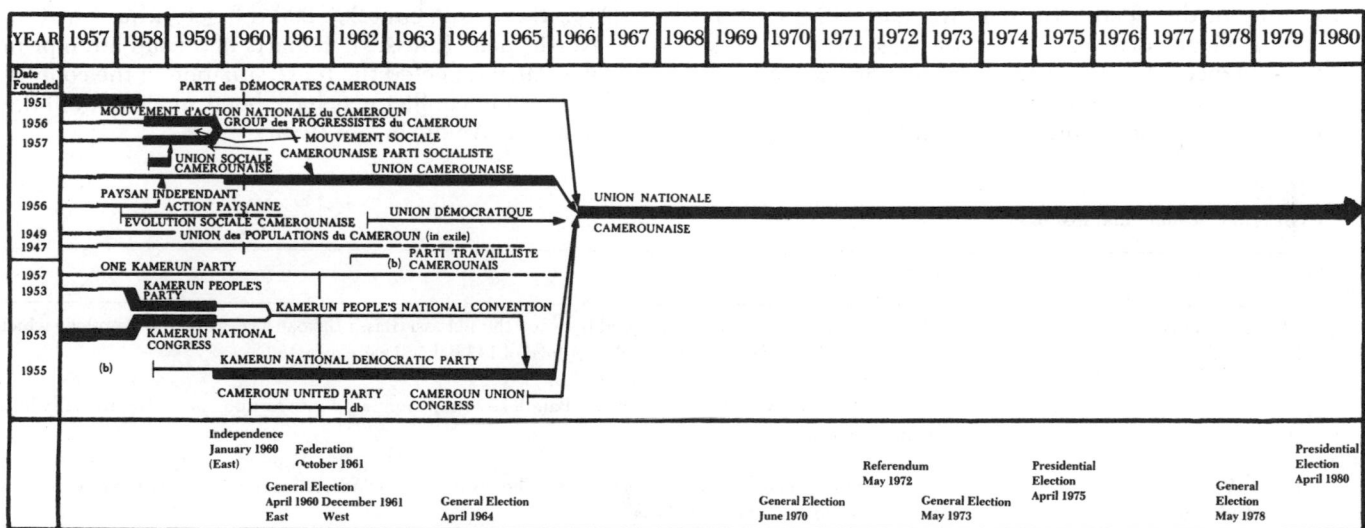

VI. National Integration and Stability

Cameroon experienced an extended period of mass instability related to demands for self-government in the years immediately prior to independence. Outlawed in July 1955 for nationalist activities unacceptable to French authorities, the *Union des Populations du Cameroun* (UPC) carried on a war of resistance which denied control by the central government over most of two provinces. Part of the unrest at the time was related to urban unemployment; and while Bamiléké and Bassa communalism were evident in the movement, we have coded UPC resistance, which continued into the post-independence period, as a "mass" phenomenon because of its multi-ethnic nature and ideological orientation. Remnants of the UPC were arrested and tried in 1970. The leader of the movement was sentenced to death and executed.

Since independence, the northern (Fulani/Islamic) based government has worked cautiously to avoid a north/south split which might occur along ethnic/religious/ecological lines. Although the Fulani are a minority in the north itself, they have ruled most of the area since the time of the Sokoto Jihad in the early 19th century. (Almost all of northern Cameroon was formerly under the influence of Adamawa—now in northern Nigeria; Adamawa in turn, paid allegiance to Sokoto.) Recently, the numerous non- Muslim Kirdi in the north have be-

gun to immigrate to northern urban centers, raising the problem of integration within the north itself. In the south, there has been an intensification of rivalry between the English-speakmng western region and the French-speaking eastern region since 1961. Within the eastern region, relations between the Bamiléké and the Beti-Pahouin groups and others have remained precariously balanced. There have been, nevertheless, only two reported instances of ethnic violence. There have been two reports of elite instability: a plot in 1962, and a plot in October 1979. The Ahidjo regime has not tolerated opposition and has strongly repressed opponents. In November 1979, a cabinet reshuffle was announced. In early 1980 Amnesty International claimed that more than 200 people were being held as political prisoners in Cameroon. They requested that the detention camps should be inspected by an international organization claiming that severe conditions and torture were being employed. In April 1980 students at the University of Yaoundé went on strike demanding scholarships. The government provided funds for 1000 students.

Also, there are about 200,000 refugees from Chad, in the North, near Kousseki. Reports of a coup attempt in October 1979 reflected the tense situation in the country and such latent conflict may have been an element in the resignation of Ahidjo in late 1982.

TABLE 5.8   Communal Instability

Event and Date	Characteristics
1. Ethnic Violence January 1, 1967	a. *Description*: Ethnic violence occurred between the Bakossi (Bassa-Bakoko Type) and the Bamiléké which resulted in 236 dead (mainly Bamiléké). A total of 143 Bakossi were arrested. b. *Participants*: Bamiléké and Bakossi peoples. c. *Apparent Causes*: Conflict caused when Bamiléké groups migrated into farming areas traditionally held by the Bakossi.
2. Ethnic Violence Date Unknown 1979	a. *Description*: Ethnic disturbances occurred in the northern province. Allegedly, security forces killed 200 people and destroyed their villages. b. *Participants*: Unknown. c. *Apparent Causes*: No specific details are known as the government is denying that this occurred. Allegedly, however, the conflict derived from a chieftancy rivalry.

TABLE 5.9   Mass Instability

Event and Date	Characteristics
1. Attempted Revolution 1955—November, 1962	a. *Description*: In 1955, prior to independence, the *Union des Populations du Cameroun* (UPC) was dissolved after it became apparent that revolutionary means were being used to take over control of government. Major fighting ended in September 1958 with the death of rebel leader Um Nyobé. The UPC, however, remained in exile and conducted sporadic attacks. According to UPC sources-in-exile, 1,975 pro-government persons were killed by guerillas, and several steam tugs and barges were destroyed during the period October 1, 1961 to December 23, 1961. On January 23, 1962, the Cameroon government reinstated its ban of the National Congress of the UPC. From February to November many of the major leders of the UPC (Emah Otu, Mayi-Matep, Prince Deka Akwa Nya) were arrested (or killed), and condemned to death or long prison terms. Occasional UPC attacks ocurred throughout the 1960's but the last of its leadership was executed in 1970. b. *Participants*: Major support for the UPC came from members of the Bassa and Bamiléké ethnic groups, especially those living in south and southwestern urban centers where trade union activity was strong. The original leadership included Felix Moumié and Reuben Um Nyobé, both of whom were killed. c. *Apparent Causes*: Initially, the UPC focused on two major isues: immediate independence and free elections. Implicit in Bamiléké and Bassa mass participation was concern over Northern Muslim domination. Government justified harsh measures in terms of national unity, including need for ethnic and religious cooperation.

SOURCES: Victor T. LeVine, "Cameroun," in *Political Parties and National Integration in Tropical Africa*, eds. James S. Coleman and Carl G. Rosberg, Jr. (Berkeley: University of California Press, 1966), pp. 132—147. Victor T. LeVine, *The Cameroons: from Mandate to Independence* (Berkeley: University of California Press, 1964), pp. 141—215. Willard Johnson, "The Union des Populations du Cameroun in Rebellion: The Integrative Backlash of Insurgency," in *Protest and Power in Black Africa*, eds. Robert I. Rotberg and Ali A. Mazrui (New York: Oxford University Press, 1970), pp. 671— 692.

TABLE 5.10   Annual Instability Events: Independence Through 1979—Cameroon

Year	'61	'62	'63	'64	'65	'66	'67	'68	'69	'70	'71	'72	'73	'74	'75	'76	'77	'78	'79
ELITE INSTABILITY																			
Assassinations																			
Plots		1																	
Attempted Coups d'État																			1
Coups d'État																			1
COMMUNAL INSTABILITY																			
Ethnic Violence							1												1
Irredentism																			
Rebellion																			
Civil War																			
MASS INSTABILITY																			
Revolt																			
Revolution	1	1																	

Year	'61	'62	'63	'64	'65	'66	'67	'68	'69	'70	'71	'72	'73	'74	'75	'76	'77	'78	'79
TURMOIL																			
Demonstrations										1		1							
Strikes (no. days)																			
Riots (no. days)																			
Terrorism	5	1	1	1			2				1								
Declarations of Emergency	1	1									1								
CABINET INSTABILITY																			
Realloc. and new appts.	9	1	2	6	13	3	9	3				4	6						
New members	11				10		2	8				4	12						
Resig. and Dismissals	3		2	6	3	2	2	6				4	6						
No. of members (max.) (maximum in year)	10	16	16	16	17	17	17	15	15	20	20	20							

VII. Selected References

BIBLIOGRAPHY

Delancey, Mark and Virginia Delancey. *A Bibliography of Cameroon*. New York: Africana, 1974.

LeVine, V. T. and R. P. Nye. *Historical Dictionary of Cameroon*. Metuchen, N.J.: Scarecrow, 1974.

GENERAL

De Lancey, M. *Cameroon*. Boulder, Colo.: Westview, 1981.

Eyongetoh, Tambi and Robert Brain. *A History of the Cameroon*. London: Longman, 1974.

Lembezat, Bertrand. *Le Cameroun*. Paris: Nouvelles Editions Latines, 1965.

LeVine, Victor T. *Cameroon Federal Republic*. Ithaca, N.Y.: Cornell University Press, 1971.

LeVine, Victor T. *The Cameroon from Mandate to Independence*: Berkeley, Ca.: University of California Press, 1964.

Mveng, Englebert. *Histoire du Cameroun*. Paris: Presence Africaine, 1963.

Rubin, Neville. *Cameroun: An African Federation*. New York: Praeger, 1971

U.S. Department of the Army. *Area Handbook for the United Republic of Cameroon*. Washington, D.C.: Government Printing Office, 1974.

POLITICAL

Ardener, Edwin. "The Nature of Reunification of Cameroon." In *African Integration and Disintegration*, ed. A. Hazelwood. London: Oxford University Press, 1967.

Azarya, Victor. *Aristocrats Facing Change: The Fulbe in Guinea, Nigeria, and Cameroon*. Chicago: University of Chicago Press, 1978.

Boyast, J. F. "One-Party Government and Political Development in Cameroun." *African Affairs*, 72 (April 1973): 125—144.

Gardinier, David E. *Cameroon: United Nations Challenge to French Policy*. London: Oxford University Press, 1963.

Joseph, R. A. *Radical Nationalism in Cameroun: Social Origins of the U.P.C. Rebellion*. Oxford: Clarendon Press, 1977.

Johnson, Willard R. *The Cameroon Federation: Political Integration in a Fragmentary Society*. Princeton, N.J.: Princeton University Press, 1969.

De Lusignan, Guy. *French-Speaking Africa Since Independence*: 121-132. London: Pall Mall Press, 1969.

Welch, Claude, Jr. *Dream of Unity*. Ithaca, N.Y.: Cornell University Press, 1966.

ECONOMIC

Clignet, R. *The Africanization of the Labor Market: Educational and Occupational Segmentation in the Cameroons.* Berkeley: University of California Press, 1976.

"Economic Development and Employment in Eastern Cameroon." *International Labour Review.* 85 (June 1962): 601—611.

Green, R. H. "The Economy of Cameroon Federal Republic." In *The Economies of Africa*, eds. P. Robson and D. A. Lury, pp. 236—286. Evanston, Ill.: Northwestern University Press, 1969.

Hugon, Philippe. *Analyse du sous-developpment en Afrique Noire: l'exemple de l'economie du Cameroun.* Paris: Presses Universitaires de France, 1968.

International Monetary Fund. "Federal Republic of Cameroon." In *Surveys of African Economies*, Vol. 1. Washington, D.C.: I.M.F., 1968.

Kendrick, Robin. *A Survey of Labor Relations in Cameroon.* Ann Arbor, Mich.: University of Michigan, 1976.

Ndongoko, Wilfred A. *Planning for Economic Development in a Federal State: The Case of Cameroon, 1960—1971.* München, Weltforumverlag, 1975.

Wells, Frederick A. *Studies in Industrialization: Nigeria and the Cameroons.* London: Oxford University Press, 1962.

SOCIAL

Ardener, Edwin, et al. *Plantation and Village in the Cameroons: Some Economic and Social Studies.* London: Oxford University, 1960.

Guillard, Joanny. *Golonpoui: analyse des conditions de modernisation d'un village du Nord-Cameroun.* Paris: Mouton, 1965.

Meek, C. K. *Land Tenure and Land Administration in Nigeria and the Cameroons.* London: Her Majesty's Stationery Office, 1957.

Vernon-Jackson, H. O. H. *Language, Schools and Government in Cameroon.* New York: Teachers College Press, 1967.

Weekes-Vagliani, W. *Family Life and Structure in Southern Cameroon.* Paris, OECD, 1976.

6. Central African Republic (CAR)

I. Basic Information

Date of Independence: August 13, 1960
Former Colonial Ruler: France
Change in Boundaries: Formerly part of French Equatorial Africa
Former Names: Ubangi-Shari, Oubangui-Chari, Central African Empire
Estimated Population (1980): 1,996,000*
Area Size (equivalent in U.S.): 240,535 sq. mi. (Texas and Minnesota)

Date of Last Census: 1975 (sample survey)
Major Exports 1978 as Percent of Total Exports: diamonds—38 percent; coffee—30 percent; wood—16 percent.

*The 1968 census figure of 2,255,536 is not accepted by international agencies.

II. Ethnic Patterns

The ethnic classification for the CAR is done at a low level of abstraction and the cultural groups selected correspond in most cases to individual identity groups. However, the Yakoma, Sango, and Gbanziri are clustered together because they share a similar ecological adaptation to a riverine environment. In addition to these peoples, the CAR has smaller populations such as the N'Zakara (3 percent), the Azande (1 percent) and a small number of Pygmies. In the extreme north, there are also small groups of Waddaiens (Rounga, Goula, Kara, Youla) and Sara (Kaba, Dagba).

TABLE 6.1   Ethnic Units Over 5 Percent of Country Population

Ethnic Units	Estimated Ethnic Population 1980	Estimated Ethnic Percentage
a. Banda	619,000	31%
1. Linda, 2. Kreich, 3. Langba, 4. Yakpa, 5. N'Gao, 6. Togbo, 7. N'Di, 8. Dakpa		
b. Gbaya (Baja, Baya)	579,000	29%
c. Mandjia (Mandja, Mangbai)	170,000	8.5%
d. Riverine Type	160,000	8%
1. Yakoma, 2. Sango, 3. Gbanziri		
e. Mbum (Bum)	140,000	7%
f. Mbaka or Bwaka	130,000	6.5%

SOURCE: Percentages based on 1959—1960 *Enquête Démographique en République Centrafricaine*. Note that this census excluded the Eastern Region (ca. 58,000 people; mainly of Azandé ethnicity). Total country population at that time was ca. 1,200,000.

III. Language Patterns

All major languages of CAR are of the Adamawa (Eastern) sub-branch of the Niger-Congo family. Such languages include Banda, Baya, Mandja Sango, Mbum, and Ngbaka. The major ethnic group, Banda, constitutes 31 percent of the population, and the Baya 29 percent. Rustow estimates the major languages to be Banda (47 percent) and Gbaya (Baya) (27 percent). Since Banda does not serve as a *lingua franca*, we limit our estimate to 31 percent. Rather, the role of *lingua franca* is performed by Sango, which is a pidgin of limited vocabulary based mainly on Ngbandi, a language of northwestern Zaire which has not only come to be the major *lingua franca* but also the official national language of CAR (although French continues as the working language of government). Knappert sugggests that Sango is the major language of CAR, although his estimate of 10 percent is probably low. Our own estimates would be Banda 31 percent, Baya 29 percent, and Sango 25 percent.

TABLE 6.2   Language Patterns

			Green-berg	Dalby
1. Primacy				
1st language	Banda	(31%)		
2nd language	Baya	(29%)		
3rd language	Sango	(25%)		
2. Linguistic classification (all ethnic units in country over 5%)	Banda		IA6	67B
	Gbaya		IA6	67A
	Mandjia		IA6	65P
	Riverine		IA6	67E, 67C
	Mbum		IA6	65P
	Mbasa		IA6	67E
3. *Lingua franca*	Sango			
4. Official language	French			

SOURCE: William J. Samarin, "Une lingua franca centrafricaine," in *Colloque sur le Multilinguisme*, Brazzaville (1962), pp. 257—266.

IV. Urban Patterns

Capital/largest city: Bangui (founded 1899)
Dominant ethnicity/language of capital
Major vernacular: Sango[1]
Major ethnic group:

Major ethnic group as percent of capital's population:

[1] Jan Knappert, "Language Problems of the New Nations of Africa," *African Quarterly*, 5 (1965): 95—105.

TABLE 6.3   Growth of Capital/Largest City

Date	Bangui
1930	20,000[a]
1940	33,000[b]
1950	60,000[c]
1960	90,000[d]
1965	150,000[e] UA
1971	187,000[f] UA
1975	302,000[g] UA
1980	709,000[h]

SOURCES:

[a]*Démographie Comparée.*

[b]*Ibid.* and *Ecyclopédie d'Outre Mer*, Vol. 2, p. 145.

[c]Thomas Hodgkin, *Nationalism in Colonial Africa*, London: Penguin, 1961.

[d]*Statesman's Yearbook*, 1960.

[e]*UN Demographic Yearbook 1967. Africa 1968* and *Europa Yearbook 1967* gives a population figure of 238,000 with no date specified, but presumably for no later than 1966. We have arbitrarily adopted the lower UNDY figure.

[f]*UN Demographic Yearbook 1972.*

[g]*Political Handbook of the World 1979.*

[h]*Europa Yearbook 1982.*

TABLE 6.4   Cities of 20,000 and Over*

City	Size	Date
Bangui[a]	709,000	ca. 1980
Bouar[b]	48,000	ca. 1978
Berbérati[b]	40,000	ca. 1978
Bossangoa[b]	36,000	ca. 1978
Bambari[b]	35,000	ca. 1978
Bangassou[c]	28,000	1968
Bria[c]	25,000	1968
Boali*	20,000	1970

SOURCES:

[a]*Europa Yearbook 1982.*

[b]*Europe Outremer* Nov. 1979, p. 65.

[c]*Census 1968 as reported in Africa South of the Sahara 1974.*

Africa South of the Sahara 1972 reports a 1968 Census figure of 2,255,536. This does not seem to have been accepted by the UN or World Bank. Consequently, where possible, we avoid using the 1968 census figures for the urban areas since there appear to be wide discrepancies. Also note, Boali is reported to have 238,000 people in the 1968 census, as reported in *Africa South of the Sahara 1972*. Dr. P. Burnham reports that the town is probably about 20—30,000 in 1971. We have taken a figure of 20,000 as an approximate estimate of Boali's population.

V. Political Patterns

A. Political Parties and Elections

Formed in 1946, the *Mouvement pour l'Evolution Sociale de l'Afrique Noire* (MESAN) has been the dominant party in the Central African Republic. The *Mouvement pour l'Evolution Démocratique de l'Afrique Centrale* (MEDAC) emerged as the major opposition party for a short time after independence until it was suppressed. From 1962 to 1966 MESAN, led by David Dacko, was the only party in what had become a one-party state. In January 1966, there was a military coup and the army Chief of Staff, Colonel Jean-Bedel Bokassa took power and declared himself President. Bokassa continued to rule in the CAE (renamed from the Central African Republic in December 1976) with no legal opposition. MESAN effectively became defunct after the coup although it was not banned. It was revived by Bokassa in 1972 in order to declare him Life President but has been allowed to wither since then. In 1977, Bokassa crowned himself emperor. There have been no elections since 1964. In September 1979, Bokassa was overthrown by David Dacko with the help of French troops. Dacko planned to establish a multi-party system but not until "tribalism" was eliminated. In March 1980 the Central African Democratic Union was created to consolidate Dacko's power and authority. All parties were outlawed after the September 1981 coup which was preceded by the March 1981 elections, substantial unrest over the electoral procedures, and the banning of an opposition party. Dacko was overthrown in September of 1981 by Colonel Kolingba.

B. Political Leadership

From independence until the coup d'état in 1966, the government of the CAR remained substantially unchanged. Since the first coup, the government has become more representative of the ethnic diversity of the country. However, there still appears to be considerable "malapportionment" in the recruitment to cabinet positions, although different groups have been more prominent in the pre- and post-1966 coup government. Cabinet reshuffles, major and minor, became a way of life under Bokassa. For example, there were cabinet reshuffles in 1968 (2), 1970 (4), 1971 (5), 1972 (3), 1973 (4), 1974 (4), 1975 (2), and 1976 (8). Part of this process was accomplished by Bokassa assuming portfolios in one shuffle and handing them out in the next, only to repeat the process in a short period. In a September 1979 coup d'état David Dacko with French backing overthrew Emperior Bokassa. The French troops remained in the CAR because of Dacko's fears of further political conflict. A successful coup came on September 1, 1981 led by Colonel Kolingba with the apparent cooperation of Dacko.

FIGURE 6.1   Political Parties and Elections   CENTRAL AFRICAN REPUBLIC

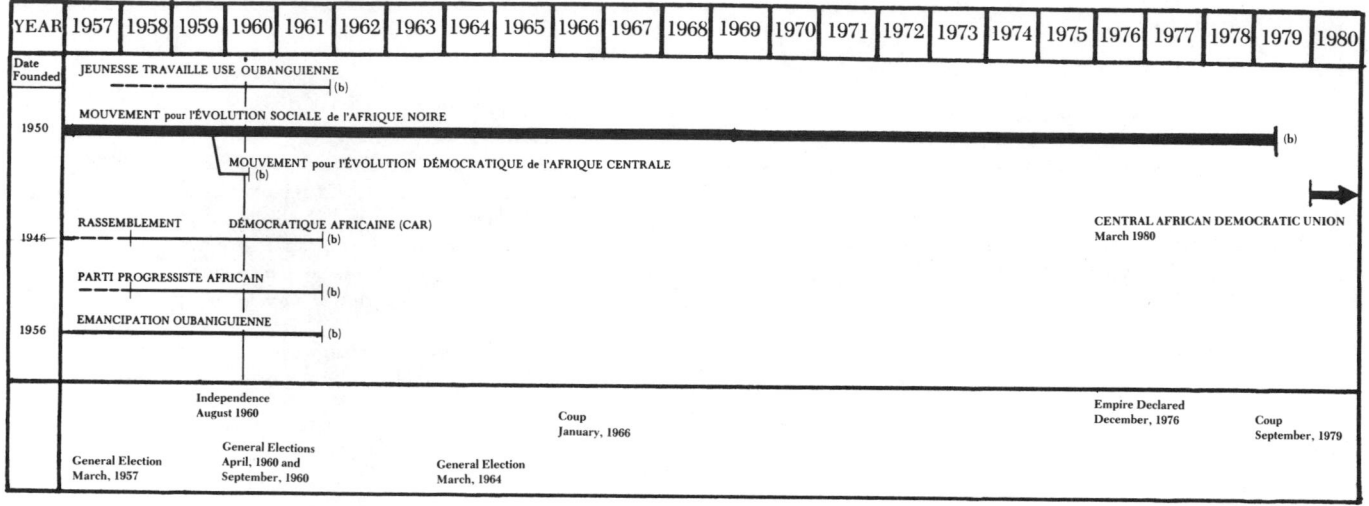

TABLE 6.5   Heads of Government (Post Independence)

Name	Dates in Office	Age 1982	Ethnicity	Education	Former Occupation	
1. David Dacko (President)	1960—1966	52	Baya	Technical- secondary in Africa (Congo)	Schoolteacher	-
2. Jean-Bedel* Bokassa (Emperor and Life President	1966— September 1979	61	Mbaka	Mission schools in the CAR and Brazzaville (Congo)	Soldier	-
3. David Dacko	September 1979—1981	52	Baya	Technical- secondary in Africa (Congo)	Schoolteacher	
4. Colonel André Kolingba Chairman Military Committee for National Recovery	November 1981— present		Yakoma		Soldier	

*For a short period, in 1976, he adopted the Muslim name, Salah Eddine Ahmed.

TABLE 6.6   Cabinet Membership: Distribution by Ethnic Unit*

Ethnicity*	Independence Cabinet	Immediate Pre-Coup Cabinet	1967 Cabinet
1. Banda (31%)	0%	11%	0%
2. Baya (29)	14	11	15
3. Mandjia (8.5)	0	11	8
4. Riverine (8)	43	44	15
5. Mbum (7)	0	0	8
6. Mbaka (6.5)	0	0	23
7. Others (10)	43	22	31
N =	8	11	15

*Ethnic units arranged in rank order of size within country with the unit's percent of national population in parentheses.

VI. National Integration and Stability

Political instability in the CAR has been characterized by conflict between elites. In January 1966, Dacko was overthrown in a military coup led by Colonel Bokassa, who has subsequently maintained control. In mid-1968 Bokassa reported the discovery of a plot purportedly backed by an unnamed foreign power. In April 1969, Colonel Banza was accused of plotting against Bokassa and was executed. In April 1973, Auguste M'Bongo was dismissed for the same reason. In October 1974, General Lingopo was arrested and sentenced to 10 years in prison for a coup planned to take place while Bokassa was out of the country. Bokassa announced the failure of plots in August 1975 and December 1976, and an assassination attempt against him failed in February 1976. Frequent reports of assassination attempts (nine within a few months in 1975—76 according to *Africa Contemporary Record 1976—77* and plots indicate that considerable disquiet existed in the country. This disquiet came to a peak in 1979. In January, there were student protests over the imposition of a school dress code. Reportedly twelve people were killed, but estimates go as high as 1,000. The miserable economic situation in the CAE was thought to be behind the student riots. In March 1979 a coup plot was uncovered and an assassination attempt was made in April 1979. After stoning the Emperor's lim-ousine approximately 100 school children were arrested and killed. There is evidence that Bokassa himself was involved in the killings. On September 20, 1979, Bokassa was overthrown and David Dacko became President. There is still much unrest in the CAR which is particularly acute because of the presence of French troops. With the increasing opposition to the Dacko regime, came increasing repression. All strikes were outlawed, a curfew was imposed, the head of the opposition Central African People's Liberation movement and former prime minister, Ange Patasse, is in prison and French troops guarded the Presidential palace. Several opposition leaders and former members of Bokassa's government were condemned to death. This opposition finally climaxed with the overthrow of Dacko by the army in September 1981.

The CAR is a relatively homogenous country in terms of language and cultural criteria. Although refugees from the Sudan civil war have migrated to the Northern part of the country there have been no apparent disturbances in ethnic relations in the country. We have coded no instances of communal or mass instability.

TABLE 6.7   Elite Instability

Event and Date	Characteristics
1. Coup d'État January 1, 1966	a. *Description*: A bloodless coup d'état staged by military officers replaced the elected civilian regime of David Dacko. b. *Participants*: High level officers of the 450-man army led by Colonel Jean-Bédel Bokassa (Army Chief of Staff). c. *Apparent Causes*: According to the military regime, Dacko's aides were concealing errors, wasting public funds, and losing touch with the masses. Other reasons may have been discontent with military appropriations, rumors that Bokassa was to be dismissed, and unrest over an austerity program which reduced government salaries by 20 percent. Immediately after the coup (January 5) Bokassa also stated that the coup forestalled a plot organized by pro-Chinese extremists in cooperation with the Chinese Embassy. The plot was suspected to have involved the Gendarmerie which was being transformed into a Presidential Guard.
2. Coup Attempt 5 February 1976	a. *Description*: An assassination attempt against Bokassa at Bangui airport occured when an army sergeant threw a grenade at Bokassa. The attackers were killed or rounded up after a six hour gunfight. b. *Participants*: Major Fidel Obrau, Bokassa's son-in-law; his brother Martin Meya; a sergeant-major Zukongo and five other army men. c. *Apparent Causes*: These people were accused of many attempts on Bokassa's life. Apparently, they were reacting to the capricious rule of Bokassa. Members of the elite were especially vulnerable to Bokassa's whims.
3. Coup d'État September 23, 1979	a. *Description*: During a 48-hour visit to Tripoli by Emperor Bokassa, French troops arrived in the capital with the new President, David Dacko. The troops patrolled the capital while Dacko announced the change in government over the radio. b. *Participants*: David Dacko with the backing of French troops and some government officials including the former Prime Minister, M. Henri Maidou. c. *Apparent Causes*: Dissatisfaction with the Bokassa regime and the outrage over reports of Bokassa's involvement in the killing of over one hundred school children in late April 1979.
4. Coup d'État September 1, 1981	a. *Description*: Colonel André Kolingba (Chief of Staff) and the Army overthrew Dacko after considerable unrest following March elections under a new multi-party constitution adopted in February 1981. b. *Participants*: The Army led by Col. Kolingba. c. *Apparent Causes*: Perception of the Dacko regime as unable to control the political pressures that it had unleashed.
5. Coup Attempt March 3, 1982	a. *Description*: Army officers take over the radio and broadcast that General Kolingba has been overthrown. They are quickly suppressed as are their supporters and political allies, particularly Ange Patasse. b. *Participants*: Army officers including Generals Bozzi and Mbaikoua, and civilian politicians led by A. Patasse. c. *Apparent Causes*: Attempt to restore civilian power. Anti-Yakoma feeling was evident which gave a basis for certain ethnic support for the attempt.

TABLE 6.10   Annual Instability Events: Independence Through 1979—C.A.R.

Year	'61	'62	'63	'64	'65	'66	'67	'68	'69	'70	'71	'72	'73	'74	'75	'76	'77	'78	'79
ELITE INSTABILITY																			
Assassinations																			
Plots						1		1	1.				1	1	1				2
Attempted Coups d'État																1			
Coups d'État						1													1
COMMUNAL INSTABILITY																			
Ethnic Violence																			
Irredentism																			
Rebellion																			
Civil War																			

Year	'61	'62	'63	'64	'65	'66	'67	'68	'69	'70	'71	'72	'73	'74	'75	'76	'77	'78	'79
MASS INSTABILITY																			
Revolt																			
Revolution																			
TURMOIL																			
Demonstrations																			
Strikes (no. days)																			
Riots (no. days)																			
Terrorism											1								
Declarations of Emergency											2								
CABINET INSTABILITY																			
Realloc. and new appts.	1	5	4	7			12	9	7	6	12	6							
New Members	1	3	2	3			7	4	5	11	11	2							
Resig. and Dismissals		1	2	2			1	4	3	5	10	6							
No. of members (max.) (maximum in year)	8	10	12	11	11	10	15	15	17	23	24	24							

VII. Selected References

BIBLIOGRAPHY

Kalck, Pierre. *Historical Dictionary of the Central African Republic*. Metuchen, N.J.:Scarecrow,1980.

GENERAL

Ballard, John A. "Four Equatorial States: *Congo, Gabon, Ubangi-Shari, Chad*." In *National Unity and Regionalism in Eight African States*, ed. Gwendolen M. Carter, pp. 231—329. Ithaca, N.Y.: Cornell University Press, 1966.

Kalck, P. *Historie de la Republique Centrafricaine des Origins Prehistoriques a Nos Jours* Paris: Berger-Levrault, 1974.

Thompson, Virginia and Richard Adloff. *The Emerging States of French Equatorial Africa*, pp, 385—425. Stanford, Calif.: Stanford University Press, 1960.

POLITICAL

de Lusignan, Guy. *French-Speaking Africa since Independence*, pp. 108—114. London: Pall Mall Press, 1969.

Kalck, Pierre. *The Central African Republic: A Failure in de-Colonization*. New York, Praeger, 1971.

LeVine, Victor T. "The Central African Republic: Insular Problems of an Inland State." *Africa Report*, 10 (November 1965): 17—23.

LeVine, Victor T. "The Coups in Upper Volta, Dahomey and the Central African Republic." In *Power and Protest in Black Africa*, eds. Robert I Rotbert and Ali A. Mazrui, pp. 1035—1071. New York: Oxford University Press, 1970.

Péan, Pierre. *Bokassa 1er*. Paris, Ed. A. Moreau, 1977.

ECONOMIC

International Monetary Fund. "The Central African Republic." In *Surveys of African Economies*, Vol. 1. Washington, D.C.: I.M.F., 1968.

SOCIAL

Lebeuf, Jean-Paul. *Bangui*. Paris, 1954.

7. Chad

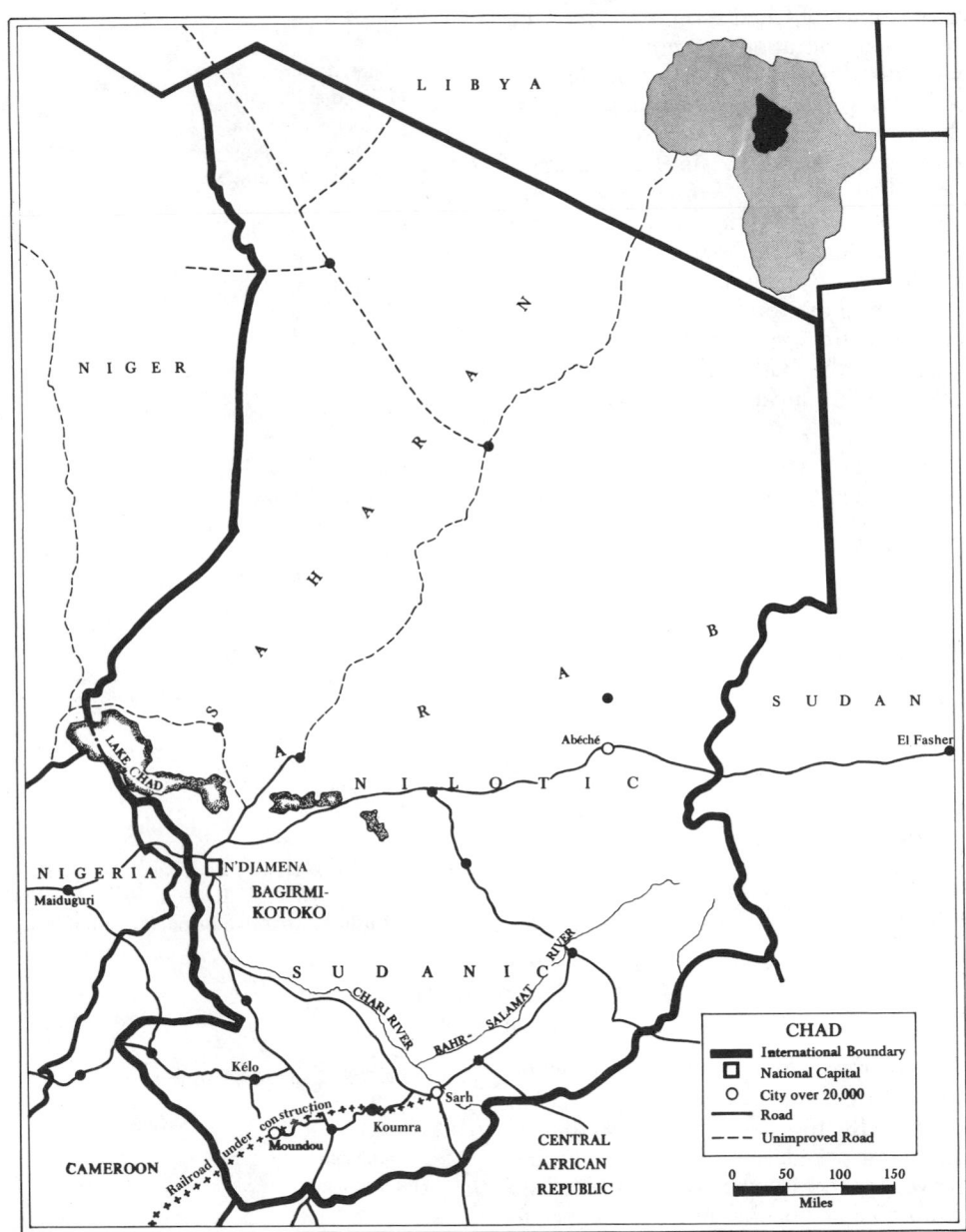

I. Basic Information

Date of Independence: August 11, 1960
Former Colonial Ruler: France
Change in Boundaries: Formerly part of French Equatorial Africa
Estimated Population (1980): 4,627,000

Area Size (equivalent in U.S.): 496,000 sq. mi. (Texas, new Mexico, and Oklahoma)
Date of Last Census: 1968
Major Exports 1978 as Percent of Total Exports: cotton—69 percent; cattle—10 percent.

II. Ethnic Patterns

Classification of the peoples of Chad is difficult since this area has a long history of migration and culture contact. Arab peoples constitute almost half the population, and are distinctive in language, culture, and identity. The Sudanic peoples bridge the zone between the rain forest and savannah area and are culturally similar to many of the Bantu peoples. The Saharan peoples live in the Sahara Desert, and are culturally similar to many of the Chado-Hamitic peoples. The term "Nilotic" is not satisfactory as a cultural label but essentially refers to people who are historically related to groups in southern Sudan. Of the ethnic units that are less than 5 percent of the population, the largest is the Bagirmi-Kotoko type (Bagirmi, Somrai, Gaberi, Bua, Fanyan, Sokoro, Kotoko).

TABLE 7.1   Ethnic Units Over 5 Percent of Country Population

Ethnic Units	Estimated Ethnic Population 1980	Estimated Ethnic Percentage
a. Arab Type	2,128,000	46%
1. Hassauna or Shuwa (Western Arabs) i. Assale, ii. Dagana, iii. Ouled Mehareb, iv. Ouled Mansour, v. Ben Wail Djoheina (Eastern Arabs) i. Hemat, ii. Salamat, iii. Rachid, iv. Myssirie, v. Djadne, vi. Khozzam, vii. Rizegat (Mahamid, Maharge, Mararit)		
b. Sudanic Cluster	1,296,000	28%
1. Sara i. Sara, ii. Barma, iii. Dindje, iv. Kaba, v. Mbai, vi. Dumra, vii. Djioko		
2. Runga, Gula, Kara, Nduka		
3. Kirdi i. Masa, ii. Musgum, iii. Tupuri, iv. Mundang	(231,000)	(5%)
c. Nilotic Cluster	440,000	
1. Wadaians (Maba) i. Wadai Kodoi, ii. Malanga, iii. Madaba, iv. Debba, v. Abissa, vi. Dekker, vii. Djema		
2. Masalit		
3. Lisi i. Bulala, ii. Kuka, iii. Midogo, iv. Abusemeu		
4. Mubi and Karbo		
5. Mesmedjé, Kenga, Babalia, Diongor, Saba		
6. Yalna, Toundjour, Torom		
d. Saharan Cluster	324,000	7%
1. Tubu i. Teda, ii. Daza, iii. Kreda, iv. Bulgeda	(204,000)	(4.4%)
2. Kanembu	(106,000)	(2.3%)

SOURCES: Pierre Hugot, *Le Tchad* (Paris: Nouvelles Editions Latines, 1965), pp. 26—27. J. C. Lebeuf, *Afrique Centrale* (Guide Bleu, 1962). G. P. Murdock, *African Summaries*, unpublished manuscript.

III. Language Patterns

Arab peoples constitute approximately 46 percent, while Sudanic peoples constitute 28 percent of the population of Chad. Knappert and Rustow seem to underestimate both the Arabic-speaking population (at 40 percent and 33 percent respectively) and also the use of Arabic as a *lingua franca*. Although not encouraged by the government until recently, Arabic would probably be understood by at least 60 percent of the population and is now used in the school system. Sara is probably the second largest of the languages in Chad and because it serves as a limited *lingua franca* we estimate it at 28 percent. (Rustow suggests Bongo-Bagirmi as the second largest language—25 percent—although there is no apparent basis for this assertion.) French is the official language.

TABLE 7.2   Language Patterns

			Green-berg	Dalby
1. Primacy				
1st language	Arabic	(60%)		
2nd language	Sara	(28%)		
2. Linguistic classification (all ethnic units in country over 5%)	Arabic		IIIA	01A
	Sara		IIE2	51A
	Nilotic		IIC	53
	Saharan		IIB	11A
3. *Lingua franca*	Arabic, Sara			
4. Official languages	French, Arabic			

IV. Urban Patterns

Captial/largest city: Ndjamena (formerly named Fort-Lamy) (founded 1900)
Dominant ethnicity/language of capital
    Major vernacular: Arabic[1]
    Major ethnic group: Arab
    Major ethnic group as percent of capital's population: 60 percent (1980)[2]

[1]Jan Knappert, "Language Problems of the New Nations of Africa," *African Quarterly*, 5 (1965): 95—105.
[2]*West Africa*, 31 March 1980, p. 566.

TABLE 7.3   Growth of Capital/Largest City

Date	Ndjamena
1940	15,000
1950	28,000
1960	80,000
1965	110,000 UA
1972	179,000 UA
1976	242,000 UA
1979	400,000 UA

SOURCE: *Démographie Comparée* and *Europa Yearbook*, various years.

TABLE 7.4   Cites of 20,000 and Over

City	Size	Date
Ndjamena (Fort Lamy)*	303,000 UA	1979
Moundou	66,000	1979
Sarh (Fort Archambault)**	65,000	1979
Abéché	54,000	1979
Kelo	27,000	1979
Koumra	27,000	1979
Bongor	24,000	1979
Pala	22,000	1979
Doba	21,000	1979

SOURCE: *Africa South of Sahara 1980—81*.
*Changed name from Fort Lamy to Ndjamena on November 28, 1973.
**Changed name from Fort Archambault to Sarh in July 1972.

V. Political Patterns

A. Political Parties and Elections

From its formation in 1946 until its dissolution in 1973, the *Parti Progressiste Tchadien* (PPT), a section of the *Rassemblement Democratique Africain* (RDA), was the dominant party in Chad. Opposition was organized by the *Groupement des Independents et Ruraux du Tchad* (GIRT) and the *Mouvement Socialiste Africain* (MSA) which merged to form the *Parti National Africain* (PNA) in 1960. After independence in 1960, the PPT and the newly formed PNA formed a coalition government known as the *Union pour le Progres du Tchad* (UPT). This coalition, however, lasted only a year and was followed by the banning of the PNA in 1962. The only other party, the *Action Sociale Tchadienne* (AST), was also banned in 1962. In 1963, after the elections, President N'Garta Tombalbaye of the PPT declared Chad to be a one-party state. In 1973, the PPT, at Tombalbaye's request, dissolved itself and a new party was formed to replace it. This new party was the *Mouvement National pour la Revolution Culturelle et Sociale* (MNRCS). At the same time, another new (and illegal) party, the

Mouvement Democratique Revolutionnaire Tchadien (MDRT), was created in Paris under the leadership of Dr. Bono who was assassinated shortly thereafter. The illegal *Chadian National Liberation Front* (FROLINAT) which represented the major anti-government forces in the civil war continued in existence but with many factions vying for dominance. All party activity was banned after the April 1975 military coup. The last elections were held in 1969. The deterioration of the Chadian political system has continued with the traditional North/South, Muslim/Christian splits gradually being replaced by factional conflicts among elements of the Northern Muslim groups. By June 1980, President Woddei who had replaced General Malloum in 1979 was locked in an intense and bloody battle with the forces of Hissen Habre, (Armed Forces of the North. Habre was appointed Prime Minister in the provisional government of national union, established August 29, 1978, and more recently the Defense Minister. Each of the several factions have political and military organizations vying for control although parties in the normal sense have ceased to exist.

TABLE 7.5   Head of Government (Post-Independence)

Name	Dates in Office	Age (1982)	Ethnicity	Education	Former Occupation
1. François Tombalbaye (President)	1960— 1975	killed, 1975, age 57	Sudanic (Sara)	Primary	Assistant Teacher, Trade-Unionist
2. General Felix Malloum	1975— 1979	50	Sudanic (Sara)	Military Schools Brazzaville, France	
3. Goukhouni Woddei (President)	1979— 1982		Tobbou		
4. Hissen Habré	1982—	40	Arab		

FIGURE 7.1   Political Parties and Elections   Chad

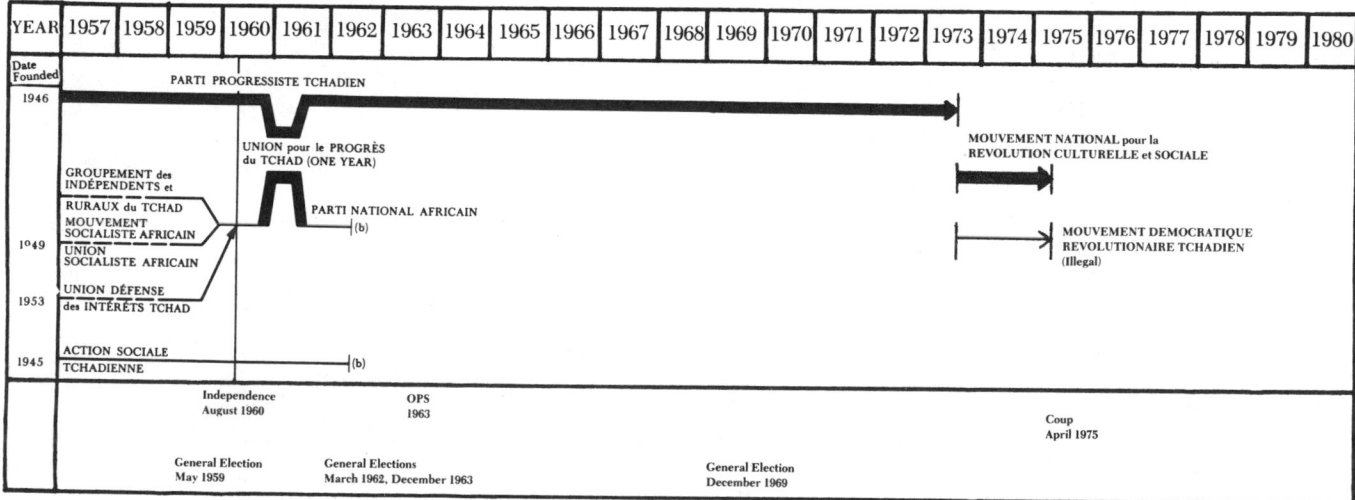

B. Political Leadership

The government of Chad was led by President Tombalbaye from independence until the coup in April 1975. During this period there were numerous changes in the personnel occupying individual cabinet portfolios, and a number of new members were brought into government office. Recruitment to office seemed to be broadly based by design, although the southern Sudanic peoples were becoming increasingly prominent in the cabinet until 1971. There were cabinet reshuffles in 1971 (twice) and 1973. In 1971, Tombalbaye promised to give 50 percent of the cabinet posts to Moslems, presumably northerners. General Malloum took power in April 1975 when the army ousted Tombalbaye. Malloum's attempts to end the civil war were ultimately unsuccessful although it appeared for a time that his readiness to negotiate with the warring groups might produce a compromise. Hissan Habre became Prime Minister in 1978 and Goukhouni Woddei of Frolinat the President in 1979 and the violence has grown precipitously since then until by mid-1980 these conflicts dominated the attempts to control the capital. Remnants of the Chadian army under the nominal Vice-President, Colonel Kamongue, were encamped outside the capital and were attacking the forces of Woddei and Habre, Attempts by the United Nation and the OAU members to mediate the conflict have been completely unsuccessful. In 1982, Habre completely ousted Woddei and took power.

TABLE 7.6 Cabinet Membership: Distribution by Ethnic Unit*

Ethnicity*	Independence Cabinet	1967 Cabinet	1972** Cabinet
1. Arab (46%)	38%	43%	50%
2a. Sudanic (Sara) (28)	38	50	50
2b. Sudanic (Kirdi) (5)	0	0	50
3. Nilotes (9.5)	0	0	50
4. Saharan Cluster (7)	0	0	50
5. Others (9.5)	25	7	50
N =	10	16	26

*Ethnic Units arranged in rank order of size within country with the unit's percent of population in parentheses.

**Estimates based on Tombalbaye's assertion in May 1971 that 50 percent of the cabinet posts would go to Moslems, presumbably Arabs.

VI. National Integration and Stability

The Tombalbaye regime dominated the political scene from independence until 1975, and during this period the major problem of national integration had been to link northern/Muslim peoples with southern/non-Muslim peoples. Plots by northern Muslim groups to overthrow the government (Tombalbaye was a southern Christian), were reported in 1963, 1965, and 1967, and were followed by arrests of northern politicians. Incidents in the east and north that began in 1965 had expanded by 1968-69 into large-scale fighting between northern Muslims and government forces (reinforced by French forces called in under the Mutual Defense Treaty). Levels of activity in the civil war had attenuated by 1972. However, in 1973 there were assassinations of two opposition politicians, M. El-Goni and Dr. Bono, and a reported plot by General Malloum, the army commander, in June 1973. General Maloum was jailed. A switch in government policy in 1974 seemed to be anti-Christian. The army ousted Tombalbaye in April 1975 and brought General Malloum to power. By October of that year, the French military garrison which had played an important role in the civil war was ousted from the country over a dispute concerning direct French contacts with northern rebels to secure the freedom of a French hostage. Rebel activity was at a low ebb in 1975 but gained momentum in 1977 and 1978. By 1977, the French military presence had increased again as they aided in the fight against FROLINAT forces. By then the civil war was raging on three fronts, North, East, and South. The conflict between Muslim northerners, backed by Libya, and the Christian southerners backed by France, continued to dominate the political life of the country and was the cause of an assassination attempt against General Malloum in April 1976. Disagreements among elements of FROLINAT groups which have regionally specific constituencies continues to make a peace agreement difficult since their demands are not uniform nor always consistent. A temporary armistice in the spring of 1978 quickly fell apart because of internal disagreements in FROLINAT. By mid-1980 the traditional conflicts in Chad had given way to one in which the Southern Christians were largely bystanders along with the French forces. The internecine and bloody fighting among the forces of President Woddei and Defense Minister Hissen Habre especially in Ndjamena increasingly turned a conflict between territorial, religious, and ethnic bases of mobilization into one where it is more of a revolution than a civil war. In 1982 Habré took power ousting Woddei.

TABLE 7.7   Elite Instability

Event and Date	Characteristics
1. Coup d'État April 12, 1975	a. *Description*: The army under General Odingar overthrew Tombalbaye, released General Malloum from prison and named him as President of the new Superior Military Council. French promises of non-involvement were important since there were 2,000 French troops in the country. b. *Participants*: General Odingar, the Chadian army, and the Gendarmerie. Others involved were Lt. Dimtoloum, Captain Tabio, and the Defence Minister Ibadaye. c. *Apparent Causes*: The mismanagement of drought relief which had affected the regimes in Niger, Upper Volta and Ethiopia was a major cause. Another reason was the alienation of important Christian support for the Tombalbaye regime because of Tombalbaye's anti-Christian campaign. The military was also dissatisfied over the perceived lack of recognition for its role in the fighting in the civil war.
2. Coup Attempt April, 1976	a. *Description*: Assassination attempt against General Malloum in which a grenade attack made against him while appearing in public fails. b. *Participants*: Followers of FROLINAT. c. *Apparent Causes*: Part of the larger dispute between the North and South.
3. Coup Attempt March 31, 1977	a. *Description*: Sixty members of the para-military Garde Nomade attacked the Presidential palace with small arms, rockets, and armoured cars. Eight people were killed but General Malloum was unhurt. b. *Participants*: Members of the Garde Nomade led by Lt. Brahim Abakar. FROLINAT appparently actively supported the attempted assassination. c. *Apparent Causes*: The North-South, Muslim-Christian conflict was the source of the discontent which led to the attack. The participants complained of the "discrimination against Muslims in the Chad armed forces."

SOURCES: *West Africa*, No. 3017, 21 April 1975, pp. 442—43; *West Africa*, 11 April 1977, p. 728.

TABLE 7.8   Communal Instability

Event and Date	Characteristics
1. Rebellion mid-1965 to 1968, Civil War 1968—72, Rebellion 1973—78, civil war, 1977—present.	a. *Description*: Despite long-standing official reticence concerning the rebellion, evidence indicates significant military action began in mid-1965 after a period of "simple banditry." At that time President Tombalbaye threatened to expel all Sudanese citizens from Chad if Sudan did not stop giving sanctuary to rebels living in Khartoum and calling themselves the "Gouvernement de la Republique Islamique de Tchad." The first notable incidents occurred in November 1965 at Mangolme (central Chad) where two high government officials were among eight illed, and at Asbel, a frontier post attacked by an armed band from the Sudan. Clashes between government and rebel forces became more frequent and intense in 1966; by August 1, 231 had been reported killed. Much of this fighting took place near the Chad-Sudan frontier in Wadai (Quaddai) Province. This prompted the government to restrict all Sudanese in Chad to within 5 kilometers of their residences. Nevertheless, insurgents battled government troops on at least two occasions (16 dead) before the end of the year. Events of February 1967 presaged further intensification of the conflict; political arrests became more common and after a serious battle at Am Timon (50 dead) in which the Prefect of Salamot and his deputy were killed, all news dispatches by foreign correspondents were censored. Thus, information on specific incidents became scarce. By the fall of 1969, the rebellion was a continuing and growing threat to the national government; opposition was no longer confined to the Chad-Sudan frontier but occurred sporadically in the north and in the southeast. Cotton crops were burned and government vehicles ambushed. French troops were called in, and there was bitter fighting in 1970 and 1971. The actual civil war had abated by 1972 although some minor activity continued. The Rebellion continued at a less active level for a few years, by 1977, three major groups had develope increased strength (Northern, Eastern, and Southern armies). French ground and air forces continued to play a major role in the fighting numbering nearly 2,000 men in 1978. By 1980 the forces of Hissan Habre and Goukhouni Woddei controlled most of the conflict which was centered in the capital, Ndjamena. The number of factions has continued to increase making a solution to the conflict more difficult.

Event and Date	Characteristics
	b.*Participants*: Rebel forces consist almost entirely of Muslim northerners who comprise about half of Chad's population. their spokesman since 1968 had been a non-northerner, Dr. Abba Sidick, Secretary General of the Chad National Liberation Front (FROLINAT). Dr. Sidick has said that rebel troops number about 2,000. The disintegration of FROLINAT's structure has made it unclear as to who represented the various interests. Until 1975, the government headed by N'garta Tombalbaye, a Protestant, was dominated by southerners. As part of his compromise formula, more northerners were brought into the government in 1971. French troops had been supporting government forces from 1968 to 1972. In the fall of 1969, approximately 2,500 French Foreign Legion troops were sent to assist the government. By the mid-1970's various splits in FROLINAT had reduced the unity of the movement and the leaders of the three main opposition groups refused to recognize any single leader. Differing positions on the legitimacy of Libya's takeover of part of northern Chad is a major element in differences among the groups in FROLINAT.
	c.*Apparent Causes*: In 1962 President Tombalbaye banned all political parties in Chad except his own, the *Union pour le Progres du Tchad* (UPT). Among the dissolved parties was the Muslim dominated *Parti National African*. It was apparently at this point that northern politicians called for extra-constitutional support from their followers who were dissatisfied as a result of the government's coercive methods of collecting taxes. The insurgent movement apparently includes a range of elements from bandits to politically motivated rebels. Tombalbaye's compromises along with a French-Chadian military offensive and cooperation of neighboring countries had largely contained the conflict by the early 1970's. However, this only led to a temporary lull in the conflict as it did not effectively deal with underlying sources of the conflict as became clear by 1980.
2.Ethnic Violence 1979	a.*Description*: Southern peoples who fled Ndjamena as it was being occupied by various factions of FROLINAT were involved in the massacre of a reported 800 Muslims in southern cities.
	b.*Participants*: Southerners reacting to the Northern-led occupation of the capital.
	c.*Apparent Causes*: Reaction to Muslim movement into Ndjamena.

SOURCES: Robert Pledge, ''France at War in Africa,'' *Africa Report*, 15 (June 15, 1970), pp. 16—19; *Africa Contemporary Record*—various years and *Africa Research Bulletin*; *West Africa* (31 March 1980), pp.

TABLE 7.10   Annual Instability Events: Independence Through 1979—Chad

Year	'61	'62	'63	'64	'65	'66	'67	'68	'69	'70	'71	'72	'73	'74	'75	'76	'77	'78	'79
ELITE INSTABILITY																			
Assassinations																			
Plots	1		2		1		1				1		1						
Attempted Coups d'État																	1		
Coups d'État															1				
COMMUNAL INSTABILITY																			
Ethnic Violence																			1
Irrendentism																			
Rebellion					1	1	1	1						1	1	1			
Civil War									1	1	1	1	1				1	1	1
MASS INSTABILITY																			
REVOLUTION																			

Year	'61	'62	'63	'64	'65	'66	'67	'68	'69	'70	'71	'72	'73	'74	'75	'76	'77	'78	'79
TURMOIL																			
Demonstrations						1													
Strikes (no days)																1			
Riots (no. days)			1		1														
Terrorism					2	5	4									2			
Declarations of Emergency			1								1								
CABINET INSTABILITY																			
Realloc. and new appts.		2	5	14		12		1			2								
New members		2	5	14		9		10			20								
Resig. and Dismissals	8	1	2	4	4	4		5	1		14	2							
No. of members (max.) (maximum in year)	10	11	14	16	16	16	16	21	21	20	26	26							

VII. Selected References

BIBLIOGRAPHY

Bibliographie du Tchad (sciences humaines) 2nd ed revue et corrigee 1970: Complemental bibliographie du Tchad 1974.

GENERAL

Decalo, S. *Historical Dictionary of Chad.* Metuchen, N.J.: Scarecrow Press, 1977.

De Proni, I. "Population, production and culture in the plains-society of northern Cameroon and Chad: the anthropologist in development projects" *Current Anthropology*, 1978 v. 9, pp. 42—57, 208—09.

Digulmbaye, Georges, and Robert Langue. *L'Essence du Tchad.* Paris: Presses Universitaires de France, 1969.

Hugot, Pierre. *Le Tchad.* Paris: Nouvelle Editions Latines, 1965.

Thompson, Virginia, and Richard Adloff. *The Emerging States of French Equatorial Africa*, pp. 426—75. Stanford, Calif.: Stanford University Press, 1960.

U.S. Department of the Army. *Area Handbook for Chad.* Washington, D.C. Government Printing Office, 1972.

POLITICAL

Ballard, John A. "Four Equatorial States: Congo, Gabon, Ubangi- Shari, Chad." In *National Unity and Regionalism in Eight African States*, ed. Gwendolen M. Carter, pp. 231-329. Ithaca, N.Y.: Cornell University Press, 1966.

Decraene, Philippe. "Chad at World's End." *Africa Report*, 13 (January 1968): 54.

de Lusignan, Guy. *French-Speaking Africa since Independence*, pp. 114-21. New York: Praeger, 1969.

Le Cornec, Jacques. *Histoire Politique du Tchad de 1900 à 1962.* Paris: R. Pichon et R. Durand-Auzias, 1963.

Lycett, Andrew. Chad's disastrous civil war. *Africa Report*, vol. 23, no. 5, 1978 pp. 4—7.

ECONOMIC

International Labour Organization. "Employment Position and Problems in Chad." *International Labour Review*, 85 (1962): 500—07.

International Monetary Fund. "Chad." In *Surveys of African Economies*, Vol. 1. Washington, D.C.: I.M.F., 1968.

World Bank. *Chad: Development Potential and Constraints.* Washington, D.C.: World Bank, 1974.

Yansane, Aguibou: Some problems of monetary dependency in French- speaking West African States. *Journal of African Studies*, vol. 5, no. 4, 1978: 444-76.

SOCIAL

Lebeuf, Annie. *Les Populations du Tchad.* Paris: Presses universitaires de France, 1959.

8. Congo

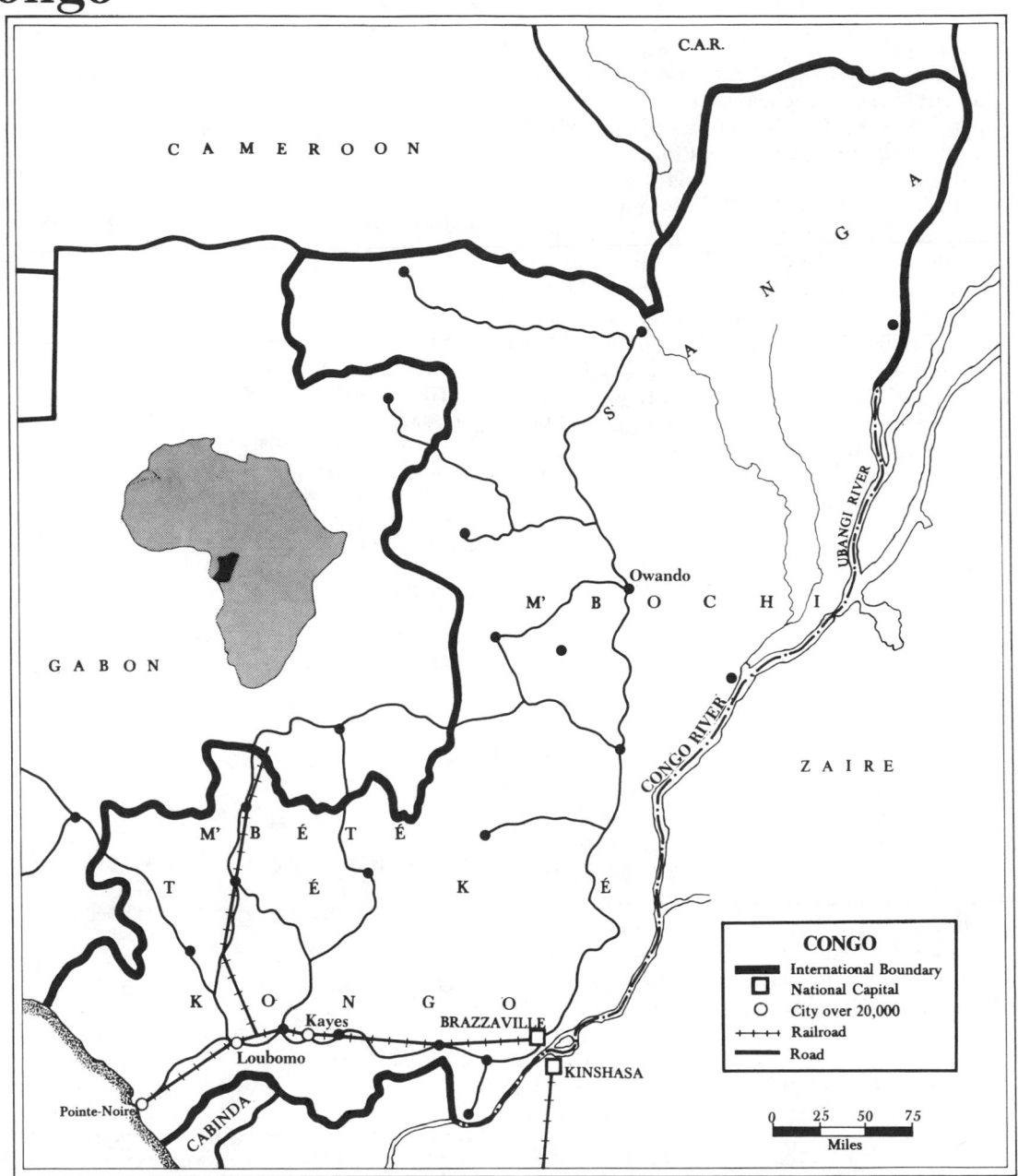

I. Basic Information

Date of Independence: August 15, 1960
Former Colonial Ruler: France
Change in Boundaries: Formerly part of French Equatorial Africa
Former Names: Moyen Congo; Congo (Brazzaville)
Estimated Population (1980): 1,544,000

Area Size (equivalent in U.S.): 132,047 sq. mi. (Montana)
Date of Last Census: 1974
Major Exports 1977 as Percent of Total Exports: Crude petroleum—53 percent; timber—17 percent.

II. Ethnic Patterns

The ethnic classifications selected for Congo as well as being based on cultural criteria, are based on locally recognized identity groups. The Kongo grouping, which constitutes nearly half the total population, is a broad group of culturally similar peoples who have historically come under the dominance of the Kongo kingdom and who speak Kikongo. They are also an important group in Zaire and Angola. It should be noted that the numerically and politically significant Lali (or Lari), although considered a Kongo group today, are of Téké origin and have formerly been classified as such. In addition to the major groups there are also Eshira peoples (4 percent), Maka (3 percent), and Kota (1 percent). Scattered Pygmy populations exist in the north. (Note: the term "M'bochi" is used in Congo census reports, but is not used by Murdock.) There were 8,000 French nationals resident in the Congo in 1977 (0.6 percent of the population.)

TABLE 8.1   Ethnic Units Over 5 Percent of Country Population

Ethnic Unit	Estimated Ethnic Population 1980	Estimated Ethnic Percentage
a. Kongo (Bakongo)	725,700	47%
1. Lali (Lari),	(324,200)	(21%)
2. Kongo, 3. Sundi, 4. Vili,		
5. Yombe, 6. Bembe, 7. Kamba,		
8. Dondo		
b. Téké	308,800	20%
1. Téké, 2. Bakoukouya		
c. M'bochi Type	169,800	11%
1. Bangi, 2. M'bochi, 3. Kuyu,		
4. Maku, 5. Furu, 6. Irébu,		
7. Libuba, 8. Linga, 9. Loi,		
10. Mboko, 11. Ngiril		
d. M'bété (M'béti)	108,100	7%
e. Sanga (Bosanga)	77,200	5%
1. Bassanga, 2. Mbimu, 3. Bombo,		
4. Konambembe, 5. Besom		

SOURCE: *Enquête Démographique de la République du Congo* (Brazzaville: 1960).

III. Language Patterns

All language groups in the Congo are Bantu. The largest are Kongo (47 percent) and Téké (20 percent). Rustow estimates the two major languages are Kongo (50 percent) and Téké (25 percent); (Knappert puts Kongo at 40 percent, which is clearly too low, especially since Kongo has become a trade language at the mouth of the Congo River). Our own estimate is Kongo 52 percent; Téké 20 percent. French is the official language.

TABLE 8.2   Language Patterns

1. Primacy		
1st language	Kongo	(52%)
2nd language	Téké	(20%)

		Greenberg	Dalby
2. Linguistic classification (all ethnic units in country over 5%)	Kongo	IA5	H1
	Téké	IA5	B7
	M'bochi	IA5	(C2, C3)
	M'bété	IA5	B6
	Sanga	IA5	L2
3. *Lingua francas*	Kongo, Lingala, Monokutuba		
4. Official language	French		

SOURCE: U.S. Department of the Army, *Area Handbook for the People's Republic of the Congo (Congo-Brazzaville)*, (Washington, D.C.: Government Printing Office, 1971), pp. 59—62.

IV. Urban Patterns

Capital/largest city: Brazzaville (founded 1883)
Dominant ethnicity/language of capital
  Major vernacular: Kongo[1]
  Major ethnic group: Kongo
  Major ethnic group as percent of capital's population:
  60 percent (1959)[2]

[1]Jan Knappert, "Language Problems of the New Nations of Africa," *African Quarterly*, 5 (1965): 95—105.
[2]Marcel Soret, *Les Kongo Nord-occidentaux* (Paris: Presses Universitaires de France, 1959), p. 2.

TABLE 8.3   Growth of Capital/Largest City

Date	Brazzaville
1930	17,000
1940	45,000
1950	84,000
1960	130,000
1965	150,000 UA
1971	200,000 UA
1974	289,700 UA
1977	310,000 UA
1980[a]	422,400

SOURCES: *Démographie Comparée*, with the exception of 1940, which is from *Encyclopédie des pays d'Outre Mer*, Vol. 2, p. 145; 1974—Census figure; 1977—*Europa Yearbook 1974*, Vol. II.
[a]*Europa Yearbook 1982.*

TABLE 8.4   Cities of 20,000 and Over

City	Size	Date
Brazzaville[a]	422,400 UA	1980
Pointe-Noire[a]	185,100	1980
Kayes*	30,600	1974
Loubomo*	29,600	1974

SOURCE: *Africa: South of the Sahara 1975*—1974 census figures.
*Dolisie was renamed Loubomo and Jacob was renamed Kayes.
[a]*Europa Yearbook 1982.*

V. Political Patterns

FIGURE 8.1   Political Parties and Elections   CONGO

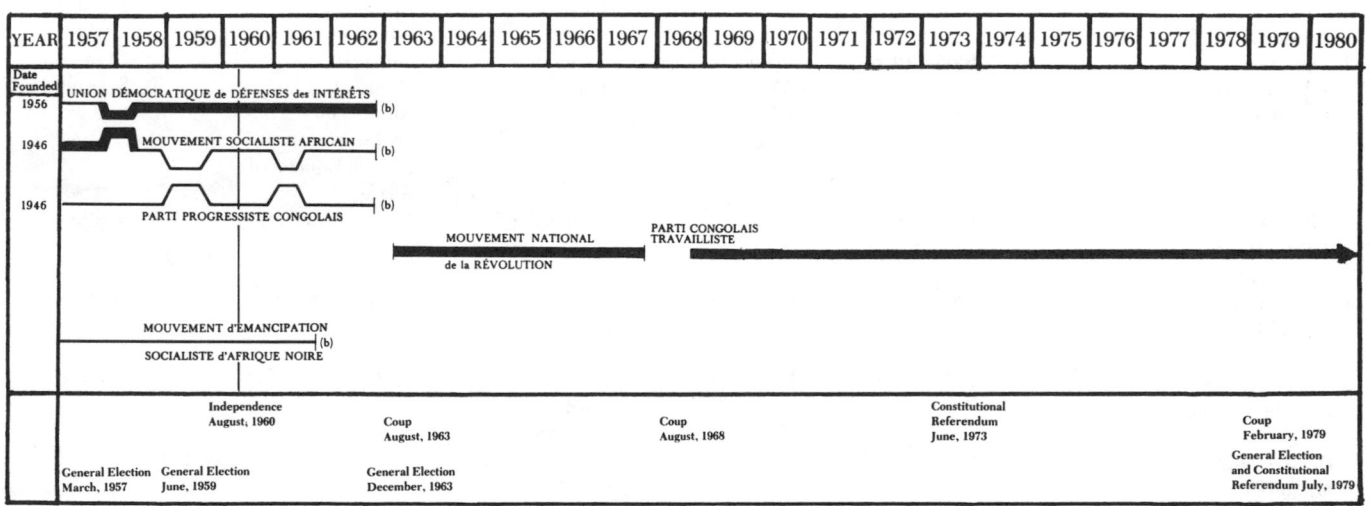

A. Political Parties and Elections

The dominant political parties in the pre-independence French Congo were: the *Mouvement Socialiste Africain* (MSA) led by Jacques Opangualt which governed from 1957 to late 1958, and the *Union Démocratique de Défenses des Intéréts* (UDDI) under Abbé Fulbert Youlou which governed from 1958 until a civilian/military coup forced Youlou to resign in August 1963. Following the coup, the *Mouvement National de la Révolution* (MNR) was formed, and selected Alphonse Massemba-Débat to form the government. Massemba-Debat continued to govern until August 1968 when his government was replaced by a military coup. The newly formed *National Council of the Revolution* (CNR) banned political activity. In December 1969, a "People's Republic" was declared, purportedly guided by Marxist-Leninist principles and the MNR was renamed the *Congolese Labor Party* (PCT). The PCT has remained in power ever since despite several attempted coups. In February 1979, there was a palace coup. President Opango was persuaded to resign and handed over his powers to a four man presidium of the PCT. Denis Sassou Nguesso was then chosen to become President. An election and constitutional referendum was held in July 1979. The turnout rate was 90% of the registered voters. The new constitution was passed and the PCT was returned to power.

B. Political Leadership

The 1963, 1973, and 1979 constitutions give strong executive power to the President, so only heads of state are given here instead of the prime ministers. In a highly pluralistic society, the cabinets of Presidents Youlou and Massemba-Débat were broadly based in terms of recruitment from the largest ethnic communities. In 1968, Alfred Raoul, the prime minister, became head of state for a short period before Marien Ngouabi assumed power as the first northern president, with Raoul as vice-president. Cabinet reshuffles in this period led to increased northern representation. On December 30, 1969 a new

TABLE 8.5   **Heads of State (Post Independence)**

Name	Dates in Office	Age (1982)	Ethnicity	Education	Former Occupation
1. Abbé Fulbert Youlou (President)	1960—1963	died in 1972 at age 55	Kongo (Lari)	Seminary in Akono (Fr. Cameroon)	Catholic Priest
2. Alphonse Massemba-Débat (President)	1963—1968	executed 1977 age 56	Kongo (Lari)	University "training college" for civil service in French Equatorial Africa	Civil Servant
3. Alfred Raoul, (Prime Minister and President)	1968—1969		'southerner'	St. Cyr (France)	Soldier
4. Major Marien Ngouabi (President)	1969—1977	Assassinated in 1977 aged 40	M'bochi (Kuyu)	French Military Academy	Soldier
5. Gen. Joachim Yhombi—Opango (President and Head, Comite Militaire du Parti)	1977—1979	43	Mbochi (born in Owando)	St. Cyr (France)	Soldier
6. Col. Denis Sassou Nguesso	1979— Present	39	Mbochi	Secondary School, French Military School	Soldier

constitution was adopted which lasted only until June 1973 when another new constitution was adopted. Both increased President Ngouabi's powers. Ngouabi continued as President throughout the period from 1968 until his assassination in 1977. There were frequent cabinet reshuffles in that period. Some of the most recent being in 1969 (2), 1970 (2), 1971 (2), 1973 (2), and 1975 (2). After the assassination, the military continued in power, appointing Col. (later General) Yhombi-Opango to succeed Ngouabi. In a coup on February 8, 1979, General Yhombi-Opango was forced to resign. The PCT chose Col. Denis Sassou Nguesso to succeed him as President. According to government reports, General Yhombi-Opango is now in prison.

TABLE 8.6 Cabinet Membership: Distribution by Ethnic Unit*

Ethnicity*	Independence Cabinet	Immediate Pre-Coup Cabinet, 1963	December 31, 1967 Cabinet
1. Kongo (47%)	43%	57%	50%
2. Téké (20)	7.1	7.1	10
3. M'bochi (11)	21	21	10
4. M'bété (7)	0	0	10
5. Sanga (5)	7.1	7.1	0
6. Others (10)	23	7.1	20
N =	14	15	11

*Ethnic units arranged in rank order of size within country with unit's percent of national population in parentheses.

VI. National Integration and Stability

Marked by three successful coups d'état, five unsuccessful attempts and numerous reported plots since independence in 1960, the political life of the People's Republic of the Congo has been profoundly complicated by external forces and influences, particularly from its neighbor to the south, Zaire. Of at least eight reported plots to overthrow the government, five can be linked to external involvement (including Portuguese, Belgian, and Zairois). The three successful coups have all involved military initiation. The second one occurring in August 1968, appears to have been precipitated by ethnic violence. This coup was not fully realized for several weeks despite the immediate diminution of Massemba-Débat's power.

Part of the problem of national integration in Congo has been that the major ethnic group, the Kongo, is split between three countries—Congo, Zaire and Angola—and there has been continuing quasi-irredentism. Tension between the Kongo and the northern peoples, most notably the M'bochi, has been an important source of strain behind events since 1968, as has been an ideological left-right struggle which was most recently manifest in the assassination of Ngouabi in 1977 and the February 8, 1979 coup. In January and February 1980 tension grew between the Congo and Zaire as Zaire charged that the Congolese government was sheltering rebels who planned to launch an invasion of Zaire.

TABLE 8.7   Elite Instability

Event and Date	Characteristics
1. Coup d'État August 15, 1963	a. *Description*: After a three-day general strike and sporadic violence, the army forced civilian President Abbé Fulbert Youlou to resign. It then supported the Christian and Communist labor leaders in their choice of a provisional government headed by Massemba-Débat and composed of radical young technician-ministers. b. *Participants*: Trade Unions, with the cooperation of the army. c. *Apparent Causes*: The unions cited unemployment and regime incompetence in the face of a growing economic crisis. Once in power, Massemba-Débat said the coup had taken place to put an end to fiscal mismanagement, extravagance in high places, despotism, tribalism, and moral corruption.
2. Coup attempt May 13, 1968	a. *Description*: It was reported that "mercenaries inspired by high finance and international reaction" led by a European took Lt. Portella and State Secretary for National Defense, Lt. Paignet, as prisoners with the aim of staging a coup d'état. The mercenaires were reportedly disarmed. b. *Participants*: Unnamed "mercenaires" led by a European named as Jacques Debreton. c. *Apparent Causes*: Unknown but implied as a reaction against a move to the left by the government.
3. Coup d'État August 3, 1968	a. *Description*: Captain Marien Ngouabi, commander of the army's paratroop battalion, was arrested by Massemba-Débat. Elements of the army overthrew the government and rescued Ngouabi from prison. Massemba-Débat, who had fled Brazzaville, was recalled to limited power by the newly constituted national Council of the Revolution. Further conflict within a couple of weeks led to Massemba-Débat's resignation and Ngouabi's eventual assumption of full power in December 1968. b. *Participants*: The coup d'état was organized by Captain Ngouabi, whose control of the paratroops was reinforced by ideological support from left-wing factions in the party and labor organizations, and by disadvantaged northerners in these institutions. The government of Massemba-Débat was brought down by the coup, and the influence of moderate and southern politicians who had supported the former president was substantially reduced. c. *Apparent Causes*: Massemba-Débat referred to the elections proposed for December, 1968, as a factor contributing to the political conflicts in the middle of the year. These conflicts appear to be related to both ideology and ethnicity. Massemba-Débat's appointment of moderate ministers, his dismissal or demotion of leading left-wing politicians, and his imprisonment of Ngouabi (a left-wing northerner) intensified these conflicts and precipitated the coup.
4. Coup Attempt November 7, 1969	a. *Description*: The government admitted an attempted coup had been carried out but gave no details as to what occurred. The coup was supposed to have originated in Kinshasa. b. *Participants*: At least 34 people were convicted of participating. Fourteen were sentenced to death including B. Kolela, D. Milongo, J. Bakama, and E. Matimba. c. *Apparent Causes*: Opposition to the Ngouabi regime and its politics. There were apparently tribal (Lari) and ideological (left) overtones. Foreign interests including the Americans and Congolese (Kinshasa) were accused of backing the coup in order to alter the country's regime.
5. Coup Attempt March 22—23, 1970	a. *Description*: A Commando unit led by Lieutenant Kikanga took over the radio station in Brazzaville. Within a few hours troops led by President Ngouabi defeated the rebels, killing their leader. On March 29, 1970, Captain Albert Miaouma, Adjutant-in-Chief of the Gendarmerie, André Nkoutou, and Sergeant Jean-Marie Mengo were executed for their part in the coup attempt. b. *Participants*: A small group of dissidents in the army. Kikanga, according to *Africa Digest*, had taken part in an earlier coup attempt in November 1969. c. *Apparent Causes*: Kikanga's grievances and political program are not known. According to *Africa Digest* the earlier coup attempt in which he participated was supported by ex-President Fulbert Youlou who was in exile in Spain.
6. Coup Attempt February 22, 1972	a. *Description*: Army units from the infantry battalion under Lieutenant Diawara seize the radio and television station and announced a coup while President Ngouabi was in Pointe Noire. Other army units, loyal to Ngouabi, arrested the rebelling army members and various politicians. Diawara escaped but others were arrested including Major Raoul (former prime minister) and various party officials. b. *Participants*: Lieutenant Diawara and elements of the infantry battalion with passive support from various army and left-wing party officials. c. *Apparent Causes*: The causes are not clear from sources available but it does appear to be a left-wing inspired coup resulting from disappointment with N'gouabi's lack of substantive movement to establish a socialist state.

Event and Date	Characteristics
7. Coup Attempt 18 March 1977	a. *Description*: Captain Kikadidi and three others including members of the palace guard penetrate the security guards at President Ngouabi's house and assassinate him. Cardinal Biayenda is also assassinated sometime later. The assassins fled into hiding. b. *Participants*: Captain Kikadidi, members of the Palace Guard, and others with the purported support of the deposed President, Massemba-Débat and other politicians and trade unionists. Some sources call these accounts into question and assert that the army had Ngouabi killed in order to prevent his rapprochement with civilian leaders which would have weakened army control in the country. c. *Apparent Causes*: According to one explanation, dissatisfaction with Ngouabi's rule from two sources. One was on the part of politicians and trade unionists that the regime was too conservative. The second was due to the resentment by the southern ethnic groups of the dominance of Northerners in the government. *Africa Confidential* asserts that the army shot Ngouabi to forestall a rapprochement with his political opponents which would have decreased army hegemony in the society. It was asserted that they then blamed these opponents for the assassination and quickly executed them including Massemba-Debat so all sources of opposition to their rule would be eliminated.
8. Coup d'État 8 February 1979	a. *Description*: An unresisted takeover of the government by the PCT occurred when General Yhombi-Opango was forced to reign. The PCT chose Colonel Denis Sassou Nguesso to succeed Opango as President. b. *Participants*: Colonel Nguesso, the PCT and certain military officers. c. *Apparent Causes*: Dissatisfaction with Opango's rule and a desire to move further to the left ideologically and to form closer ties with the Soviet Union.

SOURCES: *Africa Diary* (1963): 1327—29; *Africa Contemporary Record 1968—69*, pp. 454—57; *Africa Digest*, 17 (1970): 56—57; *West Africa* issues of 28 March, 4 April, and 11 April 1977; *Africa Research Bulletin* p. 4358.

TABLE 8.8   Communal Instability

Event and Date	Characteristics
1. Ethnic Violence February 7—11, 1963	a. *Description*: An uprising of Lali partisans of Youlou took place in Brazzaville; despite military intervention the outbreak lasted three days. b. *Participants*: Lali ethnic members who were opposed by members of revolutionary youth groups. The government accused Catholic leaders and Western embassies of inciting the uprising. c. *Apparent Causes*: Continuing discontent of Youlou supporters, many of whom were dissatisfied with the results of an election held earlier in February.
2. Rebellion August 29— September 1, 1968	a. *Description*: Following the coup d'état of August 16, 1968, resistance to the new government of Captain Ngouabi was organized by leading civilian politicians and a faction of the youth wing of the ruling party, who were armed as members of the civil militia and in training at a meteorological camp near Brazzaville. Fighting between these elements and the regular army lasted from August 29 to September 1, when the leaders of the rebellion were arrested, and their fellow insurgents disarmed. b. *Participants*: The leaders of this rebellion were leading members of the ruling party (MNR) and of its youth wing (JMNR), notably André Hombessa and Michel Bindi. The insurgents appear to have identified themselves as an ethnically cohesive group, as evidenced by their adoption of the name "Biafrans." It is not clear, however, what aims the insurgents pursued, and to what degree they represented a communal or ethnically homogenous, rather than an ideological and associational grouping. c. *Apparent Causes*: The rebellion was a reaction to the coup d'état, and the recognition of the supremacy of Captain Ngouabi and the subordination of Massemba-Débat.

SOURCES: (for 1 Ethnic Violence): John A. Ballard, "Four Equatorial States," in *National Unity and Regionalism in African States*, ed. Gwendolen M. Carter (Ithaca, N.Y.: Cornell University Press, 1966), pp. 231—335. Philippe Decraene and Mohammed Bahri, "Two Views of Congo-Brazzaville," *Africa Report*, 10 (October 1965): 35—37.

TABLE 8.10 Annual Instability Events: Independence Through 1975—Congo

Year	'61	'62	'63	'64	'65	'66	'67	'68	'69	'70	'71	'72	'73	'74	'75	'76	'77	'78	'79
ELITE INSTABILITY																			
Assassinations																			
Plots				1	2	1		1	1	1			2						
Attempted Coups d'État								1	1	1		1							
Coups d'État			1					1											
COMMUNAL INSTABILITY																			
Ethnic Violence					1														
Irredentism																			
Rebellion								1											
Civil War																			
MASS INSTABILITY																			
Revolt																			
Revolution																			
TURMOIL																			
Demonstrations			1	2		1		1			1								
Strikes (no. days)										1									
Riots (no. days)			3			1													
Terrorism					1														
Declarations of Emergency		1	1					1		2									
CABINET INSTABILITY																			
Realloc. and new appts.	6	10	10	14	21	9		2	1	3	2	2							
New members	6	2		7	5	3		12	9	4	7								
Resig. and Dismissals		2		3	5	5		11	9	6	7	1							
No. of members (max.) (maximum in year)	12	16	16	10	14	11	11	15	15	13	13	12							

VII. Selected References

GENERAL

Sautter, Gilles. *De l'Atlantique au fleuve Congo, une geographie du sous-peuplement: Republique du Congo; Republique Gabonaise.* 2 vols. Paris: Mouton, 1966

Soret, Marcel. *History du Congo: Capitale Brazzaville.* Paris: Berger-Levrault, 1978.

Thompson, V. and R. Adloff. *Historical Dictionary of Congo (Brazzaville).* Metuchen, N.J.: Scarecrow Press, 1974.

U.S. Department of the Army. *Area Handbook for People's Republic of the Congo (Congo Brazzaville).* Washington, D.C.: Government Printing Office, 1971.

Vennetier, Pierre, *Geographie du Congo-Brazzaville.* Paris: Gautheir-Villars, 1966.

Wagret, Jean Michel. *Histoire et sociologie politiques de la Republique du Congo (Brazzaville).* Paris: Librarie Generale de Droit et de Jurisprudence, 1963.

POLITICAL

Ballard, John A. "Four Equatorial States: Congo, Gabon, Ubangi-Shari, Chad." In *National Unity and Regionalism in Eight African States*. ed. Gwendolen M. Carter, p. 231—329. Ithaca, N.Y.: Cornell University Press, 1966.

Calvocoress, P. *The Congo in World Politics since 1945*, pp. 340—53. London: Longman, 1977.

de Lusignan, Guy. *French-Speaking Africa since Independence*, pp. 91—100. London: Pall Mall Press, 1969.

Gause, René with Viriginia Thompson and Richard Adloff. *The Politics of Congo-Brazzaville*. Stanford, Calif.: Hoover Institute Press, 1973.

Terrary, Emmanuel. "Les Revolutions Congolaise et Dahomeenne de 1963: Essai d'Interpretation." *Revue Française de Science Politique* (October 1964): 917-42.

ECONOMIC

Amin, Samir and Catherin Coquery-Vidrovitch. *Histoire Économique du Congo, 188—1968*. Paris: Editions Anthropos. 1969.

Bertrand, Hugues. *Le Congo: formation sociale et mode à developpement economique*. Paris: Maspero, 1975.

International Monetary Fund. "Congo-Brazzaville." In *Surveys of African Economies*, Vol. 1. Washington, D.C.: I.M.F., 1968.

SOCIAL

Andersson, Efrain. *Churches at the Grass Roots: A Study of Congo-Brazzaville*. London: Lutterworth, 1968.

Andersson, Efrain. *Messianic Popular Movements in the Lower Congo*. Uppsala: Almqvist and Wiksells, 1958.

Balandier, Georges. *Sociologie actuelle de L'Afrique Noire*, 2nd. ed. Paris: Presses universitaires de France, 1963.

Ctoce-Spinelli, Michel. *Les Enfants de Poto-Poto*. Paris: Editions Bernard Grasset, 1967.

9. Djibouti

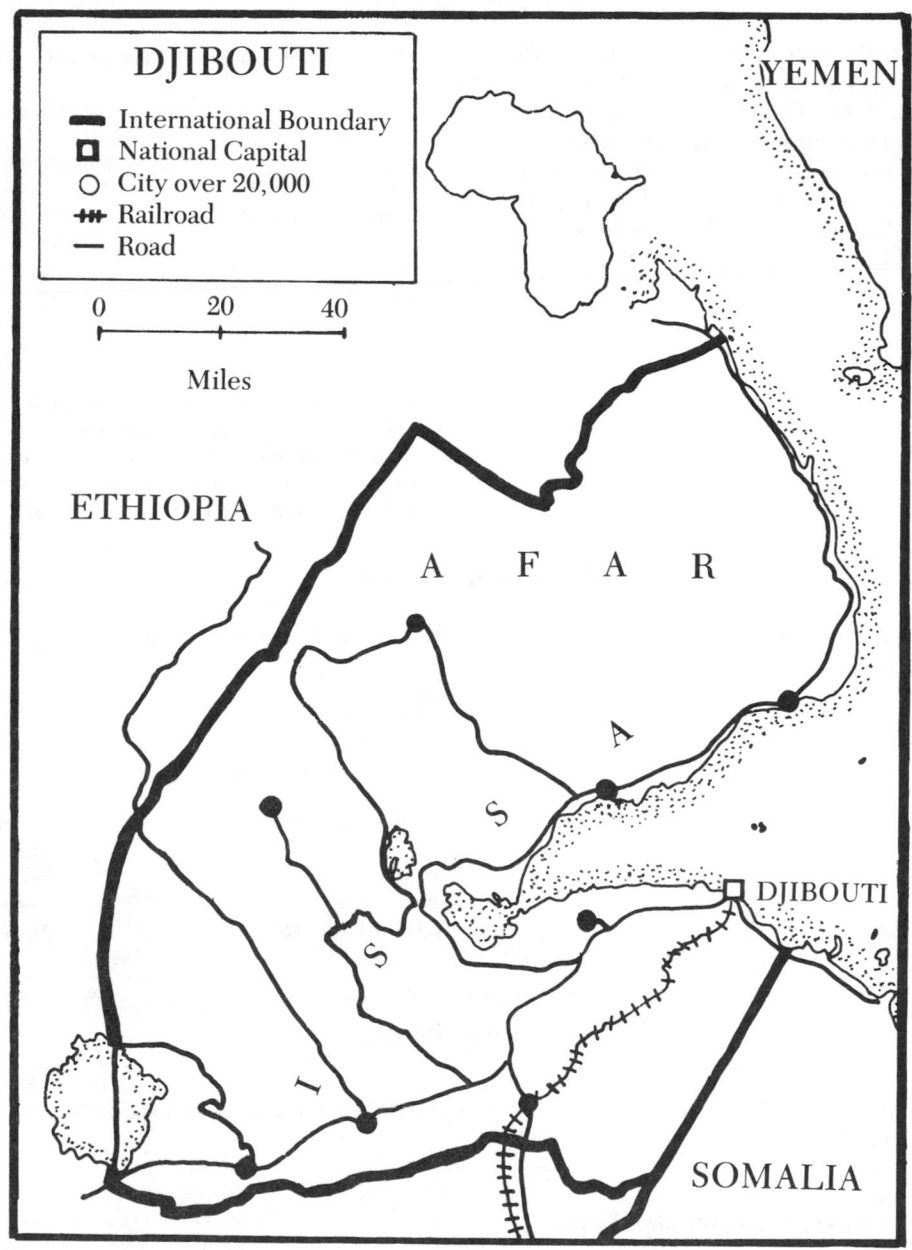

I. Basic Information

Date of Independence: June 27, 1977
Former Colonial Ruler: France
Change in Boundaries: Before independence it was known as the French territory of the Afars and the Issas.
Former Name: French Somaliland

Estimated Population (1980): 361,000
Area Size (equivalent in U.S.): 8,800 sq. mi. (New Hampshire)
Date of Last Census: 1976
Major Exports 1976 as Percent of Total Exports: skins and leather—4 percent

II. Ethnic Patterns

Djibouti's population is divided between two main ethnic groups, the Issas, who are of Somali origin, and the smaller largely nomadic Afars (Danakie), who are of Ethiopian origin. The Afars comprise 32 percent of the population while the Issas, who are concentrated in the vicinity of the capital, comprise 50 percent of the population. Somalis, Arabs, Europeans, and other foreigners make up the balance of the country's population.

TABLE 9.1   Ethnic Units over 5 Percent of Country Population

Ethnic Units	Estimated Ethnic Population 1980	Estimated Ethnic Percentage
a. Issas and other Somali	180,000	50%
b. Afars	134,000	37
c. Arabs	65,000	8
d. Europeans	25,000	3
e. Other Foreigners	18,000	2

SOURCE: Latest figures on population of country and capital from *Republique de Djibouti*, Guide d'information touristique publie par l'Office de Developpement du Tourisme—4ᵉ trimestre 1979. *Statesman's Yearbook, 1979—80. The Europa Yearbook 1980*: A World Survey (London, at the Stanhope Press, 1980), p. 217.

III. Language Patterns

Both the Afars and Issas are Muslims and speak related Cushitic languages. The official language is Arabic but French is widely spoken.

TABLE 9.2   Language Patterns

1. Primacy			
1st language	Somali	65%	
2nd language	Afar	(37%)	
2. Linguistic classification		Greenberg	Dalby
(all ethnic units in	Somali	IIID3	02A
over 5%)	Afar	IIID3	02F
3. *Lingua francas*	French, Somali		
4. Official language	Arabic		

IV. Urban Patterns

Capital/largest city: Djibouti
Dominant ethnicity/language of capital
    Major vernacular: Somali
Major ethnic group: Issas
Major ethnic group as percent of capital's population:

TABLE 9.3   Growth of Capital/Largest City

Date	Djibouti
1950	28,000
1960	56,000
1966	70,000
1967	62,000
1974	74,000
1979	180,000

*Various editions of *Statesman's Yearbook*; *Europa Yearbook 1980*.

V. Political Patterns

A. Political Parties and Elections

In 1956, the area known as French Somaliland was granted internal autonomy by France after a century of penetration; and in 1958, the voters of Somaliland elected to enter the French community as an overseas territory. The voters still chose continued association with France in the March 19, 1967 referendum. After the UN General Assembly resolution of December 31, 1975 called on France to withdraw from the territory, a second referendum was set for May 8, 1977 and the Afar president of the local Government Council, 'Ali Arif Bourhan of the National Union for Independence (UNI), resigned.[1] Representing five of the territory's major political groups, a United Patriotic Front (which acted under the name of the Popular Independence Rally) conducted the negotiations with the French that culminated in the referendum of May 8, 1977.

On May 8, 1977, 98.8 percent of the electorate opted for independence and at the same time approved a single list of 65 candidates for a constituent assembly. On June 24, Issas leader Hassan Gouled Aptidon of the African People's League for Independence (LPAI) was unanimously elected President of the Republic by the assembly; and on June 27, Djibouti was declared independent. President Gouled named Afar leader Ahmed Dini Ahmed to head a 15 member Council of Ministers on July 12.

On December 17, Prime Minister Dini and four other Afar cabinet members resigned amidst charges of "tribal repression." The duties of prime minister were assumed by the President until the designation of a new government headed by Abdullah Mohamed Kamil on February 5, 1978. Barkat Gourad Hamadou succeeded Kamil on September 30, 1978 following the dissolution of the Kamil government on September 21.

The leading parties of Djibouti are organized by ethnicity, with the African People's League for Independence (LPAI) and the Front for the Liberation of the Somali Coast (FLCS) speaking for the Issa majority; and the National Union for Independence (UNI), the Djibouti Liberation Movement (MLD), and the Popular Liberation Movement (MPL) representing the Afars. Even though the LPAI had long been the principal spokesman for the Issa majority, it was not represented in the Afar-dominated pre-independence Chamber of Deputies. Two of its members, however, did hold ministerial posts.

[1]He was replaced in July 1976 by the former Cabinet Secretary, General Abdullah Mohamed Kamil, who was appointed head of a new government, containing leading representatives of both the Afar and Somali populations.

Its leaders are Hassan Gouled Aptidon (President of the Republic and of the Party), and Moumine Bahadon Farah (Vice President).[1] Formerly outlawed and based in Somalia, the FLCS has consistently advocated that Djibouti be incorporated into a greater Somalia. Even though they participated in the negotiations with the French and were not actively opposed to independence, none of its members were presented for election to the assembly in the list of May 8, 1977. Its leaders are Abdullah Waberi Khalif (Chairman) and Omar Osman Rabeh (Vice-Chairman). Prior to independence, the UNI was split into majority and minority factions. The former was led by Ali Arif Bourhan and they elected to boycott the negotiations with the French. On April 28, 1977, however, Arif announced his "unconditional support" for Hassan Gouled's leadership and urged his followers to participate in both the referendum and the election of May 8. An illegal Marxist group based in Dire Dawa, Ethiopia, the MLD, supported independence but boycotted the pre-independence negotiations with the French as well as the legislative election of May 8, 1977. Its leader is Ahmed Bourhan Omar (Secretary General). The MPL is comprised of a group of younger Marxists who also boycotted the pre-independence negotiations and campaigned for abstention at the May 8 election. The party was declared illegal following the resignation of Prime Minister Dini Ahmed on December 17, 1977. Its leader is Mohamed Kamil Ali (President). In 1979 the Democratic Front for the Liberation of Djibouti (FDLD) was formed by merging the UNI and the MPL. The Secretary of this Afar opposition party is Mohamed Kamil Ali.

B. Political Leadership

Hassan Gouled Aptidon has been the head of government since June 27, 1977.[2] On December 17, Prime Minister Dini and four other Afar cabinet members resigned amidst charges of "tribal repressions." The cabinet named on February 5, 1978, was planned to strike a careful balance in tribal representation. The new prime minister, 'Abdallah Mohamed Kamil, is an Afar as is his successor, Barkat Gourad Hamadou (appointed September 30).

[1]In 1979 the Popular Rally for Progress (RPP) was formed to replace the LPAI, retaining Hassan Gouled Aptidon as its president.

[2]He emphasized the republic's "Arab identity, thus stressing the common Islamic allegiance of the Afar and Somalis and appealed to the powerful Arab states whose support would be necessary to safeguard Djibouti's future.

FIGURE 9.1   Political Parties and Elections   DJIBOUTI

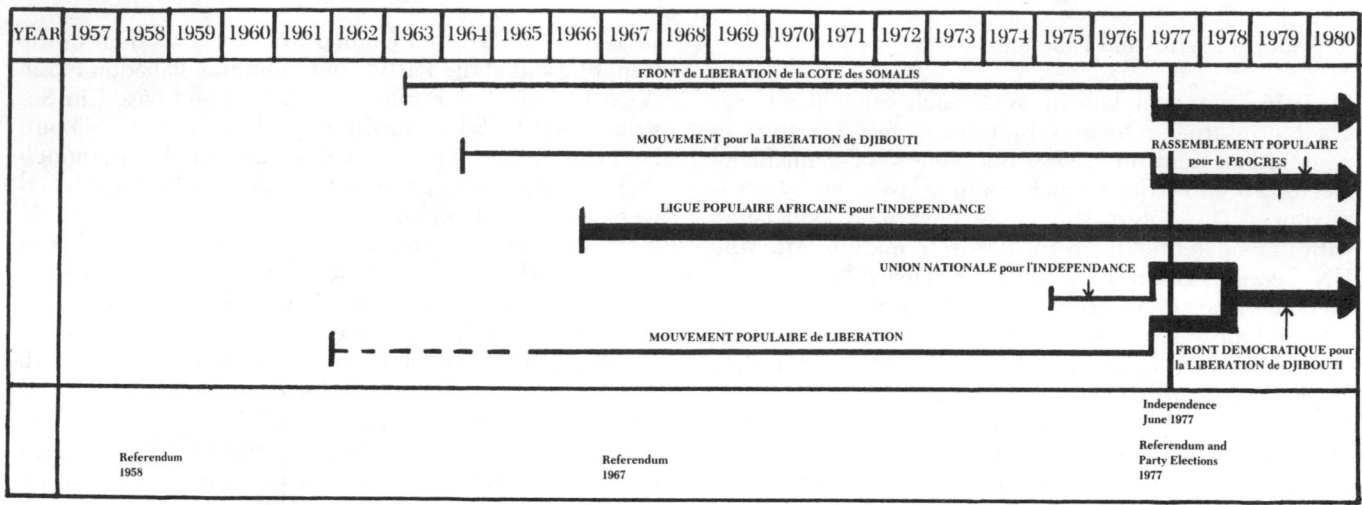

TABLE 9.5   Head of Government (Post-Independence)

Name	Dates in Office	Age (1982)	Ethnicity	Education	Former Occupation
1. Hassan Gouled Aptidon (President)	1977— present	66	Issa	No formal education	Politician

VI. National Integration and Stability

The two factors which most severely challenged Djibouti's survival were its intrinsic economic unviability and the ethnic rivalry between its Afar and Issa nationalities. In the past both Ethiopia and Somalia have claimed the territory and each have threatened military intervention if the other should threaten Djibouti's independence. The Somali population had long dominated the territory's politics. However, the less urbanized and more neglected Afar population reversed this situation in the March 1967 referendum by voting for continued association with France, while the Somali voted for independence. This outcome left a legacy of inter-ethnic bitterness. The supremacy of the Afars was consolidated in the 1968 elections for the new Chamber of Deputies when the Afar leader, Ali Arif and his "Progress Party" won 26 out of 32 seats. In subsequent years with the increase of the Somali population (especially during the 74—75 drought in Somalia) further tension with the Afars

developed. Further and violent agitation came from the banned FLCS. These pressures led to a decisive change in French policy: independence would be granted and a more harmonious relationship sought between the two ethnic groups.

Two years after independence Djibouti was still dangerously trying to steer a neutral course between the opposing forces of Ethiopian and Somali nationalism. After the full-scale war of 1977—78, the Ogaden conflict smouldered on at guerrilla level, sending economic and political shockwaves which threatened to destabilize the territory. The fragility of the Afar-Issa alliance, following the defeat of Somali forces in the Ogaden war, was underlined by a series of Afar guerrilla incidents including the kidnapping in May 1978 of a French national (who was later released by pro-Ethiopian extremists. In mid-July it was reported that Somali guerrillas had retaliated with a series of attacks on the Addis Ababa-Djibouti rail facilities less than a month after the line had been reopened to service (the previous damages to the rail facilities had resulted from earlier Somali guerrilla activity). A ban on arms trading was introduced in August. Refugees from the conflict continued to flock to Djibouti, adding an estimated 215,000 displaced persons to the politically and economically unstable territory.

VII. Selected References

BIBLIOGRAPHY

Clarke, W. Sheldon. "The Republic of Djibouti – An Introduction to Africa's Newest State and a Review of Related Literature and Sources." *Current Bibliography of African Affairs.* 10 (1977-1978), 3-31.

Clarke, W. Sheldon. *A Developmental Bibliography for the Republic of Djibouti.* (Djibouti), (1979).

10. Equatorial Guinea

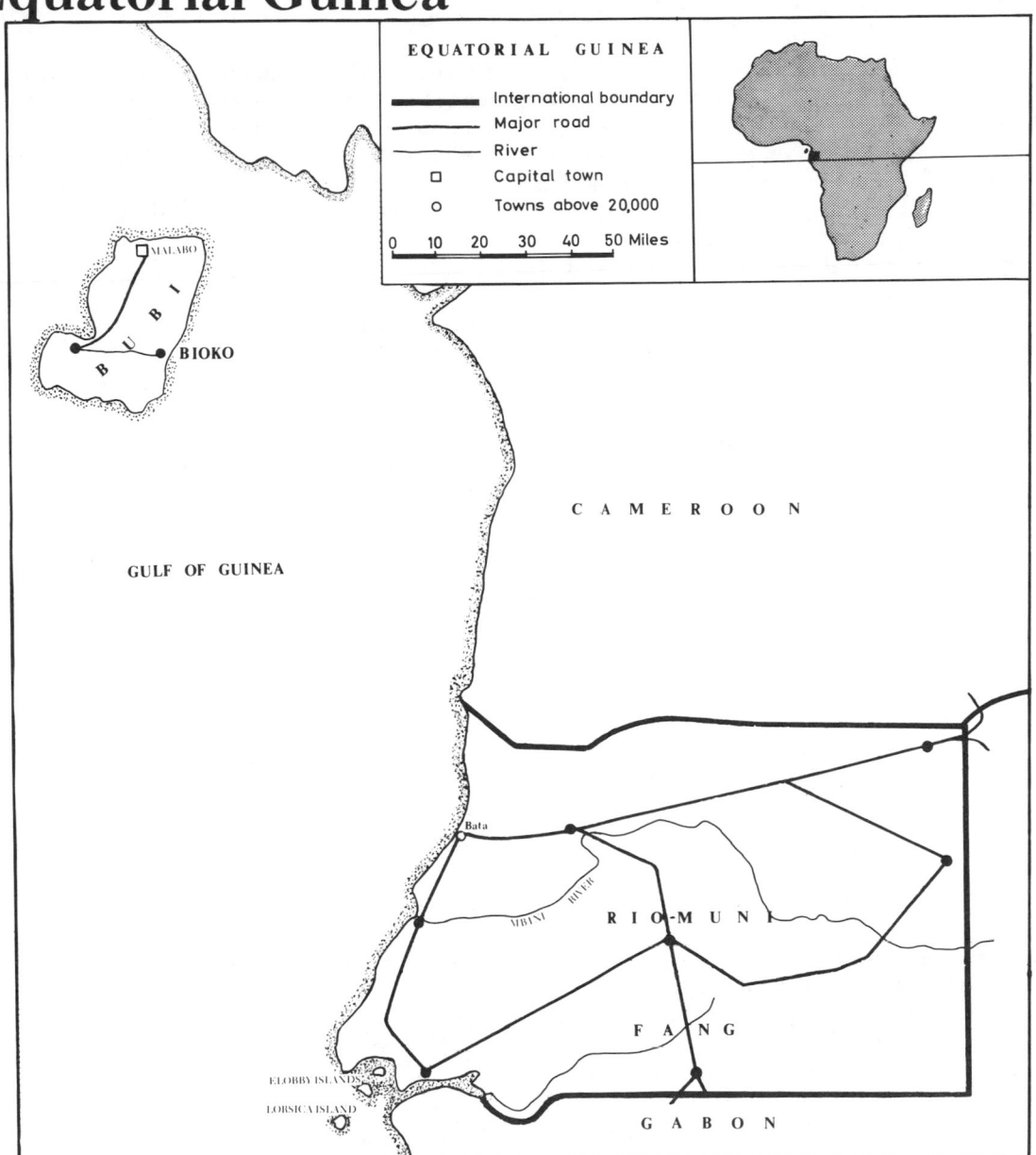

I. Basic Information

Date of Independence: October 12, 1968
Former Colonial Ruler: Spain
Change in Boundaries: The former Rio Muni and Fernando Po were merged.
Former Names: Rio Muni and Fernando Po
Estimated Population (1980): 340,000*
Area Size (equivalent in U.S.): 10,830 sq. mi. (Vermont)
Date of Last Census: 1960

Major Exports as Percent of Total Exports: no information available—principal exports are cocoa, coffee and timber

*Reports indicate that a large part of the country's population fled to neighboring countries (Gabon and Cameroon).

II. Ethnic Patterns

The major population group (90 percent) in Rio Muni is Fang. The Bubi on the island of Bioko* are the only other group in the country with more than five percent of the population. both are identity groups. There are small groups of Kombe, Balengue, and Bujeba along the Rio Muni coast. There had been a large Nigerian population (mainly from Eastern Nigeria) working on the plantations on Bioko. They numbered at least 30,000 in 1969, but this number fell to about 3,000 by 1973, and to virtually zero by 1978 because of conflicts in the country including disputes over working conditions on the plantations. In November 1975, the Nigerian government withdrew all Nigerian workers from the country because of the continuing allegations of mistreatment. Formerly a large Spanish population lived on Fernando Po and in Bata on the mainland, but virtually all had left by 1978. An important group on Bioko is the Fernandino (descendants of English-speaking Creoles) which despite its size (less than one percent) has played a major role in the history of the country until recently.

*Under the rule of Macias Nguema, the island of Fernando Po was named Macias Nguema. After his overthrow, the island was renamed Bioko.

TABLE 10.1   Ethnic Units Over 5 Percent of Country Population

Ethnic Unit	Estimated Ethnic Population 1980	Estimated Ethnic Percentage
a. Fang	289,000	85%
b. Bubi	34,000	10%

SOURCES: Murdock, *Africa*; *Africa South of the Sahara 1974*; *African Contemporary Record 1969—70*; because of the repatriation of the large Nigerian population to Nigeria, the Fang and Bubi percentages have increased from the previous 70% and 8% estimates respectively to the above estimates.

III. Language Patterns

In Rio Muni, the Fang constitute as much as 90% of the population and Fang is the primary language of the area. On Bioko, Bubi survives as a spoken language but the dominant language and also the *lingua franca* is pidgin-English (or Creole) which comes from the Fernandinos (descendants of English-speaking Creoles) and the large number of Eastern Nigerians who have traditionally supplied the main part of the labor force for the cocoa plantations which are the economic mainstay of the island. We estimated 85% Fang speakers, 10% Bubi and 5% pidgin-English. With the removal of the Nigerian workers, the pidgin percentage has decreased substantially from a previous level of 15%.

TABLE 10.2   Language Patterns

		Green-berg	Dalby
1. Primacy			
1st language	Fang (85%)		
2nd language	Bubi (10%)		
3rd language	Pidgin-English (5%)		
2. Linguistic classification (all ethnic units in country over 5%)			
	Fang	IA5	A7
	Bubi	IA5	A3
3. *Lingua franca*	Pidgin-English		
4. Official language	Spanish		

SOURCES: *Statesman's Yearbook 1974/75*

IV. Urban Patterns

Capital: Malabo (formerly Santa Isabel—founded 16th century)

Largest City: Bata

Dominant ethnicity/language of capital

    Major verncaular: Pidgin-English

    Major ethnic group: Bubi

    Major ethnic group as percent of capital's population:

TABLE 10.4   Cities of 20,000 and Over

City	Size	Date
Bata	50,000	1973
Malabo (formerly Santa Isabel)	23,000	1973

SOURCE: *Political Handbook of the World 1979.*

TABLE 10.3   Growth of Capital/Largest City

Date	Malabo (formerly Santa Isabel)	Bata
c. 1928	8,345[a]	
c. 1950	17,000[a]	
1957	20,000[a]	
1960	37,237[b]	27,000
1970	25,000[c]	
1973	23,000[d]	50,000

SOURCES:

    [a]Various editions of *Statesman's Yearbook*

    [b]*U.N. Demographic Yearbook 1972*

    [c]*Africa: South of the Sahara 1972*, p. 375

    [d]*Political Handbook of the World 1977*

V. Political Patterns

A. Political Parties and Elections

The first political party activity in Equatorial Guinea was inaugurated by left-leaning radical nationalists operating from bases in Gabon and the Cameroons about 1960. The main groups were the *Movimiento Nacional de Liberacion de la Guinea Ecuatorial* (MNLGE later renamed MONALIGE) and the *Idea Popular de la Guinea Ecuatorial* (IPGE). In 1963, the Spanish authorities allowed open political activity in the colony. The two parties based in Fernando Po were the *Bubi Union* (BU) and the *Union Democratical Fernandina* (UDF). Another new and moderate party centered around Bonifacio Ondo Edu was formed and named the *Movimiento de Union Nacional de la Guinea Ecuatorial* (MUNGE). This party held power from 1964 until independence. At independence, Macias Nguema's MONALIGE-based coalition narrowly defeated Edu's party and Macias Nguema became President. All parties were merged in 1970 by Macias Nguema into the *Partido Unico Nacional* (PUN) which later was renamed the *Partido Unico Nacional de los Trabajadores* (PUNT). No election has been held since independence in 1968, and the Fang-dominated regime under the leadership of Macias Nguema instituted a highly repressive government characterized by constant allegations of plots and attempted coups, usually blamed on foreigners or 'imperialist elements' and widespread terrorism. An illegal opposition movement, the *National Alliance for the Restoration of Democracy* (ANRD) was founded in August 1974 composed of remnants of MONALIGE, MUNGE, and the Bubi Union. Another opposition group, the *Equatorial Guinea Liberation Front* (EGLF) was formed by exiles. Since the overthrow of Nguema, political activity has been minimal.

B. Political Leadership

Macias Nguema was elected President at independence in October 1968 after his coalition narrowly won the September elections. He replaced Bonifacio Edu who had led the government from 1964 to independence. Macias' youth groups were largely responsible for the violent riots aimed at the Spanish community in February 1969. Most of the Spanish community left at this time. An attempted coup the next month was followed by a violent repression of any political opposition and the institution of a closed society which allowed no political opposition to exist. Macias was proclaimed Life President by the

PUNT in 1972 and continued to rule without legal opposition until the coup. A plot against Macias was discovered in June 1979. On August 3, 1979, however, Macias Nguema was overthrown in a bloodless military coup led by his cousin Lt. Colonel Teodor Obiang Nguema who assumed control of the country.

TABLE 10.5   **Heads of Government (Post Independence)**

Name	Dates in Office	Age (1982)	Ethnicity	Education	Former Occupation
1. Francisco Macias Nguema* (President)	1968— 1979	Executed in Sept. 1979— age 55	Fang	Local Catholic Mission Schools	Farmer, Colonial service, Party organizer
2. Col. Teodor Obiang Nguema Mbasogo (President)	Aug. 3, 1979— present	36	Fang (Essengui)	Secondary School (Bata) Military school (Saragosse)	Soldier

TABLE 10.6   **Cabinet Membership: Distribution by Ethnic Group**

Ethnicity*	Independence Cabinet	1972 Cabinet
1. Fang (70%)	64%	64%
2. Bubi (8)	36	36
3. Others (13)		
N =	11	11

*Ethnic units arranged in rank order of size within country with the unit's percent of national population in parentheses.

FIGURE 10.1   Political Parties and Elections   EQUATORIAL   GUINEA

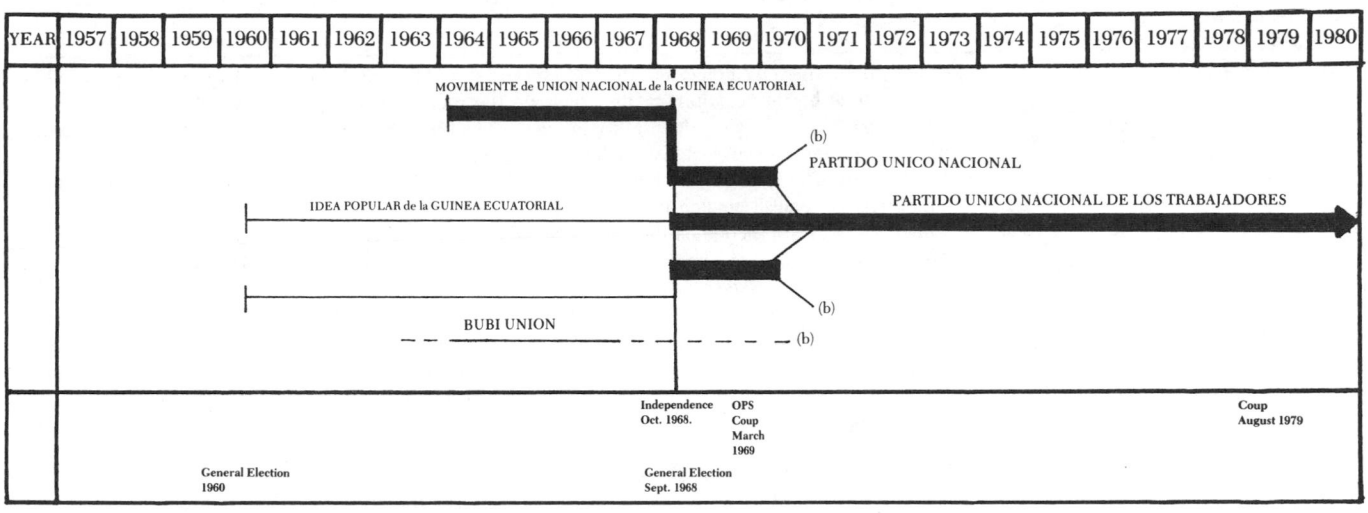

VI. National Integration and Stability

Although independent only since 1968 the country has had a history of conflict beginning a few months after independence, with clashes over the role of the Spanish community. Most of the Spaniards left the country shortly thereafter. Most Europeans, and, more recently, Nigerians have also left, leaving the economy and government in difficult straits.

An attempted coup led by the foreign minister, Ndongo, in 1969, was followed by the institution of a one-party state a year later, and the declaration of Macias Nguema as Life President in July 1972. Continuing political uncertainties deter foreign aid and investment. The ANRD asserts that 93 opposition leaders and senior civil servants were murdered by the Macias Nguema regime. Early in 1980, the UN Commission on Human Rights criticized the new government for not moving fast enough to restore democratic procedures and human rights.

TABLE 10.7   Elite Instability

Event and Date	Characteristics
1. Attempted Coup March 5, 1969	a. *Description*: Messrs. Ndongo and Ibougo returned from Spain and after an unsuccessful appeal to Macias to abide by the constitution, they blew up the radio station, took over Government House and proclaimed Ndongo as President. Macias rallied his youth movement and retook the government buildings. Ndongo and Ibougo were later killed or died in prison. b. *Participants*: The Foreign Minister, Atonasio Ndongo, the UN delegate, Saturnino Ibougo, and others supported by Spanish and non-Fang elements on Fernando Po. c. *Apparent Causes*: Reaction on the part of the non-Fang population of Fernando Po to the rapid movement by Macias Nguema to populate the civil service with Fang from Rio Muni and a campaign of terror against the Spanish, Nigerian and Bubi populations.
2. Coup March 15-20, 1969	a. *Description*: Macias Nguema suspends the constitution and takes full powers b. *Participants*: Macias Nguema backed by the "Guinean Youth" movement. c. c. *Apparent Causes*: In reaction to the attempted coup of two weeks earlier and the widespread opposition to his rule among the non-Fang population of Fernando Po (later renamed Macias Nguema).
3. Coup August 3, 1979	a. *Description*: A bloodless military coup led by Lt. Col. Teodoro Obiang Nguema overthrew Macias Nguema. b. *Participants*: Lt. Col. Teodoro Obiang Nguema and members of the military. c. *Apparent Causes*: Uncertain, but probably in reaction to the massive killings and terror tactics of the Macias regime.

TABLE 10.10   Annual Instability Events: Independence Through 1979—Equatorial Guinea

Year	'61	'62	'63	'64	'65	'66	'67	'68	'69	'70	'71	'72	'73	'74	'75	'76	'77	'78	'79
ELITE INSTABILITY																			
Assassinations																			
Plots													1						1
Attempted Coups d'État									1										
Coups d'État									1										1
COMMUNAL INSTABILITY																			
Ethnic Violence																			
Irredentism																			
Rebellion																			
Civil War																			
MASS INSTABILITY																			
Revolt																			
Revolution																			
TURMOIL																			
Demonstrtions																			
Strikes (no. days)																			
Riots (no. days)																			
Terrorism																			
Declarations of Emergency																			

Year	'61	'62	'63	'64	'65	'66	'67	'68	'69	'70	'71	'72	'73	'74	'75	'76	'77	'78	'79

CABINET INSTABILITY

	'68	'69	'70	'71	'72
Realloc. and new appts.					
New members	12				
Resig. and Dismissals					
No. of members (max.)					
(maximum in year)	10	10	10	10	10

VII. Selected References

BIBLIOGRAPHY

Berman, S. *Spanish Guinea: An Annotated Bibliography*. Washington, D.C.: Catholic University Libraries, 1961.

Liniger-Goumaz, M. *Historical Dictionary of Equatorial Guinea*. Metuchen, N.J.: The Scarecrow Press, Inc., 1979.

Liniger-Goumaz, M. *Guinea Ecuatorial: Bibliografia General*. Bern: Commu. Natu. Suisse UNESCO, 2nd. edition (no date); 1st edition (1974).

GENERAL

Great Britain Foreign Office Historical Section. *Spanish and Italian Possessions: Independent States.* New York: Greenwood Press, 1969.

Pelissier, René. *Etudes Hispano-guineennes*. Paris: 1967.

Pelissier, René. *Los Territorios Espanoles de Africa*. Madrid: C.S.I.C., 1964.

Pelissier, René. "Spanish Guinea—An Introduction." *Race*, 6 (October 1964): 117—128.

POLITICAL

"African Political Parties in Equatorial Africa, 1968." *Africa Report*, (March 1968).

Pelissier, René. "Uncertainties in Spanish Guinea." *Africa Report* (March 1968): 16—18.

ECONOMIC

International Monetary Fund. "Equatorial Guinea" in *Surveys of African Economies*, vol. 5. Washington, D.C.: I.M.F., 1973.

Kobel, Armen Eric. *La Republique de Guinée équatoriale*. Berne, Copy Quick, 1976.

Pelissier, R. "Autopsy of a Miracle." *Africa Report*, 1970, no. 75, pp. 10—14.

11. Ethiopia

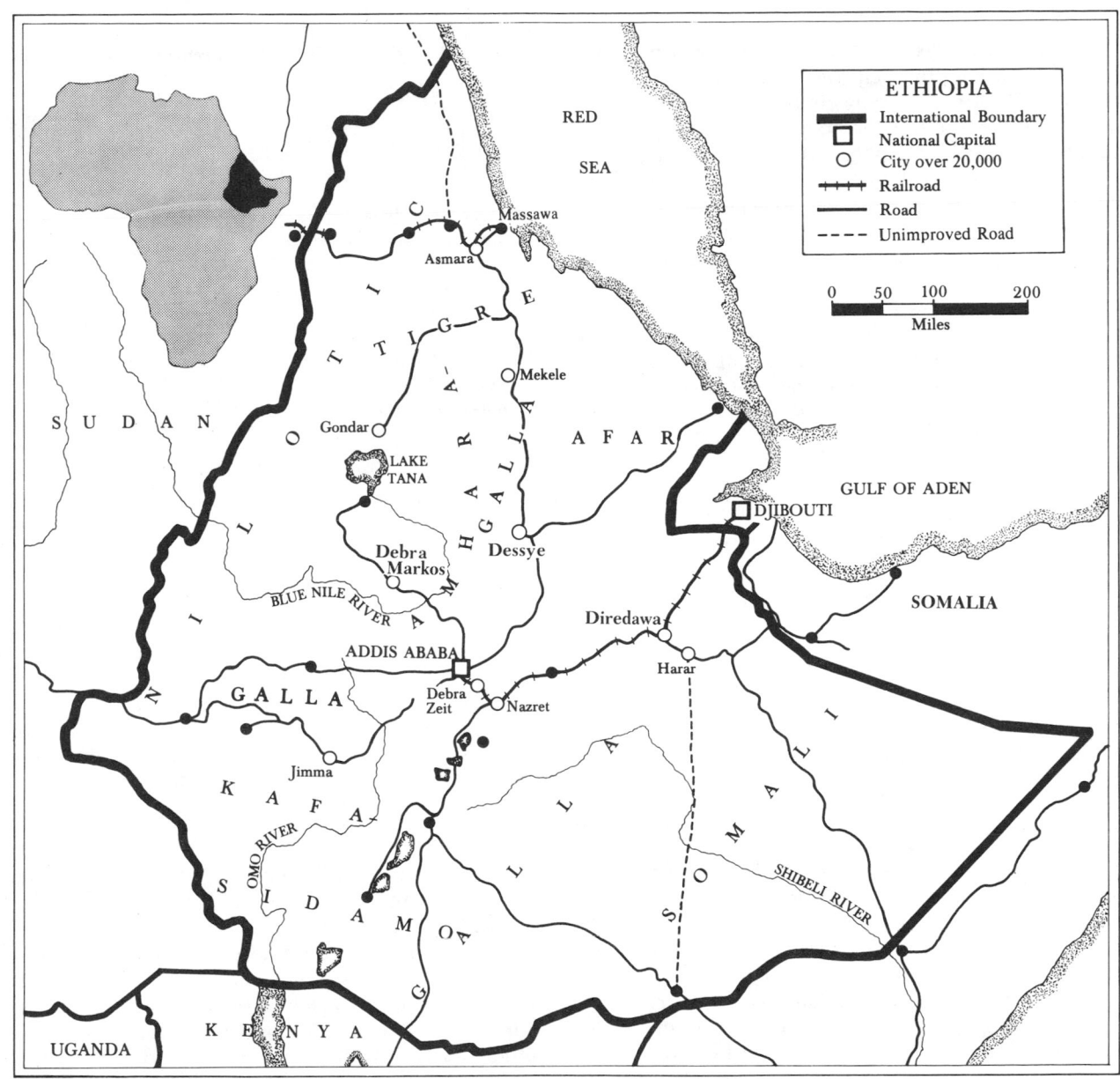

I. Basic Information

Date of Independence: Ancient kingdom
Former Colonial Ruler: None
Change in Boundaries: Eritrea added in 1952
Former Name: Both Ethiopia and Abyssinia are ancient names for the nation
Estimated Population (1980): 33,598,000

Area Size (equivalent in U.S.): 471,778 sq. mi. (Texas and Montana)
Date of Last Census: None ever held
Major Exports 1976 as Percent of Total Exports: coffee—56 percent; hides and skins—9 percent; pulses (seeds)—10 percent; oil seeds—5 percent.

II. Ethnic Patterns

The ethnic categories for Ethiopia are based on mixed levels of inclusion. In each case the groups comprising the categories are culturally and lingusitically related. The Galla (increasingly referred to as the Oromo), Somali and Afar are identity groups, as are the Amhara-Tigre (excluding the related Gurage and Harati). It should be noted that the Galla, Somali, and Afar have considerable cultural and lingusitic similarities and can be subsumed under a more general Eastern Cushitic category. In addition to these major groups there are populations of Agans (75,000), Saho-speaking peoples of Eritrea (43,000—1943 estimate), and the nomadic Ben-Amer. Since a census has never been carried out in Ethiopia, all population figures are estimates whose reliability is not ascertainable.

TABLE 11.1   Ethnic Units Over 5 Percent of Country Population

Ethnic Unit	Estimated Ethnic Population 1980	Estimated Ethnic Percentage
a. Galla (Oromo)	13,439,000	40%
1. Borana, 2. Jima, 3. Kosa		
4. Gera, 5. Guma, 6. Arushi,		
7. Walaga, 8. Wallo, 9. Yaju,		
10. Raya		
b. Amhara-Tigre (Abyssinian)	10,079,000	32%
1. Amhara, 2. Tigre,		
Related groups: 3. Gurage,		
4. Harari		
c. Kafa-Sidamo Type	3,024,000	9%
1. Bako, 2. Gibe, 3. Gimira,		
4. Janjero, 5. Kafa,		
6. Kambatta, 7. K'onso,		
8. Maji, 9. Ometo, 10. Sidamo		
d. Somali	2,016,000	6%
e. Nilotic Cluster	2,016,000	6%
1. K'unama and Barya		
2. Beni-Sciangul		
i. Guma, ii. Berta,		
iii. Koma, iv. Mao		
f. Afar (Danakil)	1,680,000	5%

SOURCE: G. F. Lipsky, *Ethiopia: Its People, Its Society, Its Culture* (New Haven, Conn.: HRAF Press, 1963), pp. 35—51; modified according to suggestions from Professor Asmaron Legesse, Boston University.

III. Language Patterns

All the major languages of Ethiopia belong to the Afro-Asiatic language family. The two main substocks in Ethiopia are (1) Semitic (e.g., Amharic, Tigrinya, Tigre, Gurage, Harari), and, (2) Cushitic (e.g., Gallinya, Beja, Somali, Afar, Agau). The two major languages of Ethiopia are Amharic and Gallinya. Amharic is closely related to the ancient language of the Kingdom of Axum—called Ge'ez—which still serves as the liturgical language of the Ethiopian Coptic Church. Amharic itself has few dialectical variations. Gallinya, by contrast, has a number of dialects: (1) Macha (spoken by ethnic groups such as the Macha, Kaffas, and Gibes—all in the west and southwest); (2) Tulama (the dialect of Shoa); (3) Eastern Gallinya (spoken by Galla groups in Harar and Arusi); (4) Southern Gallinya (spoken by the Borana). An extensive literature exists in Amharic and Tigrinya. Because of the increased use of Amharic as a *lingua franca* it is difficult to estimate its actual distribution. Kloss (1968) puts the figures at 32 percent; Demoz (1968) puts the figure at 35 percent (of whom one-third are non-Amharic peoples); Rustow puts the figure at 49 percent; whereas Knappert goes as high as 71 percent. Part of the discrepancy is ambiguity over the level, or standard, of proficiency. Likewise, with regard to Gallinya, Rustow puts the figure at 23 percent, while Kloss puts it at 44 percent. In assessing these and other sources, we have put the Amharic-speaking population at 40 percent and the Gallinya-speaking population at approximately 50 percent.

Amharic (or Amharinya) is the official language, and English has been the primary foreign language. Due to ideological changes and the new political links with the USSR and Cuba it is not clear if English will continue in its role. Amharic is used in government and trade throughout most of Ethiopia, although Tigrinya (and Arabic) is used in government and trade in Eritrea. English has been replaced by Amharic as the medium of instruction through the sixth grade, and it is likely that Amharic will be used in secondary schools as well. Tigrinya is the only vernacular other than Amharic which has a script, although Gallinya and Tigre have been written in the Ethiopic script. At present, the only vernacular (other than Amharic) used in radio broadcasting is the Somali language. On the other hand, Radio Mogadishu (Somalia) broadcasts into Ethiopia in Gallinya.

TABLE 11.2   Languge Patterns

1. Primacy			
1st language	Gallinya	(50%)	
2nd language	Amharic	(40%)	
			Green-berg	Dalby
2. Linguistic classification (all ethnic units in country over 5%)	Galla	IIID3	02B
	Amhara-Tigre	IIIA	01C
	Kafa-Sidamo	IIID3	02H
	Somali	IIID3	02A
	Nilotic	IIIE3	74, 75
	Afar	IIID3	02P
3. *Lingua francas*	Amharic, Gallinya, Tigrinya		
4. Official language	Amharic		

SOURCES: Abraham Demoz, "Amharic for Modern Use," *Journal of the Faculty of Education*, Haile Selassie University (1968), pp. 15—20. Heinz Kloss, "Notes Concerning a Language-Nation Typology," in *Language Problems of Developing Nations*, eds. Joshua Fishman, Charles Ferguson, and Jyotirindra Das Gupta (New York: John Wiley, 1968), pp. 69—88.

IV. Urban Patterns

Capital/largest city: Addis Ababa (founded 1886)
Dominant ethnicity/language of capital
   Major vernacular: Amharic[1]
   Major ethnic group: Galla[2]
   Major ethnic group as percent of capital's population: 53 percent (1952)

[1]Jan Knappert, "Language Problems of the New Nations of Africa," *African Quarterly*, 5 (1965), 95—105.
[2]*African Urban Notes*, May 1967.

TABLE 11.3   Growth of Capital/Largest City

Date	Addis Ababa
1921	ca. 50,000
1930	ca. 70,000
1940	ca. 150,000
1950	ca. 300,000
1966	640,000 UA
1971	851,610 UA
1972	912,090 UA
1974	1,046,260 UA
1975	1,120,550 UA

SOURCE: Various editions of the *Statesman's Yearbook, Africa South of the Sahara 1974, 1975,* and *1977—78* editions, and *Europa Yearbook 1979.*

TABLE 11.4   Cities of 20,000 and Over*

City	Size	Date
Addis Ababa	1,104,500	1977
Asmara	352,700	1977
Dire Dawa	80,000	1977
Nazret	70,000	1977
Gondar	68,000	1977
Jimma	63,000	1977
Harar	59,000	1977
Dessie	57,000	1977
Debra Zeit	45,000	1977
Mekele	40,000	1977
Akaki	35,000	1977
Debra Markos	34,000	1977
Humera	33,000	1977
Keren	32,000	1977
Bahs Dar	31,000	1977

SOURCE: *Africa South of the Sahara 1980—81.*

*Current populations for Ethiopian cities, other than Addis Ababa, were unavailable until the Ethiopian government began a series of sample surveys aimed at establishing the *de facto* civil population of all cities over 5,000. In 1965, 21 towns with populations of over 10,000 were covered and Addis Ababa was surveyed in 1966. For a brief report of these surveys see *Sample Surveys of Current Interest*, statistical papers series C, no. 12 (New York: United Nations, 1967), pp. 80—84.

V. Political Patterns

A. Political Parties and Elections

There are no legal political parties in Ethiopia. Political pressures were expressed through factions within and without the government of the former Emperor. Popular elections to the Ethiopian Chamber of Deputies were introduced in an Electoral Law Proclamation of 1956 and elections were held every four years from 1957 through 1973.

There are a large number of illegal and quasi-legal political groups operating in the country. One category of such groups is that associated with various secessionist movements of which there are two major movements (Eritrean and Somali secession) and several minor ones (Afar, Tigreans, Oromo [Galla]). The Eritrean opposition groups have proliferated in the 1970's. The original group, the Muslim-led *Eritrean Liberation Front* (ELF) formed in Cairo by conservative Eritrean Moslem politicians who lost their jobs when Ethiopia absorbed Eritrea in 1962, has been backed by various conservative Arab countries (Egypt, Saudi Arabia, Syria, the Gulf States and more recently the Sudan) but has been losing its membership and support to the more politically active, Marxist oriented, and originally Christian- led but increasingly Muslim, *Eritrean People's Liberation Front* (EPLF). A smaller group backed by Iraq is the ELF *People's Liberation Forces* (ELF-PLF) which split from the EPLF but it is relatively weak and has, in principle, agreed to union with the ELF under Arab and particularly Sudanese pressure. There has been strong pressure from Arab countries particularly Sudan, for the unification of all the Eritrean movements, although there does seem to be some ambiguity on the part of the conservative Arab states in having a Marxist-oriented country on the shores of the Red Sea. Many of the backers of the Eritreans are particulary concerned with the Soviet Union's presence in the area and might prefer a non-Marxist Ethiopian govenment ruling a semi-autonomous Eritrea.

In the Ogaden region in the southeast and east of the country, inhabited primarily by nomadic members of Somali ethncity, the Western Somali Liberation Front (WSLF) (renamed the *Somali Fatherland Liberation Front* (SELF) on July 30, 1977) operates with the active support of Somalia. Somalia, as a basic principle of national policy, is trying to unite all ethnic Somalis under one flag (including those in northeast Kenya and Djibouti). This group with the massive support of the Somali army had captured all of the Ogaden and some Ethiopian highland cities such as Harrar and Diredawa by early 1978 when a massive Soviet-supplied Ethiopian and Cuban force pushed them back to the Somali border. The WSLF continues to control effectively much of the sparsely populated Ogaden, however, and this threat to Ethiopian integrity continues.

TABLE 11.5   Head of Government

Name	Dates in Office	Age (1982)	Ethnicity	Education	Former Occupation
1. His Imperial Majesty Haile Selassie I (Emperor)	1930—74	d. on 27 August 1975 age 83	Amhara-Tigre (Amhara)	Private tutors	None
2. General Aman M. Andom (Chairman of Provisional Military Government)	Sept. to Nov. 1974	Murdered Nov. 1974 unknown age	Amhara-Tigre (Tigre)	Sandhurst	Soldier
3. Brigadier General Teferi Bante (Chairman of Provisional Military Administrative Council)	Nov. 1974— Feb. 1977	executed in 1977 age 50	Galla	Military School	Soldier
4. Lt. Col. Mengistu Haile-Mariam (Chairman of Dergue (the Military Provisional Administrative Council (PMAC)	Feb. 1977— present	45	Amhara-Tigre (Amhara)	Holeta Military Academy (Ethiopia)	Soldier

TABLE 11.6   Cabinet Membership: Distribution by Ethnic Unit*

Ethnicity	Independence Cabinet**	1967 Cabinet**	1972 Cabinet**
1. Galla (40%)	13%	9%	9%
2. Amhara-Tigre (30)	88	91	91
3. Kafa-Sidamo (9)	9	0	0
4. Somali (6)	0	0	
5. Nilotic (6)	0	0	0
6. Afar (5)	0	0	0
7. Other (4)	0	0	
N =	8	23	23

*Ethnic units arranged in rank order of size within country with the unit's percent of national population in parentheses.

**The "Cabinet" is taken to be the Council of Ministers and "Independence" is treated for comparable purposes as 1960.

Within the country there are several illegal groups which are actively fighting the government. They span the ideological spectrum from the far right to the left of the Marxist Dergue. The anti-Marxist front called the *Ethiopian Democratic Union* (EDU) was formed in 1975 by liberals exiled during Haile Selassie's regime and subsequently was joined by professionals; soldiers fleeing the new regime; and various elements of the semi-feudal Selassie regime including members of the old government, the aristocracy, and the Coptic Church. Primarily based in Gondar (formerly Bagemder), Tigre and Gojjam provinces, the EDU attracted local leaders, and was backed by Sudan and other Arab states who wanted to see the downfall of the Marxist Dergue. A much smaller Marxist group also operated in Tigre province and is called the *Tigre Peoples Liberation Front* (TPLF) but both the EDU and TPLF have suffered considerable losses against the Ethiopian army and the Dergue's people's military. Operating mainly in the principal cities, the illegal *Marxist Ethiopian People's Revolutionary Party* (EPRP) set up in 1976 draws its support from militant students and trade unions as well as sympathizers in the civil service and army. The PRP mounted a major urban guerrilla opposition to the Dergue which the EPRP maintains cannot lead the country to a Marxist state. Its military wing is called the *Ethiopian People's Revolutionary Army* (EPRA).

There are five quasi-legal political groups which are allowed to operate privately by the Dergue. The major group which advised the military council is the Marxist *All-Ethiopia Socialist Movement* (MASON) composed of intellectuals and trade unionists which supported a mixed civilian-military regime until sufficient civilian mobilization can take place and the military leadership is no longer necessary to the continuance of the regime's goals. MASON leaders went into opposition to the Men-

gistu regime in July 1977, however, and their leaders fled the country. A part of the group remains uder the name *Red Torch*. An offshoot of MASON is the *Revolutionary Flame* (Abyod SEDID) organized by Col. Mengistu as an elite counter insurgency force to deal with the urban guerrillas of EPRP. Other groups are the *Labor League* (WOZADER), *Revolutionary Movement for the Oppressed* (Eech-At), and the *Marxist-Leninist Organization* (MALERID). all are informally allowed to discuss political topics and circulate position papers but they are not allowed to debate publicly or solicit members. In August 1977 an attempt to consolidate these groups under an umbrella organization called the *Organization of Ethiopian Progressives* (EPD) resulted in further fragmentation and a new military-based group, the *Revolutionary Sword* (Abyot Seif), was formed as a counter to Mengistu's SEDED. Since Col. Atnafu was associated with Abyot Seif, it has been considerably weakened by his execution.

In 1978 fragmentation of political groups continued with an offshoot of the EDU, the *Ethiopian People's Democratic Revolutionary Party* (EPDRP) linking in coalition with the TPLF, and a breakaway from the EPRP was the group calling itself the *20th Century Bolsheviks*. Meanwhile the EPLF and the TPLF seemed to be coordinating their activities while purges and executions continued to be a way of life in and out of the government.

B. Political Leadership

The government of Ethiopia under Haile Selassie was difficult to compare to the governments of other African countries. Although opposition from students and intellectuals had been building since the mid-1960's the personal rule of the Emperor, Haile Selassie, had, until his overthrow in 1974, changed little for many years, although the prominence of different formal agencies—the Ministry of the Pen, His Imperial Majesty's Private Cabinet, the Crown Council, and the Council of Ministers—had changed over time. The Council of Ministers had been particularly important since the attempted coup d'état in 1960. In 1966, the Prime Minister was given the authority to "propose" ministerial appointments, and the Council obtained the ambiguous power to make decisions which do not affect "matters of policy." With the addition of two new portfolios in 1966, the membership of the Council stood at nineteen. Office-holders have always been overwhelmingly from the Amhara people. By early 1974, revolts in the military followed by labor and student strikes brought several governments down and steadily eroded the Emperor's authority until he was finally unable to prevent a total seizure of power by elements of the armed forces. Since the overthrow of Haile Seassie in September 1974 the Provisional Military Government (PMG) has held power. Power was intitally held by middle rank officers in the Armed Forces Coordinating Committee, the Dergue, who avoided public exposure. General Aman Andom was made chairman of the PMG in September 1974 after the ouster of Haile Selasie but was murdered by a group in the Dergue led by Major Mengistu after he refused to maintain a militant policy towards the Eritrean Liberation Front (ELF) and to sanction summary execution of those arrested by the army for corruption and other offenses. The execution of General Aman Andom was accompanied by a mass execution of members of the former government and the aristocracy. This turned out to be the beginning of a series of purges which continued with increasing frequency in subsequent years and which played a major role in the determining of political leadership. General Teferi Bante succeeded General Aman but the real power remained with the Armed Forces Coordinating Committee.

The major figures behind the increasingly radical orientation of the govenrment were two army Majors, Mengistu and Atnafu. In late 1976 Mengistu was shorn of many of his powers and he reacted by executing his opponents including General Teferi and becoming the new head of state. Lt. Col. Mengistu (promoted in December 1976) argued against compromise with the various Marxist opposition groups and insisted that the military must lead the way to a Marxist state. Already the society has seen massive land nationalization particularly of the large church and aristocratic holdings, organization of the society into community action groups called *Kekeles* and the eradication of any form of substantial dissent. Col. Mengistu had Col. Atnafu, his close colleague through the 1974—77 events, executed in November 1977 and rules unchallenged from within the Dergue. In February 1980 two members of the Dergue were purged, charged with corruption.

VI. National Integration and Stability

Until 1974, the ancient empire of Ethiopia was ruled by a monarchy which traces its descent from King Solomon. The Amhara people, (the Emperor was an Amhara) are only one of several major ethnic groups in Ethiopia, however. Furthermore, the fact that the Amhara are Coptic Christian, and several of the other major groups (e.g., Galla [Oromo] and Somali) are predominantly Muslim has been a longstanding potential source of cleavage. Yet, until the United Nations arranged the merger of Eritrea with Ethiopia (1952) and the birth of the Somali Republic (early 1960's), there was relatively little communal instability in Ethiopia. In this Handbook, we have coded

the long-standing secession movement in Eritrea, the irredentist movement of the Somalis, and the smaller irredentist movements of the Afar, Oromo, and Tigre which have been spawned by the revolution.

Successful elite coups (drawing on members of the royal family) have been a part of Ethiopian history. In modern times, the perseverence of the Emperor, Haile Selassie I, was legendary. Until the 1974 coup there had been only one recent unsuccessful coup attempt which was in 1960. The Ethiopian press reported several coup "plots" since 1960, but details of their magnitude are unavailable. From the mid-1960's onwards opposition to

TABLE 11.7   Elite Instability

Event and Date	Characteristics
1. Coup Attempt December 14—17, 1960	a. *Description*: Brigadier-General Mengistu Neway, Commander of the Imperial Body Guard, and his brother Germame Neway, governor of Jijiga, were the organizers of the coup. The Emperor was out of the country at the time, but returned, and—with the aid of loyal army and air force troops—ousted the rebels after a three-day battle. b. *Participants*: Imperial Body Guard, plus various younger elements in the army, government, and police. c. *Apparent Causes*: According to the Revolutionary Proclamation which was drawn up by the leaders of the coup and proclaimed over the national radio, apparently by the Crown Prince, "There has been no progress....A few self-centered persons....have chosen to indulge in selfishness and nepotism. The Ethiopia people hope to be freed from...ignorance, illiteracy and poverty." The proclamation promised land redistribution.
2. Coup d'État November 22, 1974	a. *Description*: General Aman Andom is attacked at his home and murdered. b. *Participants*: Security forces under orders from other members of the Provisional Military Government. c. *Apparent Causes*: General Aman Andom's refusals to allow summary executions by the army and to order that more troops be sent to forcibly suppress the continuing Eritrea Liberation Front's attacks. General Aman Andom was a Tigrean Christian from Eritrea.

Event and Date	Characteristics
3. Coup d'État February 3, 1977	a. *Description*: Seven officers of the ruling military council including its chairman and head-of-state General Teferi Bante as well as various civilian supporters were killed by Cols. Mengistu and Atnafu and their troops in what was described as a shoot-out but which appears to have been an execution of members of the Dergue opposed to the increasing power of Cols. Mengistu and Atnafu. b. *Participants*: Cols. Mengistu and Atnafu and troops loyal to them. c. *Apparent Causes*: In December 1976, Col. Mengistu was shorn of much of the power that he had in the ruling military council by those afraid of his increasing dominance of the regime. The coup was a successful attempt to eliminate much of the opposition to his policies and personal power. The eliminated leaders also appeared to by trying to come to some agreement with the EPRP which policy was opposed by Lt. Col. Mengistu.
4. Coup d'État November 12, 1977	a. *Description*: Lt. Col. Atnafu Abate the vice-chairman of the Provisional Military Advisory Council, the Dergue was ordered executed by Lt. Col. Mengistu. These two men had been the primary force behind the Dergue from its inception and close colleagues in the purges that had progressively eliminated opposition to their rule. Col. Atnafu remained the last obstacle to a complete concentration of power in the hands of Col. Mengistu. b. *Participants*: Col. Mengistu and his troops. c. *Apparent Causes*: Col. Atnafu while occupying the second place in the government remained a constant threat as a replacement for Col. Mengistu. By eliminating Col. Atnafu, Col. Mengistu would have no significant competitors for power within the Dergue.

SOURCES: Richard Greenfield, *Ethiopia* (New York: Praeger, 1965), pp. 337—452. See also Christopher Clapham, "The Ethiopian Coup d'État of December 1960," *Journal of Modern African Studies*, 6 (1968): 498—508. *Africa Research Bulletin.*

Haile Selasie's regime from university students had grown to major proportions. In 1969, the university and secondary-school students boycotted classes and the university was closed. In December 1969, a number of university students were killed in clashes with the police in Addis Ababa. The events leading to the September 1974 coup were particularly confusing. They began with army mutinies over pay in February 1974 followed by strikes of trade unions, teachers, priests, and sections of the armed forces through the succeeding months. Two new prime ministers were sworn in but gradually the Emperor's powers were peeled away leading to a steady diminution of his authority but without directly attacking him until his overthrow in September 1974. The events that followed the overthrow of Haile Sellasie have involved virtually every type of political instability imaginable. The irredentist conflict in Eritrea that had begun in 1962 and slowed in the early 1970's gained enormous ground and controlled the vast majority of the province by 1980. In the beginning of 1980, the two major Eritrean groups, the Eritrean People's Liberation Front and the Eritrean Liberation Front, inflicted serious defeats on the Ethiopian army forcing them to retreat to the sea. The Somali nomads in the Ogaden region began to get backing from the Somali government in 1974 and by 1980 had occupied all of the area they claimed as part of Somalia as well as some parts of the Ethiopian highlands. Reports from February 1980 state that Somali regular troops have been fighting in the Ogaden region along with the Somali no-

mads. Several new irredentist movements were encouraged by the Ethiopian Revolution, namely the groups representing the Oromo (Galla), Tigre, and the Afars.

While these communal instability events grew in magnitude so did elite instability. Purges and plots became almost everyday events in the 1974—78 period. Mass executions and coups d'état occurred. There were two plots reported by the government in 1976 but it is thought that many more existed. Strikes and demonstrations became endemic and as many as 500 university students were executed in one mass execution following a demonstration in May 1977. The Dergue has increasingly come under the direction of one man, Col. Mengistu, committed to the building of a Marxist state under military leadership. The mass instability that has resulted from attempts to mobilize the population for this goal has been enormous. Opposition both from the left and right of the Dergue's policies has made assassination commonplace throughout the years since the coming to power of the Dergue. The 1977 entry of Soviet and Cuban influence, manpower, and supplies seems to have stabilized the situation for the short run but the semi-feudal empire held together by ethnic loyalties and political skill by the Emperor has been permanently replaced by a society that will have to deal with the legacy of problems from the Emperor's regime. Large amounts of Soviet military aid, however, have not subdued the various secessionist movements in Eritrea Province.

TABLE 11.8   Communal Instability

Event and Date	Characteristics
1. Civil War and Un-successful Secession ca. 1973 to present.	a. *Description*: Eritrea was an Italian colony until 1941; a British-administered territory (1941—1952); a semi-autonomous state federated with Ethiopia (1952—1962); and a province of Ethiopia (1962—present). An Eritrean secessionist movement started a few years after the federation of Eritrea with Ethiopia in 1942 and has continued in sporadic form. Although the secessionist movement has only recently become an all-out campaign on the scale of the Katanga or the Biafra civil wars, widespread disturbances have occurred throughout the 1960's and 1970's and by 1980 all but a few cities were in the hands of the liberation groups. In 1962 the Ethiopian government abolished the federal status of Eritrea. From this time (1962), Eritrea has been a province under the centralized administration of the Ethiopian government. *The Eritrean Liberation Front* (ELF) formed in 1962 has received help from a number of Arab states including Syria, Saudi Arabia, Egypt and the Sudan. Early ELF tactics included the hijacking of an Ethiopian commercial airliner in September 1969. While the ELF seemed to be under control by the Ethiopian government by 1971, it resurfaced with renewed strength in 1973, apparently with Christian as well as Muslim support. It became increasingly effective as the revolution shook the center of the country and by early 1975 (February) was able to lay siege to Asmara, the second largest city in the country and the capital of Eritrea. By 1978, Asmara was reported to be a ghost town occupied primarily by 25,000 Ethiopian troops. A major Ethiopian offensive in 1978 forced the rebels back to the mountainous northern regions of Eritrea. During 1979 and 1980, however, the Eritreans gained substantial victories and by mid-1980 were fighting the Ethiopians along the Red Sea. Calls for peace negotiations have been made by Sudan, but their chances for success are uncertain and fighting continues in 1982. b. *Participants*: Initially, mainly the Muslim ethnic groups in Eritrea (e.g., Beni-Amer, Danakil). Now many Christians are to be found among the ELF and at least one of the top leaders is a Tigre Christian. The ELF Marxist and more politically active split-off group from the ELF called the Eritrean Peoples Liberation Front (EPLF). The EPLF was originally seen as a Christian breakaway from the ELF but it has become increasingly Muslim and the religious differences between the groups are slight. A third and much smaller group, the People's Liberation Front (ELF-PLF) is a break away from the EPLF but attempts in 1977 by Sudan and other Arab countries have produced a formal agreement of merger between the ELF and ELF-PLF, but the ideological differences with the EPLF and the increasing success of that group have, up to mid-1980, prevented the successful maintenance of a unified Eritrean liberation group. The silent partners in this activity are the various conservative and moderate Arab states in the area who want Muslim states on the Red Sea. Libya and South Yemen back the Ethiopian government but the other Arab countries each back one of the liberation groups. c. *Apparent Causes*: From the government's point of view, secession poses a threat to national unity and is interpreted as foreign (Arab) interference in Ethiopian internal affairs. Eritrea also offers Ethiopia two important seaports at Massawa and Assab. The secessionists, on the other hand, are concerned with denial of self-determination for Eritreans, and domination of Muslims by Christians. Many felt that the Federation was a failure because Eritrea was in fact governed just like another province.
2. Irredentism and Attempted Secession 1974—present	a. *Description*: Somali ethnic segments in Ethiopia, and Somali troops and "raiders" (shifta) long have been engaged in intermittent clashes with Ethiopian military forces. Since 1960 this situation has become a widely publicized issue between the two countries. Conservative estimates put the total number killed in the first five years of fighting at 1,300. A cease fire was agreed upon in July 1964, and relative peace prevailed until March 1965. Hostilities were renewed, and in the next six months of fighting 250 persons were killed. The efforts of the Organization for African Unity were successful at quelling any major activity during 1966—67, and the Somali government prior to the 1969 Somalia coup was apparently interested in a peaceful settlement. The successful prospecting for gas and other mineral resources near the Kenya-Somalia-Ethiopian border has renewed Somali interest in the area and the conflict continued at a low level until 1974. During the last half of 1979 and the beginning of 1980 the conflict increased as Somalia-backed forces have been joined by Somalia regular troops in their fighting against Ethiopian and Cuban troops. The conflict has declined but continues. b. *Participants*: The three parties to the dispute include the Ethiopian government supported by Soviet arms and Cuban troops for a period; the Somali government, also with Soviet arms; and the Somali pastoralists inside Ethiopia. The Somali irredentist groups have strong kinship and religious (Islamic) ties with Somalia. There are no predominant leaders of the Somali irredentist movement, although the governments of Somalia have been deeply committed to reunification.

Event and Date	Characteristics
	c. *Apparent Causes*: Ethiopia contends that the border with Somalia has been internationally recognized since 1897, and also claims that self-determination by Somalis in Ethiopia would be contrary to the OAU resolution of 1964. Somalis claim the border is not valid in law and that on ethnic, cultural, and historical grounds all Somalis should be incorporated into a nation-state.
3. Irredentism 1975—present	a. *Description*: Members of the Afar ethnic group bordering the Djibouti Republic have been attempting to secede to join their ethnic counterparts in Djibouti. The *Afar Liberation Front* (ALF) is leading the fight which is characterized by sporadic attacks on Ethiopian government officials, road and rail traffic going through the area, and army units. There are counter-attacks by the Ethiopian army on Afar villages. There is tacit support for the ALF from Djibouti.
	b. *Participants*: Afar ethnic groups members under ALF leadership of the Afar Sultan, Ali Mirah who lives in Saudi Arabia and his American-educated son Hanafare who lives in Somalia.
	c. *Apparent Causes*: Attempt to unite the Afar peoples and to offset the Somali population in Djibouti.
4. Irredentism 1975—present	a. *Description*: With the overthrow of Selassie's regime longstanding opposition to Amharic hegemony surfaced among the Oromo (Galla) and the *Oromo Liberation Front* was organized and has fought alongside the WSLF in an attempt to oust control of the Oromo areas to the east and south of Addis Ababa.
	b. *Participants*: Members of the Oromo ethnic group. The leadership and size of the group is not known.
	c. *Apparent Causes*: Longstanding resentment of Amharic hegemony in Ethiopia and the refusal of the regimes to allow the Oromo, the largest ethnic group in the country, to play a significant role in the country's leadership.
5. Irredentism 1975—present	a. *Description*: With the havoc that resulted from the conflicts that rocked the country, the Marxist oriented *Tigrean People's Liberation Front* (TPLF) was formed in 1975 to combat the Dergue as well as right wing groups operating in the area. Their activities are largely restricted to guerrilla operations since their numbers are small. In 1980, there were reports of cooperation between the TPLF and the larger Eritrean People's Liberation Front. The extent and durability of the relationship is unclear, however.
	b. *Participants*: Ethnic Tigreans who are opposed to the Dergue.
	c. *Apparent Causes*: Dissatisfaction with the military-led government and the progress towards a socialist state, and the desire to establish their own state.

TABLE 11.9   Mass Instability

Event and Date	Characteristics
1. Revolt February to September 1974	a. *Description*: The pressures for major social change in Ethiopia largely spearheaded by student and to a lesser extent worker's demonstrations from the mid-1960's onwards as well as the severe droughts of 1972—73 finally came to a head in early 1974. The events that led to the end of the Selassie regime began with mutinies in the armed forces over pay, strikes by various workers and students particularly in the urban areas, and even among the Coptic Church clergy, one of the major powers in the semi-feudal monarchy. This cascading series of events led to increasing pressures on the Emperor by the armed forces to make an accomodation to these demands including the right of the armed forces to approve the appointment of a prime minister. Once this process of change was set in motion there was little the aged Emperor seemed able to do to maintain control of the rapid escalation of demands throughout virtually all sectors of the society. By the summer of 1974, after the appointment of two new prime ministers in the space of a few months, a state of constitutional anarchy had developed. A committee elected from various units of the military deposed the Emperor in September and designated General Aman Andom as the nominal Head-of-State although the real power remained with the relatively junior officers in the military council whose membership was secret. The effect of this revolt was to lay the groundwork for the revolution that was to consume Ethiopia for years thereafter.
	b. *Participants*: Virtually every segment of Ethiopian society played a role in the breakdown and overthrow of the Imperial system but the armed forces performed the critical function of forcing the old system to accept the changes. Students and intellectuals provided the ideological justification for change and the pressures of inflation and drought affected most sectors of the society.

Event and Date	Characteristics
	c. *Apparent Causes*: Apparently long standing animosity towards the corruption and nepotism of the Emperor's administration was brought to a head with a combination of events including: incompetence in the handling of the drought; the rapidly incresing levels of hostilities in Eritrea; urban dissatisfaction as indicated by the widespread strikes and military mutinies; the inability of the Emperor and his Council of Ministers to deal with these problems.

2. Revolt
  Summer 1974
  to 1978
	a. *Description*: Provincial feudal leaders often supported by the Ethiopian Coptic Church fought against army units throughout the center and Northwest of the country. The resistance to the army is organized by the *Ethiopian Democratic Union* (EDU) and headed by former army officers and liberal government leaders of the Selassie regime. The resistance in Shoa province was finally ended after a ten month fight when the two brothers leading the revolt were killed but the main strength of the EDU resistance was to the northwest in Begemder, Gojjam, and the western parts of Wallo and Tigre provinces. By 1978 EDU strength seemed to be decreasing but the enormous drain on the central government from the many conflicts going on concurrently may see renewed fighting in the future.

	b. *Participants*: Provincial feudal leaders, former army officers, liberals from the Selassie regime, and parts of the rural peasant population.
	c. *Apparent Causes*: Resistance to major land reform and other political changes introduced by the ruling military council.

3. Revolution
  September 1974
  to present
	a. *Description*: After the overthrow of the Emperor, the Provisional Military Advisory Committee (the Dergue) consisting of 129 members of the armed forces elected from various units quickly divided on the policies that a new Ethiopian administration should follow. The first Head-of-State, General Aman Andom, appointed by the Dergue, was executed on the orders of the Dergue less than two months after he assumed office. This was a reflection of the severe struggle and violent disagreements which characterized the Dergue. By December 1974, a new head of state was appointed after mass executions had taken place of those in the military, aristocracy, church and civil service. Ethiopia was declared a socialist state but one determined to hold onto its territory despite the raging conflicts in rightwing (EDU) and leftwing (EPRP) groups who began retaliating with assassinations of government leaders until the bloodshed grew to massive proportions. The conflict over the radical Marxist policies continued within the Dergue as well as in the larger society and the purges of the opposition continued unabated. In December 1976, the Dergue tried to contain the growing power of the two majors who had been the principal behind the scenes leaders and directors of the Dergue's policies, Mengistu and Atnafu, by effectively demoting them. They reacted in February 1977 with the executions of the Head-of-State, General Teferi Bante, and other opposition officers in the Dergue, and civilians associated with them. The executions continued on a large scale whose numbers may never be known and the by then Lt. Col. Mengistu finally eliminated any direct threat to his control of the Dergue by the execution in November 1977 of his close colleague through all the 1974—77 events, Col. Atnafu. The various opposition groups, irredentisms, and secessionist movements continue on through 1980 with no clear direction towards a stable government and political agreement.

	b. *Participants*: Virtually every sector of the society in terms of geography, ideology, class and religion have been actively involved in this revolution. In such a searing upheaval there do not appear to be any who are allowed to be bystanders.
	c. *Apparent Causes*: The political vacuum created by the overthrow of the Emperor was accompanied by an irreversible social and political mobilization of the society and much of the previously existing social, economic, and political structure was destroyed or lost its legitimacy. While the revolt leading to the overthrow of the Emperor was not fought on ideological grounds, the new military ruling council, the Dergue, set in motion a fundamental series of changes in the society including massive land reform ultimately moving towards the abolition of private land holding, the formation of worker and peasant cooperatives, and the direction of the society by the military until such time as 'a worker's party can come into being.' These changes have generated opposition from almost all sectors of the society and from the full range of ideological perspectives ranging from the far right and liberals represented by the EDU to the far left who voice dissatisfaction with a military-led Marxist revolution which they contend should be led by civilians.

TABLE 11.10 Annual Instability Events: Independence Through 1979—Ethiopia

Year	'61	'62	'63	'64	'65	'66	'67	'68	'69	'70	'71	'72	'73	'74	'75	'76	'77	'78	'79
ELITE INSTABILITY																			
Assassinations																			
Plots						1													
Attempted Coups d'État																			
Coups d'État														1					2
COMMUNAL INSTABILITY																			
Ethnic Violence																			
Irredentism	1		1		1									1	3	4	4	4	4
Rebellion				1		1													
Civil War	1							1	1	1	1	1	1	1	1	1	1	1	1
MASS INSTABILITY																			
Revolt														1	1	1	1	1	1
Revolution														1	1	1	1	1	1
TURMOIL																			
Demonstrations					2				5		1	1							
Strikes (no. days)				5		5													
Riots (no. days)											1								
Terrorism	1	1																	
Declarations of Emergency									2	2	1								
CABINET INSTABILITY																			
Realloc. and new appts.									7	1	2								
New members									9	2	5	1							
Resig. and Dismissals									8	1	4	2							
No. of members (max.) (maximum in year)								21	22	23	24	23							

VII. Selected References

BIBLIOGRAPHY

Brown, Clifton F. *Ethiopian Perspectives: a Bibliographical Guide to the History of Ethiopia.* Westport, Conn. Greenwood Press, 1978.

Hidaru, Alaul and Dessalegn Rahmato (eds.). *A Short Guide to the Study of Ethiopia: A General Bibliography.* Washington, D.C.: African Bibliographic Center, 1976.

Marcus, Harold G. *The Modern History of Ethiopia and the Horn of Africa: A Select and Annotated Bibliography.* Stanford, Calif.: Hoover Institution Press, 1972.

GENERAL

Buxton, D. R. *The Abyssinians*. New York: Praeger, 1970.

Hess, Robert. *Ethiopia: The Modernization of Autocracy*. Ithaca, N.Y.: Cornell University Press, 1970.

Levine, Donald N. *Greater Ethiopia: The Evolution of a Multiethnic Society*. Chicago: University of Chicago Press, 1974.

Lipsky, George. *Ethiopia*. New Haven, Conn.: HRAF Press, 1962.

Ullendorff, Edward. *The Ethiopians: An Introduction to Country and People*. 3rd ed.

U.S. Department of the Army. *Area Handbook for Ethiopia*, 3rd ed. Washington, D.C.: U.S. Government Printing Office, 1981.

POLITICAL

Clapham, C. *Haile Selassie's Government*. New York: Praeger, 1969.

Farer, Tom J. *War Clouds on the Horn of Africa: The Widening Storm*. N.Y. Carnegie Endowment for International Peace 1979.

Gilkes, P. *The Dying Lion: Feudalism and Modernization in Ethiopia*. New York: St. Martin's Press, 1975.

Greenfield, Richard. *Ethiopia: A New Political History*. New York: Praeger, 1965.

Hess, Robert. "Ethiopia." In *National Unity and Regionalism in Eight African States*, ed. Gwendolen M. Carter. Ithaca, N.Y.: Cornell University Press, 1966.

Legum, C. *Ethiopia: The Fall of Haile Selassie's Empire*. New York: Africana, 1975.

Legum, C. and Lee. *Conflict in the Horn of Africa*. New York: Africana, 1977.

Levine, Donald. "Class Consciousness and Class Solidarity in the New Ethiopian Elite." In *The New Elites of Tropical Africa*, ed. P. Lloyd, pp. 212—327. London: Oxford University Press, 1966.

Markakis, J. *Ethiopia: Anatomy of a Traditional Polity*. New York: Clarendon Press of Oxford University Press, 1974.

Markakis, John and Asmelash Beyene. "Representative Institutions in Ethiopia." *Journal of Modern African Studies*, 5 (1967): 193—219.

Markakis, John and Nega Ayele. *Class and Revolution in Ethiopia*. Nottingham: Spokesman, 1978.

Ottaway, M. "Social Classes and Corporate Interest in the Ethiopian Revolution." *Journal of Modern African Studies* 14, 3 (1976): 469—86.

Ottaway, Marina and David. *Ethiopia: Empire in Revolution*. New York: Africana Publishing Co., 1978.

Perham, M. *The Government of Ethiopia*. London: Oxford University Press, 1964.

Potholm, Christian P. *Liberation and Exploitation: The Struggle for Ethiopia*. Washington, D.C.: University Press of America, 1976.

Schwab, P. *Haile Selassie I, Ethiopia's Lion of Judah*. Chicago: Nelson.

Schwab, Peter. *Decision-Making in Ethiopia*. Rutherford, N.J.: Fairleigh-Dickinson University Press, 1972.

Sherman, Richard. *Eritrea: The Unfinished Revolution*. New York: Praeger, 1980.

Trevaskis, G. *Eritrea: A Colony in Transition, 1941—52*. London: Oxford University Press, 1960.

Valdes, Vivo Raul. *Ethiopia's Revolution*. New York: International Publishers, 1977.

ECONOMIC

Bequele, A. and E. Chole. *A Profile of the Ethiopian Economy*. Addis Ababa: Oxford University Press, 1969.

Ginzberg, Eli and Herbert A. Smith. *Manpower Strategy for Developing Countries: Lessons from Ethiopia*. New York: Columbia University Press, 1967.

U.S. Department of Agriculture, Economic Research Service, Foreign Regional Analysis Division. *A Survey of Agriculture in Ethiopia*. ERS-Foreign 254. Washington, D.C.: Government Printing Office, 1969.

SOCIAL

Bender, M.L. et al. (eds) *Language in Ethiopia*. London: Oxford University Press, 1976.

Comhaire, Jean. "Urban Growth in Relation to Ethiopian Development." *Cultures et Developpment*, 1 (1968): 25—40.

Derus, Jacques. "Addis Ababa—Genese d'un Capitale Imperiale." *Revue Belge de Geographie*, 88 (1965): 283—314.

Korten, D. C. *Planned Change in a Traditional Society: Psychological Problems of Modernization in Ethiopia*. New York: Praeger, 1972.

Legesse, A. *Gada: Three Approaches to the Study of African Society*. New York: Free Press, 1973.

Levine, Donald. *Wax and Gold: Tradition and Innovation in Ethiopian Culture*. Chicago: University of Chicago Press, 1966.

Pankhurst, Richard. "The Foundation and Growth of Addis Ababa." *The Ethiopian Observer*, 6 (1962): 33—61.

Powne, Michael. *Ethiopian Music: An Introduction*.

London: Oxford University Press, 1968.

Shack, W. A. *The Central Ethiopian*: *Amhara, Tigrina, and related peoples*. London: International Institute, 1976.

Tamrat, Taddesse. *Church and State in Ethiopia*. New York: Oxford University Press, 1972.

Trimingham, John S. *Islam in Ethiopia*. London: Oxford University Press, 1952.

Ullendorf, Edward. *The Semitic Languages of Ethiopia*: *A Comparative Phonology*. London: Taylor's (Foreign) Press, 1955.

12. Gabon

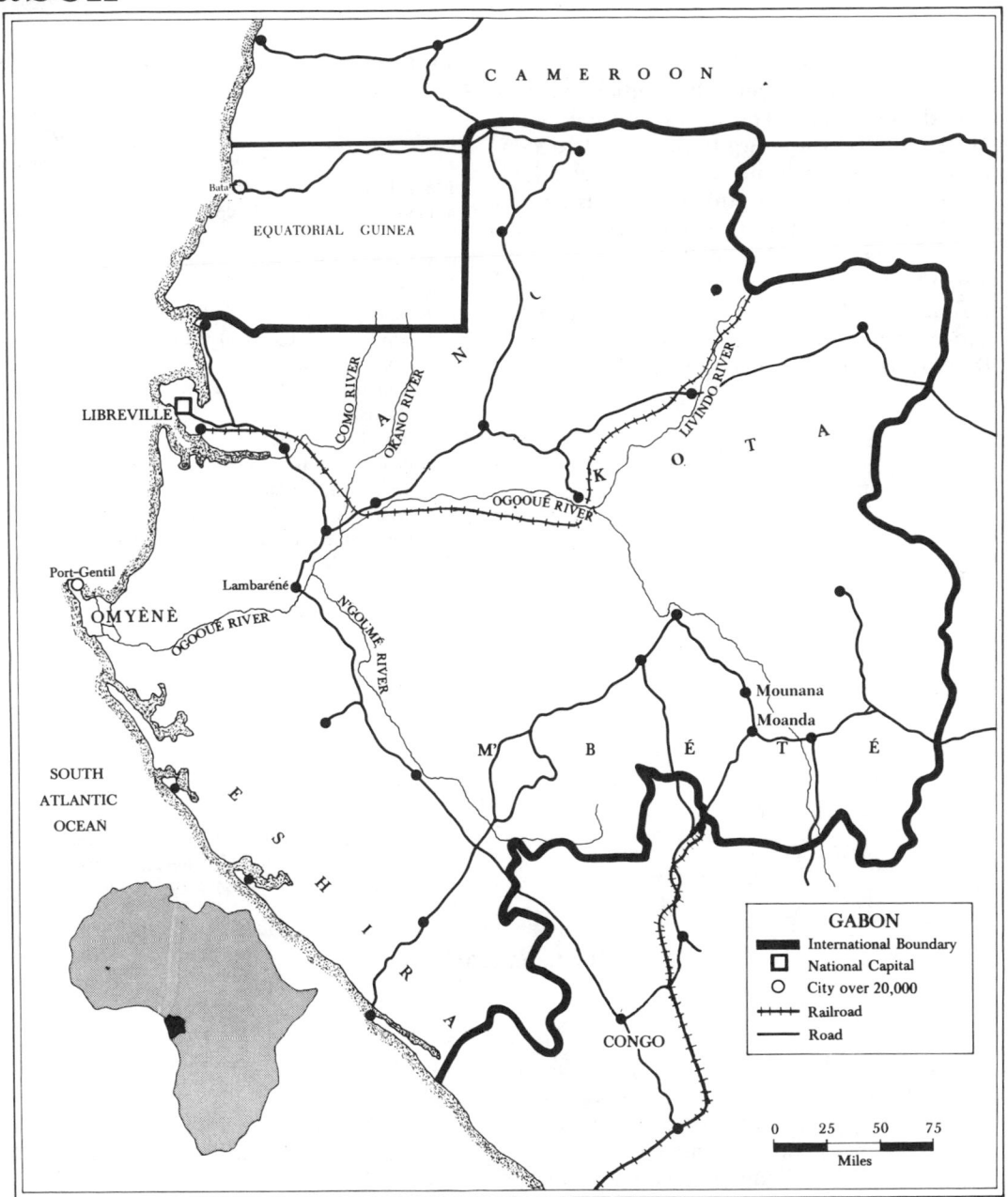

I. Basic Information

Date of Independence: August 17, 1960

Former Colonial Ruler: France

Change in Boundaries: Formerly part of French Equatorial Africa

Estimated Population (1980): 549,000 (1970 census figure of 950,000 has not been accepted by international agencies)

Area Size (equivalent in U.S.): 102,000 sq. mi. (Colorado)

Date of Last Census: 1972

Major Exports (1977) as Percent of Total Exports: crude petroleum—78 percent.

II. Ethnic Patterns

The Gabonese ethnic groups are clustered at a fairly low level of abstraction. All have essentially similar levels of socio-economic development. The major cultural variation is that the southern groups are transitional between the patrilineal belt to the north and the matrilineal belt of the Congo region. Each of the ethnic clusters is locally recognized as an identity group to some extent. In addition to the major units, there are smaller populations of Bakèlè (4 percent), Okandé (4 percent: Baptindji, Mitsogo, Pové, Bassimba, Okandé, Baveya), Séké (4 percent: Séké and Benga), and Pygmies. In 1975 it was estimated that there were 20,000 Frenchmen in Gabon.

TABLE 12.1   Ethnic Units Over 5 Percent of Country Population

Ethnic Unit	Estimated Ethnic Population 1980	Estimated Ethnic Percentage
a. Fang (Fan, Fanwe, Mfang, Mpangwe)	164,700	30%
1. Fang, 2. Ntoumou, 3. Mvaé, 4. Okak		
b. Eshira Type (Shira, Echira)	109,80	20%
1. Bapounou, 2. Eshira, 3. Ngowé 4. Bavarma, 5. Bavoungou, 6. Baloumbou, 7. Babuissi, 8. Massango		
c. M'Bété Type (M'Béti)	82,350	15%
1. Bankjabi, 2. Badouma, 3. Ambamba, 4. Bambana, 5. Mindoumou, 6. Bankaniqui, 7. Batsangui, 8. Bawandji.		
d. Kota Type (Bakota, Bandjambi, Ikota)	71,400	13%
1. Bakota, 2. Mahongwe, 3. Shake, 4. Dambomo, 5. Shamaye, 6. Mindassa, 7. Voumbou, 8. Mahouin		
e. Omyènè Type	27,450	5%
1. Mpongwe, 2. Adyumba, 3. Enenga, 4. Galoa, 5. Orungou, 6. Nkomi		

SOURCES: Brian Weinstein, *Nation Building on the Ogooué* (Cambridge: Massachusetts Institute of Technology Press, 1966), pp. 30—33. Census report in *Europa Yearbook 1967*, p. 462.

III. Language Patterns

All of the languages of Gabon are Bantu. Fang is the predominant language and ethnic group. It is increasing both as an ethnic group (due to processes of assimilation and government support), and as a *lingua franca*. Knapper estimates the Fang-speaking population at 40 percent. Rustow suggests, however, that those who speak Fang as a first language are only 30 percent. Our own estimate of Fang-speakers is 50 percent. We consider the second largest group to be Eshira (20 percent), although this language seems confined to those who use it as a first language. French continues as the official language.

TABLE 12.2   Language Patterns

		Greenberg	Dalby
1. Primacy			
1st language	Fang (50%)		
2nd language	Eshira (20%)		
2. Linguistic classification (all ethnic units in country over 5%)	Fang IA5	A7	
	Eshira IA5	B4	
	M'Bété IA5	B6, B5	
	Kota IA5	B2	
	Myènè IA5	B1	
3. *Lingua franca*	Fang		
4. Official language	French		

IV. Urban Patterns

Capital/largest city: Libreville (founded 1843)
Dominant ethnicity/language of capital
   Major vernacular: Fang[1]
   Major ethnic group: Fang[2]
   Major ethnic group as percent of capital's population:
   30 percent (1960—61)

[1]Jan Knappert, "Language Problems of the New Nations of Africa," *Africa Quarterly*, 5 (1965): 95—105.
   [2]Report of 1960—61 survey of Libreville.

TABLE 12.3   Growth of Capital/Largest City

Date	Libreville
1920	3,000
1930	7,000
1940	11,000
1950	13,000
1960	28,000
1967	57,000 UA
1970	75,000 UA
1975	125,000

SOURCE: *Démographie Comparée*, See Table 12.4, *Africa South of the Sahara 1973* and *Political Handbook of the World 1979*.

TABLE 12.4   Cities of 20,000 and Over*

City	Size**	Date
Libreville	125,000	1975***
Port Gentil	50,000	1975***

SOURCE: *Europa Yearbook 1977*, Vol. II, p. 590.

*The next largest town is Mounana-Moanda 11,000 (1971) as reported in *Africa South of the Sahara 1973*.
**The 1972 census figure of 1,027,529 for Gabon has not been accepted by international agencies. Hence, these urban figures should be treated with caution as they reflect the census. It is not known whether they are inflated figures.
***It should be noted that substantially higher population estimates have been made, e.g., Libreville 251,000 and Port Gentil 78,000 for 1975. The figures cited above seem to be more accurate, however.

V. Political Patterns

A. Political Parties and Elections

The dominant party, the *Bloc Démocratique Gabonais* (BDG) was formed in the early 1950's as a territorial branch of the *Rassemblement Démocratique Africain* (RDA), and the leader of the BDG, Leon M'Ba, was a close supporter of Houphouet-Boigny (Ivory Coast). In 1961, the BDG joined the major opposition party, *Union Démocratique et Sociale Gabonaise* (UDSG) in what (in retrospect) appears to have been a *coalition*, although some scholars suggest it was a *merger*. This coalition lasted until the national elections in April 1964, when the UDSG broke away from the BDG, and along with several splinter parties (e.g., the *Défense la Démocratique* [DD]) contested the elections. The BDG gained 31 seats, and the opposition 16 seats. During the elections, the leader of the UDSG (M. Aubame) was arrested. In Libreville, the Government received 20,556 votes, and opposition parties received 19,503 votes.

On March 19, 1967, there was another national election, in which a single list was presented. The BDG won 100 percent of the seats, and M'Ba continued as president (as well as secretary general of the BDG). Opposi-

tion groups, not being represented in parliament, joined in a loose coalition called *Parti Démocratique du Gabon* (PDG) and absorbed the PDID. In 1969 a general election was held and the PDG won another term unopposed. In February 1973, an election was held which returned President Bongo for another seven years and the PDG for another term. In this election the assembly was enlarged from 49 to 70 seats. On January 1, 1980 Bongo was reelected to his second seven-year term. Bongo was the only candidate. The parliamentary elections were held in late February 1980. Three major changes were instituted in this election in an attempt to democratize the assembly. First, independent candidates were allowed to run against party members. Second, the number of assembly seats were increased to 89. Finally, the term of office was shortened from seven to five years.

B. Political Leadership

The leadership of the government of Gabon after Leon M'Ba's death in 1967 passed to his chosen successor, President Bongo. There has been considerable change in the composition of the cabinet since independence, with a significant rise in the number of resignations and dismissals from the cabinet following the attempted coup d'état in 1964. Cabinet reshuffles are very common and most of the important portfolios are held by President Bongo. The most recent were in 1970 (2), 1971, 1972 (2),

1973, 1974 (2), 1975 (2), 1976 (3), and 1977 (1). Although the size of the cabinet has been expanded since independence, its members have become less representative of the cultural pluralism in Gabon as the Fang have become more prominent in government.

FIGURE 12.1   Political Parties and Elections   GABON

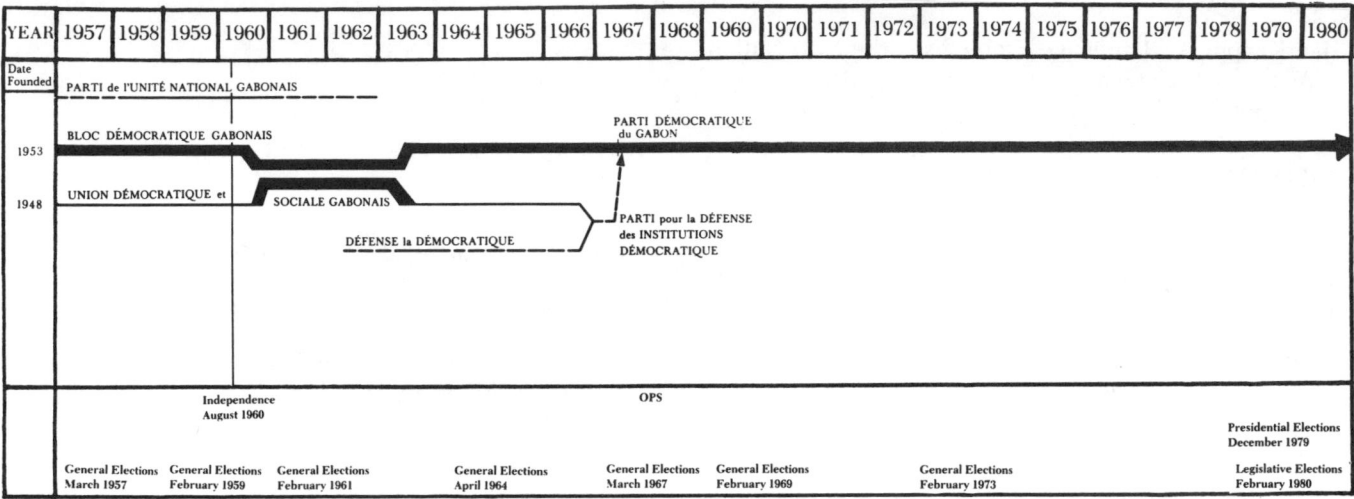

TABLE 12.5   Heads of Government (Post-Independence)

Name	Dates in Office	Age 1982	Ethnicity	Education	Former Occupation
1. Leon M'Ba (President)	1960—67	d. 1967 age 57	Fang	Catholic Secondary Gabon	Civil Servant
2. Omar Bongo (President)	1967— present	47	Téké	Brazzaville Technical College	Civil Servant

TABLE 12.6   Cabinet Membership: Distribution by Ethnic Unit*

Ethnicity*	Independence Cabinet	1967 Cabinet
1. Fang (30%)	33%	70%
2. Eshira (20)	11	0
3. M'Beté (15)	11	12
4. Kota (13)	0	0
5. Omyené (5)	0	5.9
6. Others (17	44	12
N	9	17

Ethnic units arranged in rank order of size within the country with the unit's percent of national population in parentheses.

VI. National Integration and Stability

The general pattern in Gabon has been one of political stability, despite some tensions at the elite level. According to Weinstein (1966), even during the time of the unsuccessful coup, there was no evidence of communal instability. In general, the Fang in Gabon have dominated the national life of the country, but have been "assimilative" regarding other ethnic cultures. Under the presidency of de Gaulle, France maintained especially close relations with Gabon, and the threat of French intervention, once realized in 1964, undoubtedly contributed to regime stability in Gabon. A contingent of French troops remains in the country under a treaty that was renewed in 1974. Relatively substantial wealth from natural resources has probably been an additional stabilizing factor. In May 1980 primary and secondary school teachers went on strike for higher wages, and a new salary scale was instituted in July 1980.

TABLE 12.7   Elite Instability

Event and Date	Characteristics
1. Attempted Coup Feb. 18—20, 1964	a. *Description*: Military coup led by Daniel M'bene temporarily deposed Leon M'Ba in favor of Jean-Hilare Aubame, the opposition leader. Less than 24 hours after the attempted coup began, French troops were flown from Chad and Congo to restore M'Ba to power. In heavy fighting, 19 Gabonese and 2 French soldiers were killed. b. *Participants*: M'bene and junior army officers. c. *Apparent Causes*: Army discontent with low pay and the retention of French officers in command positions. Aubame had criticized M'Ba for being authoritarian, and had objected to the slow pace of Africanization of the army and administration.

SOURCES: "Gabon: Putsch or Coup d'état?" *Africa Report*, 9 (March 1964): 12—15.   Charles and Alice Darlington, *African Betrayal*, (New York: David McKay, 1967), pp. 123—141.   Brian Weinstein, *Nation Building on the Ogooué* (Cambridge: Massachusetts Institute of Technology Press, 1966).

TABLE 12.10   Annual Instability Events: Independence Through 1979—Gabon

Year	'61	'62	'63	'64	'65	'66	'67	'68	'69	'70	'71	'72	'73	'74	'75	'76	'77	'78	'79
ELITE INSTABILITY																			
Assassinations																			
Plots																			
Attempted Coups d'État			1																
Coups d'État																			
COMMUNAL INSTABILITY																			
Ethnic Violence																			
Irredentism																			
Rebellion																			
Civil War																			
MASS INSTABILITY																			
Revolt																			
Revolution																			

Year	'61	'62	'63	'64	'65	'66	'67	'68	'69	'70	'71	'72	'73	'74	'75	'76	'77	'78	'79
TURMOIL																			
Demonstrations																			
Strikes (no. days)				5															
Riots (no. days)				2										1					
Terrorism																			
Declarations of Emergency				1						1									
CABINET INSTABILITY																			
Realloc. and new appts.	16	12	22	13	16	12	26	9	7	5	3	5							
New members	8	7	3	5	2	1	6	5	8	3	1	4							
Resig. and Dismissals	3	4	5	4	1	5	6	1	3	7		3							
No. of members (max.) (maximum in year)	13	16	14	11	18	17	17	17	22	18	19	20							

VII. Selected References

BIBLIOGRAPHY

Centre Culture Saint-Exupéry. *Ouvrages sur le Gabon.* Libreville, Centre de documentation. Saint-Exupéry, 1978.

Weinstein, Brian. "Gabon: A Bibliographic Essay." *Africana Newsletter*, 1, no. 4, 1963.

GENERAL

Bouquerel, J. *Le Gabon.* Paris: Presses Universitaires de France, 1970.

Lasserre, Guy. *La France d'Outre-mer.* Paris: Larousse, 1979.

Sautter, Gilles. *De l'Atlantique au fleuve Congo, une geographie du sous-peuplement.* Republique du Congo: Republique Gabonaise, 2 vols. Paris: Mouton and Co., 1966.

Thompson, Virginia and Richard Adloff. *The Emerging States of French Equatorial Africa*, pp. 343—384. Stanford, Calif.: Stanford University Press, 1960.

Weinstein, Brian. *Gabon: Nation Building on the Ogooue.* Cambridge: Massachusetts Institute of Technology Press, 1966.

POLITICAL

Ballard, John A. "Four Equatorial States: *Congo, Gabon, Ubangi-Shari, Chad.*" In *National Unity and Regionalism in Eight African States*, ed. Gwendolen M. Carter, pp. 231—329. Ithaca, N.Y.: Cornell University Press, 1966.

Darlington, C. and A. *African Betrayal.* New York: McKay, 1968.

de Lusignan, Guy. *French-Speaking Africa since Independence*, pp. 100—108. London: Pall Mall Press, 1969.

ECONOMIC

France Ministere de la cooperation. *Gabon: donées statistiques sur les activities, economiques, culturelles et socialles.* Paris, 1976.

"Gabon: une expansion rapide." *Europe-Franco-Outremer* (October 1969): 12—62.

Hilling, D. "The Changing Economy of Gabon: Developments in a New African Republic." *Geography*, 48 (1963): 155—165.

International Monetary Fund. "Gabon." In *Surveys of African Economies*. Vol. 1. Washington, D.C.: I.M.F., 1968.

SOCIAL

Balandier, Georges, *Sociologie actuelle de l'Afrique noire*. 2nd ed. Paris: Presses universitaires de France, 1963.

Lasserre, Guy. *Libreville, la ville et sa region (Gabon, A.E.F.): etude de geographie humaine*. Paris: Colin, 1958.

13. Gambia

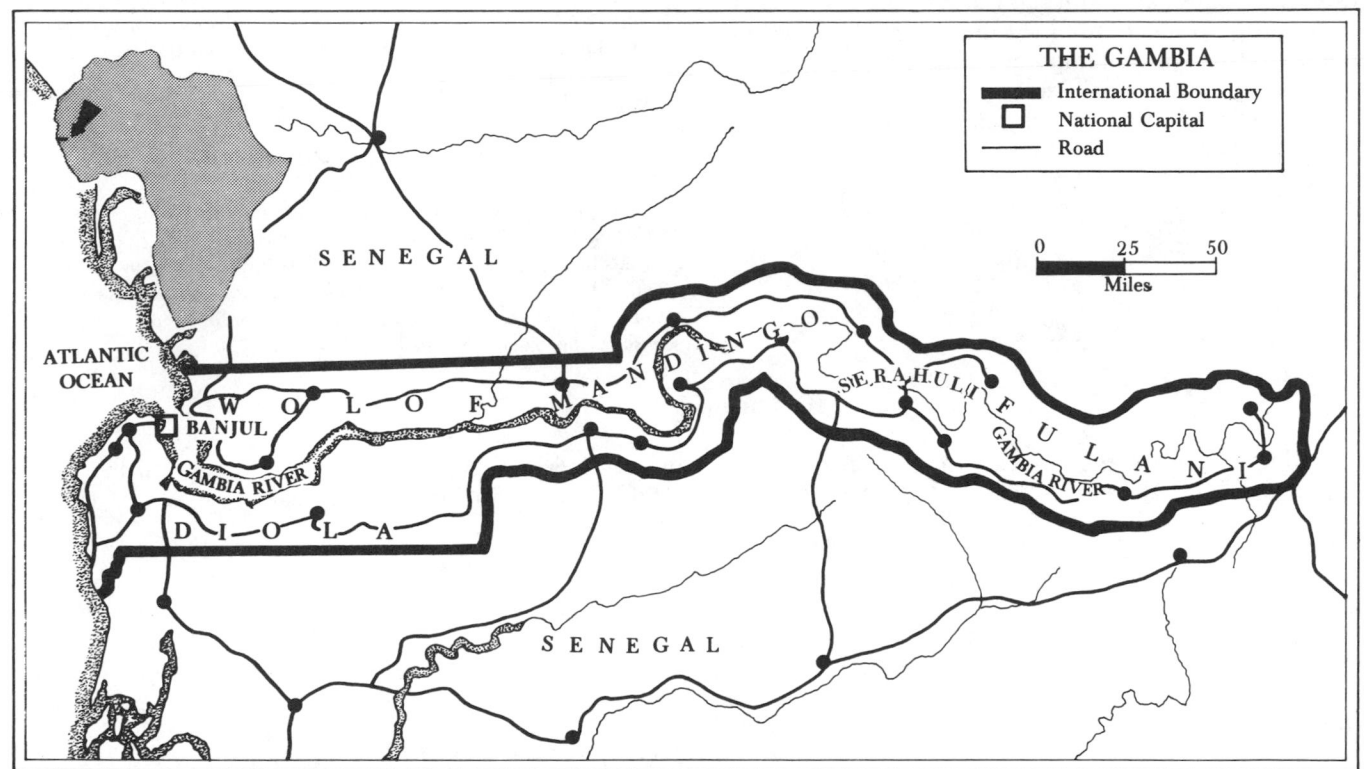

I. Basic Information

Date of Independence: February 18, 1965
Former Colonial Ruler: United Kingdom
Estimated Population (1980): 599,000
Area Size (equivalent in U.S.): 4361 sq. mi. (twice Delaware)

Date of Last Census: 1973
Major Exports 1977—1978 as Percent of Total Exports: groundnuts and derivatives—78 percent.

II. Ethnic Patterns

The ethnic classifcation of Gambia is done at a low level of abstraction. All the ethnic categories correspond to functioning identity groups. All speak different languages and have different cultural and historical backgrounds. Most groups probably entered the region within the last six centuries as a result of pressures exerted in their former homelands in contemporary Mali and Senegal. Note that the ethnic group "Diola" is not the same as the broader term "Dyula," which refers to Mandé-speaking Muslim traders.

TABLE 13.1   Ethnic Units Over 5 Percent of Country Population

Ethnic Unit	Estimated Ethnic Population 1980	Estimated Ethnic Percentage
a. Mandingo (Malinké, Manding, Wangara)	245,600	41%
b. Fulani (Fula, Peul)	80,900	13.5%
c. Wolof (Jolof, Ouolof, Wollof)	77,900	13%
d. Diola (Jola, Dyola, Yola)	41,900	7%
e. Serahuli (Soninké, Sarakolé)	38,900	6.5%

SOURCES: *Report on the Census of Population of the Gambia Taken on 17th/18th April 1963* by H. A. Oliver, Census Controller. Sessional Paper no. 13 of 1965 (Bathurst: Government Printer, 1965), p. 50. H. A. Gailey, Jr., *A History of the Gambia* (London: Routledge & Kegan Paul, 1964). *Africa South of the Sahara 1975* p. 344 reports the 1973 census as showing the population "nearly half Maninka."

III. Language Patterns

According to Weil (1968) there are three language groups in the Gambia: (1) Mandé (Western Division) (including Mandingo/Malinké, Soninké, Bambara, Dialonke, and Koranko); (2) West Atlantic (including Wolof, Werer, Diola, Fulani, Manyaka, Banyum, Temne, and Mansuanka); (3) Other languages (mainly Creole and pidgin). Weil estimates that 40 percent of the population speak Mandingo as a first language, and that it is spoken as a second language by members of most other ethnic groups. (Knappert estimates 100 percent speak Mandingo; Rustow estimates 46 percent.) We estimate 60 percent of the population speak Maningo. With regard to the second largest language, Weil estimates that about 16 percent of the populaton speak Fulani as a first language. There are seven dialects of Fulani found in Gambia: Tukulor, Futa Toro, Jombonko, Futa Jalonke, Fuladugu, Lorobo, and Aamanabi. Finally, Wolof is spoken as a first language by about 13 percent of the population. English is the official language of Gambia and is used in administration, law, education, and commerce. French is spoken by Wolof and Serer groups along the Senegal borders; Arabic is used as a religious language.

TABLE 13.2   Language Patterns

			Greenberg	Dalby
1. Primacy				
1st language	Mandingo	(60%)		
2nd language	Fulani	(16%)		
2. Linguistic classification	Maningo		IA2	31A
(all ethnic units in	Fulani		IAI	201
country over 5%)	Wolof		IA1	202
	Dyola		IAI	22A
	Serahuli (Soninké)		IA2	31B
3. *Lingua franca*	Mandingo			
4. Official language	English			

SOURCE: Peter M. Weil, "Language Distribution in the Gambia: 1966—67," *African Language Review*, 7 (1968): 101-106.

IV. Urban Patterns

Capital/largest city: Banjul (formerly Bathurst) (founded 1816)
Dominant ethnicity/language of capital
  Major vernacular: Mandingo[1]
  Major ethnic group: Mandingo[1]

Major ethnic groups as percent of capital's population: 50 percent (1973)

[1]1973 census as reported in *African Contemporary Record 1973—74*.

TABLE 13.3 Growth of Capital/Largest City

Date	Banjul*
1920[a]	9,000
1930[a]	11,000
1940	
1950[b]	20,000
1960	26,000
1966	43,000 UA
1973[c]	80,000 UA

SOURCES:
[a]O. Martens and O. Karstedt, *The African Handbook*, 2nd ed. (London: Allen and Unwin, 1938).
[b]Michael Banton, *West African City* (London: Oxford University Press, 1957).
[c]1973 Census figure for the city of Banjul and the surrounding Kombo-St. Mary area.

*Bathurst was renamed Banjul in Februrary 1973.

TABLE 13.4 Cities of 20,000 and Over*

City	Size	Date
Banjul (Bathurst)**	80,000 UA	1973

SOURCE: 1973 census figure as reported by *African Contemporary Record 1973—74*.

*The next largest city is Brikama which had a population of 4,000 in the 1963 census.

**Bathurst was renamed Banjul in February 1973.

V. Political Patterns

FIGURE 13.1 Political Parties and Elections   GAMBIA

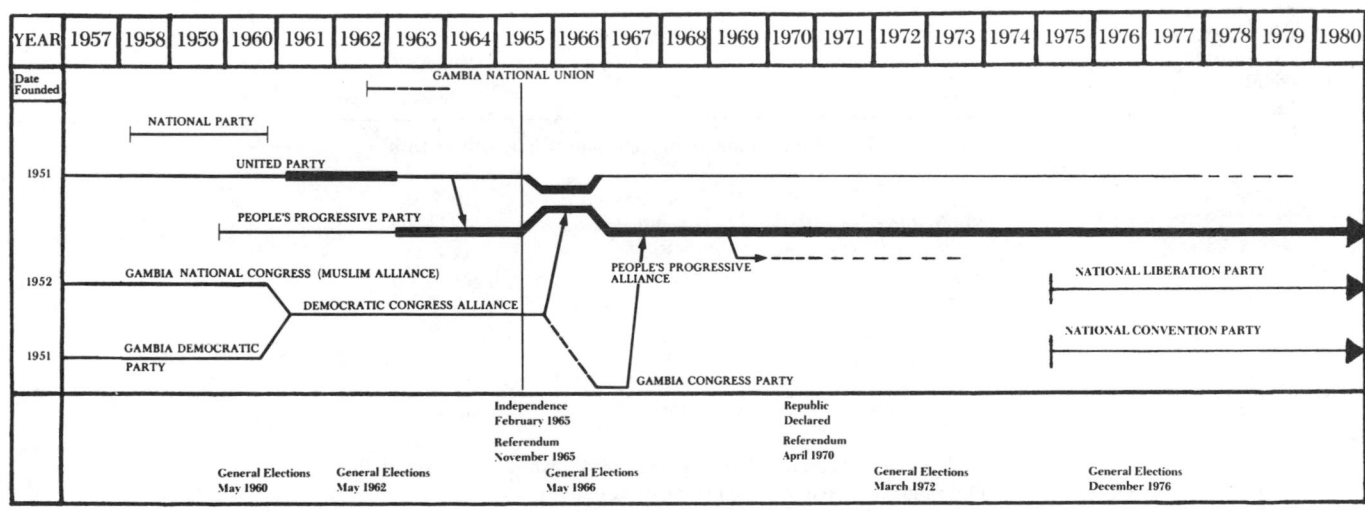

A. Political Parties and Elections

After the first Gambian elections held in May 1960, Pierre S. N'Jie was made Chief Minister. N'Jie's party, the *United Party* (UP) continued to govern Gambia until 1962 when the party was defeated by the *People's Progressive Party* (PPP) under the leadership of Dawda Jawara. In 1965 the PPP and the UP joined in a coalition government which lasted only until 1966 when the PPP assumed the sole leadership of the government. In the May 1966 election the PPP won 24 seats, and the UP/Congress won 8. the *Democratic Congress Alliance* (DCA), formed by a merger of the *Gambia Muslim Congress* (GMC) and the *Gambia Democratic Party* (GDP) in 1960, served as an opposition party until it merged with the PPP in 1966. Two referenda were held over the issue of declaring Gambia a republic. The issue was defeated in 1965, but succeeded in 1970 with a 70 percent affirmative vote. The election in March 1972 saw the PPP returned with 28 out of 32 seats and 63 percent of the votes cast. Three seats went to the UP and one to an independent. In late 1975, two new parties, the *National Liberation Party*, (NLP) and the *National Convention Party* (NCP) were formed and in the December 1976 legislative election the PPP continued its dominance of the legislature winning 28 seats and 70 per cent of the vote with the remainder going to the UP (2) and NCP (5). In a by-election in June 1977, the UP lost a seat to the PPP. And, in September 1978, the last UP member of Parliament joined the PPP.

B. Political Leadership

The Gambia became an independent state in 1965, and since that time the government of President Jawara has remained in power. In a relatively small cabinet, the number of persons of Wolof background is greater than would be expected from the proportion of Wolof in the Gambian population. The membership of the cabinet has been very stable although its size was increased from 10 to 12 in a reshuffle in 1974 and two ministers lost their seats in parliament in the 1976 election.

TABLE 13.5   **Head of Government (Post-Independence)**

Name	Dates in Office	Age 1982	Ethnicity	Education	Former Occupation
1. Sir Dawda Jawara (Prime Minister/ President)	1965—	58	Mandingo	Veterinary (England)	Veterinarian, Party Organizer

TABLE 13.6   **Cabinet Membership: Distribution by Ethnic Unit***

Ethnicity	Independence Cabinet	1967 Cabinet
1. Maningo (41%)	43%	44%
2. Fulani (13.5)	15	11
3. Wolof (13)	43	33
4. Diola (7)	0	0
5. Serahuli (6.5)	0	0
6. Others (19)	0	11
N =	7	10

*Ethnic units arranged in rank order of size within country with the unit's percent of national population in parentheses.

VI. National Integration and Stability

Until 1981, Gambia had shown no evidence of elite, communal or mass instability. The issues of national integration were far from solved, however, and the primary question is whether the thin sliver of territory surrounded by Senegal on three sides, will at some future time join Senegal in forming a new union: Senegambia.

The first steps towards this union have already been taken because of the events of July, 1981. In July of 1981, Gambia suffered from an attempted coup while President Jawara was in London. The coup resulted in the injection of Senegalese troops into the conflict and very severe damage to property and loss of life while Jawara was reasserting his authority. This event has had a profound effect on the relation of Gambia to Senegal. Shortly after the coup a movement to establish a Senegambian federation with a single army and police was hastened. The final outcome of such a move is still unclear but there are close ethnic links between the two countries and strong pressures on both sides for a more unified system exist.

TABLE 13.7 Elite Instability

Event and Date	Characteristics
1. Attempted Coup July 30-Aug 1, 1981	a. *Description*: Members of the Gambian Police Field Force take control of the country while President Jawara is in London. Jawara returns with the aid of Senegalese troops and loyal Gambian police forces. In bloody fighting he reasserts his authority in the country. The various police and political elements involved in the coup attempt are arrested and tried. b. *Participants*: Field Force members led by Kukoi Samba Sanyang and politicians including a former Vice President, Sherif Mustafa Dibo and an MP, Jibrul Jagne. c. *Apparent Causes*: The deteriorating state of the economy, worsened by droughts, and possible foreign (Libyan) encouragement of the construction of a radical left regime in the country.

TABLE 13.10 Annual Instability Events: Independence Through 1979—Gambia

Year	'61	'62	'63	'64	'65	'66	'67	'68	'69	'70	'71	'72	'73	'74	'75	'76	'77	'78	'79
ELITE INSTABILITY																			
Assassinations																			
Plots																			
Attempted Coups d'État																			1
Coups d'État																			
COMMUNAL INSTABILITY																			
Ethnic Violence																			
Irredentism																			
Rebellion																			
Civil War																			
MASS INSTABILITY																			
Revolt																			
Revolution																			
TURMOIL																			
Demonstrations																			
Strikes (no. days)																			
Riots (no. days)																			
Terrorism																			
Declarations of Emergency																			
CABINET INSTABILITY																			
Realloc. and new appts.					1	3		2	2			3							
New members					1	1		3	3	2		1							
Resig. and Dismissals					1	1		1	3	1		1							
No. of members (max.) (maximum in year)					9	9	9	8	8	9	9	10							

VII. Selected References

BIBLIOGRAPHY

Gamble, D. P. *A General Bibliography of the Gambia.* (up to 31 December 1977), Boston: G.K. Hall, 1979.

Nyang, S. S. "Politics in Post-Independence Gambia" *Current Bibliography of African Affairs*, 8, 2 (1975), 113—126.

GENERAL

Bridges, R. C. and A. Adams, eds. *Senegambia: Colloquium at the University of Aberdeen, April 1974.* Aberdeen: University African Study Group, 1974.

Gailey, Harry A. *A History of the Gambia.* London: Routledge and Kegan Paul, 1964.

Gailey, H. A. *Historical Dictionary of the Gambia.* Metuchen, N.J.: Scarecrow, 1975.

Gray, J. M. *A History of the Gambia.* N.Y.: Barnes and Noble, Inc., 1966.

Tengue, Michael. "The Gambia." *Geographical Magazine* (London), 34 (November 1961): 380—392.

Rice, Berkeley. *Enter Gambia: The Birth of an Improbable Nation.* London: Angus and Robertson, 1968.

Wright, Donald. *Oral Tradition from the Gambia.* Athens, Ohio. Ohio University, Centre for International Studies Africa Program, 1979.

POLITICAL

Daun, Holger. *Change, conflict potential and politics: two Gambian case studies.* Lunds Université, 1977.

Nyang, S. S. *The Historical Development of Political Parties in the Gambia.* Washington, D.C.: Howard University Press, 1975.

Robson, Peter. "The Problems of Senegambia. *Journal of Modern Africa Studies*, 3 (1965): 393—407.

Robson, Peter. "Problems of Integration between Senegal and Gambia." In *African Integration and Disintegration.* ed, Arthur Hazelwood, pp. 115—128. London: Oxford University Press, 1967.

Welch, Claude E., Jr. "Unlikely Gambia." *Africa Report*, 10 (Feburary 1965): 5—9.

ECONOMIC

Dunsmore, J. R. et al. *The Agricultural Development of the Gambia: An Aricultural, Environmental and Socioeconomic · Analysis.* Surbiton, Surrey: Ministry of Overseas Development, Land Resources Division, 1976.

Haswell, Margaret. *The Nature of Poverty.* London: The Macmillan Press, Ltd., 1975.

International Monetary Fund. "The Gambia." In *Surveys of African Economies*, Vol. 6. Washington, D.C.: I.M.F., 1975.

SOCIAL

Van der Plas, Charles D. *Report of a Socio-Economic Survey of Bathurst and Kombo-St. Mary in the Gambia.* New York: United Nations, 1956.

14. Ghana

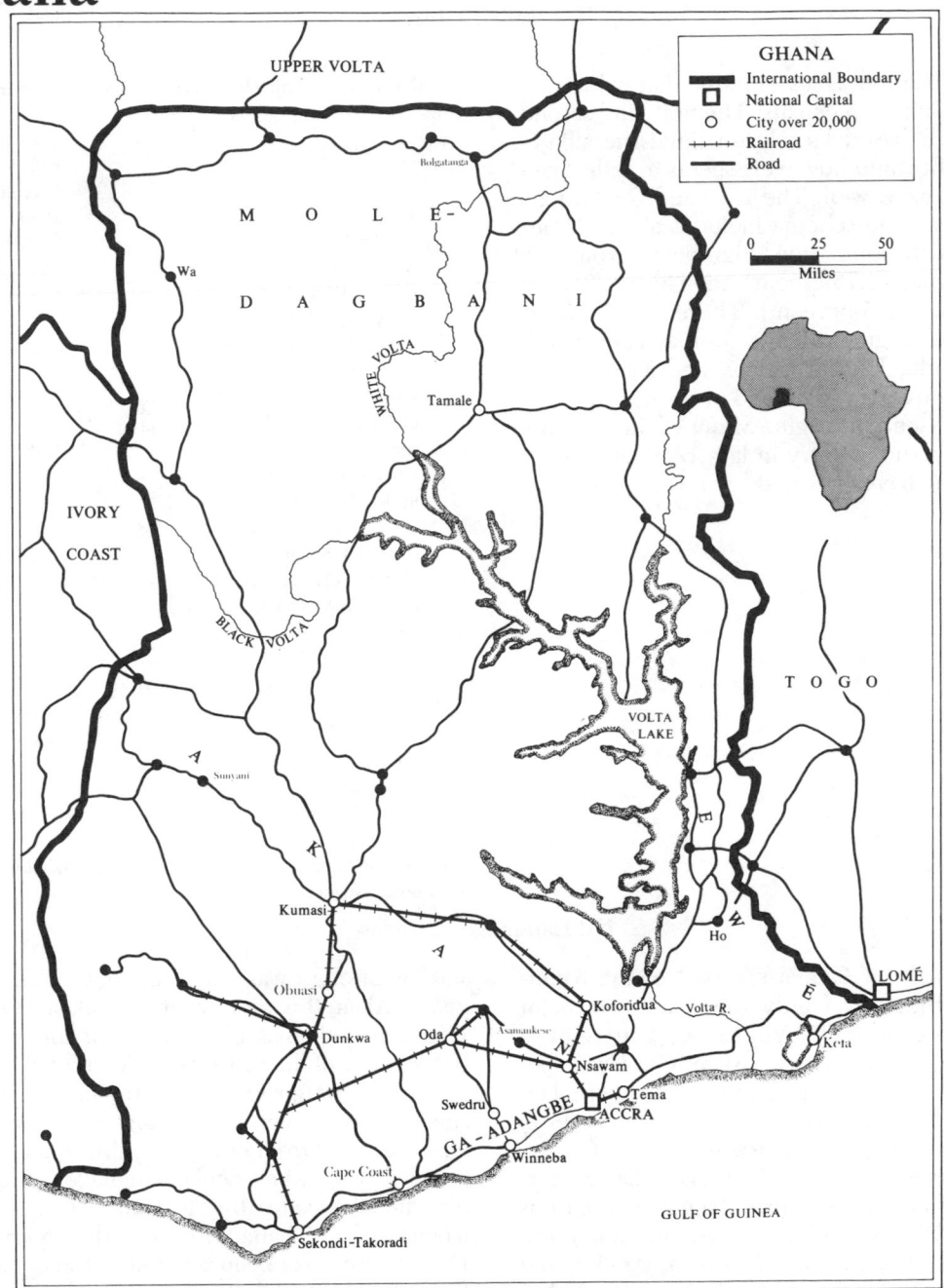

I. Basic Information

Date of Independence: March 6, 1957
Former Colonial Ruler: United Kingdom
Change in Boundaries: Addition of UN Trust Territory "British Togoland" on December 13, 1956
Former Name: Gold Coast

Estimted Population (1980) 12,128,000
Area Size (equivalent in U.S.): 92,100 sq. mi. (Wyoming)
Date of Last Census: 1970
Major exports 1975 as percent of total exports: cocoa—59 percent; logs and timber—8 percent; gold—9 percent.

II. Ethnic Patterns

Our ethnic classification is essentially that which has been used in the Ghanaian census. The first- and second-level groupings are based largely on lingusitic affinity. This basis of classification, however, seems to reflect general cultural patterns as well. The Ewé and Ga-Adangbe are identity groups. The schema includes about 82 percent of the Ghanaian population. Significant groups not included are the Guan (3.7 percent), the Gurma (3.5 percent), and the Grusi (3.5 percent). There are also an assortment of Central Togo groups, as well as Tem (Kotokoli), Songhai, Mandé, Hausa, Fulani, and Kru. In 1967 there were about a quarter million (3 percent) foreign Africans, largely of Nigerian origin. Many of these people were expelled from the country in late 1969, although it is thought that some have returned.

TABLE 14.1   Ethnic Units Over 5 Percent of Country Population

Ethnic Unit	Estimated Ethnic Population 1980	Estimated Ethnic Percentage
a. Akan Cluster	5,336,000	44%
1. Ashanti (Twi-Fanti, Twi)	(3,420,000)	(28.2%)
i. Ashanti, ii. Boron, iii. Akuapem, iv. Kwawu, etc.		
2. Fante (Twi-Fante, Fante)	(1,358,000)	(11.2%)
i. Fante, ii. Agona		
3. Nzema (Nzima)	(315,000)	(2.6%)
i. Nzema, ii. Evalue, iii. Ahanta		
4. Anyi-Bawle	(182,000)	(1.5%)
i. Sahwi (Sefwi), ii. Aowin, iii. Kyokoshi, iv. Bawle		
b. Mole-Dagbani (Mossi-Dagomba) Cluster	1,940,000	16%
1. Dagomba, 2. Dagaba, 3. Mosi, 4. Frafra, 5. Kusasi, 6. Nankansi, 7. Talensi		
c. Ewé (Ehoué, Eibe, Ephe, Krepe)	1,577,000	13%
d. Ga-Adangbe	1,031,000	8.5%
1. Ga (Gan)	1,031,000	8.5%
2. Adangbe (Adangme, Adampa)	(424,000)	(3.5%)
i. Ada, ii. Shai (Siade), iii. Krobo	(424,000)	(3.5%)

SOURCE: *1960 Population Census of Ghana, Special Report "E," Tribes in Ghana*, (Accra Census Office, 1964), pp. 1—5.

III. Language Patterns

Most of the languages of Ghana are part of the Niger-Congo family. Within this family there are two major sub-stock language groups: (1) Voltaic, or Gur (spoken mainly in the north); (2) Kwa (e.g., Akan, Ga, Ewé, spoken mainly in the south). The dominant northern language is Mole-Dagbani, and is it spoken by a number of ethnic groups: Dagomba, Mamprusi, Nanumba, Gbanyang, Nankansi, Kusasi, Talensi, Wala, Dagaba, Birifor, Namnam. The dominant southern language group is Akan, including Twi (Ashanti, Fanti, Akim, Akwapim), Anyi-Baule (Nzima, Ahanta, Sefwi, Aowin, Anufo), and Guang (Gonja, Brong, Nawuri, Atyoti, Anyanga, Nchumuru, Nkunya, Late, Afutu). Knapper estimates that 57 percent of the Ghanaian population speak "Akan"; MacDougald estimtes 62 percent; and Rustow 44 percent. Our own estimate is 44 percent based on ethnic group size, with 16 percent speaking the second language (Mole-Dagbani). It should be noted that Fanti and Twi are distinctive but mutually intelligible. (About 40 years ago an attempt was made to blend them into a new language, Akan; this was not successful; see Owiredu, 1964.) Hausa, is spoken as a *lingua franca* not only in the north, but in many of the southern cities as well.

The Ghana government after independence discouraged the use of vernacular languages in the schools (English was used from grade one), but it did extensive radio broadcasting in vernacular languages, and extensive international broadcasting in Hausa. English is the official language of Ghana. During the Nkrumah regime, French also was encouraged, and the eventual hope was to have a bilingual (French-English) state, to facilitate communications with Ghana's French-speaking neighbors. The major administrative regions within Ghana continue to be demarcated according to lingusitic criteria. In 1960, the Nationality Act required that all would-be citizens of Ghana be proficient in an indigenous language.

TABLE 14.2   Language Patterns

1. Primacy
    1st language   "Akan"   (44%)
    2nd language   Mole-Dagbani (16%)

		Green-berg	Dalby
2. Linguistic classification (all ethnic units in country over 5%)	"Akan"	IA4	44A
	Mole-Dagbani	IA3	41A
	Ewé	IA4	45
	Ga-Adangbe	IA4	407

3. *Lingua franca*   Hausa
4. Official language   English

SOURCES: R. F. Amonoo, "Problems of Ghanaian Lingue Franche," in *Language in Africa*, ed. John Spencer (London: Cambridge University Press, 1963), pp. 78—85. P. A. Owiredu, "Proposals for a National Language in Ghana," *African Affairs*, 64 (1964): 142—145.

IV. Urban Patterns

Capital/largest city: Accra (founded ca. 1550)
Dominant ethnicity/language of capital
    Major vernacular: Ga[1]
    Major ethnic group: Ga[2]
    Major ethnic group as percent of capital's population: 49 percent (1960)

[1]Jan Knappert, "Language Problems of the New Nations of Africa," *African Quarterly*, 5 (1965): 95—105.
[2]Census of 1960.

TABLE 14.3   Growth of Capital/Largest City

Date	Accra
1920[a]	38,000
1930[b]	61,000
1940[a]	100,000
1950	135,000
1960	338,000
1966[c]	600,000 UA
1970	733,498 UA

SOURCES:
[a]Michael Banton, *West African City* (London: Oxford University Press, 1957).
[b]Gold Coast census (1931).
[c]*UN Demographic Yearbook 1967*.
Other dates: census results.

TABLE 14.4   Cities of 20,000 or Over

City	Size	Date
Accra-Tema	738,498 UA	1970
Kumasi	345,117 UA	1970
Sekondi/Takoradi	160,868 UA	1970
Tamale	98,818	1970
Cape Coast	71,594	1970
Koforidua	69,804	1970
Nsawam	57,350	1970
Oda	40,001	1970
Obuasi	36,104	1970
Wenneba	36,104	1970
Keta	27,461	1970
Swedru (Agona)	23,843	1970

SOURCES: 1970 Reports are 1970 Census results as reported in *Statesman's Yearbook 1973/74, UN Demographic Yearbook 1973* and *Europa Yearbook V. II 1976*.

V. Political Patterns

A. Political Parties and Elections

The *Convention People's Party* (CPP) was founded in 1949 by Kwame Nkrumah, and was the dominant party in Ghana until the military coup in February 1966. During the pre-independence period there were a number of splinter parties. These emerged in 1957 to form the *United Party* (UP), which was led by Dr. Kofi Busia. The UP served as the "opposition" party until Ghana officially became a one-party state in early 1964. However, the country had been essentially a one-party state since the plebiscite election in April 1959, which established the republican constitution (with 89 percent of the vote), and Nkrumah as president. After the military coup, all parties were banned, and a National Liberation Council was established to govern the country. The military government scheduled elections from August 31, 1969, with the intention of returning the country to civilian rule. During the spring and summer of 1969 a number of political parties were formed in preparation for the election, but

FIGURE 14.1   Political Parties and Elections   GHANA

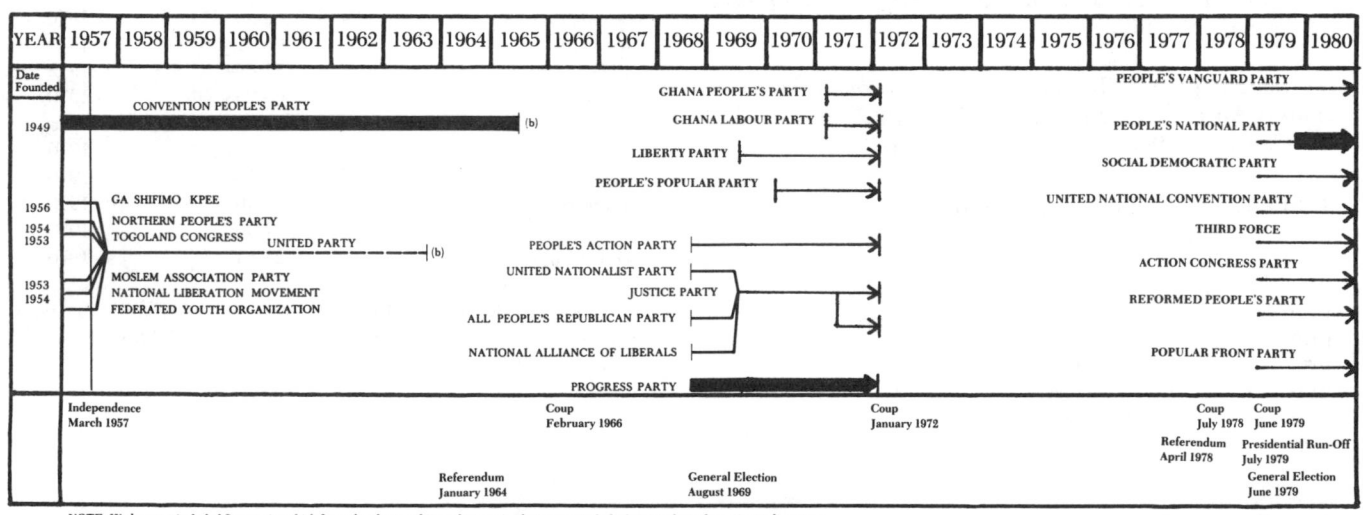

NOTE: We have not included five parties which formed and merged into other parties during a period of a few months in the spring and summer of 1969.

NOTE: The ban on political parties was lifted on January 1, 1979. We have not included several parties which formed and merged within the first few months of 1979.

the CPP was still banned. On May 1, 1969 political party activity was again permitted and 10 parties were registered but by summer mergers and banning had reduced the number to 5 groups competing in the new elections. The *United National Party* was the result of a merger in early July 1969 of four parties. The four were: *All People's Congress*; *Ghana Democratic Party*; *Nationalist Party*; *Republican Party*. The parties regrouped into two major parties, the *Progress Party* (PP), led by Dr. Busia, and the *National Alliance of Liberals* (NAL), led by K. A. Gbedemah. The results of the August 1969 elections gave control of the government to Dr. Busia. The PP won 105 of 140 seats. In October 1970 three opposition parties, the NAL, *The United National Party* and the *All People's Republican Party*, merged to form the *Justice Party*. All parties and political activity were banned in January 1972 after the military coup. In early 1976, General Acheampong stated that a program for return to civilian rule was being prepared but no date was given for the return. Subsequently plans for a combined military and civilian government were proposed. A government-sponsored and vaguely worded proposal for a combined civilian-military regime was accepted by a small margin in an April 1978 referendum which saw only a 40 percent turnout. In July 1978, a coup took place in which General Acheampong suddenly resigned and Lt. General Akuffo assumed power. Akuffo announced plans to return to a civilian government in July 1979. To this end the seven year ban on political parties was lifted, but 105 people were banned from holding public office. In spite of the order that parties could not be based on region, religion, ethnic origin, or profession, many new parties were formed. They include the People's National Party (which is associated with people from the former Convention People's Party), the Popular Front Party (formerly the Progress Party), the Action People's Congress, the Labor Party, the People's Freedom Party, and several others. Only two weeks before the elections were to be held, the government of General Akuffo was overthrown. The new government under President Rawlings announced that the elections would go on as planned on June 18, 1979, but that there would be a delay of at least three months in the transfer of power to the elected officials. Dr. Hilla Limann and the People's National Party won the election, but because Limann won only 35% of the vote, there had to be a run-off election. Limann easily won over his opponent, Victor Owusu of the Popular Front Party, in the run-off held on July 9, 1979. In late September 1979 Rawlings turned the government over to Dr. Limann.

B. Political Leadership

A coup d'état in 1966 brought an end to the government of President Nkrumah, who was succeeded by two senior military officers as head of state. Recruitment of cabinet positions before and after the 1966 coup was fairly broadly based. After three years of military rule, and the ignominious dismissal of the first leader in the military government, a civilian government under Dr. Busia ruled first at the sufferance of the National Liberation Council but on August 7, 1970 the Army's Presidential Commission dissolved itself thereby completing the return to civilian rule. In January 1972 the Busia government was ousted by a military coup led by Col. Acheampong. He continued to direct the National Redemption Council and its successor (October 1975) the Supreme Military Council until he was overthrown in July 1978. In October 1975, a major government reorganization ousted many senior government leaders including military officers and at least six antigovernment plots were reported from 1972 to 1975. Frequent government reshuffles occurred throughout the period 1972—1978. In 1978, Lt. Col. Frederick Akuffo assumed power. Akuffo announced plans to return to civilian rule by July 1979 and attempted economic reforms. Akuffo also granted amnesty to all political refugees and released those people who had been convicted by the military tribunal. An attempted coup in May 1979 was put down by the Ghanaian army. The army was unable to put down a second coup attempt on June 4, 1979 which overthrew Akuffo and put into power Flight Lieutenant Jerry Rawlings. Rawlings was appointed President by the new Armed Forces Revolutionary Committee. The elections scheduled for mid-June were held, but Rawlings said that the transfer of power to the winner, Dr. Hilla Limann would be postponed until early October. In late September, Rawlings handed the government over to Limann. Limann's tenure in office depended on his ability to control the economy and the army, and to gain support among the Ghanaian people. His lack of success was marked by the return of Rawlings and Limann's overthrow in 1981.

TABLE 14.5   Head of Government (Post Independence)

Name	Dates in Office	Age 1982	Ethnicity	Education	Former Occupation
1. Dr. Kwame Nkrumah (President)	1957—66	d. 1972 age 62	Akan (Nzima)	University & post-grad. work (United States)	Party Organizer
2. Lt. Gen. Joseph Ankarah (Chairman, NLC)	1966—69	65	Ga	Wesleyan School	Teacher, Soldier
3. Brig. Gen. A. A. Afrifa (Chairman, NLC)	1969	Executed in 1979, age 43	Akan (Ashanti)	Sandhurst (Eng.) & other Military Courses	Soldier, Infantry
4. Dr. Kofi Busia	Sept. 69— Jan. 72	d. 1978 age 65	Akan (Ashanti)	Oxford Ph.D.	University Professor
5. Gen. Ignatius Kuti Acheampong (Chairman, Supreme Military Council and Head of State)	Jan. 72— July 1978	Executed in 1979, age 48	Akan (Ashanti)	Officer Cadet School (Eng.)	Teacher, Soldier
6. General Frederick W. K. Akuffo (Chairman, Supreme Military Council and Head of State)	July 1978— June 1979	Executed in June 1979, age 42		Royal Military Academy, Sandhurst, United Kingdom	Soldier
7. Flight Lieut. Jerry Rawlings (President, and Chairman of Armed Forces Revolutionary Committee)	June 1979— September 1979	35	Scottish father Ghanaian mother (Ewe)	Military	Air Force Officer
8. Dr. Hilla Limann (President)	September 1979— 1981	58	"Northerner"	Ph.D. University (London and Paris)	Career Diplomat
9. Flight Lieut. Jerry Rawlings (President, and Chairman of Armed Forces Revolutionary Committee)	1982—	35	Scottish father Ghanaian mother (Ewe)	Military	Air Force Officer

TABLE 14.6   Cabinet Membership: Distribution by Ethnic Unit*

Ethnicity	Independence Cabinet	Immediate Pre-Coup Cabinet	1967 Cabinet
1. Akan (44%)	62%	71%	25%
2. Mole-Dagbani (16)	23	12	13
3. Ewé (13)	7.7	12	38
4. Ga (8.5)	7.7	5.9	25
5. Others (18)	0	0	0
N =	13	17	8

*Ethnic units arranged in rank order of size within country with the unit's percent of national population in parentheses.

VI. National Integration and Stability

TABLE 14.7   Elite Instability

Event and Date	Characteristics
1. *Coup d'État* *February 24, 1966*	*a. Description*: While President Nkrumah was on a state visit to the Chinese Peoples' Republic, he was replaced by an army and police coup. In all, 27 Ghanaians were killed in the coup (including Major-General Charles Bawah who was shot when he refused to support the coup). General Ankrah (retired) was asked to head a new government by the coup leaders. Dr. Nkrumah took up residence in Guinea. b. *Participants*: Colonel F. K. Kotoka, commander of the second brigade, and T. W. K. Harley, commander of the police, along with junior officers such as A. A. Afrifa. About 3,000 members of the army occupied Accra at the time of the takeover. c. *Apparent Causes*: The reasons for the coup were announced by the new regime during a broadcast on February 24: "…This act has been necessitated by the political and economic situation in the country. The concentration of power in the hands of one man has led to the abuse of individual rights and duties. He…runs the country as his own personal property. The economic situation…is chaotic."
2. Attempted Coup April 17, 1967	a. *Description*: General Ankrah reported that a plan to assassinate all senior officers was undertaken on April 17 when an army detachment on training maneuvers attacked a number of buildings in Accra. In the ensuing battle, Lt. General Kotoka and two other government officers were killed. b. *Participants*: An army reconnaissance team of 120 men, commanded by Lt. Sam Arthur. An additional squadron was also said to be involved. Lt. Arthur and Lt. Yeboah were tried, found guilty, and hanged. A third junior officer was sentenced to 20 years in prison. c. *Apparent Causes*: While the causes are unclear the role of personal dissatisfactions with army promotions and the desire for personal power seem to outweigh tribal or ideological explanations.
3. Coup d'État January 13, 1972	a. *Description*: A group of army officers led by Col. I. K. Acheampong, commander of the 1st Infantry Brigade based in Accra, seized power in a bloodless coup while Prime Minister Busia was in London for medical treatment. Cabinet ministers and two top-ranking officers were jailed. A National Redemption Council was set up headed by Col. Acheampong, parliament was disbanded, and all political parties were banned. b. *Participants*: Army officers led by Col. Acheampong. c. *Apparent Causes*: Discontent with the country's economic situation, especially the 44 percent devaluation of the *cedi* in December 1971, seems to have been the major cause. Busia's austerity budget involved cuts in military expenditures as well. Col. Acheampong accused Busia's government of extravagance and permitting widespread official corruption.
4. Coup d'État July 5, 1978	a. *Description*: Colonel Acheampong suddenly retired apparently under pressure from fellow army officers because of his inability to provide unity and stability for Ghana. Acheampong handed power over to Lt. General F. W. K. Akuffo. b. *Participants*: Army officers. c. *Apparent Causes*: Dissatisfaction with Acheampong's regime, specifically, his inability to provide the leadership necessary to unite Ghana's various factions and lead Ghana to a civilian government.
5. Coup d'État June 4—6, 1979	a. *Description*: Junior army officers led by Flight Lieut. Jerry Rawlings fought against government forces. The country was sealed off until June 6, 1979 when the new government was in place. b. *Participants*: Junior army officers. c. *Apparent Causes*: Dissatisfaction over government corruption and the severe economic problems faced by Ghana were major reasons for the takeover. Two other reasons were disagreement over Akuffo's punishment of Acheampong and the fact that Akuffo had granted amnesty for himself and members of the Supreme Military Council for the time after the return to civilian government.
6. Coup d'État December 31, 1981	a. *Description*: The Peace Regiment and the Fifth Battalion led by Flight Lieutenant Rawlings oust the Limann government, proscribe party activity, and establish the Provisional National Council, which Rawlings chairs, to rule Ghana. b. *Participants*: Flight Lieutenant Rawlings and units of the army. c. *Apparent Causes*: The marked deterioration in the economy amid widespread political corruption.

SOURCES: A. A. Afrifa, *The Ghana Coup: 24th February 1966* (New York: Humanities Press, 1966). Henry L. Bretton, *The Rise and Fall of Kwame Nkrumah: A Study of Personal Rule in Africa* (New York: Praeger, 1966). Robert Fitch and Mary Oppenheimer, *Ghana: End of an Illusion* (New York: Monthly Review Press, 1966). Jon Kraus, "The Men in Charge," *Africa Report*, 11 (April 1966): 16—20. Valerie Bennet "The Motivation for Military Intervention: The Case of Ghana" *Western Political Quarterly* 26 (December 1973): 659—674.

Except for Ewé irredentism in the early years following independence, there has been little evidence of communal instability in Ghana. Elite instability has, however, been linked to communal tension. In his autobiography, A. A. Afrifa stated that the coup against Nkrumah, who was an Nzima, was partly based on the alliance of the Ashanti and Ewé peoples. In 1967, a coup attempt led to the death of General Kotoka. After the return to civilian rule under Busia, widespread strikes, riots, and a major loss in purchasing power from a severe devaluation of the Ghanaian cedi, led to another coup under the leadership of Colonel Acheampong. There were many plots reported against the Acheampong government. In July 1978, Col. Acheampong suddenly resigned and Lt. Gen. Akuffo assumed power. Under Akuffo, attempts to reform the economy led to sharp price increases which were followed by strikes in industry and in the civil service in November 1978. A state of emergency was declared, but by January 1979 the unrest seemed to have calmed and the state of emergency was lifted. Dissatisfaction with the Akuffo regime resurfaced in a May 15, 1979 coup attempt by junior army officers. This attempt was put down by the Ghanaian army, but another attempt on June 4, 1979 was successful. Flight Lieutenant Jerry Rawlings, who had led both attempts against Akuffo, was appointed President by the new government, the Armed Forces Revolutionary Committee (AFRC). Rawlings' goal was to purge the Ghanaian army

of corruption. To this end, three former heads of state were executed in June 1979; General Acheampong, General Akuffo and General Afrifa. There were also several other executions of senior military officials and many prison sentences were handed down to those found guilty of corruption in the military, government, or business sectors. Rawlings' strict measures prompted the withdrawal of much foreign aid and trade which has worsened Ghana's already severe economic problems. Dr. Limann took office in late September 1979 and forced Rawlings and several other senior military officials to resign. President Limann continued to have problems with the army and with the economy which in late 1979 was suffering from a 70% rate of inflation. There were repeated reports of coup plots against Limann since he came to power. By mid-1980 tensions between Limann and Rawlings had intensified, Rawlings accused the state security agencies of attempting to discredit the AFRC and stir up ethnic animosities against the Ewé, Rawlings' ethnic identity. Furthermore, throughout Februrary and March, 1980, teachers, civil servants, and industrial workers staged a series of strikes demanding higher wages and better working conditions. In late March 1980 several soldiers, and one civilian were arrested on conspiracy to eliminate leading politicians and reinstate Rawlings as head of government. Rawlings was not involved in the alleged plot. Rawlings took power in a coup in 1981.

TABLE 14.8   Communal Instability

Event and Date	Characteristics
1. Irredentism ca. 1957—63 (sporadic)	a. *Description*: Certain Ewé ethnic members of the Trans-Volta region in Ghana and kinsmen in the neighboring state of Togo demanded re-unification following the UN plebiscite which placed the Trans-Volta region under Ghanaian control. Ewé irredentists from Ghana were reputed to have taken refuge in Togo. There were a series of border incidents and border closings at the Ghana-Togo border. b. *Participants*: Ewé ethnic members. c. *Apparent Cause*: Ewé irredentism. Calls for Ewé-area separation from Ghana have continued to the present, however.
2. Rebellion 1969	a. *Description*: Following a dispute over the appointment of the Ya-Na (Paramount Chief) of Dagomba in November 1968, the National Liberation Council appointed a Committee of Enquiry which reported that the installation of one of the rival candidates had been unduly influenced by Government officials, army and police in the area. The Government's order for the installation of the other contending candidate resulted in riots in Yendi in September 1969, and a state of emergency was declared. Army and police personnel stationed in Yendi killed 23 and seriously injured 40 people in a confrontation with an armed crowd. Seven hundred were arrested and 4 Dagomba chiefs were banned from Yendi in connection with this disturbance. b. *Participants*: Partisans of Dagomba royal families. c. *Apparent Causes*: Opposition to a central government decision reversing a controversial appointment to the office of Ya-Na made by the traditional authorities.

SOURCES: Claude Welch, *Dream of Unity* (Ithaca, N.Y.: Cornell University Press, 1966). Dennis Austin, "The Ghana-Togo Frontier," *Journal of Modern African Studies*, (1963): 139—146. M. Staniland *The Lions of Dagbon* (New York: Cambridge University Press, 1975).

TABLE 14.10   Annual Instability Events: Independence Through 1979—Ghana

Year	'61	'62	'63	'64	'65	'66	'67	'68	'69	'70	'71	'72	'73	'74	'75	'76	'77	'78	'79
ELITE INSTABILITY																			
Assassinations																			
Plots	1	1					1	1				1	2	1	7				
Attempted Coups d'État							1												1
Coups d'État						1						1						1	1
COMMUNAL INSTABILITY																			
Ethnic Violence																			
Irredentism																			
Rebellion									1										
Civil War																			
MASS INSTABILITY																			
Revolt																			
Revolution																			
TURMOIL																			
Demonstrations			1									2	1	1					
Strikes (no. days)	18						2	6	7										
Riots (no. days)								1	1						4				
Terrorism		5	1	1															
Declarations of Emergency			1					1	1		·	1							
CABINET INSTABILITY																			
Realloc. and new appts.	24	4	7	5	21					3		9	7						
Resig. and Dismissals	10	3		3	9				1		12		4						
No. of members (max.) (maximum in year)	14	14	19	19	19	19	16	9	19	20	20	17	15						

VII. Selected References

BIBLIOGRAPHY

Adams, Cynthia. *A Study Guide for Ghana*. Boston: Development Program, African Studies Center, Boston University, 1966.

Amedekey, E. Y. (Comp). *The Culture of Ghana: A Bibliography* . Accra:Ghana University Press, 1970.

Baynham, S. "The Ghanaian Military: A Bibliographic Essay," *West African Journal of Sociology and Political Science* 1, 1 (October 1975): 83—96.

Chand, Attar. "Ghana Since the Coup: A Select Bibliography." *Africa Quarterly* 9 (October—December 1969), 310—315.

Johnson, A. F. *A Bibliography of Ghana, 1930—1961*. London: Longmans for Ghana Library Board, 1964.

GENERAL

Aluko, Olajide. *Ghana and Nigeria, 1957—1970*. N.Y.: Barnes and Noble, 1976.

Apter, David E. *Ghana in Transition*, 2nd rev. ed. Princeton, N.J.: Princeton University Press, 1972.

Dickson, Kwamina B. *An Historical Geography of Ghana*. London: Cambridge University Press, 1969.

Fage, John D. *Ghana: A Historical Interpretation*. Madison: University of Wisconsin Press, 1959.

Foster, Philip and Aristide R. Zolberg. *Ghana and the Ivory Coast: Perspectives on Modernization*. Chicago: University of Chicago Press, 1971.

Genoud, Roger. *Nationalism and Economic Development in Ghana*. New York: Praeger, 1969.

Jeffries, Richard. *Class, Power and Ideology in Ghana: The Railwaymen of Sekondi*. Cambridge: Cambridge University Press, 1978.

U.S. Department of the Army. *Area Handbook for Ghana*. Washington, D.C.: U.S. Government Printing Office, 1971.

Ward, William E. F. *A History of Ghana*. London: Allen and Unwin, 1966.

POLITICAL

Afrifa, A. A. *The Ghana Coup, 24th Februrary, 1966*. London: Frank Cass, 1966.

Amin, Samir. *Neo-Colonialism in West Africa*. Harmondsworth, Middlesex: Penguin Books, 1973.

Armha, Kwesi. *Nkrumah's Legacy*. London: Rex Collings, 1974.

Austin, Dennis. *Ghana Observed: Essays on the Politics of a West African Republic*. Manchester: University of Manchester Press, 1976.

Austin, Dennis. *Politics in Ghana, 1946—1960*. London: Oxford University Press, 1964.

Austin, D. and F. Luckham, eds. *Politicians and Soldiers in Ghana*. London: Cass, 1975.

Bretton, Henry L. *The Rise and Fall of Kwame Nkrumah*. New York: Praeger, 1966.

Davidson, Basil. *Black Star: A View of the Life and Times of Kwame Nkrumah*. N.Y. Praeger, 1973.

Dowse, Robert E. *Aspects of Ghanaian Development: Studies in Political Sociology*. Totowa, N.J.: Frank Cass, 1979.

Fitch, Bob and Mary Oppenheimer. *Ghana: End of an Illusion*. New York: Monthly Review Press, 1966.

Harvey, William. *Law and Social Change in Ghana*. Princeton: Princeton University Press, 1966.

James, C. L. R. *Nkrumah and the Ghana Revolution*. London: Allison and Busby, 1977.

Jones, Trevor. *Ghana's First Republic, 1960—66: The Pursuit of the Political Kingdom*. London: Methuen, 1976.

Kay, G., ed. *The Political Economy of Colonialism in Ghana: A collection of Documents and Statistics, 1900—1960*. Cambridge: Cambridge University Press, 1972.

Milburn, J. F. *British Business and Ghanaian Independence*. London: C. Hurst, 1977.

Nkrumah, Kwame. *Ghana, the Autobiography of Kwame Nkrumah*. London: Nelson, 1957.

Nkrumah, Kwame. *Neocolonialism, the Last State of Imperialism*. London: Heinemann, 1965.

Nkrumah, Kwame, *Class Struggles in Africa*. N.Y.: International Publishers, 1970.

Nkrumah, Kwame. *Dark Days in Ghana*. N.Y.: International Publishers, 1968.

Ocran, A. K. *A Myth is Broken: An Account of the Ghana Coup d'État of 24 February 1966*. London: Longman's, 1968.

Ocran, A. *Politics of the Sword: A Personal Memoir on Military Involvement in Ghana*. London: Rex Collings, 1977.

Omari, T. Peter. *Kwame Nkrumah: The Anatomy of an African Dictatorship*. New York: Africana Publishing Corporation, 1970.

Owosu, M. *Uses and Abuses of Political Power: A Case Study of Continuity and Change in the Politics of Ghana*. Chicago: University of Chicago Press, 1970.

Pinkney, Robert. *Ghana Under Military Rule*. New York: Barnes and Noble, 1972.

Price, R. M. *Society and Bureaucracy in Contemporary Ghana*. Berkeley: University of California Press, 1975.

Smock, D. R. *The Politics of Pluralism: A Comparative Study of Lebanon and Ghana*. New York: Elsevier, 1975.

Staniland, M. *The Lions of Dagbon: Political Change in Northern Ghana*. New York: Cambridge University Press, 1975.

Thompson, W. S. *Ghana's Foreign Policy, 1957—1966*. Princeton, N.J.: Princeton University Press, 1969.

Woronoff, Jon. *West African Wager: Houphouet Versus Nkrumah*. Metuchen, N.J.: Scarecrow Press, 1972.

ECONOMIC

Amin, Samir. *Trois experiences africaines de developpment: le Mali, le Guineee et le Ghana*. Paris: Presses Universitaires de France, 1965.

Garlick, P. C. *African Traders and Economic Development in Ghana*. New York: Oxford University Press, 1971.

Genoud, Roger. *Nationalism and Economic Development in Ghana*. N.Y.: Praeger, 1969.

Hance, William A. "The Volta River Project: A Study in Industrial Development." In *African Economic Development*, rev. ed., by William A. Hance, pp. 87—114. New York: Praeger, 1967.

Hill, P. *Rural Capitalism in West Africa*. London: Cambridge University Press, 1970.

Howard, Rhoda. *Colonialism and Underdevelopment in Ghana*. New York: Africana Publishing Co., 1978.

International Monetary Fund. "Ghana." In *Surveys of African Economies*, Vol. 6. Washington, D.C.: I.M.F., 1975.

Killick, Tony. *Development Economics in Action: A Study of Economic Policies in Ghana*. New York: St. Martin's Press, 1978.

Killick, A. and R. Szereszewski. "The Economy of Ghana," in *The Economies of Africa*, eds. P. Robson and D. A. Lury, pp. 79—126. Evanston, Ill.: Northwestern University Press, 1969.

Lawson, Rowena. *The Changing Economy of the Lower Volta, 1954—67*. Oxford: Oxford University Press, 1972.

Leith, J. C. *Foreign Trade Regimes and Economic Development: Ghana, Vol. II*. New York: National Bureau of Economic Research, 1974.

Seidman, Ann Willcox. *Ghana's Development Experience: 1951—65*. Nairobi: East African Publishing House, 1978.

Steel, W. F. *Small-Scale Employment and Production in Developing Countries*: Evidence from Ghana. New York: Praeger, 1977.

SOCIAL

Acquah, I. *Accra Survey*. London: University of London Press, 1958.

Agbodeka, F. *Achimota in the National Setting*. Accra: Afram Publishers, 1977.

Arkaifie, R. *Bibliography of the Ewes*. Cape Coast, Ghana, 1976.

Baeta, C. G. *Prophetism in Ghana: A Study of Some "Spiritual" Churches*. London: S.C.M. Press, 1962.

Birmingham, Walter, et al. eds. *A Study of Contemporary Ghana*, Vol. 2, "Some Aspects of Social Structure." London: Allen and Unwin, 1967.

Boateng, E. A. *A Geography of Ghana*. New York: Cambridge University Press, 1966.

Brokensha, David. *Social Change at Larteh, Ghana*. Oxford: Clarendon Press, 1966.

Caldwell, John C. *African Rural-Urban Migration: The Movement to Ghana's Towns*. New York: Columbia University Press, 1969.

Curle, A. *Educational Problems of Developing Societies with Case Studies of Ghana, Pakistan, and Nigeria*. New York: Praeger, 1973.

Field, M. J. *Search for Security: An Ethno-Psychiatric Study of Rural Ghana*. London: Faber and Faber, 1960.

Foster, Philip. *Education and Social Change in Ghana*. Chicago: University of Chicago Press, 1965.

Hilton, T. E. *Ghana Population Atlas*. London: Nelson, 1960.

Kaufert, Joseph M. "Ethnic Unit Definition in Ghana: A Comparison of Culture Cluster Analysis and Social Distant Measures" in John N. Paden, (ed), *Values, Identities and National Integration*, Evanston, Ill.: Northwestern University Press, 1980, pp. 41—52.

Kay, B. *Bringing up Children in Ghana*. London: Allen and Unwin, 1962.

Levine, V. T. *Political Corruption: The Ghana Case*. Stanford: Hoover Institution, 1974.

Parsons, Robert T. *The Churches and Ghana Society*. Leiden: E. J. Brill, 1967.

Peil, Margaret. *The Ghanaian Factory Worker: Industrial Man in Africa*. London: Cambridge University Press, 1972.

Schildkrout, E. *People of the Zongo: The Transformation of Ethnic Identities in Ghana*. New York: Cambridge University Press, 1978.

Wilks, I. *Asante in the Nineteenth Century*. New York: Cambridge University Press, 1975.

15. Guinea

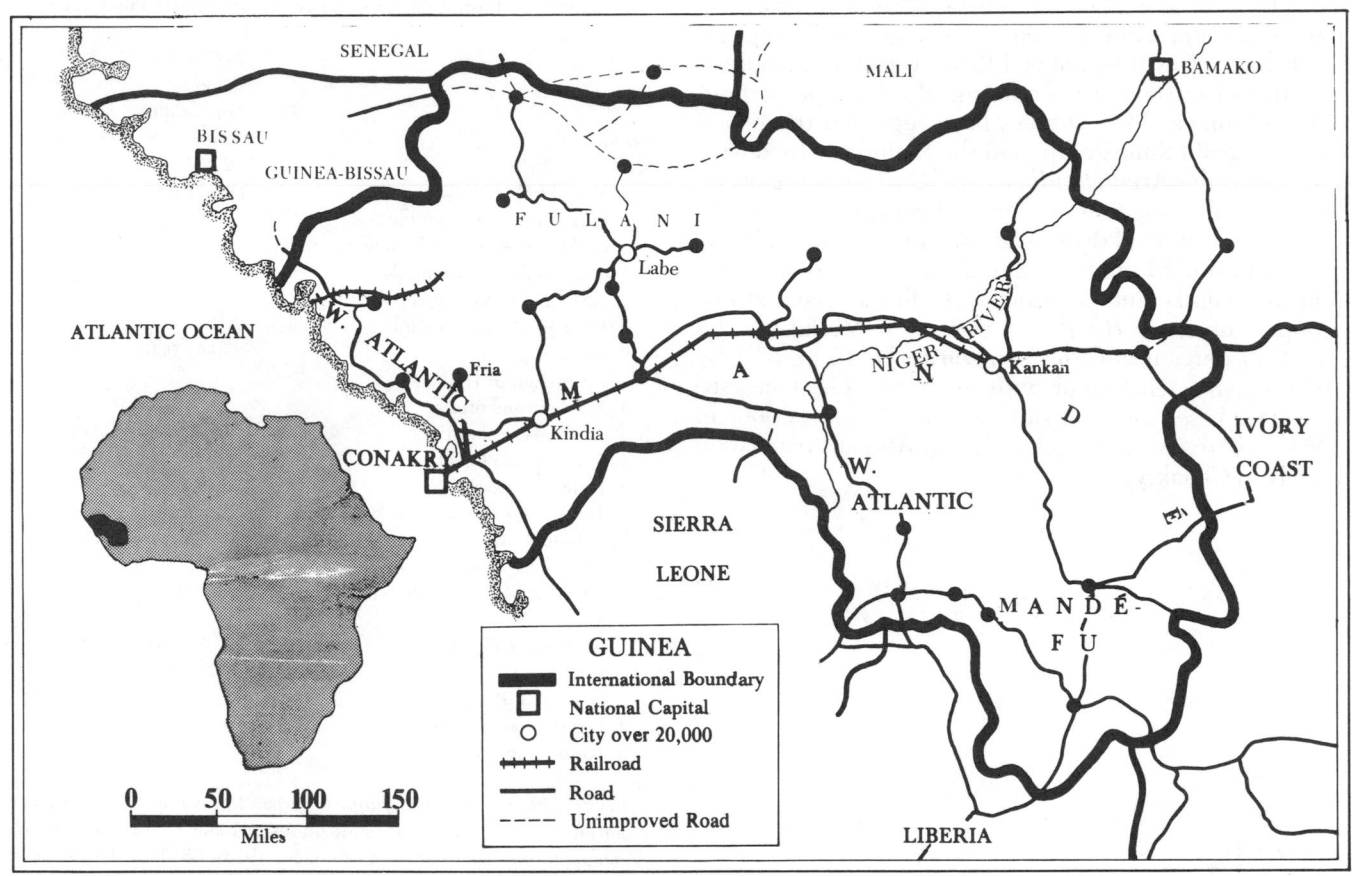

GUINEA
- ▬▬ International Boundary
- ▢ National Capital
- ○ City over 20,000
- ┼┼┼┼ Railroad
- ── Road
- ---- Unimproved Road

0 50 100 150
Miles

I. Basic Information

Date of Independence: October 2, 1958

Former Colonial Ruler: France

Change in Boundaries: Formerly part of the French West African Federation

Estimated Population (1980): 5,419,000* (the 1972 census result was reported to be 5,143,284 but this may have been for the *de jure* population including those Guineans who have left the country.

Area Size (equivalent in U.S.): 94,926 sq. mi. (Oregon)

Date of Last Census: 1972

Major Exports 1975/1976 as Percent of Total Exports: bauxite—61 percent; alumina—33 percent

*According to a report in *The New York Times* (December 1968), between 500,000 and 1,000,000 Guineans have left the country since independence. *Africa Contemporary Record 1969—70*, p. B 496, says that a population figure "in the region of 3,500,000 has been mentioned for 1967." The Europa Yearbook 1979 (Vol. II, p. 414) reported a 1978 estimate that 1,000,000 Guineans had left the country.

**A large volume of smuggling takes place across the country's borders and no information is available about its composition.

II. Ethnic Patterns

The ethnic classification of Guinea is based primarily on linguistic criteria and not on identity groups (except for the Fulani). It will be noticed that our classifcation deviates from the standard rendering of ethnic proportionality in Guinea. Most sources have regarded the Fulani as the largest ethnic group, and the Malinké second largest. Thus, the *Area Handbook for Guinea* 2nd edition, gives the following percentages that come from a 1954/55 sample survey: Peul (Fulani) 29 percent; Malinké 22 percent; Soussou 13 percent. Based on reports of assimilation by Malinké and Soussou of smaller adjacent ethnic groups, the *Area Handbook* estimated Malinké to be about 30 percent and the Soussou to be 16 percent by 1970 which is consistent with our estimates. Our estimates are based on the results of a sample survey done in 1964. There is a very small non-African population mainly in Conakry.

TABLE 15.1   Ethnic Units Over 5 Percent of Country Population

Ethnic Unit	Estimated Ethnic Population 1980	Estimated Ethnic Percentage
a. Mandé Cluster	2,601,100	48%
1. Malinké (Manding)	(1,625,700)	(30%)
i. Malinké, ii. Ouassoulonké, iii. Mikiforé, iv. Toubacaye (Diaknanké), v. Kouranko, vi. Lelé, vii. Konianke, viii. Sarakolé (Marka, Soninké)		
2. Soussou (Susu)	(867,000)	(16%)
i. Soussou, ii. Djalonké		
3. Bambara and others		
b. Peul (Foula, Fulani)	1,517,300	28%
1. Foula (Foula Djallon)		
2. Pouli (Foulacounda)		
3. Toucouleur		
c. Mandé-fu Type	596,100	11%
1. Guerzé (Kpellé)		
2. Toma, 3. Manon (G'Bema)		
4. Manon, 5. Kono		
d. West Atlantic Cluster	541,900	10%
1. Kissi	(379,300)	(7%)
2. Tcmnc, 3. Baga,		
4. Landouman (Tiapi),		
5. Bagafore, 6. Mnami		

SOURCES: *Etude démographique* (Paris: Ministère de la France d'outremer. Service des statistiques, 1956), Vol. 1. Etude démographique par sondage en Guinée, 1954—55. U.S. Department of the Army, *U.S. Army Area Handbook for Guinea* (Washington, D.C.: Government Printing Office, 1961).

III. Language Patterns

The three major language groups in Guinea are Malinké (in upper Guinea), Poular (in middle Guinea), and Soussou (in coastal Guinea). Although Malinké and Soussou are part of the same language family (Mandé), they are distinct languages. Each of the three major ethnic languages serves as a *lingua franca*, to varying degrees, in the region where it is predominant. Malinké, however, seems to be emerging as a broader *lingua franca* in the country. The local term for Malinké is Maninka. Dyula is a simplified form of Malinké.

We differ with the existing estimates as to which of the languages in Guinea is most widely spoken. Knappert estimates Fulani (33 percent), MacDougald estimates Fulani (62 percent), and Rustow estimates Fulani (39 percent) with Malinké-Bambara-Dyula second at 26 percent. Our own estimate puts Malinké first with approximately 30 percent native speakers and an additional 18 percent of second language speakers (total 48 percent). Poular (Fulani) native speakers probably comprise 28 percent; and perhaps an additional 5 percent of second-language speakers (total 33 percent).

The official language is French, which is used in government, education, and mass media. According to the second edition of the *Area Handbook for Guinea* about 20 percent of the population speak French and it is widely used as a *lingua franca*. However, broadcasting is also conducted in Poular, Malinké, Soussou, Kissi, Toma, Coniagui, Bassari, and Guerzé. It is official policy to encourage English as a second national language. Arabic is widely used as a language of religion.

TABLE 15.2   Language Patterns

1. Primacy
1st language	Malinké	(48%)
2nd language	Poular	(33%)

2. Linguistic classification (all ethnic units in country over 5%)

		Green-berg	Dalby
	Malinké	IA2	31A
	Poular	IA1	201
	Mandé-fu	IA2	31C
	West Atlantic cluster (Kissi)	IA1	25B, 25A

3. *Lingua francas*   Malinké, Poular, Soussou

4. Official language   French

IV. Urban Patterns

Capital/largest city: Conakry (founded 1885)
Dominant ethnicity/language of capital
   Major vernacular: Soussou[1]
   Major ethnic group: Soussou[2]
   Major ethnic group as percent of capital's population:
      45 percent (1952)

[1]Jan Knappert, "Language Problems of the New Nations of Africa," *African Quarterly*, 5 (1965): 95—105.
[2]O. Collfus, "Conakry en 1951—52: Etude Humaine et Economique," *Etude Guinéennes* 10/11 (1952): pp. 16—17.

TABLE 15.3   Growth of Capital/Largest City

Date	Conakry
1920	9,000
1930	7,000
1940	20,000
1950	39,000
1960	90,000
1967	197,000 UA
1972[a]	525,000 UA

SOURCE: *Démographie Comparée.*
   [a]See Table 15.4

TABLE 15.4   Cities of 20,000 and Over*

City	Size	Date
Conakry[c]	525,000 UA	1972
Kankan[a]	60,000	1970
Labe[d]	30,000	1967
Kindia[b]	25,000	1964

SOURCES:
[a]*Africa 1973* mid-1970 estimate.
[b]*Statesman's Yearbook 1967—68.*
[c]*Africa Contemporary Record.*
[d]*Area Handbook for Guinea*, 2nd ed., p. 59.

*Current urban data are generally unavailable for Guinea, making the assessment of Guinean urbanization an especially hazardous undertaking. Other main towns are: Boke, Macenta, and Kissidougou. Conakry appears to have lost population since the early 1960's according to some reports. However, in December 1972, Conakry radio reported the population for the urban agglomeration of Conakry to be 525,671. The accuracy of this statement is unknown but is in contrast to other estimates of Conakry's population which are circa 150,000 to 170,000.

V. Political Patterns

A. Political Parties and Elections

Since independence, Guinea has been a one-party state. Founded in 1947 as a branch of the *Rassèmblement Démocratique Africain* (RDA), the *Parti Démocratique de Guinée* (PDG) was Guinea's dominant party. Sekou Touré, the president of Guinea and the secretary-general of PDG, has held both positions since Guinea's independence in 1958. All members of the National Assembly must belong to the PDG. In the December 1974 election, the assembly was enlarged from 75 to 150 members. A new assembly was elected in January 1980 by regional Councils of the Revolution. The size of the assembly was increased to 210 members at this time. An illegal underground opposition party, the *National Liberation Front*, FLN, is reported to be operating against the regime. The National Council of the Revolution, the supreme governing body of Guinea elected a new central committee in September 1979. The central committee was enlarged from 25 to 75 members.

B. Political Leadership

Since independence in 1958, the government of Guinea has been led by President Sekou Touré. He has considerably enlarged his cabinet since that time and, except for the period 1963—64, there had been very few resignations and dismissals from the executive body until the 1970 coup attempt. Since that time there have been a number of purges and reshuffles of the cabinet. The most recent cabinet reshuffle occurred in June 1979 when the number of government ministers was reduced from 40 to 30. Mandé people tend to be rather more prominent in government than the Mandé proportion of the population would suggest, but cabinet membership is, nonetheless, ethnically diversified. Kwame Nkrumah, after being deposed from power in Ghana in 1966, was invited by Touré to become the co-President of Guinea, a largely symbolic arrangement which was maintained until Nkrumah's death in 1972.

FIGURE 15.1   Political Parties and Elections   GUINEA

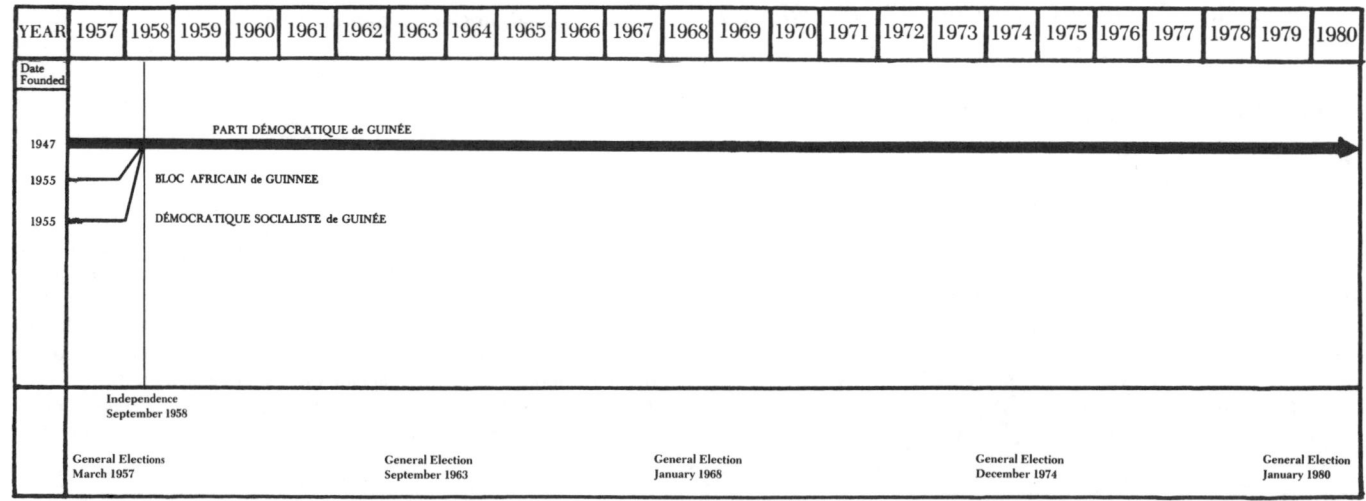

TABLE 15.5   Head of Government (Post Independence)

Name	Dates in Office	Age (1982)	Ethnicity	Education	Former Occupation
1. Ahmed Sekou Touré (President)	1958—present	60	Mandé (Soussou)	Technical-Secondary (Guinea)	Clerk, Union Organizer

TABLE 15.6   Cabinet Membership: Distribution by Ethnic Unit*

Ethnicity*	Independence Cabinet	1967 Cabinet
1. Mandé (48%)	60%	65%
2. Fulani (23)	30	27
3. Mandé-fu (11)	0	0
4. West Atlantic (10)	10	3.8
5. Others (3)	0	3.8
N =	10	26

*Ethnic units arranged in rank order of size within country with the unit's percentage of national population in parentheses.

VI. National Integration and Stability

The regime of Sekou Touré has served continuously since the mid-1950's. To some extent, the "charisma" of Touré has continued up to the present, and his broad-based political party has been successful in linking masses with elites. Tension among the various ethnic groups is carefully handled by Guinean leaders and an effort is made to represent every ethnic group in the political life of Guinea. The role of ideology and widespread Islamic culture seem to be of special importance in achieving a substantial degree of national integration. There were reports of plots in 1960, 1965, 1969 and 1976, and an assassination attempt against Touré occurrred in 1969. In November 1970, a Portuguese sponsored attack from the sea was repulsed. The invaders included dissident Guineans as well as Portuguese army officers and PAIGC dissidents from Portuguese Guinea. Of the several objectives of the invasion, one was to capture Amilcar Cabral of the PAIGC, a second was to release Portuguese prisoners, and a third was to overthrow the Touré regime. After this coup attempt several plots and waves of arrests were reported. The large number of Guineans who have left the country apparently indicates some considerable disaffection with its leadership although migration patterns and better economic prospects in some adjoining countries also play a role in this exodus. In September 1977, there were riots and demonstrations thoughout the country set off by the milita's firing on a market women's demonstration in Conakry. The market women had been steadfast supporters of the Touré regime and while information on Guinea is difficult to verify, the regime may have been seriously weakened in its base of support, in part, because of its inability to deal with the disasters of the frequent droughts during the 1970's. In response to the market demonstrations, Sekou Touré reintroduced private trade and started a program of political liberalization. In August 1979, Touré released the Archbishop of Conakry who had been imprisoned since 1970 for allegedly plotting against the government.

TABLE 15.7 Elite Instability

Event and Date	Characteristics
1. Coup Attempt February 1968	a. *Description*: The government reported that 500 Guinean nationals attempted to enter the country to overthrow the government. Among those arrested were Barry Yaya, secretary general of the banned National Liberation Front. b. *Participants*: Dissident Guinean groups opposed to the Touré regime who were living in exile in neighboring countries. c. *Apparent Causes*: Opposition to the policies and ideology of the Touré regime.
2. Coup Attempt November 22, 1970	a. *Description*: A Portuguese-sponsored 'invasion' of Conakry by opponents of the Touré regime, along with dissidents from the PAIGC, tried to overthrow Touré, to free Portuguese soldiers captured by PAIGC guerrillas in Portuguese Guinea, and to capture Amilcar Cabral and other PAIGC leaders. b. *Participants*: Dissident Guinean and PAIGC leaders along with Portuguese officers. c. *Apparent Causes*: It appears that General Spinola from Portuguese Guinea was using dissident Guineans to overthrow Touré and remove the base of PAIGC support for the war in Portuguese Guinea. (The PAIGC was the Portuguese Guinea liberation movement which came to power in 1974 in Guinea-Bissau.

TABLE 15.10 Annual Instability Events: Independence through 1975—Guinea

Year	'61	'62	'63	'64	'65	'66	'67	'68	'69	'70	'71	'72	'73	'74	'75	'76	'77	'78	'79
ELITE INSTABILITY																			
Assassinations									1										
Plots	1					1			1	2	5		2			1			
Attempted Coups d'État								1 1 1											
Coups d'État																			
COMMUNAL INSTABILITY																			
Ethnic Violence																			
Irredentism																			
Rebellion																			
Civil War																			
MASS INSTABILITY																			
Revolt																			
Revolution																			
TURMOIL																			
Demonstrations																			
Strikes (no. days)	2																		
Riots (no. days)	2																		
Terrorism									1										
Declarations of Emergency																			
CABINET INSTABILITY																			
Realloc. and new appts.	9	10	11	18	5	1	23	7	13	11	6	12							
New members	3	6	2	7			3	3	19	5	11	11							
Resig. and Dismissals			9	4		1	2	3	14	5	12	12							
No. of members (max.)	12	23	19	24	24	24	25	26	35	35	34	33							

VII. Selected References

BIBLIOGRAPHY

Organization for Economic Cooperation and Development. *Bibliographie sur la Guinee*. Paris: O.E.C.D., 1967.

GENERAL

Ameillon, B. *La Guinee: bilan d'une independence* Paris: Maspero, 1964.

Charles, Bernard. *Guinee*. Lausanne: Editions Recontre, 1963.

O'Toole, T. E. *Historical Dictionary for Guinea*. Metuchen, N.J.: Scarecrow, 1978.

Riviere, C. (trans. by V. Thompson and R. Adloff) *Guinea: The Mobilization of a People*. Ithaca, N.Y.: Cornell University Press, 1977.

Suret-Canale, J. *La Republique de Guinee*. Paris: Seghers, 1970

Thompson, Virginia and Richard Adloff. *French West Africa.* Stanford, Cal.: Stanford University Press, 1957. pp. 132—138.

Nelson, H. D. et al. *Area Handbook for Guinea 2nd edition*. Washington, D.C.: U.S. Government Printer, 1975.

POLITICAL

Adamolekun, L. *Sekou Touré's Guinea: An Experiment in Nation Building*. London: Methuen, 1976.

Amin, Samir. *Neo-Colonialism in West Africa*. Harmondsworth, Middlesex: Penguin Books, 1973.

Atwood, William. *The Reds and the Blacks*. New York: Harper and Row, 1967.

Cowan, L. Gray. "Guinea." In *African One-Party States*, ed. Gwendolen M. Carter. Ithaca, N.Y.: Cornell University Press, 1962.

de Lusignan, Guy. *French-Speaking Africa since Independence*. pp. 180—198. London: Pall Mall Press, 1969.

DuBois, Victor David. *The Independence Movement in Guinea: A Study in African Nationalism*. Princeton, N.J.: PhD. Thesis available from University Microfilms, 1963.

DuBois, Victor. "Guinea." In *Political Parties and National Integration in Tropical Africa*, pp. 186—215, eds. J. S. Coleman and C. G. Rosberg. Los Angeles: University of California Press, 1964.

Morrow, John H. *First American Ambassador to Guinea*. New Brunswick: Rutgers University Press, 1968.

Touré, Sékou. *Strategie et tactique de la revolution*. 2nd ed. Conakry, Guinea: Bureau de presse de la Presidence de la Republique, 1976.

Zartman, William I. "Guinea: The Quiet War Goes On." *Africa Report*, 12 (November 1967): 67—72.

ECONOMIC

Amin, Samir. *Trois Experiences Africaines de Developpement*: Le Mali, la Guinee et le Ghana. Paris: Presses Universitaires de French, 1965.

Berg, Elliot. "Education and Manpower in Senegal, Guinea, and the Ivory Coast." In *Manpower and Education: Country Studies in Economic Development*, eds. F. B. Harbison and C. Myers. New York: McGraw-Hill, 1965.

O'Connor, M. "Guinea and the Ivory Coast: Contrast in Economic Development," *Journal of Modern African Studies*, X, 3 October 1972, 409—26.

Voss, Joachin. *Guinea*. Bern K. Schweder, 1967.

SOCIAL

Derman, William. *Serfs, Peasants, and Socialists: A Former Serf Village in the Republic of Guinea*. Berkeley: University of California Press, 1973.

Leunda, X. "La reforme de l'enseignement et son incidence sur l'evolution rurale en Guinee." *Civilizations*, (1972/1973): 232—62.

Stern, T. N. "Political Aspects of Guinean Education." *Comparative Education Review*, 8 (June 1964): 98—103.

16. Guinea-Bissau

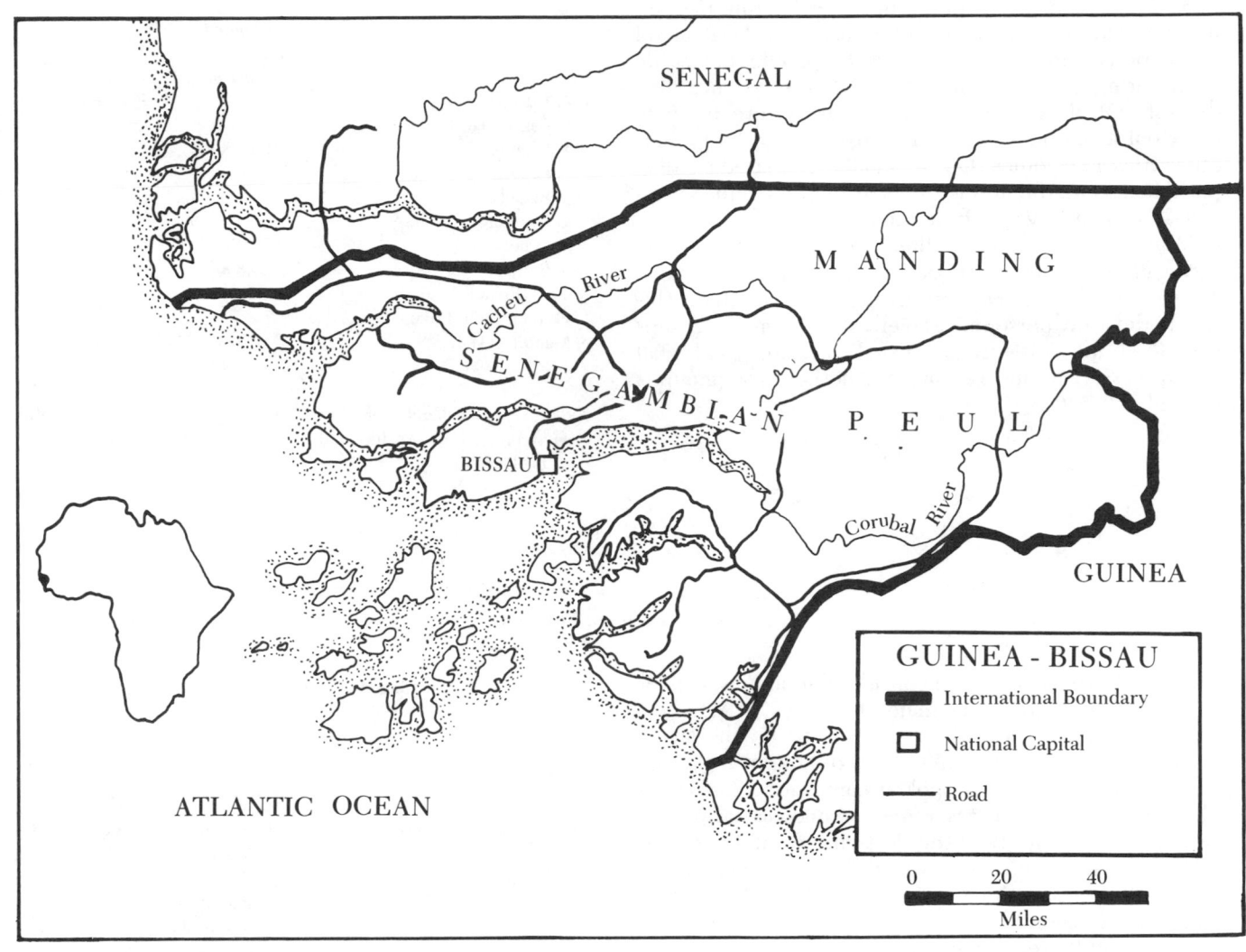

SENEGAL

MANDING

Cacheu

River

SENEGAMBIAN

PEUL

BISSAU

Corubal River

GUINEA

GUINEA - BISSAU

▬ International Boundary

□ National Capital

— Road

ATLANTIC OCEAN

0   20   40

Miles

I. Basic Information

Date of Independence: September 10, 1974
Former Colonial Ruler: Portugal
Former Name: Portuguese Guinea
Estimated Population (1980): 646,000*
Area Size (equivalent in U.S.): 13,948 sq. mi. (Mass., R.I. Conn.)
Date of Last Census: 1979

Major Exports 1977 as a Percent of Total Exports: groundnuts—60%, fish—19%, palm kernels—13%

*After independence, large numbers of refugees were reported to have returned to the country and the population may be somewhat larger than current estimates.

II. Ethnic Patterns

Because of the protracted war of liberation in the country there have been severe problems in estimating the ethnic populations. The war caused major dislocations of populations with large numbers of people fleeing to neighboring countries, and the Portuguese, since they did not control many areas in the country, were unable to carry out a complete census in 1970 as they did in their other African colonies. Our estimates are based on 1950 partial data and the observations in Jeune Afrique's *African Atlas*, and may vary from other estimates.

While the Fulani and Malinké are identity groups, the Senegambians include several distinct identity groups. There were about 2,500 Portuguese in the country exclusive of the army personnel as well as some smaller groups from the Cape Verde islands (usually mulattos) and small groups of Syrians and Lebanese. Another small group is the Felup (2%).

TABLE 16.1   Ethnic Units Over 5 Percent of Country Population

Ethnic Units	Estimated Ethnic Population 1980	Estimated Ethnic Percentage
a. Senegambian Type	387,600	60%
1. Balante	(193,800)	(30%)
2. Papel	(45,200)	(7%)
3. Biafada		
4. Banyun		
5. Mandyako	(90,400)	(14%)
6. Brame	(25,800)	(4%)
b. Peul (Fulani, Fouta Djalon, Fula)	129,200	20%
c. Manding (Malinké)	84,000	13%

SOURCES: G. Chaliand *Armed Struggle in Africa* New York: Monthly Review Press, 1969; Abshire and Samuels *Portuguese Africa: A Handbook* for 1950 census.

III. Language Patterns

Guinea-Bissau is an area of considerable linguistic diversity. Knappert gives the major language as Mandingo (20%) but since the Balante appear to be the largest group in the population (30%) it would appear that Balante is the most widely spoken language. A Creole has developed and estimates range as high as 60 percent speakers of Creole. Both the Portuguese and the PAIGC liberation movement encouraged the use of Portuguese. The estimates for ethnic population indicate that the Fulani are the second largest group in the population at 20 percent and therefore we code Fulani as the second vernacular language although Mandingo does play a role as a *lingua franca*.

TABLE 16.2   Language Patterns

			Greenberg	Dalby
1. 1st language	Balante	(30%)		
2nd language	Fulani	(20%)		
2. Linguistic classification (all ethnic units in over 5%)	Fulani		IA1	201
	Mandingo		IA2	31A
	Balante		IA1	22C
	Papel		IA1	22B
	Mandvako		IA1	22B
3. *Lingua franca*	Crioula, Mandingo			
4. Official language	Portuguese			

IV. Urban Patterns

Capital/Largest city: Bissau (founded in 16th century)
Dominant ethnicity/language of capital city
    Major vernacular: Crioulo

Major ethnic group: Senegambians
Major ethnic group as a percent of capital's population:

TABLE 16.3 Growth of Capital/Largest City

Date	Bissau
1940	
1950	18,309
1960	25,000
1971	65,000 UA
1976 (est.)	80,000 UA
1979	109,500 UA

SOURCE: Various editions of *Statesman's Yearbook, Africa South of the Sahara 1976, Political Handbook of the World 1979, Africa South of the Sahara 1980—81.*

TABLE 16.4 Cities of 20,000 and Over

City	Size	Date
Bissau	109,500 UA	1979

SOURCE: 1979 census: for Bissau district and Concelho.

V. Political Patterns

A. Political Parties and Elections

Until shortly before independence, virtually all political activity was illegal in Guinea-Bissau. The *Partido Africano da Independencia da Guine e Cabo Verde* was founded in 1956 and was lead by Amilcar Cabral until his assassination in 1972. The PAIGC led the guerrilla war against the Portuguese. In 1963, there was an alliance of several smaller groups who formed the *Frente para a Libertacao e Independência da Guineá* (FLING). This group is an illegal opposition party based in Senegal and currently has very little influence within Guinea-Bissau. The coalition of Cape Verdean groups which make up FLING are opposed to formal union with the mainland.

Elections to a legislative assembly were held in Guinea in 1973 by the Portuguese. The PAIGC held legislative elections in the liberated areas of the country in the August to October period of 1972. The PAIGC elected legislature became Guinea-Bissau's at independence. In December and January 1976—77, elections were held for "regional councils." These councils, in turn, elected 150 members to the National People's Assembly which convened in March 1977. A small opposition party, the Guinean Democratic Movement, was formed in 1974. It was banned shortly after its formation by the Armed Forces Movement in Portugal. A coup on November 15, 1980 replaced the government with a Revolutionary Council. The coup reflected ethnic and racial conflicts in the party.

B. Political Leadership

Amilcar Cabral was the unquestioned leader of the PAIGC and the presumed new leader of an independent Guinea-Bissau until his assassination in Conakry in 1972. His brother, Luis, took up the leadership of both the PAIGC and the country as it became independent from Portuguese rule in 1974. The leadership of the government was largely drawn from the membership of the PAIGC whose leadership has a large percentage of mestizoes from Guinea-Bissau and Cape Verde. This imbalance in ethnic representation was a threat to the leadership of the party, and the new military rulers are principally black Africans.

TABLE 16.5 Heads of Government (Post-Independence)

Name	Dates in Office	Age (1982)	Ethnicity	Education	Former Occupation
1. Luis de Almeida Cabral (President)	1974—1980	51	Mestizo	Nurse's training	colonial Service Accountant
2. Major Nino Vieira (President—Revolutionary Council)	1980—present		'black African'		Soldier, Politician

FIGURE 16.1   **Political Parties and Elections**   GUINEA-BISSAU

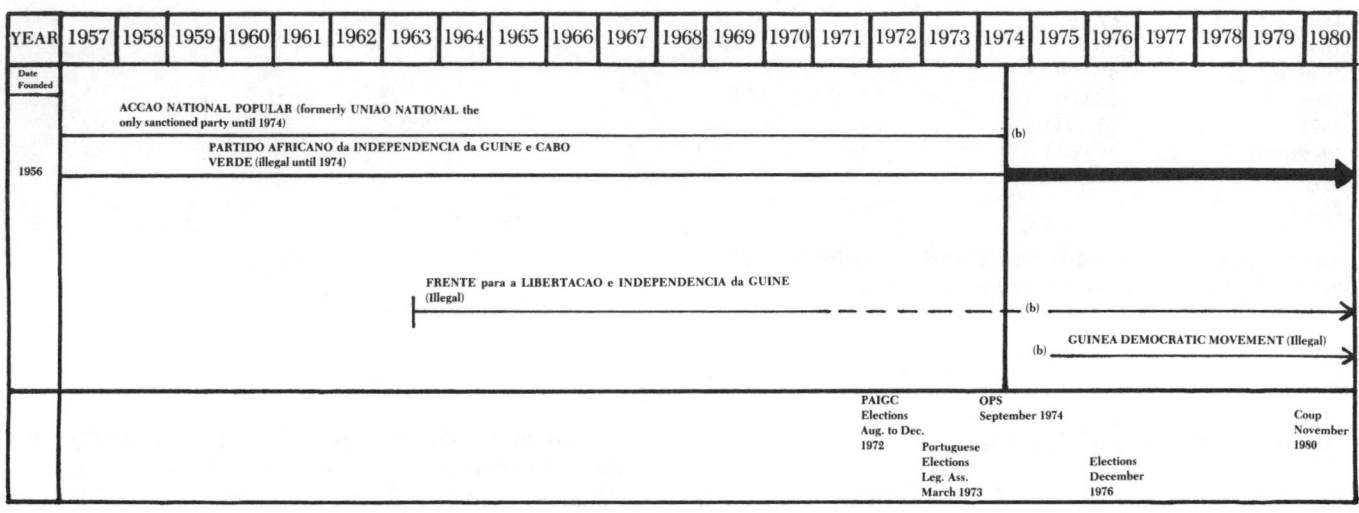

TABLE 16.7   **Elite Instability**

Event and Date	Characteristics
1. Coup d'État November 15, 1980	a. *Description*: Cabral overthrown after army occupied Bissau, and ousts his government. Two officials killed. A Revolutionary Council under Major Vieira is established. b. *Participants*: Army and Prime Minister Major Vieira. c. *Apparent Causes*: Conflict between black African leaders and the mestizo-dominated government.

VI. National Integration and Stability

In 1974 the country emerged from over a decade of guerrilla warfare against the Portuguese. By the end of that decade, much of the country was effectively under the control of the PAIGC liberation movement. In the period since independence, there have been no reported instances of mass or communal instability but there has been elite instability. A plot against the government was reported in March 1975 and a major government reshuffle took place in January 1976. A plot against the government was uncovered in November 1978 when a group of armed insurgents were captured near Bissau following a skirmish with government troops. There are border tensions with Guinea over an area believed to be rich in oil.

In July 1980, troops were dispatched to this area.

On November 14, 1980, Major Joao Bernardo Vieira, took over the government and set up a Revolutionary Council. Two senior officials lost their lives, but otherwise the coup was bloodless. The new council has nine members: six army officers and three civilians. The Vice-President is the Foreign Minister of the previous government, and Vieira himself had been Prime Minister. The fact that the two ministers killed were Mestizos, and the new ruling group is almost entirely black, has caused speculation that there was an ethnic factor in the coup. Also, the economy of Bissau has been in decline.

VII. Selected References

BIBLIOGRAPHY

McCarthy, J. M. *Guinea-Bissau and Cape Verde Islands*: *A Comprehensive Bibliography*. New York: Garland, 1977.

GENERAL

Abshire, David, and Michael Samuels. *Portuguese Africa—A Handbook*. New York: Praeger, 1969.
Duffy, James. *Portugal in Africa*. Cambridge: Harvard University Press, 1962.
Goult, Denis. *Looking at Guinea-Bissau: A New Nation's Development Strategy*. Washington, D.C., Overseas Development Council, 1978.
Lobban, Richard. *Historical Dictionary of the Republics of Guinea-Bissau and Cape Verde*. Metuchen, N.J.: The Scarecrow Press, Inc., 1979.

POLITICAL

Aaby, Peter. *The State of Guinea-Bissau: African Socialism or Socialism in Africa?* Uppsala, Scandinavian Institute of African Studies, 1978
Cabral, Amilcar. *Revolution in Guinea*. New York: Monthly Review Press, 1970.
Chaliand, Gerard. *Armed Struggle in Africa: With the Guerrillas in Portuguese Guinea*. New York: Monthly Review Press, 1969.
Chilcote, Ronald. *Emerging Nationalism in Portuguese Africa*. Stanford, Calif.: Hoover Institution Press, 1972.

Davidson, Basil. *The Liberation of Guinea*. Harmondsworth, U.K.: Penguin, 1969.
Davidson, Basil. *Growing from Grass Roots: The State of Guinea-Bissau*. London: Committee for Freedom in Mozambique, 1974.
David, Jennifer. *The Republic of Guinea-Bissau: Triumph over Colonialism*. New York: Africa Fund, 1974.
Rudbeck, L. *Guinea-Bissau: A Study in Political Mobilization*. Uppsala: Scandinavian Institute of African Studies, 1974.
Urdang, Stephanie. *Fighting Two Colonialisms, Women in Guinea-Bissau*. N.Y.: Monthly Review, Press, 1979.

ECONOMIC

Herbert, E. W. "Portuguese Adaptation to Trade Patterns: Guinea to Angola," *African Studies Review* 17 (September 1974), pp. 411—24.
U.S. Bureau of Labor Statistics. *Labor Conditions in Portuguese Guinea*. Washington, D.C.: U.S. Government Printing Office, 1966.

SOCIAL

"The Demography of the Portuguese Territories: Angola, Mozambique, and Portuguese Guinea" in W. I. Brass et. al. (eds.), *The Demography of Tropical Africa*. Princeton: Princeton University Press, 1968, p. 440—65.

17. Ivory Coast

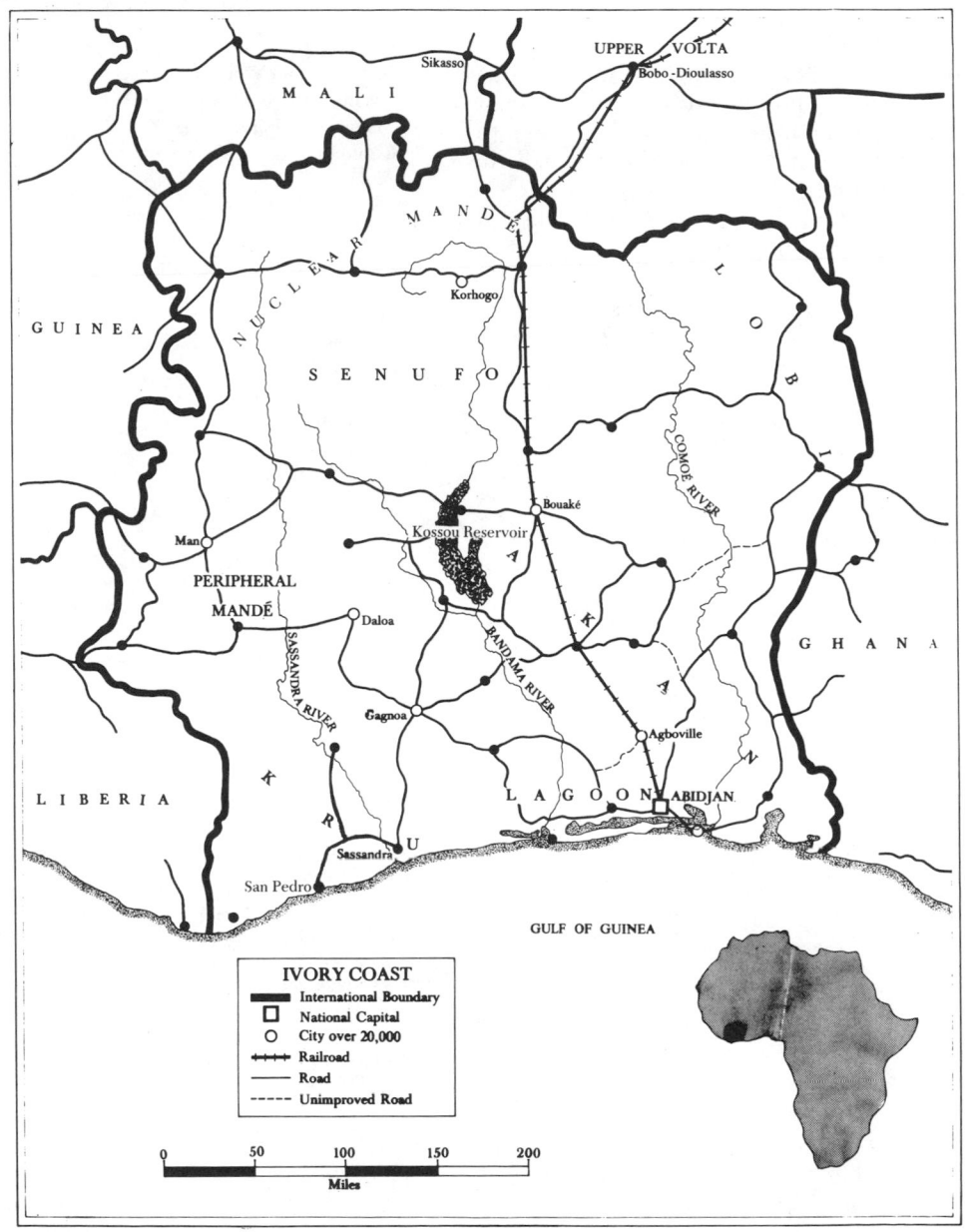

I. Basic Information

Date of Independence: August 7, 1960
Former Colonial Ruler: France
Change in Boundaries: Formerly part of the French West African Federation
Estimated Population (1980): 7,662,000

Area size (equivalent in U.S.): 124,504 sq. mi. (New Mexico)
Date of Last Census: 1975
Major Exports 1976 as Percent of Total Exports: cocoa—33 percent; coffee—25 percent; wood—14 percent.

II. Ethnic Patterns

Our classification is at a relatively high level of abstraction. It is based primarily on linguistic criteria, as well as historical, ecological, and cultural factors. These seem to be the locally accepted ethno-cultural clusters, and the classification is used both by the Ivory Coast government in official sources, and by Zolberg (1963). The extent to which these clusters form identity groups is unknown. There were 50,000 Frenchmen in the country, (1%)[*] in 1975. There are a large number of Africans from neighboring countries working in the country. Estimates of this population range between one and two million.

[*]*Africa Research Bulletin* Economic series, p. 3613.

TABLE 17.1   Ethnic Units Over 5 Percent of Country Population

Ethnic Units	Estimated Ethnic Population 1980	Estimated Ethnic Percentage
a. Akan Cluster	2,068,700	27%
1. Baule (Baoulé)	(1,532,400)	(20%)
2. Agni (Anyi)	(536,300)	(7%)
i. Agni, ii. Nzima,		
iii. Ethotilé, iv. Abouré,		
v. Abrou		
b. Kru Type (Crau, Krao, Krawi, Nana)	1,379,200	18%
1. Bété	(689,600)	(9%)
i. Kru, ii. Dida,		
iii. Gueré, iv. Wobé,		
v. Godie, vi. Neyho		
c. Nuclear Mandé Cluster	1,149,300	15%
1. Malinké, 2. Bambara,		
3. Dyula, 4. Mahon		
d. Senufo Type (Senoufo, Sene Siena)	919,400	12%
1. Senufo, 2. Minianka		
e. Peripheral Mandé Cluster	689,600	9%
1. Dan (Yacouba), 2. Gouro,		
3. Gagon		
f. Lagoon Type	613,000	8%
1. Abidji, 2. Abjukru,		
3. Ébrié, 4. Attia		
5. Abbé, 6. Alladian		
7. Avikam		
g. Lobi Type	383,100	5%
1. Lobi, 2. Djimini,		
3. Tagouana, 4. Kulango		

SOURCES: Ivory Coast, Ministère du Plan, *Inventaire économique de la Côte d'Ivoire 1947—1956* (Abidjan, 1958), p. 26. Aristide P. Zolberg, *One-Party Government in the Ivory Coast* (Princeton, N.J.: Princeton University Press, 1963), Washington, D.C.: U.S. Government Printing Office, 1973, p. xvi.

Note: The percentages used in the table are intended to characterize the distribution of the indigenous population. We assume that 1.5 million of the total population were aliens. The estimated ethnic population figures are based on subtracting tht figure from the total population for 1980 and computing percentages on an indigenous population of 7,662,000.

III. Language Patterns

There are four major language groupings in the Ivory Coast: (1) Kwa (including Akan and Kru), (2) Voltaic, (3) Mandé, and (4) Atlantic. The largest language group—the Akan—includes the Agni and Baoulé. The second largest language group—the Kru—includes Bété and Bakoué. Baoulé and Agni dialects are to some extent mutually intelligible. The Agni-Baoulé and Kru are also the two major ethnic groups in Ivory Coast, 27 percent and 18 percent respectively. Knappert estimates 30 percent for Akan speakers as a percentage of the total population while Rustow estimates 24 percent for the Agni-Baoulé cluster within the Akan. (MacDougald's suggestion that Mossi was the major language of Ivory Coast reflects the fact that at the time of his writing, Upper Volta was administered as part of Ivory Coast.) Rustow estimates Bété as the second language at 18 percent. This is in close agreement with our own estimate of Akan 27 percent, Bété/Kru 18 percent. It is important to note that Dyula, a Mandé language, is a trade language (*lingua franca*) in Ivory Coast.

The official language of Ivory Coast is French, and all education from grade one is conducted in French. Television broadcasting is also in French. There are no vernacular newspapers, but there is a limited amount of vernacular radio broadcasting. Most of the administrative units within Ivory Coast are linguistically mixed.

TABLE 17.2   Language Patterns

1. Primacy
   1st language   Akan   (27%)
   2nd language   Kru-Bété   (18%)

		Green-berg	Dalby
2. Linguistic classification	Akan	IA4	44A
(all ethnic units in	Kru	IA4	26A
country over 5%)	Mandé	IA2	31A
	Peripheral		
	Mandé	IA2	31D
	Senufo	IA3	27
	Lagoon Type	IA4	43
	Lobi	IA3	29
3. *Lingua franca*	Malinké/		
	Dyula		
4. Official language	French		

IV. Urban Pattterns

Capital/Largest city: Abidjan (founded 1903)
Dominant ethnicity/language of capital
   Major vernacular: Akan (French is the most widely spoken langue in the capital
   Major ethnic group: Akan[1]
Major ethnic group as percent of capital's population:
   15.5 percent (1965)

[1]Ministère des Finances, des Affaires Economiques et du Plan, *Côte d'Ivoire 1965: Population, Etudes Regionales 1962—1965, Synthese* (Abidjan: Ministère du Plan, July 1967).

TABLE 17.3   Growth of Capital/Largest City

Date	Abidjan
1920	5,000
1930	10,000
1940	34,000
1950	69,000
1960	180,000
1965	360,000 UA
1972	650,000 UA
1976	900,000 UA
1978	1,400,000 UA

SOURCE: *Démographie Comparée.*
   [a]*African Development* October 1973.

TABLE 17.4   Cities of 20,000 and Over

City	Size	Date
Abidjan[f]	1,400,000 UA	ca. 1978
Bouake[a]	200,000 UA	1974
Man[b]	100,000	1974
Daloa[b]	100,000	1974
Gagnoa[c]	45,000	1972
Korhogo[c]	25,000	1971
Grand-Bassam[b]	23,000	1963

SOURCES:
[a]*Europa Yearbook 1977 V. II*
[b]*Political Handbook of the World 1977*
[c]*African Development* October 1973
[d]*Jeune Afrique Atlas of Africa* New York: Free Press, 1972—1971 estimate.
[e]*Allgemeine Statistik Des Auslands Landerkurzberichte Elfenbeinkusk* (Stuttgart und Mainz: W. Kohlhammer, 1969), p. 10.
[f]*Europe Outremer* November 1979, p. 89.

V. Political Patterns

A. Political Parties and Elections

In 1946, Felix Houphouet-Boigny formed the *Parti Démocratique de la Côte d'Ivoire* (PDCI) which has continued to be the dominant party until the present time. Houphouet-Boigny also founded the *Rassemblement Democratique Africain* (RDA), an umbrella political organization of various territorial parties in the French West African and Equatorial Federations, and has been the only president of the RDA. The RDA effectively became defunct by independence. Post-independence elections were held in 1960, 1965, 1970, and 1975, but the PDCI has always controlled 100 percent of the 70 seats in the Legislative Assembly. The March 1957 national and territorial elections was the last one marked by competition. The PDCI received 80 percent of the vote, and 58 out of 60 seats in the Territorial Assembly. In the 1970 presidential election, Houphouet-Boigny received 2,003,046 (99.89 percent) of the votes and was again re-elected in 1975 and 1980. Splinter groups have developed periodically, but the Ivory Coast is a *de facto* one party state. In 1975, the size of the legislature was increased from 100 to 120 prior to the November elections. There were elections with candidates put forward by the Party in November 1980, and the size of the assembly was increased to 197 deputies. The President was re-elected with 99% of the vote.

B. Political Leadership

The government of President Houphouet-Boigny has been in power in the Ivory Coast continuously since independence. The composition of the cabinet has been enlarged in the post-independence period. Except for the marked internal reorganization and a number of dismissals from the cabinet in 1963, and 1969 the government of the Ivory Coast has been little changed. Recruitment to executive office is broadly based, although persons of Akan background have become increasingly prominent in government. In recent years, younger technocrats have been brought into the government. In May 1978, steps were taken that would reduce the political dominance of the PDCI. It was announced that the capitals of all administrative districts (except Abidjan and Bouaké) would be administered by elected mayors rather than party appointees.

TABLE 17.5   Head of Government (Post-Independence)

Name	Dates in Office	Age (1982)	Ethnicity	Education	Former Occupation
1. Felix Houphouet— Boigny (President)	1960— present	77	Akan (Baoulé)	University (Dakar)	Doctor (M.D.)

TABLE 17.6   Cabinet Membership: Distribution by Ethnic Unit*

Ethnicity*	Independence Cabinet	1967 Cabinet
1. Akan (25%)	33%	47%
2. Kru (18)	8.3	12
3. Mandé (15)	3.3	24
4. Senufo (13)	0	0
5. Peripheral Mandé (11)	0	0
6. Lagoon Type (7)	25	12
7. Lobi (6)	0	5.9
8. Others (5)	25	0
N =	12	17

*Ethnic units arranged in rank order of size within country with the unit's percent of national population in parentheses.

FIGURE 17.1   Political Parties and Elections   IVORY COAST

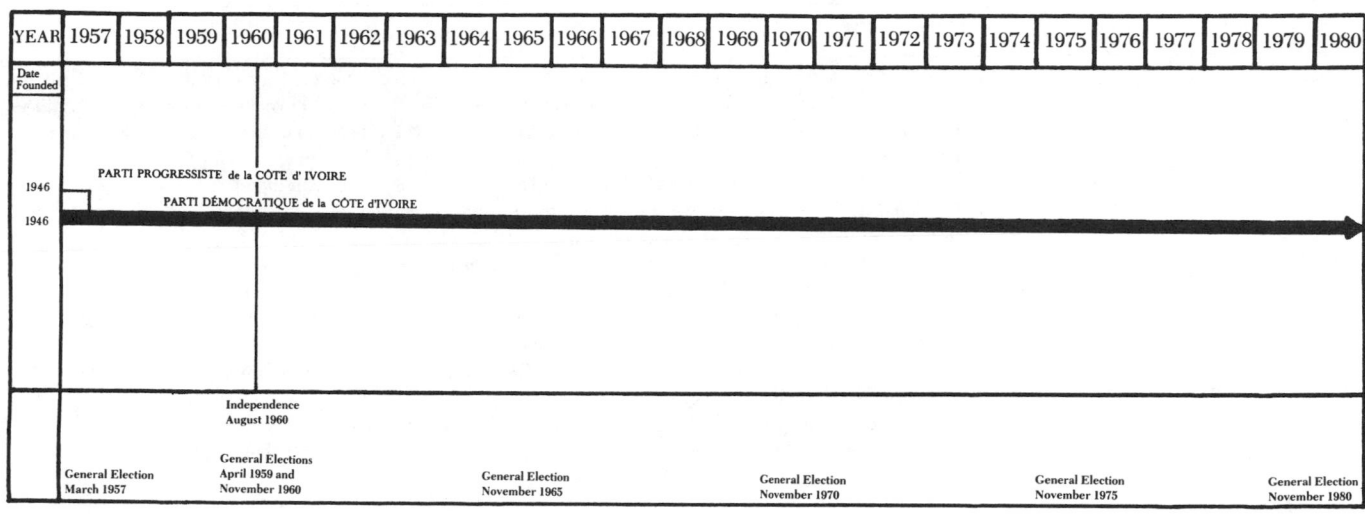

VI. National Integration and Stability

Since independence in 1960, the only evidence of elite instability was a major plot in 1963, a number of rumored plots, and a plot by young army officers in 1973. Economic prosperity seems to have alleviated some of the ususal tensions of communal competition although antagonisms are growing towards the expatriate Africans who number between one and two million and compete for jobs with Ivorians. Important sub-national identities exist, however, including a north/south regionalism which is reinforced by religious and cultural ties, and by imbalanced regional economic development. Attempts to secede were made by the Agni in 1959; these were supported by Kwame Nkrumah, and they broke out again at the end of 1969. A minor rebellion in 1970 at Gagnoa was quickly suppressed by the army. Recently, there has been unrest among students.

TABLE 17.8   Communal Instability

Event and Date	Characteristics
1. Civil War December 1969	a. *Description*: A short-lived civil war was fought in the Abiosso region in the southeast of the Ivory Coast in December 1969. The insurgents were reported to be armed, and to have been provided with shirts thought to make them invulnerable to bullets. The army of the Ivory Coast, however, succeeded in killling and wounding several people, and brought the war to an end. How severe the military action was, and how long the civil war lasted is not known since the army operation was conducted in secret. b. *Participants*: The insurgents were members of the Agni tribe, and were organized by the Sanwi Liberation Movement. c. *Apparent Causes*: The Ivory Coast Minister of Interior said that the Sanwi movement believed that because the government had recognized Biafra, it should also grant independence to the Sanwi. According to the *New York Times*, the Agni resented being ruled by a member of the Baoulé tribe and the Agni chiefs reportedly told their people that the Baoulé were going to massacre them.
2. Rebellion November 1970	a. *Description*: Gnagbe Opadjele led a group of followers in Gagnoa in an attempt to take over the country and establish himself as head of state. b. *Participants*: Led by Kragbe Gnagbe Opadjele and groups from the Gagnoa area. c. *Apparent Causes*: Unclear from available sources although referred to as a 'tribal revolt' in some sources.

TABLE 17.10   Annual Instability Events: Independence Through 1979—Ivory Coast

Year	'61	'62	'63	'64	'65	'66	'67	'68	'69	'70	'71	'72	'73	'74	'75	'76	'77	'78	'79
ELITE INSTABILITY																			
Assassinations																			
Plots			2										1						
Attempted Coups d'État																			
Coups d'État																			
COMMUNAL INSTABILITY																			
Ethnic Violence																			
Irredentism																			
Rebellion										1									
Civil War									1										
MASS INSTABILITY																			
Revolt																			
Revolution																			
TURMOIL																			
Demonstrations							1			1									
Strikes (no. days)							1		7										
Riots (no. days)									1										
Terrorism			1																
Declarations of Emergency									1										

Year	'61	'62	'63	'64	'65	'66	'67	'68	'69	'70	'71	'72	'73	'74	'75	'76	'77	'78	'79
CABINET INSTABILITY																			
Realloc. and new appts.	6	2	20	3	2	8				3	2								
New members	8		8	3	4	3				9	2								
Resig. and Dismissals		4	15			1			4	4									
No. of members (max.) (maximum in year)	15	15	13	11	15	17	17	18	16	28	25	25							

VII. Selected References

BIBLIOGRAPHY

Organization for Economic Cooperation and Development. Development Center. *Essai d'une Bibliographie sur la Cote d'Ivoire*. Paris: O.E.C.D., 1964.

GENERAL

Bernheim, M. *African Success Story: The Ivory Coast*. New York: Harcourt, Brace and World, 1970.

Foster, Philip and Aristide R. Zolberg. *Ghana and the Ivory Coast: Perspectives on Modernization*. Chicago: University of Chicago Press, 1972.

Lewis, B. *Ivory Coast*. Boulder, Colo.: Westview—forthcoming.

Roberts, T.D. et al. *Area Handbook for the Ivory Coast*, 2nd ed. Washington, D.C.: Government Printing Office, 1973.

Siegel, Efrem. "Ivory Coast: Booming Economy, Political Calm." *Africa Report*, 15 (April 1970)): 18—21.

Thompson, Virginia and Richard Adloff. *French West Africa*, pp. 117—131. Stanford, Cal.: Stanford University Press, 1957.

Woronoff, Jon. *West African Wager: Houphouet Versus Nkrumah*. Metuchen, N.J.: Scarecrow Press, 1972

POLITICAL

Cohen, Michael A. "The Myth of the Expanding Center: Politics in the Ivory Coast," *Journal of Modern African Studies*, 11, 2 (June, 1973), 227—246.

Cohen, Michael A. *Urban Policy and Political Conflict in Africa: A Study of the Ivory Coast*. Chicago: University of Chicago Press, 1974.

de Lusignan, Guy. *French Speaking Africa since Independence*, pp. 135—145. London: Pall Mall Press, 1969.

Potholm, C. *Four African Political Systems*. Englewood Cliffs, N.J.: Prentice Hall, 1970.

Wallerstein, Immanuel, *The Road to Independence: Ghana and the Ivory Coast*. The Hague: Mouton, 1964.

Zolberg, Aristide. *One-Party Government in the Ivory Coast*. Princeton, N.J.: Princeton University Press, 1964, new ed. 1969.

ECONOMIC

Amin, Samir. *Le Developpment du Capitalisme en Côte d'Ivoire*. Paris: Editions de Minuit, 1967.

Den Tuinder, Bastiaan A. *Ivory Coast: The Challenge of Success*. Baltimore: Johns Hopkins University Press for the World Bank, 1978.

Due, Jean M. "Agricultural Development in the Ivory Coast and Ghana." *Journal of Modern African Studies*, 7 (1969): 637—660.

EDIAFRIC. *L'Economie Ivorienne*. Paris: 1970.

International Monetary Fund. "Ivory Coast." In *Surveys of African Economies*, Vol. 3. Washington, D.C.: I.M.F., 1970.

Lewis, Barbara. "Ethnicity and Occupational Specialization in Ivory Coast: The Transporter's Association," in John N. Paden (ed) *Values, Identities, and National Integration*. Evanston, Ill., Northwestern University Press, 1980, p. 75—90.

Masini, J., et al. *Multinationals in Africa: A Case Study of the Ivory Coast*. New York: Praeger, 1980.

Miracle, Marvin. "The Economy of the Ivory Coast." In *The Economies of Africa*, eds. P. Robson and D. A. Lury, pp. 195—235. Evanston, Ill.: Northwestern University Press, 1969.

Roussel, L. "Employment Problems in the Ivory Coast." *International Labour Review*, 104 (December 1971): 505—526.

Sawadogo, Abdoulaye. *L'agriculture en Côte d'Ivoire*. Paris: Presses Universistaires de France, 1977.

Stryker, J. D. *Exports and Growth in Ivory Coast: Timber, Cocoa and Coffee*. New Haven: Yale University, Economic Growth Center, 1972.

SOCIAL

Berg, Elliot. "Education and Manpower in Senegal, Guinea, and the Ivory Coast," in *Manpower and Education: Country Studies in Economic Development*, eds. F. B. Harbison and c. Myers. New York: McGraw-Hill, 1965.

Clignet, Remi. *Many Wives, Many Powers: Authority and Power in Polygynous Families*. Evanston, Ill.: Northwestern University Press, 1970.

Clignet, Remi and Philip Foster. *The Fortunate Few: A Study of Secondary Schools and Students in the Ivory Coast*. Evanston, Ill.: Northwestern University Press, 1966.

Holas, Bohumil. *Changements sociaux en Côte d'Ivoire*. Paris: Presses Universitaires de France, 1961.

Holas, Bohumil. *Le separatisme religieux en Afrique noire: L'exemple de la Côte d'Ivoire*. Paris: Presses Universitaires de France, 1965.

Joshi, Heather, H. Lubell and J. Monly. *Abidjan, Urban Development and Employment in the Ivory Coast*. Geneva: International Labour Office, 1976.

Salem, Claudel. *Pluralism in the Ivory Coast: The Persistence of Ethnic Identities in the One Party State*. Los Angeles: University of California Press, 1975.

18. Kenya

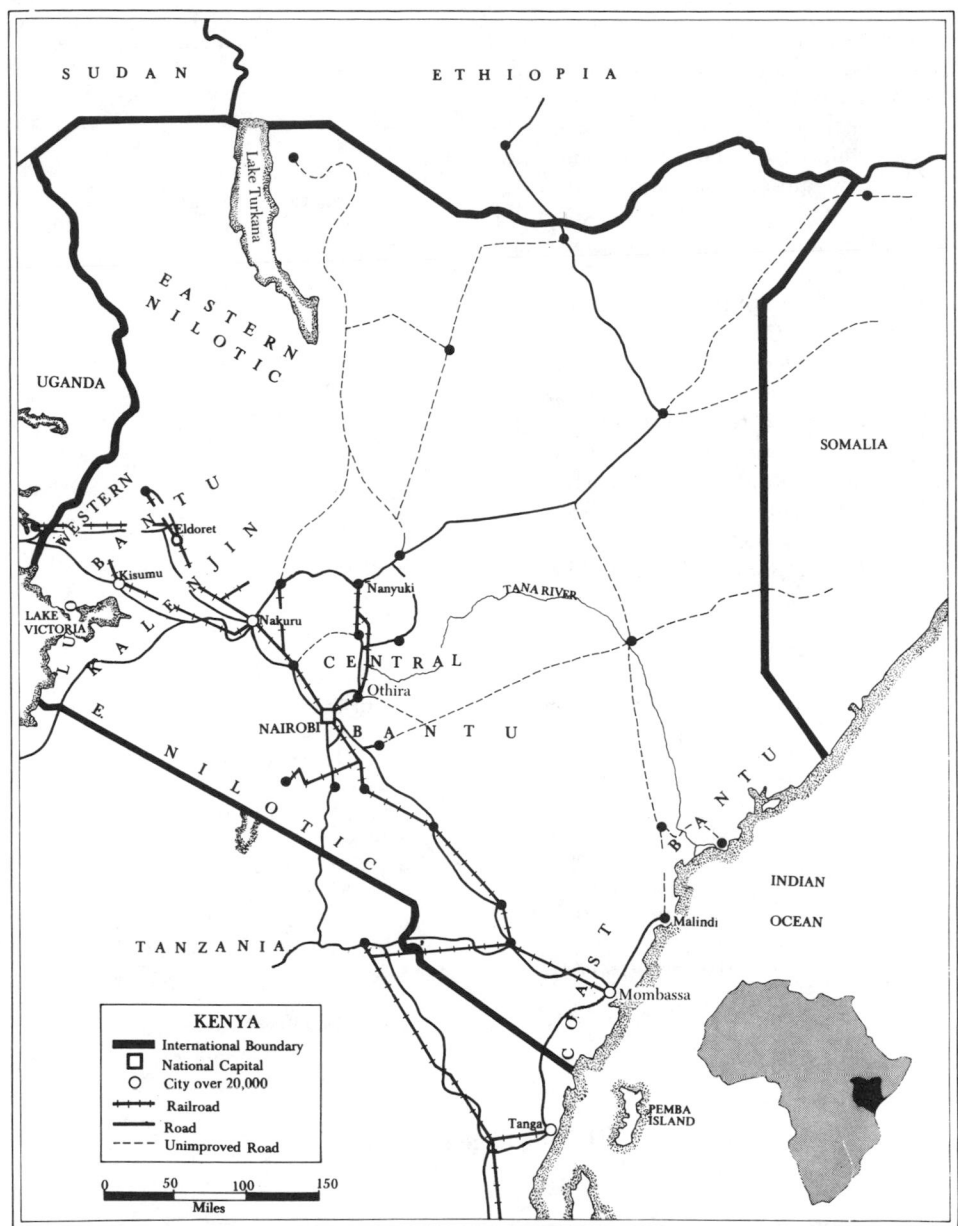

I. Basic Information

Date of Independence: December 12, 1963
Former Colonial Ruler: United Kingdom
Estimated Population (1980): 15,913,000
Area Size (equivalent in U.S.): 224,961 sq. mi. (Nevada and New Mexico)

Date of Last Census: 1969
Major Exports: 1976 (excluding re-exports to Uganda and Tanzania) as percent of Total Exports: coffee—35 percent; tea—12 percent; petroleum products—12 percent.

II. Ethnic Patterns

The ethnic classification selected for Kenya is that used by the Kenya census (1962), which states that the groupings were made on the basis of "ethnic, linguistic, and geographical considerations" and involves "somewhat arbitrary" groupings in certain cases. Thus, the Boni and Sanye, who are said to be among the oldest hunting tribes of Kenya, have been placed in their respective groups because of linguistic and geographical considerations. None of the ethnic units are themselves identity groups except for the Luo, a Nilotic people. The sub-groups are all identity groups, although the Luhya are an emerging identity group whose sub-groups have a significant sense of self-identity. Excluded here are two northern clusters: Somali-speaking Eastern Hamitic groups (Gosha, Hawiyah, Ogaden, Ajuran, Gurreh), 3 percent; and Rendille and Galla-speaking Western Hamitic groups (Rendille, Boran, Gabbra, Sakakuya, Orma), 1 percent. A large non-indigenous population continues to exist in the country (in 1969—41,000 Europeans; 140,000 Asians; 28,000 Arabs).

TABLE 18.1   Ethnic Units Over 5 Percent of Country Population

Ethnic Units	Estimated Ethnic Population 1980	Estimated Ethnic Percentage
a. Central Bantu Cluster	6,365,000	40%
1. Kikuyu	(3,342,000)	(21%)
2. Kamba	(1,750,000)	(11%)
3. Meru	(796,000)	(5%)
4. Embu	(159,000)	(1%)
5. Mbere, 6. Tharaka		
7. Chuka, 8. Igoji		
9. Miutini, 10. Mwimbi		
11. Muthambi		
b. Western Bantu (Kavirondo) Cluster	3,214,000	20.2%
1. Luhya	(2,164,000)	(13.6%)
i. Isukka, ii. Idakho		
iii. Kabras,		
iv. Nyala,v. Tsotso,		
vi. Wanga, vii. Marama,		
viii. Kisa, ix. Nyore,		
x. Maragoli,		
xi. Tiriki,		
xii. Bakhayo,		
xiii. Tachoni,		
xiv. Marach, xv. Samia,		
xvi. Bukusu		
2. Kisii (Gusii)	(1,050,000)	(6.6%)
3. Kuria		
c. Luo	2,228,000	14%
d. Kalenjin-Speaking Cluster	1,750,000	11%
1. Kipsigis	(637,000)	(4%)
2. Nandi	(318,000)	(2%)
3. Tugen	(175,000)	(1.1%)
4. Elgeyo	(159,000)	(1%)
5. Pokot (Suk), 6. Marakwet,		
7. Sabaot		
e. Coastal Bantu Cluster	796,000	5%
1. Mikikenda	(796,000)	(4.8%)
i. Digo, ii. Duruma,		
iii. Chonyi, iv. Giriama,		
v. Rabai, vi. Ribe,		
vii. Jibana, viii. Dauma,		
ix. Kambe		
2. Pokomo/Riverine, 3. Bajun,		
4. Swahili/Shirazi,		
5. Taveta, 6. Boni/Sanye		
f. Other Eastern Nilotic Groups	637,000	4%
1. Turkana	(318,000)	(2%)
2. Masai	(239,000)	(1.5%)
3. Iteso (Wamia, Elgumi)		
4. Samburu (Burkeneji)		
5. Nderobo, 6. Njemps		

III. Language Patterns

The two major language families of Kenya are Bantu and Chari-Nile (especially the Nilotic sub-branch). The two major languages, Swahili and Kikuyu are both from the Bantu family. Estimates of the percent of the total population speaking these languages varies. For Swahili, Knappert suggest 25 percent; however, many recent estimates go as high as 85 percent. As of July 4th, 1974 Swahili became the official national language in Kenya. Therefore, we have chosen a high estimate of 85 percent which is expected to increase. Kikuyu is part of the Central Bantu cluster, but as a distinct language is probably spoken by about 25 percent of the total population. (MacDougald estimates 21 percent; Rustow 29 percent).

TABLE 18.2   Language Patterns

1. Primacy
   1st language   Swahili   (85%)
   2nd language   Kikuyu   (25%)

		Green-berg	Dalby
2. Linguistic classification	Central Bantu	IA5	E5
(all ethnic units in country over 5%)	Western Bantu	IA5	E3, E4
	Luo	IIE1	71C
	Kalenjin	IIE1	72D
	Coastal Bantu	IA5	G4
	Eastern Nilotic (Masai)	IIE1	72E, 72C

3. *Lingua franca*   Swahili
4. Official language   Swahili*

*On July 4, 1974, Swahili replaced English as the official language of Kenya.

SOURCE: Lyndon Harries, "Swahili in Modern East Africa," in *Language Problems of Developing Nations*, eds. Joshua A. Fishman, Charles A. Ferguson, and Jyotirindra Das Gupta (New York: John Wiley, 1968), pp. 119—127.

IV. Urban Patterns

Capital/Largest city: Nairobi (founded 1899)
Dominant ethncity/language of capital
   Major vernacular: Kikuyu[1]
   Major ethnic group: Kikuyu[2]
   Major ethnic group as percent of capital's population:
      42 percent (1962)

TABLE 18.3   Growth of Capital/Largest City

Date	Nairobi
1920	14,000
1930	52,000
1940	65,000
1950	119,000
1960	267,000
1962	314,000 UA
1969	509,000 UA
1972	597,000 UA
1973	629,000 UA
1975	750,000 UA
1977	776,000 UA

[1]Jan Knappert, "Language Problems of the New Nations of Africa," *African Quarterly*, 5 (1965): 95—105.
[2]Census (1962).

SOURCES: Various editions of the *Statesman's Yearbook*, except for the 1950 figure which is from *East African High Commission Statistical Bulletin*, 2, no. 19: 14, *Political Handbook of the World 1977* p. 213, and the 1977 figure which is from *Europa Yearbook 1979*, V. II.

TABLE 18.4   Cities of 20,000 and Over*

City	Size	Date
Nairobi[a]	776,000	1977
Mombasa[a]	371,000	1977
Nakuru[b]	50,000	1975
Kisumu[c]	32,431	1969
Thika[c]	18,387	1969
Eldoret[c]	18,196	1969

[a]*Europa Yearbook 1979*, Vol. II.
[b]*Political Handbook of the World 1977*, estimate for 1975.
[c]Census—1969 as reported in *Africa South of the Sahara 1974*.
*Thika and Eldoret are included in the list since they probably exceed 20,000 by c. 1972.

V. Political Patterns

FIGURE 18.1   Political Parties and Elections   **Kenya**

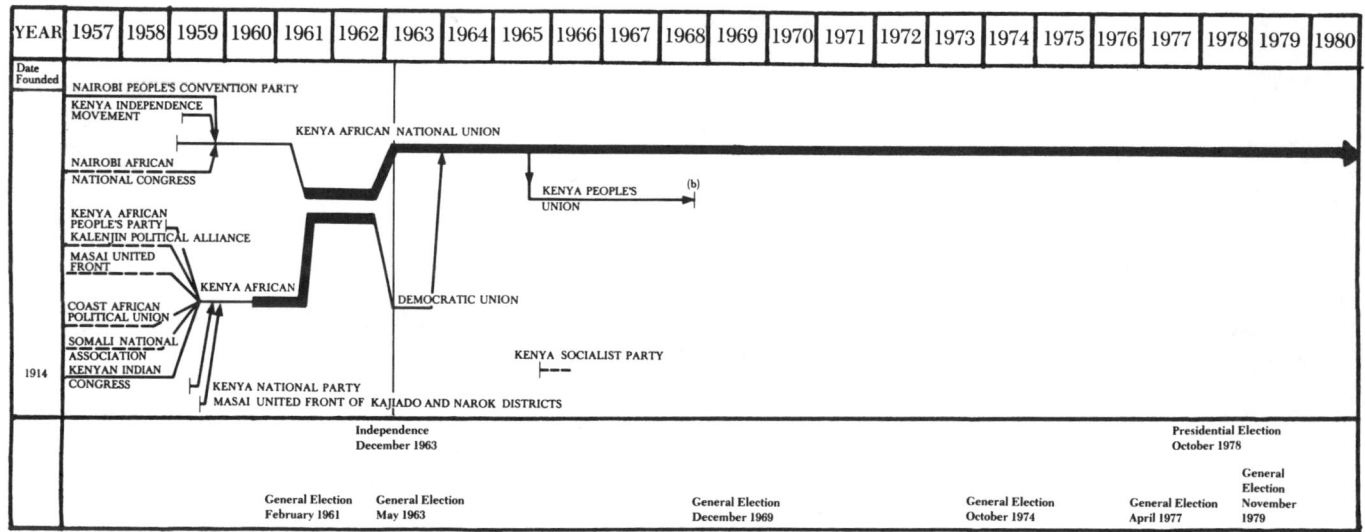

A. Political Parties and Elections

Political party life in Kenya during the 1960's was dominated by two major parties, both founded in 1960 by mergers of smaller parties. The *Kenya African National Union* (KANU) was originally led by James Gichuru and was based primarily on support from Kikuyu and Luo ethnic groups. The *Kenya African Democratic Union* (KADU) was comprised mainly of smaller ethnic groups and was led by Ronald Ngala. Although KANU won a majority in the 1961 elections, they refused to take office as long as Jomo Kenyatta was not allowed to form the government. KADU thus became the governing party until 1962 when a coalition between KANU and KADU was formed. The elections in May 1963 again gave Kenyatta and KANU a majority and he became prime minister. After independence, KANU continued to govern and in 1964, KADU merged with KANU. Kenyatta continued as president with Oginga Odinga as vice-president. Significant opposition to KANU emerged in 1966 with the defection from the ruling party of Oginga Odinga and some of his parliamentary followers and the formation of the *Kenya People's Union* (KPU). The significance of this opposition may be indicated by Odinga's subsequent house arrest and the banning of his party prior to the general election of December 1969. This election appears to have been a setback to the Kenyatta regime, since 96 incumbents (including five ministers) were defeated by other KANU candidates. Although Kenyatta maintained that opposition parties would be al-

lowed to exist, applications for registration were refused. By 1974 Kenyatta specifically prohibited opposition parties and the constitution now states that Kenya is a "de facto one-party state." Nevertheless, unlike some one-party states where a single list of candidates is presented, Kenya has followed the Tanzanaian formula of having competitive elections for parlimamentary constituencies requiring only that candidates be members of, and approved by, KANU. In the 1974 election, 88 M.P.'s out of a total of 158 were not returned to parliament. By 1978, there had been an increasing intolerance of opposition to the government and party. An example was the cancelling of the Nairobi mayoral elections when a popular opponent ran against Kenyatta's daughter. On August 22, 1978, Kenyatta died and Vice President Daniel Arap Moi became President. Following Kenyan law, a presidential election was held in October 1978 in which Moi won by a substantial margin. On November 8, 1979, a general election for a new 158 seat national assembly was held. The opposition Kenya People's Union (KPU) was banned from the election. Nevertheless, the competition was keen as there were at least 742 candidates running and some districts reported having more than ten contenders. Moi was the sole candidate for president and easily won re-election. Following the November elections, there was a cabinet reshuffle which led to an increase in the size of the cabinet from 20 to 26 members. And, in Kenyan tradition, Moi gave cabinet appointments to every region and ethnic group approximately in proportion to their populations.

TABLE 18.5   Head of Government (Post-Independence)

Name	Dates in Office	Age (1982)	Ethnicity	Education	Former Occupation
1. Jomo Kenyatta (President)	1963— August— 1978	died in office at the age of 87	Central Bantu (Kikuyu)	London School of Oriental and African Studies	Politician
2. Daniel Arap Moi (President)	August 1978— Present	58	Kipsigis	A.I.M. School and Government African School, Kapsabet	Teacher Vice President

B. Political Leadership

The government of Kenya, under President Jomo Kenyatta, was in power continuously from independence in 1963 to Kenyatta's death in August 1978. Under Kenyatta, the cabinet was enlarged, and, except for a notable increase in dismissals and resignations in 1966, cabinet membership remained stable. Recruitment to cabinet positons has been broadly based, both under Kenyatta and Moi. Prior to Kenyatta's death in August 1978, reports indicated that he was becoming increasingly isolated from public view and even from contact with other political leaders. The government appeared to be effectively in the hands of civil servants and party leaders in an increasingly repressive single party regime. With Moi's election, the government was initially more tolerant of opposition leaders apparently to assure the broadest possible base for government policies. In addition, President Moi seems to be taking a firm position of leadership within the government. For example, he has placed himself in charge of the defense of the country. In June 1980 there was a major cabinet reshuffle in the Moi government reflecting a rivalry and jockeying for position between Vice President Mwai Kibaki, and Home and Constitutional Affairs Minister (formerly Attorney-General) Charles Njonjo, the two men most responsible for Moi's easy transition to the presidency.

TABLE 18.6 Cabinet Membership: Distribution by Ethnic Unit*

Ethnicity*	Independence Cabinet	1967 Cabinet
1. Central Bantu (40%)	50%	52%
2. Western Bantu (20)	13	19
3. Luo (14)	25	14
4. Kalenjin-speaking (11)	0	4.8
5. Coastal Bantu (5)	00	4.8
6. Other Eastern Nilotic (4)	6.3	0
7. Others (6)	6.3	04.8
N =	16	21

*Ethnic groups arranged in rank order of size within country with the unit's percent of national population in parentheses.

VI. National Integration and Stability

Although there were no instances of major elite instability under the regime of Jomo Kenyatta, the assassination of Tom Mboya (Luo), and the imprisonment of Oginga Odinga (Luo) created an atmosphere of inter-elite tension between Kikuyu and non-Kikuyu leaders and, within the Kikuyu, between the various clans. In 1975, a leader in the Kenyan parliament, Keriuki, was assassinated. He was a major opponent of the government and his murderers have never been apprehended although there was a parliamentary investigation into Keriuki's death. Political arrests including those of MPs were increasingly common under the Kenyatta regime.

On January 24, 1964 two battalions of the Kenya Rifles mutinied in their barracks outside of Nairobi and Nakuru, demanding higher pay and complete Africanization of the officer corps. By January 25 the mutiny was forcibly suppressed with the aid of British troops. This event has not been classified as an attempted coup since we have no evidence that the regime itself was threatened by the army demands. Plots against the government by elements of the army and civil servants were reported in 1971 and 1972. Despite the riots following the death of Mboya, the government of Kenya—as of 1982—has been successful in preventing widespread communal instability.

The isolated instances of instability in Kenya have involved communal groups that have been engaged in attempted rebellion (the Kikuyu-based Kenya Land Freedom Army), inter-ethnic violence (the Turkana), or irredentism (the Somali). The continuing dominance of Kikuyus in the government may eventually lead to increased conflict, however, In 1974 and 1975, a series of unexplained bombings occured in Nairobi particularly after the 1974 elections. At the time of Kenyatta's death, an assassination plot against Moi was uncovered. Since Moi's succession, Kenya has seen increasing represssion after an initial period of good will. This process culminated in a series of repressive measures by the government in 1981-82 followed by a coup attempt by members of the military, principally the air force, and led by an air force private. Widespread looting and deaths associated with the coup and anti-Asian sentiments shattered the image of stability in the country.

TABLE 18.7   Elite Instability

Event and Date	Characteristics
1. Coup Attempt August 1, 1982	a. *Description*: Air Force units take over Voice of Kenya and announce the overthrow of the Moi government. The Army under General Manlingé storms the station and attempt collapses. Widespread looting and deaths reported. b. *Participants*: Air Force junior officer and members of the airforce including Sergeant Okumu and Private Ochuka. c. *Apparent Causes*; Opposition to rampant corruption and political repression of the Moi government.

TABLE 18.8   Communal Instability

Event and Date	Characteristics
1. Rebellion July 1961-1965	a. *Description*: With the formal ending of the state of emergency which existed in Kenya during most of the 1950's as a result of the Mau Mau revolution, a remnant of the Mau Mau forces continued to rebel against government forces, even after the governmental power shifted out of British hands. The Kenya Land Freedom Army continued to make sporadic attacks on European, Kikuyu, Meru, Embu, and Somali settlements. In 1961 and 1962 more than 200 persons were arrested for Land Freedom Army activities in the Rift Valley. In May 1964, 200 members of the KLFA battled the Kenya police 30 miles south of Meru. The government eventually granted amnesty to the KLFA, and most surrendered. b. *Participants*: Leadership included Gatutu Gatuthuri (arrested in July 1961) and Cheze Mwanzo (arrested in March 1962). In January 1965, the two subsequent major leaders were killled, namely Baimungi and Chui. c. *Apparent Causes*: Minority elements within the predominantly Kikuyu Mau Mau movement were dissatisfied with lack of comprehensive expropriation of European land and alleged inequity in redistribution.
2. Ethnic Violence; January 1960— August 1964	a. *Description*: From January 1960 to November 30, 1961, there were approximately 77 border incidents involving the Turkana in which 38 people were killed. In March 1962 the Kenya Ministry of Defense deployed 1,000 troops and police who tried to disarm the Turkana tribesmen. In August 1964 about 200 Merille and Dongiro tribesmen on the Ethiopia-Kenya border retaliated against the Turkana, killing 121. On November 13, 1964, the Kenya-Ethiopia Consultative Council discussed border raids from Ethiopia and both governments promised action against persons involved. b. *Participants*: Turkana tribesmen attacked groups in Kenya and Ethiopia. c. *Apparent Causes*: Traditional ethnic animosity.
3. Irredentism ca. 1962—1969	a. *Description*: In 1962 Somali tribesmen in the North-eastern Region of Kenya, which borders on Somalia, declared before an Independence Commission that they wished to secede from Kenya and join Somalia. On November 13, 1963, Somali insurgents began a series of armed raids. On December 25, 1963, the Kenya government declared a state of emergency in the North-eastern Region. The Kenya Rifles subsequently patrolled the area, resulting in a series of armed clashes between the insurgents and the Kenya Rifles. In July 1966 large sections of the Kenya army were deployed in the area. During the 1963—1966 period approximately 1600 insurgents were killed. b. *Participants*: Somali ethnic groups in Northeastern Kenya, Somali insurgents from Somalia and the government of Kenya. There were no noticeable leaders of the Kenyan Somali groups. Several Somali traditional leaders who supported the Kenya government were abducted. c. *Apparent Causes*: Somali tribesmen's claims for reunion with kinsmen in Somalia. Kenya government's demands for national unity.

SOURCES: A. A. Castagno, "The Somalia-Kenya Controversy," *Journal of Modern African Studies*, 2 (1964): 165—188. Waruhiu Itote (General China), *"Mau Mau" General* (Nairobi: East African Publishing House, 1967).

TABLE 18.10   Annual Instability Events: Independence Through 1979—Kenya

Year	'61	'62	'63	'64	'65	'66	'67	'68	'69	'70	'71	'72	'73	'74	'75	'76	'77	'78	'79
ELITE INSTABILITY																			
Assassinations															2				
Plots									1		1	1						1	
Attempted Coups d'État																			
Coups d'État																			
COMMUNAL INSTABILITY																			
Ethnic Violence				1	1				1										
Irredentism			1	1	1	1	1												
Rebellion				1															
Civil War																			
MASS INSTABILITY																			
Revolt																			
Revolution																			
TURMOIL																			
Demonstrations																			
Strikes (no. days)					11														
Riots (no. days)				1					4					1					
Terrorism									1										
Declarations of Emergency				2					2										
CABINET INSTABILITY																			
Realloc. and new appts.				15	5	10	4	5		2		2							
New members					10		6			2	1	1							
Resig. and Dismissals						4		6											
No. of members (max.) (maximum in year)				14	19	20	29	24	21	21	21	21							

VII. Selected References

BIBLIOGRAPHY

Hakes, Jay E. *A Study Guide for Kenya*. Boston: Development Program, African Studies Center, Boston University, 1969.

Howell, John B. *Kenya: Subject Guide to Official Publications*. Washington, D.C.: Government Printing Office, 1978.

Ndegwa, R. N. *Mau Mau: A Select Bibliography*. Nairobi: Kenyatta University College, 1977.

GENERAL

Harbeson, J. *Nation-Building in Kenya: The Role of Land Reform*. Evanston, Ill.: Northwestern University Press, 1973.

Kaplan, I. et al. *Area Handbook for Kenya 2nd edition*. Washington, D.C.: Government Printing Office, 1976.

Ojany, F. F. and Ogendo, R. B. *Kenya: A Study in Physical and Human Geography*. London: Longman, 1973.

POLITICAL

Arnold, G. *Kenyatta and the Politics of Kenya*. London: J.M. Dent, 1974.

Barkan, J. D. and J. J. Okumu (eds). *Politics and Public Policy in Kenya and Tanzania*. New York: Praeger, 1978.

Barnett, Donald L. and Karari Mjaja. *Mau Mau from Within: Autobiography and Analysis of Kenya's Peasant Revolt*. New York: Monthly Review Press, 1966.

Bennett, George. *Kenya: A Political History—The Colonial Period*. London: Oxford University Press, 1963.

Bienen, Henry. *Kenya: The Politics of Participation and Control*. Princeton, N.J.: Princeton University Press, 1973.

Frost, Richard A. *Race Against Time: Human Relations and Politics in Kenya Beyond Independence*. London: Rex Collings, 1978.

Gertzel, Cherry. *The Politics of Independent Kenya 1963—1968*. London: Heinemann, 1970.

Gertzel, Cherry, Maure Goldshmidt and Donald Rothschild, eds. *Government and Politics in Kenya*. Nairobi: East African Publishing House, 1969.

Kenyatta, Jomo. *Suffering Without Bitterness: The Founding of the Kenyan Nation*. Nairobi: East African Publishing House, 1968.

Kitching, G. *Class and Economic Change in Kenya*. New Haven: Yale University Press, 1980.

Murray-Brown, Jeremy. *Kenyatta*. London: George Allen and Unwin, Ltd., 1972.

Odinga, Oginga. *Not Yet Uhuru*. New York: Hill and Wange, 1967.

Rosberg, Carl G., and John Nottingham. *The Myth of Mau-Mau: Nationalism in Kenya*. N.Y.: Praeger, 1966.

Ross, Marc Howard. "Political Alienation, Participation, and Ethnicity in the Nairobi Urban Area" in John N. Paden (ed) *Values, Identities, and National Integration*, Evanston, Ill.: Northwestern University Press, 1980, p. 173—82.

Wipper, Audrey. *Rural Rebels: A Study of Two Protest Movements in Kenya*. New York: Oxford University Press, 1978.

ECONOMIC

Burrows, J. *Kenya: Into the Second Decade: Report of a Mission Sent to Kenya by the World Bank*. Baltimore: Johns Hopkins University Press, 1975.

Hazelwood, A. *The Economics of Kenya*. New York: Oxford University Press, 1980.

Holtham, Gerald and Arthur Hazelwood. *Aid and Inequality in Kenya: British Development Assistance to Kenya* London: Croom Helm in Association with Overseas Development Institute, 1976.

King, J. R. *Stabilization Policy in an African Setting*: Kenya 1963—1973. Studies in the Economics of Africa. Exeter, N.H.: Heinemann Educational Books, 1979.

Leonard, David K. *Reaching the Peasant Farmer: Organization Theory and Practice in Kenya*. Chicago: University of Chicago Press, 1977.

Leys, Colin. *Underdevelopment in Kenya: The Political Economy of Neo-Colonialism, 1964—1971*. Berkeley: University of California Press, 1975.

Obudho, Robert A. and D.R.F. Taylor. *The Spatial Structure of Development: A Study of Kenya*. Boulder, Colo.: Westview Press, 1979.

Oser, Jacob. *Promoting Economic Development: With Illustrations from Kenya*. Evanston, Ill.: Northwestern University Press, 1967.

Rempel, Henry and William J. House. *The Kenya Employment Problem: An Analysis of the Modern Sector Labour Market*. New York: Oxford University Press, 1978.

Singer, H., and R. Jolly. "Unemployment in an African Setting: Lessons of the Employment Strategy Mission to Kenya." *International Labour Review*, 107 (February 1973): 103—116.

Swainson, N. *The Development of Corporate Capitalism in Kenya, 1918—1977*. Berkeley: University of California Press, 1980.

Van Zwandenberg, R. M. A., and Anne King. *An Economic History of Kenya and Uganda, 1800—1970*. London: Macmillan, 1975.

Wolff, Richard. *The Economics of Colonialism: Britain and Kenya, 1870-1930*. New Haven: Yale University Press, 1974.

SOCIAL

Cour, D. and D. Ghai. *Education and Development*: *New Perspectives from Kenya*. New York: Oxford University Press, 1975.

Cowan, L. Gray. *The Costs of Learning*: The Politics of Primary Education in Kenya. New York: Columbia Teachers College Press, 1970.

De Bilj, Harm J. *Mombasa*: *An African City*. Evanston, Ill.: Northwestern University Press, 1968.

Gregory, R. G. *India and East Africa*: *A History of Race Relations Within the British Empire, 1890—1939*. New York: Oxford University Press, 1972.

Gutto, S. B. O. *The Status of Women in Kenya*: *A Study of Paternalism, Inequality, and Underprivelege*. Nairobi: Institute of Development Studies, University of Nairobi, 1976.

Hake, A. *African Metropolis*: *Nairboi's Self-Help City*. London: Chatto & Windus, Ltd. for Sussex University Press, 1977.

Kenyatta, Jomo. *Facing Mount Kenya*. London: Secker and Warburg, 1938.

Lamb, G. *Peasant Politics*: *Conflict and Development in Murang'a*. New York: St. Martin's Press, 1974.

Marris, P. and A. Somerset. *African Businessmen*: *A Study of Entrepreneurship and Development in Kenya*. London: Routledge and Kegan Paul, 1971.

Rhoades, John. *Linguistic Diversity and Language Belief in Kenya*: *The Special Position of Swahili*. Syracuse, N.Y.: Syracuse University, 1977.

Rothchild, Donald. *Racial Bargaining in Independent Kenya*: *A Study of Minorities and De-colonization*. London: Oxford University Press, 1973.

Sheffield, James R. *Education in Kenya*: *An Historical Study*. New York: Teachers College Press, 1973.

Soja, Edward W. *The Geography of Modernization in Kenya*: *A Spatial Analysis of Social, Economic and Political Change*. Syracuse, N.Y.: Syracuse University Press, 1968.

Whiteley, W. H. *Language in Kenya*. New York: Oxford University Press, 1975.

19. Lesotho

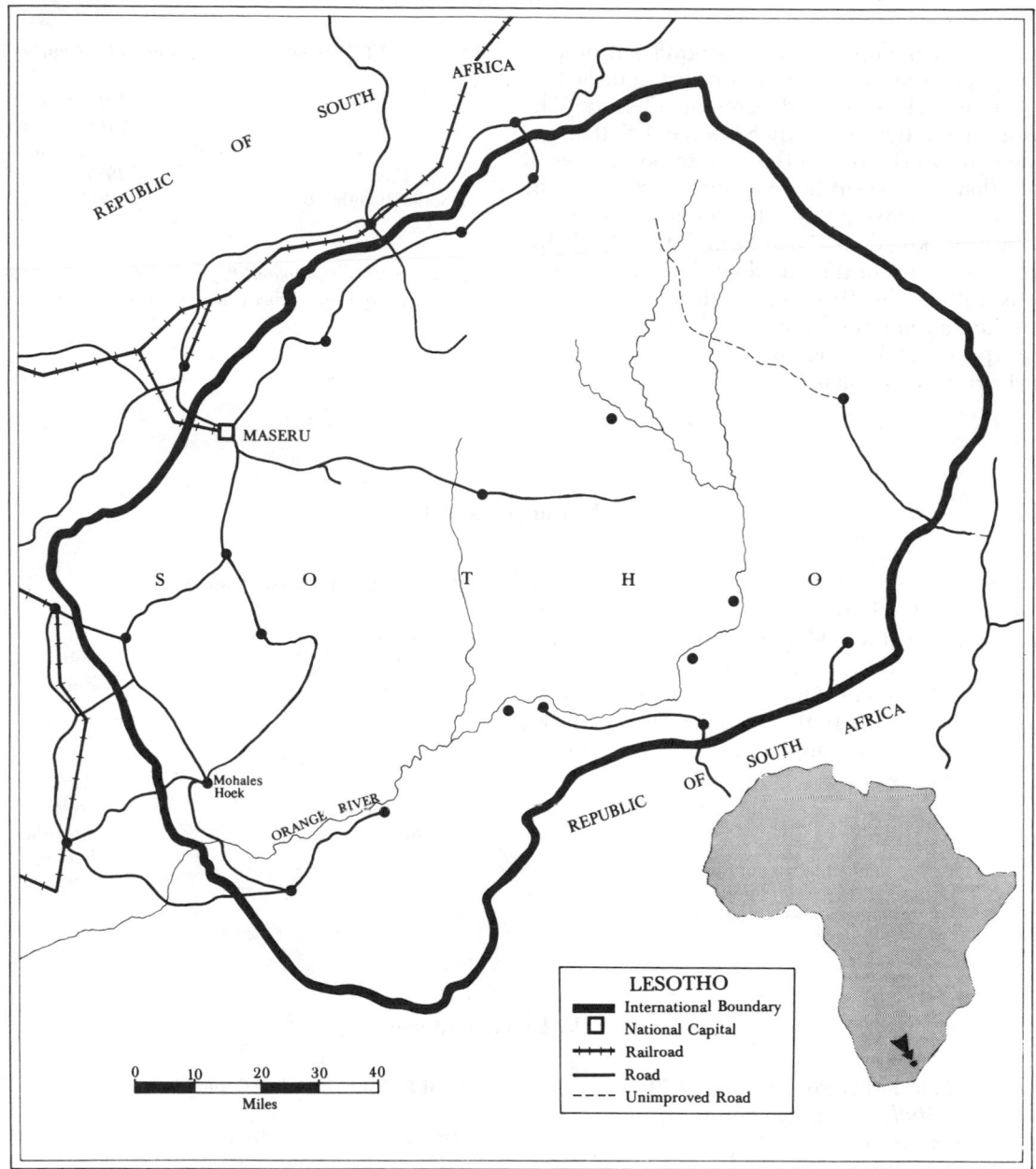

I. Basic Information

Date of Independence: October 4, 1966
Former Colonial Ruler: United Kingdom
Former Name: Basutoland
Estimated Population (1980): 1,332,000*
Area Size (equivalent in U.S.): 11,716 sq. mi. (New Hampshire and Delaware)
Date of Last Census: 1976

Major Exports 1977 as Percent of Total Exports: wool—21 percent; mohair—16 percent; diamonds—10 percent.

*Includes absentee workers (which were reported in the 1966 census as consisting of approximately 12 percent of the population).

II. Ethnic Patterns

The Sotho, who make up all but an insignificant proportion of the population in Lesotho, are distinguished by language, culture, history, and common identity. The 1956 census gave a figure of only 83 percent Sotho, and did not break down the rest of the African population. It is probable that 83 percent is a low figure. Because the Sotho are not just a kinship group but members of a politically centralized kingdom, "non-Sotho" peoples living within the boundaries of the kingdom, have come to be regarded as Sotho. The 1966 census showed that about 117,000 Sotho had migrated temporarily to South Africa for work purposes. In 1966 about .2 percent of the population was European or Asian.

TABLE 19.1   Ethnic Unit Over 5 Percent of Country Population

Ethnic Units	Estimated Ethnic Population 1980	Estimted Ethnic Percentage
a. Sotho (Basotho, Basuto)	1,319,000	99%

SOURCES: *1966 Basutoland Population Census.* J. E. Spence, *Lesotho, the Politics of Dependence* (London: Oxford, 1968).

III. Language Patterns

Sotho is used as a *lingua franca*, and both Knappert and Rustow regard virtually the entire population as Sotho-speaking (100 percent and 99 percent respectively. Rustow suggests that Zulu-Xhosa is the second largest language with only 1 percent. Our own estimate is Sotho 99 percent; Zulu 1 percent. Both languages are Bantu. English and Sotho are official languages.

TABLE 19.2   Language Patterns

			Green-berg	Dalby
1. Primacy				
1st language	Sotho	(99%)		
2nd language	Zulu	(1%)		
2. Linguistic classification	Sotho		IA5	S3
	Zulu		IA5	S4
3. *Lingua franca*	Sotho			
4. Official languages	English, Sotho			

IV. Urban Patterns

Capital/Largest city: Maseru (founded 1869)
Dominant ethnicity/language of capital
    Major vernacular: Sotho
    Major ethnic group: Sotho
    Major ethnic group as percent of capital's popultion:
    Nearly 100%

TABLE 19.3   Growth of Capital/Largest City

Date	Maseru
1920	2,000
1950	6,000
1960	9,000
1966	18,000 UA
1972	29,000 UA
1976	45,000 UA

SOURCES: Various editions of the *Statesman's Yearbook*, except for the 1976 estimate which comes from *Europa Yearbook 1979*, Vol. II.

TABLE 19.4   Cities of 20,000 and Over

City	Size		Date
Maseru	45,000 UA		1976

SOURCE: *Europa Yearbook 1979*, Vol. II.

V. Political Patterns

A. Political Parties and Elections

Until 1970, political life in Lesotho was marked by the competition of three major parties. The *Basuto Congress Party* (BCP) was dominant from 1960 to 1965. The *Marema Tlou Freedom Party* (MTFP) was formed in 1963 by a merger of the *Marema Tlou Party* (MTP) and the *Basuto Freedom Party* (BFP) under Bennet Khaketla. Along with the *Basuto National Party* (BNP), it served as opposition. In the election prior to independence the more conservative BNP, led by Chief Leabua Jonathan, won a narrow victory and elected 31 members to the National Assembly, while the BCP elected 25 and the MFP elected 4 members. In January 1970, after his leading political opponent, Ntsu Mokhehle of the BCP, had claimed victory in the general elections, Chief Jonathan suspended the constitution and took control of the government. At this time, according to *Africa South of*

FIGURE 19.1   Political Parties and Elections   LESOTHO

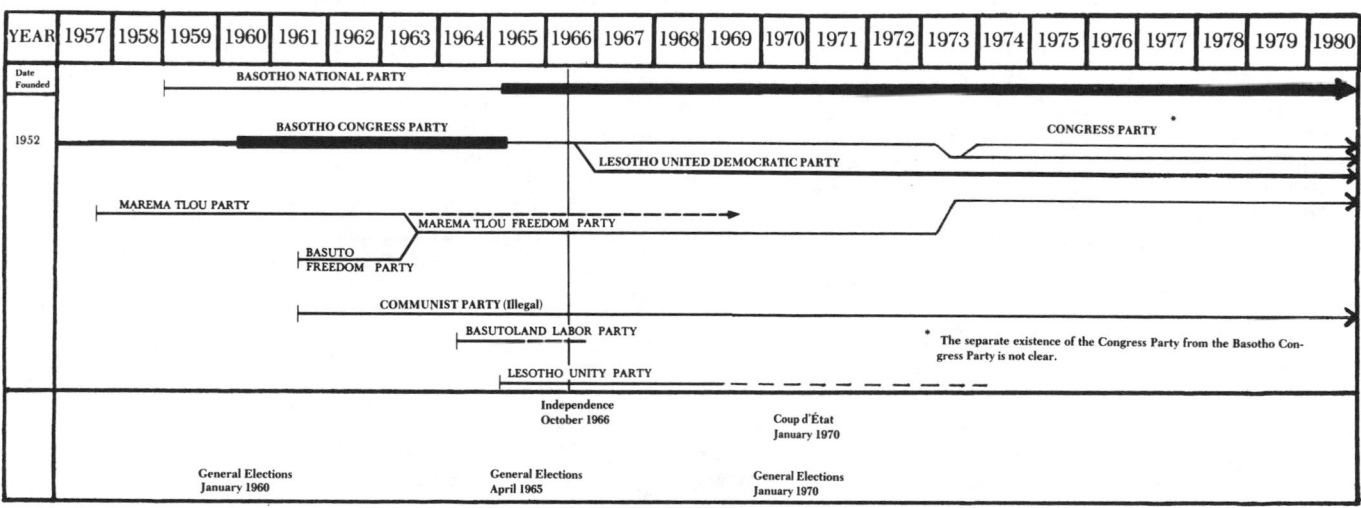

the Sahara, 1978—79 (Europa Publications, 1978), all the oppositon parties were banned. In October 1970, Chief Jonathan declared a five year 'holiday' from politics. It is not clear if parties were actually banned or whether parties were harrassed with the jailing of their leaders from January 1970 to January 1972. The conflict over the election results continued with the arrest of oppositon leaders and the declaration of a state of emergency. The latter was lifted in July 1973 and although most detainees had been released by January 1972, detention laws have continued to be used against opponents of the Jonathan regime, and the top leadership of the BCP have remained in exile. When Jonathan proposed and brought into being a new National Interim Arrangement it was boycotted by most BCP party members since it gave Jonathan's party an effective majority. In November, 1973 it was announced tht the BCP, *Lesotho United Democratic Party* (LUDP), and MTF were forming a united opposition front against Jonathan's BNP. The Congress Party, an offshoot of the Basotho Congress Party, attempted a coup in 1974, but failed and the leaders fled to Zambia. In an attempt to "effect reconciliation and full national unity," Chief Jonathan included members of the MTFP and a member of the LUDP in his ca-

binet towards the end of 1975, but this has not had any great effect on the opposition as a whole. In May and June 1979, several incidents of violence were reported to have been carried out by the Congress Party or the Basotho Congress Party. There were two bomb explosions in Maseru and later there were armed clases between the police and suspected oppositon party members. In June Jonathan and the BNP passed a bill giving amnesty to the BCP, but on an individual basis. The BCP guerrillas had claimed responsibility for various attacks, including a raid on Leribe airport.

B. Political Leadership

The government of Prime Minister Jonathan has continued in power since independence in 1966, and the cabinet, like the country itself, is ethnically homogeneous. The head of state was the young, Oxford-educated Paramount Chief Moshoeshoe II, who became a constitutional monarch in 1967 but was placed under arrest after Chief Jonathan's coup in 1970. He continued his studies at Oxford and was allowed to return to Lesotho for two months a year.

TABLE 19.5   Head of Government (Post-Independence)

Name	Dates in Office	Age (1982)	Ethnicity	Education	Former Occupation
1. Chief Leabua Jonathan (Prime Minister)	1966— present	68	Sotho	Primary, Mission School	Clerk, Storekeeper

TABLE 19.6   Cabinet Membership: Distribution by Ethnic Unit*

Ethnicity*	Independence Cabinet	1967 Cabinet	1972 Cabinet
1. Sotho (99%)	100%	100%	100%
2. Others (1)	0	0	0
N =	10	10	11

*Ethnic units arranged in rank order of size within country with the unit's percent of national population in parentheses.

VI. National Integration and Stability

There are personal and ideological conflicts among the major political leaders of the country which are complicated by Lesotho's political and economic situation vis-à-vis South Africa. On December 30, 1966, supporters of King Moshoeshoe attacked the police station at Butha Buthe in northern Lesotho. This action, which was followed by other incidents, was reputedly part of the effort of the *Basuto Congress Party* (BCP) to shift power from Prime Minister Jonathan to King Moshoeshoe which resulted in Jonathan moving against the king and limiting his political power. In January 1970 Chief Jonathan assumed extra-constitutional control following an apparent election defeat. A number of violent incidents occurred in the following months with as many as 500 persons killed. Officials of opposition parties were arrested but most were released by January 1972. Despite attempts to co-opt leaders of the opposition parties into a one-party state this idea was rejected and in January 1974 there were armed attacks against police stations by BCP supporters aimed at the overthrow of Jonathan. These attacks were unsuccessful and a state of 'suspended political animation' continues. Increasing use of force and detention by Jonathan after the 1974 coup attempt seems apparent, despite attempts to co-opt opposition party members with government positions. Incidents of violence believed to have been carried out by members of either the Congress Party of the Basotho Congress Party were reported in May and June 1979. Further pressure was put on Lesotho when, in May 1978, Transkei required Lesotho citizens to have a passport to transit to trade with South Africa. In April 1979 Ntsu Mokhehle, leader of the BCP formed the Lesotho Liberation Army and began an armed insurgency against Jonathan's government. Periodic guerrilla attacks have occurred through 1982. In the spring of 1980 Mokehele was replaced by Tseliso Makhahke.

TABLE 19.7   Elite Instability

Event and Date	Characteristics
1. Coup d'État January 30, 1970	a. *Description*: Following an election in which his party, the Basutoland National Party, was apparently defeated, the prime minister, Chief Jonathan, proclaimed a state of emergency and suspended the constitution. He arrested all the executive members and many candidates of the rival Basutoland Congress Party and placed restrictions on the head of state, King Moshoeshoe II. Reports of deaths in the takeover reach 500. b. *Participants*: The prime minister, counseled by "hard men in his party, together with some of the political appointees among the top civil servants." The police military unit under a Briton, Fred Roach and other British officers played a major supporting role. c. *Apparent Causes*: It seems that the Basutoland National Party only won 23 seats to the Basutoland Congress Party's 36 (Chief Jonathan is a strong advocate of close ties with South Africa while Ntsu Mokhehle, the head of the Congress Party, favors greater independence from South Africa). Chief Jonathan acted in order to continue in power after his electoral defeat.
2. Coup Attempt January 7, 1974	a. *Description*: Armed attacks by Basuto Congress Party (BCP) supporters on three police stations were reprted as a prelude to a counter-coup intended to return the government to its constitutional forms which had been suspended in January 1970 by Chief Jonathan. The attackers were repulsed and some were arrested. b. *Participants*: BCP supporters including Mr. Mokhehle and other officers of the party. c. *Apparent Causes*: It is unclear whether the arrest on January 6th of BCP members set off a planned attack or whether the attack came as an attempt to free their supporters.
3. Armed Insurgency April 1980—present	a. *Descripton*: Periodic armed attacks by the Lesotho Liberation Army, (military wing of the BCP) designed to disrupt the government of Chief Jonathan in hopes of its eventual downfall. b. *Participants*: BCP supporters including Mr. Mokhehle and other members of the party. c. *Apparent Causes*: Long term grievances stemming from Jonathan's coup in 1970.

SOURCES: "Lesotho Crisis," *Africa Digest*, 17 (1970): 27—28. "Lesotho Coup," *Africa Report*, 15 (March 1970): 3—4. Khaketla B. M. *Lesotho 1970: An African Coup Under the Microscope* Berkeley: University of California Press, 1972.

TABLE 19.10   Annual Instability Events: Independence Through 1979—Lesotho

Year	'61	'62	'63	'64	'65	'66	'67	'68	'69	'70	'71	'72	'73	'74	'75	'76	'77	'78	'79
ELITE INSTABILITY																			
Assassinations																			
Plots						1				1			1						
Attempted Coups d'État														1					
Coups d'État										1									
COMMUNAL INSTABILITY																			
Ethnic Violence																			
Irredentism																			
Rebellion																			
Civil War																			
MASS INSTABILITY																			
Revolt																			
Revolution																			
TURMOIL																			
Demonstrations																			
Strikes (no. days)																			
Riots (no. days)						1													
Terrorism						3													
Declarations of Emergency										1	1	1	1						
CABINET INSTABILITY																			
Realloc. and new appts.								2		5	2	2							
New members											4	3							
Resig. and Dismissals											4	1							
No. of members (max.) (maximum in year)								8	8	8	8	10							

VII. Selected References

BIBLIOGRAPHY

Gordon, Loraine. *Lesotho: A Bibliography.* Johannesburg: University of the Witwatersrand, Department of Bibliography, Librarianship and Typography, 1970.

Haliburton, G. *Historical Dictionary of Lesotho.* Metuchen, N.J.: Scarecrow Press, 1977.

Switzer, Les and Donna Switzer. *The Black Press in South Africa and Lesotho: A Descriptive Bibliographical Guide.* Boston: G. K. Hall, 1979.

Wilken, Gene C. and Carolyn F. Amiet, comps. *Bibliography for Planning and Development in Lesotho.* Fort Collins, Col.: Colorado State University, 1977.

Willet, S. M. and D. Ambrose. *Lesotho: A Comprehensive Bibliography.* Santa Barbara, Ca: Clio Press, 1980.

GENERAL

Ashton, Hugh, *The Basuto: A Social Study of Traditional and Modern Lesotho* 2nd ed. London: Oxford University Press, 1967.

Central Office of Information Reference Pamphlet. *Lesotho.* London: Her Majesty's Stationery Office, 1966.

Coates, Austin. *Basutoland.* London: Her Majesty's Stationery Office, 1966.

Halpern, Jack. *South Africa's Hostages: Basutoland, Bechuanaland and Swaziland.* Baltimore: Penguin, 1965.

Potholm, C. and Richard Dale, eds. *South Africa in Perspective.* New York: Free Press, 1972.

Sanders, Peter. *Moshoeshoe, Chief of the Sotho.* London: Heinemann, 1975.

Stevens, Richard. *Lesotho, Botswana, and Swaziland.* London: Pall Mall Press, 1967.

POLITICAL

Hammett, I. *Chieftancy and Legitmacy: An Anthropological Study of Executive Law in Lesotho.* Boston: Routledge and Kegan Paul, 1975.

Khaketla, B. M. *Lesotho 1970: An African Coup Under the Microscope.* Berkeley: University of California Press, 1972.

Spence, J. E. *Lesotho: the Politics of Dependence.* London: Oxford University Press, 1968.

Strom, Gabrielle W. *Development and Dependence in Lesotho, the Enclave of South Africa.* Uppsala, Scandinavian Institute of African Studies, 1978.

Weisfelder, Richard. *The Basotho Monarchy: A Spent Force or a Dynamic Political Factor?* Athens, Ohio: Center for International Studies, Ohio University, 1972. Papers in International Studies, Africa Series, No. 16.

Weisfelder, Richard. "Power Struggle in Lesotho." *Africa Report*, 12 (Janurary 1967): 5—13.

ECONOMIC

International Monetary Fund. "Lesotho," in *Surveys of African Economies*, Vol. 5. Washington, D.C.: I.M.F., 1973.

Leistner, J. M. E. *Lesotho: Economic Structure and Growth.* Pretoria: Africa Institute, 1966.

Manne, W. *Lesotho: A Development Challenge.* Baltimore: Johns Hopkins University Press, 1975.

Strom, Gabrielle W. *Socio-Economic Structure and Authorities in Southern Africa.* Uppsala University. Department of Peace Research, 1975.

Ward, Michael. "Economic Independence for Lesotho," *Journal of Modern African Studies*, 5 (1967): 355—368.

World Bank. *Lesotho: A Development Challenge.* World Bank Country Economic Report Series, John Hopkins University Press, 1975.

SOCIAL

Gerard, Albert S. "Literature of Lesotho." *Africa Report*, 11 (October 1965): 68—70.

Kuper, A. "The Social Structure of the Sotho-Speaking Peoples of Southern Africa," *Africa* 45 1 (1975), Part I, pp. 67—82, Part II.

Rose, Brian. "Education in Botswana, Lesotho and Swaziland." In *Education in Southern Africa*, ed. B. Rose. London: Collier-Macmillan, 1970.h Sheddick, Vernon G. J. *The Southern Sotho.* Ethnographic Survey of Africa. Southern Africa, pt. 2. London: International African Institute, 1953.

Wallman, Sandra. *Take Out Hunger: Two Case Studies of Rural Develoment in Basutoland.* New York: Humanities Press, 1969.

20. Liberia

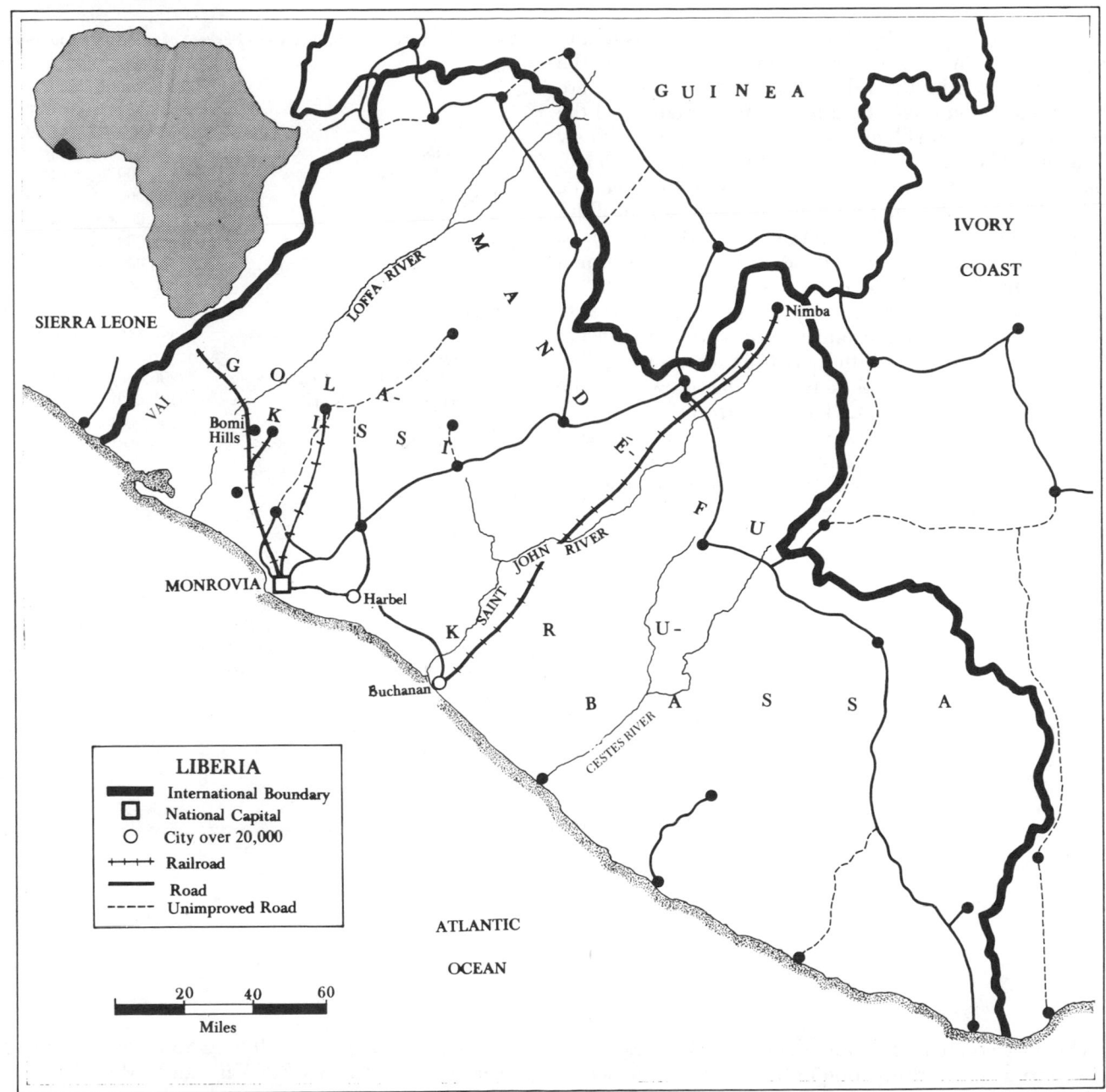

I. Basic Information

Date of Independence: 1847
Estimated Population (1980): 1,850,000
Area Size (equivalent in U.S.): 43,000 sq. mi. (Ohio)
Date of Last Census: 1974

Major Exports 1978 as Percent of Total Exports: iron ore—56 percent; rubber—14 percent; coffee—10 percent (1977); diamonds—6 percent; wood—6 percent (1977).

II. Ethnic Patterns

Liberia is an especially difficult country to classify into ethnic units. We have adopted, for the most part, the categories used by the Liberian government. These are based mainly on linguistic criteria. As an example of the complexity in individual cases, the Vai (3 percent) may be cited. They are close linguistically to the Mandingo, but many derive historically and culturally from the Gola. In addition to the units listed, there is a small intrusive population of Mandingos (about 3 percent), as well as an even smaller population of Fanti fishermen from Ghana many of whom have been expelled from the country in recent years. Some writers on Liberia refer to the descendants of the original settlers from America as "Americo-Liberians." With increasing intermarriage between the Americo-Liberians and the growth of the Westernized urban population, a sharp distinction now seems less appropriate. Locally, the urban Westernized people (including the Americo-Liberians) are now referred to as the "Kwi" and there is an increasing tendency on the part of the Americo-Liberians to emphasize "tribal" names and identities.

TABLE 20.1   Ethnic Units Over 5 Percent of Country Population

Ethnic Units	Estimated Ethnic Population 1980	Estimated Ethnic Percentage
a. Mandé-Fu Type	814,000	44%
1. Kpellé (Guerzé)	(389,000)	(21%)
2. Gio (Dan)	(148,00)	(8%)
3. Mano (Manon)	(130,000)	(7%)
4. Lorma (Buzzi, Loma, Toma)	(93,000)	
5. Ghandi (Bandi)	(56,000)	(3%)
6. Mendé		
b. Kru-Bassa Type (Coastal Cluster)	685,000	37%
1. Bassa (Basa, Basso, Gbasa)	(296,000)	(16%)
2. Kru (Crau, Krao, Nana)	(148,000)	(8%)
3. Grebo	(146,000)	8%
4. Krahn (Gueré)	(98,000)	(5%)
5. Dei		
c. Gola-Kissi Cluster (Mel, West Atlantic)	148,000	8%
1. Gola		
2. Kissi (Ghizi, Gissi, Kisi)		

SOURCES: *Liberia, Basic Date and Information* (Monrovia: Government Printer, 1966), p. 10; Colin Legum, *Africa* (New York: Praeger, 1966), pp. 231—232. S. von Gnielinski, *Liberia in Maps*, New York, Africana, 1972.

III. Language Patterns

The discussion of Liberia's language classification had centered on the distinction between various branches of Mandé which Welmers has resolved. The current discussion centers on the classification of the Kru-speaking peoples. Westermann and Bryan (1952) used the distinction between Mandé-tan (including Soninké, Maninka-Bambara-Dyula, Khasonke, Vai) and Mandé-Fu (Susu-Yalunka, Mandé, Loko, Kpellé, Loma, Bandi, Mano, Gio- Dan). Welmers suggests four categories: (1) Northern (including Susu-Yalunka, Soninké, Vai, Khasonke,

Maninka-Bambara-Dyula) (2) Southwestern (Mandé, Loko, Bandi, Loma, Kpellé), (3) Southern (Mano, Gio-Dan, Tura, Mwa, Nwa, Gan, Kweni-Guro), (4) Eastern (Sya, Samo, Bisa, Busa). Westermann did see the close relationship between the Mandé-Fu (Welmers' Southwestern group) and the Mano and Gio, calling them collectively the "Mendé- Kpellé" group. We have decided to adopt the Mandé-Fu/Kpellé groups as a language class (Mandé speakers) even though Rustow estimates that only 25 percent of the population understand Kpellé. The Mandé speakers are probably slightly larger in number than the Kru group (including Bassa). Mac-Dougald estimates Kru at 26 percent; Rustow, Kru-Bassa at 30 percent.

The Vai language has a script and a literature, which is apparently used by other groups in addition to the Vai ethnic group. The settlers from America used English, which is now related to other coastal English creole languages. English is the official language of Liberia.

TABLE 20.2   Language Patterns

1. Primacy		
1st language	Mandé	(44%)
2nd language	Kru-Bassa	(37%)
	Green-	Dalby
	berg	
2. Linguistic classification	Mandé-Fu IA2	31A
(all ethnic units in	Kru-Bassa IA4	26
country over 5%)	Gola-Kissi IA1	25C, 25B
3. *Lingua franca*	English	
	(English is the first language of the Americo-Liberians and is regarded as indigenous in this case.)	
4. Official language	English	

IV. Urban Patterns

Capital/Largest city: Monrovia (founded 1822
Dominant ethnicity/language of capital
   Major vernacular: English[1]
   Major ethnic group: Kru-speaking peoples[2]
   Major ethnic groups as percent of capital's population: 45% (1959)

[1]Jan Knappert, "Language Problems of the New Nations of Africa," *African Quarterly*, 5 (1965): 95—105.
[2]Merran Fraenkel, *Tribe and Class in Monrovia* (London: Oxford University Press, 1964), p. 36.

TABLE 20.3   Growth of Capital/Largest City

Date	Monrovia
1920	4,000
1930	10,000
1940	12,000
1950	42,000
1960	62,000
1962	81,000
1970[a]	97,000
1974[b]	180,000 UA
1978	209,000 UA

SOURCE: Merran Fraenkel. *Tribe and Class in Monrovia* (London: Oxford University Press, 1964). The 1962 Liberian Census gave 81,000 as the population of Monrovia.
[a]*UN Demographic Yearbook 1972.*
[b]*Africa Research Bulletin.*

TABLE 20.4   Cities of 20,000 and Over

City	Size	Date
Monrovia	209,000 UA	1978

SOURCE: *Europa Yearbook 1979*, V. II.

V. Political Patterns

A. Political Parties and Elections

Founded in 1860, the True Whig Party (TWP) governed Liberia continuously from 1870 until April 1980. The leader of the True Whigs and the President of Liberia from 1944—71, William V.S. Tubman, governed with the aid of a Senate (six-year term) and a House of Representatives (four-year term). Elections are held every two years for part of the legislature. Presidential elections are held at the end of a first term of eight years, and every four years thereafter. President Tolbert, who succeeded Tubman in 1971, proposed a change in the constitution to have presidents elected every four years with a maximum of two terms. Opposition to the *True Whig Party* was sporadic and disorganized, with no stable opposition party existing in Liberia until shortly before the 1980 coup.

An unofficial opposition group, the *Progressive Alliance of Liberia* (PAL) held its first congress in May 1978. In November 1979, national municipal elections were postponed when the post of mayor of Monrovia was contested. Dr. Amos Sawyer, the opposition candidate was a possible winner which threatened Americo-Liberian hegemony. In December 1978, the Probate Court ruled in favor of an application by PAL to register a new party, the People's Progressive Party. No official opposition was raised immediately by members of the ruling True Whig Party. With the call of a general strike in March 1980, however, the PPP's headquarters were raided and party members were arrested. On April 12, 1980, soldiers led by army Master Sergeant Samuel Doe overthrew the government of William Tolbert. The state of party politics and elections is uncertain at this time, but the new government said it would be at least 1983

FIGURE 20.1   Political Parties and Elections   LIBERIA

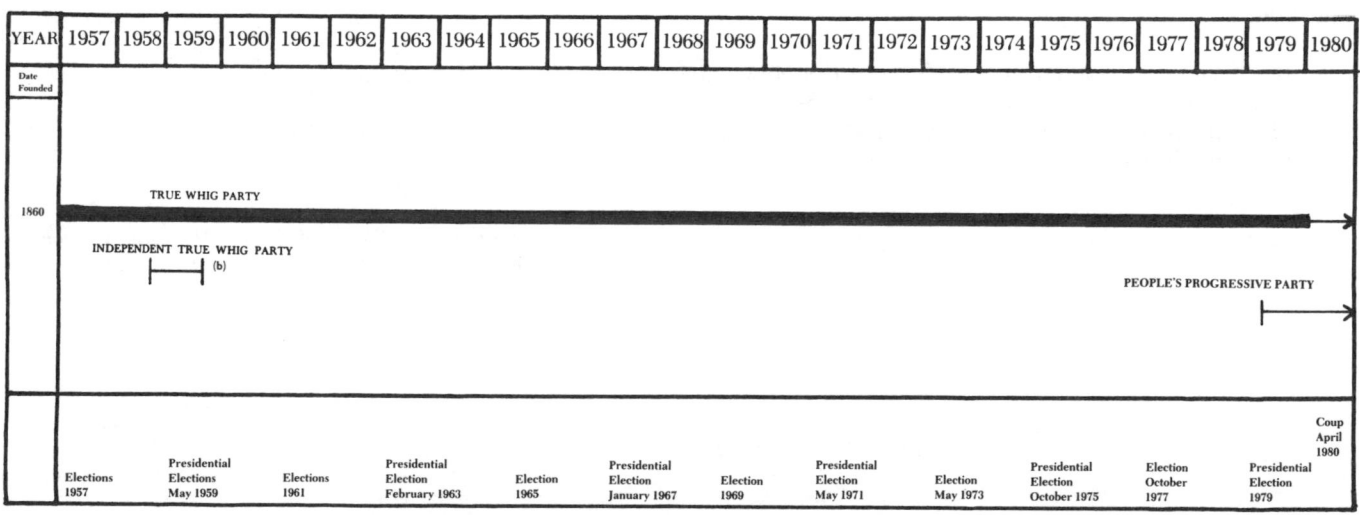

before new elections could be held. Two unofficial political parties retain influence in the new military government. These include the Movement for Justice in Africa (MOJA) led by the minister of Economic Planning Togba-Nah Tipoteh before he fled the country and the Progressive People's Party (PPP) led by Foreign Minister G. Baccus Matthews.

B. Political Leadership

The government of Liberia was led by President William Tubman without notable change from 1944 to July 1971. The composition of the cabinet changed quite frequently, notably in the periods 1957—60 and 1968—69, when the rate of dismissals and resignations was high. These changes in personnel did not, however, change the predominance of the minority Americo-Liberian group in government. William Tolbert succeeded Tubman and was elected in his own right in 1975. There was an increasing attempt to enlarge the ethnic representation in the cabinet. Master Sgt. Doe, now leads the People's Redemption council (PRC) after he led a coup in 1980.

TABLE 20.5 Heads of Government

Name	Dates in Office	Age (1982)	Ethnicity	Education	Former Occupation
1. William V.S. Tubman (President)	1944— 1971	Died 1971 age 75	Americo-Liberian	Cuttington College	Lawyer
2. William R. Tolbert, Jr. (President)	1971— April 12, 1980	Killed in coup age 67	Americo-Liberian	Liberia College	Ordained Minister, Vice-President
3. Samuel Kanyon Doe (President)	April 12, 1980— present	30	Kru	Military	Soldier (Sergeant)

TABLE 20.6 Cabinet Membership: Distribution by Ethnic Unit*

Ethnicity	Independence** Cabinet	1967 Cabinet
1. Mandé-Fu (44%)	0	0
2. Kru-Bassa (37)	0	0
3. Gola-Kissi (8)	0	0
4. "Settler" (2)	100	93
5. Vai (3)	0	6.7
6. Others (6)	0	0
N =	12	15

*Ethnic units arranged in rank order of size within country with the unit's percent of national population in parentheses.

**For purposes of comparability, "independence" is treated as 1960 although Liberia has been an independent nation for more than a century.

VI. National Integration and Stability

Under the Tubman regime, with its policy of national integration, some 'tribal' peoples had increased representation in the government, although the small Americo-Liberian dominated group continued to hold the great majority of cabinet posts. While Tolbert increased attempts to integrate the up-country groups into national political life, there was continuing evidence of tension between the Americo-Liberians and the up-country groups, which until recently had been excluded from the country's political and economic life. Evidence of elite instability, since the attempted coup d'état in 1955, included the accusation, in 1970, that the deposed army commander, General George Washington, was plotting against the government and that a plot to assassinate Tolbert was discovered in 1973. Riots in April 1979 over projected food price rises (particularly of the staple rice) destroyed the image of the country as without serious conflict. In September, a new Ministry of State Security was formed. In March 1980, the newly formed People's Progressive Party called for a general strike "to topple the government of President Tolbert" (*New York Times*, March 9, 1980). Instead, thirty-three people were arrested in a raid on the PPP headquarters in Monrovia. On April 12, 1980, elements of the Liberian military headed by Master Sergeant Samuel Doe stormed the executive mansion and shot President Tolbert. Reportedly, Doe said that "rampant corruption" prompted the coup (*Boston Globe*, April 14, 1980). In July 1980 Doe reinstated the stringent labor regulation used by the Tolbert government.

TABLE 20.7   Elite Instability

Event and Date	Characteristics
1. Attempted Coup June 24, 1955	a. *Description*: President Tubman was unharmed after an assassination attempt during the celebration of his election victory; the political assassin was seized. b. *Participants*: In all, 30 persons were charged with treason and sedition. All were reputed to be unsuccessful political candidates. c. *Apparent Causes*: The participants were associated with former President Barclay. They may have been motivated by opposition to Tubman's integrationist policies regarding the "tribal" peoples.
2. Coup d'État April 12, 1980	a. *Description*: Elements of the armed forces led by Sergeant Samuel Doe attacked the executive mansion and shot and killed President Tolbert. Other officials in Tolbert's government have been executed or are under arrest on charges of high treason. b. *Participants*: Military personnel led by Sergeant Doe who belonged to a special battalion assigned to guard President Tolbert. c. *Apparent Causes*: Doe stated that "rampant corruption" in the Tolbert government was the catalyst to the overthrow. The root cause, however, seems to be the political and economic dominance of the Americo-Liberians.

TABLE 20.10   Annual Instability: Independence Through 1979—Liberia

Year	'61	'62	'63	'64	'65	'66	'67	'68	'69	'70	'71	'72	'73	'74	'75	'76	'77	'78	'79
ELITE INSTABILITY																			
Assassinations																			
Plots	1		1			1				1			1						
Attempted Coups d'État																			
Coups d'État																			
COMMUNAL INSTABILITY																			
Ethnic Violence																			
Irredentism																			
Rebellion																			
Civil War																			

Year	'61	'62	'63	'64	'65	'66	'67	'68	'69	'70	'71	'72	'73	'74	'75	'76	'77	'78	'79
MASS INSTABILITY																			
Revolt																			
Revolution																			
TURMOIL																			
Demonstrations																			
Strikes (no. days)	7					1													
Riots (no. days)	1					1													
Terrorism																			
Declarations of Emergency						1													
CABINET INSTABILITY																			
Realloc. and new appts.		4	1	2	2		2	8	6		2	1							
New members		4	1	1	1		2	2	6		2	4							
Resig. and Dismissals		2	1	1	2	1		2	4										
No. of members (maximum in year)	11	12	12	13	13	13	13	15	17	17	17	20							

VII. Selected References

BIBLIOGRAPHY

Holsoe, Sven. *A Bibliography of Liberia*. Part I Book. Part III. Articles. Newark, Del.: Liberian Studies Association, 1971, 1976.

Holsoe, Sven. *A Study Guide for Liberia*. Boston: Development Program, African Studies Program, Boston University, 1967.

GENERAL

Buell, Raymond L. *Liberia*: *A Century of Survival, 1847—1947*. Philadelphia: University of Pennsylvania Press, 1947.

Cassell, C. Abayomi. *Liberia*: *History of the First African Republic*. N.Y.: Fountainhead, 1970.

Clifford, M. L. *The Land and People of Liberia*. Philadelphia: Lippincott, 1971.

Henries, A. Doris Banks. *A Bibliography of President William V. S. Tubman*. London: Macmillan, 1967.

Liberian Studies Journal. Newark, Del.: University of Delaware, Department of Anthropology.

Liebenow, J. Gus. *Liberia, The Evolution of Privelege*. Ithaca, N.Y.: Cornell University Press, 1969.

Marinelli, Lawrence A. *The New Liberia*: *A Historical and Political Survey*. New York: Praeger, 1966.

Smith, Robert A. *William V. S. Tubman, the Life and Work of an African Statesman*. Amsterdam: Van Ditmar, 1967.

U.S. Department of the Army. *Area Handbook for Liberia*, 2nd ed. Washington, D.C.: Government Printing Office, 1972.

Von Grielinski, S., ed. *Liberia in Maps*. New York: Africana, 1972.

Wilson, Charles M. *Liberia*: *Black Africa in Microcosm*. New York: Harper, 1971.

POLITICAL

Clapham, C. *Liberia and Sierra Leone*: *An Essay in Comparative Politics*. New York: Cambridge University Press, 1976.

Fraenkel, Merran. "Social Change on the Kru Coast of Liberia." *Africa*, 36 (1966): 154—172.

Hodgkin, Thomas. "Education and Social Change in Liberia." *West Africa*. nos. 1907—11 (1953).

Holas, Bohumil. *Mission dans l'Est Liberien*: *Resultats demographiques, ethnologiques et anthropometriques*. Dakar: L'Institut Français d'Afrique Noire, 1952.

Sawyer, Amos, "Social Stratification and National Orientations: Students and Nonstudents in Liberia," in John

N. Paden (ed) *Values, Identities, and National Integration: Empirical Research in Africa*, Northwestern University Press, 1980, p. 285—303.

Schulze, W. *A New Geography of Liberia*. London: Longmans, 1973.

Study Committee on Manpower Needs and Educational Capabilities in Africa. *Liberia: Study of Manpower Needs, Educational Capabilites and Overseas Study*, Report 5. New York: Education and World Affairs, 1965.

Liebenow, J. Gus. "Liberia." In *Political Parties and National Integration in Tropical Africa*, J. S. Coleman and C. G. Rosberg, eds. pp. 448—481. Los Angeles: University of California Press, 1964.

Lowenkopf, M. *Politics in Liberia*. Stanford: Hoover Institution, 1976.

ECONOMIC

Carlsson, Jerker. *Transnational Companies in Liberia*. Uppsala, Scandinavian Institute of African Studies, 1977.

Clower, Robert, et al. *Growth without Development: An Economic Survey of Liberia*. Evanston, Ill.: Northwestern University Press, 1966.

Dalton, George. "History, Politics and Economic Development in Liberia." *Journal of Economic History*, 25 (1965): 586—591.

Dalton, George and A. A. Walters. "The Economy of Liberia." In *The Economies of Africa*, eds. P. Robson and D. A. Lury, pp. 287—315. Evanston, Ill.: Northwestern University Press, 1969.

Hanes, William A. "Iron Ore in Liberia: A Study of the Impact of Mining on a Developing Economy." In *African Economic Development*, rev. ed., pp. 54—86. New York: Praeger, 1967.

International Monetary Fund. "Liberia." In *Surveys of African Economies*, Vol. 6. Washington, D.C.: I.M.F., 1975.

Liberia. Ministry of Planning and Economic Affairs. *Economic Survey of Liberia, 1977*. Monrovia, 1978.

McLaughlin, Russell U. *Foreign Investment and Development in Liberia*. New York: Frederick A. Praeger, 1966.

SOCIAL

Fraenkel, Merran. *Tribe and Class in Monrovia*. London: Oxford University Press, 1964.

21. Madagascar

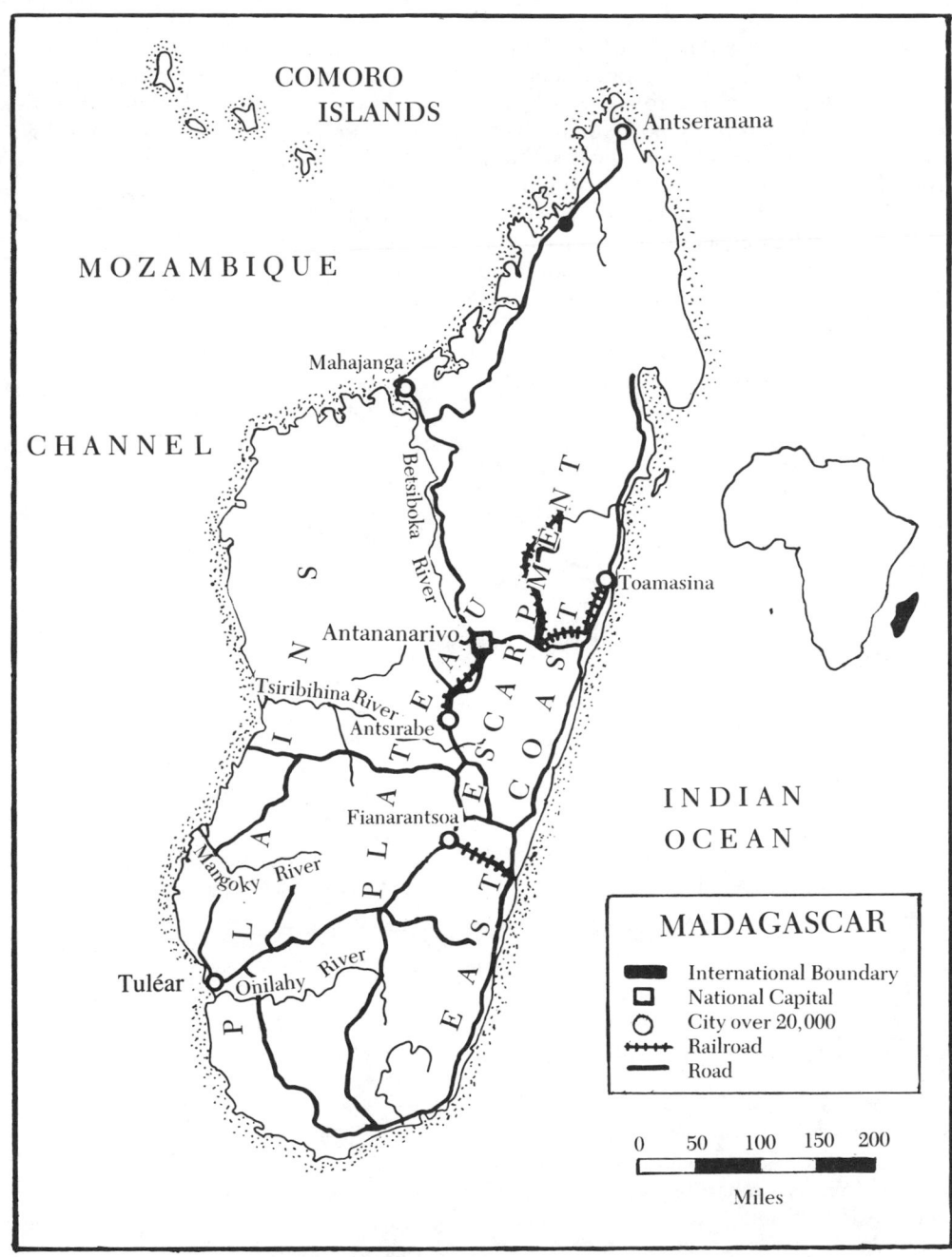

I. Basic Information

Date of Independence: June 26, 1960
Area Size (equivalent in U.S.): 226,657 sq. miles (Arizona and Nevada)
Former Colonial Ruler: France

Date of Last Census: 1975
Major Exports 1977 as Percent of Total Exports: coffee—48 percent; vanilla—11 percent; cloves—6 percent; petroleum products—6.6 percent (1976).

II. Ethnic Patterns

Most of the ancestors of the current population of Madagascar arrived after the tenth century, although some Africans may have migrated to the island from the mainland before that time. From the tenth to the sixteenth century, waves of migrations from Melo-Indonesia and to a lesser extent from the Bantu-speaking and Cushitic areas of East Africa arrived along with Arab traders. From the sixteenth century various European countries used the island as a port of call on the way to India until the French took power in the early twentieth century. Nevertheless, while there have been several cultural influences, the Malagasy language is almost universally shared. The ethnic groupings that we have constructed are based on ecological adaptation, identity, and related social and political organization. In 1972, there were 110,000 foreigners including French (31,000), Indian (18,000), Chinese (10,000), Comorian (44,000), and Reunionaire populations. By the late 1970's, these figures were considerably depleted partially reflecting the exodus of the personnel at the French naval base at Diego Suarez (now called Anteseranana) and riots against the presence of the Comorians.

TABLE 21.1   Ethnic Units Over 5 Percent of Country Population

Ethnic Units	Estimated Ethnic Population 1980	Estimated Ethnic Percentage
a. Central Plateau Type	3,377,000	39.5
1. Merina (Antimerina, Hova, Imerina, Ovah.)	(2,309,000)	(27)
2. Betsileo	(1,069,000)	(12.5)
a. Arindrano b. Ilalangina		
c. Isandra d. Manadriana		
b. East Coast Type	2,095,000	24.5
1. Betsimisaraka a. Betanimena	(1,283,000)	(15)
2. Antaisaka (Taisaka, Tesaki)	(812,000)	(9.5)
a. Antaimoro b. Antambahoaka		
c. Antifasy d. Sahafatra		
c. Plains Type	1,710,000	20
1. Antandroy (Tandruy)	(684,000)	(8.0)
a. Antanosy (Tanosy, Tanusi)		
2. Sakalava	(547,000)	(6.4)
a. Antankarana b. Antiboina		
c. Antifiherena d. Antimailaka		
e. Antimaraka f. Antimena		
g. Antimilanja h. Vezu (Veso)		
3. Bara	(351,000)	(4.1)
a. Barobe b. Imamono		
c. Sautsauta d. Timonjy		
e. Vinda		
4. Mehafaly (Mahafali)	(128,000)	(1.5)
d. Escarpment Type	1,231,000	14.4
1. Tsimihety	(641,000)	(7.5)
2. Sihanaka (Antisihanaka)	(180,000)	(2.1)
3. Tanala (Antanala)	(410,000)	(4.8)
a. Ikongo b. Menabe		
Bezamozano (Antaiva, Tankay)		

SOURCES: Murdock, *Africa*; 1971 Census reports from *Africa South of the Sahara 1974*; Heseltine *Madagascar* New York: Praeger, 1971; Nelson, H.D. et al. *Area Handbook for the Malagasy Republic*, Washington D.C.: Government Printing Office, 1973 DA Pam 550-163.

III. Language Patterns

The Malagasy Kingdom was established under the rule of Merina kings by the early nineteenth century. The language and culture of the Malagasy is universally shared and Knappert estimates Malagasy as 100 percent. While there are various dialects spoken they are all mutually intelligible, and there are no other lanaguages except for those used by non-Malagasy inhabitants of the island such as the French residents, and Arab, Indian, and Chinese traders. Dalby labels the language as Austronesian, and therefore, not an indigenous African language. He does not code Malagasy or any dialects as a result.

TABLE 21.2   Language Patterns

1. Primacy		
1st language	Malagasy	French, second most widely
2nd language	100%	spoken language, is spoken by
	no other	approximately 26% of the popu-
	vernacular	lation.
	language.	
3. *lingua franca*	Malagasy	
4. Official languages	French, Malagasy	

IV. Urban Patterns

Capital/Largest City: Antananarivo (formerly Tananarive)
Dominant ethnicity/language of capital
Major vernacular: Malagasy
Major ethnic group: Merina (Central Plateau type)[1]
Major ethnic group as percent of Capital's population: 87.1 percent in Tananarive province.[1]

[1]*U.S. Army Area Handbook for the Malagasy Republic*, p. 64.

TABLE 21.3 Growth of Capital/Largest City

Date	Antananarivo (formerly Tananarive)
1911	94,813
1926	70,847
1950	174,153
1957	193,162
1961	248,000
1966	335,149
1972[a]	366,530 UA
1976[b]	520,000 UA

SOURCES: Various editions of *Statesman's Yearbook, Africa South of the Sahara*, and the *U.N. Demographic Yearbook 1967*. [a] *Africa South of the Sahara 1974*, p. 480. [b]*Political Handbook of the World 1979*.

TABLE 21.4 Cities of 20,000 and Over

City	Size	Date
Antananarivo[a] (formerly Tananarive)	520,000	1976
Mahajanga (formerly Majunga)	67,458	1972
Toamasina (formerly Tamatave)	59,503	1972
Fianarantsoa	58,818	1972
Antseranana (formerly Diégo Suarez)	45,487	1972
Tuléar	38,978	1972
Antsirabé	33,287	1972

SOURCE: *Africa South of the Sahara 1974*, p. 480. [a] *Political Handbook of the World 1979*.

V. Political Patterns

A. Political Parties and Elections.

In 1946, the first political party was formed in Madagascar. It was the Madagascar Revolutionary Democratic Movement (MRDM) led primarily by Merina intellectuals. The MRDM was largely responsible for the 1947 revolt against the French colonial government. Its leaders were exiled or jailed, and electoral politics were banned for the next seven years. One of the main motivating factors in the revolt was the belief among the Merina leaders that they, whose forbears had been the pre-colonial rulers of the island, should be in power rather than the French. The fear of Merina domination among the rest of the country's population was to play a major role in subsequent politics in the country. The French allowed party politics to emerge again in 1954 and a large number of parties were formed during the next two years. Many of these withered or merged with other parties and Philibert Tsiranana's *Parti Sociale Démocratique* (PSD), formed in 1957, swept into power overwhelmingly in 1958 and faced only two oppostion parties by independence in 1960. They were the *Parti du Congres de l'Indépendence de Madagascar* (AKFM or PCIM) and the *Mouvement Nationale pour l'Indépendence de Madagascar* (MONIMA). After the military coup in 1972, however, a large number of new parties were created and the PSD disappeared in a merger with the *Union Socialiste Malagasy* to become the *Malagasy Socialist Party* (PSM). All parties were allowed to continue throughout the period except for the temporary banning of MONIMA in 1972. In February 1975, all parties were banned after the assassination of the newly installed head of state, Col. Ratsimandrava. They remained banned until the elections of 1977. As dictated by the 1975 constitution, a single party was formed after the 1977 election. It is the *Front National Pour la Défense de la Révolution Socialiste Malgache*.

Elections were held regularly in Madagascar from 1958 until 1972 with Tsiranana and his PSD always winning well over 90% of the legislative seats as well as the Presidency. This was in part due to the winner-take-all policy for every constituency in which one candidate received over 55 percent of the vote. The exception to this occurrence was in the capital, where the PSD could not muster a 55% majority. Under these conditons, proportional representation was used to apportion seats. After the revolt in 1972, elections were held in October 1973 to form a *People's National Development Council* to replace the old legislature. Pro-government candidates won 100 of the 144 elected seats. A referendum was held in December 1975 to confirm Ratsiraka in power and to adopt a new constitution which proclaimed Madagascar to be a "Socialist Republic". Under the new 1975 constitution, elections were held at the village, commune, communal federation, provincial, and national levels from March to June 1977. All seats were won by parties in Ratsiraka's coalition, the *Front Nationale pour la Defense de la Revolution* (FNDR) composed of the *Avantgarde de la Revolution Socialiste Malagasy* UDECMA, MONIMA, the *Mouvement pour le Pourvoir Proletarien* (MFM) and VONJI.

B. Political Leadership

Philibert Tsiranana's leadership of the country from 1958 to 1969 was unquestioned even though inter-ethnic conflicts persisted and there was growing hostility towards his closeness to France and his strident anti-communist position. He was hospitalized in France for several months in 1969—70 and from then on the struggle for succession coupled with an increasing number of strikes, riots and revolts made the continuance of his administration difficult. While he was re-elected by a near unani-mous vote in early 1972, there were accusations of widespread vote-fixing followed by the outbreak of widespread strikes of workers and students within weeks of the election. Tsiranana handed over power to General Ramanantsoa but remained as a figurehead President until a referendum later in the year deposed him as head of state. While Ramanantsoa carried out many reforms, he resisted the formation of a socialist state which was being urged on him by groups within as well as outside his government. He resigned in January 1975, but his successor Colonel Ratsimandrava was assassinated within a week after coming to power. A military directorate was established after the assassination of Colonel Ratsimandrava. Its functions were to arrest and try those accused of the assassination and to restore order in the country. Former President, Philibert Tsiranana and his party's secretary, Andre Resampa were among those tried and convicted. Most of the original 300 who were accused of complicity were pardoned, however. In June 1975, the military directorate handed over executive power to Didier Ratsiraka and continued in existence only to make broad policy goals which have been very close to Ratsiraka's stated positions when he was foreign minister in the Ramanantsoa government. Ratsiraka was confirmed in power in a referendum held in December 1975 and has directed the country in an increasingly independent path.

FIGURE 21.1   Political Parties and Elections   MADAGASCAR

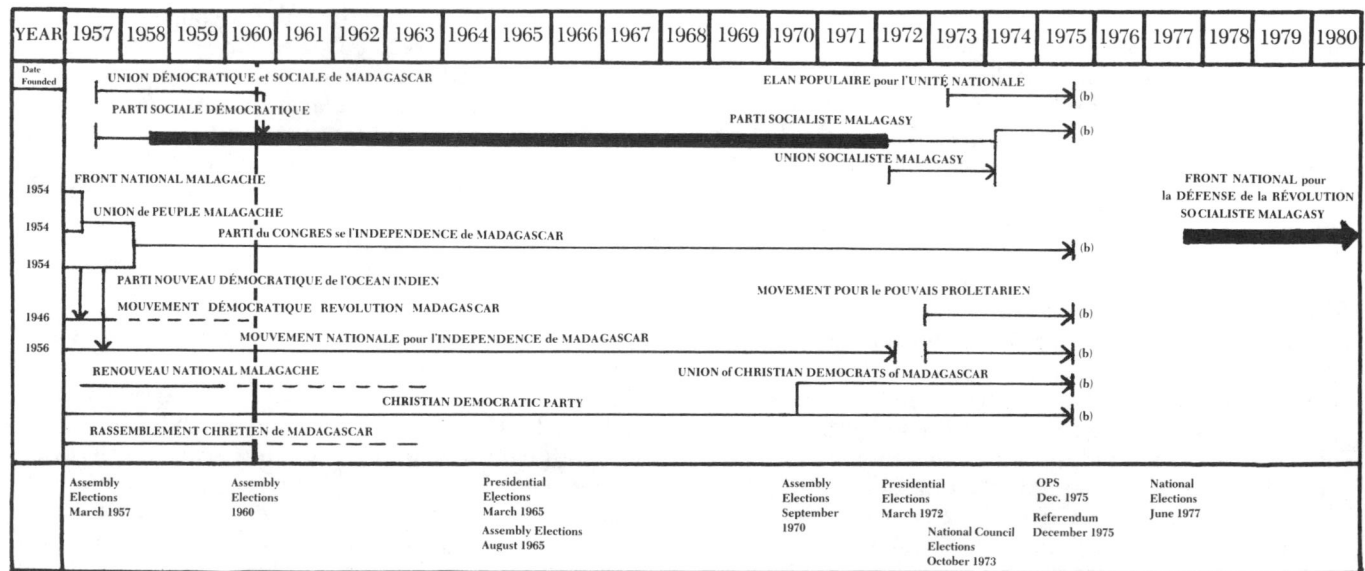

TABLE 21.5 Heads of Government (Post-Independence)

Name	Dates in Office	Age (1982)	Ethnicity	Education	Former Occupation
1. Philibert Tsiranana	1960-1972	died in 1978 aged 68	Escarpment Type (Tsimihety)	University of Montpellier (France)	Teacher
2. General Gabriel Ramanantsoa	1972-Dec. 1974	died in 1979 aged 73	Central Plateau Type (Merina)	Saint Cyr, Institute des Hautes Etudes de Defence Nationale	Army Officer
3. Colonel Richard Ratsimandrava	1975 (Feb. 5-11)	assassinated Feb. 1975 aged 44	Central Plateau Type (Merina)	Saint Cyr	Army Officer
4. General Gilles Andriamahazo	1975 Feb.-June	63	Central Plateau Type (Merina)	French War College	Army Officer
5. Commander Didier Ratsiraka (President)	1975-present	46	East Coast Type (Betsimisaraka)	Naval War College (France)	Naval Officer

VI. National Integration and Stability

Until the rebellion in the southern part of the island in 1971, the country had little manifest evidence of serious elite or communal instability during the independence period although conflict between communal groups from the central plateau and the coast had been simmering below the surface for some time. From 1971 onwards, rebellions, strikes, and riots multiplied until the overthrow of Tsiranana in 1972 and the coming to power of General Ramanantsoa. Attempts to forge a more independent foreign policy and internal economic and social reorganization led to increased strife, particularly in the ports of Tamatave and Diego Suarez, the home of a large French naval base. A plot reported to be backed by French commercial interests was uncovered in 1973. By early 1975, Ramanantsoa resigned from office in reaction to radical demands from the socialists which he was not willing to accept. His successor, Colonel Ratsimandrava, was in office only one week before he was assassinated by elements of the police force. Parties were banned but the problems of ideological differences coupled with regional and ethnic rivalries continued to make political and economic integration difficult despite the linguistic and cultural homogeneity of the population. In February 1980 President Ratsiraka announced that his government had uncovered and foiled a plot to destabilize the government and assassinate the President.

TABLE 21.7   Elite Instability

Event and Date	Characteristics
1. Coup Attempt February 11, 1975	a. *Description*: Colonel Ratsimandrava was assassinated while returning home from his office after only one week in office as the new Head-of-State. Members of the Mobile Police Comando Unit attacked his car and shot him. b. *Participants*: Elements of the Mobile Police Commando Unit led by Captains Jean Bora, Maurice Alphonse, and Laza Petit-Jean. Philibert Tsiranana and Andre Resampa were involved in the planning of the coup with the aim of returning government power to them from the military. c. *Apparent Causes*: Philibert Tsiranana and Andre Resampa, leaders of the pre-military government and its dominant party respectively, were attempting to force the military to return political power to civilians.

SOURCE: "Madagascar Power Politics" *African Affairs*, no. 44 (April 1975), pp. 16-17.

TABLE 21.8   Communal Instability

Event and Date	Characteristics
1. Rebellion April 1971.	a. *Description*: Ethnic groups in the south of the island rebel against the administration, and rioting and terrorism are finally put down by the army. b. *Participants*: Leaders of the MONIMA party as well as foreign influences were supposedly leading the peasantry of the south in rebellion. c. *Apparent Causes*: Probably a largely spontaneous uprising aimed against the arbitrary and corrupt officials of the central government and the heavy taxes they extracted. These officials were frequently Merina peoples from the central plateau.
2. Ethnic Violence December 1976	a. *Description*: Rioting erupted at Manjunja in Northwest Madagascar between immigrants from the Comoro Islands and indigenous peoples. Over 100 Comoro Islanders were killed and by some estimates as many as 1500 were killed. b. *Participants*: Immigrants from the Comoro Islands and natives of Madagascar. No clear leadership or prior planning of the violence appeared to exist. c. *Apparent Causes*: Longstanding competition between the Comorians and Malagasians over economic opportunities as well as social-political differences.

TABLE 21.9   Mass Instability

Event and Date	Characteristics
1. Revolt May 18, 1972	a. *Description*: After rioting and strikes by students and workers bring much of the economy to a standstill, Tsiranana hands over power to General Ramanantsoa while remaining the nominal President. b. *Participants*: Students, opposition political groups and workers. c. *Apparent Causes*: A cumulative breakdown of the government's ability to control the economy, and satisfy demands for greater social justice.

TABLE 21.10   Annual Instability Events: Independence Through 1979—Madagascar

Year	'61	'62	'63	'64	'65	'66	'67	'68	'69	'70	'71	'72	'73	'74	'75	'76	'77	'78	'79
ELITE INSTABILITY																			
Assassinations															1				
Plots											1		1	1					
Attempted Coups d'État															1				
Coups d'État														1					
COMMUNAL INSTABILITY																			
Ethnic Violence																1			
Irredentism																			
Rebellion											1								
Civil War																			
MASS INSTABILITY																			
Revolt												1							
Revolution																			
TURMOIL																			
Demonstrations											2								
Declarations of Emergency											1								

VII. Selected References

BIBLIOGRAPHY

Duignan P. *Madagascar (The Malagasy Republic), A list of Materials* etc. Stanford: Hoover Institution, 1962.

Fontvieille, Jean R. *Bibligraphie Nationale de Madagascar, 1956-63.* Tananarive:Université de Madagascar, 1971.

GENERAL

Bastian, Georges. *Madagascar: Étude Geographique et Economique.* Tananarive: Fernand Nathan, 1967.

Cadoux, Charles. *La Republique* . Paris: Berger-Levrault, 1969.

Deschamps, Hubert. *Madagascar*, 2nd. ed. Paris, DUF, 1976.

Deschamps, Hubert. *Histoire de Madagascar.* Paris: Berger-Levrault, 1972.

Heseltine, Nigel. *Madagascar.* New York: Praeger Publishers, 1971.

Kent, Raymond K. *From Madagascar to the Malagasy Republic.* New York: Frederick A. Praeger, Inc., 1963.

Ostheimer, John M., ed. *The Politics of the Western Indian Ocean*, New York, Praeger, 1975.

Pascal, Roger. *La Republique.* Paris: Berger-Levrault, 1965.

Ralaimihoatra, Edouard. *Histoire de Madagascar.* Tananarive: Societe Malgache d'Edition, 1966.

Thompson, Virginia and Adloff, Richard. *The Malagasy Republic: Madagascar Today.* Stanford: Stanford University Press, 1965.

U.S. Department of the Army. *Area Handbook for the Malagasy Republic.* Washington, D.C.: Government Printing Office, 1973.

POLITICAL

Comte, Jean. *Les Communes Malgaches.* Tananarive: Editions de la Librairie de Madagascar, 1963.

Gaudusson, Jean. *L'Administration Malgache* Paris, Berger Levrault, 1976.

Mannoni, O. *Prospero and Caliban: The Psychology of Colonization.* New York: Frederick A. Praeger, 1964.

Spacensky, Alain. *Madagascar: cinquante ans de vie politique.* Paris: Nouvelles Editions Latines, 1971.

ECONOMIC

Archer, Robert. *Madagascar depuis 1972*, Paris, Editions l'Harmatta, 1976.

Besairie, Henri. *Les resources minerales de Madagascar.* Tananarive: Imprimerie Nationale, 1961.

Finance Ministère de la Cooperation. *Madagascar Donnes statistique sur les activities economique culturelles et sociales*, Paris, 1976.

Gendarmen, Rene. *L'economie de Madagascar: diagnostic et perspectives de developpement.* Paris: Editions Cujas, 1960.

Minelle, Jean. *L'agriculture á Madagascar.* Paris: Librairie M. Riviers, 1959.

World Bank. *Madagascar: Economic Memorandum on Current Economic Position and Prospects and Selected Development Issues.* Washington, D.C., 1976.

SOCIAL

Gow, B.A. *Madagascar and the Protestant World*, New York: Holmes and Meier, 1980.

Ruud, Jorgen. *Taboo: A Study of Malagasy Customs and Beliefs.* London: G. Allen and Unwin, 1960.

Slawecki, L. M. S. *French Policy Towards the Chinese in Madagascar* Hamden, Conn.: Shoe String Press, 1971.

22. Malawi

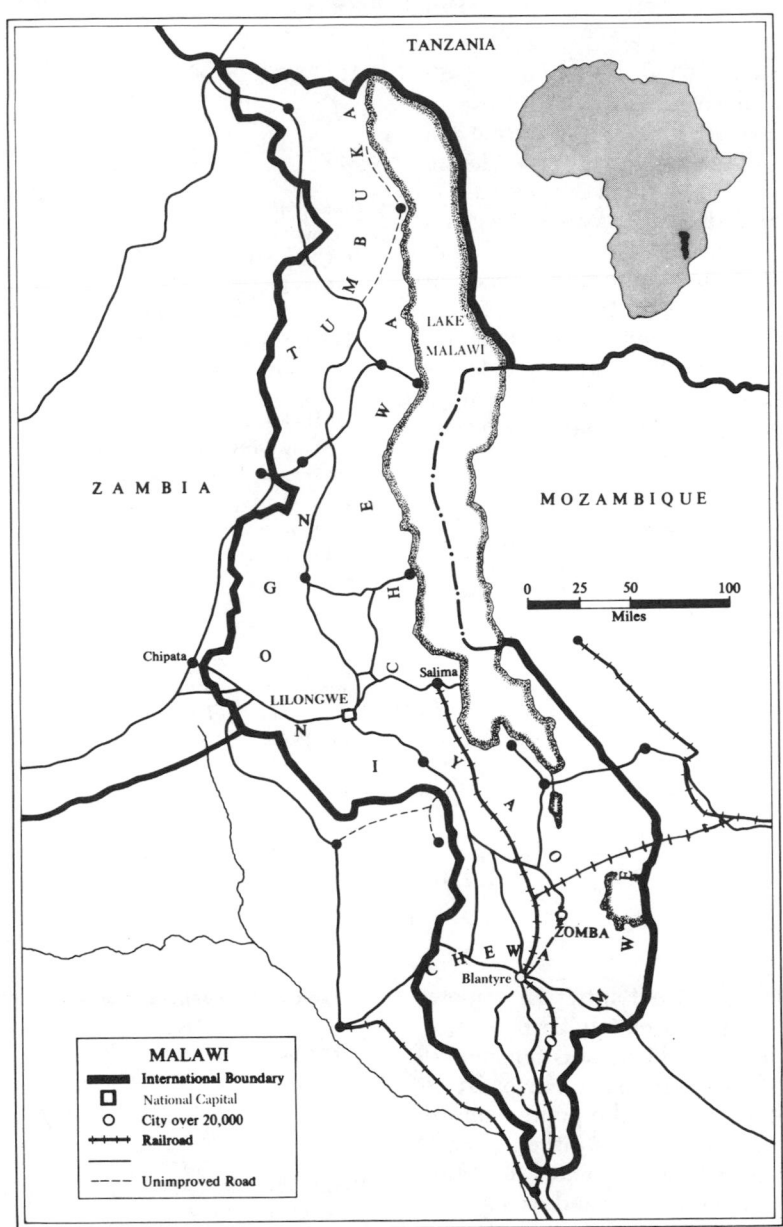

I. Basic Information

Date of Independence: July 6, 1964
Former Colonial Ruler: United Kingdom
Change in Boundaries: Formerly part of Central African Federation, 1953-1963
Former Name: Nyasaland
Estimated Population (1980): 5,734,000
Area Size (equivalent in U.S.): 45,747 sq. mi. (including 9,422 sq. miles of inland water (Louisianna)

Date of Last Census: 1977
Major Exports 1978 as Percent of Total Exports: * tobacco—57 percent; tea—18 percent; sugar—7 percent; groundnuts—3 percent.

*does not include re-exports.

II. Ethnic Patterns

As with Zambia, we have used Clyde Mitchell's classification of the Bantu of Southern Africa (1946). These are inclusive categories based on cultural and linguistic considerations. The Lomwe, Yao, and Ngoni are identity groups. In the north, there is a small Nyakyusa-type population (3 percent), consisting of Siukwa and Ngonde peoples. Other small groups are the Wandya and Lambya. It should be noted that our ethnic percentages are taken from the 1945 census, although they are assumed to be representative of the contemporary situation. There were 7,400 Europeans in 1966 and over 11,000 Asians and other non-Malawians. Asians had been ordered to do business in the major cities only and to leave the country by 1978 but many remain.

TABLE 22.1   Ethnic Units Over 5 Percent of Country Population

Ethnic Units	Estimated Ethnic Population 1980	Estimated Ethnic Percentage
a. Chewa Cluster	3,638,000	46%
1. Chewa (Achewa, Ancheya, Cewa, Masheba)	(1,606,000)	(28%)
2. Nyanja, 3. Lakeside Tonga	(860,000)	(15%)
b. Lomwe (Acilowe, Alomwe, Nguru)	1,089,000	19%
c. Yao (Achawa, Adjao)	803,000	14%
d. Ngoni Conquest States	516,000	9%
1. Mbelwe's Ngoni (Angoni, Mangoni, Wangoni), 2. Gomani's Ngoni, 3. Chiwere's Ngoni		
e. Tumbuka Type	344,000	6%
1. Tumbuka (Batumbuka, Matumboka), 2. Wenya, 3. Fungwe, 4. Phoka, 5. Fulilwa, 6. Henga, 7. Yombe, 8. Hewe, 9. Nthali, 10, Sisya		

SOURCES:*Report on the Census of 1945, Nyasaland Protectorate* (Blantyre: Government Printer, 1946), p. 15. Clyde Mitchell, *African Tribes and Languages of the Federation of Rhodesia and Nyasaland* (Salisbury: Federal Government Printer, 1964).

III. Language Patterns

All language groups in Malawi are Bantu. The Chewa group of peoples constitute approximately 28 percent of the population. Nyanja, the second largest component of the Chewa, constitutes a distinct language. Knappert estimates that as many as 83 percent of the population use Nyanja (also referred to as Chichewa) as either a *lingua franca*, or a mother tongue. Rustow estimates the figure at 36 percent. Nyanja is a *lingua franca*, and we have estimated that 60 percent of the population are able to use the language. Rustow suggests that Nguru (Lomwe) and Yao are the second largest language groups, each with 14 percent of the population. We estimate Lomwe at 19 percent. The official languages of Malawi are English and Chichewa, and most trade and governmental functions are conducted in English.

Table 22.2   Language Patterns

			Greenberg	Dalby
1. Primacy				
1st language	Chichewa	(60%)		
2nd language	Lomwe	(19%)		
2. Linguistic classification (all ethnic units in country over 5%)	Nyanja (Chichewa)		IA5	N3
	Lomwe		IA5	P3
	Ngoni		IA5	N1
	Yao		IA5	P2
	Tumbuka		IA5	N2
3. *Lingua franca*	Chichewa			
4. Official language	English and Chichewa			

IV. Urban Patterns

Capital: Lilongwe (new city, the former capital is Zomba, founded 1890)
Largest city: Blantyre (founded 1876)
Dominant ethnicity/language of largest city (Blantyre)
   Major vernacular: Nyanja [1]
   Major ethnic group: Nynaja [2]
   Major ethnic group as percent of Blantyre's population: 36% (1957)

[1]Jan Knappert, "Language Problems of the New Nations of Africa," *African Quarterly*, 5 (196f): 95—105.
[2]D. G. Bettison and P. J. A. Rigby, *Patterns of Income and Expenditure in Blantyre-Limbe, Nyasaland* (Lusaka: Rhodes-Livingstone Institute, 1961).

TABLE 22.3   Growth of Capitals and Largest City

Date	Zomba (Former Capital)	Blantyre	Lilongwe (Capital)
1940	3,000		
1950	10,000	41,000	
1960	13,000	95,000	
1966[a]	20,000	110,000	19,000
1972[b]	20,000	120,000	20,000
1973[c]	20,000	120,000	60,000
1975[d]		193,000	102,000
1977[e]	21,000	222,153	102,924

SOURCES: *Federation of Rhodesia and Nyasaland Census, 1956*, and staff estimates. Blantyre had its name changed from Blantyre-Limbe in 1966. The capital is being transferred from Zomba in the lowlying southern region to centrally located Lilongwe.
  [a]1966 Congress.
  [b]*Africa South of the Sahara 1973*.
  [c]*Europa Yearbook 1977* and *Background Notes: Malawi*, U.S. State Dept., Washington, D.C. 1974.
  [e]1977 Census.

Table 22.4   Cities of 20,000 and Over*

City	Size	Date
Blantyre	222,153	1977
Lilongwe	102,924	1977
Zomba	21,000	1977

SOURCES: 1977 census.

V. Political Patterns

A. Political Parties

The Federation of Rhodesia and Nyasaland, instituted in 1953, was dissolved in 1963, at which point Nyasaland took the name Malawi, becoming independent in July 1964. In 1964, the *Malawi Congress Party* (MCP) was founded (as the *Nyasaland African Congress*), and in August 1961 it won 23 out of 28 seats in the Nyasaland Legislature. The *United Federal party* (UFP), predominantly European, won 5 seats. The MCP has been the dominant party in Malawi since that time. The *Convention African National Union* (CANU) was established in 1962 in opposition to the MCP, but it was banned in 1966 when Malawi became a one-party state. There had been no elections since before independence. Although an election was called in 1971, no one actually went to the polls. President Banda decided on a candidate for each district from lists submitted to him and the candidates were declared winners unopposed. In the 'election,' in May 1976, this process was repeated where all seats were declared filled by unopposed candidates without an election actually being held. Elections within the one-party context were held in June 1978 for the legislature. Three externally based opposition groups exist. They are the

Socialist League of Malawi (Lesoma), the Congress for the Second Republic, and the Malawi Freedom Movement (Mafremo). Lesoma is the strongest of the three exiled groups and it apparently is perceived as a threat by Malawi's President Banda.

B. Political Leadership

The government of Malawi has been led by President Hastings Kamuzu Banda without notable change since independence in 1964. There have been marked changes in the composition of the cabinet, however, especially in 1964 when all but three ministers in the independence cabinet were dismissed. The ethnic representativeness of the cabinet has been increased by the new members, although ministers of Chewa background still predominate. The country continues under the rule of President Banda who personally involves himself in even the smallest details of political life and has ostracized anyone who has tried to establish himself as his sucessor. Banda was declared Life-President on July 6, 1971.

TABLE 22.5   Head of Government (Post Independence)

Name	Dates in Office	Age 1982	Ethnicity	Education	Former Occupation
1. Dr. Hastings Kamuzu Banda (Life-President)	1964— present	76	Chewa	Medical (United States)	Doctor (M.D.)

FIGURE 22.1   Political Parties and Elections   MALAWI

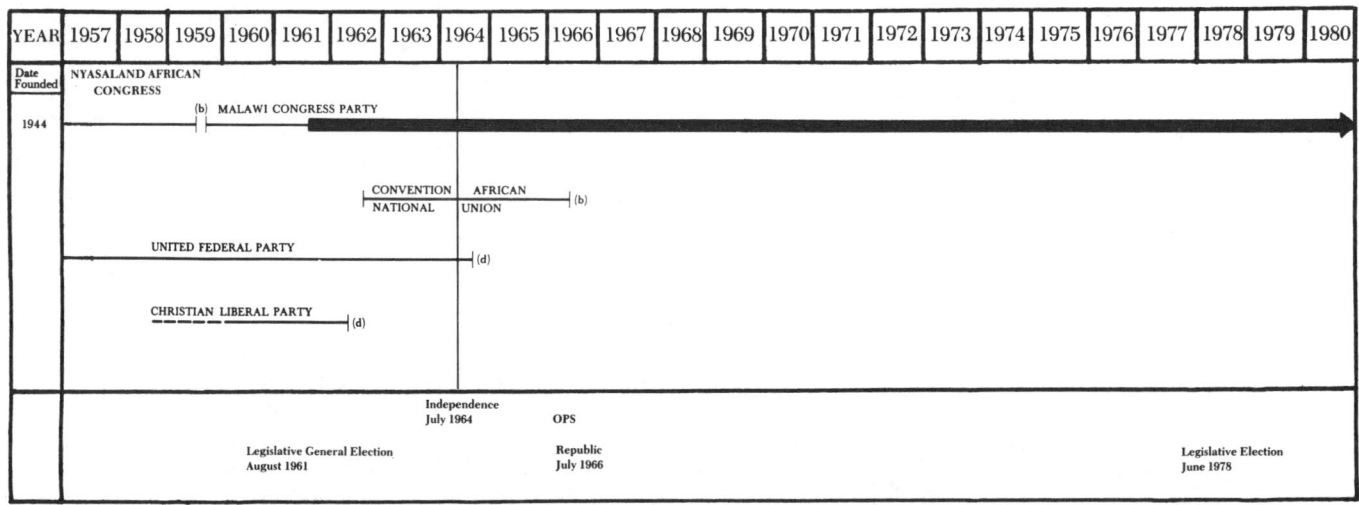

TABLE 22.6   Cabinet Membership: Distribution by Ethnic Unit*

Ethnicity*	Independence Cabinet	1967 Cabinet
1. Chewa (46%)	78%	56%
2. Lomwe (19)	11	0
3. Yao (14)	0	22
4. Ngoni (9)	11	22
5. Tumbuka (6)	0	0
6. Others (6)	0	0
N =	10	9

*Ethnic units arranged in rank order of size within country with the unit's percent of national population in parentheses.

VI. National Integration and Stability

TABLE 22.9   Mass Instability

Event and Date	Characteristics
1. Revolt September 1964— October 1967	a. *Description*: In early September 1964, a number of ministers resigned (or were dismissed) after Dr. Banda refused to accede to their policy demands. These ministers included Henry Chipembere, Yatuta Chisiza, Manoah Chirwa, Kanyama Chiume, Willie Chokani, Augustine Bwanausi. On September 28, the district headquarters of the Malawi Congress Party was attacked. In February of 1965, the supporters of the ex-ministers, led by Henry Chipembere, took control of the Fort Johnson area and launched an unsuccessful drive on the capital city—Zomba. By July of 1966 most of the dissident leaders had left the country and Dr. Banda seemed to be tightening his control. The calm was broken when Yatuta Chisiza led a rebel band into the country in October 1967. In a battle with security forces Chisiza was killed and the remaining rebels scattered. b. *Participants*: All of the ministers mentioned above were considerably younger than Dr. Banda. Support seems to have coalesced around the program and personality of Chipembere. Ethnicity does not seem to be a prime factor in this conflict. c. *Apparent Causes*: The leaders of the revolt stated their demands as follows: quicker Africanization of the civil service; abolishment of hospital fees; recognition of China. They objected to Malawian trade agreements with Portugal and to Banda's positive foreign policy toward white-dominated countries to the south.

SOURCE: John G. Pike, *Malawi—A Political and Economic History* (New York: Praeger, 1968), p. 169.

Although the political regime of Dr. Hastings Banda has continued since the pre-independence period, there have been severe dislocations within the ruling party, which later developed into a revolt. In September 1964, Dr. Banda emerged successfully from an internal power struggle in the party, and a number of important ministers were dismissed for plotting to overthrow the government (and were accused of accepting aid from Communist China). These dismissals were followed bv a revolt against the Banda regime led by the ousted ministers and their supporters. The late Henry Chipembere led forces which attempted to move on the capital from the Fort Johnson area. The revolt was crushed and the leaders fled. Rebellion again flared up in 1967 but little opposition survives the tight control of the Banda regime. Many of the more radical former ministers have gone into exile in Zambia and Tanzania. Dr. Banda has refused to support severe sanctions against the white-dominated countries of southern Africa, arguing that the geographic and economic position of Malawi makes it suicidal for Malawians to be belligerent toward these powerful neighbors. In recent years, however, Banda has improved relations with Zambia and Tanzania and other black African countries to the North. The liberation of Mozambique has presumbably weakened his arguments for close relations with South Africa. In late 1975 members of the Jehovah's Witnesses were expelled from the country. The estimates of the numbers expelled run up to 100,000. Like the Lumpa church in Zambia the Witnesses emphasize the supremacy of religious over political loyalties and this was unacceptable to the Banda regime. By 1978 there had been a general slackening of tensions in the country including the release of most political prisoners. Elections with opposition within the party was allowed. In 1979, however, Banda had apparently become quite concerned about political dissent against his regime.

TABLE 22.10   Annual Instability Events: Independence Through 1979 – Malawi

Year	'61	'62	'63	'64	'65	'66	'67	'68	'69	'70	'71	'72	'73	'74	'75	'76	'77	'78	'79
ELITE INSTABILITY																			
Assassinations																			
Plots																			
Attempted Coups d'État																			
Coups d'État																			
COMMUNAL INSTABILITY																			
Ethnic Violence																			
Irredentism																			
Rebellion																			
Civil War																			
MASS INSTABILITY																			
Revolt						1	1	1											
Revolution																			
TURMOIL																			
Demonstrations																			
Strikes (no. days)				1															
Riots (no. days)				2															
Terrorism					1														
Declarations of Emergency										1									
CABINET INSTABILITY																			
Realloc. and new appts.					3	2	4	3	2		2	9							
New members					2	2	2		4	2		6							
Resig. and Dismissals					2		3	1	3	2	2	3							
No. of members (max.) (maximum in year)					9	9	9	12	13	13	11	14							

VII. Selected References

BIBLIOGRAPHY

Boeder, R. M. *Malawi*, Santa Barbara, Ca: Clio Press, 1979.

Brown, Edward E., et al. *A Bibliography of Malawi.* Eastern African Bibliographic Series, no. 1. Syracuse, N.Y.: Syracuse University Program of Eastern African Studies, 1965.

Malawi *National Research Publications 1965—1975,* compiled by National Research Council. Lilongwe: the Council 1976.

Webster, John B. and Paulus Mohome. *A Supplement to a Bibliography on Malawi.* Occasional Bibliography no. 13. Syracuse, N.Y.: Syracuse University Program of Eastern African Studies, 1969.

GENERAL

Agnew, S. and M. Stubbs, eds. *Malawi in Maps.* New York: Africana, 1972.

Debenham, F. *Nyasaland, the Land of the Lake.* London: Her Majesty's Stationery Office, 1955.

Pachai, B. *Malawi: The History of the Nation.* N.Y.: Longmans, 1973.

Pachai, B., ed. *The Early History of Malawi.* Evanston, Ill.: Northwestern University Press, 1972.

Pike, John G. *Malawi: A Political and Economic History.* New York: Praeger, 1968.

Pike, John G. and G. T. Rimmington. *Malawi, A Geographical Study.* London: Oxford University Press, 1965.

Read, Frank E. *Malawi, Land of Promise: A Comprehensive Survey.* Blantyre: R. Parker, 1967.

Rotbert, Robert I. *The Rise of Nationalism in Central Africa: The Making of Malawi and Zambia, 1873—1964.* Cambridge, Mass.: Harvard University Press, 1966.

U.S. Department of the Army. *Area Handbook for Malawi.* Washington, D.C.: Government Printing Office, 1975.

POLITICAL

Jones, Griff. *Britain and Nyasaland.* London: Allen and Unwin, 1964.

Liebenow, J. Gus. "Federalism in Rhodesia and Nyasaland." In *Federalism in the Commonwealth,* ed. William S. Livingston. London: Cassell, 1963.

Mair, Lucy P. *The Nyasaland Elections of 1961.* London: Athlone Press, 1962.

McCracken, John. *Politics and Christianity in Malawi, 1875- 1940: The Impact of the Livingstonian Mission in the Northern Province.* Cambridge: Cambridge University Press, 1977.

McMaster, Carolyn. *Malawi: Foreign Policy and Development.* London: Julian Friedmann, 1974.

Miller, Norman N., *Malawi: Central African Paradox.* Hanover N.H. American University Field Staff, 1979.

Mufuka, K. N. *Missions and Politics in Malawi.* Kingston, Ontario: Limestone Press, 1977.

Pachai, B. *Land and Politics in Malawi, 1875—1975.* Kingston, Ontario: Limestone Press, 1978.

Short, Phillip. *Banda.* Boston: Routledge and Kegan Paul, 1974.

Spiro, Herbert. "The Rhodesias and Nyasaland." In *Five African States: Responses to Diversity,* ed. Gwendolen M. Carter. Ithaca, N.Y.: Cornell University Press, 1963.

Williams, J. David. *Malawi: The Politics of Despair.* Ithaca, N.Y.: Cornell University Press, 1978.

ECONOMIC

Hazelwood, Arthur and P. O. Henderson, eds. *Nyasaland: The Economics of Federation.* Oxford: Blackwell, 1960.

Humphrey, David. *Malawi since 1964: Economic Development Progress and Prospects,* Department of Economics, University of Malawi (1974) Occasional Paper no. 1.

International Monetary Fund. "Malawi." In *Surveys of African Economies,* vol. 4. Washington, D. C.: I.M.F., 1971.

SOCIAL

Malawi National Statistical Office *Malawi Population Change Survey: Feb. 1970-January 1972* (Zomba: Government Printer, 1973 July).

Mitchell, J. Clyde. *The Yao Village: A Study in the Social Structure of a Nyasaland Tribe.* Manchester, England: Manchester University Press for Rhodes-Livingstone Institute, 1956.

Mead, Margaret. *Children of Their Fathers: Growing Up Among the Ngoni of Malawi.* New York: Holt, Rinehart and Winston, 1960, 1968.

Rimmington, Gerald T. "Education for Independence: A Study of Changing Educational Administration in Malawi." *Comparative Education*, 2 (1966): 217-223.

Seltzer, George. "High Level Manpower in Nyasaland's Development." In *Manpower and Education: Country Studies in Economic Development*, eds. F. B. Harbison and C. Myers. New York: McGraw-Hill, 1965.

Shepperson, George. *Myth and Reality in Malawi*, Evanston, Ill.: Northwestern University Press, 1976.

Wishlade, R. L. *Sectarianism in Southern Nyasaland*. London: Oxford University Press, 1965.

23. Mali

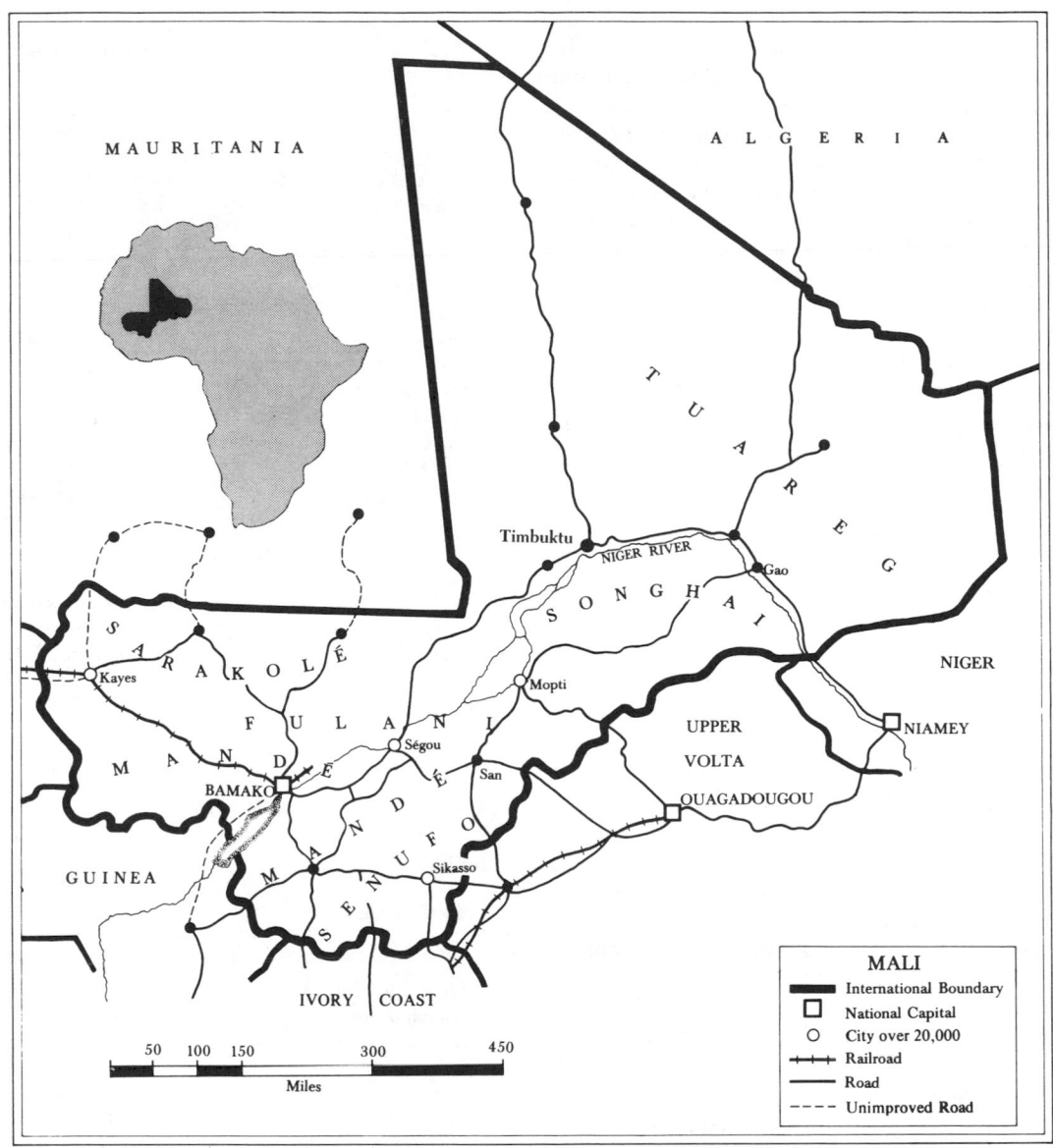

I. Basic Information

Date of Independence: September 22, 1960 (June 20, 1960 as Mali Federation)

Former Colonial Ruler: France

Change in Boundaries: Formerly part of French West African Federation. Part of the Mali Federation (formed with Senegal) from April 4, 1959, to August 20, 1960, when Senegal seceded.

Former Name: Soudan

Estimated Population (1980): 6,474,000

Area Size (equivalent in U.S.): 478,767 sq. mi. (Texas, Colorado and Nevada)

Date of Last Census: 1976

Estimated Major Exports 1976 as percent of Total Exports: cotton and cotton products—50 percent; groundnuts—16 percent; live animals—13 percent.

II. Ethnic Patterns

The ethnic classification selected for Mali is fairly inclusive. It is largely based on linguistic criteria, although cultural and identity factors strongly reinforce these criteria. The Fulani, Tuareg, and Songhai are identity groups. Within the Mande family, the Dyula are probably of Senufo origin. They have been placed with the Mandé (as was done in the Ivory Coast classification), however, for reasons of language and culture (Muslim). Mali also contains a small (1.6 percent) Moorish population. Other small groups in Mali are the Dogon (3 percent), Bobo (1 percent), and smaller numbers of Diawara, Bozo, Toucolor, Wolof, Mossi, Kagoro, Foulanke, and Dialonke. The droughts of the early 1970's depleted the desert populations, especially the Tuaregs, but to an unknown degree.

TABLE 23.1 Ethnic Units Over 5 Percent of Country Population

Ethnic Units	Estimated Ethnic Population 1980	Estimated Ethnic Percentage
a. Mandé Type	2,784,000	43%
1. Bambara	(2,007,000)	(31%)
2. Malinké	(324,000)	(5%)
3. Dyula (Diula)	(388,000)	(6%)
b. Fulani (Peul)	971,000	15%
c. Senufo (Sene, Siena) Type	971,000	15%
1. Senufo, 2. Minianka		
d. Sarakolé (Seraculeh, Soninké) Type	518,000	8%
1. Sarakolé		
2. Marka		
e. Tuareg (Touareg)	388,000	6%
f. Songhai (Songhoi, Sonhray)	388,000	6%

SOURCES: *Allgemeine Statistik des Auslandes, Landerberichte, Mali,* 1966. G. P. Murdock, *Africa* (New York: McGraw-Hill, 1959), p. 80. B. N'Diaye *Groupes Ethniques au Mali* Bamako, Editions Populaire, 1970.

III. Language Patterns

The two major languages in Mali are Bambara or Bamana (of the Mandé family) and Fulani (of the West Atlantic family). Those who speak Bambara as a first language are probably 31 percent of the total population. However, Malinke—and Dyula—speakers (11 percent) would understand Bambara, and probably another 8 percent of the population understand it as a second language. Thus, our estimate of Bambara-speakers would be 50 percent. Rustow estimates the Malinke-Bambara-Dyula speakers to be 40 percent; Knappert suggests Bambara alone consists of 23 percent; and MacDougald suggests the broader category of Mandingo at 31 percent. The second largest language is Fulani—Rustow estimates 14 percent; our estimate is 16 percent based on ethnic figures alone. French is the official language. Arabic is the language most widely used in religious matters.

TABLE 23.2 Language Patterns

			Greenberg	Dalby
1. Primacy				
1st language	Bambara	(50%)		
2nd language	Fulani	(16%)		
2. Linguistic Classification (all ethnic units in country over 5%)	Malinké-Bambara-Dyula		IA2	31A
	Fulani		IA1	201
	Senufo		IA3	27
	Sarakolé		IA2	31B
	Tuareg		IIIC	0
	Songhai		IIA	10
3. *Lingua franca*	Bambara (Malinké-Dyula)			
4. Official language	French			

IV. Urban Patterns

Capital/largest city: Bamako (founded 1883)
Dominant ethnicity/language of capital
    Major vernacular: Bambara[1]
    Major ethnic group: Bambara[2]
    Major ethnic group as percent of capital's population:
    26% (1960)[2]

[1]Jan Knappert, "Language Problems of the New Nations of Africa," *African Quarterly,* 5 (1965): 95—105.
[2]C.Meillassoux *Urbanisation of an African Community: Voluntary Associations, in Bamako,* Seattle: University of Washington Press, 1968, p. 14—report of 1960 census result.

TABLE 23.4   Cities of 20,000 and Over

City	Size	Date
Bamako	400,000 UA	1976
Mopti	35,000	1976
Segou	31,000	1976
Kayes	29,000	1976
Sikasso[a]	22,000	1972

SOURCES: 1976 Census Results
    [a]*Background Notes—Mali* U.S. State Department, Washington, D.C., 1974.

TABLE 23.3   Growth of Capital/Largest City

Date	Bamako
1920	14,000
1930	19,000
1940	26,000
1950	86,000
1960	130,000
1965	170,000 UA
1967	182,000 UA
1971	200,000 UA
1976[a]	400,000 UA

SOURCE: *Démographie Comparée.* The various population estimates for Bamako for ca. 1965 illustrate the variability of the size estimates of African cities. These range from 150,000 (*Africa 68*) to 200,000 (*Europa Yearbook* 1967). The *Statesman's Yearbook 1967* estimate is intermediate at 170,000.
    [a]1976 Census.

V. Political Patterns

A. Political Parties and Elections

The *Union Soudanaise* (US) was founded in 1946 as a territorial branch of the *Rassemblement Democratique Africain* (RDA). From 1946 until 1959, there was a two-party system in Mali. The *Parti du Regroupement Soudanais* (PRS) was founded in March 1958 from the *Parti Soudanais Progressiste* (PSP), but merged with the US in March 1959. Thus, from 1959 until the military coup in December 1968, Mali was a one-party state. It should be noted that the US broke with the RDA in 1958, and in 1959 joined with the Senegalese leaders in the Federation of Mali creating a new party, the *Parti de la Federation Africaine,* which dissolved when the Federation broke up in summer 1960. All parties and elections were banned after the 1968 coup. In a June 1974 referendum a new constitution was accepted establishing a one-party state but continuing military rule for another five years with return to civilian rule scheduled for 1979. Traoré had stated that a new party was to be formed by the end of 1975 or early in 1976 whose name would be the *Union Democratique du Peuple Malien* (UDPM), but it did not begin operating until September 1977. The UDPM was formed in order to take over the government under civilian rule. In June 1979, the UDPM held its first party Congress, at which time they established a central executive bureau to replace the military ruling committee. The Congress also elected Moussa Traoré as Secretary-General. On June 19, 1979 presidential and legislative elections were held. Ninety-four percent of eligible voters turned out to vote and Traoré, the only presidential candidate, won with 99.89% of the votes cast. Eighty-two representatives to the assembly were also elected. In July 1979, a new constitution specifying constitutional government went into effect.

B. Political Leadership

The government of Mali was led by President Modibo Keita from independence until the coup d'etat in 1968.

Following the coup, Lt. Moussa Traoré became Head of State and Capt. Yoro Diakite Head of Government. As Traoré was also the Chairman of the Military Committee of National Liberation we include him here as "Head of Government." Except for the ouster of Captain Diakite, the membership of the Military Committee was stable. The June 1974 referendum continued military rule for another five years and instituted a one-party state. On July 1, 1979 a new constitution went into effect. Mali is now under constitutional rule and Moussa Traore is President. Shortly after his election in June 1979, Traoré announced a cabinet reshuffle in which a fifteen man government composed primarily of civilians was installed. The cabinet was reshuffled in 1980.

FIGURE 23.1   Political Parties and Elections   MALI

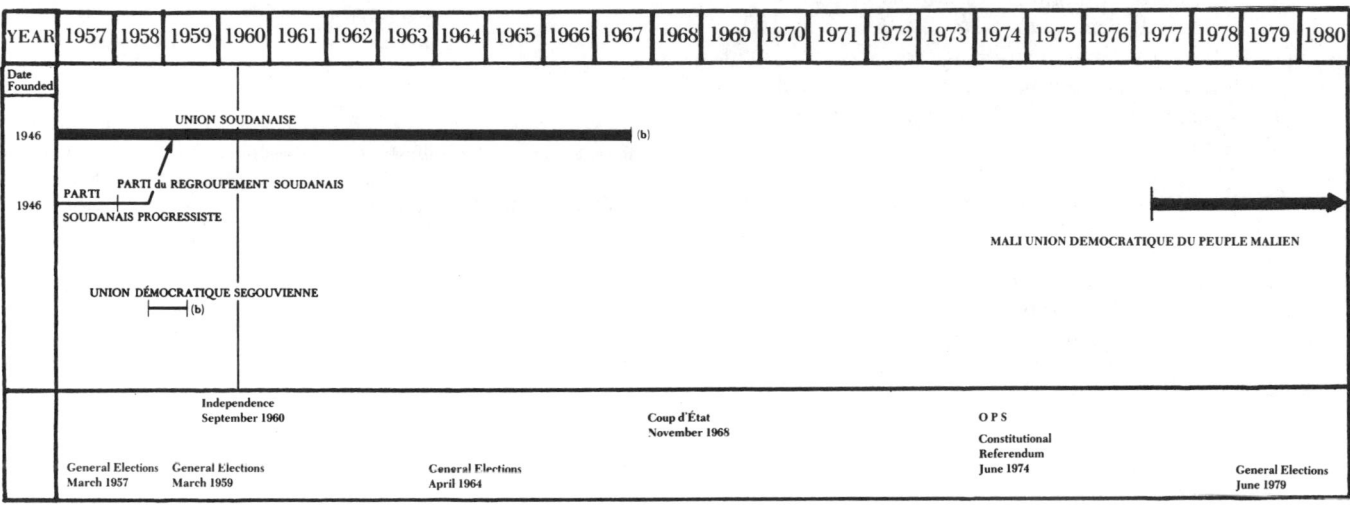

TABLE 23.5   Heads of Government (Post Independence)

Name	Dates in Office	Age (1982)	Ethnicity	Education	Former Occupation
1. Modibo Keita (President)	1960— 1968	died in detention in 1977 at age 61	Mandé (Malinké)	University Dakar	Teacher, Civil Servant (School Inspector)
2. Moussa Traoré (President) Before June 1979, President of the Military Committee of National Liberation and Head of State	1968— present	46	Mandé	Fréjus Training College in France	Soldier

TABLE 23.6   Cabinet Membership: Percent Distribution by Ethnic Unit*

Ethnicity	Independence Cabinet	1967 Cabinet
1. Mandé (43%)	43%	33%
2. Fulani (20)	43	40
3. Senufo (15)	7.1	40
4. Sarakolé (8)	0	0
5. Tuareg (6)	0	0
6. Songhai (6)	7.1	0
7. Others (2)	7.1	20
N =	15	15

*Ethnic units arranged in rank order of size within country with the unit's percent of national population in parantheses.

VI. National Integration and Stability

Mali is a relatively homogenous country in terms of basic cultural orientation. One exception has been the minority nomadic tribes, who have insisted on continuing autonomy. Tensions between Mali and France seem to have been reflected in the conflict between elites within Mali. The regime of Modibo Keita maintained power until the November 1968 coup. Signs of the tension, however, were apparent by 1962 when (on July 20) the government announced that it had discovered a plot organized by merchants and supported by the French Embassy (91 persons were accused of complicity). The plot was the result of the introduction of the Malian franc in conjunction with the declining economic situation (which also precipitated large demonstrations in Bamako). The officers who led the 1968 coup have since turned to France, as well as Eastern-bloc countries, for aid though they have left intact most of the previous regime's structures. On August 12, 1969, 33 soldiers were arrested on suspicion of conspiring to overthrow the government. In December 1969 Captains Diby Diarra and Alassane Diarra and Sergeant Boubaear Traore were sentenced to hard labor for life for their leadership of the plot. It is not known how far the plot had progressed before the arrests were made. The first Prime Minister under the military regime, Captain Diakite, was sentenced to life imprisonment in 1972 for plotting against the government in 1971. He died in prison within a year. There were anti-government demonstrations in Bamako in May and June 1977. Plots against the government were reported in 1976 and February 1978, each followed by execution of the purported plotters. The 1978 plot involved a conspiracy of leading businessmen and three members of the ruling military committee who reportedly wanted to overthrow Traore in order to maintain military rule. In June 1980, former defense minister Dankar was sentenced to death for his part in a plot.

In March 1980, there were a series of student strikes and demonstrations which stemmed from the banning of the National Union of Mali Students and Pupils and the eventual death from torture of the leader of the student organization who had been in police custody. Several students were wounded during confrontations with police. The strike ended by mid-1980 when Traore granted clemency to detained students.

TABLE 23.7   Elite Instability

Event and Date	Characteristics
1. Coup d'État November 19, 1968	a. *Description*: The main targets of the military forces were Seydou Kouyate (a former minister with a "pro-China" reputation) and other ministers including the prime minister, several labor leaders, and certain persons affiliated with the militia. b. *Participants*: Lt. Moussa Traore and a number of other junior officers in the army. Officers opposing the take-over (including the chief of staff) were arrested. c. *Apparent Causes*: The economic situation had badly deteriorated; according to Moussa Traoré "the state has been living far beyond its means" and the "demagogic and sterile radicalism" of the Keita regime has frightened away foreign investors. Also the military was being threatened by the existence of an expanding 'peoples militia' which had recently arrested several army officers.

TABLE 23.8   Communal Instability

Event and Date	Characteristics
1. Rebellion August 1963— August 1964	a. *Description*: On August 14, 1964, the government of Mali announced that for over a year an "insidious foreign power" had encouraged subversion and rebellion among the northern nomadic desert tribes. The government said that a major offensive occurred July 16, 1964, against the "last rebel stronghold," and order was restored. The government claimed that rebel elements intimidated loyal nomads by terrorism and by seizing thousands of domestic animals. b. *Participants*: Nomadic Tuareg groups. c. *Appparent Causes*: Opposition to taxes and administrative control. While Malian officials tended to minimize the importance of the rebellion, it was a strain on the economic resources of the government.

SOURCES: William I. Jones, "Economics of the Coup," *African Report*, 14 (1969): 23—26, 51—53.   Francis G. Snyder,   "An Era Ends in Mali," ibid., 16—22.

TABLE 23.10   Annual Instability Events: Independence Through 1979—Mali

Year	'61	'62	'63	'64	'65	'66	'67	'68	'69	'70	'71	'72	'73	'74	'75	'76	'77	'78	'79
ELITE INSTABILITY																			
Assasinations																			
Plots		1							1		1					1		1	
Attempted Coups d'État																			
Coups d'État								1											
COMMUNAL INSTABILITY																			
Ethnic Violence																			
Irredentism																			
Rebellion			1																
Civil War																			
MASS INSTABILITY																			
Revolt																			
Revolution																			
TURMOIL																			
Demonstrations						1													
Strikes (no. days)																			
Riots (no. days)		1																	
Terrorism																			
Declarations of Emergency																			
CABINET INSTABILITY																			
Realloc. and new appts.		2	8	4		14	1	1	2	2									
New members			4	1		8		1		6	4	1							
Resig. and Dismissals		2	1	1		4	3			5	5	1							
No. of members (max.) (maximum in year)		12	15	14	14	17	17	13	14	13	13	13							

VII. Selected References

BIBLIOGRAPHY

Brasseur, Paule. *Bibliographie Generale du Mali (Anciens Soudan Francais et Haut-Senegal-Niger)*. I.F.A.N. catalogues et documents, 16. Dakar: I.F.A.N., 1964.

Brasseur, Paule. *Bibliographie Generale du Mali, 1961-1970*. Dakar, Nouvelles Editions Africaines 1976.

Cutler, C. H. "Mali: A Bibliographic Introduction." *African Studies Bulletin*, 9 (1966): 74-87.

Imperato, P. J. *Historical Dictionary of Mali*. Metuchen, N.J.: Scarecrow, 1977.

GENERAL

Thompson, Virginia and Richard Adloff. *French West Africa*, pp. 146-54. Stanford, Ca.: Stanford University Press, 1957.

POLITICAL

Amin, Samir. *Neo-Colonialism in West Africa*. Harmondsworth, Middlesex: Penguin Books, 1973.

Barate, C. *Administration locale et socialisme dans le Mali independant*, 1977. v.31, no.3, pp. 1035.

de Lusignan, Guy. *French-Speaking Africa since Independence*, pp. 231-49. London: Pall Mall Press, 1969.

Foltz, William J. *From French West Africa to the Mali Federation*. New Haven, Conn.: Yale University Press, 1965.

Hazard, John N. "Marxian Socialism in Africa: The Case of Mali." *Comparative Politics*, 2 (October 1969): 1—15.

Rondos, Alexander G. "What Kind of Handover?" *Africa Report*, v. 24, 1979.

Hodgkin, Thomas and Ruth Schachter Morgenthau. "Mali." In *Political Parties and National Integration in Tropical Africa*, eds. J. S. Coleman and C. G. Rosberg, pp. 216-58. Los Angeles: University of California Press, 1964.

Hopkins, Nicholas S. *Popular Government in an African Town*. Chicago: University of Chicago Press, 1972.

Synder, Francis G. *One-Party Government in Mali: Transition Toward Control*. New Haven, Conn.: Yale University Press, 1965.

ECONOMIC

Amin, Samir. *Trois Experiences Africaines de Developpement: le Mali, la Guinee et le Ghana*. Paris: Presses Universitaires de France, 1965.

Jouve, Edmond. *La Republique du Mali*, Paris, Berger-Levrault, 1974.

Klaus, E. *Tradition and Progress in the African Village: the Noncapitalist Reforms of Rural Communities in Mali*. N.Y.: St. Martin's Press, 1975.

"Mali" In *Surveys of African Economies*, Vol. 7 Washington, D.C.: International Monetary Fund, 1977.

SOCIAL

Diop, Majhemouf. *Histoire des classes sociales dans l'Afrique de l'Ouest: Le Mali*. Paris: Francois Maspero, 1971.

Meillassoux, Claude. *Urbanisation of an African Community: Voluntary Associations in Bamako*. Seattle: University of Washington Press, 1968.

Milner, Horace. *The Primitive City of Timbuctoo*. rev. ed. Garden City, N.Y.: Anchor Books, 1965.

Ouologuem, Yambo. *Bound to Violence*. New York: Harcourt, Brace and Jovanovich, 1971.

Paques, Viviana. *Les Bambara*. Paris: Presses universitaires de France, 195?

24. Mauritania

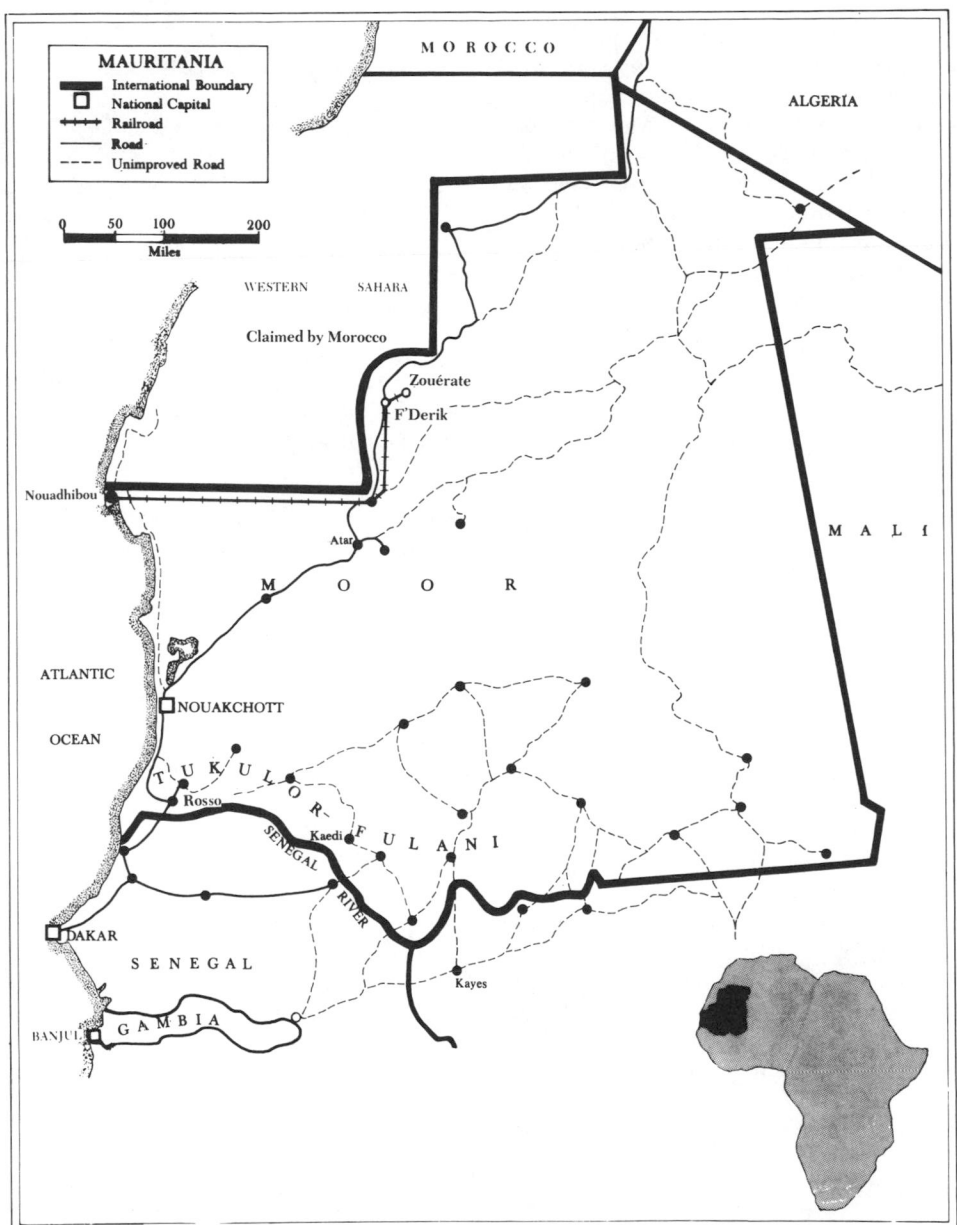

I. Basic Information

Date of Independence: November, 1960
Former Colonial Ruler: France
Change in Boundaries: Formerly part of French West Africa Federation (often grouped with Senegal for census purposes during the colonial period)
Estimated Population (1980): 1,588,000

Area Size (equivalent in U.S.): 397,950 sq. mi. (Texas, Colorado and Nevada)
Date of Last Census: 1977
Major Exports 1976 as Percent of Total Exports: iron ore—86 percent.

II. Ethnic Patterns

The many Moorish tribes represent various mixings of Berber and Arab stock. Although the distinction is made in the Mauritanian census between White Moors (54 percent) and Black Moors (28 percent), this is no longer so much a question of color, as of patrilineal descent and status difference. The Tukulor and Fulani maintain distinct identities, but share a common language and culture. There are small numbers of Wolof, Sarakolé, and Haratin peoples in the country.

TABLE 24.1   Ethnic Units Over 5 Percent of Country Population

Ethnic Units	Estimated Ethnic Population (1980)	Estimated Ethnic Percentage
a. Moore (Maure)	1,302,000	82%
1. Maaquil, 2. Lemtouna,		
3. Masoufa, 4. Tolbas, 5. Zenaga,		
6. Nemadi, 7. Imraquen, 8. Azarzir,		
9. Duaish, 10. Regeibat		
b. Tukulor-Fulani Type	206,000	13%
1. Tukulor (Takruri, Tekarir,	(127,000)	(8%)
Torodo, Toucouleur, Tukri)		
2. Fulani (Peul)	(79,000)	(5%)

SOURCES: Mauritania, Direction de l'information, *Republique Islamique de Mauretanie*. (Dakar: Grande impr. Africaine, 1963). G. P. Murdock, *Africa*. (New York: McGraw-Hill, 1959).

III. Language Patterns

The two major language groups in Mauritania are Arabic (of the Semitic group) and Fulani (of the West Atlantic group). Most of the Moorish peoples speak Arabic (although some, such as the Zenag, retain the use of Berber). The Fulani and Tukulor both speak and write the same language (Fulfulde). Our estimate is that 90 percent of the total population speaks Arabic. (Rustow estimates Arabic at 82 percent; Knappert considers the Arabic-speaking population to be 100 percent.) Thirteen percent of the population are Fulani-speaking (Rustow estimates 12 percent). Arabic is being encouraged as a *lingua franca* by the government. In 1966, when Arabic became required in government and higher education, however, significant language riots resulted (see Table 24.8). French continues as an official language although all schooling is now in Arabic.

TABLE 24.2   Language Patterns

			Green-berg	Dalby
1. Primacy				
1st language	Arabic	(90%)		
2nd language	Fulani	(13%)		
2. Linguistic classification	Arabic		IIIA	01A
(all ethnic units in	Fulani		IA1	201
country over 5%)				
3. *Lingua franca*	Arabic			
4. Official languages	French, Arabic			

IV. Urban Patterns

Capital/largest city: Nouakchott (new city)
Dominant ethnicity/language of capital
    Major vernacular: Arabic[1]
    Major ethnic group: Moor

Major ethnic group as percent of capital's population: Almost all Moors.

[1]Jan Knappert, "Language Problems of the New Nations of Africa," *Frican Quarterly*, 5 (1965): 95—105.

Table 24.3   Growth of Capital/Largest City

Date	Nouakchott
1961[a]	6,000
1965[b]	15,000
1972[c]	48,000
1973[d]	130,000
1975[e]	104,000
Dec. 1976[f]	134,000

SOURCES:

[a]*UN Demographic Yearbook 1963.*
[b]*UN Demographic Yearbook 1967.*
[c]*Africa South of the Sahara 1974.*
[d]*Africa South of the Sahara 1975.*
[e]*Europa Yearbook 1977 V.II.*
[f]*Europa Yearbook 1979 V. II.*

TABLE 24.4   Cities of 20,000 and Over

City	Size	Date
Nouakchott	134,000	1976
Nouadhibou	22,000	1976
(Port-Etienne)		
Zouérate	17,500	1976
Kaédi	20,850	1976

SOURCE:*Europa Yearbook 1979 V. II.*

Note—Other prominent towns are Atar (16,300), and Rosso (16,500). Estimates in 1975. F'Derick was estimated to have a population of 18,000 in 1972 by *Africa South of the Sahara 1974.*

V. Political Patterns

FIGURE 24.1   Political Parties and Elections   MAURITANIA

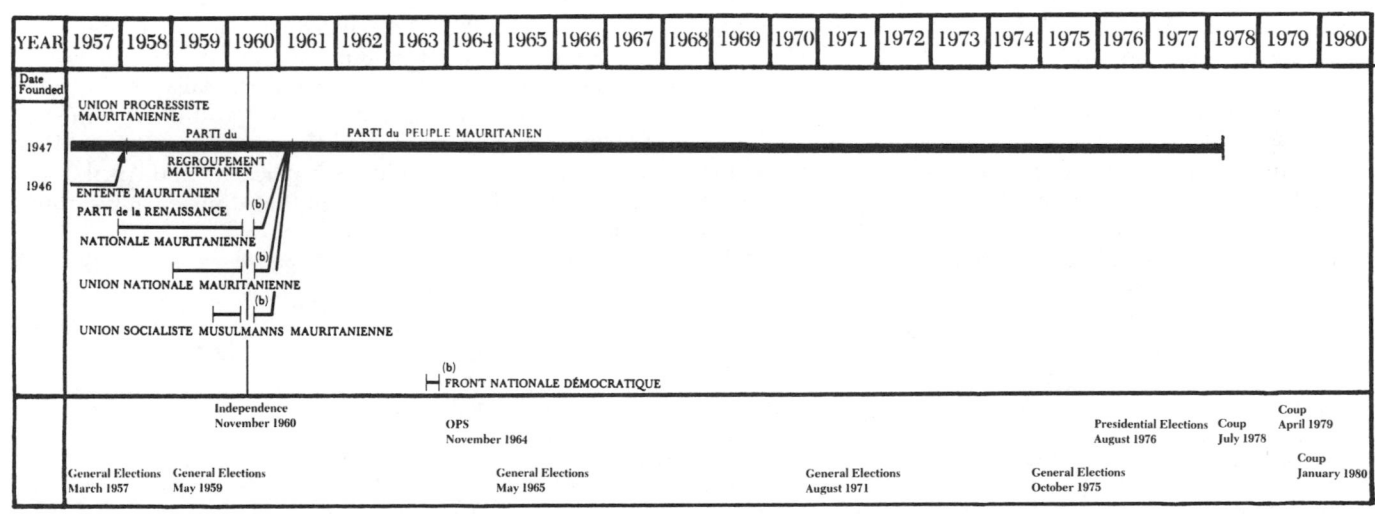

A. Political Parties and Elections

Prior to independence the dominant party in Mauritania was the *Parti du Regroupement Mauritanien* (PRM), while the opposition parties were the *Parti de la Renaissance Nationale Mauritanienne* (LeNaddah) and the *Union Nationale Mauritanienne* (UNM). On the eve of independence in 1960 LeNaddah and UNM were banned by the ruling PRM. After independence the newly revived LeNaddah and UNM merged into the PRM to form the *Parti du Peuple Mauritanien* (PPM). Mauritania was, until the 1978 coup, a one-party state under the leadership of Moktar Ould Daddah, and all members of the National Assembly were required to be members of the PPM. Elections were held to ratify the choices of the party caucus for the National Assembly. In 1973, leaflets appeared in Dakar announcing a new and illegal worker's party, the *Mauritanian Kadihines Party*, but it is not clear if this has any existence in Mauritania. In 1974, the forming of another illegal party, the *Mauritania Justice party*, was announced in Paris. The most recent legislative elections were held in October 1975. At that time the National Assembly was enlarged from 50 to 70 memebers. Elections were held to approve a single list of candidates proposed by the PPM and therefore no real competition or choice is implied in such elections. After the July 1978 coup d'etat, all parties were banned and the National Assembly was disbanded.

B. Political Leadership

Until the 1978 coup d'état, the government of Mauritania had been led by President Moktar Ould Daddah since independence. There were substantial changes in the composition of the cabinet, particularly in periods 1962-63 and 1965-66. New members of the cabinet increased the representation of the Tukulor in the executive. Daddah was reelected in August 1976. There were several cabinet reshuffles in 1977 and 1978 and Daddah tried to enlarge PPM membership, reportedly to gain support for himself and the war against Polisario. In July 1978, however, Daddah was overthrown in a coup led by Col. Moustapha Ould Salek. Upon assuming power, Col. Salek dissolved existing government bodies and suspended the constitution. A Military Committee for National Recovery was established. In March 1979, Salek assumed unlimited powers, reportedly in order to deal with the Polisario forces. Salek also announced a major reshuffle of his cabinet in early April which placed Lt. Col. Ahmed Ould Bouceif as Prime Minister. Reports stated that 'Bouceif had actually engineered a coup against the President, but Salek was not overthrown and remained in office as a ceremonial President' (Africa Report, July 1979, p. 30).

In late May 1979 Bouceif was killed in a plane crash on his way to a meeting of the Economic Community of West African States in Dakar, Senegal. At a meeting following Bouceif's death, Lt. Col. Mahmoud Ould Louly became the new head of State and Lt. Col. Mohamed Khouna Ould Haidalla became Prime Minister and Minister of Defense.

In January 1980, the governing Military Committee for National Salvation anounced the dismissal of Louly and the appointment of Lt. Col. Haidalla as the new Head of State. Haidalla has kept his position as Minister of Defense and has abolished the position of Prime Minister. A cabinet reshuffle took place in mid-April 1980 which included the dismissal of the Minister of the Interior and the Army chief of staff.

TABLE 24.5   Heads of Government (Post Independence)

Name	Dates in Office	Age (1982)	Ethnicity	Education	Occupation
1. Moktar Ould Daddah (President)	1960— 1978	58	Moor	Post-grad. professional (France)	Lawyer, Interpreter
2. Moustapha Ould Salek	July 1978— June 3, 1979		Moor	Military	Soldier
3. Mahmoud Ould Louly	June 3, 1979— January 1980	39	Moor	Military school (France)	Soldier
4. Mohamed Khouna Ould Haidalla	January 1980— Present		Moor	Military (St.-Cyr St.-Maixent)	Soldier

TABLE 24.6   Cabinet Membership: Percent Distribution by Ethnic Unit*

Ethnicity*	Independence Cabinet	1967 Cabinet
1. Moor (82%)	100%	83%
2. Tukulor-Fulani (13)	0	17
3. Others (5)	0	0
N =	10	12

*Ethnic units arranged in rank order of size within country with the unit's percent of national population in parentheses.

IV. National Integration and Stability

The government of Mauritania was led by educated Arabic-speaking elites. The government has tried to develop a multiracial society and an acceptance of the inherited state boundaries. The major internal problem of national integration has been the question of linkages between northern/Moorish/Arabic-speaking/ "Light- skinned" elements and southern/non-Moorish/non-Arabic-speaking/ dark-skinned elements. The language riots in 1966 manifested such tensions.

While there may be some irredentist sentiment in northern Mauritania for linkage with Morocco, we have not coded this as irredentism because the confrontation was almost entirely at the governmental level rather than at the popular level. It may be useful, however, to briefly review the situation. During the period 1960-1965, there were acute interstate tensions resulting from the claims of Morocco to *all* of Mauritania on the basis of pre-colonial allegiance patterns. The Mauritanian government resisted such claims and the major connective road between the two states was closed. On March 29, 1962 there was a grenade attack on a French army mess at Nema which killed 3 Frenchmen. This was later linked to attempts to incorporate all or part of Mauritania into Morocco. On August 13, 1963, four Mauritanian political leaders who had returned from self-imposed exile in Morocco were arrested on charges of subversion. In July 1965, three Mauritanians and a Moroccan were charged with treason on matters related to the Mauritanian-Moroccan dispute. The Organization of African Unity tried to settle the dispute and in 1970 at Rabat, the conflict was ended by Daddah, and Hassan, of Morocco. In 1973, President Daddah stated that a subversive underground movement existed and that a plot to overthrow the government had been discovered but no arrests were made or persons named. In late 1975, Morocco and Mauritania annexed pieces of the former Spanish Sahara, after a Moroccan confrontation with Spanish authorities led to a pullout of a Spanish presence. As a result of this action, POLISARIO, a guerrilla group committed to independence for the former Spanish Sahara, has embarked on a policy of concentrating their attacks against Mauritanian targets, the militarily weaker of the two states. This has involved attacks on the railroad transporting the iron ore to the port of Nouadhibou and attacks on military or political targets including an attack on the capital, Nouackchott. While this is a threat to the country from an external source, the resulting drain on the country's resources has been considerable and future political stability especially in the annexed territory is unclear. Daddah's policies on the conflict were primarily responsible for his ouster in July 1978 by a military coup d'etat. Since the coup, Mauritania has renounced all claims to the former Spanish Sahara and has asked Morocco to withdraw its troops from Mauritania.

In April 1980, Haidalla announced that he had uncovered a coup plot. Several members of the military and former government ministers were arrested. In May, Haidalla accused the French of fomenting disturbances and asked all French troops to leave. In June, 1980, an opposition movement in Paris known as the Mauritania Democrat Alliance was formed as an attempt to return Daddah (exiled in Paris) back to power.

TABLE 24.7   Elite Instability

Event and Date	Description
1. Coup d'État July 10, 1978	a. *Description*: A bloodless coup led by the army chief of staff, Col. Moustapha Ould Salek, deposed President Daddah. b. *Participants*: Segments of the military led by Col. Moustapha Ould Salek. c. *Apparent Causes*: Army dissatisfaction with President Daddah's policies on the POLISARIO conflict was reported as the cause of the coup.
2. Coup d'État April 1979	a.*Description*: Lt. Col. Bouceif was named Prime Minister at which time reports of a bloodless coup were made stating that Salek was only nominally President. No further details are known. b.*Participants*: Unknown. c.*Apparent Causes*: Unknown.
3. Coup d'État January 1980	a.*Description*: Louly's dismissal was announced by the Military Committee for National Salvation. He was replaced as Head of State by Lt. Col. Haidalla who had been Prime Minister and Minister of Defense under Louly's government. b.*Participants*: The ruling Military Committee for National Salvation. c.*Apparent Causes*: In their statement, the Committee said they wanted "to be rid of those who were not contributing to the national effort of reconstruction" (*West Africa*, 14 January 1980, p. 55).
4. Coup Attempt March 16, 1981	a. *Description*: Exiled army officers lead an attack against the Presidential Palace and attack government buildings in Nouakchott but are defeated by the Mauritanian army. b. *Participants*: Exiled army officers including Lt. Cols. M. Ould Abdel Kader and A. Salem Ould Sidi, and Lts. M. Niang and M. Doudou Seck. c. *Apparent Causes*: The exiled officers were living in Morocco and, with apparent Moroccan backing, tried to take over in order to turn Mauritania towards a more active anti-Polasario policy.

Table 24.8   Communal Instability

Event and Date	Characteristics
1. Ethnic Violence January 1966— April 1966	a.*Description*: In January 1966, there were widespread demonstrations in several parts of Mauritania following a new regulation establishing compulsory teaching of Arabic in secondary schools. On February 9, riots occurred in Nouakchott following the creation of a commission to study language problems in Mauritania. On February 11, fighting continued in the capital city between Arabic-speaking and non-Arabic-speaking ethnic groups. With the establishment of Arabic (in addition to French) as an official language, certain ethnic groups felt that administrative and governmental posts were less accessible. On February 16, President Ould Daddah forbade any discussion of "racial" problems in Mauritania. On March 2, certain "black" government officials were arrested for attempting to create discord between "the Negroes and the Whites." By March 7, there were 6 deaths and 70 injuries. On April 3, fighting occurred between light-skinned and dark-skinned students at the government secondary school in Nouakchott. These "school riots" resulted in many injured. b.*Participants*: Arabic-speaking Moors vs. Tukulor-Fulani/Wolof and other ethnic minorities. There was no apparent leadership, although "dark-skinned" secondary-school students and government officials were involved. c.*Apparent Causes*: Ethnic/racial/language tensions were focused on the issue of language policies.
2. Ethnic Violence May 12, 1967	a.*Description*: Violence occurred between the Sarakolé and Haratin near Selibaby (in the southeast). According to reports, 6 were killed and 20 wounded. b.*Participants*: Sarakolé and Haratin ethnic members. c.*Apparent Causes*: Not ascertainable.

SOURCE: Anthony S. Reyner, "Morocco's International Boundary," *Journal of Modern African Studies*, 1 (September 1963): 293—312.

TABLE 24.10 Annual Instability Events: Independence Through 1979—Mauritania

Year	'61	'62	'63	'64	'65	'66	'67	'68	'69	'70	'71	'72	'73	'74	'75	'76	'77	'78	'79
ELITE INSTABILITY																			
Assassinations																			
Plots													1						
Attempted Coups d'État																			
Coups d'État																		1	1
COMMUNAL INSTABILITY																			
Ethnic Violence						1													
Irredentism																			
Rebellion																			
Civil War																			
MASS INSTABILITY																			
Revolt																			
Revolution																			
TURMOIL																			
Demonstrations							1	1											
Strikes (no. days)	1			10	1		7												
Riots (no. days)							2	1											
Terrorism	1	2																	
Declarations of Emergency				1															
CABINET INSTABILITY																			
Realloc. and new appts.	10	7	10		8	21	5			6	5	3							
New members	8	3	1		3	12		4		6	9	1							
Resig. and Dismissals		10	5		5	6	1			4	8	2							
No. of members (max.) (maximum in year)	12	13	12	12	9	10	10	14	14	16	17	16							

VII. Selected References

BIBLIOGRAPHY

Van Maele, Bernard. *Bibliographie Mauritanie.* Nouakchott, Ministere de l'information et de la culture, 1971.

GENERAL

Gerteiny, Alfred G. *Mauritania.* New York: Praeger, 1967.

Heyman, J. M. "Mauritania: an annotated bibliography of bibliographies." *Current Bibliography of African Affairs.* 1978—79 p. 378-80.

U.S. Department of the Army. *Area Handbook for Mauritania*, Washington, D.C.: Government Printing Office, 1972.

POLITICAL

Chassey, F. de. *Mauritanie, 1900-1975 de l'ordre colonial: a l'ordre neo-colonial entre Maghreb et Afrique noire*. Paris:Ed. Antropes, 1978.

de Lusignan, Guy. *French-Speaking Africa since Independence*, pp. 218-230. London: Pall Mall Press, 1969.

Gaudio, Attilio. *Le Dosier de la Mauritanie*. Paris, Nouvelles Edition Latines. 1978:

Moore, Clement H. "One-Partyism in Mauritania." *Journal of Modern African Studies*, 3 (1965): 409—20.

ECONOMIC

Bradley, P., Raynaut, C., Tarrealba, J. *The Guidimaka Region of Mauritania: A Critical Analysis Leading to a Development Project*. London: International African Institute, 1977.

International Monetary Fund. "Mauritania." In *Surveys of African Economies*, Vol. 3 Washington, D.C.: I.M.F., 1970.

Westebbe, Richard M. *The Economy of Mauritania*. New York: Praeger Special Study, 1971.

SOCIAL

Stewart, Charles Cameron, and E. K. Stewart. "Islam and Social Order." In *Mauritania: A Case Study from the Nineteenth Century*. Oxford: Clarendon Press, 1973.

25. Mozambique

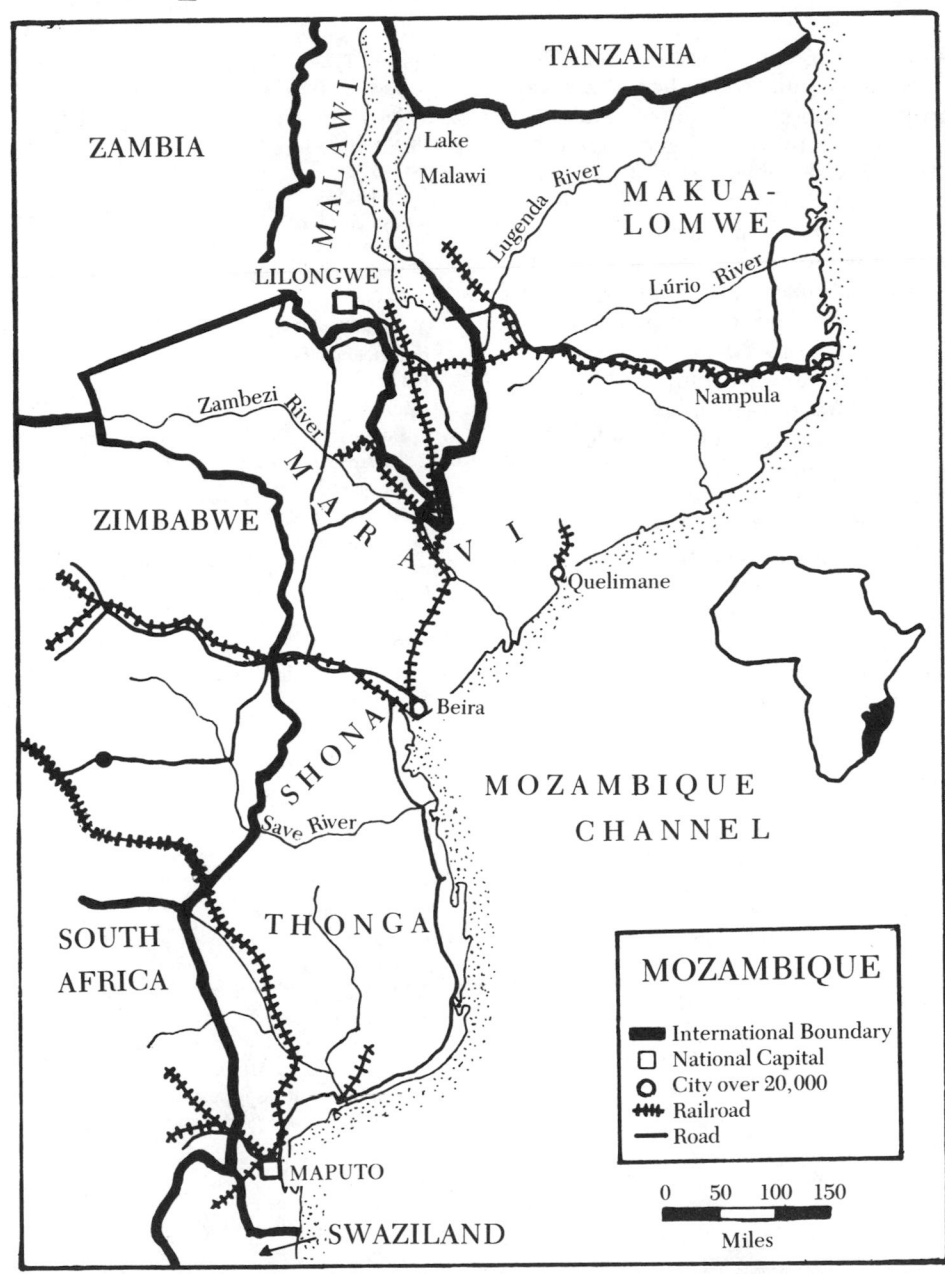

I. Basic Information

Date of Independence: June 25, 1975
Former Colonial Ruler: Portugal
Estimated Population (1980): 10,339,000
Area Size (equivalent in U.S.): 303,769 sq. mi. (Texas and Louisiana)
Date of Last Census: 1970

(Aug, 1980, a census was conducted, but results not available.)

Major Exports 1977 as Percent of Total Exports: cashew nuts—30 percent; textiles—9 percent; cotton—6 percent; sugar—5 percent; vegetable oils—4 percent; tea—8 percent; wood—3 percent.

II. Ethnic Patterns

Mozambique is a country of considerable ethnic diversity. There are seven ethnic units coded here, two associated with pre-colonial kingdoms, the Shona and Tsonga. These groupings represent the major geographical regions of the country. This classification is at a relatively high level of abstraction. It is based on a combination of cultural, historical, linguistic, and ecological criteria. Only the Shona are known to have a clear sense of common identity. This diversity may have an important bearing on the future of an independent Mozambique since there has been a history of conflict between the southern (generally patrilineal and non-Muslim) and northern (generally matrilineal and Muslim) peoples.

There was a large European population before independence, mainly of Portuguese origin (3.5%). At independence, however, there was a substantial exodus of Portuguese from Mozambique, although probably not on the same scale as in Angola. By the end of 1976, there were about 15,000 Portuguese reported to be in Mozambique but it was expected that almost all of them would leave in a few years. Other groups are the Nguni (.4%) and small numbers of Indians, Chinese, and persons of mixed European-African ancestry.

TABLE 25.1   Ethnic Units Over 5 Percent of Country Population

Ethnic Unit	Estimated Ethnic Population 1980	Estimated Ethnic Percentage
a. Makua-Lomwe Type	3,970,000	38.4
1. Makua		
2. Lomwe (Lomue)		
3. Neto		
4. Lolo (Alolo)		
5. Xirima (Acherima)		
b. Tsonga Type	2,450,000	23.7
1. Tsonga (Thonga)		
2. Ronga		
3. Shangana		
4. Tswa		
5. Helengwe		
c. Lower Zambezi Cluster	1,055,000	10.2
1. Sena		
2. Podzo (Chipango)		
3. Tonga		
4. Nhungwe (Ngunwe)		
5. Chicunda (Chikunda)		
6. Chuabo		
d. Shona	1,013,000	9.8
1. Karanga		
2. Tawara		
3. Bargue (Bargwe)		
4. Xonga (Changa)		
5. Teve (Gorongass)		
6. Manika (Manyika)		
7. Ndau (Vandau, Buzi)		
8. Tombodji		
9. Danda		
e. Maravi-Maconde-Yao Cluster	693,000	6.7
1. Maravi		
2. Senga		
3. Zimba		
4. Chewa		
5. Pimbe		
6. Nyanja		
7. Yao		
8. Maconde (Makonde)		
f. Islamic Coastal Type	662,000	6.4
1. Swahili		
2. Maca (Maka)		
3. Mvani		
g. Chopi	517,000	5.0

SOURCES: Murdock, *Africa: Africa South of the Sahara 1974* p. B550. 1950 Census results as reported in Abshire and Samuels *Portuguese Africa; Area Handbook for Mozambique.* 2nd ed. 1977.

III. Language Patterns

Considerable linguistic diversity makes estimates of languages for Mozambique difficult. Knappert gives no estimates and MacDougald estimates Makua to be 30 percent. We estimate Makua to be the most commonly spoken language at 40 percent although people in the urban areas and the south do not use it. The second language would be Thonga at 23 percent. Portuguese is widely spoken in the urban areas and serves as a *lingua franca*.

TABLE 25.2   Language Patterns

1. Primacy			
1st language	Makua-Lomwe	(40%)	
2nd language	Thonga	(23%)	
		Green-berg	Dalby
2. Linguistic classification	Makua-Lomwe	IA5	P3
(of all ethnic groups	Chewa-Nyanja	IA5	N3
with at least 5 percent	Shona	IA5	S1
of population)	Thonga	IA5	N2
3. *Lingua franca*	Portuguese		
4. Official language	Portuguese		

IV. Urban Patterns

Capital/Largest City: Maputo (formerly Lourenco Marques-founded 16th century)
Dominant ethnicity/language of capital
Major vernacular: Thonga[1]
Major ethnic group: Chopi-Thonga
Major ethnic group as percent of capital's population:

[1]J. Knappert "Language Problems of the New Nations of Africa," op. cit.

TABLE 25.3   Growth of Capital/Largest City

Date	Maputo (Lourenco Marques)
1910	9,849
1927	37,301
1940	68,801
1956	99,000 UA
1960	178,655 UA
1970	354,684 UA

SOURCES: Various editions of *Statesman's Yearbook*; *UN Demographic Yearbook*; and *Africa South of the Sahara*; *Area Handbook for Mozambique 2nd ed. 1977.*

TABLE 25.4   Cities of 20,000 and Over

City	Size	Date
Maputo (formerly Lourenco Marques)	354,686 UA	1970
Beira	130,000 UA	1970
Nampula	103,985	1970
Quelimane	66,301	1970

SOURCES: 1970 Census results as reported in *Political Handbook of the World 1977*, Arthur Banks ed. New York: McGraw Hill, 1977. The figures for Nampula and Quelimane appear to be near the 1960 census figures and it is unclear whether this signifies low rates of growth of these cities or lack of new information. Other cities for which no data was available were Xai-Xai- (formerly Joao Belo), Inhambane, Tete, Lichinga, and Pemba. The *Area Handbook* asserts that the population of these cities probably had been seriously undercounted. The masssive exodus of the Portuguese especially from the urban areas may imply a drop in the urban population if this emigration was not compensated for by immigration to the cities. No reliable information is available at this time.

V. Political Patterns

A. Political Parties and Elections

As in the other former Portuguese colonies, virtually all political activity was illegal until 1974 and the country's political life was dominated by the decade-long fight for independence led by the *Frente de Libertacao de Mocambique* (FRELIMO). FRELIMO resulted from a merger of several smaller groups in 1962. In 1965, a breakaway group, the *Commissao Revolucinario de Mocambique* (COREMO) was formed but it had little influence and did not share in the independent government. Other political groups were formed particularly after the coup in Portugal but with the Portuguese handover of power to FRELIMO, they have faded away or been banned. Mozambique is a *de jure* one-party state.

Illegal opposition groups do exist, however. The best known is the *Frente de Unidade Democratica de Mocambique* (FUMO) which supports a government in exile and claims to be operating in the northern part of the country. By late 1979, the activities of FUMO, the Mozambique National Resistance (RNM); and Africa Libre had increased with the help of the Rhodesian government which was attempting to disrupt Patriotic Front guerilla activities based in Mozambique. It was reported that the anti-government movements had staged several sabotage attacks including bombings and ambushes. It was believed that by 1980 the RNM had moved its base of operations to South Africa. The new Zimbabwe government had pledged its support to help Mozambique in its fight against the anti-government movements. Elections were held from September through December 1977 under a one-party regime in which each constituency could be competed for by any number of candidates but run-offs were held if a candidate received less than 50 percent of the vote. Above the local level all voting is indirect with each succeeding level electing representatives to the next higher level. The People's Assembly met for the first time in December 1977.

B. Political Leadership

FRELIMO was formed by Eduardo Mondlane out of a variety of anti-Portuguese groups in 1962. Under Mondlane's leadership FRELIMO's guerrilla campaign became increasingly effective against the Portuguese army. In 1969, Mondlane was assassinated, possibly by dissident elements in FRELIMO supported by the Portuguese. Nevertheless, FRELIMO was able to increase its effectiveness, finally forcing the Portuguese to capitulate and turn over the government to FRELIMO without elections or referenda in 1975. Samora Moises Machel was elected President by FRELIMO. In mid-March and early April 1980 Machel undertook two major cabinet reshuffles in an effort to deal with the country's economic problems. In order to deal with corruption and maladministration several government officials were arrested in the first half of 1980.

FIGURE 25.1   Political Parties and Elections   MOZAMBIQUE

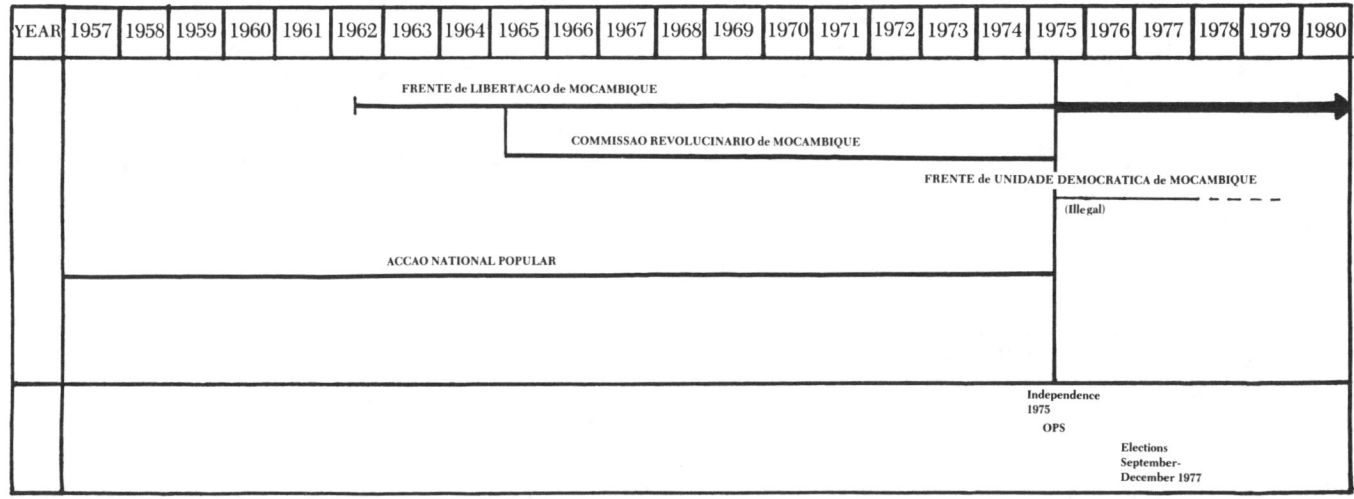

TABLE 25.5 Head of Government (Post-Independence)

Name	Dates in Office	Age (1982)	Ethnicity	Education	Former Occupation
1. Samora Moises Machel (President)	1975— present	50	Tsonga (Shangana)	Secondary School	Nurse

VI. National Integration and Stabilty

After a ten year guerrilla struggle under the leadership of FRELIMO the Portuguese handed over power to FRELIMO in 1974. On September 20, 1974, an interim government was established with ultimate power still in the hands of the Portuguese until full independence was granted in June 1975.

One of the main problems facing the new government is the integration of a country where major guerrilla operations were fought by peoples from the North albeit with a leadership drawn mostly from the South while the major population centers and industry are located in the south of the country. This division also reflects the major cultural and linguistic differentiations. This ethnic diversity coupled with considerable economic dependence on South Africa, externally and the remnants of the Portuguese community, internally, has made it difficult for the new government to function. The uncompromising ideological stands by the government have also alienated potential support. In December, 1975, an army unit mutinied in Maputo, but details of its motivation and participation remain unclear.

Apparently, anti-government activities by some army units and other groups have occurred but no details are available. There have been unsubstantiated reports of attempts on the lives of Machel and other government leaders as well. This apparent inability of the government to establish full control throughout the country may indicate that future instability is likely. The first major cabinet reshuffle took place in April 1978. In August 1978, four members of the FRELIMO central committee were expelled from the party, reportedly because they deviated from revolutionary ideology.

In 1979, Mozambique was involved in a war with Rhodesia over the issue of allowing Patriotic Front guerrilla bases in Mozambique. In July 1980, the Mozambique army launched a major offensive against the opposition National Resistance Movement capturing 300 rebels and killing 272 in the mountains near the Zimbabwe border.

VII. Selected References

BIBLIOGRAPHY

Gibson, Mary Jane. *Portuguese Africa: A Guide to Official Publications*. Washington, D. C.: 1967.

GENERAL

Abshire, David, and Michael Samuels (eds.). *Portuguese Africa-A Handbook*. New York: Praeger, 1970.
Bruce, N. *Portugal: The Last Empire*. New York: Halsted Press, 1975.
Chilcote, Ronald. *Portuguese Africa*. Englewood Cliffs, N.J.: Prentice Hall, 1967.
Egego, B. *Mozambique and Angola*. Uppsala: Scandinavian Institute of African Studies, 1977.

Kaplan, I., et al. *Area Handbook for Mozambique*, 2nd ed. Washington, D.C.: U.S. Government Printing Office, 1977.
Swift, Kerry. *Mozambique and the Future*. London: R. Hale, 1975.

POLITICAL

Gann, L. H. "Portugal, Africa, and the Future," *Journal of Modern African Studies*, 13, 1 (1975): 1—18.
Henriksen, T. H. "Portugal in Africa: A Noneconomic Interpretation," *African Studies Review* 16, 3 (December 1973): 405—16.
Humbaraci, A., and N. Muchnik. *Portugal's African Wars*. London: Macmillan, 1974.

Isaacman, Allen. *A Luta Continua: Creating a New Society in Mozambique.* Binghamton, N.Y.: Ferdinand Braudel Center, 1978.

Martins Elisio. *Colonialism and Imperialism in Mozambique: the beginning of the end.* Kastrup Denmark African Studies 1974.

Middlemas, K. *Cabora Basssa: Engineering and Politics in Southern Africa.* London: Weidenfeld and Nicholson, 1976.

Mondlane, Eduardo. *The Struggle for Mozambique.* London: Penguin, 1969.

Paul, J. *Mozambique: Memoirs of a Revolution.* Harmondsworth: Penguin, 1975.

Rees, D. "Soviet Strategic Penetration of Africa," *Conflict Studies* 77 (November 1976): 1—20.

ECONOMIC

Torp, Jens Erik. *Industrial Planning and Development in Mozambique: Some Preliminary Considerations.* Uppsala: The Scandinavian Institute of African Studies, 1979.

SOCIAL

Henriksen, T. H. *Mozambigue: A History.* London: Rex Collings, 1978.

Smith, A. K. "The Peoples of Southern Mozambique: An Historical Survey," *Journal of African History,* 14, 4 (1973): 565—80.

26. Namibia

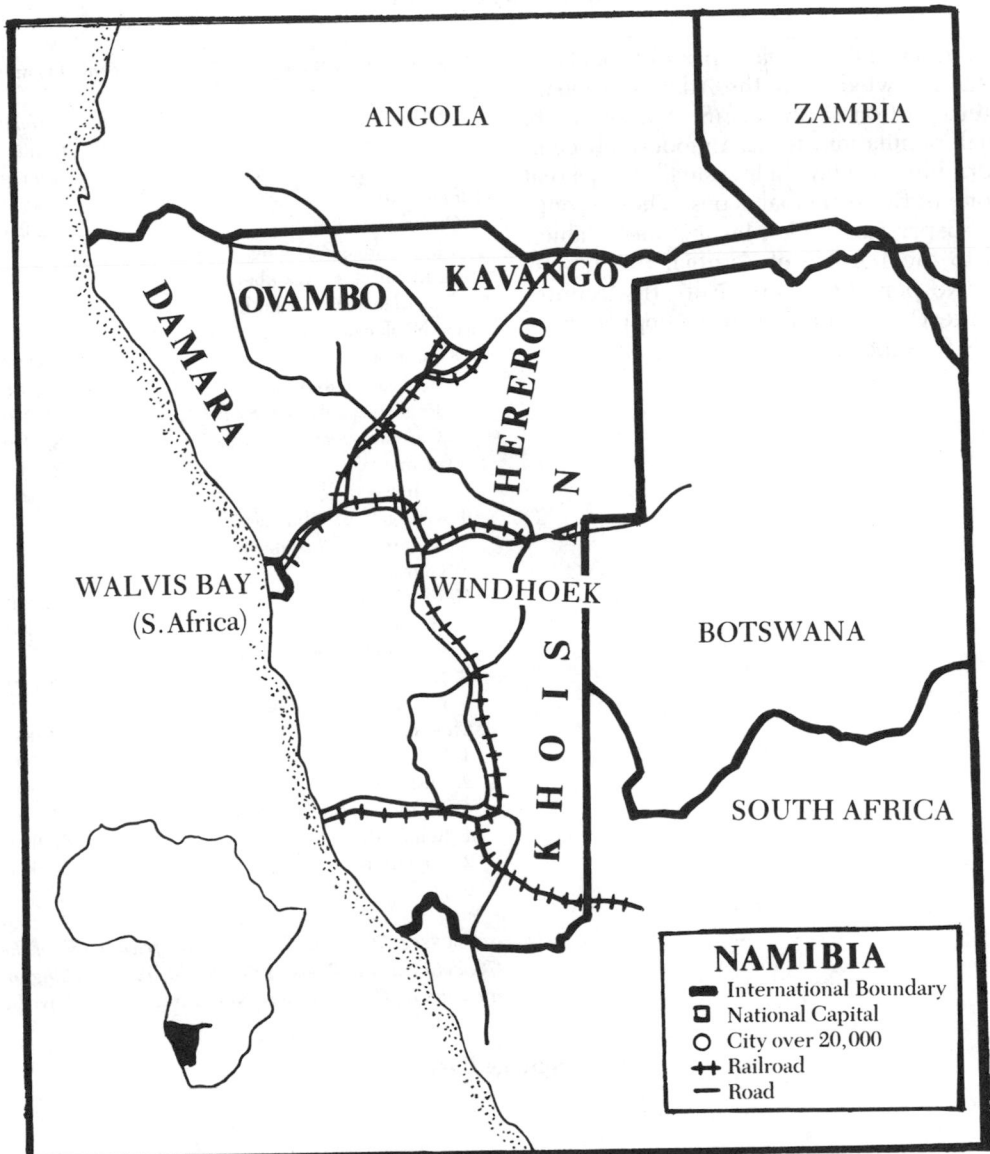

I. Basic Information

Date of Independence: Not independent as of the end of 1982
Former Colonial Ruler: Germany, South Africa.
Change in Boundaries: Former League of Nations mandated territory administered by South Africa since 1920.
Former Name: South West Africa.
Estimated Population (1980): 1,020,000
Area Size (equivalent in U.S.): 317,827 sq. miles (Louisiana and Texas).

Date of Last Census: 1970.
*Major Exports 1972 as Percent of Total Exports:** diamonds—38 percent; fish products—19 percent; livestock—15 percent; karakul pelts—14 percent.

*After 1966 no official export data were released for Namibia. Source for 1972 exports: *Africa South of the Sahara, 1978—79*.

II. Ethnic Patterns

Namibia has been described as a "vast sparsely populated desert-like country sprawled along the Atlantic seaboard in the southwestern portion of Africa." (Serfontein: 1976, 8). Despite a small population, it has a moderately complex ethnic pattern but with only a few small groups that do not fall into one of the principal types. These groups include the East Caprivians (.4% Masubia and Mafue), who are related to the Barotse of Zambia, the Tswana (.6%) and about two percent others. Note this country has by far the largest white or European population of any country in this Handbook.

TABLE 26.1   Ethnic Units Over 5 Percent of Country Population

Ethnic Unit	Estimated Ethnic Population 1980	Estimated Ethnic Percentage
a. Ovambo (Ambo)	472,000	46.3%
i. Kuanyama, ii. Ndonga,		
iii. Kuambi, iv. Ngandjera,		
v. Mbalantu, vi. Kualuthi		
vii. Nkolonkati-Eunda		
b. Europeans	120,000	11.8%
1. Afrikaaners (8.3%),	85,000	
2. English-speakers (0.8%),	8,200	
3. German-speakers (2.7%)	32,000	
c. Damara	89,000	8.7%
d. Kavango	66,000	6.5
i. Kwangali, ii. Mbunza,		
iii. Sambyu, iv. Mbukushu		
v. Geiriku		
e. Herero Type	75,000	7.4%
1. Herero	67,000	(6.6%)
i. Herero, ii. Mbandero		
2. Kaokabanders	8,000	(0.8%)
i. Himba, ii. Tjimba		
f. Khoisan	74,000	7.3%
1. Nama	44,000	(4.3%)
2. Bushmen	31,000	(3.0)
g. Coloureds and Rehoboth Basters Type	61,000	6.0%
1. Rehoboth Basters	22,000	(2.2)
2. Coloureds	39,000	(3.8%)

SOURCES: 1970 census figures from *Africa South of the Sahara, 1978—79*; *Political Handbook of the World, 1979*; Wellington, *South West Africa and Its Human Issues* (New York: Oxford University Press, 1967).

III. Language Patterns

The languages spoken in Namibia are principally Bantu with respect to the numbers of speakers. However this linguistically complex country includes the click-languages of the Bushmen and a range of European languages including English and German and their derivatives such as Afrikaans.

TABLE 26.2   Language Patterns

1. Primacy			
1st language	Ambo	(50%)	
2nd language	Herero	(10%)	
		Green-berg	Dalby
2. Linguistic classification	Ambo	IA 5	R2
(all ethnic units in	Nama-Dama	Khoisian	91A
country over 5%)	Kavango	IA 5	K5
	Herero	IA 5	R3
	Afrikaans	uncoded	99D
3. *Lingua francas*	Afrikaans, Ambo		
4. Official languages	Afrikaans, English, German		

IV. Urban Patterns

Capital/largest city: Windhoek
Dominant ethnicity/language of capital
    Major vernacular: Afrikaans
    Major ethnic group: Europeans
    Major ethnic groups as percent of capital's population: 55% (1970 census)

TABLE 26.3 Growth of Capital/Largest/City

Date	Windhoek
1951[c]	20,598
1960[a]	35,916
1970[a]	64,700
1974[a]	76,000
1978[b]	89,000

TABLE 26.4   Cities of 20,000 or Over

City	Size	Date
Windhoek	89,000	1978

SOURCE:
  [a]*Africa South of the Sahara, 1978-1979*, p. 670. [b]*Political Handbook of the World, 1979*, p. 311. [c]Census.

V. Political Patterns

A. Political Parties and Elections

Namibia as of mid-1982 was a society in which whites still dominated the electorate and in which a separate court system existed for whites as well. There are three parties representing this white population—the Federal Party, the Republican Party (RP) and the National Party of South West Africa. This system is based on the South African apartheid system and has been built up over a long period starting in the 1920's when South Africa was granted a League of Nations mandate to administer the former German colony. While the League's successor, the U.N., revoked that mandate in 1966 and was upheld by the World Court, South Africa has consistently refused to allow the U.N. to take over administration of the territory.

There are a large number of political groups and organizations that represent the interests of the non-white population, most of them with specific ethnic constituencies. The principal one is the South West African People's Organization (SWAPO) which has led the fight for independence for the last two decades and is mainly

Ovambo in membership. The South West African National Union (SWANU) is largely Herero in membership although it coordinates its activities with SWAPO. The major non-white group that is aligned not with SWAPO but with the white Republican Party is the National Unity Democratic Organization (NUDO) led by Chief Kapuao until his assassination in 1978. The Democratic Turnhalle Alliance (DTA) is a coalition of the RP and NUDO which won most of the Legislative Assembly seats in the 1978 elections.

Other parties include the SWAPO Democrats Party, an anti-SWAPO splinter group; the largely Herero, socialist-oriented South West Africa National United Front (SWANUF); the Nama Organisation for South West Africa (NOSWA); the Namibia Democratic Party (NDP), representing both Nama and Damara tribal interests; the exclusively Naman South West African United National Independence Organisation (SWAUNIO); the Damaran Namibia African People's Democratic Organisation (NAPDO); the Ovambo Independent Party (OIP); the Caprivi African National Union (CANU); the Coloured Labour Party (CLP); and the Democratic Cooperative Development Party of Ovanholava.

Elections for Legislative Assembly have been held regularly every four years. Until 1979 the National Party (NP) won regularly. In 1978 the DTA won with 82 percent of the vote and 41 of 50 seats in the Legislative Assembly.

B. Political Leadership

Namibia has been ruled directly by South Africa since September 1, 1977 when an Administrator General was appointed to supercede the previous Legislative Assembly and the largely internal white self-rule that had characterized Namibia until that time. In 1978 elections to a new legislature were won by the Democratic Turnhalle Alliance although boycotted by SWAPO and denied legitimacy by other countries and international organizations. Mr. Dirk Mudge leads that coalition.

The opposition includes many parties and individuals but SWAPO under the leadership of Mr. Sam Nujoma (and based in Angola) has led the battle for independence for the last two decades and has been almost universally recognized by the international community as the legitimate spokesman for the people of Namibia.

FIGURE 26.1   Political Parties and Elections   NAMIBIA

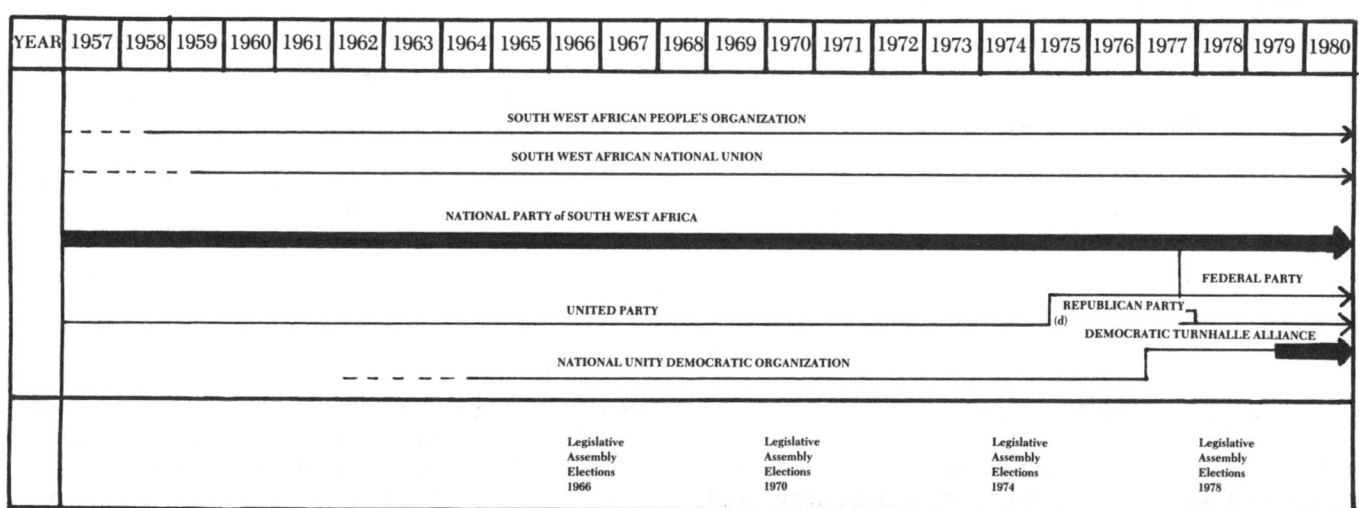

VI. National Integration and Stability

Since Namibia is not yet independent this section is not relevant in the same way as is the corresponding section in the other country chapters. While by definition, there had been no instances of *post-independence* instability, the country has been the locus of a sustained war of liberation from the control of South Africa and the white minority living in Namibia. This conflict continues at a high level of intensity that increasingly involves crossing international borders into Angola, Botswana, and Zim-babwe.

The eventual resolution of the effort will probably include SWAPO, although the form of an eventual political solution is somewhat less clear since both whites and minority black African groups are concerned about Ovambo-led domination of the polity. Any solution that does not take these issues into account is not likely to be integrative. The United Nations continues to take an active role in achieving a viable solution.

TABLE 26.9   Mass Instability

Event and Date	Characteristics
1. Pre-independence Revolution, 1966—present	a. *Description*: Military and guerrilla activity has grown in intensity since the South African rejection of the U.N. ruling in 1966 that South Africa no longer held the mandate to administer Namibia. b. *Participants*: Various African groups typically organized around ethnic groups which are sometimes under traditional leadership, but SWAPO under Sam Nujoma and a largely Ovambo leadership have been the principal participants. c. *Apparent Causes*: In 1966, the United Nations terminated the mandate to administer Namibia held by South Africa. South Africa refused to recognize the termination and continued to administer the area. SWAPO led a guerrilla campaign to force South Africa to relent.

VII. Selected References

BIBLIOGRAPHY

Bridgman, J. and D. E. Clarke. *German Africa: A Select Annotated Bibliography*. Stanford: Hoover Institution, 1965.

GENERAL

First, Ruth. *South West Africa*. Harmondsworth: Penguin, 1963.
Serfontein, J. H. P. *Namibia*. London: Rex Collins, 1977.
Winter, Colin. *Namibia*. London: Lutterworth Press, 1977.

POLITICAL

Tatemeyer, G. *Namibia Old and New: Traditonal and Modern Leaders in Ovamboland*. London: Hurst, 1974.

SOCIAL

Wellington, J. H. *Southern Africa: A Geographical Study*, London: Oxford University Press, 1978.
Wellington, J. H. *South West Africa and Its Human Issues*, Oxford, Clarendon Press, 1967.

ECONOMIC

Thomas, W. H. *Economic Development in Namibia*, Munich: Grunewald, 1978.

27. Niger

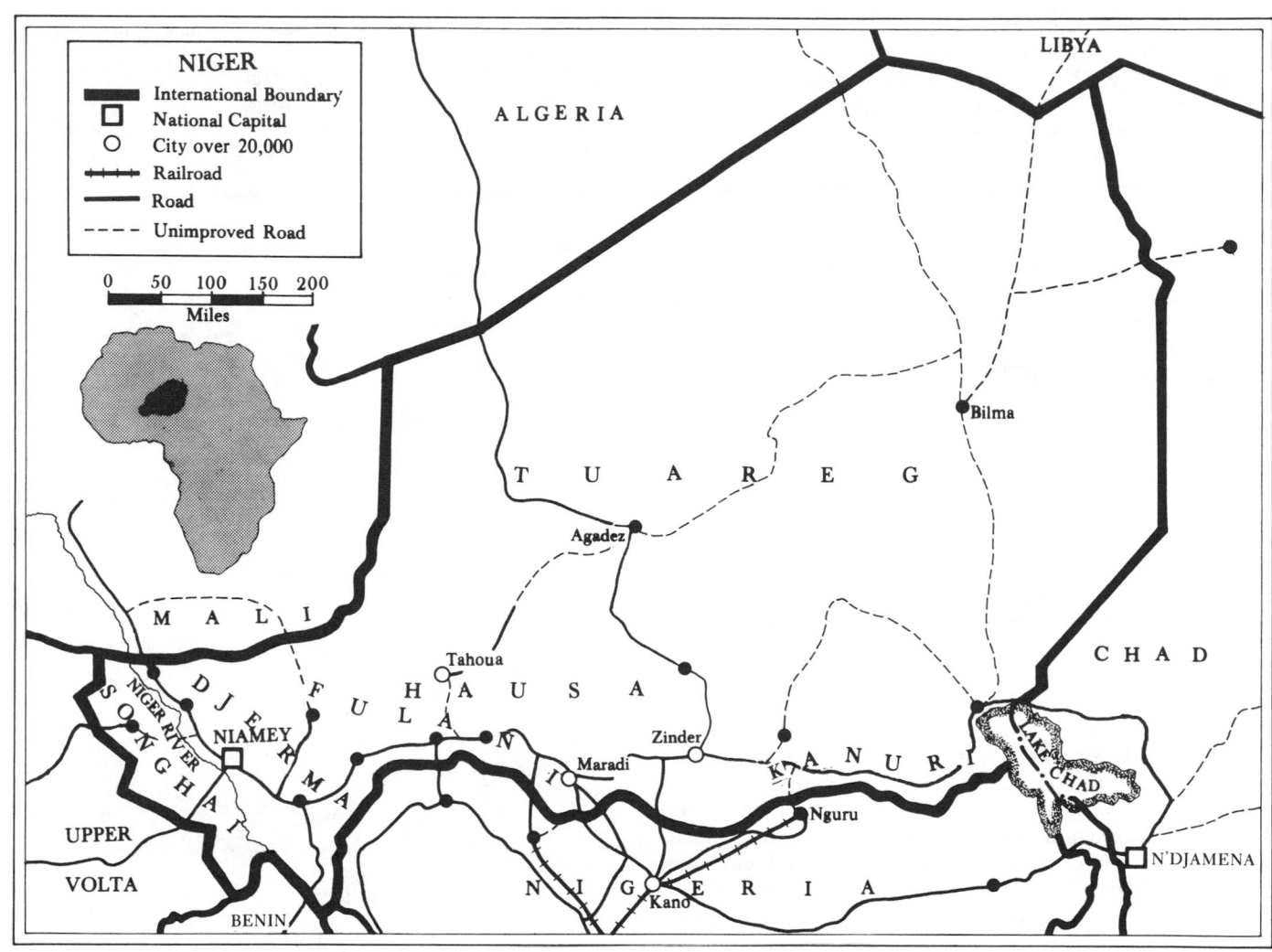

I. Basic Information

Date of Independence: August 3, 1960
Former Colonial Ruler: France
Change in Boundaries: Formerly part of the French West Africa Federation
Estimated Population (1980): 4,832,000
Area Size (equivalent in U.S.): 489,190 sq. mi. (Texas, Nevada, and New Mexico)

Date of Last Census: 1977
Major Exports 1978 as Percent of Total Exports*: uranium ore—65 percent.

*Considerable unrecorded trade takes place across the Niger-Nigeria border particularly in commodities such as groundnuts and livestock. The droughts of the 1970's exacerbated this phenomena.

II. Ethnic Patterns

Although the ethnic groupings for Niger are widely inclusive, they correspond to functioning identity and language groups. These are also the categories recognized by the Niger government. Culturally, all of the groups are relatively similar, since they have all been Muslim for several centuries. There are important ecological differences, however, especially with regard to Fulani pastoralism and Tuareg nomadism. The Tuaregs are estimated at 3 percent of the total population. Another source gives a different ethnic distribution than the one reported here. (Hausa—45 percent; Djerma-Songhai—21 percent; Fulani—18 percent; Tuareg—14 percent): see "La Republique du Niger" *Notes et studies documentation.* (Paris) July 1973, 3, 494-5, p.8.

TABLE 27.1 Ethnic Units Over 5 Percent of Country Population

Ethnic Units	Estimated Ethnic Population (1980)	Estimated Ethnic Percentage
a. Hausa (Haoussa)	2,837,000	54
1. Hausa, 2. Adarawa, Kurfei		
b. Djerma-Songhai	1,261,000	24
1. Djerma (Zerma, Zaberma)		
2. Songhai (Songhay)		
c. Fulani	578,000	11
d. Kanuri (Beriberi)	473,000	9

SOURCE: *Europa Yearbook 1977* V. II.

III. Language Patterns

The major languages of Niger are Hausa (of the Chadic family), Djerma-Songhai (of the Songhai family), Fulani (of the West Atlantic family), Tuareg or Tamashek (of the Berber family), and Kanuri (of the Saharan family). Although the percentage of total population who speak Hausa as a first language is 54 percent, at least another 27 percent (especially Fulani, Kanuri, Tuareg) speak it as a second language. Our estimate of Hausa-speakers is thus 81 percent. (Knappert, MacDougald, and Rustow estimate 32 percent, 34 percent, and 43 percent respectively.) The second largest language is Djerma-Songhai, which is spoken as a first language by 24 percent of the total population (Rustow estimates 18 percent). It is concentrated in the capital city area around Niamey, and because of the influence of French and Hausa does not really serve as a *lingua franca*. French continues as the official language although, since about 1963, radio broadcasting and adult literacy campaigns have been conducted in all major vernacular languages.

TABLE 27.2 Language Patterns

1. Primacy			
1st language	Hausa	(81%)	
2nd language	Songhai	(24%)	
		Greenberg	Dalby
2. Linguistic classification	Hausa	IIIE	03A
(all ethnic units in	Djerma-Songhai	IIA	10
country over 5%)	Fulani	IA1	201
	Tuareg	IIIC	00
	Kanuri	IIB	11A
3. *Lingua franca*	Hausa		
4. Official language	French		

SOURCE: Petr Zima, "Hausa in West Africa: Remarks on Contemporary Role and Function," in *Language Problems of Developing Nations*, eds. Joshua A. Fisman, Charles A. Ferguson, and Jyotirindra Das Gupta (New York: John Wiley, 1968), pp. 365-378.

IV. Urban Patterns

Capital/largest city: Niamey
Dominant ethnicity/language of capital
   Major vernacular: Hausa[1]

[1]Jan Knappert, "Language Problems of the New Nations of Africa," *African Quarterly*, 5 (1965): 95-105.

Major ethnic group: Djerma
Major ethnic group as percent of capital's population:

TABLE 27.3   Growth of Capital/Largest City

Date	Niamey
1920	2,000
1930	2,000
1940	6,000
1950	9,000
1960	30,000
1967	60,000
1968	79,000
1972	102,000
1975	150,000
1978	220,000

SOURCES: *Démographie Comparee*, except for the 1929 (1,000) and 1931 (3,400) figures which are given in Niger Government, *Étude Démographique de la Ville de Niamey et des Besoins Solvables en Logements*, SCET/SONUCI, 1962. All figures exclude European population; *UN Demographic Yearbook 1967*; *Africa South of the Sahara 1974*; *UN Demographic Yearbook 1975*. *Europa Yearbook 1977, Europe-Outremer* Nov. 1979.

TABLE 27.4   Cities of 20,000 and Over*

City	Size	Date
Niamey[a]	220,000	1978
Maradi	46,000	1977
Zinder	58,000	1977
Tahoua	31,000	1977
Agadez	20,000	1977

SOURCE: 1977 Census; [a]*Europe Outremer* Nov. 1979.

V. Political Patterns

FIGURE 27.1   Political Parties and Elections   NIGER

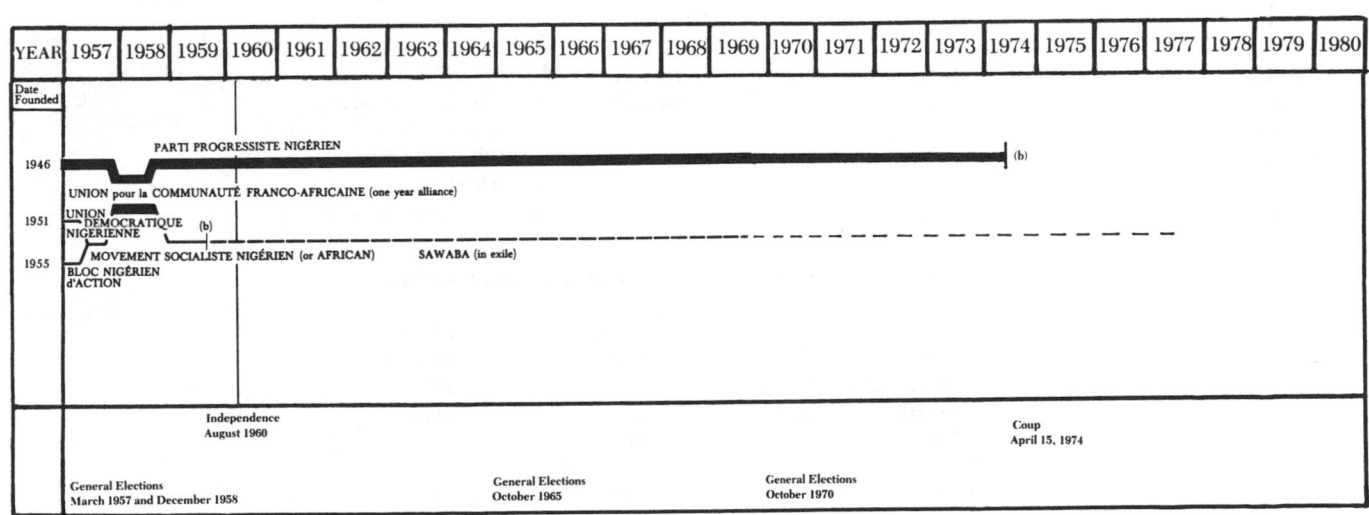

A. Political Parties and Elections

Since the 1958 vote on General de Gaulle's constitution, the *Parti Progressiste Nigérien* (PPN), which recommended a "yes" vote, had been the dominant party in Niger. Prior to the referendum, the *Bloc Nigerien d'Action* (BNA), much better known by its Hausa name "SAWABA," was dominant. Once a "yes" vote had been achieved on the Referendum, the temporary PPN/BNA coalition was dissolved, and in 1959 under the leadership of Hamani Diori and the PPN, Niger became a one-party state. The SAWABA party was declared illegal and its leader, Bakary Djibo, forced into exile. With no legal opposition Diori continued as president, with all seats in the Legislative Assembly held by members of the PPN. In April 1974, a military coup led by Lt. Col. Kountché overthrew Diori and banned all political activity.

B. Political Leadership

Hamani Diori was head of state from independence until the 1974 military coup. Although the independence cabinet tended to be overbalanced in favor of the Djerma-Songhai, the balance had generally been redressed with an increase in the number of Hausa ministers by 1967. This redistribution of ethnic representation among ministers was to some extent misleading since Djerma-Songhai dominance in the PPN and the government bureaus remained. Lt. Col. Kountché has led the country under the military regime. The early stability of the military regime was tenuous. Within eight months of coming to power there were two government reshuffles and a coup attempt in 1976 following two alleged plots against the government in 1975 and 1976. In December 1977, the number of army officers in the government was reduced. In September 1978, there was a minor government reshuffle which also placed more civilians in government. While the military regime remains in power as of 1982, a National Commission has been empowered to make proposals for a return to a civilian regime.

TABLE 27.5   Head of Government (Post-Independence)

Name	Dates in Office	Age (1982)	Ethnicity	Education	Former Occupation
1. Hamani Diori (President)	1960-74	66	Djerma-Songhai	Secondary (Dahomey) William Ponty (Dakar)	Civil Servant Teacher
2. Col. Seyni Kountché (President of the Supreme Military Council)	1974-present	51	Djerma-Songhai	French army secondary schools in Mali & Dakar Officer Training school, Paris	Soldier

TABLE 27.6   Cabinet Membership: Distribution by Ethnic Unit*

Ethnicity*	Independence Cabinet	1967 Cabinet
1. Hausa (52%)	9.1%	40%
2. Djerma-Songhai (24)	55	33
3. Fulani (11)	18	6.7
4. Kanuri (9)	9.1	6.7
5. Others (4)	9.1	13
N =	11	15

*Ethnic units arranged in rank order of size within country with the unit's percent of national population in parentheses.

VI. National Integration and Stability

The regime of Hamani Diori had survived a series of efforts by the SAWABA party to take over the government. SAWABA maintained itself in exile (in Ghana and Nigeria), and attracted younger educated elements as well as large numbers of Hausa along the border from Birnin Konni to Zinder. SAWABA supporters asserted that the Diori regime was too closely linked with Ivory Coast and France, and underrepresented the Hausa who are the dominant group in the country. Other disturbances under the Diori regime had been a series of almost endemic student strikes in the four years preceding the 1974 military coup which deposed Diori. In August 1975 a plot against the government was reported and in March 1976 an attempted coup was forestalled early into its execution. In mid-April 1980 President Kountché commemorated his sixth year in power by releasing former president Diori and Djibo Bakary, a leader of the SAWABA party.

TABLE 27.7   Elite Instability

Event and Date	Characteristics
1. Coup d'État April 15, 1974	a. *Description*: Military units under the command of Army Chief of Staff Lt. Col. Kountché arrest President Diori on the night of April 15, 1974 and take over all government facilities. Party activity was banned. Estimates of the number killed range from the official figure of 10 up to 100. b. *Participants*: Army units led by Lt. Col. Kountché and Major Sani-Souna Sido. c. *Apparent Causes*: The coup leaders stated the reasons for the coup were their dissatisfaction with the corruption of the politicians and particularly their mismanagement of drought relief supplies.
2. Coup Attempt March 14—15, 1976	a. *Description*: Army units under Major Moussa Bayere took over the radio station in Niamey at dawn. By late in the morning the radio station had been retaken by the army and those involved in the attempt arrested. The major figures were executed in April 1976. b. *Participants*: Major Moussa Bayere, dismissed as Minister for Rural Development in February, Ahmed Mouddour, secretary-general to the *Union National des Travailleurs du Niger* (UNTN), and Captain Sidi Mohammed were the apparent leaders in the coup attempt along with units of the army. c. *Apparent Causes*: The causes were unclear although inter-elite competition in the ruling Supreme Military Council which had come to a head in August 1975 with the arrest of Major Sido was probably a major factor.

SOURCE: *Africa Digest* June 1974, 52—53; R. Higgott and I. Inglestad "The 1974 Coup d'Etat in Niger: Towards an Explanation" *Journal of Modern African Studies*, 13, 3 (1975) 383—398; *West Africa* 22 March 1976 p. 373.

TABLE 27.10   Annual Instability Events: Independence Through 1979—Niger

Year	'61	'62	'63	'64	'65	'66	'67	'68	'69	'70	'71	'72	'73	'74	'75	'76	'77	'78	'79
ELITE INSTABILITY																			
Assassinations											1								
Plots			1													1			
Attempted Coups d'Etat																	1		
Coups d'Etat														1					
COMMUNAL INSTABILITY																			
Ethnic Violence																			
Irrendentism																			
Rebellion																			
Civil War																			
MASS INSTABILITY																			
Revolt				1	1														
Revolution																			
TURMOIL																			
Demonstrations																			
Strikes (no. days)														30					
Riots (no. days)																			
Terrorism				3	1														
Declarations of Emergency										1									
CABINET INSTABILITY																			
Realloc. and new appts.	18	9	10	2	8				6	13				10					
New Members	3				6					4				3					
Resig. and Dismissals			3	2	3					2									
No. of members (max.) (maximum in year)	12	15	13	13	13	13	13	14	14	16	16	19							

VII. Selected References

BIBLIOGRAPHY

Decalo, Samuel. *Historical Dictionary of Niger*. Metuchen, N.J.: Scarecrow Press, 1979.

GENERAL

Charlick, R. and J. Thompson. *Niger*. Boulder, Colo.: Westview Press, 1981.

Clair, Andrée. *Le Niger: pays á decouvrir*. Paris: Hachette, 1965.

Donnaint, P. and F. Lancrenon. *Le Niger*. Paris: Presses Universitaires de France, 1976.

Riveieres, Edmond Sere de. *Histoire du Niger*. Paris: Bergere-Levrault, 1965.

POLITICAL

Amin, Samir. *Neo-Colonialism in West Africa.* Harmondsworth, Middlesex: Penguin Books, 1973.
De Lusignan, Guy. *French-Speaking Africa since Independence*, pp. 151-59. London: Pall Mall Press, 1969.
Jouve, E. "Du Niger de Diori Hamani au Gouvernment des Militaires (1974-1977)." *Revue Français Études Politiques Africaines, 149, May 1978, pp. 19-44.*
Thompson, Virginia. "Niger." In *National Unity and Regionalism in Eight African States*, ed. Gwendolen M. Carter. Ithaca, N.Y.: Cornell University Press, 1966.

ECONOMIC

International Monetary Fund. "Niger." In *Surveys of African Economies*, Vol. 3. Washington, D.C.: I.M.F., 1970.

SOCIAL

Van Hoey, Leo F. "The Coercive Process of Urbanization: the Case of Niger." In *The New Urbanization*, eds. Scott Greer, et al. New York: St. Martins Press, 1968.

28. Nigeria

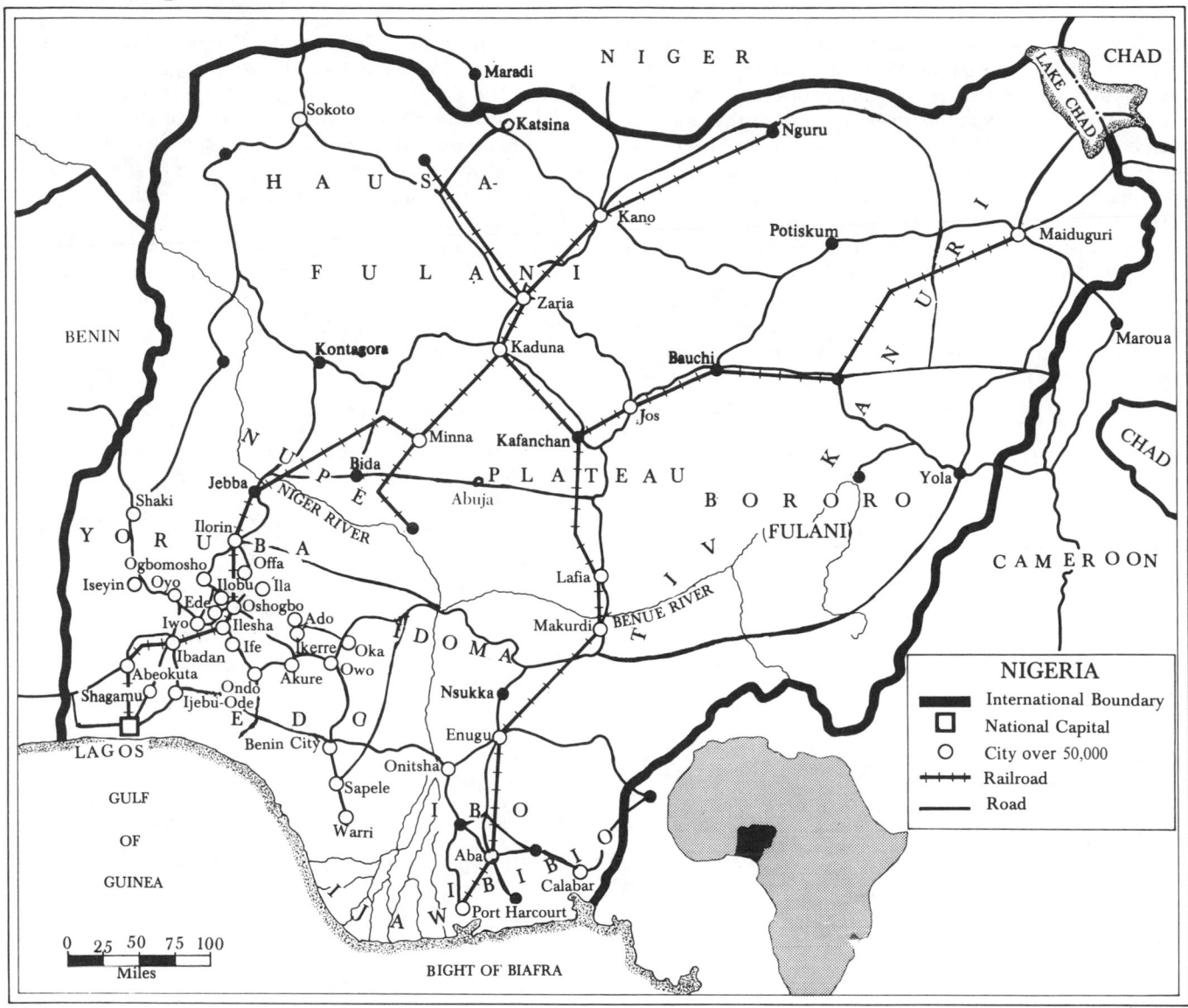

I. Basic Information

Date of Independence: October 1, 1960
Former Colonial Ruler: United Kingdom
Change in Boundaries: Addition of UN Trust Territory of Northern Cameroons on June 1, 1961
Estimated Population (1980): 72,600,000 (Note some estimates are up to 90,000,000)
Area Size (equivalent in U.S.): 356,669 sq. mi. (Texas and Colorado)

Date of Last Census: 1973 (Results repudiated by the government in August 1975—currently they use extrapolated 1963 results for government purposes)
Major Exports 1979 as Percent of Total Exports: crude petroleum—94 percent

II. Ethnic Patterns

Although Nigeria is one of the most culturally diverse states in Africa, the far northern and southern areas of the country presented few problems of ethnic classification. For the most part the northern and southern groupings have attained the state level of socio-political development, and were thus clearly bounded units. They are also locally recognized identity units and have been characterized by distinctive cultural patterns. We have grouped the urban and settled Fulani with the Hausa (as Hausa-Fulani) because of the high degree to which the Fulani have been assimilated into Hausa culture and the fact that most of them use Hausa as a first language. (We use 'Bororo' to refer to pastoralist Fulani.) The middle belt, however, is a "shatter belt" of diverse peoples who are ususally called the Plateau Peoples. We have retained this clustering though we recognize its inadequacy. The Tiv are over a million in population. Murdock subdivides these middle-belt people into three groups, but this division does not seem to have been based on culture clustering. Information is lacking to allow a more rigorous and meaningful classification at this time. Because of the large size of Nigeria, there are several ethnic groups that are less than 5 percent of the total population yet have memberships of more than half a million persons. They are included in Table 28.1. The estimated ethnic populations are based on a 1980 total population estimate for Nigeria of 72,600,000.

TABLE 28.1   Ethnic Units Over 1 Percent of Country Population

Ethnic Units	Estimated Ethnic Population 1980	Estimated Ethnic Percentage
a. Hausa-Fulani Type (plus Hausa-Fulani dominated or assimilated peoples)	21,050,000	29%
1. Hausa		
i. Daurawa, ii. Gobir, iii. Kanawa, iv. Katsinawa, v. Kebbawa, vi. Zamfarawa, vii. Zazzagawa, viii. Auyokawa		
2. Fulani, 3. Jaba, 4. Kuturmi, 5. Kagoro, 6. Janji, 7. Ninzo, 8. Kwatawa, 9. Kagoma, 10. Bugaje, 11. Kambari, 12. Dakarkari, 13. Dukkawa, 14. Fakkawa, 15. Zabermanun, 16. Gungawa, 17. Shangawa, 18. Lopawa, 19. Busawa, 20. Waja, 21. Bade, 22. Kudawa		
b. Yoruba	14,520,000	20%
1. Ahori, 2. Egba-Awori, 3. Ekiti, 4. Edo, 5. Ijebu, 6. Ijesha, 7. Itsekeri, 8. Oyo, 9. Ife, 10. Ondo, 11. Akoko		
c. Ibo	12,350,000	17%
1. Abadja, 2. Abaja, 3. Abam, 4. Alensaw, 5. Aro, 6. Awhawfia, 7. Awhawzara, 8. Awtanzu, 9. Edda, 10. Ekkpahiak, 11. Etche, 12, Eziama, 13. Ezza, 14. Ihe, 15. Iji, 16. Ika, 17. Ikwerri, 18. Ikwo, 19. Ishielu, (or Eshielu), 20. Isu, 21. Isu-Ochi, 22. Ndokki, 23. Ngbo, 24. Ngwa, 25. Nkalu, 26. Nkanu, 27. Okoba (or Okogha), 28. Onitsha-Awka, 29. Oratta, 30. Oru, 31. Ubani, 32. Ututu		
d. Tiv and Plateau Cluster	6,530,000	9%
1. Tiv, 2. Gwari (Gbari), 3. Mumuye, 4. Higgi (Kipsiki), 5. Bura, 6. Chamba, 7. Kaje, 8. Jari, 9. Eggan, 10. Kobchi, 11. Angas, 12. Birom, 13. Yergan, 14. Pangu, 15. Koro, 16. Basa, 17. Bokoro, 18. Bankal, 19. Gwandara, 20. Mada, 21, Afunu, 22. Gade, 23. Bassa Komo, 24. Burmawa, 25. Ankwai, 26. Ron, 27. Mirriam, 28. Mama Plateau, 29. rukuba, 30. Njai, 31, Gude, 32. Komma Vomni, 33. Ndorawa, 34. Glavuda, 35. Jubu, 36. Tigon, 37. Mara		
e. Ibibio and Semi-Bantu Type	4,360,000	6%
1. Ibibio, 2. Anang, 3. Ogoni, 4. Efik, 5. Ejagham, 6. Boki, 7. Ekoi, 8. Yako, 9. Ekuri, 10. Akunakuna, 11. Mbembe, 12. Ododop, 13. Orri (Ukelle)		
f. Kanuri and Kanuri-dominated peoples Type	3,630,000	5%

Ethnic Unit	Estimated Ethnic Population 1980	Estimated Ethnic Percentage
1. Kanuri, 2. Tera,		
3. Bolewa, 4. Karekare,		
5. Bede, 6. Manga,		
7. Mober, 8. Koyam,		
9. Ngizim, 10. Mandara		
g. Edo Type	2,400,000	3.3%
1. Edo (Bini), 2. Esa,		
3. Kukuruku, 4. Sobo,		
5. Urhobo, 6. Isoko		
h. Idoma-Igala-Igbirra Type	1,900,000	2.6%
1. Arago, 2. Afu,		
3. Akweya-Yachi, 4. Egede,		
5. Idoma, 6. Igala		
7. Nkum, 8. Nikim,		
9. Etulo (Utor)		
i. Ijaw	1,452,000	2%
j. Bororo (pastoral Fulani)	1,090,000	1.5%
k. Nupe	870,000	1.2%

SOURCES: G. P. Murdock, *Africa* (New York: McGraw-Hill, 1959). P. A. Talbot, *The Peoples of Southern Nigeria* (London: Oxford University Press, 1926), Vol. 3. 1963 Official Nigerian Census for Lagos, Midwestern Region, Western, Eastern, and Northern Regions. As with all population figures for Nigeria, these are extrapolations from the 1952 and 1953 censuses and do not reflect any differential growth rates.

III. Language Patterns

Following the Greenberg classification (1963), the three major language families of Africa are all represented in Nigeria, and within each family a wide variety of language sub-stocks exist. Nigeria is thus perhaps the most linguistically diverse state in Africa. The major Nigerian language of the Afro-Asiatic family is Hausa, but others exist such as Shuwa Arabic, and Tamashek (the language of the Tuareg). All seven of the sub-stocks of the Niger-Congo family are represented in Nigeria: (1) Kwa (including Ibo, Yoruba, Edo, Nupe); (2) Ijaw; (3) Benue-Niger (including Ibibio, Tiv, Jukun, and Birom); (4) Adamawa-Eastern; (4) Voltaic including the Bargu languages of the Borno state); (6) Mandingo (including the Bussa); (7) Atlantic groups (primarily Fulani). Within the Sudanic language family, Kanuri and—to a much lesser extent—Songhai exist.

The major languages of Nigeria are Hausa, Yoruba, and Ibo. Of these, only Hausa has come to serve as a wider *lingua franca*, not only in Nigeria, but in other parts of West Africa. Thus, while all scholars are agreed that Hausa is the major language of Nigeria, it is difficult to estimate the exact percentage distribution, since there are no adequate data available on multi-lingualism.[1] It is significant that Hausa in the twentieth century has come to be seen primarily as a language grouping rather than an ethnic grouping, and that a considerable number of persons have "become" Hausa through the continued use of the Hausa language. Knappert estimates the percentage of persons in Nigeria who understand Hausa at 55 percent; MacDougald estimates 36 percent; Rustow 21 percent. Kirk-Greene (1967, p. 89) estimates that 20 million persons in Northern Nigeria spoke Hausa. Our estimate for the whole of Nigeria would be about 55 percent, of whom about half use Hausa as a first language. The second language, Yoruba, is probably understood by about 27 percent of the population, primarily those of Yoruba ethnicity, although some Ibo and Hausa living in the former Western Region speak Yoruba. English con-

[1]Research at the University of Ibadan is aimed at collecting such data.

tinues to be a *lingua franca*, and the official language of Nigeria spoken by about 40% of the population. During the first civilian regime Hausa was co-equal with English as the official language of the Northern Region. With the breakup of the Northern Region, Hausa has come to be used even more extensively in some states (e.g., Kano), and less so in other states (e.g., Kwara). During the early colonial period, Hausa was the medium of instruction in the North in both primary and secondary schools. Subsequently, English was made mandatory after the fourth grade throughout Nigeria.

TABLE 28.2   Language Patterns

1. Primacy				
1st language		Hausa	(55%)	
2nd language		Yoruba	(27%)	
			Green-berg	Dalby
2. Linguistic classification		Hausa	IIIE	03A
(all ethnic units in		Yoruba	IA4	47
country over 5%)		Igbo	IA4	60
		Tiv	IA5	81
		Fulani	IA1	201
		Ibibio	IA5	62C
		Kanuri	IIB	11A
3. *Lingua franca*		Hausa		
		English		
4. Official language		English (Hausa in former Northern Region)		

SOURCES: John N. Paden, "Language Problems of National Integration in Nigeria: The Special Position of Hausa," in *Language Probelms of Developing Nations*, eds. Joshua A. Fishman, Charles A. Ferguson, and Jyotirindra Das Gupta (New York: John Wiley, 1968), pp. 199—214. Hans Wolff, "Language, Ethnic Identity, and Social Change in Southern Nigeria," *Anthropological Linguistics*, 9 (1967): 18—25. A. H. M. Kirk-Greene, "The Lingusitic Statistics of Northern Nigeria: A Tentative Presentation," *African Language Review*, 6 (1967), 75—101.

IV. Urban Patterns

Capital/largest city: Lagos (founded 1630) (A new capital is being established at Abuja in the center of the country.) The transfer of government is scheduled for 1982—83.

Dominant ethnicity/language of capital
   Major vernacular: Yoruba[1]
   Major ethnic group: Yoruba
   Major ethnic group as percent of capital's population: 59.5% (1963—64)[2]

[1]Jan Knappert, "Language Problems of the New Nations of Africa," *African Quarterly*, 5 (1965): 95—105.

[2]J. C. Caldwell and C. Okonjo, eds. *Population of Tropical Africa* (London: Longmans, 1968), p. 322. A 1974 survey by Donald Morrison found 80% of Lagos' population to identify themselves as Yorubas which probably reflects large migrations from the neighboring Yoruba states.

TABLE 28.3   Growth of Capital/Largest City

Date	Lagos
1920	100,000
1930	126,000
1940	167,000
1950	320,000
1960	560,000
1965	1,000,000 UA
1971	1,500,000 UA
1975	1,800,000 UA

SOURCES: The growth data for 1940—1960 represent staff estimates extrapolating from various sources including the 1953 Nigerian census. Metropolitan Lagos goes far beyond the administrative boundary of Lagos City into Ogun State. The estimate given here for the Lagos 1965 urban agglomeration, therefore included Mushin. The 1965 estimate is that of Pauline Baker in *African Urban Notes*, 2 (1967); 18. In 1967, when Lagos State was created, most of Metropolitan Lagos was included in the new state.

TABLE 28.4   Cities of 50,000 and Over

City	Size	Date
Lagos	1,800,000 UA	1975
(Agege)	(73,000)	1975
(Ikorodu)	(152,000)	1975
(Mushin)	(197,000)	1975
Ibadan	847,000	1975
Ogbomosho	432,000	1975
Kano	400,000	1975
Oshogbo	282,000	1975
Ilorin	282,000	1975
Abeokuta	253,000	1975
Port Harcourt	242,000	1975
Zaria	224,000	1975
Ilesha	224,000	1975
Onitsha	220,000	1975
Iwo	214,000	1975
Ado-Ekiti	213,000	1975
Kaduna	202,000	1975
Maiduguri	189,000	1975
Enugu	187,000	1975
Ede	182,000	1975
Aba	177,000	1975
Ife	176,000	1975
Ila	155,000	1975
Oyo	152,000	1975
Ikere-Ekiti	145,000	1975
Benin City	136,000	1975
Iseyin	134,500	1975
Katsina	128,000	1975
Jos	150,000	1975
Sokoto	144,000	1975
Ilobu	139,200	1975
Offa	137,600	1975
Ilawe	129,600	1975
Owo	128,000	1975
Ikirun	128,000	1975
Shaki	121,000	1975
Calabar	121,000	1975
Ondo	118,000	1975
Akure	114,000	1975
Ijebu-Ode	110,000	1975
Efon	107,000	1975
Komo	106,000	1975
Ikare	101,000	1975
Ikere	99,000	1975
Sapele	98,000	1975
Minna	96,000	1975
Warri	88,000	1975
Lafia	86,000	1975
Ikire	86,000	1975
Inisha	23,000	1975

Plus 109 cities 20,000—50,000 in size in 1963).

The 1975 estimates are from *Africa South of the Sahara 1977—78* and seem to be extrapolations from the 1963 census. These data almost certainly underestimate the rank-order size or growth rate of the capital cities of the nineteen states, particularly Benin City, Kano, Maiduguri, Lagos and Jos. With the oil wealth, there has been an extraordinary increase in urban migration in the period 1975—80, and many of the cities on our list may have doubled in size during this period.

V. Political Patterns

A. Political Parties and Elections

The pre-independence election of 1959 was based on direct suffrage in all regions, and universal suffrage except for the Northern Region where women were not enfranchised yet. The *Northern People's Congress* won a plurality of seats but not a majority. Hence they formed a coalition with the *National Council of Nigerian Citizens* (NCNC) which was in coalition with the *Northern Elements Progressive Union* (NEPU), the Northern opposition party. This coalition governed until early 1964. Just prior to the federal elections in December 1964, the coalition split and a major realignment occurred within the country. Two national coalitions emerged: the *Nigerian National Alliance* (NNA) comprised primarily of the NPC and the Western Region-based *Nigerian National Democratic Party* (NNDP); and the *United Progressive Grand Alliance* (UPGA) comprised primarily of the NCNC, NEPU, and the Western Region opposition party *Action Group* (AG). As a result of the turmoil created when certain segments of the UPGA boycotted the elections, the NNA, although they won a majority of the seats in the federal election, decided to form a national coalition by incorporating certain representatives of the UPGA (mainly former members of the NCNC) into the government. The military regime which took office in early 1966 banned all political parties and ethnic associations in Nigeria (there were 81 groups listed by name in the banning decree). Return to civilian rule was scheduled for 1976, but in October 1974, General Gowon stated that his regime would not accede to civilian rule in 1976 as had earlier been promised. The Gowon regime was overthrown in July 1975 and General Murtala Mohammed, one of the principal architects of the coup that brought Gowon to power, promised return to civilian rule no later than October 1979. Parties were to be allowed to form after October 1, 1978. A draft constitution was prepared in 1976 and in 1977—78 an elected Constituent Assembly considered the draft and prepared a final version of a new constitution which was promulgated by the

TABLE 28.5   Heads of Government

Name	Dates in Office	Age (1982)	Ethnicity	Education	Former Occupation
1. Sir Abubakar Balewa (Prime Minister)	1960—1966	Ass. 1966, age 64	Hausa-Fulani (Hausa/ Gerawa	Katsina College London School of Economics	Teacher
2. Maj. Gen. Johnson Aguiyi-Ironsi (Head Federal Military Government	1966	Ass. 1966, age 41	Ibo	School of Infantry (England)	Soldier
3. Gen. Yakubu Gowon (Head, Federal Military Government)	1966—1975	46	Plateau Cluster (Angas)	Government College, Zaria Sandhurst (England)	Soldier (Engineer)
4. General Murtala Mohammed	1975—1976	Ass. Feb. 1976 age 38	Hausa-Fulani	Sandhurst	Soldier
5. Lt. Gen. Olusegun Obasanjo	1976—1979	43	Yoruba	Military College Shrivenham (U.K.)	Soldier
6. Alhaji Shehu Shagari (President)	1979—	58	Hausa-Fulani	Kaduna teacher training college	Teacher/civil servant Politician

Federal Military Government. Local elections were held in December 1976, the first elections in the country since 1965. In the fall of 1978 the new executive federal constitution was promulgated and political parties were allowed to form and apply for registration. Stringent rules on the national character of parties as evidenced by their officers and party offices were required as well as tax and other clearances for candidates. Five parties emerged from this process, all of them led by significant political figures from the First Republic. The two dominant political figures from the south re-emerged—Awolowo led the *Unity Party of Nigeria* (UPN) and Azikiwe the *Nigerian People's Party* (NPP). The Northern politicians who had dominated the politics of the First Republic formed the *National Party of Nigeria* (NPN) and Shehu Shagari was their Presidential candidate. Aminu Kano, leader of the opposition NEPU in the First Republic formed the *People's Revolutionary Party* (PRP) and Ibrahim Waziri, cabinet minister in the First Republic formed the *Greater Nigeria People's Party* (GNPP). Each of the five parties won control of at least one state legislature and governorship. The NPN was the only party to manifest strength throughout most of the coun-

try and Shehu Shagari was elected President under a formula that not only required a plurality of the vote but at least 25 percent of the vote in at least two-thirds of the nineteen states. By a judicial decision the arithmetic was interpreted to mean 25% of the vote in 12 states and two-thirds of 25%, or 16.67% in a thirteenth state. Shagari was installed as the civilian executive President on October 1, 1979 and in the legislature an NPN and NPP coalition was able to form a majority in the Federal legislature for a time although this eventually broke up.

B. Political Leadership

The government of Abubakar Balewa held office from independence in 1960 until January 1966, after which time the leadership was military until October 1979. There do not appear to have been significant shifts in the cabinet ethnic balance between 1960 and 1966, but the cabinet turnover pattern fluctuated markedly from 1963 to 1966. General Gowon ruled with the support of the military and the government bureaucracy from 1966 to 1975, succeeding General Ironsi who was assassinated after six months in office. The only major cabinet changes in the

Gowon regime were the resignations of Awolowo (from the West) in 1971, and Tarka and Aminu Kano from the Middle Belt and North respectively, although major posts were reshuffled in 1970. General Mohammed took power in a bloodless coup in July 1975. New commissioners and state governors were installed in 1975 after the coup. Up to 10,000 senior officials and others were estimated to have been removed from office after the coup on grounds of corruption or incompetence. In February 1976, General Mohammed was assassinated in an unsuccessful coup attempt and General Obasanjo, his next-in-command, took over and continued Mohammed's programs aimed at the re-establishment of a civilian government in October 1979. Shehu Shagari, elected in August 1979 took power as the civilian President in October 1, 1979.

TABLE 28.6   Cabinet Membership: Distribution by Ethnic Unit*

Ethnicity*	Independence Cabinet	Immediate Pre-Coup Cabinet
1. Hausa-Fulani (29%)	39%	31%
2. Yoruba (20)	26	34
3. Ibo (17)	17	19
4. Tiv/Plateau (9)	4.3	3.1
5. Ibibio (6)	4.3	0
6. Kanuri (5)	4.3	9.8
7. Others (14)	4.3	3.1
N =	23	32

*Ethnic units arranged in rank order of size within country with the unit's percent of national population in parentheses.

FIGURE 28.1   Political Parties and Elections   NIGERIA

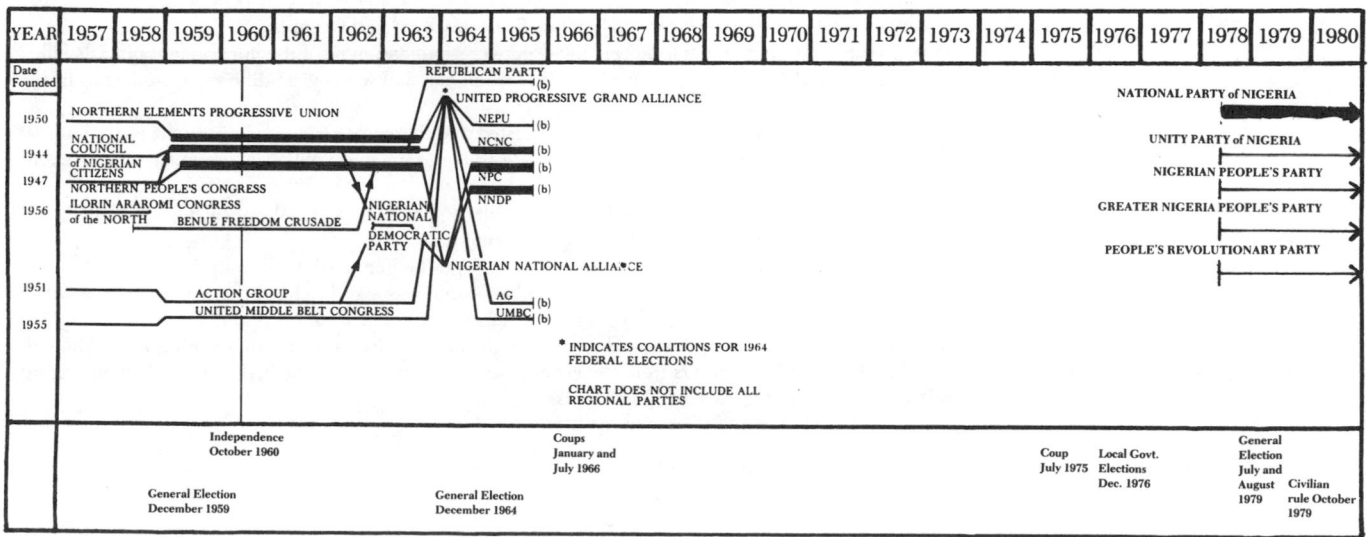

VI. National Integration and Stability

Nigeria is by far the most populous state in Africa, and the threats to national integration span the entire spectrum of African experience. Mass-elite integration was a continuing problem throughout the first civilian regime, as political leaders became increasingly remote from their constituences. Inter-ethnic integration was a problem both with regard to the three major groups—Hausa, Yoruba, Ibo—and with the multitude of smaller ethnic groups. Territorial malintegration in its primary form, was reflected in north/south regionalism. Nigeria has experienced both elite and communal types of instability and incipient mass instability. The Tiv rebellion (1960-64), the first coup (sometimes identified as two coups) (January 1966), ethnic violence (killings of Ibos and other southerners) in the North (May—October 1966). the second coup (July 1966), the civil war (May 1967—January 1970), the third coup (July 1975), and an attempted coup in February 1976 in which the Head of State was assassinated. The regroupment of government after the assassination of General Mohammed involved a major government and ruling military council reshuffle in March 1976. Although the problems of Nigeria have been formidable, the new nineteen-state federal system provides considerable accomodation of sub-national sentiment.

There have been frequent strikes by students and workers, notably the general strike of 1964, and widespread strikes and the closing of universities and other schools following the wage adjustments publication in 1974. This pattern continued in a sporadic fashion throughout the 1970s. The Agbekoya revolt of farmers in the Western State in 1971 further indicated the potential for mass rather than communal political activity in opposition to the government. The country has been ruled by decree under a state of emergency from 1966 to 1979 and arrests, while infrequent, continued with no requirement for trial. The second civilian regime (1979—present) has provided more integration and stability.

TABLE 28.7   Elite Instability

Event and Date	Characteristics
1. Coup d'État January 15, 1966	a. *Description*: Junior army officers in Kaduna, Ibadan, and Lagos killed the Premier of the Northern Region (Sir Ahmadu Bello, the Sardauna of Sokoto); the Premier of the Western Region (Chief Akintola), and two of the major federal ministers: the Prime Minister, Sir Abubakar Tafewa Balewa, and the finance minister, Chief Festus Okotie-Eboh. The remaining federal ministers turned over control of the government to a senior military officer, General Aguiyi-Ironsi, an Ibo, who suspended the constitution, and maintained order (arresting several junior officers involved in the coup). b. *Participants*: Most of the junior officers involved were Ibo, and most of the government officials killed were non-Ibo. However, there was also a generation gap and ideological differences reflected in the coup. c. *Apparent Causes*: The junior officers inolved insisted that there was no ethnic basis to the coup, but that they were trying to replace a corrupt regime, and trying to prevent politicians from using the army for political purposes.
2. Coup d'État July 29, 1966	a. *Description*: Northern army officers killed the military governor of the Western Region (Fajuyi) and General Aguiyi-Ironsi, and assumed control of the country. b. *Participants*: Troops from both the Middle Belt and from the Far North took control from national military officers and civilian advisors. Colonel Yakubu Gowon was asked to head the new regime. Murtala Mohammed, later to become Head of State, was one of the principal architects of the coup. c. *Apparent Causes*: The coup was partly a reaction by Northerners against rapid centralization, and alleged exclusion of Northerners from the government. This event could be coded as a rebellion since it reflected such considerable communal unrest.

Event and Date	Characteristics
3. Coup d'État July 29, 1975	a. *Description*: General Gowon was overthrown by a group of Nigerian army officers while he was at the Organization of African Unity (OAU) meetings in Kampala, Uganda. The coup was bloodless, apparently reflecting agreement on the action by the senior army officers. b. *Participants*: Officers in the army. Most prominent to the public was Colonel Joseph Garba, recently removed commander of Gowon's guard unit at his residence, Dodan Barracks. Who was instrumental in the coup was not clear since there appeared to be widespread consensus in the army and no units were reported to have resisted the change of leadership. General Mohammed appears to have been a major figure in the events, though, as he had been in the July 1966 coup. c. *Apparent Causes*: The generally cited causes included army dissatisfaction with Gowon's leadership and in particular with the problems of corrupton, inflation, and general mismanagement of the economy. Other aspects revolved around the failure to replace the military governors, widely characterized as corrupt, as promised, and Gowon's refusal to return to civilian rule and to consult with his military colleagues.
4. Attempted Coup February 13, 1976	a. *Description*: A group of soldiers from the physical training corps under Lt. Col. Dimka assassinate General Mohammed and his bodyguards in an apparent attempt to restore Gowon to power. They are captured and a large number of soliders and civilians are arrested. Col. Taiwo, governor of Kwara State, was abducted and murdered in Ilorin and Col. Dumuje was shot in Lagos. b. *Participants*: Lt. Col. Dimka and members of the physical training corps of the Nigerian army backed by a number of other officers in the army including Major General Bissala, the Minister of Defense, and at least 30 other officers and civilians. c. *Apparent Causes*: Radical young officers felt that the new regime was not oriented to the needs of the man on the street according to some accounts. The actual causes appear to relate more to issues of narrow self-interest including the threatened demobilization of parts of the army and the massive dismissal of civil servants since the July 1975 coup.

SOURCES: James O'Connell "The Fragility of Stability: The Fall of the Nigerian Federal Government, 1966," in *Power and Protest in Black Africa*, eds. Robert I. Rotberg and Ali A. Mazrui (New York: Oxford University Press, 1970), pp. 1012—1034. Walter Schwartz, *Nigeria* (New York: Praeger), 1968, pp. 191—231. B. J. Dudley *Instability and Political Order: Politics and Crisis in Nigeria*, (Ibadan: University of Ibadan Press, 1973). K. W. J. Post and M. Vickers *Structure and Conflict in Nigeria: 1960—65* (Madison: University of Wisconsin Press, 1973).

TABLE 28.8   Communal Instability

Event and Date	Characteristics
1. Rebellion August—October 1960; 1964	a. *Description*: In mid-1960 groups of Tiv ranging in number from 50 to 500 persons burned the houses of Chiefs and NPC members in the Benue Plateau area. By the time order was restored, thousands of people had been arrested, although not more than 25 were killed in all. In February 1961, with federal elections impending there were renewed attacks by Tiv members on government facilities and supporters. The Nigerian army engaged in a counter-attack throughout the rest of 1964, and several hundred people were killed. b. *Participants*: Tiv traditional elements with a long history of "chiefless" society and local autonomy resisted both the regional and national governments and the government-appointed Tiv chiefs. The rebellion had no predominant leadership. Although Joseph Tarka and the *United Middle Belt Congress* (UMBC) were identified with the demand for greater autonomy, there is no evidence as to their direct involvement in the rebellion (even though some UMBC supporters may have participated). c. *Apparent Causes*: Tiv elements demanded greater autonomy in the Northern Region. Much of the dissatisfaction was directed against the Native Authority and the NPC. There was no attempt to secede or take over the government.

Event and Date	Characteristics
2. Ethnic Violence May-October 1966	a. *Description*: On May 29, 1966 in most of the major far northern cities there were riots between northerners and Ibos/easterners. The riots lasted for about three days. Shortly thereafter with the successful northern counter-coup (late July), many easterners in the North began to leave for the Eastern Region. In late September and early October many of those who remained or were in the process of emigration, were killed by northern army elements. The estimate of persons killed in both May and October was put at 30,000 by the former Biafran government and around 5,000 by the Nigerian government. b. *Participants*: Ibos who had been living in the North were attacked in May, primarily by Hausa urban dwellers. In October, elements of the army were clearly involved. c. *Apparent Causes*: The May riots were partly the result of northern frustration with the Ironsi regime and resentment against the dominant position of the educated Ibos in the North. The October killings are interpreted by many as the actual origins of the civil war, since the army had been broken up by region-of-origin after the July coup.
3. Civil War May 1967—January 1970	a. *Description*: In May 1967 the former Eastern Region of Nigeria was declared to be a sovereign state. "Biafra." In July, Biafran troops crossed through the Mid-West Region and into the Western Region in an attempted attack on Lagos. Federal troops began major attacks on Biafra from the North and West and through a naval blockade from the south. By the summer of 1968 most major towns in Biafra plus most non-Ibo areas were under Federal control, although a number of important cities changed hands regularly. In the summer of 1969 Biafran counter-attacks were extended to the Mid-West Region. The civil war continued despite immense casualties and various attempts at negotiation until Biafra's surrender in January 1970. b. *Participants*: Biafrans were predominantly Ibo but received some support from minority groups (e.g., Ibibio). The Biafran leader was Lt. Col. Odumegwu Ojukwu. Nigeria had approximately a 100,000-man army. Biafrans regarded this as a total war and mobilized the entire population. Material support to the federal government came from Britain and the USSR; material support for Biafra came from France. Military casualties were estimated to be very high (over 100,000), but most deaths were the result of starvation in Biafra (estimates of the number of dead range from half a million to two million). c. *Apparent Causes*: Biafra demanded self-determination in a state which could protect the lives and properties of its citizens. Nigeria demanded national unity as a preliminary to negotiations regarding the form of civilian government (including inter-regional relations).

SOURCES: John P. Mackintosh, *Nigerian Government and Politics* (Evanston, Ill.: Northwestern University Press, 1966), pp. 498—501. *Africa Report* had a number of articles on the civil war between 1967 and 1970.

TABLE 28.10 Annual Instabilty Events: Independence Through 1979—Nigeria

Year	'61	'62	'63	'64	'65	'66	'67	'68	'69	'70	'71	'72	'73	'74	'75	'76	'77	'78	'79
ELITE INSTABILITY																			
Assassinations																1			
Plots		1		1								1							
Attempted Coups d'État																			
Coups d'État						2									1				
COMMUNAL INSTABILITY																			
Ethnic Violence						1													
Irredentism																			
Rebellion				1															
Civil War							1	1	1										

Year	'61	'62	'63	'64	'65	'66	'67	'68	'69	'70	'71	'72	'73	'74	'75	'76	'77	'78	'79
MASS INSTABILITY																			
Revolt																			
Revolution																			
TURMOIL																			
Demonstrations							5												
Strikes (no. days)			11	12	2														
Riots (no. days)		5	2	6	11	20	3	4	10										
Terrorism											4								
Declarations of Emergency		1			1	2	1	1			3								
CABINET INSTABILITY																			
Realloc. and new appts.	4	10	11	4	23	3	16				1	8							
New members	3	10		3	4	15	11				2	3	1						
Resig. and Dismissals	1	1		3	8	1					2	1	1						
No. of members (max.) (maximum in year)	15	24	24	27	28	11	11	15	15	15	17	17							

VII. Selected References

BIBLIOGRAPHY

Aguolu, C. C. *Nigerian Civil War, 1967—70, An Annotated Bibliography*. Boston: G.K. Hall, 1973.

Aguolu, C. C. *Nigeria: A Comprehensive Bibliography in the Humanities and Social Sciences, 1900—1971*. Boston, G.K. Hall, 1975.

Alati, G. A. and O. G. Tamuno, eds. *Nigerian Publications 1950—1970*. Ibadan: Ibadan University Press, 1977.

Baum, Edward. *A Comprehensive Periodical Bibliography of Nigeria, 1960—1970*. Athens, Ohio: Center for International Studies, Ohio University, 1975. Papers in International Studies, Africa Series, No. 24.

Ita, Nduntuei O. *Bibliography of Nigeria: A Survey of Anthropolotical and Lingusitic Writings from the Earliest Time to 1966*. New York: Africana, 1971.

GENERAL

Coleman, James S. *Nigeria, Background to Nationalism*. Berkeley: University of California Press, 1958, reprinted 1971.

Crowder, Michael. *The Story of Nigeria*, rev. ed. London: Faber, 1966.

Nelson, H. D. et al. *Area Handbook for Nigeria*, 4th ed. Washington, D.C.: Government Printing Office, 1982.

Onimoloye, S. A. ed. *Biographia Nigeriana: A Biographical Dictionary of Eminent Nigerians*. Boston: G.K. Hall, 1977.

Schwartz, Frederick A. O., Jr. *Nigeria: The Tribes, the Nations, or the Race—The Politics of Independence*. Cambridge: The MIT Press, 1965.

Schwartz, Walter. *Nigeria*. New York: Praeger, 1968.

Williams, G. *Nigeria: Economy and Society*. Totowa, N.J.: Rowan and Littlefield, 1977.

ECONOMIC

Aboyade, Ojetunji. *Foundations of an African Economy*. New York: Praeger, 1966.

Ayida, A. A. and H. M. A. Onitiri, eds. *Reconstruction and Development in Nigeria: Proceedings of a National Conference*. New York: Oxford University Press, 1972.

Dean, Edwin. *Plan Implementation in Nigeria, 1962—1966*. London: Oxford University Press, 1974.

Diejomaoh, Victor P. *Economic Development in Nigeria: Its Problems, Challenges and Prospects*. Princeton: Princeton University Press, 1965.

Edundare, R. O. *An Economic History of Nigeria, 1860—1960*. London: Methuen, 1973.

Hay, A. and R. Smith. *Interregional Trade and Monetary Flows in Nigeria, 1964*. London: Oxford University Press, 1970.

Helleiner, G. R. *Peasant Agriculture, Government, and Economic Growth in Nigeria*. Homewood, Ill.: Irwin, 1966.

International Monetary Fund. "Nigeria." In *Surveys of African Economies*, Vol. 6. Washington, D.C.: I.M.F., 1975.

Kilby, Peter, *Industrialisation in an Open Economy: Nigeria, 1945—1966*. London: Cambridge University Press, 1969.

Nafziger, E. W. *African Capitalism: A Case Study in Nigerian Entrepreneurship*. Stanford: Hoover Institution, 1977.

Pearson, S. R. *Petroleum and the Nigerian Economy*. Stanford: Stanford University Press, 1970.

Schatz, L. H. *Petroleum in Nigeria*.Ibadan: Oxford University Press, 1970.

Schatz, S. P. *Nigerian Capitalism*. Berkeley, Calif.: University of California Press, 1977.

Stolper, W. F. *Planning Without Facts: Lessons in Resource Allocation from Nigeria's Development*. Cambridge: Harvard University Press, 1966.

Tims, W. *Nigeria: Options for Long-Term Development*. Baltimore: Johns Hopkins University Press, 1974.

SOCIAL

Abernethy, David B. *The Political Dilemma of Popular Education: An African Case*. Stanford, Calif.: Stanford University Press, 1970.

Adeyeye, Samuel O. *The Co-operative in Nigeria: Yesterday, Today and Tomorrow*. Gottingen: Vandenhoech and Ruprecht, 1978.

Ajayi, J. F. Ade. *Christian Missions in Nigeria: The Making of a New Elite*. Evanston, Ill.: Northwestern University Press, 1965.

Ajayi, J. F. Ade, ed. *City of Lagos*. London: Longmans, 1975.

Baldwin, D. E. and C. M. Baldwin. *The Yoruba of South Western Nigeria: An Indexed Bibliography*. Boston: G.K. Hall, 1976.

Bishop, Vaughn F. "Language Acquisition and Value Change in the Kano Urban Area" in John N. Paden

ed. , *Values, Identities and National Integration*. Evanston, Ill. Northwestern University Press, 1980, pp. 183-96.

Buchanan, Keith M. and J. C. Pugh. *Land and People in Nigeria: The Human Geography of Nigeria and its Environmental Background*. London: University of London Press, 1955.

Brann, C. M. B. *Language in Education and Society in Nigeria*. Quebec City, Canada: International Center for Research on Bilingualism, 1974.

Eades, J. S. *The Yoruba Today*. New York: Cambridge University Press, 1981.

Ekanem, I. I. *The 1963 Nigerian Census*. Benin City, Nigeria: Ethiope Publishing, 1972.

Fagg, William. *Nigerian Images*. New York: Praeger, 1963.

Henderson, Richard. *The King in Every Man: Evolutionary Trends in Onitsha Ibo Society and Culture*. New Haven, Conn.: Yale University Press, 1972.

Hill, Polly. *Rural Hausa: A Village and a Setting*. New York: Cambridge University Press, 1972.

Hill, Polly. *Population, Prosperity and Poverty: Rural Kano, 1900 and 1970*. New York: Cambridge University Press, 1977.

LeVine, Robert A. *Dreams and Deeds: Achievement Motivation in Nigeria*. Chicago: University of Chicago Press, 1966.

Lloyd, P.C. *Power and Independence*. Boston: Routledge and Kegan Paul, 1974.

Lloyd, P. C., A. L. Mabogunje, and B. Awe. *The City of Ibadan*. London: Cambridge University Press, 1967.

Lucas, David and McWiliam, John. *Population in Nigeria: A Select Bibliography*. Chapel Hill, N.C.: Carolina Population Center, 1974.

Luckham, R. *The Nigerian Military: A Sociological Analysis of Authority and Revolt 1960—67*. New York: Cambridge University Press, 1971.

Mabogunje, Akin L. *Urbanization in Nigeria*. New York: Africana, 1969.

Marris, P. *Family and Social Change in an African City*. Evanston, Ill.: Northwestern University Press, 1962.

Otite, O. *Autonomy and Dependence: the Urhobo Kingdom of Okpe in Modern Nigeria*. Ibadan, Nigeria: University of Ibadan Press, 1973.

Udo, R. K. *Geographical Regions of Nigeria*. London: Heinemann, 1970.

Van den Berghe, P. L. *Power and Privelege at an African University* . London: Routledge and Kegan Paul, 1973.

POLITICAL

Adelayo, Augustus. "Policy-Making in Nigerian Political Administration," London: *Journal of Administration Overseas*, vol. 18, no. 1, January 1979, pp. 4—14.

Akinsanya, A. "The Count Down to Civilian Rule in Nigeria: The Constituent Assembly." London: *Journal of Administration Overseas*, vol. 18, no. 1, January 1979, pp. 34—45.

Arnold, Guy. *Modern Nigeria*. London: Longmans, 1977.

Baker, Pauline H. *Urbanization and Political Change*: *The Politics of Lagos, 1917—1967*. Berkeley: University of California Press, 1974.

Bienen, H. and V. P. Diejomaoh. *Political Economy of Income Distribution in Nigeria*. New York: Holmes and Meier, 1981.

Biersteker, T. J. *Distortion or Development*: Contending Perspectives on the Multinational Corporation. Cambridge, Mass.: The MIT Press, 1978.

Cohen, Robin. *Labour and Politics in Nigeria*: *1945—1971*. New York: Africana, 1974.

De St. Jorre, John. *The Brothers War*: *Biafra and Nigeria*. Ibadan: Ibadan University Press, 1974.

Dudley, B. J. *Parties and Politics in Northern Nigeria*. London: Cass, 1968.

Dudley, B. J. *Instability and Political Order*: *Politics and Crisis in Nigeria*. Ibadan: University of Ibadan Press, 1973.

Idang, G. J. *Internal Politics and Foreign Policy, 1960—1966*. Ibadan: Ibadan University Press, 1974.

Joseph, Richard. "Political Party and Ideology in Nigeria." *Review of African Political Economy*, no. 18, 1979, pp. 78—90.

Kirk-Greene, A. H. M., ed. *Crisis and Conflict in Nigeria*: *A Documentary Sourcebook, 1966—1970*, 2 vols. London: Oxford University Press, 1971.

Mackintosh, John P., ed. *Nigerian Government and Politics*. Evanston, Ill.: Northwestern University Press, 1966.

Miners, N. J. *The Nigerian Army, 1956—1966*. London: Methuen, 1971.

Murrary, D. J., ed. *Studies in Nigerian Administration*. London: Hutchinson, 1970.

Nafziger, E. W. "The Political Economy of Disintegration in Nigeria." *Journal of Modern African Studies*, 1973, pp. 505—36.

Orewa, G. O. "The Role of Traditional Rulers in Administration." In *Quarterly Journal of Administration*, vol. 12, no. 2, January 1978, pp. 151—65.

Ostheimer, J. M. *Nigerian Politics*. New York: Harper and Row, 1973.

Oyediran, Oyeleye, ed. *Nigerian Development and Politics under Military Rule, 1966—79*. London: Macmillan, 1979.

Paden, John N. *Religion and Political Culture in Kano*. Berkeley: University of California Press, 1973.

Panter-Brick, S. K., ed. *Nigerian Politics and Military Rule*: *Prelude to the Civil War*. London: University of London, The Athlone Press, 1970.

Panter-Brick, S. K., ed. *Soldiers and Oil*: *The Political Transformation of Nigeria*. London: Cass, 1978.

Peil, M. *Nigerian Politics*: *The People's View*. London: Cassell, 1976.

Post, Kenneth, W. J. and Michael Vickers. *Structure and Conflict in Nigeria, 1960—1965*. Madison: University of Wisconsin Press, 1973.

Segun, M. *Friends, Nigerians, Countrymen*. Ibadan: Oxford University Press, 1978.

Sklar, Richard L. *Nigerian Political Parties*: *Power in an Emergent African Nation*. Princeton: Princeton University Press, 1963.

Smock, Audrey C. *Ibo Politics*: *The Role of Ethnic Unions in Eastern Nigeria*. Cambridge, Mass.: Harvard University Press, 1971.

Wayas, John. *Nigeria's Leadership Role in Africa*. London: Macmillan, 1979.

Whitaker, C. S. *The Politics of Tradition*: *Continuity and Change in Northern Nigeria, 1946—1966*. Princeton: Princeton University Press, 1970.

Wolpe, H. *Urban Politics in Nigeria*: *A Study of Port Harcourt*. Berkeley: University of California Press, 1974.

29. Rwanda

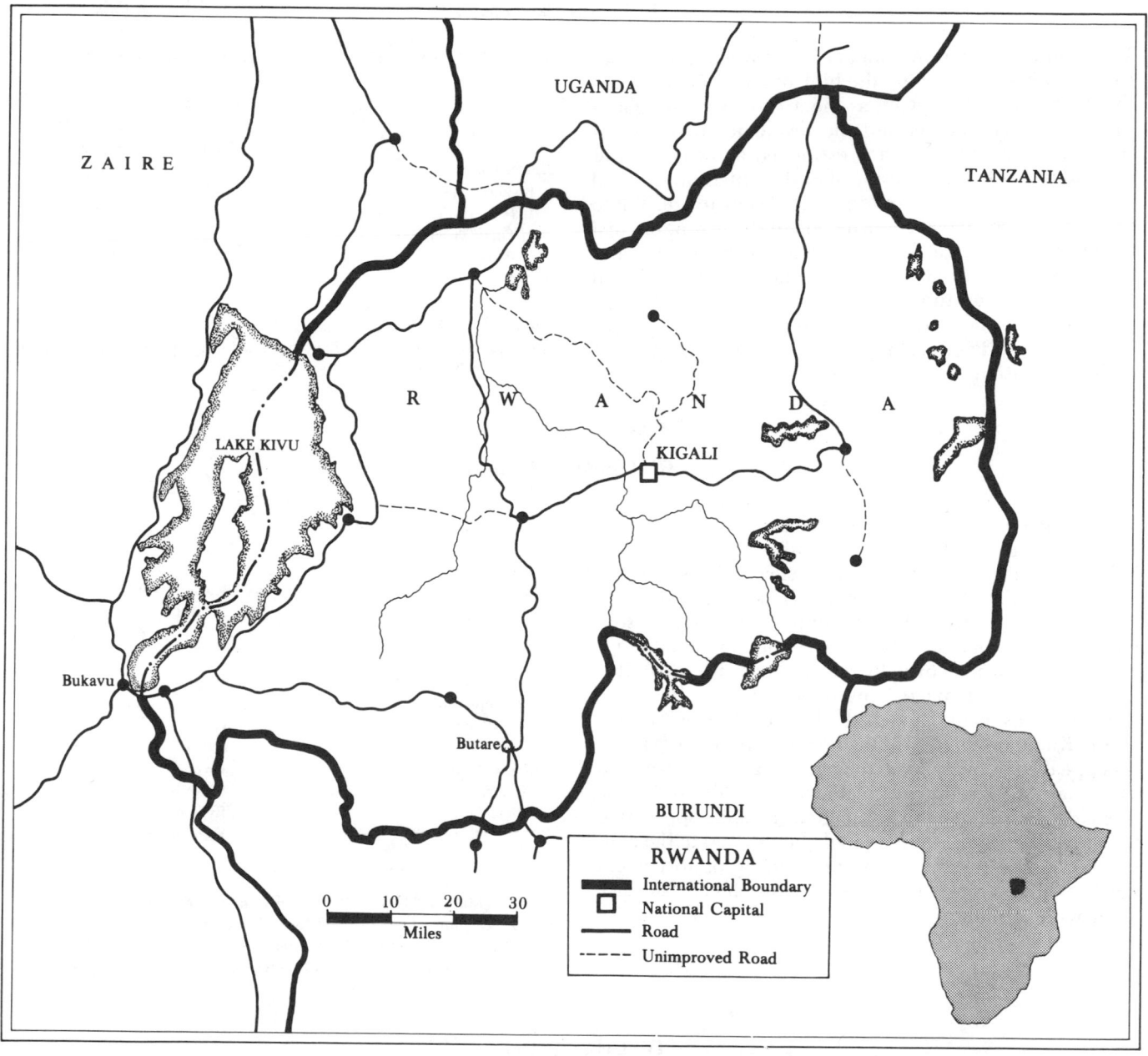

I. Basic Information

Date of Independence: July 1, 1962
Former Colonial Ruler: Belgium
Change in Boundaries: Before Independence it was part of the UN trust territory of Ruanda-Urundi
Former Name: Ruanda
Estimated Population (1980): 4,705,000

Area Size (equivalent in U.S.): 10,169 sq. mi. (Vermont)
Date of Last Census: 1978
Major Exports 1976 as Percent of Total Exports: coffee—77 percent; tea—7 percent; cassiterite (tin ore)—6 percent

II. Ethnic Patterns

The ethnic situation in Rwanda is much like that in Burundi, with Hutu forming the bulk of the population and the Tutsi formerly serving as the aristocracy. In light of the Hutu/Tutsi conflict and the resultant Tutsi emigration, the Tutsi population is estimated at 10 percent at the end of 1979. We have adjusted the Tutsi and the total population estimates here to reflect this estimate. While we do not have official confirmation of the extent of Tutsi emigration, it is clear that a large number have left and the 1973 massacres of Tutsis have undoubtedly added to the problem even though recent government policy appears to be committed to resolving the inter-ethnic conflict. The Twa (Pygmies) represent less than one percent of the population.

TABLE 29.1   Ethnic Units Over 5 Percent of Country Population

Ethnic Units	Estimated Ethnic Population (1980)	Estimated Ethnic Percentage
a. Rwanda type	4,658,000	99%
1. Hutu (Bahutu, Wakhutu)	(4,187,000)	(89%)
2. Tutsi (Tussi, Batusi, Watutsi)	(471,000)	(10%)

SOURCE: J. J. Maquet, *The Premise of Inequality* (London, International African Institute, Oxford University Press, 1960), p. 10. *Africa South of the Sahara 1975*, p. 687.

III. Language Patterns

The ethnic composition of Rwanda is sometimes viewed as Hutu (of the Bantu language family), and Tutsi (of the Nilotic language family). It is also viewed by some (see Murdock, 1959; Maquet, 1960; d'Hertefelt, 1965) as a single society—"Rwanda." In either case, both "segments" of Rwanda society share a common Bantu language, Kinyarwanda (usually referred to as Rwanda). It is clear that this language is used most widely by Hutu/Tutsi peoples who have had close contact with each other. Knappert suggests that 100 percent of the population speaks Rwanda. MacDougald suggests 79 percent. There are still groups of isolated Hutu who do not use this language, hence our estimate of Rwanda speakers is 98 percent. Swahili is increasingly being used in the eastern portion of Rwanda, and our estimate of 15 percent may be low. French continues as the official language along with Rwanda.

TABLE 29.2   Language Patterns

		Greenberg	Dalby
1. Primacy			
1st language	Rwanda (98%)		
2nd language	Swahili (15%)		
2. Linguistic classification	Rwanda	IA5	E1
(all ethnic units in	(Hutu	IA5	
country over 5%)	(Tutsi	IIE1)	
	Swahili	IA5	C4
3. *Lingua francas*	Rwanda, Swahili		
4. Official languages	Rwanda, French		

SOURCES: Marcel d'Hertefelt, "The Rwanda of Rwanda" in *Peoples of Africa*, ed. James L. Gibbs, Jr. (New York: Holt, Rinehart and Winston, 1965), pp. 403-440. J. J. Maquet, *The Premise of Inequality* (London: International African Institute, Oxford University Press, 1961).

IV. Urban Patterns

Capital/largest city: Kigali (founded ca. 14th century)
Dominant ethnicity/language of capital
  Major vernacular: Rwanda[1]

Major ethnic group: Rwanda
Major ethnic group as percent of capital's population: Nearly 100%

[1]Jan Knappert, "Language Problems of the New Nations of Africa," *African Quarterly*, 5 (1965): 95—105.

TABLE 29.3   Growth of Capital/Largest City

Date	Kigali
1950	ca. 3,000
1960	5,000*
1965	15,000
1970	54,000
1978	118,000

*UN Demographic Yearbook 1963; various editions of Statesman's Yearbook; Europa Yearbook 1977 V. II, p. 1386; and Europa Yearbook 1979. Europe Outremer, Nov. 1979 estimates Kigali's population as 118,000. 1978 figure is a census result.

TABLE 29.4   Cities of 20,000 and Over

City	Size	Date
Kigali	118,000	1978
Butare	22,000	1979

SOURCE: 1978 census.

V. Political Patterns

A. Political Parties and Elections

Political parties in Rwanda were drawn along ethnic lines, with the dominant Hutu controlling the *Parti Républicain du Mouvement d'Emancipation des Hutus* (PARMEHUTU) and the *Association pour la Promotion Sociale de la Masse* (APROSOMA). The *Union Nationale Rwandaise* (UNAE) served as the opposition voice for the minority Tutsi. By 1969 the PARMEHUTU was the only active party. The 1969 election gave the PARMEHUTU all 47 seats in the National Assembly and President Kayibanda 90.3 percent of the vote. All political activity was banned after the July 5, 1973 coup. In July 1975, Gen. Habyarimana announced the formation of a new party, the *Mouvement Révolutionnaire National pour le Développement* (MRND), and elections were held in 1976. In December 1978, a constitutional referendum was approved by 90 percent of the voters. The constitu-tion called for a return to civilian government and the establishment of a one-party state. In addition, Major General Habyarimana was re-elected President for another 5 year term. Habyarimana was the only presidential candidate and represented the MRND.

B. Political Leadership

Grégoire Kayibanda was head of government from independence to 1973. His cabinet was entirely Hutu, with frequent turnovers in membership from 1964 to 1967. When General Habyarimana took power he appointed a Tutsi as a cabinet member to symbolize his commitment to end the inter-ethnic rivalry which was the primary political force in Rwandan politics. In late April 1980, two members of the cabinet were purged on charges of corruption.

TABLE 29.5   Head of Government (Post-Independence)

Name	Dates in Office	Age (1982)	Ethnicity	Education	Former Occupation
1. Grégoire Kayibanda (President)	1962— 1973	d. Dec. 1976, age 52	Mixed Hutu/ Congolese	Grand Seminary of Nyakibanda	Teacher Newspaperman
2. Major Gen. Juvénal Habyarimana (President)	1973— present	45	Hutu	Lovanium Cadet School (Belgium) and Kigali Military College	Soldier

TABLE 29.6   Cabinet Membership: Distribution by Ethnic Unit*

Ethnicity*	Independence Cabinet	1967 Cabinet	1972 Cabinet
1. Hutu (89%)	80%	100%	100%
2. Tutsi (10)**	20	0	0
3. Others (1)	1	0	0
N =	12	13	12

*Ethnic units arranged in rank order of size within country with the unit's percent of national population in parentheses.

**At the time of independence the Tutsi amounted to some 16 percent of the population.

FIGURE 29.1   Political Parties and Elections   RWANDA

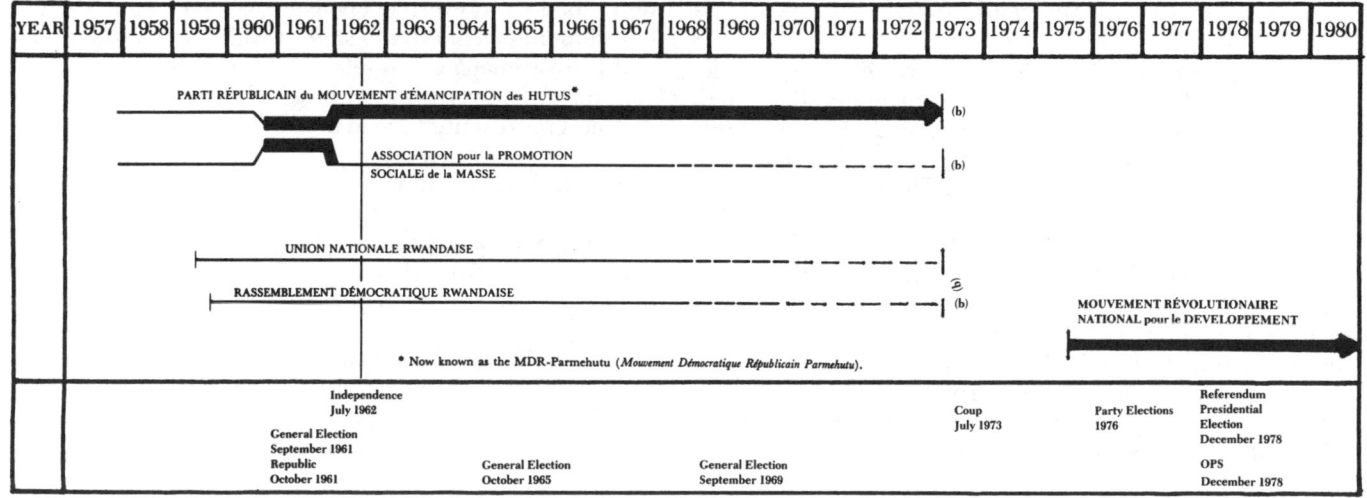

VI. National Integration and Stability

Political instability in post-independence Rwanda is a legacy of the intensive and revolutionary civil war fought in late 1959, in which the historically long-subjected Hutu majority overthrew the minority Tutsi aristocracy in a *coup d'état* at Gitarama, January 28, 1961, a year and a half before independence. Since that time there have been renewed conflicts between the Hutu, now governing, and the Tutsi, many of whom had become refugees in Burundi. The overthrow of Kayibanda was prompted by his failure to stop the spring 1973 massacres of Tutsis.

TABLE 29.7   Elite Instability

Event and Date	Characteristics
Coup d'État July 5, 1973	a. *Description*: General Habyarimana and the army depose Kayibanda in a bloodless coup.
	b. *Participants*: Army under the leadership of Major General Habyarimana.
	c. *Apparent Causes*: Habyarimana stated that the ousted government had done nothing to calm the interethnic conflict which had resulted in Tutsi massacres in the spring. It was also maintained that a massacre of certain people (presumably Tutsis) was planned. This was, in part expected to have been in reaction to the Tutsi-led massacres of Hutu in neighboring Burundi.

TABLE 29.8   Communal Instability

Event and Date	Characteristics
Civil War 1963—64, 1966, 1973	a. *Description*: In an aftermath of the pre-independence civil war of 1959, civil war again broke out in Rwanda in 1963, initiated and intensified by a series of invasions from Burundi which were led by Tutsi refugees. The refugees and some of their fellow-Tutsi still residing in Rwanda attempted to overthrow the government of their former Hutu subjects. Successive invasions on November 25, December 20 and 27, 1963, were countered by Rwandese forces, and resulted in extensive mass reprisals during the following year. Betwen 5,000 and 14,000 people are estimated to have been killed at this time. Evidence of continuing civil war is obtainable from reports of Tutsi-Hutu clashes in 1966 in which 200 were estimated to have been killed. Hostilties flared up again in 1973 with the killing of as many as 500 Tutsis and a program of expelling Tutsis from schools, government, and business employment. b. *Participants*: Although the initial action was a war between the government forces and a "foreign" invader, most of the serious violence and killing was the result of local action against Tutsi in Rwanda by Hutu officials and citizens, acting only under general instructions to take measures for their own security. c. *Apparent Causes*: There are no apparent causes apart from the desire of certain Tutsi refugees, identified only as "agitators" by a UN investigating commission, to regain their former political status in Rwanda. The massacre of Hutus in Burundi by Tutsis in 1972 and 1973 was instrumental in setting off the reaction and counter-massacres in Rwanda.

SOURCES: Aaron Segal, "Rwanda—The Underlying Causes," *Africa Report*, 9 (April 1964): 3—6; and "United Nations Findings on Rwanda and Burundi," in the same issue, pp. 7—8.

TABLE 29.10   Annual Instability Events: Independence Through 1979—Rwanda

Year	'61	'62	'63	'64	'65	'66	'67	'68	'69	'70	'71	'72	'73	'74	'75	'76	'77	'78	'79
ELITE INSTABILITY																			
Assassinations																			
Plots																			
Attempted Coups d'État																			
Coups d'État													1						
COMMUNAL INSTABILITY																			
Ethnic Violence																			
Irredentism																			
Rebellion																			
Civil War			1	1		1							1						
MASS INSTABILITY																			
Revolt																			
Revolution																			
TURMOIL																			
Demonstrations																			
Strikes (no. days)																			
Riots (no. days)																			
Terrorism			1																
Declarations of Emergency			1																

TABLE 29.10 Annual Instability Events: Independence Through 1979—Rwanda

Year	'61	'62	'63	'64	'65	'66	'67	'68	'69	'70	'71	'72	'73	'74	'75	'76	'77	'78	'79
CABINET INSTABILITY																			
Realloc. and new appts.			3	2	6	1	3	2											
New members					6		1	2			4	6							
Resig. and Dismissals			1	2	4			2				4							
No. of members (max.)																			
(maximum in year)			12	12	11	11	12	14	13	13	17	19							

VII. Selected References

BIBLIOGRAPHY

Clement, Joseph R. A. M. *Essai de Bibliographie de Ru-anda-Urundi.* Usumbura: n.p., 1959.

Levesque, Albert. *Contribution to the National Bibliography of Rwanda, 1965—1970.* Boston, G.K. Hall, 1979.

GENERAL

Lemarchand, René. *Rwanda and Burundi.* New York: Praeger, 1970.

Office de l'Information et des Relations Publiques du Congo Belge et du Ruanda-Urundi. *Ruanda-Urundi, Geography and History.* Brussels: 1960.

U.S. Department of the Army. *Area Handbook for Rwanda.* Pamphlet No. 550—84. Washington, D.C.: Government Printing Office, 1969.

POLITICAL

Chronique de Politique Étrangère. *Decolonisation et Independence de Rwanda et du Burundi.* Brussels: Institut Royal des Relations Internationales, 1963.

Codere, Helen. "Political Instability in Africa: The Case of Rwanda and Burundi." *Civilisations*, 16 (1966): 307—337.

Lemarchand, René. "The Coup in Rwanda." In *Power and Protest in Black Africa*, eds. Robert I. Rotberg and Ali Mazrui eds. New York: Oxford University Press, 1970.

Linden, I. *Church and Revolution in Rwanda.* Manchester, Manchester University Press, New York, Africana Publishing Co., 1977.

Weinstein, W. "Military Continuities in the Rwanda State." *Journal of Asian and African Studies*, 12, 1—4, Jan.—Oct. 1977, pp. 48—56.

ECONOMIC

France. *Ministere de la Cooperation Rwanda, donnees statistiques sur les activites culturelles et sociales.* Paris, Le Service, 1975.

International Monetary Fund. "Rwanda." In *Surveys of African Economies*, vol. 5. Washington, D.C.: I.M.F., 1973.

Leurquin, Philipe P. *Agricultural Change in Ruanda-Urundi, 1945—1960.* Stanford, Calif.: Stanford University Food Research Institute, 1963.

SOCIAL

d'Hertefelt, Marcel. "The Rwanda of Rwanda." In *Peoples of Africa*, ed. James L. Gibbs, Jr., pp. 403—440. New York: Holt, Rinehart and Winston, 1965.

Hanf, T., P. V. Dies, W. Mann, J. H. Wolff. *Education et Developpement au Rwanda.* Munich: Weltforum Verlag, 1974.

Harrow, Jean Paul, et. at. *Le Ruanda-Urundi: ses resources naturelles des populations.* Brussels: Les Naturalists Belges, 1956.

Hewbury, M.C. "Ethnicity in Rwanda." *Africa*, 48, 1, 1978, pp. 17—28.

Liege Universite. Foundation pour les recherces scientifiques au Congo Belge et au Rwanda-Urundi. *Le probleme de l'enseignement dans le Ruanda-Urundi.* Elizabethville: C.E.P.S.I., 1958.

Maquet, J. J. *The Premise of Inequality in Ruanda: A Study of Political Relations in a Central African Kingdom.* London: Oxford University Press, 1961.

30. Senegal

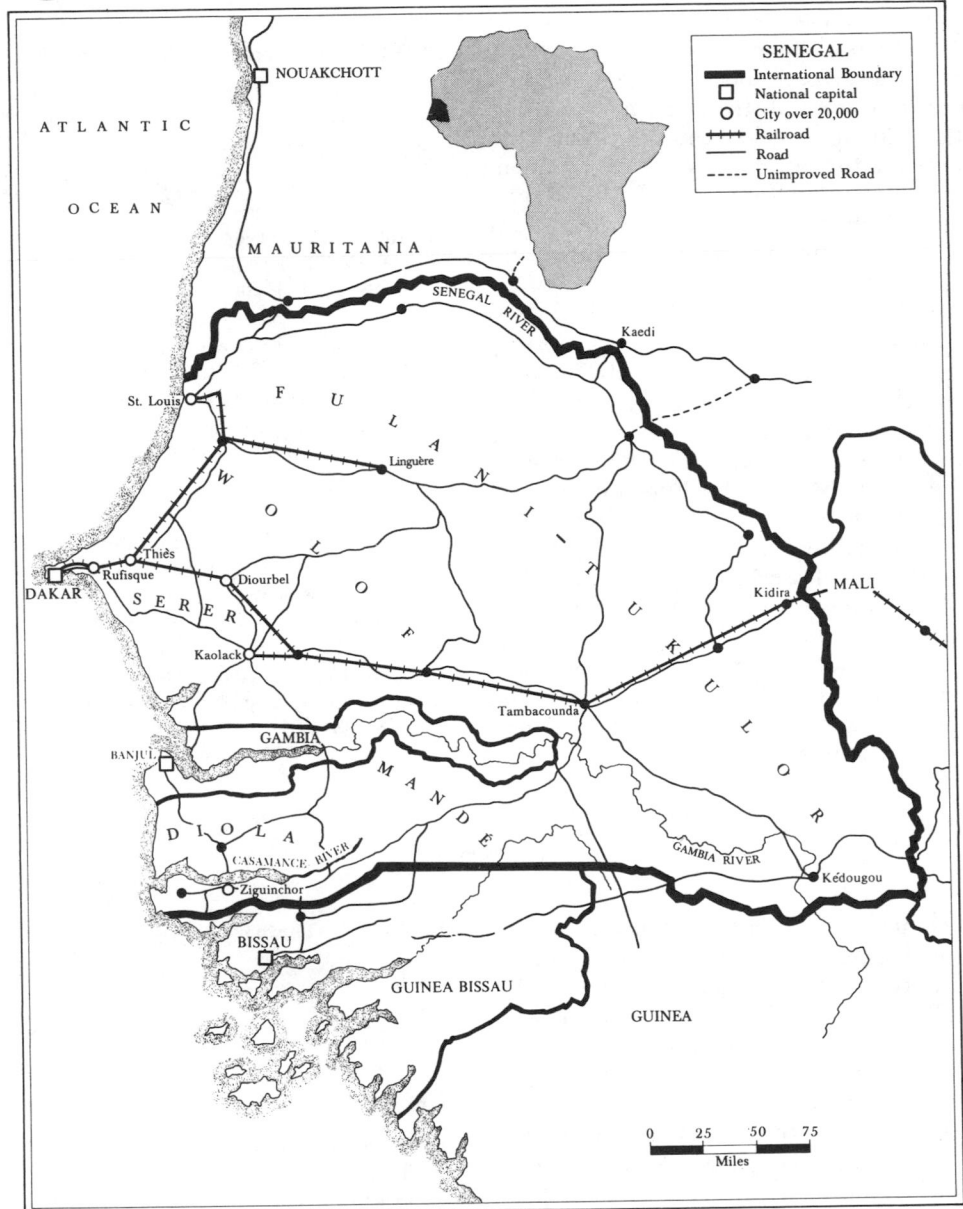

I. Basic Information

Date of Independence: August 29, 1960 (June 20, 1960 as Mali Federation)

Former Colonial Ruler: France

Change in Boundaries: Formerly part of French West African Federation. Part of Federation of Mali (formed with Mali) from April 4, 1959 to August 20, 1960, when Senegal seceded

Estimated Population (1980): 5,665,000

Area Size (equivalent in U.S.): 75,750 sq. mi. (Nebraska)

Date of Last Census: 1976

Major Exports 1977 as Percent of Total Exports: groundnuts and products—48%; phosphates—9%; oilseed cake—8% (1976); petroleum products—7% (1976)

II. Ethnic Patterns

The ethnic classification of Senegal is done at a middle level of inclusion. The Wolof and the Serer might be grouped together in a more abstract schema. It should also be noted that although the Lebou are traditionally considered a branch of the Serer, they are mixed among and assimilating into the Wolof society. All of the ethnic groups in Senegal are predominantly Muslim and there is a high degree of cultural similarity between the groups.

The percentages used by Verrière (1963) diverge somewhat from other sources (e.g. Foltz, 1964). Most notably, Verrière considers the Fulani to be only 7 percent of the population. (It will be noted that although we have grouped the Fulani and Tukulor together—since they share a common language and culture while retaining separate identities—we consider the Fulani component to be 14 percent of the total population.) Other small groups found in Senegal are the Sarakole (2 percent), Moors (1.5 percent), and Bassari (2 percent). About one percent of the population is European, one-half a percent are Lebanese and .8 percent are Cape Verde Islanders. There may be several hundred thousand Guineans in Senegal who have left Guinea for political or economic reasons but the actual figure is not known nor is permanence of their residence known.

TABLE 30.1   Ethnic Units Over 5 Percent of Country Population

Ethnic Units	Estimated Ethnic Population 1980	Estimated Ethnic Percentage
a. Wolof Type (Jolof, Ouolof, Wolof)	2,153,000	38%
1. Wolof, 2. Lebou		22%
b. Fulani-Tukulor Type	1,246,000	22%
1. Fulani (Peul)	793,000	14%
2. Tukulor (Toucouleur)	453,000	8%
c. Serer (Serère, Sarer, Kegueme)	1,076,000	19%
d. Diola Type (Jola, Dyola, Yola)	397,000	7%
1. Diola, 2. Bainouk, 3. Balanté		
e. Mandé Type (Manding, Mandinka)	397,000	7%
1. Malinké, 2. Bambara		

SOURCES: W. J. Foltz, "Senegal," in *Political Parties and National Integration in Tropical Africa*, eds. J. S. Coleman and C. G. Rosberg (Berkeley: University of California Press, 1964), p. 30. From SERESA, Rapport General (Dakar, 1960). H. Deschamps, *Le Sénégal et le Gambie* (Paris: Presses universitaires de France, 1964), pp. 26—40. L. Verrière, *Où en est, où va la Population du Sénégal?* (Paris Institut de Science Economique Appliqué, 1963). *Area Handbook for Senegal* 2nd edition, 1974. U.S. Government Printing Office. (Note: *Europe Outremer* Nov. 1979 has slightly different values.)

III. Language Patterns

The languages of Senegal fall into two categories: (1) West Atlantic (including Wolof, Serère-Siné, Serère-Non, Diola, Pulaar (Fulani), Mandjaque, Mancagne, Balanté, Bassari); (2) Mandé (Malinké, Bambara, Sarakolé/Soninké). Wolof is spoken by about one-third of the population as a first language (Knappert estimates 33 percent; MacDougald 38 percent; Rustow 42 percent). However, another third of the population probably speak Wolof as a second or third language. Arabic is widely used as a religious language.

TABLE 30.2   Language Patterns

		Greenberg	Dalby
1. Primacy			
1st language	Wolof	67%	
2nd language	Pulaar	22	
3rd language	Serer	19	
2. Linguistic classification (all ethnic units in country over 5%)	Wolof	IA1	202
	Fulani-Tukulor	IA1	201
	Serer	IA1	203
	Diola	IA2	22A
	Mandé (Malinké)	IA2	31A
3. *Lingua franca*	Wolof		
4. Official language	French (Wolof, Pulaar, Serer, Diola, Mande are national languages, however.)		

IV. Urban Patterns

Capital/largest city: Dakar (founded 1840)
Dominant ethnicity/language of capital
    Major vernacular: Wolof[1]
    Major ethnic group: Wolof
    Major ethnic group as percent of capital's population:
    35% (1955)[2]

[1]Jan Knappert, "Language Problems of the New Nations of Africa," *African Quarterly*, 5 (1965): 95—105.
[2]Senegal Service de la Statistique Général, *Recensement Démographique de Dakar* (1955) (Paris: Haut Commissariat de la République en Afrique Occidental Française, 1958), p. 17.

TABLE 30.3   Growth of Capital/Largest City

Date	Dakar
1920	30,000
1980	69,000
1940	125,000
1950	257,000
1960	375,000 UA
1965	500,000 UA
1969	581,000 UA
1976[a]	800,000 UA

SOURCE: *Démographié Comparée.*
    [a]Census result as reported in *African Contemporary Record 1976—77*, p. B698.

TABLE 30.4   Cities of 20,000 and Over

City	Size	Date
Dakar	800,000 UA	1976
Thies	117,000	1976
Kaolack	106,000	1976
Saint Louis	88,000	1976
Rufisque[a]	48,100	1969
Ziguinchor	73,000	1976
Diourbel	51,000	1976
Louga	33,000	1976
Tambacounda	25,000	1976

SOURCES: *Africa Contemporary Record 1976—77*, p. B698 report of 1976 census results.
    [a]*Statesman's Yearbook 1973/74* report of the 1969 census.

V. Political Patterns

A. Political Parties and Elections

Since its formation in 1948, the *Union Progressiste Sénégalaise* (UPS), formerly known at the *Bloc Démocratique Sénégalais* (BDS) and then as the *Bloc Populaire Senegalais* (BPS), and from 1976 as the *Parti Socialiste* (PS), has been the primary political force in Senegal. Opposition to the PS has existed in the past but the parties have either been absorbed or banned by the dominant PS, and Senegal became a *de facto* one-party state from 1967 to 1974. Among the absorbed opposition parties were the *Bloc des Masses Senegalaise* (BMS) and the *Parti du Regroupement Africain-Senegal* (PRA-S). The *Parti Africain de l'Independence* (PAI), was banned in 1960. Leopold Sedar Senghor was both President of

Senegal and the Secretary-General of the PS. Until the 1978 election all seats were held by members of the PS. The assembly was enlarged from 80 to 100 seats in 1972. In 1974 steps were taken towards a multi-party democracy. All political prisoners were freed, and new parties were allowed to form and register for elections. Senghor publicly encouraged the use of competing parties as a forum for the discussion of the country's future. The first party formed was the *Parti Democratique Senegalais* (PDS), followed by the *Parti Republicaine Senegalais* (PRS) later that year. Since legislative elections had been held in 1973, there was no opportunity for these parties to compete electorally until the December 1976 regional assembly elections and the February 1978 national elections. In 1974, Mamadou Dia, the jailed former Prime

Minister, was released from jail and he formed another party, the *International Africain Force du Developpement* (IAFD). In addition, the PAI which had been banned since 1960 was revived in 1976. The communists, the *Parti Communiste Senegalaise* (PCS), an offshoot of the PAI in 1965 continued as an illegal party throughout the period. In March 1976, a constitutional amendment was passed which established Senegal as a *de jure* three party system. Each of these parties was to reflect one of the three "currents in Senegalese political thought, socialist democratic, liberal democratic, and Marxist-Leninist. Only one party would be allowed to represent any given "current." The UPS took the label of socialist democratic, while the PAI took the label of Marxist-Leninist, and the PDS were the liberal democrats. Other parties which were denied representation in this process were the *Rassemblement National Democratique* (RND) which had come into existence in February 1976 before the constitutional amendment but had not been registered before it took effect and it was banned. The RND maintains opposition to the regime but its candidates cannot be entered onto electoral forms. The UPS in a December 1976 meeting changed their name to the *Parti Socialiste* (PS) but it has been reported that they frequently revert to the use of the old acronym (UPS). In December 1976, the elections for the regional assembly gave 85 of 87 seats to the UPS although the PDS had a considerable minority of votes. The February 1978 elections saw the UPS and Senghor maintained in power with 82 percent of the vote and capturing 83 seats (of the 100) under the proportional representation system. The PDS got the remaining 17 seats while the PAI with .32 percent of the vote got none. Senghor was also re-elected for another five year term although M. A. Wade, the first person ever to run against Senghor, got 17 percent of the vote. Subsequent to the elections, Senghor called for the recognition of a new party to represent the political right. This party is called the *Mouvement Republicaine Sénégalais* (MRS) and in December 1978, the constitution was amended thereby formally recognizing the MRS. Also in December 1978, large increases in the penalties for forming illegal associations were instituted. In 1979, El Hadj Ahmed Khalifa Niass formed an Islamic political party basing its program on the Koran. It was seeking recognition as a rightist party. In mid-May 1980 the PDS held its third party congress. Senghor resigned from office in December 1980. The limit on the number of parties was eliminated and by 1983 there were at least 13 recognized parties in the country.

FIGURE 30.1   Political Parties and Elections   SENEGAL

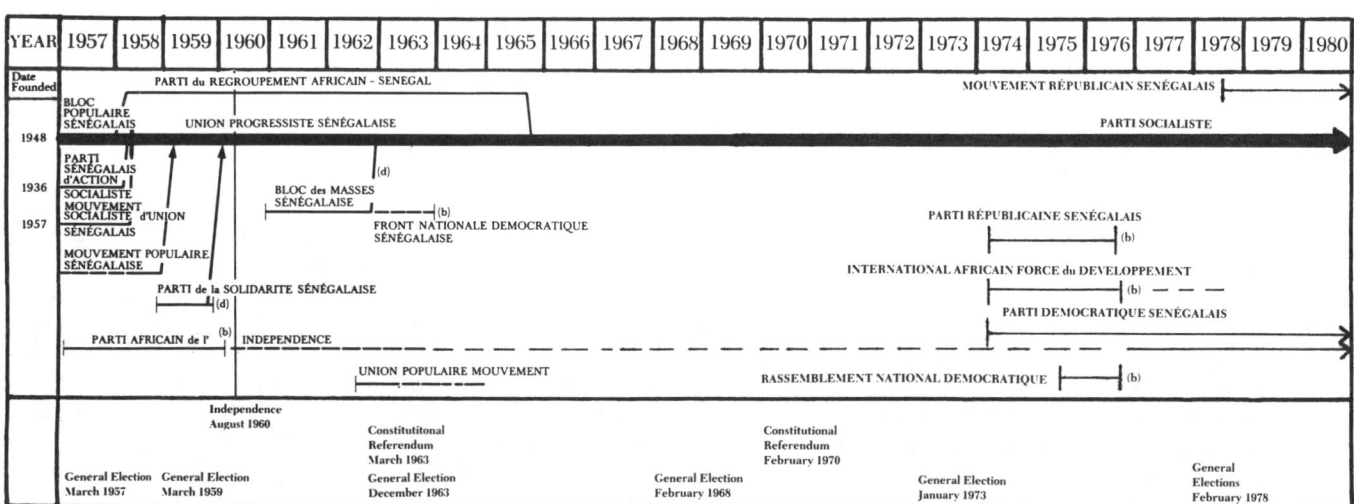

B. Political Leadership

Léopold Senghor was head of government from independence until his resignation in December 1980. The new constitution, approved by the electorate in February 1970, created the office of prime minister, which had been dropped in 1963, but the President retains the predominant share of power. There has been little shift in the cabinet ethnic balance which tends to reflect the general population. There was marked cabinet turnover in the 1962—64 period, partly reflecting the ousting of Mamadou Dia, the country's first prime minister. In recent years cabinet reshuffles have been more frequent and younger technocrats are being brought into the government. In the 1978 elections M. Abdoulaye Wade, the leader of the PDS, got 17 percent of the vote for the Presidency. He was jailed in 1980. In December 1980 Senghor resigned and was succeeded by Diouf.

TABLE 30.5   Head of Government (Post-Independence)

Name	Dates in Office	Age (1982)	Ethnicity	Education	Former Occupation
1. Léopold Sédar Senghor (President)	1960— 1980	76	Serer	University of Paris (France)	Teacher, Professor
2. Abdou Diouf (President)	1980— present	47			Politician

TABLE 30.6   Cabinet Membership: Distribution by Ethnic Unit*

Ethnicity*	Independence Cabinet	1967 Cabinet
1. Wolof (37%)	42%	44%
2. Fulani-Tukulor (24)	17	28
3. Serer (16)	17	5.6
4. Diola (9)	8.3	5.6
5. Mandé (7)	9	5.6
6. Others (7)	17	11
N =	12	18

*Ethnic units arranged in rank order of size within country with the unit's percent of national population in parentheses.

VI. National Integration and Stability

Until recent years Senegal had experienced little political instability. The conspicuous exceptions were the ambiguous clash between President Senghor and Mamadou Dia in 1962 and the assassination attempt in 1967, which was attributed to Mamadou Dia's supporters by an official inquiry. There have also been rumors of further plots against the President. The split between Dia and Senghor in 1962 may have resulted from preferences for "radical" vs. "conservative" policies respectively. Dia's (Muslim) and Senghor's (Catholic) religions also represent a potential source of conflict in Senegal, although the important traditional Muslim leaders have tended to support Senghor. To date, however, there has been no real evidence of communal instability. In 1968 and 1969, however, both unions and students staged serious protests which caused the government much concern. There were further student demonstrations and riots in 1970 which closed the University of Dakar, and again in 1973 student riots occurred. In early 1980 political tensions increased in Senegal. In January secondary students in Ziguinchor and Dakar launched a strike which developed into a large scale riot. By March 1980 the government began a crackdown on dissent. Two leaders of a clandestine Marxist wing of the PAI were detained by the government. Vigilante groups were formed with the sanction of the Socialist Party to harass dissident groups.

TABLE 30.7   Elite Instability

Event and Date	Characteristics
1. Attempted Coup December 17, 1962	a. *Description*: Prime Minister Mamadou Dia sent troops and police to evict the legislature in order to forestall a censure motion. The turning point seems to have been the loyalty of the parachutists who captured and isolated Dia and his ministers and who put a radio transmitter at Senghor's disposal. No injuries were reported. Dia stood trial and was imprisoned. b. *Participants*: President Senghor and Prime Minister Dia. One of Dia's major supporters was General Fall, Chief of the General Staff. c. *Apparent Causes*: Personal and ideological rivalry between Dia and Senghor.

SOURCE: Victor DuBois, "The Trial of Mamadou Dia," *American Universities Field Staff, Report Service*, West Africa Series, 6 (June 1963): 4—8.

TABLE 30.10   Annual Instability Events: Independence Through 1979—Senegal

Year	'61	'62	'63	'64	'65	'66	'67	'68	'69	'70	'71	'72	'73	'74	'75	'76	'77	'78	'79
ELITE INSTABILITY																			
Assassinations							1												
Plots		1					1		1										
Attempted Coups d'État		1																	
Coups d'État																			
COMMUNAL INSTABILITY																			
Ethnic Violence																			
Irredentism																			
Rebellion																			
Civil War																			
MASS INSTABILITY																			
Revolt																			
Revolution																			
TURMOIL																			
Demonstrations			1			1							2						
Strikes (no. days)	1					1		6	59										
Riots (no. days)	1		1			1	1						3						
Terrorism											1								
Declarations of Emergency	1							1											
CABINET INSTABILITY																			
Realloc. and new appt.	8	29	18	16	5	4	1	4		2	2	1							
New members	6	6	10	5	1			3		4	2	2							
Resig. and Dismissals		14		1	1	2	1	5		5	1	2							
No. of members (max.) (maximum in year)	10	17	19	19	16	16	16	16	16	15	16	17							

VII. Selected References

GENERAL

Adam, François, and others. *Atlas national du Sénégal.* Paris: Institut Géographique Nationale, 1977.

Crowder, Michael. *Senegal: A Study in French Assimilation Policy.* rev. ed. London: Methuen, 1967.

Ernst, Harold. *Senegal.* Bonn: R. Schroeder, 1965.

Fougeyrollas, Pierre. *Ou va le Sénégal? Analyse spectrale d'une nation africaine.* Paris: Editions Anthropos, 1970.

Gellar, S. *Senegal.* Boulder, Colo.: Westview Press, 1982.

Klein, Martin A. *Islam and Imperialism in Senegal.* Stanford, Calif.: Stanford University Press, 1967.

Nelson, H. D., et al. *Area Handbook for Senegal,* 2nd ed. Washington, D.C.: Government Printing Office, 1974.

POLITICAL

Behrman, Lucy. *Muslim Brotherhoods and Politics in Senegal.* Cambridge, Mass.: Harvard University Press, 1970.

Costa, E. "Employment Problems and Policies in Senegal." *International Labour Review,* 95 (May 1967): 417—451.

De Lusignan, Guy. *French-Speaking Africa since Independence,* pp. 199—217. London: Pall Mall Press, 1969.

Foltz, William J. *From French West Africa to the Mali Federation.* New Haven, Conn.: Yale University Press, 1965.

Foltz, William J. "Social Structure and Political Behavior of Senegalese Elites." *Behavior Science Notes,* 4 (1969): 145—163.

Hymans, J. L. *Leopold Sedar Senghor: An Intellectual Biography.* Edinburgh: Edinburgh University Press, 1972.

Johnson, G. Wesley, Jr. *The Emergence of Black Politics in Senegal.* Stanford, Calif.: Stanford University Press, 1971.

Markowitz, Irving L. *Leopold Senghor and the Politics of Negritude.* New York: Atheneum, 1969.

Robson, Peter. "The Problems of Senegambia." *Journal of Modern African Studies,* 3 (1965): 393—407.

Schumacher, Edward. *Politics, Bureaucracy and Rural Development in Senegal.* Berkeley: University of California Press, 1975.

Skurnik, W. A. E. *The Foreign Policy of Senegal.* Evanston, Ill.: Northwestern University Press, 1972.

Zuccarelli, François. *Un Parti Politique Africain: l'Union Progressiste Sénégalaise.* Paris: Librairie Générale de Droit et de Jurisprudence, 1970.

ECONOMIC

Bachmann, Heinz B., et al. *Senegal: Tradition, Diversification and Economic Development.* Washington, D.C.: International Bank for Reconstruction and Development, 1974.

International Monetary Fund. "Senegal." In *Surveys of African Economies,* Vol. 3. Washington, D.C.: I.M.F., 1970.

O'Brien, R. C. ed. *The Political Economy of Underdevelopment: Dependence in Senegal.* Beverly Hills, Ca.: Sage, 1980.

Peterec, Richard J. *Dakar and West African Economic Development.* New York: Columbia University Press, 1967.

Serreau, Jean. *Le Développement à la Base au Dahomey et au Sénégal.* Paris: Librairie Generale de Droit et de Jurisprudence, 1966.

SOCIAL

Cruise O'Brien, Donal B. *The Mourides of Senegal: The Political and Economic Organization of an Islamic Brotherhood.* Oxford: Oxford University Press, 1971.

Cruise O'Brien, Donal B. *Saints and Politicians: Essays in the Organization of a Senegalese Peasant Society.* Cambridge: Cambridge University Press, 1975.

Cruise O'Brien, Rita. *White Society in Black Africa: The French of Senegal.* Evanston, Ill.: Northwestern University Press, 1972.

Pfeffermann, G. *Industrial Labor in the Republic of Senegal.* New York: Praeger Special Study, 1968.

Sankale, M., L. V. Thomas, and P. Fougeyrollas. *Dakar en devenir.* Paris: Présence africaine, 1968.

Senghor, Leopold Sedar. *On African Socialism.* New York: Praeger, 1964.

Sy, Cheikh Tidiana. *La confrérie sénégalaise des Mourides.* Paris: Présence africaine, 1969.

31. Sierra Leone

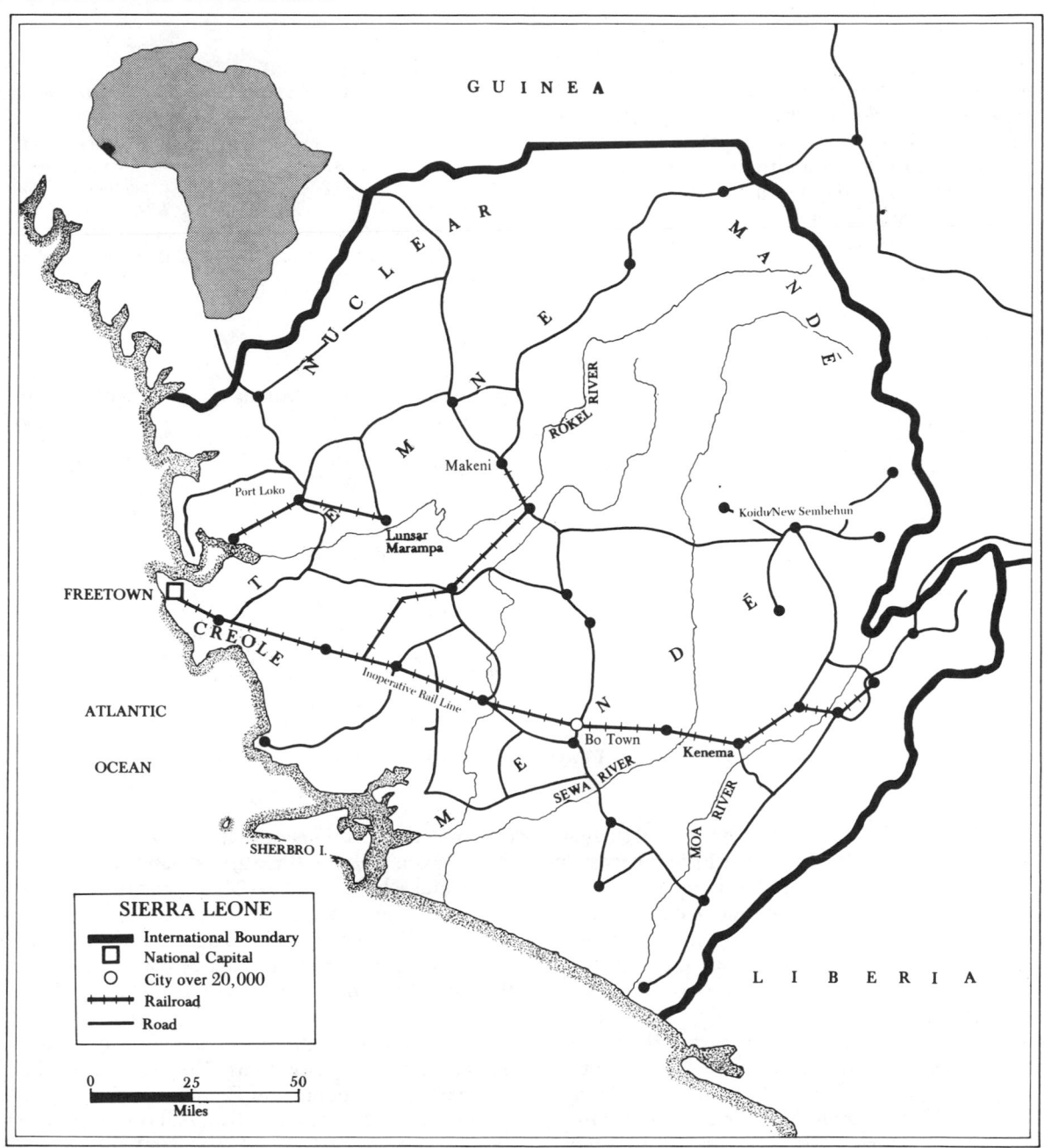

I. Basic Information

Date of Independence: April 27, 1961
Former Colonial Ruler: United Kingdom
Estimated Population (1980): 3,428,000
Area Size (equivalent in U.S.): 27,699 sq.mi. (South Carolina)

Date of Last Census: 1974
Major Exports 1977 as Percent of Total Exports: diamonds—45 percent; cocoa—13 percent; coffee—26 percent; bauxite—6 percent.

II. Ethnic Patterns

The ethnic classification of Sierra Leone is done according to the same principles used in the Ivory Coast and Liberia: the groups listed within each of the three major types are identity groups. In addition to these peoples, there are the Fulani (3 percent), the Lokko (3 percent), and the Creole (2 percent). There are also European and Asian populations of 3,000 and 5,000 respectively.

TABLE 31.1   Ethnic Units Over 5 Percent of Country Population

Ethnic Units	Estimated Ethnic Population 1980	Estimated Ethnic Percentage
a. Temne Type (West Atlantic)	1,599,000	45%
1. Temne (Timne)	(1,066,000)	(30%)
2. Limba	(284,000)	(8%)
3. Sherbro		
4. Kissi		
5. Krim		
6. Gola		
b. Mendé Type (Peripheral Mandé)	1,279,000	36%
1. Mendé (Kossa, Mendi)	(1,101,000)	(31%)
2. Kono		
3. Vai (Gallinas)		
c. Nuclear Mandé Type	355,000	10%
1. Koranko, 2. Susu,		
3. Malinké		
4. Yalunka (Jalonké)		

SOURCES: J. I. Clarke, *Sierra Leone in Maps* (London: University of London Press, 1966). G. P. Murdock, *Africa* (New York: McGraw-Hill, 1959). The 1963 census of Sierra Leone.

III. Language Patterns

According to Dalby (1962) there are five major language groups in Sierra Leone: (1) The Mande languages (including Susu, Yalunka, Mende, Loko, Bandi, Loma, Comendi, Mandinka, Koranko, Kono, and Vai or Gallinas); (2) West Atlantic languages (Temne, Banta, Bullom, Bum, Krim, Kissi, Limba); (3) the Kwa languages (Yoruba and Fanti); (4) the Kru languages (Kru and Bassa); (5) other languages (Krio—i.e., Creole—and Pidgin). Dalby notes that in the southwestern part of the country a number of distinct ethnic groups (the Sherbo, Krim, Vai and Gola) speak Mende as a first language. Within Temne, there are five dialects: Western, Yoni, Bombali, Western Kunike, Eastern Kunike. The related language of Limba has seven major dialects: Tonko, Sela, Kamuke, Wara-Wara, Keleng, Biriwa, and Safronko.

Several scholars suggest Mende is the largest language group (Knappert suggests 31 percent; MacDougald 45 percent). Rustow links Temne, Bulom, and Limba together to form 52 percent. Because of linguistic similarities, we have grouped Temne and Limba together as the largest language zone comprising 45 percent of the population, although, as mentioned above, Mende serves as a *lingua franca* in many areas. English is the official language of Sierra Leone, and French is used frequently as a trading language along the Guinea border. Arabic serves as the language of Islam within Sierra Leone.

TABLE 31.2   Language Patterns

1. Primacy
   1st language   Temne-Limba   (45%)
   2nd language   Mendé   (36%)

		Greenberg	Dalby
2. Linguistic classification (all ethnic units in over 5%)	Temne	IA1	25A
	Mendé	IA2	31C
3. *Lingua francas*	Krio, Mendé		
4. Official language	English		

SOURCE: D. P. Dalby, "Language Distribution in Sierra Leone: 1961—1962," *Sierra Leone Language Review*, No. 1 (1962): 62—67.

IV. Urban Patterns

Capital/largest city: Freetown (founded 1787)
Dominant ethnicity/language of capital
   Major vernacular: Krio[1]
   Major ethnic group: Temne type[2] (25% Limba and 17% Temne)
   Major ethnic group as percent of capital's population: 42 percent.[2]

[1]Jan Knappert, "Language Problems of the New Nations of Africa," *African Quarterly*, 5 (1965): 95—105.
[2]1963 Census.

TABLE 31.4   Cities of 20,000 and Over*

City	Size	Date
Freetown	274,000 UA	1974
Koidu	80,000	1974
Bo	26,000	1974

SOURCES: 1974 Census results as reported in *Africa South of the Sahara 1980—81*.
*The next largest city is Kenema with a population of 13,000 followed by Makeni (12,000)—1974 census *Africa South of the Sahara 1980—81*.

TABLE 31.3   Growth of Capital/largest City

Date	Freetown
1920	44,000
1930	56,000
1940	64,000
1950	85,000
1960	120,000
1963	118,000
1966	148,000
1972	196,000 UA
1974	274,000 UA

SOURCE: Michael Banton, *West African City: A Study of Tribal Life in Freetown*. London: Oxford University Press, 1957. 1963—Census; 1966 U.N. *Demographic Yearbook 1968*; *Africa 1973*; 1974 Census.

V. Political Patterns

A. Political Parties and Elections

The 1957 general election in Sierra Leone was contested primarily by the *Sierra Leone People's Party* (SLPP) led by Sir Milton Margai, and the *United Progressive Party* (UPP) led by Cyril Rogers-Wright. After the SLPP victory, Sir Milton Margai became prime minister and led the government until the constitutional conference in 1960. Opposition to his government came from the UPP and the *People's National Party* (PNP), formed in 1958 by dissident members of the SLPP and the UPP, and led by Albert Margai, younger brother of Sir Milton Margai. All parties joined in coalition in 1960, except for Siaka Stevens of the PNP who again formed a new opposition party, the *All People's Congress* (APC). The coalition called the *United National Front* (UNF) was dominated by the SLPP.

In the 1962 general elections the SLPP won 28 seats, the APC won 16 seats, the SLPIM won 4 seats and the independents won 14 seats. The general election in March 1967 was won by the APC but was followed by a military coup d'état the same week, at which time all political activity was banned. The military government of Col. Juxon-Smith was later overthrown by another military coup in April 1968. The new military group turned back power to a civilian government under Siaka Stevens whose party was shown to be the winner of the 1967 elections. At present, Siaka Stevens and the APC govern with the support of the military and, in the early 1970's, Guinean paratroopers. In June 1970, an opposition party, the *National Democratic Party* (NDP), was formed by two young cabinet ministers who quit the government to go into opposition. The NDP merged with the 'Committee of Citizens' to become the *United Democratic Party* (UDP) under Dr. John Karefa-Smart. The UPD was banned in October 1970. A republic was declared in April 1971 and Siaka Stevens became President. The May 1973 elections saw considerable harassment of the SLPP and they withdrew from the electoral campaign. The APC won 84 of 85 seats (Parliament was increased from 66 to 85 members in 1970), the remaining seat going to an independent who quickly joined the APC. Siaka Stevens was unanimously re-elected President in May 1976 by the House of Representatives. After a series of riots beginning at the University and quickly spreading through the country, parliamentary elections were held in May 1977 with the APC dropping to 65 seats and the SLPP winning l5 with 8 seats in the Bo district, a traditional area of SLPP strength, left in dispute because of election irregularities. These eight seats were later decided in a special election in September 1977 and the seats went to the APC who were unopposed. In addition, 12 seats that are held by the paramount chiefs and 3 seats filled by Presidental nomination were held by APC supporters. Stevens called for a one-party state in June 1977 and by December, four SLPP members had joined the APC after a constitutional amendment that no longer required that a member stand for election if he changed parties. A legal one-party state was officially announced in May 1978, with the passage of a new constitution in the May 1978 referendum and with the approval of the legislature. After this announcement all SLPP members

TABLE 31.5   Heads of Government (Post-Independence)

Name	Dates in Office	Age (1982)	Ethnicity	Education	Former Occupation
1. Sir Milton Margai (Prime Minister	1961— 1964	d. 1964 age 69	Mendé	Medical degree, Durham (Eng.)	Government Medical Service
2. Sir Albert Margai (Prime Minister)	1964— 1967	72	Mendé	Middle Temple, London	Lawyer, Druggist
3. Lt. Col. Andrew Juxon-Smith (NRC Secretariat)	1967— 1968	51	Creole (Mixed)	Secondary (Sierra Leone)	Soldier
4. Siaka Probyn Stevens (Prime Minister, President	1968—	77	Limba (father) Mendé (mother)	Ruskin College, Oxford	Policeman construction worker, union organiser

were forced to join the APC or lose their seats in the House. President Stevens also released political detainees and appointed several former members of the SLPP to government positions after the May 1978 constitutional referendum. In June 1978 another referendum was held after which Stevens was sworn in for a 7-year term as President.

B. Political Leadership

Leadership in post-independence Sierra Leone was initially identified with the brothers, Milton and Albert Margai. As a result of the 1967 election there was a sequence of coups d'état which eventually resulted in the civilian government of Siaka Stevens. Creole representation in the cabinet has tended to be much greater than their percentage of the population, although Stevens has attempted to maintain a wide ethnic representation in the government. In April 1971, Stevens and the APC pushed through a new constitution which Sir Albert Margai had tried and failed to do previously. Stevens declared the country to be a republic and Steven's title was changed to President. Stevens has continued as President since that time with the major issues facing the government being those of corruption and economic decline. In May 1978, in a constitutional referendum, the post of prime minister was abolished and replaced with two vice-presidencies.

FIGURE 31.1   Political Parties and Elections   SIERRA LEONE

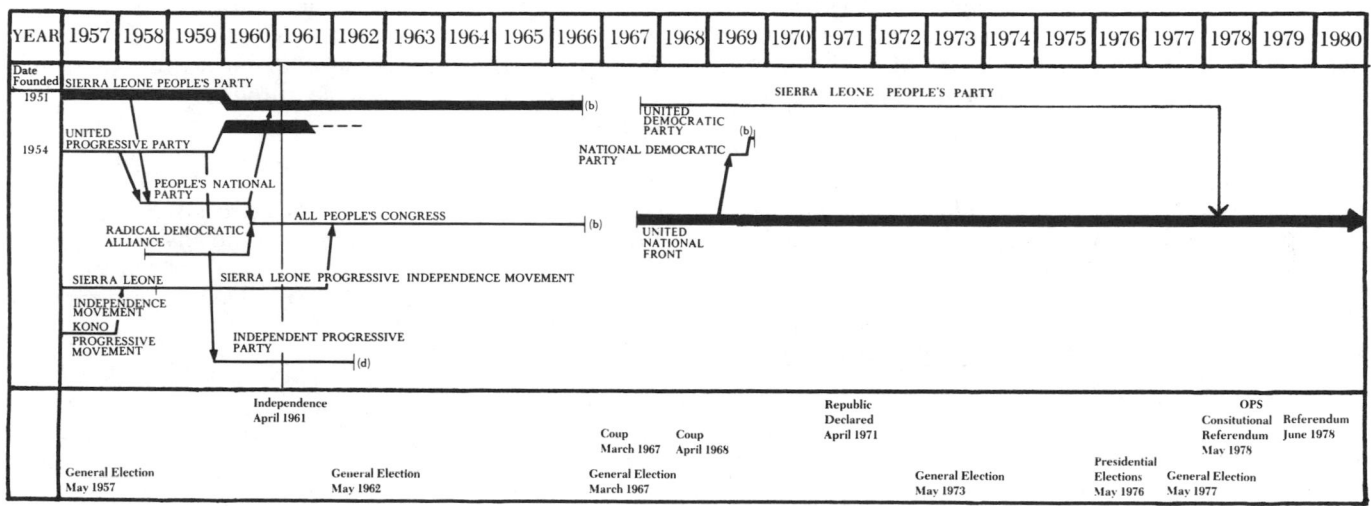

TABLE 31.6   Cabinet Membership: Distribution by Ethnic Unit*

Ethnicity*	Independence Cabinet	Immediate Pre-Coup Cabinet
1. Temne (45%)	29%	13%
2. Mendé (36)	36	62
3. Nuclear Mendé (8)	0	0
4. Creole (1)	36	25
5. Others (10)	0	0
N =	14	16

*Ethnic units arrnged in rank order of size within country with the unit's percent of national population in parentheses.

VI. National Integration and Stability

There have been continuing tensions between the ethnic groups in Sierra Leone, both in the urbanized coastal areas and the interior, with occasional riots. The patterns of elite instability which resulted from the election of Stevens in 1967 are related in part to Mende-Temne rivalry and despite Stevens' attempt to integrate the opposition into the government, strong opposition remains. On September 14, 1970, Prime Minister Stevens reacted to a challenge from two young Cabinet Ministers who quit and formed their own *National Democratic Party* by declaring a state of emergency. Reports of ethnic violence came from Port Loko and other northern towns. Stevens reported a plot by disloyal army officers and began removing Temne army officers. Stevens had already eliminated all but one of the Mende officers in 1968.

eliminated all but one of the Mende officers in 1968. There was an attempted coup by some army elements in 1971 which was put down by loyal army units. In addition, reports of army plots in 1970 and 1974 were severely dealt with. The riots in 1977 which began at the University and quickly spread throughout the country were dealt with by calling a parliamentary election. The economic crisis which gave rise to these riots in part continues and instability may re-occur. A state of emergency was declared in March 1978 but retroactive to January 1978. In February 1980, students at the Njala University College organized a strike to protest unsatisfactory conditions and facilities at the University. Demonstrations and riots broke out in early March 1980.

TABLE 31.7   Elite Instability

Event and Date	Characteristics
1. Coup d'État March 21, 1967	a. *Description*: The general elections of 1967 were won by Siaka Stevens (Limba), who was arrested shortly after he was sworn in as prime minister by Brigadier Lansana (Mendé), (Sir Albert Margai's brother-in-law). In the riots which followed this arrest, four persons were killed. Two days later, Brigadier Lansana and the former prime minister, Sir Albert Margai, were arrested by junior army officers, who also suspended the constitution, dissolved all political parties, and banned political activity. The control of the government was then offered to Lt. Col. Andrew Juxon-Smith by the National Reformation Council Secretariat. b. *Participants*: Junior army officers headed by Majors Jumu, Blake and Kai-Samba plus Mr. William Leigh, Commissioner of Police, and units of the army and gendarmierie. The officers were Mendé but anti-Margai. c. *Apparent Causes*: According to Major Blake: "We can't stress too much that we acted only to avert civil war. This was an election clearly along tribal lines, west and north against south and east. Neither party and no one tribe could command the whole country's loyalty." Another factor was the class fears of the officers who were linked to the traditional ruling families. The junior officers added that they wished to prevent Brigadier Lansana from imposing Sir Albert Margai on the country.

Event and Date	Characteristics
2. Coup d'État April 18, 1968	a. *Description*: Military and police led by army NCO's took control as the Anti-Corruption Revolutionary Movement and established a National Interim Council (NIC) led by army officers loyal to Siaka Stevens. The NIC was formed to return the country to civilian authority. Their work culminated in the appointment of Siaka Stevens as prime minister on April 29, 1968. b. *Participants*; Army and police elements led by two warrant officers—Sergeants-Major Patrick Conteh and Amadu Rogers. c. *Apparent Causes*: Sergeant Rogers charged that the leaders of the National Reformation Council (NRC—formed after the March 1967 coup d'état) had become "more corrupt and selfish than the civilian regime," that they had ignored the rank and file of the army and police, and had failed to return the government to civilian rule.
3. Attempted Coup March 23, 1971	a *Description*: Two attempts to assassinate Prime Minister Stevens by army units were made within 12 hours. The first led by Major Jawara attacked Stevens at 1:30 a.m. in his house but was beaten off by guards. The second, at his office, at noon the next day was also beaten off. Other senior army officers arrested the army commander and affirmed their loyalty to the regime. b. *particiants*: Brig. John Bangura, the army commander, and his supporters. c. *Apparent Causes*: The coup attempt followed several months of political unrest. The coup participants opposed the proposed change in the constitution. It is reported that they were also opposed to Stevens' use of Guinean troops in Sierra Leone.

SOURCE: John Cartwright, "Shifting Forces in Sierra Leone," *Africa Report*, 13 (December 1968): 26—30.

TABLE 31.8 Communal Instability

Event and Date	Characteristics
Ethnic Violence December, 1968	a. *Description*: Violent clashes between Mendé and Temne workers broke out at the Marampa iron mines, the Mokanji Hills bauxite mines, and the rutile mines in Bonthe district. In other southern towns, attacks against non-Mendé people were reported. Elections had been held the previous month, at which time there were numerous reports of ethnic clashes. b. *Participants*: The Mendé secret society was reportedly involved in organizing attacks against non-Mendé, but this is the only evidence of organizational control in this inter-ethnic violence. c. *Apparent Causes*: The clashes between Mendé and Temne do not appear to have been directed towards any immediate program for political change, although they reflected Mendé dissatisfaction with the post-coup government of Siaka Stevens, which was largely non-Mendé in composition, in contrast to the pre-coup governments led by the Mendé brothers—Sir Milton and Sir Albert Margai.

SOURCE: John Cartwright, "Shifting Forces in Sierra Leone," *Africa Report*, 13 (December 1968): 26—30.

TABLE 31.10   Annual Instability Events: Independence Through 1979

Year	'61	'62	'63	'64	'65	'66	'67	'68	'69	'70	'71	'72	'73	'74	'75	'76	'77	'78	'79
ELITE INSTABILITY																			
Assassinations																			
Plots							1			2		1		1					
Attempted Coups d'État											1								
Coups d'État							1	1											
COMMUNAL INSTABILITY																			
Ethnic Violence								1											
Irredentism																			
Rebellion																			
Civil War																			
MASS INSTABILITY																			
Revolt																			
Revolution																			
TURMOIL																			
Demonstrations																			
Strikes (no. days)																			
Riots (no. days)																			
Terrorism											1								
Declarations of Emergency	1							1			1	1	1	1					
CABINET INSTABILITY																			
Realloc. and new appts.		11	8	5	6					9	4	11							
New members		6	2					6	1	7	4	5	1						
Resig. and Dismissals		3		4		1		1	1	4	4	3	3						
No. of members (max.) (maximum in year)	16	19	11	15	15	15	6	17	20	20	23	21							

VII. Selected References

BIBLIOGRAPHY

Luke, Sir Harry C.J. *A Bibliography of Sierra Leone*, N.Y. Negro University Press, 1969.

Switzer John P. *A Bibliography of Sierra Leone 1968—1970*. Freetown, Njala University College, 1973.

Williams, Geoffrey J. *A Bibliography of Sierra Leone, 1925—67*. New York: Africana, 1971.

Zell, Hans M. *A Bibliography of Non-Periodical Literature on Sierra Leone, 1925—66*. Freetown: Fourah Bay College Bookshop, University College of Sierra Leone, 1966.

GENERAL

Abraham, Arthur. *Topics in Sierra Leone History: a Counter Colonial Interpretation* Freetown: Sierra Leone Publishers, 1976.

Clarke, J.I., ed. *Sierra Leone in Maps*. London: University of London Press, 1966.

Collier, Gershon. *Sierra Leone: Experiment in Democracy in an African Nation*. New York: New York University Press, 1970.

Dalton, K.G. *A Geography of Sierra Leone*. Cambridge: Cambridge University Press, 1965.

Foray, C.P. *Historical Dictionary of Sierra Leone.* Metuchen, N.J.: Scarecrow Press, 1977.

Fourah Bay College Library. *Catalog of the Sierra Leone Collection Fourah Bay College Library,* Boston, G.K. Hall 1979.

Fyfe, Christopher. *A Short History of Sierra Leone.* London: Longmans, 1972.

Kaplan, I., et al. *Area Handbook for Sierra Leone.* Washington, D.C.: U.S. Government Printing Office, 1976.

Kup, A. P. *Sierra Leone: A Concise History.* New York: St. Martin's Press, 1975.

Migeod, Frederick W. *A View of Sierra Leone.* New York: Negro Universities Press, 1970.

Riddell, J. Barry. *The Spatial Dynamics of Modernization in Sierra Leone: Structure, Diffusion, and Response.* Evanston, Ill.: Northwestern University Press, 1970.

Sibthorse, A. B. C. *The History of Sierra Leone.* New York: Humanities, 1971.

Walker, James W. *The Black Loyalists.* New York, Africana, 1976.

West, Richard. *Back to Africa: A History of Sierra Leone and Liberia.* London: Cape, 1970.

POLITICAL

Barrows, W. *Grassroots Politics in an African State: Integration and Development in Sierra Leone.* New York: Africana, 1976.

Cartwright, John R. *Politics in Sierra Leone, 1947—1967.* Toronto: University of Toronto Press, 1970.

Cartwright, J. R. *Political Leadership in Sierra Leone.* Toronto: University of Toronto Press, 1978.

Clapham, C. *Liberia and Sierra Leone: An Essay in Comparative Politics.* New York: Cambridge University Press, 1976.

Cox, Thomas S. *Civil-Military Relations in Sierra Leone: A Case Study of African Soldiers in Politics.* Cambridge: Harvard University Press, 1976.

Fisher, Humphrey J. "Elections and Coups in Sierra Leone, 1967." *Journal of Modern African Studies,* 7 (1969): 611—636.

Kilson, Martin. *Political Change in a West African State: Study of the Modernization Process in Sierra Leone.* Cambridge, Mass.: Harvard University Press, 1966.

ECONOMIC

Bank of Sierra Leone. Research Dept. *Charts on the Economy in Sierra Leone.* Freetown, Bank of Sierra Leone, 1975.

International Monetary Fund. "Sierra Leone." In *Surveys of African Economies,* Vol. 6. Washington, D.C.: I.M.F., 1975.

Jabati. S. A. *Agriculture in Sierra Leone.* N.Y.: Vantage Press, 1978.

Saylor, Ralph Gerald. *The Economic System of Sierra Leone.* Durham, N.C.: Duke University Press, 1968.

Van der Laan, H. L. *The Sierra Leone Diamonds: An Economic Survey Covering the Years 1952—1961.* London: Oxford University Press, 1965.

Van der Laan, H. L. *The Lebanese Trader in Sierra Leone.* the Hague: Mouton, 1976.

SOCIAL

Banton, M. P. *West African City: A Study of Tribal Life in Freetown.* London: Oxford University Press, 1957.

Fyfe, Christopher H. and Eldred Jones, eds. *Freetown: A Symposium.* Freetown: Sierra Leone University Press, 1968.

Makannah, T. J. *The Study of Internal Migration in Sierra Leone: A Review and Bibliography of Recent Literature,* Freetown: Central Statistical Office, 1977.

Porter, A.T. *Creoledom: A Study of the Development of Freetown Society.* London: Oxford University Press, 1963.

Spitzer, Leo. *The Creoles of Sierra Leone: Responses to Colonialism, 1870—1945.* Madison, Wis.: University of Wisconsin Press, 1974.

32. Somalia

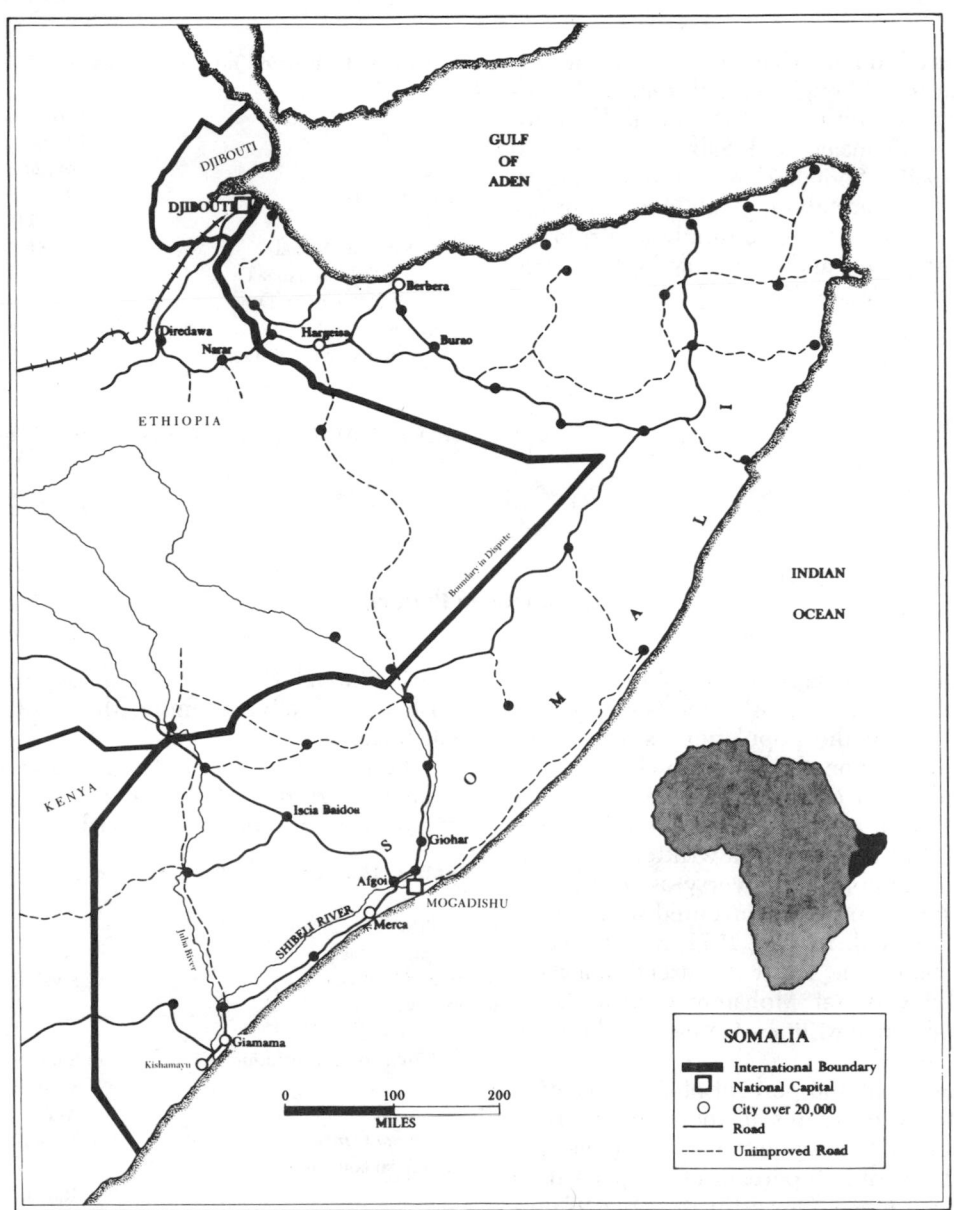

I. Basic Information

Date of Independence: July 1, 1960
Former Colonial Rulers: Italy and United Kingdom
Change in Boundaries At independence, merger of UN Trust Territory of Somaliland with British Somaliland
Former Names: Somaliland, British Somaliland
Estimated Population (1980): 3,553,000*
Area Size (equivalent in U.S.): 246,201 sq. mi. (Texas)
Date of Last Census: 1975

Major Exports 1976 as Percent of Total Exports: LIvestock, hides and skins—70 percent; bananas—16 percent.

*There have been reports that the conflict in the Ogaden has promoted the arrival of one quarter of a million refugees into Somalia. (*Africa Report*, Sept./Oct. 1980, p. 31).

II. Ethnic Patterns

The Somali peoples of Somalia share a common language and a common culture although the Sab tend to be engaged in sedentary agriculture and the Samaale in nomadic herding. The Samaale and Sab are large-scale clans within the broader Somali identity group. In addition to the Somali there are about 100,000 Bantu speaking Africans who have come to be culturally similar to the Somali, about 42,000 Arabs and Asians, and 6,000 Europeans were counted in the late 1960's.

TABLE 32.1   Ethnic Units Over 5 Percent of Country Population

Ethnic Units	Estimated Ethnic Population 1980	Estimated Ethnic Percentage
a. Somali	3,375,000	95%
1. Samaale (Somal)	(2,700,000)	(76%)
i. Darod, ii. Ishaak, iii. Hawiye, iv. Dir		
2. Sab	(675,000)	(19%)
i. Rahanwein, ii. Dighil		

SOURCE: I. M. Lewis, *The Modern History of Somaliland* (New York: Praeger, 1965).

III. Language Patterns

The major language of Somalia is Somali (of the Cushitic family) which is closely related to Afar and Gallinya. It is spoken by 95 percent of the population as a first language. The three major Somali dialects include that of the Samaale nomads, that of the Sab farmers, and that spoken along the coastal area. All dialects are mutually intelligible. Somali had never been a wriitten language, and there was considerable controversy as to whether Roman script, Arabic script, or an invented script called Usmaniya, should be used. In June 1971, a special commission set up to choose the script was urged to make a speedy decision by General Mohammed Siad Barre, President of the Supremee Military Council, and Roman script was finally selected.

Knappert suggests that 100 percent of the population speak Somali; Rustow estimates 95 percent. Approximately 1 to 2 percent of the population speak Arabic as a first language, and probably 3 percent of the population use Swahili as a *lingua fanca*. Our estimate is that 97 percent of the populaton speaks Somali. We suggest that Swahili should be considered the second language (3 percent), although the *Area Handbook for Somalia* says English is gradually becoming the most common second language.

There are four official languages in Somalia: Somali, Arabic, English, and Italian. English and Italian, however, are used primarily in official situations.

TABLE 32.2   Language Patterns

			Greenberg	Dalby
1. Primacy				
1st language	Somali	(97%)		
2nd language	Swahili	(3%)		
2. Linguistic classification	Somali		IIID3	02A
	Swahili		IA5	04
	Arabic		IIIA	01A
3. *Lingua franca*	Somali			
4. Official language	Somali, English Italian, Arabic			

SOURCE: U.S. Department of the Army, *Area Handbook for Somalia* (Washington, D.C.: Government Printing Office, 1970), pp. 65—76.

IV. Urban Patterns

Capital/largest city: Mogadishu
Dominant ethnicity/language of capital
Major vernacular: Somali

Major ethnic group: Somali
Major ethnic group as percent of capital's population:
Nearly 100%

TABLE 32.3   Growth of Capital/Largest City

Date	Mogadishu
1920	16,000
1930	32,000
1940	55,000
1950	78,000
1960	130,000
1966	170,000
1973	350,000 UA

SOURCE: Various editions of the *Statesman's Yearbook*; *African Development* (Nov. 1973); *Africa South of the Sahara, 1978—79*.

TABLE 32.4   Cities of 20,000 and Over*

City	Size	Date
Mogadishu	350,000 UA	1973
Hargesia	70,000 UA	1973
Kisimayu (Chisimaio)	60,000	1966
Merca	56,000	1965
Berbera	50,000	1966
Giamama	22,000	1964

SOURCES: *Africa South of the Sahara, 1978—79*, p. 854.

V. Political Patterns

FIGURE 32.1   Political Parties and Elections   SOMALIA

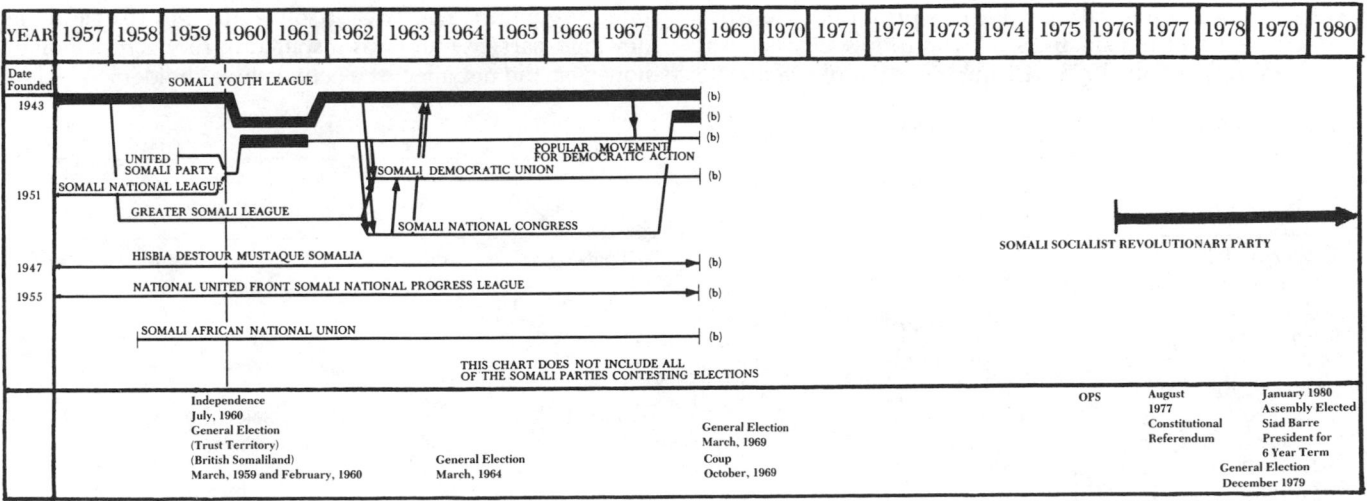

A. Political Parties and Elections

Prior to independence and merger with the Somaliland Protectorate in July 1960, the dominant party in Somalia was the *Somali Youth League* (SYL), founded in 1943 as the Somali Youth Club. Opposition to the SYL came from the *United Somali Party* (USP) and the *Somali National League* (SNL). After independence a coalition government was formed between the SYL, and a combined USP and SNL. Adan Abdulla Osman served as president and Dr. Abdirashid Ali Shermarked as vice-president. The former prime minister of the Somaliland Protectorate, Mohammed Ibrahim Egal, became the minister of education. The coalition continued to govern until the March 1964 general elections (which was a victory for the SYL) when President Osman asked Abdirazak Hussein to form a new government. After considerable difficulty in organizing his cabinet, Hussein began his government in September 1964. Hussein's government was opposed by the USP, the *Somali Democratic Union* (SDU) formed by a merger of splinter groups from the USP/SNL coalition and the *Greater Somali League* (GSL), and the *Somali National Congress* (SNC) also formed from splinter groups of the SYL, USP, and SNL. In 1967, a new government was formed after Abdirashid Ali Shermarke was elected President. Mohammed Ibrahim Egal was chosen prime minister. More than sixty parties, based mainly on clan lines, contested the 1969 election, but the SYL won a substantial majority of the seats with about 40 perent of the vote. Egal remained as prime minister until the assassination of the president in October, 1969. The assassination was followed by a coup, after which all parties were banned. General Siad Barre's promised one-party state based on the principles of "scientific socialism" was inaugurated in July 1976 with the creation of the *Somali*

Socialist Revolutionary Party but the government remained unchanged except for changes in titles. In August 1979, a referendum for a new constitution was held. This was the first constitution since the 1969 coup and was based on socialist principles. On December 30, 1979, parliamentary and local government elections were held. All of the candidates were nominated by the ruling Somali Revolutionary Socialist Party. In January 1980, the new assembly elected General Siad Barre to be President for a six-year term. These were the first governmental elections since Siad Barre took power in 1969.

B. Political Leadership

The Somali Constitution gives executive power to the prime minister. The role of the president evolved into something far more than a figurehead, however, so we present in Table 32.5 the heads of state rather than the heads of government. During the 1967—1969 regime of President Abdirashid Shermarke, he, Prime Minister Mohammed Ibrahim Egal and Minister of Interior Yassin shared power, and Egal asserted his right to control the party. The new military regime which took power following the 1969 coup set up a *Supreme Revolutionary Council* (SRC) composed of 25 officers under General Siad's presidency. Siad is a northerner and the Council has a northern-southern balance. The first fourteen-man government appointed by the SRC was composed of young, well-educated civilians and the Police Commandant, General Jama Ali Korshel, who held the post of minister of interior. There have been several cabinet reshuffles since then and more military officers have been brought into the cabinet. The SRC dissolved itself in 1976 and the new one-party regime was installed in July. This change, however, did not affect the actual power holders.

TABLE 32.5   Heads of State (Post-Independence)

Name	Dates in Office	Age (1982)	Ethnicity	Education	Former Occupation
1. Aden Abdulla Osman (President)	1960—	74	Somali	Primary	Administrator, Businessman
2. Abdirashid Ali Shermarke (President)	1967— 1969	As. in 1969, age 50	Somali	Ph.D.	Civil Servant
3. General Mohamed Siad Barre (President, Secretary General, Somali Socialist Revolutionary Party)	1969— present	63	Somali	Primary and self-taught	Soldier, policeman

TABLE 32.6   Cabinet Membership: Distribution by Ethnic Unit*

Ethnicity*	Independence Cabinet	1967 Cabinet
1. Somali (95%)	100%	100%
2. Others (5)	0	0
N =	24	18

*Ethnic units arranged in rank order of size within country with the unit's percent of national population in parentheses.

VI. National Integration and Stability

TABLE 32.7   Elite Instability

Event and Date	Characteristics
a. Attempted Coup December 10, 1961	a. *Description*: On December 6, the Minister of Health, Suk Ali Guimale, was dismissed from the government by presidential decree. He was a powerful political opponent of Presdient Usman. On December 10, twenty-three military officers failed in an attempt to seize command of an army unit in the north. The plan included seizure of local administration. All were brought to trial in Mogadishu on December 13, and were imprisoned until January 1965. b. *Participants*: Young northern military officers. c. *Apparent Causes*: Reports of the attempted coup mention the removal of Suk Ali Guimale as a contributing factor to army discontent, but this seems to be conjecture. I. M. Lewis suggests the young British-trained junior officers were angered when they were placed under the command of Italian-trained officers from the south. The officers urged a separation of north and south.
2. Coup d'État October 21, 1969	a. *Description*: Following the assassination of President Abdirashid Ali Shermarke on October 15, and conflictful debate over the choice of his successor, the army took power. A National Revolutionary Council, led by the Army commander, Major-General Mohammed Siad Barre, arrested all members of the deposed government, dissolved the National Assembly, and suspended the constitution. The coup was bloodless, and was followed by popular demonstrations supporting the new regime. b. *Participants*: Four army colonels organized the coup, and they obtained the support of the army commander and the police commissioner. These two senior officers came from the south and north respectively, and the Supreme Revolutionary Council gave balanced representation to these regions and to Somali clans. c. *Apparent Causes*: Apart from the leadership crisis brought about by the assassination of President Shermarke, the military government stressed its opposition to tribalism and corruption, and it seems that the major conflicts between Somali elites were intensified by the elections of March 1969, in which there were serious allegations of government rigging, and in which the ruling party received only 40 percent of the vote, split as it was between 64 clan-based parties.
3. Coup Attempt April 1978	a. *Description*: Army units attack key installations in Mogadishu and attempt to assassinate Siad Barre. They are defeated by army units which remained loyal to the regime. b. *Participants*: Army officers backed by certain "foreign powers" according to the government. c. *Apparent Causes*: Dissatisfaction with Siad Barre's handling of the Somalia-Ethiopia war.

SOURCE: A. A. Castagno, "Somalia Goes Military," *Africa Report*, 15 (February 1970): 25—27; *Africa Report* May—June, 1978, p. 31.

In the context of Somalia's ethnic homgeneity, the potentially divisive identities are those of the various clans and the regionalism of a mixed colonial heritage—northern vs. southern Somalia. Until 1969, the governments were successful in balancing the various groups in the country, and the most threatening conflicts were the border disputes with Ethiopia and Kenya. The president was assassinated in October 1969, however, and the army took power a week later. Plots against the military government were reported in 1970 and 1971 followed by a number of cabinet reshuffles from 1971 to 1974. The divisiveness among the population has not been eradicated. In addition, the effects of the drought which led to mass movements of nomads to sendentary life are possible sources of future conflict. In April 1978, a coup attempt led by army officers was quickly put down by troops loyal to the regime and the officers were executed. A major government reshuffle followed. The conflict with Ethiopia over the Ogaden continues at a significant level producing large numbers of refugees (about one quarter of a million by Oct. 1980) and indiscriminant violence. Thus the primary threat to the viability of the country comes from attempts to reunite the Somali peoples living in adjacent countries. There is an active war between Ethiopia and the Western Somali Liberation Front. (Note: Western Somalia is the Somali term for Ogaden.) In October 1980, a state of emergency was declared on the grounds of conflicts caused by tribalism and corrpution.

TABLE 32.8   Communal Instability

Event and Date	Characteristics
1. Rebellion April and May 1963	a. *Description*: Hergesia is the capital of former British Somaliland (now the northern province of Somalia). Demands for local autonomy and sporadic attacks had been increasing since independence in 1960. On May 2, 1963, authorities declared a state of siege in Hergesia. In the resultant clash, many government troops and civilians were injured. According to Radio Djibouti, traditional leaders in Hergesia demanded that new tax measures be rescinded or they would support a secession movement of Northern Somalia from Southern Somalia. The governor of Hergesia and the local police reportedly supported the rebels. In January 1965, several persons connected with the rebellion were given amnesty after order was apparently restored. b. *Participants*: Northern Somalia clans, the local police, and the Northern Administration. c. *Apparent Causes*: Riots started soon after the central government had imposed a number of new taxes, although underlying factors include demands for local autonomy.

SOURCE: I. M. Lewis, *The Modern History of Somaliland* (New York: Praeger, 1965), pp. 173—175.

TABLE 32.10   Annual Instability Events: Independence Through 1979—Somalia

Year	'61	'62	'63	'64	'65	'66	'67	'68	'69	'70	'71	'72	'73	'74	'75	'76	'77	'78	'79
ELITE INSTABILITY																			
Assassinations																			
Plots										1		1							
Attempted Coups d'État	1																	1	
Coups d'État									1										
COMMUNAL INSTABILITY																			
Ethnic Violence																			
Irredentism																			
Rebellion			1																
Civil War																			

Year	'61	'62	'63	'64	'65	'66	'67	'68	'69	'70	'71	'72	'73	'74	'75	'76	'77	'78	'79
MASS INSTABILITY																			
Revolt																			
Revolution																			
TURMOIL																			
Demonstrations																			
Strikes (no. days)																			
Riots (no. days)			6																
Terrorism								1	1										
Declarations of Emergency									1										
CABINET INSTABILITY																			
Realloc. and new appts.	5	7	2	18	1	7	17						2						
New members	1	4	2	8		3	11			16	11	5	2						
Resig. and Dismissals	17	6		4		4	11			20	9	6	1						
No. of members (max.) (maximum in year)	21	28	17	13	13	13	18	20	16	18	17	18							

VII. Selected References

BIBLIOGRAPHY

Krofors, C. and V. H. Narberg. *A Selection List of Literature on Somalia.* Uppsala: Scandanavian Institute of Africa Studies, 1976.

Salad, Mohamed Khalief. *Somalia: A Bibliographic Survey.* Westport, Conn.: Greenwood Press, 1977.

GENERAL

Cahill, K. M. ed. *Somalia: A Perspective.* Albany: State University of New York Press, 1980.

Castagno, M. *Historical Dictionary of Somalia.* Metuchen, N.J.: Scarecrow, 1976.

Contini, Paolo. *The Somali Republic: An Experiment in Legal Integration.* London: Cass, 1969.

Hess, Robert L. *Italian Colonialism in Somalia.* Chicago: University of Chicago Press, 1966.

Kaplan, I. et al. *Area Handbook for Somalia.* 2nd ed. Washington, D.C.: Government Printing Office, 1977.

Lewis, I. M. *A Pastoral Democracy.* New York: Holmes and Meier, 1981.

Lewis, I. M. *The Modern History of Somaliland: From Nation to State.* New York: Praeger, 1965.

Thompson, Virginia and Richard Adloff, *Djibouti and the Horn of Africa.* Stanford, Ca.: Stanford University Press, 1968.

POLITICAL

Drysdale, John C. S. *The Somali Dispute.* New York: Praeger, 1964.

Laitin, D. D. *Politics, Language and Thought: The Somali Experience.* Chicago: University of Chicago Press, 1977.

Legum, Colin and Lee Bull. The Horn of Africa in Continuing Crisis, N.Y.: Africana, 1979.

Lewis, I. M. "Integration in the Somali Republic." In *African Integration and Disintegration*, ed. A. Hazelwood. London: Oxford University Press, 1967.

Lewis, I. M. ABAAR: *The Somali Drought.* London: International African Institute, 1975.

Potholm, C. P. *Four African Political Systems.* Englewood Cliffs, N.J.: Prentice-Hall, 1970.

Barre, Mohamed Siad. *My Country and My People: Selected Speeches, 1969-74*. Mogadishu, 1974 (June).

ECONOMIC

International Labor Office. Economic Transformation in a Socialist Framework. Geneva: ILO. 1977.
International Monetary Fund. "Somalia." In *Surveys of African Economies*, Vol. 2, Washington, D.C.: I.M.F., 1968.
Quarterly Economic Review: *Uganda Ethiopia Somalia:* London, Economist Intelligence unit, 1974.

SOCIAL

Box, T. W. "Nomadism and Land Use in Somalia." *Economic Development and Cultural Change*, 19 (1971): 222—228.
Cassanelli, Lee V. "Recent Developments in Somali Studies" *Horn of Africa*, 2, 1. Jan./Mar. 1979, 36—41.
Lewis, I. M. "Conformity and Contrast in Somali Islam." In *Islam in Tropical Africa*, ed. I. M. Lewis, pp. 252—265. London: Oxford University Press, 1966.

33. Sudan

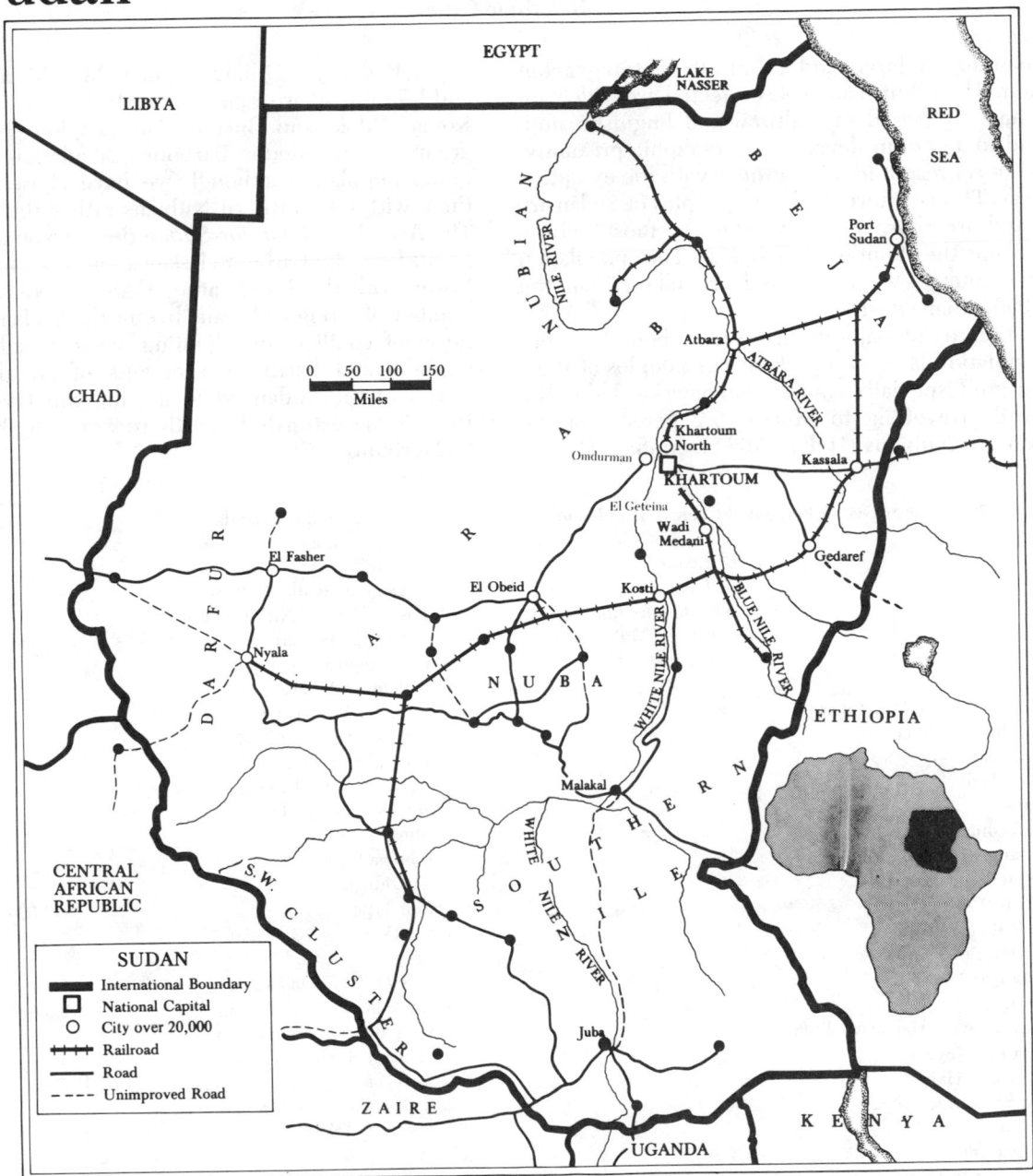

I. Basic Information

Date of Independence: January 1, 1956
Former Colonial Rulers: United Kingdom and Egypt
Former Name: Anglo-Egyptian Sudan
Estimated Population (1980): 21,590,000
Area Size (equivalent in U.S.): 967,500 sq. mi. (Alaska, Texas, and Colorado or nearly one-third the size of continental United States)

Date of Last Census: 1973
Major Exports 1976 as Percent of Total Exports: cotton and cotton product—51 percent; groundnuts—20 percent; gum hashab—6 percent; sesame—9 percent.

II. Ethnic Patterns

The Sudan has a large and ethnically heterogeneous population. The ethnic categories selected are widely inclusive, and are based on cultural and linguistic similarity, and to a certain degree on geographic proximity. They do not represent identity groups with the exception of the Beja. The northern Arabized peoples of Sudan are Muslim and are sharply distinguished by most cultural criteria from the Southern peoples. The population group percentages we have used are taken from the 1955—1956 Sudan census.

In addition to the major groups listed, about 3 percent of the population is made up of various peoples of West African origin (especially Hausa) who have settled in the Sudan while travelling to Mecca. 3.2 percent of the population are Nubians (Halfa, Sukkot, Mahas, Dongo-lawis, Bedeiriya, Dilling, Nyima, Midobi, and Birked), and 1.7 percent are Fung (Fung, Ingassana, Gule, Berta, Koma, Udok, and Burun). The last four Nubian sub-groups are included in Barbour's calculation of the Nuba group population although we have chosen to classify them with the northern Nubians rather than the Nuba. The *Area Handbook for Sudan* deviates on a number of points from the Barbour classification, e.g., including the Burun with the Fung rather than the Nilotes. A large number of foreign Africans live in the Sudan, partly because of conflicts in adjoining areas (Chad, Ethiopia, Uganda) and partly as remnants of populations that stayed in the Sudan while making the Hadj. In June 1980, it was estimated that there were 240,000 refugees in the country.

TABLE 33.1   Ethnic Units Over 5 Percent of Country Population

Ethnic Units	Estimated Ethnic Population 1980	Estimated Ethnic Percentage
a. Arab	8,852,000	41%
1. Ja'aliyin (Gaaliin) Arab		
i. Danagla Arabs, ii. Hassaniya,		
iii. Kawahla, iv. Gima,		
v. Hussaynat		
2. Guhayna Arab		
i. Jamala		
(Kababish), (Shukriya)		
ii. Baggara		
(Seleim), (Hawazma),		
(Mesiriya), (Humr),		
(Rizeiqat), (Ta'aisha),		
(Beni Rashid), (Rashaida),		
(Habaniya)		
iii. Gezira		
(Messellimiya), (Halawin), (Rufa'a)		
3. Kawahla Arab (Fezara)		
i. Kawahla, ii. Hamid,		
iii. Hamar, iv. Bedeiriya,		
v. Gawama's		
4. Zebaydiya Arabs		
5. Hawawir (Berber stock)		
i. Hawawir, ii. Jellaba,		
iii. Hawara, iv. Korobat		
6. Mixed Arab-Nubian		
i. Shaiqiya, ii. Manasir,		
iii. Rubatab, iv. Mirifab		
b. Southern Nile Cluster	4,966,000	23%
1. Western Nilotic (Nilote)		
i. Dinka, ii. Nuer,		
iii. Shilluk, iv. Anuak,		
v. Acholi, vi. Bor Belanda,		
vii. Jur (Jo Luo),		
viii. Shilluk Luo		
(Dembo, Shatt), ix. Pari		
2. Eastern Nilotic (Nilo-Hamite)		
i. Bari, ii. Mondari,		
iii. Nyangbara, iv. Pojulu		
(Fajelu), v. Kakwa,		
vi. Kuku, vii. Nyeyu,		
viii. Lokoya, ix. Luluba,		
x. Latuka, xi. Logit,		
xii. Lango, xiii. Toposa,		
xiv. Donyiro, xv. Jiye		
3. Murle Type		
i. Boma Murle, ii. Beir,		
iii. Didinga		
c. Darfur Type	1,943,000	9%
1. Fur (Keira), w. Daju and		
Beigo, 3. Beri and Berti,		
4. Masalit; Gimr, and Tama		
d. Beja (Bega)	1,295,000	6%
1. Beni Amer, 2. Amarar,		
3. Bisharin, 4. Hadendowa		
e. Nuba Type	1,079,500	5%
1. Katla and Gulud, 2. Koalib,		
3. Tegali, 4. Talodi,		
5. Tumtum, 6. Temein,		
Keiga-Girru, and Teis-um-Danab,		
7. Kadugli, 8. Heiban		
f. Southwestern Cluster	1,079,500	5%
1. Azandé type		
i. Azandé, ii. Ndogo,		
iii. Sere, iv. Mundu,		
v. Briri		
2. Moru type		
i. Moru, ii. Madi,		
iii. bongo, iv. Baka		

3. Fertit type
   i. Fertit (Mandala),
   ii. Feroge

SOURCES: K. M. Barbour, *The Republic of the Sudan* (London: University of London Press, 1961), pp. 74—87. U. S. Department of the Army, *Area Handbook for the Republic of the Sudan*, Pamphlet No. 550—27 (Washington, D.C., Government Printing Office, 1960), pp. 51—74. A. J. Butt, *The Nilotes of the Sudan and Uganda* (London: International African Institute, Oxford University Press, 1952).

III. Language Patterns

Arabic is the first language for about half of the population in the highly complex linguistic map of Sudan. (Knappert estimates 60 percent; Rustow 48 percent.) In addition, there are probably over 100 non-Arabic languages in Sudan (Knappert, 1965). The Nilotic languages (including Nubian, Jii, Dinka, and Lango) are predominant in the central non-Arab areas. In the southwest, Zandé is spoken. In the Nuba Mountains of Kordofan, a number of Kordofanian languages exist. Finally, in the northeast, a number of persons speak Cushitic languages, especially Beja. According to the Sudan census of 1955—56, about 5,276,000 persons speak Arabic; 1,591,00 speak Dinka-Nuer, 570,000 speak Darfurian.

Arabic is spoken as a second language by most of the non-Arabic populations except in the three southern provinces where probably only 1 percent is Arabic-speaking. Sudanese Arabic is a distinct dialect of classical Arabic. Even within Sudanese Arabic there are sub-dialects spoken in the Dongola, Omdurman, Gezira, and Darfur areas, plus the Baggara ethnic dialects. In the far south, pidgin English is also used as a *lingua franca*.

TABLE 33.2
Language Patterns

			Green-berg	Dalby
1. Primacy				
1st language	Arabic	(65%)		
2nd language	Dinka	(18%)		
2. Linguistic classification	Arabic		IIIA	(71B, C, 72A, 13, 73)
(all ethnic units in country over 5%)	Southern Nile cluster		IIE1	(53, 504, 11C, 11B)
	Darfur type		IID	38, 39
	Nuba type		IB5	(51C, 52A, 57DE, 68)
	Southwestern cluster		IA6	
	Beja (Bedawye)		IIID1	001
3. *Lingua franca*	Arabic, pidgin English			
4. Official language	Arabic (English is officially designated the "principal" language in the three southern provinces)			

SOURCES: Bjorn Jernudd, "Linguistic Integration and National Development: A Case Study of the Jebel Marra Area, Sudan," in *Language Problems of Developing Nations*, eds. Joshua A. Fishman, Charles A. Ferguson, and Jyotirindra Das Gupta (New York: John Wiley, 1968): pp. 167—182. Republic of the Sudan, Ministry for Social Affairs, Population Census Office, *First Population Census of Sudan*, 1955—56, p. 7.

IV. Urban Patterns

Capital: Khartoum (founded 1823)
Dominant ethnicity/language of capital
    Major vernacular: Arabic[1]
    Major ethnic group: Arab[2]
    Major ethnic group as percent of capital's population:
    42% (1955)

[1]Jan Knappert, "Language Problems of the New Nations of Africa," *African Quarterly*, 5 (1965): 95—105.
    [2]Census (1955).

TABLE 33.3   Growth of Capital and Largest City

Table	Khartoum	Greater Khartoum
1920	30,000	
1930	42,000	
1940	76,000	
1950	71,000	
1960	140,000	
1966	185,000	463,000 UA
1973	321,666	788,000 UA

SOURCES: Various editions of the *Statesman's Yearbook*; the 1966 figures are from the *UN Demographic Yearbook* 1969; 1973 census.

TABLE 33.4   Cities of 20,000 and Over*

City	Size	Date
Metropolitan Khartoum	788,000 UA	1973
a. Khartoum	(321,666)	1973
b. Omdurman	(305,308)	1973
c. Khartoum North	(161,278)	1973
Port Sudan	123,000	1973
Kassala[a]	90,000	1969
Wadi Medani	81,904	1973
El Obeid	74,109	1973
Gedaref[a]	70,000	1969
Atbara	62,407	1973
El Fasher[a]	51,000	1969
Kosti[a]	49,000	1969
Nyala[a]	39,000	1969
El Geteina[a]	39,000	1969

SOURCES: *Africa South of the Sahara 1975* report of 1973 census results.
    [a]El Sayed el Bushra *Urbanization in the Sudan* (Khartoum: Philosophical Society of the Sudan, 1972)
    *The definition of "urban place" by the government does *not* include all settlements over 20,000 in population. Villages of more than 35,000 population were omitted from the 1955/56 Census of Towns (Michael W. Khun, personal communication). Thus the list of cities given here should be regarded as incomplete. Khartoum, Khartoum North, and Omdurman each have separate town councils. The founding date of Khartoum (1823) refers to the time at which Egyptian-Turkish forces established a military post on the site. The first settlement on the site was established in 1691 by Sheikh Arbab el Agayed.

V. Political Patterns

FIGURE 33.1   Political Parties and Elections   SUDAN

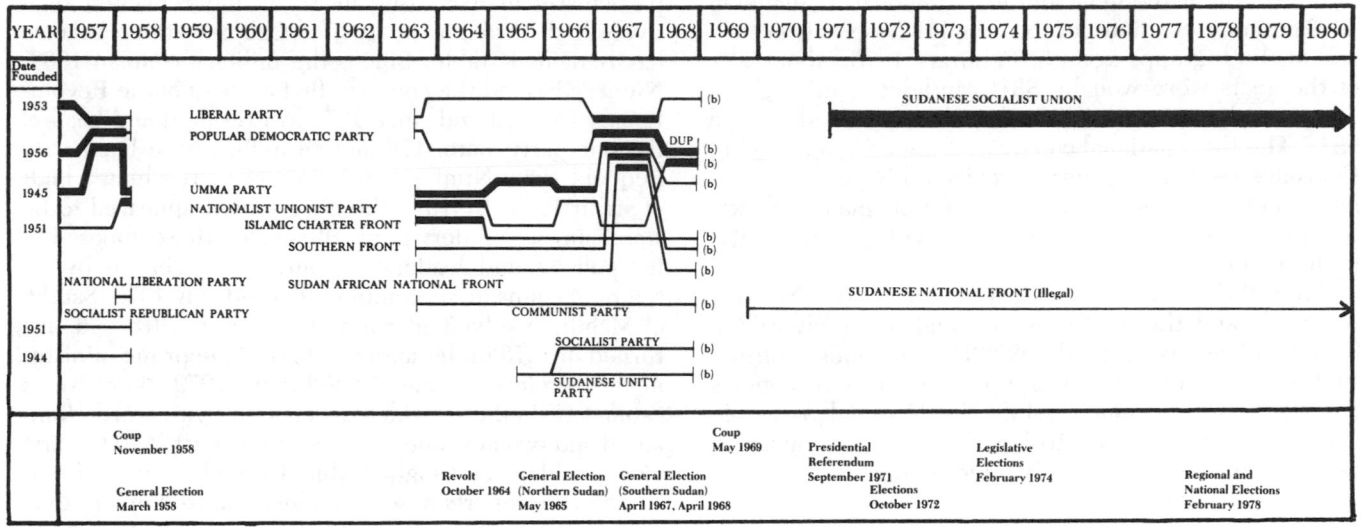

* Independence—January 1956.

A. Political Parties and Elections

The complex history of Sudanese political parties since independence has centered on many cleavages. Ethnic, relgious, and regional divisions have all had an effect on the formation of political parties. The first prime minister of independent Sudan, Ismail el-Azhari, and his *Nationalist Unionist Party* (NUP) were defeated in 1956 by a coalition of the Mirghanist-based *Popular Democratic Party* (PDP), the pro-Western *Umma Party* (UMMA), and the southern-based *Liberal Party* (LP). The new coalition, and its prime minister, Abdallah Khalil (UMMA), continued to govern until the March 1958 elections, when the NUP, under el-Azhari received a plurality and went into an unstable coalition with the *UMMA Party*. With the aid of Mr. Khalil (UMMA), the military (under General Abboud) assumed control in November 1958 and continued to rule until the revolt in November 1964. General Abboud was removed from office, and a new government led by el-Khatim el-Khalifah, a non-partisan civil servant, was formed. The cabinet was largely made up of NUP and UMMA members. Attempts were made to reconcile southern and northern partisans in 1967 and 1968 and, after having little success, the PDP and the NUP formed a coalition government—the *Democratic Unionist Party* (DUP)—in early 1969. The military coup in May 1969 resulted in the banning of all political parties. The illegal *Communist Party* is reputed to be the largest in Africa, but it is split into factions. In November 1970, following the death of Egypt's President Nasser, Egypt, Libya, Syria, and Sudan announced their intention to move towards a federation. In 1971, General Nimiery submitted a new constitution to the electorate which established him as President of a one-party state. The President would also be the leader of the sole political party to be called the *Sudanese Socialist Union* (SSU). The referendum was approved by the frequently encountered lop-sided percentage (over 99%) characteristic of such regimes in Africa and in the following year a legislature called the People's Assembly was elected. The Assembly has a complex formula which allocates seats to various segments of the population. There were elections in the south for the new Southern Regional Assembly in 1973 and new elections for the People's Assembly in 1974 and for both groups again in Feburary 1978. About 50% of the seats were won by SSU candidates although all other candidates running had to be approved by the SSU. The third national congress of the SSU was held in February 1980. The Congress reelected Nimiery as president and approved his decentralization plan to divide the north into five autonomous areas with powers similar to those in the south.

After the Congress, Nimiery dissolved the National Assembly and the Southern Regional Assembly calling for new elections in April 1980. The elections returned Alel Alier to the chairmanship of the southern region's High Executive Council, while the National Assembly became dominated by Moslem Brothers, an apparent sign of disillusionment with Nimiery's policies.

B. Political Leadership

There has been high turnover of political leadership in Sudan, both military and civilian. Cabinet turnover was particularly high starting in 1965, and remained relatively high through the 1970's. Cabinet ethnic balance has remained stable. Since, the military coup in 1969, Nimiery has led the country, first as head of the Revolutionary Council and since 1971 as President and head of the one-party state. Cabinet reshuffles have been very frequent since Nimiery came to power, reaching a high of six in 1973. By 1974 the government appeared to be stabilizing as Nimiery gradually ousted those opposed to his policies and leadership, only to be shaken by attempted coups in September 1975 and July 1976. Saddik el-Mahdi, involved in coup attempts in 1975—76, returned in 1978 under amnesty to become prime minister in the Nimiery regime. In February 1979, there was a cabinet reshuffle in which seven ministries were eliminated and two new ones created. In August 1970 the first vice-president and eight Cabinet members were fired. There were reports of several plots against Nimiery during March and April 1979, but they were uncovered before they could be carried out.

TABLE 33.5   Heads of Government (Post-Independence)

Name	Dates in Office	Age (1982)	Ethnicity	Education	Former Occupaton
1. Ismail el-Azhari (Prime Minister)	1956—1958	d. 1969 age 71	Arab	American University (Beirut)	Teacher
2. Abdallah Khalil (Prime Minister)	1956—1958	d. 1970, age 78	Darfur	Military School, Khartoum	Soldier
3. Lt. General Ibrahim Abboud (Prime Minister)	1958—1964	83	Arab	Engineering (Sudan)	Soldier
4. Sir el-Khatim el-Khalifah (Prime Minister)	1964—1965	62	Arab	Secondary (Khartoum) Exeter College, Oxford	Civil Servant
5. Muhammad Ahmad Maghoub (Prime Minister)	1965—1966	74	Arab	Law and Engineering (Sudan)	Lawyer
6. Sayed Sadik El Mahdi (Prime Minister)	1966—1967	46	Arab	Oxford	Politician
7. Muhammad Ahmad Mahgoub (Prime Minister)	1967—1969	74	Arab	Law and Engineering (Sudan)	Lawyer
8. Abubakr Awadallah (Prime Minister)	1969	66	Arab	Law (England)	Lawyer

Name	Dates in Office	Age (1982)	Ethnicity	Education	Former Occupation
9. Brigadier-General Gaafer Nimiery (President)	1969—present	52	Arab	Sudan Military College	Soldier

TABLE 33.6   Cabinet Membership: Distribution by Ethnic Unit*

Ethnicity*	Independence Cabinet	1967 Cabinet
1. Arab (41%)	56%	47%
2. Southern Nile (23)	25	20
3. Darfur (9)	0	7
4. Beja (6)	0	0
5. Nuba (5)	19	27
6. Southwestern (5)	0	0
7. Others (11)	0	0
N =	16	6

*Ethnic units arranged in rank order of size within country with the unit's percent of national population in parentheses.

VI. National Integration and Stability

The Sudan has experienced instability at the elite, communal, and mass levels. Political elite turn-over has been related to ideological, religious and regional factors, as well as to conflict over Sudanese relations to Egyptian and Arab regional politics. The revolt in 1964 was largely the result of an urban coalition of workers, students, and civil servants. Communal instability is partly the result of the colonial legacy in which many small-scale societies of Nilotic peoples in the South (who have resisted Arabization by the northern Sudanese) were attached to the predominantly Arab north. Since the 1969 coup the unsettled politics of the Sudan has continued with one major exception, the southern civil war. Nimiery agreed to substantial autonomy for the region and integrated parts of the southern rebel army into the Sudanese army. The civil war, which ended in 1972, seems to be largely a matter of the past. Nevertheless, conflict in the Sudan continues with frequent army plots, student rioting and university closures, a rebellion led by el Mahdi, and nearly successful coups d'état in 1971 and 1976.

In August and September 1979, riots, demonstrations and strikes broke out in major cities in protest of drastic increases in commodity prices. In March and again in October 1979, Nimiery escaped assassination attempts. A third attempt occurred in May 1980. This last attempt was followed by the arrest of 250—300 people including members of the National Unionist Party and Baath Party.

TABLE 33.7   Elite Instability

Event and Date	Characteristics
1. Coup d'État November 17, 1958	a. *Description*: During the night of November 17, four thousand troops under the command of General Ibrahim Abboud occupied Khartoum and arrested all the members of Prime Minister Khalil's cabinet. b. *Participants*: Lieutenant General Ibrahim Abboud (Commander-in-Chief of the Armed Forces) and several senior army officers. Acording to some reports the incumbent Prime Minister Khalil consulted with the military and suggested they take over to preserve order and stability. c. *Apparent Causes*: The army was apparently invited by Abdallah Khalil to take power to forestall pro-Egyptian elements who were gaining strength. According to a Sudanese broadcast: "The aim of the revolution is to maintain the independence of the Sudan and to raise the standard of living. Former politicians failed to do that in view of the fact that no one party had a clear majority."
2. Coup Attempt March 4—9, 1959	a. *Description*: Two provincial military commanders massed troops on Khartoum, and after their failure to take power, they demand a reshuffle of the Supreme Military Council. b. *Participants*: Brigadiers Muhyi al-Din Abdullah and Abdal-Rahim Shannan and army units. c. *Apparent Causes*: Conflict over memberhip in the Supreme Military Council. The attempt to oust Major General Ahmed Abdal Wahhab, the Defense Minister, was successful as he was retired from the Council and the army. Brigadier Hassan Beshir Nasr, the other object of the coup attempt, remained on the Council.
3. Coup Attempt May 21—22, 1959	a. *Description*: Two platoons marched on Khartoum with the intention of supporting Brigadiers Muyhi al-Din 'Abdallah, and 'Abdal-Rahim Shannan in a confrontation with Hasan Bashir Nasr, the army's deputy-commander-in-chief and minister for presidential affairs. They retreated when advised to do so by Muyhi al-Din. Muyhi al-Din and Shannan were arrested and charged with inciting to mutiny with the object of overthrowing the regime. b. *Participants*: Two platoons of troops from the eastern area (Muyhi al-Din was their former commander), several other officers, and a member of the Supreme Council. The two brigadiers had been in contact with many of the younger officers and politicians. c. *Apparent Causes*: Muyhi al-Din 'Abdallah and 'Abdal-Rahim Shannan supported the National Unionist Party (NUP) and were, therefore, not politically popular with other members of the Supreme Council. They were apparently opting for the removal of Bashir from the Council.
4. Coup Attempt November 9, 1959	a. *Description*: A mutiny at the Infantry School in Omdurman failed when expected support from the rest of the army and the populace did not develop. b. *Participants*: Young officers, mainly majors and captains, who were reportedly influenced by the "Muslim Brothers." c. *Apparent Causes*: Not ascertainable. The officers were reputedly connected with the Communists and/or the Muslim Brothers.
5. Coup Attempt December 18, 1966	a. *Description*: Soon after the High Court ruled that the government's ban on the Communist Party was unconstitutional, riots between pro- and anti-communist demonstrators erupted. In the wake of these events the government announced that it had averted a coup attempt by the armed forces. b. *Participants*: Approximately 300 trainees from the Gordon Training School led by 2nd Lieutenant Khalid Hussein. Six other officers, including the commanding officer of the Eastern Sudan Military Command, were eventually arrested. Following the announcement of the coup the leading members of the Communist Party were arrested, but their connection with the coup attempt was never made clear. c. *Apparent Causes*: No explanation for the military action was offered. The arrests of leading communists appeared to some sources to be influenced by traditional religious groups.
6. Coup d'État May 25, 1969	a. *Description*: A group of middle-ranking army officers commanding two parachute units, an infantry unit, and an armored unit, totalling some 400 soldiers, cut off communications in the Sudanese capital, arrested senior army officers, and placed President el-Azhair and the cabinet of Mr. Mahgoub under house arrest. The provisional constitution was dissolved, public meetings were banned, and a military revolutionary council and civilian cabinet were appointed. The coup was led by Col. Gafar al Nimiery, who became President of the Revolutionary Council.

Event and Date	Characteristics

b. *Participants*: The government displaced by this coup had been formed after the elections of April 1968, in which a complicated alliance between three parties produced a government headed by the pre-election prime minister (Mahgoub) and by the president (el-Azhair). In contrast to the intricate coalition before the coup, the new regime was homogenous. The organizers of the coup were a group of army majors and colonels who were members of a 10-year-old underground organization with an articulate socialist and pan-Arab orientation. These officers formed the new Revolutionary Council, and the civilian council led by Abubakr Awakallah, a former presidential candidate of the leftist bloc, included at least three other well-known Sudanese (Awadallah, a communist sympathizer although not a communist, was put out of office by Nimiery.)

c. *Apparent Causes*: The new regime, as reasons for the coup, cited the failure of the governments appointed by former President el-Azhair to solve the country's economic and political problems. In particular, they referred to the continuing civil war in the south, the failures in Sudanese agricultural policy, corruption and disorganization in civilian party politics, and the failure of the Sudan to take an aggressive posture against imperialism in the Arab world, and against Zionism in Palestine.

7. Coup Attempt
July 21—23, 1971

a. *Description*: A group of reputedly leftist army officers seized power for three days, imprisoning Prime Minister al Nimiery and other government officials. They created a seven-member command council with Lieutenant Colonel Bubiker el-Nur Osman, age 37, as chairman. Iraq immediately recognized the new government, which quickly lifted restrictions on the country's communist movement and announced a policy of regional autonomy for the south. On July 22, troops loyal to Premier al Nimiery staged a countercoup which was successful after severe fighting in which at least 30 loyalist soldiers and officers were killed. Just prior to the counter-coup, neighboring Libya forced down a British airliner which was carrying two of the coup leaders, Lieut. Col. el-Nur Osman and Major Farouk Osman Hamadallah, from London, where al-Nur Osman had been undergoing a medical checkup, back to the Sudan. The coup leaders were executed.

b. *Participants*: The coup leaders were Major Hashem el-Ata, who led the military attack; Colonel Abdel Moneim Ahmed, commander of the Third Armored Brigade; Lieutenant Colonel Osman Hussein, commander of the Republican Guards; and Captain Muaweya Abdel Hai. Lieut. Col. el-Nur Osman and Maj. Hamadallah, although part of the plot, were in London during the coup attempt. Members of the Communist Party were prominent in the leadership and approval of the coup attempt.

c. *Apparent Causes*: In November 1970, Babiker el-Nur Osman, Hamadallah and el-Ata had been ousted by Nimiery in a quarrel over plans to link the Sudan with Egypt and Libya in a federation. "General Nimiery charged that the ousted officers had fought the federation plan at the instigation of a Communist faction headed by Muhammad Mahgoub, secretary of the ostensibly banned Communist party." General al Nimiery is closely allied politically with Egypt and Libya.

8. Coup Attempt
September 5, 1975

a. *Description*: Paratroopers led by Col. Hassan Hussein Osman occupy the radio station in Khartoum and broadcast that the *National Front* has dismissed the Nimiery government because the 1969 "revolution" has failed to achieve its aims.

b. *Participants*: Lt. Col. Osman and paratroopers backed by a religious and Communist party-based group of army officers calling themselves the *National Front*. They also received general support from members of the banned UMMA Party and the Muslim brotherhoods.

c. *Apparent Causes*: Dissatisfaction with the Nimiery regime both from the left and right, the UMMA Party, and other groups who had lost power under the Nimiery regime.

9. Coup Attempt
July 2—3, 1978

a. *Description*: Army units along with other groups took major strongholds in Khartoum after the plan to assassinate Nimiery at the airport on his return from Paris was frustrated when he arrived an hour early. After hundreds of casualties the coup attempt was proved to be unsuccessful and large numbers of prisoners were taken with equipment bearing Libyan identification.

Event and Date	Characteristics
	b. *Participants*: Army units and groups trained in Libya and Ethiopia and armed by Libya. Rebel strength was estimated to be between one and two thousand men. Various civilians were involved including politicans from banned political parties such as Saddik el-Mahdi of the UMMA Party and Sharif Husayn al Hindi of the Union Party. Various other banned right wing parties of the National Front were also involved.
	c. *Apparent Causes*: Army and civilian dissatisfaction with the Nimiery regime under the single-party system which he had created.

SOURCES: Helen Kitchen, "The Sudan in Transition," *Current History*, 37 (1959): 35 —40. P. M. Holt, *A Modern History of the Sudan* (New York: Grove Press, 1961), pp. 18—90. Tariq Ismael, "Sudan Joins the Arabs," *Africa Report*, 15 (January 1970): 12—13. *The New York Times*, July 21—24, 1971.

TABLE 33.8   Communal Instability

Event and Date	Characteristics
a. Civil War: Attempted Secession 1963—1972	a. *Description*: The south was in a state of armed rebellion and civil war from 1955 through the early 1970's. Military action in the south developed during 1963 when General Abboud's regime chose force as the most likely method of national unification. Combatant deaths for 1963—1967 were reported to be over 1500 although figures as high as 500,000 have recently been cited. The secessionists could not match the armament of the central government and therefore depended on sabotage and small scale forays. The war was finally ended with the granting of considerable autonomy to the southern region and the bringing into the Sudanese army of many soldiers from the rebel army.
	b. *Participants*: The three southern provinces of Sudan (which are non-Arab) demanded separation from the Arab-dominated northern portions of Sudan. Southern distrust of northerners has its roots in 19th-century Arab slave trading. Secessionist leadership was fragmented and prone to feuds. The rebels referred to their movement as "*Anya nya*," but the degree to which they were organized cannot be ascertained. Some estimates placed southern troop strength at 12,000; the north is said to have had 18,000 troops in the south.
	c. *Apparent Causes*: Secessionists, who were drawn from black non-Muslim identity groups claimed four major grievances; (1) political domination by the Arab north; (2) attempts by the north to Arabize the south; (3) discrimination in jobs, salaries, educational opportunities; and (4) discrimination in the allocation of funds and projects for general regional development.
2. Rebellion March 1970	a. *Description*: Following an unsuccessful attempt to assassinate Premier el-Nimiery on March 27, 1970, supporters of Imam el-Hadi Ahmed el-Mahdi revolted in the city of Omdurman and on Aba Island, 150 miles south of Khartoum. Within a week the government crushed the rebellion and the Imam was killed while escaping to the Ethiopian frontier according to government sources.
	b. *Participants*: The followers of the Imam comprise the Ansar Muslim sect and number nearly two million. Some reports indicated that 1,000 or more persons died in the fighting in Omdurman and another 1,000 on Aba Island. A retired army officer, Brigadier Mohammed Abdullah Hamed was arrested and charged with training members of the Ansar sect in modern weapons, and the Imam's nephew and potential successor, Saddik-al-Mahdi, was expelled from the country.
	c. *Apparent Causes*: The Ansar sect represents a serious threat to the present Sudan government because of their size, the fact that they are influential in the army and civil service, and their opposition to government policies which they interpret as encouraging Nasserism, communism, growing secularism and the secession of the southern provinces. The government did not back away from a direct confrontation with what they regarded as a "reactionary stronghold," and it appears likely that it precipitated the conflict. This event is coded as a rebellion, although if the Ansar sect was attempting to monopolize the existing political system it would be a civil war by our definitions.

SOURCES: *Africa Digest*, 17 (July 1970): 52—53, *Africa Contemporary Record*, 1970—71, B 44—45.

TABLE 33.9   Mass Instability

Event and Date	Characteristics
1. Revolt October 20—30, 1964	a. *Description*: Civilian demonstrators forced the military government to abdicate. Reported casualties for the duration of the disorders were 36 dead and more than 100 wounded. b. *Participants*: Several thousand demonstrators from the working population of Khartoum, the judiciary and the civil service went on a general strike. Students and teachers were the first to openly defy government authority. The former political parties (UMMA, NUP, Communist Party), together with the Muslim Brothers formed the United National Front to coordinate their activities for the duration of the revolt. c. *Apparent Causes*: Discontent with the military regime was pervasive. Students resented government encroachment into university affairs; workers were burdened with tax increases; and government restrictions on political expression were generally unpopular. The military regime was also charged with nepotism and misuse of government funds. Because of the ideological foundation of the coalition, it might be coded as revolution.

SOURCES: Mohammed O. Beshir, "The Sudan: A Military Surrender," *Africa Report*, 9 (December 1964): 3—6. Yusuf Fadl Hasan, "The Sudanese Revolution of October 1964," *Journal of Modern African Studies*, 5 (1967): 491—510.

TABLE 33.10   Annual Instability Events: Independence Through 1979—Sudan

Year	'61	'62	'63	'64	'65	'66	'67	'68	'69	'70	'71	'72	'73	'74	'75	'76	'77	'78	'79
ELITE INSTABILITY																			
Assassinations																			
Plots									8	1	1	1	1	2	1				3
Attempted Coups d'État						1					1					1	1		
Coups d'État									1										
COMMUNAL INSTABILITY																			
Ethnic Violence																			
Irredentism																			
Rebellion						1				1									
Civil War			1	1	1	1	1	1	1	1	1	1							
MASS INSTABILITY																			
Revolt				1															
Revolution																			
TURMOIL																			
Demonstrations					1			1						1					
Strikes (no. days)		1		10	7														
Riots (no. days)	1			5	6	2		2	1					1					
Terrorism																			
Declarations of Emergency					1			1	3	1				1	1				
CABINET INSTABILITY																			
Realloc. and new appts.	3	10	1	1	23	16	16	1	2	6	3	7							
New members	1	3	1	1	21	8	11	8	7	6	10	12							
Resig. and Dismissals			1		27	6	11	7	8	4	7	13							
No. of members (max.) (maximum in year)	13	15	15	15	15	15	16	17	26	23	27	25							

VII. Selected References

BIBLIOGRAPHY

African Bibliographic Center, Washington. *A Current Bibliography on Sudanese Affairs, 1960—64*. Special Bibliographic Series, Vol. 3, No. 4, 1965. Westport, Conn.: Greenwood, 1965.

El Nasri, Abdal Rahman, *A Bibliography of the Sudan, 1938—1958*. London: Oxford University Press for the University of Khartoum, 1962.

Voll, John Obert. *Historical Dictionary of the Sudan*. Metuchen, N.J.: Scarecrow Press, 1978.

GENERAL

Albino, O. *The Sudan: A Southern Viewpoint*. New York: Oxford University Press, 1970.

Arkell, A. J. *A History of the Sudan*. London: Athlone Press, 1955.

Barbour, L. M. *The Republic of the Sudan: A Regional Geography*. London: University of London Press, 1961.

Collins, Robert O. *Land Beyond the Rivers: The Southern Sudan, 1898—1918*. New Haven: Yale University Press, 1971.

Conte, C. *The Sudan as a Nation*. Milan, Giuffre Editore, 1976.

El-Mahdi, Mandour. *Short History of the Sudan*. London: Oxford University Press, 1965.

Hassan, Y. Fadi, ed. *Sudan in Africa*. Khartoum: Khartoum University Press, 1971.

Henderson, Kenneth D. D. *Sudan Republic*. New York: Praeger, 1965.

Holt, Peter M. *A Modern History of the Sudan*. 3rd ed. New York:Grove Press, 1979.

Martin P. F. *The Sudan in Evolution*. Westport, Conn.: Negro Universities Press, 1970.

Oduho, J. and W. Deng. *The Problem of the Southern Sudan*. London: Oxford University Press, 1963.

Nelson, H. D. et al. *Area Handbook for Sudan*, 3rd ed. Washington, D.C.: Government Printing Office, 1973.

Voll, J. O. *Historical Dictionary of the Sudan*. Metuchen, N.J.: Scarcrow, 1978.

POLITICAL

'Abd Al-Rahim, Muddathir. *Imperialism and Nationalism in the Sudan: A Study in Constitutional and Political Development, 1899—1956*. London: Oxford University Press, 1969.

Bechtold, P. K. *Politics and the Sudan: Parliamentary and Military Rule in an Emerging African Nation*. New York: Praeger, 1976.

Beshir, M. O. *The Southern Sudan: Background to Conflict*. New York: Praeger, 1968.

Eprile, Cecil. *War and Peace in the Sudan, 1955—1972*. Newton Abbott, Great Britain: David and Charles, 1974.

Hasan, Yusuf Fadl. "The Sudanese Revolution of October 1964." *Journal of Modern African Studies*, 5 (1967): 491—509.

Howell, John. "Politics in the Southern Sudan." *African Affairs*, 72 (April 1973): 163—178.

Lees, Francis A. and Hugh C. Brooks. *The Economic and Political Development of the Sudan*. Boulder, Colorado, Westview Press, 1977.

Sylvester, A. *Sudan Under Nimieri*. London: Bodley Head, 1977.

Wai, D. "Revolution, Rhetoric and Reality in the Sudan." *Journal of Modern African Studies*, 17, 1 (March).

Wai, D. *Secessionist Politics and the International Community: The Case of the Afro-Arab Conflict in the Sudan*. Ph.D. Thesis, Harvard University, 1977.

Wai, Dunstan. "The Sudan: Domestic Politics and Foreign Relations under Nimiery." *African Affairs*, 78, 312, July 1979, pp. 297—317.

Wai, Dunstan, M., ed. *The Southern Sudan: The Problem of National Integration*. London: Cass, 1973.

Woodwar, P. *Condominium and Sudanese Nationalism*. London, Rex Collings, 1979.

Wright, P. *Conflict on the Nile*. London: Heinemann, 1972.

ECONOMIC

Adams, Martin E. and Howell, John. "Developing the traditional Sector in the Sudan." *Economic Development and Cultural Change*, 27, 3 April 1979, pp. 505—518.

Barnett, Tony. *The Gezira Scheme: An Illusion of Development*. London: Cass, 1977.

El-Hasson, Ali Mohamed. *An Introduction to the Sudan Economy*. Khartoum: Khartoum University Press.

Hance, William A. "The Gezira Scheme: A Study in Agricultural Developmenmt." In *African Economic Development*, rev. ed., pp. 31—53. New York: Praeger, 1967.

ILO. *Growth Employment and Equity: A Comprehensive Strategy for the Sudan*. Geneva: ILO, 1976.

Reining, Conrad C. *The Zande Scheme: An Anthropological Case Study of Economic Development in Africa.* Evanston, Ill.: Northwestern University Press, 1966.

Osman, Omar and A. A. Suleiman. "The Economy of Sudan." In *The Economies of Africa*, eds. P. Robson and D. A. Lury, pp. 436—470. Evanston, Ill.: Northwestern University Press, 1969.

SOCIAL

Beshir, Mohamed Omer. *Educational Development in the Sudan, 1898—1956.* London: Oxford University Press, 1969.

El Tayeb, S. D. Z. *The Students in the Sudan, 1940—1970.* Khartoum: Khartoum University Press, 1971.

Hassan, Y. F. *The Arabs and the Sudan.* Edinburgh: Edinburgh University Press, 1967.

McLoughlin, J. "The Sudan's Three Towns: A Demographic and Economic Profile of an African Urban Complex." *Economic Development and Culturual Change*, 12: Pt. 1 (October 1963), pp. 70—83; Pt. 2 (January 1965), pp. 158—173; Pt. 3 OApril 1964), pp. 186—304.

O'Null, N. "Imperialism and Class Struggle in Sudan". *Race and Class*, 20, 1, Summer 1978, pp. 1—19.

Trimingham, J. S. *Islam in the Sudan.* London: Oxford University Press, 1949.

Warburg, Gabriel *Islam, Nationalism and Trade Unionism in a Traditional Society: The Case of Sudan.* London: Frank Cass, 1978.

34. Swaziland

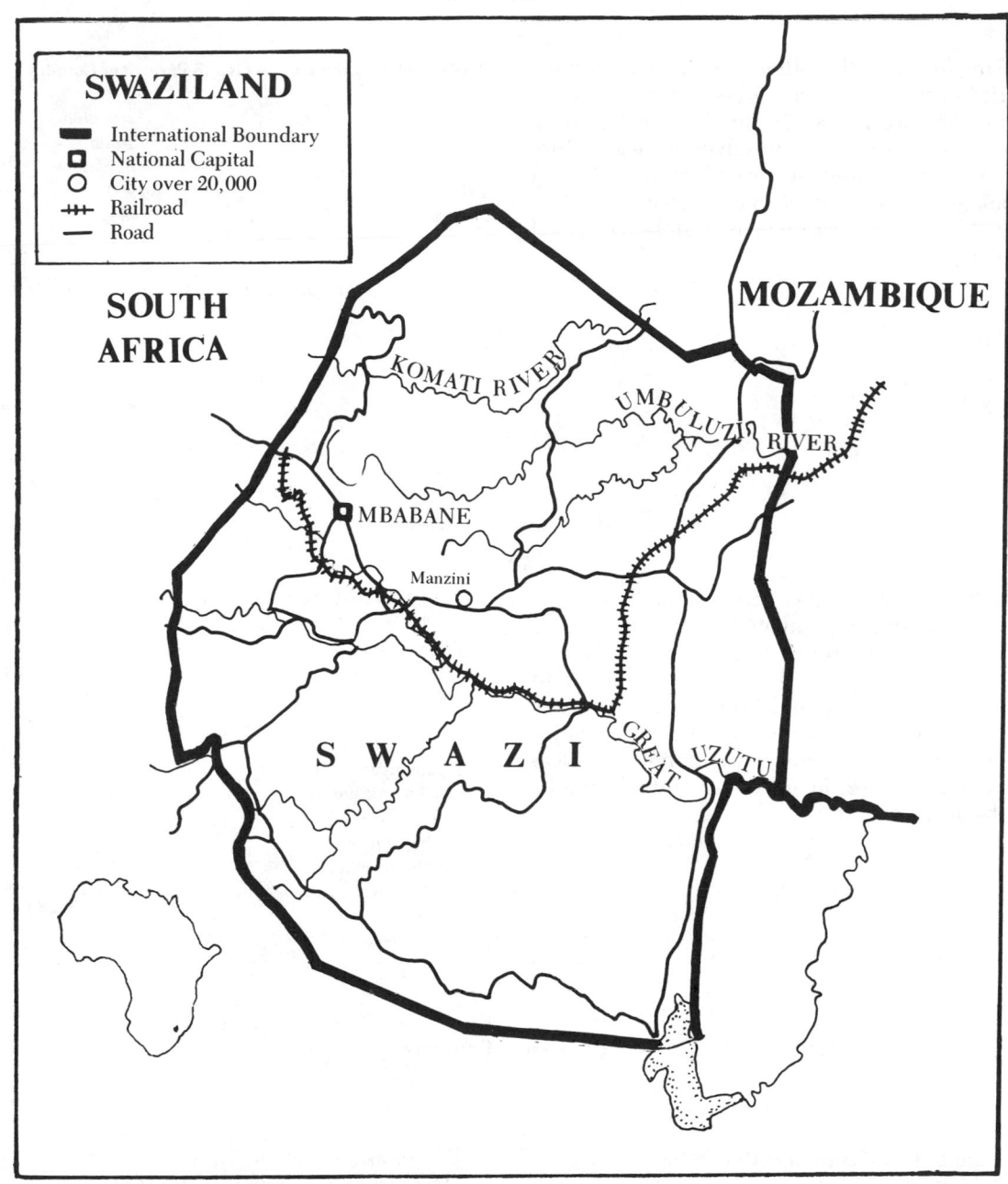

SWAZILAND

- ▬ International Boundary
- ▢ National Capital
- ○ City over 20,000
- ┼┼┼ Railroad
- — Road

SOUTH
AFRICA

MOZAMBIQUE

KOMATI RIVER

UMBULUZI RIVER

□ MBABANE

Manzini ○

S W A Z I

GREAT UZUTU

I. Basic Information

Date of Independence: September 6, 1968
Former Colonial Ruler: United Kingdom
Estimated Population (1980): 555,000
Area Size (Equivalent in U.S.): 6,704 sq. mi. (New Jersey)

Date of Last Census: 1976
Major Exports 1975 as Percent of Total Exports: sugar—54%; wood and wood products—9%; asbestos—7%.

II. Ethnic Patterns

The Swazi kingdom like the other former high commission territories in southern Africa is centered around one ethnic group, the Swazi, and the small minorities have increasingly come to identify themselves as Swazi. More than 90 percent of the population are Swazi with the rest of the population made up of small groups of Zulu, Tonga, and Shanagaan. Europeans numbered about 11,000 in 1975.

TABLE 34.1   Ethnic Units Over 5 Percent of Country Population

Ethnic Units	Estimated Ethnic Population 1980	Estimated Ethnic Percentage
a. Swazi	499,500	90%

SOURCE: *Who's Who in Africa* J. Dickie and A. Rake eds. London, 1973.

II. Language Patterns

Swati is widely used as a *lingua franca* and all estimates regard virtually the entire population as Swati-speaking. English is widespread, however, and given the relatively high level of primary education, it may be spoken by more than one-third of the population. Zulu is estimated as being spoken by about 15 percent of the population and we estimate that 95 percent of the population speak Swati. Zulu and Swati are, in any event mutually intelligible to a substantial extent.

TABLE 34.2   Language Patterns

1. Primacy			
1st language	Swati	(95%)	
2nd language	Zulu	(15%)	
		Green-berg	Dalby
2. Linguistic classification (all ethnic units in country over 5%)	Swati	IA5	R4
3. *Lingua franca*	Swati		
4. Official language	Swati, English		

IV. Urban Patterns

Capital: Mbabane (Royal capital is Lobamba)
Largest City: Manzini
Dominant Ethnicty/language of capital:
   Major vernacular: Siswati

Major ethnic group: Swazi
Major ethnic group as percent of capital's population:
   nearly 100 percent

TABLE 34.3   Growth of Capital and Largest City*

Date	Mbabane	Manzini
1956	3,428	
1960	7,250	
1962	8,390	
1966	13,803	6,081
1970	16,000	25,000
1975	24,000	25,000

SOURCES: *UN Demographic Yearbook 1962* and *Statesman's Yearbook* various editions.

*According to *Europa Yearbook 1979* V. II, the 1976 population estimates are quite different from those reported above. They are Mbabane, 22,262; and Manzini, 10,472.

TABLE 34.4   Cities of 20,000 and Over*

City	Size	Date
Manzini	25,000	1975
Mbabane	24,000	1975

SOURCE: *Europa Yearbook 1977*, V. II.

*According to *Europa Yearbook 1979* Vol. II., p. 1467, the 1976 population figures for these cities are very different from those cited above. The August 1976 figures are Mbabane 22,262; and Manzini 10,472.

V. Political Patterns

A. Political Parties and Elections

Political activity came late to Swaziland with the establishment of the *Swaziland Progressive Party* in 1960. The SPP had existed in an earlier form as the *Swaziland Progressive Association*. By 1962, the SPP had split into three groups, the *Ngwane National Liberatory Congress* (NNLC), the *Swaziland United Front* (SUF), and the *Swaziland Democratic Party* (SDP). In reaction to the growth of parties, the king, Sobhuza II, established his own party in 1964, the *Imbokodvo National Movement* (INM) and it competed in the 1964 and 1967 elections. The SDP joined the INM in 1967. The SUF and SPP declined and the NNLC remained as the only effective opposition to the royal party when independence came in 1968. In the first post-independence election, in 1972, the NNLC won three seats and nearly 20 percent of the vote although in 1971 the NNLC had split into two factions. The Ngwenyama, Sobhuza II, reacted by trying to deport an opposition MP but the courts would not accede and the king repealed the constitution and detained opposition politicians. Party activity was banned in April 1973 and the opposition leader, Dr. Zwane, was arrested and detained in November, 1975. Parliament was abolished in March 1977. In 1978, a new constitution which followed traditional law, was completed. During the summer, mounting opposition to Swaziland's close ties to South Africa led to the formation of the *Swazi Liberation Movement* (Swalimo). In October 1978, elections were held and the forty chieftancies nominated 80 members to the Electoral College.

B. Political Leadership

Sobhuza, the Ngwenyama of the Swazi, was king from 1921 until 1982 and exercised considerable control even under the British administration. After independence, he tolerated opposition at first, and then, in 1973, after the opposition had won three seats (of 24) in the National Assembly elections of 1972, he repealed the constitution, banned political parties, and formed an army, for the first time. In March 1977, the Parliament was abolished and replaced in 1978 with a system of traditional representation via the chiefs.

Except for one European, the membership of the cabinet has largely remained stable since independence. The first European in the cabinet was replaced by another European, over policy disagreements with the king.

In the spring of 1980 King Sobhuza fell seriously ill, but he recovered and ruled for two more years. There is no known appointed successor to the king except for the Queen Mother who rules in the interim until a new king can be named.

FIGURE 34.1   Political Parties and Elections   SWAZILAND

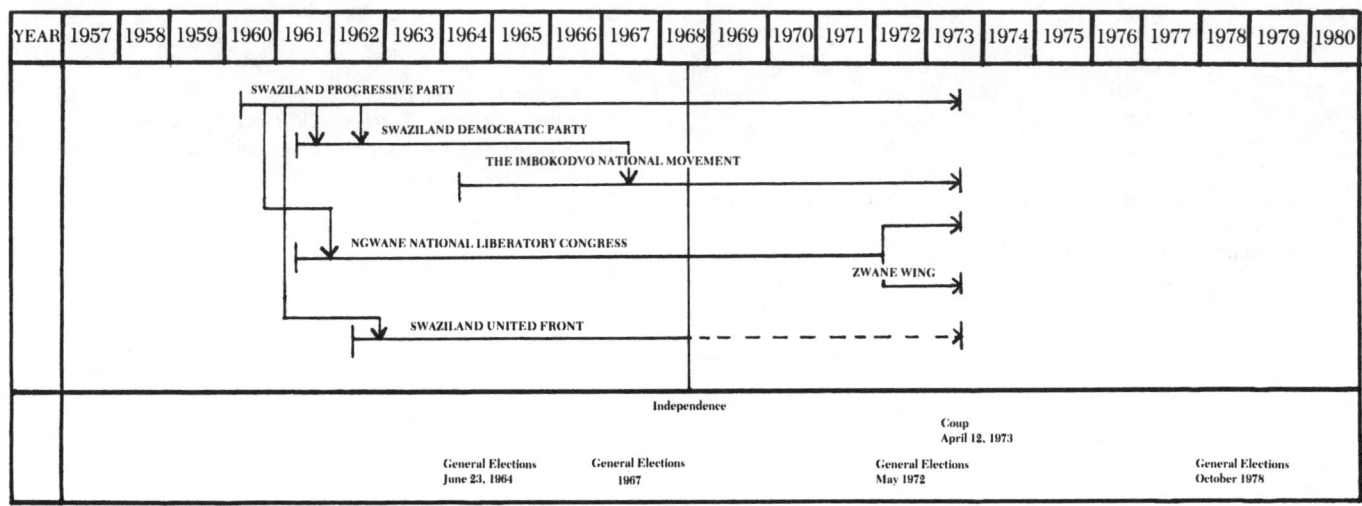

TABLE 34.5   Head of State (Post-Independence)

Name	Dates in Office	Age (1982)	Ethnicity	Education	Former Occupation
H. M. Sobhuza II (King)	1968— 1982	Died 1982 aged 83	Swazi	Lovedale College (South Africa)	King since 1921

TABLE 34.6   Cabinet Membership: Distribution by Ethnic Unit*

Ethnicity*	Independence Cabinet	1972 Cabinet
Swazi (90%)	89	89
Others (10)	11	11
N =	9	9

*Ethnic units arranged in rank order of size within country with the unit's percent of national population in parentheses.

VI. National Integration and Stability

Since Swaziland became independent in 1968, political conflict in this small ethnically homogeneous nation has evolved around loyalty or opposition to the position and policy of the Swazi King. The King, in April 1973, suspended the constitution and assumed full powers. All political activity was banned. Although Swaziland maintains good and active relations with many countries in black Africa, good relations with South Africa and rapid economic development appear to be major goals dominating the policies of the country. Opposition to Swaziland's close ties with South Africa is growing, however, and has prompted the formation of a new political group, the *Swazi Liberation Movement* (Swalimo). In October 1977, there were teachers' strikes and demonstrations. In 1980 there was increased concern by Amnesty International over the frequent usage of detention orders in Swaziland to silence political opponents.

TABLE 34.7   Elite Instability

Event and Date	Characteristics
1. Coup d'État April 12, 1973	a. *Description*: King Sobhuza suspends the constitution, assumes full powers, bans political activity, and institutes 'preventive detention.' b. *Participants*: Sobhuza, his palace supporters, and the newly formed 300 man army. c. *Apparent Causes*: After the NNLC performance in the 1972 elections and the failure to deport one of the newly elected opposition MP's, Sobhuza was concerned that the future of the royal system was threatened.

TABLE 34.10   Annual Instability Events: Independence Through 1979—Swaziland

Year	'61	'62	'63	'64	'65	'66	'67	'68	'69	'70	'71	'72	'73	'74	'75	'76	'77	'78	'79
ELITE INSTABILITY																			
Assassinations																			
Plots																			
Attempted Coups d'État																			
Coups d'État													1						
COMMUNAL INSTABILITY																			
Ethnic Violence																			
Irredentism																			
Rebellion																			
Civil War																			
MASS INSTABILITY																			
Revolt																			
Revolution																			
TURMOIL																			
Demonstrations																			
Strikes (no. days)																			
Riots (no. days)																			
Terrorism																			
Declarations of Emergency																			

TABLE 34.10   Annual Instability Events: Independence Through 1979—Swaziland

Year	'61	'62	'63	'64	'65	'66	'67	'68	'69	'70	'71	'72	'73	'74	'75	'76	'77	'78	'79
CABINET INSTABILITY																			
Realloc. and new appts.									4		2	2							
New members								8	2		1	5							
Resig. and Dismissals								4		1	3								
No. of members (max.) (maximum in year)								9	9	9	9	11							

Selected References

BIBLIOGRAPHY

Grotpeter, J. A. *Historical Dictionary of Swaziland*. Metuchen, N.J.: Scarecrow, 1975.

University College of Swaziland. *Swaziland National Bibliography 1973—1976 with current information*. Kwaluseni: University of Botswana and Swaziland, 1977.

Wallace, Charles S. *Swaziland: A Bibliography*. Johannesberg: University of Witwatersrand, 1967.

Webster, John B. and Paulus Mohome. *A Bibliography on Swaziland*. Syracuse: Program of Eastern African Studies, Syracuse University, 1968

GENERAL

Barker, Dudley. *Swaziland*. London: Her Majesty's Stationery Office, 1965.

Hailey, William Malcolm, Baron. *The Republic of South Africa and the High Commission Territories*. London: Oxford University Press, 1963.

Halpern, Jack. *South Africa's Hostages: Basutoland, Bechuanaland, and Swaziland*. Harmondsworth: Penguin, 1965.

Matsebula, J. S. M. *A History of Swaziland*. 2nd edition, London: Longmans, 1976.

Stevens, Richard P. *Lesotho, Botswana, and Swaziland: The Former High Commission Territories in Southern Africa*. New York: Praeger, 1971.

POLITICAL

Kuper, H. *Sobhuza II, Ngwenyama and King of Swaziland*. London: Duckworth, 1978.

Potholm, Christian P. *Swaziland: The Dynamics of Political Modernization*. Berkeley: University of California Press, 1972.

Rosen Prinz, B. D. *Urbanization and Political Change: A Study of Urban Local Government in Swaziland*. Los Angeles: Unviersity of California, 1976.

Szal, R. J. *Inequality and Basic Needs in Swaziland*. Geneva: International Labour Office, 1976.

Van Wyk, Adam Johanmes. *Swaziland: A Political Study*. Pretoria: African Institute, 1969.

ECONOMIC

Best, Alan C. G. *The Swaziland Railway: A Study in Politico-Economic Geography*. East Lansing: Michigan State University Press, 1966.

Fair, T. J. D., G. Murdock and H. M. Jones. *Development in Swaziland: A Regional Analysis*. Johannesburg: Witwatersrand University Press, 1969.

International Monetary Fund. "Swaziland." In *Surveys of African Economies*, Vol. 5. Washington, D.C.: I.M.F., 1973.

Jones, David. *Aid and Development in Southern Africa: British Aid to Botswana, Lesotho and Swaziland*. London: Croom Helm, 1977.

Selwyn, P. *Industries in the Southern African Periphery: A Study of Industrial Development in Botswana, Lesotho and Swaziland*. London: Croom Helm, in association with the Institute of Development Studies, Sussex, 1975.

SOCIAL

Kuper, Hilda. *The Swazi: A South African Kingdom*. New York: Holt, Rinehart and Winston, 1965.

Marwick, Brian. *The Swazi—An Ethnographic Account of the Natives of the Swaziland Protectorate*. London: Frank Cass, 1966.

35. Tanzania

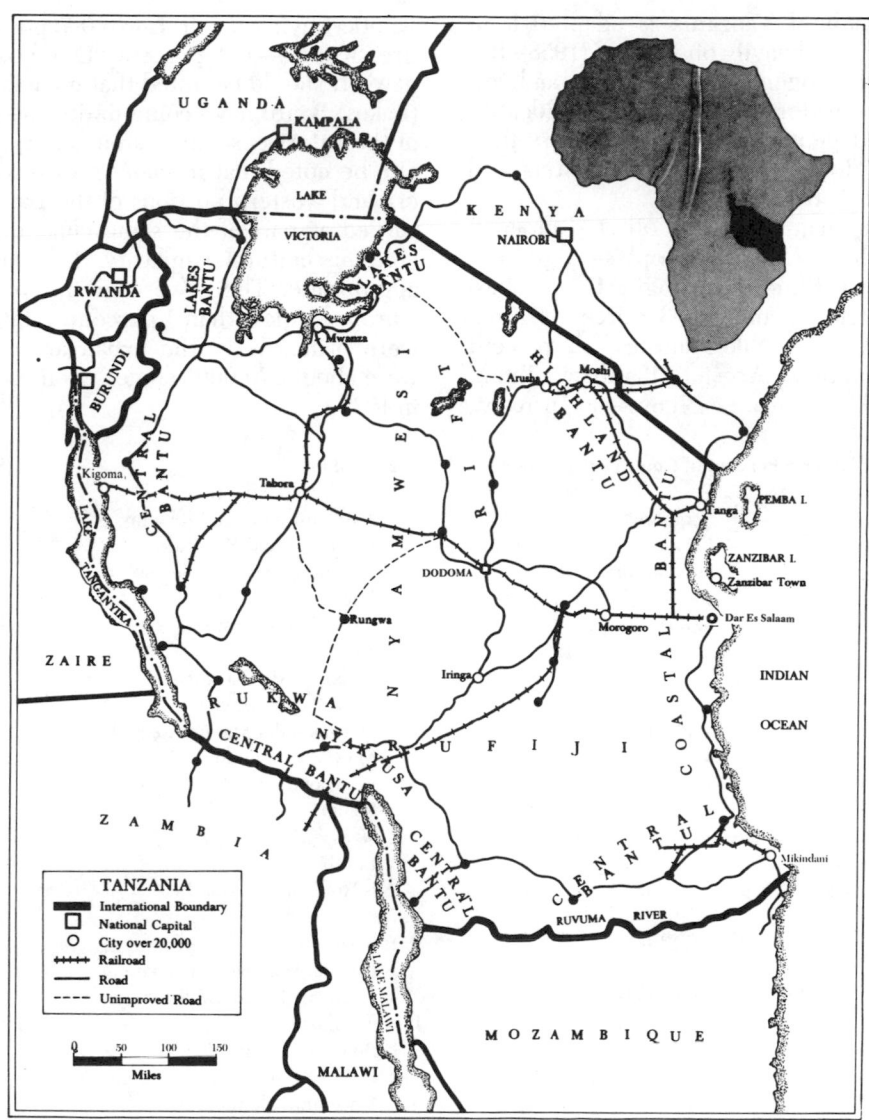

I. Basic Information

Date of Independence: December 9, 1961
Former Colonial Ruler: United Kingdom
Change in Boundaries: April 26, 1964, Tanganyika and Zanzibar became the United Republic of Tanganyika and Zanzibar; October 29, 1964, name became Tanzania
Former Names: Tanganyika and Zanzibar
Estimated Population (1980): 17,849,000

Area Size (equivalent in U.S.): 364,900 sq.mi. including inland waterways (Texas and Colorado)
Date of Last Census: 1974
Major Exports 1975 as Percent of Total Exports (excluding trade with Kenya and Uganda in locally produced goods): coffee beans—19%; cloves—13%; sisal—12%; raw cotton—12%; cashew nuts—9%; diamonds—7%.

II. Ethnic Patterns

The ethnic classification of Tanzania is adapted from Murdock (1959) and draws heavily on Moffett (1958). Because of the relative homogeneity in language and culture, despite the considerable number of identity groups, we have used geographical criteria more than usual in combining identity groups into clusters and types at a high level of abstraction.

In addition to the major groups, other Tanzanian groups include: Southern Cushitic peoples—2 percent (Iraqw, Mbulu, Gorowa, Finme, Burungi, Mbugu, Wasi or Alawa): Interlacustrine Hamites—3 percent (Hima, Tutsi, Rundi and Rwanda); "Nilo-Hamites"—2 percent (Masai, Kwavi or Lumbwa, Arusha, Barabaig, Tatog, Mangati, Kismajend, Taturu); Nguni—1 percent;

Nilotic-Kavirondo or Luo—0.7 percent; and Bushman-like peoples—0.4 percent (Dorobo, Kindiga, and Sandaw). It should be noted that many of the Interlacustrine (Lakes) Bantu have come under the political domination of the Interlacustrine Hamites (e.g., Rwanda). It should also be noted that in many previous classifications, eastern and western portions of the Lakes Bantu are not regarded as part of the same cluster. On the basis of increasing cultural similarity, however, this now seems appropriate. There were groups of Asians, Arabs, and Europeans (less than 1 percent, total) in the country who were primarily in the urban areas. In addition, there were about 170,000 refugess from neighboring countries in 1976.

TABLE 35.1   Ethnic Units Over 5 Percent of Country Population

Ethnic Units	Estimated Ethnic Population 1980	Estimated Ethnic Percentage
a. Nyamwesi Type	3,391,000	19%
1. Sukuma	(2,142,000)	(12%)
i. Sukuma, ii. Rongo, iii. Shashi		
2. Nyamwesi (Banyamwesi)	(892,000)	(5%)
i. Nyamwese, ii. Gala, iii. Galaganza, iv. Irwana, v. Nankwili		
3. Sumbwa, 4. Kimbu, Yanzi Konongo, 5. Bende, Tongwe		
b. Interlacustrine Bantu (Lakes Bantu) Type	2,499,000	14%
1. Ha	(714,000)	(4%)
i. Ha, ii. Vinza, iii. Jiji		
2. Haya	(714,000)	(4%)
i. Haya, ii. Nyambo, iii. Mwani, v. Ziba		
3. Zinza, 4. Subi, Hangaza, 5. Suba, 6. Ikizu, 7. Ikoma, 8. Jita, Kwaya and Ruru, 9. Nguruimi, 10. Zanaki, 11. Kerewe and Redi, 12. Issenye and Nata, 13. Kisii (Gusii), 14. Kuriya (Tende, Kulya)		
c. Northeast Coastal Bantu Type	1,963,000	11%
1. Zigula	(1,071,000)	(6%)
i. Zigula, ii. Luguru, Kami, Kutu, iii. Bondei, iv. Kwere and Doe, v. Nguru, Kilindi, Shambala (Sambala)		
2. Swahili	(892,000)	(5%)
i. Shirazi (Hadimu, Tumbatu, Pemba, Mbwera), ii. Zaramo and Nyagtwa, iii. Ndengereko, iv. Segeju		
3. Digo		
d. Central Bantu Cluster	1,963,000	11%
1. Yao	(1,785,000)	(10%)
i. Yao, ii. Mwera and Kiturika, iii. Makua, iv. Makonde, Matambwe and Mawia, v. Ngindo, vi. Ndonde, vii. Machinga and Songo		
2. Nyasa (Maravi cluster)		
3. Bemba		
i. Holoholo, ii. Mambwe		
e. Rift Cluster	1,785,000	10%
1. Gogo,	(714,000)	(4%)
2. Iramba, Irambi and Izanzu, 3. Nyaturu, 4. Rangi and Mbugwe		
f. Rufiji Cluster	1,606,000	9%
1. Bena, Sowe, and Vemba, 2. Hehe, Koshishamba and Zungwa, 3. Matumbi-Ndendehule, 4. Mbunga, 5. Ndamba and Pogoro, 6. Sagara, Kaguru, Kinongo and Vidungda, 7. Sangu and Poroto, 8. Rufiji and Mawanda, 9. Wungu		
g. Nyakyusa Cluster	1,071,00	6%
1. Nyakyusa (Niabiussa, Sochile, Sokile)	(536,000)	(3%)
i. Nyakyusa and Kukwe, ii. Mwamba, iii. Ngonde, iv. Selya, v. Sukwa		
2. Nyassa group	(536,000)	(3%)
i. Matengo, ii. Kinga, Panga, and Wanji		

h. Rukwa Cluster	892,000	5%
1. Fipa, Nyika and Rungu,		
2. Iwa (Nyamwanga),		
3. Lambya, Malila,		
Ndali, Tambo and Wandya,		
4. Pimbwe and Rungwa, 5. Safwa,		
Guruka, Mbwilla, Songwe		
i. Kenya Highland Bantu Cluster	892,000	5%
1. Chagga and Kahe	(536,000)	(3%)
2. Pare and Taveta, 3. Meru		

SOURCES: J. P. Moffett, ed., *Handbook of Tanganyika*, 2nd ed. (Dar es Salaam: Government Printer, 1958), pp. 283—297. G. P. Murdock, *Africa* (New York: McGraw-Hill, 1959). M. Lofchie, "Party Conflict in Zanzibar," *Journal of Modern African Studies*, 1 (1963): 185—207.

III. Language Patterns

All of the major languages of Tanzania are Bantu. Swahili has emerged as the *lingua franca* throughout the country. In 1942, MacDougald estimated that 52 percent of the population spoke Swahili. Knappert estimated 89 percent in 1965. In a sense, the entire population might be regarded as understanding some dialect of Swahili. However, Swahili has become a national language (strenuously encouraged by the government) only since the mid-1960s. It is reasonable to assume that given the age structure of the country, there are some groups (very young, or very old) who do not speak Swahili. We therefore estimated 95 percent of the population to be Swahili-speaking. The second largest language is Sukuma, spoken as a first language by 12 percent of the population. English is still widely used in Tanzania in government and higher education.

TABLE 35.2   Language Patterns

1. Primacy				
1st language		Swahili	(95%)	
2nd language		Sukuma	(12%)	
			Green- berg	Dalby
2. Linguistic classification		Swahili	IA5	G4
(all ethnic units in		Nyamwesi	IA5	F2
country over 5%)		Inter. Bantu	IA5	E1
		NE Coast. Bantu	IA5	(G1,G4)
		Cen. Bantu	IA5	(M1,P2)
		Rift Cluster	IA5	(E1,F2)
		Rufiji Cluster	IA5	(G6,F2, M1)
		Nyakyusa Cluster	IA5	(M3,N1 G6)
		Rukwa Cluster	IA5	M1
		Kenya High. Bantu Cluster	IA5	(E5,E6 G2)
3. *Lingua franca*		Swahili		
4. Official language		Swahili and English		

Note: Swahili is the language from the Northeast Coastal Bantu and is not an ethnic group from table 35.1
SOURCE: Lyndon Harries, "Swahili in Modern East Africa," in *Language Problems of Developing Nations*, eds. Joshua A. Fishman, Charles A Ferguson, and Jyotirindra Das Gupta (New York: Wiley, 1968), pp 119-127.

IV. Urban Patterns

Capital/largest city: Dar es Salaam (founded 1862)*
Dominant ethnicity/language of capital
   Major vernacular: Swahili
   Major ethnic group: Zaramo[1] (Northeast Coastal Bantu)
   Major ethnic group as percent of capital's population:

*The capital is being moved over a period of ten years from Dar es Salaam to Dodoma. Completion of the move is estimated for the mid-1980's.
[1]J. A. K. Leslie *A Survey of Dar Es Salaam* New York: Oxford University Press, 1963, p. 273.

TABLE 35.3   Growth of Capital/Largest City

Date	Dar es Salaam	Dodoma (new capital)
1930	25,000[1]	
1940	65,000	
1950	99,000[b]	10,700[d]
1960	150,000	17,000[d]
1967	273,000	24,000
1970	344,000 UA	30,000[d]
1975	517,000 UA	44,000[d]

SOURCES

  [a]O. Martens and O. Karstedt, *The African Handbook*, 2nd ed. (London: Allen and Unwin, 1938).
  [b]East African High Commission, *Statistical Bulletin*, 2 (19), p. 4.
  [c]UN Demographic Yearbook 1976.
  [d]Capital Development Authority Reports and Accounts 1, 1974, Dodoma, Tanzania.

TABLE 35.4   Cities of 20,000 and Over

City	Size	Date
Dar es Salaam[a]	51,7,000UA	1975
Zanzibar Town[b]	68,000	1967
Tanga[b]	61,000	1967
Mwanza[b]	35,000	1967
Arusha[b]	32,000	1967
Moshi[b]	27,000	1967
Morogoro[b]	25,000	1967
Dodoma[b]	24,000	1967
Iringa[b]	22,000	1967
Tabora[b]	21,000	1967
Kigoma/Ujiji[b]	21,000	1967
Mtwara/Mikindani[b]	20,000	1967

SOURCES:

  [a]*UN Demographic Yearbook 1976.*
  [b]Census—1967.

V. Political Patterns

FIGURE 35.1   Political Parties and Elections   TANZANIA

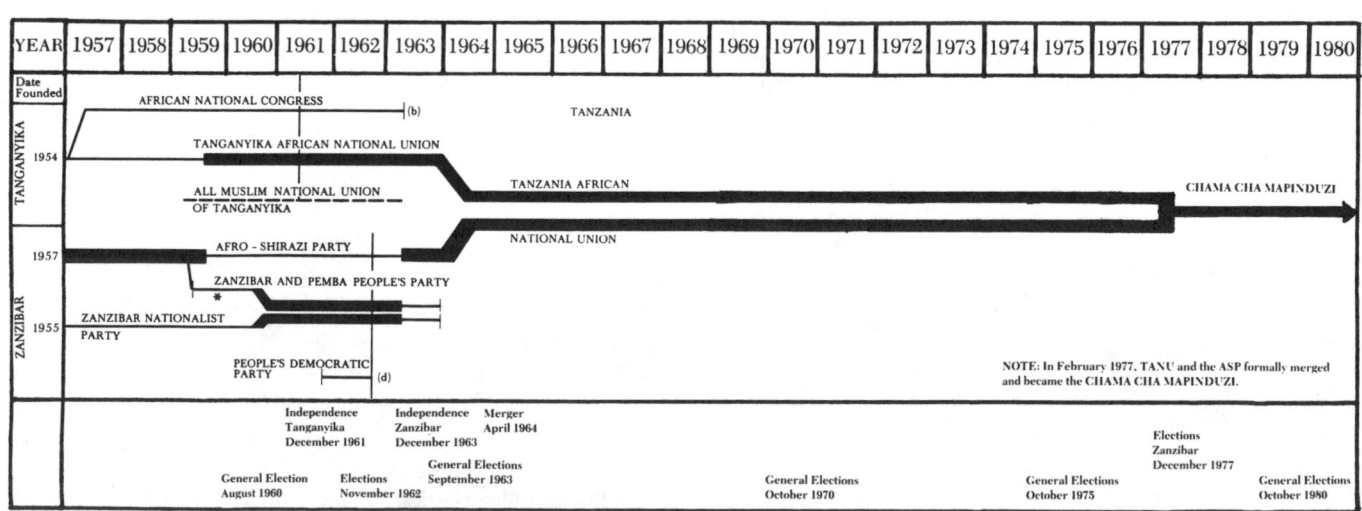

* A caretaker government was formed in early 1960 when no party won a clear majority. The deadlock was broken in July 1960 with the coalition between ZPPP and ZNP.

A. Political Parties and Elections

In elections just prior to independence the *Tanganyika African National Union* (TANU), under the direction of Julius Nyerere, achieved an overwhelming victory and continued to govern Tanganyika until 1964. At that time, a federation was formed with Zanzibar, and TANU joined with the *Afro-Shirazi Party* (ASP) of Zanzibar. Opposition to TANU came mainly from the *African National Congress* (ANC) which split from TANU in 1957 and was banned in 1963.

In Zanzibar, the ASP governed from 1957 to 1960 when they lost their majority. Political control then passed to a caretaker government until mid-1960 when the *Zanzibar and Pemba People's Party* (ZPPP) and the *Zanzibar Nationalist Party* (ZNP) formed a coalition government, with Sheikh Muhammed Shamte (ZPPP) as chief minister. A revolution in January 1964 ended the ZNP/ZPPP coalition and returned the ASP and Sheikh Abeid Karume to power as president of Zanzibar and first vice-president of Tanzania. The ASP has ruled ever since in a very tightly controlled and largely autonomous political system. Even though Karume was assassinated in 1972, the ASP continues in power although TANU and ASP have formally merged and elections were held in December 1977.

Union between Tanganyika and Zanzibar took place in April 1964 and the ruling parties of both countries joined in coalition with Dr. Nyerere as president of the Republic, Abeid Karume as first vice-president, and Rashidi Kawawa (TANU) as second vice-president. In the 1965 general elections, TANU was the only party to offer candidates. Within most of the electoral districts, however, a number of TANU candidates competed with each other. TANU was confirmed in power in the 1970, 1975, and 1980 elections although conflict between TANU and the government has occasionaly surfaced. In February 1977, TANU and ASP were formally merged into a single party named the *Chama Cha Mapinduzi* (CCM)—the Revolutionary Party of Tanzania. The first elections in Zanzibar since 1963 were held in December 1977. General elections were held in late October 1980, and President Nyerere was returned unanimously.

B. Political Leadership

Julius Nyerere has been head of government during the post-independence period winning his latest term in October 1980. Cabinet turnover was high in 1964, reflecting the federation with Zanzibar, but was very low thereafter until major changes came in 1971 and 1972 after the installation of a 'new' government in 1970. By 1974 more army officers were found in the cabinet than had been there previously.

TABLE 35.5   Head of Government (Post-Independence)

Name	Dates in Office	Age (1982)	Ethnicity	Education	Former Occupation
1. Julius K. Nyerere (President)	1961*—present	59	Interlacustrine Bantu (Zanaki)	M.A., Edinburgh Makerere (Uganda)	Civil Servant, Teacher

*Nyerere temporarily resigned from office in the period February to December 1962 to tour the country and returned to office after the November 1962 elections which changed the country to a republic with Nyerere as President. Roshidi Kawawa was Prime Minister during this period.

TABLE 35.6   Cabinet Membership: Distribution by Ethnic Unit*

Ethnicity*	Independence Cabinet	1967 Cabinet
1. Nyamwezi (19%)	9.1%	11%
2. Interlacustrine Bantu (14)	9.1	11
3. N.E. Coastal Bantu (11)	0	26
4. Central Bantu (11)	0	11
5. Rift Cluster (10)	9.1	5.3
6. Rufiji Cluster (9)	0	0
7. Nyakyusa (6)	0	0
8. Rukwa (5)	0	0
9. Kenya Highland Cluster (5)	9.1	16
10. Others (10)	64	21
N =	12	19

*Ethnic units arranged in rank order of size within country with the unit's percent of national population in parentheses.

VI. National Integration and Stability

Mainland Tanzania has experienced no communal and relatively little elite instability. In January 1964, however, there was an attempted mutiny by the 1st Battalion of the Tanganyika Rifles, who took control of Dar es Salaam while protesting pay conditions and the continued presence of British officers in the army. The 2nd Battalion mutinied at Tabora on January 21. On January 25, six hundred British Royal Marines were called in by the Tanganyikan government and the mutiny was forcibly suppressed. This event has not been classified as an attempted coup since we have no evidence that the regime itself was threatened by the army demands. Prior to its union with Tanganyika to form Tanzania, Zanzibar had a revolution and subsequently, the largely autonomous islands have had an unsettled history culminating in the assassination in 1972 of the President of the Zanzibar Revolutionary Council and first Vice-President of Tanzania, Sheikh Abeid Karume.

Mainland Tanzania has developed a remarkable degree of national unity among a very large number of relatively small ethnic groups. There is no single ethnic group which by virtue of its size is in a position to dominate the country. The ideological position of the government which tries to minimize the "mass- elite" gap, and the use of Swahili as a national language, seem to have a consolidating effect on the country. In October 1969, two civilians and four army officers were arrested for plotting a coup and in June 1972 there were bomb blasts in Dar es Salaam but no reasons are known for the incidents which were followed by arrests. Most of the conflict in the country has had external origins: Uganda's forays into

Tanzania and Amin's twice repeated threat in 1974 to invade Tanzania; the Burundi army attacking Hutu refugees as well as Tanzanians in the Tanzanian towns bordering Burundi; attacks by Portuguese troops against FRELIMO bases in Tanzania (although this has now ended); and, the closing of the Kenya-Tanzania road links by Kenya because of conflict ostensibly over the size of vehicles transporting imports into Tanzania. Only the Zaire and Zambian borders seemed to be trouble free as of 1978, but tensions mounted between Tanzania and Zambia when Zambia re-opened its border with Rhodesia in 1978. In March 1978, there were student demonstrations against increased financial benefits for politicians. Hundreds of students, including President Nyerere's son, were expelled, but were then pardoned.

On January 20, 1979 Ugandan forces attacked Tanzania at three border points. The Tanzanian army repelled the attack and joined forces with the Uganda National Liberation Front (UNLF) advancing into southern Uganda. War with Amin's Uganda continued until May 29, 1979 when UNLF and Tanzanian forces secured the last major town held by Amin forces. As of 1982 Tanzania has retained an ocupation force in Uganda. The war and the occupation army has constituted a considerable drain on the Tanzanian economy. The occupation has met with criticism within the party and army as minor party officials have been expelled for their opposition while members of the army have demonstrated, complaining that they have not been paid for services. In June 1980, discontent in Zanzibar, resulted in the arrest of 100 persons. Vice-President Aboud Jumbe announced an alleged plot, including some wealthy businesmen who were reported to be funding opposition candidates in the October elections.

TABLE 35.7   Elite Instability

Event and Date	Characteristics
1. Attempted Coup d'État April 7, 1972	a. *Description*: Sheikh Abeid Karume, President of the Zanzibar Revolutionary Council, was assassinated by Lt. Humud Mohamed Humud at the Afro-Shirazi Party headquarters as part of a planned coup d'état attempt against the government of Zanzibar. b. *Participants*: Exiled politicians such as Sheikh Abdulrahman Babu, a former Tanzanian minister, and elements of Zanzibar's army. c. *Apparent Causes*: It is not completely clear since all members of the assassination group were killed. The reasons seem to be a complex of personal ambitions to remove Karume and reaction to the highly repressive and autocratic state he was directing. Racial conflicts between Arabs, Africans and Asians undoubtedly contributed to this as well.

TABLE 35.10   Annual Instability Events: Independence Through 1979—Tanzania

Year	'61	'62	'63	'64	'65	'66	'67	'68	'69	'70	'71	'72	'73	'74	'75	'76	'77	'78	'79
ELITE INSTABILITY																			
Assassinations																			
Plots										1									
Attempted Coups d'État												1							
Coups d'État																			
COMMUNAL INSTABILITY																			
Ethnic Violence																			
Irredentism																			
Rebellion																			
Civil War																			
MASS INSTABILITY																			
Revolt																			
Revolution																			
TURMOIL																			
Demonstrations								1											
Strikes (no. days)		3																	
Riots (no. days)				1															
Terrorism										1		1							
Declarations of Emergency																			
CABINET INSTABILITY																			
Realloc. and new appts.	8	5	22	14			14	4	3		8	4							
New members	4	2	10	2			1	4			6	17							
Resig. and Dismissals	3	1	4	2			3	3	5		3	10							
No. of members (max.) (maximum in year)	12	13	13	23	21	21	21	16	20	20	26								

VII. Selected References

BIBLIOGRAPHY

Bates, Margaret. *A Study Guide for Tanzania*. Boston: Development Program, African Studies Center, Boston University, 1969.

Kocher, James E., and Beverly Fleischer. *A Bibliography on Rural Development in Tanzania*. East Lansing: Michigan State University, 1979.

GENERAL

Ayany, S. G. *A History of Zanzibar*. Nairobi: East African Literature Bureau, 1970.

Bienen, Henry. *Tanzania: Party Transformation and Economic Development*, enlarged edition. Princeton, N.J.: Princeton University Press, 1970.

Cliffe, L. *Tanzania*. New York: Praeger, 1970.

Iliffe, John. *A Modern History of Tanganyika*. New York: Cambridge University Press, 1979.

Kaplan, I. ed. *Tanzania: A Country Study*. Washington D.C. Government Printing Office, 1978.

Kimambo, I. N., and A. J. Temu (eds.). *A History of Tanzania*. Nairobi: East Africa Publishing House, 1969.

Kurtz, Laura S. *An African Education: The Social Revolution in Tanzania*. Brooklyn, New York: Pageant-Poseidon, 1972.

Kurtz, L. S. *Historical Dictionary for Tanzania*. Metuchen, N.J.: Scarecrow Press, 1978.

Yeager, R. *Tanzania*. Boulder, Colo.: Westview Press, 1982.

POLITICAL

Bailey, Martin. *The Union of Tanganyika and Zanzibar*. Program of East African Studies. Syracuse, N.Y.: Syracuse University, 1973.

Cliffe, Lionel. *One-Party Democracy: The 1965 General Elections*. Nairobi: East African Publishing House, 1967.

Cliffe, L., and J. Saul (eds.). *Tanzania Socialism-Politics and Policies: An Interdisciplinary Reader*, 2 volumes. Nairobi: East Africa Publishing House, 1972.

Duggan, William R., and John R. Civille. *Tanzania and Nyerere: A Study of Ujamaa and Nationalism*. Maryknoll, N.Y.: Orbis Books, 1976.

Glickman, Harvey. "Traditional Pluralism and Democratic Processes in Mainland Tanzania." *Asian and African Studies*, 5, 1969: 165-201.

Hatch, John. *Two African Statesmen: Kaunda of Zambia and Nyerere of Tanzania*. Chicago: Regenery, 1976.

Hopkins, Raymond. *Political Roles in a New State*. New Haven, Conn.: Yale University Press, 1971.

Hutchison, Alan. "Exorcising the Ghost of Karume." *Africa Report*, 19 (March/April 1974): 46—51.

Hyden, Goren. *Political Development in Rural Tanzania*. Nairobi: East African Publishing House, 1969.

Hyden, Goren. *Beyond Ujamaa in Tanzania*. Berkeley: University of California Press, 1980.

Ingle, Clyde R. *From Village to State in Tanzania: The Politics of Rural Development*. Ithaca, N.Y.: Cornell University Press, 1972.

Kariokia, James N. *Tanzania's Human Relation*. Univ. Park, PA. The Pennsylvania State University Press, 1979.

Liebenow, J. Gus. *Colonial Rule and Political Development in Tanzania*. Nairobi: East African Publishing House, 1972.

Lofchie, Michael F. "The Zanzibari Revolution: African Protest in a Racially Plural Society." In *Power and Protest in Black Africa*, eds. Robert I. Rotberg and Ali A. Mazrui, pp. 924—968. New York: Oxford University Press, 1970.

Maguire, C. Andrew. *Toward 'Uhuru' in Tanzania: The Politics of Participation*. New York: Cambridge University Press, 1969.

Martin, E. B. *Zanzibar: Tradition and Revolution*. London: Hamish, Hamilton, 1978.

Mazrui, Ali A. "Socialism as a Mode of International Protest: The Case of Tanzania." In *Power and Protest in Black Africa*, eds. Robert I. Rotberg and Ali A. Mazrui, pp. 1139—1152. New York: Oxford University Press, 1970.

Morrison, D. R. *Education and Politics in Africa: The Tanzanian Case*. London: Hurst, 1976.

Mwansasu, Bismarck U., and Cranford Pratt (eds.). *Towards Socialism in Tanzania*. Toronto: University of Toronto Press, 1978.

Nellis, John R. *A Theory of Ideology: The Tanzania Example*. New York: Oxford University Press, 1972.

Nyerere, Julius K. *Freedom and Development: Uhuru n Maendelco*. London: Oxford University Press, 1973.

Nyerere, Julius K. *Freedom and Socialism: Uhuru na Ujamaa*. London: Oxford University Press, 1969.

Nyerere, Julius K. *Freedom and Unity: A Selection from Writings and Speeches, 1952—65*. London: Oxford University Press, 1967.

Nyerere, Julius K. *Ujamaa: Essays on Socialsim*. Dar Es Salaam: Oxford University Press, 1968.

Pratt, C. *The Critical Phase in Tanzania, 1945—68: Nyerere and the Emergence of a Socialist Strategy*. London: Cambridge University Press, 1975.

Shivji, I. G. *Class Struggle in Tanzania*. London: Heinemann, 1976.

Samoff, Joe. *Tanzania: Local Politics and the Structure of Power*. Madison, Wis.: University of Wisconsin Press, 1974.

Smith, William Edgett. *We Must Run While They Walk: A Portrait of Africa's Julius Nyerere*. New York: Random House, 1971.

Von Sperber, Klaus W. *Public Administration in Tanzania*. Africa Studies No. 55. New York: Humanities, 1970.

ECONOMIC

Clar, W. Edmund. *Socialist Development and Public Investment in Tanzania, 1964—73*. Toronto: University of Toronto Press, 1978.

Helleiner, G. K. "Socialism and Economic Development in Tanzania." *Journal of Development Studies* (January 1972): 183—204.

International Monetary Fund. "Tanzania." In *Surveys of African Economies*, Vol. 2, Washington, D.C.: I.M.F., 1968.

McHenry, Dean E. *Tanzania's Ujamaa Villages: The Implementation of a Rural Development Strategy*.

Berkeley: University of California, Institute of International Studies, 1979.

Nyerere, Julius. *The Economic Challenge: Dialogue or Confrontation*. London: Catholic Inst. of Race Relations, 1975.

Rweyemamu, Justinian. *Underdevelopment and Industrialization in Tanzania*. New York: Oxford University Press, 1973.

Tordoff, M. *Government and Politics in Tanzania*. Nairobi: East African Publishing House, 1967.

SOCIAL

Bennett, N. R. *A History of the Arab State of Zanzibar*. London: Methuen, 1978.

Cameron, J., and W. A. Dodd. *Society, Schools and Progress in Tanzania*. New York: Pergamon, 1970.

Ranger, T. O. *The African Churches of Tanzania*. Nairobi: East African Publishing House, 1969.

Resnick, Idrian (ed.). *Tanzania: Revolution by Education*. New York: Humanities Press, 1969.

Shorter, Aylward. *Chiefship in Western Tanzania*. London: Oxford University Press, 1972.

Stren, Richard E. *Urban Inequality and Housing Policy in Tanzania*. Berkeley, Ca.: Institute of International Studies, 1975.

Sutton, J. E. G. (ed.). "Dar es Salaam: City, Port, and Region." *Tanzania Notes and Records*, 71 (1970)

Zanolli, N. V. *Education Toward Development in Tanzania*. Basel: Pharos-Verlag, 1971.

36. Togo

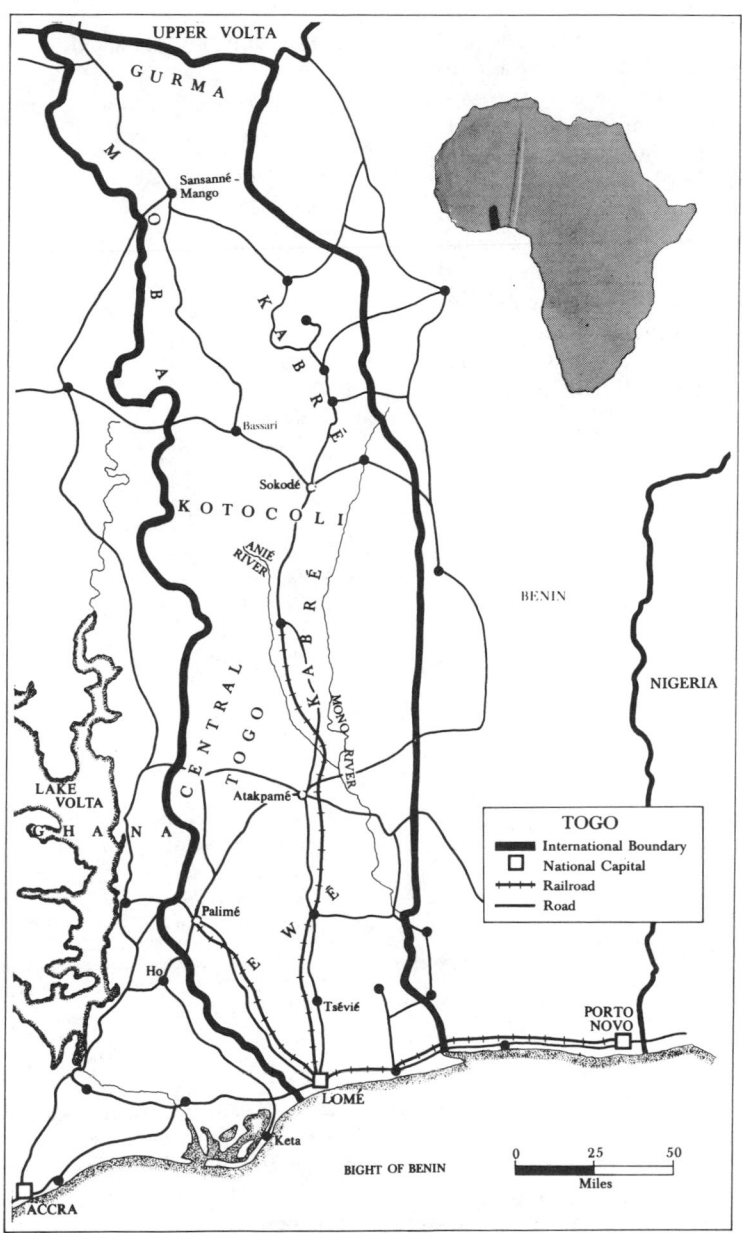

I. Basic Information

Date of Independence: April 27, 1960
Former Colonial Ruler: France
Former Name: Togoland
Population (1980): 2,596,000
Area Size (equivalent in U.S.): 21,622 sq. mi. (West Virginia)

Date of Last Census: 1970
Major Exports 1977 as Percent of Total Exports: phosphates—49 percent; cocoa—26 percent;* coffee—14 percent.

*Much of the cocoa is smuggled to Togo by Ghanaian farmers for better prices than they can get in Ghana.

II. Ethnic Patterns

The ethnic classification of Togo is fairly inclusive and is at a level of abstraction just above recognized identity groups. It classifies with the major identity groups a number of smaller groups which are related culturally. The Central Togo cluster, however, is an example of an "ethnic shatter belt," although these people are tending to assimilate to the culture of the northern Voltaic peoples. In addition to the major groups, about 3 percent of the population are Yoruba-related peoples (Ana and Nago); 2 percent are Hausa and Fulani; and 1 percent Chokosi (a people of Akan descent, but assimilating to Voltaic peoples). There were about 2,500 Europeans in Togo according to the 1970 Census.

TABLE 36.1   Ethnic Units Over 5 Percent of Country Population

Ethnic Units	Estimated Ethnic Population 1980	Estimated Ethnic Percentage
a. Ewé Type	1,142,000	44%
1. Ewé (Ethoué, Eibé, Ephé, Krepé)		
2. Ouatchi, 3. Mina,	(571,000)	(22%)
4. Fon, 5. Ehoué,		
6. Adja, 7. Pedah,		
8. Pla		
b. Kabré Type	597,000	23%
1. Kabré (Cabrai, Bekaburum, Kaburé, Kauré)		
2. Losso, 3. Lamba,	(363,000)	(14%)
4. Tamberma, 5. Mossi,		
6. Logba		
c. Moba Type	182,000	7%
1. Moba (Bmoba, Moab, Moare, Mwan)		
2. Konkomba, 3. Ngangan (Bou Bankam)		
d. Kotocoli Type	182,000	7%
1. Kotocoli (Cotocoli, Tem, Chaucho, Temba, Timn)		
2. Bassari, 3. Tchamba		
e. Central Togo Cluster	130,000	5%
1. Akposso, 2. Akebou, 3. Agnagan, 4. Adele, 5. Ahlon, 6. Bassila, 7. Buem		
f. Gurma (Gourmantche, Gourma)	130,000	5%

SOURCES: H. Attignon, *Géographie du Togo*, mimeographed text, 1965, p. 22. J. C. Froelich, *Les Populations du Nord-Togo* (Paris: Presses Universitaires de France, 1963). G. P. Murdock, *Africa* (New York: McGraw-Hill, 1959); 1970 Census results.

III. Language Patterns

The two major language groups in Togo are Ewé (of the Kwa family) and Kabré (Of the Voltaic family). Probably 44 percent of the total population speak Ewé as a first language (Rustow suggests 41 percent; Knappert and MacDougald suggest 32 percent). Since Ewé is spoken as a *lingua franca* in southern Togo, our estimate of total speakers is 50 percent. Kabré is probably the second largest language group. As a rough estimate, perhaps 20 percent of the population speak Kabré as a first language (Rustow estimates 22 percent). However, in the northern part of Togo where Kabré is to be found, Hausa serves as more of a *lingua franca* than Kabré. French continues to be the official language, but many Togolese speak English or German. Until 1963, Ewé and Hausa also served as official languages.

TABLE 36.2   Language Patterns

1. Primacy

1st language	Ewé	(50%)
2nd language	Kabré	(20%)
		Green— Dalby
		berg

2. Linguistic classification (all ethnic units in country over 5%)

	Green—berg	Dalby
Ewé	IA4	45
Kabré	IA3	426
Moba	IA3	41D
Kotocoli	IA3	46E
Central Togo cluster	IA4	46

3. *Lingua francas*   Ewé, Hausa
4. Official language[1]   French

[1]Ewé and Kabré are expected to replace French as official languages sometime in the future according to a communication from the Togo Embassy, New York.

IV. Urban Patterns

Capital/largest city: Lomé
Dominant ethnicity/language of capital
  Major vernacular: Ewé[1]
  Major ethnic groups: Ewé[2]
  Major ethnic group as percent of capital's population: 24% (1951)

[1]Jan Knappert, "Language Problems of the New Nations of Africa," *African Quarterly*, 5 (1965): 95—105.
[2]*Encyclopédie Afrique Française*, Vol. 6, p. 435.

TABLE 36.3   Growth of Capital/Largest City

Date	Lomé
1920	6,000
1930	8,000
1940	38,000
1950	33,000
1960	100,000
1966	129,000 UA
1968	135,000 UA
1971	200,000 UA
1973	225,000 UA
1977	229,400 UA

SOURCE: *Démographie Comparée; Europa Yearbook V. II 1977;* and *Africa South of the Sahara, 1978—79.*

TABLE 36.4   Cities of 20,000 and Over

City	Size	Date
Lomé[a]	229,400 UA	1977
Sokodé	33,500	1977
Palimé	25,500	1977
Atakpame	21,800	1977

SOURCE: *Africa South of the Sahara, 1978—79,* p. 1013. The next largest town according to this source is Bassari with a population of 17,500.

V. Political Patterns

FIGURE 36.1   **Political Parties and Elections**   TOGO

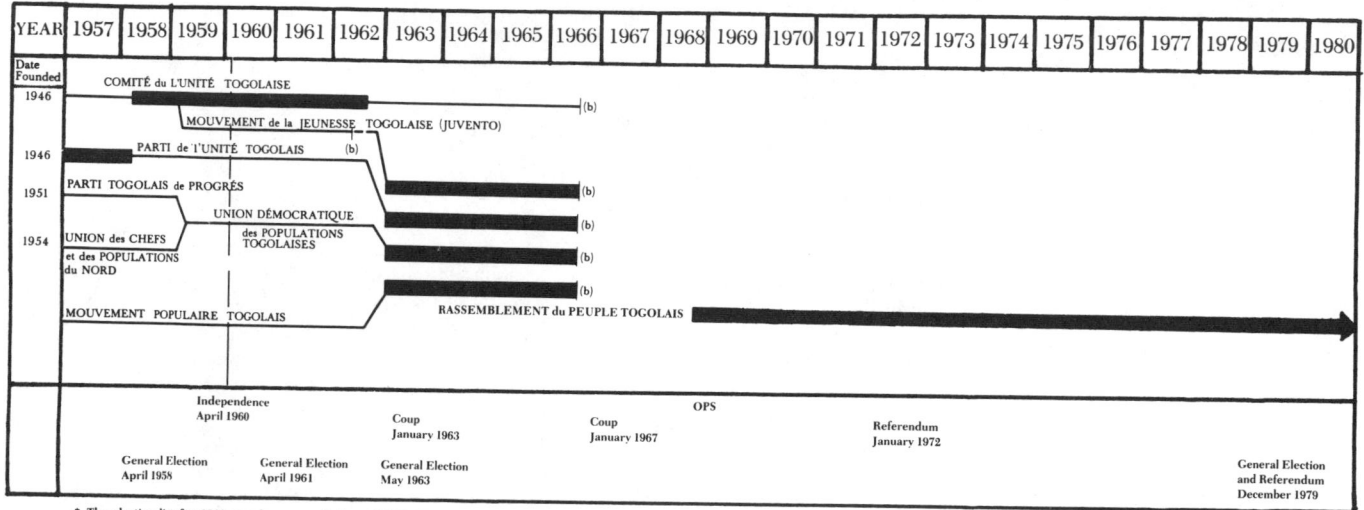

* The election list for 1963 was drawn equally from UDPT, JU-VENTO, PUT and MPT. Mr. Grunitsky was elected President.

A. Political Parties and Elections

In 1957 Togo elected its first prime minister, Nicholas Grunitsky of the *Parti de l'Unité Togolaise* (PUT), who governed until his defeat in 1958 by the *Comité du l'Unité Togolaise* (CUT). The newly elected prime minister, Sylvanus Olympio, served until assassinated by several army NCO's in January 1963. A provisional government elected in 1963 from a single slate of electors— equal numbers from the *Mouvement de la Jeunesse Togolaise* (JUVENTO), the *Union Démocratique des Populations Togolaises* (UDPT), the *Mouvement Populaire Togolais* (MPT) and the *Parti de l'Unité Togolaise* (PUT)— chose Gruntisky to head the government. Olympio's party, led by Theophile Mally, went into exile. The grand coalition continued to govern until January 1967 when a military coup, led by Lt. Col. Etienne Eyádema, removed Grunitsky and instituted military rule. In 1969, the military inaugurated the *Rassemblement du Peuple Togolais* (RPT) and Eyádema (now a Major-General) has been in power ever since under a nominally civilian sin-gle-party regime. A constitutional referendum and elections were held in December 1979. President Eyadema was the sole presidential candidate and won 99.97 percent of the vote. Turnout was over 98 percent.

B. Political Leadership

After the assassination of Sylvanus Olympio (1963) the military backed the civilian regime of Grunitsky, the pre-independence prime minister, until Eyadema's 1967 coup. Since then Eyádema has ruled as President, establishing the RPT party in 1969 and holding a presidential referendum in 1972 to confirm the one-party state. Cabinet ethnic balance has shifted from the Ewé at the time of independence to the Kabré at present. There was a particularly high turnover in cabinet membership in 1966 just prior to the coup. In January 1972, a new government was sworn in and then followed by reshuffles of the cabinet in 1973 and 1974. By 1977, Eyadema was the only soldier in the cabinet. There were two cabinet reshuffles in 1978 and another one in March 1979.

TABLE 36.5 Head of Government (Post-Independence)

Name	Dates in Office	Age (1982)	Ethnicity	Education	Former Occupation
1. Sylvanus Olympio (Prime Minister/ President	1960— 1963	d. 1963 age 67	Ewé	University of London (England)	Business Entrepreneur
2. Nicholas Grunitsky (President)	1963— 1967	d. 1969 age 56	Kabré/ German	Engineering	Transport Business Owner
3. Col. Kleber Dadjo (Chairman, Comité de Reconciliation Nationale)	1967	68	Kabré (Losso)	Secondary (Togo)	Soldier
4. Gen. Gnassingbayé* Eyádema (President)	1967— present	47	Kabré	Primary (6th grade— Togo)	Soldier

*Formerly Etienne.

TABLE 36.6 Cabinet Membership: Distribution by Ethnic Unit*

Ethnicity*	Independence Cabinet	Immediate Pre-Coup Cabinet	1967 Cabinet
1. Ewé (44%)	67%	70%	25%
2. Kabré (23)	22	20	42
3. Moba (7)	0	0	8.3
4. Kotocoli (7)	0	10	17
5. Central Togo Cluster (5)	11	0	0
6. Gurma (5)	0	0	0
7. Others (9)	0	0	8.3
N =	9	12	12

*Ethnic units arranged in rank order of size within country with the unit's percent of national population in parentheses.

VI. National Integration and Stability

The assassination of President Olympio in 1963 began a pattern of elite instability with the army intervening and withdrawing on various occasions. A military junta under the leadership of Eyadema appointed a civilian government but effective power remained with the junta. Since the 1967 coup, elite opposition to Eyadema has dwindled although plots were uncovered in 1969, 1970, and 1977. Eyadema claimed that a plane crash in January 1974 was an attempt by foreign mining interests to assassinate him. An Ewé irredentist movement in Ghana has attracted support among the Ewé of Togo. Much of the ins-

tability is related to continuing regional conflicts between north and south. A plot to assassinate Eyadema was uncovered in October 1977 according to government sources. Also, in 1977 there were violent strikes in the steel-works and at a textile factory in Ksar Helial. The exiled *Togolese Movement for Democracy* (MTD) has been working against the Eyadema regime. In January 1980, members of the MTD seized the Togolese embassy in Paris. Two sons of Sylvanus Olympio are members of the MTD.

TABLE 36.7   Elite Instability

Event and Date	*Characteristics*
1. Coup d'État January 13, 1963	a. *Description*: President Olympio was killed by non-commissioned army officers. A provisional civilian government was set up with Nicholas Grunitsky (president) and Antoine Meatchi (vice-president). b. *Participants*; Army elements, including former sergeants in the French army. Sergeants Bodjillo and Eyadema led the revolt of about 700 Togolese, recently mustered out of the French army. c. *Apparent Causes*: About 700 Togolese who had fought in the French army returned to their country in late 1962. Olympio refused to reintegrate them into the Togolese army. After the coup the size of the army increased from 250 to 1200 men.
2. Attempted Coup November 21, 1966	a. *Description*: Noe Kutuklui called for demonstrations against Grunitsky in a radio broadcast. More than 5,000 people took to the streets in the city of Lomé, but the coup attempt was aborted by the army without violence. b. *Participants*: Noe Kutuklui, Secretary General of the Union Togolaise party, and a leading Ewé politician. He was supported by many members of his party. Support for the attempt seemed to be widespread, but civilian crowds were unable to cope with the military. c. *Apparent Causes*: Ewé dissatisfaction with the government's policies and the military junta.
3. Coup d'État January 13, 1967	a. *Description*: The coup was preceded by a power struggle between President Grunitsky and Vice-president Meatchi. Grunitsky was deposed by the military. b. *Participants*: Lt. Col. Etiénne Eyadema, Chief of Staff, and the Togolese Army. c. *Apparent Causes*: Eyadema's dissatisfaction with the performance of Grunitsky and Meatchi. Grunitsky had called for the resignation of the junta after the November 1966 coup attempt. There had also been redutions in army appropriations. Eyadema decided to assume direct control instead of using civilian ministers. The coup was justified by Eyadema as necessary in order to prevent a civil war.

SOURCE: Russel Warren Howe, "Togo: Four Years of Military Rule," *Africa Report* 12 (May 1967): 6—12.

TABLE 36.10   Annual Instability Events: Independence Through 1979—Togo

Year	'61	'62	'63	'64	'65	'66	'67	'68	'69	'70	'71	'72	'73	'74	'75	'76	'77	'78	'79
ELITE INSTABILITY																			
Assassinations																			
Plots	2		1	3	1				1	1							1		
Attempted Coups d'État						1					·								
Coups d'État			1				1												
COMMUNAL INSTABILITY																			
Ethnic Violence																			
Irredentism																			
Rebellion																			
Civil War																			
MASS INSTABILITY																			
Revolt		·																	
Revolution																			
TURMOIL																			
Demonstrations																			
Strikes (no. days)																			
Riots (no. days)				2															
Terrorism		1	1				1								1				
Declarations of Emergency		1																	
CABINET INSTABILITY																			
Realloc. and new appts.	4	1	11	1		20	11			3			2						
New members		1	8				11	7	1	4			4						
Resig. and Dismissals	1			4			11	3		4			2						
No. of members (max.) (maximum in year)	9	10	11	11	11	11	11	12	12	12	12	14							

VII. Selected References

GENERAL

Corevin, Robert. *Le Togo*. 2nd ed. Paris: Presses de Universitaires Francaises, 1973.

Decalo, S. *Historical Dictionary of Togo*. Metuchen, N.J.: Scarecrow Press, 1976.

POLITICAL

Amin, Samir. *Neo-Colonialism in West Africa*. Harmondsworth, Middlesex: Penguin Books, 1973.

Decalo, S. *Coups and Army Rule in Africa: Studies in Military Style*. New Haven: Yale University Press, 1976.

De Lusignan, Guy. *French-Speaking Africa Since Independence*, pp. 170—1979. London: Pall Mall Press, 1969.

Hodges, T. "Eyadema's Unchallenged Rule." *Africa Report* (July/August 1977): 61—64.

Howe, Russell W. "Togo: Four Years of Military Rule." *Africa Report*, 12 (May 1967): 6—12.

Knoll, Arthur J. *Togo under Imperial Germany, 1884—1914: A Case Study in Colonial Rule.* Stanford: Hoover Institution Press, 1978

Thompson, Virginia. *West Africa's Counil of the Entente.* Ithaca, N.Y.: Cornell University Press, 1972.

ECONOMIC

International Monetary Fund. "Togo." In *Surveys of African Economies*, Vol. 3. Washington, D.C.: I.M.F., 1970.

SOCIAL

Aithnard, K. *Some Aspects of Cultural Policy in Togo.* Paris: UNESCO, 1976.

Debrunner, H. *A Church Between Colonial Powers: The Church in Togo.* London: Lutterworth Press, 1965

Kumekper, T. "Togo" in *Population Growth and Socioeconomic Change in West Africa.* J. Caldwell et al., eds. New York: Columbia University Press, 1975, pp. 720—35.

37. Uganda

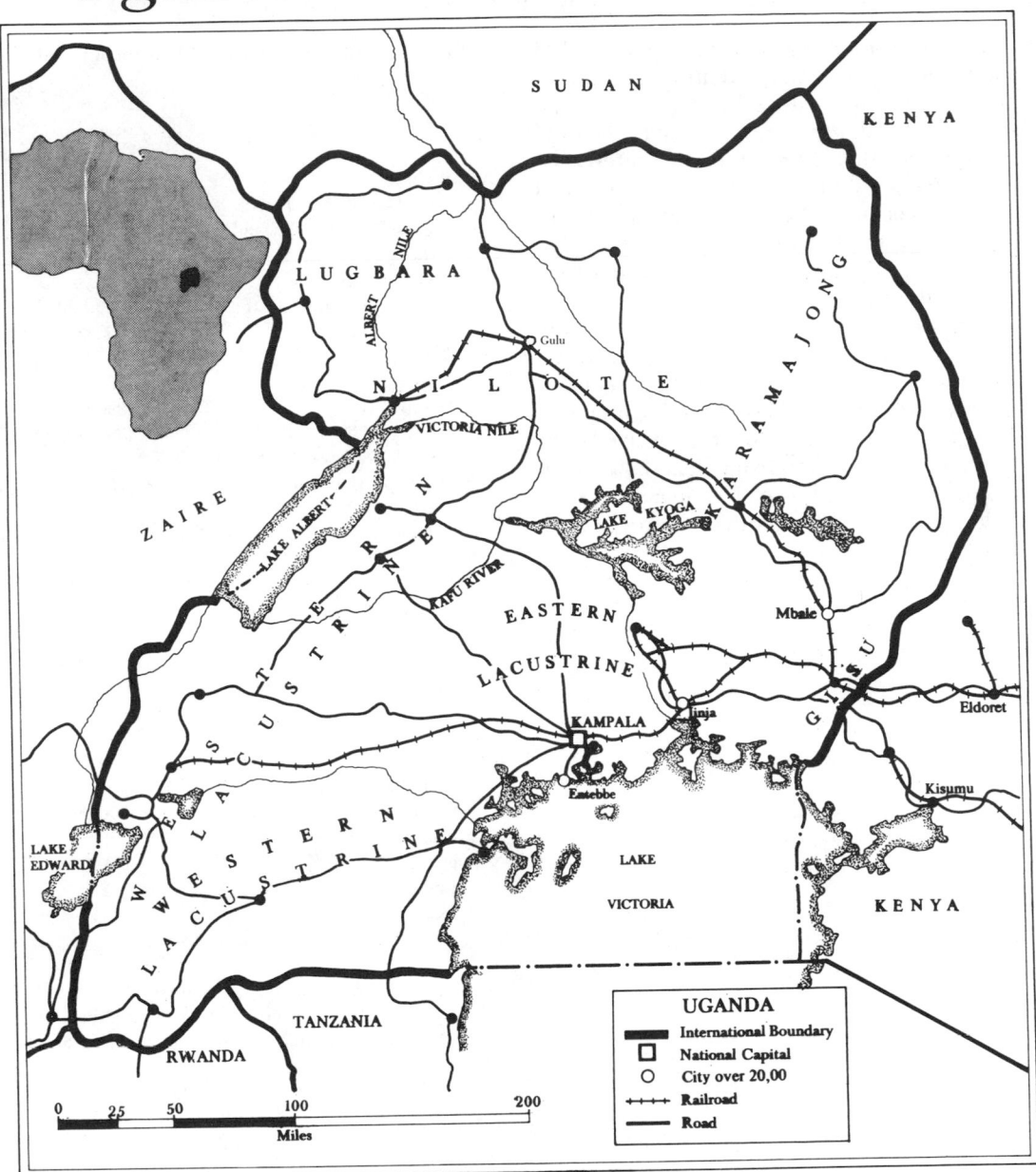

I. Basic Information

Date of Independence: October 9, 1962
Former Colonial Ruler: United Kingdom
Population (1980)*: 13,660,000
Area Size (equivalent in U.S.): 91,133 sq. mi. (Oregon)
Date of Last Census: 1969
Major exports 1977 as Percent of Total Exports: coffee—

93 percent; cotton—2 percent; tea—2 percent (excludes re-exports).

*Since there have been large numbers of refugees in adjoining countries it is difficult to estimate the country's population by extrapolating from previous census figures. Hence, this figure may be an overestimate.

II. Ethnic Patterns

The ethnic classification for Uganda is at a high level of abstraction and does not represent identity groups. In the case of the Eastern and Western Lacustrine clusters, geography is the basic differentiating criterion: it would be possible to combine the groups into the Interlacustrine Bantu. Likewise a Nilotic cluster could be devised at an even higher level of abstraction which would include the Nilote Type, Karamajong Cluster, Gisu Cluster, and Lugbara Types. The sub-categories under each type are generally identity groups. In addition to these major types and clusters, there are small populations of Nandi-like Suk and Sebei (1 percent), plus a fractional number of Twa (Pygmies). About 2 percent of the population was made up of Asians (75,000) and Europeans (9,500) according to the 1969 census. Most of the Asians and Europeans had been expelled from Uganda by 1975. In addition, an unknown number of Ugandans are refugees and reside, primarily, in countries bordering on Uganda.

TABLE 37.1   Ethnic Units Over 5 Percent of Country Population

Ethnic Units	Estimated Ethnic Population 1980	Estimated Ethnic Percentage
a. Eastern Lacustrine Cluster	3,688,000	27%
1. Ganda (Baganda, Waganda)	(2,186,000)	(16%)
2. Soga	(1,093,000)	(8%)
3. Gwere, 4. Nyuli		
b. Western Lacustrine Cluster	3,415,000	25%
1. Nkole (Nyankole)	(1,093,000)	(8%)
2. Kiga	(956,000)	(7%)
3. Toro	(437,000)	(3.2%)
4. Nyoro	(396,000)	(2.9%)
5. Konjo	(396,000)	(2.9%)
6. Rwanda, 7. Rundi, 8. Ambo		
c. Nilote Type (Luo, Lwoo)	2,050,000	15%
1. Lango	(820,000)	(6%)
2. Acholi	(546,000)	(4%)
3. Alur	(546,000)	(4%)
4. Padhola	(260,000)	(1.9%)
5. Kuman, 6. Jonam, 7. Paluo		
d. Karamajong Cluster	1,500,000	11%
1. Teso	(1,090,000)	(8%)
2. Karamajong, 3. Dodoth,		
4. Jie, 5. Tepeth,		
6. Nyakwai, 7. Kakwa		
e. Gisu Cluster	820,000	6%
1. Gisu (Bageshu, Bagish, Geshu, Masaba, Sokwia)	(700,000)	(5.1%)
2. Nyole, 3. Samia		
f. Lugbara Type	680,000	5%
1. Lugbara		
2. Madi, 3. Lendu		

SOURCE: U.S. Department of the Army, *Area Handbook for Uganda* (Washington, D.C.: Government Printing Office, 1969), pp. 77—90, and 1959 census results as reported in *Africa South of the Sahara 1977—78.*

III. Language Patterns

The two major language families in Uganda are Bantu (including Ganda, Soga, Toro, Nyoro, Rwanda, and Gisu) and Nilotic (including Lango, Acholi, Alur, Iteso, Karamajong, Lugbara). Ganda (Luganda) is probably the largest single language in Uganda, including about 16 percent of the total population who speak it as a first language, and another 25 percent who speak it as second language, mainly from the Ganda-related language groups. (Knappert estimates that 33 percent speak Luganda: MacDougald 28 percent; Rustow 28 percent.) The second most widely distributed language is probably Swahili, with a minimum of 30 percent of the population who speak it as a second or third language. English is the official language of Uganda.

TABLE 37.2   Language Patterns

1. Primacy			
1st language	Ganda	(41%)	
2nd language	Swahili	(30%)	
		Greenberg	Dalby
2. Linguistic classification (all ethnic units in country over 5%)	Eastern Lacustrine	IA5	E1
	Western Lacustrine	IA5	E1
	Nilote	IIE1	71c
	Karamajong	IIE1	72C
	Gisu	IA5	E3
	Lugbara	IE11	52A
3. *Lingua francas*	Ganda, Swahili		
4. Official language	English (Ganda was formerly the official language of the region of Buganda)		

IV. Urban Patterns

Capital/largest city: Kampala (founded in 1890)
Dominant ethnicity/language of capital
    Major vernacular: Ganda[1]
    Major ethnic group: Ganda[2]
    Major ethnic group as percent of capital's population:
    42% (1952)

[1]Jan Knappert, "Language Problems of the New Nations of Africa," *African Quarterly*, 5 (1965): 95—105.
[2]A. Southall and P. G. Gutkind, *Townsmen in the Making*, (Kampala: East African Institute of Social Research, 1957), p. 26.

TABLE 37.3   Growth of Capital/Largest City

Date	Kampala
1930	10,000
1940	24,000
1950	38,000
1960	120,000
1966	175,000 UA
1969	331,000 UA

SOURCE: Southall and Gutkind, *Townsmen in the Making* (Kampala: East Africa Institute of Social Research, 1957).

TABLE 37.4   Cities of 20,000 and Over*

City	Size	Date
Kampala	331,000 UA	1969
Jinja/Njeru*	99,400	1969
Mbale	23,544	1969
Entebbe	21,096	1969
Gulu	18,170	1969

SOURCE: 1969 census as reported in *Africa South of the Sahara 1977—1978*.
    *Includes Bugembe planning area.
    **By 1977, Kampala's population was reported to be severely depleted. Some estimates placed it as low as 40,000. (*Africa Contemporary Record 1976—77* p. B377). It can be presumed that all other cities also have lower populations by 1977 for similar reasons. Since the ouster of Idi Amin, the urban areas may have partially recovered population but it is not likely that they are up to 1969 levels in 1980.

V. Political Patterns

A. Political Parties and Elections

Uganda had its first direct elections for African representative on the Legislative Council in 1958. In March 1961, elections were held in which the *Democratic Party* (DP) won 43 seats, and the *Uganda People's Congress* (UPC), led by Dr. Milton Obote, won 35 seats, The Buganda region, however, boycotted this election, even though the *Democratic Party* originated inside Buganda (reflecting the Catholic groups, as distinct from the majority Protestants). In October of 1961, the majority of the Buganda peoples formed a party called *Kabaka Yekka*, which allied with the UPC, and this coalition won the national elections in April 1962. (The UPC won 43 out of 91 seats.) In November 1964 there was another election— the "lost counties" referendum, and by December 1965 the UPC majority had increased to 67 out of 91 seats. In February 1966 Prime Minister Obote deposed the President, Sir Edward Mutesa II, the Kabaka of Buganda, and tried to put an end to Buganda autonomy. The Kabaka died in exile in November 1969. Following the attempted assassination of Dr. Obote in December 1969, all the opposition parties were banned. The military government banned all parties after the January 1971 coup. No political activity was allowed from that time until the overthrow of Amin and the restoration of representative government. A number of clandestine groups operated in and out of the country during that period. One of these was the *Front for National Salvation* organized in 1973 with the goal of overthrowing Amin. A coalition of anti-Amin groups, the *Uganda National Liberation Front* was formed in Tanzania in March 1979 in order to overthrow Amin. They were successful and in April 1979 with the help of Tanzanian troops captured the city of Kampala and set up a new government. In October 1979, elections were held for the 127 member national assembly on a non-partisan basis.

It is generally believed that the ouster of Binaisa was an attempt to strengthen the chances of Milton Obote in the Presidential elections scheduled for September 1980. Four parties were competing in the election. The *Uganda People's Congress* (UPC), led by Milton Obote has wide ethnic representation at the top, but is primarily Lango-based at the grass-roots level. The *Democratic Party* (DP) led by Paul Semogerere is based primarily in Buganda but has widespread support among Catholics. The *Uganda Patriotic Movement* (UPM) is headed by Yoweri Museveri, the vice chairman of the military council. The UPM support comes mainly from the young, many of the intelligentsia, and those disenchanted with the old parties. The weakest party is the *Conservative Party* (CP) led by Elizaphan Mayanja-Nkanji. The CP is Baganda-based and favors decentralization. At the last minute the September election was postponed. Troops loyal to Idi Amin were reported to be back in the country and attacking key posts. In the December elections, Obote's party won with 66 of 126 seats. Most of the remainder went to the DP.

FIGURE 37.1   Political Parties and Elections   UGANDA

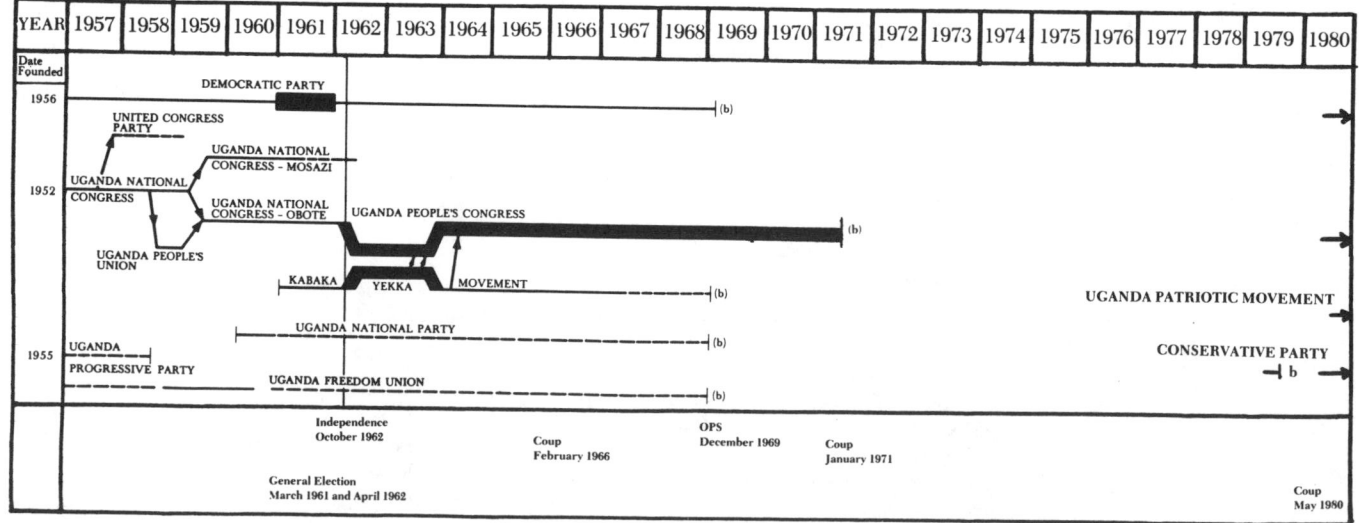

B. Political Leadership

Milton Obote was head of government from independence to January 1971. There was a rapid cabinet turnover in 1966 following the deposition of the President, Edward Mutesa (the Kabaka of Buganda). Before 1971, cabinet ethnicity remained relatively constant with a slight decrease in Ganda members and an increase in Gisu members.

During Amin's rule from 1971 to 1979, it was difficult to talk of political leadership since no stable government developed. Amin directed most of the political system himself and while the construction of a police state which ruled by terror may have been successful in keeping him in power for eight years, it is clear that the administration of the country and its economy had virtually collapsed by 1978. By then Uganda was "ruled by the gun through a military bureaucracy in which effective power was wielded by a tiny Nubian minority." (*Africa Contemporary Record, 1976—77* B372).

Many assassination attempts were made against Amin, but none succeeded. Other shocks to the regime such as the Israeli 'Entebbe rescue' in July 1976 or university student demonstrations in August 1976 also did little to threaten Amin's regime. The student demonstrations were followed by the killing of several hundred students at that time and more were killed in the massive purges in February—March 1977. Amin promoted himself to Field Marshall (1975) and to President for Life (June 25, 1976). In April 1979, a coalition of anti-Amin groups with Tanzanian backing was able to overthrow the government of Amin. On April 11, 1979, Kampala fell to the *Uganda National Libertion Front* (UNLF) and an interim government was established. Dr. Yusuf Lule was sworn in as President. Dr. Lule was replaced by Godfrey Binaisa as President with Nyerere of Tanzania playing a key role in the change. There was a cabinet reshuffle in November 1979 in which members of the UNLF were demoted. The National Consultative Council which acted as Uganda's parliament was angered by Binaisa's actions with regard to UNLF members. In early May 1980, Binaisa was overthrown and a military commission came to power. The commission sponsored multi-party elections in December 1980. At the end of May 1980, Milton Obote returned to Uganda after nine years in exile, and pre-election campaigning began. Obote's party won 66 of 126 seats in the December elections and he returned to power almost ten years after his ouster. The sectional (northern) base of power of Obote's party continues the long standing conflicts in the country, however.

TABLE 37.5   Heads of Government (Post-Independence)

Name	Dates in Office	Age (1982)	Ethnicity	Education	Former Occupation
1. Apollo Milton Obote (Prime Minister/ Executive President)	1962—1971	58	Nilote Cluster (Largo)	Makerere College	Business Entrepreneur
2. Field Marshall Idi Amin Dada (President for Life)	Jan. 1971— April 1979	57	Karamajong 57 (Kakwa)	Army Cluster Schools	Army officer Training
3. Yusuf Lule (President)	April 13, 1979— June 20, 1979	71	Ganda	M.A. Edinburgh University	Principal of Makerere College
4. Godfrey Binaisa	June 20, 1970— May 1980				Lawyer
5. Military Commission	May 1980— Dec. 1980				
6. Apollo Milton Obote	Dec. 1980—	58	Nilote (Lango)	Makerere College	Politician

TABLE 37.6   Cabinet Membership: Distribution by Ethnic Unit*

Ethnicity*	Independence Cabinet	Immediate Pre-Coup Cabinet	1967 Cabinet
1. Eastern Lacustrine (27)	41%	50%	37%
2. Western Lacustrine (25)	0	6.3	0
3. Nilote (15)	24	13	26
4. Karamajong (11)	5.9	13	0
5. Gisu (6)	18	6.3	32
6. Lugbara (5)	0	6.3	5.3
7. Others (6)	12	0	0
N =	17	16	19

*Ethnic units arranged in rank order of size within country with the unit's percent of national population in parentheses.

VI. National Integration and Stability

Through the 1960's the major problem of national integration in Uganda, both in terms of elite and communal stability, was the question of the role of the powerful and formerly autonomous kingdom of Buganda. In 1966, the power of Buganda was successfully challenged by removing the Kabaka, who was King of Buganda and President of Uganda, and establishing a unitary state. (The Kabaka died in exile in 1969.) On December 19, 1969, there was an attempted assassination of President Obote, who was overthrown by an army coup led by Amin a little over a year later. Since that coup, the chaos that followed is hard to document fully. In 1971 under the cover of alleged coups and plots large numbers of Acholi and Lango officers and soldiers were murdered. Whenever resistance was offered, it was labeled a coup attempt as some may, in fact, have been. In 1972, an invasion by pro-Obote groups from Tanzania was unsuccessful and appears to have led to further purges in and out of the military. Pro-Obote guerrilla activity continued in the country although much of this may be mislabeled and merely reflect the putative rationale for the tribal pogroms of Amin and his followers. An assassination attempt against Amin was made in February 1974 although given the contorted world of Uganda under Amin, it cannot be ignored that this might have been Amin's way to kill those who were in fact assassinated. In March 1974, there was an attempted coup by army units against Amin which failed when they were unable to locate his hiding place. Army mutinies appeared common and a major one occurred in November 1974 when most of the Airborne Division mutinied because they had not been paid. On June 25, 1976 a major assassination attempt against Amin failed and extensive purges resulted. There have been many reported plots and coup attempts but Uganda under Amin was a closed society and verified information was almost impossible to collect. There appears to have been at least two attempts to assassinate Amin in 1975, two attempts in 1976, and a major plot to kill him in January 1977 which was followed by a massive purge with at least 5,000 people murdered, many in extremely brutal fashion. Targets of the purge included army personnel, Christians, and church officials including the Anglican Archbishop of Uganda. Another attempt on Amin's life was reported in June 1977 and reports of further attempts continued until his flight from the country in 1979. The effects of the Amin period on the political future of the country cannot yet be estimated but by June 1980, two new heads of state had come and gone since Amin.

A plot by dissident army officers to overthrow Amin in early January 1979 was unsuccessful. In March 1979, several anti-Amin groups joined forces in Tanzania in order to overthrow Amin. With the help of the Tanzanian government and armed forces, the Uganda National Liberation Front (UNLF) captured the city of Kampala and set up an interim government. Dr. Yusuf Lule was sworn in as President for the interim period. In 1979 Godfrey Binaisa was named President replacing Lule. Since early 1980, there have been rumors of the growth of private armies in northern Uganda. There are also continuing reports of army and mob terrorism and looting in Kampala including activity by parts of the Tanzanian army and the Ugandan army. Under Amin, government reshuffles were frequent and almost all the important positions were held by Moslems who represent about five percent of the population in this largely Christian country.

The elections restored Obote to power in the ravaged country but it is unclear what future the once-wealthy state now has.

TABLE 37.7   Elite Instability

Event and Date	Characteristics
1. Coup d'État February 22, 1966	a. *Description*: Prime Minister Obote suspended the constitution, relieved the President, Sir Edward Mutesa (the Kabaka of Buganda), and declared himself Executive President. He ordered the arrest of five cabinet ministers. b. *Participants*: Prime Minister Obote, with the support of various police and military elements. c. *Apparent Causes*: Obote was challenged by the Kabaka Yekka Party and elements in his own party. Parliament voted to establish a commission to investigate allegations that he was involved in illegal activities in connection with the transfer of gold from Zaire. He preempted his opponents by moving first.
2. Coup d'État January 25, 1971	a. *Description*: The army seized power while President Obote was in Asia attending the Comonwealth Conference. Scattered shooting was reported in Kampala and some continuing resistance was reported in other areas of the country for a time after the coup. All political prisoners were immediately released. b. *Participants*: The army, led by Major General Idi Amin, who had risen from the ranks to become its commander in 1966. c. *Apparent Causes*: Amin stated at the time of the coup that the government's economic policies were benefiting the "rich, big men" and that Obote had developed his own home region in the north at the expense of other parts of the country., There was rivalry and infighting between officers of Obote's Lango tribe and the Acholi and other tribes culturally related to Amin's Kakwa tribe. Apparently Obote had planned to dismiss Amin from his army command.
3. Coup Attempt September 17—28, 1972	a. *Description*: Pro-Obote armed forces invade Uganda from Tanzania and are forced to retreat to Tanzania after Amin's troops repulsed the attack over a ten day period. b. *Participants*: Pro-Obote armed forces and Amin's army units. c. *Apparent Causes*: Attempt by the ousted President, Obote, and his supporters to restore him to power in Uganda.
4. Coup Attempt March 23—24, 1974	a. *Description*: Army units attacked Amin's 'command post' but Amin was not there. Amin was later able to rally loyal troops to put down the coup attempt. b. *Participants*: Brigadier Charles Arube and troops from the Malire Mechanised Battalion. Also Lt. Col. Eli and Lt. James Ayoma were implicated. c. *Apparent Causes*: Not clear but probably a reaction to Amin's anti-Lugbara moves in the army supported by opposition to his pro-Muslim, anti-Christian position. The erratic nature of the terror campaign in Uganda was probably a contributing factor.
5. Coup Attempt February 16, 1975	a. *Description*: Members of the army ambush Amin's motorcade in northern Uganda. Amin, who was following the motorcade in an unmarked car was unhurt although many in the motorcade were killed. b. *Participants*: Unnamed soldiers with possible backing from groups based in and out of the country who operate clandestine activities against Amin. c. *Apparent Causes*: As with most of the activity against Amin, the causes are presumed to be in reaction to his governmental policies and the massive violence created by his regime.
6. Coup Attempt August 1975	a. *Description*: Army units including tanks were stopped at the very beginning of an attempted coup while Amin was in Ethiopia. Details of the event are unavailable and the leaders fled into hiding. b. *Participants*: Lt. Col. Gori and other officers based at Masaka, and an unidentified Major at the Malire Mechanised Regiment at Bombo just north of Kampala. c. *Apparent Causes*: As with most other attempts against Amin, the causes are not known but are presumed to be related to his policies of rule by terror in the country at large and within the army, in particular.
7. Coup Attempt June 10, 1976	a. *Description*: While leaving a passing-out parade at the police barracks in Kampala, three grenades were thrown at Amin in his jeep. His driver, who had exchanged places with Amin (who was actually driving) was killed. Amin was apparently unhurt and mass purges followed the attack. b. *Participants*: Probably elements within the army although with the exception of one army officer, only civilians were arrested. Possibly Amin felt unable to move directly against the army at that time. The civilians were all from the southern provinces, the primary source of opposition to his regime. c. *Apparent Causes*: Opposition to Amin's policies are presumed to be the cause—especially his attempt to murder all opponents, actual or potential, who are from the south of Uganda.

Event and Date	Characteristics
8. Attempted Coup July 1976	a. *Description*: Mutiny in the army barracks at Kampala and Gulu is followed by demands of senior army and police officials that Amin resign. He locked the officers in a Kampala hotel and then had them shot. b. *Participants*: Senior military and police officers including Ali Towilli, Superintendent of Police and the four army commanders in the Kampala area. c. *Apparent Causes*: Opposition to Amin's policies in general but especially over the conflict with Kenya and the bloodbaths in the army.
9. Attempted Coup June 18, 1977	a. *Description*: Details of the event are not known. b. *Participants*: Major Patrick Kimune, Lt. Masamba and other soldiers. c. *Apparent Causes*: Opposition to Amin's rule.
10. Coup d'État April 1979	a. *Description*: On March 26, 1979, several anti-Amin groups joined together in Tanzania to plan the defeat of Idi Amin. With the support of Tanzanian forces, the Uganda National Liberation Army fought its way to and captured the city of Kampala. Idi Amin fled from the capital and now lives in exile in the Middle East. b. *Participants*: Approximately 18 anti-Amin groups united in the *Uganda National Liberation Front*. The main invasion forces were led by Obote's military commanders, Lt. Col. David Ojok and Col. Tito Okello. c. *Apparent Causes*: Opposition to Amin's rule.

SOURCES: Crawford Young, "The Obote Revolution," *Africa Report*, 11 (June 196): 8—15. Ali A. Mazrui, "Privilege and Protest as Integrative Factors: The Case of Buganda's Status in Uganda," in *Power and Protest in Black Africa*. eds. Robert I. Rotberg and Ali A. Mazrui (New York: Oxford University Press, 1970). M. F. Lofchie "The Political Origins of the Uganda Coup" *Journal of African Studies* 1, 4 Winter 1974, pp. 464—96. D. Martin, *General Amin* (London: Faber and Faber, 1974).

TABLE 37.8   Communal Instability

Event and Date	Characteristics
1. Ethnic Violence February 15— March 30, 1963	a. *Description*: On February 15th, a state of emergency was declared in the counties of Busongora and Bwanba, in Toro District (West Uganda). On March 30, 1963, Buyaga county of the so-called "Lost Counties" was declared a "disturbed" area. In March there were 43 incidents of violence: most were directed against Buganda chiefs. b. *Participants*: Bunyoro ethnic members and Buganda chiefs. c. *Apparent Causes*: Bunyoro spokesmen claimed that the "Lost Counties" in the Buganda kingdom should be returned to Bunyoro.
2. Rebellion 1962—1964	a. *Description*: Amba and Konjo people demanded autonomy from their historical overlords, the Toro. This protest was organized by the Rwenzururu movement, which demanded a separate status within Toro district, and later established a secessionist government. Ugandan troops and police were sent to the area by the central government which supported the Toro District administration. Konjo and Amba attacks on Toro chiefs were brought to an end in 1964 by a ten-day attack by Toro. Hundreds of Konjo were killed, and many others fled into the Rwenzururu mountains, before order was effectively restored in the area by the police and army. b. *Participants*: Members of the Konjo, Amba and Toro ethnic groups. c. *Apparent Causes*: The feeling by Amba and Konjo of historical exploitation by Toro, and of increased political deprivation after Uganda's independence when administrative offices remained concentrated in Toro hands.

Event and Date	Characteristics
3. Rebellion March 24—July 1966	a. *Description*: The Buganda rebellion was caused essentially by the demand of the Buganda people to maintain strong kingship (Kabakaship) and regional autonomy in the face of national government efforts to create a centralized state. After the constitution was suspended in February 1966, tension arose between Obote and Sir Edward Mutesa, the Kabaka of Buganda and former President of Uganda. Buganda demanded that the central government leave Kampala. The government attacked the Kabaka's palace on May 24 and the Kabaka fled into exile, although rebellion in rural areas continued for several days thereafter. b. *Participants*: The Buganda region which is ethnically homogeneous (Baganda) was almost completely autonomous in the colonial era and functioned under its traditional ruler, the Kabaka, who at the time of independence became the President of Uganda. Buganda has beeen the most developed region in Uganda. c. *Apparent Causes*: The Buganda perceived the central government to be dominating them, and were striving for a return to "local autonomy."

SOURCES: Martin R. Doornbos, "Kumanyana and Rwenzururu," in *Protest and Power in Black Africa*, eds. Robert I. Rotberg and Ali A. Mazrui (New York: Oxford University Press, 1970), pp1088 – 1138. Terence Hopkins, "Politics in Uganda: The Buganda Question," in *Transition in African Politics*, eds. Jeffrey Butler and A. A. Castagno (New York: Praeger, 1966): 8 – 15.

TABLE 37.10   Annual Instability Events: Independence Through 1979—Uganda

Year	'61	'62	'63	'64	'65	'66	'67	'68	'69	'70	'71	'72	'73	'74	'75	'76	'77	'78	'79
ELITE INSTABILITY																			
Assassinations																			
Plots						1	1	1			2	1	1	1	1				
Attempted Coups d'État											2			1	2	2	1		
Coups d'État						1					1								
COMMUNAL INSTABILITY																			
Ethnic Violence			2	1	1					1									
Irredentism		1																	
Rebellion			1	1		1													
Civil War																			
MASS INSTABILITY																			
Revolt												1							
Revolution																			
TURMOIL																			
Demonstrations																			
Strikes (no. days)			2																
Riots (no. days)		1			1														
Terrorism									1	2									
Declarations of Emergency			2	2	1	1			1	2									

Year	'61	'62	'63	'64	'65	'66	'67	'68	'69	'70	'71	'72	'73	'74	'75	'76	'77	'78	'79
CABINET INSTABILITY																			
Realloc. and new appts.		5	3	3	20	9	2				2	2							
New members	6	3	2	2	7	5	2				29								
Resig. and Dismissals	6	1	2				3				1								
No. of members (max.) (maximum in year)	17	17	17	17	21	21	20	20	20	18	18								

VII. Selected References

BIBLIOGRAPHY

Gray, Beverly. *Uganda: Subject Guide to Official Publications*. Washington: Library of Congress, 1977.

Hopkins, T. K. *A Study Guide for Uganda*. Boston: Development Program, African Studies Center, Boston University, 1969.

Kuria, Lucas et al. (comps.) *A Bibliography on Politics and Government in Uganda*. Occasional Bibliography No. 2. Syracuse, N.Y.: Syracuse University Program of Eastern African Studies, 1965.

Peckham, Robert et. al., (comps.) *A Bibliography on Anthropology and Sociology in Uganda*. Occasional Bibliography No. 3. Syracuse, N.Y.: Syracuse University Program of Eastern Africa Studies, 1965.

GENERAL

Col, J. M. *Uganda*. Boulder, Colo.: Westview Press, 1981.

Gertzel, Cherry. *Uganda*. London: Pall Mall Press, 1970.

Gukiina, P. M. *Uganda: A Case Study in African Political Development*. South Bend, Ind.: Notre Dame University Press, 1972.

Ibingira, G. S. K. *The Forging of an African Nation: The Political and Constitutional Evolution of Uganda from Colonial Rule to Independence, 1894—1962*. New York: The Viking Press, 1973.

Low, D. A. *Buganda in Modern History*. Berkeley: University of California Press, 1971.

Uganda Government. *Atlas of Uganda*. Entebbe: Department of Lands and Surveys, 1962.

U.S. Department of the Army. *Area Handbook for Uganda*. Washington, D.C.: Government Printing Office, 1969.

ECONOMIC

Elkan, Walter. *Migrants and Proletarians: Urban Labour in the Economic Development of Uganda*. London: Oxford University Press, 1960.

International Bank for Reconstruction and Development. *The Economic Development of Uganda*. Baltimore, Md.: Johns Hopkins University Press, 1962.

International Monetary Fund. "Uganda." In *Surveys of African Economies*, Vol. 2, Washington, D.C.: I.M.F., 1968.

Jameson, J. D. (ed.) *Agriculture in Uganda*. New York: Oxford University Press, 1971.

Richards, A. I. et al. (eds.) *Subsistence to Commercial Farming in Present-Day Buganda*. New York: Cambridge University Press, 1973.

SOCIAL

Ainsworth, Mary D. S. *Infancy in Uganda*. Baltimore, Md.: Johns Hopkins Press, 1967.

Brandt, Hartmat, et. al. *The Industrial Town as Factor of Economic and Social Development: The Example of Jinja/Uganda*. Munich: Weltforum Verlag, 1972.

Chesswa, J. D. *Educational Planning and Development in Uganda*. African Research Monograph No. 1. Paris: UNESCO. International Institute for Educational Planning, 1966.

Curley, Richard T. *Elders Shades and Women: Ceremonial Change in Lango, Uganda*. Berkeley: University of California Press, 1973.

Doornbos, Martin R. *Not All the King's Men: Inequality as a Political Instrument in Ankole, Uganda*. The Hague: Mouton, 1978.

Fallers, Lloyd A., ed. *The King's Men: Leadership and Status in Buganda on the Eve of Independence*. New York: Oxford University Press, 1964.

Fallers, Lloyd A., ed. *Bantu Bureaucracy*. Chicago: University of Chicago Press, 1965.

Parkin, David. *Neighbors and Nations in an African City Ward*. Berkeley: University of California Press, 1969. (Kampala)

Scott, Roger. *The Development of Trade Unions in Uganda*. Nairobi: East African Publishing House, 1966.

Southall, A. W. "Kampala-Mengo." In *The City in Modern Africa*. ed. Horace Miner. New York: Praeger, 1967.

Southall, A. W. "The Concepts of Elite and Their Formation in Uganda." In *The New Elites in Tropical Africa*, ed. P. C. Lloyd. New York: Oxford University Press, 1966.

Southall, A. W. and P. G. Gutkind. *Townsmen in the Making: Kampala and its Suburbs*. London: Routledge and Kegan Paul, 1957.

Tosh, John. *Clan Leaders and Colonial Chiefs in Lango: The Political History of an East African Stateless Society c. 1800—1939*. New York: Oxford University Press, 1978.

Van Zwanenberg, R. M. A. and Anne King. *An Economic History of Kenya and Uganda, 1900—1970*. London: Macmillan, 1975.

Vincent, Joan. *African Elite: The Big Men of a Small Town*. New York: Columbia University Press, 1971.

Weeks, Sheldon. *Divergence in Educational Development: The Case of Kenya and Uganda*. New York: Columbia Teachers College Press, 1967.

POLITICAL

Apter, David F. *The Political Kingdom in Uganda: A Study in Bureaucratic Nationalism*, 2nd ed. Princeton, N.J.: Princeton University Press, 1967.

Burke, F. G. *Local Government and Politics in Uganda*. Syracuse, N.Y: Syracuse University Press, 1964.

Gertzel, Cherry. *Party and Locality in Northern Uganda, 1945—1962. London: Althone Press, 1974.*

Gingyera-Pinycwa, A. G. G. *Apollo Milton Obote and His Time*. New York: NOK, 1978.

Gwyn, David. *Idi Amin: Death-Light of Africa*. Boston: Little, Brown & Co., 1977.

Hansen, Holger Bernt. *Ethnicity and Military Rule in Uganda*. Uppsala: The Scandinavian Institute of African Studies, Research Report No. 43, 1977.

Hills, Denis. *The White Pumpkin*. London: George Allen and Unwin, 1975.

Kasfir, N. *The Shrinking Political Arena: Participation and Ethnicity in African Politics with a Case Study of Uganda*. Berkeley: University of California Press, 1975.

Kiwanuka, Semakula. *Amin and the Tragedy of Uganda*. Munich: Weltforum Verlag, 1979.

Kyemba, Henry. *A State of Blood*. N.Y.: Ace Books, 1977.

Leys, Colin. *Politicians and Policies: An Essay on Politics in Acholi, Uganda 1962—65*. Nairobi: East African Publishing House, 1967.

Listowel, Judith. *Amin*. Dublin: Irish University Press, 1973.

Low, D. A. *Political Parties in Uganda, 1946—1962*. London: London University Institute of Commonwealth Studies, 1962.

Mamdani, M. *Politics and Class Formation in Uganda*. New York: Monthly Review Press, 1976.

Martin, David. *General Amin*. London: Faber & Faber, 1974.

Mittelman, J. H. *Ideology and Politics in Uganda: From Obote to Amin*. Ithaca: Cornell University Press, 1975.

Rothchild, Donald, and M. Rogin. "Uganda." In *National Unity and Regionalism in Eight African States*, ed. Gwendolen M. Carter. Ithaca, N.Y.: Cornell University Press, 1966.

Strate, J. T. *Post-Military Coup Strategy in Uganda: Amin's Early Attempts to Consolidate Political Support*. Athens, Ohio: Center for International Studies, Ohio Unviersity, 1973. Papers in International Studies, Africa Series, No. 18.

38. Burkina Faso (Upper Volta)

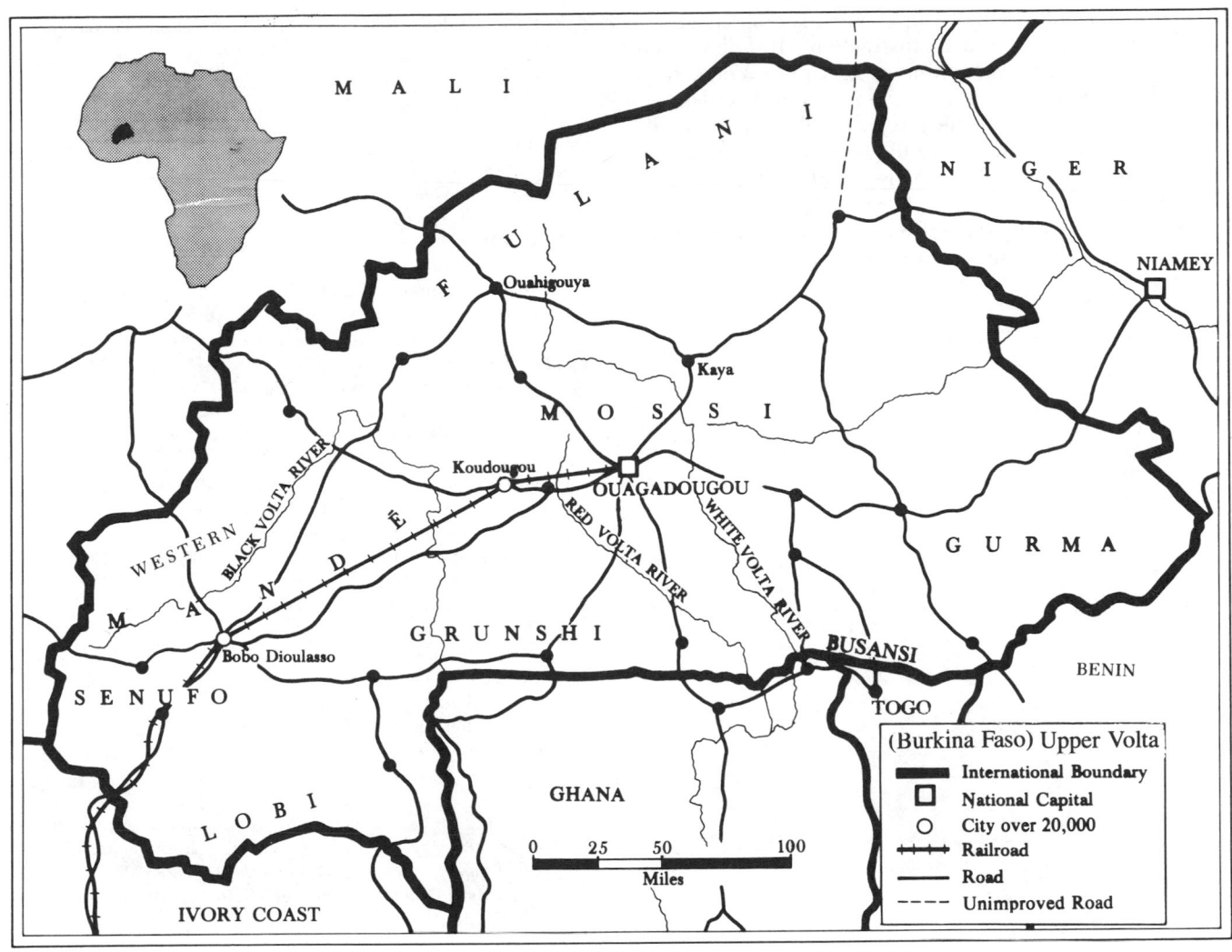

I. Basic Information

Date of Independence: April 5, 1960
Former Colonial Ruler: France
Change in Boundaries: Formerly part of the French West African Federation; administered as part of the Ivory Coast after conquest; administered separately from 1919-1932; administered as part of Mali and the Ivory Coast until 1947.

Population (1980): 6,800,000
Area Size (equivalent in U.S.): 105,870 sq. mi. (Colorado)
Date of Last Census: 1975
Major Exports 1977 as Percent of Total Exports: raw cotton—40 percent; live animals—29 percent; karite nuts and oil—14 percent.

II. Ethnic Patterns

The ethnic classification of Upper Volta is done at a middle level of inclusion and abstraction. It follows the schema used by the government of Upper Volta, who state their main criterion as follows (our translation): "The classification given here is primarily based on cultural characteristics which are likely to have an influence on demographic traits." The Mossi, Fulani, Gurma, and Busansi are identity groups. Large migrations to Ivory Coast to work, while generally temporary, leave the *de facto* population at some variance from the figure in Table 38.1.

TABLE 38.1   Ethnic Units Over 5 Percent of Country Population

Ethnic Units	Estimated Ethnic Population 1980	Estimated Ethnic Percentage
a. Mossi (Mole, Moshi)	3,400,000	50%
1. Ouagadougou, 2. Tengkedogo, 3. Yatenga		
b. Western Mandé Type	952,000	14%
1. Bobo, 2. Barka, 3. Samo, 4. Dyula		
c. Fulani (Peul)	680,000	10%
1. Fulani, 2. Rimibes (serfs)		
d. Lobi Type	476,000	7%
1. Lobi, 2. Vigne, 3. Dian, 4. Gan, 5. Dorossie, 6. Komono, 7. Birifor, 8. Dagari, 9. Wile		
e. Senufo Type (Sene, Siena)	408,000	6%
1. Senufo-Minianka, 2. Karakora, 3. Toussian, 4. Tourka, 5. Gouin		
f. Grunshi Type (Gourounsi, Gorisè, Grussi, Grunsi)	340,000	5%
1. Grunshi, 2. Koussassis, 3. Kassena, 4. Sissala, 5. Nounoumas, 6. Kos, 7. Lelas		
g. Busansi (Bisa, Bisano, Bisapele, Bousanou, Bouzantchi, Busanga)	340,000	5%
h. Gurma (Gourmantche)	306,000	4.5%

SOURCE: Upper Volta, Direction de la statistique et des études économiques. *La situation démographique en Haute-Volta; résultats partiels de l'enquête démographique 1960—61* (Paris: Ministère de la Cooperation 1962). Note—percentages add to over 100 percent due to rounding of figures.

III. Language Patterns

All of the languages of Upper Volta are in the Niger-Congo family, including the Voltaic sub-branch (Mossi, Senufo, Grunshi, Lobi, and Gurma), plus Dyula and Fulani. The major language in Upper Volta is Mossi, which is spoken by 50 percent of the population as a first language and probably by another 5 percent as a *lingua franca*. (Knappert estimates Mossi speakers at 50 percent; Rustow 54 percent.) The second largest language group is Dyula, a simplified form of Malinké (of the Mandé family). Probably 16 percent of the population speak Dyula as a first language, and probably 5 percent as a *lingua franca*. French is the official language.

TABLE 38.2   Language Patterns

1. Primacy
    1st language   Mossi   (55%)
    2nd language   Dyula   (21%)
2. Greenberg classification   Mossi   IA3
    (all ethnic units in   Western Mandé   IA2
    country over 5%)   Senufo   IA3
                               Grunshi   IA3
                               Fulani   IA1
                               Lobi   IA3
                               Gurma   IA3
                               Busansi   IA2
3. *Lingua francas*   Mossi, Dyula
4. Official language   French

IV. Urban Patterns

Capital/largest city: Ouagadougou
Dominant ethnicity/language of capital
  Major vernacular: Mossi[1]
  Major ethnic group: Mossi[2]
  Major ethnic group as percent of capital's population:
  66% (1968)[2]

[1]Jan Knappert, "Language Problems of the New Nations of Africa," *African Quarterly*, 5 (1965): 95—105.

[2]"Enquete Démographique Ouagadougou 1968," *Bulletin Mensuel l'Information Statistique et Economique*, New Series, 1969.

TABLE 38.3   Growth of Capital/largest city

Date	Ouagadougou
1920	12,000
1930	16,000
1940	24,000
1950	37,000
1960	55,000
1966	78,000
1970	110,000
1975	168,607

SOURCE: *Démographie Comparée, UN Demographic Yearbook, 1969.*

TABLE 38.4   Cities of 20,000 and Over*

City	Size	Date
Ouagadougou	168,607	1975
Bobo-Dioulasso	112,572	1975
Koudougou	35,803	1975
Ouahigouya	25,101	1975
Kaya	18,402	1975

SOURCE: *Europa Yearbook 1977*—Kaya is included since it is so close to a 20,000 population.

V. Political Patterns

A. Political Parties and Elections

The political structure and constitution of Upper Volta was almost identical to the one-party system of Ivory Coast in the early years after independence. The dominant party, the *Union Démocratique Voltaique* (UDV), led by Maurice Yaméogo, was a branch of the *Rassemblement Démocratique Africain* (RDA) led by Felix Houphouet-Boigny of the Ivory Coast. In the 1959 election the UDV won 71 out of 75 seats and subsequently gained control of the remaining four seats. There were, prior to independence, a variety of opposition parties, although many of them were banned or merged with the UDV. In 1966, the military led by Lt. Colonel Sangoulé Lamizana took control of the government and suspended all parties for four years (except for a brief period later in that year). The UDV won 37 of 57 seats in the December 1970 election, the *Parti du Regroupement Africain* (PRA) 12, the MLN 6 and Independents 2. The government formed as a result of this election was overthrown by General Lamizana in February 1974 and political parties were banned on May 30, 1974. A *National Consultative Council for Renewal* (NCCR) was set up to replace all political parties.

The NCCR created, in November 1975, the *National*

Movement for Renovation (MNR) which was to be the only party allowed in Upper Volta. In the Fall of 1977, a new constitution was accepted in a referendum which provided for a return to civilian rule under a system with up to three political parties. The ban on parties was also lifted at that time. Elections were held in April and May 1978 for the legislature and Presidency respectively. Nine parties competed in the election but only the three with the highest vote count were allowed to survive. In the April election, the UDV emerged as the clear victor with 32 of the 57 seats which had been allocated under a proportional representation system to the three parties with the largest number of votes. The other two parties who won seats were the *Union Nationale pour la Defense de la Democratie* (UNDD)—15 seats, and the *Union Progressiste Voltaique* (UPV) which was an alliance between RDA elements and the PRA—10 seats. Other parties competing in the election were the *Groupe d'Action Populaire* (GAP), the PRA, the *Union Nationale des Independants* (UNI), the *Parti du Regroupement National* (PRN), the *Mouvement des Independants du Parti du Regroupement Africain* (MIPRA) a split from the PRA. The election, however, had only a forty percent turnout of the registered voters. A coup in 1980 returned the military to power and ousted Lamizana.

FIGURE 38.1   **Political Parties and Elections**   **Burkina Faso(Upper Volta)**

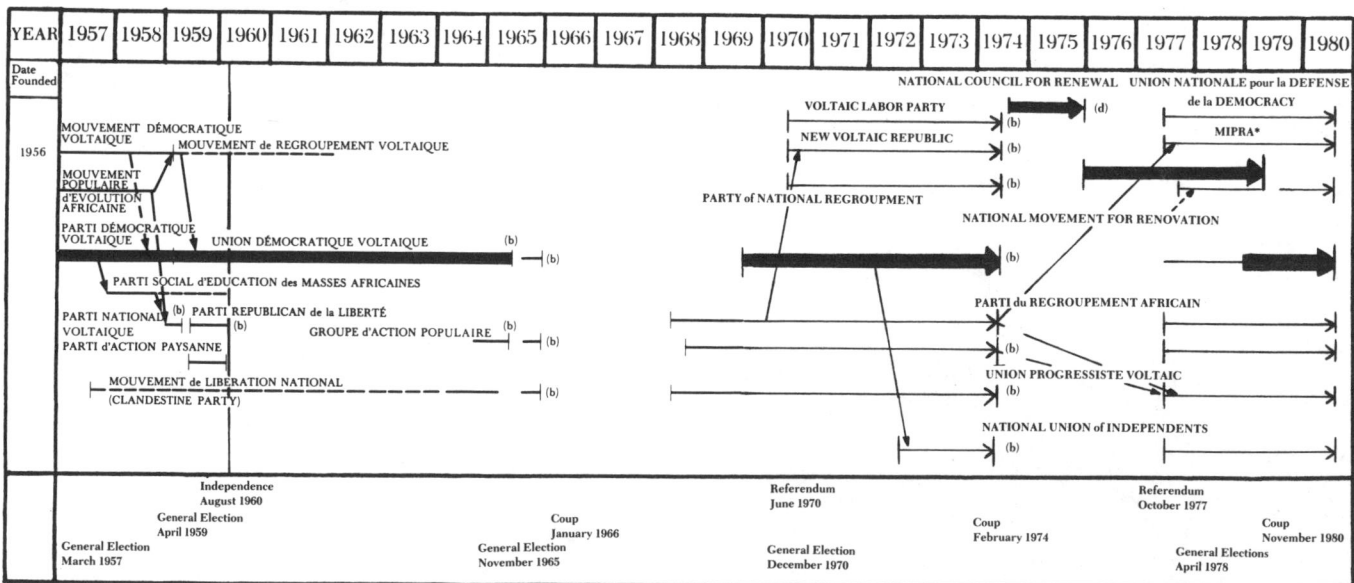

*MOUVEMENT DU INDEPENDANTS DU REGROUPMENT AFRICAIN

TABLE 38.5   Heads of Government (Post-Independence)

Name	Dates in Office	Age (1982)	Ethnicity	Education	Former Occupation
1. Maurice Yaméogo (President)	1960— 1966	61	Mossi	Secondary	Civil Servant
2. Gen. Sangoulé Lamizana	1966— 1980	66	W. Mandé	Secondary	Soldier
3. Col. Saye Zerbo	1980— 1982				Soldier
4. Maj. Jean Baptiste Ouedraogo	1982—	40	Mossi	Medical	Soldier

B. Political Leadership

Maurice Yaméogo led the government until the military coup of 1966. More than half the cabinet members have continued to be Mossi, reflecting the general population. There were rapid changes in cabinet membership in 1962 and 1966. The 1970 constitution provided for a mixed military-civilian government for a four-year interim period. Lamizana continued as a soldier-president and, following the December 1970 elections, Gerard Kango Ouedraogo, a 46-year old Mossi politician, became prime minister. This experiment in a mixed military-civilian government came to an end in February 1974 when Lamizana restored full military control and banned party activity. In January 1977, Lamizana agreed to a largely civilian government in response to labor union demands, and the return to civilian rule in 1978 after the 1977 constitutional referendum which was overwhelmingly accepted. Before the return to parties, the labor unions effectively performed many of the roles and functions of the political parties. In 1978, Lamizana was elected to head a civilian government formed under a new constitution that was accepted in a referendum in late 1977. He was ousted in a military coup led by Col. Zerbo in 1980. Colonel Zerbo was in turn ousted in November 1982 by a military coup and Major Jean Baptiste Ouedraogo was declared head of state by the *People's Provisional Salvation Council.*

TABLE 38.6   Cabinet Membership: Distribution by Ethnic Unit*

Ethnicity*	Independence Cabinet	Immediate Pre-Coup Cabinet	1967 Cabinet
1. Mossi (50%)	57%	54%	54%
2. Western Mandé (14)	21	15	31
3. Fulani (10)	0	0	0
4. Lobi (7)	0	7.7	0
5. Senufo (6)	0	7.7	0
6. Grunshi (5)	7.1	7.7	7.7
7. Busansi (5)	0	0	7.7
8. Gurma (5)	0	7.7	0
9. Others (.1)	14	0	0
N =	14	13	13

*Ethnic units arranged in rank order of size within country with the unit's percent of national population in parentheses.

VI. National Integration and Stability

Upper Volta's first coup d'état developed out of a labor-government dispute and the military returned to a modified civilian rule by 1970. The drought which severely affected Upper Volta's economy was partly responsible for the end of this experiment. A full return to military rule came in the February 1974 coup. After labor union demonstrations in 1975, Lamizana began a program for return to civilian rule that came about in the spring of 1978. Ethnic and regional bases of political mobilization continue to be an important factor in the country's political equation. In 1980, the military under Col. Zerbo overthrew the civilian regime and in November of 1982, Col. Zerbo was overthrown by another military coup and succeeded by Major Jean Baptiste Ouedraogo.

TABLE 38.7   Elite Instability

Event and Date	Characteristics
1. Coup d'État January 3, 1966	a. *Description*: Labor unions sponsored a general strike after the National Assembly, on December 30, had approved a government-backed austerity program. President Maurice Yaméogo declared a state of emergency and banned the proposed strike. Nevertheless, the strike took place as large crowds surrounded the presidential palace shouting for the army to take power. On January 3, Sangoulé Lamizana, Army Chief of Staff, took power, and on January 5, he suspended the constitution and dissolved the assembly. b. *Participants*: Colonel Lamizana (Army Chief of Staff) with support of the army and labor unions. c. *Apparent Causes*: Labor unions led by Joseph Ouedraogo, President of the *Confederation africaine des travailleurs croyants*, promoted the demonstrations to protest legislation by the National Assembly which had cut the salaries of government employees by 20 percent. The austerity budget included no reductions in the president's salary. Colonel Lamizana said that he had assumed power "to safeguard republican and democratic institutions and avoid all bloodshed."
2. Coup d'État February 8, 1974	a. *Description*: President Lamizana suspends the constitution, dissolves Parliament, takes full power and forms a National Council for Renewal. All parties are banned. b. *Participants*: General Lamizana and the army. c. *Apparent Causes*: Dissatisfaction with increasing elite political conflict and mismangagement of the state, particularly with regard to drought relief. Interethnic conflicts between Mossi politicians and Lamizana, a northerner, appeared to have played a role in the coup. In particular the army wished to prevent Maurice Yaméogo from returning to power.
3. Coup d'État November 25, 1980	a. *Description*: The army takes power in a bloodless coup, bans party activity and establishes the Committee for National Recovery and Progress led by Colonel Zerbo. b. *Participants*: Army units under Colonel Zerbo. c. *Apparent Causes*: Army and union dissatisfaction with the economic fortunes of the country under the civilian goverment.
4. Coup d'État November 7, 1982	a. *Description*: In a pre-dawn attack army units took over the capital and all communications, arrested Col. Zerbo and other leaders of the military goverment. Casualties were not known but thought to be higher than the reported five killed. b. *Participants*: Army units directed by the Council of the Voltaic Armed Forces whose membership is not known. c. *Apparent Causes*: Army dissatisfaction with the ability of Col. Zerbo to reverse the economic fortunes of the country, the ostensible purpose for the military assuming power in 1980.

TABLE 38.10   Annual Instability Events: Independence Through 1979—Upper Volta

Year	'61	'62	'63	'64	'65	'66	'67	'68	'69	'70	'71	'72	'73	'74	'75	'76	'77	'78	'79
ELITE INSTABILITY																			
Assassinations																			
Plots						1	1												
Attempted Coups d'État																			
Coups d'État						1								1					
COMMUNAL INSTABILITY																			
Ethnic Violence																			
Irredentism																			
Rebellion																			
Civil War																			
MASS INSTABILITY																			
Revolt																			
Revolution																			
TURMOIL																			
Demonstratons																			
Strikes (no. days)						3		12					5						
Riots (no. days)						4													
Terrorism																			
Declarations of Emergency						2													
CABINET INSTABILITY																			
Realloc. and new appts.	3	17	3	1	11		7												
New members	3	9	1		3		2				1								
Resig. and Dismissals		7	3		11		3							1					
No. of members (max.) (maximum in year)	14	20	20	20	13	12	13	12	10	11	17	16							

VII. Selected References

BIBLIOGRAPHY

African Bibliographic Center, Washington. *French-Speaking West Africa. Upper Volta Today, 1960—1967: A Selected and Introductory Bibliographic Guide.* Westport: Negro Universities Press, 1969.

McFarland, D. M. *Historical Dictionary of Upper Volta.* Metuchen, N.J.: Scarecrow, 1978.

GENERAL

Guilhem, Marcel. *Histoire de las Haute-Volta* . Paris: Ligel, 1964.

Grant, Stephen H. "Getting by with Nothing." *Africa Report,* 18 (May-June 1973): 29-32.

Lippens, P. *La République de Haute Volta.* Paris: Bergère-Levrault, 1972.

Pool, D. I. and S. P. Coulibaly (eds). *Demographic Transition and Cultural Continuity in the Sahel: Aspects of the Social Demography of Upper Volta*. Ithaca, N.Y.: Cornell University, International Population Program, 1977.

Thompson, Virginia and Richard Adloff. *French West Africa*, pp. 171-178. Stanford, Calif.: Stanford University Press, 1957.

POLITICAL

Amin, Samir. *Neo-Colonialism in West Africa*. Harmondsworth, Middlesex: Penquin Books, 1973.

Daniel, Raymond, *Government and Economy in Upper Volta*. Ouagadougou: African Press, 1967.

De Lusignan, Guy. *French-Speaking Africa Since Independence*. pp. 145-151. London: Pall Mall Press, 1969.

LeVine, Victor T. "The Coups in Upper Volta, Dahomey and the Central African Republic." In *Power and Protest in Black Africa*, eds. Robert I. Rotberg and Ali A. Mazrui, pp. 1035-1071. New York: Oxford University Press, 1970.

ECONOMIC

Geradin, B. *Le Développement de la Haute-Volta*. Paris: Isea, 1964.

International Monetary Fund. "Upper Volta," In *Surveys of African Economies*, Vol. 3. Washington, D.C.: I.M.F., 1970.

SOCIAL

Courel, M. F. et al. "La population de la Haute Volta au recensement de decembre 1975." *Cahiers d'Outre Mer*. 32, 125, pp. 39—65.

Levtzion, Nehemia. *Muslims and Chiefs in West Africa*. Oxford: Clarendon Press, 1968.

Rouch, Jean. "Migrations au Ghana." *Journal de la Société des Africanistes*, 26 (1956): 33-96.

Skinner, Elliot P. *African Urban Life: The Transformation of Ouagadougou*. Princeton, N.J.: Princeton University Press, 1974.

Skinner, Elliot P. *The Mossi of the Upper Volta: The Political Development of a Sudanese People*. Stanford, Cal.: Stanford Unviersity Press, 1964.

Wettere-Verhasselt, Yole Van. "Bobo-Dioulasso: Le Developpement d'une ville d'Afrique Occidentale." *Les Cahiers d'Outre-Mer*, 35 (Janvier-Mars 1959): 88—94.

39. Zaire

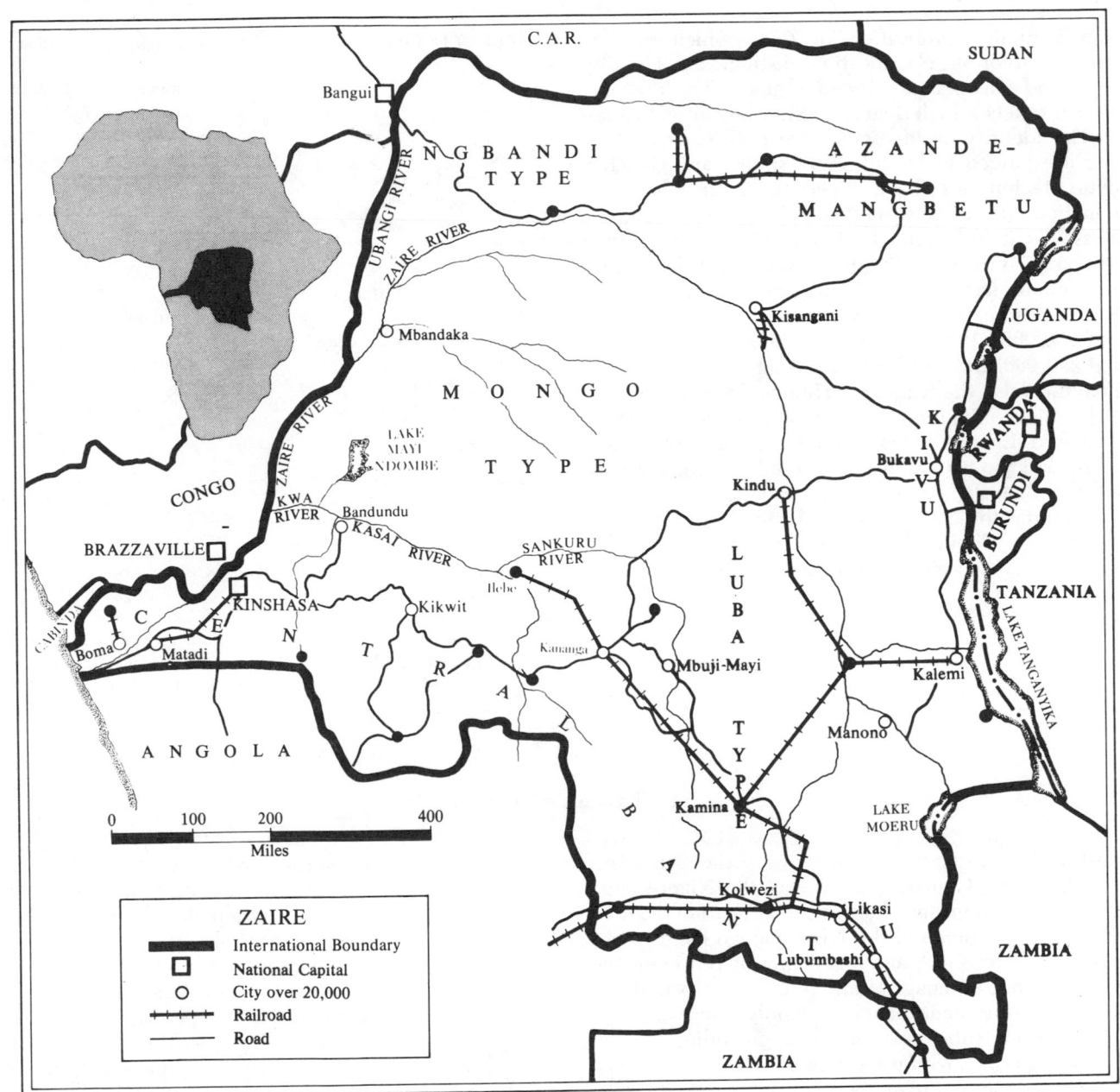

I. Basic Information

Date of Independence: June 30, 1960
Former Colonial Ruler: Belgium
Former Names: Belgian Congo, Congo (Leopoldville), Congo (Kinshasa)
Population (1980): 28,669,000
Area Size (equivalent in U.S.): 906,000 sq. mi. (Alaska, Texas, and Colorado)
Date of Last Census: 1969-70
Major Exports 1976 as Percent of Total Exports: copper—42 percent; coffee—14 percent; cobalt—13 percent; diamonds—6 percent.

II. Ethnic Patterns

Vansina's ethnic classification for Zaire, which was the starting point for our classification, distinguishes identity groups, and clusters into broad regions. The regions, however, reflect a high degree of internal cultural variation. The identity groups which we have clustered together are judged to be culturally similar and Q-factor analytic techniques have been used in this determination (for details, see the Ethnic Unit Classification essay in (in Vol. I) In addition to cultural criteria, we have also tried to assess linguistic, ecological, historical, and economic factors. Prominent groups which do not satisfy the minimum size requirement are the Téké (about 250,000), the Pendé (about 20,000), the Luimbé (about 250,000) and smaller groups such as the Yeké, the Lunda, the Yaka, the Kuba, the Hemba-Bemba, the Boa, and the Binza. Beginning in the 1880's those peoples who shared Lingala, a common trade language, have been referred to as if they constituted an ethnic group called the Bangala. President Mobutu, while born into the Ngwandi ethnic group, now claims this wider Bangala ethnicity. Population data on the ethnic units are based on 1962 data cited in the *Area Handbook for the Congo*.

TABLE 39.1   Ethnic Units Over 5 Percent of Country Population

Ethnic Unit	Estimated Ethnic Population 1980	Estimated Ethnic Population Percentage
a. Central Bantu Type	9,747,000	34%
1. Kongo, 2. Kunda, 3. Lala, 4. Ndembu, 5. Sakata, 6. Yaka, 7. Yanzi		
b. Mongo Type	4,587,000	15%
1. Kasai Luba, 2. Mongo		
c. Luba Type	3,440,000	12%
1. Katanga Luba, 2. Songye		
d. Kivu Cluster	2,580,000	9%
1. Furiiru, 2. Havu, 3. Hunde, 4. Nyanga, 5. Rwanda, 6. Shi, 7. Yira (Nande)		
e. Azandé-Mangbetu Cluster	2,007,000	7%
1. Alur, 2. Amba, 3. Azandé, 4. Mangbetu, 5. Mamvu-Mangutu		
f. Ngbandi-Ngbaka-Mbandja Type	1,720,000	6%
1. Ngbandi, 2. Ngbaka, 3. Mbandja		

SOURCES: Jan Vansina, *Introduction à l'Ethnographe du Congo* (Editions Universitaires du Congo, 1966). U.S. Department of the Army, *Area Handbook for the Congo* (Washington, D.C.: Government Printing Office, 1963).

III. Language Patterns

Almost all Zairese speak one or more of the Bantu languages (i.e., the Central sub-stock of the Niger-Congo family). A few groups may be classified as part of the Adamawa (eastern) branch of the Niger-Congo family (e.g., Pazande and Ngbandi); and a few groups represent the Central Sudanic language family (e.g., the Moru-Mangbetu). Within the Bantu language family, there are fourteen important sub-stocks in Zaire, including Kongo, Luba, Mongo, Bira-Kumu and Lega.

There are four *lingua francas* in Zaire: Lingala, Swahili (Kingwana), Tshiluba (Luba or Kiluba), and Kongo (Kikongo). Lingala is used along the river between Ubangi-Uele and Kisangani. Lingala developed in the 1880's when the commercial people on the middle Zaire River, who came to be called Bangala, developed Lingala as a trading language. Lingala later became the language of the Zairese army. Kingwana—a dialect of Swahili—developed in eastern Zaire in the late nine-

teenth century as a result of trade contact with East Africa. It is now spoken mainly in the eastern provinces of Katanga, Kivu, Kasai, and Orientale. Tshiluba, while based on the language of the Luba people of Kasai, is now widely used as a *lingua franca* in southeastern Zaire (spoken in the area between Angola and Lake Moeru). Kongo is the language of the Kongo peoples. It is widely used as a *lingua franca* in Kinshsasa Province, Lower Congo, and Kwango in the form of a simplified dialect, Kileta (or Kituba).

In order to estimate the percentage of population who speak the above languages, it is necessary to review language policy in Zaire. During the colonial period, there was no consistent linguistic planning, and vernacular languages were used in the elementary schools. Originally the armed forces (the Force Publique) used Hausa, a language principally spoken in Niger and Nigeria, and Swahili, but later adopted Lingala. Many of the missionaries, such as the White Fathers, used Swahili as the language of evangelization.

Under the Belgian colonial regime, the two official languages were French (Walloon dialect) and Dutch (Flemish dialect), although French was clearly predominant and was the language of secondary schools. In the post-colonial era, French has continued to be an official language, but five Zairean languages have official status: Lingala, Swahili, Tshiluba, Kikongo, and Kingwana. Since 1961, English has been encouraged in the schools.

Estimates vary as to which language is spoken and understood by the largest percent of the population. Knappert suggests Kongo (30 percent); MacDougald suggests Swahili (24 Percent). Rustow, apparently looking only at first-language speakers, suggests Rwanda and Luba/Lulua are co-equal at 17 percent. Our own estimate would be Lingala at 40 percent, Kongo at 35 percent and Swahili at 30 percent. These estimates are extremely tentative, and are based partly on conversations with persons familar with Zaire.

TABLE 39.2   Language Patterns

		Green-berg	Dalby
1. Primacy			
1st language	Lingala (40%)		
2nd languages	Kongo (35%)		
	Swahili (30%)		
2. Linguistic classification (all ethnic units in country over 5%)	Central Bantu	IA5	A1
	Mongo	IA5	C6
	Luba	IA5	L2
	Kivu	IA5	E1
	Azandé-Mangbetu	IA6	68A, 52C
	Ngbandi-Ngbaka-Mbandja	IA6	67C, 67A
3. *Lingua francas*	Swahili, Tshiluba, Kongo Lingala		
4. Official language	French, Lingala, Tshiluba, Swahili, Kikongo, Kingwana		

SOURCE: Edgar Polome, "The Choice of Official Languages in the Democratic Republic of the Cong," in *Language Problems of Developing Nations*, eds. Joshua Fishman, Charles Ferguson, and Jyotirindra Das Gupta (New York: John Wiley, 1968), pp. 295— 312.

IV. Urban Patterns

Capital/largest city: Kinshasa (founded 1881)
Dominant ethnicity/language of capital
    Major vernacular: Lingala[1]
    Major ethnic groups: Kongo[2]
    Major ethnic group as percent of capital's population:
      Kongo (63 percent) (1955)

[1]Jan Knappert, "Language Problems of the New Nations of Africa," *African Quarterly*, 5 (1965): 95—105.
[2]L. Baeck, "Leopoldville," *Zaire*, 10 (1956): p. 623.

TABLE 39.3   Growth of Capital/largest City

Date	Kinshasa (Leopoldville)
1920	18,000
1930	36,000
1940	47,000
1950	222,000
1960	380,000
1965	1,000,000 UA
1972	1,623,760 UA
1974	1,990,717 UA
1976	2,443,876 UA

SOURCES: From Jacque Denis, *Le Phénomène Urbain* (for 1920 and 1930) from Thomas Hodgkin, *Nationalism in Colonial Africa* (New York: New York University Press, 1957), p. 67.

TABLE 39.4   Cities of 20,000 and Over

City	Size	Date
Kinshasa[a]	2,443,876 UA	1976
Kananga[a]	704,211 UA	1976
Lubumbashi[a]	4 51,332 UA	1976
Mbuji-Mayi[a]	382,632 UA	1976
Kinsangani[a]	339,210 UA	1976
Bukavu[a]	162,396 UA	1976
Kitwit[a]	209,051 UA	1976
Likasi[a]	172,450 UA	1976
Matadi[a]	149,118 UA	1976
Mbandaka[d]	138,877 UA	1974
Bandundu[b]	74,000	1970
Kalemi[c]	29,000	1958
Boma[c]	26,000	1958
Manono[c]	20,000	1958
Kindu[c]	19,000	1958
N'Djili[c]	19,000	1958

SOURCES:

[a]*Europa Yearbook 1979*; estimated for July 1, 1976.

[b]1970 Census

[c]No 1970 estimates available. 1958 census results.

[d]*Africa South of the Sahara 1975*. Recent population estimates for Zaire's cities have been among the poorest in Black Africa. In 1970, however, a census was carried out which gives data for eleven "villes." The 1974 estimates appear to be extrapolations from the 1970 data. The 1970 data were reported in a series of issues of *L'Etoile* (August 1970) and reprinted in Leon de Saint Moulin, "Les statistiques démographiques en République Démocratique du Congo" *Congo-Afrique*, 47 (1970): 377—385. For those towns whose populations was not reported for 1970 we give data from the 1958 census. *Rapport sur l'adminstration du Congo Belge pendant l'anee 1958 presente aux Chambres legislatives* (Brussels: 1959), pp. 63—69.

V. Political Patterns

A. Political Parties and Elections

Political parties developed at a late stage in Zaire, during the 1958—59 period, just prior to independence in June 1960. By 1960 there were as many as 100 parties mostly based on ethnic or regional ties. The first national elections were held in May 1960 when the *Mouvement National Congolais* (MNC), led by Patrice Lumumba, won a plurality (41 of 137 seats in the legislature). A government was formed with the MNC in coalition with the *Alliance des Ba-Kongo* (ABAKO), led by Joseph Kasavubu, who was elected President in June 1960. After the army mutinied in July and the secession of Katanga began, the government continued until September, when the manifold constitutional crises resulted in the army—*Armee Nationale Congolaise* (ANC) led by Colonel Joseph Mo-

butu—taking over the government and then turning it over to a set of civil servants and university graduates. In November 1960, the ABAKO party was drawn into the government, and between 1960 and 1965 coalition cabinets included ministers from various political parties. The legitimacy of these regimes was strongly challenged particularly by factions allied with the former Prime Minister Lumumba, and after 1960, these factions became involved in a mass revolt against the central government. In March—May of 1965 elections were held, but the results were questioned by all sides, and in November, the army again took control of the country from the short-lived government of Moise Tshombe, ironically the former leader of the Katanga secession movement. In April 1967, Mobutu founded the *Mouvement Populaire de la Revolution* (MPR) from which the army was exluded.

The MPR held elections in 1970. Mobutu was elected President for a seven year term and a one-party legislature was voted into office. In 1975, 'elections' were held. The process involved the public reading of a list of MPR candidates in which the assembled group of voters indicated their approval/disapproval by clapping their hands. Since there was only a single list of candidates, all were elected. Mobutu claims that this is a true Zairean way of voting.

A number of clandestine opposition parties and groups operate inside and outside the country. While the opposition is highly fragmented, it is united in its opposition to the Mobutu regime. Gizenga's group is the *Forces Democratiques pour la Liberation du Congo* (FONDELICO). Other groups include the *Parti Populaire Africain* (PPA), the *Parti Revolutionnaire du Peuple* (PRP); the *Mouvement d'Action pour la Resurrection du Congo*; the MNC-L which includes the remnants of the Lumumbaist party, and the *Democratic Assembly of the Congolese People* (RDPC). the *Front de Liberation Nationale du Congo-Kinshasa* (FLNC) which is the force behind the invasions of Shaba province from Angola (1977) and Zambia (1978), is headed by Nathaniel Mbumba, and is committed to the overthrow of Mobutu and the construction of a more socialist and non-aligned state. Mobutu was re-elected in December 1977 with 98% of the votes cast. The laws of Zaire state that the President is to be elected directly by the the people for a seven-year term which is renewable only once. Constitutionally the term which ends in 1984 should be Mobutu's last term as President.

In July, 1980, five opposition groups joined together to form the Council for the Liberation of Congo. The groups include the Congo National Liberation Front (FNLC), the People's Revolutionary Party (PRP), and the Progressive Congolese Students. The front is headed by Nungul Diaka, former Minister of Higher Education and Scientific Research.

B. Political Leadership

The president and constitutional head of state until 1965 was Joseph Kasavubu. Following the coup d'état in the first year of independence, the prime ministership changed hands regularly until a second coup, in 1965. Since that time, the government appears to have become more stable. General Mobutu ruled at first with Léonard Mulamba as his prime minister, but on October 26, 1966 he dismissed Mulamba and assumed the functions of prime minister himself. In a country of the greatest cultural complexity, recruitment to governmental leadership has been considerably diversified in terms of the regional and ethnic background of cabinet members. Mobutu was elected President in 1970 under a new constitution with a one party regime. In recent years there has been considerable instability in cabinet membership as Mobutu juggles party and ministerial positions in order to maintain his pre-eminence. The considerable deterioration of the fabric of the society and economy by the mid-1970's coupled with Mobutu's ruthless suppression of any potential opposition left him still dominant but as the Shaba invasions have demonstrated, this pattern could end at any time. In February 1979, Mobutu announced a cabinet reshuffle in which the former Foreign Minister, Nguza Karl I. Bond who had been convicted of treason in 1977 was reappointed. In January 1980, another cabinet reshuffle left 13 of the 22 government ministers without their posts. At this time Mobutu brought in Kamitatu Massamba, a former opposition leader who was once head of the African Socialist Front and an ally of Patrice Lumumba. Mobutu has also made some political reforms in the hope of gaining favor with Western nations who might be able to help with Zaire's many economic problems.

TABLE 39.5 Heads of Government (Post-Independence)

Name	Dates in Office	Age (1982)	Ethnicity	Education	Former Occupation
1. Patrice Lumumba (Prime Minister)	June 1960— Sept. 1960	Murdered February 1961, aged 36	(Tetela)	Mission School, Kasai	Tax clerk, Postmaster
2. Joseph Ileo (Prime Minister)	Sept. 1960— Feb.—Aug. 1961	60	Mongo	Catholic Missions & Night School	Accountant
3. Cyril Adoula (Prime Minister)	Aug. 1961— July 1964	d. 1978 age 56	(Bulya)	Roman Catholic Secondary	Trade unionist
4. Moise Tshombe (Prime Minister)	July 1964— Oct. 1965	d. 1969 age 49	(Lunda)	American Methodist Missions	Businessman
5. E. Kimba (Prime Minister)	Oct. 1965— Nov. 1965	Hanged 1966 age 40	Luba (Katanga)		
6. General Mobutu Sésé-Séko (President)	Nov. 1965— present	52	(Ngwandi)	Secondary and Ecole des Cadres, Force Publique, Luluaborg	Journalist, Soldier

TABLE 39. 6 Cabinet Membership: Distribution by EThnic Unit*

Ethnicity	Independence Cabinet	Immediate Pre-Coup Cabinet	1967 Cabinet
1. Central Bantu (34%)	23	32	26
2. Mongo (16)	18	21	17
3. Luba (12)	18	16	17
4. Kibu (9)	14	5	4
5. Azandé-Mangbetu (7)	5	5	0
6. Ngbandi-Ngbaka-Mbanja (6)	0	5	9
7. Others (16)	23	16	26
N =	23	19	23

*Ethnic units arranged in rank order of size within country with the unit's percent of national population in parentheses.

FIGURE 39.1   Political Parties and Elections   ZAIRE

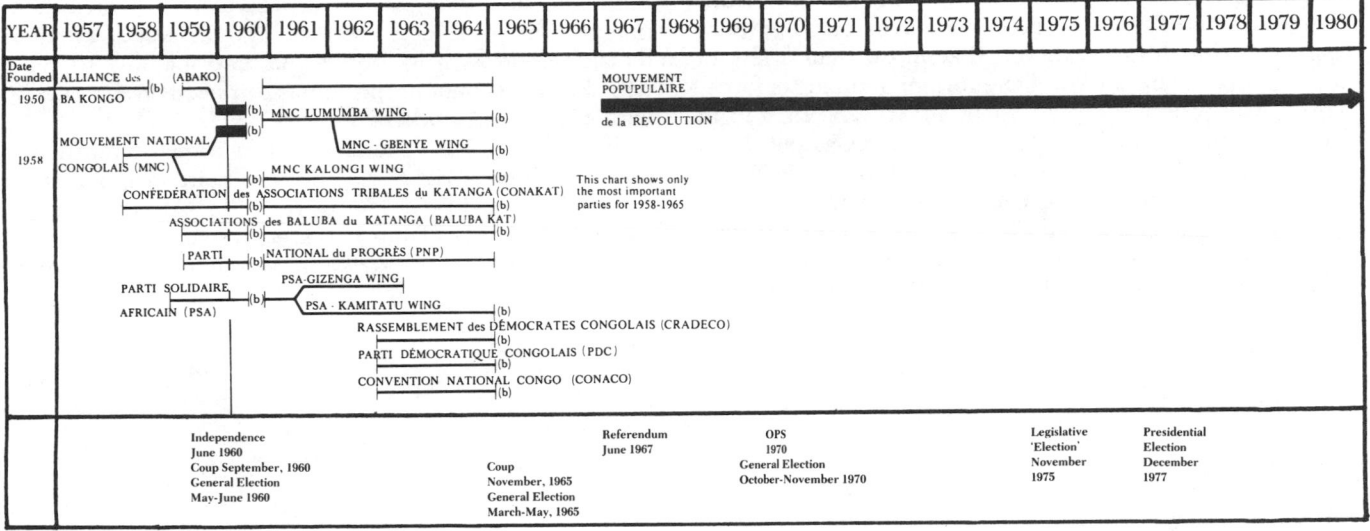

Note: The clandestine parties that exist are not included in this figure since the nature of their existence is difficult to document.

VI. National Integration and Stability

In no other African state except Chad, Sudan and Ethiopia does the combined magnitude of elite, communal, and mass instability match that of Zaire and no adequate summary of the over-all pattern of events can be given here. Two successful coups d'état (September 1960 and November 1965), along with a large number of attempted coups and (reported) plots, have been organized. In addition to elite instability, there has been a major civil war and a series of loosely coordinated rebellions marked by high levels of violence that have been potentially destructive of territorial integrity. The civil war resulted from the Katanga secession (July 1960—January 1963) and the attempted revolution was led by the *Conseil National de Libération* (mainly from January 1964 to late 1965). The Katangese secession was brought to an end by the national army and supporting UN forces, and the attempted revolution was finally put down by Mobutu's forces with assistance from mercenary forces and the parachute drop from planes provided by the United States. The only major threat thereafter was that of the exiled former Prime Minister Tshombe operating with mercenary assistance from Angola. Zaire's army defeated the mercenaries led by Colonel Schramme in October 1967. In June 1969 demonstrating students from Louvanium University were fired on by

the army and an estimated 40—50 were killed. In June 1971 the University was closed until September. It had previously been closed in 1970—71. In 1971, all students at the University were conscripted into the army although later allowed to pursue their studies while 'in the army.' The only evidence of instability in the early 1970's was minor, namely an assassination plot against Mobutu in 1971, and small scale secessionist activity in Katanga in August 1973. In June of 1975, however, a major plot was uncovered which apparently involved a very large number of people in the army, bureaucracy, and others outside of the government. At least eight generals were accused of active or passive involvement in the plot. Mobutu alleged that a foreign power (the United States) was supporting the plotters. Apparently the plot was discovered just before it was timed to begin. Two coup attempts were reported to have occured in 1976 (in March and April) but no corrobative evidence as to their existence is available (*Africa Contemporary Record 1976—77* p. B530).

On March 8, 1977, forces under Mbumba, the leader of the FLNC, invaded Shaba province (formerly Katanga) with the apparent intention of overthrowing Mobutu. They withdrew after Moroccan troops were flown to the battle scene. This group, mostly of the Lunda ethnic group, were characterized by Mobutu as former Katangese gendarmes who went into exile after the suppression of the Katangan secession movement, but there appears to be little evidence that more than a few of these people were a part of the former Kantangan force. This revolt was attempted again in May of 1978 from bases in Angola and Zambia, and again it was put down with foreign troops (French and Belgian). Since the FLNC forces were relatively untouched by these events, it should be expected that these attacks and/or guerrilla war will continue in order to overthrow Mobutu.

In February 1979, Mobutu announced a general amnesty for all Zairians who had fled to Angola during the Shaba invasions. Reports in March, however, stated that returning refugees were being massacred. Further dissatisfaction with Mobutu's rule and inability to cope with Zaire's economic problems surfaced in May 1979 with widespread workers' strikes.

In mid-May 1980 Amnesty International published a report on human rights violations in Zaire claiming hundreds of political prisoners were being held under poor conditions. Some of the detainees included University students who went on strike in March 1980 demanding higher grants.

TABLE 39.7   **Elite Instability**

Event and Date	Characteristics
1. Coup d'État September 14, 1960	a. *Description*: A military coup, led by Colonel Joseph Mobutu. Control was placed in the hands of a College of Commissioners, who served until February 9, 1961. b. *Particpants*: Military forces, under the leadership of Mobutu. c. *Apparent Causes*: The breakdown of the constitutional regime. Kasavubu and Lumumba attempted to remove each other from office.
2. Coup Attempt November 19, 1963	a. *Description*: General Mobutu and the chief of the security police, Victor Nendaka, were kidnapped by plotters, but later escaped. The *Comité National de Libération* (CNL) hoped to overthrow the Adoula regime and attempted to do so by kidnapping its most powerful supporters. b. *Participants*: The coup was organized by the CNL which was headed by C. Gbenye. c. *Apparent Causes*: Factionalism within the CNL prevented a clear statement of goals. Most, however, claimed to favor a Lumumbaist type of radical nationalism.
3. Coup d'État November 25, 1965	a. *Description*: General Mobutu displaced Joseph Kasavubu and named himself president; Brigadier General Léonard Molamba became prime minister. b. *Participants*: General Joseph Mobutu, commander in chief of the *Armée National Congolaise*. c. *Apparent Causes*: Mobutu said that he wanted to put an end to the parliamentary power struggle between supporters of Kasavubu and Tshombe: the army was reputed to fear that Kasavubu was moving away from a pro-Western position and that he was willing to negotiate with Gbenye's CNL.

TABLE 39.8   Communal Instability

Event and Date	Characteristics
1. Civil War: Unsuccessful Secession 1960—1963	a. *Description*: Katanga province had been almost completely autonomous in the pre-independence period and local administration was largely in the hands of Belgian mining companies. During the disorder following the July mutiny of the Zairese army against their Belgian officers, the mineral-wealthy province of Katanga under Moise Tshombe attempted to secede from Zaire. Secession was eventually defeated by combined Zairese and United Nations forces. b. *Participants*: The major ethnic group in Katanga (the Lunda) fully supported secession and many minority groups also appeared supportive. Moise Tshombe, the Katanga seccesionist leader, had built up a solid following in Katanga prior to independence. Although he was not a traditional ruler himself, his following depended partly on the influence and claim of his father to such authority among the Lunda. European mercenaries participated in the leadership of the attempted secession. This was essentially a soldiers' war, not a civilian war. On the government side, 6,000 UN troops participated from five African countries and India. On the secessionist side Belgian, French, Rhodesian, and South African mercenaries participated. In all, an estimated 20,000 government troops and 12,000 secessionist troops were involved. Both sides had heavy casualties. c. *Apparent Causes*: The government feared the threat to national unity, loss of natural resources in Katanga, and predominance of foreign influence in Katanga. On the other hand, secessionists wanted to use local resources to develop Katanga and not the entire country; also there was a personality and ideological clash between Tshombe and Zairese leaders. At the ethnic level, Lunda masses feared the economic consequence of increasing immigration of Luba and other ethnic groups into the urban centers of Katanga.
2. Civil War 1967	a. *Description*: In August 1967, Colonel Mongax, who had been named by the exiled Moise Tshombe as his chief of staff in exile, proclaimed a "Government of Public Safety" in Bukavu, which had been occupied by a force of 300 white mercenaries and 2,000 former Katangese gendarmes led by Colonel "Black Jack" Schramme. The military operation was apparently directed initially from Angola. The Congolese Army recaptured Bukavu on November 5, and most of the insurgents fled to Rwanda. b. *Participants*: The mercenaries and Katangese insurgents were presumably in the pay of, and acting in the interests of Tshombe, the leader of the Kantanga secession, 1960—1963, at this time in exile in Europe. c. *Apparent Causes*: The insurgents aimed to depose the existing government of Zaire in the interests of M. Tshombe's political ambitions. Although they referred to widespread resistance to the Mobutu government and the Zaire Army, there is no evidence that their support extended beyond Bukavu.
3. Ethnic Violence January and May, 1968	a. *Description*: Two distinguishable outbreaks of inter-ethnic violence occurred in 1963 in areas in which the Katanga secession was practically at an end. In January, fighting between tribes in the Kasai province caused deaths estimated between 400 and 4000. In May, inter-ethnic violence in the African quarters of Elizabethville and Jadotville cause over 50 deaths. b. *Participants*: Lulua tribesmen in the Kakenge area north of Luluabourg were invovled in the clashes in January, and the fighting in May was between Luba and Lunda tribesment. c. *Apparent Clashes*: The Kasai events were caused by rival claims to land on which a Belgian timber company operated a concession, and the Jadotville violence apparently started as the result of a rape involving two youths from different tribes.

TABLE 39.9 Mass Instability

Event and Date	Characteristics
1. Unsuccessful Revolt 1960—1966	a. *Description*: A series of revolts disrupted political authority in Zaire from 1960 to 1966. After the dismissal of Lumumba by President Kasavubu in September 1960, the vice-prime minister, Antoine Gizenga set up a rival government in Stanleyville in October. The revolt, led by Gizenga and other former ministers in Lumumba's cabinet (including Mulele as representative to Cairo), succeeded in gaining control of Orientale province, proclaimed a North Katanga province, controlled the Sankuru district of Kasai, and briefly took the Luluabourg garrison. Lumumba attempted to escape to Stanleyville in November 1960, but was captured, and murdered en route to Elizabethville. The Stanleyville revolt came to an end in January 1962, when Gizenga was arrested and sent to prison on the island of Bula-Bemba. From 1963 to 1966, a number of loosely coordinated revolts were organized in the northeast and southwest of Zaire. "Only superficially could these events be considered a single movement; on close examination the rebellions dissolved into a series of revolts, strongly influenced by local contingencies, bound together by a shifting coalition of leaders, certain common grievances on the part of the population, and common external support." (Young, 1965) The Kwilu rebellion, led by Mulele, began in January 1964, when schools, government offices, a Portuguese palm oil factory, and a mission were destroyed. In May 1964, urban terrorism was launched in Leopoldville, but was easily contained by government forces. Also in May, on the eastern borders of Zaire, Soumalot coordinated a revolt in which two ANC battalions were defeated, and he established a provisional government in Albertville. Government forces had retaken this area by August 1964, but the revolt gained new impetus from the Simba organization of Lenga, which took Stanleyville in that month, and a Peoples' Republic of the Congo was proclaimed led by Gbenye. Over 20,000 people are estimated to have been killed in this period. The Stanleyville insurgency was ended by a United States airlift of Belgian paratroops into the city in advance of regular ANC units in November 1964. For two more years there was scattered, but violent, resistance to the Congolese army and, after November 1965, to its soldier-president Mobutu. An amnesty was announced in October 1966, when 1500 rebels were reported to have surrendered, and after which date the revolt was contained by government forces. b. *Participants*: In October 1963, the *Conseil National de Liberation* was formed by former colleagues of Lumumba and Gizenga. Never a cohesive leadership, the CNL represented factions of the MNC and PSA political parties in Zaire. In the field, the insurgents were tightly organized by Mulele and Olenga, and ideological training and programs synthesizing elements of nationalist, Marxist, and syncretic religious thought were developed by the movement. Ethnic identities seem to have been less distinctive of the insurgents than organizational affiliations to individual leaders (Mulelests), parties (PSA and MNC) and movements (Simba). c. *Apparent Causes*: The government feared the threat to national unity and also foreign interference (by Chinese) in Zaire's internal affairs. The revolutionaries who identified themselves as "socialist" emphasized four issues: (1)Inequities in the distribution of the rewards of independence; (2) decline in material well-being of most Zairese since independence; (3) corrupt practices of the politicians and civil servants; and (4) the unpopularity of the *Armée Nationale Congolaise* (ANC).
2. Invasion and Revolt March—April 1977; May 1978	a. *Description*: Operating from bases in Angola and Zambia, forces of Mbumba's FLNC invade Shaba province (formerly Katanga) intending to incite the population to overthrow Mobutu. While they were apparently welcomed, they were forced to withdraw when foreign troops (Moroccan—1977; Belgian and French—1978) were brought into the battle. The conflict is fed by Lunda resentment of the use of resources by the government but a broader non-ethnic base of support was sought by the rebels. b. *Participants*: Members of the FNLC under the leadership of Mbumba. This group was originally based on exiles who were formerly members of the Katanges gendarmes who had fought for secession from Zaire but now appears to be based on more widespread anti-Mobutu elements although it is largely led by members of the Lunda ethnic group. c. *Apparent Causes*: Widespread dissatisfaction with the Mobutu regime and, in particular, resentment by the Lunda of Shaba province of the fact that their province produces most of the export wealth of the country and sees most of that wealth go to Kinshasa and foreign interests.

SOURCES: Renée C. Fox, Willy de Craemer, and Jean-Marie Ribeaucourt, "'The Second Independence': A Case Study of the Kwilu Rebellion in the Congo," *Comparative Studies in Society and History*, 7 (October 1965), 78—109. Crawford Young, "Rebellion and the Congo," in *Power and Protest in Black Africa*, eds. Robert I. Rotberg and Ali A. Mazrui (New York: Oxford University Press, 1970), pp. 969—1011.

TABLE 39.10   Annual Instability Events: Independence Through 1979—Zaire

Year	'61	'62	'63	'64	'65	'66	'67	'68	'69	'70	'71	'72	'73	'74	'75	'76	'77	'78	'79
ELITE INSTABILITY																			
Assassinations																			
Plots	1		2	1	1	1					1				1				
Attempted Coups d'État			1																
Coups d'État					1														
COMMUNAL INSTABILITY																			
Ethnic Violence			2																
Irredentism																			
Rebellion																			
Civil War	1	1	1				1												
MASS INSTABILITY																			
Revolt	1		1	1	1	1											1	1	
TURMOIL																			
Demonstrations			3		1			4											
Strikes (no. days)	2	1	3		4														
Riots (no. days)			3			1	1		1										
Terrorism			1		1					2									
Declaratons of Emergency		1	2	1	1				1										
CABINET INSTABILITY																			
Realloc. and new appts.	36	17	12	14	32	23	9	6	1	5	6	8							
New members	30	12	9	11	30	10	9	1	13	13	3	12							
Resig. and Dismissals	22	16	9	21	11	11	10	1	12	11	3	13							
No. of members (max.)	21	21	21	11	19	21	23	19	20	22	22	21							

VII. Selected References

BIBLIOGRAPHY

Bustin, Edouard. *A Study Guide for Congo-Kinshasa.* Boston: Development Program, African Studies Center, Boston University, 1971.

Liniger-Goumaz. Max. *Bibliographies Africaines.* Geneve, Editions du Temps, 1971—74, 2 vols.

GENERAL

Anstey, Roger. *King Leopold's Legacy: The Congo under Belgian Rule, 1908—1960.* London: Oxford University Press, issued under the auspices of the Institute of Race Relations, 1966.

Biebuyck, Daniel and Mary Douglas. *Congo Tribes and Parties.* Royal Anthropological Institute, 1961.

Cornevin, Robert. *Histoire de Congo (Leopoldville).* Paris: Bergère-Levrault, 1963.

Cornevin, Robert. *Le Zaire, ex. Congo Kinshasa.* Paris, P.U.F., 1972.

Merlier, M. *Le Congo de la Colonisation Belge à l'Indépendence.* Paris: Maspero, 1961.

Roth, H. M., et al. *Zaire, A Country Study,* 3rd ed. American University, Washington, D.C., 1979.

Slade, Ruth M. *The Belgian Congo,* 2nd ed. New York: Oxford University Press, 1961.

Van der Linden, Jacques. *La Republique du Zaire.* Paris. Bergère-Levrault, 1975.

ECONOMIC

Gran, Guy, ed. *Zaire, The Political Economy of Underdevelopment.* N.Y.: Praeger, 1979.

Institute de Recherches Economiques et Sociales (I.R.E.S.) *Independence, inflation, developpement; l'economie Congolaise de 1960 à 1965.* Paris: Mouton, 1968.

International Monetary Fund. "Democratic Republic of the Congo." In *Surveys of African Economies,* Vol. 4, Washington, D.C.: I.M.F., 1971.

Lacroix, Jean Louis. *Industrialization au Congo.* Paris: Mouton, 1967.

"La Republique Democratique du Congo: Economie et Developpement," *Marches Tropicaux et Mediterraneens,* No. 1269 (March 7, 1970), p. 195. (Special issue on Congo-Kinshasa's economic development.

Miracle, Marvin P. *Agriculture in the Congo Basin.* Madison: University of Wisconsin Press, 1967.

Pemans, J. Ph. "The Social and Economic Development of Zaire since Independence: An Historical Outline." *African Affairs,* 74 (April 1975): 143—179.

POLITICAL

Bustin, Edouard. "The Quest for Political Stability in the Congo: Soldiers, Bureaucrats and Politicians." In *Africa: The Primacy of Politics,* ed. Herbert J. Spiro. New York: Random House, 1966.

Bustin, E. *Lunda Under Colonial Rule.* Cambridge: Harvard University Press, 1975.

Dayal, R. *Mission of Hammarskjold: The Congo Crisis.* London: Oxford University Press, 1976.

Gann, Lewis and Peter Duignan. *The Rulers of Belgian Africa, 1884-1914* Princeton: Princeton University Press, 1979.

Gerard-Libois, Jules. *Katanga Secession.* Madison: University of Wisconsin Press, 1966.

Heiraz, G. and H. Donnay. *Lumumba: The Last Fifty Days.* New York: Grove Press, 1965

Hoskyns, Catherine. *The Congo Since Independence: January 1960—December 1961.* London: Oxford University Press, 1965.

House, Arthur H. *The U.N. in the Congo: The Political and Civilian Efforts.* Washington, D.C.: University Press of America, 1978.

Kanza, Thomas. *The Rise and Fall of Patrice Lumumba.* London: Rex Collings, 1978.

La Fontaine, J. S. *City Politics: A Study of Leopoldville 1962—1963.* New York: Cambridge University Press, 1970.

Lefever, Ernest W. *Uncertain Mandate: Politics of the UN Congo Operations.* Baltimore: Johns Hopkins University Press, 1967.

Lefever, Ernest W. *Spear and Scepter: Army, Police and Politics in Tropical Africa.* Washington, D.C.: Brookings Institution, 1970.

Lefever, Ernest W. *Crisis in the Congo.* Washington, D.C.: The Brookings Institution, 1965.

Lemarchand, René. *Political Awakening in the Congo.* Berkeley: University of California Press, 1964.

Lumumba, Patrice. *Congo, My Country.* New York: Praeger, 1962.

Nkrumah, Kwame. *Challenge of the Congo.* London: Thomas Nelson, 1967.

Schatzberg, M. G. *Politics and Class in Zaire: Bureaucracy, Business and Beer in Lisala.* New York: Holmes and Meier, 1980.

Verhaegen, Benoit. *Rebellions au Congo.* 2 vols. Brussels: Centre de recherche et d'information socio-politiques, 1966.

Weissman, Stephen R. *American Foreign Policy in the Congo, 1960—1964.* Ithaca, N.Y.: Cornell University Press, 1974.

Williams, Jean-Claude. *Patrimonialism and Political Change in the Congo*. Stanford, Calif.: Stanford University Press, 1972.

Young, Crawford. *Politics in the Congo: Decolonization and Independence*. Princeton, N.J.: Princeton University Press, 1965.

Young, Crawford. "Rebellion and the Congo." In *Power and Protest in Black Africa*, eds. Robert I. Rotberg and Ali A. Mazrui, pp. 969—1011. New York: Oxford University Press, 1970.

SOCIAL

Andersson, Efraim. *Messianic Popular Movements in the Lower Congo*. Uppsala: Almqvist & Wiksell, 1958.

Cahiers des Religions Africaines. 9, 17-18 (1975) special issue on Zaire's ethnic groups.

Caulemans, P. "Introduction de l'Influence de l'Islam au Congo." In *Islam in Tropical Africa*, ed. I. M. Lewis, pp. 174—192. London: Oxford University press, 1966.

Mabusa, Basile. "Post-Independence Education in the Congo." *Africa Report*, 11 (June 1966): 24—28.

MacGaffey, W. *Custom and Government in the Lower Congo*. Berkeley: University of California Press, 1970.

Obenga, Theophile. *Le Zaire*. Paris, Presence Africaine, 1977.

Polome, Edgar. "The Choice of Official Languages in the Democratic Republic of the Congo." In *Language Problems of Developing Nations*, ed. Joshua A. Fishman, Charles A. Ferguson and Jyotirindra Das Gupta, pp. 295—312. New York: Wiley, 1968.

Pons, V. C. *Stanleyville: An African Urban Community Under Belgian Administration*. London: Oxford University Press, 1969.

Reardon, Ruth Slade. "Catholics and Protestants in the Congo." In *Christianity in Tropical Africa*. ed. C. G. Bacta, pp. 83—100. London: Oxford University Press, 1968.

United Nations. Economic Commission for Africa. "Leopoldville and Lagos: Comparative Study of Conditions in 1960." In *The City in Newly Developing Countries*, ed. Gerald Breese, pp. 436—460. Englewood Cliffs, N.J.: Prentice-Hall, 1969.

Vansina, Jan. *Kingdoms of the Savannah*. Madison: University of Wisconsin Press, 1966.

40. Zambia

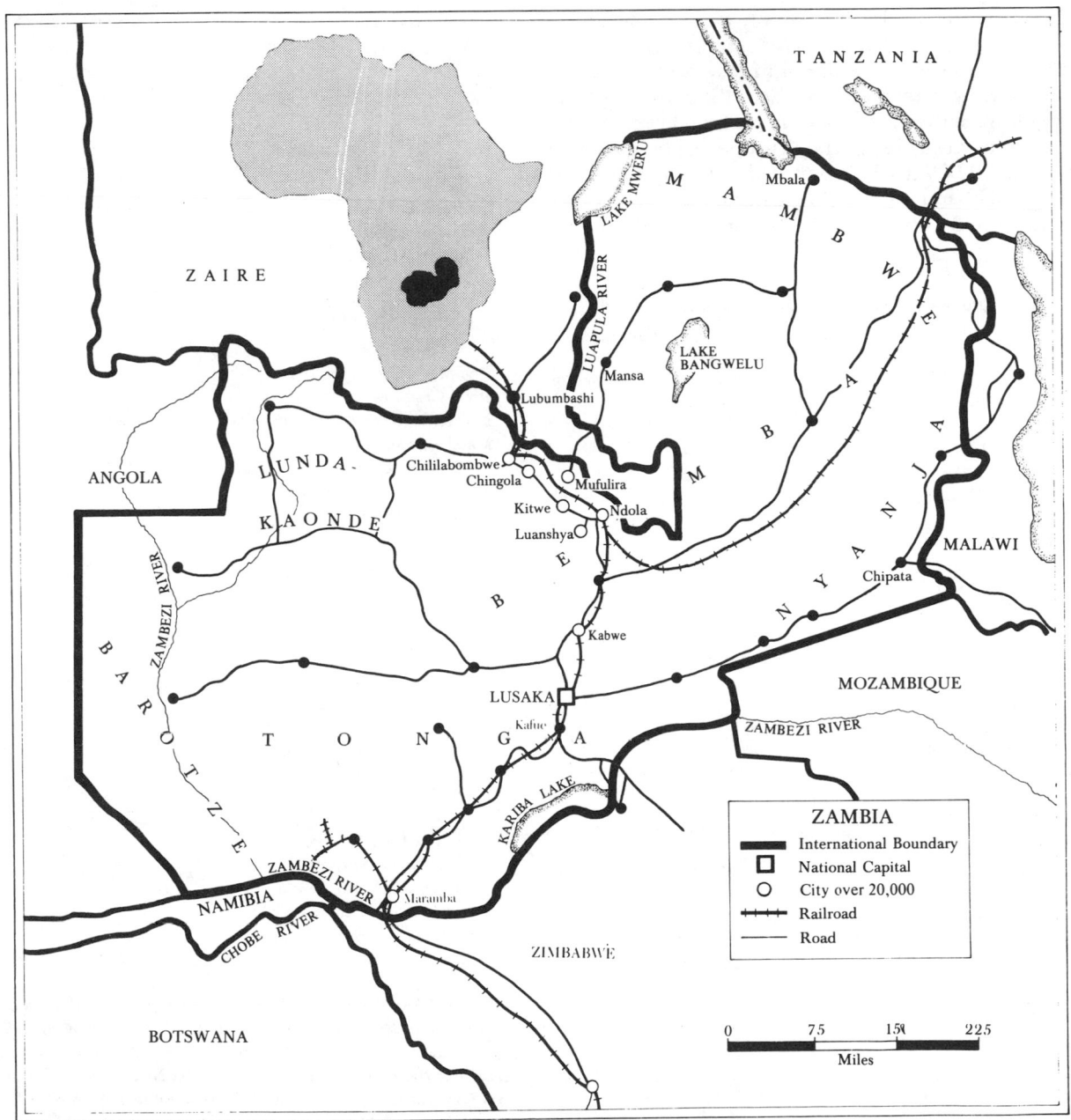

ZAMBIA

— International Boundary
□ National Capital
○ City over 20,000
╫╫╫ Railroad
— Road

0   7.5   15(22.5
Miles

I. Basic Information

Date of Independence: October 24, 1964
Former Colonial Ruler: United Kingdom
Changes in Boundaries: Part of the Central African Federation, 1953-1963.
Former Name: Northern Rhodesia

Population (1980): 5,725,000
Area Size (equivalent in U.S.): 290,586 sq. mi. (Texas)
Date of Last Census: 1969 (sample census in 1974)
Major Exports 1977 as Percent of Total Exports: copper—91 percent.

II. Ethnic Patterns

The Kay classification (1967) is largely based on linguistic criteria, while the Mitchell classification (1960—1964), which we have used, is modified to take account of cultural similarities. Our categories are at a middle level of abstraction since they are based, in part, on locally recognized identity groupings. The European population of Zambia was 70,000 in 1965, but had decreased to about 50,000 by 1972 and 1974 estimates of non-Zambian employment were 34,000 including Indians as well as Europeans.

TABLE 40.1   Ethnic Units Over 5 Percent of Country Population

Ethnic Units	Estimated Ethnic Population 1980	Estimated Ethnic Percentage
a. Bemba Cluster	2,118,000	37%
1. Bemba (Awemba, Ayemba, Babeinba, Muemba, Wemba) i. Bisa, ii. Tabwa, iii. Kunda, iv. Senga	(859,000)	(15%)
2. Luapula i. Lunda (Luapula, Kazembe), ii. Chishinga, iii. Shila, iv. Bwile	(458,000)	(8%)
3. Lamba i. Lala, ii. Lamba, iii. Ambo, iv. Lima, v. Luano, vi. Swaka, vii. Limba, viii. Seba	(458,000)	(8%)
4. Aushi i. Ushi, ii. Ngumbo iii. Mukulu, iv. Unga, v. Kabende	(401,000)	(7%)
b. Tonga Type	1,088,000	19%
1. Tonga (Batonga) i. Tonga, ii. Toka, iii. Gowa, iv. Fwe	(687,000)	(12%)
2. Lenje i. Lenje, ii. Sala, iii. Soli	(229,000)	(4%)
3. Ila i. Ila, ii. Leya, iii. Subiya, iv. Totela, v. Lumbu, vi. Lundwe	(115,000)	(2%)
c. Nyanja Type (Anyanja, Wanyanja) 1. Chewa i. Chewa, ii. Nsenga 2. Zambezi i. Chikunda 3. Ngoni	859,000	15%
d. Lunda-Kaonde Type	687,000	12%
1. Lunda-Luvale (Lunda-Alunda, Arunde, Balonde, Lounda, Valunda, Malhundo) i. Luvale, ii. Lunda (Northwestern), iii. Mbunda, iv. Luchazi, v. Mashashe, vi. Ndembu, vii. Chokwe	(515,00)	(9%)
2. Kaonde (Bakahonde, Bakaonde)	(172,00)	(3%)
e. Mambwe Cluster	458,000	8%
1. Mambwe Type i. Oungu, ii. Mambwe, iii. Winamwange, iv. Wiwa, v. Tambo	(286,000)	(5%)
2. Tumbuka Type i. Fungwe, ii. Kamanga, iii. Yome, iv. Nthali, v. Hewe	(172,000)	(3%)
3. Nkoya Type i. Lambya, ii. Wandya, iii. Nyiha		
f. Barotze (Lozi, Barotse, Barozi, Barutse, Marotse, Rotse, Rozi) Type 1. Luyana i. Kwangwa, ii. Kwandi, iii. Koma, iv. Nyengo, v. Simaa, vi. Mwenyi, vii. Imilangu, viii. Mashi, ix. Mbukushu, x. Ndundulu, xi. Lyuwa	(229,000)	(4%)
2. Lozi	(172,000)	(3%)

SOURCES: Clyde Mitchell, "The African Peoples," in *Handbook to the Federation of Rhodesia and Nyasaland*, ed. W. V. Brelsford (London: Cassell, 1960), pp. 117—181. Clyde Mitchell, *African Tribes and Languages of the Federation of Rhodesia and Nyasaland* (Salisbury: Federal Government Printer, 1964), Map. George Kay, *A Social Geography of Zambia* (London: University of London Press, 1967), p. 45.

III. Language Patterns

All of the languages of Zambia are of the Bantu family. Bemba is probably the largest of these. Although the Bemba ethnic/cultural cluster includes 37 percent of the population, those who speak Bemba as a first language are probably only 15 percent of the total population. (Knappert suggests 20 percent; Rustow 33 percent.) Denny (1963) stressed that although Bemba is the major language, it is not a *lingua franca*. This seems to be increasingly less true and we estimate 35 percent of the population understand Bemba. The second largest language is probably Tonga, although Colson says they are the largest linguistic group. Those who speak Tonga as a first language probably constitute 12 percent of the population. We estimate a total of 18 percent for Tonga. English serves as a *lingua franca* and the primary official language although seven other vernacular languages also have official status.

TABLE 40.2 Language Patterns

1. Primacy				
	1st language	Bemba	(35%)	
	2nd language	Tonga	(18%)	
			Green-	Dalby
			berg	
2. Linguistic classification		Bemba	IA5	M4
	(all ethnic units in	Tonga	IA5	M6
	country over 5%)	Nyanja	IA5	N3
		Lunda	IA5	K1
		Mambwe	IA5	M1
		Barotze	IA5	S3
3. *Lingua franca*		English		
4. Official languages		English (Bemba, Tonga, Nyanja, Lunda, Luvale, Lozi, and Kaonde are also official languages used on the radio and in other media but English is the working language of government.)		

SOURCES: Elizabeth Colson, "The Assimiliation of Aliens among Zambian Tonga," in *From Tribe to Nation in Africa*, eds. Ronald Cohen and John Middleton (Scranton, Pa.: Chandler Publishing Co., 1970). Neville Denny, "Languages and Education in Africa," in *Language in Africa*, ed. John Spencer (London: Cambridge University Press, 1963).

IV. Urban Patterns

Capital/largest city: Lusaka (founded 1913)
Dominant ethnicity/language of capital
    Major vernacular: Bemba[1]
    Major ethnic group: Bemba[2]
    Major ethnic group as percent of capital's population: 16% (1959)

[1]Jan Knappert, "Language Problems of the New Nations of Africa," *African Quarterly*, 5 (1965): 95—105.

[2]D. G. Bettison, *Numerical Data on African Dwellers in Lusaka, Northern Rhodesia* (Lusaka: Rhodes-Livingstone Institute, 1959)

TABLE 40.3 Growth of Capital/largest city

Date	Lusaka
1920	2,000
1940	20,000
1950	80,000
1960	100,000
1966	170,000 UA
1972	347,900 UA
1974[a]	401,000 UA
1977[b]	520,000 UA

SOURCES: D. G. Bettison, *Numerical Data on African Dwellers in Lusaka* (Lusaka: Rhodes-Livingstone Institute, 1959), and the 1956 census of the Central African Federation. The 1966 figure is from the *Europa Yearbook 1967*.
    [a]1974 sample census as reported in *Europa Yearbook 1977 Vol. II*.
    [b]*Europa Yearbook 1979, Vol. II*.

TABLE 40.4   Cities of 20,000 and Over*

City	Size	Date
Lusaka	559,000	1978
Kitwe (inc. Kalulushi)	310,000	1978
	+ (54,000)	
Ndola	291,000	1978
Chingola (inc. Chililabombwe)	173,000	1978
	+ (70,000)	
Mufulira	170,000	1978
Luanshya	149,00	1978
Kabwe	131,000	1978
Maramba		
(Livingstone)	72,000	1978
Kafue^a	20,000	1974

SOURCE: *Africa South of the Sahara* 1980—81

^a*Europa Yearbook 1977 V. II*—1974 sample census. The next largest town is Chipata (17,000 in 1974).

V. Political Patterns

A. Political Parties and Elections

Pre-independence Zambia was marked by a struggle over the federation with Southern Rhodesia and Nyasaland. The *African National Congress* (ANC) under the direction of Harry Nkumbula and the *United National Independence Party* (UNIP) led by Kenneth Kaunda were opposed to the federation while the *National Progress Party* (NPP) (formerly known as the *United Federal Party*) favored union. Sir Roy Welensky's NPP lost the 1962 elections and a coalition government was formed between the rival ANC and UNIP with Kaunda at its head. This coalition proved to be unstable, and the UNIP won the 1964 election and formed the new government itself. In the December 1968 elections, UNIP won 81 seats and the ANC 24 in the Zambia Parliament. The ANC's main strength was in Barotseland and the south of the country.

By 1970, much of the ANC membership had gone over to the UNIP. In 1971, Simon Kapwepwe, resigned as the country's Vice-President and began a new party, the *United Progressive Party* (UPP). Many of its leaders, excepting Kapwepwc himself, were detained by the government for several months. In December 1972, Zambia became a legal one-party state and all parties except UNIP were banned. The first elections under this new constitution were held from October to December, 1973. The turnout for the 1973 elections was the lowest in Zambian history ranging from 18 to 52 percent across constituences. The average turnout was 39 percent of the registered electorate compared to 77 percent in the 1968 elections. Elections were held again in December 1978. In September 1978, UNIP approved constitutional changes that effectively prohibited competition from the December election. Despite the lack of competition, turnout rose to 67% and Kaunda won 80.5% of the vote.

TABLE 40.5   Head of Government (Post-Independence)

Name	Dates in Office	Age (1982)	Ethnicity	Education	Former Occupaton
1. Kenneth David Kaunda (President)	1964— present	58	Bemba	Secondary, Zambia Teacher's Certificate	Farmer, Teacher

FIGURE 40.1   Political Parties and Elections   ZAMBIA

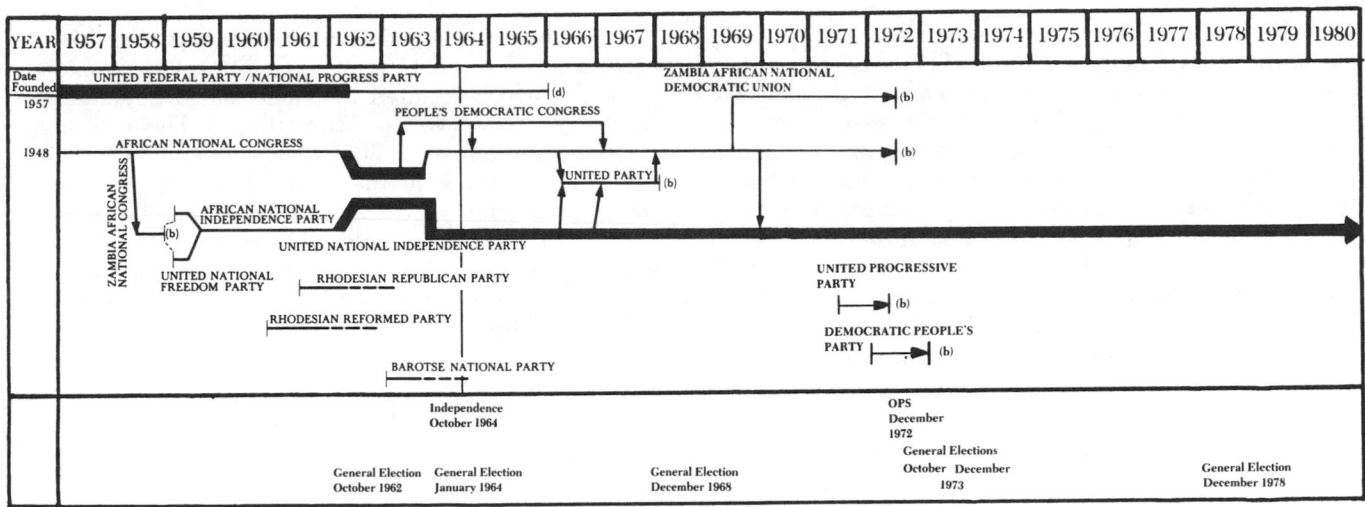

TABLE 40. 6   Cabinet Membership: Distribution by Ethnic Unit*

Ethnicity*	Independence Cabinet	1967 Cabinet	1972 Cabinet
1. Bemba (37%)	25%	29%	31%
2. Tonga (19)	13	12	12
3. Nyanja (15)	25	24	23
4. Lunda-Kaonde (12)	6	6	15
5. Mambwe (8)	0	0	0
6. Barotze (7)	25	22	15
7. Others (2)	6	6	4
N =	76	77	26

*Ethnic units arranged in rank order of size within country with the unit's percent of national population in parentheses.
SOURCE: M. Tordoff (ed.) *Politics in Zambia* Manchester: University of Manchester Press, 1974.

B. Political Leadership

Kenneth Kaunda has led the government since independence. There was marked cabinet turnover in the 1964—65 period and in 1970—72 prior to the establishment of a one-party state, but ethnic balance has remained unchanged. The military is now represented in the government. In January 1979, President Kaunda reduced the size of the cabinet from 29 to 19 and he has increasingly formed an authoritarian regime.

VI. National Integration and Stability

The only coded instance of communal instability in Zambia has been the Lumpa rebellion. Tensions between the Lozi (Barotze), Ngoni and Tongas, and the Bemba have been succesfully managed so far by the government, although the advoacy of Barotze secession has a long history in Zambia. While elite conflict has been manifest in opposition to the government, no instances of political instability have been reported although there have been a series of bomb explosions from 1972 onwards for which no satisfactory explanation has been given. Much of Zambia's history since independence has been dominated by conflicts with the white minority regimes of Rhodesia, Mozambique, and the Republic of South Africa. Zambia provided refuge and training facilities for Zimbabwe guerrillas which resulted in Rhodesian raids across the border of Zimbabwe and Mozambique. This confrontation has lessened since Zimbabwe's independence. The precipitous decline in the price of copper, the major source of foreign exchange and governmental income, has severely tested the political system and the continuing confrontation with the white-dominated regimes to the south impose a particularly high burden on Zambia's political stability.

TABLE 40.8   Communal Instability

Event and Date	Characteristics
1. Rebellion October 1964— November 1967	a. *Description*: The Lumpa Church of Alice Lenshina was founded in the 1950s as an African Christian faith-healing movement. Its main strength is among the Bemba in northern Zambia. It came into conflict with civil authorities in the pre-independence period. In the early 1960s it came into conflict with UNIP militants, and in 1963 Mrs. Lenshina forbade political activity on the part of her followers. Its religious exclusivism and its potential as a counter-force to UNIP apparently led to continued tensions which resulted in violent confrontations between the church and UNIP in 1963 and the government in July and August 1964. The Church was banned on August 3, 1964. On October 10, 1967, Mrs. Lenshina escaped from jail and more violence broke out. She was recaptured several days later. Many members of the church crossed to Zaire into exile. Mrs. Lenshina was detained or under house arrest for eleven years before she was released in December 1975. b. *Participants*: Lumpa Church members. c. *Apparent Causes*: Tension between a militant religious group and UNIP militants who demanded cooperation with the government.

SOURCES: Gerald L. Caplan, "Barotseland: The Secessionist Challenge to Zambia," *Journal of Modern African Studies*, 6 (1968): 343—360. James W. Fernandez, "The Lumpa Uprising, Why?" *Africa Report*, 9 (November 1964): 30—32. Andrew D. Roberts, "The Lumpa Church of Alice Lenshina," in *Protest and Power in Black Africa*, eds. Robert I. Rotberg and Ali A. Mazrui (New York: Oxford, 1970), pp. 513—568.

TABLE 40.10   Annual Instability Events: Independence Through 1979—Zambia

	'61	'62	'63	'64	'65	'66	'67	'68	'69	'70	'71	'72	'73	'74	'75	'76	'77	'78	'79
ELITE INSTABILITY																			
Assassinations																			
Plots													1						
Attempted Coups d'État																			
Coups d'État																			
COMMUNAL INSTABILITY																			
Ethnic Violence																			
Irredentism																			
Rebellion				1															
Civil War																			
MASS INSTABILITY																			
Revolt																			
Revolution																			
TURMOIL																			
Demonstrations													1						
Strikes (no. days)					9	3	61												
Riots (no. days)					2	1	1		1	2									
Terrorism						1		1	1				1	1	1				
Declarations of Emergency							1		1		1								
CABINET INSTABILITY																			
Realloc. and new appts.					11	7	4	2	2	3	4	2							
New members					2	2	1	1	6	6	8	2							
Resig. and Dismissals					2	2			4	3	7	3							
No. of members (max.)					18	19	19	18	20	23	25	24							

VII.   Selected References

BIBLIOGRAPHY

Grotpeter, John J. *Historical Dictionary of Zambia.* Metuchen, N.J.: Scarecrow Press, 1979.

Rau, W. E. *A Bibliography of Pre-Independence Zambia: The Social Sciences.* Boston: G.K. Hall, 1978.

GENERAL

Davis, D. H. (ed.). *Zambia in Maps.* N.Y.: Holmes and Meier, 1972.

Hall, Richard. *Zambia.* New York: Praeger, 1966.

Hall, Richard. *Zambia, 1890—1964, the Colonial Period.* London: Longman, 1976.

Kaplan, Irving, ed. *Zambia, a Country Study*, 3rd. ed. Washington, U.S. Government Printing Office, 1979.

Martin, A. *Minding Their Own Business: Zambia's Struggle Against Western Control.* London: Hutchinson, 1972.

Robert, Andrews. *A History of Zambia.* N.Y.: Africana, 1976.

POLITICAL

Arglin, Douglas G. and Shaw, Timothy M. *Zambia's Foreign Policy: Studies in Diplomacy and Dependence.* Boulder, Col.: Westview, 1979.

Bates, R. *Unions, Parties, and Political Development: A Study of Mineworkers in Zambia.* New Haven, Conn.: Yale University Press, 1971.

Bates, R. *Rural Responses to Industrialization.* New Haven: Yale University Press, 1976.

Berger, Elena L. *Labor, Race and Colonial Rule: The Copperbelt from 1924 to Independence.* London: Oxford University Press, 1974.

Bond, G. G. *The Politics of Change in a Zambian Community.* Chicago: University of Chicago Press, 1976.

Cervanka, Zdenek and R. Weiss. *Zambia: The First Ten Years 1964—1974.* Stockholm: Swedish-Zambian Association, 1974.

Epstein, A. L. *Politics in an African Urban Community.* Manchester: Manchester University Press, 1958.

Hall, Richard. *The High Price of Principles: Kaunda and the White South.* Rev. ed. Harmondsworth, U.K.: Penguin, 1973.

Kaunda, Kenneth. *Zambia Shall Be Free: An Autobiography.* New York: Praeger, 1963.

Kaunda, Kenneth. *Zambia, Independence and Beyond.* London: Thomas Nelson, 1966.

MacPherson, Fergus. *Kenneth Kaunda of Zambia.* Lusaka: Oxford University Press, 1974.

Meebelo, H. S. *Main Currents of Zambian Humanist Thought.* London: Oxford University Press, 1973.

Mulford, David C. *Zambia: The Politics of Independence, 1957—1954.* London: Oxford University Press, 1967.

Ollawa, Patrick E. *Participatory Democracy in Zambia: The Political Economy of National Development.* Elms Court, Arthur H. Stockwell, 1979.

Pettman, Jan. *Zambia: Security and Conflict, 1964—1973.* New York: St. Martin's Press, 1974.

Rotberg, Robert D. *Black Heart: Gore-Browne and the Politics of Multiracial Zambia.* Berkeley: University of California Press, 1977.

Scarritt, James R. "The Decline of Political Legitimacy in Zambia." African Studies Review, 22, 2, Sept. 1979, pp. 13—38.

Scott, I. "Middle Class Politics in Zambia." *African Affairs* (London), 77, 308, July, 1978, pp. 321—34.

Shaw, T. M. "The Foreign Policy of Zambia: An Events Analysis of a New State." *Comparative Political Studies*, 11, 2, July, 1978, pp. 181—209.

Sklar, R. *Corporate Power in an African State.* Berkeley: University of California Press, 1975.

Tordoff, W. (ed.). *Politics in Zambia.* Manchester: Manchester University Press, 1974.

ECONOMIC

Blitzer, Charles R. *Development and Income Distribution in a Dual Economy: A Dynamic Simulation Model for Zambia.* Washington, D.C.: World Bank, 1978.

Bostock, M., and C. Harvey (eds.). *Economic Independence and Zambian Copper: A Case Study of Foreign Investment.* New York: Praeger, 1972.

Dodge, D. J. *Agricultural Policy and Performance in Zambia: History, Prospects, and Proposals for Change.* Berkeley: Institute for International Studies, 1977.

Daniel, Philip. *Africanisation, Nationalisation and Inequality: Miner's Labour and the Copperbelt in Zambian Development.* N.Y.: Cambridge University Press, 1979.

Elliott, Charles (ed.). *Constraints on the Economic Development of Zambia.* New York: Oxford University Press, 1972.

Fry, James. *Employment and Income Distribution in the African Economy.* London: Croom Helm, 1979.

Gordenker, L. *International Aid and National Decisions: Development Programs in Malawi, Tanzania and Zambia.* Princeton: Princeton University Press, 1976.

Hellen, John Anthony. *Rural Economic Development in Zambia, 1890—1964.* Munich: Weltforum Verlag, 1968.

International Monetary Fund. "Zambia." In *Surveys of African Economies*, Vol. 4. Washington, D.C.: I.M.F., 1971.

Kapferer, B. *Strategy and Transition in an African Factory: African Workers and Indian Management in a Zambian Town.* Manchester: Manchester University Press, 1972.

Makings, S. M. *Agricultural Change in Northern Rhodesia/Zambia, 1945—1965.* Stanford: Stanford University Food Research Institute, 1966.

Shaw, T. M. "Zambia: Dependence and Underdevelopment," *Canadian Journal of African Studies*, 10, 1 (1976).

Simonis, H., and V. E. *Socioeconomic Development in Dual Economies: The Example of Zambia.* Munich: Weltforum Verlag, 1975.

Turok, Ben. *Development in Zambia.* London, Zed Press, 1979.

SOCIAL

Bates, R. H. "Ethnic Competition and Modernization in Contemporary Africa," *Comparative Political Studies*, 6, 4 (January 1974): 457—84.

Brelsford, W. V. *The Tribes of Northern Rhodesia*. Lusaka: Northern Rhodesia Government Printer, 1956.

Brooks, E., and V. Nyirenda (eds.). *Social Development in Zambia*: *Case Studies*. Lusaka: University of Zambia, 1977.

Heisler, Helmuth. *Urbanization and the Government of Migration: The Inter-relation of Urban and Rural Life in Zambia*. New York: St. Martin's Press, 1974.

Mitchell, J. Clyde and A. L. Epstein. "Occupational Prestige and Social Status Among Africans in Northern Rhodesia," *Africa* 29 (1959): 22—40.

Mwanakatwe, J. M. *The Growth of Education in Zambia Since Independence*. London: Oxford University Press, 1969.

Ohannessian, S., and M. Kashoki (eds.). *Language in Zambia*. London: International African Institute, 1977.

Powdermaker, Hortense. *Copper Town*: *Changing Africa. The Human Stituation on the Rhodesian Copperbelt*. New York: Harper, 1962.

Schuster, Ilsa and M. Glazer. *New Women of Lusaka*. Palo Alto, Calif.: Mayfield, 1979.

Siddle, C. J. "Rural Development in Zambia: A Spatial Analyis," *Journal of Modern African Studies*," 8 *(July 1970): 271—184.*

41. Zimbabwe

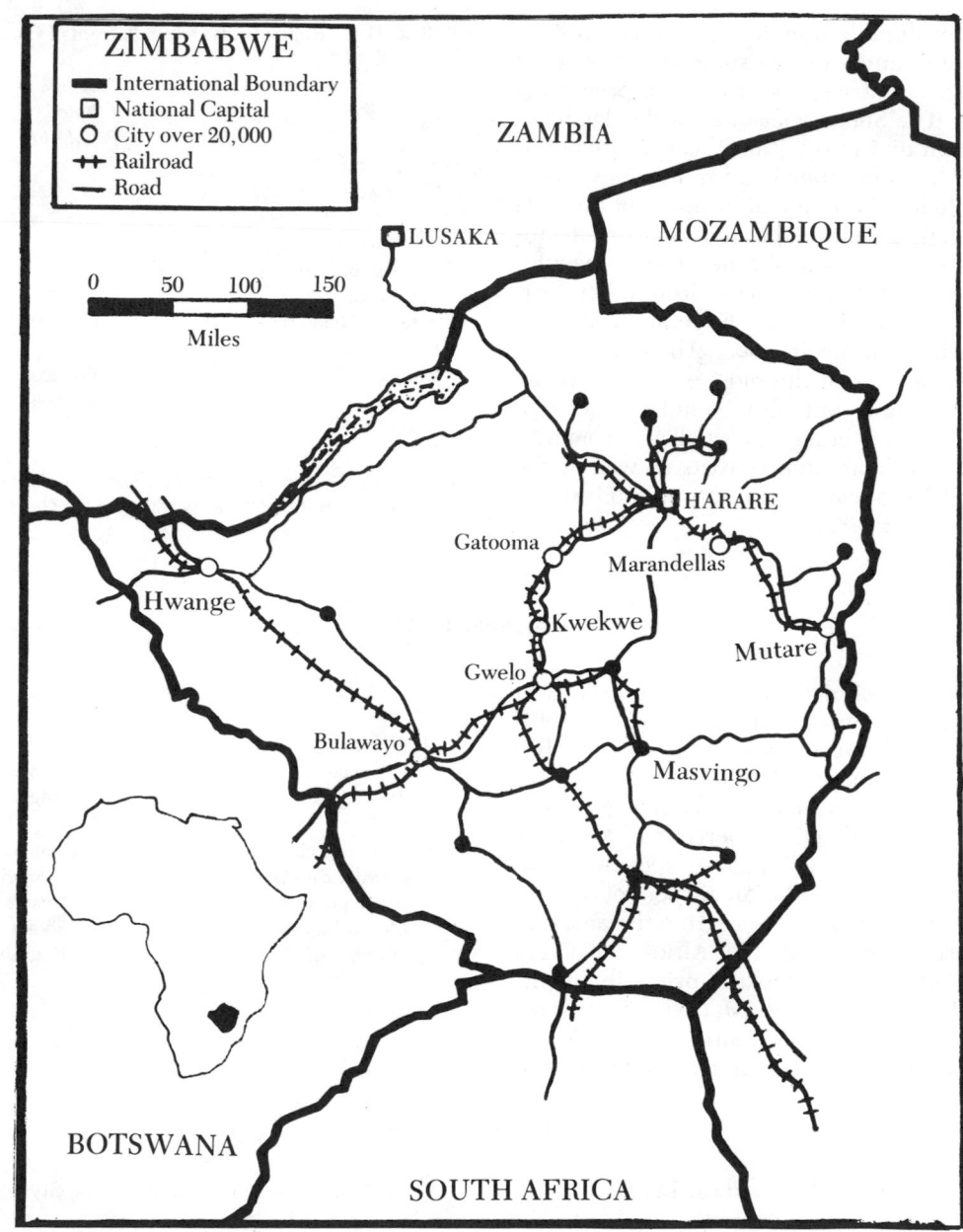

I. Basic Information

Date of Independence: April 19, 1980
Former Colonial Ruler: United Kingdom
Change in Boundaries: Member of the Central African
   Federation from 1953-1963.
Former Names: Southern Rhodesia, Rhodesia, Zim-
   babwe-Rhodesia

Estimated Population (1980): 7,820,000
Area Size (equivalent in U.S.): 150,820 sq. mi. (Mon-
   tana)
Date of Last Census: 1969
Major Exports 1978 as Percent of Total Exports: not
   known because of the war.

II. Ethnic Patterns

Because of the considerable mingling of peoples in Zimbabwe, the ethnic boundaries are somewhat less sharp than in some other countries, and are based principally on linguistic lines. The Shona-speakers are the dominant ethnic unit although divisions within this unit are politically important. The only other large indigenous ethnic group is the Ndebele who dominated much of the area that is now Zimbabwe before the arrival of the Europeans. Considerable migration of other African peoples to Zimbabwe has occurred, particularly from other partners in the former Central African Federation (Zambia and Malawi) which broke up in 1963. About 7% of the population are migrants with the most prominent being the Nyanja from Malawi but also including the Yao, Senga, Lozi, Ngoni, and others. A small but commercially significant Asian community exists as well as the formerly dominant European community which is steadily declining in size as of 1982.

TABLE 41.1   Ethnic Units Over 5 Percent of Country Population

Ethnic Units	Estimated Ethnic Population 1980	Estimated Ethnic Percentage
a. Shona type (Mashona)	5,318,000	68%
1. Shona, 2. Karanga,		
3. Zezuru, 4. Manyika,		
5. Ndau, 6. Korekore		
7. Kalanga		
b. Ndebele-Nguni type	1,173,000	15%
1. Ndebele, 2. Nguni		
c. Nyanja	391,000	5%
d. Europeans	274,000	3.5%

SOURCE: H. D. Nelson *Area Handbook for Southern Rhodesia* U.S. Government Printing Office, Washington, D.C. 1975.

III. Language Patterns

All of the languages of Zimbabwe are Bantu. Shona, a collection of various dialects of a largely mutually intelligible language predominates in most of the country. Because of the location of the capital, Harare (Salisbury), in the heart of the Shona-speaking area, Shona is used as a *lingua franca* by an estimated 10 percent of the non-Shona speaking population. Ndebele is spoken in the western third of the country and is an offshoot of the language of the Nguni who migrated here from the area that is now South Africa. A number of other African languages from outside of Zimbabwe are spoken, primarily by migrants originally from Zambia and Malawi which were, along with Zimbabwe, part of the Central African Federation. English continues to be the official language as of 1982.

TABLE 41.2   Language Patterns

1. Primacy			
1st lanage	Shona	(78%)	
2nd language	Ndebele	(15%)	
		berg	
2. Linguistic classification	Shona	IA5	S1
(all ethnic units in	Ndebele	IA5	S4
country over 5%)	Nyanja	IA5	N3
3. *Lingua franca*	Shona		
4. Official language	English		

IV. Urban Patterns

Captial/largest city: Harare (founded ca. 1890)
Dominant Ethnicity/language of capital
  Major vernacular: Shona
  Major ethnic group: Shona
  Major ethnic group as percent of capital's population:

TABLE 41.3   Growth of Capital/largest city

Date	Harare (Salisbury)
1962[a]	210,800
1972[a]	490,280
1976[b]	568,000

SOURCE:
  [a]*Area Handbook for Southern Rhodesia*, p. 65.
  [b]*Africa South of the Sahara 1978—79*, p. 757.

TABLE 41.4   Cities of 20,000 or Over*

City	Size	Date
Harare		
(Salisbury)	616,000 UA	1978
Bulawayo	357,000	1978
Gwereu (formerly Gwelo)	69,000	1978
Mutare (formerly Umtali)	63,000	1978
Kwekwe (formerly Que Que)	51,000	1978
Gatooma	33,000	1978
Hwange (formerly Wankie)	33,000	1978
Sinoia	26,000	1978
Marandellas	23,000	1978
Masvingo		
(formerly Fort Victoria)	23,000	1978
Shabani	20,000	1978

SOURCE: *Africa South of the Sahara* 1980—81.

V. Political Patterns

A. Political Parties and Elections

Zimbabwe from 1923 until 1965, had been a self-governing colony in the British Commonwealth when it declared itself to be an independent state within the Commonwealth and subsequently a Republic. From the 1920's through the end of the 1970's Southern Rhodesia, as it was then known, had a competitive party system and regular elections in a Westminster form of government. The factor differentiating this country from others was that the franchise was for the white population only and threats to its loss were the cause of the 1965 break from Britain and the increasingly bloody battle that ensued between the government and militant parties seeking the extension of the franchise to all adults.

The period before the successful end of the struggle to extend the franchise was dominated by the Rhodesian Front (RF) although various other smaller white parties and factions existed throughout the period and continue to do so. The principal black political group for most of this period in the country is the African National Council (ANC) which was founded in the late 1950's. It became an umbrella for many other black groups but was faction ridden and did not develop a genuinely effective role until the 1970's. In 1971, the United African National Council (UANC) was founded by Bishop Abel Muzorewa as the principal heir to the ANC. The UANC split into internal and external factions in 1975 led by Muzorewa and Joshua Nkomo, respectively. Nkomo, founder of the Zimbabwe African People's Union (ZAPU) in 1961 (banned in 1962) which was Zambia-based throughout most of its history, joined Robert Mugabe, who founded the Mozambique-based Zimbabwe African National Union (ZANU) in 1963 as a split off from ZAPU, to form the Patriotic Front (PF) in October 1976 in order to press the fight against the white-led regime. Further splits in the UANC led by Sithole in 1975 resulted in the African National Congress—Sithole (ANC—Sithole) and the Zimbabwe United People's Organization (ZUPO), founded in late 1976 by Chiefs Chirau and Ndiveni attempting to represent traditional ethnic interests. A number of other relatively short-lived parties, white and black, exist but have no apparent constituency for electoral effect.

The first election with an unrestricted franchise (although with the whites overrepresented) was in 1979 when Bishop Muzorewa won the election under protest from the other black leaders and became prime minister. This attempt to thwart the leaders of the Patriotic Front, Nkomo and Mugabe, in their fight against white domination of the country was unsuccessful and was not accorded legitimacy by the countries of the world. As a result, new elections were arranged under British administration in early 1980 and this time Mugabe's party, ZANU, won 57 of the 100 seats in the legislative assembly, with 20 reserved for whites, 3 to Muzorewa's UANC, and 20 to Nkomo's Patriotic Front (ZAPU). A coalition Mugabe-Nkomo government was formed but it was dominated by ZANU and Mugabe. On April 18, 1980 Zimbabwe became formally independent of Britain. Their independence was universally recognized.

B. Political Leadership

The politics of Zimbabwe has for many years resolved around the personalities of several men. They include Ian Smith, who led the white dominated regime for 15 years until 1979, Robert Mugabe and Joshua Nkomo, who led the guerrilla war against the Smith regime from outside the country, and Muzorewa, Sithole, Chirau, and others who were inside the country for most of the period. The Smith regime was replaced by Muzorewa for a short interregnum of less than a year before Mugabe was elected with a considerable majority in 1980 to lead Zimbabwe as a fully independent country.

FIGURE 41.1   Political Parties and Elections   ZIMBABWE

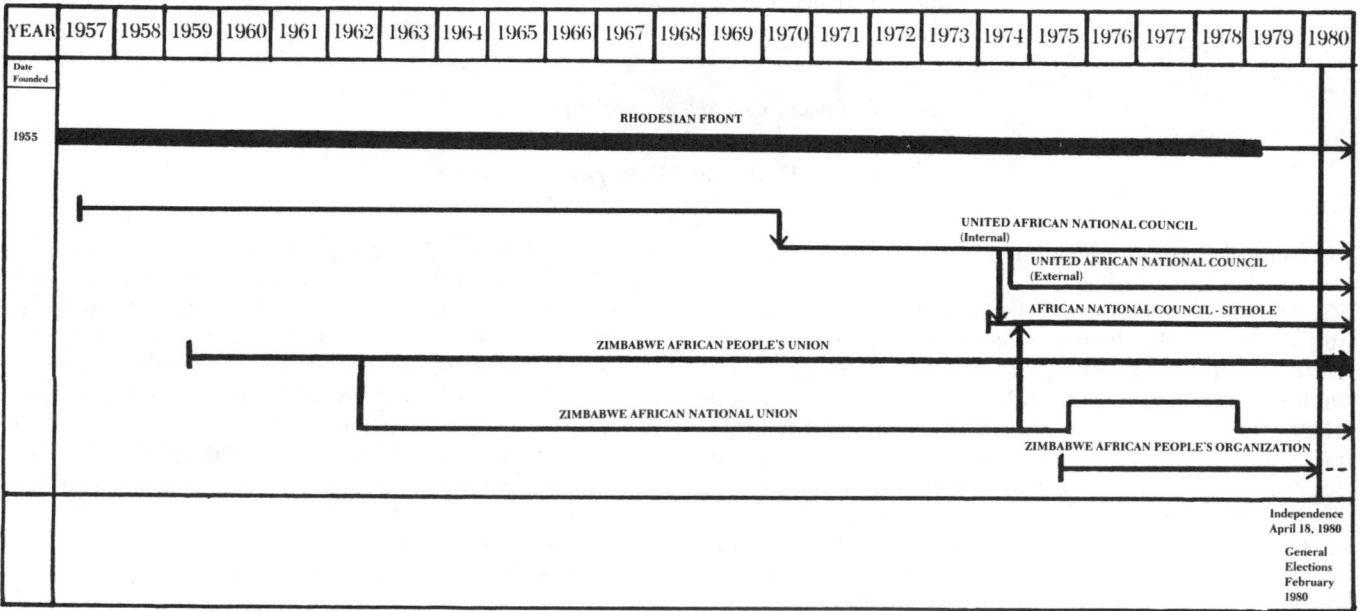

TABLE 41.5   Head of Government (Post-Independence)

Name	Dates in Office	Age (1982)	Ethnicity	Education	Former Occupation
1. Robert Mugabe (Prime Minister)	1980—	58	Shona	Fort Hare Univ. College Univ. of London	Teacher

VI. National Integration and Instability

The guerrilla war that finally gained Zimbabwe a full internationally recognized independence in April 1980 was not accomplished without considerable violence which has implications for the future of the country. While there appears to be no imminent threats to the Mugabe regime as a whole, political assassination and uncontrolled violence against whites, especially in the rural areas, has been on the increase since independence. Various factions within the Shona-speakers and the Nkomo-led opposition may pose serious threats to the future stability of the new regime. Nevertheless, as of mid-1982 there are not events of sufficient magnitude to identify in tabular format except to document the revolution leading to independence. The country has faced strikes, riots and demands for considerable acceleration in African standards of living along with demands for curtailing existing white power which may produce political stress in the future.

TABLE 41.9   Mass Instability

Event and Date	Characteristics
1. Revolution 1970—1980	a. *Description*: A white minority regime asserts independence from Britain in 1965 and black groups under various leaderships fight to establish universal franchise and the end to racially defined privilege. b. *Participants*: Whites under the leadership of Ian Smith oppose various political and guerrilla groups under Muzorewa, Sithole, Mugabe, and Nkomo. c. *Apparent Causes*: Opposition to white minority rule which became increasingly unacceptable as neighboring states overthrew their white-dominated regimes.

VII. Selected References

BIBLIOGRAPHY

Pollak, Oliver B. and Karen Pollak. *Rhodesia/Zimbabwe*. Santa Barbara, Clio Press, 1979.

Rasmussen, R. K. *Historical Dictionary of Rhodesia/Zimbabwe Metuchen*, New Jersey: Scarecrow Press, 1979.

O'Meara, Patrick and Jean Gosebrink. "Bibliography on Rhodesia." *Africana Journal*, 9,1 1978 p. 5-42 and 9,2 p. 101-112.

GENERAL

Austin, R. *Racism and Apartheid in Southern Africa: Rhodesia*. Paris: UNESCO, 1975.

Blake, R. *A History of Rhodesia*. New York: Knopf, 1978.

Cary, R. and D. Mitchell. *African Nationalist Leaders in Rhodesia: Who's Who*. Bulawayo: Bulawayo Books, 1977.

Lorey, M. *Rhodesia: White Racism and Imperial Response*. Middlesex, England: Penguin Books, 1975.

Nelson, Harold D. *Area Handbook for Southern Rhodesia*. Washington: U.S. Government Printing Office, 1975.

Rhodesia/Zimbabwe 1971—1977. New York: Facts on File Publications, 1978.

Simson, Howard. *Zimbabwe: A Country Study*. Uppsala: Scandanavian Institute of African Studies, 1979.

ECONOMIC

Clarke, D. G. *The Distribution of Income and Wealth in Rhodesia.* Gwelo: Mambo Press, 1977.

Clarke, D. G. *Foreign Companies and International Investment in Zimbabwe.* London: Catholic Institute for International Relations, 1980

Simson, Howard. *Zimbabwe: A Country Study.* Uppsala: Sandanavian Institute of African Studies, 1979.

Wasserman, Gary. "The Economic Transition to Zimbabwe." *Africa Report*, 23, 6, Nov./Dec. 1978, pp. 39—45.

Zimbabwe-Rhodesia, Government of. *Economic Survey of Zimbabwe-Rhodesia.* Salisbury, 1978.

SOCIAL

Bourdillon, M. F. C. *The Shona Peoples: An Ethnography of the Contemporary Shona, With Special Reference to Their Religion.* Gwelo: Mambo Press, 1976.

Kay, G. and M. Smout, eds. *Salisbury: A Geographical Survey of the Capital of Rhodesia.* New York: Holmes and Meier, 1977.

O'Callaghan, M. *Southern Rhodesia: The Effects of a Conquest Society on Education, Culture and Information.* Paris: UNESCO, 1977.

POLITICAL

Bull, Theodore, ed. *Rhodesia: Crisis of Color.* Chicago: Quadrangle Books, 1967.

Clements, Frank. *Rhodesia, The Course to Collision.* London: Pall Mall Press, 1969.

Good, Robert C. *U.D.I.: The International Politics of the Rhodesian Rebellion.* London: Faber, 1973.

Hills, D. *Rebel People.* New York: Africana Publishing, 1978.

Hirsch, Morris I. *A Decade of Crisis, Ten Years of Rhodesian Front Rule (1963—72).* Salisbury: Peter Dearlove, 1973.

Hutson, H. P. W. *Rhodesia: Ending an Era.* London: Springwood Books, 1978.

Lake, Anthony. *The "Tar Baby" Option, American Policy Toward Southern Rhodesia.* N.Y.: Columbia University Press, 1976.

Legum, C. *Southern Africa: The Year of the Whirlwind.* New York: Holmes and Meier, 1977.

Meredith, Martin. *The Past is Another Country: Rhodesia 1890—1979.* London: Andre Deutsch, 1979.

Nyangoni, C. and G. Nyandoro, eds. *Zimbabwe Independence Movements.* New York: Barnes and Noble, 1979.

O'Meara, P. *Rhodesia: Racial Conflict or Coexistence?* Ithaca, N.Y.: Cornell University Press, 1975.

Raeburn, M. *Black Fire! Accounts of the Guerrilla War in Rhodesia.* London: Julian Friedmann, 1977.

Sithole, N. *Zimbabwe's Year of Freedom.* Munger Africana Library Notes. 43, 1978.

Sithole, N. *Roots of a Revolution: Scenes from Zimbabwe's Struggle.* New York: Oxford University Press, 1977.

Strack, H. R. *Sanctions: The Case of Rhodesia.* Syracuse: Syracuse University Press, 1978.

Todd, Judith. *The Right to Say No.* London: Sidgwich and Jackson, 1972.

Windrich, E. *The Rhodesian Problem, A Documentary Record 1923—1973.* London: Routledge and Kegan Paul, 1975.

Windrich, E. *Britain and the Politics of Rhodesian Independence.* New York: Africana Publishing, 1978.

UNDERSTANDING BLACK AFRICA
by Donald George Morrison
with Robert Cameron Mitchell and John Naber Paden

Data and Analysis Of Social Change And Nation Building

This companion volume to BLACK AFRICA presents an overview of both historical and modern Africa and an introduction to basic quantitative cross-national research techniques used by the authors. It then goes into specific analysis of comparative patterns as well as country-by-country data for 41 nations.

TABLE OF CONTENTS

AVAILABLE APRIL 1989
(complimentary copies of the paper edition are available to instructors who request copies on their institution's letterhead, giving name of course, enrollment and next date offered)

237 pages

Cloth - $39.50
Paper - $19.95
   (minimum order quantity for paper edition-5 copies)

IRVINGTON PUBLISHERS, INC.
740 Broadway, New York, NY 10003

Copublished in the U.S. and Canada by
PARAGON HOUSE
90 Fifth Avenue, New York, NY 10011

Prices subject to change without notice.